MARRIAGE, DEATH AND LEGAL NOTICES FROM EARLY ALABAMA NEWSPAPERS, 1819–1893

Compiled

by

Pauline Jones Gandrud

Please Direct All Correspondence and Book Orders to:

Southern Historical Press, Inc.
PO Box 1267
375 West Broad Street
Greenville, S.C. 29602

ISBN # 0-89308-209-0

Printed in the United States of America

PAULINE JONES GANDRUD

The late Pauline Jones Gandrud was born May 9, 1904, in Huntsville, Alabama, the daughter of George Walter and Elvalena (Moore) Jones. Both paternal and maternal ancestors from Virginia were some of the earliest settlers of Madison County, Alabama, dating from about 1803 to 1809. After graduating from Wills Prep School in Huntsville, Alabama, in 1921, she studied two years at the Peabody Conservatory of Music in Baltimore as a piano pupil of Pasquale Tallarico and subsequently taught music for several years.

In Huntsville, Alabama, on November 29, 1930, Pauline Jones married Bennie William Gandrud, a mining engineer with the U.S. Bureau of Mines on the university campus at Tuscaloosa. They had one son, William Bentley Gandrud, born August 18, 1939, in Birmingham. A graduate of the University of Alabama with a Ph.D. in Physics from Johns Hopkins University, he is currently a physicist and supervising engineer at the Bell Telephone Laboratory in Atlanta, Georgia.

After becoming interested in the subject of genealogy at the early age of 17, she was encouraged to continue this interest by her sister-in-law, Kathleen Paul Jones. Together they collaborated in the researching and typing of Alabama county records until Kathleen's death in December, 1967.

Mrs. Gandrud has given lectures for many groups, some of which are the Virginia Genealogical Society, Richmond, Virginia; the Central Texas Genealogical Society, Waco, Texas (workshop); the Ft. Worth Genealogical Society, Ft. Worth, Texas; the Alabama Historical Society, Selma, Alabama; the East Alabama Genealogical Society, Gadsden, Alabama; the Alabama Genealogical Society, Birmingham, Alabama; the Birmingham Genealogical Society, Birmingham, Alabama; and about 15 local clubs (Tuscaloosa). Mrs. Gandrud died unexpectedly in September, 1980, at her home in Tuscaloosa.

FOREWARD

Work on this book on marriages, deaths and legal notices from Alabama
newspapers was started some three to four years ago when the publisher
and the compiler of these records discussed putting them into book form.

Previously, these valuable newspaper records had appeared throughout
the 245-volume collection of *Alabama Records* done by Mrs. Gandrud and her
sister-in-law, and therefore, one would have to scan this whole series
of Alabama books to, hopefully, find some information relating to a
member of his or her family.

Mrs. Gandrud finally decided that the best thing for her to do would
be to pull these newspaper records from each of the volumes in which they
appeared from *Alabama Records* and send them to the publisher to Xerox in
preparation for this book.

When these records were being sorted and arranged for the typist,
it was extremely difficult to decide on the exact format and arrangement
that these records should appear in, since so many different newspapers
were involved over this eighty-year period. A decision was made to try
to arrange the records in chronological order by newspaper and by
genealogical region. This format did not always follow in each instance,
but with over 1500 Xeroxed pages of copy to try to arrange, and in the
time frame allotted to do this, we did the best we could.

We have provided a table of contents listing the name of each newspaper that records were taken from and years for said paper. This does
not necessarily mean that if you see 1820-1821, that every issue for
those two years is included, as Mrs. Gandrud may have only found data on
one or two months in each of those years. Your publisher does not know
whether records for these newspapers exist in their entirety, since we
have worked only with what Mrs. Gandrud had abstracted.

TABLE OF CONTENTS

CAHAWBA PRESS AND ALABAMA STATE INTELLIGENCER

Published each Saturday in Cahawba, Dallas County, Alabama
by ALLEN & BRICKELL.

January 7, 1821
 State of Alabama-Cahawba Co.* - THOMAS TOWLIN posted before JAMES
MAHAN, a bay horse.

January 13, 1821
 Died in this place yesterday morning, Mrs. ASENATH LANE in her 29th
year, consort of EDM'D LANE, Esq. of this town...
 BETSY FRAZER, administratrix of WILLIAM FRAZER deceased.

January 20, 1821
 Died in this town last evening, Mrs. ELIZABETH CAMPBELL, consort of
the late HON. DAVID CAMPBELL of Tennessee in her 54th year. Funeral
tomorrow from her late residence on Vine St...

February 10, 1821
 Died at the residence of his brother, GEN. JOHN SCOTT, in the
variety of this place, Mr. THOMAS SCOTT of Greensborough, Geo...
 AARON FOREMAN, deceased. The Orphans Court of Dallas County, Alabama appointed DAVID MORGAN adm'r.
 THOMAS J. CAMPBELL and C. HUMPHREYS, executors and MARY H. CAMPBELL,
executrix of the will of ELIZABETH CAMPBELL of Dallas County.

February 17, 1821
 Married in Montgomery on Tuesday evening last Mr. NATHANIEL G. BROWN,
merchant of Selma to Miss ANN POWELL. In the same place on Wednesday
evening, NATHAN SARGENT, Esq. of this place to Mrs. ROSINA LEWIS of
Montgomery.
 Died at Washington City on the 11 inst. COL. THOMAS H. BOYLES of
Monroe Co. Ala.

March 10, 1821
 Married near Selma on Sunday evening last, Mr. BENAJAH KING to Miss
REBECCAH BRANTLEY.

May 26, 1821
 Married in this place Tuesday evening last by REV. LUCAS KENNEDY,
REV. JAMES L. SLOSS, Rector of Selma Academy to Mrs. LETITIA TROWBRIDGE
of this place. Note: LETITIA was nee CAMPBELL dau. of ELIZABETH. See
LETITIA's marriage to HENRY TROWBRIDGE Apr 1819 in our Vol 56; and our
Vol. 208 p. 11.

June 2, 1821
 Married in this county on Sunday evening last, Mr. WILLIAM FOSTER,
merchant of this place to Miss S(ABRINA) ROBERTS. Ancestor of Mrs.
Bettina Higdon, whose address in 1977 was Cullman, Alabama.

June 23, 1821
 Married on Tuesday evening by REV. J.L. SLOSS, WILLIAM TROTTER,
Esq. a senator from Washington County, to Mrs. PENELOPE VANDYKE of this
town.

June 30, 1821
 Married in Cahawba by REV. JAMES LONG SLOSS on Thursday evening last,
DR. THOMAS LESLY to Miss PELITIA M. LANE, daughter of EDMUND LANE, Esq.
all of this place. (See our Vol. 77 p. 36)
 Married last evening by J.B. THORINGTON, Esq. CAPT. WILLIAM BOSWELL
to Miss ELIZA LEE, daughter of CAPT. WILLIAM LEE of this county.
  State of Alabama-Green County
  ISAAC EDWARDS   )
    versus   ) Bill for Divorce
  RACHAEL EDWARDS)

*Cahawba County was established by the first Territorial Legislature and
is now Bibb County. But the town of Cahawba was in Dallas Co.

July 16, 1821
Departed this life, COL. JOHN TAYLOR, formerly of Pendleton, South
Carolina. Has been much exposed on his plantation situated on the
eastern bank of Alabama 8 or 10 miles below this town. He came on a
visit with his family to this place and on the 6th inst. died...He emigrated from Pendleton, South Carolina where he was elected to Congress
and continued to serve until he received the appointment of Receiver of
Public Monies at the Land Office. He died at the house of his brother,
GEN. WILLIAM TAYLOR from which his remains were accompanied to the burying ground by a procession of Masonic brothers...

July 30, 1821
Died at the residence of COL. M'CLELLAN about ten miles from town,
Mr. JOHN PERKINS, a young man much esteemed, who on his way from Mobile
to his place of residence at Vernon was taken sick...
Died at the residence of THOMAS A. ROGERS, Esq. about two miles from
town, MARY W. ROGERS, his eldest daughter aged 3 years.

August 6, 1821
Died in this place about 3 o'clock on Tuesday evening last in her
17th year, Miss SARAH LOWRY, daughter of JOHN LOWRY, Esq. of Maryville,
Tennessee...
HENRY WILLIAMS advertises that he is not responsible for the debts
of his wife, CATHARINE WILLIAMS.

August 13, 1821
Married in the vicinity of this place on Tuesday evening last,
THOMAS WHITE, Esq. of Cahawba to Miss ELIZABETH LEE, daughter of CAPT.
WILLIAM LEE all of this county.
Married in Pleasant Valley Thursday evening, Mr. EDWARD WOODS to
Miss CATHARINE MORRISON, both of this county. (See our Vol. 90 p. 10)
Married in Perry County, Mr. ROBERT SMITH to Miss RUTHY HUNTER.
Died in this town Sunday evening last in her 24th year, Mrs. ELIZA
KENNEDY, consort of REV. LUCAS KENNEDY.
State of Alabama-Wilcox County
"Wheras I have been unhappily married to MARY CARTER, daughter of
HEZEKIAH CARTER of Baldwin County, Georgia who has by her misconduct de-
prived me of all peace and happiness on this side of the grave I announce
to the world that we are separated forever and ever and, do hereby fur-
ther forewarn all persons from trading with her as I will not pay her
debts."   (Signed)   THORN. BROWN
State of Alabama-Greene County
NANCY HAMMON)
   versus   )   Bill for Divorce
JOHN HAMMON)

August 21, 1821
Died a few weeks ago in the vicinity of Mine Au Breton Mo. Mr. MOSES
AUSTIN, one of the earliest emigrants of that country...
Died in Mobile, CAPT. E. RUSSELL, formerly Commander of Steam Boat
Tensa.
Died at Mr. FRAZIER's on the way from Pensacola to Cahawba, EDWARD
BURROUGHS, Esq. merchant of Mobile, aged about 28 years. Native of
Boston and was highly esteemed.
Died in this town on Tuesday last, Mr. JAMES BELL, carpenter, native
of Ireland aged about 30.
Died at his residence in Tuskaloosa County on the 24th inst. COL.
RICHARDSON OWEN, Revolutionary officer in his 78th year.

August 27, 1821
Died in this place on the 24th inst...BENJAMIN W. TAYLOR, son of
BOWLING HALL TAYLOR of Montgomery County. A responsible carpenter and a
young man of benevolent character...
Died Sunday the 26th inst. DAVID DALTON, Esq. Clerk of the County
Court of this county in his 26th year. Emigrated from Bledsoe County,
Tennessee, where we understand his parents still reside...

Died in Washington County, Mrs. PENELOPE TROTTER, consort of COL. WM. TROTTER (the present member of the Senate from Washington County) and daughter of the late JUDGE CAMPBELL of Tennessee.
JESSE BEENE, attorney-at-law.

September 10, 1821
Died at Selma on the 23rd inst. WILLIAM BOOKER, of a liver complaint after an illness of three months.
Died on the 29th inst. in Pleasant Valley, THOMAS COWLES, infant son of GILBERT SHEARER, Esq. of this county aged 7 months and 10 days.
M.W. M'CLELLAN, COLONEL Com. of 22nd Regiment, A.M. JUSTUS REYNOLDS, deceased, from County Court of Bibb County, GILBERT REYNOLDS, adm'r.

September 17, 1821
Died in Tuskaloosa a few days since, Mr. WILLIAM MYGATT, printer. Emigrated from Weathersfield, Conn. to Georgia and came to this state in March last.

September 24, 1821
State of Alabama-Perry County
STEP. M'CRAW, deceased. SARAH M'CRAW, administrator and EDWARD M'CRAW, administrator.

October 1, 1821
THOMAS ROGERS, Esq. late Secretary of State, died at the house of a relation in Shelby County Saturday the 22nd of September. Himself, his wife and three children (all he had) were taken ill at his farm in the neighborhood of Cahawba about the 1st of August. Two weeks later, he lost two of his children...He was a native of East Tennessee and a Mason, Secretary of Grand Lodge of Alabama.
Died in this place Tuesday evening last, Mr. WILLIAM S. LA TOURETTE of the firm of La Tourette & Co. of Mobile.
Died on Tuesday evening last, Mr. ATHELSTON A.W. ANDREWS, a mechanic. Native of Martin County, North Carolina.
Died Thursday morning last, Mr. MICHAEL KENNY merchant tailor. Native of Ireland and lately from New York.
Died yesterday morning, Mr. JOSEPH GREEN HASKELL, carpenter, a native of New Salem, Mass.

October 15, 1821
Married Sunday evening on the 7th inst. at Claiborne by HON. REUBEN SAFFOLD, WILLIAM R. PATTON, Esq. attorney-at-law, to Miss MARY ELIZABETH SOUTL (or SCULL? - misprint)
Died in this town, Miss CAROLINE CAMPBELL, youngest daughter of the late JUDGE CAMPBELL of Tennessee.
Died of Typhus fever suddenly, Mr. JOHN H. BROOKS, late of Petersham, Mass. aged 19 years.
Died on the 11th inst. EDWARD REESE, son of REV. M.B. THOMASON aged 3 years and 4 days.
Died last evening, Mrs. EVELINE KREPS, wife of Mr. GEORGE KREPS.
Died at Green-castle, Penn. in his 69th year, GEORGE CLARK, Esq. late Collector of U.S. Revenue for that district.
Died near Sharpsburg in Washington County, Maryland, CAPT. JOSEPH CHAPLIN aged 75 years, a soldier of the Revolution.
WILLIAM DAVIS, deceased. Dallas Co. Ala. RANSOM DAVIS and PERSON DAVIS, admrs.

October 22, 1821
Married Thursday evening last in this vicinity, Mr. JOSEPH BERRY to the amiable Miss JUDITH OGLESBAY.
Died at his residence a few miles from this town Tuesday morning last, DAMIEL LORING, Esq. aged about 40 years. A Mason. He was born in Leicester, Mass. Resided for some time in South Carolina, where he married into a very respectable family and came to this country about 3 years since. Leaves an affectionate wife and an infant babe.

Note: Letter to Gandrud from Harold Delorme, Columbia, S.C. geneologist.
Aug. 25, 1954. "Do you have anything on the PITTS of Dallas Co.
say a JEREMIAH? He was of Sumter Co. S.C. His daughter married a
LORING & went to Ala. She m. DANIEL LORING of Mass. and Sumter Co. S.C.
and she was REBECCA M. PITTS, daughter of JEREMIAH and VOLUNTINE BRUNSON
PITTS of Sumter Co. S.C. The PITTS were from SE section of Va."

October 22, 1821, cont.
Died at his residence near the head of Bogue Chitto, Dallas County,
COL. THOMAS A. JONES aged about 50 years. Left a family. A native of
Virginia and had resided in this vicinity about a year.
Died of apoplexy on the 19th inst. at the house of Mr. ELI JACOBS
near Caulebe battle ground in Creek Nation. Mr. THOMAS MEANS, formerly
of Boston and late Clerk of the County Court of Perry County, Alabama
on a visit to friends in South Carolina.
Died at Louisville on the 4th inst. WILLIAM COCHRANE, Esq. Cashier
of the U.S. Branch Bank in that place. (Is Louisville, Ky. meant or
Louisville in Barbour Co. Ala?)
Died in Mobile suddenly on the 1st inst., JAMES D. MURREL, a carpenter, late of this place and emigrant from Tennessee.

October 29, 1821
Married on the 11th inst., at Pleasant Retreat, Bedford County,
Tennessee by REV. NEWTON, HENRY HITCHCOCK, Esq. of Cahawba, attorney
general of this state to Miss ANNE, daughter of COL. ANDREWS ERWIN of
the former place.
Died in this town, Mrs. MARGARET KENNY, wife of Mr. PATRICK DENNY.
Died in the vicinity of this place on the 13th inst. LOUISA ANN,
only child of JONAS BROWN, Esq. aged 7 weeks.
Died in this town, the infant child of the late COL. JOHN TAYLOR.

November 5, 1821
Died in this place Sunday morning last after a long and tedious illness, Mrs. MARGARET CAMPBELL, late of Tennessee in her 18th year.

December 17, 1821
Died...Mrs. ELIZABETH PHILIPS, consort of MAJ. A.M. PHILIPS of
Carrolton on the 20th of October last in her 27th year. Left her husband
and four small children.

January 21, 1822
Married near Claiborne on the 30th inst. STEPHEN STEELE, Esq. of
this town to Miss ELIZABETH J. RIVERS, daughter of REV. JOEL RIVERS of
Monroe County.
Note: REV. JOEL RIVERS was a local preacher - m. RHODA - from N.C.
to Monroe Co. Ala. before 1816.
Married in this town, Mr. DRURY H. WADE of Perry County, to Miss
BETSY WADDELL of this town.
Died in Washington, Autauga County, Alabama on the 13th inst. JOHN
MATTHEWS, Esq. formerly a citizen of Milledgeville, Geo.

January 28, 1822
Married Tuesday evening last by ARMSTEAD NORMAN, Esq. DUNKLIN
SULLIVAN, attorney and couseller at law, to the amiable Miss MARY
MAYBERRY, all of Perry Co.
Note: MABRY in marriage record. DUNKLIN was son of HEWLETT
SULLIVAN. In 1850 MARY was then a widow age 47 b Tenn.; in Perry Co.
Ala. See our Vol. 118 p. 6.

April 13, 1822
FOREST GREEN announces that he is not responsible for the debts of
his wife, ELIZA GREEN.
HUGH LAMB, deceased. Dallas County, Alabama. HUGH LAMB, Jr. admr.
(In 1850 Census Clarke Co. Ala. one HUGH LAMB 50, birthplace unknown,
wife ELIZ. 50 SC & 6 chn. b in Ala.

May 4, 1822
Married in the vicinity of this town on the 11th inst. by J.H.
THORINGTON, Esq. DOCT. ROCK PARSONS to Miss MARIA MORRIS.
Married in this county on Sunday last by J.H. THORINGTON Esq. COL.
EDMUND LANE to Mrs. MATILDA LORING.
Died in Winchester, Tennessee on the 4th inst. Mr. CHARLES ROGERS,
formerly a resident of this town.
JAMES MAY and wife, MARTHA H. MAY, administrators of WASHINTON
NORWOOD, deceased, of Greene Co. Ala.

June 8, 1822
Married in this town Thursday last by NATHAN SARGENT, Esq. Mr.
JOSEPH NEGUS to Miss ELIZABETH TITCOMB.

June 15, 1822
State of Alabama-Wilcox County
ANDREW THOMSON)
    versus   ) Bill for divorce - Also reversed
SALLY THOMSON) She sues him, too.

June 22, 1822
Died in this town at Cahawba Hotel yesterday at 2 p.m. MILTON TILDEN,
Esq. of Washington County, not quite 23 years old...A stranger to most
of us.

June 29, 1822
Married in Greene County, Tuesday the 18th inst. by REV. Mr. RYAN,
Mr. ISAIAH H. AYNESWORTH, to Miss NANCY ANN SEATON. (Note: Green Co.
marriages were destroyed up to 1823.)
Died in this town on Tuesday inst. of typhus fever, Mr. WILLIAM
TABELE, formerly of Philadelphia but for several years past a responsible
citizen of Mobile...
Died on Thursday last, Mr. AMBROSE II. DAY, a saddler, native of
South Carolina.

July 13, 1822
Died at Washington, Autauga County, Alabama on the 3rd of typhus
fever, Mr. EPHRAIM J. PEYTON, attorney native of Tennessee and though
but for a short time a resident of Washington was a useful citizen...

August 3, 1822
ELFENDER THOMAS, administratrix of JOHN THOMAS, deceased. Bibb
County, Alabama.
Departed this life on Friday morning at 10 o'clock after a tedious
illness, Miss MARY H. ROBERTS in her 15th year, daughter of WILLIS
ROBERTS, Esq. a merchant of this place.

August 10, 1822
Married on the 28th of February last in Greensborough, by Mr. RYAN,
Mr. ALEXANDER WEYSS, merchant, to Miss SOPHIA PECK. Note: see will of
her father, ABIJAH PECK in our Vol. 14 p. 12.
Married on March 5th, 5 miles from Greensborough by Rev. Mr. MONETT,
Mr. GEORGE BRIGGS to Miss MALINDA HOPSON.
Married on March 10th, 3 miles from Greensborough by Rev. Mr. RYON,
Mr. EZEKIEL SLAUTER to Miss ANN PENDLETON.
Married in Clarke County, Geo. on April 17th, Mr. JOHN E. GAGE, son
of MATTHEW GAGE, Esq. of the neighborhood of Greensborough to Miss ELIZA
ECTOR of the former place.
Married the last of April, 2 miles from Greensborough, Mr. K.
BENNETT to Miss HOPPER.
Married on 29th of April, 2 miles from Greensborough by Rev. Mr.
RYON, Mr. JOHN HOLDEN to Miss JUDITH RYON.
Married on 1st of May by Rev. Mr. HUNTER, Mr. EDWARD SEAMON,
merchant of Greensborough to Miss MARTHA E.R. SHACKLEFORD, daughter of
JAMES SHACKLEFORD, Esq. of Perry County. Note: See our Vol. 118 p. 7;
Vol. 87 p. 23 m. in Perry Co.

Married on May 2nd, 2 miles from Greensborough by Rev. Mr. HUNTER, Mr. E.B. WOOD of Ft. Claiborne to Miss ANNE MCKINNE.

Married the last of May, 3 miles from Greensborough by HELLEN WALDROP, Esq. Mr. ELI SEALE to Miss MABRY.

Married in Greensborough on May 17th by Rev. Mr. HUNTER, Mr. JESSE SAUNDERS to Miss ROSA CLEMENT. Note: She was dau. of EDWARD CLEMENT who d. in Sumter Co. Ala. 1840. Calls her "ROSY" SANDERS wife of JESSE P. SANDERS. A SANDERS child, ROSY living with her Clement children in 1850 Census.

Married on the same day and place by Rev. Mr. RYON, Mr. SILAS BAGGETT to Miss NICY WILLIAMS.

Married on the 4th of June by Rev. Mr. HUNTER, Mr. A.F. REES, merchant of Greensborough to Miss SARAH MATHIS of Perry County. Note: "MATTHEWS" in marriage record in Perry Co. See our Vol. 118 p. 8.

Married in Greensborough on the 27th of June by Rev. Mr. RYON, Mr. JOSEPH JOLLY to Miss MARY MILLER.

Married on the 18th by REV. DR. FLECHER, MAJ. JOHN W(HITFIELD) WILSON to Miss GLERENDA W. daughter of JACOB LENDSAY, Esq. of Marengo Co. Note: See our Vol. 29 p. 49. Ancestor of J. DEWITT COOPER, Jasper, Ala. 1877.

August 17, 1822

Married in this town Thursday evening last by Rev. Mr. SLOSS, MAJOR JESSE BEANE, attorney of this place to Miss CATHERINE BIRD, late of Georgia. Note: From Montgomery (Ala) Republican Fri. Aug. 23, 1822 "m. at Cahawba on the 15th inst. JESSE BEENE, Esq. to Miss CAROLINE BYRD."

Died in Selma, Mr. NATHANIEL L. HAYDEN, merchant formerly of Connecticut; REV. Mr. SNEAD, a member of the Methodist Church.

Died in Claiborne, DOCT. NATHANIEL ALLEN, formerly of Connecticut but for several years a respectable citizen of this state.

State of Alabama-Dallas County.

DANIEL LORING, deceased. GEORGE W. PITTS and EDMUND LANE, adm'r.

August 31, 1822

Died in Claiborne, MAJ. HENRY C. CARTER, Mr. JAMES LUNDY aged 71 years; JOSEPH CALHOUN, merchant, aged 30 years; Mr. JOSEPH ELMS, a native of Boston, aged 22.

Died in Monroe County, Mr. ROWLAND SHERMAN, merchant of Claiborne aged 25; CAPT. WILLIAM SMITH, a soldier of the Revolution aged 81; Mr. JAMES MORGAN aged 61; Mr. FARQUER R. SHAW aged 16.

Died in Clark County, Mr. WILLIAM RABURG, a native of Baltimore.

September 14, 1822

Died at Coosawda, Alabama Monday the 9th inst. Miss CAROLINE HITCHCOCK after an illness of eighteen days; had just entered her 18th year...

Died while on a visit at St. Stephens, Mr. DAVIS H. MAYHEW, Rector of Coosawda Academy and formerly of Hampshire County, Massachusetts.

Died in this town on Monday evening last, COL. ROBERT H. DRAUGHTON of Claiborne, an amiable young man...mason.

Died near Bogue Chitto, REV. E. MOSELEY.

Died at his residence near Williamsburg, Virginia on August 6th, Mr. RANDOLPH ROPER in his 61st year.

October 12, 1822

Died in this town Wednesday the 25th inst. of bilious fever, Mr. THOMAS EWING aged 51. Left numerous family.

Died, WILLIAM, only son of GEORGE KREPS aged 2 years and 9 months.

Died, Mrs. PELETIAH, wife of DR. THOMAS LESLY. Left an afflicted husband and a tender infant.

Died Thursday morning last, EMELINE ELIZA, youngest daughter of WILLIAM B. ALLEN, aged 8 years.

Died, the infant child of J.B. PATRICK.

Died, an old German engraver named JOHN LINDY BOWER.

October 19, 1822
    Married on 30th of July last by Rev. Mr. SHAFER, Mr. WILLIAM H.
MIERS of Cahawba to Miss SOPHIA BYERLY of Frederickstown, Maryland.
    Married Thursday the first by JOHN SPANN, Esq. Mr. SANDERSON SMITH
to Miss ANNE, daughter of ALEXANDER MOORE, both of Marengo Co. See our
Vol. 29 pp. 11, 49.
    Married Thursday the 15th by JOHN SPANN, Esq. Mr. OBADIAH PERKINS
to Miss SALLY MOORE, daughter of ALEXANDER MOORE, both of said co. See
our Vol. 19, pp 11, 49.
    Died on Sunday last, CHARLES MORRIS aged 17 years, a native of New
York and nearly four years a resident of this state.
    Died at Abbeville Court House, S.C., CAPT. LARK ABNEY of Claiborne,
this state. Note: In will of LARK ABNEY, of Edgefield Dist. S.C. he says
he is of Monroe Co. Ala; wife MARTHA ABNEY. Dated 6 Aug. 1822 probated
14 Jan. 1822. Box & Pkg. No. 3 did not obtain this will (WPA copy) in
State Archives of Columbia.
    Died at Milledgeville, COL. ROBERT RUTHERFORD.
    Died, Mr. OLIVER HOLMAN, merchant of Mobile and formerly of Boston.
    Died, Mr. JOHN B. HINES, one of the Editors of the Georgia Journal.

December 7, 1822
    Married in this town on Thursday evening last by Rev. Mr. SLOSS,
Mr. JOHN W. RIVERS to Miss ANN ELIZABETH TRAVERS, daughter of ROBERT
TRAVERS, Esq.

December 14, 1822
    Died at Blakeley on the 15th of bilious malignant fever, JAMES W.
PETERS, Esq...merchant.

February 22, 1823
    Married in this town on Thursday evening last by J.H. THORINGTON,
Esq. FIELDING VAUGHAN, merchant of this place to Miss MARTHA HATCHER,
daughter of JAMES HATCHER, Esq. of this county. (In 1850 census,
FIELDING was 51 b Va. MARTHA 45 b Ga.)

April 5, 1823
    Married in this place Thursday March 20th by J.H. THORINGTON, Esq.
Mr. JOSEP C. HUDDLESTON to Miss ELIZA S. ROBESON.
    Married Thursday evening last in the vicinity of this town by
N. SARGENT, Esq. Mr. WILLIAM B. HARRELSON to Miss PAMELIA BROWNING,
daughter of MAJ. WILLIAM BROWNING.

March 24, 1823
        State of Alabama Dallas County
    JAMES NALL   )
      versus   ) Bill for Divorce
    ELIZABETH NALL)
    The original bill states that they were married in Grainger County,
Tennessee September 25, 1810 and immediately removed to Bedford County,
Tennessee where they separated in 1819. Note: One JAMES NALL m. in
Grainger Co. Tenn. Sept. 18, 1806 ELIZABETH WAGGONER.
    Married in this town Tuesday evening last by JOHN H. THORINGTON,
Esq. Mr. JOSEPH CAMP to Mrs. ELIZA SUTCLIFFE.
    Died in this town Tuesday evening last, Mrs. CATHARINE TRAVERSE,
consort of Mr. ROBERT TRAVERSE, formerly of Baltimore.

May 31, 1823
    Married in Milledgeville on the 14th, Mr. EDWIN CURTIS of Cahawba
to Miss HENRIETTA B. PITTS of the former place. See our Vol. 88, p. 51.
    Married in Tuscaloosa by L. POWELL, Esq. THOMAS OWEN, Esq. attorney
to Miss DOLLY WILLIAMS, daughter of MARMADUKE WILLIAMS, Esq. all of that
place.

June 21, 1823
    Married in the vicinity of this place Thursday evening last by
WILLIAM W. GARY, Esq. Mr. WILLIAM GREEN to Miss SARAH, daughter of RANSOM
DAVIS, Esq. Note: WM. F. GREENE m. SARAH DAVIS June 19, 1823.

July 12, 1823
     Married on the 25th at Marengo Court House by REV. WM. FLUKER,
DR. JAMES KELLY to Miss JANE JORDON, daughter of Mr. JOHN JORDON,
merchant, all of said place. See our Vol. 29, p. 52.
     Died in Jonesborough, Jefferson County, Alabama, Monday the 7th
inst. MAJOR THOMAS MCHENRY of Montevallo, late candidate for Congress.

July 19, 1823
     Died in this town on Tuesday last, COL. EDMUND LANE...

July 26, 1823
     Died in this town Thursday last, Mrs. L. ALLEN, consort of WILLIAM
B. ALLEN, Esq. native of Newburyport, Mass...

August 30, 1823
     Died in this town Wednesday last, Mr. NICHOLAS CROCHERON aged 33,
formerly of New York but for the last four years a citizen of this town.

September 13, 1823
     Died in this town Tuesday last, Mr. JOSEPH MEGUS formerly of
Brattsboro, Vt. aged 25.
     Died on Saturday, the 6th inst. Mr. JOSHUA RUMPH lately from South
Carolina...Florence Gazette.

September 20, 1823
     Died in this town Friday the 12th inst. Mrs. HULDAH ALLEN aged 75,
formerly of Massachusetts.
     Died in Cahawba Valley a short time since, COL. EBENEZER LEETH, a
native of Tennessee.

September 27, 1823
     Married at Tuscumbia on August 21st, Mr. RICHARD B. BRICKELL, Junior
Editor of the Alabamian, to Miss MARGARET COMMONS (note: Should be COMAN)
     Died August 30th in Knoxville, Tennessee, Mrs. E(LIZABETH C) ARM-
ATRONG, wife of MAJ. F(RANCIS) W(ELLS) ARMSTRONG of Mobile, a bride of a
few months. Note: She was dau. of WM. AYLETT and wife, MARTHA A. POSEY;
and gr-dau. of WM. AYLETT and wife MARY MACON.
     Died in Selma on the 19th, MARY ANN, wife of DOCT. J.S.W. PARKIN...
     Died in Mobile on the 17th inst. DR. JOHN MEEKER, a native of New
Jersey but for the last six years a resident of this county, when he
moved to Mobile on February last.

October 4, 1823
     Died on the 28th in Shelby County at Montevallo, Mrs. HUMPHREYS,
consort of DR. CARLISLE HUMPHREYS, late of this place.

October 11, 1823
     Died in this town on the 21st inst. Miss ELIZABETH D. CLARK, aged 20.
     Died Tuesday the 23rd last, Miss LUCY B. ALLEN, daughter of WILLIAM
B. ALLEN aged 11 years.
     Died in this place on Monday last, GEORGE V. DICK, Esq. native of
Scotland aged about 33. He emigrated to Richmond, Virginia about 3 years
ago and became a resident of this place...

October 18, 1823
     Died at their residence, in Marengo County, HENRY WOOLF in his 78th
year and wife ELIZABETH in her 76th year, after having lived together
for nearly 60 years and raising 13 children, eleven of whom are now
living. Both fell sick on 25th of September and expired within a few
hours of each other on the 3rd and are buried in the same grave. He was
a native of Virginia and fought in the Revolutionary War; he emigrated
to this state from Kentucky in 1819, since which time he has resided in
Marengo County.
     Departed this life December 12th, COL. WILLIAM LEE of Butler County
...Among the first ranks that volunteered for service on the frontiers
of Georgia and commanded a brave company of freemen from Jones County...

November 29, 1823
    Died in Autauga County on the 19th inst. JONATHON MAXEY, Esq.
attorney, in his 21st year, son of the late DR. MAXEY, President of
Columbia College.

December 10, 1823
    Died in this town yesterday, Mrs. MARY ANN TAYLOR, consort of GEN.
WILLIAM TAYLOR and daughter of GEN. D.B. MITCHELL aged 23 years...Left
a husband and three children, the youngest only a few days old.

January 17, 1824
    Married on the 5th inst. on Bogue Chitto, Mr. SIMPSON GORMAN to
Miss MARIA VANN, both of this county. (One SIMPSON GORMAN was in 1850
Census Bradley Co. Ark.
        GORMAN, SIMPSON   45 SC
                VASHTI   45 Ga
                JOSEPH V   19 Ala
                JAS M   15 Ala
                JACKSON O   14 Ala
                MARGARET E 12 Miss
                DAVID F   8 Miss
                MARIA   6 Miss

December 27, 1823
    Married Thursday the 27th at the house of MAJOR HAYES, in Monroe
County by REV. Mr. THING, Mr. RICHARD H. HAYES of Conecuh County to
Miss ELIZA M. COLE, of Green County, Georgia.
    Married Sunday the 9th inst. CAPT. STEPHEN HERD DOSS to Miss MINERVA
BARTON, both of Marengo Co. See our Vol. 29, p. 53.

March 6, 1824
    Died on the 1st inst. SAMUEL TURNER, Esq. Chief Clerk in the
Secretary of Senate's Office.

March 12, 1824
    Died on the 18th inst. GEORGE BUCHANAN of St. Stephens...

April 17, 1826
    Married Thursday evening last on Bogue Chitto Mr. JOHN BLANN to
Miss BETSEY M'ELROY, daughter of JAMES M'ELROY.

April 24, 1824
    Married Sunday the 18th inst. by JUDGE DARGENT, WILLIS RANDLE, Esq.
to Miss TELITHA C. HUCKABY, daughter of Mr. BRITTAIN HUCKABY, both of
this vicinity. See our Vol. 208, p. 2.
    Died in Milledgeville, Georgia on the 18th of March Mrs. REBECCA
P. MITCHELL, consort of the late DAVID BRYDIE MITCHELL and daughter of
PETERSON THWEAT, Esq. in her 23rd year.

May 1, 1824
    Died in Mobile on the 17th inst. DANIEL DUVOL, Esq. formerly of
Rhode Island and for many years a resident of that place.

May 8, 1824
    Married in this town Wednesday evening the 28th inst. by REV. Mr.
MOORE, Mr. WILLIAM BOWER to Miss LOUISIANA RUTHERFORD, youngest daughter
of THOMAS N(ROOKS) RUTHERFORD, all of this county. See our Vol. 77,
p. 80.
    Died a few miles from Linden, JAMES C., youngest son of B.P. WHIT
LOW.
    Died on the 18th at Linden, Mr. CHARLES MILLER, merchant.
    Died in this place on Sunday last, Miss REBECCA TRAVERS, formerly
of Baltimore.

NOTE: These items taken from newspapers filed in the Library of Congress,
Washington, D.C.

THE HALCYON

Printed and published by THO. EASTIN every Thursday of
Greensborough, Greene County, Alabama. Note: Greens-
borough is now in Hale County but was then a part of
Greene Co.

April 24, 1823
From Huntsville, March 21st, MAJOR JOHN W. WALKER died yesterday
evening about 4 o'clock at his residence 11 miles from this place...
From Alabamian.

May 1, 1823
All persons indebted to the estate of THOMAS L. PATTERSON deceased
come forth and settle. LEWIS STEVENS, administrator and MARTHA STEVENS,
administratrix.

May 22, 1823
Married Thursday evening last by REV. J. HILLHOUSE, Mr. JAMES B.
GAGE to Miss SANDERS, daughter of CAPT. JEREMIAH SANDERS, all of Greene
County.

May 29, 1823
Departed this life Monday May 26th, Mrs. SOPHIA, consort of
PLEASANT HENDERSON of Greene County.

June 5, 1823
Married Thursday evening the 29th of May, Mr. THOMAS L. JONEGAN, to
Miss SARAH HARDIN, daughter of MARK HARDIN, all of Greene Co.
On the same day, Mr. CYRUS TORBERT, merchant of Erie to Miss HENLEY
near that place.

June 12, 1823
Married on Thursday June 5 by REV. J. HILLHOUSE, Mr. JAMES MEANS to
Miss ELIZA PATTON, all of Greene County.

July 3, 1823
Died on Saturday night last CYRUS TORBERT, Esq. Postmaster at Erie,
Mr. TORBERT had acquired the esteem of all his acquaintances...

July 16, 1823
Married Thursday last by REV. Mr. RYAN, Mr. MOSES M'WHIRTER to Miss
ELIZABETH TATUM, all of Greene Co.

July 17, 1823
Married Thursday evening the 9th, Mr. ALLEN M'DONALD of Greensborough
to Miss KISSIAH WHITSETT, daughter of L(AWRENCE) WHITSETT, Esq. of Greene
Co.
Died last night of a lingering illness, Mr. ROBERT MILLER of this
place; his friends are invited to attend the funeral from the house of
Mr. HENRY SOSSAMAN this day at 4 o'clock p.m.

July 31, 1823
Departed this life at his residence near Erie, after a short but
severe illness on the 20th, JOHN H. CARSON, Esq. He removed from South
Caroline to this county. Had inflammation of the brain. Left a widow
and two small children. See our Vol. 14, p. 6 for his will.

August 21, 1823
Departed this life, Mrs. MARTHA PICKENS, wife of Governor Pickens
at the Governor's residence near this place on the 16th at about 5
o'clock p.m...Left a husband and four helpless children.
Died Friday the 15th, DOCTOR SILAS MAGUIRE at his residence near
this place.

September 11, 1823
ANN LAWSON, administratrix of the estate of JAMES LAWSON, deceased.

September 25, 1823
Departed this life, HENRY Y. WEBB, Judge of the Third Judicial
Circuit of this state; died at his private residence in Greene County

Saturday Sept. 20 at 9:35 p.m. after a severe illness of 16 days...
Left a wife and five interesting children. As a brother, he was a brother.
        DAVID DAVIES notifies the public that he is no longer responsible
for the debts of his wife, SARAH DAVIES since she has left his bed and
board.

October 2, 1823
        SOPHIA BATES administratrix of the estate of WILLIAM BATES, deceased,
advertises for runaway slave.
        J.M. BATES, administrator of the estate of LEONARD CARDIN, deceased.

November 1, 1823
        Died at his residence near Cahawba, Dallas County, Ala. on the 20th,
JAMES S. GAINES aged about 45. In the forepart of the summer, his family
were visited with a fever of a very malignant type, which swept off his
wife and one daughter...he lost a son at St. Stephens...
        JOHN C. O'REAR, deceased. WILLIS CRENSHAW, admr.

February 21, 1824
        By a gentleman direct from St. Stephens, we hear of death of
DR. GEORGE BUCHANAN.
        ELIZA WEBB, administratrix and THOMAS WEBB, adm'r of HENRY Y. WEBB,
deceased.

GREENE COUNTY GAZETTE

        Printed and published by J.J. CRIBBS at Erie, Greene
        County, Alabama on Monday morning. This bound file of
        newspapers when copied by me (Gandrud) was in the Probate
        Office at Eutaw, Greene Co. Ala. This was in the 1930's.
        I understand it is no longer there. I do not know where
        it is now. Perhaps the Library at Eutaw.

May 17, 1830
        Married on Sunday evening the 9th instant by REV. J.H. WELLS, Mr.
JEREMIAH SANDERS to Mrs. LUCY GRIGGS, both of this county.
        CAPTAIN DENNIS MCGUIRE and those under his employ were engaged in
freighting barge, Fox at Demopolis, Marengo County. An explosion oc
curred and he died the Friday following. He was an Irishman by birth,
and formerly a resident of New York, but had resided in this state six
or seven years.
        State of Alabama-Greene County. Orphans Court, May Term 1830.
PETER GALLARD, deceased. Final settlement of estate.
        JOHN MEEK, administrator of estate of HENRY W (should be Y) WEBB,
deceased. Final settlement of estate.
        May Term 1830. Note: MEEK married the widow ELIZA WEBB in 1826.
See our Vol. 17, p. 56.

May 31, 1830
        Died Saturday, the 22nd instant in Greensboro, Alabama, Mrs. NANCY
C. HILLHOUSE in her 37th year. Left a large circle of relatives and
friends. She professed religion in 1812; was a tender wife, mother and
mistress. She left a husband and three little daughters.
        Died at his residence in this county on the 25th inst. Mr. GREEN
HILL in the 57th year of his age, leaving large and respectable
connections. (Communicated.)
        Died Saturday night, 29th inst. CAROLINE, daughter of ISAAC C. and
SARAH C. SNEDECOR, aged four months.
        Died in Tuscaloosa Tuesday 25th inst. at half past twelve Mrs. MARY
AMELIA THORNTON, wife of JAMES J(INNIS) THORNTON, Esq., Secretary of
State. She was aged 21 years and 5 months. Left a husband and two
infant female children.

June 7, 1830
        State of Alabama-Greene County, Orphans Court, May Term 1830.
HONORE BAYOL, administrator of PETER GALLARD, deceased.

11.

June 14, 1830
Mr. JOHN MOCK, residing in Bogue Chitto, Dallas County was murdered on the 28th ult. He was a native of North Carolina.

June 21, 1830
Died in this county on the 18th inst. WILLIAM P. MCDOWELL, Esq. highly respected citizen and a promising member of the Bar. Native of Fayette County, Kentucky, where his father and numerous relations still reside. The funeral will be held with Masonic honors at the residence of his brother, in this county on the 19th inst.

June 28, 1830
Died on Monday the 21st ult. at his residence near Springfield, MAJOR WILLIAM CHILES aged 56 years.
Married on 18th BY OBADIAH HAMPTON, Esq. Mr. WILEY DICKERSON to Miss NANCY SWIFT, all of this county. See our Vol. 17 p. 88 for marriage license which says "WILLY P. DICKISON" & m. on 19th.
Married in Perry Co. on the 19th inst. DR. L.B. BARTLE, formerly of Louisiana to Miss ____ RODDY of that county. See our Vol. 198 p. 17 for marriage record of "LAMBERT" B. BARTLE to JANE RODDY 19 June 1830.

July 5, 1830
Married in this county on the 29th inst. by THOMAS RIDDLE, Esq. Mr. WILLIAM BOYKIN of Springfield to Miss WILLY RICHARDSON of this Co.

July 19, 1830
Married on Thursday evening last by W.N. MOFFETT, Esq. Mr. JOHN D. RICHARDS, merchant of Carthage, Tuscaloosa County to Miss FRANCES MOUNGER of Greene County.
Died Thurs. evening on the 15th inst. Mrs. NANCY KENNARD, wife of JAMES P. KENNARD of this vicinity.

July 26, 1830
Died on the night of the 20th inst. in this vicinity, Miss ELIZA D. STEELE aged 14 years, daughter of JAMES D. and MARY STEELE, all of Jones County, Georgia (Communicated).

August 2, 1830
Died at her residence in this county on the 28th ult. after a painful illness, Mrs. VIRGINIA BAYOL in her 19th year.
Married on Thursday evening, the 22nd inst. by REV. JAMES HILLHOUSE, REV. THOMAS ALEXANDER of Dallas to Miss MARGERY, second daughter of CAPT. ROBERT BELL of Perry County.
ELIJAH MOORE)
   versus   ) Bill for Divorce
SARAH MOORE) March Term 1830

August 16, 1830
Married on 12th inst. by R.M. CUNNINGHAM, Esq. Mr. ____ CONROE to Miss BETSEY M'COWAN, both of the vicinity of Carthage, Tuscaloosa County. See our Vol. 25 p. 45.
Notice: Commissioners appointed by the Orphans Court of Greene County, Alabama to examine claims of creditors of ABSALOM ALSTON, deceased.
    JOHN MARRAST
    JOHN MALONE

August 13, 1830
EDWARD JAY OSBORNE Estate of JOSEPH HEARNE deceased.

August 30, 1830
Died on the 20th at the residence in Greene County. SAMUEL ARCHIBALD, Esq. aged 68 years and 3 months, of pulmonary consumption; native of North Carolina and when very young man, an active soldier in the Revolutionary war and for many years a number and elder in the Presbyterian Church (Communicated).
Died at DR. WILLIAM PURNELL's in Greene County Saturday 31st of July, DR. E.P. STEELE, late from South America. His sister will hear something much to her interest by applying to DR. WILLIAM PURNELL. Editors of <u>Kentucky Reporter</u> and <u>St. Louis Beacon</u> please publish.

Married on the 18th inst. by WILLIAM A. FORTSON, Esq. Mr. JAMES R.
DUNLAP to Miss MARY BOND, all of this county.
Married on the 19th inst. by REV. JOHN H. GRAY Mr. J.C(ANFIELD
BUNNELLE of Springfield to Miss ELIZA K. DUNLAP of this county.
State of Alabama-Greene County. Orphans Court, August 16, 1830.
JACOB ATKINSON, deceased. JETHRO HARRISON and MILBERRY ATKINSON, ad-
ministrator and administratrix.
Married Tuesday 17th inst. at the residence of JOHN C. PERRY near
Cahawba (or Chawba) by HON. REUBEN SAFFOLD, Mr. THOMAS H. WILEY, Editor
of the Intelligencer to Miss LOUISA PERRY of Dallas County.

September 6, 1830
Died on the 10th of August near Washington City, GEORGE GRAHAM, Esq.
Commissioner of General Land Office.
WILLIAM P. MCDOWELL, deceased. JOHN N. MCDOWELL, administrator.

September 20, 1830
EPHRAIM P. STEELE, deceased. HORTENSIUS Q. PURNELL, administrator.
15 September 1830.

October 25, 1830
Died on the 11th at the residence of his mother in this county,
Mr. WILLIAM SANDERSON, native of Pennsylvania, in his 41st year. He
emigrated to this state at an early period of its settlement. (Communicated.)
State of Alabama-Greene County. Orphans Court. WILLIAM B. ALLEN,
executor in right of his wife, MARY C. ALLEN, and MARY L. ALLEN, executrix of will of JOHN H. CARSON, deceased. October 4, 1830.

November 15, 1830
WILLIAM BELL, administrator of estate of JOHN W. RABB, deceased.
WILLIAM L. BROWN, deceased. BREWSTER H. JAYNE, administrator.

December 13, 1830
Married on the 2nd inst. by REV. Mr. CUNNINGHAM, Mr. JAMES COLEMAN
to Miss MARTHA ANDERSON, all of this county.
Married on Sunday evening 12th inst. by REV. S.K. JENNINGS, Esq.
Mr. LAWRENCE HILYER to Miss SYLVIA LANGFORD, all of this vicinity.
Obituary..Died on the 10th ult. at his residence in Greene County,
Mr. DANIEL W. TILMAN in his 30th year etc.

December 20, 1830
Married on the 15th inst. Mr. JOHN HILLHOUSE to Miss (JANE) LAWSON,
all of the vicinity of Greensboro
Married on the 16th by T.F. MOODY, Esq. Mr. JAMES SHACKELFORD of
Perry County to Miss NANCY ATKINSON of this place.
BENJAMIN COOPER, deceased. GEORGE HAYS, adm'r.
MATILDA SANDERSON, administratrix of estate of WILLIAM SANDERSON,
deceased.
JOSEPH HUTTON, deceased. WILLIAM HUTTON and AMOS TIMS, executors
of will.
Circuit Court of Greene County Alabama
ANN M'JOHNSON   )
   versus   ) Bill for divorce
SOLOMON M'JOHNSON   )

December 27, 1830
Married on the 30th of November in Batavia, New York by HON. SIMEON
CUMMINGS, Mr. GEORGE W. HARRIS to Mrs. LUCINDA, widow of the late
celebrated WILLIAM MORGAN.

January 10, 1831
Married on the 9th inst. by DR. H.L. KENNON, Esq. Mr. JAMES B.
M'DONALD to Miss SUSAN GAINS, all of this vicinity.

January 24, 1831
JOHN KENNARD, administrator of estate of CADER STALLINGS, deceased
to make title to FREDERICK PECK, executor of will of ABIJAH PECK, late
of said county, deceased.

January 31, 1831
JEREMIAH SANDERS, administrator of estate of BENJAMIN WILSON,
deceased.

February 7, 1831
Married on 2nd inst. by REV. J(OHN) H. GRAY, DR. A(QUILLA) D.
HUTTON to Miss ELIZABETH TUTT, all of the vicinity of Clinton, Greene
County.
Died in Greene County on 4th January 1831, JAMES H. SMITH of
lingering pulmonary disease (Communicated).

February 21, 1831
CHRISTOPHER C. SCOTT, administrator of estate of TURNER D. BELL,
deceased.
THOMAS H. GORDAN, deceased. JEFFERSON GORDAN, administrator and
CAROLINE GORDAN, administratrix.
DANIEL THOMPSON, administrator of estate of FLORA THOMPSON, deceased.

March 10, 1831
Married on Tuesday the 22nd inst. Mr. THOMAS WILSON to Miss EMILY
LONGMIRE, all of this county.
Married on _____ by REV. J.H. GRAY, Mr. HINESBERRY BONDS to Miss
ANN KENNEDY all of this county.
Married on _____ by REV. J(OSEPH) P. CUNNINGHAM, Mr. JOHN HERRIN to
Miss ELIZABETH CAMPBELL all of the vicinity of Havanna.
Married on _____ by REV. R.G. CHRISTOPHER, Mr. LUKE WILLIAMS to
Miss NANCY DICKINSON, all of this county.
Married on _____ by _____ Mr. JAMES BRYAN to Miss MOURNING BATTEN.
Married on Tuesday 1st inst. by Mr. JAMES HILLHOUSE, Mr. ERASMUS
WYNNE to Miss SEMPHRONIA ANDERSON, all of this county.
Married on the 9th inst. by HON. T.F. MOODY of this place, Mr.
MATTHEW TALBOT to Miss HARRIET S. GAYLE, both of the vicinity of
Springfield.

March 24, 1831
JOHN W. SMITH and WRIGHT W. SMITH, executors of will of JAMES H.
SMITH, deceased.

April 21, 1831
State of Alabama-Greene County. Orphans Court WILLIAM L. DUFPHEY,
administrator of estate of WILLIAM DUPHEY, deceased.
JAMES F. MAY and JOHN MAY, administrators of estate of JOHN MAY,
deceased.

April 28, 1831
Married on 5th inst. by REV. JOHN H. GRAY, THOMAS RIDDLE, Esq. to
Miss ELIZABETH M. CHILES, eldest daughter of Mr. THOMPSON CHILES, all of
the vicinity of Springfield.
FREDERICK PECK, administrator of estate of THOMAS PECK, deceased.

May 5, 1831
RICHARD B. WALTHALL, executor of last will and testament of DAVID W.
EASLEY, deceased.

May 19, 1831
Married on the 11th inst. by HON. T.F. MOODY, DR. FRANCIS L.
MERIWETHER to Miss ELIZABETH J. LONG, both of the vicinity of Springfield.

May 26, 1831
ANN PERRY, administratrix of estate of JOSIAH PERRY, deceased. His
late residence on the road leading from Greensboro to Havanna for sale.

June 2, 1831
Died on Tuesday the 24th at his residence in this county, Mr. EDWARD
FINCH at an advanced age.
Died at Springfield on the 25th inst. Mr. PHILIP WEAVER some time
a resident of that place.
Married at Prairie Bluff on 19th inst. by REV. JOHN W. WILSON,
Mr. WILLIAM J. DEXTER to Miss JULIET ATWOOD, sister of Mr. HENRY S.
ATWOOD respected merchant of that place.
Married on 29th inst. by S.K. JENNINGS, Esq. Mr. JAMES GAIDY (GEDDY
in marriage record) to Miss CATHARINE PHARES, both of the vicinity of
this place.

June 23, 1831
Married on the 19th inst. by HON. T.F. MOODY, Mr. SEABORNE DUKE to
Miss ELIZA SHEPHERD all of this vicinity.

June 30, 1831
Married on Thursday, the 23rd inst. by REV. JOSEPH CUNNINGHAM, Mr.
WILLIAM M. MURPHEY, attorney at law of Erie to Miss AMANDA MALVINA,
daughter of Mr. BAKER HOBSON of Carthage, Tuscaloosa County.
Married on Monday the 27th inst. by SAMUEL K. JENNINGS, Esq. Mr.
GREEN B. STALLINGS, late of Georgia to Mrs. SARAH STALLINGS, widow of Mr.
CADER STALLINGS, of this vicinity.

July 14, 1831
Married on Thursday 7th inst. by HON. T.F. MOODY, Mr. REUBEN SEY
(SEAY) to Miss ANN M'GEE, both of the vicinity of this place.
Married on the 7th inst. by _____ Mr. R. FORTSON to Miss HARRIET,
daughter of Mr. JOSIAH RICKS, all of this county.
On the same day, WILLIAM PERTEET to Miss CALLIHAM NELSON both of
this co.

July 21, 1831
Married on Tuesday 19th inst. by REV. R.G. CHRISTOPHER, Mr. WILLIAM
MCALPIN, to Miss ANN WATSON, all of this county.

July 28, 1831
Died on the 24th inst. at her residence in Springfield, Mrs. ELIZABETH
HORNER, consort of Mr. BENJAMIN HORNER. Death caused by mental
derangement, veiled in darkest mystery.
Paper in mourning for death of JAMES MONROE.

August 4, 1831
Died in Mobile after a short illness on the 22nd ult. Mrs. CORNELIA
L. SANFORD, consort of Mr. THADDEUS SANFORD, Editor of the Register in
her 26th year.

August 25, 1831
Died, Mr. CARSON, a young man lately from Kentucky and also Mr.
RICHARD S. LEWIS, from same state. Mr. CARSON died Thursday evening last
of bilious fever. Mr. LEWIS died Saturday last of the same disease.
FREDERICK RAVESIES, administrator of estate of JOSEPH ETIENNE
GARDIEN, deceased.

September 15, 1831
Died on Monday, 5th of September, MAJOR WILLIAM M. MARR, at Blount
Springs. Highly respected citizen and one of early settlers in this
town. He was born in Pittsylvania County, Virginia, was educated as a
physician, emigrated to Tennessee in 1798 and from thence to this place
in January 1819. He was 49 in May last. Volunteer officer in the Creek
War of 1813, 1814. Left a wife and eleven children (From Spirit of the
Age, Tuscaloosa).
Married on the 8th inst. by HON. T.F. MOODY, Mr. JAMES A BEAL,
Deputy Marshall of Southern District of Alabama to Miss MARTHA ANN,
eldest daughter of Mr. JAMES YEATES, Clerk of the Circuit Court, all of
this place.

Married on Thursday evening, 8th inst. by REV. RECTOR of Christ Church of Tuscaloosa, EDWARD BAYAL to SYLVANIA, eldest daughter of FRANCIS STOLLENWERCK, all of this county.

Married on the 8th inst. by REV. CUNNINGHAM, Mr. THOMAS BRADFORD, Jr. to Miss NANCY MARTIN, all of the vicinity of Havanna.

September 22, 1831
ELIZABETH S. GORDAN, administratrix of estate of POSEY GORDAN, deceased.

September 29, 1831
Married on Tuesday evening 27th inst. by Rev. Mr. _____Mr. ROBERT CAROTHERS of Tuscaloosa to Miss MELINDA HATTER of this county. BELINDA in Tuscaloosa Records.

ISAAC W. WRIGHT, administrator of estate of THOMAS WRIGHT, deceased.

October 6, 1831
Married on Sunday 25th inst. by S.K. JENNINGS, Esq. Mr. JOSEPH HALEY to Miss ELIZA RONEY, all of this county.

October 20,1831
Died on 7th ult. of bilious fever, Mrs. ANN HARRIS, consort of REV. ELEAZAR HARRIS of Greene County. A lovely daughter of Erin, where she was ANN DUNN (Communicated).

October 27, 1831
Died at Cambridge, Guernsey County, Ohio on the 26th inst. Mrs. MARY WHITE, aged 110.

Married on the 24th inst. by S.K. JENNINGS, Mr. EMBERSON LOW to Miss MARTHA SPRAGGINS, all of the vicinity of this place.

November 3, 1831
Married near Havanna Tuesday the 25th ult. by REV. J.P. CUNNINGHAM, T.L.R. WHITEHEAD attorney and counsellor at law of Greensboro to Miss ELIZABETH C. WILLIAMSON.

DELILAH WRENN, deceased. VINCENT LEE, administrator.

DRURY CADE, deceased. SARAH CADE, executrix.

November 10, 1831
Married on Thursday November 3 by REV. ELEAZOR HARRIS, Mr. HUGH HENRY of this county to Miss ELIZABETH, daughter of Mr. JAMES MCMULLEN, deceased.

Married on Tuesday 18th inst. by REV. J.H. GRAY, Mr. ROBERT H. BEAUFORT to Miss C(YNTHIA) M. SHAW, all of the vicinity of Clinton.

HUGH BARNETT, deceased. Orphans Court of Greene County, Alabama.

THOMAS GANNON, deceased. PHILOMON KIRKLAND, adminstrator.

November 17, 1831
Married on Thursday 10th inst. by REV. ELEAZER HARRIS, Mr. WILLIAM HENRY to Miss MARY, daughter of Mr. HENRY FULLERTON, all of this county.

Married on 10th inst. by REV. E.V. LIVERT, Mr. JAMES R. WYNN to Miss MARGARET C. MITCHELL, all of Greene County.

Funeral of Mrs. PICKENS will be preached at Greenwood, the residence of the late Governor PICKENS on Monday next.

November 24, 1831
Married at Ashville, North Carolina on Tuesday evening October 24th by REV. Dr. DICKSON, ROBERT HETT CHAPMAN, Esq. attorney at law of Greene County to Miss CLARISS EMALINA CHUNN, daughter of COL. SAMUEL CHUNN of the former place.

December 8, 1831
Married by REV. JAMES MONETT this evening, Mr. DAVID S. WIER to Miss ANN ELIZABETH, daughter of D. PUCKETT all of this county. (One DABNEY PUCKETT was in 1830 Census of Greene Co. Ala).

Notice: On 10th of January 1832 we will offer for sale at the late residence of GEORGE CHERRY, deceased, 1 mile from Greensboro the perishable property, belonging to estate of said deceased, to wit: 3 head of horses, 40 head of hogs well fattened, together with some hogs, 20 head of cattle, 700 bushels of corn and 1000 lbs. of fodder. All the farming utensils, household and kitchen furniture, all of which will be sold on a 12 month credit. Bonds and approved security will be required of the purchasers.

JOHN D. ARINGTON, adm'r
PENELOPE CHERRY, adm'x
Dec. 1, 1831 32ts.

December 1831
Married on Thursday evening last by H.L. KENNON, Esq. Mr. NIVEN PHARES to Miss ____(ELIZABETH) M'DONALD, daughter of Mr. ELI MCDONALD, all of this vicinity.
Married on Thursday last by HON. T.F. MOODY, Mr. ____(EDWIN) SHEPHERD to Miss SARAH QUINBY, all of this vicinity. See our Vol. 20 p. 83 for marriage record which says QUIMBY.
JONATHON and DEMSEY COCKRELL, administrators of the estate of NATHAN COCKRAN deceased. (Note: COCKRELL in previous records).

December 29, 1831
Married on Thursday, 8th inst. by REV. Mr. ADAIR, Mr. THOMAS J. GANNON to Miss ELIZABETH MORGAN both of Perry Co.
Married on Thursday the 22nd inst. by REV. Mr. LAMBETH, Mr. JAMES SHORT to Miss ANN DERDON, all of Greene County.
Married on the same day by REV. JAMES MONETT, Mr. ELLIS LINDSEY to Miss SARAH B. THOMPSON, all of Greene Co. See our Vol. 2 p p. 83 for marriage record says ELIAS LINDSEY and MARTHA THOMPSON. MARTHA is correct.
A few days since at Pleasant Ridge in this county, Mr. JAMES G. GEORGE to Miss PERMELIA A. HUTTEN.

January 5, 1832
Married on Sunday evening last by REV. JAMES MONETT, Mr. JACOB HAISCH to Miss PATIENCE WINGATE, all of this county.
Died on Monday morning last after a short illness, Mr. CHARLES FRIES, for some time a resident of this place.

January 12, 1832
HENRY PRICE, deceased. GEORGE ROBINSON, administrator.
Married on the 29th of December last by T.L.R. WHITEHEAD, Esq. Mr. SIMEON BAIRD to Mrs. ELIZABETH HUGHS, all of this county.

January 26, 1832
Married on the 12th by BURREL HUGGINS, Esq. Mr. SHEMMI FLEMING to Miss HARRIET CARTER, all of this county.
Married this evening by REV. J.H. GRAY, Mr. WILLIAM KARR to Miss SARAH DIAL.
At the same time and place by same minister, Mr. BENJAMIN J. MITCHELL to Miss NANCY DIAL, all of this county.
JOSHUA RODEN, deceased. Orphans Court of Greene County.

February 2, 1832
Married on 31st instant by HON. T.F. MOODY, Mr. WILLIAMSON LOW to Miss ELEANOR MAGEE, all of this vicinity. See our Vol. 20 p. 84 for marriage record which says "MCGEHEE".
Died on the 27th instant Mr. WILLIAM LEWIS at the residence in Flat woods of influenza in the 37th year of his age. He left a wife and six small children.
Died on the 30th ult. of influenza, Miss ELIZABETH SANDERLAND.

February 16, 1832
Married in Tuscaloosa Sunday the 5th inst. by REV. B.M. CUNNINGHAM, Mr. JOHN R. HAMPTON, one of the proprietors of the Spirit of the Age to Miss FRANCES ANN WEBB.

February 23, 1832
    AMASA CALLOWAY deceased. LEMUEL CALLOWAY, adm'r.
    BENJAMIN BROWN, deceased. STITH EVANS, adm'r.
    Orphans Court of Greene County.

March 8, 1832
    Married on 1st instant by REV. JAMES MONETT, Mr. DUNCAN M'CLAURIN
to Miss ELIZABETH PAMELIA MADISON, all of this vicinity.

March 29, 1832
    WILLIS PULLIAM, deceased. DANIEL B. SAMPLE, administrator. Orphans
Court of Greene County.

April 5, 1832
    Died in Erie on Saturday the 31st of March last after a short ill-
ness, ELEONORA EDGERLY, second daughter of Mr. D(ANIEL) W. and Mrs.
E(LEANORA) K. EDGERLY, aged 18 months.
    SAMUEL WILLIAMS, executor of the last will and testament of REUBEN
LONG deceased. State of Alabama-Greene County Orphans Court.

THE ALABAMA SENTINEL

        Printed and published at Greensborough, Greene County,
        Alabama each Saturday by DANIEL F. BROWN.

April 16, 1836
    Married in this place Thursday evening last by REV. Mr. BESTOR,
Mr. HAYWOOD PARKER, late of North Carolina to Miss MARIAH LAWRENCE,
daughter of Mr. HAYWOOD LAWRENCE of this place. Note: Called "JOHN H.
PARKER" in marriage record.

May 14, 1836
    Married near this place Thursday evening last by REV. Mr. LEVERT,
Mr. WILLIAM M'LATHAM to Miss MINERVA CLEMENT, all of this county. See
our Vol. 34 p. 24.

May 17, 1836
    Died Saturday night last near this place, Mrs. MARY BECK, consort
of CAPTAIN ALFRED BECK in the 42nd year of her age. She has left a
husband and a large family of children to lament her loss.

June 4, 1836
    Married in Clarksville, Tennessee Wednesday the 11th instant, Mr.
JOHN M'GINNIS of this place to Miss MARTHA MATLEY of the former place.
    Died in this place on Wednesday last after a long and severe indis-
position, Mr. JOSIAH DOWNING, an old and respected inhabitant of this
town.
    Died at the residence of Mr. WILLIAM BREWER in Sumter County on the
28th instant, Mr. JOHN D. SMITH, Senior editor of the Sumter Gazette in
the 23d year of his age. He was a native of Maine and a young man of
great talents...

July 2, 1836
    Married in this place on Thursday evening last by HENRY WATSON, Esq.
Mr. DAVID K. WOODALL to Miss ELIZABETH BYERS, all of this place. See
our Vol. 34 p. 24.
    Note: Letter to Gandrud from Mrs. Elliott M. Jantz, Rt. 1 Box 1453,
Waco, Tex. 76710. "I think I have located the father of DAVID KALIAH or
(KELITA) WOODALL. DAVID m. ELIZ. BYARS in Greene Co. Ala. 1736 where
that that MASTIN WOODALL (shown on most records as MARTIN WOODALL) is
the father. MASTIN lived in Johnston Co. N.C. was m. there ca 1795
(Marriage rec. not dated) to JUDITH GILES. He rec'd land grants around
1800 & bo't several tracts. He sold all of his land at different times,
the last being in 1815. DAVID named his 1st son JOSEPH MASTIN WOODALL.
This from a Family Bible. MASTIN had a son in right age bracket to be
DAVID. Was MASTIN ever in Ala?"

Died in Erie (Greene County) on the 23d instant at the residence of
CAPTAIN PEASE after a short but severe illness, Mrs. ELIZA CAROLINE LA
VERGY, consort of Mr. PHILANDER LA VERGY and eldest daughter of DR.
WALTER O. BICKLEY. She left her husband, mother and many relations to
mourn her loss.

July 23, 1836
    Married near Clinton in this county on Tuesday the 4th instant by
HON. WILLIAM B. STREET, Mr. JAMES D. M'ALLISTER to Mrs. MARY C. FLEMING.
Note: She was dau. of JOHN & MARY (LEWIS) MOORE & widow of JOHN FLEMING.
See our Vol. 87 pp. 25 & 89.
    Also at the same time and place, Mr. ULYSSES M'ALLISTER to Miss
SARAH F. FORTSON, all of this county.

July 30, 1836
    Died in Perry County on the 25th ult. Mr. G.W. CHARLES, late of
North Carolina in the 18th year of his age. He died from an accidental
discharge of his gun.

August 13, 1836
    Married near this place on Thursday evening last by REV. Mr.
WITHERSPOON, Mr. JAMES MCCANN, formerly of Abbeville, South Carolina to
Miss SUSAN M'DONALD daughter of Mr. JAMES M'DONALD of this county.
    Married at Mr. WILLEFORD's at the Baptist Institute near this place
on the same evening by REV. Mr. LOWERY, Mr. MILTON CALLOWAY to Miss
CAROLINE M. SMITH, all of this county. See our Vol. 87 p. 25 for
marriage rec. which says CATHARINE. In 1850 Census Sumter Co. Ala. he
40 b Ga., she 36 b S.C.
    Died at his residence near Erie (Greene County) on Sunday morning
last after a few days illness, Mr. THOMAS WILLIAMS, formerly of North
Carolina, but for the last ten years a resident of this county.
    Died near Marion in Perry County on the 1st instant of bilious
fever, Mr. JOHN HILLHOUSE, for many years an inhabitant of this place.
    Died at Mr. TARVER's Wood Landing on Alabama River, on the 3rd
instant, a stranger left by the Steamboat Pioneer.

August 20, 1836
    Married in this place on Thursday evening last by REV. Mr. HATCH,
Mr. GEORGE NOBLE, Merchant, to Miss ELIZABETH SIMS, all of this place.
See our Vol. 87 p. 25.
    Died at Livingston, Sumter County on Friday the 12th instant after
a few days illness in the 29th year of her age, Mrs. ELIZABETH MARRAST,
consort of Mr. WILLIAM MARRAST, formerly of this place. She was a
member of the Baptist Church. She left a husband and infant daughter.
    State of Alabama-Greene County. HENRY S. MASON, administrator
with will annexed of MARTIN M'CALL, deceased.

August 27, 1836
    Died in this place Tuesday morning last after a short illness, Mrs.
L. MOORE, consort of Mr. S. MOORE, late of Connecticut.

September 3, 1836
    Died at his residence 8½ miles southeast of Tuscaloosa of inflamma-
tory bilious fever, REV. H(ENRY) W. HART, son of JOHN and MARY HART,
aged 38 years and 22 days, native of Richland District, South Carolina;
served an apprenticeship in the coach-making business in Columbia, after
which he moved to Edgefield village, where in 1822 he married HARRIET W.
BEAMS, daughter of JAMES and REBECCA BEAMS and on the Friday following,
he joined the Baptist Church. In 1826, he moved to Tuscaloosa County,
Alabama. In 1834, he was licensed to preach, the next year ordained to
preach by the Gilgal Church and had pastoral charge of Little Sandy
Church when he died.

September 10, 1836
    Married on Thursday evening last by REV. Mr. HATCH, Mr. SAMUEL
COWEN of this place to Miss MARTIA EVANS, daughter of Mr. STITH EVANS of
this county. See our Vol. 87 p. 26.

Died at Shelby Springs in this state on the 24th ult. in his 38th year, COL. ROBERT DUNLAP of Dallas County, late of Newberry District, South Carolina.

Died at the residence of Mr. BARNABAS MATT in the Canebrake, Monday the 5th instant, Mr. CHARLES STILTS of this place, late of Sumner County, Tennessee.

September 24, 1836

Died at his residence near this place Friday night the 16th instant, Mr. BRYANT RHODES after a long and severe illness in the 40th year of his age.

Died on Monday the 10th instant at his residence near this place, Mr. DANIEL BOOKER, formerly of North Carolina.

Died on the 2d of September about 3 p.m. of croup, Isaac P., infant son of ISAAC C. and SARAH C. SNEDECOR, aged 11 months and 6 days. Of six children the parents have lost five.

Died at 3 a.m. Wednesday the 13th of September, after a severe attack of bilious fever, which lasted eleven days, ELIZA ANN PEARSON, wife of GEORGE C. PEARSON and daughter of COL. JAMES SNEDECOR, aged 19 years. She left a husband and two small children.

VOICE OF SUMTER

Published at Livingston, Sumter County, Alabama and filed in the Probate Office at Livingston, Ala. Published each Tuesday. Name of WARREN BARNES written on paper. THOMAS & TROTT, editors.

March 29, 1836

PETER DOTY-attorney at law.

JAMES HAIR-attorney at law.

WILLIAM H. GREEN and MURRAY F. SMITH, law partners.

April 5, 1836

GEORGE S. PICKLE advertises 275 acres of land for sale 7 miles Northwest of Livingston.

DAVID E. BOTHWELL advertises 1672 acres near Marion, Lauderdale Co. Miss.

Estate of WILLIAM S. CHAPMAN, deceased. COZIAH ANN CHAPMAN, executrix and ROBERT H. CHAPMAN, executor. (In 1850 Census COZIAH CHAPMAN age 37 born in N.C.) - Vol. 154 p. 80.

EDWARD J. WILLIAMS, administrator of DAVID HOOKS, deceased. Advertised in Orphans Court, Sumter Co. Ala.

April 12, 1836

Died on the 1st inst. in Greene County, REV. ZADOK BAKER, a native of North Carolina, but had been a resident of this State several years. Baptist preacher...(Note: One ZADOK BAKER's credentials as minister "in the Holy Church of Christ" 15 August 1815 Madison Co. Ala. P.J.G.)

Died at Mount Pleasant in this county, JAMES, son of WILLIS I. ROAN aged 12 years. Death certificate of MARTHA ANN ROAN b Sept. 11, 1838 shows b Ala., father WILLIS I. ROAN b. Ala., mother ANNA PRIUTE b Ala.

On 5th at the residence of his father, WASHINGTON, son of JOEL HERDS, Esq.

April 19, 1836

Communicated. Died on Wednesday evening last, after an illness of 4 days, Mrs. ELIZABETH WHITE, wife of Mr. JOSEPH WHITE, aged about 29 years...member of Methodist Episcopal Church. Signed O.B.W.

Died at his residence 8 miles south of this place, GEORGE W. FREELAND Esq. aged about 30 years, one of our most respected citizens.

April 26, 1836

Married in this vicinity on Wednesday evening last by HON. PETER DOTY, Mr. JAMES MCMILLIAN of Tuscaloosa County to Miss NANCY J. daughter of DANIEL GREEN Esq. of this county.

Married in this county at Payneville by REV. Mr. CAMPBELL on
Thursday evening last, Mr. JOHN K. ELLIOTT to Miss NANCY PAYNE. (In
1850, JOHN K. ELLIOTT was age 37 born in Tenn.; NANCY T. aged 34 born in
Ala. and next foor was ANNA ELLIOTT aged 57 born Tenn.)
    DANIEL M. NOBLE)
       versus   )— Divorce - Defendant is a non-resident of
    ELIZABETH NOBLE)   this state.

May 3, 1836
    Died in this county on Sunday evening 1st inst. Mr. WASHINGTON
TERRELL, son of Mrs. MARY ANN TERRELL aged about 19 or 20 years, a worthy
and respected young man.
    Died-a few days since in Lauderdale County, Mississippi, Mrs. SARAH
CALHOUN, after an illness of 12 hours of apoplexy, consort of Mr. DUNCAN
CALHOUN, a worthy and esteemed lady. She has left a husband and family
of small children...

May 10, 1836
    Married in this county on the 19th by REV. WILIE W. STANTON, Mr.
JOHN N. HUTTON of Greene County to Miss ELLA WATKINS, daughter of LEVEN
WATKINS, Esq. Marriage not in Sumter Co. (Note: In 1850 Census Greene
Co. Ala. JOHN N. HUTTON shown as age 43 born in SC, wife ELIZA J.age 30
born Ala. Register of Graduates & Students of University of Ala. 1831-
1901 by THOMAS WAVERLY PALMER shows that AUGUSTUS CALDWELL HUTTON, class
of 1861, enrolled from Hopewell, Greene Co. 1860, son of JOHN NEWTON
HUTTON, West Greene Co. and ELIZA JANE WATKINS, A.C.H. born Sept. 23,
1841, Private in Co. B 36th Ala. Reg. CSA, died in Tuscaloosa Jan 8,
1898. Did JOHN N. HUTTON marry two sisters, or were ELLA and ELIZA the
same? P.J.G. (This marriage not on record in either Greene or Sumter
Co.)
    Died on Saturday evening, 30th ult. in Greene County at her resi-
dence, Mrs. MARY BECK, consort of ALFRED BECK, Esq. in her 42nd year...
Many children and fond husband have met with a loss. Communicated.
(U of A 1845 says she was MARY MCKINNEY.)
    State of Alabama) ANDREW H. RAMSEY, administrator of OBEDIAH
    Sumter County) WIMPEY, deceased. Estate insolvent.
    BRYANT RICHARDSON, deceased. CURNY RICHARDSON and WILLIAM O'NEAL,
administrators.

May 17, 1836
    Married in this county on the 10th, Mr. WALTER L. CHILDS to Miss
ISABELLA MCKINZIE, both of this county. Vol. 117
    Died in this place on 13th inst., of strangulated hernia, Mr. M.C.
WARD, journeyman, tailor, a native of New Jersey
    Died on 12th of scarlet fever, JAMES GORDON aged 10 years. Also on
15th, GEORGE W. GORDAN, aged 5 years, both sons of Mrs. JACKSON BREWER
of this place. Communicated.
    Died in this vicinity of 14th of scarlet fever, Miss EMILY MIMMS,
daughter of SEABORNE MIMMS, Esq. aged about 15 years...Methodist church.
    CHARLES W. LINN, deceased. WILLIAM MCKELLETT, administrator.

May 24, 1836
    Law notice - JNO. EDMONSON.
    SAMUEL B. BOYD - attorney-at-law.
    Married in the vicinity of this place on Tuesday evening, the 17th,
by P.S. GLOVER, Esq., DOCT. H.F. ARRINGTON to Miss MARY JEMISON.
Vol 117, p. 54 (1850 Census shows HENRY F. ARRINGTON age 39 born Ga.,
MARY aged 32 born Ga.)

May 31, 1836
    Married in this county on Thursday evening last by WM. B. OCHILTREE,
Esq., Mr. DAVID BOYD to Miss SARAH CLARK. (1850 Census shows him aged
45 b. S.C.; her 38 b Ga.) Vol. 117 p. 53
    Married in Perry County on Tuesday evening the 10th by REV. ROBERT
NALL, Mr. THOMAS ALEXANDER SANDERS of Sumter County to Miss ANN JONES,
daughter of COL. HARWOOD JONES of Perry.
    JAMES B. MAY, administrator of SAMUEL MONETT, deceased.

June 7, 1836
Died in this place on the 2nd, Mrs. _____ BINNS, consort of CHARLES
BINNS, Esq.
BENJ. W. JOHNSON, deceased.

June 14, 1836
Died on Sunday night the 12th inst. in this place of scarlet fever,
ELIZABETH, daughter of JAMES SAVAGE, Esq. in her 9th year.

June 21, 1836
Married on Sunday evening the 19th inst. by W.B. OCHILTREE, Esq.
Mr. WILLIAM JOHNSTON, merchant of this place to Miss MARGARET, daughter
of CAPT. DRUMMOND of this county.

June 28, 1836
Died in this place on Wednesday morning the 22d, MARY ELIZABETH
SCOTT aged about 4 years (poem).
Died in this town on Tuesday the 21st, ELIZABETH, daughter of Mr.
and Mrs. JOHN CLARK aged 6 years.
Died in this county on 18th inst. CALVIN H. DAVIS in 12th year, son
of Mrs. CHRISTOPHER DAVIS.
Died in this county on 22d inst., COL. THOMAS HENDERSON in the 50th
year of his age. Native of Rockingham County, North Carolina. Very soon
after he attained his majority, he removed to the city of Raleigh and
became editor of The Star...The family of COL. HENDERSON are remarkable
for intelligence, different members for a long time have been the pride
of the bar and bench of his native State...About 1819 he emigrated to
Madison County, Tennessee, where he lost his amiable companion...In the
autumn of 1835 he removed to this county. His health continued gradually
to decline until he received intelligence of the death of his son,
LIEUT. RICHARD HENDERSON of U.S. Army, who fell with MAJOR DADE in the
Seminole War, since which time he delicned rapidly until the period of
his dissolution.

July 5, 1836
Died in this place Wednesday the 29th, ISABELLA S. beautiful and
interesting little daughter of S.B. BOYD, Esq. aged 5 years.
Died Thursday the 30th, ANDREW JACKSON, infant son of JAMES SAVAGE,
Esq. of this place.
DARLING MASSY, deceased. ANN MASSY, administratrix.
GEORGE W. FREELAND, deceased. ELEANOR FREELAND to have lands
belonging to estate sold to pay debts. Orphans Court sale. (See our
Vol. 17 page 48 for marriage of GEORGE W. FREELAND to NELLY STALSWORTH,
28 Sept. 1835.)

July 12, 1836
Died at the residence of her father in this place on the 6th, Miss
DORINDA, daughter of Mr. WILLIAM EARBEE in her 15th year...Methodist
Episcopal...

July 19, 1836
Married in this county on 12th, Mr. MEREDITH PUGH of Clark (Co.) to
Miss CATHERINE JANE, youngest daughter of CAPT. STEPHEN NOBLE. Also on
same evening by WADE R. THOMAS, Esq. Mr. DANIEL E. HARPER to Miss
ELIZABETH GORMAN. Vol. 117, p. 54. On 14th, Mr. JAMES HAGAN to Miss
MARY MARTIN. (See our Vol. 17 p. 57 for marriage of JAMES HAGANS to
REBECCA MARTIN July, 1836.)
Died in Greene County on 13th, Mrs. CAROLINE KIRKPATRICK, aged 21,
consort of Mr. WILKINS KIRKPATRICK, and daughter of the late WILLIAM
DILLIARD, Esq. of Orange County, North Carolina...Methodist Episcopal...
Died in this place Tuesday, the 12th, CAPT. WILLIAM L. RUSH aged
about 25. Left an affectionate wife and 2 children.

July 26, 1836
Died in this place this morning, JOSEPH son of JAMES SAVAGE, Esq.,
aged about 10 years.
LEVIN WATKINS advertises he is no longer responsible for debts of
his wife HENRIETTA WATKINS, lately HENRIETTA WHITE, as she has left no
bed and board.

August 2, 1836
    Co-partnership of RIX, RICH & Co. dissolved.
                                    GEORGE RIX
                                    REUBEN RICH
                                    WILLIAM RIX

August 9, 1836
    Died on Monday morning the 8th inst. after a short illness,
PLEASANT N. WILSON, Esq. formerly of Tuscaloosa...
    Died near this place on the night of 7 August, Mrs. JULIA ANN TARTT,
consort of Mr. JAMES B. TARTT in her 20th year, daughter of REV. Mr.
TOWNS of La Grange, Alabama, and was raised and educated with all that
pious care of her devoted parents...

August 16, 1836
    Died in this place on 12th in accouchment, Mrs. ELIZABETH MARRAST,
consort of WM. MARRAST, Esq. Deceased was a lady of accomplished mind
and heart... Leaves affectionate husband and infant daughter.
    Died at residence of his father in this county, Mr. ASEL MAY in his
25th year. Native of Tenn. which state he left and settled about 3 years
ago in Ala. He has left a wife and 3 small children.

August 30, 1836
    Died in the vicinity of Livingston on 29th after a few days illness,
Mrs. MATILDA CHAPMAN, consort of HON. SAMUEL CHAPMAN...

September 6, 1836
    REDDICK SIMMS, deceased. JAMES SIMMS, administrator.

September 13, 1836
    Died in this place on 9th of inflammation of the liver, DAMIEL
WOMACK, Esq. in 25th year; emigrated from Washington County at early
period of settlement of Sumter. He filled the office of Clerk of County
Court with general approbation...

September 27, 1836
    Died in the vicinity of this place on the 20th, Mr. FRANCIS ASBURY
SHUTE, a native of Washington, Beaufort County, North Carolina. Supposed
to be about 25 years of age and was travelling to the west, perhaps to
Texas. He was taken ill before he arrived at Mr. MIMM's 2 miles from
Livingston, where he died. Remains were decently interred in public
burying ground in this place.

October 4, 1836
    Died at the residence of his father, in this vicinity on Saturday
the 1st inst., Mr. JOHN C. CUSACK, merchant of this place, in the 25th
year of his age. Was among the first who cast destinies in our bereft
village...Leaves wife and infant son.

October 11, 1836
    JOHN D. MIERS - saddler's business in Livingston.
    Married on 9th by W.P. JONES, Esq. Mr. WM. HENRY KNOX to Mrs.
JENNETTA C. DOTSON, daughter of JOSIAH DABBS, Esq. all of this county.
(In 1850 Census Wm. H. was aged 35 b. NC and she was 37 b. Va.) See
our Vol. 117 p. 55 for marriage record.
    Died in this vicinity on Friday last, Mrs. PRISCILLA CUSACK, amiable
consort of THOMAS CUSACK, Esq. in her 60th year... It was but last week
that we announce the death of the only son of the above aged couple.
    Died in Gainesville on Friday evening last of apoplexy, COL. MOSES
LEWIS in his 66th year...
    Died on 27th at residence of COL. HOWARD JONES, in the vicinity of
Marion, Perry County, COL. ALANSON BROWN of this county in his 26th
year.
    Died in the town of Clinton, Alabama on the 20th, Mrs. MARY JANE
JORDAN, consort of BURRELL P. JORDAN, in her 20th year...

October 18, 1836
    PETER WELBURN, deceased. BLAKE LITTLE, administrator.

23.

October 25, 1836
    1 page missing, where obituaries would be.

November 1, 1836
    Married by W.P. JONES, Esq. on 27th, Jr. JAMES M. GUNN to Miss
SARAH C. BARBER, all of this county. (See our Vol. 177 p. 56 for
marriage of JAMES MADISON GUNN to SARAH C. BARBER 21 Oct. 1836. In 1850
Census Choctaw Co. Ala. he was 35 b. Tenn. and she 33 b. SC.)

November 8, 1836
    Died in this place on 1st after lingering illness, Mrs. MILLY (or
NELLY? - blurred) HANCOCK in her 68th year.
    Died in this place on Thursday the 3d Mrs. DERLINDA WILEY, consort
of Mr. TAYLOR WILEY, in her 45th year. Leaves husband and several small
children. (1840 T. Co.)
    Died in this place on Monday evening last aged 9 months, RICHARD
ARNOLD, interesting child of Mr. and Mrs. COUNCIL R. WRIGHT.
    Died at the residence of A(LEX) H(AMILTON) FALCONER, Esq. in the
Fork, Greene County, on Saturday the 29th, Miss MARY PUGH FALCONER,
youngest daughter of the late ALEXANDER FALCONER, Esq. of Franklin County,
North Carolina. Miss FALCONER emigrated to this state last winter in
company with her brother and family... (1850 Census Greene Co. Ala.
shows one ALEXANDER H. FALCONER aged 50 b. N.C.)
    Died at the family residence in Kemper County, Mississippi Wednesday
12th October last in 27th year, Mrs. SUSAN A. DAVIS, consort of THOMAS
DAVIS, Jr. Her illness was of a bilious character, but so stubborn that
it baffled the skill of the physicians and on the 8th day of the attack,
her spirit took its everlasting flight... No public profession of religion. (See our Vol. 117 page 39 for marriage of THOMAS DAVIS to
SUSAN DAVIS, 3 August 1834)

November 15, 1836
    Died on 7th at residence in the vicinity of this place, CAPT. ALFRED
BECK in his 52nd year...
    DANIEL WOMACK, deceased. JESSE WOMACK, administrator.
    CHESLEY R. GUIN, deceased. (1830 Perry Co.)

November 22, 1836
    ELI TOOL (1830 Dallas Co.) deceased. His late residence in
Lauderdale County, Mississippi near Alamuchie Olt Town to be sold.
Administrators: DAVID and JOSEPH TOOL and A.P. MCCURDY. (1830 Dallas
Co.) (1 DAVID m. in Perry Co. in 1833.)
    DR. WILLIAM D. JEFFERSON (late practitioner of medicine in Virginia)
advertises that he will practice in Sumter and Greene near Jones Bluff.
(1850 Census Sumter Co. Ala. shows DR. WILLIAM D. JEFFERSON aged 35 born
in Va. and family.)

November 29, 1836
    Married at the house of SEBORNE MIMS, Esq. in this vicinity on
Thursday evening last, Mr. WILLIAM A. MIMS to Miss MARY JANE DILLIARD,
daughter of the late WILLIAM DILLIARD, Esq. of Orange County, North
Carolina. (1850 Census shows WM. A. MIMS aged 32 b. Ga.; MARY J. age
30 b. NC; also see our Vol. 117 p. 57 for marriage record.)
    Died at his residence in Talladega on 14th, HON. SAMUEL W. MARDIS,
formerly Representative in Congress from this District.

December 13, 1836
    JAMES R. BATTLE advertises 200 acres of land 4 miles East of
Livingston.

December 20, 1836
    Married on 25th by W.P. JONES, Esq. Mr. JOHN SMITH to Miss NANCY
ARNOLD, both of Sumter County. (See our Vol. 117 p. 57 for marriage.)
    Died at the residence of ALEXANDER CHAPMAN, Esq. of this vicinity
on Friday morning last, Mr. GEORGE TODD, formerly of Caroline County,
Virginia in the 23rd year of his age...
    Died in Lauderdale County, Mississippi on the 14th, JOHN C. infant
son of THOMAS H. DAVIS, Esq. aged 20 days.

January 3, 1837
Married in Greene County on the 27th Mr. WILLIAM D. MOORE, merchant
of this place to Miss ARABELLA SMITH of the vicinity of Greensborough.
(1850 Census Greene Co. shows WM. D. MOORE aged 44 born in N.C. and
ARABELLA M. MOORE aged 38 born Va. Also see our Volume 69 page 32 and
Vol. 87 p. 33.)
Married in Lauderdale Co. (Miss?) on 17th ult., Mr. JOHN R. LEATH,
merchant of Daleville to Miss DORINDA ADAIR.
ANN SIMMONS advertises that a horse was stolen from her on the 27th.
State of Alabama-Sumter Co. Petition of ANN MASSEY, widow and
relict of DARLING MASSEY, deceased, who died seized of FE fractional
section quarter of Section 1 Township 17 Range 2 West etc. The following
minor heirs: JAMES O. MASSEY, JOHN D. MASSEY, WILLIAM MASSEY and FRANCIS
MASSEY.
JAMES UNDERWOOD, deceased. JOHN EZELL, administrator.
THOMAS PETEATE, deceased. WILLIAM JOHNSTON, adm'r.
ARTHUR PATTON, deceased. JOHN D. ROGERS, administrator.
ROBERT COLVERT, deceased. JOHN H. ANDERSON, administrator.

January 10, 1837
ELIZABETH FREELAND, administratrix of estate of GEORGE W. FREELAND,
deceased, petitions for dower in E½ of SE¼ of Section 30 Township 18
Range 1 West.
ROBERT COLVERT, deceased. ELIZABETH COLVERT, administratrix,
petitions for dower in land in Section 22 Township 20 Range 2 West.

January 24, 1837
Married on Thursday the 19th by REV. PETER DOTY at Mr. WM. GODFREY's,
Mr. ASBURY MYERS to Miss S.E. MCCREA all of Sumter. (See our Vol. 117,
p. 58 for marriage of ASBERRY MYERS to ELIZA MCREA 19 Jan. 1837 - she
(SARAH ELIZA MYERS married 2. (1847) ROBERT L. HUNTER) In 1850 Census
ROBERT L. HUNTER was age 38 n. NC and wife SARAH E. was 31 b. Ala.
Land for sale - RACHAEL BRASHEARS offers for sale the remainder of
her Reserve, adjoining the Black Bluff.
ELIZABETH CALVERT, widow of ROBERT CALVERT, deceased.

January 31, 1837
JOHN BOND, deceased. Sale of Real Estate. Heirs: GEORGE W.
WALKER, LOUISA BOND and THOMAS BOND, the former husband of REBECCA,
formerly REBECCA BOND, and wife of JOHN BOND, deceased and the two
latter said to be heirs of the said JOHN BOND, deceased, are not residents of Alabama.

February 7, 1837
Co-partnership of DAVID A. TORRY and DELANA ELLIS dissolved-merchants.

February 14, 1837
Dissolution of partnership of WILLIAM R. HORTON and A.W. HORTON,
Mobile. 29th Dec. 1836.

February 21, 1837
Married on Tuesday evening the 16th by P.S. GLOVER, Esq., Mr.
WILLIAM P. POSEY to Miss NANCY M. daughter of DR. FLUKER, all of this
county. (Note: See our Vol. 117 p. 59 for marriage record; WILLIAM
PINKNEY POSEY was born Nov. 4, 1814 (Bible record) son of JESSE HAMIL-
TON POSEY and wife, ELEANOR BROOKS: NANCY MADISON FLUKER was daughter of
DR. WILLIAM FLUKER and she later 19 June 1842 married PHILLIP E. EDMONDS.
In 1850 Census she was Mrs. EDMONDS, and age 29 born in Ala.
Married in this county near Jameston Thursday evening the 11th, by
REV. WILLIE J. STANTON, Mr. JOSEPH HUDSON to Miss MARGARET HARPER. (Not
listed in Sumter Co. marriages.)
Married at same time and place (see listing before this), Mr. CALVIN
MCDANIEL to Miss ELIZABETH HARPER. (Not listed in Sumter Co. marriages.
CALVIN MCDANIEL 1850 Prs 31 N.C. wife MARTHA.)
Also on Thursday the 18th by REV. WILLIE J. STANTON, Mr. WILLIAM
MORRIS to Miss LUCINDA WINDHAM, daughter of W. WINDHAM, Esq.
Died in Pickens County on 12th, Mrs. MARGARET BARNES, consort of
Mr. JOHN R. BARNES.

March 14, 1837
     This paper cut out and torn.

March 21, 1837
     MARY PETETE, widow of THOMAS PETETE, deceased. Administrator's
notice.

March 28, 1837
     Advertisement - SUSAN PARKER, as widow and relict of SHERROD H.
PARKER, late of Marengo County, Alabama, petitions for dower in land in
Sumter Co. Ala.

April 4, 1837
     JAMES W. HUBBARD, deceased. CATHARINE A. HUBBARD, administratrix.
Letter from Mrs. S.E. GODFREY, Jr., P.O. GODFREY, Jr., P.O. Box 221,
Eufaula, Ala. May 19, 1965. "JAS. W. HUBBARD b. Va. m. CATHERINE ANN
ELLIS b. 1810 S.C. Wilcox Co. Ala. m. 8 Aug. 1833, they had 1 child
CATHERINE. JAMES HUBBARD b. 1836 Wilcox Co. m. F. SPURLEN in Camden,
Ala. 1855. JAS. W. HUBBARD d. before 1840, because in that year
CATHERINE ANN ELLIS HUBBARD m. WM. JAS. DEXTER of Camden."

April 11, 1837
     PHEBE JUZAN advertises for all persons to file claim on estate of
CHARLES JUZAN, from Orphans Court of Lauderdale County, Mississippi.

April 18, 1837
     PETER P. SCALES, deceased. JOSEPH LAKE, executor.

April 25, 1837
     Departed this life on the 25th at his residence in this place, DR.
JOHN L. MCCANTS in the 33rd year of his age... Pride of his aged
parents in S.C.
     HUGH CRAVY, deceased. CHARLES H. STEPHENS, administrator.

February 28, 1837
     NATHAN J. COCKRELL advertises store house for sale.

March 7, 1837
     Departed this life Sunday the 5th inst. Mrs. ELIZABETH HAIR, consort
of JAMES HAIR, Esq. of Livingston, after a lingering illness of many
months... Presbyterian... (See our Vol. 44 page 10; Vol. 70 page 30 and
Vol. 57 page 3.)
     GEORGE W. WALKER and wife REBECCA (formerly REBECCA BOND, wife of
JOHN BOND, deceased), will petition for dower.

May 2, 1837
     ALANSON BROWN, deceased. SARAH J. BROWN, executrix.

May 9, 1837
     Died in the vicinity of this place Wednesday the 3d ROBERT A. BATES
in his 55th year.

May 16, 1837
     Died in this town Wednesday the 10th, Mrs. MARGARET JOHNSTON in
22nd year of her age, consort of WILLIAM JOHNSTON, Esq., Sheriff of
Sumter Co...

May 16, 1837
     ROBERT A. BATES, deceased. JAMES A. BATES, administrator.
     SAMUEL A. R. DABBS, deceased. ANDREW H. DABBS and WILLIAM P.
MARTIN, administrators.

May 23, 1837
     WM. H. JAMES, deceased. WM. W. CAPERS, administrator.

May 30, 1837
    Died at Payneville in this county on Tuesday 23rd inst. COL. CALVIN
R. BLACKMAN about 36 years of age, formerly of Wayne County, North
Carolina but for the last 2 years an inhabitant of this State. Raleigh,
N.C. papers please copy. (Vol. 101, p.92.)
    Died in Gainesville the 21st, Miss CAROLINE M. BUGBEE, daughter of
OLVORD BUGBEE of Hartford, Vt. aged 15 years 5 months and 6 days.
    MICAJAH FRAZER - attorney-at-law. (See Vol. 122 p. 38.)

June 6, 1837
    Married on Wednesday the 17th by REV. JOHN ALLEN, MAJOR JOHN J.
WALKER to Miss MARIA M. HOPKINS, daughter of JUSGE A.F. HOPKINS, all
of Huntsville. (M. in Madison Co., Vol. 153 p. 40.)
    DAVID W. WALL, administrator of JESSE BRASHEARS, deceased.

June 13, 1837
    Married on 24th by REV. D.P. BESTOR, Mr. JOHN G. MOORE of Mobile
to Miss MARY DUGGER of Marengo County.

June 20, 1837
    Obituaries cut out.

June 27, 1837
    Obituaries cut out.

July 4, 1837
    Obituaries cut out.

July 11, 1837
    Married in Gston on 2 July, Mr. JOHN TOW to Miss CHERRY LANGFORD.
(See marriage record in our Vol. 117 page 66.)
    Married in Kemper County, Mississippi on Thursday evening the 6th,
by REV. ASA WRIGHT, Mr. BENJAMIN F. PARKE, merchant, Daleville, Lauderdale County, Mississippi to Miss ALATHA ADAIR, daughter of Mr. ZADOCH
ADAIR.
    DANIEL E. HARPER of Sumter County having determined to remove to the
city of Mobile, the ensuing season, begs to offer his services to his
friends as a commission merchant.

August 1, 1837
    Married in this county on Thursday evening the 27th at the residence
of CAPT. WM. DRUMMOND by CLEVELAND ROBBS, Esq. Mr. JOHN J. DENMARK to
Miss HARRIET DESHON. (See marriage record in our Vol. 117 page 63)
    In this county on 16th by REV. Mr. ROSS, JOHN V. WELSH, Esq. (1812
pension) to Mrs. MARTHA M(OUND) TARTT wid. of ELNATHAN TARTT   (In 1850
Census she was age 45 b. N.C. See our Vol. 117 p. 63 for marriage record.)
    Died in this place on 27th, JAMES RANDOLPH infant son of Mr. JAMES
A. and Mrs. SARAH T. ABRAHAMS aged 10 months and 10 days.
    Died on 24 whilst on a visit at residence of JOHN C. PHARES, Esq.
Mrs. CHARLOTTE DUNCAN in the 51st year of her age. Left husband and
children...
    Died at the residence of THOMAS B. WALLACE Esq. near Gaston, on
25th, JOHN Y. HALLUM of Erie, Greene County, in 21st year...(Vol. 180)
    Died at his residence near Kintebish with a pulmonary affection
which had prayed on him for many years, Mr. JOHN TAYLOR...

August 2, 1837
    The four following deaths occurred on the plantation of CHARLES
GIBBS, 6 miles from this place in the family of his overseer, all by
congestive fever.
    July 26 - LEONARD GIBBS aged 6 yrs.
    July 27 - Mrs. CLARISSA GIBBS, consort of FRANCIS GIBBS, aged 28
    Aug. 1 - WILLIAM GIBBS aged 9 yrs.
    Aug. 2 - FRANCIS GIBBS aged 33 yrs.
    Died in this town on Wednesday last, HENRY F. infant son of Mr.
ROBERT ARRINGTON aged 8 months.
    DAVIS WALLACE, deceased. RAUL S. DELAMAR, administrator.

August 15, 1837
JOHN G. DECOSTO, deceased. JOHN T. MORAN, administrator.

August 22, 1837
Married in the vicinity of this place at the residence of Mr. FISH, on Thursday evening last by HON. HENRY F. SCRUGGS, Mr. WILLIAM C. LAND, Jeweller, to Miss LYDIA MCCANTS. (See marriage record in our Vol. 117, p. 64.)

August 29, 1837
Nothing of interest.

September 3, 1837
Died in this place on 22nd, ANN EUNICE aged 7 years eldest daughter of Mr. ROBERT ARRINGTON.
Married in this county in the vicinity of this place Thursday evening last, Mr. DANIEL GOULD to Miss ELIZA ANN, eldest daughter of W.D. LANGHAM, Esq. (In 1850 Census DANIEL was aged 35 b. Ala., his wife 27 b. Ala. See our Vol. 117 p. 64 for marriage record.)....she copied mar. 28 July 1837.

September 12, 1837
SEBASTIAN HOUPT, deceased. Court ordered to notify MATILDA HOUPT, executrix and all others concerned that peition for final action is to be held. (Note: In 1850, MATILDA was aged 56 b. Ga.; she married again March 15, 1846 to MERRETT HODGINS. SEBASTIAN "HOUGH" married in Clarke Co. Ala. Aug. 21, 1817 MATILDA BREWSTER.

September 26, 1837
Married on Wednesday evening the 13th, Jr. JOHN OVERSTREET to Miss EMILY HILLIARD, daughter of WILLIAM HILLIARD, (2d wife...his 1st was ELIZABETH), all of this county. (See marriage in our Vol. 117 page 66). (Client of L.L. McNees, 1860. Client is Alberta Overstreet Powers, 5508 Ave. M, Birmingham, Ala.)
Married at Gaston Tuesday evening the 19th, DR. ROBERT L. HUNTER to Miss MARY LOUISA, eldest daughter of THOMAS B. WALLACE, Esq. of that village. (See our Vol. 117 p. 65 for marriage record. In 1850 Census he was age 38 b. N.C.)
Married in this county on Wednesday evening last by W.J. STEELE, Esq. Mr. WILLIAM LONG to Miss MARTHA ANN, daughter of JOHN J. BURTON, Esq. (See our Vol. 117, p. 66 for marriage record.)

October 3, 1837
Married in the vicinity of Jameston, on Thursday evening last by REV. WILIE J. STANTON, Mr. JONES SOUTH to Miss SARAH, daughter of MITCHEL WADKINS, all of this county. (See our Vol. 117 p. 67 for marriage record where it looks like JAMES H.C. SMITH) SOUTH in newspaper, SMITH in marriage record. JAMES H.C. SMITH plain in marriage record.)
MEREDITH COLLINS of Gaston to Mrs. SIDNEY W. BIGGS. (Note: See our Vol. 117 p. 64 for marriage record. She was widow of WM. S. GIBBS of Hyde Co. N.C. In 1850, he was 60 born in Ky, she was 47 b. N.C. His former wife was MARIA A.; was son of ELISHA COLLINS, Revolutionary soldier of Greene Co. Ala.)
Married in Marengo County, Tuesday evening the 19th, DR. DAVID M. DUNLAP of Clinton, Greene County, to Miss ELIZABETH THOMPSON of Marengo. (In 1850 Census Choctaw Co. Ala. he was aged 43 b. S.C.; she was 30 b. Ala.)

October 10, 1837
Died in the vicinity of this place today, Mr. SAMUEL M. BERRY, late of Jackson County in this State but for the last several months an esteemed citizen of this place, aged about 23... He was taken with a violent fever whilst on his return from Mobile... Editor of Bellefonte Star and Huntsville Advocate please copy.

October 30, 1837
Died in this vicinity Friday morning last, Mr. ROBERT CAMPBELL, a worthy and respectable young gentleman.

October 17, 1837
    Married Thursday evening last in the vicinity of this place by
RICHARD YARBOROUGH Esq., Mr. JOSEPH MCGOWIN of Mississippi to Miss NANCY,
eldest daughter of Mr. ROBERT BELL. (Note: See our Vol. 117 p. 68 for
marriage record.)
    Married on Wednesday evening the 11th by Mr. GRAY, DR. M.B. POSEY,
to Miss FRANCES WINSTON, daughter of COL. JOHN J. WINSTON of Greene Co.
(See our Vol. 20 p. 54. MADISON B. POSEY in 1850 was aged 38 b. Ala. and
was living in Greene Co. Ala. with his 2nd wife, SARAH HARRIETTE
THOMPSON.)
    NANCY HALSALL, relict of THOMAS HALSALL, deceased.
    JOHN M. WESTON, administrator of JOHN U. GUYGER? deceased, or
GRIGER. (Blurred and letters missing.) Could it be GEIGER?
    ARCHIBALD GRAHAM, deceased. WILLIAM D. MOORE, adm'r.

October 24, 1837
    Married Thursday night last by REV. Mr. HILL, DR. ALFRED ANDERSON
to Miss ELIZABETH, daughter of Mr. HENRY BOLING, both of this county.
(See our Vol. 117 p. 68 for marriage record.)
    THOMAS G. BRIGHT, deceased. NANCY BRIGHT, administratrix.

October 31, 1837
    Nothing of interest.

November 6, 1837
    Married in this county Tuesday evening the 24th at the residence of
COL. L.V. UNDERWOOD by P.S. GLOVER, Esq. MICAJAH FRAZAR Esq. of Sunter-
ville to Miss SUSAN A.R. COBB. (See our Vol. 117 p. 69 for marriage
record.)
    Married in the village of Gaston, Sumter County, on Wednesday even-
ing last at the residence of Mr. EDWIN PECK by THOMAS B. WALLACE, Esq.
JOHN GAYLE, Ex-governor, to Miss CLARISSA PECK. (See our Vol. 117 p. 69
for marriage record.)

November 14, 1837
    This paper has many things cut out, probably otituaries.
    KESIAH MYERS, deceased. JAMES A WIMBERLY, administrator.

November 21, 1837
    1 page missing.

November 28, 1837
    Cut out.

December 5, 1837
    Married in the vicinity of this place Tuesday the 21st by C. ROBBS,
Esq. Mr. R(ADFORD M(ADISON) GUNN to Miss STACY, daughter of DANIEL
GREENE, Esq. (See our Vol. 117 p. 70 for marriage record of RADFORD
MADISON GUNN to Miss STACY F(LOYD) GREEN.)

December 12, 1837
    Married in this county Thursday evening the 7th by WADE R. THOMAS,
Esq. Mr. LEWIS PARHAM of Wilcox County to Miss PAMELIA B. daughter of
JOHN E. ANDERSON, Esq. (See our Vol. 117 p. 69 for marriage record.)

December 19, 1837
    Married Tuesday the 12th by REV. L.D. HATCH, DR. JAMES L. TUNSTALL
to Miss ELIZA ANN CROOM both of Greensboro, Alabama. (In 1850 Census
Greene Co. Ala. he was 40 b. Va., she 31 b. Ala. See our Vol. 20 p. 47;
Vol. 34 p. 86; Vol. 69 p. 46)
    Married on Wednesday night the 13th by REV. F.C. LOWRY, Mr. JAMES
ALBERT HENDON to Miss MARY SMITH HOGUN, all of Greensborough. (See our
Vol. 20 p. 25; in 1850 Census Greene Co. he was 54 b. N.C.; she was 30 b.
Ala.)
    Married on Tuesday in Greene County by C.CHESTER, Esq. Mr. GEORGE
REEVES of Pickens County to Miss CANDACE, daughter of JESSE HORTON, Esq.

December 26, 1837
    Died in this town the 19th after a few hours suffering with paralysis, JAMES SAVAGE, Esq., clerk of Circuit Court in 58th year of his age. His youth passed amid agitations of his native Ireland until the year 1800 when he became a citizen of the United States...last 20 years Clerk of Circuit Court of Clarke and Sumter Counties...
    BENJAMIN CHENEY, adminstrator of JOHN TAYLOR, deceased.

January 2, 1838
    Married in this county on 26th by WILLIAM C. DENMARK, Esq., MARTIN P. REINHARDT, Esq. to Miss MARY JANE, daughter of JOHN H. WILSON, Esq. (Vol. 117, p. 72)

Januray 9, 1838
    Married in this place Tuesday evening the 2nd by REV. Mr. HADDEN, JESSE WOMACK, Esq. Sheriff of Sumter County to Miss JULIA ANN BROWN. (See our Vol. 117 p. 72 for marriage record.)
    Married in this vicinity on Thursday evening the 4th, by JOHN A. COWAN, Esq. CLEAVELAND ROBBS, Esq. to Miss JANE DENMARK. (See our Vol. 117 p. 73 for marriage record.)

January 16, 1838
    JAMES SAVAGE, deceased. PRICE WILLIAMS, administrator and ELIZABETH SAVAGE, administratrix.

January 23, 1838
    Nothing of interest.

January 30, 1838
    Married on Tuesday evening last by HON. HENRY F. SCRUGGS, Mr. THOMAS CUSACK to Mrs. MARTHA HAND, widow of the late OBADIAH HAND, deceased. (She was nee CLANTON and OBADIAH was a (not legible)) (See our Vol. 117, p. 7 for marriage record. In 1850, he was 64 b. Ireland, she 48 b. N.C.)
    Married on 28th by ARCHIBALD H. GRIFFIN, Esq. Mr. LLEWALLEN LEWIS of Payneville to Miss SARAH ANN, daughter of Mr. JAMES SAMPLE. (See our Vol. 117 p. 75 for marriage record.)
    Married in Greene County on Thursday evening last by REV. Mr. MANNING, WILLIAM W. PASCHAL, Esq., Editor of the Gainesville Reporter, to Miss PHEREBE, daughter of COL. WILLIAM HINTON. (See our Vol. 69, p. 10; Vol. 20, 0 26. In 1850 Census Greene Co. he was age 32 born Ga.; she was 35 b. N.C.)

January 30, 1838
    Departed this life at 9 p.m. on 16th inst. at house of his brother, CEPHAS L. WILSON at Salubria, Pickens County, Alabama, Mr. FRANCIS H. WILSON. He was a young man of high respectability...aged 21 years 1 month 10 days. Raised in Lunenburg County, Virginia where his parents now reside. Left that country in the fall of 1835 for this State; he had never since returned...

February 6, 1838
    Nothing of interest.

March 13, 1838
    HENRY WELCH deceased. ARCHIBALD A. MCNEILL, administrator.

March 20, 1838
    Nothing of interest.
    This is the last issue of the bound volume of newspapers, on file at the Probate Office of Livingston, Sumter Co. Ala. 1856.

SUMTER DEMOCRAT

A newspaper published at Livingston, Sumter Co. Ala. each Saturday by HENRY W. COLLIER and SAMUEL W. INGE.

May 3, 1851 (torn)
    Married at Gainesville on the 1st by REV. JOHN L. KIRKPATRICK, Mr.

ALBERT B. HOLCOMB to Miss CAROLINE A. HUTCHINS, all of this county.

May 10, 1851   (torn)
May 13, 1851   (torn)
May 24, 1851
     Married in Mansfield, DeSoto Parish, Louidiana, Mr. CHARLES W.
GIBBS to Miss SUSAN M. BONEAU of the same place on 19th March last.
     Died in this place Saturday evening last after a short illness,
BETTY ANN, infant daughter of CHRISTOPHER S. and JACQUELINE S. MCCONNICE.
     Died in this place on 17th the infant son of JOHN F(OSTER) and
AMARINTHA VARY (BROOKS). See Vol. 39, p. 99.

May 31, 1851
     Died in this place Wednesday last at the residence of W.M. SHEARER,
Esq. after an illness of 5 days, JOSEPHINE, daughter of WILLIAM BOLTON
of this county, aged 14 years.

June 7, 1851
     Married at the residence of Mr. NATHAN AMASON by B.B. THOMAS, Esq.
on the 4th, Mr. A.W. RICHARDSON to Miss MARTHA A.E. KNIGHT, all of
this county.

     Lone Star State, Lewis Pub. Co. 1892. JOHN T. GILL b. 1819 Franklin
Co. N.C. d. 1876 Freestone Co. Tex. m. MARY BONNER, dau. of REUBEN W.
BONNER b. Ala. Came to Tex. 1852. Clin. RB JOHN H. of Childress Co.
Tex.; CALLIE; WM. HUBB b. Freestone Co. Tex. 1854.

June 14, 1851
     Married in Butler County on 29th by REV. SAMUEL OLIVER, Mr. JOHN
T. GILL of Sumter County to Miss LOUISA M., daughter of R.M. BONNER,
Esq. of Butler Co. Ala.

June 21, 1851
     Nothing of interest.

June 28, 1851
     SARAH TERRELL deceased. MATTHEW C. HOUSTON, executor of will. (In
1850 Census, she was aged 90 born in N.C.)

July 5, 1851
     Married in this place at Episcopal Church on 1st by REV. J.H.
TICKNOR, GEORGE B. SAUNDERS Esq. to Miss MARY T. GIBBS, daughter of
CHARLES R. GIBBS, Esq. all of Livingston.
     Died at the residence of her husband in this county, Mrs. ELIZABETH
BELL wife of Mr. JOHN W. BELL. (In 1850 Census she was aged 19 b S C and
he was 25 b. S.C.)

July 12, 1851
     Married in this county on 10th by DAVID HITT, Esq. DR. C.F.
WILLIAMS of Oxford to Miss MARTHA daughter of G.W. CHANDLER Esq. at the
residence of the latter.
     Died at his residence in this county on the evening of the 5th
DANIEL GOULD in the 37th year of age. Husband and father. Baptist...

July 19, 1851
     Nothing of interest.

July 26, 1851
     Nothing of interest.

August 2, 1851
     Married at Gaston on the 21st by JESSEE J. SHEID, Esq., Mr. WILEY
JONES to Miss JANE VEIL, all of this county.
     Died of congestion of the bowels at his late residence in this
county on the 29th, RICHARD HARRIS in his 64th year... Native of
Abbeville District (to the L), South Carolina and in the year 1836 re-
moved to this county...devoted family.
     Died on 30th ROBERT RANDOLPH infant son of JAMES W. and R(ACHEL) K.
MAURY aged 2 months 14 days.

August 9, 1851
    Nothing of interest.

August 16, 1851
    Nothing of interest.

August 23, 1851
    Nothing of interest.

August 30, 1851
    Nothing of interest.

September 13, 1851
    Married in Choctaw County on the 3rd by REV. ALEXANDER MCBRIDE,
DR. WILEY BROWNRIGG of this county to Miss MARY E. PRINCE of the former
county.

September 20, 1851
    Married at Eutaw Friday morning the 12th by S.J. CHAPMAN, Esq.
Mr. WM. H. HUNT to Miss ELLA J. BOND all of Lauderdale County, Miss.
    Married on 18th September by REV. JAMES O. WILLIAMS, Mr. WALLEN W.
WAINRIGHT to Miss JULIETT A. GRAHAM, all of this county.

September 27, 1851
    Nothing of interest.

October 4, 1851
    Married at Gainesville Wednesday 1st of October by REV. JNO. L.
KIRKPATRICK, WILLIAM O. WINSTON, Esq. to Miss AMANDA MORRISON both of
this county. (In 1850 Census, he was aged 41 born in Tenn.)
    On Thursday evening, October 2nd, by REV. J.L. KIRKPATRICK, Mr.
JAMES H. HOUSTON to Miss MARY AMANDA SMITH all of this county.

October 11, 1851
    Nothing of interest.

October 18, 1851
    Departed this life near Sumterville on Friday morning the 10th,
AMARANTH MARY, wife of HARRIS W. KILLEN and daughter of CAPT. JAMES
PARKER aged 29 years 5 months and 27 days...congestion of the brain...
Family burying ground at CAPT. PARKER's...Episcopalian...(In 1850, she
was 27 b. Ala.)
    State of Alabama-Sumter County. JOSIAH WRENN, administrator with
will annexed of estate of ANNA EDWARDS, deceased. Non-resident heirs:
GEORGE WRENN, ABRAHAM FISHER in right of his wife SARAH, SHERROD HOWELL,
JANE HOWELL and the heirs of WILLIAM WRENN, deceased. (Note: In 1850
Census, one JOSIAH WRENN was aged 36 b. N.C.)

October 25, 1851
    Nothing of interest.

November 1, 1851
    Married on Thursday 30th October by JAMES BEAVERS, Esq. Mr. WILLIAM
J. POOLE to Miss MARY BILLUPS, all of this county. (She was daughter of
THOS. M.)
    Died in the neighborhood of Jones' Bluff in this county, VERNAL
LOWERY on 28 October 1851 (injuries from a fall). (In 1850, he was 43
born in N.C.)

November 8, 1851
    Died at the residence of her husband on Thursday the 20th of last
month, Mrs. SUSAN E. STUART wife of Mr. RICHARD E. STUART of this
county in 18th year of age...

November 15, 1851
    Nothing of interest.

November 22, 1851
    Married on 16th by REV. WILLIAM WOODARD, Mr. WILLIAM H. STOUTTON to
Miss MARY Y. SEALE at the house of her father in this county.
    Departed this life after a lingering and painful illness, MARGARET
ELIZABETH, eldest daughter of MARY W. and late JOEL WHITSITT. Born
25 December 1835 died aged 15 years 10 months 14 days...

November 29, 1851
    Nothing of interest.

December 6, 1851
    Married on 26 November last by REV. F.B. LOFTIN, Mr. HIRAM BROWN
to Miss ELIZABETH FOSTER, all of this county.
    Died near Intercourse in this county on 17 November last, WILLIS
THORN in 29th year. (In 1850, he was 27 b. N.C.)

December 13, 1851
    Died in Montgomery on December 2, 1851, Mrs. GEORGENA R. RIGGS, wife
of JOEL RIGGS in 29th year. (In 1850 Census Montgomery Co. she was 26
b. N.C.)

December 20, 1851
    Died at Downieville, Forks of the Yuba, California, October 14th,
MAJ. JEREMIAH MANASCO of Alabama aged 39...Mason. (m. Miss PHOEBE HILL
11 Feb. 1846, Sumter County.) (Mrs. Guttery writes, 1962, "Our Jeremiah
Manasco went to Sutter's Mill California with his nephew, CALTON MANASCO
in 1849. This was JOHN's bro. as CALTON W. was his son.)

January 10, 1852
    Died at Mrs. BINGHAM's near Gaston on the 5th, REV. ROBERT W(ILSON)
HADDEN in 28th year of his life and 3rd year of his ministry...(Note:
He married 1850 LOUISA JANE BINGHAM, daughter of Mrs. MARY BINGHAM.)
(Received his education at Nassau Hall (now Princeton) and his theological
education at Columbia, S.C.)

January 17, 1852
    Married in this county on 7th by REV. D.P. BESTOR, Mr. ANDREW
MILLER to Miss MARY M. daughter of JUDGE BOOTH of Louisville, Mississippi.
    Died on 1st after a lingering illness, Mr. GEORGE M MALLORY, native
of Virginia and for many years past a highly respected merchant. (Mobile
Herald)

January 24, 1852
    Married on the 15th in Greene County by REV. Mr. MITCHELL, Mr.
PHILLIP P. MAY of this county to Miss JANE TINDALL.
    On 15th January by REV. GEORGE W. BOGGS, Mr. JNO. T. SMITH to Miss
CORNELIA E. daughter of M.C. HOUSTON, all of this county.
    In this county on 21st by REV. Mr. CLEMENT, Mr. THOMAS M. HILL, to
Miss MARY MAY, daughter of R(ICHARD) B. MAY, Esq.
    In the Parish of Caddo, Louisiana on 17th December last by REV.
WILLIAM SCALL, of the Episcopal Church, DR. R.T. GIVVS, of Mansfield,
to Miss EMILY C., daughter of FLABEL FOSTER, Esq.

February 21, 1852
    Married at the residence of DR. H.F. ARRINGTON on the morning of
the 17th by REV. J.O. WILLIAMS, Mr. JOSIAH MOORE to Miss SARAH REBECCA
WARD, all of this county.

February 28, 1852
    Departed this life on the 18th about noon at her father's in the
village of Gaston, Sumter County, Mrs. HARRIET, consort of J.J. WATSON
aged 25 years 12 days, second daughter of PLEASANT and FRANCIS WHITE.
She was born near Greensboro, Greene County, Alabama February 7, 1827.
Baptist. Married November 22, 1847...
    Died at Capan Grey, Missouri (Mrs. JENKINS copied at Miss) on
31 December last, Mrs. SOPHIA H. consort of TULLY R. CORNICK, Esq.
formerly of this place, aged about 30 years. Well known.

March 13, 1852
    Died at Tompkins at 8 o'clock on the morning of the 20th after a
short illness, PETER C. DINKINSON aged about 40 years. Raised near
Coffeville, Clark County, Alabama, where many of his near relations now
reside. Settled in Tompkinsville in 1839. (Note: 1850 Census Choctaw
Co. Ala. he was aged 40 b. Va.)

March 20, 1852
    Died in Livingston Monday evening Mar. 8th, WILLIAM DUKE aged 19.
Raised in this county.

March 27, 1852
    Married in this county on 21st at the residence of ALBERT LANCASTER
by THOMAS B. WETMORE, Esq. Mr. ADDISON HORDE to Miss JOSEPHINE COCKRELL.
    Died in this vicinity, WILLIAM BREWER aged 76. (In 1850, aged 76
b. N.C.)

April 3, 1852
    Married in Kemper County, Miss. on the 10th by REV. Mr. WOODS, DR.
MATTHEW TALBERT to Miss SARAH, daughter of MAJ. ALEXANDER C. POWE. (Copy
of Barry W. Talbot, 1968 says Sarah was daughter of ALEX CRAIG POWE and
wife MARY ALLEN (CHAPMAN)) (From Lone Star State, Lewis Pub. Co. 1983
(Navarro, Anderson, Freestone, Limestone and Henderson Co. Tex.), MATHEW
TALBOT b. Ala. d. 1863 med. Dr. md. SARAH POWE b. Miss d. 1875 chn.
HARRY CRAIG b. Aug. 22, 1859 Kemper, Miss. and ANNIE BARRY 1885
Navarro Co. Tex. (Tex. in 1870). Several words ellegible. Note: H.C.
TALBOT was raised by an uncle, REV. A.R. SCARBOROUGH.) (After MATTHEW d.
she married a Mr. REYNOLDS and had chn. - girls, he thinks.)

April 17, 1852
    Departed this life on 9th of April in her 44th year. Mrs. AZUBAH K.
POST, wife of Mr. A. POST of Gainesville... (In 1850 Census, she was
age 41 b. Conn. and her husband, ACKMON POST was aged 55 b. Conn.)
    This is the last issue in the bound volume of newspapers and are
on file in the Probate Office of the Court House at Livingston, Sumter
County Alabama 1956.

LIVINGSTON JOURNAL

Extracts, printed and published in Sumter County, Ala.

July 9, 1875
    Died at the residence of her son in law, Mr. J(OSEPH) G. COLEMAN
(32T) at Lauderdale Sta. Miss. on the 15th of June, 1875, Mrs. ELIZABETH
M. HARRIS (52SC). She was born in Greenville District, South Carolina
May 3 1798 and was married to Mr. RICHARD HARRIS (62SC) March 12, 1818.
She moved with her husband to Alabama in 1835 and settled in Sumter Co.
In 1836 where she continued to live until a few years since when from
old age and infirmity she made her home with her daughter and son in law.
Joined the Presbyterian Church in S.C. more than 50 years ago...S.J.B.

July 16, 1875
    Mr. JOHN HARE. brother of the late WILLIS V. HARE sends us a sample
of red wheat.
    J.G. HARRIS, administrator of WYATT HARPER (49G), deceased.
    E.A. MCMILLAN, administrator of HUGH MCMILLAN.

July 30, 1875-Friday
    HIMIE NICHOLS (see HIRAM p. 10), son of Mrs. ROSANNA NICHOLS, aged
about 6 years, died of congestive chill last Saturday.
    Administrator's Notice-Sumter County, Alabama
    JULIETTE VANDEGRAFF (45G), deceased. E(LIZA) J. V(ANDERGRAFF)
BALDWIN, admrx.

August 6, 1875
    State of Alabama-Sumter Co. MICHAEL GRADY, administrator of estate
of ARMISTEAD GATEWOOD, deceased.

August 13, 1875
    Mrs. ELIZABETH R. STARNES (8A), wife of Mr. F.L. STARNES and oldest
daughter of JAMES H. BELL, Esq. died at her residence in Warsaw, Sumter
Co. Tuesday the 27th of July aged 33 years 9 months and 25 days. It was
at Salem, N.C. she laid the foundation of a practical education. At.
Greensboro, N.C. she received all the accomplishments of a more popular
education...Mrs. STARNES 5 months before her death stood by the bedside
of a departing brother. She leaves a husband, father, sister and 3
brothers...A.G.G.
    Tribute of Respect - Mrs. LILLY R. STARNES, who died 27 July in 34th
year by Johnson Grange No. 233.

August 20, 1875
    Mr. W.E. PERT of Pike, 71 years of age, walked 6 miles to Troy on
election day to cast his vote.

August 27, 1875
    ELIAS and JENNIE MURPHREE of Murphree's Valley, celebrated their
golden wedding the 20th. REV. DEFOREST ALLGOOD, JEREMIAH ELLIS and Mrs.
PATSY ELLIS, witnesses to their marriage 50 years ago were present.

September 3, 1875
    R.G. MCMALION, Jr. aged about 16 years, son of Mr. A.W. MCMALION
met with a fatal accident on the 21st.

September 10, 1875
    Notice to non-residents -
    State of Alabama-Sumter Co. Probate Court. TO: WILLIAM JOHNSON,
HARVY JOHNSON, SUSAN HARRINGTON, JULIA A.G. JOHNSON and CATHARINE
JOHNSON. Take notice that WILLIAM LARKIN has filed the will of LEWIS
JOHNSON, late of this county deceased.

September 17, 1875
    Ex-Governor, THOMAS H. WATTS was married on the 3rd to Mrs. E.C.
JACKSON of Princeton, N.J.

September 24, 1875
    Died in Livingston Friday, the 17th, PEARL, daughter of D.W. and
A(NNIE) P. MITCHELL aged about 1 year.
    A(UGUSTUS) E. BROCKWAY, deceased. M(ANTHA) E. BROCKWAY, administra-
trix.

October 1, 1875-Friday
    Mr. WILLIAM KIRKLAND, an old citizen of this place died suddenly on
Wednesday near town. Had been in bad health for some months. Leaves a
large family.

October 8, 1875
    Several deaths have occured in our county within a few days. We.
have heard of the following: Mr. J.D. COWAND, Mr. A(RNOLD) A. POWELL,
(39SC), Mr. W.I. ALLEN, Mr. NICHOLAS SWILLEY, Mrs. G.W. TORRY, and Mrs.
JOHN R. BARNES. (NANCY 27K)

October 15, 1875
    Choice Groceries - E. & T.E. LOCKARD.

October 22, 1875
    Mortgage Sale. Mortgage made by THOMAS H. DILLARD (3A), NANCY (39T)
J. DILLARD. Their share of estate of JOHN J. DILLARD (52V), deceased.
Mortgage dated 22 Dec. 1870.

October 29, 1875
    Mr. B. WHITE, an old and much respected citizen of Warsaw died a few
days ago.
    Died on the 14th, WILLIAM ALLISON, son of N.B. and M.M. BULLOCK
aged 4 mo. 3 days.

Married on 12th at residence of bride's mother, by REV. J.S.
FRIERSON, Mr. NAT. KENNARD (3As of Jasp) and Miss PATTIE C. JOHNSON,
all of this county.

November 5, 1875
    Died in Livingston on the morning of 3rd of hemorrhagic malarial
fever, MAGGIE, daughter of THOMAS & LUCY L. COBBS in her 16th year.
    Married on the 14th at the residence of S.M. SILLIMAN, Kemper Co.
Miss. by REV. S.J. BINGHAM, Mr. J.B. PANKEY and Miss M.E. ALEXANDER.

November 12, 1875
    Died on the 2nd near Jones' Bluff, SUSAN B. wife of JAMES B. LEE
aged 54.
    Died on night of 1st at Jasper, Tenn., CHAS. WESENBERG.

November 19, 1875
    Married on 16th at residence of bride's mother by REV. C.M. HUTTON,
Mr. JAMES T. BELL and Miss JULIA MCDONALD, all of this county. (death
of DANIEL A? Vol. 158, p. 53)
    Married on 11th at Gainesville by REV. A.A. MORSE, Mr. A.M. WOODS
and Miss HESSIE GRATTAN BELL, all of this county.
    Resolutions on death of MARGARET COBBS who died on 3rd. Livingston
Lodge #12, I.O.G.T.

December 3, 1875
    Died at residence of (wife of WM. PEMBERTON GOULD) Mrs. M(ARITA)
P(ENDLETON) GOULD (she was sis. of JEMIMA) on evening of 12 of November
of consumption, Mrs. J(EMIMA) O. WARREN (14A), wife of J(OHN) M. WARREN
(23SC) of Texas and youngest daughter of the late R(ICHARD) B. MAY (53NC)
aged 38 years. Funeral preached by REV. A.R. SCARBOROUGH.
    State items - HENDERSON KETCHUM of Blountsville died on the 23rd
of wounds inflicted by FRANK GABLE.
    Mr. J.E. GRIFFIN writes to the Moulton Advertiser of his visit to
an aged couple in Winston County: "On the 11th of November I dined with
Mrs. SELIVA (SELINA?) WALKER of Winston, who is 103 years old. She informed me she had 12 living children, 9 boys and 3 girls - 62 grandchildren and 28 great grandchildren. Her husband, BUCKNER WALKER is 104
and attends to his mill." (In 1860 Winston Co. Ala. BUCKNER WALKER 54 b.
Tenn., SELETA 35 b. Ga.) (Anc. of Wm. H. Taylor, 502 Church St., George-
town, Ill. 61816. Feb. 19, 1978. BUCKNER WALKER b. Ga. 1806 Ga. d.
Winston Co. Ala.? m. SALETA FREELAND, Resident of Lumpkin Co. Ga. 1832.)

December 10, 1875
    Married at the residence of CAPT. T.H. LAKE, Mobile, Ala. by REV?
S.U. SMITH, ADDISON G. SMITH, Esq. of Livingston, Ala. to Miss FLORENCE
D. HOPKINS of Stockton, Cal.
    We regret to learn that Mr. G(REEN) B. MOBLEY (50SC), an aged and
respected citizen of Gainesville had one of his arms mutilated in a gin.

December 17, 1875
    L.F. WHITEHEAD offers plantation for sale.

December 24, 1875
    Estate of CATHARINE MCMILLAN, deceased. M.J. DOVE, adm'r.
    Estate of ISABELLA GILMORE, deceased. A.J. DERBY, adm'r.

January 7, 1876
    Mr. E(REN) N. BRYANT (37NC), an old citizen of this county died in
Sumterville neighborhood Monday night. He was the father of Mrs. (SARAH
J.) (5A) E.H. WARD (m 1866 E.H. WARD), whose husband's death is noted
in another place in today's paper.
    We regret to learn that CAPT. E.H. WARD, who was shot by JOHN GRAY
in Choctaw last week died from the wound received.

January 14, 1876
    Married at the Methodist Church in Belmont by REV. JAMES M. PATTON
on the 9th, Mr. ROBERT B. FLOWERS and Miss ANNIE CALDWELL, all of Sumter.

Mr. and Mrs. THOMAS SIMMONS of Chilton Co. have buried 24 children in one graveyard. Only one of them lived to maturity. The aged couple live alone.

January 21, 1876
Married on the 17th at residence of Mr. R.H. HALE by REV. C.M. HUTTON, Mr. ALBERRY W. OWENS and Miss LIZZIE MCALPINE, both of this county.

Died at the residence of his father, Mr. JAS. W. MAURY (27V) in Kemper Co. Miss. Dec. 24, 1875 in his 27th year, RICHARD HARRIS MAURY (1A). Educated at Spring Hill College near Mobile... In 1871 he entered U of Va. and graduated the same year in literature and in 1873 in law. Soon after his return home, he removed to Ark., settled in Little Rock. On 16 Dec. last, he came on a visit to his father, where he anticipated spending a happy Christmas with his parents and brothers.

State Items - On the night of 5th, the wife of CAPT. BENJAMIN R. HARRIS living near New Hope committed suicide.

February 4, 1876
Mr. GREEN B. LOWE (25A), a well known citizen of South Sumter died suddenly near Black Bluff some three weeks ago.

J.M. MASON, a Henry County planter was drowned in Alabama River week before last.

February 11, 1876
Married on the 3rd, by REV. J.S. FRIERSON at the residence of bride's father, DR. D.D. BRIGGS, Mr. T.O. RHYNE of Sumter Co. Ala. and Miss C. BRIGGS of Kemper Co. Miss.

Tribute of respect. Of our beloved brother WILLIAM I. ALLEN who died Oct. 2, 1875. Sumpter Lodge #166. Copy sent to widow.

DR. J.H. TAYLOR and Miss FANNIE MOSBY of Gainesville were married on the 1st.

February 18, 1876
Married on the 10th by REV. J.M. PATTON at residence of Mrs. WIMBERLEY in Sumter Co., Mr. A. HINKLE and Miss EUGENIA WILSON.

Mr. I.D. HOIT, an old citizen of this county left Wed. for Texas accompanied by son WILLIAM.

Mrs. S.M. REAVIS, widow of the late JUDGE REAVIS of this county, has removed to Natchez, Miss. her former home.

Mr. JOSEPH HERRING of Gainesville died of typhoid pneumonia last wee,

State Items - COMMODORE VICTOR M. RANDOLPH died at residence of his son near Blount Springs a few days ago.

February 25, 1876
Notice to Non-residents
B.A. SIMMONS   )
    versus   )
THOS. J. CARVER &   )   In Chancery, Sumter Co. Ala.
ULRICA E. CARVER   )
The CARVERS reside in New Orleans, La. (This was REV. THOMAS J. CARVER, Methodist minister probably born in 1828, married 1849 Mobile. (1) LAVENIA daughter of THOMAS STRONG married (2) 1860 Sumter Co. - Mrs. ULRICA E. (THOMPKINS) LEVERT.)

March 3, 1876
Married on the 12 Jan. 1876 in Bellevue, La., Mr. JAMES H. GRIFFIN (formerly of Gainesville, Ala.) and Miss JULIA V. MCSPADDEN.

March 10, 1876
Married on 29 at residence of Mr. J.F. WILLIAMSON by REV. J.M. PATTON, Mr. WILLIAM CARROLL and Miss VIOLA CURRY, all of this county.

On the 24th at residence of bride's mother, by REV. J.S. FRIERSON, Mr. JOHN J. ALTMAN, Esq. and Miss CORA A. LOCKARD, all of this place.

Miss MARY CRIGGS and Mrs. JOHN CALLOWAY died in Gainesville week before last.

March 17, 1876-Friday
 Died near Brewersville Feb. 16, MARY E., daughter of FELIX and DORA
MCMILLAN...
 The wife of Mr. HENRY MCDANIEL (48NC, wife in 1850 was DELILAH 44T)
died last Friday at Sumterville of paralytic stroke.
 Mr. G.W. ROGERS aged about 30 died at the residence of his father
in law, Mr. D(AVID) W. HOODS (29SC) on the 9th. (Married to MARY S.
HOODS (1848-71))
 CAPT. JESSE A GIBBS (37V) who took a prominent part in movement to
establish a city court at Gainesville is writing a history of his even-
ful life. Extracts: "I was born in Prince Edward Co. Va. May 29, 1812...
My mother was a RANDY and married my father in Prince Edward Co. near
Burksfield, 40 miles west of Richmond. I left there with my uncle when
he came there to draw his legacy from his grandfather. My uncle lived
in Kentucky. I went with him home. I was 7 years old when I left my
parents' house."...

March 24, 1876
 Notice to Non-residents - State of Alabama-Sumter Co. TO: MARY A.
LAND (4A) and husband, HENRY G. LAND. Take notice that JUDITH KESIA (22A)
SIBLEY and SAMUEL W. SIBLEY have this day filed the will of SAMUEL B. (46V)
SIBLEY, deceased. (1850 Marengo Co.)
 State Items - THOMAS R. ADAMS, a soldier of the War of 1812 died in
St. Clair Co. on the 6th in the 83rd year of his age.

April 7, 1876-Friday
 Mr. PHILIP WILLINGHAM (41NC), an old and respected citizen of
Ramsey's Station neighborhood died on Monday. Had been in feeble health
for some months.
 Notice to Non-residents-
 Citizen's Mutual Insurance Co.
 versus
GEORGE A. BROWN, Sr. & Jr., WILLIAM L. BROWN, GEORGE W. HINTON
GEORGE W. BATES and AMANDTINE R. ALLEN, executrix etc. Each defendant
is of full age; WILLIAM L. BROWN resides in Tenn.; GEORGE A. BROWN, Sr.
and Jr. reside in West Point, Lowndes Co. Miss.; GEORGE W. HINTON
resides in Brookville, Noxubee Co. Miss.

April 14, 1876
 Mr. G. SID. WHITE, living near Gaston and one of the most respected
citizens of South Sumter was drowned.
 A number of our citizens went to Meridian Tuesday to attend the
golden wedding of Mr. and Mrs. R(OBERT) F. HOUSTON (48NC, wife ANN 48T),
former residents of this place. Yesterday was the 50th anniversary.
 DR. ISAAC F. PEARSON of Gainesville died on the 31st aged 39.

April 21, 1876
 Notice to Non-residents-
 TO: MARTHA R. HARRIS, wife of ROBERT HARRIS, SALLIE V. (1A) wife
of LEVI HURLBUTT (M. 1869) and FANNIE LEE EARLY. TAKE NOTICE THAT Mrs.
CARRIE WILLINGHAM has filed the will of PHILIP WILLINGHAM.
 Died at his late residence in Sumter Co. on 3 April, GREEN W. GRANT
(D in Con-46SC). Born in Greenville District, S.C. 6 January 1803 and
emigrated to Greene Co. Ala. at an early age and from thence he removed
to Sumter about 1836...

April 28, 1876
 Married on the 25th at residence of Mrs. BILLUPS, in Sumter Co. Ala.
by REV. J.M. PATTON, Mr. CHARLES E. HAGEN and Mrs. JANE SWANN.

May 5, 1876
 Little EDDIE WINDHAM aged 4 months and little MARY WINDHAM aged
3 years died, the former on the 4th and latter on the 10th of Oct. 1875.
Poem dedicated to Mrs. M.A. WINDHAM.

May 12, 1876
 Married on the 20th, Mr. FRANCIS L. STARNES and Miss AGGIE BARNES,
both of Warsaw, this county.

DELILAH MCDANIEL (44T) was born in Davidson Co. Tenn. April 27, 1807. Her parents, JOHN and MARGARET HARRIS moved to Washington Co. Ala., then a part of Mississippi Territory and settled in the vicinity of St. Stephen. On Feb. 20, 1827 she was married to HENRY MCDANIEL of North Carolina, who survives her; united with Methodist Church June, 1831 under joint ministry of REVS. JOHN A. COTTON and A.A. DICKENSON. About 1835, with her husband, she removed to Sumter Co. Ala. recently purchased from the Choctaw Indians and were among the first settlers of Sumterville, and, we may say, of the county. Their names were the first enrolled on the record of the Methodist Church in that village, BRO. WILEY THOMAS preaching. She died March 10, 1876...To her only living daughter she said "Train your child right." To a son in Texas: "Tell ASBURY to meet me in heaven." Turning to Mrs. WILSON she said: "You must pray now for ASBURY in my stead."

  Estate of HENRY D. OATES (M. in Con. - 30NC), deceased.
  Estate of SUSAN LYNCH, deceased.
  Estate of W.W. PAYNE, deceased.
  Estate of JESSE HUTCHINS, deceased.
  Estate of J.B. RAMBO (26A), deceased.

May 19, 1876
  GEO. U. WALKER, Esq. and Miss CORNELIA RUSSELL of Gainesville were married on the 2nd.

May 26, 1876
  Mr. ROBERT W. BREWER (31A), a former well-known citizen of this place, but for several years a citizen of Wilcox, died of meningitis on 9th.

June 2, 1876
  Mr. W.W. CROOME, the father of Mrs. E.W. BELLAMY of Gainesville died in Rome, Ga. and was buried in Eutaw, Ala. on the 2nd.
  Married on 17th at residence of Mr. J.W. THETFORD by REV. ROBERT CALDWELL, Mr. JAMES W. LEE and Miss S.E. HOPPER, all of this county.

June 9, 1876
  COL. R(OBT.) G. MCMAHON (36V) contributes to the Dispatch copies of two letters written by his grandfather and dated respectively Sept. 26 and Oct. 28, 1774. The writer, JOHN MCMAHON was then serving in the Colonial army in Virginia, fighting the Indians.
  MAJ. SIMON HALL (28NC) has shown us a pocket-book over 100 years old. It is in possession of Mrs. ANN M. WARD (40G-wife of THOS. B.?). It was made for one of her North Carolina ancestors and bears the name and date "ENOCH WARD, May 21, 1776" wrought in needlework.

June 16, 1876
  REV. GEORGE B. WETMORE of North Carolina, brother of our townsman, COL. T.B. WETMORE (29NC), will deliver a free lecture on temperance.

June 23, 1876
  We had a pleasant visit this week from our venerable friend, HENRY MCDANIEL, one of the earliest settlers of Sumter.
  State Items - The wife of PROF. E.Q. THORNTON of Marion died on the 8th.

June 30, 1876
  Married on the 27th in Episcopal Church, Livingston, Ala. by REV S.U. SMITH, Mr. JNO. S. JOHNSTON and Miss M.V. THORNTON.
  We are pained to learn that the wife of E(DWIN) K. FULTON, Esq. (11A; son of WM. F.) formerly of Sumter but now of Birmingham died at the latter place on 23rd.

July 7, 1876
  Married in Bryan, Texas May 11, 1876 DR. F.M. HALL and Miss ELLA GILLESPIE (6A-daughter of JOHN C), the latter formerly of Livingston, Ala.

Married in Atlanta, Ga. at residence of bride's brother, W.B. LOWE, Esq. by REV. Mr. COOK, Mr. J(OSIAH) L. SCRUGGS (34) of Livingston, Ala. and Mrs. FANNIE C. GARY. (nee LOWE 1822-96)

The health of JONA. BLISS (50Vt.), Esq. of Gainesville had improved sufficiently to enable him to start on his annual visit to his native state, Massachusetts. (Born Randolph, Vt.)

July 14, 1876

Married on the 9th at residence of bride's mother by REV. J.M. PATTON, Mr. JOSEPH B. PATTON and Miss W.A. BEVILL.

July 21, 1876

DANIEL CARROLL died in Calhoun Co. June 16 aged 99. He was a pensioner for services in War of 1812.

Mr. JOHN N. SOWELL, a citizen of Conecuh Co. was shot and killed on night of 3rd by parties unknown. He was a Member of Democratic Executive Committee.

July 28, 1876

Died on the 2nd, the infant of S.V. and MOLLIE HORN. The wife of MAJ. THOMAS K. JACKSON of Gainesville died on the 13th. Daughter of the late JUDGE REAVIS and she leaves a family of several children most of them of a tender age.

ELIZABETH M. HARRIS, deceased. RICHARD M. HARRIS, adm'r.

August 4, 1876

Married on the 19th by REV. J.M. PATTON, Mr. W.W. GARLAND and Miss M.J. GRADY, all of this county.

Died in Livingston on the morning of 31st of typhoid fever, Miss MALLIE C. daughter of Mrs. E.J. UNDERWOOD in her 19th year. (See p.7)

August 11, 1876-Friday

Married on the 2nd by LEWELLIN LEWIS, Esq. at the residence of the bride's father, Mr. S. FORRESTER, Mr. JAMES A BRAKEFIELD and Mrs. MINERVA SWINDLE, all of this county. Each had been twice married previously and each has two children.

Mrs. ASA AMASON (45NC), one of the oldest and most respected citizens of Sumter died on the 8th after a lingering illness. (M. Nov. 20, 1838 SARAH H. SIMMS. See Vol. 128, p.5.)

Mr. ELNATHAN TARTT (34NC), a former citizen of Sumter died at Lauderdale, Miss. Sunday last after a protracted illness.

State Items - Mrs. TOWNSEND, an old and highly respected citizen of Mobile and mother in law of BISHOP MCTYEIRE of the Methodist Episcopal Church South, died recently in Nashville, Tenn.

August 18, 1876

Died on the 13th at the residence of her brother in law, DR. A(LEX) M. GARBER near this place, Miss CONSTANCE L., daughter of Mr. JAMES RHODES.

Notice to Non-residents - State of Alabama-Sumter Co. Probate Court, Aug. 9, 1876 TO: JAMES E. JENKINS, MARTIN L. JENKINS, M.R. JENKINS (devisee, legatee and transferree of ELIAS JENKINS), WILLIAM M. JENKINS, FRANKLIN P. JENKINS, BENJAMIN C. JENKINS, HENRY JENKINS, HATTIE JENKINS, ROBERT B. JONES, JEFFERSON B. ALLGOOD, DEFORREST ALLGOOD, JEFFERSON B. GRAHAM, DEFORREST GRAHAM, NANNIE S. GRAHAM, WIOLIAM GRAHAM, ELIZABETH PIERCE and JOHN PIERCE.

This day dame LEWIS M. STONE, administrator and NANNIE A STONE, administratrix of MARTHA W. HAIR, deceased.

August 25, 1876

Mr. W.H. NEVILLE of Preston Beat and aged 90 years was carried to the Polls on the 7th and voted the Democratic ticket. (Goodspeed's Miss. Memoirs, 1891. WM. H. NEVILLE b.S.C. 1812 (son of WM. and WLIZA-BETH (LINDSAY) NEVILLE). Moved to Sumter Co. Ala., m. SARAH SPENCER 1848. He died in Ala. in 1887.)

State Items - CAPT. P.U. MURPHY of Mobile died of apoplexy a few days ago. M.E. MACARTNEY, Esq., County Solicitor of Mobile died last week. Mr. BILLY WARD, aged 88, of Conecuh Co. walked 6 miles to the polls on the 7th. COL. SAM WELBORN of Russell Co. died some months ago. Left his wife and family $35,000 insurance.

September 1, 1876
Mr. JOHN H. GARNER (38NC) who died in Mobile last week was formerly a citizen of Gainesville. He resided there from 1837 to 1845. (1850 Census of S. Co.)

Visit from Mr. HENRY MCDANIEL, bordering on 4 score years. Revisited many localities in West Alabama and East Mississippi with which he was familiar some 40 years ago.

Died of diphtheria at the residence of their parents, J.Z. and KINNIE TUTT near Belmont, Sumter Co. Ala. on the 14th of August, little LAURIE aged 4 years 7 months 19 days and BIRDIE.

Miss C(ONSTANCE) L. RHODES, daughter of JAMES and ELIZABETH RHODES died at the residence of DR. A.M. GARBER, Sumter Co. Ala. Sunday morning Aug. 13, 1876 in her 43rd year...From childhood was under hand of affliction...

September 8, 1876
CASWELL EADS, Mobile, Ala. advertises his plantation near York for rent.

September 22, 1876
A veteran, Mr. JABAL FAULKNER (52SC), of York Beat and upwards of 80 years of age rode to town last Friday to hear the Governor.

Died in this county on the 8th, Mrs. ELIZABETH PHARES (45T), widow of the late Mr. J(OHN) C. PHARES (53NC) in her 72nd year. (She was daughter of REV. JAS. MONETTE and 2nd wife RACHEL FLETCHER.)

Died on the 12th at Warsaw, this county, Miss KATE BAKER aged about 20.

On the 14th near Sumterville, in this county, Mr. SLATER DOZIER.

Notice to Non-residents

RICHARD M. HARRIS (19SC)
            versus
RICHARD H. JEMISON et al. In Chancery, Sumter Co. Ala. RICHARD HARRIS JEMISON, MARGARET E. WALKER, ROBERT BORDEAUX (THOS. BORDEAUX married 1838 LAURA HARRIS, daughter of RICHARD), CLITUS BORDEAUX, SAMUEL K.HARRIS, ROBERT W. HARRIS, RACHEL K. MAURY (24SC, wife of JAS. F. 27Vt), EMILY A. COLEMAN (17SC), MARY E. BELL, ELIZABETH COLEMAN, and HARRIS COLEMAN are non-residents; JEMISON, WALKER, BORDEAUX, E.A. COLEMAN and BELL are over 21 and reside in Lauderdale Co., Miss.; MAURY, over 21, resides in Kemper Co., Miss., Shuqualak is her P.O.; ELIZABETH and HARRIS COLEMAN under 21 and reside with their mother, E.A. COLEMAN; SAMUEL K. HARRIS and ROBERT W. HARRIS, over 21 and reside in New Orleans, La.

October 6, 1876
W.B. PARHAM and E.C. HUTTON, law partners, Gainesville, Alabama.

October 13, 1876
Married at Ioncy, Choctaw Co. Oct. 4, 1876 by REV. W.H. WILD, Mr. HENRY MCDANIEL of Sumterville, Sumter Co. to Miss PERMELIA HARRIS of Isney.

Died near Coatopa Sta. on 10th, Mr. GEORGE MORRIS (48NC), an old and highly respected citizen of Sumter.

JOSIAH MOORE, deceased. R. CHAPMAN, Jr., administrator.

October 20, 1876
Died near Cuba Sta. on morning of 16th, Miss SARAH BROWN aged 96.

State Items - Mrs. CHARITY UPTON died on Sand Mountain the other day aged 99 years 8 months and 7 days. (Widow of REV. SOL. GEO. UPTON.)

October 27, 1876
Mr. JOSEPH PATTON (53NC), one of the oldest and most respected citizens of Sumter died at his residence near Brewersville a few days ago.

Our former citizen, Mr. JOSEPH ARRINGTON, now of Coahoma Co. Miss. is on a visit to Livingston.

November 2, 1876

Died on the 17th, the infant daughter of LEWIS and EMMA MCLEAN aged 4 months and 6 days...

Mr. JOSEPH PATTON was born in N.C. Dec. 20, 1797 and died at his home in Sumter Co. Ala. Oct. 20, 1876. His parents emigrated to Tennessee about 1808 and thence came to Alabama in 1811 and settled in Washington Co. He spent the early part of his life in Mobile, Baldwin and Marengo Counties. In the winter of 1831, he moved to Sumter Co. where he continued to reside until his death. On account of privations of new and unsettled country he was deprived of early educational advantages...Methodist Church at Brewersville in 1847...He leaves an aged widow and several children among them, REV. J(AMES) M. PATTON...

November 10, 1876

Married at the residence of Mr. JOSEPH JENKINS on the 1st, by REV. J.M. PATTON, Mr. J.C. ARRINGTON and Miss W.A. JENKINS, all of Sumter Co. Ala.

Died Sept. 19, 1876, S.C., Jr. son of S.C. and SUSIE COLEMAN, aged 2 years and 7 months.

Notice to Non-residents - TO: PATTON T. BLACKSHEAR, MATTIE O. PARKER wife of JAMES PARKER, NANNIE K. PHILLIPS wife of H. PHILLIPS and LULA BLACKSHEAR, all residents at or near Opelousas, Parish of St. Landry, La. TAKE NOTICE THAT JAMES M. PATTON, THOMAS A. SCALES, SAMUEL P(ATTON) HAND and DAVID U. PATTON have propounded for probate the will of JOSEPH PATTON, deceased. (SAMUEL P(ATTON) HAND born Jan. 5, 1835, married MARTHA ANN PATTON. SAMUEL P(ATTON) HAND was son of OBADIAH HAND and 4th wife MARTHA L. CLANTON.)

November 17, 1876

Mr. ISAAC MOORE was murdered last week near Uniontown.

November 24, 1876

Married on the 9th in Mobile, Ala. at the residence of Mr. R.G. HOUSTON by REV. DR. PALMER, Mr. J(OSEPH) O. SCRUGGS (1A-son of J DIAH L.) of Livingston and Miss ETTA HOUSTON of Mobile.

Died on the morning of 4 Nov., GEORGE MONETTE, son of RICHARD and MARY E. FELDER, aged 2 years 3 months and 25 days.

Died on morning of Nov. 19 at 3:15, MOLLIE E., wife of RICHARD FELDER and daughter of CAPT. J.W. and EMMA MONETTE and niece of L. BREWER, Esq.

Notice to Non-residents - TO: NANCY OWENS, MILICENT OWENS, W.R. OWENS, BETSY ROGERS and husband ARTHUR ROGERS, MAHALA WEBB, MARGARET MATTHEWS, ARMANDA WELLS, MATILDA BELL, MIRANDA CHERRY and husband JESSE B. CHERRY, LUCINDA GALLOWAY, ADELINE RITTER, AUZY JONES and husband JAMES JONES, all of whom reside in N.C. and LEWIS RITTER, who resides in Arkansas. TAKE NOTICE THAT W.G. LITTLE, Jr., administrator of JOHN RITTER, deceased, filed application to sell real estate.

Notice to Non-residents - TO: WILLIAM KIRKLAND, residence Corpus Christi, Texas; MARY A. BAILEY and husband, AUGUSTUS BAILEY, residence unknown; SALLIE B. PARDOM and husband WILLIAM PARDOM, residence Columbus, Ky.; ROBERT KIRKLAND, residence unknown and FANNIE KIRKLAND, residence unknown. TAKE NOTICE THAT Mrs. MARTHA H. KIRKLAND has filed application to probate the will of WILLIAM KIRKLAND, late of this county deceased.

Notice to Non-residents - TO: Heirs of SALLIE PARKER, whose names are unknown and who reside near Canton, Miss.; Mrs. FANNIE WATSON, residence Shubutam, Miss.; heirs of JOHN MORRIS, who reside in N.C.p heirs of ABRAHAM MORRIS, who reside in Monroe Co., Miss.; heirs of JAMES MORRIS, who reside in West Tennessee. TAKE NOTICE THAT Mrs. HARRIETT MORRIS (32NC, wife of GEO.) filed application to probate the will of GEORGE MORRIS, late of this county deceased.

THOMAS GREENE aged 72 of St. Clair Co. raised 500 bushels of corn.

WILLIAM REDDEN of Cherokee Co. recently murdered his wife age 67.

S.S. MONTGOMERY aged 23 accidentally shot himself fatally in Fayette Co. on the 10th.

December 1, 1876
    Notice to Non-residents - TO: JOHN L. UNDERWOOD, CAMILLA, Mitchell
Co. Georgia; TAKE NOTICE THAT BENNETT B. THOMAS and JOHN M. RAMSEY, administrators of estate of L(AUNCELOT) V. UNDERWOOD, deceased filed application to sell real estate.

December 8, 1876
    State Items - CHIEF JUSTICE BRICKELL and Miss MARY B. GLENN of
Montgomery married on the 29th.
    REV. JOS. C(UNNINGHAM) MCAULEY, member of the Presbyterian Church
and a citizen of Calhoun Co. was killed by train a few nights ago.

December 22, 1876
    Married at residence of bride's father in Livingston, Sumter Co. on
14th Dec. by REV. A.R. SCARBOROUGH, Mr. WILLIAM W. SMITH and Miss MAGGIE
J. TROTT.
    Married at residence of bride's father in Sumter Co. Ala. on 13 Dec.
by REV. A.R. SCARBOROUGH, Mr. J.M. SAIN and Miss B.B. MCGOWEN.

December 19, 1876
    REV. A.B. JONES of Clay Co. Missouri is visiting his brother,
CAPT. W.A.C. JONES of this place.

January 5, 1877
    KEARNEY C. HALL (29NC-KENNY C. in Census), deceased.

January 12, 1877
    Married in North Sumter on the 20th, Mr. L.D. NORVILL and Miss
FLORENCE WARE, all of this county.

January 19, 1877
    Died on the 15th near Payneville, this county, Mr. MATTHEW H. BOYD
(49SC), aged 68.
    Resolutions on death of JORDAN H. SHORT (33NC) by Livingston
Council #1, F of T.
    State Items - REV. JAMES M. SCOTT, a Baptist minister of Macon Co.
reached his 100th birthday on Jan. 8.

February 2, 1877
    Married at residence of Mr. JOE JENKINS on Jan. 10 by REV. C.R.
WILLIAMSON, Mr. A.B. HARRISON and Miss ELLA C.H. PHILLIPS, all of
Sumter Co.
    Married at the residence of Mr. J.T. SCRUGGS on Jan. 25 by REV.
C.R. WILLIAMSON, Mr. HENRY T. ANDREWS of Hale Co. and Miss ANNIE B. HILL
of Livingston, Sumter Co.

February 9, 1877
    Married on Monday Jan. 24 at Shady Grove Church by REV. H.H. MCNEAL,
Mr. C.M.A. ROGERS and Miss LIDA J. ROGERS, all of Sumter Co.   Selma
papers please copy.
    Died recently at his residence in Red River Parish, La. Mr. JAMES
M.N. ARRINGTON aged 54, brother of Mrs. L.F. WHITEHEAD and was raised
in Sumter.   In 1848 he removed to La. where he has resided ever since.
    DR. J.G. MICHAEL, late of Belmont has removed to Citronelle, Ala.
Physician and gentleman.
    J.C. BENNETT, deceased.   R. CHAPMAN, Jr., administrator.
    JANE MCELROY   )
      versus   )   Chancery Court, Sumter Co. Ala.
    BEDFORD MCELROY)
    The respondent is a non-resident.
    MATTHEW H. BOYD, deceased.   M.C. KENNARD, adm'r.
    Mr. GREEN HOLLY of Henry Co. dropped dead a few days ago.
    REV. JACOB WATSON, a Baptist minister died in Tuskegee in Dec. last
in his 97th year.
    Mrs. REBECCA PAUL of Butler Co. (to Mrs. GLENN) is in her 96th year.
She was married in 1801 and is still quite vigorous.

The St. Clair Aegis trots out Mr. WARREN DAVIS of St. Clair Co. as the champion old man of the state. He is now 100 and 10 years ago married his second wife.

February 16, 1877
Died in Sumterville, this county, on the 4th, Mrs. SARAH ELIZABETH HATTEN aged 26-1-22.

February 23, 1877
Married on the 15th at Cuba Sta. by REV. GEO. BANCROFT, Mr. EDWARD HALL and Miss LENORA KNOTT, all of this county.
Married at the residence of Mrs. N.A. STONE in Warsaw, Sumter Co. Ala. on 7th by REV. N.A. MCNEIL, Mr. W.H. ROGERS of that place and Miss HALLIE R. WILLIAMS, daughter of Mr. JOHN B. WILLIAMS, Sr. late of Greensboro, Ala.
Died on 5 Feb. infant daughter of FELIX and DORA MCMILLAN aged 10 mo.

March 2, 1877
Married Feb. 1, in Washington Co. by REV. J.C. JOHNSON, DR. JNO. D. JOHNSTON of Sumter and Miss OLIVA L. HOOKS of the former col
Mr. NATHAN AMASON (49NC), one of the oldest and most respected citizens of this county died suddenly of heart disease Sat. last at his residence near Sumterville aged 77.
COMER B. JONES, guardian of ANNIE B. HILL; final settlement of guardianship.
MATTHEW H. BOYD, deceased. M.C. KINNARD, adm'r.

March 9, 1877
Died in Livingston Sat. eve Feb. 24, little PETER, infant son of A.P. and J.H. EVANS aged 1 year 16 days. Bristol (Tenn.) News and Mansfield (La.) Reporter are requested to copy.
Died at the residence of DR. PERKINS in Oktibbeha Co. Miss. Feb. 20, 1877, CAPT. GEORGE WASHINGTON... Born in Edgefield District, S.C. on 24 Sept. 1826 and was at the time of his death in his 51st year. Graduated with honor at University of Alabama before he was 21. Then studied law with JUDGE ORMAND of Tuscaloosa and entered upon practice at Carrollton, Pickens Co. Ala. Afterward moved to Louisville, Miss. and formed a partnership with JUDGE ROBERT S. HUDSON and sometime thereafter formed a partnership with HON. J.A.P. CAMPBELL, now one of the Associate Judges of Supreme Court of Miss. with whom he practiced for several years in town of Kosciusko... Married Miss MARGARET S. CROMWELL, daughter of P.S. CROMWELL, formerly an esteemed citizen of Sumter Co. Ala. He settled and commenced farming and from thence forward to time of his death led the quiet life of planter in Oktibbeha Co. Miss. In 1861, he entered ranks of Confederate army, commanded a company of Miller's Regiment of Cavalry. Surviving are his mother, wife and children...
State Items - JOHN COX, residing near Ashville fell dead on 20th. CAPT. FRANK M. JOHNSON, the oldest of Mobile's River Men died in Birmingham last week. JAMES T. SMITH has been appointed Tax Collector in Greene Co. vice J.D. KIMBROUGH, dead. Miss ELIZA WHITFIELD, a demented sister of PROF. H.S. WHITFIELD, was accidentally burned to death in Tuscaloosa last week, aged about 65. Mr. BRANTLY STEPHENS was run over by a train near Fleming's Sta. a few nights ago and instantly killed.

March 16, 1877
Married on the 18 at residence of S.W. BARNES by REV. A.G. GROVE, Mr. JNO. W. BELL and Miss MAGGIE BARNES, all of this county.
Died on 12 near Intercourse (Sumter Co.), JOHN A. MCDONALD aged 33.
Died near Belmont, Sumter Co. Tue. Feb. 20, Mrs. ELIZA MCREE (30A-wife of WM.), nee GILLESPIE in her 59th year. Member of M.E. Church South....J.M.G.
JOHN M. WESTON (52SC), deceased. THOMAS S. WESTON (14A), adm'r.
J.M. MITCHELL, guardian of JAMES and MINNIE KENNARD.

Notice to Non-residents - TO: Mrs. MARY A. GILBERT (or SPEIGHT) who resides in Forest, Miss.; ELI WARD, resides in Wahalak, Miss.; HENRY WARD, resides in Forest, Miss.; JOE WARD, resides in Smith Co. Miss.; Mrs. ELLEN FOY (23NC) and husband WILLIAM FOY (25SC), resides in Forest, Miss.; SARAH A. MOORE and EVELINE ELLIS, who reside at Brandon, Miss.; MARY E. FARR and husband, DR. R.S. FARR, who reside at Centreville, Leon Co. Texas; TAKE NOTICE THAT D(AVIS) FOY (39SC) and T(HOS.) T. FOY (3/12A) have filed the will of NATHAN AMASON, deceased.

T(HOMAS) P. LEWIS, jeweler, an old resident of Tuscaloosa, died there on the first.

In Covington Co. lives Mrs. RAINER aged 113, whose youngest child is 75.

March 23, 1877
Died of consumption at residence of his mother near Intercourse, Sumter Co. March 12, Mr. JOHN A. MCDONALD aged 33-5-27...Presbyterian.

Died on 19th at residence of ROBERT MASON, of whooping cough, WILLIE, son of LEWIS and S.A. LANCASTER in 8th year.

R. CHAPMAN, Jr. GUARDIAN of S. RUTH WIER, PETER WIER and CHARLES N. WIER, minors; also administrator of MARY E. MCKERALL, deceased.

March 30, 1877
Married Tue. morning the 20th by REV. C.B. DUBOSE at residence of bride's father, J.L. TURRENTINE, Esq. and Miss TENIE, daughter of CAPT. J(ESSE) A. GIBBS, all of this county.

Died in Gainesville on the 18th, CALVIN WIGGINS. Had been a resident of that place since 1832.

April 6, 1877
DR. R.L. SEALE, an old and prominent citizen of South Sumter left a few days ago for Johnson Co. Texas to reside.

State Items Between Feb. 29 and Mar. 3, ZACHARIAH, DANIEL, VIRGINIA and JACKSON CHANDLER, all of one family died in East Perry of pneumonia.

April 13, 1877
Mrs. MARY MCRAE MAY (1A), wife of Mr. R.C. MAY died at her home on Indian River, Florida on 21st. Daughter of the late DR. WILLIAM P. MCRAE (28Miss) of this county and step-daughter of our townsman, CAPT. W.A. JONES. She was married in 1868 (1866) and in 1873 removed with him to Florida. She has left a husband and three children...

Funeral sermon of the late JOHN A. MCDONALD was preached in Siloam Church last Sunday by REV. A.J. SHELTON.

Died on the 9th, near Gaston, W.R. HORN.

Mrs. MARY E. LEE, guardian of J. MARSHALL and I.H. LEE.

A.R. SCARBOROUGH, guardian of ADELAIDE, JAMES, MOLLIE and ALICE BILLUPS.

State Items - DR. and Mrs. F(RANCIS) L. CONSTANTINE (46 France) of Birmingham celebrated their golden wedding on the 27th. (Greene Co. 1850 Census wife CLEMENTINE C. 36 NC, daughter of WM. R. and ELIZABETH HAMLETT.) MAJ. JOHN M. MOREY, formerly of Mo. and for many years widely known business man of Selma died in Dallas, Texas on the 29th.

April 20, 1877
Died on the 9th, Miss SALLIE A. SLEDGE, daughter of the late A(LBERT) G. SLEDGE aged 18.

Died at her home on Indian River, Brevard Co. Fla., March 21, Mrs. MARY MCRAE MAY in her 29th year. Daughter of the late WILLIAM P. MCRAE of this county and step-daughter of CAPT. W.A.C. JONES, who married her widowed mother. She married Mr. R.C. MAY of Sumter in 1866 (right) and in 1873 removed with him to Florida. Previous to her marriage she was a Presbyterian, but joined the Baptist Church with her husband... Leaves her husband and 3 children, one to whom she gave birth but 3 days before her death.

Died near Sumterville, March 21, Mrs. MARY ALEXANDRIA JACKSON aged 22-3-14, daughter of Mr. and Mrs. R.P. BOBBITT and granddaughter of Mrs. MARY SLEDGE. Methodist. Married Mr. C.M. JACKSON Feb. 10, 1875. Only child of her widowed mother, leaving a babe only 2 weeks old.

PETER HANDLEY (36K), deceased. L.T. ORMAND, adm'r.

State Items - S(TANDWICK?) W. HAYES (63SC), who resides 6 miles east of Blount Springs is 95 and has twice been married and is the father of 21 children. CAPT. W.A. ROBINSON, a prominent citizen of Hale Co. was drowned last week while returning from a visit to Demopolis. Swollen Stream.

April 26, 1877

DR. WILLIAM MCPHERSON, a prominent citizen and physician of this county died of pneumonia Monday morning at his residence at Belmont in prime of manhood.

Died in South Sumter Sunday the 22nd, Mrs. EDA HAMMONDS, aged 70.

Died in South Sumter Sunday the 22nd, Mr. DAVID PIPKIN, aged about 21.

DAVIS FOY, executor of NATHAN AMASON, deceased.

State Items - REV. W.H. BIGGS who moved from Pike Co. to Texas last year recently died from poison with wine, of which he was forced to drink by some "roughs." (1860 Census Pike Co. Da. Western Densyn p. 68 Po. China Grove, July 18, 451-451. BIGGS, WILLIAM H. 35 Ga. clergyman Meth. Epis. - $2,000, $2,000.; MARY 30 Ga., THOMAS 9 Ga.; JOHN 7 Ga.; WILLIAM 5 Ala.; ELIZABETH 3 Ala.; ALFORD, GEORGE 28 Ala., farm labor.)

May 5, 1877

WILLIAM ELROY BOYD, eldest son of ROBERT and REBECCA BOYD was born near Paynesville in this county February 4, 1851 and departed this life near the home of his childhood March 30, 1877 aged 26. Left fatherless at the age of 12, he provided for his mother and younger brothers and sisters...Presbyterian. Married November 12, 1873 Miss ALICE RHYNE, and also an infant...

Mr. WILLIAM F. TURNER (29V), an old and substantial citizen of Sumter died Thursday last after an illness of several months.

HON. R(OBT.) B. WALLER (44V), one of the oldest and best citizens of Greensboro died of paralysis of the heart on the 20th.

May 11, 1877

SALLIE ALBERTA SLEDGE was born in Sumter Co. near Horn's Bridge February 7, 1858. Methodist, since August 21, 1876. Died at residence of her uncle, DR. W(M.) H. SLEDGE near Sumterville April 9.

Died at her residence in Sumter Co. April 27, Mrs. E(LIZA) A. THORNTON (47V, wife of JAS.), born in Orange Co. Va. Feb. 4, 1804. Excellent wife and mother.

Mrs. MARY VENTRESS, an aged lady of Bullock Co. was burned to death.

May 18, 1877

Died in Meridian, Miss. on the 13th, infant son of F.E. and ADA W. HULL.

Died of pneumonia at his residence 8 miles west of Livingston, on the 13th, DR. WM. H. SLEDGE (28T), in his 58th year, son of JOSHUA and MARY L. SLEDGE and was born in Tennessee. While quite young he removed with his parents to North Alabama and in 1843 located in Sumter Co. where he resided up to time of his death. In 1848 he married Miss A. M(ELVINA) SIMMONS (18A), daughter of Mr. LEWIS SIMMONS, Sr. an honored citizen of Marengo, who with 6 children survive him. DR. SLEDGE had been a practicing physician for many years and also a planter...Was in the Confederate army.

May 25, 1877

Married in Starkville, Miss. on 16th, COL. E.K. FULTON of Birmingham, Ala. and Miss NENA MONTGOMERY of the former place.

Died at his residence in Preston Beat, this county, on 3rd, COL. WM. NEVILLE in his 91st year.

Died on 17th of heart disease, Mrs. A. M(ELVINA) SLEDGE, wife of
the late DR. WM. H. SLEDGE. Only last week we published a notice of
death of her husband, who died on 13th.

June 1, 1877
　　Died May 5 of paralysis at residence of REV. J.M. PATTON, Sumter
Co. Ala. Mrs. MARY H(ARRIET EATON) FALCONER aged 66. (Widow of ALEX.
HAMILTON FALCONER. Daughter of WM. born 1843 and MINERVA EATON born
1834, both married by REV. JAS. PATTON in Greene Co.)
　　Mr. THOMAS MAXWELL of Tuscaloosa has a curiosity in form of old
book printed in London in 1609 giving an account of DeSoto's expedition
in this country.

June 15, 1877
　　Mr. R(ICHARD) W. RYLAND (43V), an old citizen of Tuscaloosa was
found dead in bed on 4th.

June 22, 1877
　　W.F. TURNER, deceased. JOHN S. TURNER, administrator.

June 29, 1877
　　Mrs. C.A. BELL died at Warsaw on 24th. Mother of a large family
of children. She had just passed her 54th year.
　　Masonic burial service was read at grave of ROBERT HORN at Elizabeth
Church by Gaston Lodge.
　　Livingston Lodge #41. Resolutions on death of WILLIAM F. TURNER.

MONTGOMERY WEEKLY MAIL

Printed and Published in Montgomery, Ala.

March 30, 1860
　　"From Selma Sentinel: Alabama Medical Society make resolutions on
death of DR. ROBERT J. DICKERSON. JAMES KENT, M.D. president; E.J.
KIRKSEY, M.D. secretray."

April 20 1860
　　Montgomery County, Ala. Homicide in Sumter Co. of ENOS TERTT at
hands of THOMAS SIMMS on Monday last at SIMM's house 6 miles west of
Sumterville and 8 miles east of Gainesville Junction on Mobile and
Ohio Railroad. SIMMS claimed TARTT had stolen his wife.

June 1, 1860
　　A.B. MCCURDY (A.P. in Census - 50 NC), an old citizen of Dallas
Co. died on the 24th.
　　JACOB MORGAN, another old citizen of Dallas Co. died recently.
(See ts, died May 1860, born in Richmond Co. NY.)

July 13, 1860
　　Died at her residence in Dallas County, Mrs. MARY SAFFOLD (56G),
widow of the late HON. REUBEN SAFFOLD in her 67th year.

January 18, 1861 - Copied from Selma Reporter, 15th
　　Death of REV. A(DNER) G(AREYS) MCCRAW (47SC, Perry Co.), died in
this city yesterday morning aged 58. (Bapt. g.v.)

January 11, 1861 - Copied from Cahaba Slaveholder
　　Sudden death. Miss HARRIETT FAGAN, daughter of our esteemed friend,
ENOCH FAGAN, Esq. of Marion fell dead in the floor last night. Aged
about 18.

Published and printed in Elmore County, Alabama (Court-
esy of Department of Archives)

May 15, 1839
    It is with deep regret that the citizens of Wetumpka are called
upon to pay the final tribute of respect to the memory of their late and
highly esteemed fellow citizen, M.D. SIMPSON, Esq. late Editor of the
"Argus and Sentinel" published in this city, who departed this life after
a long and lingering illness on Tuesday the 7th inst., aged 33 years.
Mr. SIMPSON was a Scotchman by birth, born at Dundee Scotland AC 1804
and came to this country accompanied by his family in 1831 and has been
a resident of this city for the last four years, during which time many
offices of public trust were confered upon him, the duties of which he
invariably discharged with honor to his adopted country and credit to
himself. He was ardently devoted to the Democratic cause, but while he
was firm in the support of his political views, he ever demeaned himself
with a generosity and a spirit of amenity, that won for him alike the
approbation and affection of his friends and opponents. He was an esteemed citizen, and kind and affectionate husband, an indulgent father
and a devoted friend, few men indeed could have left a better recollection and a purer name. He has left an esteemed and amiable wife, and
three promising children, to mourn his bereavement and his loss! A
numerous concourse of our most respected citizens, preceded by the military and the Masonic brethren accompanied the body in procession to the
place of interment, where was consigned to the keeping of the dust the
last sad remains of mortality; bedued by the tears of regret and consecrated by the greeting emblem of Masonic Brotherhood. Which shall
convey him to realms of perrenal light. So mote it be.
    Died on Sunday the 12th of May 1839 in the city of Wetumpka, ELIZA
ALBERTHA, daughter of M.B. and SARAH A. MCCOY, aged one year and eleven
days

                Read ye that run the awful truth
                With which I charge my page
                A worm is in the bud of youth
                And at the root of age
                No present health can health ensuer
                For yet an hour to come
                No medicine though it oft can cure
                Can always balk the tomb
                Like crowded forest trees we stand
                And some are marked to fall
                The axe will smite at God's command
                And soon shall smite us all.

May 22, 1839
    Died on Saturday afternoon at the residence of his father, WILLIAM
JONATHAN, infant son of WILLIAM J. and LAVINIA D. COUCH aged 2 months
and 5 days. Page 3, column 4.

May 29, 1839
    Died in this city on Saturday morning 26th instant, Mr. LAWRENCE
SPINNACUTA, Printer, aged 45 years. The Savannah, Ga. papers are requested to copy the above. Page 3, column 5.

June 19, 1839
    A meeting of the friends and acquaintances of H. BARROW, deceased,
was convened at the Council Chamber, on Friday, 14th inst., when DR. J.
BEALL was called to the chair, and J.N. LIGHTNER requested to act as
Secretary on motion of W.W. MASON, Esq., a committee, consisting of
DR. J.T. REESE, W.A. MCCLUNG and M.M. GORMAN were appointed to draft
a paper expressive of the regret of the meeting for the death of Mr.
BARROW and of their respect for his memory, the committee after retiring
reported as follows: The committee in discharge of their melancholy duty
in offering this last tribute of respect to the worth of their departed
friend and associate, WILLIAM H. BARROW, can but express their unfeigned
grief for his untimely loss; nor can they let this opportunity pass
without offering their condolence to his immediate friends and acquaintance, and to his relatives and parents at a distance. The deceased had
for some time been ardently engaged in the study of medicine and in pre-
paring himself for future usefulness to his fellow creatures; had he

lived, science might have claimed him as one of her brightest ornaments,
but an all wise being has ordained it otherwise. Though he died at a
distance from those connected with him by the closest ties of our nature,
all that kindness, attention, and medical skill could do to avert the
hand of the destroyer was extended to him by surrounding friends and the
faculty that one so young in life, and who was just about to enter on
its active stage, should have been so suddenly snatched away by the rude
archer, as if to signalize the certainty of his triumphs over all mortality created in our bosom an anguish which only the remembrance of his
real virtues can mitigate by the hope that those virtues will secure to
him in another and better world a bliss that knows no ending. To us
remains now only the privilege of doing justice to his memory, and
commingling our griefs with those of his bereaved parents and relatives,
and condoling with them in their loss and affliction,
"But can storied urn or animated bust
Back to its mansion call the fleeting breath
Can honors words provoke the silent dust,
Or flattery sooth the cold dull ear of death."
On motion. Resolved that the proceedings of this meeting be signed by
the chairman and Secretary, and published in the city papers, and that
a copy be forwarded to the parents of the deceased.
J. BEALL, Ch'n
J.N. LIGHTNER, Sec'y   Page 3, column 2.
        Died in this city on Thursday, 13th inst. ADA BYRON, only child of
GEO. R. and SARAH J. HOWE, aged 13 months and 8 days.
        Her spotless Soul from pain and sorrow free,
        Suffer those little ones to come to me.
        Forbid them not for such surrounds my throne.
The New York City papers will please copy. Page 3, column 2.

July 24, 1839
        Died on the 18 inst. at his residence in this City, ALDERMAN JAMES
W. YARBROUGH in the 38 Year of his age. Thus in the meridian of his
life and usefulness has death robbed us of one of our most useful and
worthiest citizens. Mr. YARBROUGH emigrated from Jasper County in the
State of Georgia to this city in the spring of the year 1837 where by
the urbanity of his manners and his upright deportment he won the esteem
and confidence of all that knew him. At the first charter election for
the city, he was elected Alderman of the ward in which he resided, which
office he continued to fill with usefulness to the City and honors and
dignity to himself. His heart was the sacred temple of all the social
virtues and his home was emphatically the home of hospitality and kindness. The public demonstration of the City Authorities and his numerous
friends was but a just tribute to his worth and merit and the proud
motto of the poet may be justly inscribed upon his monument. "An honest
man, the noblest work of God." (From the Independent Monitor) Page 3,
column 1.
        Respect to the late REV. ROBERT M. CUNNINGHAM. Pursuant to Notice
the citizens of Tuscaloosa assembled at the Town Hall, on Thursday,
July 11, 1839 at 11 o'clock, A.M. to take into consideration the most
suitable means of paying proper respect to the memory of the late REV.
ROBERT M. CUNNINGHAM, when on motion of Mr. C.S. PATERSON, GEN. THOMAS
D. KING was called to the chair and R.T. CLYDE appointed Secretary.
After the object of the meeting had been stated from the chair on motion
it was Resolved that a committee of three be appointed to carry out the
intentions of this meeting. Messrs. ERASMUS WALKER, R.M. GARVIN and
M.D.J. SLADE were appointed said committee and on motion Messrs. JOHN
D. PHELAN and JOEL WHITE were added to the committee. On motion, Resolved that the Committee retire and report immediately. The committee
after a short retirement reported the following resolutions, which were
unanimously adopted: Whereas, We have recently received intelligence of
the deceased of the REV. ROBERT M. CUNNINGHAM. Resolved. By this
meeting that we feel it our duty on the melancholy intelligence of the
death of our late REV. ROBERT M. CUNNINGHAM, to meet together to give a
public expression to the profound respect and high admiration in which
we hold the memory of the deceased, and to bear testimony to his spotless
character and useful life. As a man, his integrity was above reproach
as a christian minister, he was a bright and shining light through a long
life: but it as one of that cherished remnant who fought the battle of
American liberty in the days "that tried men's souls", that our hearts

contemplate the venerable departed worthy; with the loftiest sentiments of love and gratitude. Resolved that we deeply sympathize with his family in their affliction. Resolved that a copy of these resolutions be forwarded to the family of the deceased. Resolved that the citizens of Tuscaloosa, the clergy of the city, the Professors and students of the University, the officers of the State, and the several societies, trades and Professions be respectfully requested to join the procession agreeably to the order of proceeding published by the committee of arrangements at 4 o'clock this afternoon; and that in token of respect to the virtues of the deceased, it be respectfully requested that the stores may be closed, and business suspended at that hour. Resolved, that if it be agreeable to the family of the deceased that the Tuscaloosa Guards be respectfully requested to join the procession in military order. Resolved that a committee of --- be appointed by the Chair to superintend and direct arrangements for the funeral. Whereupon, the chair appointed Messrs. CRABB, KING, BATTLE, J.D. PHELAN, CLYDE J. WHITE and MAJOR LEWEN. Resolved that these proceedings and resolutions be published in the paper of Tuscaloosa.   THOMAS D. KING, Chairman
                        R.T. CLYDE, Secy.
    Died in this city on the 17th inst., Mr. WILLIAM HUTCHINSON.

August 11, 1839

Died at Washington City, on the 25th ult. COMMODORE DANIEL T. PATTERSON, Commandant of the Navy Yard at that place. His illness was violent and of short duration. The deceased was in the Naval service about forty years, and was a midshipman in the Philadelphia frigate, when she was lost on the Tripolitan Coast in the year 1803. Commodore Patterson was a native of Long Island and at his death was about 58 years of age. General Naval Order: As a Mark of respect to the memory of COM. DANIEL T. PATTERSON, late of the United States Navy, who died at Washington on the 25th inst., the flags of the Navy yard, Stations and vessels of the United States Navy are to be hoisted half mast and nineteen minute guns fired at noon on the day of the receipt of this order. J. CHAUNCEY, Acting Sec. of the Navy, Navy Dept. Army Order: Adjutant General's Office Washington August 27, 1839. The Officers of the Army on duty near the War Department, and those who may be now at the seat of government, are requested to attend in uniform, the funeral of the late DANIEL T. PATTERSON, Commandant of the Washington Navy Yard at 4 o'clock on Wednesday, the 28 inst. R. JONES, ADJUTANT GENERAL.

August 21, 1839

Died on Sunday morning, 11th inst. in Mobile the HON. HENRY HITCHCOCK, in the 48th year of his age.
    Died at Windsor, the residence of COL. PAUL FITZSIMMONS, near Augusta, Ga. on the 12 inst., COL. DAVID W. ST. JOHN.

August 28, 1839-Same p. 3, column 2.

Died in the city of Mobile on the evening of the 16 inst., Mrs. ELIZA CASEY, relict of the late DR. THOMAS CASEY of that city.

September 11, 1839

Died in Augusta on Thursday morning the 4th inst., after a short illness, Mrs. SARAH WALTON, relict of the late JOSIAH WALTON and sister of the late GOVERNOR CLARKE of this state in the 72 year of her age. She had been an exemplary member of the Baptist Church for about thirty five years and contemplated her approaching dissolution with that tranquil resignation and peace of mind, which evinced her preparation for a change of worlds. She retained her senses to the last moment of her existence and aware that her end was approaching, she expressed her willingness to depart in the full assurance that she was about to enter upon higher enjoyments than the present world could possibly afford her. Her children and grandchildren and those who knew her in life will long retain an affectionate remembrance of her worth.

October 2, 1839
    Died yesterday morning about two o'clock at his residence in
Summerville, Mr. EPAPHRAS KIBBY, Junior Editor of this paper, aged about
27 years. (Mobile Register of the 16th inst.)

Date of paper, 1839
    Died in this city on the evening of 22 ult., GEORGE W. MAGHER, Esq.
in the 24 year of his age. He was a native of the State of New York.
    The death of a young, vigorous and promising man affects our minds
and feelings much more than the death of one who has lived his.
    "Three score years and ten" one departs as it were, because it is
reasonable that after having run a long race he should be at rest and
that having long battled in the conflicts of each he should be permitted
to retire from the field and allowed the opportunity of enjoying the
blessings of heaven. He seemed to go, because having performed the duties imposed upon him in this world, he is ready to take upon himself
duties of a higher and holier character in another and a better world,
but when a young man one who is just entering upon the way is taken from
amongst us we are filled with wonder and dismay. When to youth is added
health, strength, beauty and grace of person commanding talents, the love
of his intimate acquaintance, the good will of all and success in his
pursuits; when he possesses all that can render the present agreeable and
flattering and all that betokens a bright and brilliant future, when one
so gifted and so favored is taken from us before the sun has cleared
away the morning twilight of his existence. We feel an utter inability
to comprehend the wisdom of the great disposer of human events. Such
are our feelings when contemplating the fate of this young man.
    He came to this city in Feb. 1838 and soon after commenced the prac-
tice of the law. He was very early marked by our observant citizens, as
a man eminently calculated to attain success in the great business matters of life. His handsome, graceful and gentlemanlike person, his
winning manners, his amiable temper, his knowledge of the world, his intelligence, his talents, his professional knowledge remarked in one so
young, his energy, his elevated and honorable bearing in the discharge
of his social and (can't find the rest).

December 11, 1839
    Married at Abbeville Village on Tuesday morning, 19th ult. by the
REV. DR. BARR, COL. JOHN CUNNINGHAM of Laurens to Miss FLORIDA CALHOUN
NOBLE of Abbeville Village, daughter of his Excellency GOVERNOR NOBLE.

WETUMPKA ARGUS

Printed and published Elmore County, Alabama

August 5, 1840
    Died in Athens, Ga. on the 21st ultimo, MOSES WADDEL, D.D. late
President of Franklin College aged 70.

August 12, 1840
    Died in Autauga County at the residence of his father after a pain-
ful illness of 26 days, WM. B. ROBINSON in the 23 year of his age.

August 19, 1840
    Died of congestive fever on the 14th instant, Mrs. ELIZABETH SORELLE,
consort of S. J. SORELLE in the 32 year of her age. Esteemed by all who
were privileged with her acquaintance, her loss will no doubt be deeply
felt by her relatives and friends, especially in the removal afflictive
to her husband and numerous family of children.
    Few women discharged more fully the relative duties of wife, mother,
and mistress of a family; affection, industry and economy were marked
traits in her character. As a christian she gave the brightest evidences
of fervent piety. In the fall of 1832, she united with the Baptist
Church at Old Town Creek, Dallas County. Since that time it may be said
that the house of God was literally her home and the love of Jesus the
theme upon which above all others she delighted to dwell. When about a
year since, it pleased the Lord to visit this city with showers of

refreshing from his presence none was more active, none more ardently
engaged at a throne of Grace, than she, who, we thrust, is now united
with the worshiping assembly in heaven. During all her illness she retained full possession of her mental faculties. She was sensible sometime previous to her dissolution that death was near, and in answer to an
enquiry of her husband, replied, I am perfectly willing to die, I can confidently commit the keeping of my soul into the hands of my Savior, con-
tinuing from time to time, to express her confidence in an Almighty Power,
at 9 o'clock P.M. she fell asleep in the arms of Jesus.

And I heard a voice from heaven saying unto me, write blessed are
the dead that die in the Lord henceforth! Yea saith the Spirit, that
they may rest from their labors and their works do follow them." Amicus.

The papers at Cahawba and Selma will please copy.

September 4, 1839
Died at the residence of his father in Coosa County on the 21 inst.,
JAMES A. WALL aged 30 years. He had for the last nine years been severely afflicted with the rheumatism, but permitted at times to enjoy short
intervals of ease; his last illness which was of three months duration,
was unusually severe, yet not a murmur escaped his lips. Conscious of
the near approach of death, he evinced no fear, but on the contrary
hailed it as a welcome messenger, as a deliverance from this world of
pain and woe to one far more glorious eternal in the skies; never did
man die more perfectly resigned to the will of his maker. As a son he
was all the parent wish never during his life, giving the least cause for
regret; as a neighbor and friend, kind and benevolent to a fault, he was
truly the friend of all, possessed of an active and enterprising disposition, with a mind well cultivated, he bid fair, had health been granted
him of being an honor to his family and country; but he is gone and that
too it is hoped and believed to the bright abode of the just made perfect;
long will his loss be felt by his family and numerous friends. The
Huntsville Democrat will please copy the above. A Friend.

September 11, 1839
Died in this city on Monday night last at 8 o'clock of billious
fever, ROBERT L. WHARTON, aged 23 years formerly of Fauquier County,
Virginia. In this dispensation of Divine Providence a young wife has
been thoroughly bereaved of a kind and affectionate husband, to whom she
had been united but a few short months. Mr. WHARTON was a well known
and highly esteemed citizen -- industrious, upright and honorable in all
his intercourse with his fellow beings, he gave promise of extended usefulness and a long life, which have been cut short by the hand of death.
The writer of this short notice has known the subject of it intimately
for several years, and can truly say that in all the varied relations of
life his character has been irreproachable without a stain. His death
is as much regretted by his numerous friends and associates as his life
has been upright and useful. But who shall scrutinize the dispensation
of the author of our being? L.

The Va. Times and the McMinnville, Tenn. will please copy the above.

September 23, 1840
Died of congestive fever at the residence of his father near Wetumpka on Sunday Evening 13th instant, AYDELOTT SYNDENHAM, eldest and only
son of DR. SAMUEL H. and MARY H. BILLING, aged six years and five months.

He suffered a severe and unremitted illness of five or six days,
without murmur or complaint, thus exhibiting the most remarkable patience
for one of his age. He was in life amiable, intelligent and dutiful, his
father's hope, his mother's joy. But the destroyer came, and claimed him
for his own. His spirit has gone hence to swell the angelic choir of the
redeemed, and his parents loss is his eternal gain.

"Ere sin could blight, or sorrow gain
Death came with friendly care
The opening bud to Heaven conveyed
And bade it blossom there."

September 30, 1840
Died on Sunday evening 19 inst. of congestive fever, JAMES S. TUCKER
in the 29th year of his age.

September 30, 1840
    Died on Wednesday evening 23 inst. after a very short illness, Mr.
JOHN GRAY, JR. aged 20 years.

October 28, 1840
                Leaves have their time to fall
                And flowers to wither at the north wind's breath
                and stars to set but all are thine
                Thou hast all seasons for thine own, O Death."
    Died in this place on Wednesday morning late, Mr. JOHN D. MORAN aged
about 24 years. Mr. M was a native of Ireland but had been a resident of
this city for about three years and by his upright deportment and unassuming manners, had won the friendship and esteem of all who knew him. He
was interred with military honors by the Wetumpka Borderers, of which
Corps he was a member and his funeral services attended by a large concourse of citizens. New York papers will please notice.

November 11, 1840
    Died at her father's residence in this city of nervous fever, after
an illness of twenty-six days, Miss LOUISA JANE, daughter of HENRY VAN
BIBBER aged 15 years 7 months and 26 days. Selma Free Press please copy.
    Died - It is our painful duty to record the death of the REV. R. A.
MONTGOMERY, late principal of the Female Academy. He died on the morning
of the 9th instant after a painful illness of ten days.

November 18, 1840
    Died at his residence in this city on the 13th inst., of nervous
fever, after an illness of twelve days, Mr. JOHN R. DUE (1812 peusemer)
aged 48 years. Columbia S.C. papers will please notice.
    Died at Hayneville, Ala. on Wednesday evening the 4th instant of
congestive fever after two weeks' illness, WILLIAM B. SAFFOLD, Esq. aged
27 years.

November 25, 1840
    Died in Forsyth on the 29 ult. ROBERT COLEMAN, Esq. aged 56 years.
He was one of the earliest settlers of this city and still resided in
the vicinity. He ever sustained the character of a worthy and enterprising citizen.

February 3, 1841
    Died in this place on Friday night the 23rd instant after a long
and protracted illness, Mrs. ELIZA R. SMITH, consort of JUDGE E. T. SMITH
in the 36th year of her age leaving a husband, three children and many
relatives and friends to deplore her loss. The deceased was born in the
village of Greenville, South Carolina and was the eldest daughter of
GEORGE WASHINGTON EARLE, a name well known to many of our citizens and
connected with some of the first families of that state. After her
marriage, Mrs. S. removed with her husband to the period of their removal to this place in the autumn of 1837.
    With a disposition the most amiable with a mind highly cultivated
by a finished education and the refinements of the accomplished society
with which she had been associated, it is not strange that during the
three brief years which she has resided among us, she had drawn around
her a circle of friends and acquaintances who will long continue to cherish the pleasing recollection of her virtues, her accomplishments, her
unassuming manners and the ardent and tender attachments of her friendship.
    In the month of August of the past year Mrs. SMITH became a member
of the Methodist Episcopal Church. During the few months which have
elapsed since that connection her influence and the force of her example
have been directed to adorn the doctrine of the Christian Religion. In
the dispensations of an overruling Providence it does seem on some occasions at Last that lovely and gentle spirits are prepared by the sanctifying influences of God's grace for that heavenly home which a Saviour
knows they will shortly occupy. Too good for each, that are first
marked with the blood of Sprinklin and then beckoned away to the society
of God and Angels.
    Though "Death has sadly triumphed" over the Mortal existence of our
departed friend, his icy hand has not and cannot chill the ardent and
enduring attachments of a disconsolate husband, and children, and friends,

until they too shall fall his victims - no, not ever then united again in the blissful Paradise of God, their bright spirits will live and love throughout eternitys never ending years.

The bereaved family which she has left are not the only suffers by this mournful event. A numerous list of acquaintances, both in town and in the country, deeply and justly feel that our society one has departed whose peace cannot be easily supplied, if indeed the loss be not irremediable.

> There lurks a dread in all delight,
> A shadow near each ray
> That warns us then to fear their flight
> When most we wish their stay.
>
> And sadder still the pain will stay-
> The bliss no more appears;
> As rainbows take their light away
> And leave us but the tears
> Jacksonville Republican

The funeral of Mrs. JUDGE SMITH which took place in the village on last Sunday, we were gratified to learn, was attended by a much larger concourse of persons than has ever before attended on any similar occasion in this section of country. Being absent from home on that and several preceding days, we were denied the melancholy privilege of paying the last tribute of respect to the mortal remains of one than whom none stood higher in our own estimation.

February 3, 1841
        Died in Columbus, Geo. on Saturday morning last, Mrs. ALPHIA COLQUITT, consort of the HON. WALTER J. COLQUITT.

March 17, 1841
        Died in this city on Saturday night, the 13th instant, Mrs. EMELINE E. B. wife of DR. S. V. WATKINS in the 26 year of her age. It is not the intention of the writer to eulogize the dead; for sensible he is, that fought which he can say in relation to the many christian moral and domestic virtues which were so eminently and happily combined in the character of the deceased, could serve to perpetuate or endear her to the memory of her relations and friends. Her early demise has created a breach in the religious and social circles which time will all the healing opiates it can administer to the fondest recollection will be slow to repair, the vacuum in the affections of her relatives and friends can be closed by nothing earthly.

She was a consistent member of the Baptist Church an ornament to her profession and died with a brilliant hope of a glorious immortality beyond the grave. Life was open before her with all its assiduous and fascinating smiles, and the choicest blessing which earth can afford, contributed to render her existence pleasing and desirable; yet, she meekly bowed to the mandate of her Lord and Master and calmly acquiesced to the will of Heaven. Death to her was shorn of all its terrors - for she was prepared to meet its cold embrace. To her numerous friends and associates her example in life and triumph in death seem to say from the tomb "be ye also ready".

> Thus pass the hopes of earth away
> Like fallen leaves before the storm
> The object which we love today
> Tomorrow seems a transcient form
> E'en morning's brightest beams are oft
> Eclipsed in gloom and dark ere even;
> And nature whispers loud, but soft
> that there is "nothing true but heaven".
>
> Rest, sleeper, rest, Thy toil is O'er
> Thy pilgrimage, though short, is done;
> Thou'rt on a holier, brighter shore
> To wear the crown so nobly won;
> 'Tis thine to see, to feel, to know
> That which to mortals is not given;
> Thou has exchanged this world below
> For everlasting joys in Heaven.

Rest, sleeper, rest, these vines will bloom
in vernal beauty ever wave,
They're planted here around thy tomb,
To shed thy fragrance O'er thy grave
Perchance in autumn's chilly breath
As thou hast been they may be risen
Like thee, they'll break this seeming death
They, here to bloom, and thou, in heaven.

(Com)

April 7, 1841

Died of consumption after a painful illness of several months, on
the morning of the 4th inst. at the residence of COL. HENRY H. COOK in
this city, Mrs. ANN B. relict of the late F. S. COOK aged 37 years. She
has left six children to mourn their irreparable loss.

The deceased was a lady of highly cultivated mind, amiable in all
the relations of private life and greatly esteemed by those who knew her
and in her death our society has sustained a loss which it will be difficult to repair. She had been for many years a member of the Baptist
Church; and it is grateful to be friends to remember that in her last
moments the cheering influence of the Christian religion, shed a softening light over the otherwise rugged scenes of the death bed. A Friend.

July 7, 1841

Death of MAJOR GENERAL MACOMB. Our Washington letter announces the
death of this distinguished officer of the last war with Great Britain.
He was a gallant commander and an amiable man. The victory of Platts-
burg crowned him with laurels on the plain.

July 14, 1841

Died at his residence in Russel Co., Ala. on the 20th ult, DR.
BURWELL INGRAM after an illness of six days in the 31st year of his age
leaving a widow and two children and a numerous circle of friends and
relatives to mourn their irreparable loss. He was born in the County of
Dinwiddie, Virginia and with his father removed to the county of Hancock,
Ga. in the year 1818. After completing a thorough medical education,
DR. INGRAM commenced the practice of his profession and his skill and
fidelity will long be remembered by the citizens of Hancock. Once elected
to the house of Representatives (in 1835) and twice to the Senate of the
State (in '36 and '37). He discharged his public duties with credit to
himself and advantage to his constituents in 1839, he settled upon his
farm in this state.

In the character of our deceased friend, there was a rare union of
gentleness and firmness, of nice perceptions of honor and a tender regard
for the feelings of others; of modesty and of courage, of confidence in
himself, and a liberal and just appreciation of his fellow men. He was
kind and sincere in all the domestic and social relations of life. And
as a master, was obeyed more from the attachments of his dependents than
from their fears. In his professional character, the afflicted hardly
knew which most to admire, the clear judgement and medical skill which
he exercised or his gentleness of manner and kind sympathies which fall
upon the fainting spirit of the sick man. "Like due." He died calmly
and with a strong assurance of future happiness. He lived without reproach and he died without fear. Russell County, Ala. Geo. Argus

August 4, 1841

Death of a Hero - GEN. SAMUEL DALE, one of the bravest of the pioneers of the Southwest died at his residence in Lauderdale County,
Mississippi on the 23 of April. A writer in the Natchez Free Trader re-
lates the following incidents in his life:

As a scout - a pilot to the emigrants who blazed the first path
through the Creek Nation from Georgia to the Tombigbee, with arms in
their hands; and subsequently as a spy among the Spaniards at Pensacola
and as a partisan officer during the most sanguinary epochs of the late
war present at every butchery remarkable for hair breadth scapes; for
caution and coolness in desperate emergencies; for exhibitions of gigan-
tic personal strength and undaunted moral courage - his story is shudded
over with spirit stirring incidents, unsurpassed by anything in legend
or history. His celebrated canoe fight, where unaided in the middle of
the Alabama river then in its spring flood, he fought seven warriors with

clubbed rifles and killed them all, and rowed to shore with the corpse of his late antagonist under his feet, would be thought fabulous if it had not been witnessed by twenty soldiers standing near the bank, who not having a boat, could render him no assistance.

Some years ago he was attacked by two warriors who shouted their warwhoop as he was kneeling down to drink, and made a rush at him with their tomahawks. He knifed them both and though bleeding from five wounds he retraced their trail nine miles, crept stealthily to their camp, brained three sleeping warriors, and cut thongs of a female prisoner, who lay by their side. While in this act, however, a fourth sprang upon him from behind a log taken at a disadvantage and exhausted by the loss of blood, he sank under the serpent grasp of the savage, who with a yell of triumph drew his knife, and in a few moments would have closed the contest at that instant however the woman drove a tomahawk deep into the head of the Indian, and this preserved the life of her deliverer.

August 11, 1841
     Died at the house of Mr. J. A. PYLANT of this county on the 6th instant of consumption, Mr. WM. A. WALL, aged about 23 years, formerly of Madison, Indiana but lately of this city.

August 18, 1841
     Died in Autauga County at the residence of Mr. MIMMS, while on a journey in the country, Mr. HARVEY COE, formerly of Connecticut, aged about 23 years. Although he was among strangers when taken sick every means which skilful physicians and kind friends could suggest were used, but without success. The grim tyrant had marked him for his own, and he has gone down to a premature grave. His modest deportment and agreeable manners had secured to him a large share of friends who deeply lament his loss. Connecticut papers will please copy.

September 1, 1841
     Died at his residence in this city on the 21st instant, CAPT. JEREMIAH M. FRION, of wound from a Bowie knife. The deceased was a native of Newbern, N. C., but for the last 7 years a resident of this place, during which time his conduct was such as to merit the approbation of all who knew him. He was a man of industrious, temperate habits and sedate disposition and had it pleased Divine Providence to have screened him from the unfortunate accident for a few more years, his exemplary habits would have proved him one of our most useful citizens. But since it has pleased the Almighty disposer of human events to thus permit his removal from his family and our midst, afflicting as it is, yet we will bow with humble submission to his stern decree. To his distant connection and friends it will be gratifying to hear that every attention was bestowed upon him, both by skilful physicians and his numerous friends, and that he was interred with appropriate honors by the fraternity of Masons to which he had long been attached together with the citizens. He has left an affectionate wife and four infants to deplore their loss yet may they be comforted with the reflection that time at last sets all things even. And that to the meek and humble in spirit will be meted out justice by him who alone can give and take away. The papers at Newbern will notice. Communicated.

October 6, 1841
     Tombstone, Elmore Co. - Mrs. MARY B., wife of B. EASTERLING and daughter of JAS. B. and ELIZABETH C. ROBINSON. She was born Nov. 25th, 1820 and died Sept. 20, 1841.
     Obituary - Died at her residence in Autauga County, on Monday, the 20th ult, Mrs. MARY B. EASTERLAND, in the 21st year of her age. Mrs. EASTERLAND was the second daughter of JAMES ROBINSON, Esq. of Autauga and had been married but little more than a year to her now bereaved husband. To behold an amiable and interesting lady thus cut off almost at the very moment when girlhood, with all its joys and sorrows, its hopes and fears have been laid aside, and she was just entering upon the untried scenes of domestic life, with its weightier cares, its more staid and sober enjoyments, is an event which all may truly mourn. To her friends, her companions and particularly to her afflicted family, it is indeed a stunning blow. How at such a moment does memory come thronging back, bringing in her train all the happy hours they have spent with her whose death they so deeply mourn? How at such a moment does recollection

fondly cling to all the little incidents which chequers the path of girl-hood and tinges so many of its spots with hues of golden sunlight? But alas! Death comes to all, and we mourn that we shall see her face no more. Removed from the troubles and disappointments of life at the moment of entering upon its stern realities, she is gone, we trust, to that bright spirit land of the blest," where she will dwell forever in the presence of her God.

October 6, 1841
Died at his residence in Clark County, on the evening of the 21st ult JOHN MURPHY, aged 56 years. Mr. MURPHY served two terms as Governor of Alabama and was subsequently a representative in Congress from the 5th district.

October 13, 1841
Died at his residence in this city, on the 6th inst. of congestive fever, Mr. ELIAS ROBERTS, formerly of Bristol, Ct. in the 64th year of his age, a faithful and devoted husband - a kind and affectionate father a good and an upright citizen, his death is mourned by all as it becomes us to mourn when a good man dies. He was interred with Masonic honors by the Lodge, of which he was a worthy and efficient member. At a meet-ing of the Wetumpka Lodge of Free and Accepted Masons, on the Occasion of the death of Brother ELIAS ROBERTS, it was resolved that the members of the Lodge wear the customary badge of mourning thirty days and that the Secretary cause the same to be published in the city papers.
E. Randall, Secretary. The Hartford papers will please copy.

March 30, 1842
Departed March 23, Steamboat JNO. DUNCAN with 220 bales of cotton.
Departed March 26, Steamboat FORMOSA with 80 bales of cotton.
Departed March 26, Steamboat FACTOR with 300 bales of cotton.

November 30, 1842
Departed this life on the 10th inst. Mrs. L. A. C. SMITH, wife of Mr. ALEXANDER SMITH of Coosa County in the 30th year of her age.
Mrs. SMITH was the daughter of the late JOHN MCMILLAN of Cumberland County, North Carolina. She was the affectionate wife, the tender mother, the faithful friend, the cheerful consistent Christian. Throughout the whole of life her meek and placid countenance exerted a cheering influ-ence over all around her; and retaining her native serenity until her dying hour, showed then by her faith in Christ, that there was substan-tial bliss even amid the pains of death. Her life afforded an example worthy of imitation, and her death afforded conclusive evidence that to the truly pious penitent heart, death has no sting and the grave can claim no victory. G.
The Fayetteville (N.C.) Observer will please copy.

December 14, 1842
Died on the 4th inst of pulmonary consumption at the residence of GEORGE GRAY in Coosa County, Miss MARY C. BULL of Talladega County in the 19th year of her age.

December 21, 1842
Died in Talladega County on the 6th of November, Mrs. MARY WATSON, consort of the REV. ALEXANDRIA WATSON, aged 43 years. The partialities of friendship not infrequently prompt extravagant praises of the dead. There are multitudes whose lives exhibit nothing, who, after death, are lauded as having professed uncommon excellencies; yet nevertheless there are those among the departed who were excellent, and who constitute the best subjects for eulogy. To this no one more properly belongs than the lady whose death we have announced at the commencement of this article. Seldom has it been our happiness to enjoy the acquaintance of one so interesting and lovely, for all those virtues which confer peculiar sweetness upon the female character, Mrs. WATSON was surpassingly dis-tinguished. In the social and domestic relationships of life, that sphere which Providence has assigned to woman and where many shine with the brightest lustre, we have known but few more amiable - none more exemplary. She was a consistent member of the Baptist church for 20 years and it may truly be said she was a pious Christian, the affection-ate wife, and the kind Mother, yes, and I may add she was a preacher's

wife indeed. When her husband's spirits would faint within him, and
would sometimes be almost persuaded to give up the arduous task of preaching, she would often say to him in words as follows: "Your company's
sweet, your union's dear, your words delightful to mine ear, but my husband leave me - yea, leave me, and go and preach the Gospel to dying
sinners and I will remain at home lifting up my prayers for your success
while my hands are employed for the support of 12 little children, hoping
that she that tarries at home shall divide the spoils," Ps Ch 68 vs 12.
     But the precious woman is gone and gone to glory, leaving many dear
friends, a dear church, a fond and affectionate husband and 13 weeping
children to lament her loss.
     "And I heard a voice from Heaven saying unto me write henceforth,
blessed are the dead who die in the Lord; yea, saith the spirit that they
may rest from their labors and their works do follow them."

> Give Joy or grief, give ease or pain,
> Take wife or friends away
> But let me find them all again
> In that eternal day.
>   T D A

January 4, 1843
     Died in this city on the 2d instant, after a lingering illness,
HARRIETT, consort of JAMES MCFARLIN, in the 28th year of her age.

January 4, 1843
     Died on the 9th ult, in LeGrange, Geo. at the house of her brother,
the REV. JOHN E. DAWSON, MARY FRANCES, consort of the late COL. HENRY H.
COOK of this place, aged 35 years and 10 months.
     This event had long been expected, yet the occurrence has brought
sadness to many a heart, which has sympathised deeply with that afflicted
and lovely woman. Although "consumptions ghastly form" had fixed its
signet upon her frame for years previous to her death - though an adverse
fate seems to have thwarted the fortunes of her family, and though her
death came to embitter her few remaining days in a form, in which all
that we know, or dream, or fear of agony----" was concentered - by first
snapping the chord of life in the bosom of her only son and 'ere the
mourner had returned from his sepulchur by prostrating the manly form of
her husband, yet though all, though stricken in heart and mellowed by
grief she exhibited the same mild, yielding and sweet disposition, which
had made her an ornament to society in her prosperity and a solace and a
pride to her friends in adversity. She is now dead! The mother and the
wife has followed to the grave the son and the husband. What truer or
nobler epitaph can a bereaved friend indite to thee, departed spirit,
than that thou was't the modest confiding wife - the tenderest mother -
the sweetest friend.

May 16, 1843, May 17, 1843
     Died at his residence in Dadeville, Tallapoosa County WILLIAM L.
JUSTISS, clerk of the Circuit Court of said county, at half after ten
o'clock on the 5th of May 1843.
     His last moments were solemn and impressive - the terrors of death
making no impression on his mind to disturb his peace in his expiring
moments. Being in his senses he declared that he died in the fearless
hope that God was reconciled to him and that he should rest in peace.
     On Saturday the 6th, His Honor JUDGE ELI SHORTRIDGE presiding, the
body of the deceased being brought into the court room, numerously attended by the gentler sex as well as others to mourn his loss, the presiding Judge explained the object of the meeting after which LEROY
GRESHAM offered the following preamble and resolutions which were
adopted (viz):
     Whereas, the melancholy news of the death of WILLIAM L. JUSTISS,
Clerk of the Circuit Court, has been announced to us at this Term of the
Court; in evidence of the high regard and esteem we entertain for the deceased.
     Resolved That the members and officers of this court wear the usual
badge of mourning thirty days.
     Resolved That the court do now adjourn, that we may attend the
funeral services about to be performed and the interment.

Resolved That the bereaved family of the deceased be furnished with a copy of the proceedings and resolutions of this meeting in token of our respect.

Resolved That the foregoing proceedings and resolutions be spread upon the minutes of the court, and that the same be published in the East Alabamian and the Wetumpka Argus.

After the foregoing proceedings were had the REV. FREDERICK P. NORSWORTH (Meth. Min. - left Troup Co., Ga. and settled in Dallas Co. then in Tallapoosa Co. where he died before 1850. Was in Hayneville Circuit then in Lowndesboro Circuit. Was expelled from ministry. See West's p. 541-543.) performed the funeral services with that solemnity, eloquence and ability, which ever characterize the time-worn servant as a minister of God.

May 31, 1843

Died in this city on the 28th inst. Mrs. ELIZABETH, wife of FREDERICK COFFMAN, in the 20th year of her age.

July 5, 1843

Died in Autauga County on the 23d May 1843, Mr. HIEL CASTON, aged 27 years.

August 9, 1843

Died in Coosa County on the 15th of July, MARK C. LIVELY in the 30th year of his age. The deceased was a resident of this city for the last three years and commanded the esteem and regard of all that knew him. (One MARK C. LIVELY married in Benton Co., Ala. 7 March 1838. She m. (2) Aug. 12, 1845 MEMORY ALLEN in Benton Co. - m. 1850. She was 33 SC and had LIVELY chin. 10,826.)

August 23, 1843

Mr. Editor - Indulge me with room enough in your columns to render an offering of homage to the character of an interesting and estimable gentleman-which I could not undertake while he was living without offending my own sense of propriety and violating his amiable modesty. The death of DR. HORATIO NELSON MORRIS, who departed this life on the 31st ult at Wetumpka, claims a more extended notice than a fugitive announcement in the obituary list of a newspaper. From the writer of this article his memory demands under imperative obligations, an acknowledgement of the devoutest affection. For the last ten years during the evolution of which I intimately knew him, he was a source of delight to his friends-a star that sparkled with mild and unclouded lustre, from a horizon of great serenity and beauty. There was neither malice, guile, hipocrisy, envy or hatred in his bosom-frankness and generosity were sovereign traits in his character - his soul was all manliness and his heart all magnanimity. DR. MORRIS was a man of superior learning and extensive reading in the standard work of his profession, and yet his erudition was so covered over with practical good sense, that it required close observation to detect in him, what other gentlemen of the cloth with great pomp and circumstance strive to exhibit. He had been diligently trained in the medical schools and hospitals of Philadelphia and his intimate knowledge of the principles of the healing art rendered his promptness and success in their practical application to invalid cases almost miraculous. His buoyancy of spirits and an unaffected glow of native benevolence rendered him a welcome visitor to a sick bed - shed a ray of sunshine into hearts shrouded with melancholy and dissipated the gloom which collects and thickens in the apartments of distress. His shop was a dispensary from which poverty and affliction were supplied with unstinted bounty - and his heart was never shut to the whispers of charity and duty. His liberality to his friends was unhesitating, prompt, profuse, peerless and princely.

But it was in the warmth of unguarded fraternal intercourse and the hush of private friendship, that the charming attributes of DR. MORRIS' character were most successfully developed. His face was the summer morning and his voice musical - roses and violets sprung up spontaneously about his footsteps - his path was a flower garden, and a salient spring of perrennial cheerfulness rendered his conversation eminently fascinating - his presence an ornament to every domestic circle and his society courted by every well disposed and benevolent mind. Tread lightly on his ashes ye men of genius - for he was your kinsman. Weed clean his grave, friends of humanity - for he was your brother.

September 13, 1843
    Died at Rockford, Coosa County, on the 8th ult in the 24th year of
her age, Mrs. SOPHIA CAROLINE CHERRY, wife of ROBERT M. CHERRY, Esq. and
daughter of DR. ABNER CRENSHAW, all of this place.
    Though called suddenly and unexpectedly, her friends are not as
those "who sorrow without hope". The deceased was a subject of the religious revival here in 1839; after having weighed the subject, she thus
wrote to a friend: "It has indeed been a struggle for one so devoted to
gayeties, and pleasures of this life, to determine to renounce all and
espouse the cause of Christ! To this determination I have finally come,
but I distrust myself so much, that I know if the Divine influence were
withheld I should again turn to a state of estrangement from God. O for
courage! O for strength! May this determination to come forward as one
supplicating a share in the benefits of a Saviour slain, be unalterable!"
    She attached herself to the Presbyterian Church, soon after, and
though sorely tried since by much suffering from ill health we have
reason to believe she ever looked to Heaven for strength to support her,
under her very severe afflictions. She seemed to have an humble sense of
her own imperfections in the sight of God.
    Some months before her death, she remarked to a friend, that she
wished to dedicate her daughter to God in baptism and after having expressed considerable anxiety to train her up in a way she should go, she
said with a pensive look, "I remember, my mother seemed to feel an in-
creased confidence that God would take care of us after she had performed
that duty."
    Possessed of a well cultivated mind and agreeable manners she was,
until borne down by disease, the life of the circle, in which she moved.
She was an affectionate daughter, a devoted wife, a tender mother, and
a warm hearted friend. Her physicians can bear testimony to her gratitude.
The writer has often heard her speak of them, with an affection, which
proved she was not one of the cold and heartless.
    She is gone! We shall miss her in the church; we shall miss her in
the social circle; but we confidently hope that clothed in a Saviour's
rightness, she was welcomed into Heaven, and that her entrance there was
hailed by her deceased pastor, who was the instrument in her conversion
and by the many pious friends, who had preceded her.

        Thou art gone to the grave - we no longer behold thee
        Nor tread the rough paths of the world by thy side
        But the wife arms of mercy are spread to enfold thee,
        And we too will hope in the Saviour that died.

September 13, 1843
    Died at the residence of the Editor of this paper in this city, on
Saturday evening last (August 26) in her 31st year, Mrs. MARTHA JANE,
consort of the REV. SEMOUR B. SAWYER, of Wetumpka Station, Alabama Conference.
    Mrs. SAWYER was the daughter of THOMAS and LAVINIA BROTHERS and was
born in Colleton District, S. C. June 7, 1813. She was principally raised
and educated in Montgomery, Alabama where she was married to her now bereft husband November 3, 1834.
    Her health, for the last 12 months had been very feeble. About the
last of May, brother SAWYER left home on a travel to Indiana for the purpose of recruiting his wife's health and visiting his aged mother. He
reached this place about the 1st of July when Mrs. SAWYER was unable to
proceed any farther. Every effort was made for her restoration; but all
was fruitless. She gradually wore away until her body sunk in death, and
her spirit returned to God.
    She was converted under the ministry of the REV. Mr. CUNNINGHAM of
the Presbyterian Church in her 17th year; but her parents being Methodists,
she united herself with that church, whose doctrines she fully believed
and whose discipline she heartily approved. She was always given somewhat to despondency on the subject of religion, growing out of the fact
that she was not fully satisfied with evidence of her conversion. This
she often overcame, and then, under the influence of temptation, was to
a certain extent robbed of her enjoyment.
    When it was first announced to her that she was near to her end,
she expressed some doubts; but in a few moments, having joined with her
in prayer, the cloud broke away, and her spirit was filled with the love
of Christ. She praised God aloud and talked in strains of eloquence of

the great goodness of God. A brighter scene we never witnessed. She spoke affectionately of many of her friends, and sent a special message to some of them who had been laboring under similar temptations with herself. She said, "Tell them to doubt no more." She exhorted her husband and the writer to go on and preach Jesus, till called to our reward. She said much which we cannot here record. She died calmly, and doubtless has gone to heaven. Her funeral was preached by the writer of this brief sketch at the McKendree church, on Sunday at 3 o'clock, P.M. when her body was deposited in the city burying ground to await the resurrection of the just.

> "Happy soul, thy days are ended,
> All thy sorrowing days below
> Go, by angel bands attended
> To the arms of Jesus go"

September 20, 1843
Died on Friday the 8th inst in the 12th year of his age, JAMES A. HOBDAY, son of STARK and ELIZA HOBDAY of Coosa County. The deceased was first taken with a headache and sick stomach then with a bilious fever and cold extremities. Two physicians were called in, who gave their medical aid, and applied their usual treatment; but all medical skill, the efficacy of medicine, as well as the care and unremitting attention of relatives and friends proved unavailing to effect his recovery. After about twelve days sickness he gradually declined and finally the spirit left the tenement of clay. When the symptoms of death began to appear, he was told by an aged friend to give himself up to the care of the Saviour and to trust to Him and His merits, and that he need not dread the terrors of death. He was asked by mother if he felt willing to die; he answered in the affirmative. She asked him if he wished to tell his Father (who was from home at the time) that he was willing to die, and to meet him in Heaven; he replied again in the affirmative. He was naturally of a mild and pliable disposition; obedient to parents, affectionate to friends, inoffensive and unassuming among his acquaintance. He has left behind him an affectionate father and mother, several sisters, an infant brother with other relatives and friends to bemoan their loss; yet they would not give vent to their sorrows like those who have no hope, but would acquiesce to the Divine will and would say with one of former days who passed through the furnace of affliction, "The Lord gave, and the Lord hath taken away, blessed be the name of the Lord."

> Thy life how short, O! mortal man
> Thy days are measured by a span

October 4, 1843
Died in this city on the 22nd ult, GEORGE S., son of Mrs. A. SIMPSON in the 10th year of his age.

October 25, 1843
Died on the 19th inst in Tallapoosa County, THOMAS BROTHERS, son of REV. S. B. SAWYER aged 15 months.

November 8, 1843
Died in Columbiana, Shelby County, Alabama on the 29th of September 1843, NOEL MASON, Esq. Clerk of the County Court, aged about 31 years.
At a meeting of the citizens of Columbiana and the vicinity at the Court house on the 30th of September to take into consideration the subject of this dispensation of Providence, on motion of GEORGE S. GRASTY, Esq. HON. CHARLES R. GIBBS was called to the chair and Y. A. CARR was appointed Secretary.
On motion of S. BRASHER, Esq. a committee was appointed by the chair to prepare and report suitable resolutions expressive of the sense of the meeting consisting of WADE H. GRIFFIN, J. M. McCLANAHAN, S. BRASHER, L.P. BRASHER and M. J. HORTON, who retired and in a short time reported the following preamble and resolutions:
1. Resolved That we regard his death as a public loss - that we sympathize deeply and sincerely with his friends and relatives in their affliction.
2. Resolved That we regard the deceased while living as a faithful public officer, a kind and affectionate relative and an honest man.

3. Resolved That a copy of these resolutions be handed to the family of his relatives in which he lived and died and that the chairman and Secretary be required to perform that duty.

4. Resolved That the officers of the Court of which he was clerk and his friends general wear the usual badge of mourning ten days.

5. Resolved That the proceedings of meeting be published in the Democratic Watchtower, Flag of the Union and the Wetumpka papers after being signed by the President and countersigned by the Secretary.

CHARLES R. GIBBS, Pres.

Y. A. CARR, Secy.

December 20, 1843

Died suddenly at his residence in Coosa County on the night of the 7th inst, COL. JOHN McNEILL, supposed to be congestion of the head and lungs.

The deceased was a native of Moore County, North Carolina. In 1819-20 he moved to Autauga County in this State, where he resided until 1838, when he removed to the place of his late residence.

One of the first settlers of this part of the State, after its admission into the Union, he was, on several occasions, sent to Cahawba, the then seat of Government by his fellow citizen in a Representative capacity to aid in setting in motion the machinery of our State Government under its new organization. Since that time, he has preferred the retirement of a private life, ambitious only in being counted an honest man, and meriting the favor of his neighbors and friends, in the kindly interchange of social duties. Uniformly hospitable, strangers as well as friends, found a ready welcome at his table. Naturally cheerful and buoyant in disposition, sad melancholy and gloomy misanthropy were never visible within his domestic circle. Such in belief and feebly given in the character of one whose death a bereaved widow mourns, and whose loss numerous relatives and friends lament.

He died suddenly and unexpectedly; but a few minutes before his spirit took its departure, he was conversing freely and with his usual cheerfulness of the certainty of his recovery by the next morning. But to him that morning never came. What food for calm and serious reflection is furnished us in the sudden death of our friend and companion and relative the destiny of us all. What an admonition that we "also be ready" for verily in the "midst of life we are in death."

January 17, 1844

Died in the town of Kingston, Autauga County on Thursday, the 4th inst, MAJ. SAMUEL SIMMONS, aged 52.

January 17, 1844

Mr. McALPIN-

Permit one who knew and appreciated the virtues of MAJOR SAMUEL S. SIMMONS, deceased, to give to his memory a tribute of friendship.

About the year of 1821 MAJOR SIMMONS removed to Autauga County, Ala. in which county he resided until his death. He moved amid the various and strong temptations which the speculations of the first settlement of this State and the political arena afforded, uncorrupted, the upright man, the honest politician, the dignified senator, the faithful officer, the modest and consistent christian. As a husband, father, neighbor and friend, he had no superiors. Untutored in academic lore, his mind naturally strong, generally took correct and strong views of important subject. This trait in his character, together with his well established candor and integrity secured him high confidence of his acquaintances and no inconsiderable portion of influence in society. He amassed a large estate and mingled for many years in the turmoil of political life, without having made a single personal enemy, known to the writer of the article.

An aged and highly respected fellow-citizen, who witnessed the death scene remarked that had he assurance that he would die like SAMUEL SIMMONS, death would have no terror for him.

On Thursday morning before day light, on finding the premonitory symptoms of rapidly approaching death, he calmly dictated his will - requested Mrs. SIMMONS to be composed - stating that he felt no pain; that he had a firm belief in his Saviour's love; that though he did not feel those rapturous glows which some have experienced, yet he "saw his way clear and he was about to die, without any pain of body or mind." Having signed his will he requested his wife to remove the pillow from

his head and let him pass off - he died immediately without a single
evidence of a death throe- surely

> Jesus can make a dying bed
> Feel soft as downy pillows are
> Whilst on his breast I lean my head
> And breath my life out sweetly there

January 9th, 1844

Died in this city on the 5th instant after a lingering illness, Mrs.
L. JORDAN, consort of ELIJAH JORDAN, in about the 30th year of her age.

The deceased was a native of Virginia, of respectable parentage and
a few years since a resident of Henry County, Georgia, where she married
Mr. JORDAN. She left four helpless children entirely dependent on the
bounty of strangers, her husband having basely abandoned her and family
after squandering what little property she had. He is now supposed to
be in Macon County in this state. For sometime before the death of Mrs.
J. from the lone and wretched condition in which she was left, she suffered many privations until her neighbors discovered her situation and
relieved her wants.

Should this meet the eye of any relatives or friends in Georgia,
they would be doing an act of kindness to make enquiry and take these
helpless and abandoned children under their charge. Any information can
be obtained by addressing the Editor of this paper or E. WILLIAMSON at
this city, who has with true christian charity given the children a home
and ministered to their wants like those of his own family. Georgia
papers please copy.

February 28, 1844

Died at his plantation in Montgomery County on the 9th inst. Mr.
GEORGE M. RIEVES of the house of Rives, Battle & Co.

Died in Mobile on the 14th inst, of small pox, Mrs. MARCIA S. D.,
wife of DARIUS CLOCK, Esq. in the 22nd year of her age. The death of
this estimable lady deserves more than a passing notice. She was a native of Brunswick in the State of Maine; and about the 1st of December
last, in that distant section of our country - in the full enjoyment of
health - in the bloom of early life - with fond hopes clustering around
her heart and the blow of promise brightly spanning the almost cloudless
future - she stood at the altar with the man of her choice, a loving,
hoping, trusting bride - scarcely two months had passed away ere she was
laid in the cold and silent grave. Death came upon her suddenly and in
the most unwelcome form, not only far away from the care and sympathy of
her friends, but under circumstances which deprived her even of the ordinary attention of sympathising strangers - and more than this, which
denied to her those consolations, so dear to a christian in the dying
hour - the personal attentions and communion of her christian friends.

Death is at all times an unwelcome visitant to the young; it must
have been so to our departed sister. How painful to be called away just
as another and holier tie had been cemented around her heart. But not-
withstanding all, her death was a triumphant one. She had put her trust
in Him who could never leave or forsake her. She had made peace with God,
and was calmly resigned to his holy will - Having made religion her
choice when the blessings and favors of heaven were around her, she was
permitted to enjoy its consolation in this her trying hour. Her afflictions she knew would be brief and she felt assured they were out. A
prelude to the eternal fruitions of another and a better world. Feeling
and hoping thus, she could patiently endure all that might be ordered and
without a murmur bear her father's chastening rod.

One of her first acts on coming among us was to unite herself with
the Second Presbyterian Church in this city and to assume a part in the
duties and responsibilities of the Sabbath School and all can bear testimony to the consistency of her christian walk, and the zealous discharge
of the christian duties during her brief sojourn among us. Up to the
time when her Master called her, she was prompt - we believe faithful in
his service; and we have no doubt she has heard the gracious commendation,
"well done, thou good and faithful servant." But once with us, was she
permitted to come to the table of her Lord, and partake of the memorials
of a Saviour's dying love, ere she was called to sit down with that
Saviour in the kingdom of his Father.

As a Sabbath School Teacher, none was earlier in their places, or
seemed to labor with more earnestness than our departed sister, to point

the children of her class to that Heaven to which she had soon led the
way. Her labors on earth are ended. In life and in death she bore a
pleasing testimony to the sanctifying and sustaining power of the grace
of God; and through a large circle of near and dear friends will lament
her early death yet are permitted to enjoy the consoling hope that their
loss is her unspeakable and eternal gain - that from the toils and trials
and sorrows of earth, she has gone to rest forever in the bosom of her
God.
        Also part of the obituary of Mrs. MARTHA MARIA HAYNIE, who died 16th
November 1842. Obituary written by her step-daughter. Wetumpka Argus
November 23, 1842.

GAINESVILLE NEWS

        Published each Saturday, Sumter County, Alabama by J. D.
        COWLAND, publisher. On file in the Probate Office,
        Livingston, Sumter County, Alabama.

        (Note: I skipped about, copying only the most important
        genealogically. A history of Sumter County was running
        serially, and I tried to get most of these.)

July 15, 1869
        Died at Gainesville, Alabama July 7, 1869, LENA HARRIS, daughter of
the late Mrs. EMMA WILLIAMSON, aged 12 months. Memphis papers copy.

November 4, 1869
        Died at Lower Peach Tree, Wilcox County, Alabama, on 16 October,
Mrs. ELLA McLEOD, wife of JOHN McLEOD and daughter and eldest child of
A. G. HORN of Lauderdale, Mississippi. (Meridian Mercury)

December 4, 1869
        History of Sumter County - Chapter VI.
        Rev. WILLIAM WOODWARD born November 15, 1792 in York District, South
Carolina. Circumstances of his father were humble. Elder children were
girls, so the subject of this memorial was reared to labor on the farm.
Married when 21 and moved to Chester District in 1820. Elected to representative branch of the Legislature but after serving 3 years removed to
the frontier of Georgia. In 1828 joined the Baptist Church. Settled in
Greene County in 1834 and in 1838 to Sumter County in that portion of it
which became Choctaw. Ordained a minister. In 1842 nominated by the
Democratic party for a seat in the legislature...(Long, did not copy
more.) (Judge says this was real old history that was re-published.)

December 11, 1869
        Death of a stranger. Died at the residence of JOSEPH FERGUSON near
Holly Grove, Walker County, Alabama on 2 October 1869, JOHN G. HAMILTON,
supposed to be about 35, medium size, dark hair, eyes and complexion.
Stated before he died he had been in Texas and was married to a lady
named LOOPER. She lived in Blount County. He had not seen her in 2 or
3 years. Left some property which relatives can obtain.

December 25, 1869
        History of Sumter County - Chapter VII
        JAMES HARVY THOMPSON born at Mt. Sterling, Kentucky, but when he
reached adolescence, he moved to Morgan County, Alabama, where he passed
several years employed as clerk in a store. Removed to Gainesville in
1838 and in 1843 was Sheriff... Died 1854 at Livingston. (Note by
Gandrud: Tombstone says died March 1855 aged 37.)
        WILLIAM S. TUREMAN was born in Lawrence County, Alabama about 1825,
removed with his father to Gainesville a few years after it was settled.
His father, "OLD ZAC" was for years one of the institutions of Gainesville. Many fancied he was the only one in the State that could shoe a
horse properly. WILLIAM S. TUREMAN was County Clerk under PRICE
WILLIAMS. In 1850, was defeated for Circuit Clerk...etc. But his mind
suddenly darkened and he is now in the asylum at Tuscaloosa. (Note: 1850
Census shows him aged 22 born in Alabama.)

December 25, 1869
        Died in Tuscaloosa, Alabama December 7, 1869, Mr. JOHN PICKFORD,
formerly of Gainesville aged about 36 years. A soldier in the Confederate army during the war. Silversmith by trade and native of Nova Scotia.

January 8, 1870
        History of Sumter County - Chapter VIII.
        GEORGE AMASON, Esq. born in Edgecombe County, North Carolina about
1823, removed to this county along with his father in 1835... Fair education... Tall, stout and corpulent. Face oval, dark hair, blue eyes,
gait slouchy and dress untidy, yet a man of great humor. He died in 1854.
        PHILIP S. GLOVER was quite an early settler in Sumter County. A
lawyer. Social, frank, lively and gentlemanly. In 1847, was nominated
to the legislature. Died in Montgomery before the close of session aged
about 40.
        GEN. JAMES T. HILL, born in Madison County, Virginia, removed to
Sumter County in 1843, locating in Livingston. For several years was a
law partner of HON. S. W. INGE. In 1849, was elected to the legislature.
Died in Livingston about 1854 after a brief illness aged about 45. (Note:
In 1850, was aged 40 b. Va.) Tombstone says died 1851, but 1 and 4 often
look alike and could be 1854, as age checks.
        HON. BENJAMIN J. H. GAINES born in Tennessee, removed in early man-
hood to Sumter, settling near Black Bluff. In the fall of 1857, removed
from Livingston to Tennessee and then to NorthEast Arkansas, where he
now resides.
        JAMES P. KENNARD born in Tennessee but in early manhood, he removed
to Greene County. Among the early settlers of that county. After remaining a few years in Greene, he settled in Sumter. Clerk of Sumter Circuit
Court. Is now living on his plantation near Livingston. Methodist.
(Note by Gandrud: 1850 Census says aged 29 born in Nelson Co. Va.
Tombstone says born July 3, 1820 died Feb. 20, 1883.
        REUBEN THOM born in Virginia, settled in Sumter about 1842. Clerk
of Circuit Court. (Note: age 20 b.Va. in 1850 Census)
        JORDAN H. SHORT, a native of North Carolina. Sheriff of Sumter in
1852. Died at his home in Livingston in 1862. (Note: Someone copied
death date as 1877 from his tombstone.)

January 15, 1870
        History of Sumter County - Chapter X
        HON. WILLIAM WINTER PAYNE born in Fauquier County, Virginia in 1805,
removed to Tuscumbia, Alabama in 1825. In June 1826 he married Miss
MINERVA WINSTON, daughter of COL. JOHN J. WINSTON. In 1833 settled in
North Sumter... 1841, elected to Congress (very lengthy...).
        DANIEL BROWN WYATT died Thursday morning. Born in Portsmouth, New
Hampshire 24 September 1808. In the winter of 1836, moved to Mobile
where he died.
        Died near LaGrange, Tennessee January 10, 1870, MAJ. EDMUND WINSTON
aged about 70 years.

January 29, 1870
        History of Sumter County Chapter XI
        DR. ROBERT LARKIN born in Hanover County, North Carolina April 1,
1810. Graduated in medicine at Lexington, Kentucky and soon after settled
in Montgomery County, Alabama. In 1832, moved to Perry County and formed
a partnership with an elder brother, DR. SAM LARKIN. On 31 January 1833,
he married Miss MARY A. TRIGG and removed to Sumter County in 1836,
settling near Brewersville... 1851 elected to Legislature.

February 26, 1870
        Funeral of DR. H. W. HENRY, a citizen of Montgomery. Held at
Protestant Methodist Church yesterday, the Presbyterian church of which
he is a member being closed for repairs. For the past 2 or 3 years, DR.
HENRY has resided in Baltimore, where his youngest daughter was attending
school. He died in that city a few days ago, and his remains here Tuesday
night. With one exception, Mr. NEIL BLUE, who still survives him, DR.
HENRY was doubtless the oldest citizen of Montgomery, having settled here
in 1819. Age nearly 80 years (Montgomery Advertiser, 22d).

April 23, 1870
    In Memoriam. Mr. TAYLOR BRADSHAW, son of Mr. ROBERT BRADSHAW, of
this place, was born in Lexington, Virginia 4 March 1841 died in St. Louis
on 27 March 1870 aged 29 years 23 days (lengthy article).

June 18, 1870
    Died in this town Monday afternoon June 13, 1870 after a long and
wearisome illness, Mrs. REBECCA HARTSFIELD in her 68th year, one of the
oldest citizens of Gainesville. Relict of COL. SIHON J. HARTSFIELD, who
departed this life here in 1850. She was a native of Wake County, North
Carolina... (In 1850 Census was age 47 born in NC.)

July 16, 1870
    Departed this life at St. Stephens, Washington County, Alabama on
28 June, Mr. BURRELL PITMAN BRANTLEY aged 69 years 6 months 28 days.
Born in Halifax County, North Carolina, removed to Alabama in 1828 and
settled at old St. Stephens in Washington County, where he resided about
4 years. In 1832, he removed to Gainesville and was a citizen of this
place until the last of January, when he removed back to St. Stephens.
He was therefore one of the earliest residents of this town...for 30 years
Deacon of the Baptist Church in this place... (In 1850 Census was age
48 born in N.C.)

October 22, 1870
    Died at the residence of her son-in-law, Mr. JOHN ALEXANDER in
Gainesville of yellow disease on Monday evening October 17, Mrs. M. J.
MASSENGALE in 42d year of her age.
    At the family residence in North Sumter, Alabama on the morning of
the 5th, of pulmonary consumption, AMANDA, wife of S. P. TOMPKINS in 42d
year of her age. Mobile and S.C. please copy.

November 26, 1870
    Miss CARRIE CHILES, daughter of Mrs. CHILES, formerly of Gainesville,
died one day this week at her mother's residence in Greene Co.
    Mrs. ELIZABETH GATES, an estimable lady and old resident of Gaines-
ville died very suddenly at her residence last Wednesday night of paral-
yses. (Note: Age 45 b.N.H., in 1850 Census.)
    We learn with sorrow that REV. C. A. STILLMAN, late Pastor of the
Presbyterian Church in this place but now of Tuscaloosa, was bereft by
death on Thursday last of a beloved daughter, Miss MARY STILLMAN, aged
about 22. She died in Tuscaloosa, where her father had but recently
moved, of hemorrhagic malarial fever.

December 3, 1870
    On Wednesday night last, Mrs. REAVIS, estimable wife of HON. TURNER
REAVIS departed this life at her family residence in Gainesville. (Other
records show she died 30 November 1870.)

January 7, 1871
    We learn from Livingston Journal that Mr. DANIEL L. AYRES, Tax Col-
lector of this county died Monday night, old citizen of Livingston.
(1850 Census, age 39 b.N.J.)
        JAMES FERRELL born Ca. 1771 N.C. Married (1)   (2) SUSAN
          , in Greene Co. December 1840.
        Children
        1. SALINA, dead in 1860, married J
        2. REBECCA, born S.C. March 13, 1804, died Oct. 10, 1853, married
           THOMAS L. SPIVEY born Ca. 1806 S.C.
        3. WILLIAM A., married in Greene Co., Ala. 12 Oct. 1839 Miss SELINA
           ANN FERRELL.
        4. BENJ. P. born Ca. 1808 N.C. Married in Greene Co., Ala.
        5. BENNETT, born Ca 1811 N.C. Married in Greene Co., Ala. Jan.16,
           1834, Miss MARSHA H. FREEMAN born Ca 1799, N.C.
        6. EMILY, married in Greene Co., Ala. Jan. 9, 1845 to WM. B. BOYKIN.
        7. MAHALA ANN HELEN, born Ca. 1820 N.C., married in Greene Co., Ala.
           Nov. 1, 1838 to JOHN W. HARRIS, born Ca. 1816 N.C. She died
           Nov. 13, 1868 at 48-8-7.

THE LIVINGSTON JOURNAL

Published at Livingston, Alabama, Sumter County, every
Saturday evening by BEN F. HERR.

July 15, 1865
Died, COL. JOHN R. McCLANAHAN, founder and editor of the Memphis
(Tennessee) Appeal. Killed in that city on the night of the 28th by
falling from the 4th story of Gayoso House....

August 5, 1865
Married at the residence of the bride's father on the 19th instant
by REV. W. C. HEARN, Mr. A. B. JONES of Louisiana to Miss BETTIE PHARES,
daughter of JOHN C. PHARES, Esq. of Marengo County.

August 12, 1865
Married on the 3d instant by REV. NEWMAN at the residence of the
bride's father, Mr. JAMES M. KELLY of Missouri to Miss MARY E. DANIEL of
Lauderdale County, Mississippi.
Died at Brewersville, Sumter County, on the night of 12th of July,
Mrs. FANNIE K. MURPHY, wife of Mr. W. W. MURPHY aged 29 years. She was
born in Alexandria, Virginia and at the time of her death, was a refugee
from Washington, D. C.
Tribute of Respect - At a meeting of Livingston Lodge #41 of Free and
Accepted Masons, held on 5th of August, a committee was appointed to draft
resolutions expressive of their respect for the memory of CAPTAIN LUCIUS
S. BOLLING, member of a Lodge in Missouri.

S. W. MURLEY)
THOMAS COBBS) COMMITTEE
J. L. SCRUGGS)

August 19, 1865
Dissolution of partnership, JAMES COBBS having been appointed Judge
of the 7th Judicial Circuit, JAMES COBBS and THOMAS COBBS now dissolve
partnership. THOMAS COBBS will continue practice of law in Livingston.
W. M. CUNNINGHAM, Cabinet Maker
JAMES C. USTICK, Watch Maker

August 26, 1865
Married on Tuesday the 15th instant in Lauderdale County, Mississippi,
Mr. M. N. CRAWFORD of Jackson County, Missouri to Miss MARY A. ARMSTRONG
of Hanover County, Virginia.
Candidates - S. W. MURLEY for sheriff
- GOERGE B. SAUNDERS for Probate Judge
- ZACHARIAH TUREMAN for Circuit Clerk

September 2, 1865
Married the 31st instant at the residence of the bride's father in
this county by REV. A. R. SCARBOROUGH, Mr. B. L. MITCHELL of Missouri to
Miss ARBORETT LYNN.
Administrator's Notice - Letters of Administration on the estate of
ROBERT S. LAVENDER, deceased granted to H. E. LAVENDER.
HON. C. S. McCONNICO, Judge of Pro-
bate Court
Accounts of DR. C. M. FRANCE have been left in my hands to collect.
J. L. SCRUGGS
Livingston Female Academy, H. J. CARTER, Principal. Music and Orna-
mental Branches in charge of Mrs. H. J. CARTER. Trustees: M. C. HOUSTON,
R. D. WEBB, R. F. HOUSTON, A. W. DILLARD, P. G. NASH, J. L. SCRUGGS.

September 9, 1865
H. L. BENNETT for Sheriff
All persons indebted to the estate of H. H. HARRIS, deceased call
upon THOMAS COBBS, my attorney. SOC PARKER, adm'r
MATTHEW SANTRY advertises brick for sale.

September 16, 1865
Died on the 14th instant, WILLIE LOU, infant daughter of JAMES and
REBECCA BRANCH of this county.

Candidates - J. C. HOUSTON for Sheriff
         - THOMAS S. HUNTER for Probate Judge

September 23, 1865
    Married on the 17th instant by REV. CHARLES MANLY at Mount Moriah
Church, Mr. THOMAS B. SPAULDING of Missouri to Miss EMMA WRIGHT of this
county.
    Candidates - DANIEL L. AYRES for Tax Assessor
             - REUBEN CHAPMAN, Jr. attorney at law
    Mrs. NARCISSA MAY advertises personal property for sale.

September 30, 1865
    J. C. GILLESPIE for Probate Judge
    HENRY C. JOHNSON for Circuit Clerk
    ROBERT ARRINGTON for Justice of the Peace
    Administrator's Notice - Letters of Administration on the estate of
JAMES M. ALEXANDER, deceased granted to OLIVER WYLIE.
    Final Settlement - This day came M. C. HOUSTON, guardian of AMANDA
DELOACH and filed account of guardianship for final settlement.
    Notice - To MARY L. BOYD (Later spelled BOYETT): You are hereby
notified that A. H. SMITH, administrator of the estate of ROBERT H. MOORE,
deceased, has filed a petition praying for the sale for the purpose of a
distribution of estate among the heirs.
                         Attorneys-at-Law
    WILLIAM M. BROOK   P. G. NASH
    Marion, Alabama   Partners   Livingston

October 7, 1865
    JAMES CREWS, candidate for Probate Judge.

October 14, 1865
    Candidates - JOHN T. FOSTER for State Senator
             - B(ENJ.) N. GLOVER of Choctaw County for State Senator
             - JOHN McINNIS for Representative from Sumter County
             - J. A. ABRAHAMS for Representative from Sumter County
             - LEWELLEN LEWIS for Representative from Sumter County
             - NEWTON W. HODGES for Circuit Clerk
             - T. S. RHYNE for Tax Collector
             - WILLIAM BEGGS for Tax Collector
             - JAMES COBBS for Judge of 7th Judicial Circuit
             - COL. E. S. GULLY for Probate Judge

October 21, 1865
    Candidates - HON. WILLIAM R. SMITH of Tuscaloosa for Governor
             - MAJOR J. A. SLEDGE for Representative from Sumter County
             - THOMAS B. CANNON for County Commissioner
             - E. W. DILLARD for Sheriff
    Administrator's Notice - Letters of Administration on the estate of
HENLEY R. WEBB, deceased granted to WILLIAM H. WEBB.
    Final Settlement - Came P. G. NASH, administrator of estate of OLIVA
JENKINS, deceased, for final settlement. P. G. NASH, administrator of
estate of LUCY GLASSCOCK, deceased.

October 28, 1865
    Candidates - HON. GEORGE D. SHORTRIDGE of Shelby County for Repre-
                 sentative from 4th Congressional District.
             - SAMUEL P(ATTON) HAND for County Commissioner
             - W. V. HARE for Representative from Sumter County
             - F. M. CROOKS for Tax Assessor

November 4, 1865
    Died of typhoid fever on the 30th of September, Miss CORA ELLA
BLACKSHER aged 16 years 11 months and 20 days. She was a Methodist.

November 11, 1865
    Died on the 4th instant, HOGAN ADAMS, only son of C. C. and M. E.
HAINSWORTH aged 1 year 5 months and 8 days....
    Notice - FANNY D. MARSH, administratrix of the estate of EDWARD
MARSH, deceased.

November 18, 1865

WILLIAM J. POOL, guardian of the heirs of ELIZABETH SANDERS, deceased, filed accounts.

WILLIAM J. POOL, guardian of the minor heirs of JAMES POOL, deceased, filed accounts.

Died on the 12th instant in this county, little ELIZABETH JANE, daughter of M. P. and N. S. HOWIE aged 3 years 1 month and 3 days.

FANNY L(ITTLEPAGE) MARSH, administratrix of the estate of EDWARD MARSH, deceased, filed account for final settlement of the guardianship of PETER MARSH, minor.

November 25, 1865

To DAVID S. LAVENDER and NANCY G. PORTER, wife of JOHN C. PORTER. You are hereby notified that H. E. LAVENDER, administrator of the estate of ROBERT S. LAVENDER, deceased has filed a petition praying for the assignment to MARGARET LAVENDER, widow of said deceased, her dower interest.

December 9, 1865

LEWELLEN LEWIS, administrator of the estate of OBEDIENCE LEWIS, deceased.

P. G. NASH, administrator of the estate of WILLIAM B. SAUNDERS, deceased.

LEWELLEN LEWIS, guardian of THOMAS R. LEWIS, JR.

December 16, 1865

ELIHU C. HOPSON, administrator of the estate of BINFORD HOPSON, deceased.

ISAAC DICKINSON, guardian of JOHN H. E. DICKINSON.

To JOSEPHINE BENY and GEORGE BENY: Take notice that JAMES F. WILLIAMSON, administrator of the estate of ALEXANDER WILLIAMSON, deceased filed a petition praying for division among heirs.

To HENRY P. DANCE, JAMES DANCE, JOHN S. DANCE, HENRY DANCE, and MARTHA, wife of GEORGE W. DUFF: Take notice that the will of RHODA TALBOT, deceased has been filed.

December 23, 1865

Married on the morning of the 18th instant by REV. S. U. SMITH at the residence of the bride's father, Mr. J. W. TARTT to Miss MARY ELIZABETH, daughter of JAMES R. SMITH, Esq. all of this county.

Married in Eutaw (Greene County), Alabama at the residence of the bride's father on the morning of the 21st by REV. S(TEPHEN) U. SMITH, Mr. JAMES C. USTICK of Livingston to Miss MARY E., daughter of ALEXANDER JARVIS of the former place.

Pay accounts due the estate of ALEXANDER DALLAS, deceased, to A. W. COCKRELL.

HOWELL WHITSETT, administrator of the estate of LAURA WHITSETT, deceased.

DEMPSEY COCKRELL, administrator of the estates of NATHAN E. COCKRELL and MARTHA A. E. COCKRELL, deceased.

December 30, 1865

Died at Jones' Bluff on the 24th, COL. R(ICHD) J. EPES in his 49th year.

J. P. HILLMAN, guardian of PHILIP A. HILLMAN, minor; also guardian of JUDSON J. HILLMAN, minor.

L. H. HARE, executor of the estate of JAMES SIMPSON, deceased.

To FRANCIS W. EPES, REBECCA SMITH, BEVERLY McCORMICK, DANIEL McCORMICK, EPES BEVERLY, wife of ROBERT BEVERLY and VIRGINIA A. HATCHETT: You are hereby notified that JOHN W. EPES, executor of the will of RICHARD EPES has filed will.

B. G. COOK, administrator of the estate of JOHN M. GOULD, deceased.

SARAH W. GOWDEY, administratrix of the estate of S(AMUEL) M. GOWDEY, deceased. Greene Co.

January 6, 1866

P. G. NASH, administrator of the estate of NIEL S. YARBROUGH, deceased.

Died at the residence in Sumter County on 2nd of December last, DAVID DRUMMOND in his 52nd year.

Died at her residence near Jones' Bluff, Sumter County on the 25th of December 1865, HELEN AMELIA wife of ANDREW J. ARRINGTON aged 28 years 2 months and 5 days. Left a husband and three little children. Died with tuberculosis.

January 13, 1866
Married at the bride's father's on the morning of the 20th by REV. E. PHILLIPS, Mr. T. W. WELLER of Nashville, Tennessee to Miss MATTOE, daughter of WILLIAM McREE.

Married on the 26th instant at the residence of Mr. L. HOUPT by REV. E. PHILIPS, LIEUT. J. Z. TUTT to Miss C. M. TAYLOR, all of this county.

Died on the 17th of December in Wilmington, North Carolina, JOHN A. KIRKLAND, formerly of Livingston, Alabama. He was a native of Greensboro, North Carolina but moved at an early age with his parents to Alabama. Editor and proprietor of Livingston Messenger. Married in 1863 and directly after returned to his native state and has been there ever since. He served until disabled as lieutenant in the 5th Alabama Regiment. Left a wife and infant child.

H. W. KILLEN, executor of the estate of ISAIAH MOORE, deceased; also of A. J. BROWN, deceased.

P. G. NASH, guardian of SARAH L. HINES.

H. W. KILLEN, executor of the estate of M. A. KING, deceased.

January 20, 1866
Married the 18th instant at the residence of his mother, by REV. R. A. MASSEY, Mr. NEWTON W. HODGES to Miss SALLIE J. LAVANDER, all of this county.

HON. JOSHUA MORSE of Choctaw County candidate for Judge of 7th Judicial Circuit.

January 27, 1866
This day came GEORGE J. COLGIN, guardian of CLARINDA M. TAYLOR (now TUTT) for final settlement of guardianship.

ELNATHAN TARTT, administrator of the estates of J. R. T. EASON and T. H. EASON, deceased.

STEPHEN HORTON, executor of the estate of WYATT HARPER, deceased.

PRESTON G. NASH, administrator of the estate of EDWARD S. BELL, deceased.

N. J. HAMMILL, Dentist. Livingston, Alabama. "Having studied and practiced Dental Art for three years with my father, DR. R. G. HAMILL."

TURNER REAVIS, Complainant)
        versus   )   Bill to foreclose Mortgage
GODFREY S. WILDER, adm'r)
of H. F. D. GILBERT et als
The defendants, JAMES W. GILBERT, ELIZA BOUNDS, wife of JOHN BOUNDS, JOHN BOUNDS, DAVID GILBERT and SUSAN F. GILBERT are of lawful age and residences are unknown; EZEKIEL CHERRY, another defendant, resides in Louisiana, but in what part is unknown.   GEORGE B. SAUNDERS, Register and Master of Chancery Court of Sumter County.

February 3, 1866
Married on the 30th instant at the residence of Mr. I. C. BROWN by REV. D. P. BESTOR, Mr. THOMAS M. TARTT to Miss ANNE M. JONES, all of this county.

February 10, 1866
Married Tuesday morning the 30th instant by REV. A. R. SCARBOROUGH and at his residence, COL. JAMES M. LEE to Miss MARY H. HUNTER, all of this county.

O(CTAVUS) L. CREWS and JAMES CREWS, executors of the estate of THOMAS R. CREWS, deceased.

THOMAS JARMAN, JR. guardian of the minor heirs of ELIZA HEARN, deceased.

THOMAS JARMAN, JR. guardian of MARY E. and WILLIAM T. HEARN.

Livingston Female Academy. H. J. CARTER, Principal and teacher of Literary and Scientific Depts., Miss NELLIS C. GIBBS, Intermediate Dept., Miss PANTHIA S. McSWAIN, Primary Dept., Mrs. E. J. CARTER, Music and French.

W. K. USTICK, Licensed Auctioneer.

February 17, 1866

Married on the 15th instant by REV. J. F. MARSHALL at the residence of the bride's father, Mr. W. H. JOHNSON of Choctaw to Miss ANNA MURLEY of this place.

Married on the 15th ult. at the residence of the bride's father by REV. A. R. SCARBOROUGH, Mr. GEORGE W. MASON to Miss ANNA FARR, all of this county.

REV. S. J. BINGHAM, candidate for Supt. of Public Schools.

Febryary 24, 1866

Married on the 30th instant by REV. PARKER, Mr. E. M. VANDIVER of Missouri to Miss S. J. CRAVEY of this county.

Died on the 29th of January in this place of pulmonary consumption SAM H. CHILES in his 29th year. Native of Petersburg, Va. but had for many years been a citizen of this place.

Died at his residence in Sumter County January 7, 1866, THOMAS RICHARD CREWS aged 52 years 6 months and 15 days. He was born in New Haven County, N. C. (New Hanover?) on 22nd of June 1813. Removed from his native state in 1837 and settled near Lauderdale Springs, Miss. In 1846, he removed to Gaston, Sumter County....People returned him to the Legislature from this county to the session of 1849. In May, 1862 he was elected Probate Judge. Became a Methodist in 1847. Affectionate husband and father.

W. K. USTICK, candidate for Justice of Peace.

J. G. COATS, administrator of the estate of ANN COATS, deceased.

J. G. COATS, administrator of the estate of WILLIAM BATES, deceased.

JOSEPH ARRINGTON, executor of the estate of MARY J. ARRINGTON, deceased.

P. G. NASH, administrator of estate of R. A. BROWN, deceased.

P. G. NASH, administrator of estate of THOMAS R. McGOWAN and of JAMES R. McGOWAN, deceased.

A. H. SMITH, adm'r of estate of ROBERT H. MOORE, deceased.

THOMAS B. CANNON, guardian of WILLIS H. PETETE and MARY E. MANLEY.

W. C. LITTLE, administrator of estate of E. G. SPEIGHT, deceased.

GEORGE J. COLGIN, guardian of MARY and MARTHA HARREL, minors.

GEORGE J. COLGIN, guardian of minor heirs of PETER JOHNSON, deceased.

March 3, 1866

Married on the 28th instant by REV. J. F. MARSHALL at the residence of the bride's father, Mr. ROBERT B. CARR of New Orleans to Miss S(ARAH) VIRGINIA, daughter of W. K. USTICK, Esq. of this place.

WILLIAM BEGGS, Candidate for Town Marshal.

P. G. NASH, guardian of JOHN F. WATSON.

JOHN W. SWILLEY, guardian of J. W. JACKSON.

A. A. COLEMAN, executor of BENJAMIN IVY, deceased.

JOHN W. HARRIS, administrator de bonis none of estate of N(ORFLET) T. HARRIS, deceased. Also of JAMES FERRELL, deceased.

March 10, 1866

Married on the 6th instant by REV. W. H. PASLEY, Mr. D. B. MILLER to Mrs. MARY A. E. McCAIN, both of this county.

Died at his residence in this place on 20th of January Mr. SAMUEL H. CHILES in 29th year. Born in Petersburg, Virginia and when only 3 years old, came to Alabama with his parents and settled in Livingston.... Married at early period in life....Left wife and two little boys.

JOSEPH K. DIAL, administrator of estate of JAMES C. DIAL, deceased.

To JOSEPHINE BERRY and her husband, GEORGE BERRY and JOHN WILLIAMSON. You are hereby notified that JAMES F. WILLIAMSON, administrator of the estate of ALEXANDER WILLIAMSON, deceased has filed petition for division of estate.

A. A. COLEMAN, administrator of the estate of ELIZA M. MARKHAM, deceased.

J. M. GODFREY, guardian of HARRIET UNDERWOOD.

JAMES I. GORDON, adm'r of the estate of WILLIAM A. LUMMUS, deceased.

March 17, 1866

Died in Livingston, Sumter County, Thursday March 1, 1866, in her 32nd year, Mrs. REBECCA SOUTHALL CHAPMAN, wife of REUBEN CHAPMAN, JR. Esq. and only daughter of ROBERT and PATIENCE ARRINGTON. Born in Halifax County, North Carolina on 16th of January 1835 from whence she came with

71.

her parents to this town in 1837, where she has continued to reside. To
her mother and father, to her husband and those two pledges of her affection which she has left in his care, and to her two brothers, her death
is a great loss....Protestant Episcopal.
    E. SLOCUMB GULLEY withdraws from race for Probate Judge.
    J. M. GRAYSON, adm'r of estate of YOUNG W. GRAYSON, deceased.
    R. S. HARPER, administrator of estate of CATHERINE C. HARPER, de-
ceased.
    J. T. DAVIS, administrator of estate of RICHARD J. WALTON, deceased.
    THOMAS COBBS, administrator of estate of RICHARD WOOTEN, deceased.
    WILLIAM McPHERSON, executor of estate of CYRUS McPHERSON.

March 24, 1866
    STEPHEN HORTON, administrator of estates of JOHN W. W. HORTON and of
MARGARET A. HORTON, deceased.
    E. A. SAMPLE, administratrix of estate of R. T. SAMPLE, deceased.
    J. C. H. JONES, administrator of estate of E. JONES, deceased. Also
guardian of LUCIEN A. JONES.
    WILLIAM BIRD, administrator of estate of JAMES C. PEYTON, deceased.
    GEORGE M. WRENN, executor of estate of SAMANTHA A. WRENN, deceased.
    D. H. WILLIAMS, administrator of estate of ELIZA J. GRIFFIN, de-
ceased.
    W. A. A. and M. E. JONES, guardians of MARY L. and WILLIE A. McRAE.
    P. G. NASH, guardian of THOMAS BOHANNAN.
    WILLIAM HOWARD, administrator of estate of WILLIAM A. MAY, deceased.
    N. P. DEAN, administrator of estate of ALEXANDER DEAN, deceased.
    NARCISSA THOMAS, formerly NARCISSA ANDERSON, administratrix of
WILLIAM S. ANDERSON, deceased.

March 31, 1866
    SAMUEL ESKRIDGE, administrator of JOHN J. SMITH, deceased.
    S. W. MURLEY, administrator of SAMUEL H. CHILES, deceased; also of
ELIZABETH R. CHILES, deceased.
    Notice to MARY C. WHITFIELD and her husband, RICHARD A. WHITFIELD:
Note that JAMES G. WHITFIELD, executor of the will of NICHOLAS P. CROOM,
deceased, filed the will of G. S. WHITE, administrator of JOHN W. WHITE,
deceased.
    Estate of SIMON M. WILSON, deceased. M. C. HOUSTON, administrator,
filed allegation of insolvency.

April 7, 1866
    Married on the 4th inst. at the residence of the bride's father in
Gainesville by REV. C. A. STILLMAN, LIEU. C. S. ANDERSON of St. Louis,
Mo. to Miss MARY H. FLEMING of this county.
    Estate of JOSEPH C. INMAN, deceased. F. P. SNEDICOR, administrator,
filed allegation of insolvency.
    G. B. MOBLEY, administrator of H(UMPHREY) F. EATON (36NH), deceased,
makes partial settlement.
    T. A. HAINESWORTH, guardian of BETTIE LARKIN, minor.

April 14, 1866
    Died on the 6th at the residence in Brewersville, DR. S(AMUEL) J.
ARRINGTON (23 NC) in his 39th year. Graduate of Medical School in Philadelphia in 1852 and since that time has successfully practiced his profession. Volunteered in CAPT. STONE'S Company of "Sumter Mounted Guards"
and served some time in Virginia campaigns. Health failing, he returned
home and resumed practice of his profession... Leaves wife and three
children. (Son of GEN. JOSEPH)
    MARY F. ADAMS (39 V), daughter of WILLIAM and MARGARET ROUTT was
born in Orange County, Virginia September 18, 1813; married JAMES COCKRELL
in 1834; moved to Alabama in 1839 and in 1843 (Aug. 21, 1842, marriage
record) married a second time to AARON ADAMS of this county. Twice was
left a widow with orphan children. In 1841, she joined the Baptist Church.
Though she was poor in this world's goods, she was rich in faith... On
the 23 of February, death came suddenly by an electric stroke...
    DAVID M. RUSSELL, JR., executor of DAVID M. RUSSELL (55 NH), SR.,
deceased, filed accounts for final settlement of his testator's administration on the estate of ANSON BRACKET (46 Vt), deceased (dead in 1857).

JAMES CREWS withdraws from the Probate Judge race.
SAMUEL H. SPROTT, administrator of ROBERT SPROTT, deceased.
JOHN McINNIS, administrator of MARIUS MARTIN, deceased.
SAMUEL ESKRIDGE, administrator of JOHN J. SMITH, deceased.

April 21, 1866
BENJAMIN LANCASTER was born in Orange County, Virginia July 23, 1778 and moved to Sumter County, Alabama in 1838. He settled about seven miles from Livingston, where he resided until his death. Member of the Baptist Church for 50 years. Having reached the extraordinary age of 87 years 7 months and 9 days (although afflicted many years with paralysis), he died on the 14th of February. Left a large family of children.
B. E. DuBOSE, guardian of WILLIAM R. HORN.
M. C. HOUSTON, guardian of AMANDA and JOHN and AUGUSTA DeLOACH.
S. H. FERGUSON, administrator of MATTHEW QUIMBY (28 NC), deceased.
SOC PARKER, guardian of MARY POOL's heirs.

April 28, 1866
Married on the 23rd inst. at the residence of the bride's father by Mr. MARSHAL, Mr. W. D. BATTLE, JR. to Miss LUDIE SCRUGGS, both of this place (could this be LOUISA daughter of JOSIAH L.)
Estate of BEN B. LITTLE, deceased. WILLIAM LITTLE, executor. Estate insolvent.
"We, the undersigned, late members of Co. "D", Jeff Davis Legion, C.S.A. and only surviving ones who are citizens of this county desire THOMAS S. HUNTER for Probate Judge:

A. K. RAMSEY, Capt.	J. J. HILLMAN
A. ARMSTRONG, 1st Lieutenant	J. L. HODGES
R. S. MASON, 3d Lieutenant	E. L. HODGES
J. L. BROWN, 2d Lieutenant	W. H. HODGES
L. F. BINNS	J. W. JACKSON
J. M. COOK	H. C. KNIGHT
R. CURRY	L. A. KNIGHT
J. C. ELLIOTT	F. A. LOONEY
S. L. ESKRIDGE	G. W. MASON
J. P. HAGLER	E. F. MASON
W. H. HAWKINS	R. C. MAY
J. M. SCARBOROUGH	C. L. SUMMERLIN
THOMAS B STONE	J. C. WILLIAMS

May 12, 1866
J. W. BREWSTER)
versus) Bill for Divorce
NANCY BREWSTER)
The defendant is over 21 years of age and she resides in Lauderdale Co. Miss.
Letters of administration on estate of SAMUEL J. ARRINGTON, deceased, granted to JOSEPH ARRINGTON.

May 19, 1866
Married in the Methodist Church on the evening of the 16th by REV. J. F. MARSHALL, Mr. W. B. McRAE of Missouri to Miss ANGIE TUREMAN of this place. (ANGELINE 3 A, d. of MARY A.)
DAVID WATSON, administrator of DAVID ROBINSON, deceased.

May 26, 1866
Died at his residence on Saturday morning last, Mr. WILLIAM H. JEMISON (45 G) in his 62nd year.
Letters of administration on estate of PLEASANT (53 G) WHITE, deceased granted to W. W. COATS.
WILLIAM H. COLEMAN, guardian of JEROME C. THOMPSON: also of RUFUS K. THOMPSON.

June 9, 1866
Married Thursday evening May 31st by REV. J. F. MARSHALL, Mr. ROBERT HATTEN to Miss SARAH FRANCES SPEAKMAN, all of this county.
PHILIP MAY, executor of MARY BUCHANAN, deceased.

```
GREEN B. MOBLEY                          )
     versus                              )
JANE CARPENTER (34 NC) (widow of)    In Chancery
     THOMAS, 39 NC)                      )
et al                                    )
```
The defendants, ALLEN CARPENTER and LOUISA HICKS and her husband, JAMES HICKS are severally over age of 21 and reside in Lauderdale County, Mississippi; JAMES CARPENTER, another defendant, is also over 21 and resides out of this state, but where is unknown. .

June 16, 1866

THOMAS B. CANNON, administrator of JAMES BEABERS (1 JAS. BEAVERS @ 39 NC), deceased. Also administrator of JOHN P. PETEET, deceased and of WILLIAM PETEET, deceased, MARK TIDMORE, deceased and of JAMES W. HALL (17 A), deceased.

JOHN McINNIS, guardian of minor heirs of A. THETFORD, deceased.

```
L. F. WHITEHEAD                 )
     versus                     )
W. T. & G. W. PARKS, def'ts )     Attachment suit
C. B. WOOTEN et al, gar.    )
```

June 30, 1866

P. G. NASH, administrator of GEORGE W. BLAIR, deceased advertises land for sale.

W. A. JEMISON, administrator of W. H. JEMISON, deceased.

RICHARD H. WHITFIELD, administrator of THOMAS GEE, deceased. Also of THEODRIE J. GEE (38 V), deceased and of JOHN S. NAUVLE, deceased.

A. Y. SHARP, administrator of THOMAS J. McCORMICK, deceased.

July 7, 1866

Died on the 30th of June at the residence near Sumterville of paralysis occasioned by being thrown from a horse, ROBERT L. BROWN (25 NC) aged 41. Native of Marlborough District, South Carolina but for many years a prominent and successful planter of this county. Had spent last winter in an extensive tour through the southern portion of Brazil and was making preparations to remove thither with his family....Baptist.

July 21, 1866

VIRGINIA A. ESKRIDGE was born December 15, 1842 and died June 24, 1866 aged 23 years and 7 months. Left a husband and a daughter.

P. G. NASH, administrator of LEWIS HOUSTON, (40 NC), deceased and of RICHARD JENKINS (53V), deceased. (Married 1822 JANETTE of JOHN WMS. of Henirco County, Va. See minors dead in 1852.)

July 28, 1866

Married at Murfreesboro, Tennessee the 12th by REV. RANSOM, Mr. Z(ACK) Tureman (17 A, s. of Zach.) of this place to Miss KATE H. BROWN of the former place. We were well aware of our friend's Zac's efficiency as Circuit Clerk but did not know he could issue a writ of attachment that would hold good in Brownlow's dominions.

August 4, 1866

Married Thurs. the 2d. at the residence of MARK PARKER, Esq. by REV. S. BINGHAM, Mr. L. B. HUMPHRIES of Handsboro, Miss. to Miss JULIA HINES (74 daughter of ELIZ.) of this county.

WILLIAM A. WOODALL administrator of JAMES M. WOODALL (17A son of LITTLE), deceased.

August 11, 1866

Married at the residence of the bride's father on the 27th by REV. S. J. BINGHAM, Mr. T. H. TURNIPSEED of Pickens Co. Ala. to Miss JENNETT BOYD.

JAMES H. MARTIN says he is not responsible for the debts of his wife, MARY F. MARTIN.

M. C. HOUSTON and MARTHA W. HAIR (50 NC), executors of estate of JAMES HAIR (58 Pa), deceased.

CYNTHIA SHIELD, administratrix of J. J. SHIELD, deceased.

August 18, 1866
    Married at the residence of the bride's father in Choctaw County the
9th by REV. S. J. BINGHAM, Mr. OLIVER WYLIE to Miss GEORGIA ABB CURRY (3A
daughter of JOHN).

August 25, 1866
    Married at the residence of the bride's mother on the 15th by REV.
A. R. SCARBOROUGH, Mr. W. H. BROWN (he was of Sumter) to Miss KATE B.
HENEGAN, all of this county. (CATHERINE BILLINGSLEY HENAGAN...She was
daughter of EPHRAIM L. and ANN (McINNIS) HENAGAN. See letter from MAJ.
GEN. JOHN C. HENAGAN.)
    Letters of administration on estate of JAMES H. BARTEE (Dillon, S.C.,
Jan. 9, 1958), deceased granted to HARRIET J. BARTEE.

September 1, 1866
    Died on the 23rd at her residence near Pushmataha after a short ill-
ness, Miss MARGARET PEARSON, sister of DR. R. N. PEARSON of Choctaw County.
    COL. JAMES M. NORWOOD of Arkansas died in this county at the resi-
dence of his brother-in-law, D. O. WHITE, Esq. on the 22d inst. after a
protracted illness. Native of Perry County, Alabama, where he has many
friends and relatives. Moved to Mississippi at an early period of his
life. Served in the Confederate army....
    Letters of administration on estate of WILLIAM HOWIE (53 NC), de-
ceased granted to MICHAEL P. HOWIE (17 A).

September 15, 1866
    P. G. NASH, administrator of JOSEPH RUFFIN, deceased.
    W. G. LITTLE, administrator of JOHN T. JENKINS, deceased.
    ISAAC R. McELROY, Sen., administrator of THOMAS E. JAMES, deceased.
    Estate of JARED WATSON, deceased (49 G). THOMAS F. WATSON, adminis-
trator.
    Letters of administration on estate of JAMES C. BENNETT, deceased
to WILLIAM H. BENNETT.
    Estate of JOHN P. BLANN, deceased. ISAAC R. McELROY, administrator.

September 22, 1866
    Married on the evening of the 12th at the residence of the bride's
brother in Pickens County by REV. S. J. BINGHAM, REV. W. B. BINGHAM of
this place to Miss ELIZABETH E. TURNIPSEED.
    ROBERT TANKERSLEY, executor of estate)
        of GEORGE G. TANKERSLEY, Senr.   )
        (See his will in Vol. 164, p. 52))   In Chancery
                   versus   )
    Heirs of said estate   )
JAMES H. TANKERSLEY (9 A) over 21 and HARRISON TANKERSLEY (7 A) over
21 reside in Brazoria County, Texas, Sandy Point P.O., FANNIE A. TANKERS-
LEY, widow of FELIX TANKERSLEY (6 A) deceased and their child, WILLIAM
TANKERSLEY about 3 years old reside in Chapel Hill, North Carolina.
    MAJ. W(HITMELL) K. BULLOCK (52 NC), an old and highly respectable
citizen of our county died yesterday aged about 70.
    Married at the residence of the bride's mother on the 27th inst. by
REV. S. J. BINGHAM, COL. E. S. GULLY to Miss R. HINES (Is this REBECCA
9 A daughter of ELIZABETH?), all of this county.
    Tribute of respect to WM. E. CHILES (35 SC), deceased by Livingston
Lodge #41, P. G. NASH, W. M. and J. L. SCRUGGS, Sec'y.

October 6, 1866
    A. W. RICHARDSON, deceased. W. R. RICHARDSON, administrator.
    LEWIS M. STONE, administrator and N. A. STONE, administratrix of
GEORGE W. STONE, deceased.
    JAMES G. BENNETT, deceased. Notice to CHARLES WILLIAM H. BENNETT,
NARCISSA B. TILLMAN, OLIVER P. BENNETT, C. C. McCASKILL and ELIZA A.
McCASKILL his wife, E. R. LILES, WM. RAMSEY and ADELA RAMSEY his wife;
W. H. BENNETT, administrator of JAMES C. BENNETT, deceased has this day
filed petition to sell land.
    Tribute of respect to WILLIAM HOWIE, deceased by Quarterly Conference
of which he was a minister. S. H. COX, P. E. and P. G. NASH, Sec'y.

October 13, 1866
     Married on the 3d inst. by ELDER A. R. SCARBOROUGH, JOHN KENNEDY of
New Orleans and ELLEN McBRIDE (12 A, daughter of JAMES) of this county.
     Died on the 30th in Greene County, Alabama after a short illness,
Mr. SAMUEL WRIGHT, son of P. T. (PLEASANT T.?) WRIGHT, Esq. aged about
20 years.

October 20, 1866
     Executor's sale---H. W. KILLEN, executor of JOSIAH MOORE's (45 T)
estate advertises property for sale. "I will sell at my residence 5
miles southwest of Sumterville certain stock, corn (etc.) and also rent
the plantation for ensuing years--200 acres of open land." Signed MARIA
L. G. EASON.

October 27, 1866
     Married Tuesday evening the 23rd by ROBERT ARRINGTON, Esq. Mr. GEORGE
WILSON to Miss JULIA A. ANDERSON (12 A, daughter of PLEASANT H.) all of
this county.
     THOMAS I. McCORKLE, deceased. P. G. NASH, administrator.
     JOHN DANIEL, deceased. JOHN DANIEL, administrator.
     RICHARD WOOTEN, deceased. THOMAS COBBS, administrator.
     SAM THOMPSON, deceased. H. L. BENNETT, Sheriff, administrator.
     HENLY B. WEBB (39 SC), deceased. WILLIAM H. WEBB, administrator.
     JOSEPHINE PEYTON, deceased. J. G. HARRIS, administrator.
     WILLIAM E. CHILES, deceased. R. M. BRASSFIELD, administrator.
     W. B. MASTERS, deceased. JOSEPH B. MASTERS, administrator.

November 3, 1866
     JEFF. BOYD, guardian of the minor heirs of ROSINI HODGES, deceased
(in a later issue, the name is spelled "ROZENA").
     JEFF. BOYD, guardian of MARGARET LAVENDER.
     ELISHA C. HOPSON, administrator of BLUFORD HOPSON, deceased.
(BLUFORD HOPSON married in Perry County, March 27, 1831, SUSAN R. CARLISLE
Vol. 198, p. 38.)

November 10, 1866
     Died in this county on the morning of the 3rd inst. JOHN E. BROWN,
JR. (6 A), only son of JOHN E. (41 SC) and MARY JANE (34 A) BROWN, aged
22 years and 8 months....
     Resolutions on the death of JOHN E. BROWN, JR. by Hermon Lodge no.
16, JAMES D. HARWELL, Secretary pro tem.
     Died in Wilmington, North Carolina on the 20th of congestive fever,
Miss PAULINE F., daughter of WM. KIRKLAND, SR. of this place in her 19th
year....
     Sale of personal property of ROBERT L. BROWN, deceased by I. C. BROWN
executor. Residence 2 miles south of Sumterville for sale.

November 17, 1866
     Married at the residence of the bride's father on the 13th ult. by
REV. WM. CHERRY, Mr. R. W. LAWLER to Miss M. V. GILLESPIE, all of this
county.
     Died in this county on Saturday the 10th at the residence of H. L.
BENNETT, Esq. Mr. JOSEPH B. GREENLEES (7 A) aged 23 years and 10 months.
     Died in this county on the 6th of November 1866 at his residence,
CAPT. RICHARD DUNFORD SHACKELFORD (56 V) in his 74th year. Born in
Pittsylvania County, Virginia November 11th, 1792. He served during the
war of 1812 and after the close of it, moved to this state, settling in
Perry County. Afterwards he moved to Sumter County, where he lived for
a number of years, a highly esteemed, honorable and reliable citizen.
As a husband and father, he was kind and affectionate.... Like others,
he had his faults, but his goodness of heart outshone all....

November 24, 1866
     THOMAS B. BILLUPS, deceased. J. G. HARRIS, general administrator.
     ROBERT M. BEGGS, deceased. WILLIAM BEGGS, administrator.
     "Under order from Probate Court of Greene County, Alabama, I will,
as administrator of WILLIS P. RIDDLE, deceased, sell to the highest
bidder certain lands in Sumter County." Signed
                                   T. C. CLARK, administrator.

December 1, 1866

Married on the 28th at the residence of the bride's father in Livingston by REV. A. R. SCARBOROUGH, R. C. MAY and Miss MARY L. McRAE (1 A, daughter of WM. P.), daughter of Mrs. W. A. C. JONES.

Married on the 21st near Sumterville by REV. WM. PASLEY, E. H. WARD of Choctaw to Miss SALLIE J. (5 A), daughter of E(UEN) N. BRYANT, Esq.

VERNAL LOWRY (43 NC), deceased. PRUDENCE LOWRY (40 T), executrix.

GEORGE MORRIS, guardian of ALSON BLAKENEY.

JOSEPH ARRINGTON, JR., administrator of SAMUEL J. ARRINGTON, deceased.

December 8, 1866

Married at the residence of the bride's father on the 4th inst. by REV. W. H. PASLEY, Mr. GEORGE M. HIBBER to Miss MARY A. KENNEDY (9 A, daughter of JOHN) of this county.

Married on the 6th ult. in this place by ROBERT ARRINGTON, Esq. Mr. H. M. DAVIS to Miss A. L. JOHNSON.

State of Alabama-Sumter County. 6 December 1866. Probate Court-Special Term. TO: ELIZABETH MAHONEY, ELIAS MAHONEY (husband of said ELIZABETH). EVELYN ARCHER and DELLA L. and NANNIE ARCHER, minor heirs of LINEOUS ARCHER, deceased--You are hereby notified that ANDERSON LIPSCOMB, executor, has filed the will of YANCY MITCHELL, deceased.

WILLIAM P. BREWER, executor of SERENA JONES, deceased.

Plantation belonging to estate of W. DRAKE, deceased, for rent by A. E. BROCKWAY, administrator.

WILLIAM P. BREWER, executor of WILLIAM H. JONES, deceased.

THOMAS W. SMITH, administrator of ROBERT B. SMITH, deceased.

December 15, 1866

M. F. BOLTON, deceased. S. E. BOLTON, administratrix.

December 22, 1866

H. W. KILLEN, executor of M. A. KING, deceased.

H. W. KILLEN, administrator of A. J. BROWN, deceased.

JAMES F. WILLIAMSON, administrator of ALEXANDER WILLIAMSON (66 V), deceased.

December 29, 1866

Married on the 16th inst. by REV. A. SCARBOROUGH at the residence of J. A. FARROW, Mr. J. A. JONES to Miss MARY JENKINS, all of this county.

Married on the 20th by same at the residence of GEORGE MORRIS, Mr. J. JACKSON to Miss ELIZA BLAKENEY all of this county.

Married on the 20th inst. by REV. A. SCARBOROUGH at the residence of J. MUNDELL, Mr. R. J. PEAVY to Miss MARY MUNDELL (4 Miss., daughter of JOHN), all of this county.

Died on the 7th of December at her residence near Gaston in this county, Mrs. W(ILMOTH) M. JONES, relict of W(ILLIAM) D. JONES in her 65th year. Native of South Carolina but for the last 25 years a resident of this county. Member of Methodist Episcopal Church and was uniformly beloved and respected. She sent an only son to the army in defense of her native south, who fell a victim to disease. She leaves a bereaved and much afflicted family.

Departed this life at his residence in this place on the 22nd at 8 o'clock P.M., DR. NEWTON J. HAMILL. He was born in Eutaw, Greene County, Alabama March 31, 1836 and 9 years since removed to this place where for several years he taught school. Having graduated at an early age in Dentistry....Husband and father....In a conversation with his kinsman, REV. A. R. SCARBOROUGH, he said that his greatest regret was to leave his wife and little children. (Ancestor of CARR COLLINS, Dallas, Texas, 1960, says he married 1860 as her 1st husband, SUSAN A. PORTER.)

January 5, 1867

Married on the 13th of December, 1866 at the residence of the bride's father by REV. W. H. PASLEY, Mr. JAMES T. WREN to Miss C. W. COCKRELL (is this CORNELIA 11 A, daughter of HILLSMAN?), all of this county.

RICHARD D. SHACKELFORD, deceased. S. C. COLEMAN and ABRAM LARKIN, administrators.

January 12, 1867
    Died in Tompkinsville, Choctaw County on the 31st of December 1866,
CAPT. CHARLES EUGENE RHODES in his 26th year. Native of Sumter County,
Alabama. He was an only son. He succeeded in raising a company of
cavalry for the war. At the battle of Lafayette he was captured and remained some 12 months in captivity on Johnson's Island....
    Wanted: Mr. R. H. YARBROUGH, a disable Confederate soldier wants
some information of his father, JAMES YARBROUGH (65 SC, Barton County),
who emigrated to this state (Texas) from Calhoun County, Alabama in 1862.
Address: R. H. YARBROUGH, Bonham, Fannin County, Texas.

January 19, 1867
    Probate Court--TO: MARY RINGER, wife of P. H. RINGER, E(LLINGTON,
5 A) EVENS, non-resident heirs, and WILLIAM McDONALD, minor and non-resident heir of ELLINGTON EVANS (73 V), deceased. You are hereby notified
that ABNER P. EVANS (16 A), executor, has filed the will of ELLINGTON
EVANS, deceased.

January 26, 1867
    Married at the Baptist Church at Meridian on the 10th ult. by REV.
S. J. BINGHAM, assisted by REV. A. L. KLEIN of Columbia, Tennessee, Mr.
G. C. OSBORNE of Tennessee to Miss E. TOURNIER EMERSON, daughter of REV.
W. C. EMERSON of Meridian.
    Married on the 17th inst. by REV. JOHN MORGAN, Mr. SETH LITTLE to
Miss MARY E. ROGERS, all of this county.

February 2, 1867
    Married on the 23rd at the residence of the bride by REV. T. A. C.
ADAMS, Mr. J. B. ROACH of Choctaw to Mrs. ROSINA TANKERSLY of this county.
    SARAH E. TUREMAN, deceased. Z. TUREMAN, administrator.
    M. G. WOODALL, guardian of W. A. WOODALL filed her account of
guardianship.

February 9, 1867
    Married on the 23rd at the residence of the bride's father by REV.
GERALDUS GAY, Mr. GEORGE B. GAY to Miss SALLIE HARE all of this county.
    Married on the 7th at the residence of the bride's mother by REV.
W. H. PASLEY, Mr. D(AVID) L. BENNETT (13 A, son of SARAH E.) to Miss
FRANCES P. POYTRESS all of this county.
    WELLINGTON A. MURLEY, deceased. S. W. MURLEY, administrator.
    M. G. WOODALL, guardian of MELISSA WOODALL.

February 16, 1867
    Died at his residence 4 miles north of Livingston on the 18th day of
December 1866 of pneumonia, SAMUEL ESKRIDGE (53 SC) in his 68th year.
Born in Spartanburg District, South Carolina in the year 1798, where he
resided until 1820 when he emigrated to Greene County, Alabama where he
lived until 1835 when he moved to this place at which he died. Best
citizen, kind husband and father....honest, sober, industrious and economical. At 18, he joined the Baptist Church....
    WILLIAMSON JORDAN, deceased. C. S. McCONNICO, administrator.
    N. B. SHERARD, deceased. SOC PARKER, administrator.
    MARGARET TARTT, deceased. ELNATHAN TARTT, administrator.

February 23, 1867
    Died near Secoba, Kemper County, Mississippi Friday morning the 15th
inst. at about 20 minutes after 12, HUGH DALE (49 Me), Esq. in his 67th
year....Mobile Times copy.
    SARAH J. JONES)
        versus   )   Bill for divorce
    EDWARD D. JONES)
    The defendant is over 21 and resides out of this state; he is be-
lieved to be now in Maine, P. O. Unknown.
    JOHN P. BLANN, deceased. ISAAC R. McELROY, administrator.
    W. A. LUMMUS, deceased. S. H. SPROTT, administrator.
    THOMAS J. McCORMICK, deceased. S. H. SPROTT, administrator.

March 2, 1867
    Died, CAPT. F. N. SMITH of pulmonary consumption in Livingston on
the 14th at 9 A.M. Disease was acquired by exposure and hardships of im-
prisonment at Ship Island during the recent war. Of his private life,
little can be said, as he passed almost direct from his graduating class
to camp. He sleeps in the Livingston graveyard beside a brother and
other relatives....
    Departed this life, DR. JOHN L. HADLY (48 T), who was born May 11,
1802 near Gallatin, Sumner County, Tennessee and died at his residence in
Avoyelles Parish, Louisiana on January 20, 1867....He emigrated to Greene
County, Alabama in 1837, where he practiced his profession with success.
In 1845 he moved to Sumter County. Here he abandoned his profession and
was a planter. In 1863, he moved to Louisiana....
    Departed this life---Mrs. HARRIET A. KENNEDY (44 NC), born in Jones
County, North Carolina November 8, 1805, died December 28, 1866 after an
illness of only a few hours. Was in comparatively good health, when she
suffered a paralytic stroke....Wife and mother.

March 9, 1867
    DR. B. HAWKINS--Dental Surgeon.

March 16, 1867
    Died on the 14th inst. at the residence of Mrs. ELIZABETH McMILLEN
in this county, DR. JAMES H. McDONALD in his 35th year.

March 23, 1867
    Departed this life--MEREDITH WEBB LYNN (30 A), who was born in Morgan
County, Alabama November 19, 1819. In the year 1833 or 1836 he came to
this county a poor, friendless youth without advantages of liberal education...He soon attracted the attention of the late JAMES PARKER. His
business qualities as overseer rendered him indispensible...He married in
18-- Miss LANCASTER (ACNESS E. 29 V), who with 6 children survive him. In
1860 he became connected with the Baptist Church. After the death of Mr.
PARKER, Mr. LYNN moved to Bear Creek where he died of typhoid pneumonia
March 2, 1867 in his 47th year....

March 30, 1867
    In memory of Mrs. ELIZABETH McCAIN (52 SC), who departed this life
on 15th of March 1867 aged 69 years and 2 days. She was born in Fairfield
District, South Carolina March 13, 1798 and moved to this state about 1826
and had been a resident of this county about 34 years. She died suddenly
during the night. She was blessed with pious parents. Member of the
Baptist Church.

April 6, 1867
    A. M. BROWNING, deceased. E. F. BROWNING, administrator.

April 13, 1867
    Married in Brazoria County, Texas on the 2nd by REV. Mr. SHEPPARD,
W. A. WAYNE to Miss SALLIE ABRAHAMS (9 A, daughter of JAS. A.), both of
this place.
    Married on the 28th at the residence of the bride's father in Madison
County, Mississippi by REV. W. C. CRANE, GEN. S.A.D. GREAVES to Miss
JENNIE, daughter of COL. W. F. BATTLEY.

April 20, 1867
    Married on the 11th at the residence of Mr. ASA AMASON near Sumter-
ville by B. B. THOMAS, Esq. Mr. I. R. WILSON of Missouri to Miss M(ARTHA)
O. LEWIS of this county. As one of the few survivors of the Old Brigade,
we congratulate "Ike".
    ARMSTEAD GATEWOOD, deceased. MICHAEL GRADY, administrator.

April 27, 1867
    JOB MEADOR (45 NC), deceased. CALEB J. LANDRUM, administrator.

May 4, 1867
    BRYAN CROOM, deceased. A. M. CROOM, administrator.
    DAVID S. BURTON, deceased. NANCY J. BURTON, administratrix.
    W. H. COLEMAN, guardian of JEROME C. THOMPSON.

May 11, 1867
    Married on the 2nd inst. by REV. J. H. MORGAN at the residence of the
bride's father in Warsaw, Mr. ANDREW ARRINGTON to Miss MAGGIE L. BELL,
all of this county. (His 1st wife, HELEN A. died Dec. 25, 1865.)

May 18, 1867
    Married on the 15th by REV. A. R. SCARBOROUGH at the residence of
the bride's mother, DR. B. BEN SEALE to Miss M. F. McMILLEN, all of this
county.
    Married on the 15th by REV. T. A. S. ADAMS at the residence of COL.
WILLIAM W. STONE in this place, Mr. M. L. JENKINS to Miss BERTIE HOUSTON.

May 25, 1867
    WILLIAM A. McCLURE, deceased. C. S. McCONNICO, administrator.
    JOHN C. MILLER, deceased. C. S. McCONNICO, administrator.

June 1, 1867
    Married on the 27th at the residence of the bride's father by REV.
T. A. S. ADAMS, Mr. W. W. LAWLER of Mississippi to Miss NORA PARRENT of
this place.

June 15, 1867
    ALEXANDER DALLAS, deceased. DANIEL F. SANFORD, administrator.

June 22, 1867
    Married on the 20th inst. at the residence of the bride's father,
Mr. E(DWARD) H. USTICK by REV. T. A. S. ADAMS, Mr. DAVID AKIN of Demopolis
(Marengo County) to Miss ANNIE TERHUNE USTICK of this place.

June 29, 1867
    Died in Bryan, Brazos County, Texas on June 6, 1867, Mrs. SARAH A.
DODSON, wife of WESLEY C. DODSON.

July 27, 1867
    Died on the 8th at his home in Johnson County, Mo. COL. JAMES McCOWN,
formerly commander of 5th Missouri Infantry, 1st Missouri Brigade, Confederate States Army.
    Died on the 8th, REV. W(ILLIAM) S. LARKINS (13 NC, son of SUSAN E.)
of South Sumter.

August 3, 1867
    THOMAS DONALD, deceased. ELIZABETH DONALD, executrix.
    SARAH ANDERSON, deceased. J. G. HARRIS, general administrator.

August 17, 1867
    Married in Meridian, Mississippi at the residence of DR. N. B.
KENNEDY at 6 A.M. Wednesday August 7th by REV. Mr. THOMAS, Mr. JOHN P.
HAGLER of Sumter County, Alabama to Miss SALLIE A. MARTIN of Meridian,
Miss.
    Married on the 15th inst. by REV. A. R. SCARBOROUGH at the residence
of JOSEPH McGOWEN, JOSEPH L. DEWIT of Mississippi to MARY A. McGOWEN of
this county.
    Died on the 12th of congestion of brain and lungs at the residence
of J. M. HORD in this county, Miss IDA COUCH, daughter of DANIEL and MARY
COUCH in her 14th year. Selma and Marion papers please copy.
    Died at her residence near this place Monday the 12th after a short
illness, Mrs. MARY R. KIRKLAND, wife of WILLIAM KIRKLAND, SR. in her 37th
year. Elyton Herald, Pensacola Observer, Blountsville paper, Talladega
Reporter and Watchtower and Forrest Miss. Reporter copy.
    Died at the residence of J. G. HARRIS in Livingston on the morning
of the 10th, EVENDER B. STEWART, only son of Mrs. CHARLES S. STEWART, aged
8 years 5 months and 6 days.
    JOHN C. EPES, deceased. JOHN W. EPES, administrator.

August 24, 1867
    Died on the 17th at the residence of J. M. HORD near Sumterville,
Mrs. S. J. ELLIOTT of this county.

August 31, 1867

Died on the 27th in this place of congestion of the brain, WILLIE ERNEST, infant son of WILLIAM J. and ANNIE M. RAWLS. WILLIE was born December 13, 1866....

September 7, 1867

Died of inflammation of the stomach on the 15th in Lauderdale County, Mississippi at the residence of her husband, SARA, wife of OWEN PIGFORD in her 61st year. Left a husband and children and large circle of friends.

September 21, 1867

Died in this county on the 6th, SARAH, consort of Mr. SAMUEL POND in her 61st year. She was born in Anson County, N.C. and moved to this county with her husband in 1847. Baptist. Leaves large family....

September 28, 1867

Died at father's residence in Hale County on the 12th of congestive chill, WILLIAM PEMBROKE, oldest son of Mr. F. L. and Mrs. J. T. SIMS aged about 6 years.

Died at her residence in Sumter County, Mrs. SARA J. wife of J. C. ELLIOTT and daughter of JEFFERSON and HULDAH HORD. Born in Spotsylvania County, Virginia October 7, 1835, moved with her parents to Alabama and in 1857 joined the Baptist Church. Leaves a husband and two little children and many relatives....

October 5, 1867

Died in Livingston on September 16, 1867 after a long and painful illness, ROBERT ARRINGTON (49 NC), who was born in Nash County, North Carolina on March 8, 1801, was married to P(ATIENCE) A. WRIGHT (43 NC) on June 17, 1824. The deceased moved to Sumter County, Alabama in 1837 and continued to reside here until his death...Sympathy to widow.

October 12, 1867

Died of congestive fever at Gaston, Alabama on September 27, 1867, ELIZABETH (44 G), wife of MATTHEW A. MARSHALL (46 G), after a brief but exceedingly painful illness. Born in Jones County, Georgia November 3, 1807 but had resided for many years in Sumter County...Methodist for 25 years...Good wife and mother.

November 9, 1867

Married Tuesday morning, October 15th at the residence of and by REV. E. PHILIPS in Sumter County, Mr. CHARLES C. CROUCH of Selma to Miss JEANNIE P. SMITH of Sumter County.

Married on the evening of the 22nd, by REV. E. PHILIPS at the residence of the bride's father, Mr. GEO. NEATHERY (7 A, son of JAS. S.) of Mississippi to Miss FLORENCE McREE (3 A, daughter of WM.) of Sumter County.

Died in this county at the residence of her parents Thursday Oct. 31, little JIMMIE, youngest daughter of COL. I. JAMES and SUSAN L. LEE aged 5 years 6 months and 12 days. Tuscaloosa Monitor copy.

November 16, 1867

Died on 24th of sudden and severe illness, MARY ADELAIDE, daughter of WM. A. and MARY W. SILLIMAN aged 9 years 1 month and 21 days...

November 23, 1867

Died on the 18th near Bennett's Station, Sumter County, JOHN E. BAKER, formerly of Missouri and aged about 40. Tribute of respect by Livingston Lodge #41.

Died October 18, 1867 near Gainesville, MARTHA SPEIGHT, wife of ROBERT E. HIBBLER and only daughter of the late HON. EDWARD G. SPEIGHT aged 21.

Died at her residence in Sumter County on the 20th at 4 A.M. Mrs. ELIZA H. SLEDGE, wife of A(LBERT) G. SLEDGE (38 T) in her 51st year. Member of Protestant Methodist Episcopal Church...Leaves husband and children and relations.

December 7, 1867

Married on the 26th at the residence of W. SHELBY by REV. S. J. BINGHAM, Mr. WM. BELL and Miss M. J. SHELBY.

At the same time and place by same, Mr. F. RUMLEY and Mrs. P. A.
ALLISON. (FRED RUMLEY 1844-1924 buried in cemetery at York, wife BELL
1842-1908?)
Married on the 27th at the residence of the bride's father by B. B.
THOMAS, Esq., Mr. W. J. GREGORY and Miss NANNIE AMASON of this county.
Married on the 26th at the residence of W. R. RICHARDSON by REV. T.
Y. RAMSEY, Mr. JAMES S. POYTHRESS and Miss MATTIE G. RAIFORD, all of this
county.

December 14, 1867
Married on the 12th at the residence of JOHN HARVISON by HUGH GREENLEE,
Esq., WM. R. BELL and Mrs. MARY JANE JONES, all of this county.

December 21, 1867
Died in this place on the 14th, MAGGIE B., daughter of B. B. and
B. A. SAUNDERS aged 3 years 5 months and 21 days.

January 11, 1868
Died at the residence near Brewersville in this county on the 8th,
DR. H(ENRY) F. ARRINGTON (39 NC) aged about 57.

January 18, 1868
Died on the 6th near this place, SARAH A. wife of R. C. KNIGHT aged
40.

January 25, 1868
Married on the 22nd by DR. B. HAWKINS, Mr. WALTER SCOTT to Miss
MARTHA DRUMMOND (7 A, daughter of DAVID), all of this county.
At the residence of the bride's father in this county on Monday the
20th inst. by REV. PARKER, Mr. COMER B. JONES of Marengo County and Miss
C. LOUTIE, eldest daughter of Mr. PHIL. MAY, SR.

February 15, 1868
Died February 5, 1868, LUCINDA, wife of GA(S?)WELL EADES (CASWELL in
Census, 44 V) at York Station, Sumter County, Alabama aged 63 years 5
months and 26 days.
Married on the 12th by J. W. HARRIS, Esq. at the residence of T. A.
JOHNSON, Mr. J. L. PEEL of Mississippi to Mrs. M. J. PRAYTOR of this
county.

February 22, 1868
Departed this life at the residence of Mr. H. S. LIDE in Sumter
County, Alabama on Monday the 10th inst., Mr. JERE H. BROWN (BROWNE)
(48 SC) in his 67th year. Native of Darlington District, S.C. and graduated in that state in Columbia in 1824. Removed to Alabama and became
a resident of Sumter County in 1834. Deacon in Baptist Church. Left 2
daughters and 1 son. Has gone to join a pious wife and his little
children....
Departed this life, DR. A(UGUSTUS) E. BRECKWAY (36 Conn) February 15,
1868. Resolutions on his death, by Gaston Lodge no. 66.

February 29, 1868
Departed this life February 9, 1868 Mrs. BETTIE UNDERWOOD at her
home in Perry County. Only daughter of Mr. J. L. LARKIN, deceased of
Sumter County and was born January 2, 1844. Left an orphan in early
childhood, she received care from a maternal aunt...It is but 14 months
since her husband, J. B. UNDERWOOD led her to the bridal altar...Joined
Presbyterian Church at Marion of which her husband was a member on
March 2, 1867...
Departed this life, A. A. BEALL. Resolutions on his death by Gaston
Lodge No. 85.

March 7, 1868
Married on the 25th ult by WM. M. FARRAR at the residence of the
bride's father, Mr. JOHN D. FAULKNER (9 A, son of JABEL) of Sumter County
to Miss MOLLIE L. FARRAR of Lauderdale, Miss.
Married on the 25th ult. by WM. M. FARRAR at the residence of the
bride's father, Mr. JOHN D. FAULKNER of Sumter County to Miss MOLLIE L.
FARRAR of Lauderdale, Mississippi.

Died in Gainesville, Alabama January 19, 1868, Mrs. EMMA, wife of
A. M. ARMSTRONG, formerly Miss WRIGHT of Greene County, Alabama and a native of Livingston, Sumter County, Alabama where she was born November 21,
1836. Left without a mother at a tender age, she afterwards referred
with infinite kindness of an aunt, Mrs. DOWOH, who embraced her at once
by adoption...Her precious children, a little girl and a boy are too young
to appreciate the goodness they have lost, while the husband alone is to
bear the bitterness of his grief. A Methodist...W.H.A.

    ELLITT & ALLISON)
      versus   )   Attachment
    JOHN A. JOHNSTON)
    JOHN A. JOHNSTON is a resident of Lauderdale, Miss.
    S. S. ESKRIDGE, deceased. S. H. SPROTT, administrator.
    REBECCA GULLEY, deceased. EZEKIEL S. GULLEY, administrator.
    LEWIS M. SCOTT (32 NC), deceased. J. A. MOORING, administrator.
    NOTICE TO M. A. HADDEN, wife of LEWIS HADDEN, Opelousas, La. You
are hereby notified that L. P. HARPER has this day propounded for Probate
in this office a paper purporting to be the will of SOPHIA HARPER, deceased.

March 14, 1868
    E. A. ESKRIDGE, deceased. S. H. SPROTT, administrator.

March 21, 1868
    Married at the residence of WM. J. CANTWELL, Esq. February 24, 1868
by REV. FATHER KEILTY, AUGUSTIN J. BEAKEY to Miss CADDIE F. CLINTON, all
of St. Louis, Mo.
    W(ILLIAM) H. DANDRIDGE (48 V), deceased. F. P. SNEDECOR, administra-
tor, filed a report that the estate is insolvent. J. A. ABRAHAMS, Judge
of Probate Court.

March 28, 1868
    M. C. KINNARD advertises a mare for sale.
    W. H. BROWN, licensed auctioneer.
    A. M. CROOM, administratrix of Bryan Croom, deceased, petitions to
sell land.
    ROBERT CRAWFORD--attorney-at-law.
    J(AMES) C. USTICK--watchmaker and jeweller.
    C. S. McCONNICO--attorney-at-law.
    THOMAS B. WETMORE and R. CHAPMAN, JR., law partners.
    J. G. HARRIS--attorney-at-law.
    W. COLEMAN and W. G. LITTLE--attorneys-at-law.

April 4, 1868
    Drowned March 16, NICHOLAS COBBS, youngest child of WILLIAM and
ELLENORE G. WADDILL of Selma, aged 16 years 6 months and 13 days...
    JERE H. BROWN, deceased. J. A. MOORING, General Administrator for
the County.

April 11, 1868
    S. C. COLEMAN and A. LARKIN, administrators of R. D. SHACKELFORD,
deceased filed accounts.
    J. G. HARRIS, administrator of LEWIS HOUSTON, deceased petitions for
an order allowing him to compromise a note due said estate made by JOHN
J. HOUSTON, BERNETTY HOUSTON (PERNETTA in Census), JESSE C. HOUSTON and
W. V. WARE.
    E. G. SPEIGHT, deceased. W. G. LITTLE, Jr., administrator with will
annexed.
    GEORGE W. GREEN, administrator of ABA GREEN (43 NC), deceased.
(Ancestor of AUBREY D. GREEN, 1978.)

April 25, 1868
    Died in Brewersville, Sumter County, Alabama on March 6, 1868, Mrs.
LODNSKY J. WOODWARD aged 35, daughter of WM. REID and was born in Perry
County, Alabama. Subsequently she moved to Demopolis, where in 1851 she
married Mr. JOHN H. WOODWARD. Mrs. WOODWARD left a husband and seven
children.

```
     LAVENIA S. HIGH)
        versus    )          Bill for Divorce
     CALVIN M. HIGH )
```
     The defendant, CALVIN M. HIGH is over 21 and resides in Kemper County,
Miss. (From Raleigh Register, August 26, 1834, CALVIN M. HIGH of Alabama
married LAVINA SARAH JETER of Raleigh August 21 in Raleigh.)
     GEORGE SOMERS (SUMMERS in Census) (54 Germ.), deceased. WILLIAM
SMYLEY, administrator.
     THOMAS DANIEL (45 NC), deceased. JOHN DANIEL, administrator.
     JAMES MOORE, deceased. J. A. MOORING, administrator.
     H. F. ARRINGTON, deceased. R. H. ARRINGTON, administrator.
     DR. B. B. SEALE---Dentist.

May 2, 1868
     M. E. BROCKWAY, administratrix of A. E. BROCKWAY, deceased, filed
accounts and vouchers for the final settlement of A. E. BROCKWAY's
guardianship of ROBERT, BERNICE and S. P. McSWEEN.
     JACOB DRISKELL (62 Del), deceased. S. H. SPROTT, administrator.

May 9, 1868
     H(ENRY) G. JOHNSON, (27 at sea), deceased. J. A. MOORING, adminis-
trator.
     R. F. STEWART, deceased. J. A. MOORING, administrator.
     Married on the 30th ult at the residence of the bride's father by
REV. A. R. SCARBOROUGH, Mr. ROBERT GREENLEE to Miss LIZZIE C. JOHNSON.

May 16, 1868
     Tribute of respect to the memory of STEPHEN W. MURLEY (37 SC) of
Livingston Lodge no. 41.
```
               SAMUEL H. SPROTT )
               J. G. HARRIS     )     Committee
               C. S. McCONNICO  )
                                   J. L. SCRUGGS, Secretary
```
     ELIZABETH LITTLE, deceased. R. E. MOFFITT, administrator.
     SOPHIA HARPER, deceased. R. S. HARPER, administrator.
     R(OBT.) S. LAVENDER, deceased. ELNATHAN TARTT, administrator of
MARGARET TARTT, deceased has filed a petition in which he alleges he was
a creditor of the estate of R. S. LAVENDER and that H(UGH) E. LAVENDER,
administrator of R. S. LAVENDER deceased has removed from this state without having made a settlement.
     GREEN B. MOBLEY, administrator of H. F. EATON, deceased.
     WM. McPHERSON, executor of the will of D. M. TAYLOR, deceased.
     Estate of R. D. SHACKELFORD, deceased. TO: WILLIAM H. WARREN,
HENRY M. WARREN, DAVID O. WARREN, RICHARD D. S. WARREN and ALICE WARREN,
who reside in Leon County, Texas; SUSAN W. WOODING (formerly SUSAN W.
WARREN), now wife of N. H. WOODING, who resides in the State of Virginia.
You will take notice that S. C. COLEMAN and ABRAM LARKIN, administrators
of RICHARD D. SHACKELFORD, deceased have this day filed in court their
petition for citations to issue to heirs of said decedent requiring them
to make a report of advancements made to them during his lifetime and
alleging among other things that ELIZA WARREN, your ancestor, who was a
daughter of said decedent, received from him in her life time property to
the value of $30,000. (ELIZA WARREN married in Perry Co., Ala. 29 March
1832, DAVID O. WARREN, brother of ELIZA WARREN of Madison Co., Ala., Vol.
198.)

May 23, 1868
     (Letter from RAYMOND J. ROWELL, Sr., 1640 Sterner Ave., S. W.
Birmingham, Alabama, January 7, 1962. "I write stories for publication
in Confederate Postal System, Postmasters, etc. I am writing a story on
Livingston 5¢ Postmaster Provisional, which Mr. STEPHEN W. MURLEY had
printed in 1861. He was Postmaster of Livingston during the Civil War.
I want to trace his descendants; hoping they have in their possession that
would show who printed this stamp and when.")
     STEPHEN WELLINGTON MURLEY was born in Charleston, South Carolina in
1813 and removed to Selma, Alabama in 1837. From Selma he removed to
Livingston, Sumter County, Alabama in 1841, where he resided until his
death, which occurred May 7, 1868 after a protracted illness. He was
married August 28th, 1838 in Fayetteville, North Carolina to Miss ANN
BEEBE, who died April 24, 1852 leaving her husband and four children,
three daughters and one son. The son was just approaching manhood when

the war called him to the field of battle. He was killed while defending
his native South at Atlanta in August, 1864. His sisters remain to mourn
the loss of brother and father...Mr. MURLEY was married a second time to
Miss H. D. GILDERSLEEVE February 14, 1854, she of Marengo County, Alabama,
who with four daughters and two sons survive him...Soon after his first
marriage, he connected himself with the Protestant Episcopal Church...W.
        WILEY DUNNING, deceased. J. A. GIBBS, administrator.
        W. P. HILMAN (33 V), deceased. J. A. GIBBS, administrator.

May 30, 1868
        Died on the 24th inst. at the residence of R. M. BRASFIELD in this
county, Mrs. E(LIZ.) L. CHILES (62 NC) aged 81 years.

June 6, 1868
        M(ADISON) B. TAYLOR (38 G), deceased. WM. McPHERSON, executor of
the will of D. M. TAYLOR, deceased, filed accounts for the final settlement of D. M. TAYLOR's administration on the estate of M. B. TAYLOR, deceased.

June 13, 1868
        ELIZA C. DURFEY, deceased. R. CHAPMAN, Jr., administrator.
        ROBERT ARRINGTON, deceased. R. CHAPMAN, Jr., administrator.

June 20, 1868
        Died at the residence of her son-in-law, DR. JOHN H. JOHNSON in
Navaro County, Texas, Mrs. NANCEY MITCHELL (37 SC), widow of BENJ. J.
MITCHELL (41 SC), deceased in her 56th year. She was born December 2d,
1812 and died May 1st, 1868. Native of Newbery District, South Carolina.
In early childhood, her parents moved to what was then Greene County,
Alabama, now Hale County. While young, she connected herself with Mount
Zion Presbyterian Church then under the care of REV. ISAAC HADDEN. In
1832, she married Mr. BENJ. J(AMES) MITCHELL with whom she lived and
raised a large family of children; her companion was taken away April 1st,
1859 (Mrs. JENKINS book has his tombstone, died April 1857.) For a
number of years before her death, she was afflicted with a lingering and
painful disease from which she never expected to recover...

June 27, 1868
        Died in Greensboro on the 13th of inflammation of the bowels, MACCIE
WARD, infant daughter of Mr. G. G. and Mrs. L. H. WESTCOTT aged 10 months
and 3 days.
        J. C. BENNETT, deceased. WILLIAM H. BENNETT, administrator.
        A. J. STUART, deceased. J. A. MOORING, administrator.

July 4, 1868
        A. E. BROCKWAY, deceased. Former guardian of MARY McSWEEN.

July 10, 1868
        Married on the 2nd by REV. S. M. THAMES, Mr. CASWELL EADS of York
Station to Miss MARY WILDER of Sumter County.
        At the residence of the bride (date not given) by REV. A. R. SCAR-
BOROUGH, CAPT. J. V. TUTT to Mrs. HARRIET BARTEE.
        JOHN C. MILLER, deceased. J. G. HARRIS, administrator.

July 17, 1868
        Died at Bladon, Alabama June 20, 1868, ROBT. P. WILEY, native of
Montgomery County, North Carolina, born May 9, 1840. Aged 28 years 1
month 11 days...He enlisted as private in "Sumter Co. Guards" 5th Alabama
Regiment...Wounded at Chancellorsville May, 1863...He returned from the
army in extremely bad health. He married Miss MANNA HORN near Gaston
February, 1866. Visited Bladon for his health...

August 14, 1868
        Livingston Lodge no. 41 prints Tribute of respect to memory of C. S.
McCONNICO, who has been suddenly stricken down by death in the strength
of his manhood while on a visit to Missouri with his family.
                G. W. BROWN   )
                J. L. SCRUGGS)   Committee
                S. E. SPROTT)

Died at Gaston August 4, 1868 little NETTIE CANNADY, born February 5, 1867; aged 1 year 5 months and 29 days.
Estate of JAMES C. BENNETT, deceased. TO: CHARLES W. BENNETT, ELIZA A. McCARKILL and her husband, C. C. McCARKILL, NARCISSA B. TILLMAN, OLIVER P. BENNETT, ADILLA RAMSEY and her husband H. RAMSEY and the children of HELLEN M. LILES, deceased, whose names are not shown.

August 28, 1868
Death of ALMA A. FEW, daughter of AUGUSTUS and Mrs. VIRGINIA FEW, who after a brief illness departed this life August 16, 1868 aged 11 years, 9 months and 7 days...
WILLIS A. WILSON, deceased. EDWARD McCALL, administrator.

September 4, 1868
HENRY McELROY (45 G), deceased. J. A. MOORING, administrator.

September 11, 1868
LEMUEL T. ORMAND, executor of the will of THOMAS ORMAND (42 NC), deceased.
Died near Sumterville, Alabama at the residence of J. M. HORDS of congestion, little CORNIE, eldest daughter of J. C. and S. J. ELLIOTT aged 4 years 8 months and 24 days...

October 2, 1868
THOMAS J. McCORMICK, deceased. SAMUEL H. SPROTT, administrator.

October 9, 1868
Married on the 5th by REV. C. H. BROWN, Mr. JOHN W. THETFORD to Miss MARINDA G. RHYNE all of this county.
Died at the residence of her parents in Sumter County on September 17, 1868, GERTRUDE TOMPKINS aged 14 years.
CHARLES HOLDER (62 NC), deceased. WILLIS CURL, executor.
WILLIAM A. LUMMAS, deceased. S. H. SPROTT, administrator.
WILLIAM H. JEMISON, deceased. W. A. JEMISON, administrator.

October 16, 1868
Married on the 12th by REV. J. W. PHILLIPS, Mr. WM. KIRKLAND to Miss MARTHA H. PUGH, all of this county.
Estate of WILLIAM A. LUMMAS, deceased: S. H. SPROTT filed a petition Praying the court for an order assigning to REBECCA LUMMAS, widow of WILLIAM A. LUMMAS, deceased, her dower.

October 23, 1868
CHESLEY HOLDER, deceased. WILLIS CURL (born March 10, 1820, died February 25, 1901, wife PENELOPE C. (1829-97) buried in cemetery at York), administrator.
WILLIAM R. McCAIN (18 A), deceased. A(DAM) S. McCAIN (14 A, daughter of ELIZ.), administrator.

October 30, 1868
Died on the 2nd of September, 1868 at her home in this county, Mrs. MARY HARVY MAY (26 G), wife of REV. JOHN P. MAY (29 A), and daughter of the late WILLIAM H(ARVEY) (59 G) and CAROLINE TALBOT aged 44 years 3 months and 14 days, native of Jones County, Georgia but removed at an early age with her parents to this state. At the age of 17, she professed religion, joining the Missionary Baptist Church. She married July 9, 1843, her husband becoming a member of the Primitive Baptist Church...She talked to her husband and children at the last...(MARY was born May 18, 1824, daughter of WM. HARVEY TALBOT and first wife CAROLINE (TALBOT). See marginal note in Vol. 94. WILLIAM H(ARVEY) was born Washington County, Ga., Sept. 5, 1790, died Sumter County, Ala. Jan. 3, 1863.)

November 6, 1868
Died on September 18th near Gaston, Mr. ELLIS LINDSEY aged 62. (See Choctaw Co., Ala. 1850 Census @ 45 G m. 1831 in G. Co.)

November 27, 1868
Died on November 13th in Livingston, Alabama, Mrs. M(AHALAH) A(NN) H(ELEN) HARRIS (30 NC), consort of J(OHN) W. HARRIS (34 NC) aged 48 years 8 months and 7 days. (m. in Greene Co. Nov. 1, 1838. she was daughter of JAS. FERRELL.)

December 4, 1868
	Mr. TILMAN HICKS (52 NC Greene Co. Census), an old and esteemed
citizen of Greene County died on the 24th inst. (Note: See Alabama
Records Vol. XX, p. 27 and Vol. XXXIV, p. 46. Son of ASA, see deeds.)

December 18, 1868
	JAMES DYE (66 SC), Sen. died lately in Talladega aged 86 years hav-
ing been married 53 years to his wife, who survives him.
	HON. A. B. FANNIN for many years a prominent Georgian died of apo-
plexy in Montgomery on the 10th.
	HON. LEWIS L. CATO, a well-known lawyer of this state died at
Eufaula on the 4th.

December 25, 1868
	Married in this place at residence of the bride's mother on 23rd by
REV. W. B. BINGHAM, SAM'L. H. SPROTT, Esq. and Miss NONIE A. BROCKWAY.
	Died, Mrs. L. C. BELL, consort of JOHN W. BELL and daughter of CAPT.
JOHN and ANNIE TERRELL. Born in Albemarle Dist. S.C. (Albemarle Co. N.C.
or Abbeville Dist., S.C.?) Jan. 29, 1836. Soon after her marriage she
removed to Sumter County, Alabama thence to Lauderdale County, Miss.,
where she died November 20, 1868. She had long been a prey to disease...
	ALLEN ELSTON (68 NJ), one of the first settlers of Talladega County
died a few days ago aged 86 years.

January 8, 1869
	Married on the 31st at the residence of the bride's mother at Jones'
Bluff by REV. A. R. SCARBOROUGH, Mr. WM. WINSLETT to Miss MATT. SMITH all
of this county.
	REV. BASIL MANLY, for many years President of the University of
Alabama died a few days ago in Greenville, S. C.
	COL. JAMES DENFORD PORTER, formerly of Marengo County died in Brazil
on the 25th of November.
	Mr. JACK MASON of Lauderdale County was killed by accidental dis-
charge of gun
	On the night before Christmas, CAPT. ELIJAH STAMPS (67 NC) of
Talladega County died aged 86 years; and a few hours later on the same
day, his wife (ELIZ. 57 G) with whom he lived for over 60 years died also.

January 22, 1869
	Died in this place on the 9th, BETTIE GAINES, daughter of THOMAS and
LUCY L. COBBS aged 10...
	Mr. JOHN D. PHELAN has located in Moulton, Lawrence County.
	Mr. and Mrs. B. S. BIBB of Montgomery celebrated their 50th wedding
anniversary on the 19th.

February 5, 1869
	GEN. N(ATHAN) B(RYAN) WHITFIELD of Demopolis died some days ago.

February 12, 1869
	REV. MURRELL ASKEW, a Baptist preacher of Lauderdale County, while
under the influence of whisky or in a fit of insanity a few days ago
terribly abused his family and attempted to kill his wife.

February 19, 1869
	Married on the 15th at the residence of the bride's father near
Paynesville by REV. J(AMES) W. PHILLIPS, Mr. NEWTON PRESTWOOD (18 A, son
of AUSTIN) and Miss MARY ANN MOORE of this county.
	COL. JOSEPH J. COOK of Pickens County committed suicide by shooting
himself January 31st.
	MAJ. F. W. RAGLAND of Decatur was shot through a window and killed
on the night of the 9th while sitting with his family.
	Mr. H. V. COUCH, son of REV. A. B. COUCH of Mobile killed a man
named HENRY JACOBS in that city.
	JAMES ALLEN PEARSON, a resident of Mississippi aged 106 visited his
grandson in Calhoun County, Alabama last week. He was accompanied by a
daughter, the youngest of 16 children and now 50 years old.

February 26, 1869
	Married Feb. 18th at the residence of the bride's father by REV. JOHN
A. ALLEN, Mr. M. B. McDONALD to Miss M. A. HALE, all of Sumter County.

JUDGE A(LEX.) B(ARON) CLITHERALL (29 SC), a well-known citizen of this state died at his residence near Montgomery on the 17th.

The Meridian Mercury states that DR. N. B. KENNEDY of that place and formerly of this county has removed to New Orleans.

WILLIAM P. PHIFER (34 SC), an old and respectable citizen of Tuscaloosa was shot down in his own yard Monday night of last week. He died the next day. Murderer unknown.

March 5, 1869

Married February 23 by REV. A. R. SCARBOROUGH, Mr. J. F. WIATT and Miss LEW E. COLE, all of this county.

COL. HARRY MAURY, a well-known citizen of Mobile and former commander of the 15th Confederate Cavalry died last week.

JAMES HILL shot and killed his nephew of the same name in Bibb County on the 17th. Dispute about land.

Mr. P(HILLUP) J. SIMPSON (8 A, son of JOHN P.) of Washington County living near Choctaw line was killed last month by J. H. JORDAN. SIMPSON leaves a wife and three children.

March 12, 1869

Died on the morning of the 9th at the residence of WM. KIRKLAND near this place, BERNARD WINFREE (37 V) aged 56 years, native of Virginia and a printer, having learned the art in Richmond under FATHER RITCHIE. He had been a resident of this place about 18 years and of Alabama nearly 30 years.

Mrs. ANNA LUSK died in Madison County last week at the age of 107 years.

CAPT. JESSE J. COX, an old Alabama river steamboatman died in Mobile last week.

JOHN T. FOSTER, Probate Judge of Choctaw County.

HIRAM PIERCE has been appointed Sheriff of Butler County and IRA SCOTT Tax Collector, both old citizens and worthy men.

Mr. B(ECKMAN) D. PALMER (31 NC, Greene Co. Census) of Eutaw died on the 3rd from injuries received on the 27th. Two intoxicated young men threw a brickbat, fracturing PALMER's skull. Leaves a wife and 6 children.

March 19, 1869

Married on the evening of March 15th at the residence of the bride's father by REV. A. R. SCARBOROUGH, DR. P. D. COULSON of Texas to Miss ETHELDRA A. JOHNSTON of this county.

PAYTON BAUGHN, Probate Judge of Winston County was killed by a man named GARRISON week before last.

March 26, 1869

Died on the 8th of March at his late residence near Belmont, Sumter County, THOS. L(UDWELL) BEVILL (38 A, son of WOODLIFF BEVILL, ancestor of Mrs. W. B. SMITH, Nash, Tenn.), late Sheriff aged about 54 years. Eutaw Whig and Meridian Mercury copy.

April 2, 1869 - Friday

THOS. M. JOHNSTON (48 NC), an old and highly respected citizen of Greensboro died Thursday of last week.

JOHN A. DOUGLAS, who killed JOHN W. WEAVER in 1865 was tried at late session of Circuit Court for Madison County at Huntsville and acquitted.

Dwelling of Mrs. NANCY WEATHERFORD at Red Hill, Wilcox County was burned March 15th.

April 9, 1869

Died near Sumterville on the 5th, Mrs. MARTHA O., wife of ISAAC R. WILSON.

Town of Stevenson (Jackson County) has been incorporated. GEORGE W. RICE, Mayor.

REV. J. D. EASTER, former Rector of Christ Church, Tuscaloosa, has accepted a call to Rectorship of Trinity Church, St. Louis, Mo.

Mr. GEO. H. CRAIG has been appointed Sheriff of Dallas County to fill a vacancy.

April 16, 1869

Married March 31, 1869 in Lowndesboro by REV. E(THELBERT) S(PENCER) SMITH, COL. W. BREWER and Miss MARY, daughter of the late GEN. D. W. BAINE, both of Lowndes.

Died in Gainesville on Thursday morning April 8th, 1869, Mr. JAMES B. TARTT (49 NC), an old citizen of Sumter County. Mr. TARTT was born in Edgecomb County, North Carolina on the 12th day of November, 1800 and was the W, Master of the 1st Masonic Lodge established in this county.

WILLIAM B. JONES has been elected Mayor of Demopolis.

Tuscaloosa Monitor says there are now three students at the state university.

COL. JOHN G. COLTART (25 A, son of SAMUEL) was buried at Huntsville on the 7th. He died in Tuscaloosa.

Dwelling of Mrs. ANN E. SANDERS at Tuscaloosa was destroyed by fire a few days ago.

ROBERT W. MAYRANT has been acquitted of the charge of murdering WM. M. MOORE of Mobile.

JOHN HUTCHISON of Montgomery and a conductor on the Florida Railroad fell from cars a few days ago and was killed by train running over him.

An old man named REUBEN ANDERSON living near Spanish Fort, Baldwin County, was murdered by 4 negroes on the 8th.

Former residence of JOHN C. PHARES, deceased, in Greensboro was destroyed by fire on the morning of the 4th. Building was occupied by DR. JOHN H. PARRISH and was considered one of the best in Greensboro.

April 23, 1869

TROTT & STONE--Real Estate Agents.

April 30, 1869

THOS. J. CROW (50 K), one of the oldest citizens of Florence died in that place on the 20th. He settled in Florence in 1821.

Miss CHARLOTTE THOMPSON, the accomplished actress, a resident of Lowndes County, will depart for California to fill a professional engagement.

May 7, 1869

The Huntsville Advocate says that several cases of small pox have occurred in Morgan County nearly opposite Whitesburg and that two old and respectable citizens, STEPHEN DUKE (42 K, married SARAH DITTO) and WM. DITTO (44 K) have died from it.

May 14, 1869

JOHN P. SOUTHWORTH, Esq. of Selma has received appointment of U. S. District Attorney for Alabama.

WM. FOWLER, an ex-Conductor on the M. & C.R.R. while crazy from liquor a few days ago, jumped from the train near Tuscumbia and was killed.

May 21, 1869

Married on the 13th at the residence of the bride's father by REV. A. R. SCARBOROUGH, Mr. JOHN R. LARKIN to Miss SUSAN A. LEE, daughter of COL. JAMES M. LEE (30 A) all of this county.

THOS. W. ROBERTS, Esq. was admitted a member of the Bar of Greene County last week.

Mrs. LEVISA DANIEL was killed at Evergreen on the 7th being thrown from a buggy.

Mr. FRANCIS E. HARRIS of Madison County was killed a few days ago by a limb falling from a tree and fracturing his skull.

The Mobile Tribune announces the death in that city of DR. S. MORDICAI, the oldest physician in the place, having commenced practice there in 1823.

ALLEN HARPER, a night policeman of Huntsville has mysteriously disappeared. His family are in ignorance as to the cause of leaving home.

It is believed REV. JAMES M. McKEE (1850 Census Lowndes Co. 36 born S.C., 1860 Census Pike Co., 45 SC), a Presbyterian minister of Montgomery was drowned during a recent freshet. His horse and buggy were found a short distance below the road in a swamp.

May 28, 1869
    Died in this county on the 21st, Mrs. MARY ARRINGTON (38 T), consort
of the late COL. WM. ARRINGTON (48 SC) of this county, member of the
Baptist Church. Leaves 3 sons.
    ANDREW J. MITCHEM was killed by PETER SIMMONS in Madison County last
Thursday week. Difficulty grew out of settling some business affairs.
    On Monday night of last week, JAMES E. HARRIS shot and killed his
brother-in-law, R. R. BAILEY in Montgomery. Self defense.

June 4, 1869
    JOHN HURTEL, one of the old French citizens of Mobile died a few days
ago.
    JUDGE C(URTIS) N(ASH) WILCOX (34 Miss), formerly of Choctaw has re-
moved to Meridian, Miss.
    Residence of A. T. RHODES at Talladega was consumed by fire on
Monday of last week.
    C. W. HATCH appointed Postmaster at Greensboro vice Mr. W. S. KELLY,
removed.
    A. R. DAVIS, Probate Judge of Greene County.
    Residence of DR. J. BREITLING three miles south of Butler, Choctaw
County destroyed by fire last week.
    DEMPSEY WILLIAMSON of Northport, Tuscaloosa County, while laboring
under mental aberration hung himself on Tuesday of last week.

June 11, 1869
    Married on the 1st at Meridian, Mississippi, Mr. THEODORE STURGES of
that place to Miss ALLIE McINNIS of this county.
    Married on May 31 at the residence of the bride's father near
Ramsey's Station, Mr. LEVI G. HURLBUTT of Meridian, Miss. to Miss SALLIE
V. WILLINGHAM (1 A, daughter of PHILLIP) of this county.
    Tribute of Respect - Western Lodge No. 222, Cuba Station, Alabama,
June 5, 1869. "Brother ALFRED OWEN departed this life on 4th of May;
native of South Carolina and removed to Alabama and became a resident of
Sumter County some years ago, where he pursued planting interest with
success...copy be sent to bereaved widow." THOMAS JARMAN, JR., chairman
of committee.
    Also tribute of respect to memory of HENRY ALTMAN, who departed this
life on Tuesday May 18; native of South Carolina and at an early age removed to Alabama. Copy be sent to Bro. J. W. ALTMAN. J. J. McELROY,
Chairman of committee.
    F. C. BROMBERG has been appointed Postmaster at Mobile vice B. R.
PIERCE removed.

June 18, 1869
    Mr. WM. KNOX, one of the oldest citizens of Montgomery and formerly
President of Central Bank of Alabama died in that city a few days ago.
    MICHAEL WHELAN, an old citizen of Selma committed suicide last week
by jumping in the river and drowning.

June 25, 1869
    Married at Gaston, Alabama on the 22nd by REV. S. M. THAMES, COL.
W. B. GERE of Chicago, Ill. to Mrs. AUGUSTA M. CROOM of Gaston.
    We learn that ARTHUR A. SMITH, brother of Judge LUTHER R. SMITH has
been appointed Superintendant of Education for Greene County.

July 2, 1869
    Married on the 23rd by REV. G. W. BROWN, G. W. ROGERS to Miss MARY S.
HOOKS all of this county.
    The West Alabamian announces the death of DANIEL J. HARGROVE (58 NC),
an old and highly esteemed citizen of Pickens County.
    Mrs. NANCY STROUD of Lee County died a few days ago aged 84. Had
been married 66 years and her husband is still living.
    COLUMBUS LEE (39 G) of Perry County died at his residence near
Uniontown on the 23rd. For many years an active politician and had extensive acquaintance in East Alabama.

July 9, 1869
    Married at the residence of the bride's father June 29th by REV. W.
H. PASLEY, Mr. J. F. ORMAND to Miss ELLA, youngest daughter of E. N.
BRYANT, Esq. all of this county.

List of registered voters is printed in this issue.

July 16, 1869
Married at Enterprise, Mississippi on the 7th by REV. S. U. SMITH, Mr. HENRY C. GOWDEY of this county to Miss MANIE R. BIRD of the former place.

AUGUSTUS FLETCHER MIMS was born in Sumter County, Alabama November 12, 1840 and died July 4, 1869. For 15 years he has been languishing under wasting hand of disease...

JOHN D. SANDERS (50 SC), an old and valued citizen of Pickens Co. died on the 2nd, aged 70.

On the 5th, JOHN B. STEWART shot and killed SAMUEL FRANCIS at Decatur. Justifiable homicide.

WILEY W. CROOK, an old citizen has been appointed Deputy Collector of Internal Revenue for counties of Calhoun, Cherokee and Claiborne.

July 23, 1869
Died--MAJ. THOMAS C. PRINES, a former citizen of this place, who left in bad health some years ago, died and was buried in Mobile on Tuesday.

Residence of REV. J. A. FONVILLE, Lowndes County burned.

July 30, 1869
Died in Sumter County on 28 July 1869, ROSA KNOX, infant daughter of JOHN M. and MARY McDANIEL.

Died in this county on the 20th, PRESTON N., son of DRURY McMILLAN in his 18th year.

August 6, 1869
Married at the residence of Mr. L. F. WHITEHEAD near Livingston on the 5th by REV. A. G. GROVES, Mr. J. A. MOORING to Mrs. T. A. HAINSWORTH, all of Sumter County.

The 50th wedding anniversary of CAPT. WM. L. (56 SC) and JANE R. McDOW (58 SC) (1812 Vol.) last Thursday the 29th celebrated with a dinner for all their children, grandchildren and neighbors. Fifty years ago, CAPT. McDOW rode on horseback 20 miles to marry his present wife. They were then poor. They soon removed to this state and settled in Greene County. From there they came to Sumter County. By dint of industry, energy and economy, CAPT. McDOW made a fortune.

Mrs. LOUISA KAELIN of Selma took poison.

W. H. WEBB, a son of MAJ. W. P. WEBB of Eutaw has been nominated for District Attorney by Democracy of Monterey Co. Cal.

COL. JOHN T. ABERNATHY, one of the oldest and most respected citizens of North Alabama died at his home near Leighton on the 27th.

August 13, 1869
Died at Oxford, Mississippi on the 26th, Mrs. ELIZABETH HINES (40 NC), aged 60. Baptist.

Mr. PHILLIP WOODSON, the founder and for 33 years conductor of Huntsville Democrat died in that city on the 4th aged 78.

CHARLES CULP, son of AMOS CULP of Huntsville died on Saturday of week before last of lockjaw.

Mr. JOHN BONHAM and Mr. JOSIAH PALMER, two old citizens of Montgomery died recently, their respective ages being 84 and 82. Both were natives of South Carolina.

A Mrs. PICKETT of Girard, Alabama was killed a few days ago by mistake of druggist who sent the wrong prescription.

August 27, 1869
AUGUSTUS BAYALL was drowned on the 15th.

Mr. JEFF BURGIN living near Elyton killed last week by accidental discharge of gun.

Mr. G. W. SKINNER of Washington County accidentally killed his sister-in-law, Miss MARGARET HILL a few days ago since. She was the niece of GEN. A. P. HILL of Virginia.

September 3, 1869
MAJ. JAMES T. DENT, one of the heroes of Lundy's Lane died in Tuscaloosa last week aged 80.

September 10, 1869
    Married on the 1st at the residence of Mr. I. W. HORN by REV. A. R.
SCARBOROUGH, Mr. JOHN W. BLACKNEY to Miss ROBERTE E. CAMPBELL, all of
this county.
    Departed this life near Warsaw, Sumter County, Alabama September 1,
1869, Mrs. LUCY P. LITTLE, consort of DR. W. G. LITTLE. Born October 19,
1837, married January 7, 1857...
    Tribute of respect to memory of Brother J. T. WOOD, who died 27th
inst.   Sumter Lodge No. 166. Gaston, Ala., Aug. 28, 1869.   M. E. TARVIN,
Secretary.

September 17, 1869
    Married on the 12th at the residence of the bride's father by REV.
VAUGHN, Mr. JOHN ALEXANDER TO Miss DELLY BROWN, all of this county.
    Married on the 12th by M. GRADY, Esq., Mr. J. C. DeVANE to Miss
ARTEMESIA HINTON, all of this county.
    SID. WOMACK, Circuit Clerk of Greene County died on Tuesday of last
week.

September 24, 1869
    Tribute of respect--To memory of J. T. WOOD who died on the 27th ult.
at his residence in this county.   Gaston Chapter no. 85 held Sept. 8,
                                     1869.
                                     R. L. SEALE   )
                                     M. E. TARVIN   )   Committee
                                     C. F. THREADGILL)
    DR. NOLAN killed a Mr. FEARS at Tuskegee Friday night by shooting
him.
    GOVERNOR SMITH offers a reward of $400 for the capture of WADE BYNUM,
colored, the murderer of a Mr. BOUNDS, who lived near Florence.
    A man named JACK CARPENTER was shot and instantly killed by BILL
EATON in Eutaw last week.
    An altercation occurred between JACOB PALMER and JOHN GRUBBS living
near Eufaula last week, which ended in the killing of PALMER.
    Two hand cars collided on railroad near Demopolis on the 15th re-
sulting in the death of a young man named ROBERT E. ALSTON from Marion
Station and wounding of two others.

October 1, 1869
    Married on the 18th at the Presbyterian Church in Payneville by REV.
E. ANDERSON, Mr. J. T. ORMAND and Miss ROXANA ELLIOTT, all of this county.
    ISAAC W. SANDERS of Madison County accidentally shot and killed him-
self while hunting last week.
    RUFUS J. REID (See Vol. XXXIV, p. 65) of Marion, late Solicitor for
Dallas Circuit has been indicted by Grand Jury of Dallas County for
bribery.
    Mr. JAMES LEAKE of Montgomery County was thrown from his buggy on
Sunday of last week and died from effects of the injury the next day.
    CAPT. E. G. FLEMING has been required to give a $2500 bond for
stabbing GEORGE W. FISHER (See Vol. XXI, p. 32) in front of the Methodist
Church in Huntsville a few days ago.

October 8, 1869
    Married on the 30th at the residence of the bride's father by REV.
A. R. SCARBOROUGH, Mr. J. L. MITCHELL of Texas to Miss BETTY A. HORD of
this county.
    At the same time and place by same, Mr. W. H. COLEMAN of Mississippi
and Mrs. JUDITH A. HEISLER of this county.
    On the evening of the 29th in St. James' (Episcopal) Church in
Livingston by REV. F. R. HANSON, Mr. OLIVER C. ULMAN and Miss SADIE
TANKERSLEY, all of Choctaw.
    Departed this life in Livingston on Tuesday morning the 28th,
MARGARET ANN (25 A), wife of DAVID H. TROTT (38 NC). The deceased was
the daughter of JOSEPH and JANE (64 NC) JEMISON and was born in Perry
County, Alabama June 24, 1824. Married near Livingston August 26, 1841.
Joined the Episcopal Church in 1856. Leaves a husband and children to
mourn her loss...

October 15, 1869
    Mrs. ANN PEAGLER aged 102 died in Butler County last week.

Gin house on plantation of WINFIELD S. BIRD 8 miles south of Eutaw burned.

CALVIN TINKER of DeKalb County, Alabama was killed by the cars on the 25th and DR. JACK seriously injured.

A. A. SMITH, Esq. of Eutaw was appointed Clerk of the Circuit Court of Greene County in place of SIDNEY WOMACK, deceased.

October 22, 1869

A train of cars ran over and killed a Mr. HENDRICKS near Tuscumbia a few days ago.

CHANCELLOR COCKE died very suddenly in Greenville on the afternoon of the 10th inst. (U of A 1863, COCKE, JOHN BINION, 1861, Montgomery, son of CHANCELLOR COCKE: b. Nov. 15, 1846.)

ANDERSON MOSS, an old and highly respectable citizen of Talledega County was recently sent to lunatic asylum at Tuscaloosa. (Son of E. MOSS, REV. SOL.)

Mr. JAMES H. DUVALL, one of the former proprietors of the Battle House has assumed its management since the death of CAPT. GODFREY (Mobile).

ISAAC COOK, mailing clerk in Selma Times office was killed a few days ago by accidental discharge of gun in hands of a friend.

CAPT. A. M. GODFREY, proprietor of the Battle House, Mobile, committed suicide a few days ago.

Mr. JAMES M. SLEDGE and lady, Mrs. JOSEPH BORDEN, whose husband is now in that state and Mr. ALEXANDER MAULDIN, all of Hale County left Greensboro last Monday week for California.

GEN. DANIEL MORGAN BRADFORD of Huntsville died on the 13th aged 76. He was Capt. of "Carroll's Life Guard" at the battle of New Orleans and was appointed by PRESIDENT JACKSON Receiver of Land Office at Huntsville, a position which he held until removed by GRANT.

On last Friday night, Mr. JAMES CARPENTER, a useful and highly respectable citizen of this county was shot and killed by an unknown. From Eutaw Whig.

Married on the 19th at the residence of the bride's father by REV. A. R. SCARBOROUGH, Mr. J. M. SULLIVAN to Miss O. H. TERRELL, all of this county.

Died on the 18th in South Sumter after a short illness, MATTIE ALMA, daughter of W. A. and M. A. SILLIMAN aged 4 years 1 month and 2 days.

October 29, 1869

ANDREW HENRY SMITH, a young man living near Huntsville suicide on the 14th.

November 5, 1869

Married on the 2nd by REV. W. H. PASLEY, Mr. EWD. B. TARTT to Miss JOSEPHINE BULLOCK (14 A), all of this county.

Married on the 3rd by REV. J. K. RYAN, Mr. Z. M. HOIT to Miss M. E. SCARBOROUGH, all of this county.

Died on Saturday, October 30 near Belmont, LEONIDAS RUSHING aged about 42.

November 12, 1869

Died in Warsaw, October 18, 1869 at the residence of his step-father, BENJAMIN WHITE, Esq. after a brief but severe illness, THOMAS E. AMASON, son of the late GEORGE AMASON of Greene County, Alabama aged 20 years and 25 days...

WM. D. HUMPHREY, Democrat has been elected to the legislature from Madison County.

TRENTON FOSTER was killed near Tuscaloosa a few days ago by being thrown from a buggy.

CAPT. WILLIAM FORREST, brother of GEN. FORREST killed a Mr. JOHN S. SOUTH at Marion last Monday night.

An old and respectable citizen named WATKINS residing near Opelika was murdered and robbed by one of his hired negroes on the 28th.

November 26, 1869

JESSE COX, a citizen of Talladega County was killed by a negro on Monday of last week.

Miss JENNIE BOYD died in Eufaula on the 15th from overdose of chloroform to relieve toothache.

A plantation in Greene County known as the "Montague Place" and containing 800 acres was sold for $25.50 per acre.

A personal difficulty occurred in Eutaw Monday the 8th between JAMES SHEPPARD and SAMUEL B. BROWNE, which resulted in the shooting and severe wounding of the former by the latter.

December 3, 1869
Married at the residence of GREEN W. GRANT on the 25th by REV. A. R. SCARBOROUGH, JOHN W. BELL of Lauderdale County, Mississippi to Miss MARY E. MANLIE (1 A, daughter of NARCISSA E.) of this county.

Married on the 25th by LEWELIN LEWIS, Esq., Mr. JOHN A. HARBINSON to Miss MARTHA A. HAGGARD, all of this county.

Married on the 18th by REV. J. K. RYAN at the residence of the bride's mother, THOMAS J. LEE to Miss M. A. WOODALL.

JAMES A. OWEN, an old citizen of Choctaw County was struck down with paralysis last week.

Reward of $1,000 offered for the arrest of GILES C. EFURD, charged with killing CALVIN SMART near Louisville, Barbour County.

EX-GOVERNOR PATTON is about to become a citizen of Montgomery. His property in Florence, where he has resided for many years is offered for sale.

The widow of NEWELL E. THOMAS (who was murdered by the Attorney General of Alabama), late Editor of the Choctaw Herald is teaching school in Butler.

An estate of $500,000 for the relatives and heirs of JOHN C. CLARK, who removed in the year 1825 or thereabouts to Alabama or Mississippi and thence to Texas is advertised.

Mr. MEYER CRAMER, the oldest man we personally ever knew died in this place on Monday the 8th in his 102nd year. Native of Asselheim, Bavaria. Fought as a soldier under the 1st Napoleon all through his numerous campaigns, was in the disastrous retreat from Moscow and remained in the French army until the fall of the great Capt. and his final banishment to St. Helena. He then settled in Germany and emigrated thence to America in 1850. From Eutaw Whig.

December 10, 1869
Married in Greene County on the 2nd by REV. S. U. SMITH, Mr. W. L. GARRETT to Miss M. W. GLOVER.

In this place on the 8th by REV. G. W. BROWN, Mr. H. O. VOSS to Miss BETTIE MASON.

The wife of JUDGE S. F. RICE died in Montgomery on the 30th.

December 17, 1869
Married at the residence of the bride's mother on the 7th by REV. A. R. SCARBOROUGH, Mr. D. W. MITCHELL to Miss ANNIE P. LOWERY, all of this county.

At the residence of the bride's father on the 29th of November by REV. JAMES W. PHILLIPS, Mr. H. R. FOSS to Miss SARAH FRANCES JENKINS (5 A, daughter of JOS. W.), all of this county.

December 24, 1869
Mrs. DR. BYRNE of Mobile, a lady 63 years old is giving literary readings in Montgomery.

RICHARD MOORE, one of the eldest and best citizens of Calhoun County was killed a few days ago by being struck on the head by a stone thrown by one LUNEY THOMPSON.

Died in this county on the 19th, THOMAS AUGUSTUS (23 T), son of THOMAS A. SEALES (2 A) aged 22. Consumption...

At his residence in Sumter County on the 16th, THOS. JARMAN, SR. (14 NC) aged about 72. (See will in our Vol. 32.) Born in Onslow County, North Carolina and moved to Alabama about 35 years ago. Though uneducated, he possessed a strong and well-balanced mind...A kind father but kinder grandfather, he supported and tenderly cared for the largest family of orphaned grandchildren in the county...His wife survives him, stricken with age...

December 31, 1869
Married on 21st by REV. A. R. SCARBOROUGH, Mr. JOSEPH CATES and Mrs. SALLIE A. HUNTER, all of this county.

94.

Died in Mobile on the 4 November, 1869, Mrs. SARAH AUGUSTA FLETCHER,
wife of COL. RICHARD M. BECK in the 54th year of her age.

January 7, 1870
        Married on the 23rd by LEWELEN LEWIS, Esq., Mr. T. F. FORD and ANN E.
JOHNSON, both of Greene County.
        At the residence of the bride's father on the 20th by REV. A. R.
SCARBOROUGH, Mr. ROBERT A. ESTES of Marengo County to Miss SUSAN M. MARTIN
of Sumter County.
        DR. A. B. COLLINS charged with murder of DR. HAUGHEY broke jail at
Moulton on the 17th.

January 14, 1870
        A daughter of Mrs. SALTMARSH of Camden was burned to death last week.
        CAPT. JULIAN McKENZIE of Eufaula was drowned on the 4th. He was
Captain of Eufaula Light Artillery during the war.

January 21, 1870
        On the 10th, a Mr. PATTERSON killed JAMES SIMMONS in Somerville.
Both fond of whiskey.
        REV. J. M. SPALDING, (died Jan. 14, 1870, born Jan. 27, 1833) a
Baptist minister for several years past a resident of Huntsville died in
that place a few days ago.

January 28, 1870
        Married on the 25th at the residence of the bride's father by REV.
J. W. PHILLIPS, Mr. JOHNSON C. WILLIAMS and Miss BETTIE M., (4 A, N. in
Census) daughter of JOHN C. GILLESPIE (34 V).
        WILLIAM GILBERT (37 NC, son of WM., Sr.) was born in Jones County,
North Carolina July 23, 1813 and died in Sumter County, Ala. January 12,
1870. Was an honest, industrious and economical man and had accumulated
a handsome property...Left a wife and 5 little children...
        Departed this life January 8, 1870 near Intercourse, Sumter County,
Alabama, MARY ELEANOR LOWE (20 A), consort of C(REENE) B. LOWE (25 SC)
aged 40 years 9 months and 18 days. Dutiful wife, genial companion and
affectionate mother. In 1847, she professed religion and joined the church
at Ellis' Chapel in this county...Leaves her husband and 5 children, 4
girls and 1 boy.
        Mr. E. J. BELSER shot and killed W. H. HOGAN in Montgomery last week.
BELSER charges HOGAN with having seduced his daughter whom he had been engaged to marry. He subsequently married another lady.

February 11, 1870
        Married on the 3rd at the residence of the bride's father by REV.
W. H. PASLEY, Mr. ISAAC R. WILSON and Miss MARY WRENN.
        WADE R. THOMAS, Esq. formerly of this county has removed to Meridian
where he has purchased a residence.
        RYLAND RANDOLPH, Editor of the Tuscaloosa Monitor was married last
week to Miss KATIE C(LAY) WITHERS of Tuscaloosa.
        The Montgomery papers announce the death from pneumonia of Mr. E. J.
BELSER, who was under bond for killing JAMES H. HOGAN in that city some
3 weeks ago.

February 18, 1870
        Married on the 8th by REV. A. R. SCARBOROUGH at the residence of the
bride's father Mr. EDWARD CARROL (1 EDMOND, 1 son of JACOB P.) and Miss
ALICE M. COATES, all of this county.
        On the 10th by REV. W. H. PASLEY, Mr. GEORGE H. McCAIN (21 A) of
Mississippi to Mrs. MARGARET RICHARDSON of this county.
        On the 1st, a Mr. BULLARD shot and killed JOHN CHITWOOD in Jackson
County.

February 25, 1870
        Dwelling of Mrs. MALCOLM SMITH near Prattville destroyed by fire.
Loss $8,000.
        Deputy Sheriff ROGERS of Franklin County shot and killed HORACE
SUMMERHILL, JR. of Lauderdale County last week.

March 4, 1870
    Married on the 28th at the residence of the bride's father in Livings-
ton by REV. J. W. PHILLIPS, Mr. D. L. KIRKLAND and Miss IDA E. LOCKARD.
    Mr. JOHN H. GARY, an old citizen of Sumter and more recently of
Mobile has opened a business house in Meridian.
    An old lady named PATTERSON who lived near Cross Roads in Madison
County fell down a stairway of her house the other day and was killed
instantly. She was over 90 years of age.
    The Oxford Rising Star of the 26th says: "Mr. ROBERT PRESKNEL was
brutally murdered on Saturday last and his wife is in a serious condition."

March 18, 1870
    Married on the 10th at the residence of Mrs. ORR in Livingston by REV.
A. R. SCARBOROUGH, REV. JOHN P. MAY and Mrs. A. P. BROWN, all of this
county.
    C. C. CROWE of Perry County has been appointed Register of Land
Office, Wyoming Territory.
    There is a letter in the Selma Postoffice addressed to "DR. BLAKE,
formerly of North Carolina, who went on a bridal tour to New Orleans Xmas."
    REV. DR. W. M. CUNNINGHAM, an able and learned divine of the Presby-
terian Church and President of Oglethorpe College died of pneumonia at
La Grange on Thursday of last week.

March 25, 1870
    In Memoriam: At term of Commissioner's Court for Sumter County held
on 21 March 1870, the HON. J. A. ABRAHAMS presiding. Resolutions on death
of W(ILLIS) V. HARE, an honored man of this court...

April 1, 1870
    Married on the 29th inst. at the residence of DR. D. HENAGAN by REV.
A. R. SCARBOROUGH, Mr. M. C. GOWDEY of Sumter and Miss FANNIE MILES of
Bennettsville, S. C.
    Died at the residence of her father in this county on the 23rd of
February last, SARAH FRANCES (5 A), wife of H. F. FOSS and daughter of
JOSEPH W. (32 V) and JANE L. JANKINS (19 A); born in Greene County,
Alabama on March 8, 1846 and had almost completed her 24th year. Married
on 29 November 1869.
    Mrs. JUDGE A. J. WALKER died at her residence in Montgomery on the
20th.
    The remains of two sons of EX-GOVERNOR PATTON killed during the war
were re-interred in Huntsville last week.
    The State Journal records the death of HON. WM. RICE, member of the
Legislature from Talladega; and brother of HON. S. F. RICE, which sad
event occurred in Talladega Wednesday.
    Residence of GEN. C. A. POELNITZ near Linden, Marengo County was
destroyed by fire. Loss $50,000.

April 8, 1870
    Died on the 27th in St. Louis, ROBERT TAYLOR BRADSHAW (son of R.
BRADSHAW, Esq. of Gainesville, Ala.) in his 29th year.
    In Mobile on the 2nd, Miss P(ERNETIA) M. GARY (2/12 A), daughter of
JOHN H. and ELIZA GARY, formerly of Sumter.
    Several North Carolina families have settled on the NUCKOLL's place
east of Huntsville.

April 15, 1870
    Mrs. T. B. REYNOLDS, widow of the late publisher of Athens (Ala.) Post
who died recently, is now conducting the above journal as administratrix.

April 22, 1870
    DR. GEORGE B. SMITH of Randolph County was killed by lightning on
Wednesday of last week. Wife and little daughter knocked down by same
bolt.
    BRADFORD JONES of Bullock County disappeared from his home very sud-
denly about a month ago. Was known to have considerable sum of money with
him so foul play is suspected.

April 29, 1870
      Married on the 20th by REV. A. R. SCARBOROUGH at the residence of
the bride's father, THOMAS H. HAWKINS, Mr. JOHN M. SCARBOROUGH to Miss
MARY C. HAWKINS, all of this county.

May 6, 1870
      Mr. TAYLOR BRADSHAW, son of ROBERT BRADSHAW of Gainesville, Ala. was
born in Lexington, Virginia on 4 March 1841 and died in the city of St.
Louis 27 March 1870 aged 29 years and 23 days...
      Tribute of respect by Livingston Lodge #41 on death of L. B. HUMPHRIES.
"The lodge has lost a faithful member, his wife a true and devoted husband,
his family an affectionate brother."   SAMUEL H. SPROTT)
                                WILLIAM G. LITTLE) Committee
                                J. L. SCRUGGS   )
      ELIJAH HENDON "the beaver trapper" of the Coosa died in Calhoun
County recently in his 83rd year. (See 1812 pension. Married in Putnam
County, Ga. 1821. SUSAN E. PHILLIPS who applied for pension in 1878 while
a resident of Cleburne County, Alabama.)

May 13, 1870
      LYNN BOYD HUMPHRIES was born in Livingston, Madison County, Mississip-
pi December 25, 1842 and died at Gaston, Sumter County, Alabama April 24,
1870. His parents were from South Carolina. In 1845 his father, T. J.
HUMPHRIES moved from Madison to Handsboro, Miss. where he now resides. In
1861, L. B. HUMPHRIES joined the Confederate army and surrendered with his
little band of soldier-comrades from Sumter at the last post held by Confederate army east of the Mississippi River...In August, 1866, he married
Miss JULIA HINES, who survives him. For the past two years, her life has
been one of sorrow. She has mourned a mother and two infant children and
now her husband...

May 20, 1870
      Married on the 10th at the residence of ROBERT LAWLER by REV. J. F.
EVANS, Mr. FELIX G. McMILLAN and Miss DORA GILLESPIE, both of this county.
      On the 17th by same at the residence of Mr. A. D. FORTNER, Mr. THOMAS
H. HAWKINS and Miss SUSAN M. BURNOUGH, both of this county.
      Married on the 12th in Marengo County by REV. W. H. PASLEY, Mr. M. W.
DAVIS of Sumter and Miss LUCY SIMMONS of Marengo.
      Mr. WM. ROWE of Greenville fell dead on the sidewalk a few days ago.
      The Huntsville Advocate says that on the night of the 3rd in Blounts-
ville, Mr. WM. HIGGINS, a jeweler was called to his door and shot dead by
some unknown persons.

May 27, 1870
      Married on the 19th at the residence of Mrs. S. ESKRIDGE by REV. C. B.
DuBOSE, DR. L. E. FORD of Mississippi and Miss E. E. ESKRIDGE.

June 17, 1870
      Married near Mayesville, Sumter District, South Carolina on the 12th
by REV. J. L. WILSON, D.D. Mr. JOHN S. MOORE of Sumter County, Alabama
and Miss SALLIE M. COIT of Cheraw, S. C.
      Died near Lauderdale, Miss. May 20, 1870, Mrs. E. K. EASON in her
33rd year. In her 12th or 13th year she joined the Presbyterian Church.

June 24, 1870
      ALBERT LANCASTER (40 V), native of Orange County, Virginia was born
May 10, 1810 and died at his residence of pneumonia on 19 May 1870.
Joined Baptist Church at Jones' Creek in this county in August, 1850...

July 8, 1870
      Married on 30 June at the residence of REV. J. P. MAY by REV. A. R.
SCARBOROUGH, Mr. T. W. MAY and Miss ANNIE A. BROWN all of this county.
      Died on 22 June in Livingston, JULIA, wife of Mr. GEORGE WILSON in
her 23rd year.
      Tribute of respect on death of Bro. A(DAM) S. McCAIN (14 A, son of
ELIZ.) by Hermon Lodge no. 106, Sumterville (dated June 11, 1870). Tender
sympathy to the widow and children.

July 22, 1870
Married at West Newton, Mass. on the 19th, Mr. J. CHEEVER FULLER and
Miss LAURA EAVES. Mr. FULLER will be remembered here as having formerly
had charge of the Railroad Depot at this place.
THOMAS J. BALLARD of Pickens County was killed on the 5th.

July 29, 1870
Married on the 27th at the residence of the bride's parents by REV.
C. B. DuBOSE, Mr. R. CHAPMAN, JR., Esq. and Miss KATE SCRUGGS, all of
this place.

August 5, 1870
HON. GEORGE D. SHORTRIDGE died at his residence at Montevallo on the
27th.
Died at his residence in Choctaw County on the 23rd, ALLEN C. WALTERS,
former Capt. of Co. "E", 43rd Regiment Alabama Volunteers of C.S.A.

August 23, 1870
Married on the 18th at the residence of Mr. R. A. PAYNE by REV. C. B.
DuBOSE, Mr. R. C. KNIGHT and Mrs. ELIZABETH KELLY, all of this county.
Married on the 16th at Cuba, Sumter County by REV. C. B. DuBOSE, Mr.
JOHN KENNARD and Miss SALLIE J. BURTON, all of this county.
Died in Livingston on the 24th, Mrs. AMANDA KENNARD, wife of JAMES P.
KENNARD in his 59th year.
In Memoriam: This Lodge is called together to mourn the loss of our
aged and beloved brother, ELBERT AMASON, originally of Joseph Warren Lodge
no. 92, Stantonbury, Edgecomb County, North Carolina and at the time of
his death a worthy member of Hermon Lodge no. 106...Kind husband, affectionate father...   W. R. HIGH)
                                      J. D. THOMAS)   Committee
                                      J. R. RAMSEY)

September 2, 1870
Married on the 27th in Livingston by REV. A. R. SCARBOROUGH, Mr. C.
T. ROAN and Mrs. SUE A. HAMILL (she was widow of NEWTON J. HAMILL, p. 20),
all of this county.
Died on the 16th in Perry County, Alabama, Mr. HENRY JEMISON in his
62nd year (JAMESON in Census Perry County, 41 G, son of JOSEPH and JANE
JEMISON).

September 3, 1870
Died on September 13, 1870, Mrs. CHRISTINE, wife of Mr. J. W. PHILLIPS
of this county in her 32d year. The deceased was born in Demopolis, Ala.
August 22d, 1839. She was left an orphan at the age of 14, but was for-
tunate in finding a friend who cared for her with true parental affection
until her 14th year, when her protector died. She married in Feb. 1857.

October 7, 1870
Married on the 29th by REV. A. R. SCARBOROUGH, DR. D. HENAGAN and
Miss KATE ETHRIDGE, all of this county.
Tribute of Respect: Livingston Lodge #41 mourns death of ABRAM LARKIN
and sends condolence to the widow and fatherless.

October 14, 1870
Died on the 4th at Cuba in this county, Mr. D. V. PATTERSON aged
about 60 years.

October 21, 1870
Died at the family residence in North Sumter, Ala. on the morning of
the 5th of consumption, AMANDA F., wife of S. P. TOMPKINS in her 42nd year.
Mobile and South Carolina papers please copy.
Died near Jones Bluff September 9, 1870 after a brief but severe illness, JAMES DUFFEY, eldest son of H. C. and S. J. KNIGHT aged 2 years 11
months and 22 days.

October 28, 1870
Married at the residence of the bride's father on the 20th by REV.
W. H. PASLEY, Mr. W. R. ARRINGTON and Miss LUCY BELL, all of this county.
Married on the 12th by REV. E. BELL at the residence of the bride's
uncle, C. P. WHITT, Esq. in Dallas County, Mr. E. N. BRYANT, Jr. of Sumter
and Miss LIZZIE C. WHITT of Dallas County.

November 11, 1870
     Tribute of Respect: Livingston Lodge #41 mourns death of D. IRWIN
RAST, which took place in New Orleans September 29, 1870. Copy to be
sent to widow.   J. L. SCRUGGS)
                                      T. B. STONE)   Committee
                                      H. O. VOSS   )

November 18, 1870
     Married on the 13th at the residence of Mr. J. R. SMITH, by REV. C. B.
DuBOSE, DR. J. P. BEESLEY of Ouachita, La. and Mrs. KATE VAUGHAN of this
county.
     Died at the residence of her father, WM. P. GOULD on the 8th after a
short illness, ELLEN, wife of P. W. PARKER of this place...Leaves a husband and a little son.

November 25, 1870
     Married on the 17th by REV. B. M. EMANUEL, Mr. MOSES MARX of Mobile
and Miss REBECCA ZIMMERN of Livingston.
     The Eutaw Whig of the 18th says: "On last Thursday night, Mr. STEPHEN
COBB of this vicinity came to his death in the following manner...killed
by a cow."
     The Greensboro Beacon says: "Mr. CHARLES JOHNSON, oldest son of Mr.
ANDREW JOHNSON, an old and worthy citizen of Greensboro lost his life
Tuesday. Horse ran away with him."

December 9, 1870
     Died on the night of the 30th inst. in Gainesville, Sumter County,
Alabama, Mrs. REAVIS, wife of HON. TURNER REAVIS (38 NC). (Mrs. REAVIS,
MARY S., 38 V.)

December 16, 1870
     Died on November 9th at the residence of her husband in Choctaw
County, SUSAN LIGHTFOOT FLUKER, wife of C. S. WARD aged 18 years 4 months.
     Died in Sumter County November 27, 1870 of pneumonia, JOHN W. PHILLIPS
aged 43. In less than 3 months, three of the family have died; the wife
in September, a child in October and the husband as above stated. They
have left a daughter twelve and a son ten...Previous to his death, he
left the children to care of Mr. and Mrs. JOSEPH W. JENKINS...

December 23, 1870
     Departed this life at the residence of her husband near Livingston
on the 10th, Mrs. SARAH L. LAKE, wife of T. H. LAKE, Esq. in her 35th
year, daughter of M. C. HOUSTON, Esq. She resided in and near Livingston
the greater portion of her life though for several years Mobile was her
home...After the death of Mr. JAMES LAKE of Georgia, his children were
confided to the care of the above...

January 6, 1871
     DANIEL L. AYRES (39 NC), an old and well known citizen of this place
and for many years Tax Assessor died on Monday night. He had been ill
for several weeks.

January 13, 1871
     Married on the 3rd at the residence of WM. H. JOHNSON near Butler,
Choctaw Co. by REV. TURNER, Mr. W. F. GREEN of Holmes County, Miss. and
Miss LINDA B. MURLEY of Choctaw, formerly of Livingston.
     At the same time and place by same, Mr. GEORGE E. JOHNSON and Miss
BETTIE R. MURLEY, all of Choctaw, the latter formerly of Livingston.

January 20, 1871
     Married at the residence of Mr. ROBT. HATTEN in Tuscaloosa on the
28th by REV. G. H. HUNT, Mr. W. PENN LYNCH and Miss JOSEPHINE SPEAKMAN.
     NORA J. LAWLER, daughter of L. PARRENT in the 20th year died Dec. 10,
1870 near Brownsborough, North Alabama.
     Estate of NATHAN LOVE (38 V), deceased. HELEN D. NOBLE, administra-
trix.
     ROBERT P. NOBLE, administrator. Jan. 17, 1871.
     Estate of NANCY J. BURTON, deceased. CHARLES H. BULLOCK, administra-
tor.

January 27, 1871
    Estate of JOSIAH MOORE, deceased. H. W. KILLEN, executor.
    P. B. CALHOUN versus LODECIA ALLISON.
    W. G. LITTLE, Jr. adm'r of)
    D. BLACKSHEAR, deceased   )
            versus   )   Attachment
    T. W. TALIAFERRO, defendant)   and
    R. H. CLARKE, adm'r of   )   Garnishment
    BENJAMIN TALIAFERRO, dec'd)
    garnishee   )
    MARY S. HARRIS, guardian of minor heirs of H. H. HARRIS
                        versus
    JOHN M. BOYD, LODESIA ALLISON and R. R. MOORE.
    "Levied upon as property of Mrs. LODECIA ALLISON."
    The wife of PRICE WILLIAMS, SR. died in Mobile a few days ago after
a brief illness.

February 3, 1871
    WALLACE S. NEALE, deceased. F. P. SNEDECOR, administrator.
    BENJAMIN HARRISON, administrator of M. J. RICKERSICKER,
                        versus
    THOMAS B. McKERRALL-Circuit Court of Greene County, Ala.

February 10, 1871
    Tribute of respect by Livingston Lodge no. 41 on death of Brother
DANIEL L. AYRES, one of its oldest and best members. Copy sent to widow.
                        G. W. DAINWOOD)
                        W. A. C. JONES)   Committee
                        BEN F. HERR   )
    Married on the 1st at the residence of the bride's father, Mr. JOSEPH
GREENLEE by REV. W. H. PASLEY, Mr. WM. RILEY and Miss ELIZABETH GREENLEE,
all of this county.
    Married on the 25th of Jan. at the residence of Mrs. C. JACKSON by
REV. A. R. SCARBOROUGH, Mr. S. A. WIMBERLEY and Miss EMMA JACKSON all of
this county.
    At the residence of Mr. M. H. BOYD by REV. W. P. McBRYDE, Mr. J. L.
DAVENPORT and Miss S. P. SILLIMAN, all of Sumter County.
    Estate of J. W. PHILLIPS, deceased. JOSEPH W. JENKINS, adm'r.
    A. J. STEWART, deceased. J. A. MOORING, adm'r.

February 17, 1871
    FELIX TANKERSLEY, deceased. REUBEN CHAPMAN, Jr., adm'r.
    GEORGE DENTON, deceased. STEVE. TOMPKINS, adm'r.

February 24, 1871
    Married on the 17th at the residence of Mr. ASA MAY in Jefferson Co.
Florida by REV. Mr. QUIMBY of Monticello, Mr. F. M. CUNNINGHAM of Livingston, Ala. to Miss ALICE I. COLE of Jefferson.
    JOEL PEARSON, deceased. M. L. STANSEL, adm'r.
    SALLIE WOOTEN, deceased. SAMUEL H. SPROTT, adm'r.
    To CORNELIA SMITH and her husband, JOHN T. SMITH, ADDISON SMITH,
STEPHEN SMITH and WALTER SMITH--TAKE NOTICE that T. H. LAKE has this day
filed application to probate the will of SARAH L. LAKE, deceased.
    REBECCA GILBERT, administratrix versus L. H. HARE and CHARLES SIMPSON.
    DR. R. MILLER, a leading physician and one of the most highly esteemed
gentlemen of Mobile died there on the 18th.
    GIDEON B. FRIERSON, deceased. W. G. LITTLE, JR., administrator of
C. S. McCONNICO, dec'd, who was adm'r. of G. B. FRIERSON.

March 10, 1871
    Tribute of respect to a member of our beloved Grand Master, WM. P.
CHILTON of Grand Lodge of our State, by Belmont Lodge #372, Belmont, Ala.
                        J. G. MICHAEL)
                        J. G. COATS   )
                        ED. ARRINGTON)   Committee
                        JNO. ZAC. TUTT)
    Estate of JACINTH JACKSON (53 G), deceased. ASA AMASON, executor of
will.
    T(HOS.) R. CREWS (36 NC), deceased. O(CTAVIUS) L. CREWS (13 Miss),
executor of will.

March 17, 1871

ROBERT HILL, deceased. ELIZA HILL, administratrix.

A. W. RICHARDSON, deceased. W. R. RICHARDSON, administrator.

THOMAS J. DONALD, deceased. E. C. SLOAN, executrix.

Mr. ED. MILLS, formerly of Mass. committed suicide near Bladon Springs last Friday by shooting himself.

Mrs. DAWKINS and child were killed near Clayton in Barbour Co. last week by a falling limb.

WM. STILLINGS, a printer formerly employed in the Commonwealth office at Marion was knocked down by a negro about a month ago and died on the 13th.

March 24, 1871

Livingston Lodge #41 - tribute of respect on the death of NATHAN LOVE.

P. G. NASH)
WM. BEGGS) Committee
R. D. WEBB)

On the 15th, Mr. NEIL BLUE of Montgomery, now 78, celebrated his 52nd anniversary of his arrival at the site of that city.

March 31, 1871

Married on the 25th at the residence of the bride's mother by REV. W. H. PASLEY, Mr. H. M. DANIEL and Miss VIRGINIA SCOTT, all of this county.

F. W. RICHARDSON (FANNY W? Census, 33 NC), deceased. BRYANT RICHARDSON, (25 NC), adm'r.

THOMAS HART CLAY, son of HENRY CLAY died on the 18th at his residence in Fayette County.

April 7, 1871

C. V. SILLIMAN, guardian of SUSAN P. SILLIMAN.

A few days ago the family of Mr. J. FLEM. CROSS was poisoned. Mrs. CROSS died and others recovered.

April 14, 1871

Estate of THOMAS CUSACK (64 Ire.), deceased. S(AMUEL) P. HAND, executor.

SUSAN LEE, deceased. J. A. MOORING, adm'r. de bonis non with will annexed.

JAMES BALLARD (37 NC), deceased. CLARISSA J. BALLARD (24 NC), administratrix.

JOEL WATT (32 SC), deceased. CHARLES SIMPSON, administrator.

April 21, 1871

Married in Livingston on the 20th by REV. C. B. DuBOSE at the residence of J. W. HARRIS, Esq. (the bride's father), Mr. ISAAC A. CHILDS of Meridian and Miss NANNIE P. HARRIS of this place.

J. A. MOORING, guardian of CHARLES N., PETER and SUSAN R. WEIR.

J. A. MOORING, guardian of MATTIE A. HARE.

Our community recently sustained a serious loss in the death of Mrs. SUSAN SPRATT COCKRELL, Esq. (8 A) and daughter of ROBERT D. SPRATT, Esq. (43 SC). She was born March 9, 1842; married November 8, 1860 and died on the 10th instance...

In Chancery - JOHN F. WIATT versus LUCINDA E. WIATT. The defendant resides in Tehula, Holmes County, Mississippi.

April 28, 1871

Married on the 19th by REV. A. R. SCARBOROUGH at the residence of Mrs. C. JACKSON, Mr. J. V. TUTT and Miss BETTIE JACKSON, all of this county.

Married on the 20th by REV. A. R. SCARBOROUGH at New Prospect Baptist Church, Mr. R. C. HALLEY of North Alabama and Miss FANNIE GOULD of this county.

May 5, 1871

EMILY BILLUPS (called AMELIA in Census, 44 NC), widow of THOMAS M. BILLUPS (64 NC), deceased, petitions for dower.

May 12, 1871
    JACOB DRISKILL, deceased. S. H. SPROTT, administrator. Non-resident
heirs are: LEWIS DRISKILL, CAROLINE MATTHEWS, VIAN DRISKILL, G. W.
PRAYTOR and W. J. PRAYTOR.
    THOMAS M. BILLUPS (64 NC), deceased. EMILY BILLUPS (44 NC), widow.
Notice of petition be given to W. A. J. BILLUPS, EMILY BRANTLEY and her
husband, J. A. BRANTLEY, W. T. POOL, EMILY POOL, J. R. POOL, R. J. POOL,
THOMAS BILLUPS, JESSE BILLUPS, ROBERT BILLUPS, CLUNY BILLUPS, SUSAN
BILLUPS and JOHN BILLUPS,
    JAMES SIMPSON, deceased. CHARLES SIMPSON, administrator.

May 19, 1871
    JOHN J. DILLARD (52 V), deceased. W. O. WINSTON, administrator.

May 26, 1871
    ELISHA WOOD, guardian of J. A. GREEN filed vouchers for final settle-
ment of guardianship; also of S. D. GREEN for annual settlement of guardianship.

June 2, 1871
    Tribute of respect--Worshipful Master Hugh McMILLAN, deceased.
                              J. G. MICHAEL   )
                              C(ALEB) J. LANDRUM)   Committee
                              ZAC. TUTT   )

June 9, 1871
    YANCEY MITCHELL, deceased. ANDERSON MITCHELL, executor of will.
    M. A. KING, deceased. S. H. SPROTT, administrator.

June 16, 1871
    Married on the 8th at the residence of the bride in Livingston by
REV. J. S. FRIERSON, Mr. R. S. MASON and Mrs. A. McCONNICO.
    THOMAS LINDSAY, an elder brother of GOVERNOR LINDSAY died in Liver-
pool, England a few days ago.

June 23, 1871
    Married in Natchez, Miss. June 3 at the residence of C. W. BABBITT,
Esq. by REV. J. B. STRATTON, D.D., HON. TURNER REAVIS of Gainesville,
Alabama and Miss SALLIE MOSLEY of Natchez. Montgomery Advertiser please
copy.
    Married on the 6th at the residence of the bride's father by REV.
A. R. SCARBOROUGH, Mr. J. W. CURRY and Miss EDNY MATTHEWS, all of this
county.
    Married on the 8th at the residence of the bride's father by REV.
A. R. SCARBOROUGH, Mr. T. D. JAMES and Miss E. L. NUFFER, all of this
county.
    Married on the 15th at the residence of the bride's father by REV.
J. S. FRIERSON, Mr. C. M. BAUMAN of Knoxville, Tenn. and Miss IDA G.
CUNNINGHAM of this place.
    J. G. HARRIS, guardian of LILLY B. and JERRY J. BROWN files vouchers
for annual settlement of guardianship.
    J. G. HARRIS, administrator of R. S. NICHOLSON, deceased.
    J. G. HARRIS, administrator of D. S. BURTON, deceased.
    J. G. HARRIS, administrator of SARAH ANDERSON, deceased.
    JAMES KILDUFF fell down a stairway in Mobile and broke his skull.

June 30, 1871
    ELIZABETH LITTLE, deceased. R. E. MOFFITT, administrator with will
annexed.
    Petition to Probate Will -- To RICHARD R. MORGAN of Salisbury, Md.
TAKE NOTICE that this day A. G. GROVES has filed petition to probate the
will of JOHN MORGAN, deceased.
    In Chancery -- JOHN PARKER versus LAURA A. M. LIDE, ADDIE B. WHITE et
al. One of the defendants, JULIA A. GREER is a non-resident; she resides
in Meridian, Lauderdale County, Miss. and is believed to be over 21.

July 7, 1871
    JOSEPH PATTON, guardian of JOSEPH B. and DAVID W. PATTON files
vouchers for annual settlement of guardianship.
    DR. D. G. GARDNER of Pickens Co. died at Bridgeville on the night of
14th.

W. O. WINSTON, guardian of ANNA B., ED. A., JOHN W., LAVINIA and WM.
B. GILBERT, filed vouchers.
ALEXANDER SHACKELFORD, deceased. ROBERT THOMPSON, administrator.

July 21, 1871
Married by REV. A. R. SCARBOROUGH near Livingston on the 19th, Mr.
W. T. McKNIGHT of Clinton, Miss. to Miss MAGGIE SPROTT of this county.
Died at her home near Payneville, Ala. on 11 July 1871, Mrs. PATTIE
(MARY M. in Census 9/12 A) RENFROE, eldest daughter and child of DR.
WILLIAM H. (28 T) and MALVINA (18 A) SLEDGE. Born near Sumterville
Nov. 17, 1849, she married STEPHEN S. RENFROE Dec. 1, 1869...Joined
Missionary Baptist Church at Marion, Ala...J.D.J.
PLEASANT WHITE (53 G), deceased. W. W. COATS, executor of will.
M. M. WOOTEN, deceased. JOSEPH ARRINGTON, executor of will.
JOSEPH ARRINGTON, guardian of JOHN H. SHERARD, a minor.
NEWTON PRESTWOOD, administrator of JOHN PRESTWOOD (23 A), deceased.

July 28, 1871
Married by REV. A. R. SCARBOROUGH on the 25th at the residence of the
bride's father, Mr. G. W. FLUKER to Miss E. K. JOHNSTON, all of this
county.
Died at Butler, Choctaw County on 15th, ROSINA WINSTON, infant
daughter of OLIVER C. and SADIE T. ULMER aged 1 year 5 days.
JUDSON J. HILMAN (1 A, son of NIMROD W., 43 V), deceased. J. G.
HARRIS, administrator.
W. O. WINSTON, guardian of HENRIETTA M., TEXANA A., W. C., FRANKLIN
and WALTER R. BALLARD, made final settlement of guardianship of MARY ANN
BALLARD.

August 4, 1871
Estate of WILLIAM A. DRINKARD, deceased. WASHINGTON DRINKARD, ad-
ministrator.
PLEASANT L. DRINKARD (13 A), deceased (Choctaw Co.). WASHINGTON
DRINKARD (38 SC), administrator.

August 11, 1871
Died at the residence of her father, DR. A. M. GARBER Tuesday the
8th of congestion, JULIET ELIZABETH GARBER aged 7 years 3 months.
Stanton Valley Virginian please copy.
Died in McKinley (Marengo Co.), Ala. July 29 after a short illness,
KATE LUCRETIA, only daughter of DR. W. T. and ANNIE K. ABRAHAMS aged 4
years 6 months and 1 day.
ISADORE BAILEY, deceased. S. H. SPROTT, administrator.
JARED W. (JARRET W. in Census, 54 Miss.) CHERRY, deceased. WILLIAM
J. CHERRY, executor of will.
NOTICE TO NON-RESIDENT HEIRS: LUCINDA J. WARE, wife of HENRY A.
WARE, ELIZABETH CHERRY (20 A), EZEKIEL CHERRY (33 K), ROBERT L. CHERRY,
MARGARET I. ANDERSON, wife of B. ANDERSON, MILTON B. SMALL, MARY CAMPBELL
and the children of JOSHUA CHERRY, deceased are next of kin of JARED W.
CHERRY, deceased.
WILLIAM E. WILLIAMSON, deceased. JAMES F. WILLIAMSON, executor of
will.
WILLIS V. HARE, (36 A) deceased. J. A. MOORING, administrator.
JOHN C. EPES, deceased. JOHN W. EPES, administrator
Mr. WILLIAM OATES, father of COL. (GOVERNOR) W(ILLIAM) C(ALVIN)
OATES died at his residence in Pike County on the 28th.
Mr. CHARLES TEE was killed by lightning on the 6th in READ HORTON's
Store at Spring Hill.
Mr. GRIGG, son of ELISHA GRIGG was killed near Catoma Bridge Monday
evening last by Mr. FLEMING GILMER.
COL. THORINGTON of Montgomery died. Law partner of the late distin-
guished JUDGE CHILTON.

August 18, 1871
Mrs. MARY S. ROGERS, consort of G. W. ROGERS and daughter of D(AVID)
W. (29 SC) and M(ARGARET) A. HOOKS (20 NC) died July 12, 1871 at the residence of her father near Livingston. She was born July 23, 1848. Member of Methodist Episcopal Church, South.

REV. JEREMIAH PEARSALL of Pontotoc, Miss. will preach the funeral
sermon of REV. R(OBERT) R. SHELTON (d. Jan. 8, 1870), deceased on the
second Sabbath in September at Siloam Church 5 miles south of York Station (Bapt. min. m. 1. _____ 2. RACHEL STURGIS. Anc. of Mrs. JACK
BULLARD, Jefferson, Tex. 1955 who says he m. in Lauderdale Co. Ala. 1820
JANE MARLEY and Aug. 26, 1830 in Lauderdale Co. Ala. RACHEL C. STURGEON
probably dau. of JOHN C. STURGEON. RACHEL d. April 9, 1891. Family
tradition says JANE left Va. in 1810. Bapt. min., he had 12 children.
AVA's husband ISAAC JAMES. Mrs. MARION W. (ERMA COLEMAN) THORNE, 2454
40th Avenue, Meridian, Miss. 39301, Sept. 12, 1977, "My husbands anc.
ROBERT ROAN (ROWAN) SHELTON b. Va. 25 May 1796 d. in Sumter Co. Ala.
Jan. 8, 1870. Spent much of his early married life in Ala. Wife RACHEL
CYNTHIA STURGES b. NC 20 July 1810, 2d child b. 1830 Ala. His dau. AVA
MYRILLA was my husband's ggm b. 28 Nov. 1839. Next child b. Miss. 1841.
He was in Pontotoc Co. Miss. until Civil War, then moved to Sumter Co.
where both d. We have visited the graves in Chestnut Grove Cemetery."
    Married on the 13th by REV. C. C. VAUGHAN at the residence of the
bride's mother, Mr. HENRY McELROY (see his obit. on p. 27) to Miss LULA
WOOD, all of Sumter.

September 1, 1871
    Died Aug. 28th near Belmont in this county, JOHN HENRY, son of DR.
F. E. and HELEN M. DAVIDSON aged 12 years 4 months and 18 days.
    R. T. SAMPLE, deceased. E. A. SAMPLE, administratrix.
    JAMES O'BANNON, deceased. J. G. HARRIS, administrator with will
annexed.
    Mr. J. P. HARRIS was shot and killed last Sat. in Oxford by Mr. SAM
MORGAN.

September 8, 1871
    Married on 31 August in Livingston at the residence of G. W. DAIN-
WOOD by REV. C. B. DuBOSE, Mr. JOHN A. COLLIER of Columbia, Miss. to
Miss R. E. DAINWOOD, daughter of HENRY B. DAINWOOD of Columbia, Tenn.
Columbia Herald please copy.
    Married at the residence of the bride's father by REV. C. B. DuBOSE
on the 31st, Mr. B. C. HUNTER of Kentucky to Miss ANNA J. TROTT of this
place.
    GEN. THOMAS W. McCOY of Mobile died in Baltimore on 1st. In Madison
Co. on 17th, JOHN MARKHAM, while sitting at supper was killed by shot
through window.

September 15, 1871
    A few days ago, DANIEL HAWKINS was drowned in Choccolocco Creek.
    In Dekalb Co. Aug. 24, BEN WHEELER shot and killed KINNEY KEAN.
    On 17th, near Blount Springs, DAVID LANDINGHAM was cut and mortally
wounded by a Mr. HAYS.
    An old man named McVAY was found dead near Montgomery and Eufaula
Depot in Montgomery on 1st.

September 22, 1871
    M(EREDITH) W. LYNN (30 A), deceased. A(GNES) E. LYNN, administratrix.

September 29, 1871
    Married at the residence of the bride's mother by REV. S. J. BINGHAM,
Mr. R. H. HALE to Miss M. C. McDONALD, all of this county.
    The wife of PETER M. BOX, member of Congress from the 5th District
died near Huntsville on 12th Sept.
    JUDGE A. H. HUTCHINSON, editor of Tuscaloosa Observer died in that
city last Sat. after an illness of some weeks.
    Mr. THOMAS NICHOLS, a planter living in upper portion of Clark Co.
was killed by a negro a few days ago.
    Died at Beckley's Landing on 15th, J. N. COOK, son of DR. J. M. and
MARY E. COOK aged 15 years 5 months and 15 days.

October 6, 1871
    FANNIE HAMMOND and her husband, M. R. HAMMOND filed a petition
alleging they are joint owners in common with ISABELLA CHILES, wife of
WALTER L. CHILES, ISABELLA DEARMAN, wife of THOMAS DEARMAN, JOHN McKINZY,
CHARLOTT BREWSTER (24 NC), wife of HIRAM BREWSTER (27 A), MARGARET GRAHAM,
MARGARET SYLVESTER, wife of NATHAN SYLVESTER and NANCY JACKSON of certain
real estate.

SAMUEL SWILLEY (53 G), deceased. N. SWILLEY, adm'r.
H. J. HAZLEWOOD, guardian of HENRIETTA HAZLEWOOD.
FRANK A. LESLIE, an estimable citizen of Mobile died in that city on
the 28th. He had resided in Mobile since 1847.

October 13, 1871
DR. WILLIAM R. KENNARD of this place left last Tuesday for Texas
where he intends to make his future home.

October 20, 1871
JOSEPH LANCASTER was born October 13, 1850 and died on the evening
of 23 September 1871. Since the death of his father, ALBERT LANCASTER
(40 V), which occurred in May, 1870, he had care of his widowed mother
and two sisters.
FREDERICK HINES, deceased. J. P. HICKEY, adm'r.
DEMPSEY GRAHAM (41 SC), deceased. SAMUEL POND, adm'r.
Mrs. BALDWIN (27 A), (nee CELIA FITZPATRICK), wife of COL. M(ARION)
A(UGUSTUS) BALDWIN for many years Attorney General of Alabama died near
Montgomery a few days ago.

October 27, 1871
Married by REV. A. R. SCARBOROUGH on 25th inst. at the residence of
T. A. JOHNSTON, Mr. A. L. KORNEGAY to Miss J. A. SHERARD, all of this
county.
By REV. A. R. SCARBOROUGH on the 18th at the residence of the bride's
father, E. E. MIMS to Miss NANNIE McGOWEN, all of this county.
By Esquire SILIMAN on the 9th at the residence of Mr. JOE McGOWEN,
Mr. SAMUEL HALSELL to Mrs. FANNY PRATER.
Died at the residence in this county on Wednesday 11th of October,
1871 of yellow chills, WILLIAM R. DAVIS aged 40 years. Born in Greene
Co. Ala. and removed to this county when an infant, where he continued
to reside until his death. Leaves one daughter aged about 13 and a large
circle of distressed relatives. The writer of this sketch knew the de-
ceased for many years and can say that he was true and generous hearted
friend, an obedient son, a kind father and pure patriot...
State of Alabama-Sumter Co. Probate Court Oct. 25, 1871. H. H.
STEPHENS, guardian of CASWELL M. STEPHENS filed accounts for annual
settlement of guardianship.
JESSE A. GIBBS, administrator of WILEY DUNNING, deceased, advertises
land for sale.
NOTICE TO NON-RESIDENTS:
W. W. COATES, executor of)
PLEASANT WHITE, deceased)   Chancery Court of
           versus   )   Sumter Co. Ala.
FRANCIS C. WHITE, et al   )
One of the defendants, AMERICA SHURLEY, wife of THOMAS SHURLEY
and CAROLINE P. WILLIAMS, wife of SOLOMON WILLIAMS reside out of Alabama.
Their residence is near Meridian, Miss., Lauderdale Co. and to the best
of belief are over 21.
WILLIAM R. RICHARDSON, guardian of WILLIAM C. RICHARDSON, a minor.
JESSE A. GIBBS, administrator of WILLIAM P. HILLMAN, deceased.
J. P. HICKEY, administrator of FREDERICK HINES, deceased.
SAMUEL POND, administrator of DEMPSEY GRAHAM, deceased.

November 3, 1871
Married Thursday morning the 19th at Alabama Insane Hospital by REV.
Mr. HUNT, Mr. ROBERT E. BAIRD of Tuscaloosa and Miss MARY E. PUGH, form-
erly of Missouri. (Son of ALEX and SARAH W. (EMOND) BAIRD.)
COL. THOMAS McC(ARROLL) (45 NC) PRINCE of Choctaw died at Mt. Ster-
ling on the 13th ult.
At his residence in the city of Tuscaloosa on Monday night the 16th
of Oct. 1871 the spirit of ROBERT JEMISON quietly passed away.
HENRY T. LINDSAY, guardian of ROBERT and MARTHA J. LINDSAY.
HENRY T. LINDSAY, adm'r of ELLIS LINDSEY, deceased.
Estate of WILLIAM P. HILLMAN, deceased. McDUFFIE HILLMAN, one of
the heirs is a non-resident of this state and a minor.

November 10, 1871
Died at her home in this county on 16 Oct. 1871, Mrs. EUGENIA C.
ARRINGTON, consort of JOSEPH ARRINGTON aged 39 years 10 months and 26

days. Member of Methodist Episcopal Church South. Leaves a devoted
husband, one child and a large circle of relatives...
    Valuable plantation near Moscow belonging to Mrs. L. H. ADAMS for
sale.
    Estate of EDWARD W. LOVE, deceased. R. P. NOBLE and HELEN D. NOBLE,
adm'rs.
    S. H. SPROTT, administrator of THOMAS J. DONALD, deceased offers
property for sale.
    W. L. McDOW (1812 sol), deceased. Land for sale. E. P. SNEDECOR,
administrator de bonis non.
    J. G. HARRIS, administrator offers land for sale belonging to estate
of DAVID S. BURTON situated near Peyneville; WYATT HARPER situated near
Belmont; THOMAS M. BILLUPS situated near Intercourse.
    LARKIN EASTER, a Radical Candidate for Constable in Madison Co. has
been arrested for assaulting a woman.
    Mrs. A. S. WAYES of Springfield, Washington County, Kentucky wants
the address of relatives of J. J. GAMBLE, a Confederate soldier from
Alabama who died at her house in the fall of 1862.

November 17, 1871
    Estate of Mrs. ELIZABETH D. HARWOOD (55 V), deceased. (ELIZ. D.
ELLYSON, w. of SAMUEL M. HARWOOD will in Sumter Co.) JAMES HART, execu-
tor of the will. SUSAN E. HART, wife of JAMES E. HART; CORDELIA F.
PEARSON (18 A), wife of W. E. PEARSON; REUBEN E. MEREDITH; ELLISON
MEREDITH; HORAN H. DUKE, JAMES H. DUKE and ROBERTINE H. CARR wife of
        CARR are heirs at law and all reside out of this state.
    NOTICE TO NON-RESIDENTS:
    MELISSA A. LEE, complainant)   In Chancery
            versus   )   Sumter Co. Ala.
    MARY G. WOODALL, et al   )
        By affidavit of EDWARD W. SMITH, Esq., Solicitor for the com-
plainant that WILLIAM JONES, one of the defendants, is a minor and resides
out of this state, viz: in the state of Tennessee, P. O. unknown; and
that SALLY SYLVESTER, JAMES SYLVESTER, and JOHN SYLVESTER, other defendants are also minors and reside in Scott Co. Miss. with their father,
N. B. SYLVESTER, P. O. unknown.

November 24, 1871
    Died in this county near Belmont on the 11th, SAMUEL MILLON, eldest
son of EDWARD and MARY JANE ARRINGTON in his 19th year...
    NOTICE TO NON-RESIDENTS:
    JOHN PARKER, complainant)   In Chancery
            versus   )   Sumter Co. Ala.
    LAURA A. M. LIDE, et al)
    JOSIAH THOMAS and JULIA A. THOMAS are non-residents; they reside at
Meridian, Miss.
    W. E. BEGGS, attorney-at-law. Advertisement.
    L. D. COCKRELL, attorney-at-law. Advertisement. Office at Eutaw.
    State of Alabama-Sumter Co. MARY E. LEE, guardian of WILLIAM R.,
SUSAN B., JOHN H. and JAMES M. LEE petitions to sell property.
    Estate of BLUFORD SEALE (59 SC), deceased. R. L. SEALE, administra-
tor.

December 1, 1871
    Estate of HUGH McMILLAN, deceased. ELIZA A. McMILLAN, administra-
trix.
    Petition to probate will of ALEX. GEIGER, deceased by WILLIAM M.
GEIGER; notice to Mrs. A. C. NEUFFER, ISABELL M. GEIGER, JOHN A. GEIGER,
FRED ANN GEIGER, HENRY J. GEIGER, JOHN WESTON and others interested.
    ELNATHAN TARTT, guardian of MARY E. and SARAH TARTT.
    R. L. SEALE, administrator of BLUFORD SEALE (BLUFORD SEALE b. 1789
in S.C. S. of THOS. 1st w. RACHEL BAXTER), deceased filed a petition
for assignment of dower to ELIZA SEALE (Gen. Query in Wash. paper),
widow of said deceased. Notice to ELIZABETH BAGGET (m. 7 Jan. 1839,
Vol. 128, p. 10) and her husband, JOHN BAGGET, SUSAN B. SEALE (27 A),
SALLIE STRUTTER and CORINE STRUTTER.
    A. TANNENBAUM   )
            versus   )   In Circuit Court
    DANIEL PRICE, defendant)   Sumter Co. Ala.
    E. HERNDON, et al, gar.)
    DANIEL PRICE, a non-resident.

STEPHEN TOMPKINS, administrator of GEORGE DENTON (49 T), deceased.
Petition for dower to SALLIE B. DENTON (38 SC), widow of said GEORGE
DENTON, deceased; notice to JOHN W. DENTON (18 A), ISAAC DENTON (16 A),
JAKE (JACOB) DENTON (5 A), JIM DENTON (2 A), SALLIE SPARKMAN (6/12) and
her husband, JESSE R. SPARKMAN, JOHN HILL, GEORGE HILL, BENNIE HILL,
NANNIE HILL and TAYLOR SNEAD, non-resident heirs.

December 8, 1871
       Married on the 22nd by REV. A. E. CLEMENS at the residence of the
bride's mother, DR. A. B. DELOACH of Rusk Co. Texas (formerly of Livingston, Ala.) to Miss FANNIE E. YOUNG of Marshall, Tex.
       DR. J. M. MAYES of York Station in this county, a most estimable
gentleman and good physician died on last Wednesday the 6th of malarial
hemorrhagic fever.

December 15, 1871
       Died on 17 November 1871 little MILESON, only daughter of L. L. and
CAROLINE CLARY aged 2 years 11 months and 27 days...
       Died Oct. 15, 1871 near St. Stephens, Ala. after a lingering illness,
Mrs. JENNIE C. SPEED, wife of JAMES SPEED of Sumter Co. Ala. Leaves a devoted husband, two children and a large circle of relatives. M. E. Church.
       MAJOR W. S. KNOX (1812 sol.-q.v.), for many years an honored citizen
of Selma, died on night of 6th at Carlowville, Dallas Co., Ala.

December 22, 1871
       Married on the 19th by REV. A. R. SCARBOROUGH, Mr. JOSEPH ARRINGTON
to Miss MARY E. DuBOSE, all of this county.
       In Mobile on the 18th, Mr. A. W. COCKRELL of Livingston to Miss EVA
NASH of Mobile, formerly of Livingston.
       On the 20th at the residence of the bride's mother by REV. C. C.
VAUGHAN, Mr. GEORGE W. ADAMS to Miss SUSAN S. ROLAND, all of this county.
       REGISTER'S SALE:
       PATTIE C. JOHNSTON, executrix)
       of B. P. HUNTER, deceased   )   Chancery Court
                     versus   )   Sumter Co. Ala.
       HENRY C. GOWDEY   )

December 29, 1871
       JOEL HUNNICUTT (66 SC) of Shelby Co. aged about 95 killed a buck,
hams of which weighed 20 and 24 lbs. respectively.

January 5, 1872
       SKETCH OF JOHN ANTHONY WINSTON (37 A), EX-GOVERNOR OF ALABAMA.
Tribute to his Memory. Born in Madison Co. Alabama about 1811. Oldest
child of WILLIAM and MARY WINSTON. His mother was MARY COOPER (15 A),
a sister of WILLIAM COOPER and L. B. COOPER, distinguished lawyers of
North Alabama. ANTHONY WINSTON, grandfather of GOVERNOR WINSTON was born
in Hanover Co. Va., and was a captain in the Revolutionary War. He moved
from Va. to Tennessee and settled about 1 mile from the Hermitage. JOHN
ANTHONY WINSTON married in early manhood, MARY JONES of Madison County,
Ala. a sister of his partner, JOEL W. JONES. She was mother of GOVERNOR
WINSTON'S only child, Mrs. AGNES W. GOLDSBY, now of Mobile; but she died
when her daughter was only a few years old. GOVERNOR WINSTON married
again, but had no children. In 1834 he moved from Franklin County to
Sumter Co. near Gainesville (gives political record in detail). Was
COLONEL of 8th Alabama regiment and served in campaign of peninsula of
Williamsburg and Seven Pines...He will be buried beside the mother of
his child.
       A. F. HENDERSON, late joint proprietor and editor of the Montgomery
Mail committed suicide at Tuskegee on the 22nd.

January 12, 1872
       WILLIAM HUNTINGTON (he was son of ROSWELL, Rev. sol.), jeweller of
Marion, 79 years old, has just engraved perfectly formed letters on a
finger ring made for himself.
       Mr. PAUL LYONS of Mobile Co. died on the 21st aged nearly 111 years.
He was the oldest man in Mobile Co. and leaves a large number of descendants.

January 19, 1872
    Married at the Baptist Church in Gainesville on the 11th by REV.
J. B. HAMBERLIN of Meridian, Miss. REV. L(EWIS) M. STONE to Miss MARY G.
HIGH.
    By REV. A. R. SCARBOROUGH on the 4th at the residence of Mrs. BILLUPS,
Mr. G. W. BRANTLEY to Miss P. McSWAIN, all of this county.
    By REV. A. R. SCARBOROUGH on the 11th at the residence of H. B.
LEITCH, Mr. W. C. ARMSTRONG to Miss N. GILMORE, all of this county.
    Death of Mrs. BETTIE JOHNSTON, who died at the residence of her hus-
band, GEO. JOHNSTON on Dec. 25, 1871...Episcopal Church...there with
loved parents to wait a little while till husband, sisters and loved ones
join her...
    WILLIAM RIPLEY killed JAMES WHITLOCK at Ladiga on the 15th. RIPLEY
now in Calhoun Co. jail.
    JOHN BIRD HALL of Cherokee Co. aged 70 married to Miss CAGE aged 17.

January 26, 1872
    Married by REV. S. BINGHAM on 15th at residence of Mrs. JANE AIKEN,
Mr. W. G. HOLDEN of Kemper Co. Miss. to Miss MARY E. TARTT of this county.

February 2, 1872
    Died Dec. 21, 1871 at the residence of Mrs. ANN WOOD, his mother-in-
law, near Cuba Station, HENRY W. L. McELROY (see his marriage on p. 14)
aged 20 years and 20 days. Youngest child of I(SAAC) R(ANSOM) (45 G)
and Mrs. NANCY McELROY (47 or 42? G) and was born in Sumter Co. Ala.
His remains rest in the family graveyard in sight of the house he first
drew breath in. Baptist. Fall from a horse caused concussion of brain.
Left a devoted wife, fond parents and other relatives.

February 9, 1872
    Married on 30 Jan. at the residence of the bride's father in Demopo-
lis, Ala. by REV. A. R. SCARBOROUGH, Mr. S. C. COLEMAN of Sumter Co. to
Miss SUE McCARTY of Demopolis.
    BRYANT RICHARDSON, adm'r of F. W. RICHARDSON, deceased.
    W. V. STANTON, guardian of WILLIAM W. STANTON, FANNIE L. STANTON,
and SUMMERVILLE STANTON. Final settlement of guardianship of SUMMERVILLE
STANTON and annual settlement of other two.

February 16, 1872
    Married at the residence of CAPT. L. OLIVER, the bride's grandfather
in this county on 6th Feb. 1872 by REV. Mr. BARDWELL, E. M. WATSON, Esq.
of Holly Springs, Miss. to Miss LILLIE P. MOORE of Noxubee Co. Miss.
    Another old citizen gone! On Monday night the 12th, JUDGE GEORGE B.
SAUNDERS (34 V), a resident of Livingston for the last 30 years died at
his residence near this place. For a number of years he was Register in
Chancery and after the war was elected Probate Judge for this county.
    Estate of MARIAS MARTIN, deceased. JOHN McINNIS, administrator.
    Estate of SAMUEL SWILLEY, deceased. NICHOLAS SWILLEY, administrator.

February 23, 1872
    Married on the 31st at the residence of the bride's father by REV.
WILLIAM A. SHAPARD, Mr. ALLSON R. WILSON to Miss MARY KATE BYRNES,
second daughter of THOMAS BYRNES, Esq. all of Mobile. (1 REV. WM.
SHAPARD, cred. in Madison Co. M. E. Ch., 1858---same one?)
    Died in Livingston on the 2 Feb. 1872, MAJOR EDWARD HERNDON (50 V)
after a long and painful illness. Born in Spotsylvania Co. Va. Sept. 17,
1799 and grew up to manhood in the neighborhood of Fredericksburg. In
1817, MAJ. HERNDON removed to St. Stephens, Ala., then the capitol of the
Territory and the point to which most immigrants directed their steps.
Remained there as clerk in a store some 18 months....In 1819, he removed
to Greene Co. Ala. settling at Erie on the Warrior. In a few years he
was elected to office of Clerk of County Court of Greene. In 1830, he
removed to the neighborhood of Clinton, Greene Co. and engaged in planting and merchandising and after a couple of years lived in town of
Clinton. In 1840, he became a citizen of Gainesville and with the exception of one year passed in North Carolina, he was been a citizen of Sumter
for 32 years. Was several times chosen Intendant of Gainesville; was
County Treasurer from 1857-1863 and was at time of his death Register in
Chancery and Clerk of Circuit Court of Sumter...Mason...Elder in Presbyterian Church...His wife was an invalid for long years. Of the adult

inhabitants of Gainesville in 1840 when MAJ. HERNDON settled among us, not over a half a dozen---REAVIS, BLISS, LEWIS and the McMAHONS---remain.

Still another old citizen gone! Mr. M(ATTHEW) C. HOUSTON (51 T), who has resided in Livingston for last 35 or 40 years died very suddenly at his residence in this place yesterday morning. Funeral from the Presbyterian Church.

March 1, 1872
Estate of ELBERT AMASON, deceased. ELI AMASON, executor of will.

March 8, 1872
Another old citizen gone! Mr. J. W. HARRIS who has resided in Livingston for last 36 years died on last Sat. morning. This makes four of our oldest citizens who have died in 4 weeks.

March 15, 1872
CAPT. J(OSEPH) J. LITTLE born in Edgecomb Co. N. C. May 8, 1820, met with violent death in Warsaw in this county Thursday 22 Feb. 1872 (killed by C. E. TARTT. March 1 issue gives account of it.). Leaves wife and 9 children, five of whom are helpless.

Estate of W(ALLACE) S. NEALE (27 NC), deceased. F. P. SNEDECOR, administrator.

March 22, 1872
Mrs. AMANDA M. POWELL, wife of HON. E. A. POWELL died in Tuscaloosa on 9th.

Death of Mr. STEPHEN WEDGEWORTH, an old and respected citizen of Hale is announced.

COL. CHARLES FORSYTH, commercial Editor of Mobile Register and son of its Editor-in-Chief died in Mobile a few days ago.

JAMES NOBLES was shot and killed by some unknown party near his house in Bullock Co.

Mr. JOHN F. BONDURANT and Miss SALLIE DRAKE were married in Marion on 29 of Feb. 1872 (Gadsden Times).

March 29, 1872
Death of HON. R. H. SLOUGH, ex-mayor of Mobile is announced. Mr. JOHN ROBINSON, an old and respected citizen of Montgomery died suddenly in that city on 21 of heart disease.

REV. FATHER CORNETTE for long time professor of Mathematics in Spring Hill College died in Mobile on 21st.

April 5, 1872
Died at the residence of Mr. THOMAS B. CANNON on Feb. 24, Mrs. LEVINA LUMMUS (wid. of JOHN D., Vol. 180, p. 37) in her 77th year. Native of South Carolina but had resided in this state over 50 years. M.E. Church.

Died in Gainesville on 2nd in 75th year, ROBERT BRADSHAW, Esq., a citizen long and well known and greatly respected.

Death of COL. CHARLES R. GIBBS (63 V). Another old citizen gone! Died at his residence near this place yesterday morning. Approaching close of 86th year. Been a resident of this community for 36 years. (See 1812 pension.)

April 12, 1872
HON. SHELDON TOOMER, late Representative from Lee Co. in the Legislature died in Opelike on 25 of last month.

April 19, 1872
Mr. JAMES HUTCHINS, an old citizen of this county died near Sumterville on 6th aged 78.

Petition to probate will of JAMES L. HUTCHINS (56 SC), deceased. L. T. PORTER and L(EMUEL) T. ORMAN, executors. Notice be given to AMANDA KENDALL and her husband, T. R. KENDALL and CATHARINE LEMMON and her husband, W. J. or M. J. (sic) LEMMON.

April 26, 1872
Estate of ELIZABETH D. HARWOOD, deceased. SAMUEL B(ERNARD) M(AYJOR) HARWOOD, administrator with will annexed.

May 3, 1872

Married by REV. A. R. SCARBOROUGH on 25th at the residence of Mr. GEO. MORRIS, Mr. J. P. HANCOCK to Mrs. E. PARKER, all of this county.

We were in error in our issue on 12th inst. in speaking of death of Mr. WILLIAM GARRETT, formerly of this county in saying that he committed suicide. Verdict "accidental death from drowning."

May 10, 1872

Died near Sumterville on 6 of April, 1872, Mr. JAMES HUTCHINS aged 78. Brother HUTCHINS was born in South Carolina Jan. 28th, 1794. In 1820, he emigrated to Greensboro, Alabama, where he married and joined the Baptist Church. In 1835, he moved to Sumter Co. Ala. Soon after the Surrender, he was attacked with paralysis. Interred in graveyard at Gainesville. Bereaved family.

May 17, 1872

On Friday last at York Station, Mr. JOHN BRADSHAW, a former employee on A & CRR was found dead in his bed. Supposition is that he died of apoplexy.

Estate of ROBERT BRADSHAW, deceased. JOHN W. BRADSHAW, executor of will.

Estate of JOHN W. HARRIS, deceased. J. E. CUSACK, adm'r.

Estate of WILLIAM J. GREGORY, deceased. ASA AMASON and DAVIS FOY, administrators.

Married in Tuscaloosa on Tue. 30 April 1872 by REV. CHARLES A. STILLMAN, DR. TRUEHEARD of Galveston, Tex. to Miss ELLA STREET.

May 24, 1872

Mr. WILLIAM LOCKARD (45 SC), another old citizen, one of the first settlers in this community died on morning of 22nd after a long and painful illness.

Estate of THOMAS M. BILLUPS, dec'd. J. G. HARRIS, administrator.

Estate of ABRAM LARKIN, dec'd. IRENE LARKIN, administratrix.

Estate of DAVID S. BURTON, dec'd. J. G. HARRIS, administrator.

June 14, 1872

Died in San Francisco, Cal. on 20th, Mrs. LOUISA E. INGE (30 NC), relict of HON. SAMUEL W. INGE (33 NC) who represented 4th Ala. District in Congress for 4 years commencing in 1845 or 1847. She was born in Warrenton, N. C. and was the oldest daughter of REV. W. W. and Mrs. ANNE HILL, who moved from Warrenton, N. C. to vicinity of Greensboro in fall of 1834. She leaves 2 sons, the older a citizen of Greensboro, the younger of San Francisco; two brothers and two sisters besides other relatives. Her age was about 50 years.

June 21, 1872

Again the people of Sumter are called upon to mourn the loss of one of its oldest citizens, JUDGE (TURNER) REAVIS (38 NC). For last 30 or 35 years, he has been identified with all the interests of our country. Died very suddenly on 14 at his residence in Gainesville.

June 28, 1872

Estate of S. G. ESKRIDGE, deceased. S. H. SPROTT, administrator.

July 5, 1872

Married on 24 June at St. John's Church, Stockton, Cal. by REV. Mr. BIRDSALL, Mr. T. H. LAKE of Mobile and Mrs. BETTIE GAINES of Stockton, Cal.

Estate of R. S. NICHOLSON, deceased. J. G. HARRIS, administrator.

July 12, 1872

TRIBUTE TO JUDGE TURNER REAVIS: Died at Gainesville on 13...Born June 18, 1812. He spent 34 years in Ala.

Estate of JOHN W. PHILLIPS, deceased. JOSEPH W. JENKINS, administrator.

ELIZABETH SKINNER, guardian of JOSEPH N., SUSAN R. and ANDREW J. STEWART filed vouchers for final settlement of guardianship.

WALTER H. DANIEL, guardian of JAMES T., NANCY E. and JOHN W. STEWART filed vouchers for final settlement of guardianship.

R(OBT.) M. BEGGS, deceased. WILLIAM BEGGS, adm'r.

July 19, 1872
     W. J. NICHOLS, deceased. ROSENA M. NICHOLS, administratrix.

July 26, 1872
     We are glad to know that CHARLES COOKE, Esq. formerly of Gainesville
and son-in-law of late HON. T. REAVIS will soon return to this county to
make his residence. Will resume his law practice.

August 9, 1872
     THOMAS A. DILLARD and   )
     NANCY DILLARD   )   In Chancery
          versus   )   Sumter Co. Ala.
     WM. O. WINSTON, executor of)
     JOHN J. DILLARD, deceased)
     Affidavit of THOMAS COBBS, Esq. one of Solicitors of complainants,
that in his belief, EDMUND W. DILLARD, one of defendants is a non-resident of Alabama; that when last heard from, he was at Jefferson, Texas
and is over 21.

August 16, 1872
     MARCUS PARKER   )   Chancery Court
          versus   )   Sumter Co. Ala.
     RACHEL SHELTON et al)
     Affidavit of THOMAS COBBS, Esq. one of Complainant's Solicitors that
in his belief, M(ARION) M. SHELTON, J. L. SHELTON, E(VELINE) H. FRAZIER
(m. JOHN FRAZIER) and A. J(ANE) PERVIS (m. ISAAC PURVIS), defendants are
non-residents of Alabama; that they reside at New Albany, Miss. and are
over 21; that N(AOMA) M(ALISSIA) BLACKBURN (w. of JESSE DANIEL BLACKBURN),
a defendant resides at Marshall, Tex. and that she is over 21.   (N. M.
BLACKBURN b. Aug. 2, 1831, d. Sept. 5, 1899.)

August 30, 1872
     JOHN RITTER (48 NC), an old citizen of this county died in Birming-
ham on the 22nd. He resided in the northern portion of this county and
had been on a visit to the neighborhood of Birmingham for several weeks.
Death was very sudden.
     Estate of BRYAN CROOM, deceased. A. M. GERE and husband W. B. GERE
(she formerly being AUGUSTA M. CROOM), administratrix.

September 6, 1872
     On the morning of Sept. 1st, Mr. WILLIAM K. USTICK (43 V), one of
our oldest citizens died. Had been a citizen of Livingston for the last
36 years.
     Died on the night of Sept. 1 at the residence of her father, Mr.
CHAS. BALL near this place after a long and painful illness, Miss LENA
BALL in her 19th year.
     Tribute of respect to W. K. USTICK, deceased, by Board of Councilmen
of Livingston held Sept. 2; states he moved from Virginia to Livingston
in 1836. Has for many years acted as Magistrate in our town. Impartial
and honest judge.

September 13, 1872
     Mrs. HANNAH HYDEN, who has for a long time been an invalid at the
residence of her sister, Mrs. W. K. USTICK died there last Tue. the 10th.
     REV. JOHN W. BOOTH died in Mobile a few days since at the age of 86.
He labored extensively in the ministry in Ala. and Miss. and was the first
to organize a society of the Methodist Episcopal Church in Mobile,
     COL. M. J. WILLIAMS of Selma died at Shelby Springs where he had gone
for his health. Formerly proprietor of the Selma Times, one of the most
esteemed citizens.

September 20, 1872
     Died in Birmingham August 21, 1872 in his 69th year, JOHN RITTER
(48 NC) of this county. Born in Edgecomb Co. N. C. and moved to this
state about 1834.
     WILLIAM J. SIMS, deceased. Notice to W. A. SIMS, ELIZA J. COX and
her husband, G. A. COX, non-resident heirs. Petition to probate will.

September 27, 1872
  Died at Gainesville Aug. 29th, ANNE B., second daughter of Mr. and
Mrs. F. P. SNEDECOR aged 5 years and 6 months.

October 25, 1872
  Died October 1st, TAYLOR BARNES born December 14, 1860, son of
SAMUEL W. and HATTIE BARNES of Warsaw, Ala.

November 15, 1872
  Married on Wed. the 6th at the residence of the bride's father by
REV. E. P. PALMER, Mr. RICHARD FELDER to Miss MARY E. MONETTE, all of
Mobile.
  MAJOR GENERAL MEADE of Union Army died on 30th.
  Died on 8th at his residence near this place, Mr. JAS. BRANCH,
  JOHN SUMMERFIELD GREENE, for many years employed in the Counting Room
of Mobile Register died suddenly on the 8th.
  Mrs. LOWERY, wife of REV. Mr. LOWERY, Pastor of the Presbyterian
Church at Selma died in that city on the 3rd. Had been in ill health a
long time.

November 22, 1872
  Died Saturday last at his residence near this place, Mr. THOS. A.
JOHNSTON. Had been a citizen of Sumter and held office of County Treas-
urer for one or more terms. Buried by Masonic Fraternity.
  NOTICE TO EDMONIA N. McWHORTEN and her husband, D. O. McWHORTON and
BETSEY H. MOSBY. Petition to probate will of CAROLINE M. BARRET, deceased.

November 29, 1872
  ELIZABETH P. PARKER   )   Register's Sale of
       versus   )   Town Lots
  PHILANDER W. PARKER et al)   Livingston, Ala.

December 6, 1872
  Married in Gainesville Nov. 19, 1872 by REV. ALBERT A. MORSE, Mr.
ALLEN W. HILL and Miss FANNIE ST. CLAIR BELL.

December 13, 1872
  Married in Opelousas, La. Wed. evening Nov. 28th at the residence of
the bride's father by REV. RICHARD F. FANCHER, Mr. E. S. ANDRUS to Miss
IDA HADDEN and Mr. THOMAS B. SMITH to Miss LENA HADDEN. Mr. SMITH and
Miss HADDENS were formerly of this county but now reside in Opelousas, La.

January 3, 1873
  Married on the 19th at the residence of the bride's father, JOHN
TOMPKINS near Warsaw this county by REV. Mr. KELLIS, Mr. JOHN FLORA of
Noxubee, Miss. and Miss EMMA TOMPKINS of this county.
  On the 19th at the residence of the bride's father in Noxubee, Miss.
by REV. Mr. HAMILTON, Mr. WALTER D. WINDHAM of Pickens Co. and Miss MARY
F. HIBBLER, of Noxubee Co. Miss.
  Died on the 5th near Warsaw, this county, Mrs. TEMPE LITTLE (41 NC),
wife of WM. LITTLE (45 NC) aged about 60.

January 10, 1873
  Died December 30, 1872, CHARLES HOOKS, son of DAVID W. and M. A.
HOOKS aged 19 years 8 months and 30 days.

January 17, 1873
  Married on the 15th at the residence of the bride's mother, by REV.
J. M. PATTON, Mr. GEO. H. BUNCH of Meridian, Miss. and Miss MARY A.
BEVILL of this county.
  Died on Dec. 30 near Warsaw this county, JOSEPH ROGERS aged about 63.
  Died on Dec. 26 near Warsaw, this county, JAMES I. WINDHAM.
  Died on 10th near Warsaw, this county, A. IRBY aged about 21.
  Died on 14th near Warsaw, this county, Mrs. MARY ANN CUNNINGHAM.
  Died, Mrs. EVA NASH COCKRELL (5/12 A), wife of A. W. COCKRELL Dec.
26, 1872 in her 23rd year. Daughter of JUDGE P(RESTON) G. NASH (29 Nelson
Co. Va.) and Mrs. LAMPETER NASH (27 NC). Born and raised in Livingston.
  Died in Sumter Co. Nov. 22, 1872, Mrs. MARTHA WATSON, wife of
THOMAS F. WATSON (Gainesv.) aged 33. (S. of JARRED WATSON of T21.)

January 24, 1873
Married on the evening of Jan. 16th at the residence of L. F.
WHITEHEAD, Esq. in the vicinity of Livingston by REV. J. SIMPSON FRIERSON,
Mr. JOHN SPROTT and Miss MARY A. V. EVANS.
Died in Sumter Co. Nov. 2, 1872 after a painful illness, PATRICK
BOGEN MAY, SR. (51 NC). Born in Anson Co. N. C. April 3, 1799. Moved to
Ala. in 1817 and settled near St. Stephens. Subsequently moved to Greene
Co. and from there went to Belmont, Sumter Co. where he resided more than
30 years. Joined the Primitive Baptist Church over 30 years ago.

January 31, 1873
ROBERT JOHNSON, an old and well-known citizen of Livingston died
suddenly Tue. night. Was at work a few hours before his death.
The wife of W. J. GILMORE, deceased, died in Montgomery last Friday.
HON. N. W. NORRIS, ex-member of Congress from the 3rd Ala. District
died in Montgomery last Sunday night.

February 14, 1873
Resolutions on the death of BRYANT RICHARDSON (25 NC). (Herman
Lodge #106 F & AM. Sgn by C. S. HENAGAN and J. P. McINNIS.)
C. W. DORRANCE died in Mobile a few days ago.
Mr. JOSEPH WARD (70 Del.), the oldest inhabitant of Huntsville died
a few days ago aged 93.

February 28, 1873
Married by REV. A. R. SCARBOROUGH at the residence of the bride's
father, Mr. H. R. FOSS to Miss BETTIE M. MASON, all of this county.
Tribute of respect to ALBERT H. IRBY, who lately died.
Died at Ramsey's Station, Sumter Co. Sunday Feb. 16, of meningitis,
W. O. SIMMS aged 20 years 2 mo. and 2 days. (S. of W. T. and HARRIET
(GRAY) SIMMS.)

March 7, 1873
Petition of PRISCILLA LONG, widow of RICHARD B. LONG for dower.
THOMAS M. LONG, executor of will of RICHARD B. LONG.

March 14, 1873
Married on 6th at the residence of Mr. D. W. HOOKS near Livingston
by REV. J. M. MASON, Mr. GEORGE W. ROGERS and Miss GEORGIA A. HOOKS.
Died in Livingston on 6th, Miss LIZZIE HOUSTON, daughter of the late
M. C. HOUSTON.
On the 1st in Greene Co. Mr. D(AVID) B. PHILLIPS (28 T), a former
citizen of Sumter.
At Ramsey's Station, Sumter Co. Tuesday the 4th of meningitis, Mrs.
HARRIET (GREY) SIMMS (20 SC), wife of W(ILLIAM) T. SIMMS (43 NC) aged
about 45.
Mrs. MARY S. HARRIS left yesterday for a temporary residence in
Missouri.

March 21, 1873
Died in Gaston, Sumter Co. of paralysis, MARTIN RUMLEY (Vol. 20, p. 6,
1850 Perry Co., 42 NC) on the morning of 11th aged 66 years 1 mo. and 22
days. Native of Beauford, N. C. where he lived to manhood. In 1835, he
moved to Greene Co. Ala. where he married and resided till the fall of
1856, when he moved to Sumter Co. Left a devoted wife and four children.
(M. in Greene Co. Ala. 1840 ELIZABETH, d. of FREDERICK TOLSON, Vol. 108,
p. 7, Vol. 20, p. 6.)
A few mornings ago, Mr. WM. GREEN (53 SC), an old citizen of Calhoun
Co. suddenly fell down dead.
Married in this county Tuesday the 18th by D(AVID) H. TROTT, Esq.
Mr. ROBERT T. RODGERS to Miss ELIZABETH A. FREEMAN.

March 28, 1873
Died in this county on 27th, Mrs. HARRIET PIPKIN (36 A, w. of ARCH.)
aged 68. (She m. GODFREY HOLLEY (1.). She was dau. of W. BYRD.)
Residence of Mrs. ELIZA HILDRETH in Pickens Co. burned on the 13th.
L. V. B. MARTIN, Esq. died in Tuscaloosa last Sat.

April 4, 1873
    Died in Livingston 22 March of bronchitis, Mrs. PATIENCE A. ARRINGTON, (43 NC), widow of the late ROBERT ARRINGTON (49 NC), Esq. in 65th year.
    Mrs. TEMPIE M. SCRUGGS (30 NC), daughter of GEN. JOSEPH (61 NC) and MARY J. ARRINGTON (60 NC) was born in Nash Co. N. C. Sept. 29, 1817. In childhood, she removed to Sumter Co. where she married JOSIAH L. SCRUGGS (34 V) May 17, 1838. (Mrs. JENKINS copied March 17, may be she is right.) Joined the M. E. Church in 1844 and died of pneumonia at her residence in Livingston March 31.
    Died in this place on 13 March, DR. BLAKE LITTLE aged 80 years and 3 months. Born in Edgecombe Co. N. C. December 13, 1793. First moved from N. C. to Greene Co. Ala. in 1823; subsequently moved back to N. C. and again moved to Ala. in 1830 and located in Pickens Co. and in 1832 settled in Sumter Co. In 1848 he moved to the West where he lived until about three years ago when becoming helpless from paralysis he returned to Alabama. Last 6 months spent with his daughter, Mrs. CAROLINE A. BELL. Served in Legislature of Alabama in 1839, 40 and '41. Mason, Methodist Protestant Church.
    WILLIAMSON JORDAN, deceased. SAMUEL SPROTT, administrator de bonis non.
    HILLIARD J. FINCHER (29 NC), deceased. SAMUEL SPROTT, administrator de bonis non.
    M. A. KING, deceased.
    Died, HON. WM. TAYLOR of Sumter Co. Ala. Born Ponhatan Co. Va., went to W. Va. where he lived 30 years; migrated to Belmont 1857, Presbyterian; member of House of Representatives 1869 to fill unexpired term of BENJ. INGE; elected in 1892 by 800 majority.

April 11, 1873
    Montgomery Advance of 6th contains sketches of two negro legislators.

April 18, 1873
    Died near Livingston on 26 March, Mrs. EDNA M. RHODES (34 NC), wife of JAMES RHODES (45 NC) aged about 57.
    On 2 (2 Mar as Mrs. J. copied it) of consumption in Gainesville, Mrs. HENRIETTA MOBLEY (50 Vt.), wife of GREEN B. MOBLEY, (50 SC) Esq. aged 73. (Article from Tuscaloosa News dated April 14, 1978: The Magnolia, an antebellum home owned by Mrs. DAISY McLELLAND FALLS, will be open for tours today, Saturday and Sunday. The home is located in Gainesville in Sumter County. The Sunday tours are from 1 p.m. to 5 p.m. and on the other days from 10 a.m. to 5 p.m. The admission charge is $3 and the proceeds will go to cancer research, Mrs. FALLS said. Shown is an exterior view of the home with its giant white columns. (News photo by CALVIN HANNAH). The giant mirror (shown on left) is among the features of the hallway of The Magnolia, the antebellum home of Mrs. DAISY McLELLAND FALLS in Gainesville. Open House is being held Friday, Saturday and Sunday at the home with a $3 admission charge which will go to cancer research. The home was built in 1832 by COL. GREEN B. MOBLEY.)
    Miss ANNIE E., (6A) youngest daughter of the late T(HOS. McCARROL) C. PRINCE of Choctaw died at Mt. Sterling on 8th.
    LOUIS CARYELE said to be 108 years old died in St. Stephens last week.
    DR. J. H. MURFEE, formerly of Tuscaloosa has removed to Okolona, Miss.

April 25, 1873
    Married on the 16th at the residence of the bride's father by REV. C. B. DuBOSE, Mr. D. L. KIRKLAND and Miss MINNIE SEELEY all of this county.

May 2, 1873
    Married on the 30 by D. H. TROTT, Esq. Mr. PINKNEY MORRIS and Miss ELLA FAIR JOWERS all of this county.

May 9, 1873
    Tribute of respect. JAMES P. KENNARD (46 T) died at ripe old age of 69. Livingston Lodge #41.   W. G. LITTLE)
                                         W. A. C. JONES) Committee
                                         A. D. FORTNER)

May 16, 1873
    Letters testamentary on estate of HARRIET S. PIPKIN.

W. T. HARWELL, deceased. J. G. HARRIS, adm'r.
     Mr. HENRY ENGLISH, formerly ticket agent of the West Point Rd. died
in Montgomery on night of 10th.
     Mr. JOHN WILSON, a citizen of Tuscaloosa residing near the Fayette
Co. line was called from his home and killed.

May 23, 1873
     Married on the 20th at St. James' Church by REV. S(TEPHEN) U. SMITH,
Mr. S. T. PRINCE of Choctaw Co. to Miss HELEN RHODES of this place.
     N(ATHANIEL) P. DEAN, deceased. (Clarke Co. Ala. Rev. sol. JOHN
DEAN had a son, U. P. DEAN. 42 A.) JOHN R. LARKIN, special administrator.
     JAMES P. DIAL, deceased. ELIZABETH DIAL, administratrix.
     HUDSON P. LIPSCOMB, SR., deceased. H. P. LIPSCOMB, Jr. adm'r.
     WASHINGTON BRYANT, deceased. E. W. SMITH, adm'r.
     JAMES I. WINDHAM, deceased. ROBERT HIBBLER, adm'r.
     Died at his residence near Intercourse, Sumter Co. Ala. on 5 May
1873, Mr. LEMUEL B. HALE (40 NC). Born in Marion District, S. C. in
October, 1809, came to Alabama 1824 and was in his 64th year. He was a
man of strong will and was remarkably tenacious of his opinions, which he
never yielded without convincing argument. He was a good man. Member of
church since he was 18.
     In memory of WILLIAM JABAL PRAYTOR (6/12 A, s. of JAS. T. and MARY C.)
born December 30, 1849 in Sumter Co. died in Birmingham, Alabama April 27,
1873. Half orphaned by the war, he lived with his widowed mother and
brothers and sisters. (Was engaged by Southern Express Co.)
     Mr. C. D. ARMSTRONG was drowned in Beach Creek, Dallas Co. last week.
     Mrs. MASSEY, wife of REV. DR. (J. A.) MASSEY, Rector of Trinity
Church, Mobile died very suddenly on 13th.

May 30, 1873
     Mr. JAMES P. KENNARD (46 T) died at the residence of his son-in-law,
DR. M(ICHAEL) C(LAIBORNE) KENNARD (m. his ___ SARAH KENNARD) in Livingston
on 3 May 1873. He was born 27th November 1803 (Mrs. J. copied 1801) in
Williamson Co. Tenn. and was therefore in his 70th year of his age. His
parents being comparatively poor could not give him the advantages of a
good primary education; and so, while quite young, he was placed in a
mercantile house. He was among the first settlers in this county. Having
moved to it in the fall of 1830. He was elected Circuit Court Clerk in
1838 and re-elected in 1842 and 1846, thus filling the office 12 years.
This office was a very lucrative one; and he was thus enabled, by using
strict economy and great industry to pay off a large old debt and accumu-
late a handsome property. He was a kind, obliging and efficient officer.
He was conscientious, honorable, high-toned and Christian gentleman. His
honesty was proverbial. As husband, brother, father and master, he was
ever kind and provident. Joined the Presbyterian Church in this town in
1839; and a few months afterwards was elected Deacon.
     HELEN D. and R. P. NOBLE, adm'rs of EDWARD W. LOVE, deceased.

June 6, 1873
     Died on Sunday morning, June 1, Mr. HENRY OTTO VOSS born in
Berlinchen, Prussia; aged 33. During the war, he was a member of Scott's
La. Cavalry. Merchant.

June 13, 1873
     In Memoriam. THOMAS P. WIGGINS died 17 March 1873. Resolutions by
Western Star Lodge #222.
     COURTNEY BAKER, son of GENERAL ALPHEUS BAKER of Eufaula died sudden-
ly at his father's residence in that city some days ago of congestion of
the brain, aged 20.

June 20, 1873
     JUDGE COCHRAN, a very prominent citizen of Eufaula died suddenly of
cholera morbus a few days ago.

June 27, 1873
     Mrs. FLORENCE FULLER, a sister-in-law of PROF. CONNERLY died at
Summerfield last week. Widow.

July 4, 1873
     Married on 26th at residence of JNO. M. ALEXANDER by R. H. HALE, Mr.
WM. R. ASHLEY to Miss JOSEPHINE A. LOWE.

Died, JOHN MOORE SLEDGE, infant son of MARCUS P. and SUE C. SLEDGE, June 24.

Died on Monday evening the 23, Mr. WM. J. McKERRALL of this county in Tuscaloosa. He was awaiting the graduation of his three daughters at Tuscaloosa Female College. Just one year ago, Mr. McKERRALL lost his wife, who was before her marriage a Miss MONETTE of Hale Co. Ala. We suppose he was about 40 years (Mrs. J. copied 41) of age. We knew him about 15 years ago.

An old citizen of Mobile, AUGUSTUS GIRARD, a man of more than ordinary scientific attainments was drowned accidentally last week.

July 11, 1873

Died at this place Sat. the 5th, LAURA, youngest child of I. C. and M. A. BROWN aged 1 year and 10 months.

Mr. R. W. LAWLER, a former resident of this county died in Coahoma Co. Miss. on June 1. Left a wife and five children who "purpose" returning to Sumter.

July 18, 1873

COL. FRANK L. MILHOUS, a member of the Mobile firm of MILHOUS, SHIELDS & MORRING died in Dallas Co. on 11.

July 25, 1873

JOEL M. KEY, deceased. J. G. HARRIS, administrator.

August 1, 1873

On 23, Miss MATTIE DENT, a former resident of this place was married to CAPT. D. M. CURRIE of Miss. CAPT. CURRIE was formerly employed in the engineering dept. of the A & C Railroad Co. and spent some months in Livingston.

The wife of SENATOR ROBINSON of the Chambers District died on 20th.

Mrs. SALLIE BROWN of Conecuh Co. aged 104 is in good health and quite active.

August 8, 1873

NOTICE TO NON-RESIDENTS:

W. G. LITTLE)	In the Chancery Court
versus)	of
ANN E. SPENCE, et al)	Sumter Co. Ala.

The complainant believes ANN E. SPENCE and her husband, THEODORE SPENCE are non-residents of this state and reside in the state of Arkansas, Argento P.O.; and that ALICE CROOK and her husband MADISON CROOK, EVA GLENN and her husband, JAMES GLENN, MOLLIE MARR and her husband, JAMES MARR and WILLIAM P. HEBBARD are non-residents of this state and reside in West Point (White Co.), Arkansas, except ALICE CROOK and husband, whose P.O. is unknown; and that MOLLIE MARR is under 21 and over 14 and that WILLIAM P. HEBBARD is over 14 and under 21.

August 15, 1873

MELISSA A. LEE)	
versus)	In Chancery
MARY G. WOODALL, et al)	Sumter Co. Ala.

JOHN M. LANSDON of Butler Co. (to Mrs. GLENN) is 96 years old and is still an active farmer. He has a son 70.

There are 13 survivors of the War of 1812 residing in Butler Co., the youngest of whom is 77.

August 22, 1873

Death of CHANCELLOR JAMES B. CLARK. A primitive letter from Blount Springs brings information that HON. JAMES B. CLARK died at that place on Sunday morning of cholera. He filled a prominent place in the Judiciary of the State for many years and the records of the Chancery and Supreme Courts bear testimony of his worth and ability. He was a native of Pa. Bedford County 1796 and was 77 years old at the time he died. Came to Alabama in 1822, having been licensed to practice law a short time previously and settled in Bibb Co. He subsequently settled in Cahaba after having filled one term in the Legislature from Bibb. Engaged in practice of law in Cahaba 8 years and met with great success. From Cahaba he moved to Eutaw, of which place he continued to his death a citizen. In 1863, CHANCELLOR CLARK resigned his office and became a private citizen and after the close of the war, engaged in the practice of law with his son,

116.

MAJ. T. C. CLARK. CHANCELLOR CLARK was perhaps as widely known as any man in Alabama and was universely respected for his honesty and integrity. On the Bench, he was a stern Judge, yielding nothing and compelling the most implicit obedience. As a private gentleman, he was affable and sociable and it was hard to realize that CHANCELLOR CLARK on and off the Bench was the same man. He was a man of untiring application and observed the greatest system in his business and professional engagements. While living, he was honored and respected by the people of Ala. (Selma Times)

HON. WM. M. MEREDITH, Secretary of Treasury under PRESIDENT TAYLOR died on 17th.

JAMES B. IVEY (32 V), an old and prominent citizen of North Sumter died a few days ago.

MOSES MELSEN, a Dallas Co. planter was killed by lightning last week.

MR. BALL, Sheriff of Washington Co. died of apoplexy a few days ago.

DR. W. D. F. KELLY has removed from Birmingham to Demopolis where he has opened a drug store.

On Sat. the 9th, HON. J(OHN) G. PIERCE (24 V) died at the residence of his father, HON. WM. F. PIERCE (48 V) in Eutaw; and on the following Monday, his father died. The son had gone to Blount Springs to recruit his health but growing worse, his father went thither and brought him home. On his return the father contracted cholera at Birmingham or some other point and died.

August 29, 1873

Livingston Female Academy
Miss NELLIE C. GIBBS)
Mrs. M. C. SHORT   )   Principals
            Mrs. M. A. HEDLESTON, music

September 5, 1873

The wife of GOVERNOR WATTS died in Montgomery last Sunday.

JOHN J. YERBY and family have returned from Texas to Pickens Co.

September 12, 1873

Died at her residence near Horn's Bridge, Sept. 6, Mrs. HETTY (HESTER) NIXON, wife of JAMES NIXON, formerly of N. C. and niece of HENRY McDANIEL of this county. She was seriously ill only one week. A faithful and loving wife and mother.

(Orphan's Court Book, 1833, 39 p. 391. Heirs of WM. McDANIEL's est. were ELIZ. C., SARA H., JAS. HOWARD, HESTER HOWARD, HULDY HOWARD, p. 530 gives the wid. as PENELOPE McDANIEL and HENRY McDANIEL and NANCY NOBLE, consort of JEREMIAH NOBLE, both of full age and JAS., HESTER A. and HULDY HOWARD all of whom live outside of the state. Mrs. Jenkins book p. 124. J(OHN) W(ILLIAM) NIXON was born near Wilmington N.C. 16 Nov. 1858. Came to Sumter Co. Ala. when he was 13. His relatives, the McDANIELS had already come to Sumter Co. 1. WILLIAM McDANIEL, father of 2. HULDY McDANIEL, m. CAPT. JOHN HOWARD, mother of 3. HESTER HOWARD, m. JAS. M. NIXON, parents of 4. JOHN WM. NIXON, m. ALICE BOYD.)

NOTICE TO NON-RESIDENTS:
FOSTER M. KIRKSEY, et al)
        versus   )   In Chancery
FRANK P. 3NEDECOR & W. G.)   Sumter Co. Ala.
LITTLE, JR., adm'rs et al)

Believes MARTHA HIBLER, ISAAC SESSUMS, MARTHA SESSUMS and POLLY H. SESSUMS are all non-residents and reside in Miss. MARTHA HIBLER resides somewhere in Noxubee Co. Miss. and the others somewhere in Octibbeha Co. Miss.

MICHAEL GARMAN said to have been 103 died in Calhoun Co. a few days ago. He had been a soldier of the War of 1812.

Mr. ASA HOLT a well-known saloon keeper of Mobile died on Tuesday.

September 19, 1873

Married on the 17th at the residence of the bride's mother by C. S. HENAGAN, Esq. W. W. MITCHELL and MARY A. ESKRIDGE.

Died at Jones' Bluff on 13, ANNIE ROBERTA, youngest child of D. W. and P. A. MITCHELL aged 1 year one month and 17 days.

Died near Bennett's Station Sept. 5, RUFUS REED, infant son of W. T. and M. C. JARMAN aged 1 year 2 months and 1 day.

RUFUS GREENE at one time Grand Master of Masonic Fraternity in this state died recently.

September 26, 1873
    Married on 24th at residence of Mr. I. W. HORN by REV. A. R.
SCARBOROUGH, COL. E. S. GULLEY and Miss CYMANTHA CAMPBELL, all of this
county.
    Died at his residence 10 miles northwest of Gainesville, Ala. Aug. 17,
1873, Mr. JAMES B. IVY (32 V) in his 55th year. Native of Southampton Co.
Va. and remained in that state until 21 years of age when he moved to Tenn.
and from there to Pickens Co. Ala. in 1842. Left an orphan at an early
age. Had few advantages of education. Faults were but human.
    Died Monday night last, WILL LITTLE (45 NC), an old citizen of this
county aged about 67. Was last of four brothers who came to Sumter from
N. C. in 1832.
    REV. THOMAS WALLACE of Congregational Methodist Church residing in
Cleburne Co. aged 65 died on 11th from bite of a rattlesnake.

October 3, 1873
    Mr. U. A. HARRIS of Union, who emigrated to Texas about 12 months
ago has returned to Greene, satisfied "to fight it out on the Alabama
Line."

October 10, 1873
    Mr. FEISTER FOY (32 SC), one of the early settlers of Sumter Co. and
since the war a citizen of Meridian died in that city on the 1st.
    Mrs. McLEROY of Shelby Co. was killed a few days ago by being thrown
from a buggy.

October 17, 1873
    Tribute of respect to Miss ELLA LYNN, who died suddenly; by CUBA
GRANGE of the Patrons of Husbandry.
    On 10th of Nov. the administrator will sell lands of J. C. BENNETT,
deceased.

October 24, 1873
    We regret to learn that COL. L(AUNCELOT) V. UNDERWOOD (41 NC), an
old and prominent citizen of Sumter died a few days ago after a brief
illness.
    Mr. CHARLES WILLIAMS, formerly of Selma was murdered by a negro in
Marengo Co. a few days ago.

October 31, 1873
    From Demopolis News-Journal: Died in Baltimore Oct. 21 of heart
disease, REV. F(RANCIS) R. HANSON. Came to Ala. in early days of her
history. (Prot. Epis. - Cred. in Greene Co. June 1839. Rector of St.
John's Church, b. Greene Co. 1845.)
    Dr. KENDALL, Lowndes Co. and his sister of Dallas Co. have become
heirs to $40,000 in La.
    Mr. ALEX. P. HOGAN, who left Tuscaloosa many years ago for a western
state has returned to his old home satisfied there is no better country
than this.
    MAJ. S. F. MILLER, a gentleman well-known in this state died last
Wed. at Columbus, Ga. He was many years editor of a Whig paper at
Tuscaloosa.

November 7, 1873
    Estate of PRUDENCE LOWRY (40 T, w. of VERNAL, 43 NC), deceased.
D. W. MITCHELL, adm'r.
    HON. THOMAS J. JUDGE (Lowndes Co., 34 SC) has removed from Montgomery
to Greenville.
    On 20th, the wife of DR. McGEHEE near Fayetteville died from effects
of burns, from kerosene lamp.

November 14, 1873
    Married by REV. A. R. SCARBOROUGH on the 6th at the residence of the
bride's father, Mr. L. A. McLAIN to Miss EMMA TURNER all of this county.
    Lands of the estate of JOHN RITTER, deceased near Warsaw for sale.
    Mr. M. F. COKER a Tuscaloosa carpenter who had been putting up some
buildings here died last week.
    Mrs. SARAH HALL aged 103 died in Conecuh County the other day.

November 21, 1873
    Died on the 18th near Livingston, Mrs. MARY A. V. SPROTT, wife of
JOHN SPROTT in her 21st year.
    MAJ. E. C. ELMORE, Ex-Treasurer of the Confederate States died in
Pensacola on the 13th.

November 28, 1873
    PRUDENCE LOWRY, deceased. Joint owners of land: D. W. MITCHELL,
administrator; PRUDENCE MITCHELL (5 A), S. E. MITCHELL, CATHARINE KENNEDY
(@ 13 A), VERNAL LOWRY (7 A) and the children of MARY KENNARD (20 Miss.),
deceased. Land in South Carolina.

December 5, 1873
    Married on the 25th, Mr. JAS. A. ALLEN of Birmingham and Mrs. SUSAN
LANG of Ramsey's Station, this county.
    Mr. JAMES R. SMITH (34 NC), lately an old resident of Sumter died
on Deer Creek, Miss. on 19th after a brief illness.
    REV. C. P. RODEFER, who some 3 years ago had charge for a short time
of St. James' Parish, Livingston is now located in Franklin, Tenn.
    FRANK A. MONROE, editor of Conecuh-Escambia Star was married on the
20th to Miss NURSIE A. AUTREY.
    Estate of HUDSON P. LIPSCOMB, SR., HUDSON P. LIPSCOMB, JR., adm'r.

December 12, 1873
    Married at the residence of Mrs. CATHARINE DEAN, this county on 10th
by REV. J. S. FRIERSON, CAPT. M. V. MITCHEL of Polk Co. Mo. and Mrs. JULIA
E. HUMPHRIES of Sumter.
    Died of pneumonia in Livingston on 7 Dec. DR. JOSEPH A. SMITH (35 NC)
aged about 61. A second time within a few weeks has death visited the
family of which he was a member. On Nov. 19, JAMES R. SMITH, formerly of
this county died on Deer Creek, Miss. at the age of 58. Remains deposited
alongside grave of his mother. Graduate of U of Pa. 1834, department of
medicine. In 1836, he removed from Wayne Co. N. C. the home of his ancestors to Livingston, Ala.
    MAJOR A. J. PHARES, formerly of this county is now enroute to Sumter
Co. Florida.
    JOSEPH J. LITTLE, deceased. Estate insolvent.
    CHARLES COOKE, administrator of V. R. SOULE (is this Va., w. of
JOHN M.?), deceased. Final settlement of estate.
    Mr. ROBERT HATTEN of Tuscaloosa, formerly of Livingston has opened
a branch of his saddlery establishment in Meridian, Miss.

December 19, 1873
    Married by REV. A. R. SCARBOROUGH on 17th at residence of the bride's
father, Mr. J. C. GILES of Mississippi to Miss FANNIE LEARD of this county.
    Died on the 9th, Mr. AUSTIN PRESTWOOD (53 G) in his 77th year, at
the residence of his son, NEWTON PRESTWOOD (18 A) near Livingston.
    Sale of personal property of ASA JOHNSON, deceased. HAMILTON P.
SNOW, administrator.

December 26, 1873
    Sale of personal property of WILLIAM J. McKERALL, deceased. 7. W
WOODRUFF, administrator.

January 2, 1874
    Married on 28 December 1873 at M. E. Church South, Belmont, Ala. by
REV. J. M. PATTON, Mr. JOHN C. PHARES to Miss BELLE TUTT, all of Sumter
Co.
    Married on the 29th December 1873 at the residence of Mrs. PHARES by
REV. J. M. PATTON, Mr. H. H. HOPPER of Mobile to Miss E. O. PHARES of
Sumter Co.
    Z. W. WOODRUFF, administrator of MARY E. McKERRALL, deceased.

January 9, 1874
    Married on 23rd in Mobile by REV. DR. BURGETT, D. P. BESTOR and
NELLIE, daughter of G. W. TARLETON.
    From Los Angeles (Cal.) Express of Nov. 28 we copy the following
notice respecting the death of a former citizen of Sumter, well known to
many of our readers: "Funeral of ANDREW GLASSELL (57 V), Sr. took place
this morning from the residence of his son and was attended by a large

concourse of friends. Mr. GLASSELL was 80 years and 6 months old at the time of his death and had lived in this city about 6 years. Born in Virginia, he served in the War of 1812 and at the time of his death was one of the veteran pensioners of that war. Well preserved old gentleman and retained his full faculties to the end. His recollection of the stirring events of his early years was remarkable and his reminiscenses were invested with deep interest by clearness of his faculties and his graphic powers of relation."

January 16, 1874
Married on the 1st at the residence of the bride's father near Warsaw by REV. JAMES SOMMERVILLE, Mr. J. K. SPENCE of Pickens and Miss BETTIE STANTON of Sumter.
Married on the 1st near Warsaw by REV. A. C. GROVE, Mr. MAJOR LYON of Pickens and Miss ELLA WESTON of Sumter.
On the 21 at the residence of the bride's father, JOHN E. BROWN by REV. L. M. STONE, Mr. A. C. REYNOLDS of Mobile and Miss ELLA BROWN of Livingston.
On the 8th at the residence of Dr. W. G. LITTLE near Warsaw by REV. J. S. FRIERSON, Mr. C. J. BROCKWAY and Miss CARRIE LITTLE, daughter of the late BEN B. LITTLE, Esq. all of Sumter.

January 23, 1874
DR. GASTON DRAKE of Selma has removed to Florida where he will join his son and his son-in-law, A. J. PHARES of Sumter.
U. H. USTICK died in Walker County, Texas on the 21st. We have no doubt the person referred to in the above notice from an exchange is EDWD. H(ARRIS) USTICK (37 V), a former old and well known citizen of this county; inasmuch as he was living in Walker Co. Texas and had long been suffering from a chronic disease. He was an old time printer and a brother of our late townsman, W(ILLIAM) K(ING) USTICK, Esq. (Sons of JOHN GANO USTICK and wife JANE BERRY; grandsons of JAS. and ELIZ. BERRY. See USTICK chart in REV. MOSELEY's records.)
Mr. JOHN KENNEDY (33 NC), a former citizen of this county, who settled in Sumterville neighborhood some 40 years ago died last Sunday night at the residence of his son, DR. S(IDNEY) P. KENNEDY (19 A) at Lauderdale, Miss.
Estate of ROBERT BRADSHAW, deceased. JOHN W. BRADSHAW, executor of will.

January 30, 1874
JOSEPH ARRINGTON, one of Sumter's most industrious planters has determined to move to Coahoma Co. Miss. where he recently purchased a plantation.
Estate of JOSEPH A. SMITH, deceased. Sumter Co. Ala. Notice to JOHN T. SMITH, S. A. E. SMITH, MARY A. HOUSTON, KATE W. BEASLEY, MOLLIE TARTT, R. B. S. SMITH, EVELINE SMITH, LANGDON SMITH, EDWARD SMITH, MATTIE SMITH, STEPHEN EARNEST SMITH, JOSEPH SMITH and HELEN SMITH, non-resident heirs.

February 6, 1874
EDMOND JOURDAN, who recently died in Etoway County was 105 years old. (1 EDWD. JORDAN @ 71 b. N.C. lived in Dekalb Co. 1850 Census.)

February 13, 1874
MAJ. J. B. GRAYSON, a former worthy citizen of Sumter has removed to Demopolis.

February 20, 1874
GEN. QUARLES of Tennessee has been spending some days in Livingston visiting his son, G. M. QUARLES, Esq.

February 27, 1874
HON. E(DWD.) W. SMITH (23 NC), an old and distinguished citizen of Livingston and Representative from Sumter County in the Legislature 1870-1871 died at his residence in this place on Wed. night.
Tribute of respect to memory of EDWARD W. SMITH, who died yesterday, Feb. 25th. Bar of Livingston.

Mr. I. M. LANDSON(JOHN M. LANSDON on p. 51), an aged citizen of Butler County aged 94 was found dead about 2 miles from his home on the 14th. Greenville Advocate makes mention of his children.

March 6, 1874
Estate of GEORGE DENTON, deceased. STEPHEN TOMPKINS, adm'r.
JOHN W. SWILLEY, deceased. F. P. SNEDECOR, adm'r.
GEN. C. A. BATTLE has removed to Texas.

March 13, 1874
Died in this county on the 8th, THOMAS A. KENNARD (17 A, THOMAS O. in Census), son of the late JAMES P. KENNARD (46 T) in his 41st year.
DR. JAMES C. HOUSTON, formerly of this place but now of Mobile is spending a few days with Livingston friends.

March 27, 1874
JOHN C. GILLESPIE, formerly of this place is living in Bryan, Texas.
Died in Gainesville, Ala. March 16th, Mrs. DORA O. HARRIS, wife of YOUNG W. HARRIS.
Mrs. M. M. GARROTT of Marion has removed to Texas.

April 3, 1874
Married in Meridian on the 22nd by Elder L. M. STONE, Mr. ELNATHAN TARTT and Miss DELIA WALKER both of Lauderdale, Miss.
IN CHANCERY: FRANCES OLIVER versus JESSE OLIVER. JESSE OLIVER is a resident of Lauderdale Co. Miss. and is over 21.
SARAH E. BOLTON, administratrix of M. F. BOLTON, deceased.

April 10, 1874
Died in Sumter Co. Ala. on March 30 at the house of his father-in-law, Mr. MARK PARKER (25 A), EDWIN CHURCHILL GIBBS (6 A), oldest son of the late EDWIN (30 V) and LOUISA GIBBS (30 V). Born Feb. 3, 1844 and was married January 10, 1872 to Miss MARY PARKER. Cumberland Presbyterian. For a time, he was the chief stay of his widowed mother and her children.

April 17, 1874
COL. W. M. STONE, of Meridian (formerly of Livingston) spent a day or two here.
Married at the residence of the bride's father, Mr. JOHN E. BROWN on the 14th by REV. J. B. HAMBERLIN assisted by REV. L. L. LURTON, Mr. E. B. LURTON of Clarkesville, Tennessee and Miss CLARA R. BROWN of Livingston.
Married in Choctaw County on the 25 of March, BENJ. W. LANCASTER, youngest son of J. L. and A. C. LANCASTER to Miss ELIZA JOHNSON, youngest daughter of the late SAMUEL JOHNSON. (She is buried in cemetery at York, "Mrs. ELIZA H., wife of B. W. LANCASTER. b. Perry Co. Ala. Nov. 26, 1850 d. at York Oct. 5, 1884.)
NOTICE TO NON-RESIDENTS:
ELIAS MIDDLETON)
    versus   )   Sumter Co. Ala.
CHARLES SIMPSON)   Attachment
CHARLES SIMPSON resides in Meridian, Miss.
ANDREW M. WINDLE (56 V), an old citizen of Pickens County died on the 5th in his 80th year.
Mrs. ELIZA WEST of Marion, Perry Co. died suddenly Thursday morning with apoplexy.

May 1, 1874
CAPT. BLASSENGAME NABORS (65 SC Shelby Co. Census 1850), for many years a citizen of Shelby County died on the 5th in Bibb County aged 87.

May 8, 1874
Estate of EDWIN C. GIBBS, deceased. Notice to non-resident heirs: STITH GIBBS (2 A), ALICE SILLIMAN and her husband, W. A. SILLIMAN, CHARLES GIBBS and ANN GIBBS. MARY E. GIBBS produced the will for probate.

May 15, 1874
JAMES KERR (42 Scot.), an old citizen of Pickens County died on the 3rd.

May 22, 1874
Mr. JOEL EARLY MATTHEWS (40 G), a citizen of Dallas since 1831 died in Selma on the 11th.
Married on the 13th at the residence of REV. A. R. SCARBOROUGH, by REV. J. M. PATTON, Mr. WM. H. HAWKINS and Miss ALICE G. SCARBOROUGH, all of this county.
ELIZABETH D. HARWOOD, deceased. SAMUEL B. M. HARWOOD, administrator with will annexed.

May 29, 1874
S(IDNEY) T. PRINCE and wife of Choctaw clebrated the anniversary of their marriage among relatives in this place last night.
Aunt POLLY THOMAS (47 SC) of Calhoun County aged 73 walks 9 miles and carries produce for sale.
Mr. F. M. WEEMS of Butler County (to Mrs. GLENN) was lying at the point of death a few days ago from effects of a wound received in the battle of Sharpsburg more than 10 years ago.

June 5, 1874
Married on the 28th at the residence of the bride's father, F. B. MOORE by REV. CALDWELL, Mr. S. P. BURKE of Garner's Station, Miss. and Miss SALLIE P. MOORE of Sumter Co. Ala.
W. E. COOKSEY near Seale is 87; and his wife is 77. They were married in 1816. (1 WM. E. COOKSEY rec'd land grant, was of 1812. See Vol. 121, p. 10. 1 WM. COOKSEY in 1850 Russell Co. 63 NC.)

June 12, 1874
Died (57/1817) of pneumonia near Warsaw, June 3, Mrs. TABITHA ROGERS (33 NC), consort of JOSEPH ROGERS (44 NC) aged about 57, Greenville (Mrs. GLENN) papers please copy.
Mr. THOMAS H. KENNEDY has removed to Little Rock, Ark. He was of Meridian and formerly of Sumter Co. Ala.

June 19, 1874
Died on the 15th at his residence in Sumter County, Mr. HUGH LEMON in his 48th year.

June 26, 1874
Married June 14 at Soule Chapel, M. E. Church South by REV. ALEX. HOOD, DR. HAMET PINSON, late of Arkansas and Miss ANNIE GILBERT of Sumter Co.

July 3, 1874
Mr. WILLIAM R. RAMSEY (14 A, s. of AMBROSE K. 55 NC) died near Ramsey's Station on the 26th.
ARCHIBALD TYSON (45 NC) an old citizen of Lowndes died June 23, of cancer of the face.
JAMES BRANTLEY, a citizen of Escambia County was shot and killed by JAMES HAYS at Garland on the 18th.

July 10, 1874
DR. R(EUBEN) P(ARKER) VAIL (35 NC), a former resident of Sumter died in Meridian last Sunday.
Mr. W. L. CAIN of Gadsden on the 17th took a fatal dose of strychnine through a mistake for quinine.
GEN. JAMES CANTLEY, a well known citizen of Alabama died at his house in Russell County on the 30th (From Mobile Graphic).
The venerable DR. LOVICK PIERCE, 90 years old and foremost in the Southern Methodist Church is seriously ill at Macon, Ga.

July 17, 1874
HENRY HENDRICK (45 NC), an old and esteemed citizen of Choctaw Co. died on the 3rd.
DR. H. H. HIPPLE of Hale Co. was drowned on the 2nd.
MARION F. LEEMAN, MISSOURI M. LEEMAN, JAMES LEEMAN, non-residents and next of kin of HUGHEY LEEMAN, deceased. NANCY A. LEEMAN, widow of deceased filed petition to probate will.

July 24, 1874
Mr. K(ENNY) C. HALL, an old citizen of this county died at Cuba Station last Sunday aged about 58.

July 31, 1874
CAPT. J. A. MOORING, of the House of Shields & Mooring, Mobile, died week before last. Remains brought to Sumter for burial. Was old and well known citizen of Sumter. Was one of our Representatives in the Legislature 1870-71.

August 7, 1874
Estate of VIRGINIA R. SOULS (21 A, w. of JOHN M. 36 Maine), deceased. ROBERT HIBBLER, administrator.
Estate of J. V. BARRET, deceased. ROBERT HIBBLER, administrator.
Estate of JAMES I. WINDHAM, deceased. ROBERT HIBBLER, administrator.
DR. B. HAWKINS, Dentist. Advertisement.

August 14, 1874
Mrs. BETTIE M. WILLIAMS, formerly Miss PINK. GILLESPIE of Livingston died in Bryan, Texas on the 30th.
THOMAS BASS killed CARROLL BAXTER in Madison Co. a few days ago.
W. H. ELLIS found dead in his field on 31st.
Mr. and Mrs. DeVANE of Greenville (to Mrs. GLENN), for several years divorced, were re-married last week.

August 21, 1874
Mr. and Mrs. JOSEPH AKERMAN of Selma died last week, one on Sunday and the other the next day.

August 28, 1874
We have been shown a letter from Mr. JOS. ARRINGTON, formerly of Sumter, now of Coahoma County, Mississippi in which he gives a gloomy account of the drouth.
CAPT. J. W. MONETTE, a former resident of Livingston, now of Mobile spent a few days here with old friends.
SAMUEL THOMPSON, deceased. F. L. STARNES, administrator.
J. A. MOORING, deceased. T. A. MOORING, administrator.
NOTICE TO NON-RESIDENTS:
CHARLES COOKE and wife SUSAN)
                versus   )   In Chancery Court of
JOHN V. MOORE and   )   Sumter Co. Alabama
JOHN R. MOORE   )
JOHN V. MOORE is a non-resident; resides in New Orleans, La.
CANDIDATES:
T. W. BROADHURST, NEWTON PRESTWOOD, SIMON HALL, R. H. HALE, SAMUEL WILLIAMSON, For Tax Collector.
J. E. WESTCOTT, ZAC. TUREMAN, JAMES M. HENEGAN, JOSEPHUS WALLACE, G. BEDFORD SAUNDERS, For Circuit Clerk.
TURNER D. BELL, J. L. LANCASTER, EUGENE M. SHAW, W. R. DELOACH, For Tax Assessor.
D. W. MITCHELL, J. E. CUSACK, W. D. BATTLE, For Sheriff.
G. W. DAINWOOD, R. S. MASON, J. L. SCRUGGS, For County Treasurer.
GEORGE WILLIAM TORRY, CHARLES COOKE, COL. I. C. BROWN, B. B. THOMAS, WILLIAM BEGGS, A. R. SCARBOROUGH, E. H. NELSON, For Probate Judge.

September 4, 1874
Commissioner's Sale of Land on 31 October. Certain land in Sumter County, the following named being joint owners thereof: WILLIAM MEADOR, CORA E. LANDRUM, J. W. LANDRUM, MARY AGNES LANDRUM and SALLIE G. LANDRUM. J. G. MICHAEL, WM. McPHERSON, WM. McRAE, JACOB SPIDLE, R. D. HOOT, Commissioners.
Estate of ISABELLA GILMORE (see XLV 36, Tenn. III 68), deceased. A. J. DERBY, administrator. Sale of land.
JAMES A. POWELL, deceased. REUBEN CHAPMAN, JR., administrator.

September 11, 1874
THOMAS B. STONE, County Treasurer.
NORVAL E. DINKINS--school for little children.

September 4, 1874
CAPT. JOHN B. STONE, now residing in Texas but formerly of Dallas has given CAPT. DEDMAN's Selma Co. $900 with which to equip themselves.

September 18, 1874
Final settlement of guardianship. WILLIAM O. WINSTON, guardian of
ANNIE B. GILBERT, a minor who has intermarried with one HAMMET PINSON
filed accounts.
Final settlement of estate of WILLIAM GILBERT, deceased by
WILLIAM O. WINSTON, administrator.

September 25, 1874
Married on the 8th by REV. J. M. PATTON, Mr. L. A. PREWETT and
MISS L. O. PUGH, all of Sumter Co.
DR. A. G. GROVE of Warsaw will preach in the Methodist Church at
Livingston next Sunday.
J. V. BARRETT, deceased, CHARLES COOKE, adm'r.
WILLIAM O. WINSTON, guardian of FLANK C. BALLARD filed accounts
and vouchers for final settlement of guardianship.

October 2, 1874
Died on the 14th at her residence in this county, MRS. NANCY TIDMORE
(31 A, wife of MARK 40 SC) in her 57th year. Greensboro Beacon and
Marion Commonwealth copy.
MR. WM. E. WASHINGTON (45), an old and widely known citizen of
Sumter died at his residence at Washington's store on the 24th ult.

October 9, 1874
MR. JOHN SPROTT, an estimable citizen residing near this place died
Wednesday morning.

October 16, 1874
Died near Butler, Choctaw County September 27th after a protracted
illness, ANNA S. (11A) wife of MR. W. H. JOHNSTON. Deceased was a
daughter of the late S(tephen) W. MURLEY (37 SC) of Livingston and was
greatly esteemed for her many virtues. Her family has our sincere
condolence.
Estate of WILLIAM E. WASHINGTON, deceased. Notice to
JOHN WASHINGTON and JAMES WASHINGTON and to the other children of
JOSIAH WASHINGTON, deceased whose names are unknown, all of whom are
non-residents and next of kin of WILLIAM E. WASHINGTON, deceased. You
will take notice that JOHN B. WASHINGTON has this day filed his petition
praying the court to probate a certain paper purporting to be the last
will and testament of W. E. WASHINGTON.
ELISHA FLETCHER COX, SARAH WIGGINS, by next friend, CALVIN WIGGINS
versus W. H. NEVILLE, as adm'r et al., Chancery Court Sumter Co., Ala.
By affidavit of T. D. COBBS; states he believes that MARTIN V. LACY
and JOHN BROWNING are non-residents, but that their residence is
unknown.
MR. CHARLES BALL, an honest man, a worthy citizen and obliging
neighbor died at his residence near this place last Sat. Tribute of
respect to his memory by Livingston Lodge #41. "Kind husband and
indulgent father."

October 20, 1874
W. E. BARRINGER will repair wagons, carriages etc. Livingston,
Alabama.
J. G. WHITFIELD offers his residence in Livingston for sale.

November 6, 1874
For rent--a valuable plantation of about 500 acres on Sumterville
and Livingston Road. Apply to J. C. HODGES, living near said place;
or to A. W. COCKRELL, Esq., Livingston; or to MRS. F. L. McCAIN at
Sumterville.

November 13, 1874
Married October 29, 1874 at the residence of the bride's mother at
Garrett's Mills by REV. L. M. PATTERSON, MR. JOSEPH J. HILMAN of Sumter
and MISS EMMA R. GARRETT of Greene Co, Eutaw, Ala. Whig and Observer
please copy.

November 27, 1874
J. C. RICHARDSON, formerly Principal of Livingston Male Academy was
married in Greenville on the 12th to MISS BETTIE McCALL.

Estate of JOHN P. EVANS, deceased. This day came THEODOSIA A. MOORING, executrix of will of J. A. MOORING, deceased and filed vouchers for final settlement of her testator's administration on estate of J. P. EVANS.

A. G. SMITH, administrator de bonis non of NANCY E. SMITH, deceased.

D. J. GAINES of Conecuh Co. was killed on the 15th by parties unknown.

FELIX E. REID (14 A s of A. M. REED) of Butler Co. died on the 3rd from effects of accidental burn.

GABRIEL MATHIS of Dale Co. is 91 and his wife is 86 and they have been married 64 years.

MR. JAMES CUNNINGHAM of Mobile took an overdose of morphine on the 17th and died shortly afterward.

December 4, 1874
Died at Brewersville Nov. 27th of complicated meningetis and diphtheria, B. B. SEALE, JR., youngest son of B. B. and M. F. SEALE aged 2 years 7 months.

Married on the 3 at residence of bride's mother in Livingston, by REV. A. J. COLEMAN, MR. W. K. PICKENS and MISS FANNIE W. SHORT, all of this place.

Estate of NANCY E. HOUSTON, deceased. A. G. SMITH, adm'r. Married on the 25th in Kemper Co. Miss. by REV. H. D. WHITE, MR. J. J. GREENLEE of Sumter Co. and MISS CORA McCAIN of Kemper Co. Miss.

December 11, 1874
Married Thursday Nov. 12 at the residence of the bride's father by REV. W. F. POND, DR. JAMES H. O'HARA to MISS ROSA WALTON, all of Choctaw Co.

At the residence of the bride's mother on 9 December by REV. J. M. PATTON, DR. D. U. PATTON and MISS ALICE BOLTON all of Sumter Co.

Died on 7 Nov. at his residence near Gaston in this county, SOLOMON WARD (39 NC, Greene Co. Cen) aged 64. Born in Carteret Co. N. C. and married in Greene, now Hale Co. Ala. ANN HALL (28 NC) a niece of ARCHIBALD HALL (58 NC, Sumter Co. cen), an old and respected citizen who lived for many years and died in Sumter Co. His wife and several children live to mourn his loss (see marriage in vol. 94, p. 32, m. in Greene Co., lic. dated 23 Dec., 1839).

Sale of real estate and personal property under the will of RICHARD B. LONG, deceased late of Sumter Co.
THOMAS M. LONG, executor
PRISCILLA LONG, executrix

December 18, 1874
Married on 13th at Jones' Bluff by L. LEWIS, Esq., MAJOR CHARLES PAXTON of A & C. R. R. and MRS. ROSA SHIRLEY of Georgia.

Died on the 12th near Sumterville, MR. W(illiam) M. Hale (35 T), an old and esteemed citizen.

SHERRIFF'S SALE:
ANN K. DUKE versus PHIL. May et al.
JULIETTE VAN DE GRAFF deceased. JOHN McINNIS, adm'r.
WILLIAM O. WINSTON, guardian of MARTHA HIBBLER, who has recently intermarried with one W. A. COOK filed vouchers for final settlement of guardianship.
Estate of N. J. DILLARD, deceased. GEORGE A. DILLARD, admr.

December 25, 1874
Married on the 17th at the residence of the bride's father by REV. GEORGE BANCROFT, MR. J. M. ALEXANDER and MISS HELEN McALPINE, all of this county.

Died at her home on December 15 after a short illness. CAROLINE M. CLARY, wife of LEONIDAS CLARY aged 34. Left a husband and 2 children.

Tribute of respect to memory of WILLIAM M. HALE, deceased by Hermon Lodge, F. A. M.

After a residence of several years in Louisiana, MR. JOHN T. SMITH again becomes a citizen of this county.

MR. B. S. BARKER, Intendant of Livingston died at early hour Monday morning. Health had been failing several months.

MR. W. P. BREWER who moved to Louisiana soon after the surrender, this week returned to Sumter to stay.

NOTICE TO NON-RESIDENTS:

JOHN McINNIS, Admr. of   )   In Chancery Court
JULIETTE VAN DE GRAFF   )   Sumter Co.
      versus   )   Ala.
WM. FLEMING et al   )

The defendants, WILLIAM FLEMING, MARY C. ORME and her husband, HENRY ORME are non-residents; that Fleming resides in Woodford Co., Ky., Midway P.O.; said MARY C. and HENRY ORME reside in Los Angeles, Cal. and that Los Angeles is their P.O.

January 1, 1875

JONES BASS of Crenshaw Co. has 26 living children.

MR. JOHN PARISH of Perry Co. was killed last week by a horse falling on him.

MR. JOHN CLAYTON ot Pickens Co. is 86; was married to his present wife in 1814 and at the late election rode several miles to vote the Democratic ticket.

"GRANDMA" BULLARD of Bullock Co. aged 81 was about starting for Texas last week, but on reaching the depot at Union Springs she broke her leg and trip was postponed.

NOTICE OF APPLICATION:

To JOHN C. EVANS (5 A), HALLY wife of W. B. W. GEORGE, THOMAS J. EVANS, FRANK M. EVANS and MARY S. EVANS, heirs-at-law of JOHN P. EVANS, deceased.

Married on the 23rd at the residence of the bride's father, in Livingston by REV. JOSHUA HEARD, MR. J. B. CHAPFIELD of Meridian, Miss. and MISS IMOGENE NORVILL of this place.

HON. LUTHER R. SMITH has removed to Bladon Springs.

MR. GEORGE R. REYNOLDS (45 K) of Pickens County has over 100 living descendants, 14 children, 90 grandchildren and great grandchildren. Has 11 sons-in-law.

January 8, 1875

Married on 31 at Cuba Station by REV. A. L. McBRYDE, MR. R. P. CLAY and MISS ELLA HALL. Selma papers please copy.

January 1, 1875

Last Sunday BISHOP MARVIN (M. E. Church) preached the funeral sermon of the late JUDGE WM. E. BYRD (com E 375 C) in Selma.

January 15, 1875

IRENE LARKIN, guardian of WILLIAM R. LARKIN, MARY C. LARKIN, MARY C. LARKIN and BETTIE LARKIN, minors. Petitions the court to sell real estate in Mobile belonging to said minors.

January 22, 1875

Estate of JOSEPHINE SIMS, deceased. Sheriff's Sale.

HON. R. H. ERWIN, Senator from Wilcox died a few days ago.

January 29, 1875

We learn that JAMES D. TUREMAN died at the residence of MR. LIPSCOMB a few miles from town on the 16th. Had been a most gallant Confederate soldier; was a good mechanic and well-disposed man, but unfortunately had an uncontrollable appetitie for strong drink, which marred his usefullness.

Married on the 21 at residence of MR. ----PREWITT, Sumter Co. by L. LEWIS, Esq., MR. WILLIAM TUCKER and MISS ALICE RHINEHART.

Died on the 9th near St. Stephens, Washington Co., REV. THOMAS I. FLLIOTT (58 T) aged 76 years and 6 days. For 30 years, the deceased resided near Gaston, this county.

February 5, 1875

On Monday, MR. JOHN HALL, watchman for the R. R. Bridge at Jones' Bluff lost his life. Drowned, Native of Greene Co. and had been a member of Capt. Gould's Co. 20th Alabama Regiment.

MR. NAT. ROBINSON was found dead near Opelika last week. Head was lying in a branch and it was supposed he drowned.

February 12, 1875
     Tribute of respect to memory to RICHARD E. FAIRES by Western Star Lodge #222.
     WILLIAM WELDON shot and killed his father in Chilton Co.
     REV. JAMES DeLOACH (46 SC) of Pickens Co. died on 26th.

February 19, 1875
     MR. JEREMIAH HORN (Tenn II 67, sent to Gwen Horn), father of COL. A(lex?) G. HORN (sold printing press 1838), Editor of Meridian Mercury died in this county on night of 9th aged 82. Native of Edgecomb (now Wilson) Co. N. C. and moved to this county in 1834. Some 25 years ago, he removed to East Miss. where he resided up to time of his death. He was a man of great probity of character and enjoyed the respect of all who knew him.
     JUDGE (illeg) L. B. STRANGE (38 SC; m in Mtgy Co. 1840 Hemutial Westmoreland) died suddenly near Tuskegee a few days ago.
     Will of JACOB HORN - Edgecombe Co. N.C. probated 1827 the names
     Daus. MELICENT FARMER, MOURNING COBB, EDI SIMMS
     Sons JEREMIAH, THOMAS, HENRY, JOSIAH R., WILLIAM
     Gr-son THOMAS HORN and his sister SALLY
     G-dau POLLY TUCKER ARMSTEAD
     STEPHENS CROOM, Esq. was married to MISS MARY H. MARSHALL in Mobile on 3rd.
     MRS. W. A. COPE of Bullock Co. was fatally burned week before last.
     MRS. ELIZABETH HOWELL of Pickens County aged 80 has 9 sons and 5 daughters living and all members of the church. Seven of her sons were in the Confederate army.

February 26, 1875
     Married on the 17 at the residence of MR. JOS. GREENLEE by REV. A. R. SCARBOROUGH, MR. THOS. FITZPATRICK and MISS BELLE GREENLEE, all of this county.
     PATTIE C. JOHNSON, administratrix of B. P. HUNTER, deceased. Administratrix sale.

March 5, 1875
     JOHN McINNIS (42 NC), an old citizen of Sumter and former Representative on the Legislature died at his residence 10 miles north of this place Tue. night last.
     HARRIET S. PIPKIN, deceased. ABNER R. SCARBOROUGH, executor of her will.
     M. C. KINNARD, guardian of SUSAN F. BURTON, a minor.
     L. B. HALE, deceased. JOHN W. HALE, admr.
     JAMES M. MAYES, deceased. JOHN W. ALTMAN, admr.

March 12, 1875
     MARCUS PARKER versus RACHEL SHELTON et al.
     D. R. KIRKLAND-confectioner.
     DR. WILLIAM DALE (43 SC) of Wilcox was killed on 24th by falling tree.
     DR. S. N. FERGUSON, a pioneer citizen of Pickens Co. committed suicide on 17th.

March 19, 1875
     On 3rd, MR. BEN W. LITTLE of Sumter married MISS EMMA F. SOMERVILLE of Pickens Co.
     DR. JAMES R. MILLS of Choctaw Co. has removed to Dallas, Texas.
     EMMET L. WOOTEN, a printer died in Marion on 9th. Young man of promise.
     MRS. PRATT, widow of the late DANIEL PRATT died recently in Prattville, Ala. Native of New Hampshire, aged 74.

March 26, 1875
     MR. ALEXANDER S. WILSON, son of MR. GEORGE WILSON, who was stricken with paralysis last summer died from an apoplectic stroke Sunday night.

March 12, 1875
    "HON. BEN. EDWARDS GRAY died at Bellevue, Dallas County on the
night of the 1st."

April 2, 1875
    "GEN. T. E. McIVER died in Dallas Co. on the 8th aged 98."
    "MRS. ELIZABETH CLAY died in Dallas County on the 21st in her 80th
year."
    Married on 31st at residence of MR. BASSEN near Livingston by
REV. J. S. FRIERSON, MR. HUGH W. GREENLEE and MISS KATE C. COBLENTZ,
all of this county.
    MISS RODY BYNUM (62 SC; seems to be w. of John Bynum) of Blount Co.
aged 88 has removed to Texas.
    Elder Z. H. GORDON, the father of Senator GORDON of Ga. is a
resident of Seale, Russell Co. Ala. He has been in Baptist ministry
over 50 years; is 79 years of age and has baptised over 1000 persons.

April 9, 1875
    Married on 9th at residence of bride's father by REV. J. S.
FRIERSON, MR. A. P. EVANS and MISS J. H. JENKINS, all of this co.
    Estate of YANCEY MITCHELL, deceased. ANDERSON LIPSCOMB, executor
of will.
    JAMES B. STANSEL of Pickens Co. has removed to Macon (Noxubee Co),
Miss.
    M. A. GRISSOM under indictment for murder died in Mobile jail
Monday.
    On 26th, THOMAS CANTWELL was killed by W. B. NOLAND in Pickens Co.

April 16, 1875
    "MRS. MARY L. HARDEE of Dallas Co. widow of the late GENERAL HARDEE
died in St. Augustine, Fla. on the 6th."
    "COL. GEORGE W. GAYLE (44 SC), an old and prominent citizen of
Dallas, died last Saturday."
    MR. H. MEARS and family have removed from Port Huron, Mich. to
Huntsville, Ala.

April 23, 1875
    Died Feb. 10th at residence of her father, MR. J. C. DAVIDSON near
Belmont, this county, MRS. VIRGINIA CARDEN aged 21.
    WILLIAM O. WINSTON, guardian of TEXANNA BALLARD, WALTER R. BALLARD
and WILLIAM C. BALLARD, minors. Final settlement of guardianship.
    JOHN LAWLEY of Coosa Valley is father of 21 children, 11 he has
seen married.

April 30, 1875
    MRS. ISABELLA RAVESIES, widow of late F. P. RAVESIES and her 3 sons,
MESSRS, EDMUND, A. H. and FRED RAVESIES and her daughter, MISS MINNIE;
MR. HENRY McRAE, wife and 3 children; MRS. EUGENIA, wife of
CAPT. A. H. RAVESIES and servant; and two of MR. EDMOND RAVESIES'
children left Greensboro last week for Florida. They purpose settling
in Hernando Co. Fla. (Marengo Co. Ala marriages book I, p. 281--F. P.
Ravises to Isabella Strudwick--June 11, 1833--vol. 186, p. 17)

May 7, 1875
    Died on 2nd at his residence near Brewersville, THOMAS J. WIMBERLEY
(42 NC) in his 67th year.

May 14, 1875
    "JOSEPH N. ESKRIDGE who killed Brantley in Mississippi two or
three years ago is to be hanged on 18th of June. Both were from
Dallas Co."
    An interesting daughter of MR. R. W. ENNIS aged about 6 years
died of diphtheria on 28th
    DR. JOSEPH BORDEN, a son-in-law of MR. JAMES RHODES of Sumter died
in Fresno Co. Cal. on 9th. Had been a citizen of Cal. for several years.
    REV. JESSE TOMLIN, Primitive Baptist treasurer of Dale Co. is 86.

May 21, 1875
    Died of meningitis near Brewersville on 6th DRU aged 1 year 4 months,
son of F. G. and DORA McMILLAN.

Estate of JOSEPH J. LITTLE, deceased. W. G. LITTLE, JR. and
FRANKLIN P. SNEDECER, admrs.

May 28, 1875
    DAVID CUCHEN, an aged citizen of Henry Co. died at dinner table
week before last.
    Estate of KERNEY C. HALL, deceased. R. CHAPMAN, admr.
    "JAMES D. CRAIG (47 SC) of Dallas at the age of 75 removed to
California."

June 4, 1875
    Regular Beef Market--B. M. EMANUEL.

June 11, 1875
    A. MRS. YOUNG of Cleburne Co. is 43 and the mother of 24 children.
    REV. JOHN NOBLE (John Noble @ 60 SC living in St. Clair Co. 1850)
aged 88, for over 60 years a Baptist preacher died in poor house in
Etowah Co. a few days ago.

June 18, 1875
    WYATT HARPER (49 G), deceased, J. G. HARRIS, admr. de bonis non.
    HUGH McMILLAN, deceased. E. A. McMILLAN, admr.

June 25, 1875
    Married on 2nd near Black Bluff by REV. MR. BANCROFT, MR. GOODMAN
FLOWERS and MRS. M. L. PEARCE.

July 2, 1875
    I. D. HOIT advertises well known plantation for sale.

July 23, 1875
    Administratrix Sale--PATTIE C. JOHNSTON, administratrix of
B. P. HUNTER, deceased. By Probate Court of Greene Co. 8 Feb. 1875
order of sale.

SELMA TIMES

May 9, 1860
    "On Sunday night, MRS. J. P. AYLETT, a resident of Virginia,
but for some time past on a visit to her daughter, MRS. CABELL of this
place died suddenly of apoplexy at the residence of DR. P. H. CABELL,
her son-in-law. She was quite advanced in life."

June 22, 1860
    "W. R. MACON, R. R. Agent at the Columbiana Depot died quite
suddenly at his residence near that depot on Sunday last."

CAHABA GAZETTE

June 7, 1860
    "MR. JOHN HATCHER (40 G), one of our oldest citizens died at his
residence in this county yesterday morning."

SHELBY GUIDE

Columbiana, Shelby Co. Ala.

July 6, 1871
    WILLIAM HALLIS, administrator of REBECCA ANDREWS, deceased
15 April 1871

July 13, 1871
    FRANK JORDEN, residing in lower part of county died very suddenly
Tues.

MRS. LOOMIS, relict of the late JOHN Q. LOOMIS died at Wetumpka on Sat. last.

MRS. MOLLIE POND wife of MR. GEORGE POND died at Fayetteville, Talladega Co. on 2nd.

July 20, 1871
Died in Talladega on 4th, June, MRS. MARY L. NASH aged 58.

July 27, 1871
Death of C. R. RICE, a former gallant member of the Scouts attached to 8th Alabama Regiment. Died early yesterday morning after a short illness and his remains will be interred in Magnolia Cemetery (Mobile Register, July 19)

August 3, 1871
Died-THOMAS R. HUNNICUT at Calera last Monday.

August 10, 1871
Death of COL. JACK THORINGTON, an old and honored citizen of Montgomery. Died yesterday morning at half past 2 o'clock. Softening of the brain (Montgomery Advance, Aug. 3).

August 17, 1871
LT. FILLEBROWN, an account of whose death is given in another column had a wife and 5 children, one of whom he had never seen.

August 24, 1871
Death of SAMUEL LEEPER, Esq. of Shelby County died at the residence of his son, JUDGE LEEPER in Columbiana on Thur. last. One of early settlers of Talladega County. He aided in establishing and was 1st Superintendant of Sabbath School ever organized in the county. In every respect a good man. He had been a Ruling Elder in the Presbyterian Church for more than 40 years and died as he lived--a true christian. (Talladega Reporter)

September 7, 1871
W. P. MASSEY, a lawyer of Marion died at Elyton on 29th of consumption.

The many friends of MR. ALEX. SMITH of Coosa County will regret to learn that he died at Talladega Springs on 30th. Old and very highly esteemed citizen extensively known throughout this and adjacent counties. (Rockford Sentinel)

September 14, 1871
MR. PETER E. HARRIS, residing a few miles from Dadeville, Tallapoosa County, committed suicide on Tue. last.

September 21, 1871
Death of COL. D. H. HUYETT last Sat. morning last at his residence 4 miles East of this place.

MR. JOSEPH SAVORY died in Selma on 6th in 84th year. From an obituary notice in Southern Argus we learn he was born in Dunkirk, France near coast of Flanders on 2 December 1787 and grew to manhood among stormy scenes of French Revolution. When scarcely more than a boy he served as drum major in famous army of Italy and was not yet 19 when he followed Napoleon in the terrible passage of the bridge of Lodi on 1 May 1791. In 1811 he came to America first landing at Philadelphia but afterwards came to Alabama to join colony of French emigrants who settled in Marengo County. Had lived in Alabama ever since.

HON J. F. DOWDELL, prominent citizen of Alabama died at his residence in Auburn Thr. morning. Served 6 years in Congress. During the war he commanded 37th Ala. Regiment. (Montgomery Advertiser 14th)

October 5, 1871
Married at Harpersville on 28th MR. AUGUSTUS W. McGRAW to MISS LAURA McCLANAHAN, daughter of the late JUDGE McCLANAHAN of this co.

Near Montevallo on 4th, MR. ROBERT D. HARRIS to MISS NANNIE A. WOOD, daughter of ALMATH WOOD.

October 12, 1871
Died, MR. D. T. VINCENT, an esteemed citizen of this county at
Harpersville on 6th. Remains carried to Plantersville for interment.

October 19, 1871
NANCY CUNNINGHAM deceased. J. F. M. WELCH, adm'r.

October 21, 1871
RILEY H. HONEYCUTT, adm'r of JAMES HONEYCUTT, dec'd. October 17,
1871.

November 2, 1871
DAVID A. BAKER candidate for Commissioners

November 9, 1871
Died on Lowndes Co. at res. of MRS. M. O. ROBINSON.
On --- MRS. CORA MORGAN, wife of DR. J. R. MORGAN of this place.
WILLIAM OZLEY, executor of will of MRS. ELIZA ROACH.

November 16, 1871
Nothing of interest

November 23, 1871
MR. JOSEPH D. NEELY, an old citizen of this co. 1 Nov. a. res. of
La. was here yesterday.

December 7, 1871
Death of MISS MARY LEEPER, sister of our Probate Judge and a
daugher of the late SAMUEL LEEPER, at half past 3? Cancer.

April 10, 1873
Married at the Campbell House, Calera, on Tue. 8th inst. by
REV. W. H. McAULEY, COL. M. C. STOKES of Montgomery to MISS MARY C.
CAMPBELL.
MR. JOHN SCOFIELD, an old citizen of this county died at his
residence near this place at age of 76.

January 30, 1873
Married Jan. 23d near Columbiana by REV. BRUCE HARRIS, MR. THOMAS
W. TINNEY to MARTHA L. SIMPSON.
At Shelby Iron Works, Jan 22d by REV. BRUCE HARRIS, MR. JOHN ANCHORS
to MISS ROXANA HORTON.
MRS. CAROLINE DUPRIEST sister of F M. MANN of Wetumpka was burned
to death near that place on 17th.
GEN. SAM G. HARDAWAY died in Montgomery last Sun. He was one of the
few who escaped murder at the hands of Indians who captured a stage
coach between Montgomery and Columbus. He was in the war which
achieved independence of Texas, a member of the American army in
Mexico also a member of the 6th Alabama in the late war (vol. 202, p. 33).

February 13, 1873
MAJ. W. L. LANIER took possession of Selma, Rome and Dallas
Railroad as Receiver last Monday.
REV. JAMES L. COTTEN many years a citizen of Dallas County and
member of the Alabama Methodist Conference died at Durant, Texas on the
4th inst.

February 27, 1873
Died near Shelby Iron Works on 7th, of pneumonia, MRS. SALLIE A.
DUNLAP.
Married in the place Tue. morning 25th at the residence of MRS.
M. S. BRASHER the bride's mother, by REV. BRUCE HARRIS, MR. WILLIS W.
WALL, to MISS LIZZIE BRASHER, all of this place.

March 6, 1873
Married in St. Clair County on 20th, MR. ABNER CROW and MISS
ELLEN HODGES.
MICAL TAUL, Esq. of Talladega died at Tampa, Fla. on 13th of
consumptions. He was respected and honored by all who knew him and for

several terms served as Secretary of Senate and was Secretary of the
State during GOV. PATTON's term of office.

March 20, 1873
    DR. G. T. DEASON of Elyton died on the 13th inst of small pox.
REV. ALBERT WILLIAMS a Baptist minister for many years past, a citizen
of Montgomery died on 8th.
    We regret to learn that DR. DAVID MOSELEY had his new residence
near Bibb Mills which was nearly completed, burned Tue. night.
    THOMAS E. MASON, a son of the late GEO. L. MASON of Wetumpka
was drowned at that place on 17th.

    MRS. GOTHARD, a very old lady living in lower end of this county
was run down and killed by a Passenger train from Montgomery last
Thurs. about 2 miles below Calera. She and her daughter were crossing
trestle.

April 17, 1873
    Married at residence of bride's father near Montevallo on 16th by
REV. W. H. MEREDITH, MR. THEODORE M. ALLEN to MISS MATTIE M. PERRY.
    Died at residence in Montevallo on morning of 20th, JAMES ADAMS an
old and respected citizen of this county for many years identified with
Central Alabama and was known generally to have been a man of great
energy and sound mind and good christian character.

May 1, 1873
    JAMES R. MARSH of Chambers Co. is dead, leaving a wife and
several children.

May 8, 1873
    Married at Evansville, St. Clair Co. on 10th Apr. MR. JESSE G.
WAITS to MISS MINERVA SHELLY (1843), daughter of MAJOR W. P. SHELLY.
    DR. JOHN H. PARISH, a most highly esteemed citizen of Talladega
has removed to Gallatin, Tennessee. DR. P was for many years an
honored citizen at Greensboro.

May 15, 1873
    Died at his residence 2½ miles west of Columbiana on 9th inst.
MR. DANIEL GARDNER. We, his children and our mother...

June 12, 1873
    Married in Talladega on 10 at residence of bride's father.
MR. WAILES W. WALLACE of this co. to MISS MARY CATHERINE HENDERSON.
    On the same day, in Presbyterian Church by REV. P. L. EWING,
MR. EDWARD BAILY of Mountain Home to MISS EMMA MOSELY daughter of
DR. R. A. MOSELEY.
    On the same day in Baptist Church at Alpine, Talladega Co.,
MR. JORDAN R. STONE of the Raleigh (NC) Standard to MISS MATTIE WELCH.
    In Talladega Co. June 3, MR. JOHN B. McCAIN to MISS OTHELLA BROCK.

June 19, 1873
    Died in this county on 13th of dropsy, MRS. LOUISA HOLMES, wife
of WM. HOLMES.

July 10, 1873
    Married at Shelby Iron Works on 8th, by REV. V. O. HAWKINS,
G. W. WILSON of Jacksonville, Alabama to MISS LAURA WILSON.
    COL. R. B. RHETT, editor of New Orleans Picayune and JUDGE COOLEY,
counsel for presecution in a recent libel suit against that paper
fought a duel last week. JUDGE COOLEY was killed at the 2nd fire.
    CHANCERY NOTICE:
    MARY A. JONES pr pro ami
    WM J. PARKER
        versus
    JORDAN JONES et al
    In Chancery 9th District of Middle Chancery Division of the State
of Alabama. Defendants LUCY CAROWAY wife of CALVIN CAROWAY of full age
and BENSON C. JONES, a minor, are non-residents of this state and their
residence is in Mississippi, that defendants JOHN J. JONES, MARY A JONES,

LUCY N. JONES, WALTER G. JONES and BENJAMIN N. JONES, minors under 21
are non-residents, and reside in Rusk County, Texas.

July 17, 1873
    Married at Montevallo yesterday evening at residence of GEORGE R.
ALLEN, the bride's father, by REV. W. H. MEREDITH, MR. HENRY WILSON,
Esq. to MISS AUGUSTA ALLEN.
    CHANCERY NOTICE:
    HENRY MILNER   ) In Chancery 9th district Middle Chancery
        versus   ) Division of State of Alabama
    LOVICE P. RAMSEY)
    LOVICE P. RAMSEY, administrator of estate of B. B. RAMSEY deceased
is a non resident, a resident of Lee County, Mississippi and he is over
21.

July 31, 1873
    Died near this place Tuesday morning at residence of MR. JAMES
McGOWAN, MRS. MARGARET JOHNSON.
    Married in Talladega County on 10th, MR. FRANK MALLORY to
MISS LIZZIE HENDERSON daughter of REV. SAM HENDERSON.

August 14, 1873
    MRS. ROSE, widow of the late COL. HOWELL ROSE, died at her residence
in Wetumpka on 4th.
    MR. WILLIAM DALE, a citizen of Calhoun Co., died on 7th.

August 28, 1873
    Married at St. Johns Church, ELYTON at 9 o'clock yesterday,
Wednesday morning by REV. P. H. FITTS, MR. FRENCH NABORS of Montevallo
to MISS SARAH E. HAWKINS of the former place.
    Married in Yallobusha County, Mississippi August 10, 1873,
MR. DAVID RICE to MRS. M. A. OZLEY, formerly wife of W. T. OXLEY of
this co. (OZLEY seems to be right)

September 4, 1873
    Married in this place at residence of the bride's father on
evening of 2nd by JUDGE J. T. LEEPER, MR. W. M. NABERS to MISS ADDIE
ELLIOTT all of this place.
    MISS THEODOSIA RENFROE, daughter of REV. J. J. D. RENFROE, pastor
of Talladega Baptist Church, died a few days ago.
    RUFUS GREEN, well known throughout the state died at the residence
of MRS. ELMER, his wife's stepmother near Wetumpka on 26 August aged 60.

September 11, 1873
    CAPTAIN A. N. PORTER died in Selma on 2nd. He was a nephew of
JUDGE T. A. WALKER of Calhoun.
    MR. THOMAS JENKINS, a Selma merchant, committed suicide in that
city Thursday (excessive drinking).
    Married in Wetumpka on 2nd, MR. F. ELBERT TAYLOR of Birmingham to
MISS LYDIA SMITH.

September 18, 1873
    Dead--HIRAM BUTLER for many years a resident of this county and
a merchant of Montevallo died at his residence in Meriden, Conn on 30th.

September 25, 1873
    State of Alabama Shelby County. Probate Court AMOS M. ELLIOTT,
administrator of WILLIAM HUGHES, deceased. Sept. 6, 1873

October 2, 1873
    As REV. J. McLEROY and wife from near Harpersville were going from
this place to Primitive Baptist Association at Mt. Olive Church 2 miles
west of this place last Sat. morning the mule scared at a stump...MRS.
McLEROY died Sat. night.
    MR. A. GARRETT, an old citizen of this county died at his residence
3 or 4 miles west of this place last Fri. night.
    MRS. MISSOURI FOUST, wife of W. N. FOUST, died last Sat. night of
consumption at their residence 4 miles east of this place.
    State of Alabama-Shelby County. Probate Court Sept. 1, 1873
NOAH HAGGARD deceased. ALAMATH WOOD executor.

MRS. CYNTHIA V. HONEYCUTT, administratrix of THOMAS R. HONEYCUTT, deceased.

October 9, 1873
The wife of COL. OSCEOLA KYLE of Wetumpka died at that place last week, MR. C. M. CABOT and COL. BENNET S. GRIFFIN both prominent citizens of this place died there a few days ago.
Married in Selma at Baptist Church on 2nd by MR. E. B. TEAGUE, MR. MERRITT BURNS to MISS E. E. PHILPOT.
Married on 3 October at Alamo House in this city by REV. C. C. ELLIS, MR. THOMAS NETTLES of Montgomery to MISS MARY McCALL of Saluria, Shelby County (Birmingham Independent)

October 16, 1873
MR. THOMAS ABERCROMBIE, brother-in-law of the late GEN. JAMES H. CLANTON and 1st Lieutenent in Co. I 1st Alabama Cavalry Regiment died at his residence near Rayville, Louisiana on 20th.
MAJ. WILLIAM McDUFF, a soldier of the War of 1812, under GEN. FLOYD and a resident of Leak County, Mississippi died at the residence of MR. A. J. CROSS, Sr. in Cahaba Valley on 25 September. MAJ. McDUFF was 88 years of age last June. He was father-in-law of MR. CROSS and was on a visit to friends and relatives in this section. He was born in Union District, South Carolina and his father was a soldier under GEN. WASHINGTON.
NOTE: HARRIET BELL McDUFF (1816-1875) married ANDREW JACKSON CROSS.
W. T. OZLEY has opened a Dry Goods and Grocery store at Shelby Springs.

October 23, 1873
W. H. FELLOWS, administrator advertises lands of estate of EXUM B. MELTON, deceased, for sale.
MRS. RANDALL, widow of the late BENJAMIN RANDALL, died near Montevallo last Thursday.
NOTE: MRS. NANCY RANDALL (1815-1873)

October 30, 1873
MR. JOHN W. JONES, son-in-law of DANIEL McLEOD of this county died at Cropwell, St. Clair Co. last Saturday.
Died near Shelby Iron Works last Friday, SAMUEL BAKER brother-in-law of H. C. NABORS.
Died in Tuscaloosa on 15th, ALICE VIRGINIA, infant daughter of HON. B. B. and ROSE GARLAND LEWIS aged 6 mo.

November 6, 1873
MRS. HORTON, wife of RANSOM HORTON of this county, died last Sat. at their residence.

November 13, 1873
Only one page there. End of bound volume.

FRANKLIN ENQUIRER

Published at Tuscumbia, Franklin County
every Wednesday morning by Richard B. Brickell

April 7, 1824
Died at his residence in Mobile on the 5th instant in his 48th year, GEN. TURNER STARKE.
Married Thursday evening the 8th instant, EDMUND DILLAHUNTY, Esq., one of the Editors of the Columbia Reporter, to MISS SARAH G. LOONEY of Maury County (Tenn.).

May 19, 1824
Married in this place Tuesday evening the 11th instant by REV. JOSEPH WOOD, MR. MICHAEL DAVIS to MISS ANN M'CANN, daughter of THO. M'CANN of this town.

Married Thursday evening the 13th instant by REV. JACOB PECK,
COL. BARTLEY COX, merchant of Huntsville to MISS ELIZA A. FREEMAN of
this place.

September 1, 1824
    JOSEPH MERRILL, assignee)
        versus   ) attachment
    LYDAL WILKINSON   )
    FRANCIS GHOLSON, JOSEPH JAMMERSON
        versus
    Heirs of MARGARET JAMMERSON, deceased
    Petition to sell real estate
    ASA GOUGH   )
        versus   ) Bill for Divorce
    SALLY GOUGH)
    SARAH R. SWANSEY)
        versus   ) Bill for Divorce
    JAMES N. SWANSEY)

September 8, 1824
    Died in this town on Saturday the 4th instant in her 57th year
MRS. NANCY JOHNSON, consort of RANDALL JOHNSON, Esq.

February 14, 1825
    ROBERT THOMPSON and ELLIS ISBELL, administrators of the estate of
JOHN ISBELL, deceased.

March 14, 1825
    Died in Tuscumbia on Thursday the 10th instant, MR. JAMES HANCOCK,
aged 27 years, a native of Londonderry, Ireland.

April 18, 1825
    Died at the residence of ED. PEARSALL, Esq. Sunday night the 10th
instant, MRS. NANCY SHERON, wife of MR. THOMAS SHERON, in the 16th year
of her age.

May 19, 1824
    Letter from LEROY POPE, followed by a letter addressed to the
Pension Department dated May 7, 1822: "Please pay to BENJAMIN BLACKBURN,
an invalid pensioner on the rolls of your agency at $8 a month" etc. and
signed by J. L. EDWARDS.

May 26, 1824
    Married on 13th inst. in Franklin Co. MR. JOHN JONES of Madison
County to MISS MOORMAN, daughter of COL. M. MOORMAN of said county.
    Married in Limestone County on 13th inst. by REV. DR. FAVORS,
DR. CASTLETON B. AKE of Tuscumbia to MISS RACHEL SIMS of Limestone Co.
(see our Vol. 35, p. 17 which says they m. in Tuscumbia)
    Married in Huntsville on 18th inst. by REV. M. THOMPSON, GEORGE
FEARN, ESQ. attorney at law to MISS ELIZABETH BURRUS, daughter of the
late COL. CHARLES BURRUS of Madison Co.

THE TUSCUMBIAN

September 17, 1824
    Married on Monday 22nd ult in Prince George County, Md. MR. LUKE
HOWARD, merchant of this place, to MISS HARRIETT, youngest daughter of
the late HENRY BROOKE, Esq., of said county.

October 7, 1824
    Married in this place on Sunday 3rd inst. by REV. A. A. CAMPBELL,
MAJOR HUGH PETITT to MISS LUCINDA, daughter of MR. CHARLES TONEY of
this place.

October 15, 1824
    Advertisement--NANCY DEATS appointed administratrix of GROVER S.
BEATS' estate.

December 3, 1824
Advertisement--Plantation of R. B. CUNNINGHAM, deceased for rent.
GEORGE S. SMITH, adm'r.

December 17, 1824
Advertisement--HENRY POWELL appointed administrator of estate of
JOHN W. TURNER, deceased.

December 24, 1824
WILLIAM THOMPSON, deceased. WILLIAM PRIDE, JOHN MONTGOMERY and
J. J. BENHAM, commissioners.
JOHN COOK, administrator of estate of DAVID COOK deceased. Non
resident heirs are: THOMAS COOK, WILLIAM H. COOK, LEMUEL COOK and
JOHN GILLELAN and wife, REBECCA.

January 31, 1825
Married in Russellville on Sunday evening 23rd inst. by his honor
JUDGE DAVID, PHILIP GATES, Esq. of Russellville to MRS. MARGARET HENLEY
of this county.

February 7, 1825
SILAS FUQUA, administrator of estate of JACOB FUQUA, deceased.
Sale of land by Orphans Court. ROBERT THOMPSON and ELLIS ISBELL,
administrators of estate of JOHN ISBELL, deceased. Non-resident heirs
are: JAMES ISBELL and SUSANNA ISBELL.

February 23, 1825
Letters of administration granted to ENOCK BRIANT on estate of
JAMES MMORE, deceased in Marion County, Alabama. Sale of personal
property to be held at house of WILLIAM RAGSDALE, Marion Co.

March 14, 1825
Advertisement--GEORGE D. DAVENPORT left Pensacola, Florida 12
months ago--supposed to be in Alabama--to communicate with brother,
J. D. DAVENPORT, Pensacola.

March 28, 1825
Died at his residence in this county on 16th inst. MAJOR WILLIAM
RUSSEL aged about 63. "An officer in late Creek and Seminole Wars."
Died at South Florence in this county Thursday the 24th inst.
MR. JOHN JOHNSON aged 29, a native of Belfast, Ireland.

June 6, 1825
Advertisement--Commissioners EPPS MOODY, B. McKERNON, E. BATES,
HENRY ELLIS and HENRY DAVIS to record claims against the estate of
EDMUND JEFFERSON, deceased.

July 18, 1825
Married in Tuscumbia on last Thursday by DOCTOR CAMPBELL,
MR. JOHN KENNEDY, merchant to MISS SARAH LOUISA, only daughter of
MR. DAVID GOODLOE, all of this place.

August 8, 1825
Died in this place Friday 29th ult. MR. ALEXANDER McFADDIN, Jr.,
partner of the house of JOHN SIMPSON and Co. in 30th year Jr. of his
age.
Died in Williamson County near Nashville Sunday the 31st ultimo,
MR. WILLIAM H. MERRILL, second son of MR. JOS. MERRILL of this place
in his 23rd year.
Died on Wednesday last MRS. .... ANDERSON, wife of JOHN ANDERSON,
Esq. of this neighborhood.

August 15, 1825
Advertisement--Information wanted by an old soldier. DAVID
CHANCELLOR asks help to prove service in Revolutionary War. He was in
the Virginia line in February 1777, CAPTAIN HOLDMAN Rice's Company to
guard troops of Burgoyne, then prisoners of war; was in said company
eight months, then transferred to CAPTAIN MERIWETHER'S Company where he
served 15 months. COLONEL FRANCIS TAYLOR commanded the regiment. He

was honorably discharged May 2, 1779. Was also at the siege of Yorktown. MR. WILLIAM ROUNDTREE and MR. DANIEL KNEAVES who a few years ago lived in Mercer County, Kentucky were in the same company with him, but they have moved, he cannot learn where. From age and helpless situation, he needs help of his country. Information to be communicated to COL. STEPHEN F. OGDEN, Yellow Banks, Davies County, Kentucky.

August 22, 1825
Citation issued to CONSTANT PATTERSON, DAVID PATTERSON, JOSEPH PATTERSON, DICEY BAKER, wife of JOHN BAKER, heirs of SARAH FERGUSON, late wife of ATHEL FERGUSON, and ELIZABETH HITTLE, deceased, late wife of SOLOMON HITTLE, to show why WILLIAM T. PATTERSON, JOHN T. PATTERSON and GEORGE T. PATTERSON should not probate the will of JOHN S. PATTERSON, their deceased father. County of Marion, State of Alabama.
Died, JAMES GALLIGAN, a native of Ireland.
WILLIAM B. LONG, Esq., late senior editor of the "Democrat" (Huntsville) is no more; died 17th inst of bilious fever. Was an affectionate husband and father.
Died on Saturday last in 26th year, MRS. JOHN BAKER of this place; left affectionate husband and four infant children.
Died on 18th inst. MR. JOHN ADAMS, about 19th years of age, a native of Ireland.

October 3, 1825
Advertisement--"Owing to death of my brother in North Carolina, I expect to be absent. My affairs are to be in hands of THOMAS WOOLDRIDGE of Tuscumbia, WILLIAM B. MARTIN of Florence and PETER MARTIN and JAMES DAVIS of Russellville." L. L. ALSOBROOK
WILLIAM S. PATTERSON, administrator of estate of JOHN S. PATTERSON, late of Marion County deceased. "Pay subscriber in Franklin County of H. ROBERTSON of Marion Co" Note: Evidently WILLIAM PATTERSON lived in Franklin Co.

November 7, 1825
Advertisement to sell land of JOHN S. PATTERSON, deceased of Marion Co. by administratrix, CONSTANCE PATTERSON. Note: At foot of advertisement is signed PATIENCE PATTERSON)

December 5, 1825
Died 2d inst. at father's residence in this county, MR. JOHN TONEY, aged 22/

December 12, 1825
Died suddenly at the residence of her father, DOCTOR A. W. MITCHELL, MRS. ISABELLE ELLIOT, consort of JAMES ELLIOT of this town "in bloom of her youth"
Died in this town on Saturday last, MRS. ALDRIDGE, wife of COL. THOMAS ALDRIDGE, left children

January 16, 1826
Citation to the heirs of ANTHONY WHITE, deceased who are unknown.

February 6, 1826
Letters of administration to ISAAC WILEY and JAMES WOODDELL on estate of EVAN S. WILEY. 2 December 1824. Final settlement of estate.

February 13, 1826
Died at Cabin Row, Montgomery County, Tenn. JOHN M'ALISTER, Esq. late of Frederick Co. Virginia in 74th year of his age (communicated)

February 27, 1826
WILLIAM THOMPSON versus BENJAMIN HUDSON, adm'r of estate of WILLIAM THOMPSON, Sr. who before his death, contracted to sell land. JOSEPH WOFFARD, Clerk of Circuit Court.
Advertisement of G. H. MALONE and Co. "Late of Huntsville."

July 5, 1826
Married Tuesday evening 27th June in Franklin Co., DR. DILLARD of Tuscumbia to MISS NANCY WINSTON, daughter of COL. ANTHONY WINSTON.

On same evening, MR. WINTER PAYNE of Franklin Co. to MISS MINERVA
WINSTON, daughter of COL. JOHN J. WINSTON. On 29th ult. MR. ISAAC HOOKS
to MRS. HOLT, both of Florence.
Died at the residence of JAMES JACKSON, Esq., on Saturday 25th
ult. MR. ALEXANDER JACKSON aged 50, a native of Ireland, a resident of
New Orleans for 20 years.

July 12, 1826
Married in Warren Co. North Carolina on 9th inst. LUNSFORD L.
ALSOBROOK, Esq. attorney of law at Tuscumbia to MISS TEMPERANCE EATON
of Warren County.

October 25, 1826
Died 16th inst. in this place, MR. DEMPSEY FULLER, Drugist, a
native of Lynchburg, N.C.
Married 3rd inst. MR. PHILIP O'RILEY of Russellville to MISS
TRALUCIA H. LESTER of Lawrence Co. (Letter to us from a descendant says
Tralucia was b Mar. 1805 daughter of FREDERICK LESTER and wife DOLLY
(ROBERTSON) POLLARD and widow of THOMAS POLLARD.
Married 5th inst. MR. JOHN J. ORMAND, Esq. to MISS MINERVA,
eldest daughter of WILLIAM BANKS, Esq., both of Lawrence County.

November 8, 1926
Died in this place 6th inst. MR. SOLOMON MATHEWS, native of Virginia;
left bereaved wife and eleven children.
Petition of WILLIAM RUSSELL, administrator of estate of WILLIAM
RUSSELL, Sr. deceased to sell land.

November 22, 1826
Letters of administration granted to ARTHUR S. HOGUN and JOHN HOGUN
on the estate of MASON RONNALDS, deceased (17 Oct. 1826 date of granting)
Advertisement of sell personal property of JAMES SMITH, deceased
at his house at Lagrange by ARTHUR S. HOGUN and JOHN HOGUN, administrators, who were appointed 11 Oct. 1826.
JOHN JONES appointed administrator of estate of DEMPSEY FULLER,
deceased.

November 29, 1826
Died at Florence, 22nd inst. SAMUEL H. BARR, native of Ireland,
a young man.

December 13, 1826
Married Thurs. eve. last by REV. DOCTOR CAMPBELL, CAPT. JAMES
INGLISH of Jefferson Co. to MISS CYNTHIA CRAWFORD of this place.

December 20, 1826
Adv. sale of personal property of CALEB B. JONES, deceased on
Spring Creek 2 miles south of Tuscumbia, ISAAC WINSTON administrator
(letters of administration granted Nov. 23, 1826)

January 3, 1827
Obituary of WILLIAM MACON TUREMAN--native of Franklin Co. Kentucky,
but soon removed to Maysville. As a young man, came to Tuscumbia;
set out for home to die among his people, but died 25th December at
house of DR. BARNES HOLLOWAY 25 miles south of Pikeville. Left
relations in Kentucky.

TUSCUMBIA (ALA) TELEGRAPH

October 31, 1827
Died on Saturday 27th inst. ay one o'clock MR. FAQUHAR MATHIESON,
native of Inverness, Scotland; left wife and three children.
Depart this life in 15th year, MISS ELIZA EDINGTON, only daughter
of MR. JAMES EDINGTON of Limestone Co.
Died at his residence in Tuscumbia Monday 29th inst. MR. JOHN D.
FARNESWORTH, native of Virginia, but for last two years of this place--
loving and affectionate husband and fond father.

Died at the residence of his father in Scott County, Ky. on Monday last, HON. DANIEL P. COOK, late representative of the state of Illinois in U.S. Congress.

Died on 7th inst. after a short illness of a fatal disease prevailing in Wilks Co. MATHEW TALBOT, Esq., candidate for the place of Governor in opposition to JOHN FORSYTH, Esq.

An appeal to the friends of missions-contributions to be given to WILLIAM S. JONES, Russellville, JOHN HAYNIE of Tuscumbia, ROBERT B. CARY, Courtland and NATHAN KIMBLE, Decatur. JAMES SAUNDERS, ALEXR. SALE and FINCH P. SCRUGS, traveling preachers.

November 14, 1827

County Court of Franklin, State of Alabama. JESSE VANHOOSE, administrator of estate of WILLIAM WILSON.

Died at residence of COL. ANTHONY WINSTON on 8th inst. CAPT. ANTHONY WINSTON, Senr. in 78th year of his age. Deceased was a native of Virginia and emigrated to Tennessee at an early period. "It is due to his memory to state that during the gloomy hours of '76 he fearlessly arrayed himself on the side of his country and struck for the liberty which we now enjoy. Left a large and respected family."

Died suddenly Tuesday evening last, GEORGE WHITE, youngest son of COL. JOHN J. WINSTON aged 2 years and 4 months.

Departed this life on 11th inst. GEORGE SUTHERLAND, JR. aged 5 years, youngest son of MAJOR GEORGE SUTHERLAND.

November 28, 1827

Married at LaGrange on Sunday 25th inst. by REV. D. B. BESTER, MR. CORNELIUS POWELL to MRS. ELIZABETH WHITMILL.

County Court of Morgan, State of Alabama, GEORGE SUTHERLAND, administrator of estate of THOMAS SUTHERLAND, deceased late of said county.

January 9, 1828

Married on Thursday eve. the 3 inst. by REV. MR. ASHBRIDGE, MR. GEORGE W. CARROLL to MRS. LUCY LOCKHART, daughter of CAPT. A. JONES.

January 30, 1828

Married on Tuesday evening last by REV. MR. OWENS, MR. MARQUIS L. BROWN, publisher of the Tuscumbia Patriot, to MISS MARTHA FRANKLIN.

On same evening, MR. LEWIS DICKSON, a partner in the office of the Tuscumbia Patriot to MRS. ANN MOORE, all of this place.

February 6, 1828

Franklin County--Chancery Court. October Term 1827 CAROLINE S. HESLEP, ANGELINE H. HESLEP, CLINTON HESLEP and J. HESLEP, infant heirs of JOSEPH HESLEP, deceased, by guardian, THOMAS KIRKMAN versus PETER MARTIN, MARTIN S. GRAY, THOMAS WHITESIDE and DAVID WHITESIDE, heirs of JENKIN WHITESIDE, deceased and JOSHUA COX.

Chancery suit Oct. 1827--RICHARD S. JONES versus JOHN C. WELLS, administrator of THOMAS WELLS, deceased and EDMUND N. SALE.

JOHN N. SHIELDS and JOHN A. CUMMINGS, administrators of estate of GEORGE W. SHIELDS, deceased.

February 13, 1828

Married 7th inst. by REV. JOHN HAYNIE, MR. R(OBERT) G. CROZIER to MISS SUSAN H(ENNINGTON) HARDY, all of this place. Note: She was dau of JONATHAN HARDIE of Madison Co. Ala.

February 27, 1828

Married Thursday 14th inst. by REV. LEWIS McLEOD, MR. EDMOND WINSTON of Tuscumbia to MISS MARTHA ANN W., daughter of CAPT. THOMAS J. COCKE of Fayette Co. Tenn.

April 2, 1828

Died at his residence near Tuscumbia on Wednesday last, MR. WILLIAM DICKSON in 23 year.

QUINN MORTON IS CANDIDATE for legislature.

Published by Mont I. Burton, prop.

January 6, 1876
      Married at Presbyterian Church in this city on 5 at 12 M by
REV. DR. C. A. STILMAN, MR. FRANK S. MOODY and MISS MARY F. MAXWELL,
all of this city.
      Marriages in Ala.:
      Married in this co. on 23, MR. JUNIUS T. SIMS and MISS FANNIE E.
McKERALL (Ala. Beacon)
      Married on 29, MR. R. C. WALKER and MISS M. ALICE CORY all of
Eufaula, Ala.
      Married in this city on 20, CAPT. HENRY W. STRICKLAN and MISS MARY,
daughter of DR. W. H. ROBERT (Troy Enquirer)
      Also in Crenshaw Co. on 23, MR. JOSEPH W. DICKEY and MISS MOLLIE
HORN. Ib.
      MR. S. A. RAWLINS and MISS ADA DENNIS were married on 23 ult all
of this co. ib.
      "Married in Dallas County December 23rd, JAMES F. STEWART of
Wilcox County to MISS MARTHA A. SMITH" (Selma Argus)
      "Married in this county on the 2nd, T. J. DRISKELL and MISS KATIE
WATSON" (Selma Argus)
      Died in this county on the 28th, MR. ISAAC C. WHEELER for 30 or more
years an esteemed citizen of East Green County, what is now Hale County;
for the last 2 or 3 years a resident of this county.

January 13, 1876
      Died in Mobile on morning of 4 at residence of her mother,
MRS. P---(fade) FISHER, TOULIE G. wife of DAVID P. WOOD (there was a
DAVID P. WOODRUFF in T.) (faded out) of Chattanooga, Tenn.
      Married at the Methodist Church in this city on eve of 12, by
REV. B. F. LARRABEE, MR. D. PATTON KENNEDY and MISS SALLIE B. MITCHELL,
all of this city.
      Married in Chambers Co. on 30, MR. J. M. THWEATT and MISS J. BAILEY.
      News Item:
      THOMAS SIMMONS and wife residing in Chilton Co. have 24 children
buried in one graveyard. They are old and now childless.
      Married in Jefferson County recently, MR. JOHN ALEXANDER and
MISS MARY MORGAN, all of St. Clair Co.

January 20, 1876
      "Married at St. Paul's Church in this city on Tuesday the 11th,
by RT. REV. R. H. WILMER, Bishop of Ala., DR. RICHARD P. HUGEE of
Tuskaloosa and MISS MARY C. ALLSTON, daughter of D. L. L. ALLSTON of
this county." (Selma Times)
      Married in Wetumpka on 5th, MR. ROBERT WILLIAMS and MISS MARY MOORE.
      "Died in Dallas County on the 10th, MR. ALEXANDER SNEED."
      Married in this city on morning of 13 by REV. C. A. STILLMAN,
MAJ. J. T. HESTER of N.Y. and MISS SARAH ELLEN MAXWELL of this city.
      At residence of bride's mother in Northport on 18 by REV. MR.
BRANDON, MR. T. A. NIXON and MISS A. G. HALL.
      In this city on 18 by REV. C. A. STILLMAN, D. D., MR. CHARLES R.
ASHLEY, of Montgomery to MISS ELLA BOYNTON, daughter of PROF. W. S.
WYMAN of U. of A.
      Marriages and Deaths in Ala.:
      Married in Troy, Ala. on 5, MR. E. G. CHAFFIN and MISS SABINA A.
BARROW.
      In Orion, Pike Co. last week, MR. J. S. COPELAND and MISS ANNIE L.
HINDRICK.
      In Mobile on 3, MR. WILLIAM McCREERY and MISS MARY F. MERVIN.
      In Choctaw Co. on 5, REV. J. F. FREEDMAN and MISS L. C. BROCK.
      In Mobile on 5, MRS. ELIZABETH DAUDRILL died.
      News Items:
      JOHN EVANS of Clayton was found dead in his house last week and is
supposed to have been killed by his son, CHARLTON EVANS.
      "Married in Dallas County on the 11th, MR. WALTER CRAIG and
MISS ANNIE SHIELDS."

"Married in Selma on the 6th, REV. MR. BROWNING and MISS A. E.
CLARK."
"Married in Carlowville on the 4th, MR. THOMAS E. LIDE and
MISS KATIE KNOX."
"Died in Dallas County on the 10th, MR. ALEXANDER SNEED."

January 27, 1876
Married at Hot Springs, Ark. on morning of 27 at residence of
bride's uncle, DR. W. H. GRAY, MR. MONT I. BURTON, Ed. and Prop. of the
Gazette of Tuskaloosa to MISS FANNIE A. ROSS of Little Rock, Ark.
Married in Marion on 13, MR. JOHN P. TILLMAN and MISS SALLIE HURT.
Married in Tuskegee on 18, MR. A. H. GRAHAM and MISS NELLIE LIGON.
In Mobile on 14, MR. STEPHEN D. SHERIDIAN died aged 19.
In EuFaula on 14, MR. SAMUEL BARNARD.
News:
MR. H. A. WILSON of Selma Republican was married to MISS EMMA
LOUISE GARDNER of Montgomery on 20th.
MR. P. T. WAGNER, publisher of Shelby Sentinel and MISS JENNIE
LEEPER were married in Columbiana on 20th.
A lady by name of PULLEN, aged 60 years of age committed suicide
at Jemison (Chilton Co.) by overdose of laudanum.
Married in Autauga County on the 19th, MR. W. T. DAUGHTRY and
MISS M. M. HOUSTON.
Married in Jefferson Co. on the 19th, MR. ROBERT F. WALKER and
MISS BESSIE N. McADORY.

February 3, 1876
Married in Greene County on the 17th MR. ALFRED TURNER and
MISS MARY JANE LYLES. In the same county on the 20th, MR. J. T.
BOUCHILLON and MISS BETTIE GILMORE.
Married in Birmingham on the 25th, MR. JOHN C. HENLEY and
MRS. ANNIE L. MATTHEWS. Also on the 16th MR. E. R. PALMER and MISS
DORA HAGOOD.
Married on Sun. 30th at residence of bride's mother by REV. J. C.
FOSTER, MR. Y. H. FOSTER and MISS CORNILE FOSTER all of Tuskaloosa Co.
News Items:
MRS. CECELIA BOWEN of Mobile took an overdose of morphine,
mistaking it for quinine on 24 and died.

February 10, 1876
Died near Blount Springs, Ala. on 28 Jan. 1876 CAPT. VICTOR M.
RANDOLPH (MRS. SUE WATSON, Chattanooga, in 1954 says VICTOR M. RANDOLPH
was son of EDW'D BRETT RANDOLPH). Born in Culpepper Co. Va. July 24,
1797, was commissioned from that state a midshipman in U.S. Navy in the
year 1814 and sailed under CAPT. STEPHEN DECATUR. He served with great
credit during the fierce conflicts with the Algerine pirates that
ended in their extermination. He was with the late CAPT. JOSIAH TATTNALL
at the bombardment of Vera Cruz and caught the latter in his arms when
he fell dangerously wounded by a Mexican missile.... For more than
40 yrs a member of Episcopal Church. His remains sent to Columbus,
Miss. and interred by side of his beloved wife.
Died at Brewton (Escambia Co.) on 29, MRS. REBECCA LOVELACE. Also
at same place on 29, GEO. D. JERNIGAN on same day.
Died on the 2nd near Selma, MRS. H. LANGFORD.

February 17, 1876
Died in Selma on the 8th, MRS. MATILDA W. COCHRAN (45 NC) aged 71.
Died in Selma on the 9th, MRS. CYNTHIA C. WARNER aged 87.

February 10, 1876
Married in Greene County recently, MR. A. J. UPCHURCH and
MISS N. A. LEE.
At Alpine, Ala. on the 2, REV. J. T. TICHENOR and MRS. McGRAW.
(In another item, REV. ISAACC TAYLOR TICHENOR m. on 4th, MRS. EPPIE
REYNOLDS McCRAW).

February 17, 1876
Married in Mobile on 7 by REV. THOMAS J. BEARD, DR. RICHARD WILDMAN
and MRS. CHRISTINA S. HOGG.

Died at his residence in this city at 1 p.m. on yesterday (Feb. 16)
MR. DAVID WOODRUFF aged 78.
  In North Port on morning of 12 of consumption, JOSEPH SELF in his
26th year.
  On Feb. 9 near Tuskaloosa, JOHN P. PATTERSON in 41st year. Miss.
papers please copy.
  Married in Gainesville on 1, DR. J. TAYLOR and MISS FANNIE MOSBY.
  Died near Marion Junction (Dallas Co.) on 3, MR. THORNTON B.
GOLDSBY.

February 24, 1876
  Married in Bibb Co. on 9, MR. W. C. FARRINGTON and MISS C. A.
WOOLEY.
  In Madison Co. on 13, MR. W. L. JONES and MISS NANNIE J. TAYLOR.
  In Mobile on 16, MR. J. F. TURNER and MISS M. A. KEIRNAN.
  News Items:
  EBEN MATTHEWS, formerly of this city died in Selma on 15 of
consumption aged about 22. Remains brought to Tuskaloosa and interred
in the old cemetery.

March 2, 1876
  Married at Plantersville, Dallas County on the 17th ult.,
MR. J. R. RAWLINGS of Chattanooga and MISS A. J. HARVILL.
  MR. STEPHEN EDWARDS of Knoxville, Greene County, was found dead
near Mantua Sunday night.
  Married at Auburn on 23, MR. J. M. RILEY of Montgomery and MISS
JENNIE E. CLOWER.
  In Elmore Co. on 24, MR. CHARLES R. WILLIAMS of Montgomery and
MISS KATE E. McKEITTAN.
  In Houston Co. Ga. on 23, REV. THOMAS K. ARMSTRONG (12 Autauga Co.)
of Montgomery and MISS CARRIE F. JOHNSTON of Houston, Ga.
  Died in Mobile on 17, JOHN KING, and old citizen.

March 9, 1876
  Died on 3 of typhoid pneumonia, W. K. MABRY in 34 the yr.
KELLY MABRY served in Confederate army.
  Married in Uniontown on 22, MR. W. H. THOMAS and MISS SALLIE S.
McMURRAY.
  Married in Marion on 20, MR. WASHINGTON DOBBINS and MRS. MARTHA
McGEE.
  Daily Dots:
  MR. JOE RICHARDS and MISS FOWLER were married in Northport last
week.
  MRS. I. L. LAWRENCE died on 2, one of oldest and most highly
respected ladies of Tuscaloosa. Funeral from Baptist Church Sat.
  Sorry to announce the death of MR. HIRAM PETERSON, father of
MR. H. D. PETERSON. Died at his home about 16 miles NE of Tuskaloosa
on Tue. last. He was one of the oldest citizens of the county, being
about 80 years of age and was a soldier in Indian War of 1835. Remains
brought to this city and buried yesterday evening.
  Died in Selma on the 28th, MISS ANNA POTTS.

March 16, 1876
  Daily Dots:
  MRS. HAMILTON, widow of the late REV. DR. JEFFERSON HAMILTON is
at DR. R. C. McLESTER'S and will spend several weeks here.

March 23, 1876
  Married in Shelby Co. on 8, MR. GEORGE W. SUGGS and MISS MARTHA A.
DAY.
  In Tuskegee on 9, MR. W. W. FELTS and MISS DELLA DANCY.
  In Dallas Co. on 9, MR. J. L. SMITH and MISS NANCY E. DAY.
  In Elmore Co. on 15, MR. JOHN W. LEA of Montgomery and MRS. EMMA E.
YOREE.

March 30, 1876
  DR. JAMES W. STRUDWICK died at residence of his mother in Demopolis
on 19. He resided near Havana, Hale Co. and was well known in Tuscaloosa.

Marriages in Ala.:
In Lawrence Co. on 16, MR. HENRY OWEN and MISS ADELINE PRIUTT (Pruitt).
In Talladega on 22, MR. D. B. RISER and MISS BETTIE WILSON.
In Union Springs on 22, MR. B. T. ELEY and MISS WILELLA FIELDER.
In Macon Co. on 23, MR. FRANCIS A. TRAMMEL of Union Springs and MISS WILLIE E. MOTLEY.
In Briarfield (Bibb Co.) on 16, MR. J. C. SIMMONS of Shelby Springs and MISS KATE CURTIS of Briarfield.
Near Prattville on 23, MR. WM. S. McVORY and MRS. CARRIE O. SMITH.
In Greensboro on 23, MR. Z. E. HOLT of Miss. and MISS LAURA JONES.
State Items:
JAMES GRAYSON of Jackson Co. was killed by being thrown from his wagon a few days ago.

April 6, 1876
Married in Marion on 29, MR. W. M. JONES and MISS MARY B. JOHN.
Married in Greene County at Mount Hebron, MR. F. D. PARHAM to MISS KATE MASSEY.
Died in Eutaw on the 28th after a lingering illness, MRS. MARY B. HAWKINS aged 61.
Died in Eutaw on the 27th, MRS. JANE R. CALVIN.

April 13, 1876
Married in Tuscaloosa on 6 by REV. W. H. WILLIAMS, MR. JOHN C. WILKERSON to MISS JESSIE A. MILLER.

April 20, 1876
MR. PATRICK McNEILUS (McNelis in Times) killed in accident, aged 37.
Married in Shelby Co. on 9, MR. SANDERS and MISS PILGRENE.
In Birmingham, on 13, MR. JOHN B. RODEN and MISS CORA J. GILLIAM.
In Birmingham on 13, MR. JOHN H. RANDALL and MISS ELIZA DILL.
Died at Warrior Sta. on 7, MR. THOS. PLATT aged 77.
In Fayette Co. on 1, MRS. MILLS.
In Madison Co. on 9, MRS. C. C. COBB.
In St. Clair Co. on 6, JAMES TREECE aged 24.
In Bibb Co. on 22, MRS. NANCY McSPADDEN aged 86.
In Birmingham on 13, CLARA WILSON.
In Mobile on 11, FRANCIS HENRY GAINES.
In Tuscumbia on 6, MRS. LOUISA B. MEREDITH aged 63.
In Demopolis on 9, LEWIS B. McCARTY aged 65, a citizen of that place for more than 40 years.
State Items:
BASIL HAYES of Lawrence Co. Ky. was born 1804. Father of 20 children, grandfather of 98, great grandfather of 17.

April 27, 1876
Married at residence of M. J. EDDINS on Tue. by REV. GEORGE H. HUNT, COL. JAMES D. RADCLIFFE and MISS PATTIE EDDINS. (see Times).
Died on 15 at residence of MRS. SARAH A. MARTIN near Macon, Miss., LEMUEL HOGAN in his 82nd year; servant in family of late JOSHUA L. MARTIN, deceased of Tuscaloosa.
Elder J(ONATHAN) P(ARKER) THOMPSON (s of (illeg)) was born in N.C. 1795. At age of 5 his father moved to State of Ohio, where resided for 5 years and again removing, settled in Lancaster District, S.C. where the subject of this notice lived 37 yrs. At age of 22, he married MISS SARAH CROXTON (d of JOHN)--12 children, 10 sons and 2 daughters, 7 of whom, together with the aged mother, still reside. At 23, joined Baptist Church. In 1842 he moved with his family to Ala. and settled in Tuscaloosa Co. where he resided until time of his death. Died 18 Dec. 1875 in 80th year.
Married in Fayette Co. Ala. on 13, MR. FARGUHAR (FARQUHAR) and MISS HARRIS.
Died in Sumter Co. on 3, MR. GREEN W. GRANT.
In Montgomery Co. on 20, LIZZIE ELBERT, infant daughter of MR. and MRS. JOHN W. SIMPSON.
In Eutaw, on 9, of typhoid pneumonia, JOS. A. HALL aged 17.
In Winston Co. on 7, MRS. NANCY ROMAINE.
In Selma on 15, MR. JOHN KEITH of Talladega aged 56.
In Selma on 15, HENRY T. STONE after a long illness.

News Items:
A lady 94 years old in Randolph Co. has a daughter who is 75.
MR. LARKIN WILLIS died at Elmore, S. & N. Railroad on 19 from an overdose of morphine.

May 4, 1876
Married in Hale County on the 25th, MR. ROBERT W. WITHERS and MISS MARY C. PICKENS.

ALABAMA BEACON

Greenesboro, Ala.

January 16, 1847
Died on the 6th inst. in the 87th year of his age, JOHN PARR.
MR. PARR emigrated from Fairfield District, SC to this state about twelve years ago and has since resided in this county till his death.
He entered into the service of his country at the age of sixteen in the Revolutionary war and served two campaigns. No man has left behind him a more unblemished character. Note: See our Vol. 20 p. 31 for the will of JOHN PARR.

TUSKALOOSA GAZETTE

May 4, 1876
Died on 27 in this co. MRS. SARAH E. SMITH, daughter of MR. and MRS. A. D. SANDERS.
Died on 30, a short distance above Tuskaloosa, MR. AARON BOYD (51 SC; Times also says 86) aged 86.
Married in Ala.:
In Mobile on 19, MR. E. V. HEWTER and MISS EMMA E. HERNDON, daughter of COL. THOMAS K. HERNDON.
At Hayneville on Sun. 23, MR. JOHN SPANN and MISS NANNIE WITCHER.
News Items:
Abbeville (Henry Co.) Register 28. CHANCELLOR GRAHAM last week in Dale Chancery Court in case of W. O. BETHUNE versus JOHN E. LITTLEFIELD held that act of Legislature exempting 160 acres of land from levy and sale was unconstitutional.
Died in Selma on the 20th, MRS. HENRIETTA J. WALKER (she was nee Chambless. Her sis. EVALINE m. ROBT. L. DOWMAN, according to ADMIRAL INGERSOLL)
Married in Birmingham on the 26th, MR. JOS. R. SMITH, JR. to MISS KATE J. MOULTON.
Married in Jefferson Co. on the 20th, MR. JOHN A. DAVIS to MISS JANE SMITH.

May 11, 1876
Marriages and deaths in Ala.:
In Shelby Co. on 30, MR. GEORGE NICHOLS and MISS NANNIE PERRY.
In Birmingham on 4, MR. W. L. SCOTT and MISS LIZZIE LINN.
In Montgomery on May 4, REV. A. C. HUNDLEY of Autauga and MISS ANNIE BARNES.
Died in Mobile May 3rd, MRS. JENNIE A. HUGGINS.
Died in Mobile May 3rd, MRS. SUSAN WHITLEY.
In Huntsville on 23, JAMES B. SEAT aged 20.
At Union Springs April 20, COL. JAMES F. GATCHETT.
In Selma on 2, MRS. W. G. JAENS.
In Mobile on 1, MR. CHARLES R(OBT) LABUZAN aged 64 (b. CULPEPPER Co Va July 23, 1813, son of CHARLES and CHARLOTTE SLAUGHTER LABURZAN. m Oct 14, 1846 (in Mtgy Co Ala) SARAH ELIZ. MARSHALL 3-18-1817 Richmond Co Ga, d of GREEN BERRY & FRANCES COLE--Marshall, Data from LOUIS M. F.)
We regret to learn MR. T. J. DURRETT is determined on removing to Tex. He expects to leave in a couple of weeks.
MR. IRA J. OSBORNE and MISS GERTRUDE GRAY were made one by REV. F. L. ROUSSEAU in Northport at residence of MR. G. H. TIERCE on 6.

News Items:
GEORGE SHAVER and his son RUFUS were drowned in Terrapin Creek, Cherokee Co. on 11th.
Paint Rock Valley, Jackson Co. can boast of having among its residents, MOSES SWAINE aged 76, who is father of 25 children, 16 boys and 9 girls.

May 18, 1876
Died near this city on 16 of typhoid fever, MISS LETHIE JONES aged 19, only daughter of MR. and MRS. Z. W. JONES.
Married in Wetumpka on 10, MR. W. J. BENSON of Little Rock, Ark. and MISS WILLIE READY of Wetumpka.
In Cullman on 7, MR. H. W. EBERLY and MRS. JOSIE BRINDLEY.
In Huntsville on 9, HON PETER M. DOX and MISS MARGARET SIMPSON.
In Montevallo on 4, MR. W. K. STARR of Opelika and MISS PAULINE CARY.
In Cherokee on 4, MR. JAMES EAST and MISS SALLIE BURTON.
In Burnesville (Dallas Co.) on 10, MR. W. E. McCASKEY of Selma and MISS E. LEE PERRY of Dallas Co.
Died in Ala.:
In Montgomery on 10, CICERO M. LEDBETTER
In Tuskegee on 30, R. N. KEELING, SR.
Near Cherokee on 6, MRS. T. W. THOMPSON of congestive chill
In Dallas Co. on 5, MR. JEFF. CAMPBELL
In Selma on 6, JANE PICKENS, infant
In Selma on 6, MR. CHARLES COLLIER, a most estimable gentleman and good citizen.
In Montgomery on 10, MR. JACOB HASSELTON.

May 25, 1876
Died near this city on 16 of typhoid fever, MISS LEATHEY JONES aged 19, only daughter of MR. and MRS. Z. W. JONES.
MRS. MARY WILLINGHAM, wife of MR. E. WILLINGHAM, died on 14 at her residence about 6 miles from town, on Bear Creek Road.
Married in Hale Co. on the 11th, MR. JAMES H. WILKINSON and MRS. E. J. BONDS.
Married in Eutaw on the 11th, MR. SYD. MOORE and MRS. M. E. HUTTON.

June 1, 1876
Married in Selma on the 17th, MR. CHARLES MASSEY and MISS LIZZIE SANDERS.
A. MR. PATTERSON (his name was CHA__ PATTERSON and word was nee CYNTHIA HAYNES; see person in vol. after 168) living about 25 miles from Tuskaloosa, an old man 76 years of age and a pensioner of the War of 1812 was in town Tue. and was robbed. The old man and his wife were in town and drew the pension and a negro held them up.
A prominent active Democrat in Shelby Co. is 87 years of age-- MR. LOFTIN QUINN.
MRS. RADCLIFFE nee MISS PATTIE EDDINS and MRS. WATTS nee MISS JOHNNIE EDDINS are in the city on a visit to their mother, MRS. M. J. EDDINS.
Died on 14 in Uniontown, ROBERT CHRISTIAN.
Married in Dallas County on the 22nd, MR. L. D. MULLEN and MISS ALICE DENNARD.
Married near Clinton, Greene County on the 14th, MR. A. H. PIPPIN and MISS SALLIE F. DUNLAP.

June 8, 1876
Married in Eutaw on the 30th, MR. ALBERT C. HILL and MISS MAMIE SCEARS.
Married in Birmingham on the 25th, MR. HENRY BEHRENS and MISS MARY SCHMETT.
Married in Selma on the 30th, MR. SAMUEL SMART and MRS. I. R. OLIVER.
Married in Dallas County on the 25th, MR. JAMES R. GRIBBLE and MISS PRUDENCE S. SHELBY (SNC; d of J M)
Died in Selma on the 22nd, JOSIAH HOBBS aged 82.
Married at residence of W. R. K. BECK in Camden on 25 by REV. MR. HUNTER, EDWARD N. JONES, Esq. and MISS MOLLIE M. BECK, all of Wilcox Co. MR. JONES is a brother of MRS. W. C. RICHARDSON of Tuscaloosa.

Died at her residence in this county on 5, MRS. HARRIET PHIFER
aged about 70. (She was wid of WM. P. PHIFER, and also of HARRY W. HART--
see Gilga Church Register)
News:
JOHN CARTER was killed by lightning at Allenton last week (28)
Butler Co.

June 15, 1876
Died near Huntsville on 4, MR. WILLIAM ROWE aged 85 years.
In Huntsville on 6, MISS MARY C. FIGG
In Mobile on 4, NANNIE SLOAN POE, infant
On 6 in Baldwin Co., MRS. C. SHORT
In Eufaula on 1, MR. R. C. ROSS and MISS IDA C. ROSS
In Bangor, Blount Co. on 7, MR. ANDREW HUGHES and MISS MARINDA JETT
News:
MR. JOHN C. ROBERTSON of Fayette Co. sailed from N.Y. for Scotland
on 27 on a visit to relatives.
Married at Elyton on the 6th, MR. THOMAS S. SMITH and MRS. LUCY E.
WALKER (see below).
Married on the 2nd at Meridian, Mississippi, MR. G. BROWN of Selma
and MISS NINA SMITH.
Died in Dallas County on the 4th, DR. THOMAS HUNTER, a distinguished
physician.
Died in Selma on the 6th, MR. MIKE FITZGERALD.

June 22, 1876
Died in Selma on the 12th, MR. MARDIS L. WOOD (to A. LEECY), a
resident of Dallas Co. from childhood.
Married in Elyton on the 7th, MR. THOMAS SMITH and MISS LUCY WALKER.
Married in Greensboro on the 5th, MR. CLARENCE DERRICK of Washington,
DC and MISS OCTAVIA HALMAN.
Died in Hale County on the 14th, MR. JOHN WARREN aged 92.
Married in Marion Co. on 7, MR. WALTER STURDIVANT and MISS CALLIE
KING.
In Newbern on 8, MR. JAMES A MAULDIN and MISS GILIAN H. HUGGINS.
Died in Mobile on 8, MR. GEORGE OTIS HALLETT.
News:
MR. S. DENNIS of Tallapoosa Co. aged 84 recently walked 8 miles and
hoed an acre of cotton in one day.

June 29, 1876
Married in Dallas County on the 13th, MR. R. K. JONES and MISS MARY
P. RUSSELL.
Married in Dallas County on the 13th, CAPT. FRED H. SMITH and
MRS. R. E. COCHRANE.
Died in Dallas Co. on the 19th, MRS. T. M. REESE.
Married in Tuskegee on 20, MR. C. U. YANELY and MISS IDA WOOD.
Died in Mobile on 20, MRS. MARY T. HERPIN.
Tribute of respect--Big Sandy Grange No. 103. Tuscaloosa Co.
June 17, 1876.
Resolutions adopted on death of our beloved sister, HARRIET W. PHIFER
who died 5 June, 1876.
News:
MR. MOSES SPENCER and family fresh from England have come to
Tuscaloosa and will make their home here. He will go in mining business
with KELLOG & SPENCER.
MRS. ROBERT HATTEN, wife of our esteemed townsman died on last
Fri. On Wed. preceding MR. HATTEN buried a little child.
JAMES D. HARTSFIELD was drowned at Decatur on 11.

July 6, 1876
News:
NATHAN'L KING, an old citizen of this county, died at his residence
near Windham Springs on 20.

July 13, 1876
Died in Lockhart Tex. on 2, HENRY WILMER, only son of J. H. &
ADA GLASCOCK aged 10 mo. 24 days.

The little son of MR. and MRS. ALFRED BATTLE died at their home near the Miss. line on Sat. last. MRS. BATTLE is herself dangerously ill.

DANIEL CARROLL who died in Calhoun Co. last week would have been 100 years old in Sept. next.

July 20, 1876
Died in Sanford Co. on 22, MR. JEPTHA SEAY aged 60.

MR. JOHN L. MAXWELL, an old and respected citizen of this place died Tue.

W. P. STEDMAN killed ALBERT HUBBARD near Forkland, Greene Co.-- cause: whiskey.

Married on the 22nd in Birmingham, MR. WM. VINES and MISS AMANDA NEWMAN.

Died in Springville on the 23rd, MRS. LAURA FULTON of Elyton.

July 27, 1876
Married in Calhoun Co. on 1, JAS. E. ADERHOLT and MISS ANNIE READ.

In Mobile on 3, WALTER JONES of Selma and MISS JOHNSON.

In Bullock Co. on 13, M. C. DAVIS and MISS S. G. BOZEMAN.

Near Peaks Hill, Calhoun Co. on 8, OSCAR A. FINCH and MISS MARY E. MORRIS.

Died in Henry Co. on 11th, JOHN PARKER

In Mobile on 8th, BERNARD LUSCHER, SR.

Died near Uniontown on 11, MRS. SUSAN J. POOL aged 54

Near Hanna Springs on 4, JAMES BROWN aged 92

Near Faunsdale on 17, MRS. ELIZABETH ALEXANDER aged 67

News:

MR. MILES STEVENS of Hale Co. was killed by lightning a few days ago. He was a very poor man and leaves a widow and 7 helpless children.

August 3, 1876
MRS. MARY NEILSON died at residence of her son, DR. R. NEILSON in Northport on Fri. 28. aged about 87. Body interred in the old cemetery on this side of the river.

Married in Shelby Co. on 20, MR. JNO W. PAYNE and MISS LOUCILLA SEALE.

In Selma on 25, MR. WARNER and MISS M. C. KINKLE.

Died at Blount Springs on 28 infant son of MR. and MRS. ROBERT L. WATT of Montgomery.

In Mobile on 27, LOUIS EDWIN McKINNEY

In Selma on 24, JAMES MACKIN

In Selma on 22, NELLIE DAVIS aged 14

News:

DR. SAMUEL CARTLIDGE of Clay Co. was called to his door on night of 15 and killed by unknown party.

WILLIAM HOWELL, an old and greatly respected citizen of Marion was found dead in bed Fri. morning 21st.

August 10, 1876
Married on Thursday August 3 by REV. R(ICHARD) FURMAN (Bapt.) at his residence in Tuscaloosa MR. JOE. (Wm. J. in Times) DAFFRON and MISS ELIZA E. BURK, all of this county.

Marriages and Deaths in Ala.:

Married in Blountsville on 30, MR. JOHN M. DOYLE and MISS MARY A. WOOTEN.

Died in Livingston on 31, MISS MATTIE C. UNDERWOOD aged 19.

In Clanton (Chilton Co.) on 2, infant of MR. BOWDEN.

In Montgomery on 5, MILLARD B. CAMPBELL aged 10 mo.

In Butler Co. on 1, DR. JESSE R. RAY aged 66.

News:

Death of MRS. HENRY COST (a daughter of MR. R. A. GARNER) which occurred near Birmingham on 27. Left infant twins.

JUDGE STERRETT of Shelby Co. suicided by shooting on 29. Mind impaired by softening of the brain. (This was ALPHONSO ANDERSON STERRETT, son of ROBT. and SALLY (BROOKS) STERRETT)

August 17, 1876
Married in Livingston on 29, MR. W. W. GARLAND and MISS N. J GRADY.

Died in Montgomery on 10, SAMUEL S. CARRAWAY.
In Shelby Co. on 1, MRS. CATHERINE MOORE aged 70.
In Pickens Co. on 29, EDWARD L. NOLAND aged 2.
In Pickens Co. on 8, MOSES J. COOK.
On 1 at Dadeville, MRS. M. J. FURGUSON.

August 24, 1876
Married in Selma recently, A. KAYET and MARY A. SHORES of
Summerfield.
MR. MELVILLE WALLACE, son of REV. A. J. WALLACE was killed in
Clayton by falling of a well bucket some days ago.

August 31, 1876
News:
On 18 MR. W. D. LORD living in Montgomery and a party went seining.
MR. LORD caught a fish and held its head between his teeth; fish
jumped down his throat producing death almost instantly.
Died in Elyton on the 19th, MR. J. D. HUSH.
Died in Jefferson Co. on the 22nd, MRS. SARAH NAVE.

September 7, 1876
Died in Hale County of yellow disease on the 25th, MRS. KATE B.
MOORE aged 23.
Died in Eutaw on the 17th, MRS. E. F. CAMPBELL.
Died in Eutaw, August 24th, MRS. REBECCA WHITE, aged 75.
Died in Birmingham on the 31st, MRS. MARY HUGHES.
On 16 in Blount Co. PROF. MANOAH V. HENRY and MRS. HENRIETTA B.
VAUGHAN.
News:
A MRS. DEAN of Talladega Co. was killed a few days ago by a limb
falling from a tree.
MR. WALTER L. JOHNSON of Rocky Mount, Crenshaw, while ill with
typhoid fever and insane with its effects, cut his own throat and died
last week.

September 14, 1876
Married at Christ Church in this city on 13, by REV. GEO. H. HUNT,
MR. W. F. FITTS and MISS ANNIE SPILLER, all of this city.
News:
GEORGE SANDERS has moved to Pleasant Grove. Pickens Co.
REV. B. W. BUSSEY, Pastor of Huntsville Baptist Church has resigned,
with view of removing to Ga.

September 21, 1876
News:
Last week we recorded the death at hand of an assassin of POWELL
BOLTON in Northport. On last Sat. night, MR. JESSE MABRY, an uncle of
MR. BOLTON was assassinated at Blount Springs. Remains of MR. BOLTON
were brought down on the train Mon. and buried in the old cemetery.

September 28, 1876
Married at residence of bride's father on 21 by REV. MR. GOODWIN,
MR. B. L. OWEN of Tuscaloosa and MISS TENNIE WATSON of Columbus, Miss.
News:
The father of our townsman, MR. JOHN PRITCHETT died in N.Y. a few
days ago whither he had gone from his home in Iowa for medical treatment
for dispepsia. He was about 70 years old.

October 5, 1876
MR. JOHN R. MAXWELL was stricken with yellow fever and died in
New Orleans while on a few days business trip. We extend to bereaved
wife and relations our sincere sympathy. Telegram to MR. THOMAS MAXWELL.

October 12, 1876
MR. LEMUEL B. PEEBLES, who resided near Union, Greene County, was
killed a few days ago by kick of a horse.

October 19, 1876
MRS. CHARITY UPTON died on Sand Mountain the other day aged 99-8-7.

October 26, 1876
 Married in this city on 25 by REV. G. H. HUNT, MR. ROBERT JEMISON and MISS GENIE SORSBY.
 MRS. PARISH, widow of the late R. C. PARISH, died on 18. MR. P was for several years Circuit Clerk and died about 18 mo. since. Two small children, girl and boy are left orphans. MR. PARISH'S brother, who resides in another state, will probably take them.
 MR. W(ILLIAM) A(LLEN) MILAM (45 SC), with 22 sons and grandsons of age, will all vote for TILDEN. MR. M. has 108 grandchildren (Moulton Adv)

November 2, 1876
 Married at Presbyterian Church in this city at 7½ o'clock Wed. eve, Nov. 1, by REV. DR. STILLMAN, MR. JESSE M. MAXWELL and MISS SALLIE J. THOMAS, all of this city.
 News:
 COL. JOHN HARPER, formerly of Romulus neighborhood in this co. died in Morehouse Parish, La. of yellow chills about 1st Oct. COL. HARPER was a useful citizen of Tuscaloosa Co. for nearly half a century. Last request was that his remains might be laid to rest near his old home at Romulus.
 Married on the 30th October near the line of Tuskaloosa in Jefferson Co. by REV. N. W. BLALOCK, MR. ASBERRY CROWNOVER and MISS M. DENTON.

November 16, 1876
 FRANK BRADLEY, late Tax Collector of Dallas County, died in the penitentiary the other day.
 ISAAC MOORE, living near Uniontown, was murdered by unknown parties.

November 23, 1876
 State of Alabama-Tuscaloosa Co. Probate Court Nov. 5, 1876. Came A. H. SANDERS, JR., admr. of estate of SARAH E. SMITH and filed petition. SARAH E. SMITH died seized of certain real estate. It appearing from said petition that JOHN J. SANDERS, LYDIA A. LAWLEY, wife of ELISHA LAWLEY, GEORGE W. SANDERS, all over 21, and residing in Texas, and ASA D. SANDERS, petitioner, WILLIAM P. SANDERS, both over 21, THOMAS A. SANDERS, JAMES M. SANDERS, both under 21-last 4 residing in Tuscaloosa Co. are only heirs of said SARAH E. SMITH, dec'd.

November 30, 1876
 Register's Notice--Tuscaloosa Co.
 SENIE R. MARLOWE by next friend and husband NICHOLAS P. MARLOWE versus NEWTON N. CLEMENTS and EGBERT RUSH CLEMENTS, executors et al. Early CLEMENTS, defendant, is a non-resident--resident of Miss. and is over 21.

December 7, 1876
 Married on 23 near Marcumville this co., MR. J. T. LONG and MISS MARGARET LUNCEFORD.

December 21, 1876
 Married in Mobile at residence of bride's mother on Thursday, Dec. 14, by REV. DR. BEARD, DR. WILLIAM SMALLWOOD and MISS SALLIE SULLIVAN.

TUSCALOOSA TELEGRAPH AND PATRIOT

June 21, 1828
 Petition for sale of land by JOHN ATKINSON, adm'r of estate of EDWARD ATKINSON, deceased.

ALABAMA SENTINEL

Printed and Published by Thomas B. Grantland of Tuscaloosa, Ala.

March 10, 1826
Notice: DAVID LINDLEY, administrator of estate of JOHN RACKLEY, late of Tuscaloosa County, deceased; also WILLIAM TATUM, administrator of estate of JESSE TATUM, deceased.

March 24, 1826
Adv. Bibb County 6 March 1826. JOHN HUNT, one of executors of will of ZEPHANIAH CLEMENT, deceased with WILLIAM CLEMENT and THOMAS CLEMENT to make final settlement.

April 7, 1826
Married on Thuesday evening last by REV. MR. CURTIS, MR. CHARLES DRUMMOND to MISS ELIZABETH TALIAFERRO, all of this co.

April 21, 1826
Died at his residence in New Town on Monday night, 17th inst. CAPT. GEORGE COX, formerly of the US Navy; left amiable wife and several small children.

April 28, 1826
Married on Tuesday evening 24th inst. by REV. MR. CURTIS, HENRY W. COLLIER, attorney at law to MISS MARY ANN BATTLE all of this place.

May 5, 1826
Departed this life at late residence in this place on Sunday morning 30 ult. after lingering illness, MRS. HANNAH FEW, formerly of the state of Georgia; embraced religion at early age of 13, Methodist Episcopal; left family of several children.
Died in Pickens County in 25th year after prolonged illness, DR. HARRIS BREWTON, late of South Caroline (communicated).
Divorce notice filed by EVELINA SPENCER versus JOHN SPENCER.

May 12, 1826
Letter from HAMILTON states that on April 16, house of JAMES BOAL was struck by lightning. "MR. BOAL was deprived of his wife and two children and a widowed mother, MRS. PERRINE, of a daughter." There were four others in the room, three of MR. BOAL'S children and the daughter of MRS. McCARRON.

May 12, 1826
Bibb County, ROBERT HILL, administrator in right of his wife, ALEXANDER HILL and ROBERT COLEMAN, administrators of estate of WILLIE COLEMAN, deceased to make final settlement.

May 26, 1826
WILLIAM B. GILES of Amelia County has been elected a representative in the Virginia Legislature.
Advertisement of ALEXANDER McCARTNEY of Winchester, Tenn. for a runaway slave.

June 3, 1826
Married 28th ult by REV. JAMES BAINES, MR. JAMES RICE to MISS MARIA T. FILES, daughter of MANLY FILES, SENR. all of Tuscaloosa Co.

June 17, 1826
Married Thurs. eve. last by LEVEN POWELL, Esq. MR. WILLIAM THOMAS to MISS MALINDA MOORE all of this county.
Jefferson County--JOHN BROWN, administrator of the estate of ANTHONY LABRUZAM.

July 1, 1826
Greene County--Original Bill in Chancery filed February Term 1826--

WILLIAM and BENJAMIN SIMS versus GEORGE SIMS and MILES GREENE, the latter not an inhabitant of this state.

ALABAMA STATE INTELLIGENCER

Published each Saturday at Tuscaloosa, Ala by Wiley, McGuire and Henry

April 17, 1829
        On night of 15th inst. the dwelling of MR. JEREMIAH WATTS of Butler County burned. Four of his children, one grandchild and a traveller perished, two others fatally injured (Mobile Register 30th ult)

April 24, 1829
        Died in Cahawba on 14 inst. DR. THOMAS LESLEY, formerly of Abbeville District, SC

May 17, 1829
        Final settlement of estate of WILLIAM PICKENS of Greene Co. Commissioners are: J. B. STICKNEY, JOHN MAY and WILLIAM L. DUFPHEY.

June 5, 1829
        Bibb County, CIVILL KORNEGAY versus DANIEL KORNEGAY--suit for appointment of trustee. Complainant by her solicitor, DANIEL KORNEGAY non resident of the state.

June 12, 1829
        Departed this life at 9 o'clock evening of 2nd inst. MR. WILLIAM JEMISON in 51st year after severe illness of nine days. Left wife and several children.
        Before LAWRENCE CARR, J. P. in Bibb County appeared MICHAEL PIRTLE and WILLIAM CLEMENT and swore to description of horse taken up by WASHINGTON CLEMENT.

July 3, 1829
        Died in vicinity of Greensborough lately, MR. WILLIAM H. BARRON, printer aged about 19.
        In Greensborough on 17th June, DR. JOHN HUNTER, formerly of Pendleton District, SC

July 10, 1829
        Letters of administration on estate of WILLIAM JEMISON granted to ROBERT JEMISON, JR. and ROBERT JEMISON, SR.
        HENRY CHILES, administrator of estate of Hatch Dent, deceased of Marengo County.

July 17, 1829
        Married in this place on Thursday evening 9th inst. by REV. DR. CHRISTOPHER, THOMAS CHILES, Esq. of Greene Co. to MRS. THIRZY DELOACH. Note· This is THIRZA (HAGOOD) CRAWFORD, widow who m. SAML DELOACH, JR. who d. 1822. She was THOS. CHILES 3rd wife.
        Died in Williamson Co. Tenn. at residence of her father, COL. N. T. PERKINS, on 24th ult. MRS. SARAH M. SNOW, late of Tuscaloosa.

August 7, 1829
        Married on Thursday evening July 30 by REV. JAMES HILLHOUSE, MR. JOHN BURK to MISS HANNAH GARRETTSON, both of Marengo Co. (see our Vol. 39 p. 13)
        Married at Berkley, Charles City County, Va. on the 8th ultimo, CO.. ANDREW PICKENS of Dallas County, Ala. to MISS MARY W. NELSON of the former place.
        Married on Tuesday 28th ult. by REVD. T. ALEXANDER, JOSEPH PICKENS, merchant of Selma to MISS CAROLINE J. HENDERSON of Pleasant Valley.
        Died in this town 23 ult. ELIPHALET, second son of DR. A. L. ACEE aged 7 years.
        Died on 30th ult. SAMUEL FARNESWORTH, Esq. native of Groton, Mass. aged 39 years.
        Died 31st ult. infant son of REV. R(OBERT) L(EWIS) KENNON.

151

January 1, 1831
Married Thursday evening the 16th inst. by HON. N. E. BENSON,
MR. GEORGE WHITMAN, merchant of Montgomery to MISS HARRIET P. BRAIME
(Vol. 172, p. 39 for mar).
Married in the vicinity of Greensborough on the 15th inst.,
MR. JOHN HILLHOUSE to MISS JANE LAWSON.
Died near Washington, Autauga County, Alabama on the 9th,
MR. JAMES B. MATHEWS, clerk of the County Court aged 31.
Died on the 9th inst. near Montgomery, MRS. MARGARET wife of
COL. JOHN TAYLOR in her 61st year.
Died suddenly of apoplectic fit between Stanton and Warm Springs,
MAJ. DANIEL SHEFFY of Augusta County, Virginia.

January 8, 1831
Married at the University by REV. MR. KENNON on Tuesday evening
last, COL. ELISHA YOUNG, Representative from Perry County in the
legislature to MISS MARTHA STRUDWICK of Hillsborough, N.C.
On the same evening in the vicinity of this place by REV. MR.
WILLIAMS, MR. P(HILIP) P. WRIGHT to MISS S(OPHIONA) MITCHELL.

January 26, 1831
Died at Indian Queen Hotel in this place on the 21st inst.,
MR. JAMES WEBB of Limestone County.
THOMAS J. ABBOTT, attorney-at-law

February 9, 1831
Died on Thrusday morning last, MRS. CATHARINE COMEGYS, wife of
E(DWARD) F. COMEGYS, Clerk of the Bank.

March 23, 1831
Died in this place on the 17th inst. of consumption, MR. L. H.
M'NEIL, printer, aged about 36 years.
Died at her residence in Halifax County, Virginia on the 15th
MRS. DOROTHA WINSTON, widow of the celebrated PATRICK HENRY. Her last
husband was the late JUDGE EDMOND WINSTON.

April 13, 1831
Married Thursday last in Marengo County, Alabama, MR. MATTHEW
PARHAM to MISS ELIZABETH M'FARLAND.
Died recently in Florida whither he had repaired for recovery of
his health, MR. THOMAS PECK, merchant of Greensborough, Ala. Had been
married but a few months. (m. 14 Sept. 1830 NOVALINE A. KENNARD.
She m. WM. B. OCHITTA 1834 Sumter Co.)
WILLIAM M. MARR--attorney

May 25, 1831
Married in Mobile Thursday evening the 5th by REV. JOSEPH P.
CUNNINGHAM, W. M. BERRIEN (Jas Wm in mar rec), Esq., of Sparta, Ga. to
MISS CATHARINE JANE, daughter of DR. THOMAS CASEY. From The Spirit of
the Age.
Died in this town Wednesday night, the 11th inst., MARY GRIFFIN,
infant daughter of MR. CHARLES S. PATTISON aged 1 year and 5 months.
Advertisement of JACOB WYSER and WILLIAM WING--coachmaking.

June 1, 1831
Married in the vicinity of this place Tuesday evening the 24th
inst. by REV. RECTOR of Christ Church, DR. CHARLES SNOW of this city to
MISS VIRGINIA PENN.
Married in Dallas County Wednesday last by REV. THO. O. SMITH,
MR. JOHN G. SIMS of this place to MISS ELVIRA M. PINSON.
Married in this vicinity on Thursday the 27th inst. by DR. M.
THOMPSON, COL. MARTIN BINION (50 G Pux Co.) to MISS MARGARET DEAL (36 SC;
1st wife Goodspeeds Miss. memories says ALEX DEALE of SC 1782,
d Noxubee Co. Miss 1844 m. MARGT LAURENCE to Ala 1818 to Miss 1832)
daughter of ALEX. DEAL, all of this county.
Married Thursday the 19th inst. by REV. FRANCIS PORTER, MR. JOHN R.
GOREE (39 SC; Perry Co.) to MISS SARAH ELIZABETH (33 Ga), eldest
daughter of COL. E. D. KING (Ind. was q. v.) all of Perry County.

Died at the house of MR. JAMES CANTEE (from Selma Courier) in this
town, on Tuesday afternoon last after a painful illness of about 4
weeks, MR. JOHN W. DONALDSON in his 28th year. Had for 2 or 3 years
been Clerk on Steamboat Amazon. His remains were yesterday followed to
the burying gound near this place by a parent and brother who reside
in Tuscaloosa.
State of Alabama--Marengo County. Circuit Court.
WOODEN M. BURGE)
    versus   ) Petition for Divorce
NANCY BURGE

June 4, 1831

Died on Tuesday evening last at the residence of her father,
MR. W(ASHINGTON) J(OHN) WASHINGTON, MRS. CAROLINE NEAL, consort of
MR. ROBERT NEAL.
MRS. CATHARINE P. HUNTER, Greensborough, Alabama. Advertisement
for house of entertainment.

June 11, 1831

Died in Lowndes County on 21st, MRS. PARTHINA RUGELEY, consort of
CAPT. JOHN RUGELEY.

July 2, 1831

GARMER DE SAINTS, deceased. Sale of land by FREDERICK RAVESEES;
CHARLES D. CONNER, BENAJAH P. WHITLOW, commissioners.

July 9, 1831

Married Tuesday the 23rd inst. by REV. JOSEPH CUNNINGHAM,
MR. WILLIAM M. MURPHY (47 NC), attorney-at-law (Greene Co.) of Erie to
MISS AMANDA (35 G) MALVINA, daughter of MR. BAKER HOBSON of Carthage,
Tuscaloosa Co.
Lands of ALPHONSE GARNIER, deceased, for sale.

August 6, 1831

Married in Dallas County on the 28th inst. by REV. MR. MOORE,
MR. SAMUEL F. JONES, merchant of Selma to MISS MARY GIVHAN.
Died in Mobile on the 22nd inst. MRS. CORNELIA L. SANDFORD,
consort of MR. THADDEUS SANFORD, Editor of the Commercial Register.
Died on the 28th of June last at his residence in Suggsville in
his 32nd year, HON. WILLIAM MOBLEY (sent to Hynson), late Representative
to Legislature from Clarke County.

August 13, 1831

Married in this town Tuesday evening by REV. ALVA WOODS, PLEASANT
N. WILSON, Esq. to MISS CATHARINE L. DRISH.
MRS. MAHALE PATE: Take notice that on 12th of September next,
I, JACKSON PATE will attend at house of HENRY BREWER, Fayette County to
take deposition of HENRY BREWER and THOMAS BREWER and on the 15th of
same month, I will attend house of THADDEUS WALKER in Marion County to
take deposition of MARK E. PATE and on 17th of same month, I will attend
at house of E(LDRIDGE) MALLARD in Walker County to take deposition of
ALFRED G. LANE and ELIZABETH M. LANE, all to be read in evidence in a
suit in Chancery in Circuit Court of Walker County, Alabama, at which
times and places you may attend if you think proper.

August 20, 1831

Died at the residence of B. B. FONTAINE of this place on Wednesday
last, MR. LEWIS KERR aged 23.

August 27, 1831

Died of a short illness in Marengo County, Alabama on the 16th,
MR. ALLEN GRIMES, gentleman of high standing and has left a wife and
2 children.

September 3, 1831

Died in Montgomery County Sunday the 21st inst. MR. JOHN ASHURST
in his 53rd year, a native of Virginia and for many years a citizen of
Alabama.
Died on the 21st inst. in the same county, MAJ. JAMES PINKSTON,
long a respectable citizen of that county.

Died on Monday last at Blount Springs in this state, MAJ. WILLIAM M.
MARR, a respectable citizen of this town in his 49th year. Born in
Pittsylvania County, Virginia and emigrated to Tennessee in 1798 where
he married and resided for more than 20 years. He removed to this
state in 1819 and was one of the first settlers of Tuscaloosa. For
several months past he has been afflicted with dispepsia.... Left a
wife and 11 children to mourn his loss.

September 17, 1831
    Married Thursday evening the 8th by REV. RECTOR of Christ Church,
Tuscaloosa, EDWARD L. BAYOL (42 Pa), Esq. (Greene Co.) to SYLVANIA
(39 NY), eldest daughter of FRANCIS STOLLENWERK, all of Greene Co. Ala.
    (Letter from MISS FLOY WATES--610 Church, Lufkin, Tex.
February 24, 1964 "Trying to find where in Ala. my ggf NAPOLEM B. GARNER
was b & reared & what was name of his wife ANN before she m. GARNER left
Ala. & came to Tex (San Augustine) in 1841. Tex Census 1850. Shows his
wife ANN was from Tenn. He was killed in 1842. "I have it by word of
mouth that he came from Tuscaloosa.")

October 1, 1831
    Married Tuesday evening last by REV. THOMAS A. SMITH, MR. ROBERT
CARUTHERS (must be dead, 1850 Census) to MISS BELINDA HATTER (@ 45 in
1850 SC) both of this place.
    Married in Fayetteville, Tennessee on the 12th inst. MR. NAPOLEON B.
GARNER of Selma, Alabama (Dallas Co.) to MISS ANN L. McCONNELL, daughter
of the late JOHN P. M'CONNELL of the former place (see Vol. VIII, term
pp 7, 8)
    Died on the 24th inst. at MAJ. LEWEN's Hotel in this place after an
illness of ten days, MR. HENRY HARSEIM of Eisenach, Grand Duchy of
Weimar in Saxony. Had arrived in this country in the company of two
friends about 3 months since. Object was to find a suitable place for
settling for himself and some of his countrymen.
    Departed this life on Saturday night last after a short and
afflicting illness, JOSEPH, eldest son of MR. H. M. ANDREWS aged 3 years
11 months and 16 days.
    BENJAMIN STOVALL, deceased. JAMES STOVALL, administrator.

October 8, 1831
    Died Thursday the 29th inst. SARAH, daughter of MR. BAKER of this
place.
    Died Friday the 30th, GEORGE, son of MR. G. SALTONSTALL.
    Died Saturday the 1st inst., MR. SAMUEL M'CRORY of this place.
    Died Sunday the 2nd inst., ELIZA H(OUSTON), daughter of MR. SAMUEL
VANCE of this town (see card of Mis. ROBT. W. HARPER, JR. 1964)

October 15, 1831
    FRANCIS H. HICKIMBURG advertises Alabama Coffee House under
management of ALEXANDER BLACKWELL.

October 22, 1831
    Died lately near Centreville, Bibb County, Alabama, MR. JACOB
DOMINACK, a worthy and esteemed citizen.

October 29, 1831
    Died on the morning of the 15th inst. MRS. HARIET MOORE, wife of
DR. DAVID MOORE of Madison County, Alabama. MRS. MOORE was the daughter
of the late JUDGE HAYWOOD of Tennessee, formerly of North Carolina and
was born in the latter state April 23, 1790. Methodist.
    Died lately in Centreville, Bibb County, Alabama, MRS. LOUISA ADAMS,
wife of MR. GEORGE ADAMS.
    Departed this life on the 26th inst. MILDRED, youngest daughter of
CONSTANTINE and ELIZA PERKINS.

November 5, 1831
    Married lately in Falmouth, Virginia by REV. E. C. M'GUIRE,
JAMES INNIS THORNTON (49 v), Esq., Secretary of State of Alabama to
MISS ANNE AMELIA (38 V), daughter of the late GEORGE SMITH, Esq. of
Dumfries (Fred Arena)..

154

Married on the 27th inst. near Havana, Greene Co. Ala. by
REV. J. P. CUNNINGHAM, T. L. R. WHITEHEAD, Esq. of Greensborough to
MISS ELIZABETH C. WILLIAMSON (40 T, Greene Co.).
    Married on the 27th inst. in this county (not in rec.) by
REV. MR. WALKER, MR. JOHN H. LEE (Isaac) to MISS AGNES JINKINS (Jas).
    Married in this place on the 27th ult. by LEVEN POWELL, Esq.,
MR. JOHN W. LANDEN to MISS NANCY TAYLOR.
    Married on the 27th inst. by REV. MR. COPP, COL. THOMAS M'ELDERRY,
Senator from Morgan County to MRS. FRANCES EDMONDS of Madison County.
    Married on the 4th inst. near Church Hill, Lowndes County, Ala.
by REV. MR. CAMPBELL, MR. DAVID A STEELE (48 V, Loundes Co.) to
MISS JULIA ANN, daughter of MAJ. WILLIAM BROWNING, all of said county.

November 12, 1831
    Married in Montgomery on the 27th by B. D. HASSELL, Esq.
MR. BANJAMIN L. POWELL of Virginia to MISS CECELIA C. MONGIN of New
York. (vol 174, p 20--see mar rec.)
    Died lately near Centreville in Bibb County, MRS. MARY CRAWFORD,
consort of HON. THOMAS CRAWFORD in her 43rd year.
    Died lately in Greene County, MRS. MARY PICKENS, consort of
COL. SAMUEL PICKENS.
    Departed this life on the 5th inst. at the residence in Dallas
County, REV. WILLIAM MOORE, a member of the Cumberland Presbyterian
Church in his 40th year.

November 19, 1831
    Departed this life in her 22nd year, MRS. MARY E., consort of
COL. SAMUEL PICKENS and daughter of DR. R. E. MEADE of Greene County.
    DR. S. W. COMFORT--surgeon-dentist.

November 26, 1831
    Died at St. Rosa, Pensacola on the 10th, MR. WILLIAM MORTON aged
38, formerly of Grange County, Virginia (from Pensacola Gazette)
    Died in St. Clair County, Thursday, the 10th of November,
ANDERSON C. M'AFEE of billious fever after an illness of 13 days on
his return from Edgefield District, South Carolina.

December 10, 1831
    Married at the residence of MR. JABEZ CURRY in Perry County on
Tuesday evening the 29th by REV. THOMAS ABERNATHY, MR. JOHN S. JEMISON
of Tuscaloosa County to MISS JANE ANN JORDAN, youngest daughter of
MAJOR BURWELL JORDAN, deceased (mar rec says MARY JANE vol 198 p 38).
    Died at his residence in this county on the 5th inst., HUME R. FEILD,
Esq. in his 59th year, former Judge of County Court of Tuscaloosa and
for several years a resident Trustee of the University of Alabama.

December 24, 1831
    JAMES B. CLARK--attorney
    Female Boarding School--NANCY WALSH in charge
    Cabinet Manufactory--GEORGE KREPS

THE DEMOCRATIC GAZETTE & FLAG OF THE UNION

1837-1844--Published at Tuscaloosa, Ala.
Samuel A. Hale, editor

June 14, 1837
    State of Alabama--Tuscaloosa County. Orphans Court. Final settle-
ment of estate of JOHN E. BROWN, deceased. CHARLES MONTGOMERY and
WILLIAM BROWN, adm;rs.

May 25, 1837
    State of Alabama-Pickens County. Creditors of HENRY M. STORY and
WILLIAM W. STORY notified that they will attend court 1 August 1837 to
settle debts.
    Creditors of JOHN H. EZELL notified that he will appear in court
to pay debts 17 July 1837.

NOTICE: At a meeting of the Orphans Court of Jefferson County, I was appointed administrator ex-officio of estate of WILLIAM EASLEY, deceased. All persons having claims should present them to me.
P. ANDERSON
State of Alabama-Tuskaloosa County May 25, 1837. Final settlement of estate of DAVID MITCHELL, deceased. JOHN MITCHELL, administrator.
At meeting of Orphans Court held at Linden, Marengo County 1 May 1837; final settlement of estate of JOHN PAGE, deceased. DAVID CURRY, Sheriff, adm'r.
Administrator's notice. All persons having claims against estate of JAMES DOUTHITT deceased to present same.
HUBBARD P. DOUTHITT, admr.

June 21, 1837
WASHINGTON MOODY, attorney at law
HARVEY W. ELLIS and JOHN D. PHELAN, attornies at law
Partnership of E. W. PECK and LINCOLN CLARK, lawyers
Partnership of H. W. ELLIS and E. W. PECK dissolved
Partnership of JOHN E. RIAL and ROBERT LACY dissolved
ROBERT LACY and JAMES H. MITCHELL advertise goods.
P. L. SINK states he has bought out the interest of E. A. PRINCE and will sell goods cheap.
WILLIAM VAN WYCK having this day taking joint interest with JOHN D. TERRELL and NEWTON L. WHITFIELD in mercantile business.
J. PAYSANT and Co. partnership dissolved. Signed
J. PAYSANT
J. J. WEBSTER
WASHINGTON R. WARE, HENRY S. BARRINGER and JOHN J. WEBSTER form partnership in business.
DEERMAN DEER (TEER) and DANIEL TEER, partnership dissolved at Pickens Co.
During my absence, MR. MARTIN RICHARDS is authorized to settle my business in North Tuscaloosa.
JAMES PATTERSON
Dissolution of partnership of JAMES PATTERSON and JAMES McCRIGHT.
HARVEY W. ELLIS, Esq. candidate for Representative in Congress from 3rd Congressional District.
HON. JOAB LAWLER, candidate for re-election to Congress from this District.
PLEASANT H(UGH) MAY, Esq., candidate to represent Tuskaloosa Co. in legislature.
ALEXANDER B. MEEK, candidate to represent Tuskaloosa Co. in the Representative branch of Legislature.
JOLLY JONES, candidate to represent Tuskaloosa Co. in Legislature.
G. W. MITCHELL, candidate to represent Tuskaloosa Co. in next Legislature.
M(ARMA) D(UKE) WILLIAMS, candidate to represent Tuskaloosa in Legislature.
CHARLES S. PATTISON, candidate for Representative of Tuskaloosa Co.
DR. W. C. TURNER, candidate to represent Tuskaloosa Co. in Repr. Branch of Legislature.
WILLIAM SIMONTON, Esq., candidate to represent Tuskaloosa Co. in Legislature.

June 28, 1837
GEN. G. W. CRABB, candidate to represent Tuskaloosa Co. in senatorial branch of next Legislature.

July 5, 1837
ALEXANDER MARTIN informs the gentlemen of Tuskaloosa that he has opened a shop in No. 2 on Row of Washington Hall where hair dressing and shaving will be done.
C. MORRISON'S Drug Store. Advertisement.
B. F. PORTER, candidate for Representative in State Legislature.
SAMUEL C. FRIERSON candidate for State Senate
"I have sold my entire stock of goods, with books and accounts to JAMES H. THOMASON, who alone is authorized to collect for said accounts."
JOHN I. THOMASON

Bill for divorce--NANCY JACKSON versus STERLING JACKSON. Defendant
is not an inhabitant of this state. See our Vol. 3 p. 76 for marriage
of STERLING JACKSON to NANCY RINGER, 1831; One STERLING JACKSON m.
SARAH J. CARTER, 1849.
The 2nd Battalion, 18th Regiment will parade at the house of
JOHN HUDSON on Saturday, 15th of July at 11 o'clock.
JOHN M. TALFORD, MAJOR
Committed to the jail of Tuscaloosa a slave who says he belongs to
MR. JOHN F. JOHNSON of Pickens Co.
Committed to the jail of Tuscaloosa Co. a slave, who says he belongs
to MR. HARRINGTON BURDEN of Green Co.
Committed to the jail of Fayette Co., a slave who says he belongs
to MRS. TERRY of Jefferson Co. Miss.
Committed to the jail of Tuscaloosa a negro, who says he belongs
to JESSE EDWARDS of Wilcox Co.
R. W. BARBER, Jailer

July 12, 1837
Committed to the jail of Pickens County a slave, who says he
belongs to DAVID G. MOORE and ROBERT MOORE, near Benton, Yazoo County,
Miss.
Committed to the jail of Pickens County a slave, who says he belongs
to ANDERSON WILKINS, Benton Co. Ala.
G. B. FRIERSON, attorney at law
JAMES ABBOTT--Barber and hair cutter

July 19, 1837
Obituary of NATHANIEL MACON, North Carolina statesman. Died in
Warrenton, NC June 29th, 1837 in his 83rd year.
Died in this city on Friday last, COL. CHARLES WRIGHT, an old
and respectable citizen.
Died on 21st ult. at the residence of his father in this vicinity,
DAVID S. MORTON, Esq., son of MAJ. QUIN MORTON aged about 24 years
(North Alabamian)
Died on 4th inst. at his farm 3 miles from Tuscumbia, MAJOR QUIN
MORTON, one of our oldest citizens and for many years one of our most
valuable public servants.
Administrator's Notice:
Property belonging to the estate of JAMES McCULLOUGH, deceased,
will be sold.
MOSES McGUIIRE, administrator

July 26, 1837
Married on the 20th inst. by REV. WILLIAM H. WILLIAMS, DR. REUBEN
SEARCY of this city to MISS MARY ANN A. FITCH formerly of Vermont.
JOHN B. CAMP, advertises for runaway slave.

August 2, 1837
Co-partnership of JAMES M. NORMENT and JOHN IVY in North Tuscaloosa
dissolved 29th June 1837.
J. D. BLACKBURN resolved to go to Texas, wishes to sell land 11
miles Northeast of Tuscaloosa.
Administrators of JEREMIAH DOUGHTY, deceased petition to sell land.
JAMES CADDELL in right of wife is one of legatees and does not reside
in this state.
Orphans Court--Tuscaloosa County. Administrator of estate of
ALLEN CARTER, deceased, petitions to sell land. It appearing to the
court that ELIAS STORY, who in right of wife ELIZA (late ELIZA CARTER)
is a distributee and does not reside in the state.
Orphans Court--Tuscaloosa County. The executors of will of
JAMES CHILDRESS, deceased, petition to sell land. JAMES SMITH, in right
of wife, MARY P. SMITH, is one of the legatees and does not reside in
the state.
The University of Alabama will commence the third Monday of
September. Board $16 a month in advance.

August 9, 1837
Notice:
All persons having claims against the estate of ALEXANDER CARTER,
deceased, will present them within time prescribed by law.
BURCH DARD. admr.

August 16, 1847
Married in this place on Tuesday evening last by the REV. DANIEL
BAKER, MR. JAMES L. CHILDRESS to MISS SUSANNA L. L. BRUEN.
Obituary:
Departed this life in this county on Wed. morning on 2nd inst.
RACHAEL, consort of THOMAS G. BIRDWELL and daughter of ROBERT and
NANCY OLIVER of bilious dysentery aged 27 years 10 months and 23 days.
The subject was born in Davidson Co. Tennessee. Her parents moved
from thence to Giles County at an early period of her life and lived
there for many years.... She has left a bereaved husband and four small
children and numerous relations. Trumpet of Liberty, Pulaski, Tenn.
please copy.

August 23, 1837
Married in this place on Wednesday evening last, the 16th inst. by
REV. MR. WILLIAMS, MR. JOHN B. REED of Huntsville to MISS SUSAN W.
CHILDRESS of this vicinity.

September 20, 1837
State of Alabama-Fayette County. Orphans Court, September Term
1837. JOHN D. MORROW, one of administrators of estate of AQUILLA
CAVANAH, deceased, appeared in court and exhibited a statement of
accounts for settlement.
State of Alabama-Fayette County. Orphans Court, September 1827
(1837?). JOHN D. MORROW, one of administrators of estate of
JOHN W. CAVANAH dec'd, appeared in court and requested a settlement of
estate.
Candidates:
CAPTAIN JOHN TATOM of Morgan Co. for re-election for doorkeeper to
House of Representatives.
CHARLES BEALE, Esq., of Tuscaloosa for doorkeeper.
JAMES RATHER of Tuscaloosa for messenger to House of Representatives.
DANIEL PEYTON, Esq., as engrossing Clerk to House of Representatives.
M. P. WILLIAMSON for Engrossing Clerk.

October 4, 1837
State of Alabama-Tuscaloosa County. Orphans Court September 4, 1837.
Final settlement of estate of WILLIAM GAMBLE, deceased. LUCINDA
GAMBLE, executrix.
State of Alabama-Tuscaloosa County. Orphans Court Sept. 4, 1837.
JAMES M. MURPHY, administrator of estate of ROBERT PERRY reported
estate to be insolvent.
Notice:
Letters of administration on estate of CHARLES PATE, deceased,
granted to ISHAM PARKER Aug. 31, 1837.

October 11, 1837
Married on 28th ult. by ELDER J. C. KEENEY, MR. J(OHN) C. WILLINGHAM
to MISS ELIZA DURRETT, all of this county.
Married on 1st by same, MR. ELISHA THORNTON of Pickens County to
MRS. ELIZABETH H. BURROUGHS of this county.
Married in this county on 28th inst. by REV. R(OBT) OLDHAM,
W(INSTON) J(AMES) BROWN, Esq., of this place to MISS LOUISA L., daughter
of ISAAC LEA, Esq.
Died in this place on 27th ult, of congestive fever, SARAH L.,
daughter of COL. THOMAS B. and MRS. MARIA A. H. CHILDRESS, aged 4
years 2 days.
Notice:
All persons indebted to estate of THOMAS BLASSINGAME, deceased,
are requested to come forward and make payment.
WILLIAM A. LELAND, adm'r
Letters of administration on estate of DANIEL SIMPSON, deceased,
was granted to WILLIAM COLE and TRUSTEN NEWSWORTHY (later written
(NORSWORTHY) by Judge of County Court of Fayette on Aug. 9th.

October 18, 1837
Dissolution of partnership of GEORGE S. GAINES and JONA. EMANUEL,
Factorage business.
State of Alabama-Tuscaloosa County. Orphans Court, Sept. 22, 1837.
WILLIAM BRAZEAL, administrator of estate of ELIHU BRAZEAL, deceased,
reports that estate is insolvent.

October 25, 1837
ABRAM PERKINS says his wife, LUCY, has left his bed and board so
he is not responsible for her debts.
State of Alabama-Fayette County. Orphans Court, Oct. Term 1837.
PLEASANT MAY, administrator of estate of THOMAS MAY, deceased, petitions
to sell land. JOHN MAY, SEN., DAVID MAY, SUSAN MAY, WILLIAM MAY,
GEORGE MAY, HAMPTON MAY, ROBERT MAY and PLEASANT MAY are heirs of said
deceased; and that WILLIAM MAY resides without the limits of the state.
JAMES M. ELLIS advertises land for sale.
DR. J. R. CREAL--Dental surgery will visit Tuscaloosa 6th November
17th Regiment Alabama Militia notified to attend for Regimental
Muster
RICHARD JONES, Colonel

November 1, 1837
State of Alabama-Tuscaloosa County. Orphans Court, Oct. 21, 1837.
Administor of estate of ABNER WINN, deceased, petitions to sell land.
Published in paper to notify GENUBATH WINN, JOHN A. WINN and JAMES R.
WINN, heirs who do not reside in the state.
State of Alabama-Tuscaloosa County. Orphans Court, October 27,
1837. All persons having claims against estate of JAMES McCOAL,
deceased, to file with Clerk of County Court, ANDREW McCOAL, admr.
Administrator's Notice:
JOSEPH WOODRUFF, administrator of estate of GEORGE L. MEDLOCK,
deceased of Shelby Co.

September 8, 1837
Obituary:
Departed this life in this place on 6th inst. MR. AUGUSTIN SLAUGHTER
in 55th year of his age. Native of Virginia. Resided for many years
in the city of Augusta (Ga).... Two years ago he removed to New Orleans
and at time of his death was a member of mercantile firm of SLAUGHTER,
PICKET and BANKS. Although he died at a place remote from his residence,
yet he was surrounded by friends.

November 29, 1837
Died in the town of Montgomery on 23d inst. after a lingering
illness, the HON. WILLIAM D. PICKETT, Judge of 8th Judicial Circuit of
this state.
I. H. KELLY--attorney at law

December 6, 1837
Married in this city on Tuesday 5th inst. by REV. DR. KENNON,
MR. WINFIELD S. STOKES of Petersburg Va. to MRS. MARY ANN WOODRUFF of
Philadelphia, Pa.
Notice:
Letters of administration on estate of SAMUEL MOSES, deceased,
granted to MEREDITH MOSES and JOHN MOSES.
State of Alabama-Pickens County Orphans Court, July Term 1837.
MARY RICKMAN petitions for dower as widow of WILLIAM RICKMAN, deceased.

December 12, 1837
Letters of administration granted to ANDREW SMITH on estate of
CHRISTOPHER VANNER, deceased.

December 20, 1837
Married by REV. MR. OLDHAM on 13th inst. MR. DUET COOPER to
MISS SARAH PEARSONS, all of this co.
Married by same on 14th inst. MR. ELISHA HAYS to MISS BINA N.
NEWTON, all of Bibb County.
Died at his residence in this county on Sunday last, MR. ROBERT
McADORY aged 29.

January 10, 1838
    Married on Tuesday evening 26th of Dec. last by REV. MR. CATER,
MR. H(UBBARD) P(EEBLES) DOUTHITT of Tuscaloosa to MISS ELIZABETH R.,
daughter of COL. WILLIAM McGEHEE of Benton County.

January 17, 1838
    Died on 7th inst. in 76th year of her age, MRS. SARRAH MORRIS,
consort of MAJ. JAMES ROBERTSON known as HORSESHOE ROBERTSON. For about
40 years she had been a member of Baptist Church and was an affectionate
wife and tender mother.
    Died in Columbus, Miss. Tue morning 9th inst. of affection of the
lungs where he was attending Methodist Conference...DR. R. L. KENNON.
Has been a resident of this place since its earliest esistence, occa-
sionally absent for a short time...Independent Monitor.
    State of Alabama-Fayette County. Orphans Court, Jan. Term 1838.
JAMES SMITH, one of the administrators of estate of HUGH E. SMITH,
late of said County deceased petitions to sell land. JAMES SMITH,
MARY, wife of MOSES ALLIN, SARAH, wife of THOMAS SLONE, JOHN SMITH, JR.,
ELIZABETH, wife of JOHN SLONE, TABITHA, wife of MATTHEW SLONE, NANCY,
wife of THOMAS BARRON, RANDIL SMITH, THEBY SMITH, wife of deceased,
H. R. SMITH, WILLIAM SMITH, ESTHER SMITH, WASHINGTON SMITH and MARTHA
SMITH, husband of said deceased, of whom SARAH SLONE, ELIZABETH SLONE
and TABITHA SLONE reside beyond limits of state. Note: There is a
typographical error, but it appears the same way in ten different
editions of this paper (at different dates).
    State of Alabama-Tuscaloosa County. Administrator's sale. Estate
of ROBERT McADORY. GEORGE COBB, executor.

February 28, 1838
    Married in this city on 13th by REV. J. H. DeVOTIE, MR. DAVID
J. J. W. FULTON to MISS MARY P. BRALY.
    Married on 21st inst. in this place by REV. DANIEL BAKER, MR. JOHN
NEWTON to MISS ROSINE HIERNMALL of this city.
    Married on Tuesday evening last by REV. J. H. DeVOTIE, MR. WILLIAM
G. THOMPSON of Lawrence County to MISS MARY E. GILBERT of Franklin
County.
    Notice:
    At Orphans Court held at Jefferson County 11 December, 1837,
PETER ANDERSON was appointed administrator of estate of CHARLES P. JONES
and HUGH PIERCE, deceased. Also on 6th of February, 1838 of estate of
JAMES TATE, deceased.
    Died at the North Tuscaloosa Female Academy on Monday last,
REV. JOSEPH WOOD.

March 2, 1838
    Married on Tuesday evening 14th inst. by REV. J. C. KEENY, MR.
FRANCIS HATFIELD of Demopolis to MISS HARRIET A. SMITH. .
    Married on 8th inst. by REV. J(AMES) H. THOMASON of Tuscaloosa,
MR. R(OBT) B. MONTGOMERY of Elyton to MISS NANCY, eldest daughter of
JOHN CAMP of Jefferson Co. See our Vol. 18 p. 69.

March 28, 1838
    CAPT. GEORGE A. KITCHENS, candidate for LT. COL. in 18th Regiment,
A. M. to fill vacancy occasioned by resignation of COLONEL MULLINAX.

April 4, 1838
    State of Alabama-Bibb County. Orphans Court, Feb. 1838. JOHN E.
GREEN petitions for division of estate of JOHN GREEN, late of said
county deceased. SAMUEL P. GREEN, EZEKIEL C. GREEN, BENJAMIN S. GREEN,
GEORGE S. GREEN, JOSELUM B. GREEN, JAMES H. GREEN, THOMAS REESE, in right
of wife CAROLINE (late CAROLINE GREEN), JAMES THOMPSON in right of wife,
ELIZABETH and the petitioner, JOHN E. GREEN, and the minor heirs of
MARY WOODS, to-wit: ELIZABETH WOODS, JANE WOODS and JAMES L. WOODS,
all heirs of JOHN GREEN.
    Remains of our esteemed fellow citizen, MAJOR MIMS JEMISON, who
was killed at battle of Clonotahassa in Florida 27 April 1836 were
brought to this place yesterday for burial.

April 11, 1838
Died in this place Friday last, MRS. NANCY GILLASPIE, daughter of
MAJ. CHARLES LEWEN.

April 18, 1838
Married 12th inst at residence of R. ROCKETT, SEN. near Jonesboro,
Jefferson County by REV. T. W. COX, DR. A(LVA) J. HOLCOMBE of Tuscaloosa
to MISS MARY T. ROCKETT of the former place. See our Vol. 18 p. 69.
Died Sunday the 1st April at her father;s residence in Tuscaloosa
County, MRS. ELIZA HARDWICK, wife of MR. GEORGE HARDWICK and eldest
daughter of MR. JAMES GRAY in her 23d year. See our Vol. 2 p. 71.
State of Alabama-Jefferson County. Orphans Court 7 Apr. 1838.
LUCY TURNER, administratrix and THOMAS M. ADAMS, adm'r of estate of
WILLIAM TURNER, deceased.

April 29, 1848
Died at his residence near Bolin Chissa, Clark County, Mississippi
on January 26th the HON. THOMAS S. STERLING, Judge of the 5th Judical
Court of said state.
Died at Hill's Landing, Washington County, Ala. 27th of January of
wounds received by accidental discharge of a pistol on Jan. 1st, MR.
JAMES BRADY, of firm of Cato and Brady.
J. M. WITHERS, attorney-at-law
State of Alabama-Tuscaloosa County. Orphans Court Jan. 2, 1839.
THOMAS BUCHANAN, administrator of estate of WILLIAM BUCHANAN, deceased.
State of Alabama-Walker County. Orphans Court. 26 Jan. 1839.
ABSALUM BARTON, one of administrators of estate of JOSHUA HENSON, late
of said county, deceased.

May 2, 1838
Married on Wed. last in Bellefonte, Ala. by HON. T. M. RECTOR,
MR. ROBERT A. ETON (or Easton?) of Tuscaloosa to MISS LYDIA J. GILL of
former place.

May 9, 1838
CATHARINE CONNERLY versus DENNIS KENSALL and others, Pickens
County; DENNIS KENSALL, JOHN RAGAN and THOMAS JONES are not inhabitants
of this state.
Letters of administration granted by Orphans Court of Fayette
County to HAGAN YEARBY on estate of STEPHEN GEORGE deceased. Note:
Letter to us from MRS. L. E. STONE, Provo, Utah 1956. "STEPHEN GEORGE
of Fayette Co. Ala; wife, SUSANNE BARBEE GEORGE. They had a dau.
REBECCA b 1826 in Tuscaloosa Co."
JOSHUA HENSON, late of Walker County. ABSALUM BARTON and ELIZABETH
HENSON, adm'r and adm'x.

June 6, 1838
Died Tuesday 22d ult. MR. SAMUEL L. MILLER.

June 13, 1838
Departed this life on Saturday morning last, HUGH FRANKS, a native
of North Carolina in 24th year, after an illness of two weeks.

June 20, 1838
State of Alabama-Pickens County. Orphans Court June 12, 1838.
ROBERT JEMISON, JR. petitions that the executors of the will of
WALTER W. GILKEY, late of Pickens County, deceased by compelled to make
title to real estate. WILLIAM M. GILKEY and ALFRED GILKEY, executors.

July 4, 1838
Married in New Town in this vicinity on Thursday evening 28th inst.
by REV. MR. CLANCY, MR. ERASMUS COOPER to MISS SARAH ANN, daughter of
MR. THOMAS CUMMINGS.

July 11, 1838
Married in this city, 3d inst. by REV. D. BAKER, MR. CHARLES J.
FIQUET, late of Baltimore and formerly of New York to MISS MARY ANN
FOSTER of Burlington, New Jersey. See our Vol. 2 p. 53.
T. C. RICHARDSON states that he has purchased from his brother,
JOHN RICHARDSON the steamboat "Ophelia."

July 18, 1838
     Married the 10th inst by REV. B. L. DEFREESE, W(M) C. HENRY,
Esq. to MISS ELMINA C. HARRISON, all of Centreville, Bibb County.
See our Vol. 160 p. 47.

July 25, 1838
     Administrator's Notice 18 May 1838. Judge of County Court of
Chambers County granted letters of administration on estate of
JAMES McLAIN, deceased, to MARIA McLAIN and JOHN McLAIN.

August 1, 1838
     Married on 19th inst. by REV. J. C. KEENEY, MR. JOHN MILLER to
MISS MELVINA A. CARTER, both of Tuscaloosa. See our Vol. 8 p. 51.

August 8, 1838
     Married on the evening of 31st ult. by REV. MR. DeVOTIE, MR. GEORGE
D. PEARSON of Greene County to MISS SARAH, daughter of HENRY T. ANTONY,
Esq. of this city. See our Vol. 9 p. 18.
     Died on Monday 30th of July in her 24th year of perpureal fever at
the residence of her brother-in-law, HON. JOHN G. CREAGH, near Clarkesville, Clarke County, Ala. MRS. ANN D. CREAGH, consort of MR. ALEXANDER
CREAGH of Clarke County. Also left infant son seven days old. Her
aged widowed mother, brothers and sisters also survive.

August 15, 1838
     TABITHA SHIELDS versus JOSEPH SHIELDS. Defendant is not a resident
of this state.

August 29, 1838
     Married 21st inst. by REV. THOMAS A. SMITH, JAMES HAIR, Esq. of
Livingston, Sumpter Co. Ala. to MISS MARTHA W. JENKINS of this city.
     Died in this city Monday evening last, ROSWELL, son of V. HART
aged about 5 years.
     Died Saturday 4th of August at his residence in Marengo County
after a painful illness of a few days, DANIEL HENRY TILLINGHASTE,
formerly of South Carolina, but for many years a highly respectable
inhabitant of this state.
     JAMES T. BURDINE, administrator of estate of JOSEPH MARTIN,
deceased late of Pickens Co.

September 12, 1838
     Married in this city Thursday evening 6th inst by REV. DANIEL BAKER,
CAPT. H(OLLIS) C. KIDDER to MISS MARY C. (S) WASHINGTON. See our Vol. 8
p. 38.
     Obituary:
     JOSEPH MARTIN was a native of Union District, South Carolina. He
was born November 26, 1802 and with his father and mother and other family
connections emigrated to the west in 1821, then being about 19. His
father, with whom he had always lived, settled near Yorkville, now is
in Pickens County, where he has ever since resided. When the call for
volunteers to protect Florida from horrors of savage warfare came,
MR. MARTIN, then Major of battalion, volunterred as a private soldier
and was elected Captain of Volunteers from Pickens County.... After
his return, he was in 1836 elected to the Legislature, re-elected in
1837 and 1838 and on the very day of his death was chosen for third
time a Representative. He died 7th of August, 1838 at 2 o'clock.
     Died in this city on 28th, WILLIAM MORRISON, an old and worthy
citizen.
     Died in this vicinity on 3rd inst at her father's residence,
HENRY S. SIMONTON, Esq. MISS CECELIA SIMONTON after a protracted
illness.

September 19, 1838
     State of Alabama-Bibb County. Orphans Court Sept. Term 1838.
WILLIAM H. WILSON and JOHNS LATHAM, administrators of estate of JOHN
WILSON, deceased JOHN WILSON, ROBERT WILSON and HARRIET LATHAM, wife
of BAILEY LATHAM, ENOCH M. BROWN, E. P. SMITHERMAN, MARTHA A. SMITHERMAN,
ROBERT D. SMITHERMAN, LUIZA J. SMITHERMAN, HARRIET SMITHERMAN and
ANDREW SMITHERMAN, all heirs of deceased. JOHN and ROBERT WILSON and
HARRIED LATHAM reside beyond limits of the state.

September 26, 1838
    Married in this city Thursday night 20th inst. by REV. J. H. THOMASON
of the Methodist Episcopal Church, MR. ELIAS PURSINGER of North Port
to MISS LOUISA S. daughter of MR. GEORGE CURLIN of the former place.
See our Vol. 9 p. 18.
    Died in this city 25th inst. MR. JOHN CLARE in his 26th year.
Funeral from his brother's (WILLIAM CLARE) dwelling.
    Died in this city of fever on 21st inst. the REV. CHARLES HARDY,
Pastor of the Methodist Episcopal Church in this city.
    Died at Mount Vernon, Ala. on 6th inst. MR. JOHN C. RAGSDALE,
Printer. Died of remittant fever. Papers in North Alabama requested
to copy (Stockton, Ala. Minor).
    Obituary:
    Departed this life on 11th inst. at age of 28 years and 9 months,
MRS. JANE KELLY, consort of DOCT. JAMES KELLY, of Jefferson County, Ala.
    Obituary:
    Died on 14th of July last in 27th year at Blount Springs (which
place he visited for his health) in 27th year, FRANCIS C. D. BOUCHELLE,
who was connected with Franklin College at Athens, Ga. in 1829 and 1830.
He was born in South Carolina. Graduated from the University of Alabama
in August, 1833. Note: FRANCIS CUMMINS DECATUR BOUCHELLE, grad.
U oc Ala. 1833, son of JESSE C. & REBECCA (CUMMINS) BOUCHELLE; b 1814
d. 1838 at Blount Springs.

October 3, 1838
    Married in the Cado Purchase, near Shrieve's Port, La. on 6th
ultimo, MR. CHARLES W. LEWIS, formerly of this city of MRS. PRESCOT
of the former place.
    Married on Tuesday evening, 25th ult. by REV. R. B. McMULLEN,
WILLIAM TASKER, Esq. to MRS. SARAH T(HOMAS) CUNNINGHAM, all of Clinton,
Ala.

October 1-, 1838
    Married in this city on the 2d inst. by REV. THOMAS A. SMITH,
MR. DAVID G. FULTON of Gainesville to MISS DORITHEA MASSENGALE of this
city. See our vol. 2 p. 53.
    Obituary:
    Departed this life at Pickensville, Ala on 13th Sept. 1838 in
33rd year, MRS. MATILDA ANN KELLY, consort of GERSHOM KELLY. For last
10 or 12 years a member of Baptist Church.

October 17, 1838
    Married on evening of 9th inst. by REV. T. A. SMITH, MR. STEPHEN B
COMBS to MISS MARTHA M. MASSENGALE, both of this city. See our Vol. 2
p. 30.
    Married in Courtland, Ala. on 26th ult REV. W. R. HOLCOMBE of
Athens to MRS. M. FINDLEY of the former place. Note: Lawrence Co.
marriages show: WM. H. HOLCOMBE to MARTHA J. FINDLEY Sept. 20, 1838.

October 31, 1838
    Married 23d inst. by REV'D I. C. KEENEY, MR. WILLIAM McLAUGHLIN to
MISS RUTH BUCHANAN, all of this co.

November 7, 1838
    Married in this city on Thursday, 1st inst. in Christ's Church by
REV. MR. KNAPP, MR. JACOB SALEE, of Vienna, Ala. formerly of Maysville,
Va. to MISS ELIZABETH S. WILLIAMS of the former place and originally
from Newbern, NC. See our Vol. 13 p. 20.

November 14, 1838
    State of Alabama-Bibb County. Orphans Court Nov. Sitting 1838.
BRANDON (should be BRANSON) LAWRENCE/LARRENCE, NOAH LARRENCE, MARTHA
LARRENCE, NANCY LARRENCE, JESSE GATLIN, in right of wife ELIZABETH
(formerly LARRENCE), ZACHARIAH DAVIS in right of wife, AMY (formerly
LARRENCE), ALSTON GARNER, in right of wife, POLLY (late LARRENCE),
JAMES SAMPLE, guardian of minor heirs viz: JONATHON LARRENCE, WILLIAM
LARRENCE, EDWARD LARRENCE, AMANDA LARRENCE, MARGARET LARRENCE and
CATY LARRENCE, all heirs of EDWARD LARRENCE, deceased. Heirs ordered to
appear in court to show why commissioners should not be appointed to
sell land belonging to estate.

November 28, 1838
    Executors Notice--Orphans Court of Chambers County. Granted
letters testamentary, will of ABSALOM JACKSOM, late of said County to
ABIGAIL JACKSON and JOHN F. SHARP.

December 5, 1838
    Died in this city 29th ult. GEORGIA ANN, daughter of COL. PETER
DONALDSON aged 21.
    Died Tue. 27th ult. VIRGINIA infant daughter of SAMUEL G. FRIERSON,
Esq.

December 26, 1838
    Married on the 29th inst. by REV. EDWARD MOBLEY, Esq., MR. GEORGE
W. MITCHELL to MRS. MARGARET ANN McDOW, all of this co. See our Vol. 8
p. 51.
    Married in Bellefonte on 14th inst. CAPT. NORRIS, Editor of
Jacksonian, to MISS NANCY, daughter of COL. WILLIAM SAXTON.
    Also at the same time, MR. JACOB HIENA to MISS BRADY all of
Jackson Co.
    HARVEY W. ELLIS, candidate for Congress.

January 2, 1839
    Married at the Famale Institute in this city by REV. WILLIAM H.
WILLIAMS, MR. SAMUEL McKEE STAFFORD, Professor in the University of
Alabama to MISS MARIA B. BROOKS of Westmoreland, New Hampshire.
See our Vol. 13 p. 20.

January 9, 1839
    Died of consumption in Clark County, Ala. on 15th ult. EDWARD B.
CLAPP, native of South Carolina. Charleston Courier please notice.
    Administrator's Notice:
    Letters of administration on estate of BENJAMIN BOX deceased, late
of Fayette County, granted to LILES BOX.

January 16, 1839
    Died at MRS. HERBERT'S in this city on Monday evening last of
influenza, HON. URIAH GRIGSBY, Member of the House of Representatives
from Dallas County. He was born in Newberry District, SC on 14th
January, 1799 and died aged 40.
    Died Thursday 10th January at Woodlawn in Greene County in 19th
year MRS. SUSAN CAROLINE, consort of DR. A. D. POPE.

February 13, 1839
    Obituary:
    Killed on night of 28th ultimo by a pistol shot through the head,
MR. MICHAEL DAILY, a native of Ennis, County Clare, Ireland aged 28
years. Left a wife and one orphan child. He was a Catholic.
    Died Monday 28th Jan 1839 of a protracted illness, MRS. MARGARET
WILSON, wife of WILLIAM P. WILSON, principal of North Tuscaloosa
Female Academy. Affectionate consort and mother.

February 20, 1839
    Melancholy Accident:
    Died A. L. R. THOMPSON, Esq. by accidental discharge of his own
gun, while hunting. Native of New York, where he was born 17th May,
1816. Recently a member of the profession of law. Member of Presbyterian
Church.

April 24, 1839
    Candidates:
    HARRIS MITCHELL for Sheriff
    GEORGE T. WASHINGTON for sheriff
    JOSEPH L. HOGG for sheriff
    ALEXANDER LACY for sheriff
    THOMAS G. BIRDWELL for sheriff
    FRANCIS R. BAKER--Esq. for sheriff
    R. W. BARBER for sheriff
    WINSTON J. BROWN for sheriff

Letters of administration on estate of BENJAMIN M. GREEN deceased granted to THOMAS MERRET and B. B. GREEN 18 Dec. 1838.

THOMAS CUMMINGS and ERASMUS COOPER dissolved partnership.

GIDEON B. FRIERSON and JOHN W. WOMACK attorneys

State of Alabama-Bibb County Orphans Court. JACKSON CREEL, one of administrators of estate of JOSHUA CREEL, deceased.

ROBERT T. CLYDE, attorney

ROBERT LEACHMAN and STEPHEN S. SORSBY, attorneys

JOHN D. PHELAN, attorney

GEORGE W. CRABB and WILLIAM COCHRAN, attorneys

W. B. and H. L. MARTIN, attorneys

S. A. HALE, attorney

State of Alabama-Pickens County, Orphans Court. SAMUEL G. COCHRAN states that EDWARD KING in his lifetime sold him land. NANCY KING, administratrix.

State of Alabama-Pickens County. Orphans Court. SAMUEL BASS petitions that JOHN CARSON sold him land. ARCHIBALD SHAW, JR. adm'r.

May 1, 1839
State of Alabama-Pickens County. Orphans Court. JAMES GARNETT, administrator of estate of RICE GARNETT, deceased. Some of the heirs reside out of the state.

Married at Brookland near Greensborough on 10th inst. by REV. WITHERSPOON, HON. HENRY COLDTHWAIT, one of Justices of Supreme Court of this state to MISS ELIZA I. (J) WITHERSPOON, daughter of DOCT. JOHN R. WITHERSPOON.

May 8, 1839
Died Tuesday evening 7th inst by a sudden casualty, MISS MARY ANN L. BARBER in 17th year and L. B. YOUNG aged 23 both of Tuscaloosa. They were to have been married.

WILLIAM BRALY and THOMAS ADKINS, candidates for Sheriff.

May 15, 1839
State of Alabama-Fayette County. Orphans Court. GEORGE W. TOMLIN, deceased. GEORGE COLLINS, administrator says estate cannot pay debts without sale of land (after reserving widow her dower).

May 22, 1839
Married Thursday evening 2nd by HON. JUDGE MORRISON, CAPT. JOHN J. CLARK of North Carolina to MISS E.(LIZ.) S. STAFFORD of Marengo Co. See our Vol 215 p. 74.

Died M D SIMPSON, Esq. late Editor of "Argus and Sentinel" Tuesday 7th inst. aged 35. He was a Scotchman by birth. Born at Dundee, Scotland in 1804 and came to this country with his family in 1831. Has been a resident of this city for last four years. Affectionate husband and father (Wetumpka Argus).

May 29, 1839
Married Wednesday evening by REV. MR. LYNCH, MR. ADAM W. POOL to MISS ELIZABETH ANN LEMMON, all of this city.

June 12, 1839
Letters of administration on estate of HUGH HENRY, deceased, granted to JOHN HENRY by Orphans Court of Bibb County on 25 December last.

To JOHN PETERS:
Dear Son: Your long absence from Brownsville connected with your silence have occasioned your old and afflicted parent with apprehension. Should you be in Alabama, to which state I understood you removed, I hope it will influence your immediate return.
MARGARET PETERS
Brownsville, Pa. Jan. 30, 1839"

April 3, 1839
Married in this city on last evening by REV. J. H. DeVOTIE, MR. S. H. BRALY to MISS OCTAVIA M. BROWNE.

State of Alabama-Fayette County. Orphans Court. CORNELIUS HOLIMAN, administrator of estate of WILLIAM RAINSWATERS, deceased. Note:

CORNELIUS HOLIMAN was 1812 pensioner. He m. 2 in Fayette Co. Ala. June 23, 1839 ELIZABETH RAINWATERS, according to pension. He d. in Marion (or Lamar) Co. Ala. 26 Oct. 1862.

July 1, 1840
MATTHEW W. LINDSAY, attorney-at-law
Administrator's Notice:
Letters of administration with will annexed on estate of WILLIAM WRAY, deceased, late of Fayette County granted to CATHARINE WRAY.
Married on Thursday evening, 18th inst. by REV. D. MANLY, SWAN H. SKELTON, Esq. of this city to MISS DIANA A. LEE, daughter of ISAAC LEE of this county. See our Vol. 13 p. 21.

July 15, 1840
State of Alabama-Bibb County. Orphans Court July Sitting 1840. LEWIS CAMMACK, administrator of estate of MARGARETT CAMMACK, deceased petitions to sell land, in Sumpter County. She left following heirs: DAVID CAMMACK, MICHAEL CAMMACK, MARGARET GRIFFIN, late CAMMACK, MARY WYATT, late CAMMACK, wife of ZADOC WYATT, SARAH OWENS, late CAMMACK, wife of WILLIAM OWENS, BENJAMIN EVANS, in right of wife ANN, late of CAMMACK and SAMUEL CAMMACK.

August 5, 1840
Died of consumption on Wednesday evening 29th ult. MISS HARRIETTE TRIPLETT MARTIN aged 18 years and 9 months only daughter of HON. PETER MARTIN of this city.

August 12, 1840
Died at his residence near this place of congestive fever on morning of 4th inst. after a few days illness, MR. EDWARD SIMS aged 57 years. Native of North Carolina then resided in Elbert County, Ga. and for last 20 years has been a resident of this county.

August 6, 1840
Died in this city Wednesday 19th inst. HELEN VIRGINIA, daughter of JOHN and ANN W. MARRAST aged 8 years 5 months and 16 days.
Died Wednesday last at Linden after a short illness in 19th year EDWARD OSCAR, eldest son of MR. MATHEW HOBSON of this place.
Died in this city last night, MR. MICHAEL GLEASON, formerly of Philadelphia, Pa. in 20th year.

September 9, 1840
Died of congestive fever after illness of five days in this city on Sat. 5th inst. MRS. HARRIETT B. NEAL in 26th year, consort of LEONARD B. NEAL. Affectionate wife and mother. Warrington, Va. Times and Hillsborough Recorder, NC please copy.
Died in this city on 27th ult. CHARLES LEWIN, son of ARMSTEAD R. and ELVIRA THOMAS after illness of 7 years and 9 mo.

September 23, 1840
Died at the residence of his father in Tuscaloosa County on 16th Sept. of congestive fever, ALGERNON S. KENNON in 23rd year. Graduate of LaGrange College in this state.
Died on yesterday morning 22d inst. after short but severe attack of congestive fever aged 45 years, MR. PATRICK MxAULIFFE, native of City of Cork, Ireland and resident of this city about 3 years (communicated)

September 30, 1840
Administrator's Notice:
Estate of JOHN WILSON, deceased. JAMES B. WILSON and MARY WILSON, administrator and administratrix.

October 7, 1840
State of Mississippi--Noxubee County. RICHARD M. CROWSON versus EMILY CROWSON, administratrix and CHARLES KICHARDS and DAVID ABERNATHY, administrators of estate of THOMAS CROWSON, deceased.
Administrator's Notice:
Letters of administration on estate of BENJAMIN GILPIN, late of Fayette County, deceased, was granted to RICHARD GILPIN.

September 8, 1840
    Administrator's Sale:
    Late residence of JOHN WILSON, deceased, to be sold. JAMES B.
WILSON and MARY WILSON, adm'r and adm'x.
    GEORGE B. SAUNDERS, book agent
    Holcombe, Brother and Co. Factors, Commission Merchants, Mobile.
                        JOHN C. HOLCOMBE
                        HENRY B. HOLCOMBE
                        GEORGE G. HOLCOMBE

October 21, 1840
    Died in this city on Monday the 19th inst. of billious fever,
WILLIAM GAINES McDANIEL aged 15 years. This young mam had been for
several months in the employ of this office.
    Proclomatiom:
    JAMES C. RAYMOND, late of Tuscaloosa County murdered EUGENE FANNILL,
Reward offered by Governor

October 27, 1840
    Private Boarding for young ladies by MRS. CANTLEY, widow of the
late MAJOR JOHN CANTLEY, deceased.
    Married at the Episcopal Church in this city on Thursday 22d
inst. at 7 o'clock by REV. MR. KNAPP, DR. L(UTHER) L. SKINNER to
MISS SOPHIA PERRY, daughter of HON. SION L. PERRY. See our Vol. 13 p. 23.
    We are pleased to learn by last news from Texas that WASHINGTON D.
MILLER, Esq., formerly of this city and a graduate of the University of
Alabama has been elected a member of Congress from the county of
Gonzales. MR. MILLER emigrated to Texas about 12 months since.

November 4, 1840
    PETER DONALDSON advertises rates of Bell Tavern.
    Obituary:
    Died on 20th ult. at residence of his father, ROBERT WALKER, JUN.
after a long and painful illness aged 27 years, 8 months and 2 days.
Left behinds an effectionate wife and two little sons.

November 11, 1840
    Married in this vicinity 5th inst. by REV. J. L. DACC, MR. N(ICHOLAS)
W. PRINCE to MISS MARY HILL, daughter of JAMES FOSTER, Esq. all of this
county. The fair bride has our respectable compliments for the generous
slice of cake which accompanied this notice. See our Vol. 9 p. 19.
    Administrator's Notice:
    State of Alabama--Pickens County. Orphans Court 5 Oct. 1840.
Letters of Administration granted to CYNTHIA JONES and SAMUEL W. EDDINS
on estate of JOHN B. JONES, deceased.

November 18, 1840
    Died on Monday 16th Nov. at the Mansion House in this city,
Virginia, infant daughter of DR. DAVID MOORE of Madison County aged 13
months and 4 days.

December 2, 1840
    DR. DAVID MORROW, dentist.

December 9, 1840
    Another Revolutionary soldier gone!
    Departed this life in Pickens County, Ala. on 23d of November last,
MR. JAMES McCRORY, a native of Ireland. He was born on 15th of May,
1758 at Larga on the River Bann in the County of Antrim, Ireland. He
sailed from Belfast in the year 1775 and landed at Baltimore 1st July
same year. In 1776, he settled in Guilford County, North Carolina and
the same year enlisted in continental service as it was then called.
He was at the battle of Bradywine under GEN. WASHINGTON, at battle of
Germantown under GEN. WASHINGTON and wintered at Valley Forge in Pa.
He fought under GEN. GREENE at Guilford; was at battle of Eutaw Springs
and at battle of Stono. He was with GEN. GATES at his defeat and with
Morgan at battle of the Cowpens. For courage, services and good conduct,
he was promoted to the rank of Ensign in GEN. WASHINGTON's Corps of
Force (or Life Guards) and while belonging to the Corps was taken

prisoner and marched to south of Cape Fear River and kept confined on
board a prison ship for six months. At the close of the Revolution, he
retired to labors of private life and early became one of citizens of
the Territory, now the state of Alabama. For last 25 years of his life,
he was a worthy member of the Church and in the cheerfulness and con-
tentment of his mind seemed to anticipate that future happiness....
    Communicated:
    Died in this city on evening of 2d inst. MR. CHARLES W. COZENS,
late of Columbia, SC in his 36th year.

December 23, 1840
    Obituary:
    A patriarch has been taken from amongst us...ALLEN GLOVER. A
few minutes after 11 o'clock on Thursday 3rd inst. in 72d year, he
closed his eyes in death after a protracted and painful illness. He
was the head of a numerous and highly respected family. In February,
A D 1820 he emigrated from Abbeville District, SC to Alabama and located
himself in the dense forest upon what was then called White Bluff on
Tombeckbee river, now Dempolis. One of earliest settlers in this
quarter of state, he remained a permanent citizen.
    Administrator's Notes:
    Estate of ABRAHAM HOUSTON, deceased late of Fayette County.
JAMES M. MORROW, adm'r

December 30, 1840
    State of Alabama--Jefferson County. Estate of JUDITH VAUGHAN,
deceased. RICHARD HUDSON, adm'r. 28 Nov. 1840.
    Administrator's Notice:
    State of Alabama-Fayette County. Estate of ABEL WHITE, deceased.
JOHN WHITE, JEPTHA WHITE, executors.

January 6, 1841
    Died in this town on Friday last, MR. GEORGE HAMPTON, formerly of
Charlotte, NC in his 63d year.

January 13, 1841
    Married at Madison College near Marion on 5th inst. A(RNOLDUS) V.
BRUMBY, Esq. to MISS A(NN) E. WALLIS, daughter of DR. J(OHN) F. WALLIS.
Note: DR. BRUMBY was in 1850 Census of Macon Co. Ala. ae 35 b Md she
27 Ga.

January 20, 1841
    Married in the vicinity of this city on evening of 12th inst. by
REV. W. A. SCOTT, SAMUEL D. J. MOORE, Esq. attorney at law to MISS ANNA
MARIA, daughter of MAJ. D. M. FORNEY. See our Vol. 8 p. 52.

January 27, 1841
    Died at Sweetsen's Tavern in North Tuscaloosa on Wednesday 20th
inst. HARDIN P., youngest son of B. TRAWEEK, Esq., in 22d year of his
age.

February 3, 1841
    Married in this city on Tuesday last week by REV. JOHN OWEN,
WILLIAM D. MARRAST, Esq. to MRS. SUSAN M. (should be N(eel) MAHER all
of this co. See our Vol. 8 p. 52.
    Died in Madison Co. on 23d ultimo, HON. SAMUEL WALKER, late
Speaker of House of Representatives which office he was compelled to
resign by reason of ill health.
    Notice:
    Whereas my wife, ANNA has left my bed and board I am not responsible
for her debts.
                        JOHN A. T. DURRETTE
    Tuscaloosa, Ala. Jan. 31, 1841. Note: JOHN A. DURRETT m. Jan.
1840, ANNA B. EVANS.

February 10, 1841
    Married on Wednesday evening February 3d by REV. J. L. DAGG, MR.
SAMUEL M. FARRAR to MISS ELIZABETH J. HAMNER.

Administrator's Notice:
Estate of WILLIAM RICHARDSON, deceased late of Walker County.
JOAN (JOHN?) RICHARDSON and WILLIAM PIKE, administrators.

February 17, 1841
        AUGUSTIN LYNCH, cabinet and sofa manufacturer
        DR. L. S. SKINNER, dentist

February 24, 1841
        Married in vicinity of this city on Sunday 21st inst. by
REV. DR. MANLEY, CAPT. P(HILANDER) LaVERGIE of Steamboat "Hercules" to
MISS MARY V(IRGINIA) BICKLEY of Greene Co.

March 3, 1841
        Died at White Plains, Benton County, Ala. on 17th ult. VIRGINIA
ELIZABETH, last daughter and child of COL. WILLIAM GARRETT of this
place aged 1 year 11 months and 17 days. The last link which joined
together a devoted father with a wife and four children, who have gone
before it....

March 10, 1841
        Died in this city on 4th inst. at residence of her son-in-law
JUDGE ORMAND, MRS. MARY BANKS after a long and painful illness, which
she bore with resignation and fortitude. Note: See her will in our
Vol. 2 p. 83. She was dau of THOS. JENKINS & wife MARY WASHINGTON.

March 17, 1841
        In Chancery:
WASHINGTON ERLAND et al versus RACHEL MABRY, WILLIAM MABRY,
BENJAMIN MABRY, SARAH MABRY, FRANKLIN MABRY, DANIEL MABRY and CAROLINE
MABRY, defendants reside without the limits of the state.
        JAMES JOHNSON versus HENRY JOHNSON
        Administrator's Notice:
        Estate of CHARLES H. JONES, deceased of Fayette County.
LEVI LINDSEY, JAMES M. MORRIS, ALVIS DAVIS, commissioners.

March 31, 1841
        Administrator's Notice·
        Estate of ROBERT MORROW, deceased, Pickens County. MARTHA MORROW,
administratrix and SAMPSON NOLAND, adm'r.

April 14, 1841
        State of Alabama-Pickens County. Orphans Court March #22, 1841.
CYNTHA T. JONES, administratrix and SAMUEL EDDINS, administratrix of
estate of JOHN B. JONES, deceased.
        Register's Sale:
        JOHN BOARDMAN
             versus
        MARY JUGE et al

May 5, 1841
        Married in vicinity of Livingston, Sumter County on evening of
25th March by REV. S. WITHERSPOON, GIDEON B. FRIERSON, Esq. to MISS
SARAH A. BECK.
        Married in this vicinity on Thursday evening 15th April by
REV. DR. MANLEY, MR. RICHARD FURMAN to MISS MARGARET CAMMER, both of
this city. Note: She was dau of PETER CAMMER. See our Vol. 79 p. 25.
        Married in this vicinity on 6th inst. by REV. WILLIAM HOOD,
COL. THOMAS G. BIRDWELL to MRS. TERXA HESTER. Note: She m. 1.
(June 21, 1825) DAVID HESTER & was nee McCOWN. His former wife
(BIRDWELL'S) RACHAEL OLIVER, d. 1837.
        In this city 27th inst. by REV. DR. MANLY, MR. JOHN PARKER of
Cockermouth, England to MISS LUCINDA A(NN) HART, of this city. See
our Vol. 9 p. 19.
        Administrator's Notice:
        State of Alabama--Bibb County
        ABISHA CAMP, deceased.
        WILLIAM L. CAMP)
        J. C. D. TROTT   ) Executors
        ELSEY CAMP   )

Note: 1 ABISHA CAMP m. in Bibb Co. 6 Aug. 1837 ALSEY ALLEN.
See our Vol. 160 p. 15.

April 27, 1841 (date of above

May 26, 1841
   Married in vicinity of this city on Friday 21st inst. by
E(LIJAH) M. BURTON, Esq., MR. SAMUEL TEMPLE to MRS. NANCY HALL.
   Married near Montgomery Tuesday 11th inst. by REV. DR. WEST,
WASHINGTON MOODY, Esq., of Tuscaloosa to MISS ELIZABETH BOWDON,
daughter of SAMUEL BOWDON, Esq., of Shelby Co. (Note: m. in Shelby Co.
5-11-1841.)
   Died in this city 18th inst. of consumption after a protracted
illness, MRS. HELEN E. wife of RICHARD WHITING, Esq., of this city.

June 9, 1841
   Married on Wednesday 26th ult. by REV. MR. BYERS, JAMES THOMASON,
Esq., of Springville, St. Clair County, to MRS. JANE HAMLBETON of
Jefferson Co. (See our Vol. 26 p. 87)

June 30, 1841
   Died in this city of hemorrhage of the lungs the 29th inst.
PETER EARLY DONALDSON aged 25 years 9 months and 16 days, son of
COL. PETER DONALDSON of this city. This is the sixth deprivation of a
similar character, which this afflicted family has suffered in four
years. The friends of PETER and NANCY DONALDSON are invited to attend
the funeral at the Methodist Church at 4 o'cluck at 4 o'clock this
evening.
   Died in this city on Tuesday 22d inst. MRS. NANCY IRVIN, daughter
of MR. GEORGE KERR.

July 7, 1841
   Married on the 20th ult. by REV. MR. STANTON, JOHN G. CLARKE, Esq.,
of Fairfield, Pickens County, to MISS RACHEL JANE, daughter of COL. A.
DEAL, of Noxubee Co. Miss.

July 14, 1841
   Administrator's Sale:
   State of Alabama--Chambers County--Orphans Court 7 June 1841.
Negroes belong to estate of BENJAMIN DOLES, deceased of Halifax County,
N C will be sold for benefit of heirs of DEMPSEY JOHNSON, deceased,
late of Coweta County, Ga.
                    DAVID J. JOHNSON, adm'r
   Married in North Tuscaloosa on 6th July by REV. ZACHIUS DOWLING,
the REV. MARTIN SIMS of Fayetteville, Ala. to MRS. SARAH A. RICE of
North Tuscaloosa. See our Vol. 13 p. 22.

July 21, 1841
   Married in this city on the 16th by REV. JOHN OWEN, E(LIJAH) M.
BURTON, Esq. to MISS MARGARET HEARN, all of this city. See our Vol. 2
p. 11.

July 28, 1841
   Married by REV. BASIL MANLY on 20th inst. GEO. Y. BROWNE of Mobile
to MARY FRANCES, daughter of REV. J. L. DAGG of this city. See our
Vol. 2 p. 12.
   Died in this city on Saturday last the 24th inst JULIETTE,
daughter of DR. WILLIAM A. LELAND aged three years and nine months.

August 4, 1841
   State of Alabama--Autauga County. Orphans Court. Personally
appeared before us, A. W. GRAY and GEORGE NELSON, Justices of Peace for
said county, ANN LIVINGSTON (formerly ANN SHANNON), LUIS SHANNON and
LEMUEL SHANNON, who deposeth that HENRY M. G. LARY used ANN's name to
get money out of the State Bank. Note: WM. LIVINGSTON m. May, 1841
NANCY SHANNON. See our Vol. 224 p. 72.
   Died in Pickens County at the residence of her father, on Saturday,
17th inst. of hemorrhage of the nose, MERIAM IRBY, aged 14 years,
daughter of JOHN O. CUMMINS, Esq., formerly of this city.

August 11, 1841
    (Communicated)
    Died of a bilious attack at his home near Jonesboro, Alabama on
31st ult. REV. HOSEA HOLCOMBE aged 61 years and 11 days. The disease
came came on while he was traveling at a distance of 75 or 80 miles
from home and with much difficulty, he reached his residence on the
third day, after which he lay 8 days and bore his affliction without a
murmur. The subject of this notice had been for about 40 years an
indefatigable laborer in the Gospel Church. He was the author of
several small publications and of the history of the Baptists in
Alabama.... Left a widow and many friends.

August 18, 1841
    STEPHEN ELLEDGE on the night of 17th of July murdered HENRY FRANKS
in Tuscaloosa County. Reward offered by Governor. ELLEDGE described
as being about 40 years old.
    Reward offered for arrest of WILLIAM RUFF, who on 23rd February
1839 murdered DANIEL HENDRICK, late of Tuscaloosa Co.
    Married at Starkville, Miss. by REV. J. C. KEENEY, MR. JAMES BELL
to MISS REBECCA A. MONTGOMERY, both of Starkville, Miss.
    Died in Perry County on 26th ult. DR. JOHN F. WALLIS aged 58 years
formerly Professor of Moral Philosophy in University of Alabama.

August 25, 1841
    Married in vicinity of this city on 19th inst. by REV. JOHN OWEN,
MR. EDWARD A(UGUSTUS) HAUG to MISS MARY TEMPERANCE WARE. See our Vol. 2
p. 72.
    Married in Pickens County on 15th inst by REV. GEORGE SHAFFER,
COL. NATHANIEL SMITH, formerly of Madison County to MRS. FRANCES ANDERSON
of Pickens County. Huntsville Democrat please copy.
    At a meeting of the officers of the 5th Brigade, 2nd Division
A.M. and the volunteers who served in the Florida campaign in 1736 to
pay respects to the late COL. CHARLES LEWIN, deceased. He accompanied
the Alabama Volunteers in 1836 to Florida as Quartermaster General.
                    GEO. W. CRABB, Chairman
                    W. JOHN WHITING, Sec'y

September 1, 1841
    Died in this city on Friday last, the 27th ult. MR. JOHN S. ANDRESS.
    Died in this county on Sunday, the 8th inst. MRS. E(LIZ.) H.
NORSWORTHY aged 64 years, wife of SAMUEL NORSWORTHY. During her
affliction of eight days she suffered great pain. She was a devoted
wife and mother.
    Another Revolutionary Patriot Gone:
    Died on 14th inst. at his residence in Granger County, Tennessee,
WILLIAM CLAY, Esq., father of the HON. C. C. CLAY, Senator in Congress
from Alabama. The deceased was born in the county of Chesterfield, in
the state of Virginia on the 11th day of August 1760. Consequently,
when he died he was within one week of completing his 81st year. He
entered the Revolutionary army at the early age of 16, served several
tours of duty with the militia of his native state and aided in the
closing scene of the War of Independence by his services at the seige
of Yorktown and the capture of LORD CORNWALLIS.
    Went off:
    From Chester District, South Carolina last winter, JAMES LAND and
BENJAMIN NICKELS, who are settled somewhere in Alabama in Cherokee
County near Leesburg P. O. Said men went off without paying their
debts to merchants and others and may do so again. This is to warn all
honest men to take care and not credit them.
                    THOS. McCULLOUGH & SON
    Fairfield District, S C July 29, 1841
    Monument erected to memory of JONATHON CILLEY by friends of
deceased in Elm Grove Cemetery in this town cost $500.
                    Thomaston Recorder

September 11, 1841
    Married on Thursday, 2d inst, by REV. MR. LAMBERT, MR. JAMES WATSON,
of Greene County to MISS ELIZABETH, daughter of BLANTON McALPIN, Esq.
of Mobile.

                              171

September 15, 1841
Died at his residence near this city on Tuesday evening the 14th
inst. MR. P. B. HEALY.

September 22, 1841
(Communicated)
Died on Tuesday evening at his residence in vicinity of Tuscaloosa
of bilious feverm MR. P(ERCIVAL) B. HEALEY in 36th year of his age.
MR. HEALEY was a native of County Carlow Ireland and for some time was
a resident of this city. He was a son of well known integrity and also
of industriuos and enterprising habits. He left a wife and interesting
children.

September 29, 1841
Married on 31st ult by the REV. J. C. KEENEY, MR. JAMES A.
MONTGOMERY of Oaktibbeha County to MISS ASCENATH R. and daughter of
COL. BENJN. WILLIAMS of Yallobusha County, Miss.
Died on 18th inst. JULIA MARIA, infant daughter of CAPT. JAMES H.
DEARING of this city aged 11 months.
A slave belonging to estate of WILLIAM A. AIKIN, deceased, late of
Madison County murdered a slave belonging to MRS. PHOEBE BLACKBURN of
Madison County. 25 Aug. 1841. Reward offered for arrest of said slave.

October 6, 1841
Information wanted concerning the children of JOHN and ROSANNA S.
DIVEN, formerly of Winchester, Va. MR. DIVEN moved from Winchester to
Knoxville, Tennessee in 1811 where on the 26th of August of that year,
MRS. DIVEN died leaving two surviving children: MARY and SUSAN.
MR. DIVEN shortly afterwards moved from Knoxville to Mobile, Ala. where
he again married. The girls, MARY and SUSAN, who had been left near
Knoxville were then taken on to Mobile, since which time their friend
in Winchester having received no information from them, except that in
a letter from MRS. ELIZA RAMSEY, dated Athens, Tenn. May, 1838 to
DAVID DEADRICK, Esq. of Knoxville. They were referred to a MR. PHILIP
or G. S. GAINES of Mobile, who MRS. RAMSEY said could give information
concerning them. Should these children be living, information of
importance can be furnished them.
                      JOHN FLETCHER
    Winchester, Va. Aug. 25, 1841 (See our Vol. 92 p. 36 for lawsuit.)
    Died on 23rd inst. MRS. FRANCES SCOTT CRENSHAW aged 22 years 2
months and 17 days, the wife of MR. J. W. CRENSHAW.
    Died in 19th ult. THOMAS T. son of MR. ELIJAH and MRS. MARTHA
WILSON, of Selma in 16th year of his age.
    Died on 15th ult. at residence of MRS. MARY BOYKIN in Dallas
County, MRS. MARY C. BOYKIN in 23rd year of her age, wife of BURWELL
BOYKIN, Esq., of Mobile and daughter of the HON. ELI SHORTRIDGE of
Talladega.
    Died at his residence in Clarke County on 21st ult. HON. JOHN
MURPHY aged 56 years. MR. MURPHY served two terms as Governor of
Alabama and was subsequently a Representative in Congress from that
District.

October 13, 1841
Obituary:
Died at the residence of her uncle, C. A. CHANDLER, Esq., in
Columbus, Miss. on Sat. morning the 25th ult. MISS MARIA C. GOFFE aged
12 years and 14 days....
    Died in this city on Saturday last of whooping cough, aggravated
by influenza, CHARLES FOX aged 2 years, son of HON. JOHN J. ORMAND.
    While the family of DR. ALFRED MOORE of Madison County were
returning home, a large limb from a tree, killing a daughter of
DR. MOORE, aged 6 or 7 years and the driver.
    Administrator's Notice:
    Estate of FRANCES CROWLEY, deceased of Fayette County, R. H. POE,
admr.

October 20, 1841
Died in North Tuscaloosa on 15th inst. of an attack of fever,
THOMAS B. STONE.

October 27, 1841
    Married in this city on 25th inst. by REV. JOHN OWEN, JOHN B. GAILEY
of Lawrence County to MISS NANCY CORLEY (COOLEY in marriage record) of
this city.
    Notice:
    Estate of JOHN MORROW, deceased, late of Walker County. MARY MORROW
adm'x.

November 3, 1841
    Letters of administration on estate of WALLER J. JONES, deceased,
late of Tuscaloosa County granted to RICHARD COLE.
    Died at the residence of MR. L. B. PIPPEN in this place on 18th
inst. at 8 P.M. MR. JAMES P. GLEASON of bilious fever, after a lingering illness of 23 days. Aged 28 years...Philadalphia papers requested
to copy.

November 24, 1841
    Tribute of Respect:
    Death of AMAZIAG DUDLEY HARGROVE, who died 18th inst. at the
residence of his uncle, MR. DANIEL J. HARGROVE in Pickens County in
his 19th year. We sympathize with his afflicted parents.
    Departed this life on 18th inst. FLORENCE AMELIA, daughter of
S. M. & ANN A. MEEK, aged 1 year 11 months and 8 days.

December 1, 1841
    Delegates from Agricultural Societies
    DAVID MOORE   )
) Madison County
    GEORGE T. JONES)

    JOHN L. HUNTER) Barbour County

    HENRY W COLLIER   )
    B. MANLY   )
    R. JEMISON, JR.   ) Tuscaloosa County
    BENJAMIN WHITFIELD   )
    Nov. 13, 1831 (1841?))
    Died in New Town in this vicinity on 18th inst. WILLIAM B. ALLEN,
Esq., an old and highly respected citizen. Many years ago, he published
"The Press" at Cahawba and was State Printer before the removal of the
seat of Government.
    Died at LaGrange House in this city on 20th inst. DAVID WHITE,
Esq., of the city of Mobile. On his way to the seat of Government, he
became exposed to weather and took cold, which was the immediate cause
of his illness, though he labored under a slight affection of the
liver.
    Died at the residence of his brother in Irwinton, Barbour County on
17th inst. of Typhus congestive fever, HARVY BUFORD, a youth of 14.

December 8, 1841
    Married in Bibb County on 2d inst. by CHARLES H. COLLIER, Esqr.,
MR. A. R. P. CONWILL to MISS SARAH WOOD, all of that county.

December 16, 1841
    Died in Tuscaloosa on 9th inst. REV. RANDOLPH STONE. He was sick
about three weeks of bilious fever. MR. STONE preached for a number of
years on the Reserve during its early history. He was one of the most
efficient members in prepatory measures, which led to erection of
Wester Reserve College. He was editor of the new Ohio Observer for
several years.

December 22, 1831
    Administrator's Notice:
    Letters of administration on estate of MARY DRENNON, dec'd late of
Walker County granted to WILLIAM GRAVLEE.

December 29, 1841
    Married in Greensboro on 8th inst. by REV. THOMAS S. WITHERSPOON,
HON. SYDENHAM MOORE to MISS AMANDA, daughter of MATHEW HOBSON of
Greene County.

January 5, 1842
Died in this city on 31st December last, PLEASANT D. E. QUARLES in
26th or 27th year of his age. MR. QUARLES was a native of Aylette,
King William County, Va.... It will be a consolation to his mother and
numerous relations in King William to learn that he was highly esteemed
in Tuscaloosa. Richmond Enquirer copy.
Notice:
Estate of ALLISON JONES, deceased. Land offered for sale by
JAMES STEWART, WILLIAM WOMMACK, WILLIAM MADDOX.

January 12, 1842
Married by REV. MR. GLADNEY at Fairfield, Pickens County on 33rd
(23rd?) ultimo, MR. BIRD IVY to MISS ELIZABETH STONE, daughter of
COL. WILLIAM D. STONE.

January 19, 1842
Married on Tuesday 11th inst. by REV. J. HAMILTON of this city,
WILLIAM C. BIBB of Lowndes Co. Miss. to MISS PRISCILLA A. SIMS, daughter
of MRS. SARAH SIMS of this county.

January 26, 1842
Died on consumption in this county on the evening of 16th inst.
MRS. NANCY R. consort of REV. JAMES H. THOMASON in 32d year, leaving
a husband, four little children and a weeping mother. Methodist.

February 2, 1842
Married Monday evening last by REV. J. L. DAGG, ROBERT E. LOVE,
Senior Editor of Marion, Perry County Herald to MISS LAURA A. CONE of
this city.
Married at Irwinton, Ala. on 11th inst. by REV. ROBERT C. SMITH of
the Presbyterian Church, COL. JOHN COCHRAN of the House of Representa-
tives to MISS CAROLINE E. WELLBORN, only daughter of GEN. WILLIAM
WELLBORN of Irwinton.

February 9, 1842
Married on the evening of 4th inst. by REV. W. A. SCOTT at resi-
dence of JUDGE PERRY near Tuscaloosa, JAMES J. FOSTER to MISS MARIAH
CUSACK.
Married in Greene County on 11th Jan. by REV. MR. BRADSHAW, MR.
WILLIAM R. PATTON of Huntsville to MISS MARY C. THOMAS of Greene County.
See our Vol. 120 p. 15.
Death of DR. JAMES SOMERVILLE
Died of apoplexy about 12 o'clock Thursday last. Left behind a
most interesting family. Camt to this city with his family in 1837.
Eminent physician. By Legislature of 1839, he was elected trustee of
State University....

February 16, 1842
MRS. MARGARET SMITH, relict of the late HON. WILLIAM SMITH, died
in this place on 24th ult. at a very advanced age. She possessed all
the sterling virtues of the ladies of olden times. From Huntsville
Democrat.

February 23, 1842
Married on Monday evening last by REV. MR. HAMILTON, MR. GEORGE D.
PURCELL of Virginia to MISS MARY L. AVERY to Tuscaloosa Co. (Letter
to us from MISS RUTH EVANS, Box 147, Butler, Ala 36904 Apr. 5, 1969
"My father, JAMES SLICER PURCEL b Tuscaloosa July 25, 1843. In 1856
his parents, GEO. DOWELL PURCELL & MARY LUCINDA AVERA moved to Black
Hawk, Miss. Carroll Co. J. S. P. volunteered in Civil War."
Died in this city on Friday the 18th inst. MRS. MARY HAWN, wife of
WILLIAM HAWN, Esq., in her 30th year.... A few weeks ago, the deceased
gave birth to a lovely baby. As a mother, as a daughter, as a sisterm
she was the pride of her aged parents and to her brothers an object of
purity. She left a husband, four young children and other relations,
among them an aged father and mother.

March 2, 1842

Married at Dummerville on evening of 22d, ult, by REV. MR. HAMILTON, I)J) P(ENNINGTON) BORDEN, Esq., of Greene County to MISS ELIZABETH H. daughter of DR. JOHN MARRAST.

March 9, 1842

ETHEL alias ELLIS DRED PORTER in August 1841 murdered STARNES M. WELBOURNE. Reward to deliver him to sheriff of Marengo County. PORTER described as being about 35 or 40 years old.

Administrator's Notice:
Estate of DANIEL HERRIN, deceased. HENRY HERRIN, administrator.
Married Thursday evening 3rd inst. by REV. DR. JOHN OWEN, DR. JOHN H. NEILSON to MISS MARY JANE, daughter of JOHN HARGROVE, all of this county.

Obituary Communicated:
Died at the residence of her father in New Town Friday morning last, MISS MARGARET CUMMINGS in her 15th year. Killed when a tornado razed the house.

March 16, 1842

Died at his residence in Clarke County, Ala. on 1st of March, CAPT. WILLIAM ARMISTEAD, native of Virginia aged about 83. Fought in battles of Monmouth and Stony Point.

State of Alabama--Fayette County. Orphans Court. POLLY JONES, administratrix of CHARLES H. JONES, deceased.

Political letter from GEORGE T. JONES, first of series.

March 23, 1842

Thursday evening last, a man by name of JACOB TARVER stayed all night at my home. When called to breakfast, he appeared unwell and mentally deranged and later died. From two letters found in his possession, he resided in Irwinton, Henry County, Alabama. Has a brother and sister living in Jackson County, Florida. Had been traveling in Texas and Arkansas and was on his way back to Alabama.
G. N. LANGFORD
Brandon, Miss., March 2, 1842

March 30, 1842

Died on morning of 20th February in 41st year of her age, MRS. LUCY BINNS FLETCHER, consort of MR. JOHN J. FLETCHER of Limestone County.... Left husband, five small children (all daughters, one of which was born about two weeks ago) and numerous relations.

State of Alabama Bibb County. WILLIAM BARNETT, administrator of estate of SAMUEL BARNETT, deceased.

State of Alabama--Tuscaloosa County. G. W. MITCHELL, administrator of estate of ABNER WINN, deceased.

April 6, 1842

Another political letter from GEORGE T. JONES.

Married in this county on 4th inst. by E. M. BURTON, Esq., BENJAMIN D. HASSELL, Esq. to MISS HESTER ANN McCLENDON, both of Montgomery.

Married last evening 12th inst. by HON. J. J. ORMAND, MR. WILLIAM BILLINGSLEA of Montgomery to MISS KETURAH GUILD, daughter of DR. JAMES GUILD of this city.

Died on Wednesday, 30th ult. at his residence in Wilcox County, COL. THOMAS B. CREAGH in his 75th year. Native of Virginia, but for twenty years a resident of this state. Note: He was son of THOS. & KEZIAH (BREVARD) CREAGH.

April 20, 1842

Letter of GEORGE T. JONES from JEREMIAH CLEMENS.

May 4, 1842

Married in this city on Thursday evening last by REV. DR. JOHN OWEN, JOEL RIGGS, Esq. to MISS GEORGENA R. MOORE, eldest daughter of JUNIUS A. MOORE, Esq., all of this city.

May 11, 1842
Married on 24th of April by REV. BASEL MANLY, DR. GEORGE A. PARKER
to MISS MARION CONROW, both of this city.

May 18, 1842
Married near Centreville on 5th inst. by REV. CHARLES YALE,
DR. L. W. WILSON to MISS NANCY C. DUFF, only daughter of WALTER C. DUFF,
Esq., all of Bibb Co.
Information wanted of IRVIN HOLCOMBE, who left Greenville District,
South Carolina in 1833 and has not been heard from since 1836, wh en he
was was in Tuscumbia, Ala.
                                JORDAN HOLCOMBE
Merrittsville, S C
May 1, 1842

May 25, 1842
Administrator's Notice:
JAMES WHITSON, deceased. WILLIAM T. WHITSON, administrator
NATHANIE; J. F. DOUTHITT, administrator of estate of JAMES DOUTHITT,
dec'd.

June 1, 1842
Another Revolutionary Soldier Gone!
Died at his late residence seven miles north of Tuscaloosa on 25th
of May last, WILLIAM BINION, Esq., in his 79th year. He was born in
Buckingham County, Virginia August 28, 1763. But a little above above
tender age of 16, he entered the American army in which he served during
latter part of Revolutionary struggle. Engaged in battle of Camden and
also at th seige of York....

June 8, 1842
Married at Cahawba on Thursday, 26th ult. by REV. MR. CAMPBELL,
W. W. FAMBRO to MISS ELIZABETH JACOBS of that place.
Communicated:
Died at Barryton, Washington County Friday May 6th MRS. MARTHA W.
HOUSTON of pneumonia wife of HON. S. S. HOUSTON.... (Tombstone--
cemetery at old Barrytown "MRS. MARTHA W. HOUSTON d. May 26 1842 aged
27 years")

June 15, 1842
Another letter from GEORGE T. JONES.

June 22, 1842
Married on 21st inst. by REV; WILLIAM A. SCOTT, RICHARD WHITING to
MISS MARTHA M. MURRELL, both of this city.
Obituary:
Departed this life in this city Sunday night last 19th last.
MR. PATRICK REDMOND aged about 39. Drowned while bathing. -inexperienced
swimmer; native of Philadelphia, but resided in this city about 9 years.
He was Register in Land Office for this District under administration
of VAN BUREN and at the time of his death filled office of Pension Agent
and was Discount Clerk in Bank of State. Philadelphia papers please
copy.

June 29, 1842
Died at the University on night of 22nd ult. CAROLINE BREVARD,
infant daughter of Professor R(ICHARD) T. BRUMBY aged 10 months. Note:
He m. MARY ISABELLA BREVARD. He was b. Aug. 4, 1804 d. Oct. 6, 1875.
Reward for arrest of GEROGE W. LORE, convicted of murder of
HENRY BLAKE of Barbour County on 23rd of May last.
    Candidates for Legislature-Representatives
    GENERAL JAMES G. CARROLL
    W. P. MERIWETHER
    WILLIAM H. OGBURN
    ROBERT M. GARVIN
    Candidates for Sheriff of Tuscaloosa County:
    DANIEL CRIBBS
    SAMUEL HOLLOWAY
    ISAAC COLE
    D. J. W. FULTON

THOMAS P. MITCHELL
Administrator's Notice:
Letters of administration on estate of MOSES DUKE, late of Fayette
County, sdeceased granted to B. S. DUKE 12 Aug. 1841.
NEWTON L. WHITFIELD, Mayor of Tuscaloosa
Reward for arrest of JOSEPH B. JENNINGS, who on 17th of August 1841
murdered JEREMIAH FRION in Coosa County; description of Jennings--
5 ft 8 in. tall, stout built, dark complection, curly hair of sandy
brown color and about 24 years of age.

June 15, 1842
Administrator's Notice:
JAMES WHITSON, deceased. WILLIAM T. WHITSON appointed adm'r.
JAMES M. DUNLAP and W. MILLER, new mercantile firm.
BARNARD & HARRINGTON for Daguerrotypes
ALEXANDER B. FORNEY now in firm of JONES M. WITHERS and ROBERT T.
CLYDE, lawyers
STERRETT & STEVENS--law firm (A. A. STERRETT, A. W. STEVENS)
HENRY STITH, attorney--Pickens Co.

July 6, 1842
Letters of administration on estate of PATRICK REDMOND, deceased
granted to WILLIAM G. PARISH admr.
To be continued.
Departed this life after a long and painful attack of palsy on the
2nd day of June last, ELIZABETH DARDEN, consort of GEORGE DARDEN of this
county and vicinity in the 76th year of her age. MRS. DARDEN has long
been a citizen and resident of this county and vicinity and needs but
to be named to be recollected by most of our citizens.... She was an
affectionate wife, a tender mother.... For 33 years she was a member
of the Baptist Church. She left an aged husband and numerous posterity.
New Stage line from Tuscaloosa to Livingston. S. G. FRIERSON & Co.

July 13, 1842
Died in Philadelphia on the 27th of June, THOMAS W. KORNEGAY of
this city aged about 27 years. Native of North Carolina. Died o
pulmonary consumption, with which he was afflicted for a long time....
Obituary:
Departed this life on Friday morning the 25th of June at the house
of her son, near the line of Mississippi, MRS. JANE BINION, aged and
amiable relict of the late WILLIAM BINION, Esq., of Tuscaloosa County.
She survived her husband one month and was under much indisposition
at the time of her husband's death. After his death, she retired with
her sons to spend the remainder of her days with them and their families
She was born in 1764 or 1865 of respectable parentage and brought up
in Caswell County, North Carolina. She received more than an ordinary
education for the custom of that time. She married in the year 1784
and not long after removed with her husband to Georgia and settled in
Columbia County. She professed religion in May, 1803.... Was interred
with her husband and some of her children.... Note: Her husband,
WM. BINION was a Rev. War soldier.
Administrator's Notice:
Letters of Administration on the estate of THOMAS A. HEARD,
deceased late of Walker County, Alabama granted to ABSALOM BARTON.
Jasper, June 10, 1842
Law Notice:
SAMUEL F. RICE & THOS. D. CLARKE--partnership in Huntsville office
of Rice at Jacksonville, Ala. Office of CLARKE at Talladega, Ala.
June 22, 1842.

July 20, 1842
List of Post Offices in Alabama

Postoffice	Postmaster	Distances from Tuscaloosa
AUTAUGA COUNTY		
Chesnut Creek	AKLEN RAY	81 mi
Hamilton	JAMES SHARP	95
Independence	HENRY D. HUFFMAN	96

Postoffice	Postmaster	Distance from Tuscaloosa
Kingston C. H.	M. P. HOLMAN	90
Milton	WILLIAM H. ROBERTS	100
Mulberry Creek	SANFORD H. McGRAW	105
Vernon	LEWIS SIMPSON	114
Washington	BENJAMIN F. TARLETON	105
Wetumpka	WILLIAM J. COUCH	110

BALDWIN COUNTY

Blakely	JOSEPH RANDALL	225
Stockton	GERALD BYRNE	198
Tensaw	EDWARD D. HALLEY	180

BARBOUR COUNTY

Clayton	BENJAMIN PETTY	185
Emorysville	JAMES WOOD	205
Fullersville	JOSH H. DANFORTH	190
Glennsville	MASSILON M. GLENN	230
Irwinton	WILLIAM S. TAYLOR	220
Louisville	DANIEL S. McKENZIE	193
Midway	SAMUEL FAIGIN	205
Pea River	FRANCIS JOHNS	192
White Oak Springs	A. FERGUSON	196
Williamson	JOHN W. MOORE	198

BENTON COUNTY

Alexandria	EDMUND PENDLETON	160
Cane Creek	URIAH BARNETT	165
Corn Grove	JOSHUA TEAGUE	163
Cove Creek	WILLIAM P. REED	160
Goshen	THOMAS R. WILLIAMS	165
Jacksonville	E. L. WOODWARD	151
Kemp's Creek	NORMAN PERENDA	175
Ladiga	JAMES MONTGOMERY	161
Ohatchie	PHILIP GEE	126
Ten Islands	H(AZEL) LITTLEFIELD	160
White Plains	ARTHUR T. CROZIER	166

BIBB COUNTY

Centreville	MORGAN HOWARD	40
Maplesville	WILEY BUCHER	65
Mars	JOHN A. BAGBY	25
Randolph	K. MORRISON	56
Scottsville	JUSTIN HOUGHTON	31

BLOUNT COUNTY

Blount Springs	JAMES C. LUCY	90
Blountsville	THOMAS SHERRER	110
Brooksville	JEREMIAH CHANEY	120
Locust Fork	ALEXANDER COOKE	90
Martin's Stand	JAMES MARTIN	131
Murphy's Valley	H. CORNELIUS	121
Stouts	JAMES R. SPARKS	98

BUTLER COUNTY

Greenville	JOHN F. JOHNSON	152
Kirksville	ZENO PERKINS	150
Manningham	ROBERT S. WARE	138
Middleton	JOHN HUGGINS	165
Millville	ANGUS BROWN	160
Ridgeville	W. B. WATERS	135
Starlington	STARLING PARKER	168

CHAMBERS COUNTY

Chambers C.H.	JOHN A. FRAZIER	170
County Line	NATHANIEL CATCHING	156
Cusseta	JAMES OATES	174
Fredonia	JOHN A. HURST	178
Gold Hill	WILLIAM CARTLEY	161

```
Mount Jefferson        WILLIAM A. ADAMS           185
Oak Bowery             H. W. KIDD                 171
Poplar Valley          P. J. TRAMMELL             170
Sharon                 THOMAS SHANNON             169

CHEROKEE COUNTY
Ball Play              JOHN ROBINSON              195
Cedar Bluff            JAMES V. HOGG              160
Culstia Creek          JOHN DOHERTY               170
Deep Springs           HENRY JACKSON              175
Double Springs         HENRY McCOY                135
Spring Creek           EMORY COOLEY               156
Terrapin Creek         JOHN SNIDER                163
Turkey Town            JOHN G. MEANS              136
Gaylesville            JOHN WILKINSON             163
Leesburg               CHARLES P. HENSLEE         146

CLARKE COUNTY
Air Mount              DAVID A. HOUSTON           125
Clarkesville           JOHN A. COATE              140
Coffeeville            JAMES W. FIGURES           135
Gosport                SAMUEL FORWOOD             147
Grove Hill             ISHAM KIMBLE               131
Jackson                PETER DUBOSE               163
Mechanic Grove         NATHANIEL BRADFORD         135
Motts                  STEPHEN HEARON             120
Suggsville             GEORGE CLOTHIER            156

CONECUH COUNTY
Bellville              MILTON AMES                160
Brooklyn               JOHN D. LEIGH              185
Evergreen              BLANTON P(OWELL) BOX       175
Nathansville           JOHN L. LANSON             193
Sparta                 AUSTIN J. ROBERTSON        180

COOSA COUNTY
Harquin                ABNER BAKER                 95
Nixburg                HENRY LEE                  131
Rockford               SIGNAL M. SMITH            126
Sockapotoy             WILLIAM WINSLETT           138

COVINGTON COUNTY
Cawlcysville           JAMES PARKER               205
Montezuma              JAMES G. DONNELLY          191

COFFEE COUNTY
      This county was created by act of December 29, 1841 and its
Postoffices are included under Dale.

DALE COUNTY
Bridgeville            BARTLEY M. TUCKER          220
Dale Court House       ALLEN G. CARTER            230
Geneva                 JAMES THURRELL             215
Saw Mill               JOHN ARD                   211

DALLAS COUNTY
Barnes                 JOHN E. BARNES              98
Bougue Chitto          JOHN J. CREENING           99
Burnsville             WARREN B. ANDREWS           85
Cahawba                JOHN McELROY               93
Cambridge              CLAUDIUS M. COCHRAN        86
Liberty Hill           J. R. JOHNSON              81
Pleasant Hill          GREEN UNDERWOOD           109
Portland               ALEXANDER HALE             95
Richmond               A. W. COLEMAN             110
Selma                  JOHN M. STRONG             87
Valley Creek           JAMES V. PETTIBONE         81
Woodlawn               WHEELER RANDALL            86
```

```
DEKALB COUNTY
Annawake                      JAMES HUGHES                    130
Lebanon                       CHARLES D. GEORGE               131
Mount Zion                    CHARLES P. MALONE               133
Rawlingsville                 JESSE G. BEESON                 160
Valley Head                   JOHN K. HOGE                    168
Van Buren                     S. C. NEWMAN                    140
          (No town underscored for county seat)

FAYETTE COUNTY
Ashbury                       JOHN MARMBY                      56
Fayette C.H.                  AZOR VAN HOOSE                   42
Millport                      WILLIAM W. TAGGERT               68
Sheffield                     H. P. LEONARD                    40

FRANKLIN COUNTY
Buzzard Roost                 WILLIAM DICKSON                 150
La Grange                     JAMES KENNERLY                  140
Newburg                       PLEASANT M. BOLIN               130
Russelville                   NOBLE R. LADD                   116
Tuscumbia                     JONAS J. BELL                   145

GREENE COUNTY
Boligee                       SAMUEL E. JOHNSTON               53
Clinton                       JAMES H. SIMS                    42
Daniel's Prairie              JOSEPH W. GALL                   44
Erie                          BRYANT GULLY                     54
Eutaw                         THOMAS C. CHILES                 37
Forkland                      WILLIAM A. GLOVER                41
Havanna                       JOHN W. WILLIAMSON               26
Hinton's Grove                WILLIAM W. PASCHALL              43
Hopewell                      ROBERT CRAIG                     55
Greensboro                    JOHN STREET                      41
Knoxville                     MATTHEW KNOX                     28
Nixenburg                     CHARLES A. SPEAR                 43
Mount Hebron                  Z. P. McALLISTER                 51
Newbern                       ALFRED SEXTON                    53
New Prospect                  JAMES HANNA                      57
Pleasant Ridge                ANDREW BROWNLEE                  48
Smith's Ferry                 DANIEL CAMPBELL                  60
Springfield                   MOSES HUBBARD                    33
Union                         WILLIAM MILLER                   38

HENRY COUNTY
Abbeville                     GEORGE H. TUTTLE                220
Columbia                      SAMUEL S. COLEMAN               243
Franklin                      RICHARD C. SPANN                225

JACKSON COUNTY
Bellefonte                    ALVA FINLEY                     170
Bolivar                       JAMES M. McLENNEHAN             190
Griffin's Hollow              WILLIAM L. GRIFFIN              210
Langston                      LANGSTON COFFEE                 170
Larkins' Fork                 W. P. ROBERTSON                 180
Larkinsville                  DAVID LARKIN                    175
Rocky Spring                  WILLIAM J. PRICE                191
Santa                         JAMES SMITH                     164
Trenton                       S. P. PADGETT                   186
Woodville                     S. J. ROUNDTREE                 180

JEFFERSON COUNTY
Cedar Grove                   CLAYTON THOMPSON                 98
Elyton                        THOMPSON CAMP                    56
Green's                       BENJAMIN TARRANT                 63
Jonesboro'                    SAMUEL A. TARRANT                45
Little Cahawba                RICHARDSON FRAZIER               80
Mount Pinson                  ZACHARIAH HAGOOD                 71
Rockville                     ANDREW S. HAMILTON               56
Trussville                    ROBERT A. HAGOOD                 75
```

LAUDERDALE COUNTY
Barton's	ROSS HOUSTON, JR.	160
Bellview	JOHN M. DAVIS	130
Cherry Grove	CHARLES McCLUSKY	150
Cotton Gin	K. PATE	151
Florence	JOSHUA D. COFFEE	158
Lexington	E. P. WESTMORELAND	160
Marmion	JAMES WILLIAMS	140
Masonville	JOHN HARRISON	147
Rogersville	G. N. HARROWAY	139
Waterloo	JAMES HUMPHREY	166
Young's X Roads	THOMAS K. YOUNG	151

LAWRENCE COUNTY
Brickville	WILLIAM WALLIS	143
Camp Springs	WILLIAM A. MELAM	96
Courtland	S. W. SHACKLEFORD	128
Hillsborough	ROBERT ELLIOTT	139
Leighton	WILLIAM LEIGH	136
Moulton	C. McDONALD	108
Mount Hope	WILLIAM W. DOWNS	126
Oakville	GREEN SLADE	120

LIMESTONE COUNTY
Athens	THOMAS BASS	164
Gilbertsborough	LEWIS NELSON	178
Mooresville	JOHN A. HUNDLEY	156
Shoal Ford	WILLIAM M. DONALDSON	170

LOWNDES COUNTY
Benton	RUSSELL W. HILL	98
Bragg's	PETER M. BRAGG	125
Church Hill	RICHARD B. CARTER	103
Farmersville	JOSEPH SOLES	116
Hayneville	MORGAN B. HINKLE	120
Mount Willing	HENRY ADAMS	121
Prairie Hill	WILLIAM GORDON	122
Sandy Ridge	WILLIAM PAYNE	138

MACON COUNTY
Aberfoil	DAVID FARRIOR	160
Auborn	GEORGE B. NUCKOLLS	180
Bainbridge	JYRES S. TURPIN	160
Cubehatchee	HENRY L. BUTTS	144
Calagee	HARDY R. JACKSON	150
Cross Keys	JOHN A. HOWARD	152
Fort Decatur	CHESLEY D. STRANGE	165
Fort Henderson	JAMES DELBRIDGE	167
Pine Grove	J. LEE BEARD	151
Society Hill	JAMES TORBERT	171
Soouchahatchee	JAMES McALLISTER	156
Tuskeegee	JOHN BEDELL	156
Union Springs	H. H. SMITH	158
Uphaupee	WILLIAM MYRICK	150
Valverdi	JOHN W. DEVEREAUX	153

MADISON COUNTY
Cobb's Store	BRYANT COBB	160
Hazle Green	ROBERT ERWIN	172
Huntsville	GEORGE COX	160
Loweville	A. W. HADEN	168
Madixon X Roads	MATTHEW DAVIS	175
Meridianville	JOHN KIRKLAND	171
New Hope	GEORGE RUSSELL	152
New Market	E. ECHOLS	173
Oakley	WILLIAM LESLIE	180
Trianna	EDMOND TONEY	146
Whitesburg	JAMES H. ROANE	163

MARENGO COUNTY
Antioch	ADOLPHUS S. CADE	90
Boston	JOHN T. BURWELL	73
Dayton	JOHN C. DANSBY	80
Demopolis	ROWAN A. SMITH	66
Faransdale	B. M. PEARSON	80
Laurel Hill	WILLIAM DORSEY	96
Linden	JAMES N. HILL	80
McKinley	ELLIS W. KING	98
Macon	JOHN PATTERSON	57
Montpelier	BENJAMIN DUBOSE	80
Nanafalia	HENRY G. LEONARD	110
Pickens Mills	JAMES PICKENS	53
Pineville	JOHN BATES	115
Pleasant Plains	BOWEN SEABROOK	90
Shiloh	THOMAS HOSEA	100
Spring Hill	RUSH FULLER	75
White Hall	RICHARD WOOTEN	96
Woodwardsville	CHARLES C. WOODWARD	110

MARION COUNTY
Moscow	WILLIAM E. TROTTER	90
Pikeville	JOHN D. TERRELL	71
Toll Gate	CHARLES THOMAS	81

MARSHALL COUNTY
Aurora	WILLIAM G. JORDAN	165
Cottonville	GEORGE LOY	152
Claysville	W. H. C. WHEELER	150
Dodsonville	JACOB GROSS	150
Hillian's Store	ABSALOM HILLIAN	158
Marshall C. H.	BENJAMIN S. PARSONS	156
Miltonsville	A. J. DOWNS	175
Red Hill	ALEXANDER DONALDSON	151
Warrenton	JAMES CHILDRESS	160

MOBILE COUNTY
Mobile	JOHN W. TOWNSEND	226
Mount Vernon	JAMES M. MORGAN	195

MONROE COUNTY
Bell's Landing	JAMES M. BURGESS	135
Burnt Corn	ISAAC BITTS	150
Claiborne	RICHARD STEPHENS	151
Monroeville	ALDEN CLARK	158
Mount Pleasant	WALTER R. ENGLISH	160
Turnbull	THOMAS M. RILEY	150

MONTGOMERY COUNTY
Argus	JAMES M. STAGGER	146
Carter's Hill	ALEXANDER W. CHAPMAN	136
Hickory Grove	FRANKLIN ARMSTRONG	135
High Hill	JAMES JONES	131
Line Creek	PEARLY S. GERALD	150
Montgomery	NEIL BLUE	122
Mount Meigs	JAMES STOGNER	131
Pine Level	GEORGE SHEARERS	150
Pintlala	JOHN BONHAM	130
Sharrsville	WILLIAM SHARP	130
Tiara	ZEPH JONES	136

MORGAN COUNTY
Cedar Plains	JAMES HERRING	130
Decatur	JAMES A. PATTERSON	140
Houston's Store	JOSEPH HAMPTON	120
Lacey's Spring	THOMAS H. LACEY	143
Mount Hill	SAMUEL HASLETT	145
Somerville	CHRISTOPHER WELCH	136

PERRY COUNTY
Hamburg	WEST T. JOHNSON	68
Jericho	WILLIAM WRIGHT	58
Perry Court House	N. W. FLETCHER	59
Perryville	BENJAMIN FORD	56
Plantersville	T. S. DRISKILL	80
South Cane Brake	PETER VANORDEN	71
Uniontown	RICHARD CLARK	61

PICKENS COUNTY
Benevola	BARTLETT UPCHURCH	34
Carrollton	ANDREW M. WINDLE	42
Cochran's Mills	S. G. COCHRAN	40
Fairfield	MOSES J. WICKS	58
Hope	JAMES S. GARDNER	60
Pickensville	WILLIAM CHALMERS	56
Pleasant Grove	W. R. KING	29
Providence	WILLIAM C. HENRY	75
Reform	JAMES B. CLADNEY	38
Vienna	REUBEN WEAVER	56
Yorkville	ALEXANDER BROWNLEE	70

PIKE COUNTY
China Grove		
Gainer's Store	CHRISTOPHER TOMPKINS	151
Missouri	WILLIAM D. DARBY	185
Monticello	MALCOLM BLUE	173
Prospect Ridge	BENJAMIN COLLIER	168

RANDOLPH COUNTY
Beaver Dam	WILLIAM McKNIGHT	180
Eastville	GEORGE H. COOPER	175
Factory Shoal	THOMAS ASHCROFT	151
McDonald	JOSEPH BENTON	165
Oakfuskie	ARCHIBALD SAWYER	160
Roanoke	WILEY M. McCENDON	181
Weehadlee	F. W. CHANDLER	190
Arbacoochy	JOHN GORDON	170

RUSSELL COUNTY
Crockettsville	JOHN T. RILEY	185
Dover	MARK McCUTCHEN	196
Fort Mitchell	ENOCH JOHNSON	235
Girard	JAMES B. COX	210
Opellikan	WESLEY WILLIAMS	180
Salem	HENRY M. CROWDER	191
Sand Fort	ROBERT ALLEN	190
Uchee	JOHN B. TATE	198
Wacoochee	T. J. COOCKE	190

SHELBY COUNTY
Columbiana	ALPHONSO H. STERRETT	80
Harpersville	WILLIAM POSEY	96
Kamulga	LEWIS S. FRELAND	98
Montevallo	DAVID W. PRENTICE	65
Waxahatchee	BRYANT RUSHING	90
Wilsonville	JAMES O'HARA	86
Woodsboro	WILLIAM WOODRUFF	68

ST. CLAIR COUNTY
Ashville	JAMES ROGAN	98
Bennettsville	GEORGE HALLOWAY	125
Branchville	ADAM W. BYERS	110
Broken Arrow	FRANCIS B. WALKER	112
Cropwell	RUSSELL J. ALLEN	112
Kelly's Creek	GEORGE M?DUKE	110
Mount Niles	WILLIAM H. SHOTWELL	96
Springville	WILLIAM H. ETHRIDGE	86

```
SUMTER COUNTY
Bellmont            BURWELL BLANTON          80
Berlin              JOHN C. McGREW           86
Big Rock            WILLIAM H. PHILLIPS     128
Bluffport           THOMAS DUER              76
Gainesville         R. G. McMAHON            56
Gaston              CHARLES A. SHELDON       91
Intercourse         ISHAM DANIEL             87
Jamestown           BENNETT B. BELL          65
Jones' Bluff        FREDERICK STEWART        62
Livingston          ROBERT T. HOUSTON        68
Payneville          THOMAS J. GEORGE         82
Sumterville         GEORGE RIX               68
William X Roads     SAMUEL WILLIAMS         101

TALLADEGA COUNTY
Brownsville         DUNCAN BROWN            148
Chinnibee           GREENVILLE W. PENN      150
Crooked Creek       GLOVER McCANE          135
Fayetteville        JOHN M. LAURIE          90
Fife                THOMAS J. CRAVEN        130
Hickory Level       LEWIS PYLES            141
Hillabee            REUBEN PHILLIPS        150
Kelly's Springs     WILLIAM CURRY          130
Mardisville         STEPHEN SMITH          115
Mineral Springs     ISAAC M. THOMAS         91
Mountain Springs    WILLIAM DAVIS          142
Syllacauga          ALLISON RAMSEY         100
Talladega           JAMES LAWSON           130
Weewahaville        ADAM RISER             117

TALLAPOOSA COUNTY
Dadeville           T. HATCHER             142
Dudleyville         JAMES A. BARR          156
Horse Shoe Bend     JAMES W. BALEY         175
Pinckneyville       WILLIAM RODGERS        150
Tallassee           ELI B. SCARLOCK        151
Youngsville         REUBEN G. YOUNG        143

TUSCALOOSA COUNTY
Buck Creek          WILLIAM ARCHIBALD       20
Carthage            WILLIAM P. FULLER       17
Foster's            JOHN L. FOSTER          13
Jena                DANIEL TEER             23
McMath's            ELISHA McMATH           32
New Lexington       F. W. WOODWARD          26
Northport           LEWIS ETHRIDGE           1
Romulus             JOHN SANDERS            13
Tuscaloosa (Capital)  WILLIAM D. MARRAST   ---

WILCOX COUNTY
Allenton            JAMES ROBINSON         125
Barges              JOHN BARGE             130
Bethel              S. C. DUMAS            110
Black's Bluff       JAMES A. TATE          105
Canton              ELEAZAR HALE            95
Lower Peach Tree    HENRY W. BRYAN         123
Mount Moriah        SILAS W. WOOTEN        135
Norrisville         BENJAMIN DULANEY       108
Pine Hill           GEORGE SHELDON         105
Prairie Bluff       HENRY S. ATWOOD         91
Rocky Mount         HENRY C. PEARSON       125
Snow Hill           JAMES L. BENSON        120
Wilcox Court House  JOHN B. FARLEY          98
Womack's            WATKINS SALTER         125
```

WALKER COUNTY
Eldridge	Eldridge Mallard	54
Thorn Hill	J. W. WALKER	76
Jasper	J. D. BEAUCHAMP	56

WASHINGTON COUNTY
Arrarat	JOSEPH McCARTY	135
Barryton	WILLIAM CHAPMAN	150
Huberta	JOHN EVANS, JR.	151
Isney	JOHN EVERETT, SR.	161
Mount Sterling	S. E. CATTORLIN	119
New Wakefield	MOSES WICKWISE	171
Pleasant Valley	ROBERT F. HAZARD	160
St. Stephens	JAMES MAGOFFIN	151
Tuscahoma	S. S. SCOGGINS	125
Warrior Bridge	JOSEPH A. HUBER	141
Washington Court House	PETER MYER	154

Note: Tuscaloosa was then Capital of the State.
Distributing Offices: Huntsville and Florence
Number of Offices: 398
Distance calculated from Tuscaloosa (seat of government) by the nearer
mail route.
Note: Many of these towns are no longer in existence and some others
have changed the name. For instance, in Madison Co. Loweville is now
called Maysville.
Benton County (now Calhoun) was created in 1832 by the Creek Cession/
    Reward offered for the arrest of JAMES HENDERSON, JR. who murdered
GEORGE BOGGAN of Clarke County. 19 May 1841. HENDERSON is described
as being about 22 years old.

July 27, 1842
    Died on the 25th instant at the residence of DANIEL CRIBBS,
MRS. PAULINA ANN WYNNE, consort of WILLIAMSON WYNNE of Greene County.
    $200 reward for the arrests of CRAWFORD A BROWN and JAMES C. RAYMOND,
who broke jail in this county on Monday last.

August 3, 1842
    Married in this vicinity last evening by REV. DR. MANLY, MR.
WILLIAM C. WALKER, Printer of this county to MISS MARTHA B. WILLIAMS
of this county.
    Note: Many of the marriage bonds for Tuscaloosa County were
evidently lost or not recorded, as the above marriage and many more are
not to be found recorded in the Marriages books now.
    At the same time and place by REV. DR. MANLY, MR. BENJAMIN F.
MORRISON, formerly of Baltimore, to MISS ELENOR ROSS, late of Staunton,
Virginia, but now of this city. See our Vol. 8 p. 52 for marriage
record.
    In Greene County, on Monday evening last, by REV. W. A. SCOTT,
THOMAS MAXWELL, Esq. formerly of Cockermouth, England (now of this
city) to MISS SUSAN C(HARLOTTE) FARLEY, formerly of Massachusetts.
    Died in the city of New York, on the 16th ult. of consumption,
MAJ. GOVENEUR V. BARTINE aged 36 years, late of this city.
    Died in Sumter County on the 11th instant, MR. HENRY W. SHACKELFORD,
Esq.
    Died in Sumter County, on the 22d of July, MR. THOMAS JOHNSTON,
formerly of Georgia, aged about forty years.
    Died in Wahalak, Mississippi, MR. JESSEE WRIGHT, of billious fever,
aged about thirty years, leaving a wife and two children.

August 10, 1842
    Married in this city on Thursday morning last by REV. MR. HAMILTON,
MR. LEONARD B. NEAL to MISS HARRIET SAUNDERS, youngest daughter of
HON. MARMADUKE WILLIAMS, all of this city.
    Death of WILSON COBB, of Fayette. Died in Fayette County on
Saturday the 31st ult. WILSON COBB, late member of the House of
Representatives from said county. He was killed instantly by a falling
limb. He was a native of South Carolina. A wife and children mourn
his loss. Etc.

```
        Election Returns
        From 38 counties.  Whigs are msrked thus *
                           Senators
        COUNTY                              SENATOR
Autauga & Coosa                            HALL
Barbour & Russell                          BUFORD*
Benton                                     WALKER
Blount & Marshall                          BRINDLEY
Butler & Pike                              ARRINGTON*
Cherokee & DeKalb                          FOSTER
Clarke, Baldwin & Washington               CREAGH
Dallas                                     PHILLIPS*
Greene                                     THORNTON*
Franklin                                   HUDSON
Henry, Covington & Dale                    McALLISTER
Jackson                                    WILSON
Lawrence                                   RODGERS
Lauderdale                                 McVAY
Limestone                                  TERRY
Lowndes                                    HUNTER*
Macon & Tallapopsa                         DAILEY
Madison                                    FLEMING
Marengo                                    MOORES*
Marion & Fayette                           WILSON
Mobile                                     TOULMIN
Montgomery                                 OLIVER*
Monroe & Conecuh                           WATKINS
Morgan & Walker                            McCLANAHAN
Perry                                      WALTHALL
Pickens                                    KING*
Randolph & Chambers
Shelby & Bibb                              WATROUS*
St. Clair & Jefferson                      BAYLOR
Sumter                                     JONES
Talladega                                  McCONNELL
Tuscaloosa                                 DENT*
Wilcox                                     ROSS*

   21 Democrats 11 Whigs 1 District to be heard from.
                   Representatives
Autauga                             MORGAN, MITCHELL*
Baldwin                             GASQUE
Barbour                             PETTIT*, JACKSON*
Benton                              ABERNATHY, MARTIN
Bibb                                HILL, MORRISON
Blount                              HORTON, FOWLER
Butler                              HENDERSON, WATTS*
Coosa                               KENDRICK
Conecuh                             JONES*
Cherokee                            HENSLEE, COOPER*
Dallas                              CALHOUN, NORRIS*
DeKalb                              WINSTON, LANKFORD
Fayette                             MARCHBANKS, MORRIS
Franklin                            GARLAND, RICHESON,
                                       NORMAN
Greene                              ERWIN, JONES*,
                                       YOUNG*
Jackson                             FINLEY, MUNDY,
                                       WILLIAMS, SCOTT
Jefferson                           EARLE*, McMILLION
Lauderdale                          DOUGLASS, SMITH,
                                       KENNEDY
Limestone                           TATE, ENGLISH
Lowndes                             HARRISON, DUNKLIN
Lawrence                            WALKER, HUBBARD,
                                       VALLIANT
Macon                               OLIVER*
Marengo                             HENLEY*, PICKETT*
Marshall                            GRIFFIN, FLETCHER
```

186

Madison	ROBINSON, MOORE, CLAY, McCLUNG*
Morgan	ROBY, RICE
Mobile	DUNN*, ERWIN*, McCOY*, CAMPBELL
Montgomery	WARE*, CAFFEY
Perry	BARRON*, MOORE, MIREE
Pickens	GARDNER*, SMITH, WILLIAMS
Shelby	STORRS*, KIDD*
Sumter	WINSTON, DORTCH, WOODWARD
Talladega	BARCLAY, BISHOP
Tallapoosa	GRESHAM*
Tuscaloosa	BANKS*, MERIWETHER, SMITH*, PORTER*
Walker	CAIN*
Washington	TURNER
Wilcox	DEAR*, BRIDGES

57 Democrats, 27 Whigs, 12 counties to be heard from.

Married at Oxford, Mississippi on the 2d instant by REV. MR. HOLCOMBE, MR. GUSTAVUS HOPKINS of Tuscaloosa to MISS REBECCA R. LANDON of Guilford, Connecticut.

August 24, 1842
Died at the residence of her son-in-law in Pickens County on the 19th inst. MRS. SUSANNAH BRUMBY aged 68 years.

Died near this city on Saturday last, WILLIAM H. aon of ARMSTEAD THOMAS.

MARCUS McMILLION, candidate for messenger to the House of Representatives.

August 31, 1842
Married on Tuesday the 9th instant by REV. WILLIAM A. SMITH at the residence of DR. N. LYON in Perry MISS HENRIETTA M. AIREY of Perry County, formerly of Philadelphia.

Married in this county on Tuesday the 16th instant by REV. MR. WILLIAM HOOD, MR. JAMES ROBERTSON to MISS PERMELIA ANN SANDERS.

September 7, 1842
Reward for the arrest of ALEXANDER COSSELIN, who murdered his wife, MARY A. COSSELIN in the city of Mobile on 11th of July last.

Died at Pleasant Grove, Pickens County on the 31st of August, WILLIAMSON R. KING in his 32nd year. Death caused by wound received by fall from scaffold. Left a wife and six small children....

September 14, 1842
Married at New Britain, Conn. on the 24th of August by REV. CHARLES A. GOODRICH, Professor EDWARD D. SIMS, of the University of Alabama to MISS L. ANNE ANDREWS, daughter of Professor E. A. ANDREWS.

Obituary:

Died in this city on Saturday the 10th instant, BENJAMIN FRANKLIN COCHRAN, son of the late HIRAM P. COCHRAN in his 20th year, after an illness of four days....

Died on Saturday last, CHARLES L. A. THOMAS, son of A(RMSTEAD) R. and ELVIRA THOMAS.

Died at his residence in Sumter County on Sunday the 21st ult DANIEL GREENE, Esq, an old and respectable citizen.

Died on the 1st instant at his residence near Cahawba of a lingering and painful disease, MAJ. URIAH G. MITCHELL, an old and respected citizen of Dallas County in his 63rd year....

September 28, 1842
Obituary:

Died in this city on Saturday the 24th instant, WILLIAM LOWNDES PARISH in his 20th year, eldest son of COL. WILLIAM G. PARISH....

Died in this county on the 19th instant, WILLIAM DUNLAP, Esq. aged 65 years, an upright and valued citizen.

Died in Shelby County on Saturday the 10th instant of congestive fever, MRS. NANCY KING, consort of MR. EDMUND KING in her 50th year.

Died in Noxubee County, Mississippi on the 29th ult. MRS. CHARLOTTE M. MASSENGALE aged 24 years; after three weeks and four days illness of bilious fever. She was a resident of Gainesville and had gone on a visit to her father's with intention of returning in a short time.... Left a husband and one child.
    Note: JOHN W. MASSENGALE married in 1840 CHARLOTTE M. WEATHERED. See our Vol. 52)

October 5, 1842
    Died in this city on the night of the 28th of September of bilious fever, CLARISSA CRANE KNAPP, wife of the REV. NATHANIEL C? KNAPP, formerly of Brooklyn, Long Island, aged 30 years.

October 19, 1842
    Married in Huntsville on the 10th inst. by REV. THOMAS MADDIN, MR. WILLIAM H. SMITH, Editor of the Tennessee Telegraph to MISS MARY JANE GLASCOCK of said place.
    Died at Fairfield, Pickens County on the 5th instant at the residence of her father, WILLIAM D. STONE, MRS. ELIZABETH ANN IVY, consort of MR. BIRD IVY in her 17th year.
    Died at his residence near Trussel's Ferry on Beckbee River in Greene County, Alabama Sunday the 9th instant, MR. RICHARD HATTER, aged 62. He was amongst the first settlers of this section of the country, having emigrated from South Carolina to Greene County in 1819. (From Eutaw Whig)

October 26, 1842
    Died yesterday morning at his residence in this county, CAPTAIN JAMES G. BLOUNT, former Sheriff of this county.
    Died in this city on Thursday morning last, HENRY W. SPENCER, printer, late of Columbia, Tennessee.
    Died in Gainsville on the 27th of September last at the residence of her uncle, N. E. CHANDLER, FANNY D. WIGGINS aged about 9 years (From Gainsville Pilot)

November 2, 1842
    Died at the residence of JOHN T. PRIMM in Shelby County on the 20th of October, MR. JOHN NETTLES of Wilcox County aged 24 years and 8 months. Victim of liver complaint...Member of the Baptist Church.
    Obituary:
    Departed this life on the 24th instant at his residence in Tuscaloosa County, REV. JOSHUA HALBERT in his 57th year. For many years a member of the Baptist Church and for the last four years a minister... Columbia South Carolinian please copy.

November 9, 1842
    Married in this city on Thursday evening last by REV. DR. JOHN OWEN, MR. THOMAS CUMMINGS, JR. to MISS CATHERINE ISH.
    Married in Bibb County on the evening of the 23d instant, KENNETH MORRISON, Esq. Representative from said county, to MISS ELIZA OAKLEY.
    Died in this county on the 15th ult. ROBERT WALKER, Esq, in his 75th year. Native of Georgia and had resided in Tuscaloosa County for the last 23 years. For the last forty years he was a member of the Methodist Church...Was public spirited and useful, a good neighbor and esteemed by all who knew him. A large and affectionate family mourn his loss....
    Died on the 3d inst. at Benevola, Pickens County, MR. J. H. HARRIS.
    Obituary:
        Masonic Hall Oct. 28, 1842:
    At a meeting of Rising Virtue Lodge No 4 the following resolutions were adopted conserning the death of our brother, JAMES G. BLOUNT,....
                (Signed) HENRY McGOWN, W M
                        C R HARRISON, Secretary
    Candidates:
    COL. SAMUEL H N DICKSON for Assistant Secretary Senate
    COL. JAMES CHILES of Greene Co. for assistant clerk of House of Representatives
    JAMES H MOSLEY for Principal Clerk of House of Representatives
    CAPT. D H BINGHAM for Asst Secy of Senate

WILSON C BIBB of Madison County for re-election as Engrossing Clerk, House of Representatives

TALIAFERRO F SAMUEL for Engrossing Clerk of House of Representatives

JOSEPH PHELAN- for Principal Clerk of House of Repr.

COL. B A PHILPOTT for re-relection as Secy of Senate

ALEX B CLITHERALL of Pickens County for Assistant Clerk of House of Representatives

MARCUS McMILLION for Messenger of House of Representatives

JAMES H. OWEN for re-election as Doorkeeper of House of Representatives

CROCKETT G. DAVIS for re-election as messenger of House of Representatives

C C DONOHO for re-election as Doorkeeper of Senate

GEORGE B. CLITHERALL for Secretary of Senate

A R THOMAS for Doorkeeper of Senate

THOMAS M GLEASON for Messenger of House of Representatives

Florida Volunteers and citizens generally are invited to attend a meeting at the Court House to respect the memory of our lately deceased fellow citizen CAPTAIN JAMES G. BLOUNT.

November 16, 1842

Meeting of the citizens to pay respect to the memory of the late HARVEY W. ELLIS deceased (Paper in mourning for same)

Died at his plantation near Fairfield in Pickens County on Saturday the 12th inst. HARVEY W. ELLIS, of this city in his 41st year. His remains were brought to the city and interred on yesterday morning from the Presbyterian Church. REV. DR. MANLY, President of the University preached an eloquent and most appropriate sermon upon the occasion.

Married in Kemper County, Mississippi, MR. SAMUEL HARMON of this county to MISS ADELINE SIMS, daughter of WILLIAM SIMS, late of this county.

Married in this city on Thursday evening the 27th ult. by REV. J. HAMILTON, WILLIAM P. HATTER, Esq. of Mobile to MISS MARY C. SIMS, daughter of the late EDWARD SIMS, Esq.

Dissolutoin of the partnership of GEORGE W. CRABB and WILLIAM COCHRAN, law firm.

R. H. POE, Sheriff, advertises slave committed to jail who says he belongs to RHODAH HORTON near Huntsville and ran away from HORTON's plantation in Marengo County.

J C VAN DYKE advertises for runaway slave.

Committed to the jail of Marengo County, a slave who says he belongs to JAMES QUARLES of Woodford County, Kentucky about twn miles from Lexington.

J. P. BLASS, Jailer

Committed to the jail of Tuscaloosa County a slave who says he belongs to NATHAN B. WHITFIELD of Marengo County.

WILLIAM JENNINGS, Jailer

Committed to the jail of Tuscaloosa County a slave who says he belongs to THOMAS TUCKER of Knoxville, Tennessee.

WILLIAM JENNINGS, Jailer

State of Alabama-Bibb County

Taken up by MADISON RASBERRY on the 14th of May, 1842 a mare, appraised by JAMES H. ATKINSON and ISAAC LAWHORN to be worth $35.

WILLIAMS CADDELL, Clerk

November 23, 1842

Married in Kemper County, Mississippi on Thursday the 3d instant by REV. MR. SHELTON, MR. SAMUEL R. HAMNER of Tuscaloosa to MISS ELIZABETH ADELINE GUNN, daughter of WILLIAM GUNN, formerly of this county.

Died in this city on Monday the 14th instant MRS. LYDIA NEAL, formerly of Orange County, North Carolina.

Tribute of Respect:

At a meeting of the Wetumpka Borderers, who served in the Florida Camppaign in 1836, CAPTAIN W J COUCH announcd the object of the meeting. Resolutions on the death of CAPTAIN JAMES G. BLOUNT.

Committed to the jail of Tuscaloosa County a slave who says he belongs to JAMES CORBIN of Claiborn County, Miss.

Committed to the jail of Bibb County a slave who says he belongs to JOSEPH NOBLES of Shelby County.

Administrators Notice:
   Letters of administration on estate of JAMES HILL, deceased granted
to ROBERT and JAMES HILL.
   Land belonging to estate of LEWIS J. HENDRIX deceased advertised
for sale by SETH BROWN, JOLLY JONES and ALEXANDER KYLE, commissioners.

November 30, 1842
   Committed to the jail of Fayette County a slave who says he belongs
to GEORGE BARNES of Halifax County, North Carolina.

December 7, 1842
   BURR W. WILSON, trustee= estate of JESSE VANHOOSE, deceased of
Fayette County. Negroes for sale.
   Married in Pickens County on Wednesday evening, November 30th
by REV. GEORGE SHAFFER of Columbus, COL. WILLIAM K. DAVIS of Fairfield
to MISS FRANCES A. H. BURDINE, second daughter of JAMES T. BURDINE,
Esq. of this county.
   Married in Boston, Mass. on Thursday evening, 17th of November by
REV. F D HUNTINGTON, MR. JOHN N. WALTHALL of Perry County, Alabama to
MISS CHARLOTTE A. PHIPPS of Boston.

December 14, 1842
   Married on Thursday evening, December 1st by REV. MR. HAMILTON of
Tuscaloosa, the HON. WALTER R(ALEIGH) ROSS, Senator from Wilcox County
to the amiable and much admired MRS. ANN BOZMAN of Greene County.
Note: He was a pensioner of War of 1812.

December 28, 1842
   Died on the 10th of December last in Pickens County, OBADIAH
STRICKLAND, SENR. aged 79 years and 11 months, formerly of Franklin
County, North Carolina. Member of the Baptist Church for 30 years.
   Notice:
   Letters of administration on the estate of JEREMIAH W. WALKER,
deceased, late of Walker County, granted to LUCY M. WALKER.

January 11, 1843
   Alabama Conference
   Station of Preachers for the Year 1843

Mobile District	J. BORING, P.E. (Presiding Elder)
Mobile-F St and West Ward	L. PIERCE, J C KEENER
Saint Francis St.	J. HAMILTON
Tombigby	THOMAS KILLOUGH, J T CURRY
Linden	WILLIAM A. SMITH
Spring Hill	JESSE P PERHAM
Gaston	P(ETER) HASKEW
Winchester	JOHN D. FISHER
Chickasawha	J. W. BROXSON, H. J. HUNTER
Mount Vernon	JAMES McLEOD
Pensacola District	G. GARRETT, P E
Cedar Creek	T. L. DENSIER, W K NORTON
Belleville	JAMES SHANKS, W A TARLTON
Greenville	D. FOWLER
Claiborne	JOHN D. LOFTIN
Escambia Mission	A S DICKINSON
Mount Pleasant	C(HARLES) B EASTMAN
Cahawba	W. H. McDANIEL, J W T LEE
Pensacola	F. A. McSHAN
Troy	JOHN T. ROPER, J. WELLS
Irwinton District	T. LYNCH, P E
Irwinton & Glennville	S. PILLEY
Glennville Circuit	JOHN HUNTER
Choctawhatchee	JAMES PEELER, T G GILMORE
Mariana	G R W SMITH
Spring Creek	H T HILL
Apalachicola	CHARLES STRIDER
Pea River	T D BARR
Walton Mission	Z(ACHIUS) DOWLING
Montgomery District	J W STARR, P.E.
Montgomery	W(M) B NEAL

Line Creek	A B ELLIOTT
Tuskegee	SAMUEL ARMSTRONG, R R DICKINSON
LaFayette	T J WILLIAMSON, JAMES H. LANEY
Russell	E W STORY, one to be supplied
Dadeville	J STARR
Woodley Bridge Mission	JOHN BOSWELL, H. STERNS
Chattahoochee Mission	J A McBRIDE, L. RUSH
Hayneville	P. R. McRARY
Talladega District	E PEARSON, P E
Wills' Valley	WILLIAM RHODES
St. Clair Mission	W. J. REAVES
Jefferson	JAMES P. McGEE, G. L. PATTON
Jacksonville	H. BAILEY, JOHN JONES
Randolph	J. KUYKENDALL, one to be supplied
Coosa	JESSE ELLIS, H. Y. GARRISON
Harpersville	B. L. WEST, A. PEARCE
Talladega & Mardisville	T. MOODY
Tuscaloosa District	C. McLEOD, P.E.
Tuscaloosa	T. H. CAPERS
Big Sandy	L. G. HICKS
Brush Creek	T. H. P. SCALES, C. McLEOD
Greensborough	T(HOMAS) W DORMAN
Marion	W. MOORES
New Lexington	N. P. SCALES
Warrior Mission	JOHN A. SPENCE
Prairie Creek Mission	A P HARRIS
Walker Mission	JOHN FOUST
E(d'wd) D Sims, Professor in University of Alabama)	
Selma District	E V LEVERT, P E
Selma and Valley Creek	T F SELBY
Washington	W J SASSNETT
Wetumpka	S B SAWYER
Centreville	V(ARNUM) L. HOPKINS, R. COURLIE
Jones Valley	JOHN BOLDING
Blount	J C STRICKLIN
Columbus District	W(M) MURRAH, P.E.
Columbus	R S FINLEY
Eutaw	J T HEARD
Greene	L. B. McDONALD
Ebenezer & Trinity	To be supplied
Carrollton	ACTON YOUNG, J. A. CLEMENT
Fayetteville	J W LANEY, W VAUGHAN
Athens	A S HARRIS, J G GILMORE
Pikeville Mission	JEFFERSON BOND
Gainesville District	W. WIER, P E
Sumterville	J. O. WILLIAMS
Macon	GEORGE SHAEFFER
Prairie Hill	E. CALLOWAY, one to be supplied
Kemper	H. WILLIAMSON, J. W. ELLIS
Lauderdale	J. L. DANIEL, T. ARMSTRONG
Livingston & Bellemonte	E. J. HAMMILL
Livingston Circuit	J. L. SANDERS

Agent for Centenary Institute and LaGrange College-
E. HEARN

The next conference meets December 27, 1843. Increase of the M.E. Church within limits of Alabama Conference during the past year- 5,156

Administrator's Notice
Letters of Administration on estate of PHILIP PAGE, deceased, late of Shelby County, granted to MATILDA PAGE.

Letters of administration on estate of PATRICK REDMOND, late of Tuscaloosa County, deceased, granted to WILLIAM G. PARISH. Saturday Evening Post of Philadelphia insert four times.

January 18, 1843
MR. WILLIAMS of Pickens County rose and addressed the House of Representatives: "My colleague, REUBEN GARDNER, Esq. died at his residence in Pickens County on the 12th day of this month.... He was a native of South Carolina and emigrated to this state at an early date.

He resided in Pickens County about fifteen years, has several times been honored with a seat in the House of Representatives and when he died he was about 47 years old. A kind husband and father."

February 1, 1843
Reward for the arrest of a slave named WADE, property of HENRY HURT, SENR. of Russell County who assaulted HENRY HURT, JR. with intent to kill.

February 8, 1843
Married on Wednesday evening last by REV. THOMAS CAPERS at the house of HON. HENRY W. COLLIER in this place, COL. CLEMENT C. CLAY, JR. of Huntsville to MISS VIRGINIA C. TUNSTALL only daughter of DR. PEYTON R. TUNSTALL. Note: This is the noted MRS. VIRGINIA CLAY-CLOPTON, a famous belle of the fifties.
Death of THOMAS W. WHITE
Founder and Editor of "Southern Literary Messenger" Died Tuesday morning in his 55th year, He was several weeks since attacked with paralysis in the city of New York (From the Richmond Enquirer Jan. 21st)

March 22, 1843
Died at Centreville on the 10th of March 1843 JOHN HENRY in his 48th year.

April 5, 1843
Married on Monday, the 3d instant by REV. DR. MANLY, PROFESSOR JAMES C(OVINGTON) DOCKERY of the University of Alabama to MISS MARY A. WHITFIELD of this place. Note: He d. Nov. 3, 1863 in DeSoto Co. Miss. (tombstone) b. Richmond Co. NC. She probably d. ab 1854-5 dau of BENJ. & MATHILDA WHITFIELD.

April 19, 1843
Died in DeKalb County, Alabama on the 1st instant, MR. PALMER CLAYTON, eldest son of MR. SAMPSON CLAYTON aged about 18 years.

April 26, 1843
Married in Tuscaloosa on the evening of the 20th instant by REV. J. H. THOMASON, MR. LUCIUS N. HOLBERT of Aberdeen, Mississippi to MISS M. E. SHORTRIDGE of the former place. (A genealogist in Aberdeen says his name was really HALBERT not HOLBERT. He was made gdn of minor heirs of JOSHUA HALBERT, 1844, Monroe Co. Miss. MARY HALBERT.)
Married on the 25th instant by REV. J. P. McMULLEN, MR. ROBERT G. MARTIN to MISS EMMA J. McCLARY, both of this co. (a genealogist thinks they moved to Oktibbeha Co. Miss.)
State of Alabama-Bibb County
Taken up by WASHINGTON HULLUM a mule appraised at $40 by HENRY STRICKLAND and J. W. THRASHER.
                    WILLIAMS CADDELL, Clerk

May 3, 1843
Married in Mobile on the 22nd of April by REV. J. HAMILTON, COLONEL WILLIAM GARRETT of Tuscaloosa, Secretary of the State of Alabama to MISS JULIA B(RUNETTE) HENRY of Mobile, daughter of the late MAJ. WILLIAM HENRY of St. Stephens, Ala.
Married in this city on the 27th ult. by REV. DR. MANLY, MR. HARRIS OLCOTT to MISS LOUISA C. AVERELL.

May 10, 1843
Married on Thursday evening last, 4th of May by REV. MR. CAPERS, MR. JOHN P. BOYLE of Philadelphia to MISS CATHERINE H. CURLING, daughter of GEORGE CURLING, Esq. of this city.
Died near Centreville, Bibb County, MRS. MARTHA JAMES, consort of FREDERICK JAMES, Esq. in her 41st year, Beloved and esteemed by all who knew her as an estimable companion and affectionate mother (Communicated)
Administrator's Notice:
Letters of Administration on the estate of ROBERT N. MOORE, deceased, late of Fayette County, granted to WILLIAM O. MOORE on 3d of October last.

May 17, 1843
     Died on board Steam Boat Fashion on the 11th instant on her
passage from Mobile to New Orleans, DR. TRUEMAN WOODRUFF, of this city,
late of Batavia, New York, aged about 50 years. DR. WOODRUFF had
resided in this city about seven years for the benefit of his health.
His intelligence, integrity and gentlemanly deportment caused him to
be highly esteemed by all who knew him; and will cause his death to be
no less generally regretted.
     Obituary:
     Died on the 23d, ult, at the residence in Montpelier, Baldwin
County, Alabama, COLONEL LEE SLAUGHTER in the 48th year of his age.
In early life, he devoted himself to attainment of military acquirements.
Having received the appointment of Lieutenant in the regular army he
emigrated to the South and was promoted to Adjutant under command of
COLONEL KING of the 4th Regiment of United States Infantry; in all
offices, he discharged his arduous duties with honor and dignity to
himself and patriotic cause in which he was engated "never shrinking
as a soldier from any duty assigned him." After his retirement from
the army, he acted in various civil and public capacities--sheriff of
County and a representative in the legislature of his adopted state.
And in all his social and business relations, he sustained the character
of an honest, liberal and high minded gentleman. Amiable and candid
as a friend- honest, upright and manly as a citizen- tender and devoted
as a husband- kind and affectionate as a father- feeling and humane as
a master- his death created a chasm in those relations which years
cannot fill. Carried forward by his own exertions without the aid of
any splendid patrimony, without influence and interest of powerful family
connections, he acquired an ample and independent estate and established
a character, which would do honor to any man in any country.
     He left an affectionate wife, five children and a large circle of
friends and acquaintances....E D M

May 24, 1843
     $400 reward for the arrest of JOHN BOLES, ANNA BOLES, JOHN W. BOLES
and JONATHON BOLES, who murdered QUINNA C. YELVERTON, a citizen of Dale
County on the 18th of May, 1843. JOHN BOLES described as being about
45 or 50 years of age, blue eyes, light hair, ANNA BOLES, wife of said
JOHN BOLES, aged about 45. JOHN W. BOLES, son of said JOHN BOLES aged
about 22. JONATHON BOLES, son of said JOHN BOLES aged about 16.
     Reward for the arrest of WILLIAM H. SMITH and JAMES W. HILL, who
murdered BURRELL B. TOMPKINS in Russell County. HILL is described as
being about 23 or 24 years of age; has dark eyes, fair skin. SMITH is
about 24 years of age, has brown hair and grey eyes.

June 7, 1843
     EDMUND ROURKE & Co. advertise muslins and fashionable goods for
ladies.
     Candidates:
     BACKUS W. HUNTINGTON for House of Representatives
     WILLIAM R. SMITH for Senate
     B. S. THOMPSON for Tax Collector
     SWAN H. SKELTON for Clerk of Circuit Court

June 14, 1843
     Married on Wednesday evening last by REV. MR. SMYTH, MR. STEPHEN B.
COMBS to MISS MAHALA ROBERTSON of this city.
     Candidates:
     W. P. MERIWETHER for House of Representatives

June 21, 1843
     Married in Wilcox County on the 7th instant by W. W. RIEVES, Esq.
DR. I(SAAC) F(OOTE) DORTCH of Sumter County to MISS MARY ANN ROSS of
Wilcox Co. See Owen's Dict. of Ala. Biog. Vo. IV p. 1467.
     Married at the residence of JOHN S. BEALLE, Esq. in this county on
Thursday evening, the 15th instant by REV. B. MANLY, E(LDRED) B. TEAGUE
to MISS SOPHIA N(ELSON) BLOUNT, daughter of the late CAPT. JAMES G.
BLOUNT. (In 1850 Census Sumter Co. Ala. ELDRED B 30 b S C SOPHIA 27
S C & 3 chn b Ala

June 28, 1843
    Reward offered for the arrest of JAMES M. KING, who on the 21st
of November 1842 did murder BRITTON FARROW in the county of Lauderdale.
KING is described as being about 40 years of age, dark, reddish complexion, and a very hard drinker.

July 5, 1843
    Married at Providence Church, Sumter County, Alabama near the
residence of REV. S. S. LATTIMORE at 5 o'clock, P.M. on Sunday, the
25th of June by REV. B. L. BARNES of Wahalak, Mississippi, MR. MATTHEW
LYON, Printer of the Pickensville Register to MISS SUSAN MUSCOGEE,
daughter of REV. LEE COMPERE of Tippah County, Mississippi.
    Married in North Tuscaloosa on the 23rd instant by WILLIAM THOMPSON,
Esq. DR. SAMUEL N. McMINN to MISS ANN NUCKOLS.
    Also on the 25th instant by same, MR. THOMAS H. WALKER to MISS
ELIZABETH OWEN.

July 12, 1843
    Reward offered for the arrest of ROLAND J. JOHNSON, who did murder
ANGE WILSON in the County of Marshall on March 1st, 1841. JOHNSON is
described as being about 25 years of age and has sandy hair and blue
eyes.

July 19, 1843
    Petition to sell real estate. State of Alabama--Marion County.
JAMES B. BANKHEAD, administrator and JANE BANKHEAD, administratrix of
the estate of JOHN BANKHEAD, deceased.
    versus
JOHN H. BANKHEAD and others, heirs of said JOHN BANKHEAD, deceased.
JAMES B. BANKHEAD, one of the administrators made affadavit in court,
showing that ELIZABETH METCALF, wife of JAMES METCALF, JOHN B. BARTON,
SAMUEL BARTON and DAVID BARTON are non-residents of this state.
                            EDWIN G. MOZLEY, Clerk C C

July 26, 1843
    Died near Warsaw in Sumter County on the 9th instant, MRS. MINERVA
BAKER, wife of the HON. ROBERT A. BAKER. She died as she lived- a
Christian. She has left a large family of children, her husband and an
extensive circle of acquaintances (Gainesville Pilot) Note: ROBT. A.
BAKER m. in Madison Co. Ala. 1823 MINERVA LAMPKIN (1st wife). He m. 2d
MRS. POTTS.
    Notice:
    MR. NELSON SMITH will deliver an address in the Presbyterian
Church on Tuesday evening. Subject: "Cultivation of Taste"

August 9, 1843
    (From Eutaw Whig)
    Died near Clinton on the 25th of July, JESSE HARBERT HORTON aged
23 years 8 months and 3 days, amidst tears of father and mother,
brothers and sisters....
    LaFayette

August 16, 1843
    State of Alabama--Tuscaloosa County.
    HENRY POTTER filed petition praying for an order to compel
HARDIN PERKINS, administrator and ELIZA A. PERKINS, administratrix of
the estate of CONSTANTINE PERKINS, deceased, to make title to 20 acres
of land sold during PERKINS' lifetime to one HIRAM P. COCHRAN.
                            MOSES McGUIRE, Clerk
    Died in this city on Saturday evening, the 12th instant at 5
o'clock ANN, daughter of LEVI B. and ANN H. WINDHAM, aged about 4 years.
    Died on the morning of the 31st instant at the residence of her
father in Greene County, Alabama of scarlet fever, after a short but
severe illness, MISS SARAH LOUISA GLOVER, eldest daughter of WILLIAM A.
and AMELIA T. GLOVER in the 17th year of her age.
    Obituary:
    Death of DR. HORATIO NELSON MORRIS, who departed this life on the
31st ult. at Wetumpka... He had been diligently trained in medical
school and the hospitals of Philadelphia....

A. R. THOMAS, candidate for Doorkeeper of the Senate

Proceedings of the City Council (Tuscaloosa) Present: RO. S. INGE, Mayor---MESSRS. COOPER, EATON, FOSTER, SKELTON and WHITING

Accounts allowed: CHARLES BEALL'S (Marshal) account and quarterly salary $145.75

ROBERT S. INGE (Mayor account and quarterly salary: $48.00; T. F. SAMUEL (Secretary) $27'; OTIS DYER's account for hire of servant, 32 days: $24; JAMES HULLUM for same, $9.75; JANE POWELL's account for same, $3.75; THOMAS CUMMINGS' account for same, $8.25; H. G. DONOHO's account for same, $2.35; JOHN FORRESTER's account for three days work, $2.25; HENRY T. ANTHONY's account, 4 days work, $3.00.

The Board proceeded to elect a watchman. The names of ADAM POOL and JAMES O'BRIEN were in nomination and JAMES O'BRIEN having received all the votes, was declared duly elected watchman for the term of one month.

MR. SKELTON, alderman from the 1st ward, offered his resignation, which the Board refused to receive.

By a private letter from Centreville, Bibb County, we learn of an encounter between EZEKIEL HENRY and CROCKETT G. DAVIS, in which the latter received nine stabs with a knife (Wetumpka Times)

Since reading the above, we learn that DAVIS has died of wounds. Many of the citizens will remember DAVIS as Messenger of the House of Representatives in 1840.

Melancholy Tradegy. On Tuesday last, MR. WILLIAM NEIL was killed in this place by a man named HENRY GEE. MR. NEIL left a large family of children, whose mother died about a year ago (Gainesville Pilot)

August 23, 1843

Married at her father's residence near Blount Springs, on the 17th instant by HON. THOMAS SHEARER, ALEXANDER EWING, Esq. to MISS ROBERTA ANN, daughter of DR. HENRY W. RHODES.

Candidate:

GEORGE B. CLITHERALL for re-election to office of Secretary of State.

August 30, 1843

Reward for the arrest of EZEKIEL HENRY, who murdered CROCKETT G. DAVIS in the County of Bibb on the 7th of August, 1843. HENRY is described as being about 23 years of age, and has dark hair and blue eyes.

September 6, 1843

State of Alabama--Bibb County. Orphans Court. JOHN W. SUTTLE, sheriff, administrator de bonis non, of estate of JAMES PAGE, deceased, showing to the court that he had received from DANIEL E. DAVIS $269.92 belonging to said estate and that part of the heirs of said estate reside beyond the limits of this state.

WILLIAMS CADDELL, Clerk

Administrator's Notice:

DANIEL CRIBBS, sheriff, administrator de bonis non, of estate of JOHN PARKER, deceased, Tuscaloosa County.

September 13, 1843

Died in this city on the 9th instant, MRS. CAROLINE SUSAN MILLER, aged 24 years, consort of MR. WILLIAM MILLER and daughter of COL. PETER DONALDSON.

S. B. COMBS, candidate for Messenger of House of Representatives.

September 20, 1843

Obituary:

Died in this city on the 9th instant, MRS. CAROLINE SUSAN, consort of MR. WILLIAM MILLER in her 24th year....Survived by parents, husband and two little children...(Communicated)

State of Alabama--Bibb County. Orphans Court. DAVID S. LIPSCOMB, administrator of the estate of WILLIS BROWN, late of said county deceased. Estate is insolvent.

JOHN W. SUTTLE, Clerk

We announce with pain, the death of HON. JOHN G. CREAGH of Clarke County. He died at his residence near Clarkesville on Friday, the 25th of August in th 52d year of his life. He was favorably known throughout the state, having formerly represented Clarke County in the Legislature, Also recently, Judge of County Court of Clarke County and he occupied many other stations of honor. He left a large family and numerous relatives.

September 27, 1843
    Married in this city on Thursday evening last by REV. DR. JOHN OWEN, MR. GEORGE B. QUINN to MISS SUSAN T. MASSENGALE.
    Obituary:
    Departed this life a few days since, near Tuscaloosa, MISS ELIZABETH CALDWELL aged about 65 years, She was a native of Ireland and emigrated to South Carolina about 1787, and in 1818 moved with her parents to this state and has lived in or near Tuscaloosa since that time... Presbyterian....So lived and so died this dear lady and as we hope, child of God.
    Died in Mobile on Sunday the 17th of congestive fever, after an illness of two weeks, JOSEPH VOKES, Printer, formerly of Warrenton, North Carolina.
    Candidates:
    JOSEPH PHELAN for Clerk of House of Representatives
    WILSON C. BIBB for Engrossing Clerk of   "
    ALEXANDER B. CLITHERALL for ass't Clerk   "

October 4, 1843
    Alabama Female Institute
    N. M. HENTZ, Principal
    C. L. HENTZ, MARY CHAPMAN, JOANNA SMITH (latter of this city will supply place of MISS LINSLY, who was prevented from coming)
    Musical Department- AMAND P. PFISTER
    Board of Trustees- P. MARTIN, President; A. V. BRUMBY, Secretary; J. H. DEARING, JOHN C. CUMMING, C. MORRISON, H. C. KIDDER, DANIEL M. FORNEY.
    Obituary:
    Died in this city on Wednesday, the 26th ult. COLONEL PETER DONALDSON, an old and highly respected citizen; COL. DONALDSON was born at Cheraw, Chesterfield District, South Carolina on the 15th of May, 1777 A D. He removed to Augusta, Georgia in 1795 and in 1809 was elected sheriff of Richmond County, Georgia. This office he filled until 1818, also having served as colonel in the militia. In 1818, he removed to Indian Springs, Georgia and thence to this city in 1824, where he has since been known as an enterprising, public-spirited citizen and as the worthy host of the Bell Tavern. In his private circle, COL. DONALDSON had been familiar with intense affliction. Cut of ten children, eight on full flush of youth, had preceded him to an untimely grave.....Buried on Thursday last with Masonic honors. Sermon was preached by REV. MR. CAPERS of this city.

October 18, 1843
    Died at his residence in this city on Saturday, the 14th inst. MR. STEPHEN B. COMBS, formerly of Philadelphia.
    Obituary:
    Died in Columbiana, Shelby County, Alabama on the 29th of September 1843, NOEL MASON, Esq. Clerk of the County Court, and aged about 31 years.
    Bill for Divorce:
    State of Mississippi- Choctaw County
    JANE SMITH, complainant
            versus
    HENRY SMITH, Defendant
    Dancing School- MR. JAMES A. IRVINE in a room situated above the store of MR. JOHN E. ROYALL.
    Administrator's Notice:
    State of Alabama-Tuscaloosa County
    Letters of administration on the estate of JOHN MILLER, late of Tuscaloosa County, deceased granted to MALVINA A. MILLER, administratrix and STEPHEN MILLER, adm/r.
    Administrator's Notice:
    State of Alabama-Tuscaloosa County. Orphans Court. Letters of administration on estate of WILLIAM LUNDBERG, late of Tuscaloosa County, deceased. DANIEL CRIBBS, sheriff, admr de bonis non.

October 25, 1843
Married in this city on the 23rd instant by REV. J. H. THOMASON,
MR. THOMAS A. MORRIS of Hinds County, Mississippi to MISS REBECCA JANE
MORRIS of St. Clair Co. Ala.

November 1, 1843
Indian Queen Tavern. WILLIAM CLARE, proprietor. MRS. DONALDSON
informs her friends that she will continue to open the house of her
late husband COL. PETER DONALDSON, as a private boarding house.

Boarding per month, with lodging:	$20.00
without lodgins	13.00
Man and horse per day	2.00
Dinner	.50
Supper	.37
Lodging	.25
Breakfast	.37
Horse feed	.37
Horse per month	12.00
Spirits or wine, none except by quart or gallon	

Jefferson Hotel (formerly known as Covey's Bank Coffee House).
RICHARD MURPHY, prop.
MR. JOHN WORD- Dancing School. All fashionable dances taught.
Cotillons, waltzing, Spanish dances etc.

November 8, 1843
Died in this city on Saturday evening, the 4th instant, MISS
AMANDA MASSEY in her 17th year.
HON. BENJAMIN F. PORTER, candidate for Major General of the 2nd
Division, A.M. composed of Counties of Tuscaloosa, Pickens, Bibb and
Shelby. Vacancy caused by resignation of Maj. Gen. GEORGE W. CRABB.

November 15, 1843
Obituary:
Died in Greensboro on Saturday, the 22d of July, MISS JULIA ERWIN,
daughter of COL. JOHN ERWIN, aged 16 years.
COL. FRANCIS W. BOSTICK of Pickens County, candidate for Major
General.
State of Alabama-Tuscaloosa County. Orphans Court. CHAPMAN A.
HESTER, executor of the last will and testament of SAMUEL M. FARRAR.
Estate insolvent.
State of Alabama Tuscaloosa County. Orphans Court. NANCY HUDSON
petitions for dower from the estate of her late husband, JAMES HUDSON,
deceased. 9 Oct. 1843.
State of Alabama-Tuscaloosa County. Orphans Court. 9 October 1843.
JOHN HUDSON, administrator in right of wife, of the estate of JAMES
HUDSON, deceased. Notice is hereby given to JOB H. BINION and LEWIS
HUDSON, heirs of said estate.

November 22, 1843
E. B. TEAGUE states that he is a graduate of the University of
Alabama. Class of 1840 and that he has since that time engaged in
teaching; that he designs opening a school to prepare boys for college.
Terms, $25 per session of 5 months. Reference: Faculty of the
University, EDMUND PRINCE, Esq. and M. D. J. Slade, Esq.
JOSHUA STORRS Prep. School
Obituary:
Died in Carthage on the 10th instant after a most painful illness,
COL. ELIAS FRIERSON in his 70th year. He was born in Williamsburg
District, South Carolina from whence he removed to Tennessee in the
year 1806 and was one of the earliest settlers in the dense forest
of the "Duck River country" in that state. After having resided there
about thirteen years in 1818, he removed to this state, then a territory,
where he resided until his death....Humble, unpretending, kind,
benevolent...Kind father, neighbor and friend.
Died on the 12th instant at Carthage, in Tuscaloosa County, MRS.
LAVINA M. QUARLES, consort of DR. M(OSES) QUARLES in the 33d year of her
age after a protracted illness of several weeks, leaving a husband and
infant daughter, besides a number of relatives. (Communicated) Note:
She was LAVINIA M. AYLETT m. 1841 MOSES QUARLES.

It becomes our melancholy duty to record the death of our most
valuable citizen, ALVA FINLEY, Esq. who died about 9 o'clock this
morning, the 13th instant...Left a wife and child...(Jackson County
Democrat) Note: tombstone at Bellefonte- d Nov. 13, 1843 aged 38
yrs 27 days

November 29, 1843
    Married at the residence of THOMAS LEE in Tuscaloosa County on
the 2ed instant by E. A. MONTGOMERY, Esq. WILLIAM R. SMITH, Esq. of
this city to MISS JANE ELIZABETH BINION.
    Died in this city on Wednesday the 22d instant, MARTHA ANN ELIZA,
aged 5 years, daughter of HON. H. W. COLLIER....

THE DEMOCRATIC GAZETTE

Printed and Published by R(OBT) A. EATON
each Wednesday Tuscaloosa, Ala.

January 17, 1844
    Died in this city Friday evening last, the 12th instant, THOMAS,
aged 2 years and 8 months. On Sunday the 14th instant in the afternoon,
JAMES aged 5 years. On the evening of the same day, LEWIS aged 3 years
and 7 months, all children of ROBERT A. EATON, proprietor of the
Democratic Gazette. All died of scarlet fever. We extend our sympathy
to the mourning mother.

January 31, 1843 (misprint or odd copy?)
    Died in this city Thursday evening last, ROBERT HARRIS, only
child of R. A. EATON, aged 9 months. Note: The date should be 1844.
    Obituary:
    Died on the 31st of December in his 87th year, ELIJAH McGUIRE in
Tuscaloosa County. He was born in Cumberland County, Virginia on the
19th of January, 1857; from thence moved to South Carolina. At an
early age, he enlisted as a soldier in a regiment commanded by COL.
WILLIAM THOMPSON and was one of the company of CAPTAIN JOHN BUCHANNAN.
The post of danger at the time was the city of Charleston, and hastening
with his companies to defence of that city, he was taken prisoner of
war at the capitulation. Immediately on his exchange, he attached
himself to a troop of light horse, commanded by GENERAL SUMTER and
continued in active service until the war was concluded. He was
distinguished for ardent patriotism and eminent courage and was
connected with many daring and perilous enterprises in defense of his
country. After the war, he married MISS EVERETT WILLIAMS, with whom he
lived a happy life for upwards of 60 years and who, now, a widow in
her 83rd year of age, mourns his loss. They were both Baptists for
nearly half a century....

February 7, 1844
    Died on the island of Cuba, whither he had gone for health,
OSCAR F. RAINEY, Esq. aged 23, formerly of Eutaw, Alabama. From
Independent Monitor of Wednesday last.
    The subject was well known here. He finished his professional
studies here and was admitted to practice....
    E. G. FORREST advertises his tailoring business.
    Committed to the jail of Tuscaloosa County, a slave who says he
belongs to the estate of HANNON PRUDE, late of Noxubee County, Mississippi deceased.

March 13, 1844
    MRS. CLITHERALL's Seminary for Young Ladies.
    Advertisement.

March 20, 1844
    Obituary:
    Departed this life on the 12th ult. at his plantation on Second
Creek after a painful and protracted illness, COL/ HENRY A. GARRETT,
a native of Tennessee, but for several years past, a citizen of Madison

and subsequently of Adams County in this state. As a member of the Bar, he had a high reputation. In social and domestic circles, he was greatly admired (From Natchez Miss. Free Trader)

The deceased we understand was a brother of COL. WILLIAM GARRETT, Secretary of State, and of T. G. GARRETT, Solicitor of this Judicial Circuit (From Talladega Watchtower)

April 10, 1844
Administrator's Notice:
DANIEL CRIBBS, administrator with will annexed of the estate of PETER DONALDSON, deceased. Also, administrator of the estate of STEPHEN M. STINSON, deceased.

May 1, 1844
Died in this city Sunday night last, very suddenly, of congestive fever, JOHN H. COCHRAN, Esq. aged 24 years and 6 months......Buried with Masonic honors.

Committed to the jail of Tuscaloosa County, a slave who says he belongs to NANCY McDANIEL, of Noxubee County, Mississippi, near Macon.

May 23, 1844
Married at Spring Hill in this county on Tuesday evening last by REV. T. F. CURTIS, JAMES D(ABNEY) SPILLER, merchant of this city, to MISS FRANCES J(ANE) I. CARUTHERS, daughter of ROBERT CARUTHERS, Esq.

Ice cream and Soda Water at Drug Store of JOHN LITTLE, Adv.

June 6, 1844
MARY L. BRADFORD   )
     versus   ) Bill for Divorce
THOMAS M. BRADFORD)
Abandonment charged. The defendant is a non-resident of this state.

Died i n this city on the 2d instant of dropsy in the chest, JUNIUS A. MOORE, Esq. aged about 40 years. Formerly of Newbern, North Carolina, a man of fine acquirements and great integrity.

Died in this county on the 30th instant, MRS. CYNTHIA TERRELL, wife of WILLIAM H. TERRELL, Esq. aged 53 yearsmx nine months and nine days.

Sudden death:
MR. GEORGE DARDEN, a very respectable citizen of Tuscaloosa died. very suddenly in this place on the 30th ult.

The deceased reached here from Tuscaloosa on the day of his death and was apparently well a few minutes before his attack, which occurred whilst he was returning to the house of MR. JOHN KERR, with whom he was walking at the time. He breathed only a few seconds after he felt the first symptoms. We learn MR. DERDEN was over 80 years of age and that he has left a large circle of children and grand-children to lament his death. (Evidently quoted from another paper, but name of paper not stated)

June 13, 1844
The REV. MR. HACKETT (Catholic Priest) will deliver a lecture on Temporal Power of the Pope on next Sunday evening at early candle light.

Reward offered for escaped prisoners.
STEPHEN ELLEDGE- 5 ft. 9 in. spare made hair, eyes and complexion dark, aged about 45; charged with murder.

DEMPSEY SANDERS- 6 ft. large size; hair, eyes and complexion dark, with a peculiar cast in his eyes; aged about 43 or 42; a blacksmith by trade; charged with larceny.

JOHN T. CHAMBERS, 5 ft 8 in. medium size; fair complexion, light hair and blue eyes; aged 21 or 22 convicted of a penitentiary offence.

A. W. ALLEN, 5 ft 8 in. medium size, dark hair, high cheek bones, light complexion and blue eyes; aged about 30 years; charges with robbing the Post Office in Clinton, Greene Co.

DANIEL CRIBBS, Sheriff
Committed to the jail of Tuscaloosa County by LEWIS ETHERIDGE, Esq. a slave who belongs to MARTHA KNOX of Greene Co.

Committed to the jail of Tuscaloosa County by C. LEWIS WILLIAMS, Esq. a slave who says he belongs to ELISHA SKULL of Lowndes County, Mississippi.

Also by N. L. WHITFIELD, Esq. a slave who says he belongs to
HORATIO L. BAILEY of Lowndes County, Mississippi.
STEPHEN N. STINSON, deceased. DANIEL CRIBBS, administrator of
estate.
L(UTHER) SKINNER, surgeon and mechanical dentist
Advertisement.
Law Notice:
SION L. PERRY and JOHN H. COCHRAN
Committed to the jail of Tuscaloosa County a slave who belongs to
CHRISTOPHER ORE, living near Houston, Chickasaw County, Mississippi

August 1, 1844
Obituary:
Died in this city on the 24th ult, MARY G. E. J. SPILLER, aged 4
years 7 months and 6 days, only daughter of JAMES S (D) SPILLER, Esq.
Sad bereavement has fallen upon the family of DAVID WOODRUFF, Esq.
On Sabbath afternoon, his lovely little daughter FLORENCE, aged about 7
was playing near a well and fell in.

August 8, 1844
Died in this city last afternoon after a long illness, MR. WILLIAM
GLEASON aged 64 years, a native of Ireland and formerly a resident of
Philadelphia.
Died in this city yesterday morning of congestive fever, MR. PATRICK
FALLAN aged 23 years, a native of Leitirim County, Ireland.
After sixteen days suffering of consuming fevers, departed this
life on the 2d of August, a few moments before 2 o'clock, A.M.
LOUISA WHITFIELD, aged 13 years 7 months and 2 days, daughter of
BENJAMIN and MATILDA WHITFIELD.
Married in this city on Wednesday of last week by REV. MR. FORBES,
SAMUEL B. JONES, Esq. of New Orleans to MISS MARY L. SOMERVILLE of this
city.

August 22, 1844
Married in Benton County on the 6th instant by REV. MR. PACE,
MR. JOHN CLASCOCK, merchant of this city to MISS ANN IRWIN, daughter
of COL. WILLIAM McGEHEE.
Died at the residence of his grandmother, MRS. BANKS in this
vicinity on the 17th instant, MR. ELBERT B. JONES aged about 23 years
of Marengo County.
Died in this city on the 16th instant of congestive fever,
MISS FRANCES SCOTT BANKS aged 18 years, daughter of WILLIS BANKS, Esq.

September 4, 1844
Married on the 22nd ult, by REV. ROBERT OLDHAM, MR. AEZOR HAYS
to MISS HANNAH A. LOWRY of Bibb County.
WILLIAM MARTIN, deceased, Letters of administration on estate
granted to DANIEL B. SAMPLE.
Candidates:
SAMUEL A. HALE for Secretary of Senate
S. H. BACON for Clerk of County Court
ROBERT P. BLOUNT for Clerk of County Court
A. R. THOMAS for Doorkeeper of Senate

September 12, 1844
Married in this city on the 4th instant by REV. MR. HACKETT,
LEWIS McGEHEE, Esq. to MISS CATHARINE GLEASON, all of this city.
Died at his residence in this city on the 4th instant, HON. THOMAS
CRAWFORD in the 60th year of his age.

September 25, 1844
Died in this vicinity on the 23d instant, MR. DANIEL HAMER aged
about 65 years.
J. F. MARRAST candidate for assistant Secretary of Senate

October 10, 1844
Died in New York on the 18th ult, MISS MARY WALTHALL, eldest
daughter of R(ICHD) B. WALTHALL, Esq. of Perry Co. Ala.

October 17, 1844
    Married in this city on Sunday evening last by REV. T. J. (F)
CURTIS, MR. MILTON TANNEHILL to MISS MARY, daughter of MR. RICHARD
MURPHY.
    Died in this city on Friday the 11th instant of an inflammatory
bilious attack of about two weeks continuance, MRS. ELIZABETH A.
FOSTER, wife of HON. ARTHUR FOSTER, aged 42 years.
    Died in this city on the 10th instant, CHARLES HENRY MORRISON,
aged 3 months, infant son of BENJAMIN F. and ELLEN MORRISON.
    MRS. ARMSTRONG, formerly of New York has opened an academy for
instruction for Young Ladies in Music and Painting.

THE REPUBLICAN BANNER

Published at Tuskaloosa by DENNIS DYKOUS, prop.

June 25, 1870
    Married on the morning of the 20th at Elyton (Jefferson Co.) at
the residence of the bride's mother by REV. J. F. SMITH, MR. WILLIAM H.
DOUTHIT and MISS JENNIE M. SAMUEL.
    State of Alabama-Tuscaloosa Co. Estate of W. H. SUGG, deceased.
MOSES McGUIRE filed application stating that he is guardian ad litem of
------SUGG, a minor child of said decendent; that MRS. C. A. GILLIGAN,
wife of JAMES GILLIGAN the administratrix has removed out of the state
without having completed her administration of said estate.
    State of Alabama-Tuscaloosa County. Estate of A. G. GOOCH, deceased,
MRS. MARGARET GOOCH, administratrix.

July 2, 1870
    Died May 31 (Mdgo. M. says d June 1; see Vol. 184 p. 27) from
effects of measels, MISS MARY SPILLER, daughter of ROBERT SPILLER in
her 22nd (28th yr Independent Monitor) year; on June 1, JIMMY, son of
ROBERT SPILLER in his 13th (19th? 12th yr, in Independent Monitor)
year; on June 5, MISS ALICE, daughter of ROBERT SPILLER in her 20th
year.

July 16, 1870
    JAMES WHITE, administrator of M. T. GROSSLAND, deceased.

July 23, 1870
    Died in this city on July 16, PHILIP HENRY MAXWELL, infant
daughter of JOHN L. and MARY ANN MAXWELL aged 8 months.

July 30, 1870
    Died at the residence of MR. C. E. TILKINS in Marysville (Calif),
July 4, 1870, DR. LaFAYETTE GUILD. Native of Alabama and removed
from Mobile to San Francisco in Nov. 1869. Very eminent in his profession (see Indep. Monitor).

August 6, 1870
    Died in this city on the evening of the 2nd of August, MRS. JENNIE
M. consort of W(M) H. DOUTHIT in her 20th year. Just weeks before,
MR. DOUTHIT claimed her for his bride and brought her hither from
Elyton (Jefferson Co.) where lives her mother and other relatives.
(see Indep. Monitor)
    Died in Tuscaloosa Aug. 1, MRS. WEALTHY JANE BOYD (26 A), relict
of FRANK BOYD, Esq. aged about 47. She was born if I mistake not in
Tuscaloosa Co. and resided in the town of Tuscaloosa for a number of
years prior to the war. Devoted wife and affectionate mother. (see
Indep. Monitor)

August 13, 1870
    Married on the evening of 7th at residence of bride's father by
REV. GEORGE H. HUNT, MR. JOSEPH VOYLE and MISS GENEVIEVE SELLICK, all
of this city.
    Estate of S. P. JOHNSON, deceased, divided between ELIZABETH,
DAVID and HARVEY JOHNSON, minor heirs.

August 20, 1870
State of Alabama- Tuscaloosa Co. Aug. 16, 1870. A. C. HARGROVE
and H. CLAY VAUGHAN, administrators of E(DWD) BRACY VAUGHAN (1798-1868),
deceased filed a petition to sell real estate belonging to said
deceased. Following heirs to be notified: SAVILLA B. wife of WM. H.
HARGROVE, daughter of said dec'd, resides in Lowndes Co. Miss; FRANCIS
MARION VAUGHAN, son of dec'd, resides in Lowndes Co. Miss; CARRIE
VAUGHAN, wife of GEORGE W. VAUGHAN, dec'd, resides in Rankin Co. Miss.;
JOSEPH BRACIE VAUGHAN and MARIA VAUGHAN, minors under 14, children
of said GEORGE W. VAUGHAN, dec'd, said JOSEPH resides with his uncle,
F. M. VAUGHAN in Lowndes Co. Miss and said MARIA resides with her
mother, the said CARRIE VAUGHAN in Rankin Co. Miss.
State of Ala-Tuscaloosa Co. J. H. FITTS and S. J. LEACH, admr's
of D. H. AVERY, dec'd petition for dower of JULIA K. AVERY in lands of
which her husband died seized of. Notify JULY C. AVERY, CHARLES and
EDWARD AVERY, heirs at law of said estate.

August 27, 1870
Died in this city (vol 184, p 29) on morning of 25th of croup
(see Indep. Monitor), EDMONDS MASON MARTIN, 4th son of JOHN M. and LUCY
C. P. MARTIN aged 3 years.
On Sat. 20th at 9 P.M. in 19th year, JOHN DONOHO (see Indep.
Mon.), son of MONROE DONOHO....
In this city on Aug. 16th, ANNA E. daughter of MR. P. and MRS. MARY
McNULTY (see Indep. Mon.).

September 10, 1870
Died in this city on Sat. Sept. 3, THOMAS BLOUNT, son of B. and
CATHARINE SLADE aged 8 years...(see Independ. Mon.).
State of Ala- Tuscaloosa Co. Will of ELIZABETH DEASON (can't find
will recorded), dec'd filed. Notify MARY WRIGHT, BEATRICE DEASON,
ELIZABETH WRIGHT, SARAH ANN DEASON, RODY ANN DEASON and JOHN DEASON,
who are non-residence and next of kin of deceased. (Oc 11 - p 25
ELIZ. DEASON dec'd 27 Aug 1870. Next of kin WM, EDWD & MIDDLETON DEASON,
Tuscaloosa Co. MARY, BEATRICE & ELIZ. WRIGHT, Pontotoc Co. Miss
SARAH ANN, RODY & JOHN DEASON, Miss SUSAN NIX - Ala.)
Notice:
E. A. POWELL, adm'r of JOHN PICKFORD, dec'd who died in Tuscaloosa
on or about the 9 of Dec. 1869. It is reported that he was born in
Nova Scotia. Unable to ascertain any lawful heirs.

September 17, 1870
Died--SUSANNAH CAROLINE, daughter of DANIEL and MARGARET LOGGINS;
born in Tuscaloosa Co. Mar. 9, 1860 and died in Austin Co. Tex. Aug. 10,
1870...

September 24, 1870
Died in this city on 20th, JOHN S. FITCH (57 Mass, 1792-1870),
a native of Norwich, Conn. in his 78th year. Emigrated to Tuscaloosa
in 1821 about the time the city was laid out with lots and streets,
so he was truly one of our eldest citizens. Man of gravity and
sedateness of character....(see Indep. Monitor).
Died in North Port on 19th, ROSCO (see Indep. Monitor), son of
R. and P. H. SIMPSON.
State of Alabama-Tuscaloosa Co. Will of DANIEL M. CLARK (d 1870),
dec'd. Notify ELIZABETH WELCH (widow), residing in Boston, Mass. and
WILLIAM CLARK (residence unknown), who are non-residents and next of
kin of dec'd.
Married in this city on 21st by REV. C. D. OLIVER, MR. ROBERT A.
CHILDRESS and MISS MOLLIE C. MURPHY, all of this county (see I. M.).
Also in this city on 22nd by REV. J. H. FOSTER, MR. HENRY COST and
MISS MARY J. GARNER, all of this county.

October 1, 1870
Died on 19th Sept. MR. DANIEL M. CLARK, long a citizen and merchant
of this city....(see Indep. Monitor).
Died at residence of MRS. B. F. EDDINS near this city on Thurs.
the 22, little LOLLIE, infant daughter of J. A. and NONIE OGBURN.

Died in this city on morning of 26, HARRY PEGUES MARTIN, son of
MR. and MRS. L. V. B. MARTIN aged about 1 year (see Indep. Mon.).

October 8, 1870
    Died, W. T. SARTIN in 37th yr., at residence of MRS. S. S. L.
COCHRANE on Oct. 2, 1870 (see Indep. Mon.).

October 15, 1870
    Died in this city on Tuesday, 11th, IRBY, infant son of T. B. and
C. SLADE.
    Also in this city on 13th after lingering illness, WILEY B.
THOMPSON in 27th year (see Ind. Mon.).
    On 13th, MRS. MINORA SPILLER (Ind. Mon.), wife of HENRY L. SPILLER
in 38th yr.

October 22, 1870
    Died Thurs. 20th, at Mansion House in this city at 10½ o'clock
A.M. of typhoid fever, JOHN W. HOYT (supposed aged about 25). Comparatively a newcomer here....(see Ind. Mon.).

October 29, 1870
    Died on 25th at residence of MR. THOMAS P. LEWIS, CAPT. H(OLLIS)
C. KIDDER (@ 50 in 1858 b M), one of our oldest and most respected
citizens.

November 5, 1870
    Died in Mobile on 20th, MISS LIBBIE C. PEARCE, daughter of
MRS. R. C. PEARCE, formerly of this city.
    Died in Charlotte, N.C. on 26th after a very short illness,
DR. JAMES YOUNG BRYCE aged 23 yrs and 4 months. Spent many months of
last year in this vicinity assisting his brother, DR. PETER BRYCE at
Insane Hospital....
    Married in Christ Church, Tuscaloosa by REV. GEO. H. HUNT on eve.
of Nov. 2, MR. JOSHUA T. HAUSMAN to MISS R. CANNIE LYNCH, all of
Tuscaloosa.

November 12, 1870
    Died of pneumonia at his residence near Foster's Settlement on
11th, WILLIAM B. ELLIOTT, highly esteemed citizen of this county.

November 19, 1870
    Married by REV. J. T. YERBY at residence of bride's father on
Nov. 17, MR. WILLIAM W. PRUDE, JR. and MISS AMANDA ROBERTSON all of
Tuscaloosa Co. (Ind. Mon.).

November 26, 1870
    Died in this city on 24th of malarial haematuria, MISS MARY
STILLMAN aged 23, daughter of REV. C. A. STILLMAN. Presbyterian
(Ind. Mon.)

December 10, 1870
    Married in this city on 7th by REV. GEO. H. HUNT, MR. WILLIAM A.
LELAND and MISS ELLA McLESTER (Indep. Mon.)

TUSKALOOSA OBSERVER

January 7, 1871
    Died in this city at 5 o'clock Monday evening Jan. 2, THOMAS H.
RALPH aged about 38. Has resided here for more than 15 yrs...Leaves
widow and 3 small children.
    Married 28 Dec. 1870 at residence of MR. ROBERT HATTEN, by
REV. GEO. H. HUNT, MR. W. PENN LYNCH and MISS JOSEPHINE SPEAKMAN,
all of this city.

January 14, 1871
    Died in Tuscaloosa Ala. Jan. 2, 1871 after a short illness,
THOMAS H. RALPH; born in Minola Co. Mago, Ireland-aged 39 years.

January 21, 1871
    Married in this county on 17th by REV. J. T. YERBY, MR. D. M. FARMER
and MRS. AGNES DAVENPORT----no cake.
    Married in the jail of this county on 18th by Hon. Judge of
Probate, SERGEANT SOWERS, 2d U.S. Infantry and MISS FANNY WALKER.

February 18, 1871
    Married at residence of CAPT. J. B. EDDINS on Tuesday Feb. 14,
by REV. T. M. BARBOUR, MR. JAMES C. BEAN to MISS JOSEPHINE EDDINS.

March 25, 1871
    Died in this city on 18 of measles, MRS. WILLINGHAM, wife of
BRADFORD WILLINGHAM, Esq.

April 1, 1871
    Married in this city at residence of bride's mother on 27th by
REV. GEO. H. HUNT, MR. JOHN P. BARTEE and MISS EMILIE DOUTHIT.
    Married last evening at Broadway Methodist Church, LOGAN P. KENNEDY,
Esq. to MISS HANNAH J. LITHGOW, daughter of HON. JAMES LITHGOW, ex-mayor.

April 8, 1871
    Married at residence of MR. JOHN GROGAN by REV. J. T. YERBY on
2 April, MR. JAMES WILSON to MISS MARY GROGAN.
    Also by same on 4 April at residence of MR. DANIEL CRIBBS,
MR. W. N. WILLIAMS to MRS. MARY A. MILLER, daughter of DANIEL CRIBBS,
all of Tuscaloosa Co.
    Died near this city on 26 March, MISS JULIA A. BLOUNT in 17th year;
as an only daughter, she greatly endeared herself.

April 22, 1871
    Married in Assumption Parish, La. at residence of bride's mother
on 11th, MR. JOHN E. GUERIN to MISS MARY E. LEFTWICH.
    Died in this city on Fri. the 21st of consumption, MISS MARIA R.
DEARING.

May 6, 1871
    Died at Taylorville on the 1st, HENRY HAYS, infant child of
DR. W. H. and REBECCA ARMSTRONG.

May 27, 1871
    Died in this city on Thurs. the 18th, WILLIAM C. SAMUEL aged
about 37; died from effects of a gunshot wound received in his breast
about 16 days before. Confederate soldier.
    Died in this city on 17th, MRS. THERESY LOVEMAN, wife of MR. E.
LOVEMAN of firm of FRIEDMAN & LOVEMAN of Tuscaloosa.

July 22, 1871
    Died in this city Monday night the 17th of congestive fever,
SION P(ERRY), elder son of LUTHER and SOPHIA SKINNER (she was d of
SION L. PERRY, see d of g 1846) aged 24 years.

August 5, 1871
    Died at her residence about 18 miles from this city on 28th of
July, MRS. HARGROVE, wife of W. H. HARGROVE, Esq. of this county.
    Died in this city on afternoon of 28th of July, SIDNEY WALLACE,
infant son of F. P. and M. K. TURNER.
    Died in Tuscaloosa on Fri. the 4th of congestive fever, GEO. DALLAS
JOHNSON, aged about 20 years.
    Married in Northport on 24 July at residence of bride's mother,
by REV. T. M. BARBOUR, MR. J. G McGEHEE to MISS M. L. HALL, all of
Tuscaloosa Co.
    Married at St. John's Church, Mobile on 25 July by REV. DR. R. D.
NEVINS, ANDREW C. McCLEAN to MISS NORA TOUMEY.
    Married in this city at residence of MRS. BURKE on 31 July by
REV. DR. HAMILTON, REV. F. M. GRACE of Tenn. to MISS KITTY GREEN of
Jefferson Co. Ala.

August 12, 1871
    Death of COL. JOHN H. BURTON who resided in Hale Co. more than 35
years. Died at residence of his son near Elyton (Jefferson Co.)

August 19, 1871
    Died at his residence on Sipsey River in this county recently,
MR. GEORGE WASHINGTON (son of Wash'n John Wash'on; @ 50 in 1850, b Va.,
Bible says d Aug 9, 1871) who was upwards of 70 yrs. Worthy citizen
and was a lineal descendant of the great WASHINGTON.
    Died August 3 at residence of her husband in Trousdale Co. Tenn.
MRS. MARGARET C. SIDDONS, wife of DR. W. M. SIDDONS and daughter of
MR. and MRS. NELSON A. CRAWFORD of Eutaw (Greene Co. Ala.) aged 28
years. The deceased and her husband resided in Tuscaloosa for about
2 years, having removed to Tenn. less than a year ago.

August 26, 1871
    Died after a short illness at his residence in this county on
19th, WILEY G. W. HESTER aged about 31 years.

September 2, 1871
    Married at residence of bride's father by REV. R. S. COX on
Sunday Aug. 27, THOMAS M. BARNETT and MISS SALLIE A. HAGLER, all of
Tuscaloosa Co.
    Died in the city of Baltimore on 18 Aug. of consumption at house
of her uncle, JOHN M. ELY, MRS. MARY OLIVIA GOLIBERT, eldest daughter
of our townsman, PROF. F(RANCES) S. WALTER aged 36 years.
    Died in Northport Aug. 26, LEONA; also on 28, LENORE, infant
children of L. F. and E. C. BURKS.

September 9, 1871
    JOHN and ELIAS WILSON, administrators of WILLIAM WILSON, dec'd;
petition for division of estate. Notify children of WILLIAM WILSON,
son of deceased, who is also deceased; WILLIAM E. WILSON, JOHN H. WILSON,
SARAH F. WILSON, JAMES E. WILSON, reside with their guardian, WILLIAM
DODSON and their mother, MRS. WILLIAM DODSON--non-residents of Ala.

September 16, 1871
    Died in Elyton (Jefferson Co.) Aug. 7, ANNITA PRENTICE DEASON,
daughter of DR. G. T. DEASON aged 1 yr. and 9 days.
    Married on morning of 7th at residence of WILLIAM FARMER, Esq.
by REV. WILLIAM H. ARMSTRONG, ELIJAH C. SMITH and MISS ELVIRA HALL,
all of Tuscaloosa Co.

October 21, 1871
    Will of JOHN E. CHAMBERS, dec'd presented by S. M. CHAMBERS.
Notify SAMUEL T. CHAMBERS, Campbell Co. Va; WM. M. CHAMBERS, Roxborough,
N.C. and LUCY R. HAMLETT, -------Va. all non-residents

October 28, 1871
    Married on Oct. 25 at residence of bride's mother by REV. FATHER
KIRWAN, J. W. GAUDIN and ANNIE E. COLLIER.
    Died at his late residence in Foster's Settlement on Thursday
Sept. 28 A.D. 1871, Deacon F. H. NIX (@ 49 m 1850, b SC); born in S.C.
about 1793. Has lived about 40 years in this settlement. Useful
citizen. Had 6 sons in Confederate service, four of whom died in
service. Deacon of Grant's Creek Baptist Church many years.
    MRS. REBECCA HASSELTINE FOSTER, wife of J. LUTHER FOSTER died very
suddenly at residence of her husband on 18th in her 32nd year; daughter
of ELISHA and ELIZABETH H. THORNTON, late of Green Co. Ala; member of
Grant's Creek Baptist Church. Affectionate mother.
    MRS. ELIZABETH MAHARREY (@ 28 in 1850 b NC), relict of JOSEPH P.
MAHARREY (@ 49 b Md.) died at her late residence in August last. For
several years a member of Grant's Creek Baptist Church.

November 4, 1871
    Married near Forkland at residence of bride's mother on 25th Oct.,
NORFLEET HARRIS, Esq. of Tuscaloosa to MISS BETTIE BLOCKER of Greene Co.
    Died in this city on 1st inst. LEIGHTON, youngest son of the late
RT. REV. N. H. COBBS.

November 25, 1871
    Died near Newbern on 8th inst. at residence of MR. SAMUEL NICHOLS,
MRS. ELIZA M. REATTY in her 70th year. Native of N.C.

December 16, 1871
      Died in Summerfield on 21st, MRS. MASSEY, wife of PROF. JOHN MASSEY,
Principal of Centenary Male Institute.
                              From Marion Commonwealth

December 23, 1871
      Obituary of NORMA JONES from Athens Post, Limestone Co. Ala.

TUSCALOOSA TIMES

TAYLOR A. WARD, prop.

January 17, 1872
      Married at Carthage church on 28th Dec. 1871 by REV. JOHN C. FOSTER,
MR. J(AMES) A. BURGIN (his 1st wife, MARY CAROLINE HICKMAN d. 10-2-1878)
of Pickens Co. (49G) to MRS. H. S. GLADNEY of Hale Co.
      Married in Tuscaloosa on morning of 4th, by REV. C. A. STILLMAN,
MR. D. FORNEY MOORE to MISS HELEN L. GORREE.
      Married at Eutaw (Greene Co.) on ----- by REV. S. W. SMITH MR. J. M.
SMITH of New Orleans to MISS MARY LYNCH of Tuscaloosa.

January 24, 1872
      Married at the residence of bride's father Dec. 31 by REV. JOHN C.
FOSTER, DR. A. B. C. NICHOLLS and MISS MARY ELLEN FOSTER, all of
Foster's, Ala.
      By same at residence of MR. WOODWARD, step-father of bride on
Jan. 2, DR. E. CLAY ELLIS and MISS MARY D. TAYLOR, all of Tuscaloosa Co.
      By same at residence of bride's father, MR. WILLIAM R. BEALLE of
Tuscaloosa Co. and MISS SOPHIA WHEELER of Hale Co.
      Married at residence of bride's father on 18 by REV. R. S. COX,
MR. JAMES G. BELL and MISS REBECCA A. NAUGHER.
      THOMAS J. NIX, adm'r of F. H. NIX, dec'd filed petition that
dower be allotted to MARY C. NIX, the widow.
      W. G. COCHRANE, adm'r de bonis non of WILLIAM SUGGS, deceased,
petitions to sell land. This is to notify G. A. GILIGAN and her
husband, ----GILIGAN, heir of said estate.
      PHILLIP RHODES   ) TERYLLA, a non-resident; probably resides
          versus   ) in Arkansas.
      TERYLLA RHODES   )

January 31, 1872
      ISABELLA LYNCH, administratrix of AUGUSTIN LYNCH, deceased.
Petition to sell land. This is to notify AUGUSTA J. FOWLER wife of
L. M. FOWLER and MARY W., wife of JAMES M. SMITH, non-resident heirs.

February 7, 1872
      CALVIN STACKS, adm'r of ROBERT GRAY, dec'd. Final settlement.
J. H. FREEMAN, adm'r of W. B. GRAY, dec'd.
      Died at the residence of his father near Carthage, Ala. on Jan. 22,
1872, WM. D. MILLER in his 35th year.

February 14, 1872
      Married at the residence of bride's mother by REV. JNO. T. YERBY
on morning of 6th, MR. SAMUEL W. JACK of Hale Co. to MISS ADELIA E.
MILLER of Tuscaloosa Co.

February 21, 1872
      Died in this city on 16th of pneumonia, CHARLES FOSTER WOODRUFF
aged 45.
      J. J. GLOVER, deceased. J. F. WILLIAMS, adm'r.

February 28, 1872
      Died Wed. night 21 Feb. of pneumonia, JOHN HENDRIX in his 64th
year. (see Cen 1850 p 26)
      This day was presented to Probate Court for probate by BASIL M.
THOMAS, a paper purporting to be the last will and testament of
S. A. SWOOPE, dec'd. This is to notify MARY FIELDS, wife of WILLIAM

FIELDS, who resides in the state of Missouri; GEORGE W. SWOOPE, resides
in Owensburgh, Ky; SARAH E. HENRIETTA, CHARLES, ANNIE, ESTHA, DOUGLAS and
ALVA SWOOPE, who reside in Falmouth, Ky; H. S. MASON and ANTOINETTE
PLEASANTS, who reside in Richmond, Texas; all non-residents and next
of kin of S. A. SWOOPE, deceased.

March 6, 1872
GEORGE A. SEARCY & Co.-wholesale & retail. Dealers in books etc.

March 13, 1872
Died at the residence of her husband in this county on evening of
Feb. 18, MARY JANE HOLMES, 2nd daughter of MR. and MRS. C(HAS) K.
OLIVER (see Cen 1850 p 115). She was born March 5, 1848 and married
Apr. 20, 1870 to W. T. HOLMES. Methodist since 14 years of age....
Died near North-Port, Ala. on eve. of Mar. 9, MRS. AMANDA M. POWELL,
wife of E. A. POWELL, Esq. in her 48th year.
Married at residence of bride near Wetumpka on morning of Feb. 29
by REV. D. W. GWIN, MR. J. T. HARRIS to MISS ANNIE TERRELL.
ISAAC ROBERTSON, administrator de bonis non of DAVID ROBERTSON,
deceased.

March 20, 1872
Died at the residence of his son, JAMES HUFFMAN, Jan. 29, ALEXANDER
HUFFMAN in his 70th year (see later); Deceased was a citizen of
Tuscaloosa Co. for nearly 40 years and highly respected by all who
knew him. (see Cen 1850 p 226)

March 27, 1872
Died at residence of his son, JAMES HUFFMAN, Jan. 29, ALEXANDER
HUFFMAN in his 90th (right, as was 66 in 1850) year (see above).
Deceased was a citizen of Tuscaloosa Col for nearly 40 years and was
highly respected by all who knew him.

April 3, 1872
ED. CHRISTIAN, adm'r of MARY CHRISTIAN, deceased.

April 10, 1872
Died at Finches Ferry, Greene Co. on 29 Mar., GEORGE WILLIE,
infant son of MRS. JANE MARONA aged 11 mo.
E. A. POWELL, adm'r of LINDSAY G. GRIFFIN, dec'd.
E. A. POWELL, adm'r of THOMAS L. CARSON, dec'd.
State of Ala-Walker Co. In Chancery.
WILLIAM McDONALD   )
       versus   ) DELILAH is a non-resident; she resides in
DELILAH McDONALD) Lawrence Co. Tenn.

May 8, 1872
Chancery Sale---SARAH E. SMITH)
          versus   )
        E. J. SMITH   )

May 22, 1872
Married on 14th near Carson's Landing, Miss. by REV. W. C. HEARN
of Little Rock Conference, CAPT. A. CORBIN BURTON of Ala. and MISS MARY E.
BLANCHARD of Bolivar Co. Miss.
W. B. THOMPSON, deceased. S. T. PALMER, adm'r.
A. H. HUTCHINSON, deceased. JOHN J. HARRIS, adm'r.
WILLIAM M. MARR, deceased. W. S. FOSTER, adm'r.
EDMUND PRINCE, deceased. C. M. FOSTER, adm'r.

May 29, 1872
Died in this city on 26th, EDWARD WARREN, youngest child of
MR. and MRS. B. F. LARRABEE.

June 5, 1872
Married in this city at residence of MRS. M. J. EDDINS, the
bride's mother at 11 A.M. Wed. 29th, by REV. GEO. H. HUNT of Episcopal
Church, MR. EDWARD S. HULL and MISS ELLA EDDINS...

This day was presented by Probate Court by WILLIAM SLAYTON a
paper purporting to be the will of OBADIAH SLAYTON, deceased. This is
to notify SARAH HASTY (m. 1858 COLLINS WM. HASTEY), JAMES D. SLAYTON
and MARY BLOCKER wife of W. G. BLOCKER, non-residents and next of kin.
(m. 1. 1839 GEO AGNER or EGNER Z. 1840 WM. G. BLOCKER.)

June 12, 1872
        Married on 23rd at residence of bride's father, HON. THOS. M.
GABBERT, deceased by HON. JOHN BROWN, Judge of Probate, MR. McGUIRE
SPEARS to MISS ARABELLA R. GABBERT, all of Jasper, Walker Co. Ala.

June 19, 1872
        Died in this city on Fri. 14th, ELLA LIVINGSTON, daughter of
ROBT. and FANNY HATTEN aged 1 yr. and 6 days.
        Married in West Point, Miss. on 6th by REV. MR. COOPER, MR. L. F.
BRADSHAW to MISS SALLIE M. McEACHIN, sister of our townsman,
A. B. McEACHIN, Esq.

June 26, 1872
        Died, JOSEPH SMITH, son of JAMES and SILVY SMITH; born in Fauquier
Co. Va. April 4, (1801) (yes--cen 1850 p 113 b Va). Baptised in Long
Branch Baptist Church in 1830; removed to Ala. 1832 and united with
Beulah Church by letter; was a member of Shiloh Church at death.
Married MISS MARY LEAVELL Dec. 24, 1834, by whom he had 10 children,
7 still alive... (MRS. OPHELIA PHILLIPS says MARY was sis of SARAH
LEAVELL who m. 1841 BALONS JENNINGS.)
        Died in this city on 25th, EMMET LEE, infant son of ROBERT and
FANNY HATTEN aged 1 year and 16 days.

July 17, 1872
        Married at University of Miss. on 10th by REV. MR. WADDELL,
DR. EUGENE A. SMITH and MISS JENNIE GARLAND, daughter of DR. L. C.
GARLAND (note: EUGENE A. SMITH was State Geologist of Ala.)

July 24, 1872
        Married at Providence, Grenada Co. Miss. on 5th, REV. JOHN C. FINNELL
and MISS WILLIE GRIER.

July 31, 1872
        Death of HON. B. I. HARRISON. We are pained to learn by a private
letter from his son to a citizen of this place that B. I. HARRISON
formerly of Summerfield, afterwards for 2 yrs. Principal of the
Female Academy at this place, died at his residence in Tuskaloosa on
Sun. night last... From Jacksonville Republican.

August 14, 1872
        Married at the residence of A. C. HARGROVE, Esq. in this city, on
Mon. eve. the 12th by REV. P(HILIP) A(UGUSTIN) FITTS (Enos min),
W. G. COCHRANE, Esq., County Solicitor, to MISS LILLEY TAYLOR, daughter
of JOHN TAYLOR, Esq. of Mobile. An elegant reception was given at the
residence of the bridegroom's mother, MRS. S. L. COCHRANE of New Town.

August 27, 1872
        In memoriam- MARY EMMA, infant daughter of CAPT. A. F. & S. PRINCE
of Tuscaloosa Co. who died Aug. 11, 1872.
        Died after a protracted illness at residence of his father in
Foster's Settlement, Tuscaloosa Co., W(M). RUFUS QUARLES, son of
S(AML) W. QUARLES, Esq. aged 33 yrs. 5 mo. and 24 days.

September 4, 1872
        Married Aug. 13th in Mobile by RT. REV. R. H. WILMER, DR. SID B.
SMITH of Birmingham and MISS FANNIE, daughter of DR. W. H. BEATTY of
that city.
        Death of MAJOR M. J. WILLIAMS of Selma, died suddenly near Shelby
Springs on 29th; well known over the state.

September 11, 1872
        Married on 4th by REV. E. H. KESSLER at residence of the bride's
father, MR. H. G. PARKS and MISS IDELLA HARPER, all of Tuscaloosa Co.

Died of a protracted illness at his late residence in Foster's
settlement, MR. WILKERSON V. WARD on Sat. Sept. 7 in 59th yr.
Died at his late residence in Southwestern portion of this co.
Sun. Sept. 8, ELIAS BARTON, Esq. aged about 72.
In this city on 9th, MARY EMMA, daughter of REV. and MRS. C. W. BUCK.

September 18, 1872
Married at residence of bride's father, JUDGE WM. MILLER in
Tuscaloosa on 11th by REV. DR. STILLMAN, MR. FLETCHER ROPER of Prattville,
Ala. and MISS KATE S. MILLER.
Died at Oxford, Miss. on the 8th, MISS ALICE, daughter of PROF.
and MRS. L. C. GARLAND aged about 16.
Died in this city on the 12th, MRS. MARTHA C. wife of J. A. SKELTON.
Died in Tuscaloosa on the 12th, MARY EMMA, daughter of REV. and
MRS. C. W. BUCK, aged about 5 years.
Died at his residence a few miles west of North Port on Sunday the
15th, S. F. MOSES, for many years a highly respected citizen of this
county.

September 25, 1872
Died in Birmingham on the 21st, MISS HATTIE WATKINS, formerly
of this city.
MARK TATUM, administrator of WILLIAM TATUM, deceased. Notify
JANE BROWN, JESSE TATUM, J. C. BURCHFIELD and children of WILLIAM
BURCHFIELD, deceased (names unknown) and children of MARY BURCHFIELD,
deceased (names unknown), non-resident heirs of said estate.

October 2, 1872
Married at residence of bride's father on Sept. 17, ALONZO HILL
of Ala. to SALLIE B. daughter of JUDGE WILLIAM J. ROBERTSON of
Charlottesville, Va.
Died in this city on 25th of pneumonia, MRS. JULIA A. DEARING,
relict of the late JAMES H. DEARING.

October 9, 1872
Married near Woodstock, Bibb Co. at the residence of the bride's
father on 4th inst. at 6 o'clock by JOHN GREENE, Esq. DR. J. U. RAY
to MISS LEVINIA E., daughter of JOHN RODGERS.
Death of MRS. JAMES B. HAYS (MARY JANE HEMPHILL).
Married at residence of bride's mother by REV. J. T. YERBY on
Oct. 3, MR. T. J. PERRY to MISS MARIETTA MILLER, all of Tuscaloosa Co.
Also by same at residence of MRS. HARRIET PHIFER on 8th, MR. S. W.
HINTON to MISS S. E. JAMES.
Died in this city on 10 of diphtheria, TOMMY, eldest son of MR.
and MRS. P. FERRELL aged about 6 yrs.

October 23, 1872
Died in Savannah, Ga. on Oct. 3, ROSA BELL WOODRUFF aged 15 mo.

November 13, 1872
Married at residence of bride's father, MR. R. C. McLESTER in this
city, Tuesday morning the 12th by REV. GEORGE H. HUNT, MR. EDWARD SNOW
to MISS CARRIE McLESTER.

December 4, 1872
Died, HON. NEWTON L. WHITFIELD, one of Representatives from this
county to Legislature; died of pneumonia in Montgomery at half past
2 o'clock A.M. Mon. last, 2nd inst.. Paper in mourning for him.
Mr. Editor: We have in our county a family that is worthy of
notice. That family is old MR. CHANDLER MADDOX (@ 70 in 1850 b SC)
and his wife. They are both 96 years old, about 3 weeks difference in
their ages. (Wife LUCINDA @ 66 b SC. Letter from HUBERT L. PERRY,
P.O. Box 414, Caldwell, Tex 77836 Aug. 23, 1971 - My Maddox came from
SC to Ga & then thru Ala. I have a LAWSON or LOSSON MADDOX & his bro.
CHANDLER who were both in Albert Co. Ga 1820. CHANDLER was in Girnnett
Co. Ga 1840 & Tuscaloosa Co. 1860. There was a JOHN MADDOX as well as
thus in Tuscaloosa Co. in 1840 & 1850 thus JOHN was son of LAWSON, was
in Fayette Co. Ala as was his father LAWSON MADDOX
Their oldest son is living, of about 76 years old. They have a

granddaughter living who is herself a great grandmother. Six generations of that family live in this county.

December 11, 1872
Married in North Port at residence of bride's mother on 10th, by REV. T. M. BARBOUR, DR. R. NEILSON and MISS AMY PARKER.
Married by REV. J. D. ANTHONY at the residence of MR. JONATHON SHIRLEY in Northport on Dec. 13, 1872, MR. RUFUS C. PARKER to MISS SUSAN SHIRLEY, all of Tuscaloosa County.
Married in First Baptist Church, Macon, Ga. on evening of 10th, Dec. 1872, MR. T. S. LOWRY of Marion, Ala. to MISS MARY GUILD BATTLE, daughter of DR. A. J. BATTLE, formerly of Marion.

December 27, 1872
Married at residence of bride's motheron 19th by J. W. THOMPSON, Esq., M. J. T. RYAN and MISS NELLIE P. NORWOOD, all of this county. (Letter from MRS. H. M. SMYLY, Knoxville, Texas 1961. "A great aunt of mine & a gd of DANIEL NORWOOD says that she remembers her gf had a sister by name of NELLY RYAN. Her husband's name was JEFF or JESS RYAN. She had 2 sons named JOHN RYAN, & SID RYAN.)
Died on 18th in Foster's Settlement, MRS. ELVIRA QUARLES MAHARRY, wife of JOSEPH A. MAHARRY, aged 23.
Died in Mobile at the Church Homes for Orphans on 18th, SISTER JANE WILLIAMS, a lady who was well known to citizens of Tuscaloosa for her many Christian virtues.

NORTHPORT SPECTATOR

Published by A. B. PERSINGER, Tuscaloosa Co. Ala.

November 3, 1871
In Memoriam--Death of ROBERT JEMISION, JR... As a legislator, vigilant in his duties...Lawyer.

November 16, 1871
Married in Tuskaloosa on 15th, MR. J. B. HAYS and MISS JENNIE HEMPHILL, all of that city.

November 23, 1871
State Items:
In Madison Co. Sat. THEODORE SCOTT was shot and killed accidentally by WM. T. JOHNSON, JR.

December 14, 1871
Married at residence of bride's father on Sabbath 3 P.M. Nov. 5 by REV. JOHN C. FOSTER, MR. JAMES ROBERTSON to MISS JULIA LIVERMAN, all of Tuskaloosa Co.
On 21 Nov. at house of bride's mother by same, MR. J. P. PARK and MISS JULIA A. HICKMAN, all of this county.

December 21, 1871
Married by H. K. POWELL on 19th at residence of bride's father at Kennedale, MR. MARCUS JENNINGS to MISS MARTHA CRAWFORD, all of this county.

December 28, 1871
Died in Mobile Dec. 21, HON. JOHN ANTHONY WINSTON, ex-Governor of Ala. aged about 59 yrs.

February 29, 1872
MR. JOHN MARTIN, an inhabitant of Canon Co. Tenn. is reported to be 119 years old.

March 14, 1872
Died near Northport on evening of Mar. 9, MRS. AMANDA M(ELVINA) POWELL, wife of E. A. POWELL, Esq. in her 48th yr; member of Methodist Church over 30 years. Did her duty as wife and mother.

April 13, 1872
    Died in Northport on 10th after a few days illness, JOHN D. HALEY
aged 37.

May 18, 1872
    In Chancery:
    JEREMIAH DUNKIN   )
         versus   )   MARY ELIZABETH DUNKIN, a non-resident;
    MARY ELIZABETH DUNKIN   )   believed to reside in Miss.

May 25, 1872
    Married in Carson, Bolivar Co. Miss. on 15th, A. CORBIN BURTON of
Tuscaloosa to MARY F. BLANCHARD to REV. M (W?) C. HEARN.
    MAJ. JAMES ROBINSON in open court Sat. morning announced death of
WILLIAM ASKIAN, one of eldest members of Huntsville Bar and who thru
50 years practiced and sustained unsullied reputation.
    Died in Northport May 21 of typhoid pneumonia, ARISTIDES ROYCROFT
in 21st year of his age.

June 1, 1872
    Married by REV. MR. HUNT at residence of bride's mother on 29th
EDWARD T. HULL to MISS ELLA EDDINS, all of this city.

June 7, 1872
    Death of H. G. NABORS, Esq. late of Pickens Co. which occurred
at Birmingham at residence of his brother on 28th May; was a young
lawyer of fine promise and had but recently settled in Birmingham.
Had been Clerk of Circuit Court of Pickens Co...Brave soldier in late
war...

June 29, 1872
    Died in Tuscaloosa on 23rd inst. MRS. MILLICENT E. BATTLE, wife
of ALFRED BATTLE.
    Death of HON. TURNER REAVIS which occurred at his residence in
Gainsville on 13th...was withint 5 days of 60 years of age having been
born on June 18, 1812. Spent 34 yrs. in Ala...

September 14, 1872
    Married at residence of bride's father, JUDGE WILLIAM MILLER in
Tuscaloosa on 11th inst. by REV. DR. STILLMAN, MR. FLETCHER ROPER of
Prattville and MISS KATE S. MILLER.
    Died in Tuscaloosa on 9th, MARY EMMA, daughter of REV. C. W. BUCK
aged 5.
    Died near Foster's Store in this county on 7th, W. V. WARD aged
about 60 and respected citizen of that neighborhood.
    Died near Hickman's P.O. in this county on 8th, ELIAS BARTON aged
about 75. Highly respected citizen of the county.
    Died in Tuscaloosa on 12th, MRS. MARTHA C. (@ 19 in 1850 b SC)
wife of J(AMES) A. SKELTON.

September 21, 1872
    Died in Tuscaloosa on 14th, GERTRUDE, infant daughter of MR. &
MRS. C. C. SEED.
    Died at his residence a few miles west of this place on Sunday
1th, S. E. MOSES.
    Married at Greene Springs, Male Co. on 3, MR. C. N. MERRIWETHER
and MISS KITTIE A. TUTWILER.

September 28, 1872
    Died in Tuscaloosa on 25 of pneumonia, MRS. JULIA A. DEARING,
relict of late JAMES H. DEARING, aged 73.
    Died in Birmingham on 21, MISS HATTIE WATKINS.

October 5, 1872
    Married at residence of bride's father, on 23, by J. E. SHIRLEY,
MISS MARTHA EEDS and ALFRED SLOANE.

November 2, 1872
    Died in Northport on 29th inst. MRS. LOU T. BROWN--devoted wife
and mother...

January 6, 1874

Died in this city at residence of his brother MR. GEORGE GREEN on 5th after a long and painful illness, MR. HENRY P. GREEN. Young man of great promise. Leaves widow and 2 little children. Remains will be carried to Jasper for interment.

January 14, 1874

Married at Baptist Church, Tuscaloosa on New Years Day by REV. WM. H. WILLIAMS (Presbyterian), CAPT. A. R. MEGRUE and MISS MARY A. BERRY.

January 20, 1874

DR. E. J. SMITH, a well known resident of this co. died in a fit at his residence about 7 miles from this city on night of 11th (Blade).

January 27, 1874

Married at residence of bride's father, MR. THOS. N. HYCHE by REV. D(ANIEL) S(ONLI) McDONALD (Meth), MR. JAMES H. RICH and MISS WINNIE HYCHE.

At residence of MR. W. W. PRUDE (bride's father) in this city on night of 21, HON. NEWBERN H. BROWNE and MISS M. E. PRUDE.

Died in this city on 18 at an advanced age, MRS. -----THOMAS, widow of the late JOHN THOMAS, who died here last summer. MRS. T. was a sister of the late MISS SALLY SWOOPE.

Died in this town on 25, MRS. REBECCA SMITH (58 G), relict of the late JOHN SMITH at advanced age of 86. She was a resident of this county about 55 years having settled here in 1818. Her husband was 1st Sheriff of Tuscaloosa Co. MRS. SMITH survived her husband many years and has received the devoted attention of 3 of her children whom she now leaves to mourn her loss.

February 17, 1874

Married at Methodist Church in North Port on 10 by REV. J(EREMIAH) M. BOLAND, REV. SIDNEY R. PROPST to MISS MISSOURI A. POWELL.

Married on 10 at Methodist Church in Tuscaloosa by REV. B. F. LARRABEE, MR. ETHEL PHILLIPS to MISS MARY C. BENAGH, both of Tuscaloosa.

Married at residence of PROF. W. S. WYMAN in Tuscaloosa on evening of 11, by. REV. C. A. STILLMAN, D.D. MR. GEORGE A. SEARCY to MISS ALICE DEARING, both of Tuscaloosa.

At residence of REV. P(HILIP) A(UGUSTUS) FITTS (Epis) in Birmingham by RT. REV. BISHOP WILMER, MR. B. E. GRACE, JR. to MISS ANNIE E. WALKER, daughter of C. A. WALKER of Elyton.

Died in Carthage on 7 of consumption, HENRY B. FORCE an esteemed citizen of Hale Co. Civil Engineer of N.E. & S.W. (now A.C. & C.) Railroad and during war, a member of Warrior Guards aged about 45.

Died in Tuscaloosa on Sunday morning 15th after a protracted illness, CL. MICHAEL A. KING in --year of age. Came to this co. some 15 years ago and settled in agricultural pursuits. Native of Madison Co. and commence life there as a lawyer. Several times elected to represent Madison Co. in State Legislature.

March 3, 1874

Married in North Port on 2 JAMES CAIN Esq. to MRS. POLLY COX all of this co.

Died in this co. on ---MRS. EVA BROWN, wife of REV. JOHN BROWN in 35th yr.

Died in North Port at residence of her husband, WM. THOMSON, Esq. on 24, MRS. NANCY THOMSON aged 68. Methodist.

March 10, 1874

Death of MR. PATRICK BRADY of Tuscaloosa. Shot himself on March 9. Funeral from Catholic Church.

March 24, 1874

Died in North Port on 20 at residence of P. F. M. COMERFORD, MRS. MAHALA A. ODOM aged about 57.

March 31, 1874
    Obituary:
    MRS. MAHALA ANN ODOM, relict of the late RICHARD ODOM died on 20
of yellow chills...aged 56-10-10. Baptist.

May 26, 1874
    News of death of MRS. J. F. PARKER nee JULIA HART reached Tuscaloosa
by telegraph from Milen, Gilson Co. Tenn. where deceased lived. Born
and reared in this place, only daughter of MRS. S. O. HART. She
appeared in Baptist Church as a bride July 15, 1873...
    Death of MRS. RICHARD H. CLARK nee MISS MARY BURKE formerly of
Tuscaloosa. Died at her home in Linden, Marengo Co.

June 16, 1874
    Died in North Port very suddenly MRS. E. NORIS, nee MISS CHRISTIAN.
    In Tuscaloosa on 10, LYDIA, daughter of PROF. and MRS. D. L. PECK
aged about 14 months.
    In Tuscaloosa on night of 8 of typhoid fever, MISS VIRGINIA DONOHO,
daughter of MR. and MRS. MONROE DONOHO.
    In Tuscaloosa on 4 at residence of her brother-in-law, DR. JOHN
LITTLE, SR. MISS MARY KERR aged about 74.

July 21, 1874
    Married at Catholic Church in Tuscaloosa on morning of 11 by
REV. FATHER KIRWIN, MR. CON MURPHY to MISS JENNIE RAYMOND, all of
Tuscaloosa.

August 22, 1874
    Died in Tuscaloosa on Sun 3, JOHN A. WYNN, Esq. in 79th year.
Highly esteemed and worthy citizen.

September 26, 1874
    Died suddenly in Eutaw on Mon. morning 21, A. S. NICOLSON, Esq.
Man of ability, superior attainments as a scholar, excellent lawyer,
gentleman. Remains brought to this city yesterday and interred in our
city cemetery.

October 10, 1874
    Died suddenly at residence of DR. JOHN MARRAST near Tuscaloosa on
2, MARRAST STURDIVANT aged 12 years, son of MRS. IDA STURDIVANT and a
grandson of DR. MARRAST.

October 24, 1874
    Died in this city on 18, MRS. SARAH SIMS, relict of the late
FRANK SIMS, aged 83...
    Died on 15 at her late residence 2 mi. from Tuscaloosa, MRS. E. A.
EDDINS, relict of the late CAPT. J. B. EDDINS (only confederate soldier
killed here by Yankees when a Croxton raid occurred)...Baptist.
    Died at her late residence near this city on 19, after a lingering
illness MRS. SARAH W. BAIRD (47 of Va.; wid of ALEX BAIRD) aged 71...
    In Northport on 14 of bilious fever, ROBERT ADAMS aged about 17,
son of the late REV. ROBERT ADAMS, formerly of this co.
    At his residence in this co. on 19, RUFUS H. WILLINGHAM aged 28.
Mason.
    Died in Birmingham on eve. of 16 of typhoid fever, MR. A. J. SILVEY
in 24th year.

November 16, 1874
    Died on night of 7th, MRS. SARAH RICHARDSON. Born in Ky. Dec. 1785,
consequently was nearly 89 years of age. Left 3 sons, all distinguished
scholars. A. W., W. C. and W. G. RICHARDSON. (Is this the same
SARAH RICHARDSON who belonged to Gilgal Bapt Church?)

JACKSONVILLE (ALA.) REPUBLICAN

(Calhoun County)

Copied for us by MRS. JOHN C. LESHER from papers
in State Archives at Montgomery, Ala.

June 8, 1852
WILLIAM GOGGANS, Esq. soldier of the Revolution died in Carroll Co.
Ga. 21 March 1852. Born in Richmond Co. Va. 14 Jan. 1758.

June 6, 1852
ISAAC BREWER, Revolutionary soldier 90 years old died in Talladega
25 May 1852.

August 3, 1852
Died at her residence Tuesday night last, MRS. AMY LAIRD (72 NC),
wife of WM. LAIRD (62) of Jacksonville. She was in her 76th year.

August 10, 1852
MARY WALKER (45 SC), wife of JOHN WALKER (53 SC) died 29 July 1852
in her 48th year.
MRS. SOPHIA MONTGOMERY (59 V w of JOHN P.) died 27 July 1852 in
her 64th year.

August 16, 1852
JAMES J. BUSH died 5 Aug. 1852 at Oxford.

August 31, 1852
REV. HARRIS TAYLOR (42 K) died 21 Aug. 1852 aged 46 years.

October 19, 1852
NANCY COKE, daughter of BENJ. H. and EMMA E. RICE, granddaughter
of F. FORNEY aged 9 mo.

October 20, 1852
EDMUND TOWNES son of WM. L. and SOPHIA A. TERRY died Oct. 17, 1852
in Tallade Co. aged 19 years.

October 26, 1852
Died in Oxford Oct. 9, MRS. ANN LIKENS aged 77 yrs. 11 mo. native
of Montgomery Co. Va. a member of the Presbyterian Church. MRS.
L(UCINDA) D. WILSON, a daughter. (WILSON, LUCINDA D. 30 Tenn, 5 clin &
LIKENS, SARAH R. 51)

December 14, 1852
Died at Pickensville on Nov. 19, MARY ADELLE, infant daughter of
MAJ. ALBERT P. and SARAH A. BUSH.

January 25, 1853
Died in Oxford, Ala. Jan. 5, JOHN FREDERICK, son of DR. S. C. (32
S.C.) & M(ARY) A. WILLIAMS (22 NC).

March 8, 1853
Died in Jacksonville, Mar. 17, MRS. PARTHENA ANN WHATLEY (28 SC),
daughter of the late JAMES CROOK and wife of GEORGE C. WHATLEY (29 G),
Esq. aged 31.

May 17, 1853
Died at Alexandria May 10, ELIZABETH GREEN (36 SC) aged 40, wife
of JACOB R(OSS) GREEN (40 SC), Esq.

May 24, 1853
Died near Talladega, Ala. Apr. 2, 1853, REV. T. H. P. SCALES.
He was born April 9, 1797.

November 15, 1853
Died Nov. 5, SAMTEL WARE (69 V) aged 74 years.

Died at FINNE LOCKO, Randolph Co. Ala. Oct. 22, HON. ARCHIBALD
SAWYER, aged 66 years. Born in Rowan Co. N.C. Served in War of 1812
under COL. PEARSON. Belonged to Masons.

December 13, 1853
         Died at Rocky Mount, DR. JAMES J. SKELTON (25 SC) aged 32 years.
         Died at J. C. BAIRD's, MISS CORDELIA M. MARABLE aged 20 yrs.

February 14, 1854
         Died of catalepsy Jan. 23 at Oxford, MARY J. daughter of JOHN and
MARY SPENCER.

March 31 (?), 1854 or April
         Died March 24, 1854 GEORGE SPENCER, son of the late JESSE and
ELIZABETH SPENCER aged 7 years.

August 8, 1854
         MRS. MARY SANDLIN died about August 8, 1854.
         Died at Jacksonville, Ala. Aug. 3, 1854, MR. HENRY GILDER (57 Eng)
aged 67 years. He was a teacher and a Mason.

August 22, 1854
         Died July 15 in Chocollocco Valley, MRS. SARAH STAFFORD, wife of
D. J. STAFFORD.

September 24, 1854
         REV. JOHN HOWEL (62 SC), who was born in 1789 in Lawrence Dist.
S.C. died. He was a Methodist minister.

November 7, 1854
         Died in Benton Co. Oct. 28, 1854 aged 51 years, GEORGE BROYLES
(48 T; sent to MR. WILHITE), born in Blount Co. Tenn.
         Died in Arbacoochee, Randolph Co. Oct. 26, 1854. H. M. CAGHREN
of Masonic Fraternity.
         Died in Randolph Co., WM. PINKNEY OHARROW Oct. 22 aged 24 years.

November 17, 1854
         Died Nov. 10, JOSEPH REED, son of J. B. and MARY E. FORNEY aged
11 months.

April 10, 1855
         Died in Ashville, St. Clair Co. Ala. March 22, MR. MOSES DEAN
(46 SC) aged 50 years.

June 5, 1855
         Died, MRS. PAINTER June 3, 1855.
         Died in Jacksonville, Ala. ELIZABETH ANN (21 T), wife of
MARIDETH P. HENDERSON (25 SC) and daughter of JOHN LINDSAY (V) aged 25
years.
         Died at Oxford, Ala. May 2, MISS SARAH R. LIKENS (51 T) aged 57
years.

June 12, 1855
         Died in Benton Co. May 28, 1855, MRS. MARY P. CASTLEBERRY, wife
of DANIEL CASTLEBERRY, aged 38 years.

August 15, 1855
         Died north of Jacksonville, Aug. 7, 1855, NANCY A. ROWLAND (41 SC),
born Feb. 22, 1808.

August 29, 1855
         Died in Jacksonville Aug. 19, EDIE CLARA WARE aged 1 year.
         Died in Rome (Floyd Co.), Ga. in home of her uncle, COL. SAMUEL
FARRER, ANN VIRGINIA E. LASSITER, daughter of MR. J. S. and CAROLINE
LASSITER aged 7 years.

November 13, 1855
         Died in Benton Co. Ala. Nov. 5, 1855, PRESLEY SELF aged about 100
years. (In Blount Co. Ala. 1830 Census 60-70.)

Died in Walker Co. Ga. Oct. 28, DR. SPENCER W. SKELTON (22 A),
son of A(SA) SKELTON (44 G) of this county aged 28 years.

January 22, 1856
      Died in Jacksonville Jan. 14, MRS. LUCINDA WILSON (36 SC), wife
of CRAVEN WILSON (52 SC) aged 41 years.

February 5, 1856
      Died Feb. 1, ADA JANE DAILEY, infant daughter of J. G. and
S. A. DAILEY.

February 12, 1856
      Died Jan. 22, 1856, Cherokee Co. N.C., JACOB F. ABERNATHY aged
60 years.
      Died Feb. 7, 1856 in Jacksonville, MRS. NANCY E. WHITE (60 V),
wife of SAML B. WHITE (50 SC). She was born in Lunenburgh Co. Va.
July 3, 1790.

April 22, 1856
      Died in Monroe Co. Miss. Feb. 16, 1856, MR. HIRAM TAYLOR.
      Died in Alexandria April 14, MRS. MARTHA A. HUNTER, wife of
REV. A. C. HUNTER.

August 19, 1856
      Died in Jacksonville Aug. 10, 1856, DANIEL HOKE, Sr. (76 Pa)
in his 83rd year. Born in York, Penn. in 1773, married BARBARA RAMSOUR.
      Died in Alexandria, Aug. 5, MRS. HARRIET GOODLETT (see tombstone;
47 SC; She was HARRIET HUGHES), wife of MR. ZION GOODLETT (see tombstone;
62 SC) aged 53 years.
      Died in Alexandria Aug. 7, PYRENA, daughter of MR. and MRS. DICKSON
aged 1 yr.

October 7, 1856
      Died in Benton Co. Sept. 5, JOHN BOYD (60 T) aged 67 years.
Born in Tenn. in 1789.

October 28, 1856
      Died in Benton Co. Oct. 11, MRS. MARGARTE ANN ELIZABETH THOMAS
(24 SC), wife of ATHEY THOMAS, JR. daughter of THOMPSON (63 SC) and
MAHALA HODGES (55 SC) aged 28 years.

January 27, 1857
      Died Jan. 26, 1857 JAMES BERRY (60 V) aged 69.

February 11, 1857
      Died in Jacksonville Feb. 6, 1857 MARTHA JULIET, daughter of
W(ILLIAM) C. & J(ULIET) A(DELINE) ELSTON aged 4 years.
      Died Feb. 6, 1857 MARGARET INGLEDOVE (or INGLEDORE?) daughter of
MRS. INGLEDORE aged 11 years.

February 18, 1857
      Died in Benton Co. Feb. 2, 1857 SAMUEL MORGAN (71 NJ) aged 77
years. Born in New Jersey and moved to Ga. with parents.

February 26, 1857
      Died in Fayette Co. Tex. Feb. 3, MRS. E. R. SCALES, aged 54,
widow of REV. T. H. P. SCALES.
      Died in Jacksonville Feb. 17, MRS. SARA E. McCAMPBELL (24 SC),
wife of JAMES A. McCAMPBELL (32 T) and daughter of MAJ. JOHN (49 SC)
& JULIET FINDLEY (43 SC) aged 32. Born in S.C., Chester District.

March 4, 1857
      Died in Benton Co. at residence of B. MURPHREE, Feb. 16, 1857
JOHN MADDOX (65 V) aged 72 years. Born in Culpepper Co. Va.

March 18, 1857
      Died March 13, 1857, WM. K. SINGLETON aged 13 years, son of
MRS. SARAH SINGLETON.

May 27, 1857
   Died near White Plains, Benton Co. May 16, 1857, HENRY B. MARTIN
(8 A), son of CHARLES M. (39 G) and SARAH E. S. MARTIN (31 V) aged 16
years.

July 15, 1857
   Died at residence of DR. C. C. PORTER (38 NC) of Jacksonville
May 20, 1857, JOHN H. PORTER (60 NC) of N.C. born Feb. 8, 1790.
   Died in Oxford June 29, 1857 ANDREW PICKENS son of DR. S. C. &
M. A. WILLIAMS aged 1 yr.
   Died in Catawba Co. N.C. June 30, 1857 MRS. SUE WALKER wife of
W. J. WALKER, daughter of JOHN J. SHUFORD.
   Died in Jacksonville July 6, 1857 THOS. W. infant son of THOS.
and NANCY C. RODEN.
   Died in Benton Co. July 3, 1857 JOHN HORACE, son of WILLIAM C. and
JULIET A. ELSTON aged 2 yrs.

July 29, 1857
   Died in Trenton (Gibson Co.) Tenn. on May 7, 1857 MRS. HOUSTON,
wife of MAJ. M. M. HOUSTON. (tombstones 4 mi Meth Ch.)
   Died in Benton Co. July 19, 1857 MRS. HUMPHRIES, wife of
G. W. HUMPHRIES, Esq. (ZELLA K. d. July 19, 1857 in 52 yr)
(d Apr 3, 1802; d Mar 24, 18)

August 5, 1857
   Died in Jacksonville, Ala. July 29 GEORGE WEIR (65 V) aged 74
years, one of the first comers to the county from Tenn.
   Died July 23, 1857 THOMAS B. WILLIAMS (11 A) son of J(AMES) A.
WILLIAMS (56 SC) at White Plains, Benton Co. Ala.

August 12, 1857
   Died Aug. 7, 1857 in Jacksonville, Y. C. WOODWARD (10 A, y Crutan
e) son of E. L. (43 V) & M. E. WOODWARD (35 T) age
   Died in Alexandria, Ala. July 26, 1857 NANCY CAROLINE GLADDEN,
infant dau. of JAMES A. & MARTHA GLADDEN.
   Died July 24, JAMES GLADDEN aged 4 years.

   FROM HUNTSVILLE ADVOCATE MADISON COUNTY, ALABAMA

            in Files at Library of Congress

February 4, 1825
   Died in Triana on the 24th, DOCT. JOHN A. H. HERRING in his 23rd
year.
   Died in this county on the 25th, MR. FREDERICK W. JAMES aged 52.

February 11, 1825
   Died in Coosawda, Alabama on the 21st of pulmonary complaint,
JAMES S. WALKER, Esq. brother of the late JOHN W. WALKER, Esq. of
this county.

February 18, 1825
   Married on the 9th inst. by REV. MR. THOMPSON, MR. JOHN B. ELDRIDGE
of this town to MISS ELIZABETH M. BROWNING of this county.
   Married on the 10th by REV. MR. ALLAN, WILLIAM G(REEN) HILL, Esq.
of this town to MISS MARY C(ATHARINE) HALL (see vol. 147 p 21, 22),
daughter of E(LIHU?) S. HALL, Esq. of Nashville, Tenn.

March 18, 1825
   Married lately in Mecklenburg County, Virginia, MR. STITH B.
SPRAGGINS of this county to MISS ELIZA GREEN, daughter of GRIEF GREEN,
Esq. of the former place.

March 25, 1825
   Married in Elyton (mar rec 19 Feb. 1825 (sd 20th), Alabama on the
10th by REV. THOMAS A. SMITH, the REV. MARCUS C. HENDERSON to MISS
SUSAN L. HARRISON, daughter of MR. NICHOLAS HARRISON. (MRS. ELIZ. JONES,

Aberdeen Miss May 18, 1978 "I have a client whose ancestor is MARCUS C. HENDERSON, a Meth. man--He was in 1850 census Monroe Co. (Miss) & later went to Holly Spr--His oldest dau, MAY L. was b Ala & youngest (nex 2 in Tenn) in Ky. It seems he moved around quite a bit. He wrote to Ministers Records from Lake Junaluska NC & they told him he m. in Ala in 1825 but did not give town or Co. He was b in Tenn, wife SUSAN in Va.")

April 8, 1825
        Died at his residence near Hazlegreen, MR. CHARLES CABANESS, an old and respectable citizen of this county.

April 22, 1825
        Married in this town on the 14th by REV. MR. HOLLAND, WILLIAM M'CAY, JR., Esq. to MRS. SARAH O'REILLY, both of this place.
        Died in Limestone County on the 13th, MRS. ELIZA CHAMBERS, wife of DR. HENRY CHAMBERS.

MISCELLANEOUS DEATHS FROM HUNTSVILLE (ALA.) NEWSPAPERS

        JOHN BUFORD--Killed on 5 Jan. 1867 by ANDY HANNAH.
        JOSEPH F. BAILEY died 9 Mar. 1867--old and well-known citizen.
        MRS. NANCY BYRNE died 27 May 1867 aged 100 years 5 mo. 21 days. Born Halifax Co. Va.; emigrated to this state 1837.
        MRS. ANN BROOKS died 22 June 1867 in 71st year.
        ANDREW J. BEARD died 17 July 1869 aged about 73 resides near Maysville for near 45 years.
        ELDER REUBEN W. CRUTCHER died Jan. 15, 1867--Southern Advocate.
        EVERETT COONS, son of DR. SAMUEL W. and MARTHA E. COONS died aged 21; d. May 9, 1867 in Phillips Co. Ark. (Bobbie)
        CHARLES M. CANTERBURY died Nov. 24, 1867 near Madison Station aged 62 years 6 mo. and 25 days.
        GEN. T. O. COLLINS, brother-in-law of WILLIAM McCAY died in Crockett, Tex. 5 July 1869, formerly of this county.
        MRS. REBECCA COX died near Sulphur Springs in this co. June 1880 in her 68th year. Baptist.
        ISAAC COOK died Dec. 3, 1888 aged 80; born in N.C. July 10, 1808. His father came to this county and settled a few miles below New Market when he was a little boy. Raised a large family.
        BYRD HAMLET died 8 Nov. 1867 aged about 50. Leaves many relatives.
        MOSES HILL died 5 Oct. 1867 near New Market aged about 75. Died suddenly while out hunting deer.
        MARY ELIZABETH HAMBRICK, daughter of JOSEPH HAMBRICK died 13 Sept. 1867 aged about 22.
        MISS D. C. HUNTER, youngest daughter of REV. D. K. HUNTER died 4 Sept. 1867 aged 25.
        ROBERT H. HUGHS died at Burleson, Ala. 12 Mar. 1867 aged 56, formerly of Madison Co.
        MRS. ELIZABETH JACKSON, formerly of this co. died 14 Sept. 1867 in Desoto Co. Miss. aged 49.
        DR. J. M. LEWIS died 23 Apr. 1867 in 38th year at home of brother, GEO. W. LEWIS, of consumption.
        S. E. MORROW of Whitesburg died 11 Aug. 1867
        JOHN A. R. MOSELEY, formerly of this county died 11 Sept. 1867 in Franklin Co. Tenn. aged about 48.
        MRS. ROXANA WILLIAMS, wife of R. J. WILLIAMS and daughter of REV. DANIEL WADLEY died 18 June 1867 aged 23 yrs. 4 mo.; and infant daughter, REBECCA SUSAN WILLIAMS died 19 Apr. 1867 aged 14 days.

HUNTSVILLE ADVOCATE

Published each Friday

June 16, 1866
        Died in Lincoln County, Tennessee on the 7th instant, MR. CHARLES BRIGHT aged about 75; also on the 9th, JOHN H. STEELMAN, Esq. aged about 48.

June 27, 1866
    Died near Helena (Phillips Co.), Arkansas on March 1st 1866,
CALEDONIA E. wife of DR. B(RIGHT) NUNNALLY, formerly of this county
aged about 37, and on the 26th of May, WILLIAM B. son of DR. B. B.
NUNNALLY aged 17 years 11 months and 14 days.

July 7, 1866
    Died in Memphis on the 7th, MR. T. FULLER MARTIN, formerly of this
city. (son of THOMAS & SARAH (IRBY) MARTIN gs of WM. W. IRBY)
    Died at the residence of her father near Mooresville (Limestone Co.)
on the 26th, MISS LAVENIA V. TUCKER aged 26 years 9 months and 17 days.

July 21, 1866
    Died on the 3rd instant, JEREMIAH BROWN (51 NC; Owens says b. 1800
d 1868), prominent citizen of Jackson (to Christian) County.
    Died, MR. JAMES A. YOWELL; MISS CYNTHIA E. BRIGHT; MRS. WILSON
GROCE, all of Lincoln Co. Tenn.

July 25, 1866
    Died in Mooresville (Limestone Co.) on the 16th, ANNA, daughter
of Greenville and JANE FOGG aged 16.

August 8, 1866
    Died on the 1st, MRS. MARGARET ELLIS, wife of MR. ----- ELLIS of
this county.
    Died at his residence in Tuscumbia on the 29th of inflammation of
the brain, MR. JOHN C. McMAHEN, formerly of Lauderdale Co.

August 15, 1866
    Died on the 11th of congestive chill, MR. CHARLES A. BAKER of this
city.
    Died on the 13th at the residence of MR. GEORGE A. McBRIDE, MISS
UNITY DANDRIDGE LEWIS of this county.

August 18, 1866
    Died in this city on the 15th, CHARLES BURRITT, son of JOHN P. and
NANCY G. BRANHAM.
    Died in Florence (Lauderdale Co.) on the 9th instant, WALTER GLENN,
SR. The deceased was born in County Donegal, Ireland December 14, 1780
and was in his 86th year.

August 29, 1866
    Died at Mobile on the 21st, MRS. SUE HOPKINS, wife of CHARLES
HOPKINS, Esq. and daughter of the late WILLIAM McDOWELL of this city.

September 1, 1866
    Died in Marshall County on 1st of June of consumption, MISS MARY
ANN COLLIER aged 19 years and 6 months.
    Died near Moulton, Ala. (Lawrence Co.) on the 9th ult. MR. R. M.
WHITE aged 71 years 3 months and 6 days.
    Died near Florence on the 22nd, MR. JAMES S. BODDIE aged 37.
    Died in Franklin County, Alabama on the 21, R. J. MOODY aged 28.

September 5, 1866
    Died--MRS. SALLIE HILLIARD and MISS ANNA DAVIDSON, both of Lincoln
Co. Tenn.

September 8, 1866
    Died in this city on the 7th at the residence of MRS. M. A. CAROTHERS,
JOHN McFERRAN aged 17 months, infant son of MR. E. R. GLASCOCK of
Nashville, Tenn.
    Died--MR. BENJAMIN FOX; MR. THOMAS ALBERT McKINNEY, both of
Lincoln County, Tenn.
    Married on the 4th instant by REV. W. BURR, MR. FLEMING J. RIGNEY
to MISS LAURA E., daughter of DR. ISAAC SULLIVAN, all of this county.

September 19, 1866
     Died in Lincoln Co. Tennessee on the 10th of congestion,
MR. HENRY KELSO aged about 50.

September 22, 1866
     Died on the 21st, WILLIAM ANDERSON, son of MR. and MRS. D. A.
RAMSEY of this place.

September 26, 1866
     Died on the 23rd, MISS SALLIE DONOHUE, an aged lady of this place,
old and feeble... (SARAH DONAHO @ 50 in 1850 b Tenn)

October 20, 1866
     Died on the 11th near Florence (Lauderdale Co.) COL. G. G. ARMISTEAD
aged 56.
     Died in Florence (Lauderdale Co.) on the 17th, MARGARET SHELTON,
daughter of STRINGER and MARY WHITE aged 38 years.

November 10, 1866
     Died in Lincoln County, Tennessee on the 27th, MRS. ELIZA, wife
of MR. JAMES WILSON aged about 60.

November 25 number missing

December 1, 1866
     Died in Florence (Lauderdale County) on the 25th, MRS. ANN CAMPBELL
aged 57.
     Died in Tuscumbia on the 9th, MRS. G. W. GILLESPIE and on the 11th,
MISS MARTHA F. DICKEY.

December 11, 1866
     Died on the 20th, GREEN F. BRAZELTON, son of JASON M. BRAZELTON
in his 24th year.
     Died on the 30th in Shelbyville (Bedford Co. Tenn.) of cholera,
MR. JAMES H. CASTLEMAN, formerly of Fayetteville (Lincoln Co. Tenn.)
aged about 42.
     Died on the 30th in Petersburg, Tenn. DR. H. H. REEVES aged about
45.
     Died on the 2nd near Florence, MR. JAMES A. TURNER aged 63 years.

January 4, 1867
     Married on the 2nd instant by REV. M. E. JOHNSON, MR. DAVID H.
FRIEND to MISS ELVIRA G(OLD) ROPER, all of this county.

January 11, 1867
     JOHN B. FITZ (ancestor of MISS MABEL YOUREE GUZZARD, Waxahachie,
Tex 1953) died at his home at Madison Station in this county on the
5th quite suddenly. Was Postmaster and merchant of that village. Had
been a citizen of this county for 54 years. Member of Baptist Church
for 20 years. Was one of the best men that ever lived...

January 15, 1867
     Died on the 27th at the residence of his father, J(OHN) C(ALVIN)
GOODLOE (32 NC), Esq. (Franklin Co.), DAVID S(HORT) GOODLOE, JR. in
his 19th year. (see tombstone in vol. 56 p. 27)
     Died on the 18th, MR. ROBERT ROGERS, an old and respected citizen
of this county.
     Died in Fayetteville, Tennessee (Lincoln Co.) on the 7th, MR. JOHN M.
PERRYMAN aged 30.

January 18, 1867
     Died in Florence (Lauderdale Co.) on the 14th inst., MRS. ROSANNA
MUNN aged about 70.
     Died in New Orleans on the 1st, MR. JAMES J. HANNA aged 66.

January 22, 1867
     Died in Lincoln County, Tennessee on the 8th, MR. JOSEPH G. WEST
aged about 40.

Died in Huntsville of consumption on the morning of the 19th, DeFOREST B. TOMLINSON, eldest son of MAJ. D. C. TOMLINSON in his 23rd year. He left his home in Watertown, New York a few weeks ago for the purpose of spending the winter with his father in northern Alabama....

January 29, 1867
CAPT. DUDLEY SALE was born in Amherst County, Virginia October 25, 1781 and moved to Georgia with his parents when quite young. Emigrated to Madison Co. Ala. in 1814 when it was but newly settled. First settler on Beaver Dam Creek near Meridianville. Soon afterwards, he purchased his present place. Here he raised a family of 12 children... Member of Methodist Episcopal Church South for more than 40 years. Died January 16 leaving his wife, 3 children, 13 grandchildren and many great grandchildren....
Died at Florence (Lauderdale County) on the 23rd, DUNCAN R. FOSTER, son of JUDGE B. F. FOSTER in his 15th year.

February 1, 1867
Died on the 30th near Madison Station, FANNY, daughter of MRS. ELIZA HOPKINS.

February 5, 1867
Died in Lincoln County, Tennessee on the 25th, MR. WILLIAM G. MOORE aged 56.
Died on the 20th in Marshall County, Miss., MR. RICHARD H. McCRAVEY (McCRARY--@ 42 T), formerly of Jackson Co. (to Christian) (Ala.)
Died in this city on the 3rd of dropsy, MR. MIKE SULLIVAN.

February 12, 1867
Died on the 11th, MR. LEWIS M. KENNARD (38 T), an old and well known citizen.

February 15, 1867
Died on the 10th at his father's residence 7 miles northwest of Huntsville, MURRAY ROBERTSON KING in his 24th year.

February 26, 1867
Died in Lawrence County on the 2nd, MRS. MARY R. EGGLESTON aged 50.

March 8, 1867
Died on the 2nd of consumption, WILLIAM B. JOHNSON of this city.
Died on the 5th in Florence (Lauderdale Co.), PROF. A. E. TETLOW.
Died on the 4th of consumption, MR. CRAWFORD M. HUMPHREY.
Died near Tuscumbia on the 24th, MR. JOSIAH RICHARDSON aged 38.
Died on the 19th, MR. L. P. GUY, an old citizen of that vicinity.

March 12, 1867
Died near this place on the 9th, MR. JOSEPH F. BAILEY, an old and well known citizen of this vicinity.

March 14, 1867
Died on the 6th instant at his residence near Bell Factory of erysipelas, MR. MORRIS MOORE aged 66. He was a native of North Carolina and came to Madison County, Alabama some 50 years ago and has resided here ever since. Member of the Cumberland Presbyterian Church. Wife and many children and grandchildren survive.
Died in this county on the 11th of consumption, MR. DICKSON GRAHAM aged 30.

April 2, 1867
Died on the 12th at Burleson, Alabama, MR. ROBERT H. HUGHS aged 56, formerly of this county.

April 5, 1867
Died on the 2nd instant of consumption, MR. RICHARD L. ELLIOTT aged 44 years, 4 months and 5 days. For a long time, he was a citizen of this place. He leaves an interesting family.

April 30, 1867
    Married in Slema, on 23rd by RT. REV. R. H. WILMER, COL. HILLARY A.
HERBERT of Greenville to ELLA W. daughter of HON. W. M. SMITH.

May 7, 1867
    DR. ISAIAC MORGAN of Selma died on the 29th.

August 2, 1867
    JAS. R. FAIRBANKS of Selma died on the 26th. He was U.S. Commis-
sioner.

May 17, 1867
    State Items:
    GEORGE L. MASON, editor of Wetumpka Standard died on the 2nd.

August 20, 1867
    REV. C. C. CALLAWAY of Methodist Episcopal Church died on 11th in
Greensboro, Ala.

October 11, 1867
    Married on 8th in Wetumpka by REV. C. D. OLIVER, MR. B. H. SCREWS
of Montgomery to MISS EMMA, daughter of MRS. E. McNEIL of Wetumpka.

October 15, 1867
    DR. P(LEASANT) W. KITTRELL, formerly of Greene Co. Ala. died in
Texas a short while ago of yellow fever.

November 8, 1867
    The venerable REV. DR. P. J. SPARROW of the Presbyterian Church
died in Dallas Co. on the 30th.

November 19, 1867
    Married in N.Y. City on the 25th, MR. JAMES L. BLISS, formerly
of the firm of FRY, BLISS & Co. of Mobile, to MRS. P. W. CABELL, widow
of the late DR. CABELL of Selma, Alabama.

December 6, 1867
    Died on 22 near Greensboro, Ala. of pneumonia, MRS. MARIA MENEEOS
(nee WITHERS) wife of REV. MANEEOS in her 49th year. Note: m. in Madison
Co. Ala. ANASTASIUS MANAEOS to MARIA WITHERS 2 Feb. 1860 (see our
Vol. 185 p. 99- a Greek)

December 2, 1867
    On 12 near Frankfort, Ala. by HON. S. S. ANDERSON, SIDNEY R. KING
of Green Co. to MISS NANCY L. HESTER, daughter of ROLAND HESTER, Esq.

January 3, 1868
    Died on the 31st ult. at the residence of COL. ED. TONEY in this
place, MRS. ADELAIDE ROGERS. Woman of fine attainments....

January 10, 1868
    Died on the 5th instant, WILLIAM HODGES of this county.
    Died on the 5th instant, W. J. BYRNE of Brownsboro in this county.
    Died on the 6th instant of congestion of the brain, MR. WILLIAM H.
BRIDGES, a worthy and respected citizen.
    Married at the Church of Nativity in this city, January 8, 1868
by REV. J. M. BANISTER, MR. CHARLES ROBINSON of Jackson, Mississippi
to MISS VIRGINIA P. daughter of COL. JAMES L. WATKINS of this city.
    Married on December 23, 1867, MR. H. F. CRAWFORD to MISS IDA
PATTERSON, both of Tuscumbia, Ala.
    Married on 31st inst. by REV. W. N. MOORE, MR. W. P. JENKINS to
MISS MATTIE R. BENNETT, all of this county.

January 14, 1868
    Married on the 22nd of December by A. G. WESTMORELAND, Esq.,
MR. LEVI H. HENDERSON to MRS. LOUISA C. MILLER, all of Limestone Co.
    On the 24th of December by same, MR. JOSEPH CROUCH to MISS MARTHA
BROOKS, all of Limestone Co.

On the 3rd instant by REV. JOHN TURRENTINE, MR. J. C. CLARK to
MISS SARAH A. BLACKSHEAR, all of Limestone Co.

January 17, 1868
    Married on the 13th instant, by ROBERT W. FIGG, Esq. at his office,
GEORGE HUBERT of the U.S.A. to MISS SARAH WELCH of this city.
    Married on the 2nd instant by REV. H. P. TURNER, MR. JOHN E.
WINSETT to MISS MARY L. RUSSELL of this county.

January 21, 1868
    Married on the 15th instant at the residence of the bride's mother
in Montgomery by REV. DR. PETRIE of the Presbyterian Church, COL.
CHARLES POLLARD BALL to MISS ANNA MARY, daughter of the late COL. J. J.
SEIBELS, all of that city.

January 24, 1868
    Died on the 14th instant, HETTIE ANN, daughter of WILLIAM H. and
MARY E. WEBSTER aged 16 months and 3 days.
    Died on the 6th inst. of congestion of the brain, WILLIAM T. HODGES,
an acceptable member of the Madison Station Lodge no 329 of Free and
Accepted Masons.
    Married on the 16th inst. by REV. M. B. DeWITT, MR. BENJ. LEE
COYLE to MISS SOPHIA C. NASH, all of this county.
    On the 22nd inst. in Cumberland Presbyterian Church at Meridianville
by REV. M. B. DeWITT, MR. ALEX. G. NOWLIN to MISS SOPHIA T. OTEY.

January 31, 1868
    Died in Limestone County on the 11th inst. MR. WATSON DAVID in
his 72nd year. Was one of the first settlers of the county and leaves
a large circle of friends to mourn his loss.

February 4, 1868
    Died on the 2nd instant, BELLE, infant daughter of MR. and MRS. JOS.
C. BRADLEY of this place.
    Married on Thursday evening the 30th instant, by REV. JOHN M.
BANNISTER, MR. JACOB W. BATTLE to MISS KATE ROBINSON, daughter of
MAJ. JAS. ROBINSON of this place.
    Resolutions of respect on the death of JAMES P. CALLAGHAN by the
Printers of Huntsville.

February 7, 1868---missing

February 11, 1868
    Married in Montgomery by REV. J. M. MITCHELL, MAJ. EMMET SEIBELS
to MISS ANNIE GOLDTHWAITE, daughter of HON. GEORGE GOLDTHWAITE of that
city.
    Married on the 4th instant in Columbia, Tennessee by REV. J. M.
GALLAWAY, MR. THOMAS PRIDE of Decatur, Ala. (Morgan Co.) to MISS JENNIE
NEILY of Columbia, Tenn.

February 18, 1868
    Died at Madison Station in this county on the 13th, MR. WILLIAM P.
VAUGHAN aged 57.
    Died on the 14th inst. at Madison Station in this county, MRS.
SARAH LIPSCOMB aged 68 (wid of RICHARD dau of ALLEN McCARGO)
    Married--MR. DAVID F. GRABB to MISS RUTH STEPHENS; MR. ROBERT
JOHNSTON to MISS LUCY T. INMAN; MR. JAMES A. McKINNEY to MISS MARTHA J.
WICKS; MR. JAMES P. HAMILTON to MISS MARTHA J. CARTER; MR. JOHN HELMS
to MISS JANE BLAIR, all of Lincoln County, Tenn.

February 21, 1868
    Died in Coffeeville, Clarke County, Alabama on the 14th instant,
after a short illness, JOHN W. FIGURES, brother of the Editor of the
Advocate. He was born September 23, 1810... He lived and died where
he was born and raised... Leaves wife and child.
    Died on the 28th instant at the residence of his mother near
New Market, Alabama, GEORGE T. JONES aged 21 years, 8 months and 22 days.
    Died on the 5th instant in Limestone County, MR. THOMAS NESBIT,
an old and highly esteemed citizen.

February 25, 1868
        Died on the 24th inst. MRS. L. ELIZABETH EDWARDS, wife of
MR. W. W. EDWARDS of this place.
        Married--MR. ISAAC B. MOORE to MRS. L. C. C. PARKINSON;
MR. W. A. BARNES to MISS R. A. GEORGE; MR. C. D. HAWKINS to MISS S. S.
BIRDSONG; MR. A. L. CORPIER to MRS. S. M. FINNEY; MR. JOHN C. SMITH to
MRS. L. McLAUGHLIN; MR. J. L. HARRIS to MISS E. R. STANLEY; MR. SEABORN
STILES to MISS M. A. FRANKLIN; MR. WALTER HOLT to MISS SUE V. MOTLAW;
MR. E. P. BOBO to MISS BETTIE BROADWAY; MR. J. T. WEAVER to MISS NANCY A.
BUCHANAN; MR. HENRY WILSON to MISS AGNES BLACK; MR. W. K. BOYD to
MISS MARY J. ALLEN, all of Lincoln Co. Tenn.

February 28, 1868
        Died on the 17th instant in this county, MISS EMILY McCALLUM in
her 70th year.
        Died on the 23rd instant, MR. BENJAMIN OSBORNE, an old and respected
and well known citizen of this county.
        Married on the 19th ult. in Colbert County by REV. W. H. MITCHELL,
CAPT. ROBERT McFARLAND of Florence (Lauderdale Co.) to MISS KATE
ARMISTEAD.
        Married on the 19th instant by same, CAPT. Z. N. ESTES of Memphis
(Tenn.) to MISS NETTIE COLLIER of Florence (Lauderdale Co. Ala.)
        Married on the 27th instant by REV. M. B. DeWITT, MR. THOMAS B.
DUNCAN of Corinth, Miss. to MISS JULIETTE E. ELGIN, daughter of MR.
FRED ELGIN of this place.

March 10, 1868
        Married the 27th ult. in Calhoun County by REV. GORDON MINATT,
MR. JOHN M. CRITCHER (CRUTCHER?) of Guntersville (Marshall Co.) to
MISS CARRIE MINATT.

March 27, 1868
        Married on the 10th instant by REV. JOEL WHITTEN, MR. BENJAMIN E.
HOWELL to MISS SALLIE WITHERSPOON, all of Lauderdale.
        Married on the 13th instant by REV. THOMAS DUNNAVENT, MR. SIDNEY
GIBSON of Courtland (Lawrence Co.) to MISS LIZZIE S. ANDERSON of
Blount Co. Ala.

April 3, 1868
        Married on the 24th instant by REV. JAMES WALSTON, MR. MICHAEL
MALONE to MISS E. J. WALSTON, daughter of JUDGE JOHN WALSTON, all of
Lauderdale.
        Married in Courtland (Lawrence Co.) on the 26th instant by
REV. B. W. SAWTELLE, COL. THOS. E. CANNON of Columbus, Miss. to
MISS MAGGIE E. JONES of Courtland.

April 7, 1868
        Married on the 5th instant at Madison Station by REV. W. T. ANDREWS,
MR. JAMES DILLARD of Triana to MISS SALLIE HALSEY, daughter of MR. W. J.
HALSEY of this place.

April 10, 1868
        Died on the 7th instant, PHILIP CALLAGHAN, son of M. CALLAGHAN,
Esq. of this city.
        Died on the 8th instant, ALICE NORVELL, infant daughter of
THOMAS and M. E. JOHNSON.
        Married in Memphis (Tenn.) on the 2nd ult. by REV. B. N. SAWTELLE,
MR. CHAS. B. CREAMER of Tuscumbia to MISS ANNIE L. MARGERUM of Memphis.
        Married in Colbert County on the 2nd instant by REV. JOHN S. DAVIS,
DR. W. AMES of Starkville, Miss. to MISS LUCY O. RAND of Colbert Co.

April 14, 1868
        Died on the 14th instant, MRS. JULIA A. CLARK, wife of MR. S. S.
CLARK of this place.
        Died on the 8th instant, MRS. ELIZABETH B. COOPER, wife of
WM. COOPER, Esq. of Tuscumbia.
        Died on the 23rd instant, SAM'L B. HARRIS of Colbert Co. aged 22.
        Died in Jackson (to Christian) County on the 17th, MR. JOHN B.
GURLEY, an old and respectable citizen.

Married on the 14th instant in Decatur (Morgan Co.) by REV. A. S.
LAKIN, CAPT. C. R. BROWS to MISS CARRIE LEMON, all of that place,
formerly of Ohio.
Married on the 15th instant at the residence of the bride's father
by FATHER P. McMAHON, MR. JOSEPH H. CONNER to MISS SUSAN ELLEN GREEN,
daughter of THOS. U. GREEN.

April 21, 1868
Died in Tuscaloosa on the 16th instant, COL. JOHN G. COLTART of
this place aged 42 years.
Died on the 29th inst. HOLLIE CRUTE aged 3 years, 4 months and
11 days.
Died on the 2nd inst. MRS. MARY M. KENNEDY, an aged and highly
esteemed lady of this city.
Married at the residence of MRS. E. E. HOLT on the 29th inst. by
REV. DR. PETRIE, MR. WM. BERNEY to MISS LIZZY J. TAYLOR, daughter of
DR. W. P. TAYLOR, all of Montgomery.

May 8, 1868
Died on the 6th instant in Lauderdale County, MR. JAMES ROBERTS
aged 45.

May 12, 1868
Died in Jefferson County on the 4th, MR. G(EORGE) J. ROEBUCK aged
50.
Died in this vicinity on the 9th, ROBERT, infant son of COL. ROBERT
and ELIZA FEARN.
Died on the 28th of Jan. 1868 in his 74th year, JOSEPH PICKENS,
Esq. Born in N.C. on 31 Aug. 1794 and had been a citizen of Madison
Co. over 50 years. Quiet, useful, good citizen, beloved by all who
knew him and an earnest, faithful Christian. (son of ANDREW & MARGARET
(DONDLE) PICKENS--anccotoro of MRS. HARRY C. WHITE, Homewood, Ala. 1952--
He m. 1818 SELINA BROWN BRAZELTON, d of HENRY, LYDIA (LEDBETTER)
BRAZELTON; gd of JACOB & HANNAH BRAZELTON & of JOEL LEDBETTER)
Married on Tuesday the 5th instant by REV. MR. T. TANNEN, MR. JOHN W.
DOUGLASS of Jackson (to Christian) County to MISS MARY F. R. HILL,
daughter of MR. JOHN HILL of Rutherford Co. Tenn.

May 15, 1868
Married on the 14th at the residence of COL. S. W. HARRIS by
REV. DR. F. A. ROSS, MR. YANCEY P. NEWMAN (Fin Cen 6 A FARANCIS II.) to
MISS MARY WATKINS, daughter of the late ROBERT H. WATKINS, all of
Huntsville.
Died on the 14th at his residence in this city, DR. TOLBERT,
formerly of Louisville, Ky.

May 26, 1868
OSMOND T. JONES of Perry Co. Ala. was killed last week by a kick
from a mule.

May 29, 1868
Married in this city on 27th by REV. F. P. SCRUGGS, MR. J. OTEY
ROBINSON to MISS IRENE SCRUGGS, both of this city.
On 25th by REV. W. BURR, DR. A. G. ISAACS of Texas to MISS ALICE
O'NEAL of this county.
On 27th at bride's residence by REV. FATHER TRECY, MR. JAMES CONWAY
to MRS. ANNIE E. DAVIS, both of this city.
On 26th by REV. FATHER TRECY at his residence, JOHN BYRON, 15th
Regiment, U.S.I. to NANCY EVERELL of Nashville and JOHN ADAMS of the
same regiment to AMANDA VICK.
Died in this city on 24th, MRS. CATHARINE CHEWNING (52 V--in 1818
THADEUS CHEWNING)
On 28th, MR. JOHN A(?) MURRELL (43 V), an old and well-known
citizen of this place aged about 67.

June 2, 1868
MASTER JAMES BIBB of this place was killed near Corinth (Alcorn Co.)
Miss. last week as is supposed by a man named STEWART and then robbed.

June 9, 1868
CHARLES A. FULLER, grand secretary of Masonic orders in Tennessee died last week.

June 12, 1868
Married on the 4th by REV. DAVID JACKE, MR. EDWARD M. RICE to MISS FRANCES M. RODGERS, both of this county.
On the 4th at Broyles Church by REV. J. J. BURDINE, MR. JAMES FANNING aged 82 yrs to MISS BRAGG aged 50, both of this county.
Died on the 9th in Big Cove, MRS. PEGGY MULLEN aged 84.
On the 14th, MRS. SARAH MATTHEWS, wife of SAMUEL MATTHEWS, Esq. of this city.

June 16, 1868
Advertisement of WILLIAM FRYE, portrait painter

June 19, 1868
Died on the 14th, HATTIE ANN COLLIER, daughter of MARY S. and JO. C. COLLIER aged 2 years 3 months and 15 days.

June 23, 1868
Died on the 20th after a short illness, MRS. MARY H. ALLISON, wife of ALEX. ALLISON, Esq. of this place. Her remains were taken to Knoxville for interment.
On the 14th, JULIA HENTZ MILLER, infant daughter of BURGESS M. and ELIZABETH M. MILLER of this county.
On the 15th, GEORGE WILLIAM SMITH, son of JOSHUA and CAROLINE SMITH died aged 2 years and 6 months, living in Big Cove.
Died on the 18th, MELTON BYRD, infant son of REV. J. H. and MARY DRAKE of this county.

June 26, 1868
Married Tuesday evening by REV. DR. F. A. ROSS, CAPT. JAS. O. STANAGE of the firm of STANAGE, SAUNDERS & Co. of Cincinnati to MISS MARY M. BRADLEY (4A), daughter of COL. JOSEPH C(OLVILLE) BRADLEY (40 V) of Huntsville, Ala.
Died on the 23rd, COL. E. C. PYNCHON aged 64. Native of Mass. and moved to Georgia when 21, where he resided until 1838, when he removed to Huntsville. Man of strong sense, much information and of strict integrity.

June 30, 1868
MICHAEL RINEHARDT of Shelby County, Alabama was killed last week while threshing wheat.
SEABORN JONES was killed at Notasulga (Macon Co.), Ala. on 25th by NICK FERRELL. JONES was a railroad engineer.

July 3, 1868
Died on the 30th, KATE, infant daughter of C. C. and MARY J. DART aged 5 mo. and 8 days.
Died on the 2nd, HARRIET McCALLEY, wife of REV. JEFFERSON McCALLEY of this place aged 35.
MAJ. S. B. MARKS, a prominent citizen of Montgomery died last week.

July 10, 1868
Died on the 6th, MRS. GEORGIANN NORVELL (31 A; nee BEALE m 1842), wife of MR. R(EUBEN) B. NORVELL (41 V) of this place. MRS. N. was a true woman in every sense of the word educated, accomplished, refined. A firm friend, a devoted wife, a fond and faithful mother, an humble Christian; and there was a daily beauty in her walk and conversation such as is rarely seen but always appreciated by the discerning. Her sad death is a grievous loss to her family and a large circle of friends and acquaintances.

July 14, 1868
Died, JOHN OWEN SCHRIMSHER (4 A), son of ALFRED SCHRIMSHER (39 T) on the 9th aged about 25.
COL. ROBERT MITCHELL of Macon Co. Ala. died a few days ago.

July 17, 1868
   Married on the 5th by ELDER J. A. MILHOUS, ELDRIDGE R. HAWKINS to
MISS MILLY F. McCALEB, both of this county.
   Married on the 15th in Edgefield, Tenn. at the residence of
GEN. WM. B. BATE by REV. DR. HANNER, MR. C. DuPRE of Nashville to
MISS MARY IRBY PEETE (12 A) of Huntsville.
   Died on 16th, MOLLIE, infant daughter of MR. T. J. CHILDRESS of
this city.

July 21, 1868
   JOHN YORK, an old citizen of Nashville died on the 18th.

July 31, 1868
   Married on the 30th at the Methodist Church by REV. R. K. BROWN,
HON. JAMES H. SCRUGGS (30 A, m. before) to MRS. REBECCA ROBINSON,
all of this city.

August 4, 1868
   REV. H. C. FURGURSON, an old citizen of Bedford Co. Tenn. died
last week.
   MRS. JAS. WEBB of Cherokee Co. Ala. died last week of sunstroke.

August 7, 1868
   Died on the 25th at the residence of LEVI HINDS, Esq. MRS.
HULDAH HINDS aged 96 years 7 months and 17 days. Baptist for 54 years
and had resided in Madison Co. 60 years...
   Died near Maysville on 18 Apr. in 23rd yr. MISS MARY PARKER,
daughter of W. & E. PARKER, deceased.
   Tribute of respect to memory of DR. HENRY M. ROBERTSON (44 Md),
deceased by Doctors of Huntsville.
   DR. HENRY M. ROBERTSON, an old physician and citizen of this place
was found dead in his office having died during the night....

August 11, 1868
   Died near Cluttsville on 2nd, MR. JOHN SMITH aged about 40.
   Also on the Sat. preceding, MRS. SMITH, wife of the above.
   JACKSON MULLANY was accidentally killed in Fayetteville, Tenn.
last week.

August 25, 1868
   Married on the 20th by REV. R. K. BROWN, ROBERT H. WILSON, Esq.
to MISS SUE P. daughter of DR. G. R. WHARTON, both of this county.
   Married on the 6th by REV MR. INGLE in Frederick City, Md.,
ELMORE J. FITZPATRICK, Esq. to MISS ELIZABETH THORNTON, daughter of
MR. WILLIAM M. MARKS of Montgomery City.
   COL. L. P. SAXON (47 SC), late State Treasurer died in Wetumpka on
19th,

September 1, 1868
   MR. JOHN L. McINTOSH (16 T; Wm N.) of Triana died Friday last.
   MR. W. H. TANCRE died near this place yesterday. From Wisconsin.

September 4, 1868
   Died on 24th in this county of congestion of brain, MARY EMELINE,
daughter of ZACHARIAH BAILEY aged 10 years.
   Also on same day of same disease, ELLA, daughter of JOSEPH CHORMLEY
aged 7 years.
   MR. PAT BOONE (is this Albert P?) (30 T), a well known and good
citizen of this county died on the 2nd near Triana.

September 8, 1868
   Died September 6 in Triana, IRENA SAMPSON (45 NC, w of Chas, nee
Smith in 1822) aged 63.

September 11, 1868
   Married on Aug. 23 by REV. JAMES A. ORMAN, MR. JOSEPH ERWIN of
this city to MISS FANNIE C. SMITH of Marshall Co. Tenn.

September 18, 1868
 Died on the 9th at the residence of her mother, MRS. BETTY MILLS,
consort of PRESTON MILLS and daughter of JOSEPH and SELINA PRESTON in
her 40th year. Leaves two orphan boys.
 Died on the 17th of congestive chill, JAMES BROWN aged about 15
of this city.

September 22, 1868
 COL. F. M. WINDES of this state died in Lynchburg (Campbell Co.),
Va. on the 16th. He commanded a regiment of cavalry under GEN. RODDY
and was a gallant officer.
 JACOB D. SCHRIMSHER (9 A) of this county was drowned in Duck River
below Columbia, Tenn. on the 15th aged 26, son of A(NDREW) J. SCHRIMSHER
(35 NC). Methodist. Leaves wife and one child.
 WEBSTER GILBERT, one of the early settlers and Indian fighters in
this state died last week in Butler Co. aged 85.

September 25, 1868
 Married on 23 at residence of the bride's father by REV. M. B.
DeWITT, MR. JAS. E. CAIN to MISS ANNA GILL.
 Married on 23 at residence of MRS. SCHLACK by REV. M. B. DeWITT,
MR. GEORGE W. BERRY to MISS MATTIE W. SCOTT.
 On 17, by REV. E. R. BERRY, MR. THOMAS M. J. AUSTIN to MISS MILDRED
P. MITCHELL, all of this county.
 On 17 by REV. E. R. BERRY, MR. LeROY P. CAMPBELL to MISS ELIZA E.
DUNCAN, all of this county.
 Died in Maysville on 13, J. WILLIE DERRICK, eldest son of
WILLIAM M. and JANE DERRICK aged 19 years 4 months and 3 days.
 At residence of H. H. HADEN, Aug. 28, LULA, daughter of
WILLIAM P. and SARAH J. SMITH and granddaughter of H(ORATIO) H. HADEN,
Esq. aged 8 months.
 On 16, H. H. KIRKLAND aged 31 years and 8 days; of 4th Ala. Reg.
 In Maysville on 15th, JOHN M. eldest child of W. C. HALL aged 11.
 SMITH ADAMS (54 Pa), Esq., for many years a magistrate of this
place and an old citizen died on 23 after a short illness.
 DERUSHA DAFFIN, Esq. for 18 years, Clerk of Circuit Court of
Clarke Co. Ala. died on 27th.

September 29, 1868
 Died on 26th, MRS. MARY G. IRBY (41 V, d of FRANCIS MASTIN),
relie of late DR. E(DMUND) IRBY (60 V) of this place.
 DR. D. C. GLENN, a prominent politician and lawyer of Mississippi
died last week.

October 2, 1868
 Remains of MR. W. G. BIBB will be buried at 4 o'clock. Service
from Episcopal Church by REV. MR. BEARD.

October 6, 1868
 Died on 5th, MRS. MARY TONEY (26 Pa), wife of COL. ED. TONEY (43 V).
Funeral will take place this afternoon at 4 o'clock from Episcopal
church.
 On 3rd near Triana, MRS. ELIZABETH KIRBY (43 NC) at advanced age.
Familiarly known as "Aunt Betsy" (wid of WM. KIRBY, 1812 sol who d 1847)
 REV. B. F. PERRY, Methodist preacher in Hayneville died last week.

October 9, 1868
 Died on 4, NELLIE, infant daughter of L. E. and MARY R. (or B- ink
worn off) BAKER of this city.

October 13, 1868
 Married at Donegan Hotel in this city on 12 by REV. M. B. DeWITT,
MR. W. P. HARPER (HOOPER) of Yanceyville (Caswell Co.), N.C. to
MISS MATTIE (MARTHA ANN; 10 A) daughter of THOMAS S. McCALLEY (39 V),
Esq. of this vicinity.
 Died on 11th, KATIE DOWNS, infant daughter of MR. and MRS. CARL
NEWMAN aged 11 months and 12 days.
 CAPT. ROBERT HARRISON, 33 Regiment U.S.I. died here Sunday after
a short illness. Remains to be taken to Chattanooga for interment in

National Cemetery there. Well known here and elsewhere in the state.
From Ky.; entered army as private and rose to captain.
     MR. TAZ. W. NEWMAN of Franklin Co. Tenn. died on 2nd.

October 20, 1868
     Died on 19th, JAMES W. son of J(AMES) V. A. HINDS (40 A) of this
city.
     Died on 16 near Madison Station, MRS. SARAH BIBB, widow of
REV. JAMES BIBB aged 85.
     Died on 13th on Sugar Creek of a congestive chill, MR. JOSEPH GRAY
aged 60.

October 23, 1868
     Married on the 20 at the residence of the bride's mother near
this city by REV. THOMAS J. BEARD of Episcopal Church, DR. J. LUCAS
RIDLEY, Murfreesboro, Tenn. to MISS FANNIE J. ROBINSON.
     In the Episcopal Church on Tuesday evening 20th by REV. THOMAS J.
BEARD, MR. BURT LOGWOOD to MISS ELLEN BENTLEY, daughter of MR. ALBERT
BENTLEY, all of this place.
     MRS. JULIA A. McAFEE of Pike Co. drowned herself on 6th.

October 27, 1868
     Married on 22nd by W. M. BALCH, Esq. MR. ROBERT E. HOGWOOD to
MISS ELVERMINE A. BARNES, all of this county.
     Died on 14, MRS. MALINDA GRAVETT (39 NC), relic of late VINCENT
GRAVETT (44 V).
     JAMES H. HAUGHTON, formerly of this county died at his residence
near Aberdeen, Miss. on 18.
     CAPT. JOHN M. BRAINARD, an old steamboat man died on 20th in
Mobile.

October 30, 1868
     Died on 24, MRS. ELIZA HOUK, wife of M. D. HOUK, Esq.
     Married on 22 by REV. MR. ANDREWS, MR. WILLIAM DAVISON to
MISS CALLIE A. LIPSCOMB, both of this county.
     On 19 by REV. JOHN TURRENTINE, MR. B. F. MALONE to MISS SARAH E.
JOHNSON.

November 10, 1868
     Married on 29 by REV. A. J. HALL, MR. JOS. C. VANN of this county
to MISS SUE M. FULLER of Dyer Co. Ala. (must mean Tenn.)
     Died on 30 Oct. at residence on Brier Fork in this county,
MR. WILLIAM MURPHY (56 SC) aged about 77. Baptist. He is the last of
the early settlers of that neighborhood. Raised a large family of
children, all of whom are grown and highly respected. Wife survives
him.

November 13, 1868
     Married on 28th in Marion, Ala. by REV. R. H. RAYMOND, M. B. P.
YEATMAN, formerly of this city to MISS SALLIE E. JOHNSON of Macon.
     MR. JOHN McKINNEY to MISS DENA KELSO; MR. J. F. MOORE to MISS
MARY E. FARRISTON; MR. J. A. NEWMAN to MISS MARY SEISS; MR. J. T.
BINNINGTON to MISS MARGARET A. WELCH; MR. B. W. RHOTON to MISS SARAH J.
MOORE; MR. G. W. ANDERSON to MISS LOUISA SETLIFF, all of Lincoln
County, Tennessee.
     Died on 22nd, MR. ISAAC MILLER (54 V) aged 74, for many years a
respected citizen of this county.
     REV. DR. PHILIP PHEELEY of Methodist pulpit died in Mobile on 9th.

November 17, 1868
     Married on the 3rd in Gadsden, Alabama by REV. J. RUSSELL,
CAPT. SAM B. ECHOLS to MISS JODA M. POPE, daughter of the late
JUDGE B. T. POPE.
     In Corinth, Mississippi on the 10th by REV. MR. FREEMAN,
MR. D. A. TIMBERLAKE of Huntsville to MISS MINNIE DUNCAN of Corinth.
     Died on 13th, MR. JOHN G. CLAPP, son of MR. S. S. CLAPP of this
city after a long illness aged about 18. Formerly of South Bend, Ind.
     On 13, MR. WILLIS BLANKENSHIP (34 A, s of HANNAH) aged about 50.
Baptist and Mason.

In Auburn, Alabama on 4th, MR. EDWARD F. MONTAGUE of this county and formerly of Virginia.

On 15th at residence of MR. A. F. STEELE 10 miles north of Huntsville, MR. JAMES E. ALEXANDER (49 A) in 71st year.

WILLIAM P. HILLIARD, son of REV. H. W. HILLIARD died two weeks ago in Columbus (Muscogee Co.), Geo. brilliant young man.

BENJAMIN GOSS drowned in Coosa river, Cherokee County, Ala. on 8th.

November 24, 1868
Married on the 10 by REV. JOS. E. CARTER at the residence of MR. M. E. BATTLE, DR. J. P. HAMPTON of Mississippi to MISS. M(ARY) T. BATTLE (6 A) of this county, daughter of the late MR. JOSIAH D. BATTLE (38 NC).

COL. JOHN SIMS, formerly of this state died in Texas recently.

November 27, 1868
Tribute of respect to the memory of B. G. BURNETT to Madison Lodge #25, I. O. O. F.

December 1, 1868
GEN. N. G. EVANS, late C. S. A. died in Macon County, Alabama on the 24th.

JUDGE W. L. HARRIS of Miss. died on 26th.

CAPT. JOHN G. FISHER, formerly cashier of Bank of Tennessee died last week.

COL. JOSEPH TAYLOR, formerly of Madison Co. died in Phillips Co. Ark. on 16th.

December 4, 1868
Married on 2nd in Methodist Church by REV. R. K. BROWN, MR. WILLIAM M. ERSKINE (3 A Alex) to MISS SUE RAGLAND, all of Huntsville.

On 2nd by REV. F. A. ROSS, MR. WILLIAM THOMAS BARHAM to MISS KATE JOLLEY (7 A), daughter of COL. B(ENJ) JOLLY (40 V), all of Huntsville.

December 11, 1868
Married on 9th at residence of COL. S. W. HARRIS by REV. R. K. BROWN, MR. HARRIS TENEY to MISS MARY ALEXANDER.

MR. HENRY B. MORGAN to MRS. MARY ANN PEECE; MR. JOHN T. ROWE to MISS SARAH A. WOODARD; REV. JOHN P. FUNK to MISS MEDORA A. HOWARD; MR. JOHN J. RAWLS to MISS MADALINE BEARDEN; MR. ANANIAS WATKINS to MISS MARTHA E. WRAY; MR. J. J. NEWMAN to MISS MARY E. SMITH; MR. ENOCH STEPHENS to MISS ELIZABETH BEECH, all of Lincoln Co. Tenn.

December 15, 1868
State of Alabama--Marion Co. Estate of ISAAC T. MIXON (22 A), dec'd. ROBERT BROWN, adm'r.

State of Alabama--Marion Co. OLIVER P. MATHUS, administrator of GEORGE HALLMARK, deceased.

State of Alabama--Marion Co. LEMUEL FRANKS (555 C), deceased. H. P. DAWNUM, administrator.

Married on the 12th at residence of JACOB KUNZ, Esq. in Chattanooga, Tenn. by Pastor of M. E. Church, REV. JONATHON L. MANN, MR. ERNEST DENTLER of Huntsville to MISS WILHEMINA LEISER of Brooklyn, N.Y.

On 15th by REV. JOSEPH SHACKELFORD, MR. G. W. CONNER to MISS HATTIE WHEELOCK of Iuka, Miss.

Died at residence of DR. DAVIS MOORE near Vienna on the 5th, MRS. BETTIE MOORE, wife of JAMES MOORE after a protracted illness.

January 5, 1869
Died December 25, 1868 near Maysville, MR. MARY F. MARTIN, wife of MR. E. T. MARTIN. She was born August 25, 1839.

MATTIE LEE, infant daughter of E. T. and MARY E. MARTIN died near Maysville, Ala. December 11, 1868, aged 1 yr. 2 mo. 1 day.

DR. JOHN T. DeBOW (30 A) of this place died Saturday night after a short illness. He was a kind, gentle, sensible, honest man, a good citizen and a skillful physician. Left many friends in this county.

WILLIAM NOLAN was killed on 27th at Mossy Crrek, Tenn. by ROBERT BLEVINS who fled.

January 8, 1869
    Married on 22 by REV. S. M. CHERRY, MR. WILLIAM C. BENNETT to
MISS NANNIE POTTS.
    On 6th by REV. WILLIAM S. MITCHELL, MR. GEORGE S. HOUSTON, JR.
(8 A) of Athens to MISS MAGGIE IRVINE, daughter of the late JAMES IRVINE,
Esq.
    In Memphis on 31, MR. A. W. SOUTHWORTH, formerly of Fayetteville,
Tennessee to MRS. KATE YELL, late of Ark.
    In Fayetteville, Tenn. by REV. JAMES WATSON, MR. JOHN A. FORMWALT
to MISS MAGGIE MURPHY.
    Married in Lincoln County, Tennessee on 31st by REV. ALEXANDER
SMITH, REV. A. B. COLEMAN to MISS H. B. TAYLOR.
    In Lincoln County, Tennessee on 24 by REV. M. R. TUCKER,
MR. WILLIAM A. PITTS to MISS MATTIE J. BROWN.

January 12, 1869
    Married on the 24th at the residence of the bride's father,
HON. JAMES WILLIAMS by REV. JAMES COX, MR. W. H. SELLS to MISS M. M.
WILLIAMS.
    Married on the 3rd at residence of GEORGE VAUGHN near Cluttsville
by REV. MR. HARDIN, MR. SIMPSON BALLARD and MISS SALLIE VAUGHN.
    Died near Cluttsville in this county, MR. PHILLIP HILLIARD (bet
this should be PHILEMON as PHILEMON d 1868 @ 63) of pneumonia aged 60
years. An old citizen.
    On the 8th in this city of consumption, MRS. SARAH ADAY, wife of
DOW ADAY, Esq.

January 15, 1869
    Married on 13th at Huntsville Female College by REV. R. K. BROWN,
A. E. GARNER, Esq. of Springfield (Robertson Co.), Tenn. to MISS ADDIE E.
MORRIS of this city.
    On 17th in Lincoln Co. Tenn. by REV. A. S. RANDOLPH, MR. N. P.
SMITH to MISS EMALINE KOONCE.
    Died in Lincoln Co. Tenn. at the residence of her son-in-law,
JOHN MOORE, Esq., MRS. DAVIS aged about 84.
    State of Alabama--Marion Co.--WILLIAM J. NEAL, deceased.
MARSHAL McLEOD, adm'r.
    Married on the 7th in Bowling Green, Ky. by REV. FATHER DEARIES,
MR. JOHN W. WRIGHT of Huntsville, Alabama to MISS KATE GERHARDSTEIN of
Bowling Green, Ky.

January 22, 1869
    Married on 20th at residence of bride's father, DR. GEORGE R.
WHARTON by REV. J. R. PLUMMER, MR. H. T. PHILLIPS of Atlanta, Ga. to
MISS BETTIE WHARTON.
    Married on 10th inst. MR. WILLIAM T. LINDSEY to MISS MARGARET E.
PRICE, all of Cherokee.
    On 14th by REV. DR. STEADMAN, HON. THOMAS A. BLAIR of Miss. to
MISS A. E. ROSS, daughter of CAPT. W. J. ROSS.
    On 10th near Cluttsville by REV. MR. HARDEN, MR. W. CLUTTS to
MISS ELIZA A. HILLIARD, both of this county.
    On 18th by REV. R. K. BROWN, MR. HENRY B. ROPER to MISS CORNELIA A.
CLOPTON, both of this county.
    On Saturday night last, 16th inst. MR. SAMUEL CHILDRESS was shot
and killed in the northwest part of this county by MR. JERE DORTRY.
    In Baton Rouge, MR. JOHN WAX to MISS RHODIE M. PINE--the knot that
ought to stick.
    Died on 23 at residence of her father, CHARLES W. STRONG (45 V)
of consumption, MISS NANNIE STRONG (4 A) aged about 20.

January 29, 1869
    Married on Tue. evening the 26th at residence of the bride's
father, REV. J. H. SPALDING by REV. JOSEPH E. CARTER, MR. ROBERT A.
MILLER to MISS CHRISTINA F. SPALDING, all of this city.
    On 18th at residence of THOMAS H. CAWTHON in this county by
REV. MR. BURR, MR. LEROY P. RUTLAND of Nashville, Tenn. to
MISS MARTHA W. CAWTHON, of this county.
    In this county on Wed. Jan. 27 at 10 A.M. by REV. R. K. BROWN,
DR. J. J. DEMENT to MISS CORNELIA C. BINFORD (5A), daughter of
DR. HENRY A. BINFORD (38 NC), all of Huntsville.

February 2, 1869
    Married on 28th at residence of bride's mother by ELDER G. W.
CARMICHAEL, MR. WILLIAM T. BRUNLEY to MISS MARY BRUCE BRANAUGH all of
this county.
    On 28th by REV. R. H. TALIAFERO, MR. W. A. POWER to MISS ELIZABETH
RICE, both of this county.
    On 26th at residence of bride's mother by REV. JOSEPH SHACKLEFORD,
MR. THOMAS H. GIBSON to MISS MATILDA GANNON.
    Died in Denver City, Colo. Dec. 26, 1868, DR. EDWARD C. STRODE
of apoplexy aged 28.

February 5, 1869
    HENRY GREEN of Lincoln Co. Tenn. aged 30 fell dead on 27th.

February 9, 1869
    Married on 7th at New Market by J. W. DAVIS, magistrate, MR. HENRY
GILBERT to MISS MARTHA JANE LITTLE.
    MR. EDWARD DOUGLAS died suddenly at residence of MR. JAMES LANDMAN
Sunday night.

February 12, 1869
    Married on 11th by REV. R. K. BROWN, MR. GEORGE ALLEN to MISS
ANNIE E. ASHWORTH, all of this city.

February 16, 1869
    Married on 9th at residence of bride's father, MR. ALLEN STEGER
in Tishomingo Co. Miss., DR. JOSEPH S. MACON (recently of N.C.) to
MRS. MARY E. WRIGHT, both of Madison Co. Ala.
    On Thursday evening 11th inst. at residence of bride's father,
MR. J. ANDREWS by ELDER J. S. COLLINS, MR. WILLIAM TURNER to MISS NAOMA S.
ANDREWS, all of this county.
    Died on 13th at her residence in this city, MRS. SARAH ANN NEVILL
(48 V) aged 67. Cumberland Presbyterian. Has left many to mourn her
death.
    On Sunday morning of consumption, MRS. HESTER A. wife of I. J.
PARSON of this city. Cumberland Presbyterian.
    At 2 o'clock Sat. night Feb. 13 aged 75, MRS. MARY WILLICK,
mother of MR. JAMES A. WILLICK of this city. Native of Baltimore, Md.
Member of Protestant Episcopal Church.

February 19, 1869
    Married Wednesday evening the 18th by REV. MR. BANNISTER, MR. LOUIS
H. MAYER to MISS EDMONIA TENEY, daughter of COL. ED. TENEY, all of
Huntsville.

February 23, 1869
    Married on the 10th in New Orleans by REV. DR. PALMER, MR. WILLIAM L.
MALONE of North Alabama to MISS ALICE NELSON, daughter of S. O. NELSON.
    GEN. HENRY MAURY of Mobile is dead.

March 2, 1869
    Died on the 28th after a long illness, MRS. ANN HENRY SIBLEY,
wife of MR. FELIX W. SIBLEY and daughter of MR. and MRS. STEPHEN HAYNES
of this vicinity, aged about 23.
    CAPT. JESSE COX, an old Alabama steamboat officer died in Mobile
on the 2nd.

March 12, 1869
    Married on the 10th at the Cumberland Presbyterian Church by
REV. M. B. DeWITT, MR. JAMES C. LEFTWICH (son of JOBEZ N) to MISS AGGIE
P. SCOTT, all of Huntsville.
    Married on the 10th by REV. M. B. DeWITT at the residence of the
bride's father, MR. WILLIAM M. COWAN of Cowan (Franklin Co.), Tennessee
to MISS BELLE JOHNSON of this city.
    The oldest editor in Georgia, R. M. ORME died on the 8th in
Milledgeville.

March 16, 1869
    Married at the Baptist Parsonage at 4 P.M. Friday 12th by REV.
JOSEPH E. CARTER. MR. SAMUEL F. LEE to MISS ELLEN F. MILLER, all of
Madison Co.

On the 11th at the bride's residence by REV. HENRY P. TURNER,
MR. MILAS R. NEEVES to MRS. FRANCES E. McCAFFEY, all of Madison Co.
    Married in this city on the 15th by REV. R. K. BROWN, MR. CLARK S.
JAMES to MISS SARAH E. KENNARD, all of Huntsville.

March 19, 1869
    Married on the 10th by REV. J. G. WILSON, MARTIN J. VAUGHN, Esq.
to MRS. FANNIE LEFTWICH, all of this county (d of JAMES & JULIA
(HATTON) Landman-)
    Married on the 16th by L. M. DOUGLASS, Judge of Probate,
MR. WILLIAM PEMBERTON to MISS JANE SCHRIMSHER, all of this county.
    Married on the 15th by REV. J. J. BURDINE, MR. PIPKIN EARP(?) to
MISS MARY J. WILKES.
    Died on the 16th in this city, MRS. MARY LAUDER, wife of GEORGE
LAUDER of the 33rd U.S. Infantry.

March 23, 1869
    Married on the 4th in Lawrence Co. Tenn., MR. A. T. WHITE, late of
Ala. to MISS R. E. OLIVER of Lawrence Co. Tenn.
    MRS. ELLEN HUNT, wife of MRS. CHARLES H. HUNT and daughter of
MR. and MRS. THOMAS W. WHITE of this place died near Grand Junction
(Hardeman Co.), Tenn. on Friday.

March 26, 1869
    MR. ARCHELAUS M. BRADLEY died in this county on the 23rd at an
advanced age. He was a well-known citizen, a skillful mechanic and
possessed of considerable architectural taste and had been a successful
builder. Man of good character, good sense and genial nature and in the
earlier days of this section was a prominent citizen. (related to
FRANK BRADLEY, N.Y. Public Library who said ARCHELAUS was son of
ARCHELAUS & SUSANNA (LYON) BRADLEY who m 3 Feb 1980 Henrico Co. Va.)

March 30, 1869
    Married on the 29th at the Church of Nativity by REV. J. M. BANISTER,
MR. THOMAS HELM of Jackson, Mississippi to MISS LAURA PATTON, daughter
of MR. JOHN PATTON of this city.
    Married on the 18th at the residence of PARKS TOWNSEND, Esq by
REV. M. E. JOHNSON, MR. ED F. DOUGLASS to MISS LOTTIE COOVER.
    Died on the 28th in this county, MR. JAMES DAMASCUS aged 16.

April 2, 1869
    MR. ISAAC M. JAMISON, one of the oldest citizens of Columbia
(Maury Co.), Tennessee died in that place last Wed. morning.

April 6, 1869
    Obituary:
ARCHELAUS M. BRADLEY, Esq. was born in Charles City County, Va.
December 17, 1796 and emigrated to this place in 1817, which was then
Mississippi Territory. Formerly warden of the Penitentiary, Justice of
Peace and for many years Secretary of Lodge, Chapter etc. of Free
Masons in different parts of our state. He was once quite "well off,"
in fact, comparatively wealthy.... Did service in the war of 1812 in
Virginia (although he never applied for a pension. Died March 23, 1869
aged 73 years 3 months and 4 days.

April 9, 1869
    Married on the 8th at the residence of the bride's father by
REV. R. K. BROWN, MR. HENRY DELP to MISS BETTIE A. WARE, all of this
city. (Parents of MRS. BOYD, MRS. E. C. LANDENS, JAMES DELP, Huntsville)
(see obit of MRS. BOYD)
    Remains of COL. JOHN G. COLTART, who died in Tuscaloosa last year
were brought home and interred in the graveyard here Wednesday with
Masonic honors and the military band of 33 regulars supplied music. He
was a good officer and soldier on the Confederate side.

April 16, 1869
    Died in this city on the 11th(?), WILLIAM, infant of J. B. (or H?)
and L(?) H. BUCKALEW aged 8 months. Print very dim.

April 23, 1869
   Married on the 21st at the residence of MR. NASH. MALONE in this
county by REV. M. B. DeWITT, MR. J. T. LONG of Meridian, Miss. to
MISS SALLIE EWING of this vicinity.

April 27, 1869
   Died in this county on the 23rd of congestion of the brain and
spinal column, LESLIE, second son of J. M. and 'ADELIA P. MOSS. Born
Jan. 5, 1853 in Boone County, Illinois; in 1854 moved to Waverly, Iowa
and in 1866 to this county.

April 30, 1869
   Died in this city on the 26th, YOUNG HUMES aged about 19 months,
son of JAMES and SUSIE C. WHITE.
   MRS. REBECCA ELOISA WITHERS, wife of GEN. JONES M. WITHERS died in
Mobile on the 22nd.
   MR. JOSEPH ANGELL, formerly of this place died in Brooklyn, N.Y.
April 24th aged 61. Baptist.

May 4, 1869
   Married on the 29th by J. J. PITTS, PETER G. HASTEN, formerly of
Giles Co. Tenn. to MISS LIZZIE A. PHILLIPS of Madison Co. Ala.

May 7, 1869
   Married in the Presbyterian Church Thursday evening in this place
May 6th by DR. F. A. ROSS, DR. ROBERT L. HALLONQUIST of Lowndes Co. to
MISS HATTIE FIGURES, eldest daughter of W. B. FIGURES of Huntsville,
Ala.

May 11, 1869
   Died on Sunday morning the 9th in this city, LULA MARIA, daughter
of MR. and MRS. JAMES A. PICKARD aged 4 years, 9 months and 7 days.
   JOHN G. BLACKWELL was appointed Receiver of Public Moneys at
Huntsville on the 7th; GEN. D. M. BRADFORD is the present incumbent.
GEN. BRADFORD is one of the Union patriarchs of this region, a veteran
of the War of 1812, an opponent of secession revolutionary democracy;
a good officer.
   COL. A(UGUSTINE) J. WITHERS, an old and well known citizen of this
vicinity died on Friday last in his 64th year.

May 15, 1869
   Married in St. Clair County on the 6th by HON. THOMAS N. MONTGOMERY,
HON. H. J. SPRINGFIELD to MISS MARY E. C. FRANKLIN.
   (m in St. Clair Co. 12-24-1861 MARY C. MOSTILLO--con. of mother,
CATHARINE SPRINGFIELD wit H. B. SPRINGFIELD; m. 2-28-1866 JOICIE L.
SIMPSON; groom m before)
   Married on the 20th on White's Creek (Davidson Co.), Tennessee by
REV. MR. WILLI(S?) MR. W. F. TURK to MISS BOBELL FULGHAM of Huntsville.
   Died on the 20th in Franklin County, Virginia, MRS. ANN JUDSON
SMITH, wife of REV. H. P. SMITH of this city.
   MRS. HARRIET B. MACOMB, wife of the late GEN. MACOMB is dead aged 86.

June 1, 1869
   Married on the 27th in Chickasaw Co. Miss. at the residence of
CAPT. G. R. KIDD by REV. DR. EGBERT, MAJ. S. A. JONAS of Aberdeen to
MISS JULIA JORDAN of this city.
   Died on the 29th after a short illness, MRS. HARRIET FARISS, wife
of the late DANDRIDGE FARISS, Esq. in her 63rd year. Native of
Philadelphia and came to Hutnsville nearly 50 years ago, where she
continued to live up to her death. She was a Presbyterian, having
attached herself to it when DR. JOHN ALLEN was its Pastor...
   JOHN RUSSELL (m. 1860 DEKALB 64 T, m 1850 54 T) of DeKalb Co. Ala.
died on the 22nd aged 73.
   B. S. HAMILTON, an old merchant of Nashville died there last week.

June 8, 1869
   Married on the 28th near Flint Factory by Esq. R. A. PETTEY,
MR. PLEASANT W. MILES to MISS SARAH C. COUCH, all of this county.

Died on the 19th of May at the residence of her son, CAPT. JOHN
CLARKE at Campbellton (Jackson Co.), Fla., MRS. SUSAN CLARKE, mother of
MRS. WILLIAM MASTIN and MRS. J. C. BRADLEY of this city, in her 70th
year. We have known her since our early boyhood... Presbyterian...

June 5, 1869
        DR. SAMUEL BRECK, formerly of this place died in Canton (Madison Co.)
Miss. on the 30th. Possessed of fine sense, excellent attainments,
genial manners.

June 18, 1869
        Married on the 16th at the residence of CARVER KING, Esq. by
REV. R. K. BROWN, THOMAS H. HEWLETT, JR. to MISS VIRGINIA KING, all of
this county.
        Died on the 13th at the residence of her husband, DR. J. W. PETTY
in the vicinity of New Market, MRS. ANNA PETTY in her 72nd year.
Baptist.

June 22, 1869
        Died near Brownsboro on the 2nd of consumption, NANCY SANFORD,
youngest daughter of JOHN SANFORD.
        Died on the 21st of acute enteritis, MARY ALICE, daughter of
CAPT. S. W. and MRS. SUE E. FORDYCE aged 19 months.

June 25, 1869
        Married at the Church of Nativity June 24th by REV. J. M. BANNISTER,
Rector, COL. WILLIAM F. MASTIN to MISS FANNIE MOORE, both of this city.
        Died at Hazle Green on the 17th of pneumonia, MRS. ANN WILBURN,
relict of ELIAS (Rev. Sol) WILBURN (or son of Rev Sol) aged about 60.
(Note: I think this should be WELBORN.P.J.G.)
        CAPT. THOMAS B. MILLS, formerly of this place died in Montgomery
on the 21st. Son of the late COL. A(RCH'D) E. MILLS, was an officer
in the Navy and then a captain in the Confederate navy.
        DR. DRU TANNER was killed this week near Markham's Mills in this
county by a young man named HALL.

July 2, 1869
        Died in Nashville on the 29th, MRS. ELVIRA FACKLER NICHOL, daughter
of MR. JOHN J. FACKLER of Huntsville, and wife of DR. WILLIAM T. NICHOL
of that city. Remains were brought here for interment.

July 9, 1869
        Married on the 30th by REV. J. H. DRAKE, MR. WILLIAM B. HAYNES to
MISS ELIZA G. SIBLEY, all of this county.
        Married on the 5th by REV. J. H. DRAKE, MR. HENRY TUCK to MISS
LUCY J. DAVIS, all of this county.
        Married in this city on the 7th at the residence of the bride's
father by REV. FATHER TRECY, MR. H. A. WRENCH of Dalton (Whitfield Co.),
Ga. to MISS FRANCIS REBMAN of this city.
        Died on the 7th near this city, MRS. SUSAN J. ROBERTSON, wife of
J. MURRAY ROBERTSON.
        Died on Saturday the 26th of consumption, MRS. ANN ELIZA TONEY,
widow of ELIJAH TONEY, deceased aged 35. Methodist. Leaves 5 small
children.
        Died on Sunday the 4th, EVA WEDEMEYER, daughter of FREDERICK and
FRANCES WEDEMEYER aged 7 years and 8 months. PROF. WEDEMEYER is leader
of the military band of U.S. Infantry stationed here.

July 13, 1869
        Married on the 12th by ROBERT W. FIGG, Esq. at the residence of
F. ARNAL, CHRISTOPHER WOOLF to MISS BETTY HURLEY, all of this county.
        MAJ. W. T. GUNTER of Dale Co. was killed.
        REV. DR. THOMAS W(ILMER) DORMAN, a prominent (b Oct 13, 1804)
minister of the M. E. Church died in Mobile on the 3rd. (news says d 2d)

July 16, 1869
        Died on the 17th near this city, MRS. MARY WALTER PLEASANTS, wife
of SAMUEL PLEASANTS, Esq. and youngest daughter of JOHN ROBINSON, Esq.

July 27, 1869
Married on the 25th by R. W. FIGG, Esq. MR. BERTIE V. JENKS to
MISS JOSEPHINE PARKER of this city.
Married on the 22nd at the CORNELIUS place 8 miles north of
Huntsville by REV. J. J. PITTS, MR. J. N. CAPS to MISS CHARITY A. TAYLOR,
all of this county.
ANDREW J. MORGAN, administrator with will annexed of JOHN HATHCOCK,
deceased.
Estate of MARY M. JORDAN, deceased. MORRIS K. TAYLOR, adm'r.
JAMES L. RIDLEY, administrator de bonis non of LUCY A. M. HORTON,
deceased.
MORRIS K. TAYLOR, guardian of CYNTHIA F., WILLIAM L. and
ROBERT HAMLET, infants.

July 30, 1869
WILLIAM TANCRE, deceased. WILLIAM H. TANCRE, administrator.

August 3, 1869
"MRS. LOUISA KALIN of Selma committed suicide on the 26th."

TUSKALOOSA GAZETTE

January 6, 1876
"Married near Selma, FRANK A. BATES of Marion to MISS ADDIE L.
PHILLIPS on the 21st." (Selma Times)

HUNTSVILLE (ALA.) ADVOCATE

August 3, 1869
Died on the 28th of July 1866 (misprint?) JOHNSON B., son of
P. L. and ELIZABETH C. HARRISON aged 2(?) mo.
Died on the 28th of consumption, MRS. ELIZABETH THOMPSON in her
28th year.
MASTER CHARLES CULP, son of MR. AMOS CULP, died on Saturday of
lock-jaw.

August 6, 1869
Married on the 3rd near this city by REV. R. K. BROWN (s of ISAAC--
census), MR. JOHN D. GROOMS to MISS ANNIE W. CARTER.
Died on the 24th of July in St. Louis, Mo., AGNES LOUISA, infant
daughter of JACOB P. and MAGGIE J. CROOKER aged 1 year 7 months and
22 days. Nashville papers please copy.
Died on 3 June near Brownsboro, NANNIE SANFORD, daughter of
MR. JOHN SANFORD. M. E. Church.

August 10, 1869
Married on the 5th by REV. VAN HOUSE, G. S. NUCKOLL, M.D. of
Huntsville to MISS MARY E. JORDAN, daughter of E. L. JORDAN, Esq. of
Murfreesboro, Tenn.
Died on the 6th in this city, JAMES, son of W. D. and ELVIRA ROWTON
aged 6.

August 13, 1869
Died in this city on the 11th of flux, MR. JACOB HERZ aged 29.

August 17, 1869
W. R. HUDSON aged 82 hung himself in Madison County, Tennessee
last week.

August 20, 1869
Died on 11th of July last, MR. JAMES A. M. HUNTER (s of REV. DANULK--
census) aged 41 years 5 months and 9 days. Good man and useful citizen.
MR. JEFF. McCALLEY, one of the members of the Legislature from this
county died yesterday in the northern portion of the county as we

learn. He was, for his opportunities possessed of good sense and
judgment.
    In Franklin Co. Ala. on the 13th, JOHN NORMAN was killed by
ED. MASTIN, who fled.

August 24, 1869
    Died in this place on the 22nd, MISS LUCRETIA WARWICK, sister of
MR. GEORGE H. WARWICK.
    At Grand Junction (Hardeman Co.), Tenn. on the 22nd, JAMES WHITE,
infant son of CHARLES M. and ELLEN W. HUNT. Burial will take place at
half past 5 from the residence of THOMAS W. WHITE.
    THOMAS WILKERSON was killed and W. J. ESTES and J. C. WILSON
wounded in Calhoun Co. the other day.

August 31, 1869
    State of Alabama--Madison County. Aug. 19. Probate Court.
MORRIS K. TAYLOR, administrator of EZEKIEL W. MATKIN, deceased.
Non-resident heirs: JAMES D. MATKIN, RUA A. LANSDEN and her husband,
WILLIAM T. LANSDEN, MARY T. HENTZLY and her husband, RUFUS HENTZLY,
WILLIAM T. MORRIS, ELAM M. MORRIS, DRAKE MORRIS, AUGUSTA L. MORRIS,
ANDREW H. SIVELY, ELIZA MATKIN, JOHN MATKIN, THOMAS MATKIN, MALINDA
MATKIN, LEVI F. MATKIN, ANDREW F. MATKIN and MARGARET MATKIN.
    State of Alabama--Madison Co. Probate Court, August 11th.
ELIAS WELLBORN, deceased. DEKALB LIPSCOMB, executor. Non-resident
heirs: NANCY E. GRAY and her husband, SEVIER T. GRAY, ELIAS WELLBORN,
SAMUEL S. WELLBORN and ALFRED C. WELLBORN.

September 3, 1869
    Married on the 31st at Valhermoso Springs, Alabama by REV. T. J.
BEARD, COL. LEE CRANDALL of New Orleans to MISS MARY HARRIET GIERS.
    Married on the 2nd in this city by REV. R. K. BROWN, MR. CHARLES J.
NEELY of LaFayette (Christian Co.), Kentucky to MISS TENNIE CONNER of
Huntsville.
    Died on the 2nd in this city, MRS. HANNAH MANN aged 65. Funeral
will take place from the Methodist Church (w of THOMPSON MANN--mar 182_).
    State of Alabama--Madison Co. Probate Court, Aug. 12. WILLIAM P.
GLOVER and JONATHON W. GLOVER, administrators of JONATHON GLOVER,
deceased. Heirs who are non-residents of Ala: ADJET McG. B. GLOVER
and JAMES W. GLOVER.

September 7, 1869
    State of Alabama--Madison Co. Probate Court. JERUSHA LAYMAN,
deceased. JAMES M. WILDER, administrator.
    MR. PETER S. BAKER, an old and respected citizen of this county
died at his residence near New Market Sat.
    State of Alabama--Madison Co.--Probate Court, Sept. 4.
JAMES JOHNSTON, executor of WILLIAM JOHNSTON, deceased. Heirs who are
non-residents of Ala: JOHN T. SMITH and wife MARY, WILLIAM F. STANDIFER,
JOHN NEWMAN and wife DUANNA, LEONIDAS F. STANDIFER, QUINTERIA STANDIFER,
CECIL STANDIFER, CYCELIUS STANDIFER, JEROME STANDIFER, PERRY EAGLE and
wife CRUCY, JOHN JOHNSTON and JAMES JOHNSTON.

September 14, 1869
    MR. WILSON FARISS (s of DANDRIDGE--census) died on the 13th of
congestion after a short illness. He was born here on September 15, 1826,
was a printer but for many years was a bookkeeper. Principal clerk in
the Post Office at the time of his death. Emphatically an honest and
good business man. Leaves a family and many friends.

September 17, 1869
    Funeral Notice--Friends of the late ALLEN COOPER and of JAMES L.
and JOHN W. COOPER are invited to attend the burial of the former
from the residence of J. W. COOPER this afternoon.
    MR. ALLEN COOPER died yesterday at his son's residence, MR. JOHN W.
COOPER. He came here in 1819 and was in his 70th year. Member of
M. E. Church and a respected citizen.

September 21, 1869
    CAPT. W. A. MAYO, who formerly resided here died in Munroe County,
Tenn. on the 10th.

ISAAC W. LANDERS while out hunting near Madison Station was killed. State of Alabama--Madison Co.--Probate Court, Sept. 13. JOSEPH M. HAMBRICK, administrator of HENRY WHITMAN, deceased. Heirs who are non-residents of Alabama are: SARAH EVANS, wife of HARRISON EVANS and JIMMIE WHITMAN.

September 24, 1869
Married Wed. eve. September 22nd at the Methodist Church by REV. J. G. WILSON, MR. ELLIOTT R. MATTHEWS to MISS FANNIE, daughter of J. W. SCRUGGS, Esq. all of Huntsville.

October 12, 1869
Died on the 8th in this city, MR. WILLIAM N. PRESTON in his 49th year. Born in Prince Edward County, Virginia April 13, 1821. Came to this city several years before the war and has resided here ever since, except two years spent at Corinth, Miss. Affectionate husband, good citizen, Mason.

October 15, 1869
Married on the 14th in this city by REV. R. K. BROWN, MR. JAMES E. FLETCHER to MISS SALLIE S. MATTHEWS, daughter of SAMUEL MATTHEWS, Esq.
Died near Meridianville in this county on 24 Sept. MR. SAMUEL A. THOMPSON aged 23.
HON. N. W. COCKE, late Chancellor died in Greenville, Ala. on Sunday last.
JUDGE JOS. W. FIELD of Columbus, Miss. died on the 2nd aged 70.

September 28, 1869
Died on the 11th in Cherokee County, MR. JOHN W. TRIPPE an estimable citizen aged 38.

October 19, 1869
Died on the 11th, ROBERT D. youngest son of MR. and MRS. A. J. SCHRIMSHER of this vicinity aged about 15 years.
On the 14th, ANDREW HENRY SMITH, son of SENEA SMITH committed suicide near Vienna in this county.

October 22, 1869
Married at the Church of Nativity October 21st by REV. MR. BANISTER, MR. OLIVER BEIRNE PATTON to MISS BETTY IRVINE WHITE, daughter of COL. ADD. WHITE, all of Huntsville.
MR. GEORGE W. NEAL, a well-known citizen died on Tue. night aged about 57. For a long time a druggist and then a banker of this place. Liberal and public-spirited and a man of strong practical sense and leaves many friends.
"ISAAC COOK, a clerk in the Selma Times was accidentally killed on the 16th."

November 16, 1869
"Married on the 10th at the residence of THOMAS J. CARSON near Huntsville by REV. JOSEPH E. CARTER, MR. AUGUSTUS H. FINNEY of Houston Co. Ga. to MRS. MARY E. GOFF of Selma, Ala."

October 29, 1869
Married on the 27th at the residence of the bride's father by REV. ROBERT K. BROWN, MR. HENRY P. TURNER to MISS FANNIE LEE ELLIOTT all of this county. (Note: This should be "ELLETT")
Married at the Church of our Saviour in Brooklyn, N.Y. at 12 o'clock M., Oct. 21st by REV. MR. POSTLETHWAITE, MR. ALBERT H. ANGELL, formerly of this city to MISS FLORENCE A., daughter of ELISHA DeWOLFE, Esq. formerly of Horton, Nova Scotia.
Died on the 9th at Bell Factory, WILLIE, son of MARGARET L. FLUELLEN aged 8 years 6 mo.
Died on the 24th, JAMES A. ESSLINGER, son of MR. LEVI W. and MRS. MOLLIE D. ESSLINGER aged 1 year 9 mo. 2 days.

November 2, 1869
Married on the 29th at Huntsville Hotel by REV. J. G. WILSON, WILLIAM P. KRAMER, Esq. to MISS MARY BYRD of Cynthiana (Harrison Co.), Ky.

Married in Pickensville, Alabama on the 28th by REV. DR. MURRAH, MR. WILLIAM P. McCLUNG (s of JAS WHITE McCLUNG & w MRS. JANET E.) of Madison Co. to MISS JENNIE ANDERSON, daughter of MAJ. W. B. ANDERSON.

November 5, 1869
Married on the 2nd at JOHNSON'S WELLS by REV. M. E. JOHNSTON, MR. SAMUEL C. BLANCHARD of Miss. to MISS ELVIE McCOY of Madison Co. Ala.
Married on the 28th by REV. S. M. CHERRY, MR. J. T. CASPER, JR. to MISS SUE E. BARTON, all of the vicinity of Dickson, Ala.
Married on the 20th by REV. MR. PEARSON, ALONZO W. QUINN (b Talladega Co. (or Lure? Co.) 1839, s of E. W. & LUCINDA (GREENWOOD) QUINN), Esq. of Union Co. Ark. (Alfortzo m. Valeria) to MISS LENA SEVIER, eldest daughter of DR. BENJAMIN B. SEVIER of Baldwyn (Lee Co.), Miss. (gd of SAM'L SEVIER, son of GOV. SEVIER; Check 1850 census and Goodspeed Ark. history)
Died on Wednesday, Nov. 3, 1869 at the residence of MR. H. G. BRADFORD in this county of paralysis of the brain, MR. JAMES M. WILSON aged 52. MR. WILSON was born in York County, S.C. and removed to Madison County, Alabama at an early age. In his decease, we lose a most estimable quiet, inoffensive and high toned gentleman.
Died in this city October 31st, MRS. VIORA C. (she was VIRA C. STUBBS see Vol. 111 p. 83) wife of A(NDREW) J. BOLTON. Her disease was cancer against which she employed all the skill of physicians in vain. Member of M. E. Church.
Died in Gadsden, Ala. on the 18th, EVA THERESA, infant daughter of R. B. and M. KYLE aged 6 mo.

November 23, 1869
Married on the 16th at the residence of MR. HENRY SHELTON in Jackson, Tennessee by REV. J. A. EVANS, MR. JOHN YOUNG DYSART of New Orleans to MISS MOLLIE ROBINSON of this city.

November 19, 1869
Died in this county on the 17th, MRS. ELIZA JANE MANSON, wife of MR. W. W. MANSON and daughter of MR. A. J. SCHRIMSHER aged about 24.

November 23, 1869
Died in this city on the 19th, MRS. RESA C. BRANDON (m. 1863 ROSALIE (CALDWELL) Christian d of DR. JOHN D. CALDWELL), wife of JOHN D. BRANDON, Esq.
Died in this city on the 22nd, MISS MATILDA E. ERWIN aged 20. The friends of MR. and MRS. JOHN A. ERWIN are invited to the funeral of their daughter from the Baptist Church.

November 26, 1869
Married in Tishomingo Co. Miss. on the 2nd by REV. W. S. McMAHON, MR. WM. M. ROSS to MISS JENNIE R. LEDBETTER, daughter of T. W. LEDBETTER, Esq. formerly of Fayetteville, Tenn.

December 3, 1869
MR. FRANCIS J. LeVERT died here on the 30th after a short illness in his 79 year. Old citizen of Huntsville.
Near Meridianville on the 1st, MR. ED S. DOUGLASS was shot and killed by B. R. THOMPSON, both well known citizens.
MR. SAMUEL F. RICE died in Montgomery on the 30th.
RUSSELL CAMPBELL was killed in Blount County, Alabama last week by WILLIAM DUNN.

December 6, 1869
Married at St. Paul's Church, Spring Hill by BISHOP WILMER of Ala., MR. HARVEY E. JONES to MISS MARION WILMER, daughter of the officiating Bishop.

December 10, 1869
Married in Madison County, Alabama near New Market Tue. the 16th by REV. DAVID TUCKER, DR. JAMES C. FLYNT to MISS L. O. GRIMMETT.
Died in Memphis on the 1st, MR. ALBERT M. HINES, brother of CAPT. J. J. HINES in his 19th year.

December 14, 1869
    Died on Sunday the 5th at Loudon, Tennessee, MRS. LUCRETIA JULIAN,
mother of MR. C. H. JULIAN of this city.

December 17, 1869
    Married on the 16th in this city at the residence of MR. SAMUEL
COLTART by REV. DR. BANISTER, MR. WILLIAM H. FARRIS to MISS HELEN
NESBIT.
    Married on the 15th at the residence of MR. F(REDK) O. SCHAUDIES
by REV. JOS. E. CARTER, MR. LAFAYETTE SMITH of Reddersville, Tenn. to
MISS ANNA M. SCHAUDIES.
    At P. N. SOTHERLIN'S Dec. 9th by J. N. GREEN, Esq. S. A. CASS to
LUCINDA WARDO.

December 13, 1869
    MR. WILLIAM H. FOWLER, an old citizen (76) of this county died a
few days ago at his residence.
    MR. ISAAC WILLIAMS died in Columbus, Miss. on the 17th aged 76.
He resided here from 1820 to 1835 and was a good man.
    Died on the 18th at his mother's residence near Brownsboro,
MR. WILLIAM J. LAWLER in the 31st year of his age.

December 24, 1869
    Married at the residence of COL. W. D. HUMPHREY Dec. 22nd by
REV. M. G. DeWITT, MR. JAMES DRAKE to MISS BELLE JONES HUMPHREY, all
of this county.
    In Blount County, Ala. this week, GEORGE SHELTON (@ 30 A) was shot
and killed by a MR. HENRY.

December 21, 1869
    WILLFORD SULLIVAN, deceased. M. K. TAYLOR, administrator.
    Married on the 15th by REV. MR. SANDERS, MR. JNO. CAWTHORN to
MISS CHARLOTTE, daughter of MR. L. F. LAMBERSON, all of this co.
    Died on 19th (? says d Nov. 26, 1869), REV. WILLIAM GREEN (Meth.;
b Dec. 10, 1800) aged about 73. Old citizen of this county. Much
beloved by all who knew him. Life was one of honest toil and practical
usefulness. Leaves many to lament his death.

December 6, 1869
    COL. STEPHEN W. HARRIS of this place died on Sunday after a linger-
ing illness. He formerly represented this county in the Legislature
and was a gentleman of intelligence, culture and moral worth.

May 13, 1870
    MR. B. R. THOMPSON died here on the 4th at the residence of
DR. J. J. DEMENT from wounds he received on the night of March 9th at
the hands of disguised men at his own residence about 9 miles north of
Huntsville.
    Tribute of respect--Madison Lodge 25 I.O.O.F. "Our worthy and
esteemed brother, SAMUEL S. CLARK, Past Grand Master of this Lodge."
ISAIAH DILL, JAMES E. SEAR and C. A. JORDAN, committee.
    Died in this place on 11 May 1870, WILLIAM F. ELGIN in 43rd year.
    On the 4th inst. at the residence of her son-in-law, LOGAN R.
GLOVER in this city, MRS. NANCY McCLEHANY (w of DAVID--census) aged
about 76 years. Native of Virginia but for many years a resident of
this county and consistent member of the Cumberland Church.
    Died at his residence in this place May 6, 1870, MR. SAMUEL S.
CLARK aged 53 years 3 months and 6 days. Florence, Ala. and Auburn,
N.Y. papers please copy.
    Married on the 1st inst. by REV. U. S. BATES, MR. JEFFERSON ECKELS
of Tennessee to MISS LOUISA S. GORMLEY of this county.

May 20, 1870
    Married on 2nd inst. in Nashville, Tennessee by MR. KANTRO VIEZ,
MR. GERSON MEYER to MISS GUSTA GILDZINSKI of Nashville.
    Died on the 13th inst. at the residence of MR. J. MAYHEW,
JOSEPH W. DURYEE aged 18.

May 27, 1870
Married on the 18th in Huntsville by REV. M. B. DeWITT, MR. WILLIAM
L. J. WINSTON to MISS MARY E. ENNIS.
Died on the 17th of April 1870 of consumption, MRS. RUTH D. LANDMAN,
wife of ROBERT LANDMAN in her 23rd year.
We regret to state that BENJAMIN TYSON MOORE, Esq. died on the
25th at the residence of his brother, HON. WILLIAM H. MOORE of this
place. Born in North Carolina. Graduated at the State University
there. 67 years of age and had resided in Huntsville about 45 years.

June 3, 1870
Tribute of respect by Huntsville Bar on death of friend and fellow
member, CHARLES A. DONEGAN, Esq. W. W. GARTH, chairman, WILLIAM RICHARDSON,
sec'y.
Married in this city May 25, 1870 by REV. M. B. DeWITT, MR. ORRIN
A. WHITE of Wyoming Territory to MISS VIRGINIA B. THURSTON, daughter
of MRS. A. H. THURSTON of this city.
Married at Church of Nativity June 1, 1870 by REV. DR. BANISTER,
MILTON HUMES, Esq. to MISS ELLA LEE, daughter of Ex-governor REUBEN
CHAPMAN.
Married on the 27th ult. in Pulaski, Tennessee at the residence of
the bride's mother by REV. MR. McFERRIN, MR. CHARLES T. ROBINSON of
this city to MISS DORA REYNOLDS of Pulaski.
Married on 17 May 1870 by REV. M. PORTER in Tupelo (Lee Co.),
Mississippi, MR. BRANHAM MERRILL to MRS. SUSAN A. SAMPLE.
Died on 27 May 1870, MRS. SARAH ANN WILSON (nee GLENN) in her
32nd year. Consistent member of the Baptist Church, Step-daughter of
MORRIS K. TAYLOR.
Died at the residence of DR. H. A. BINFORD in this city on the
28th inst. MRS. LOUISA H. BURTON, relict of the late COL. THOMAS O.
BURTON of Henrice County, Virginia aged 67 years. She was a meek,
gentle amiable old Virginia lady and communicant of the Episcopal Church.
Died in Germantown, Pa. May 22, 1870, SAMUEL HAZZARD, formerly a
highly respectable citizen of Huntsville and one of the original members
of the Presbyterian Church of Huntsville.

June 17, 1870
Married on the 6th inst. by REV. J. H. DRAKE, MR. JAMES M. GINN to
MRS. MARY MARTIN (this county). On the 4th inst. by same, MR. GEORGE W.
SMITH to MISS MARY MARCUM (this county).
Married on the 15th at the Church of Nativity by REV. DR. BANISTER,
MR. GILBERT C. GREENWAY of Abingdon (Washington Co.), Va. to MISS ALICE
WHITE, daughter of GEN. ADDISON WHITE.
Died in this city on the 11th of consumption, MRS. ROSA B. O'NEAL,
relict of the late JAMES O'NEAL in her 56th year. Affectionate and
faithful wife, loving mother, kind friend and a true Christian woman.
Tribute of respect--Pleasant Hill Sabath School--JOSEPH W. DURYEE,
son of the late JAMES W. and MRS. MILDRED DURYEE of Huntsville, Ala.
died at his mother's residence 5 miles Northeast of Huntsville on 13 May
1870 aged 17 years 5 months and 31 days. Left a widowed mother and two
little sisters. Signed by WILLIAM M. ROPER, Supt., HENRY B. ROPER,
E. BOLEN, J. H. BRYANT.

July 1, 1870
MR. CHARLES McCALLEY died on the 25th at his brother's residence
of this vicinity, MR. THOMAS S. McCALLEY. Native of Virginia and
resided here about 20 years and was 59 years of age.

July 8, 1870
MR. ROBERT HAMLET, JR. died in this city on the 29th ult.

July 15, 1870
Married on the 18th near Trinity by REV. A. L. DAVIS, MR. R. P. FORD
to MISS ELIZA C. FULLER.
Married on the 5th inst. by REV. R. J. C. HALE, HON. JAMES M. MORAGNE
to MISS MARY HUGHES, all of Gadsden.
Died on the 9th inst. at Johnson's Wells in this county, MRS. MARY R.
BAKER, wife of L. E. BAKER and daughter of DR. C. A. JORDAN of this
vicinity.

Died on the 8th inst. of pulmonary consumption, ADA, daughter of the late JAMES NEELY aged 20 years and 4 months.

July 29, 1870
Married on the 26 of July in Columbia, Tennessee by REV. WILLIAM ESTES, MR. J. H. EWING of this city to MRS. MARY A. HILLIARD of Columbia.

Married on 30 June 1870 by REV. J. H. DRAKE, MR. GEORGE W. WEBSTER to MISS CAROLINE SADDLER all of this county.

August 5, 1870
Tribute of respect by Chapter 91, Royal Arch Masons to JOHN A. GIBSON. J. M. HAMBRICK, GEORGE C. SAUNDERS, J. W. DAVIS, committee.

Married on 26 July by REV. MR. GRAY, MR. EDD. D. STRONG of Madison County to MISS SALLIE REESE of Lincoln Co. Tenn.

August 12, 1870
MR. JAMES R. BLOUNT died here on the 10th of consumption. Good man and good citizen.

Married on 20 July at the residence of the bride's mother in Clarke Co. Ala., MISS CORNELIA P. FIGURES to MR. R. A. GILBERT of Summerfield, Ala.

Married on 2 July in Corinth, Mississippi by REV. J. W. WHITTEN, REV. THOMAS F. BROWN of the Tennessee Conference to MISS FANNIE E. KENNEY.

Died on the 6th inst. in this city, MRS. CASSANDRA SHOENBERGER, wife of MR. GEORGE SHOENBERGER.

August 19, 1870
Married on the 31 ult. near Trinity, Alabama by REV. A. L. DAVIS, MR. JAMES PHILLIPS to MISS SALLIE R. JOHNSON.

August 26, 1870
Married on the 18th by L. R. GLOVER, Esq. MR. ANDY J. HANNA to MISS SUSAN T. BRAZELTON, daughter of MR. SILAS M. BRAZELTON in this co.

Married on the 18th inst. by REV. J. H. DRAKE, MR. ELI B. SMITH to MISS ELIZABETH ANYAN, daughter of CAPT. B. S. ANYAN, all of this county.

September 9, 1870
MR. RICHARD KAVANAUGH, a most intelligent man raised here and beloved by all who knew him died in Missouri a few weeks ago. Was a son of CORTEZ D. KAVANAUGH.

Married on the 23rd in Elyton at the residence of the bride's father, HON. W. S. MUDD by REV. J. F. SMITH, MISS JENNIE T. MUDD to WILLIAM A. WALKER, JR. Esq.

Died on 7th of consumption, MRS. EMMA J. WALKER, formerly EMMA J. DeBOW and wife of ELIJAH F. WALKER of this county aged 19.

September 16, 1870
MR. WILLIAM POWERS, an old and highly respected citizen of this city died on the 14th. Born in Virginia in 1787 but had been a resident of Ala. since 1818 and was a soldier of the War of 1812.

Died on the 7th inst. near Nashville, JOHN E. TUCKER aged 58, formerly of this city.

September 30, 1870
Died in Meridianville on the 21st inst. MR. JOHN G. BENTLEY in his 66th year. MR. BENTLEY was one of our oldest and most respected citizens, having moved to this state from Virginia in 1825. He was a member of the M. E. Church South from early youth.

October 14, 1870
Died near Tibbee, Mississippi on the 9th inst., MRS. MATTIE JONES, wife of DR. RICHARD JONES, formerly of Huntsville. Remains will be buried in the cemetery here at 3 o'clock this afternoon from the Episcopal Church.

October 21, 1870
Died on the 16th, MR. WILLIAM A. McGAHA aged about 46. Left a wife and children.

Died on the 10th, MR. SAMUEL MOON aged 38.
Died on the 17th, MRS. MARY C. FOWLER, wife of MR. JOHN FOWLER
aged about 80.
Died on the 16th, MRS. LYDIA SANFORD, wife of MR. ALLEN SANFORD
aged about 55.

November 4, 1870
Died Oct. 28th, MRS. FELICIA CHAPMAN, wife of Ex-Governor
REUBEN CHAPMAN.

November 11, 1870
Died on 8th in this vicinity, MRS. SUSAN S. HOBBS, wife of
MR. ISHAM H. HOBBS.

January 6, 1871
Married in Nashville, Tennessee on the 3rd by REV. R. A. YOUNG,
D. D., MR. F. M. YOUNG to MISS LUCY LEE, daughter of W. HY. SMITH.
On the 22nd ult. in Louisville, Ky. MR. MALCOLM M. HANNAH of
Florence, Ala. to MISS JOSEPHINE CASTLEMAN of Louisville, Ky.
On the 22 of Dec. 1870 by REV. G. B. SAUNDERS, JAS. D. BRAZLETON
to MISS ANN ELIZA OWEN, all of this county.
On 23 Dec. 1870 by LOGAN R. GLOVER, Esq. MR. ROBERT F. HUNT to
MISS REBECCA E. ELLETT, all of this county.
On 20 Dec. 1870 by REV. ALEX PENLAND, MR. JAMES B. STOGNER to
MISS THEODOSIA P. GARDNER, all of this county.
On 21 Dec. 1870 by REV. ALEX PENLAND, MR. ALBERT R. ARNETTE to
MISS AMANDA GRANTLAND (20 A Wm T), all of this county.
On 8 Dec. 1870 at the residence of the bride's father near
Brooksville (Noxubee Co.), Miss. by REV. MR. WEBB, MR. G. MURRAY ROBERTSON,
formerly of this city to MISS E. O. HERRON, daughter of MR. JAMES HERRON.
In Jacksonville, Ala. on 23 Dec. 1870 by REV. MR. SMITH, MR. WM. T.
ALEXANDER to MISS JENNIE FRANK
Chancery Sale--LAWRENCE GARDNER et al versus VIRGINIA GARDNER et al.

January 13, 1871
Married Wed. the 11th by REV. ANSON WEST, DR. FRANK M. HUDSON of
Blountsville to MISS PERMELIA E. DOYLE (2 A), daughter of JOS. P. DOYLE
(26 A), Esq. of this place.
On the 11th by REV. JOHN G. WILSON, MR. EDWARD M. NEAL of Lebanon
(Wilson Co.), Tenn. to MISS BLOSSIE WHARTON, daughter of DR. G. R.
WHARTON of this vicinity.
Died Nov. 20, 1870, WILLY MAY WISHARD, daughter of STEWART and
OLIVE E. WISHARD aged 2 years and 9 mo.
Died at the residence of J. M. KENNEY in this county Dec. 28,
1870, MISS NANCY CAIN (50 V) in her 75th year.
Death of MAJ. HICKMAN:
MAJ. EDWIN HICKMAN died in this city on the 19th at the advanced
age of 85. Born in Nashville, Tenn. in 1785 just after the close of
the Revolution. We believe he spent the earlier part of his life in
the vicinity of his birthplace, a while in Huntsville, Ala. but our
first knowledge of him was at Memphis, Tenn. over which city he presided
as Chief Magistrate for many years, giving universal satisfaction. He
came to San Antonio in the year 1853, where he resided over after with
respect and love of all who ever knew him. He was not, we believe a
professor of religion, but he was a man of true noble principles and
sentiments and the soul of honor, a fine, perfect gentleman of the
old school. (From San Antonio, Tex. paper)
State of Alabama--Madison Co. Probate Court. Dec. 30, 1870.
FELIX J. JONES, executor of the will of ANN TILLER (47 V, w of BENJ.),
deceased. The following names heirs-at-law are non-residents of Ala:
ELIZABETH J. (21 A), wife of WM. ROBINSON, LUCY C. SEVERS (15 A), wife
of JOHN W. SEVERS (25 A, DAN'L H.), ABRAM L. TILLER (6 A), residing in
Phillips Co. Ark.

January 20, 1871
Married on the 17th at the residence of the bride's father by
REV. M. B. DeWITT, MR. W. W. HUMPHREY to MISS RACHAEL B. CUMMINGS.
On the 17th at the residence of the bride's father by REV. M. B.
DeWITT, MR. CHARLES M. HUMPHREY to MISS AMANDA CUMMINGS.

On the 16th at the residence of the bride's father by REV. C. B.
SANDERS, MR. SAMUEL M. STEWART to MISS KATIE A. TAYLOR, both of
Maysville, Ala.
At the residence of MR. CHARLES W. STRONG on the 12th by REV. M. B.
DeWITT, MR. GEO. SHOENBERGER to MRS. FANNIE P. DAVIS, all of this city.
On the 12th by REV. A. B. TOMLINSON, MR. ANDREW C. BAILEY to
MRS. JULIA E. CALLAHAN, all of this county.

January 27, 1871
Married on the morning of the 25th in the Presbyterian Church by
DR. F. A. ROSS, HON. ROBERT M. HOOKE of Chattanooga, Tenn. to MRS. ADA F.
STEELE of Huntsville, Ala.
Married on the 12th by REV. J. L. PAYNE, MR. JNO. M. MEADOWS to
MISS MARY F. PAYNE, all of this county.
On the 22 Dec. 1870 by REV. J. H. DRAKE, MR. JESSE F. MULLINS to
MISS JANE BELL, all of this county.
On the 18th by REV. J. H. DRAKE, MR. RICHARD GINN (2 A Jas) to
MRS. ALICE C. FOSTER, all of this county.
Died in New Market, Dec. 24, 1870, CARA, infant daughter of
MR. and MRS. ALFRED HAMBRICK aged 1 yr. and 2 mo.

February 3, 1871
Married on the 26th at Hazle Green, Ala. by REV. J. R. MORRIS,
MR. JAS. J. FOSTER to MISS ANNA S. ELLIS.
On the 26 Jan. 1871 by R. W. FIGG, Esq. at the residence of
MR. MAYHEW in this vicinity, MR. CHARLES BARRETT to MISS NELLIE MILTON.
On the morning of the 25th in the Presbyterian Church by REV. F. A.
ROSS, HON. ROBERT M. HOOKE of Chattanooga, Tenn. to MRS. CEDA (ADA) F.
STEELE of Huntsville, Ala.
Died in this city Sunday Jan. 29th, WOODSON WITHERS, infant son
of JAMES B. and SUSIE C. WHITE aged 14 months.
Died after long and useful life, COL. WM. O. WINSTON (46 V--DeKalb
census) at his residence at Valley Head, DeKalb Co. Ala. on 18th Jan.
at 6 a.m. in 67th yr. Paralysis that rendered him helpless and speech-
less. About 11 yrs. ago he associated himself with 1st Presbyterian
Church in Chattanooga, Tenn... Bereaved wife and children...

February 10, 1871
Married on the 26th by REV. JOS. R. MORRIS, MR. JAMES J. FOSTER to
MISS ANNIE T. ELLIS, all of this county.
On the 25th by REV. L. H. GRUBBS, MR. SAMUEL CANNON to MRS. CLARISSA
READING, all of this county.
On the 1st by REV. H. M. WELCH, MR. WM. G. JAMAR to MISS LOUISA
OWEN, all of this county.
On the 1st by REV. G. W. CARMICHAEL, MR. J. M. WILSON (should be
NELSON) to MISS WILLIE A. CLUNN, all of this county (Vol. 54-57;
J. M. WILSON should be NELSON--as in infor have a deed proving it also)
On the 2nd inst. by ELDER DAVID (illegible) MISS ESTHER F. CAMPBELL,
all of this county.
In Memphis, Tennessee on the 26th, MR. SAMUEL W. COOPER of
Somerville, Tennessee (Fayette Co.) to MISS EMMA WALKER NELSON, daughter
of COL. THOMAS A. NELSON.
On the 26th near Cherokee (Colbert Co.), Ala. by REV. S. H. FORD,
CAPT. J. H. FIELDS of Columbus, Miss. to MISS SALLIE MALONE.
Died in this city on the 2nd of consumption, MISS AMANDA J.
CARMICHAEL aged 16 years.
Married, MISS SALLIE POLK PILLOW, daughter of GEN. G. J. PILLOW to
MR. MELVILL WILLIAMS of Nashville on 19th.

February 17, 1871
Married on the 14th at the residence of the bride's mother in this
city by REV. FATHER McGINNIS, MR. CHRIS. McDONALD to MISS KATE CALLAGHAN,
(Y 12 A), daughter of the late MICHAEL CALLAGHAN (37 Ire), all of this
city.
At residence of MR. LEVI DONALDSON by REV. JOS. R. MORRIS,
MR. AUGUSTUS D. RODGERS (3 A Robt) to MISS ZORA F. VAUGHN, all of this
county.
On 18th near Hazle Green by REV. JOS. R. MORRIS, DR. J. B. W. NOWLIN
of Tenn. to MISS BETTIE MAUPIN of this county.

Died on the 10th, the infant son of MR. and MRS. J. F. BROWN of this city. Funeral from Cumberland Presbyterian Church Sat. eve. at 4 o'clock.

February 24, 1871

Married at the Catholic Church on 21 Feb. 1871 by REV. FATHER McGINNIS, MR. ALBERT SWEENEY to MISS CATHARINE NAGLE, both of Huntsville, Ala.

Married on the 15th by REV. F. M. PROCTOR, MR. JOHN H(ENRY) BRYANT to MISS ANN ELIZA McGAHA (8 A, d of Jas), all of this county. (BETTY's grandparents)

On 14th by REV. C. B. SANDERS, MR. JOSEPH B. KELLY to MISS MOLLIE KELEN.

On 2nd by OTHNIEL RICE, Esq., MR. SILAS THOMPSON to MISS ELIZA J. C. CAMPBELL.

BOWERS
Census of 1850 p 206 (see Vol 54)
Pro Rec 42 p 345. Petition for division of land of DAVID BOWERS who died 9 Sept. 1902. LIZZIE D. BOWERS purchased the interest of W. D. BOWERS, a son, as shown by deed of W. D. BOWERS and wife LULA. The following children of sd DAVID BOWERS are each entitled to a 1/7th interest of the estate.

1. EDWARD L. BOWERS of Mooresville. (Census is T; will have to check)
2. NANNIE MOORE, Hillsboro, Tex. (She m HEZEKIAH P. MOORE, 1865)
3. JESSE BOWERS, Madison, Ala.
4. LIZZIE V. BOWERS by right of purchase from W. D. BOWERS.
5. The children of SARAH FARRALD dec'd, over 21:
   WILL FARRALD, supposed to be in Va.
   JOHN   "   "   " " " Hillsboro, Texas
   JIM   "   "   " " " Purdom, Texas
   IDA   "   "   " " " Madison, Ala.
   OLA   "   "   " " " Memphis, Tenn. m. GEORGE BELOTE
   BOWERS   "   "   " " " (minor) Madison Ala...another
                                  place says over 21
6. The children of FANNIE RUSSELL dec'd
   OLEN RUSSELL, a minor, Russellville, Indian Territory
   HERMAN   "   "   "
7. The children of MARY AKERS dec'd
   HOUSTON AKERS, Dawson, Texas
   CHESTER   "   "   "
   NINA   "   "   " (a minor)
   Other children, minors, at Dawson, Tex. but unable to secure their names.
       Petition signed by T. J. BOWERS, 16 Feb. 1905
   I have on my census record his dates as d 1902 and hers as b 6/8/22 and d 10/6/03 (obit)

Married in Lincoln Co. Tenn. on 8th by REV. T. T. JONES, MR. GEORGE J. COBLE and MISS SUSAN VIRGINIA FREEMAN.

Married in Lincoln Co. Tenn. on 9th by J. G. LAXSON, Esq., MR. ROBERT SMITH to MISS MARY L. HOBBS.

In Lincoln Co. Tenn. by R. N. BERRY, MR. JAMES HENRY HONEY to MISS MARTHA J. WICKER on 12th.

March 3, 1871

Married on 16 Feb. by REV. H. M. WELCH, MR. ETHELRED Q. JAMAR to MISS SALLIE PENLAND (1853-1888), all of this county. (she was d of REV. ALEX PENLAND--see preacher index; buried at Ebenezer Church. Cen notebook XIV p 26).

On 15 Feb. by REV. M. E. JOHNSON, MR. BENJ. F. McDONALD (McDOWELL) to MISS MARGARET A. JOHNSON (RAMBERSON), all of this county. (see p 59 - 15 Feb by M. E. JOHNSON. BENJAMIN F. McDOWELL to MARGARET A. LAMBERSON - (That printer was drunk! or else so badly written he couldn't read it))

On 15 Feb. 1871 by REV. J. W. WHITTEN (see Vol 123 p 40) MISS PAULINE P(OCAHONTAS?) MORRISON. (see vol 123 p 40, 3 P & B(RIDGET) ALEX. C. CHISHOLM)

Died in Madison Co. on 18th, ELLEN DOUGLASS BOWERS, daughter of EDWARD and ROMANIA T. BOWERS.

Died on 16th near Cherokee, Ala. MR. GOODLOE MALONE (52 NC, Franklin Co. Census), formerly of this city. (of Colbert Co.--see vol 56 p 70)

State of Alabama-Madison Co. Probate Ct. Feb. 27, 1871. This day came A. A. CARY and wife, CATHARINE T. CARY (28), legatee and heir-at-law, and propounded for probate instrument of writing purporting to be the last will and testament of MILES KING (12 A, JOHN D). The following named heirs-at-law are non-residents of Ala. viz: JOHN W. KING, resides at Covington (Kenton Co.), Kentucky; MARY PRICE (23 A) and her husband, --------PRICE, resides in San Francisco, Cal; MRS. SALLIE McGEHEE, wife of A. F. McGEHEE and ROSALIND KING (8A) in Panola Co. Mississippi; JENNIE BEALE and SHEPPARD BEALE, residence unknown; and JAMES KING, residence in Mississippi; JENNIE BEALE and JAMES KING are minors (bros & sisters of MILES KING).

JAMES B. JAMES aged 80 and PLEAS. WHITECOTTON aged 33 died in Cherokee Co. last week.

March 10, 1871
Married on the 23rd by REV. J. J. BURDINE, MR. JOSEPH R. WALKER to MISS MARY D. SLOAN, all of Madison Co.

Died on 5th of pneumonia, LEROY P. McCRARY, son of B. P. and LAVINIA McCRARY aged 17 years 10 mo.

March 17, 1871
Died at Whitesburg, Alabama March 5, 1871, MRS. ELIZABETH JANE RADFORD aged 37 years 11 days.

On the 10th after a short illness, MR. C(HRISTOPHER) B. WILLIAMS (s of WM. & MARTHA K) of this vicinity. He was a good man and a quiet orderly citizen and had many friends.

March 24, 1871
Resolutions on death of BRO. C. B. WILLIAMS by I. O. O. F. Lodge no. 25.

HON. S. L. RUGG of Indiana, father of COL. D. C. RUGG of this place died on 28th aged 65. Stood high as a man and was the father of the public school system in Indiana.

April 14, 1871
Married on the 4th by REV. M. B. DeWITT, MR. C(HARLES) H. CUMMINGS to MRS. MARY HARRIS, all of this city.

Died at the residence of her mother, MRS. SALLIE WATKINS near Jackson, Mississippi Mar. 24, 1871, MRS. MARIAN SHELBY ROSS, wife of COL. F. W. ROSS, daughter of the late DR. MILES S. WATKINS, formerly of Huntsville.

April 21, 1871
Married on the 12th at the residence of the bride's mother in this city by REV. ANSON WEST, MR. ANDREW TANNOCK, JR. to MISS SUE W. CAROTHERS (9A JOSEPH), all of this city.

April 28, 1871
ALEX. EDDINS died in Lincoln County, Tennessee on the 13th aged 72; and MRS. MARY HILL on the 19th aged 76.

In DeKalb Co. Tenn. MOSES BLYE was killed and SAMPSON TRAMWELL whipped by disguised men.

Married on the 30th by REV. J. W. BROWN, MR. WM. A. STEWART to MISS MARTHA McCLURE all of this county.

On the 6th by REV. ALEX. PENLAND, MR. W. D. GARDNER to MISS MARY STOGNER, all of this county.

Married on the 6th by REV. W. WEAKLEY, MR. THOMAS B. LEE to MISS PARTHENIA GIBSON, all of this county.

Married on the 16th by REV. A. S. LAKIN, MR. WM. C. WELLS to MISS EMMA EZELL, all of this county.

On the 16th by REV. M. B. DeWITT, MR. JACOB HORSCH to MISS SENA (or Soma?) HORN, all of this county.

On the 20th by R. D. WILSON, Esq., MR. JAS. A. HOOK to MISS BETTIE MOFFITT, all of this county.

"MAJ. WELDON of Selma died on the 22nd."

May 5, 1871
    Married on the 20th by REV. M. B. DeWITT, MR. JNO. H. JAMES to
MISS ALLIS CONNERLY.
    On 29th by REV. M. B. DeWITT, FERDINAND BANGEST to MISS MARY J.
HORTNER.
    On 20th by JOHN S. BRONAUGH, Esq., MR. JOHN SMITH to MISS BETTIE
FREEMAN.
    On 16th by REV. J. S. COLLINS (V), MR. SAMUEL H. WALKER to
MISS ROSANNA BOSTICK (3 A N).
    On 26th Apr. by REV. DR. H. STRINGFELLOW in Episcopal Church,
REV. W. R. C. COCKE of Virginia to MISS CLARA VERNON, daughter of
COL. CHARLES T. POLLARD of Montgomery, Ala.
    Died on 25 Apr. near Madison, Ala. MRS. MARY F. TROTMAN (42 T,
w of SAM'L) aged 63.
    (Letter from MRS. W. R. CARTER, 5021 Wooddale Lane, Minneapolis,
Minn 55424 Aug. 30, 1963. "Do you have death notice of MRS.
WILSFORD, grandmother of JAMES A. P. SKILLERN, d. July 21, 1873 near
Pulaski, Tenn. It might have been in a Hr paper. How about death
notice of JAMES A. P. SKILLERN, alive in 1880 & later hotel keeper at
Pulaski.")

May 12, 1871
    Married on the 3rd by REV. J. G. WILSON, D.D., FELIX W. SIBLEY
(10 A, ABRAM H), Esq. to MISS SALLIE E. FERGUSON (6 A, ROBT), all of
Madison Co.
    At Church of Nativity on 4th by REV. DR. BANISTER, MR. SAMUEL
PLEASANTS to MISS MARIE BLEDSOE, daughter of DR. D. SHELBY, all of
this city.
    On 2nd in Giles Co. Tenn. by REV. C. MITCHELL, MR. J(AMES) A. P.
SKILLERN to MISS IDA B. daughter of REV. R. CALDWELL.
    On 3 at Concord (Knox Co.), Tenn. by REV. MR. BROWN, MR. MARK PATE
of Concord to MISS EMMA SHANKLIN of this city.
    On 3rd by REV. M. P. BROWN, MR. J. W. JEFFRIES, formerly of
Virginia to MISS MOLLIE E. CLOPTON of Winchester, Tenn.
    On 13 April at residence of her father in Madison Co., MRS. MARY E.
(3 A), wife of GEORGE H. BRITTON (12 A, GEO. H.) and daughter of
OTHNIEL (53 NC) and MARY RICE (35 T) died aged 24 years 3 months and
20 days; of consumption.

May 19, 1871
    MR. GEO. T. JONES (1790-1871) of this county died at his residence
near New Market on the 4th inst. aged 81 years. He was for a great
many years a prominent and useful citizen taking a lively interest in
public affairs and had been a member of the Legislature. He was noted
for his energy, good sense and probity.
    COL. HAL. C. CHAMBERS of Miss. died a few days since. Native of
Huntsville.

May 26, 1871
    Married in Fayetteville, Tenn. on the 11th by REV. MAT. M. MARSHALL,
MR. S. W. CARMACK to MISS MATTIE G. ROSS.
    Died on the 23rd at residence of his mother near Huntsville of
consumption, LOUIS T. POLLARD (G in census; 13 V) aged 34.

June 2, 1871
    Married on the 23rd in this city by REV. MR. BUSSEY, MR. JOHN C.
ENNIS to MRS. SALLIE ANN SPAULDING, all of Huntsville.
    Married on the 16th at Falmouth, Ky. by REV. MR. BARBEE, MR.
G. J. DAWSON of Dawson Bros. & Co., Huntsville, to MISS ALICE ROBERTS.
    At Vidalia (Concordia Par), La. on 10 May by HON. THOMAS RIBER,
WILLIAM J. SLATTER of Tennessee to MISS BERTA BARROW of La.
    Died at his residence in this city on Thursday evening May 25,
1871 CHAS. W. CUMMINGS, formerly of Wilson Co. Tenn.
    HON. J. J. CHAPEL died in Lowndes Co. last week in his 90th year.
He was the oldest ex-member of Congress, having served several years
from South Carolina.
    DR. ROBT. M(ASON) CLARK (55 NC--Lawrence Co. 1850 Cen), father of
JUDGE J. S. CLARK died on the 11th in his 81st year. He was a soldier
in the War of 1812; a Mason, an honest man and a Christian.

Died in Lincoln Co. Tenn. MRS. FOSTER, aged 80; MR. RUFUS D. FLAUTT aged 38 and MR. AMOS GORE aged 72 died last week. (MRS. TOMMIE BRITTAIN, Pasadena, Tex 1970 asks about AMOS GORY, GOREE or GOREY who m. a dau of JOHN BRITTAIN.)

June 9, 1871
    Married on the 7th by REV. M. B. DeWITT, JESSE B. SHIVERS, Esq. of Marion, Ala. to MISS MARIA LOUISA, daughter of JAMES B. ROBINSON, Esq. of this place.
    On 25 May by B. W. BUSSEY, MR. DAVID A. WOOLDRIDGE to MISS ELIZA J. WILLIAMS.
    At Presbyterian Church in Oxford, Ala. on 23 by REV. MR. McLAIN, DR. W. W. HARRISON of Madison Co. to MISS ANNIE GLADDEN, daughter of MR. JAMES A. GLADDEN of Oxford.
    Died on the 26th in New Orleans, MRS. SYLLA WITHERSPOON, wife of CAPT. H. E. WITHERSPOON and daughter of GEN. JONES M. WITHERS.
    A. P. WIMBISH of Clark Co. Ala. was killed a few days ago by MR. CHAPMAN.

June 16, 1871
    In Lincoln Co. Tenn. MR. L. W. NELSON was married to MISS J. E. KING; MR. JOHN H. SCOTT to MISS SUSAN P. MINSETT and W. T. ROSS to MISS ANNIE W. MILLER; and MINOS CANNON aged 24 years and MRS. MARTHA J. SHORT aged 47 died.
    MYERS FISHER a well known citizen of Mobile died on the 5th.
    Married on the 7th by REV. OLIVER WELCH, HON. JAMES CROOK of Calhoun Co. to MISS JENNIE P. daughter of the late WALKER REYNOLDS of Talladega Co.
    Died on the 15th, HOLLIS BARCLAY, son of MR. and MRS. WM. P. NEWMAN of this place aged 2 years 10 mo. and 19 days.
    On the 12th of congestion, SAMUEL P. son of ROBERT W. and MATTIE COLTART.
    In Wetumpka, Ala. on 6th of chronic liver complaint, MRS. LUCY JANE ROOT, wife of REV. TIMOTHY ROOT in her 67th year.

June 23, 1871
    Married on the 15th at the residence of the bride's father, MR. WM. C. WINSTON, MR. WILLIAM A. HUNT to MISS FANNIE A. WINSTON of this city.
    Married on the 7th by REV. J. H. DRAKE, MR. ANGELO R. ALLISON to MISS SALLIE C. ANYAN, all of this county.
    Married on the 9th of Mar. 1871 by REV. J. H. DRAKE, MR. BLUFORD HYMEN to MISS FRANCES M. McPETERS, all of this county.
    On the 18th by REV. L. HENSLY GRUBBS, DR. JOSEPH M. PHILLIPS to MISS FANNIE J. daughter of MR. JAMES ARNETT.
    Died at Bay of St. Louis, Miss. June 10, 1871, MRS. MARY SMITH CALHOUN (40 SC), relict of the late MEREDITH CALHOUN (50 Pa) and granddaughter of the late JUDGE WILLIAM SMITH, formerly of this city. Member of Protestant Episcopal Church.
    C. L. VALLANDDIGHAM dead--was born in 1822; a man of decided ability.
    "LEWIS B. MOSELEY (49 G), a prominent citizen of Selma is dead."

June 30, 1871
    Married on the 20th by REV. J. A. MILLHOUSE, MR. YANCEY P. TROTMAN (s of SAM'L Vol 59 p 222) to MRS. SARAH E. CRUTCHER.
    Married on May 23 by DICKSON COBB, Esq., MR. GEO. VANN to MISS JULIA LEDBETTER.
    Married on 25th May by DICKSON COBB, Esq., MR. ASBERRY CARMACK to MISS MARY A. D. R. VANN.
    Married on 7 May by DICKSON COBB, Esq., MR. WM. D. OWEN to MISS ELIZA J. GLASS.
    Married on May 20 by ELDER JOHN N. BROWN, MR. HUGH TAYLOR to MISS NANCY E. WILHELMS.
    Married in Natchez (Adams Co.), Miss. June 3 by REV. J. B. SCRATTON, D.D., HON. TURNER REAVIS of Gainesville, Ala. to MISS SALLIE MOSBY of Natchez.
    Married at Jacksonville, Ala. on the 19th by REV. JAMES M. McLEAN, HON. A. J. WALKER, late Chief Justice of Supreme Court of Ala. to MISS CLARA NESBIT of Jacksonville, Ala.

Died in this city on the 26th, ARTHUR HAMPTON, son of JAMES H. and FRANCIS M. LANDMAN, a few weeks old.

Died in this county on the 23rd, CHARLIE ANN, daughter of LEVI W. and MARTHA D. ESLINGER aged about 11 mo.

Died at the family residence on Franklin St. on the 22nd, MRS. ISAPHEENA BASSETT aged 60 years, wife of the late DR. JOHN Y. BASSETT.

July 7, 1871

Married on June 26 in this county by H. H. HARTON, Esq. MR. WM. .G. JOHNSON to MISS ANNIE M. CHUNN, all of Madison Co.

Married at the residence of the bride's father, GEN. E. W. PETTUS in Selma Tue. June 27 by REV. MR. LOWRY of the Presbyterian Church, MR. THEOPHILUS LACY, JR. of Huntsville to MISS MOLLIE N. PETTUS.

Died on 22 June near Madison Roads, Alabama, MARK H. CROCKER, an old and highly respected citizen of this county, after lingering 14 years with chronic rheumatism. He was about 52. Brandon (Rankin Co.) (Miss.) Republican please copy.

WILLIAM FRAZIER was scalded to death in Dallas Co. Ala. last week by bursting of a saw mill engine.

July 21, 1871

DR. JAMES B. ALEXANDER of Mobile died on the 13th aged 47.

July 28, 1871

Married on the 23 by DICKSON COBB, Esq. MR. WM. C. POOR to MISS MARY L. CRAFT, daughter of the late JOHN CRAFT, all of this county.

Died in this city on 22nd, GEORGE BEIRNE PATTON, son of MR. WM. PATTON in his 20th year.

Died on the 16th in this city, GEORGE W. JR. infant son of GEO. and SARAH J. HERBERT aged 6 months and 6 days.

Died on the 18th at the residence of COL. THOMAS H. HEWLETT in Madison Co. Ala., MARY LOUISA, infant daughter of C. H. and MYRTICE BANKS of Marianna (Lee Co.), Ark. (to McLane)

August 4, 1871

Married on 2 August in the Methodist Church by REV. J. G. WILSON, MR. BENJAMIN S. TURNER to MISS ADDIE M. JORDAN, daughter of DR. C. A. JORDAN, all of this place.

Married on 19 July at the residence of DR. BURKE in Meridianville, by REV. J. R. MORRIS, MR. RICHARD A. CHUNN to MISS MARY E. BURKE.

Married on 29 June by REV. JOHN W. BROWN, MR. JOHN D. OWEN to MISS MARTHA E. J. VANN, all of this county.

Died at his residence in this place on Sunday night 30 July of consumption, CAPT. DAVID H. TODD, formerly of Kentucky, but for last six years a resident of Huntsville, in his 40th year. Served in the Mexican War, was engaged in a Revolution in Chili and visited Japan etx. and was a Captain in the Confederate army.

Died at the residence of his sister, MRS. CLARISSA H. TONEY, MR. GEORGE W. NOBLE, formerly a printer in Huntsville. We think he served his initiate in Southern Advocate office under the late DANDRIDGE FARISS. He was about 60 years of age, a good printer and a man of amiable character.

August 11, 1871

Married on the 3rd at Tennessee House in Pulaski, Tennessee by REV. L. HENSLEY GRUBBS, MR. JAMES R. SPRAGINS to MISS SALLIE KATE, daughter of the late JAMES H. BIBB, all of Madison, Ala.

Married on July 12 by REV. J. H. DRAKE, MR. JOHN M. McNIEL to MISS MARTHA M. BRAZELTON, all of this county.

August 25, 1871

Married in Pulaski, Tennessee on the 10th by REV. JAMES BRADLEY of Columbia, PROF. Z. WHITFIELD EWING to MISS HATTIE JONES, daughter of MAJ. THOMAS M. JONES of Pulaski.

September 1, 1871

Married on 17th by OTHNIEL RICE, Esq. MR. DEMPSEY HALE to MISS AMANDA C. SHEPHERD.

Married on the 13th by LOGAN R. GLOVER, Esq. MR. GEORGE P. FULERMANN to MISS HARRIET MOORE.

Died on the 26th August in this city, MRS. RUTH CROSS aged 72. Affectionate mother. For about 40 years a member of the M. E. Church.

September 8, 1871

Died on the 6th in Corinth, Mississippi of pulmonary consumption JAMES H. NORVELL, son of MR. R. B. NORVELL, formerly of this city aged 20 years.

Died in this city on the 4th, ARCHIE, son of GEORGE P. and MARY F. LANDMAN aged 19 months.

September 15, 1871

Married on the 27th at Wayland Springs, Tennessee by JAMES A. STEWART, J.P., MR. PLEASANT SMALLWOOD to MISS A. C. JOHNSON.

Married on Sept. 5 at the residence of the bride by REV. H. P. TURNER, MR. BURWELL C. GARNER to MRS. ELIZABETH BURNETT, all of this county.

Married on the 7th at the residence of the bride's mother, by REV. JAMES S. BARTEE, MR. WILLIAM M. GORMLEY to MISS MARY ELLEN SULLIVAN all of this county.

Married on the 6th at the residence of COL. ANDREW ERWIN of Lafayette (Chambers Co.), Ala. by REV. S. C. HEARN, MR. JAMES RENDER DOWDELL to MISS ROSA TURNER, niece of MRS. ANDREW ERWIN (nee ELVIRA SEARCY). (see Tenn Vol 7 p 69--d of DAN'L B. TURNER & wife SUSAN D. SEARCY)

Died in this city on the 11th, VIOLA YOUNG, infant child of MR. and MRS. WILLIAM LAWLER aged about 6 weeks old.

We regret to learn that MRS. MATILDA WALKER DOX, wife of HON. P. M. DOX of this place died here on the 13th.

GEN. THOMAS McCOY of Mobile died on the 1st aged 64.

In Baldwin Co. MISS ELIZABETH S. DADE died on the 27th aged 94 years 6 months.

September 22, 1871

Married in Frederick City, Maryland on 6 Sept. by FATHER SMITH, MR. J. H. WHITE of the firm of COXE & WHITE of this city to MISS S. BIRDIE JOHNSON of Frederick City.

Married on 14th at the residence of the bride's father in this city by REV. ANSON WEST, MR. CHARLES A. GILL to MISS SUE C. BLAKEMORE.

Married on the 13th in Cincinnati, O., MR. ISAIAH WEIL of this city to MISS EMMA L. WERTHEIMER of Cincinnati.

Married in Arkadelphia (Clark Co., to McLane), Ark. August 27th by REV. J. F. CARR, MR. JAMES D. TATUM to MRS. MATTIE T. RUSSELL (nee SANFORD).

Died in Coahoma Co. Miss. on 10 Sept. JOHN J. WEBSTER, formerly of this county, son of JAMES L. WEBSTER, aged 32 years 11 months and 7 days, leaving a wife and 4 small children.

Died on the 10th near Meridianville, ROBERT WALTER PRUITT, son of MR. JOHN W. PRUITT aged about 25.

HON. JAMES F. DOWDELL, Col. of 37th Ala. Regiment during the late war died at his residence in Auburn (Lee Co.), Alabama on the 12th.

HON. JAMES F. DOWDELL of Chambers Co. died last week. He was formerly a Member of Congress.

MAJ. MACE T(HOMAS) P(ARGNE) BRINDLEY (he was bro of ASA REGGS BRINDLY of Cherokee Co.) of Blount died about 2 weeks ago at an advanced age; for many years a member of both Houses of the Legislature. Also JUDGE JOHN C. GILLESPIE, for many years Clerk and Probate Judge of Blount. Both were old citizens.

September 29, 1871

Died on the 17th in this county, TOMES O. BURTON, son of THOMAS O. and MINNIE BURTON aged nearly 12 years.

HON. WM. WOODWARD (@ 58 SC; b York Dist SC Nov 15, 1792 moved to Chester Dist 1820 to Ga 3 yrs later, to Greene Co. Ala 1834 to Sumter Co.1838) of Choctaw, for many years a member of the State Senate died last week aged 78. Baptist minister. (d. Sept. 7, 1871)

REV. E(UGENE) STRODE, formerly a Baptist minister here and a man of decided ability, earnestness and usefulness died in Springfield

(Robertson Co.), Tennessee on the 24th. Remains were brought to
Huntsville for interment. (gf of HUDSON STRODE)

October 6, 1871
    Married in this city September 28th at the residence of
MR. WILLIAM R. RISON by REV. J. M. BANISTER, D.D., MR. FRANK S. HORTON,
of Mobile to MISS AMANDA N. COLEMAN, daughter of the late JOHN J.
COLEMAN of Huntsville.
    Died in this city on the 4th, MISS NELLIE LEE JOLLEY, daughter of
BENJAMIN and CAROLINE E. JOLLEY aged 16 years 4 months and 3 days.
    Died on the 30th at his residence near Meridianville, MR. CHARLES
THOMAS, an old and well-known citizen.
    Died on the 1st after a long and painful illness, MRS. AMERICA
GERON, wife of MR. C(LAIBORN) C(OLE) GERON of this place. (Bible says d
2 Oct 1871--buried in Huntsville on family plot)

October 20, 1871
    Married at Cumberland Presbyterian Church in Maysville, Ala. at
8½ P.M. October 15th by REV. C. B. SANDERS, D. C. GORDON, Esq., Sheriff
of Phillips County, Arkansas (to McLane) to MRS. COOSIE JONES.
    Married in Madison, Ala. Oct. 9th at the residence of DR. G. R.
SULLIVAN by REV. L. HENSLY GRUBBS, MR. JAMES M. DOUTHIT to MISS SUSAN E.
DEDMAN.
    Died on the 18th in this place, WILLIAM R. infant son of JAMES W.
and CALEDONIA POLLARD.

October 27, 1871
    Married at Nashville, Tennessee October 18th by REV. DR. KELLEY,
COL. L. H. SCRUGGS of this city to MISS EMMA COOLEY of Nashville.
    Died on the 24th of heart disease, MR. JAMES W. BURWELL in his
69th year. Good citizen of the county, had lived here for over 20
years. (b Westmoreland Co. Va. Jan 1, 1803 d 1871 Huntsville, Ala.
m. 1. VIRGINIA BROOKS SALE b 1808 - 2. ANNE WALKER SALE, sister of Va--
J. W. was son of JAMES & JUDITH (BALL) BURWELL; gr-son (JONAS) BURWELL,
etc. Data from a prof. gen. L. L. M. S. NEES, Lexington, Miss)
    MRS. JULIA B. GARRETT, wife of COL. WM. GARRETT died last week in
Coosa Co. Ala.
    CAPT. JOE WALKER of Mobile died last week.
    COL. THOMAS McC(ARROLL) PRINCE of Choctaw Co. Ala. died on the
13th. He was one of the old Whig leaders of former days.

November 3, 1871
    Married at the residence of MR. F. MASTIN in the vicinity of
Huntsville October 24th, MR. EDWIN J. AMISS of Blacksburg (Montgomery
Co.), Va. to MISS REBECCA E. W. MASTIN.
    HON. JOHN A. LEWIS of Russell Co. Ala. died last week. He had
been Probate Judge and served in the State Senate.

November 10, 1871
    Married on the 1st in Holmes Co. Miss. MR. ROBERT NANCE OF
Madison County, Alabama to MISS FANNIE BINFORD.

November 17, 1871
    Married on the 15th at Huntsville Hotel by REV. J. M. BANISTER,
MR. MARK GRAYSON to MRS. JENNIE GILBERT REESE, both members of Gilbert
Dramatic Troupe.
    Married on the 13th by ROBERT W. FIGG, Esq. MR. WM. F. WILSON to
MISS ADELAIDE POWELL, both of this city.
    On the same day by same, MR. JAMES R. WOOLDRIDGE to MISS SARAH J.
MOONEY.
    Married on the 7th at Simmsport, Aveyelles Parish, La. by F. M.
PAVEY, J. P., CAPT. W. E. FLETCHER to MISS ANNIE M. LEIGH.
    At Methodist Church in this city, Thursday evening the 9th by
REV. J. G. WILSON, MR. THOMAS B. TROTMAN to MISS ETTIE COOPER, daughter
of JOHN W. COOPER, Esq., Sheriff of the county, all of this city.
    Married on the 7th at the residence of JUDGE NATHAN GREEN in
Lebanon (Wilson Co.), Tennessee by REV. MR. DARNELL, MR. H. L. BENTLEY
of Union City (Obion Co.), Tennessee to MISS ALICE M. GREEN of Lebanon,
Tenn.

Married in Memphis, Tennessee October 11th, MR. THOMAS H. BROCCHUS
to MISS F(?)anthe(?) PENN, formerly of this city.
Died in New Market October 11, MR. EDWARD DARNABY aged 70.   An
old citizen of this county.

November 24, 1871
Married on the 16th in Lynchburg (Campbell Co.), Virginia by
REV. DR. GREENFIELD, MR. JAMES O. WILSON of this city to MISS AMERICA V.
CRAIG of Lynchburg, Va.
Married in this county on the 8th at the residence of the bride's
mother by REV. M. E. JOHNSTON, MR. WM. E. D. STEGER to MISS IDA DAVIS
(note: In our records, it is "ADA" DAVIS.P.J.G.)
On the same day by same at the bride's residence, MR. JEROME A.
WINSTON to MISS IDA FERGUSON, all of this county.
Died on the 20th of consumption, MRS. ELLA BURKE, wife of DR. BURKE
of Meridianville in this county.

December 1, 1871
Married on the 28th of November at the residence of J. SHEFFER by
ROBERT W. FIGG, Esq. MR. HENRY JAGER to MRS. ELIZABETH ALLEN, both of
this county.
Married on 15 November by REV. M. B. DeWITT, MR. ROBERT J. MOORE
to MISS SALLIE L. WHITNEY, all of this county.
Married on 16 November by REV. JOHN N. BRAGG, MR. ROBERT SMITHEY
to MISS JANE FITCH, all of this county.
Married on Sunday, Nov., at residence of REV. L. HENSLEY GRUBBS
at Madison, Ala. MR. LAFAYETTE SAUNDERSON to MISS SARAH A. PATRICK.
Married on the 22nd at the residence of the bride's father by
REV. DR. ROSS, DR. J. A. GREAVES of West Tennessee to MISS GRACIE D.
COLTART of this city.

December 8, 1871
Married on the 6th at the residence of MR. WILLIAM SPRAGUE by
REV. ANSON WEST, MR. SKILTON SMITH of Jackson, Tennessee to MISS BETTIE
ROBINSON of this city.
Married on the 8th at the residence of the bride's father,
MR. HENRY STEPHENS, MR. JAMES M. McKINNEY to MISS M. M. STEPHENS, all
of this county.
Married in Staunton (Augusta Co.), Virginia on the 28th by
REV. WILLIAM BAKER, MR. V. A. NUCKOLS of this county to MISS SUE ALLEN.
Married on the 15th in Grove Hill, Clarke Co. Ala. DR. BRYAN
BOROUGHS to MISS LIZZIE M. DICKINSON, daughter of ex-Congressman,
JAMES S. DICKINSON, CSA.
Died on the 23rd at Madison Station, DR. WM. B(ARHAM) DUNN (43 NC),
an old and much respected citizen.   (son of JOHN of Teale Co., see
Vol 104; m. 1. (1829) ELIZA ANN DUNN d of JOHN, 2. JACKEY G. DUNN
Dec 1841, Lauderdale Co. Vol. 230 p 2)
Died on the 3rd, MR. RICHARD A. WIGGINS (40 NC), well-known by all.
MRS. RICHARD ROBERS was thrown from a horse in DeKalb Co. Ala.
last week and killed.
SAM ANTHONY of Jefferson Co. killed himself accidentally last week
with a gun.

December 15, 1871
Married at the residence of the bride's father on the 7th by
REV. H. P. TURNER, MR. WM. J. JONES to MISS MARY S. NEAVES, all of
this county.
Married on the 10th by WM. M. ROZELL, Esq., MR. JOHN S. HARBIN to
MISS ALICE LANGLEY, all of this county.
Married on the 30th by REV. T. REDCOAT, MR. RANDOLPH McHIEAILES
to MISS NANCY DANIEL, all of this county.
Married on the 6th by ELDER T. G. MILLER, MR. THOMAS J. MERRING to
MISS MARY A. LAWLER, daughter of MR. JAMES H. LAWLER of this county.
Obituary:
MRS. JOHN J. FAEKLER (ELIZABETH W. TURNER; M. in mar rec) died.
She was born in Caroline County, Virginia August 11, 1804.   Removed to
Huntsville in 1823, was married to JOHN J. FACKLER January 17, 1826,
became a member of the Presbyterian Church under the ministry of

REV. DR. JOHN ALLEN in 1829; died Dec. 11, 1871 at 11 P.M. aged 67 years
and 4 months...

Died on 9th Dec. at the residence of his parents on Monroe St.,
North Nashville, JOHNNIE, infant son of JOHN W. and LYDIA WATKINS aged
17 months.

SOLOMON SEAGROVES (@ 73 NC) of Chambers Co. Ala. died on the 4th
aged 107. His wife (SARAH @ 62 NC) is still living and is over 100.

In Monroe Co. Ala. on the 29th, two old and respected citizens,
ENOCH RILEY (@ 39 SC) and JEHIAL COTTON (@ 39 SC) killed each other.

COL. JAMES McADORY, an old citizen of Jefferson Co. Ala. died on
the 3rd.

ARTHUR McCLUNG, Esq. formerly of Huntsville was married to MISS
MARY E. LEE of Pickensville, Ala. at that place on 23 November.

December 22, 1871

Married in this city on 21st by REV. FATHER BAAZAR, CAPT. P(?) H.
FLOOD of Washington, D.C. to MISS IDA L. FRYE of Huntsville.

Married on the 6th at the residence of the bride's father in Mobile
(MARY BURTON HALE'S grandparents) by REV. DR. BURGITT, MR. WM. E. MATHEWS
of this city to MISS CARRIE M. TARDY, daughter of BR. TARDY, Esq.

Married on the 14th at the residence of L. H. LANIER, Esq. in
Nashville, Tennessee by REV. DR. A. J. BAIRD, MR. TOM MANEY to
MISS IDA MORRIS.

Married in Mobile on the 12th by W. E. JENNINGS, Esq. MR. JEREMIAH
McCLELLAN of Austin (Travis Co.), Texas to MISS VIRGINIA BEEMAN of this
city.

Married on the 12th by REV. B. W. BUSSEY, MR. EDWARD C. STRONG to
MISS BETTIE ALLEN, all of this county.

Married on the 12th by REV. JOHN A. BRYAN, MR. JOHN W. IKARD, JR.
to MISS MARY E. CLARKE, all of this county.

December 29, 1871

Married in this city on the 21st by REV. FATHER BAAZAR, CAPT.
P. H. FLOOD of Washington, D.C. to MISS IDA L. FRYE of Huntsville.

Married near Madison, Ala. on the 20th by REV. J. G. WILSON, D.D.,
WILLIAM J. GLADISH, JR. to MISS LILLIAS N. CURTI(S?), all of this
county.

Married at the residence of the bride's mother (MRS. H. G. PORTER),
on the 20th by REV. THOMAS MADDIN, D.D., THOMAS M. STEGER to NANNIE G.
EAKIN.

MR. BENDALL S. ANYAN died on the 24th at an advanced age. A
well-known citizen.

January 5, 1872

Married on the 27th by REV. J. H. DRAKE, MR. FREDERICK BENNETT to
MRS. SUE PHIPPS, all of this county.

Married on the 13th by R. W. FIGG, Esq., MR. GEORGE G. EDWARDS to
MISS MARTHA ANDREW, all of this county.

Married on the 20th by REV. T. G. MILLER, MR. JOS. M. STEGER to
MISS CALLIE D. LAWLER, daughter of MR. JOHN LAWLER, all of this county.

Married on the 20th by DR. F. A. ROSS, MR. WM. A. BOYD to MISS
BETTIE G. HUEY, daughter of MR. JOHN HUEY, all of this county.

Married on the 26th by REV. ANSON WEST, MR. AUGUSTUS KEMPER to
MRS. ELIZABETH P. ADAY, all of this county.

Died on the 29th in Blount County of apoplexy, MR. GEORGE W. WEAVER
of this place aged about 30. Well known and had many friends and
relatives.

Died on the 1st after a short illness, MR. CHRIS. B. DONEGAN of
this place. Had a most brilliant mind, many noble qualities and hosts
of friends. Served in the 4th Ala. and was a gallant Confederate.

COL. GEO. W. DENT, late CSA is dead.

January 12, 1872

Married on the 3rd at the residence of the bride's mother in this
city by REV. W. D. F. SAWRIE of Nashville, MR. JOHN A. MEADORS of
Nashville to MISS SALLIE CAROTHERS of Huntsville.

Married on the 1st by REV. M. B. DeWITT at the residence of the
bride's father, MR. GEORGE O. KELLER of Dayton, Ohio to MISS EMMA E.
SPEAKMAN of this place.

Married in this city on the 10th by REV. FATHER KIRWIN, MR.
JAMES M. CLELAND to MISS HENRIETTA LEONARD, all of this city.
Married on the 4th by F. T. BUTLER, Esq. MR. JNO. W. HODGES to
MISS MARY MOON, all of this county.
Married on the 31st by WM. MOON, Esq. MR. ISHAM H. McABEE to
MISS MARY M. COBB, all of this county.
Married on the 28th by G. B. STRATHER, Esq. MR. WM. H. McCURRY to
MISS MARY ANN RATLEY, all of this county.
Married on the 26th by REV. L. H. GRUBBS, MR. RUFUS J. HILLIARD to
MISS SARAH J. SANDERSON, all of this county.
Married on the 22nd by REV. D. JACKS, MR. JAMES C. DAVIS to
MISS SARAH J. CAMPBELL, all of this county.
Married on the 15th by REV. JAMES HORNER, MR. BENJ. McCRARY to
MISS LUCY ANN DAVIS, all of this county.
Married on the 27th, MR. JAMES C. AUSTIN to MRS. MILDRED J. DURYEE,
all of this county.
COL. JAMES BISHOP died at Cedar Bluff (Cherokee Co.), Ala. on the
24th aged 92.
MR. JAMES A. ARNETT died at Madison in this county on the 23rd.

January 19, 1872
Married on the 16th by REV. F. M. PROCTOR, MR. REUBEN C. WEBSTER to
MISS MARY J. WILLIAMS, all of this county.
Married in this county on the 3rd by REV. F. M. PROCTOR, MR. JAS. S.
McGAHA to MISS WILLIE E. BRANNON.
Married on the 10th at the residence of the bride's mother by
REV. JOS. R. MORRISS, MR. J. PEYTON POWELL to MISS CORNELIA W. STRONG,
daughter of the late MR. CHARLES W. STRONG, all of this vicinity.
Married on the 10th by REV. M. E. JOHNSTON, MR. JOHN BAYLESS to
MISS SUSAN E. McCALEB, all of this county.
Died in this city on the 16th, MINNIE W. HAWKINS, daughter of
MRS. I. M. HAWKINS in her 9th year after a short illness.
WILLIAM GLENN died in Williamson Co., Tennessee on the 7th aged 106.

January 26, 1872
Married on the 4th by B. P. HUMPHREY, Esq. MR. WILLIAM F. EAST to
MISS MARY E. ALLEN.
Married on the 9th by REV. C. (G?) A. MORRING, MR. DAVID K. WADE to
MISS VIRGINIA E. HILLIARD.
Married on 16th by FATHER ED. KERNAN, MR. JOHN MYERS to MISS
HONORA LYONS.
Married on the 17th by REV. L. HENSLEY GRUBBS, MR. WM. P. McCREARY
to MISS MATTIE J. daughter of JOHN CLIFF, Esq. all of this county.
Died on the 23rd, CHARLEY, son of MR. and MRS. C. W. HEREFORD of
this place.

February 2, 1872
Married on the 31st in Cumberland Church in Huntsville by REV.
M. B. DeWITT, DR. JOHN W. BARCLAY to MISS KATE BALDRIDGE.
Married on the 25th in the Episcopal Church by REV. J. M. BANNISTER,
MR. LeROY H. WILSON to MISS ELLEN T. WARD, daughter of the late
J(OHN) J. WARD, all of this city.
COL. JAMES S. WATKINS of West Tennessee died in Texas in December
aged 86.

February 9, 1872
Married on the 1st by REV. J. H. DRAKE, MR. GEORGE A. MILLER to
MISS AMANDA FOX, all of this county.
Married on the 1st by R. W. FIGG, Esq. MR. REUBEN LEMLEY to
MISS ELIZA J. MELTON, all of this county.
Married on the 1st by REV. M. E. JOHNSON, MR. JOSEPH M. BAILEY to
MRS. MARTHA CLEVELAND, all of this county.
Married at the residence of the bride's mother on the 7th by
REV. ANSON WEST, MR. ENOCH M. McCARTY to MISS AMANDA BIBB, all of
this county.
Married at Pride's Station, Ala. on the 1st, MR. D. D. MANEY of
Tennessee to MISS MARY D. BRYAN.
MRS. CATHARINE HALE, the venerable and aged widow of the late
CAPT. WM. HALE of this city (one of the veterans of 1812) died on
Monday night.

THOMAS PRITCHETT of Monroe Co. Ala. died on the 30th aged 106.

February 16, 1872
    CAPT. ED. F. SHIELDS, an old citizen of Mobile died on the 10th.

February 23, 1872
    Married on the 16th by REV. M. B. DeWITT, MR. WARREN J. BRIDGES
to MISS ELIZABETH G. DICKSON.
    Married on the 16th by REV. M. E. JOHNSON, MR. CASWELL H. ANDERSON
to MRS. SALLIE G. McIVER.
    Married on the 3rd by K. T. DANIEL, Esq. MR. EDMOND SMITHWICK to
MISS NANCY STYLES.
    Married on the 1st by JOHN D. RAGLAND, MR. SAMUEL L. ROWAN to
MISS MARY JANE GILBREATH.
    Married in this county on the 20th by REV. T. S. CAMPBELL, MR.
JOHN LEMLEY to MISS ELIZABETH BAULDIN.
    Married on the 15th by REV. MR. RICE, MR. PRES. N. DRAKE of
Huntsville, Ala. to MISS KATE A. BURNETT of Franklin, Tenn.
    Died in this city on the 15th, MRS. LUCY PRIDE, daughter of
DR. GREEN, formerly of Columbia, S.C.
    Died on the morning of the 17th, EVA, infant daughter of S. A. and
M. I. BAILEY aged 4 months and 14 days.

March 1, 1872
    Married on the 20th by REV. THOMAS S. CAMPBELL, MR. JOHN LEMLEY to
MISS ELIZABETH BOULDIN, all of this county.
    Married on the 20th by REV. B. W. BUSSEY, MR. BENJ. F. WILMORE to
MISS LUELLA BENSON, all of this county.
    Married at the residence of the bride's father. COL. E. H. McCORD
in Pulaski, Tennessee on 19th February by REV. DR. MITCHELL, MR. JOHN H.
KIRK, formerly of this city to MISS KATIE McCORD.
    Died on 18th in San Marcus (Hays Co.), Texas, REV N J TAYLOR
of the Cumberland Presbyterian Church.

March 8, 1872
    Married on the 4th in this place by ROBERT W. FIGG, Esq. MR. S. JAMES
STARKEY to MISS MARGARET C. DOBBS, all of this county.
    Married on the 29th in this city by ROBERT W. FIGG, Esq. JOHN T.
McCAY to MISS BETTIE JENKINS, all of this county.
    Died on March 1 at 3½ o'clock P.M. MRS. MATILDA W. wife of
JAMES M. VENABLE.
    Died on the 1st at the residence of MR. R. S. NORRIS in this
county, MRS. SARAH B. ROBERTS aged 63. Cumberland Presbyterian Church.
    MR. ALFRED HUGHES, an old citizen and generally known died on
Sunday.

March 15, 1872
    Married on the 6th by REV. B. W. BUSSEY, MR. BENJAMIN E. BAYLES
to MISS MARY SMITH, all of this place.
    Married on the 3rd by REV. THOMAS RIDEOUT, MR. JAMES W. BURCHFIELD
to MISS JULIA FAUGHT, all of this county.
    Married on the 29th by LEVI W. ESSLINGER, MR. CALVIN HUGHES (s of
HENRY--census) to MISS MOLLIE KING, all of this county.
    Married at Prospect (Giles Co.), Tenn. on the 24th REV. RICHARD P.
RANSOM to MISS ANNIE WESTMORELAND.
    Married on the 28th by REV. J. H. DRAKE, WILLIAM ELLIOTT to
MISS MARY A. CLARKSTON, all of this county.
    Died in this city on the 9th, MORRIS, infant son of MR. and MRS.
MORRIS BERNEY.

March 22, 1872
    Married in this county on the 13th by REV. M. E. JOHNSTON,
MR. GATES McMAHAN to MISS ELIZA JANE MASSENGALE.

March 29, 1872
    Married on the 20th at the residence of the bride's mother by
REV. ANSON WEST, MR. WILLIAM H. WOOLDRIDGE to MISS MOLLIE M. WILLIAMS
all of this city. (dau. of MARGARET WILLIAMS--& gr-dau of DEBORAH HALL--
see Vol. 159 p. 81)

Died on Thursday evening in this vicinity of typhoid fever, JOHN S. son of HENRY F. HALSEY, Esq. in his 17th year.

Died on the 26th after a short illness. MRS. MARY E. BATTLE of this county, widow of the late JOSIAH D. BATTLE. Baptist.

April 5, 1872

COL. WALTER DRANE (@ 54 Ga), an old citizen of Lowndes Co. died on the 24th aged 76.

SHELDON TOOMER, member of the late Legislature from Lee Co. died on the 26th.

WILLIAM LARKIN and THOMAS DANIEL, old citizens (80 yrs) of Franklin County, Tennessee died last week. Also CAPT. JOHN BENNETT at Tullahoma (Tenn.).

April 12, 1872

Married on the 12th by REV. JOHN M. HAMER, MR. GEORGE M. DUNN to MISS JESIE SOLOMON.

Married on the 21st by REV. E. R. BERRY, MR. STEPHEN J. STONE to MISS MARY J. SMITH.

Married on the 4th by REV. ALEXANDER PENLAND, MR. ISHAM H. HOBBS to MISS MATILDA E. PARKER, all of this co.

Died in Brownsboro, Ala. on the 10th, J. F. SANFORD, son of SAMUEL W. and ELIZA J. SANFORD aged 5 years 4 mo.

MR. WM. H. WORTHAM died in Maysville in this county on the 7th after a short illness. He had resided in this county for many years and was an active, enterprising, sensible citizen having many friends. He possessed many amiable qualities and was widely known.

MARTIN COLE, Esq. died on the 3rd in Cross Roads neighborhoods aged about 85, an honest, respected citizen, having been constable or magistrate much of the time and a constant member of the Baptist church.

ROBERT S. HATCHER (48 G), formerly State Senator from Dallas and Wilcox was killed by cars last week.

April 19, 1872

Married on the 13th by FATHER KIRWAN, MR. WM. T. W. MORTON of Washington, D.C. to MISS EASLEY of this city.

Died on the 11th, MR. BENJ. THOMPSON aged 65 and for many years a citizen of this county.

JOHN ASH, formerly State Senator from St. Clair died on the 1st.

May 3, 1872

HUGH W. FRIZZELL, formerly of Winchester (Franklin Co.), Tennessee died in Nashville last week aged 45.

Married on the 24 April at residence of J. M. KERR by REV. J. B. GRAVES, ROV. R. B. CAVITT to MISS D. A. SUTTON, all of Monroe Co. Ark. (to McLane)

Died on the 29th, MRS. SALLIE PICKETT, wife of MR. S. F. DARWIN of this place.

State of Alabama-Madison Co. Probate Court Apr. 30, 1872. Estate of GARRET S. NUCKOLLS (s of SAM'L; m cen), deceased. VIRGIL A. NUCKOLLS, adm'r.

CAPT. A. J. EDMONDSON of Memphis a veteran under JACKSON is dead.

COL. JOHN W. DAWSON, a prominent citizen of Memphis died on the 29th.

DR. DAVIS MOORE died at his residence near Vienna in this county on Sat. Sept. 27th. Man of fine sense, an experienced physician, was well known, had many friends and was about 75.

Our fellow citizen and friend, MR. JOSIAH SPRINGER of this county is a member of a Delaware family and a direct descendant of one whose will has been discovered owning property where Wilmington stands.

May 10, 1872

Married near Whitesburg, Ala. Apr. 25th at the residence of the bride's father by REV. ALEXANDER PENLAND, MR. WILLIAM A. STOGNER to MISS SARAH E. GARDINER, all of this county.

Died on 29th March, MRS. M(ARIANNA) FORD at her residence near Meridianville at an advanced age having been born Aug. 4, 1812, widow of the late JOHN FORD, so long a citizen of Madison Co; and she was a most excellent woman, a devoted mother and a kind neighbor.

Married on 16 July by REV. J. H. DRAKE, MR. SILAS A. L. BRAZELTON
(s of SILAS M.--census) to MISS MOLLIE SCHRIMSHER, daughter of
MR. ALFRED SCHRIMSHER, all of this county.
Married on 18 July by WM. M. ROZELL, Esq. MR. ROBERT FISK to
MISS DICEY A. PRUITT, all of this county.
Married on 21 July at Catholic Church in this city by ED. KIRWAN,
R.C.P., MR. GEORGE C. MARCHAND of Pleasant Hill, Mo. to MISS MARY
ELIZABETH MORGAN, of Huntsville.
Married on 10 July by REV. G. W. CARMICHAEL, MR. MEREDITH MILLER
to MISS MATTIE F. PETTY, daughter of D. H. PETTY, Esq. all of this
county.
Married on the 18th at residence of the bride by REV. ANSON WEST,
MR. BENNETT W. PETTY to ------(paper torn)
SOLOMON SPURLOCK (@ 52 G in 1850) died in Barbour Co. on 9th,
several months over 100.

August 2, 1872
WYLIE M. SIMPSON died at Hillsboro (Lawrence Co.), Ala. on the
12th aged 32.
Married on 18 July at residence of the bride's mother in Shannon
(Lee Co.), Miss. by REV. A. V. BELL, CAPT. R. C. TOPP to MISS BENNETT S.
BOGGESS, formerly of this county.
Married on 25 July by F. T. BUTLER, Esq. MR. JOSEPH S. MAPLES to
MISS MARTHA J. CARMACK.
Married on 23 July at the residence of MR. JOSEPH K. SANFORD by
REV. J. R. MORRIS, MR. WILLIAM D. STEGER to MISS MARGARET F. SANFORD.
Also at same time and place, MR. JOSEPH F. JINKINS to MISS RHODA A.
SANFORD, all of this county.
Died on 23 July on Monte Sano near Huntsville, CORA LEE, daughter
of MR. and MRS. W. T. NICHOLS--an infant bud.

August 9, 1872
Died in this county July 25, NANCY ALLISON (w of JOHN--census)
aged 61 years 5 months and 4 days. Life long resident of this county
and for many years a true and consistent member of the Cumberland
Presbyterian Church.
Died in this city on the 30th, MRS. ELIZA R(ACHAEL) POOSER
(b Sept 26, 1807, d July 29, 1872, nee ELIZA RACHEL WAMER--
says b Orangeburg Dist SC), mother-in-law of REV. G(EORGE) W. F. PRICE,
President of Huntsville Female College in her 61st year.
Died in this city on the 4th, MRS. PRICE (she was ELIZ M. POOSER
tombot-b Jan 22, 1827, d Aug 4, 1872), wife of REV. G. W. F. PRICE.
Died on the 3rd at the residence of MR. THOMAS S. McCALLEY of this
place, MRS. ANN C. LANFORD, widow of the late ROBERT LANFORD aged 83.
Born in Augusta (Richmond Co.), Ga. December 17, 1789 and had resided
in this vicinity about 60 years. Methodist.
Died in Marion (Cuttenden), Ark. on 15 February, SUE HINDS,
daughter of MR. LINSEY HINDS, formerly of this county, in her 17th year,
having been born Jan. 17, 1856.

August 16, 1872
Married at Church of Nativity in Huntsville on 8th by REV. J. M.
BANISTER, DAVID D. SHELBY, Esq. to MISS ANNIE E. DAVIS, daughter of
COL. Z. P. DAVIS, all of this city.
Died on 6th at his residence near Jonesboro, Ala. REV. W. B. MOORE
(d 1872 @ 75 SC); also on 7th, his wife. There was only 12 hours between
their deaths and both were buried on the 8th in the same grave. (former
w LUCY A d 1859 m. 63 yr.)

August 23, 1872
Died on 17th of consumption, MRS. JENNETTE SWASEY, wife of
MR. JOHN SWASEY. Devoted wife and mother.

August 30, 1872
MR. JOHN SANFORD, an old and good citizen of this county died on
the 22nd at his residence in Brownsboro.
Married on the 8th at the residence of the bride's mother by
REV. I. HENSLEY GRUBBS, MR. WOODSON C. SAUNDERS to MISS EMILY P.
CANTERBURY all of this county.

Died on the 23rd near this place after a long illness, MRS. NANCY
L. SCHRIMSHER wife of MR. A. J. SCHRIMSHER; born in Virginia March 17,
1811 and came to this county when only 9 years old. Faithful wife,
devoted mother.
MRS. AURELIA FITZPATRICK, widow of the late GOVERNOR BENJAMIN
FITZPATRICK died on the 25th.

September 6, 1872
Died near Cypress Landing, Desha Co. Ark. (to McLane) Aug. 23rd,
MRS. E. J. LEWIS (Eliz?), wife of MR. GEO. W. LEWIS, formerly of this
county aged 43 years 5 months and 11 days.
Died on 27 August in this place, WILLIE A. JONES aged about 8
years, son of MR. JAMES P. and MRS. SARAH J. JONES. Baptist. Congestive
chill.

September 13, 1872
(From NASHVILLE UNION AND AMERICAN)--"THOMAS PINION of Montgomery
County, said to be 118 years of age and a soldier of the first Revolution
arrived here yesterday for the purpose of drawing his pension. He
came in a wagon accompanied by two sons and two daughters, the youngest
of his children being 75 years of age. MR. PINION, his advanced age
being considered, exhibits remarkable traces of physical and mental
vigor. He gets about with almost as much activity as either of his
children and speaks of events of recent and ancient occurrence with a
wonderful degree of animation and accuracy. He distinctly remembers
the battle of Stony Point and is still able to give a vivid description
of that engagement and other events of Revolutionary memory. MR. PINION
has not drawn any portion of his pension money since the commencement
of the late war, and says he thinks there is a 'right smart coming to
him just about now'"
Died in this city on the 7th at the residence of her sister,
MRS. MARTHA CAYTON, MISS ADELINE MOSELEY.
Died in Richmond, Va. Aug. 24 of consumption, MRS. ELLEN A. wife
of MR. W. H. JARVIS of this city.
Died last week, JOHN ANTHONY CARR of Clay Co. Ala.--suicided.
On Sunday last, 1st inst. in Bedford Co. Tenn., REV. MR. LANDRUM.
a Baptist preacher suddenly fell dead in the pulpit.

September 20, 1872
Married on the 10th in Madison Ala. by REV. L. HENSLY GRUBBS,
MR. WILBURN PERRY of Madison Co. to MISS EMILY J. LAWRANCE of Morgan Co.
We regret to learn that MR. LUCIEN T. MATTHEWS of this city, who
has been ill for several months died yesterday the 18th.
MR. WILLIAM MATKIN, an old. well-known and highly esteemed citizen
of this county died on the 14th after a long and painful illness.
MR. ZACH. DRUMMOND was killed by lightning in Mobile on the 9th.
ABEL PHILLIPS, an old citizen of Calhoun Co. died last week.

October 4, 1872
(Paper in mourning for WILLIAM B. FIGURES, editor of Huntsville Adv)
REV. PETER CARTWRIGHT, the well-known pioneer Methodist preacher died
in Illinois on the 25th.
P. H. WHETSTONE, late assessor for Autauga Co. died on 20th.
Married in Attala 19th Sept. by REV. JOHN POTTER, MR. JOHN B. ROGERS
to MISS S. CORNELIA PICKENS, all of Etowah Co.
Died in this city on 21 September of pneumonia, HARRIET ELIZA,
infant daughter of MR. and MRS. J. F. PHELPS.
Died on 27 September in New Market of hemorrhage of lungs,
MR. HENRY COCHRAN, brother of JAMES G. COCHRAN, Esq. of this city aged
about 23.
MR. AARON WRIGHT, a well known citizen of Nashville died last
Monday aged 73.
Testimony of respect to WILLIAM B. FIGURES, Register in Chancery,
by Printers and publishers of Huntsville; Huntsville Bar; Mayor and
Alderman of Huntsville etc. He died at his residence in this city at
2½ o'clock morning of the 1st; born March 6, 1820 and commenced
publication of his paper in 1838.... Consolation to his widow and
orphan.
HON. BUSH JONES of Perry Co., presidential elector of 4th District
died in Uniontown Sept. 27.

CHARLES HALL, an old citizen of Barbour Co. died in Eufaula last week aged 81. He served with GEN. JACKSON in Indian War.

HON. JOHN P. GRAHAM of Marion died last week. He was a soldier of 1812 under JACKSON and was a member of the State Senate one or two terms.

State of Alabama--Madison Co. GEORGE W. WELLS, administrator of ELIZABETH SLOAN, deceased. Following named heirs are non-residents, viz: THOMAS SLOAN, MARY P. SPELTS, WILLIAM SPELTS, HARRIET L. SLOAN, WILLIAM R. SLOAN, SARAH E. SLOAN, SAMUEL A. SLOAN, JAMES C. N. SLOAN, BETHIAH POWER, ALMIRA POWER, MARY POWER, ROBERT POWER, ALABAMA POWER TENNESSEE POWER, who reside in Ark; MARTHA E. wife of --- WATSON, LEANDER JEFFERSON MASENGALE, DEMPSEY THOMAS MASENGALE, MARY VIRGINIA HILL, wife of --- HILL, LODINA KETURAO MASENGALE, ANNE E. MASENGALE, THOMAS EPISON, who reside in Texas.

October 11, 1872
MR. WILLIAM PAYNE, an old citizen of Lowndes Co. died last week aged 76.

Tribute of respect to COL. GEORGE ANDERSON GORDON by Church of Nativity.

COL. NATHANIEL TERRY, well-known throughout North Alabama died in Texas recently.

MRS. PHOEBE HAMLET, an old, well-known and highly esteemed lady died at her residence near this city Friday last aged 92.

October 18, 1872
MR. WILLIAM WELLS, County Treasurer died this morning Sat. about 7 o'clock.

Married in the vicinity of Huntsville Oct. 10 by REV. MR. STAINBACK, JAMES A. MOORE of Marion, Ala. to MISS SALLIE, daughter of JAMES B. ROBINSON of Madison Co.

Married on the evening of the 10th at Church of Nativity in this city by REV. J. M. BANISTER, GEORGE S. GORDON, Esq. to MISS MATTIE EASON, daughter of the late ALCUIN EASON.

We regret to learn that MR. JAMES P. SPRINGER, son of our old friend, JOSIAH SPRINGER died at the residence of the latter near Triana on the 10th.

J. M. PROVINE, one of oldest citizens of Memphis died on the 10th aged about 60.

October 25, 1872
Married on the 17th at the residence of the bride's mother in Madison, Ala. by REV. MR. ROBERTSON, MR. THOMAS B. HOPKINS to MISS VIRGINIA HARRIS.

Married on the 16th by REV. DR. J. M. BANISTER, MR. JOHN BARBER to MISS KATE GRAVES, all of this city.

Died in Pleasant Hill on the 12th, a little daughter of DR. A. G. CLOPTON, formerly of Madison Co. Ala.

WILLIAM C. PENICK, Past Grand Master of Masonic Grand Lodge of Ala. died at Wetumpka on the 16th aged 72.

November 1, 1872
ROBERT DAVIS of Butler aged more than 90 years died in Lowndes Co. on 4th. He helped to erect the first house that was built at Montgomery.

November 8, 1872
Married on 30 Oct. in Nashville, Tenn. by REV. DR. R. A. YOUNG, MR. LEONARD F. DAVIS to MISS BESSIE K. SAWRIE, youngest daughter of REV. DR. W. D. F. SAWRIE, formerly of this city.

MR. ALFRED H. DICKERSON, an old citizen of Eufaula died there last week.

November 15, 1872
Married on the 7th at the residence of the bride's father by REV. DR. F. A. ROSS, MR. F. P. COUSINS of Memphis, Tenn. to MISS SUE JOLLY, daughter of MR. BENJ. JOLLY of this city.

Died in this county on 30 Oct. of congestion of brain, MR. ROBERT M. LYNE, an old citizen of this county aged 54.

November 22, 1872
Married at the residence of the bride's mother on 14th by
REV. DR. BANISTER, MR. P(RESTON) Y(EATMAN) GERON to MISS MATTIE J.
HEREFORD, all of this county.
Married on 14th at residence of WILLIAM R. RISON of this city by
REV. ANSON WEST, MR. WALTER N. PHARR of Ark. (to McLane) to MISS
AGGIE JONES of this county.
By ELDER J. L. LATTIMORE at the residence of J. D. SPEAR (or
SPEAK?) near Oakville on 31st, MISS LUISA LINDSAY to MR. JASPER N. WADE
of Trinity.
Died in this city on 17th, MRS. LILLIAN DeWITT, daughter of
DR. and MRS. R. T. SEARCY.
Died at Grand Junction (Hardewan Co.), Tenn. Oct. 26, MRS. MOLLIE
LUCAS, formerly MISS MOLLIE RAGLAND.
Died at Longview, Tex. Oct. 12 of congestion of brain, MANIE,
daughter of J. LEE and BELLE ABLE aged about 4 years.
Died near Landersville (Laurence Co?), Ala. on 12 Aug. MRS. MARY
E. C. WILLIS aged 27.
JOHN S. GREENE of Mobile Register died on 8th.
GEN. STERLING JACKSON, formerly of Athens, Ala. died in Pulaski,
Tenn. on 7th aged about 88. He was a good man.
CAPT. IRA W. STOUT, formerly Tax Assessor of Butler Co. (to MRS.
GLENN) died on 1st in that county.

November 29, 1872
WILLIAM H. SADLER, a prominent citizen of Mobile died there last
week.

December 6, 1872
Married at the residence of DR. A. L. LOGAN in this county by
REV. J. R. NORRIS, MR. C. W. CHADICK to MISS CHARLOTTE C. BELL.
HON. N. L. WHITFIELD, member of Legislature from Tuscaloosa Co.
died in Montgomery on 3rd.
MATTHEW D. MOORE, Esq. died near Prattville last week. Native of
Talladega.

December 20, 1872
Married on the 11th at Tulip St. Church, Edgefield, Tenn. by
REV. R. K. BROWN, MR. GREEN MORROW to MISS MAGGIE HENDERSON, formerly
of this city.

January 3, 1873
Died in Memphis, Tenn. on Christmas morning, KATE, youngest
daughter of GEORGE and MARY HARPER, formerly of this city.

January 10, 1873
Married in Lynchburg, Va. Dec. 18, 1872 by REV. MR. SHELD,
CAPT. WILLIAM RICHARDSON of this city to MISS LIZZIE B. RUCKER of
Lynchburg, Va.

January 24, 1873
Married in this city at the residence of the bride's father on
12 Jan. by LEVI HINDS, Esq. MR. SILAS M. LEDBETTER of Miss. to
MISS SARAH C. MAPLES, daughter of REV. PETER MAPLES.

February 7, 1873
Married in this county on 30 Jan. by L. W. ESSLINGER, Esq.
MR. ROBERT GOWAN to MISS NANCY TALIAFERRO.
Married on 26 Dec. 1872 in this county by L. W. ESSLINGER, Esq.
MR. J. W. HUGHES to MISS LEONORA LYONS.

February 14, 1873
Married on 3rd inst. at residence of bride's father by
REV. L. H. GRUBBS, MR. FERDINAND M. TROTMAN to MISS SARAH E. McGAHA,
daughter of MR. J. M. McGAHA.

February 7, 1873
Married on 24 Dec. 1872 in this county by L. W. ESSLINGER,
J. W. McKINNEY to MISS MARY McMULLEN.

February 28, 1873
    Married on 17th inst. by ROBERT W. FIGG, Esq., BASCOMB W. ANDREWS
to MISS MARY M. WEST, both of this county.
    On 17th inst. by R. W. FIGG, JOHN ANDREWS to MISS MARGARET CUNNINGHAM
both of this county.

March 7, 1873
    Married in this county on 1 Jan. by REV. B. W. BUSSEY, MR. M. O.
STRONG to MISS GERTRUDE MOSS, daughter of MR. J. M. MOSS.

March 21, 1873
    Death of COL. ROBERT FEARN (s of ROBT--census). Died at his
residence on Monte Sano near this city on Wed. evening the 12th inst.
Although he had been for several years in poor health and recently quite
ill, his death was sudden and unexpected. But sudden as the summons
was, it found him ready and waiting. He was kind and affectionate in
his family, hospitable to his friends and neighbors, charitable to his
enemies. He rests beside his noble ancestors who left him a name and
character pure and spotless and well he has preserved it. To his
broken hearted wife and little orphan children, we feel authorized to
tender the heart felt sympathies of our community.

March 28, 1873
    Died in Barnwell, S.C. on the morning of the 20th inst. MRS.
HATTIE FIGURES HALLONQUIST, daughter of the late WILLIAM B. FIGURES
and wife of DR. ROBERT L. HALLONQUIST. A few months ago left here with
her husband to try their fortunes in S.C. Was a good wife, an affectionate daughter. Her devotion to her little boy was beautiful and none
will miss her more than he.

April 4, 1873
    Died in Madison Station, Ala. Mar. 2, 1873 at his mother's residence.
MR. E. M. FITTZE aged 4--(blurred) Years 11 mo. and 15 days.

April 18, 1873
    Married in this city on 10th inst. at residence of MR. WILLIAM
SPRAGUE by REV. B. B. ROSS, MR. J. M. SNOW of Jackson, Tenn. to MISS
NELLIE ROBINSON of this city.

April 25, 1873
    Death of W. HENRY SMITH. The death of this good man is deeply
regretted by many of the old citizens of this city. He began his
newspaper career in this city and was once Associate Editor with the
late WILLIAM B. FIGURES in 1838. He left here for Nashville where he
has since remained in the newspaper business. He died on the 17th in
Nashville.

May 9, 1873
    Sudden and unexpected death of MR. O. D. SLEDGE, which sad event
occurred Sat. A.M. MR. SLEDGE was one of the oldest citizens and most
prominent merchants. As husband, father and friend, was ever loving
and kind.
    Died in McMinnville (Marion Co.), Tenn. on 2nd inst. MRS. JENNIE
WHITSON nee MISS JENNIE CHADWICK of this city.

May 23, 1873
    Married in Church of Nativity in this city on 19th inst. by
REV. DR. BANISTER, MR. JAMES H? PATTON to MISS SALLIE K. WATKINS.
    Died on 18 April at residence in Macon, Miss. after a long and
painful illness, MRS. ELIZA L. BOGUS (BOGGASS), formerly of this county.
Kind and affectionate mother and true friend.

May 30, 1873
    Married May 22, 1873 at the residence of the bride's father by
REV. H. P. TURNER, MR. JACOB VITTERNER to MISS MARY J. KIRKLAND, all
of this county.

June 5, 1873
    Married in Church of Nativity in this city on 31st by REV. DR. J. M.
BANISTER, MR. H. P. HUFF of Va. to MISS MARY WOODSON WITHERS of this city.

June 19, 1873
    Married in Church of Nativity in this city on 17 by REV. DR.
BANISTER, HON. DANIEL COLEMAN of Athens, Ala. to MISS CLAUDE LeVERT
of this city.

June 26, 1873
    Tribute of respect by Madison Lodge #25 I.O.O.F. to beloved
brother, ABNER GRAHAM, deceased. Committee: LEWIS M. DOUGLASS,
J. P. SPENCER, J. VANVALKENBURG.
    Tribute of respect by Mayor and aldermen regarding the death of
ex-alderman, SAMUEL COLTART. WILLIAM J. HUMPHREY, City clerk.

June 26, 1873
    Regret to learn that MR. WILLIAM NANCE, formerly of this city died
of cholera in Nashville on Friday last.

July 3, 1873
    We are sorry to chronicle the death of MR. FRANK MASTIN on Tues.
morning last, an old and highly respected citizen of this city.
    HON. STEPHEN H. MURPHY died at his mother's residence in this city
on Sat. June 28, 1873 aged 36 years. Was a member of 4th Regiment Ala.
Volunteers, Army of Northern Va. Represented his native county in the
state senate.

July 17, 1873
    Died in this city on 13th inst. of typhoid fever, MISS JULIA SMITH,
eldest daughter of DR. C. G. SMITH.
    Died at the residence of MRS. CAROTHERS in this city on 15th,
MR. ANDREW J. TANNOCK in 28th year.
    Died at Johnson's Wells in this county on 11th of cholera,
MR. SAMUEL PLEASANTS of this city.

July 31, 1873
    Married on 24th by REV. S. L. SANFORD, DR. M(ILTON) C. HAMER of
New Hope, Ala. to MISS MOLLIE L. GOGGIN of Bedford Co. Tenn.
    Died on 22 Dec. 1871 (misprint?) in Crocket (Houston Co.), Texas,
MR. WILLIAM McCAY formerly of this city.

August 14, 1873
    Married on 31st at residence of bride's father, MR. JOHN L. BUCK
by REV. E. M. WAIR, MR. JAMES N. BARHAM of this city to MISS ANNIE BUCK
of Pine (Jef Co.) Bluff, Ark. (Pine Bluff Press)
    Died on 9th, MR. HUGH EASLEY of this city.
    Obituary:
HAZEL GREEN, Ala. Aug. 6, 1873. MR. D. SKAGGS' death of heart
disease at residence of MR. P. S. TOWNSEND in Madison Co. Ala. on 31 July
1873 in 30th year. Leaves widow and one child. Louisville Democrat,
Bowling Green (Warren Co.) and Franklin (Simpson Co.), Kentucky papers
please copy.

August 28, 1873
    Departed this life Wed. A.M. 20th inst. MARY J. wife of SAMUEL A.
BAILY and daughter of WILLIAM C. IRWIN aged 29 years, of typhoid fever.
Native of Pa.

September 11, 1873
    Died on Wed. Aug. 27, FELICIA PICKETT, daughter of MAJOR STEPTOE
PICKETT at home at Madison Station from inadvertently swallowing a
glass bead. She was about 12 years of age and a bright and interesting
child.
    Died Aug. 12 of consumption near Madison X Roads, MRS. SARAH
ELIZABETH, wife of P. J. GREEN. She was born in Pt. Pleasant, Clermont
Co. Ohio and was in her 39th year. Faithful and affectionate wife,
true friend and mother and sincere Christian. Cincinnati, Salem and
New Albany, Ind. papers please copy.
    Married in this city on Thurs. the 10th at residence of the bride's
father, JOHN T. STRATTON by REV. T. H. BOWMAN, MISS KATE J. STRATTON of
Memphis to WILLIAM B. LEEDY of Huntsville, Ala. (From Memphis Avalanche)
        Copies missing to Oct. 23.

October 23, 1873
    Married on the 28th of October 1873 at the residence of the bride's
father, MR. JOHN W. POLLARD by REV. G. W. F. PRICE. MR. JOHN R. ----
(rest cut off)
    Died at his residence in Big Cove, Madison Co. on Oct. 21 after a
long and painful illness, MRS. SARAH SCHRIMSHER aged 68 years 18 days.
Consistent member of Baptist Church. Mentions children.

October 30, 1873 (copy missing)

November 6, 1873
    Married on Tues. Nov. 4, 1873 at residence of A. F. MURRAY of
this city, MR. FRANK WATKINS to MISS MINNIE MURRAY, all of this city.

November 13, 1873
    Married on 6th inst. at residence of bride's mother by ROBERT FIGG,
Esq. DANIEL RICHMOND to MISS FANNIE BARBER, both of this county.
    Married on 6th at residence of bride's father near Madison X Roads
by FATHER E. KIRWAN, MR. WILLIAM M. CLARKE to MISS MINNIE E. GREEN.

December 4, 1873
    Married at residence of bride's mother Nov. 5 by REV. C. B. S. ---
MR. L. B. CARTER to MISS SALLIE LOBLE (?) all of Red Hill.
    Died in this county Thurs. Nov. 27 GLASGOW W. JORDAN of congestive
chills. MR. J. was a young man, much respected by all who knew him.
    Died near Red Hill, Ala. on Tues. Nov. 25, JAMES BERRY (56 NC,
MARSHALL W) in his 81st year. MR. BERRY was born in S.C. and when quite
young removed to Ala. He was father of 18 children and had up to the
day of his death, 79 grandchildren. Consistent member of Baptist
Church.

December 18, 1873
    Married in this city on 17th inst. at residence of the bride's
father, MR. W. J. HALSEY by REV. DR. STAINBACK, MR. HARRISON LYLE of
Triana to MISS LAURA A. HALSEY. No cards.
    Married on 9th at residence of bride's mother near Pulaski, Tenn.
by REV. G. W. MITCHELL, MR. R. M. SLEDGE of this city to MISS ANNA
LINDSAY of Giles Co. Tenn.
    Died in this city on 17th, MRS. ALICE JAMES, wife of JOHN JAMES.
Funeral service from Cumberland Church.
    Died on 16th November in this city, MRS. LUCY CROSS, consort of
JOHN M. CROSS of congestive chills.

January 8, 1874
    Died in this city on Monday last, the 5th instant, MR. J. W. DAVID.
He moved to this city about the close of the late war from Columbus,
Ga. A Baptist and Mason Left a wife and children.

January 29, 1874
    Married on Thursday, January 8th at the residence of the bride's
mother in New Orleans, La. by REV. HENRY M. SMITH, JOHN WALKER COLEMAN
to ANNIE H., daughter of the late JOHN BROWNLEE, both of that city.
WALKER is well and favorably known in this community as son of the late
JOHN J. COLEMAN, once editor and proprietor of the Huntsville Advocate.

February 12, 1874
    Tribute of respect. Whereas on the 1st day of January 1874, it
pleased the Architect to the Universe to remove from our midst our
worthy brother, JOHN T. HADEN aged 61 years. Masonic Northern Lodge
#278.

February 19, 1874
    From Minutes of Board of Directors of National Bank of Huntsville
24 February 1874: "Since last meeting of this board, THEOPHILUS LACY,
beloved and worthy cashier of the National Bank of Huntsville died at
his residence within those walls on Thursday night, 10th day of
February, 1874 at the age of 70 years 1 month and 10 days. Leaves
widow and fatherless children." By JOSEPH MARTIN, Cashier.

March 19, 1874
    Died in Marysville, Cook County, Texas on the 1st day of February
last, WILLIAM M. CROSS. He was born in Huntsville, Ala. about the
year 1816. Removed to Texas in 1858. Single man. Died at the residence
of his cousin, JAMES P. CROSS. (From Talladega Reporter)

May 7, 1874
    Died April 9, 1874 in Dekalb Co. Ala., MRS. SUSAN C. WILLIAMS,
wife of REV. URIAH WILLIAMS. Formerly lived in Madison County.
(Meth. Rev m says he m 1834 Sept. in Morgan Co SUSAN C. RIGNEY)

May 4, 1874
    Died on the 5th instant at his residence near Scottsboro (Jackson
Co.), MR. JOHNSTON HARRISON in his 78th year. Came to this county from
St. Louis and resided here many years. One of the first Commissioners
of Jackson Co. (to Christian) (Tombstone--Center Point, Missionary
Bapt Church, 3 mi from Scottsboro "Founded 1842"--JOHNSON HANISON b in
Christian Co. Ky--Mar 11, 1797, d May 5, 1874; ANN G. wife of JOHNSON
HARRISON b Apr 21, 1804, d Dec 22, 1872)

June 4, 1874
    Died in this city on the 29th ult., MRS. M. B. GILL, wife of
THOMAS C. GILL aged 63 years. Methodist.

June 11, 1874
    Married at the residence of the bride's father on evening of the
13th ult. by REV. G. T. STAINBACK, MR. WILLIAM BROCK to MISS JOSIE
BRYANT, all of this city.

January 6, 1876
    JOHN J. FOWLER, deceased. L. M. PEEVY, administrator.

January 13, 1876
    Died in this city Monday, January 11, 1876 after a lingering
illness, GEORGE W. YUCKLEY in his 52nd year. Was raised here, and
leaves a wife, family and large circle of friends. Commenced life as
a printer, serving apprenticeship in this office and faithfully guarded
its interests for nearly a quarter of a century. Afterwards followed
other vocations.
    Married in Chattanooga, Tennessee Monday evening January 10 by
ESQUIRE WILCOX, MR. DAVID TACHOPIK of this city to MISS CEBELLA LAZARD
of Chattanooga.

January 20, 1876
    JAMES HARRISON and MISS MARY C. ROTTENBURY married in Limestone Co.
on the 26th.

February 3, 1876
    Married at the residence of the bride's mother near Columbus,
Georgia Wednesday January 26th by REV. J. N. EMERY, MR. GEORGE B. GILL
of Nashville, Tennessee to MISS OCTAVIA J. SCROGGINS of Columbus, Ga.
    Married at the residence of the bride's father Thursday night
December 30, 1875 by REV. DR. BUSSEY, MR. HENRY DAHN to MISS ROSA
FROMM, all of this city.
    Married at the residence of the bride's father Thursday night
December 30, 1875 by REV. R. N. TINNON, MR. J. M. AMMERMAN to MISS
NETTIE McDEVIT, all of this city.

March 2, 1876
    Died near Whitesburg February 6 of hemmorage, SARAH F. wife of
P. W. LYNE in her 22nd year.

March 9, 1876
    Death of THOMAS J. JUDGE (34 SC, Lowndes Co.):
    Death of this distinguished jurist occurred at his home in
Greenville (Butler Co.) last Friday after a painful illness borne with
heroic fortitude. He was born in Richmond District, North Carolina
November 1, 1815. While yet a child, his parents removed to this state
and settled in Butler County. Commenced life as a printer, afterwards
edited a paper, studied law, entered the political arena, joined the

array and was recently elected to the Supreme bench of the State.
Buried in Greenville Tuesday morning.

March 16, 1876
JOHN D. TANNER, deceased. HARMON HUMPHREY, administrator.

March 23, 1876
CELIA BLACKBURN, deceased. HARMON HUMPHREY, administrator.

May 25, 1876
Married at the Methodist Church Tuesday evening by REV. DR. PRICE,
MR. JOHN S. CORBETT to MISS TEA MONTGOMERY all of this city.

June 15, 1876
Died in Chattanooga, Tennessee at 6 A.M. June 3, 1876, CHARLES
WALTER VAN HORN from internal injuries received the day previous from
being run over by a street car. He was the son of MAJ. and MRS. M. D.
VAN HORN, who formerly resided in this city and was born in Stevenson,
Alabama (to Christian) (Jackson Co.) February 4, 1873.
Obituary of MISS MARY C. FIGG....

June 20, 1876
Married at the Cumberland Presbyterian Church in this city Thursday
June 22 by REV. MR. TINNON, MR. JAMES LEE of Corinth, Mississippi to
MISS OLA HEREFORD of Huntsville.

July 6, 1876
MRS. SARAH BLACKBURN, widow of an old and esteemed citizen of
Madison County, MR. DAVID BLACKBURN, died of consumption in that place
last Friday night.

July 13, 1876
Died--DR. THOMAS S. MALONE, old and greatly respected citizen and
physician died at the home of his daughter in Athens (Limestone Co.)
Friday evening. One of our oldest and best citizens. (From Athens
Post)

August 24, 1876
Died in this city Wednesday morning August 24 of cancer, in 44th
year, AMATUS ROBBINS BURRITT, born near Springville, Illinois. His
father, DR. ALEXANDER H. BURRITT was one of the pioneers of homeopathy.
Seeing his fitness for medicine, he received his medical education at
Cleveland, Ohio, graduated 1853 and soon after located in this city,
being associated with DR. RICHARD ANGELL. In 1866, he married MISS
MARY K. ROBINSON and leaves an interesting family.... Funeral from
Church of Nativity (Episcopal).

August 31, 1876
Died at Madison Station Friday night the 18th, MRS. SARAH CLAY
aged about 50 (w of THOS? J.--census?)
Obituary of DR. BURRITT:
Born April 19, 1833.... His father now resides in New Orleans.

September 7, 1876
From Moulton Advertiser (Lawrence Co.). MR. L(EVI) F. WARREN
(49 SC), 76 years old died at his home 5 miles south of this place on
the 26th of typhoid fever. He was here when this county was nothing
but a canebrake.... Married at the residence of the bride on the 24 of
August, MR. J. O. NORWOOD to MRS. SARAH ELKINS, all of this county.
The groom is 78 and the bride is 40.

September 21, 1876
Limestone Co. news:
MRS. WILLIAM EGGLESTON died at Bibb's Lane Sunday the 10th.

October 19, 1876
Married in this city Tuesday the 17th by REV. R. M. TINNON, MR.
LEWIS HALL of M & C.R.R. and MISS MAUD MATHER, all of Huntsville.

Married in this city on Tue. the 17th by REV. R. M. TINNON, MR.
JAMES CUNNINGHAM of Cherokee Co. and MISS CLORENDA DAVIS of Huntsville.
Died at Byhalia (Marshall Co.), Miss. Friday the 13th, MISS MOLLIE
BETTIE SPILLMAN, daughter of MR. C. G. SPILLMAN of this city aged 19;
vising DR. HAYS family.

October 26, 1876
Died in this city Tue. the 24, MRS. MARY J. wife of DR. J. D. FOSTER.

November 2, 1876
Died at Grand Junction (Hardeman Co.), Tenn. on the 20, GEORGE
GRAHAM, a former citizen of Huntsville. Remains brought to Huntsville
and interred Sunday the 22nd.

November 9, 1876
HENRY DELP (27 Germ; wife was ELIZ. WARE--see obit of MRS. BOYD--
or this may be father of other HENRY), one of the oldest citizens of
Huntsville died at his residence Thursday last the 2nd after an illness
of one week. Aged about 53. Disease was congestion of the lungs.
(HENRY m. ELIZ. WARE 1869 & had at least 3 chn.)

November 23, 1876
Married in this city Thursday morning last, 16 Nov. by REV. DR.
BANISTER, JOHN GRIMBALL, Esq. of N.Y. City and MISS KATE MOORE of
Huntsville.
Married in this city Thurs. evening last 16 by REV. DR. BANISTER,
CAPT. HARRY P. RYAN, assistant Supt. of M & C.R.R. to MISS ALICE,
daughter of COL. JOHN VAN VALKENBURG, all of Huntsville.
Died, WILLIAM I. HALSEY (30 A), one of the oldest inhabitants of
this city; died at his residence on Tue. morning last in 57th year;
of dropsy of the chest. Native of Huntsville....
HARRY F. CHRISTIAN died at his residence in Eastern part of the
county Thursday morning last, 16th, in 41st(?) year....
MRS. ELIZABETH SYDNOR (53 V) died at the residence of her son-in-
law, ISAIAH DILL (43 Pa), Esq. in this city on Thurs. Nov. 16, 1876 aged
82 years 4 months and 16 days. Native of Goochland County, Virginia
and removed to and settled in Huntsville in 1820 where she lived up to
the time of her death, 56 years. Presbyterian for 40 years.

December 7, 1876
Married at the residence of the bride's father, MR. F. C. ESTES
in this city on Thurs. 30 by REV. B. W. BUSSEY, MR. B. F. LUDWIG and
MISS ANNIE A. ESTIS, all of Huntsville.
At St. John's Church, Thursday by REV. HORACE STRINGFELLOW,
HON R. C. BRICKELL, Chief Justice of Supreme Court of Alabama and
MISS MARY B. GLENN of Montgomery.
On Monday Nov. 20 at Zion Church, New York, by REV. JOHN N.
GALLAHER, J. SHEPHERD CLARK to SADIE B. HOUGHTON.

December 16, 1876
Married near Ripley (Sippah Co.), Mississippi on 7th at residence
of the bride's father, AUGUST M. GAILLIARD, MR. FRED J. MO----- and
MISS CARA A. GAILLIARD by REV. JOS. H. GAILLIARD.

December 23, 1876
Died 13 December at residence of his father on Wynn Island,
Richland Parish, La., MR. ABE JANIER aged 37 years and 8 mo....
Married at the Church of Nativity in this city on 19th by REV. DR.
BANISTER, IRVINE WHITE, Esq. and MISS LUCY MATTHEWS, all of this city.
On 10 by REV. J. H. DRAKE, JAMES MITCHELL, Esq. and MISS MARY E.
SCHIMSHER, all of Madison Co.
Near Meridianville in this county Wednesday the 19th by REV.
J. R. MORRIS, MR. GEORGE W. BENTLEY and MISS EMMA WARE.
In the same vicinity on Wednesday the 19th by REV. J. R. MORRIS,
MR. ED. GILFS and MISS PUSS THOMPSON, all of this county.
NOTE: GEORGE W. BENTLEY above should be GEORGE M. BENTLEY; he was
born April 6, 1848, son of JOHN GAY and JUDITH (THOMSON) BENTLEY.

January 6, 1877
     Died at her residence near Corinth, Miss. on the 2nd, MRS. ELIZABETH
COX, widow of the late GEORGE COX and mother of MRS. JOHN D. CHADICK
of this city. MRS. COX was a former resident of Huntsville and was
highly esteemed for her truly benevolent and Christian virtues. Her
demise was very sudden, dying within one hour after being taken.
     Married in Como, Miss. on 3rd at residence of bride's father by
REV. DR. WHITE of Memphis, MR. CHARLES R. BROWN, formerly of this city
and MISS JENNIE McGEHEE.

January 13, 1877
     News from New Hope--WILLIS CARPENTER, living near here is probably
the oldest man in the county. He is 99.

January 20, 1877
     Married at the residence of the bride's father on Jan. 14, MR.
SIMON EMRICH of Huntsville to MISS SARAH SOMMER of 542 5th St. New York
City.
     The many friends of HERMON HUMPHREY, Esq. of this city will regret
to learn of the death of his mother, MRS. SUSANNAH H(ERVEY) HUMPHREY,
which occurred on 13th. (she was d of HERMAN B. SNEED & wife of
BOYLE P. HUMPHREY) (Bible says d Jan 13, 1875 & so does tombstone)
("The many friends of HERMON HUMPHREY Esq. of this city, will regret
to learn of the death of his mother, MRS. SUSANNAH H. HUMPHREY, which
occurred on the 13th inst. The family have our sincere sympathy in
their bereavement." Huntsville Advocate, Saturday, Jan. 20, 1877.
Want it certified?)
     MRS. SHELLEY, wife of GEN. C. M. SHELLEY, congressman-elect from
4th district is dead.

January 27, 1877
     We learn with regret that CAPT. JOE THOMAS, formerly of Huntsville
died recently in Little Rock (Pulaski Co.), Ark. (to McLane) of
consumption. He was a brother of MRS. JOHN W. COOPER of this city.
He was in the Confederate army as an officer under GEN. JOE SHELBY.
     We regret to learn of the death of two estimable ladies of Madison,
MRS. THOMAS CAIN aged about 40 and MRS. SARAH FARLEY in her 81st yr.
     Tribute of respect--SAMUEL WISE by Forest Home Range #514
     Married at the residence of the bride's mother near Whitesburg on
24th by REV. ALEX. PENLAND, MAJ. D. C. B. DUNLAP and MISS JOSIE MILLER.

February 3, 1877
     Married at residence of bride in this vicinity on 25 Jan.,
MAJ. J. W. ELDRIDGE, late of Mo. and MRS. M. S. DRAKE of vicinity of
Huntsville.
     Married Jan. 13th, MR. NELSON to MISS MARY M. BROWN, both of
Rockford, Ill.
     Married in Dallas, Tex. on 24 Jan. by RT. REV. BISHOP, A. C. GARRET,
of Tex. MR. FRED MANGET and MISS HATTIE TROTMAN of Dallas.
     Died, one of our old friends, J. TROTMAN, a well-known merchant
of this city.

February 10, 1877
     Married in the Cumberland Presbyterian Church in this city on
Thurs. evening Feb. 8th by REV. R. M. TINNON, MR. ROBERT L. O'NEAL and
MISS KATE ELLIOTT, all of Huntsville.
     In the Presbyterian Church in this city on evening of 8th by
REV. DR. RAYMOND of Marion, Ala. assisted by REV. J. DeWITT BURKHEAD,
MR. WM. M. RAYMOND of Selma and MISS DICIE PATTON, daughter of JOHN
PATTON, Esq. of this vicinity.
     Married on 7 Jan. last by REV. J. H. DRAKE, WILLIAM A. SADLER, Esq.
and MISS JULIA C. CLINTON.
     MRS. CHARLOTTE WARREN died near this place at the residence of
JOHN POE Tue. morning 30th of consumption. Sixteen years ago the
deceased was a young and lovely girl.... LOTTIE LAMAR was the pros-
pective mistress of 80 slaves. Her father and young husband are both
now dead.... (Explains how she lost everything in the war and had to
work in Bell Factory to earn a living. Lint got in her lungs)

February 17, 1877
    Married, REV. B. W. BUSSEY, the popular pastor of the Baptist
Church of this city married in Central Baptist Church, Memphis, Tenn.
on 18 Jan. to MISS MAGGIE L. LANDRUM of Memphis, REV. DR. LANDRUM
officiating.
    Departed this life on 8 Jan. at Homestead Place, Big Cove,
Madison Co. Ala. JOHN C. McGAHA in 43rd year. Son of JAMES and ELIZABETH
McGAHA deceased after a lingering illness of about 3 years of consumption.
Left a large circle of friends and relatives. Sympathy extended to
brothers and sisters.
    Early History of Madison Co. to be written. DR. GEORGE D. NORRIS
and COL. W. B. JONES propose furnishing many valuable incidents
connected with New Market.

February 24, 1877
    DANIEL JOHNSON, one of oldest and most respected citizens of our
city died at his residence on Greene St. Sat. night last. Born in Va.
Aug. 16, 1800 and was consequently in 77th year. Emigrated to Ky with
his father when a boy and soon afterwards came to this county. About
1837, he became an inhabitant of Huntsville, from which time he has
continually resided here.... "UNCLE DANIEL" as he is familiarly known
in this section was repeatedly entrusted with office of County Treasurer
for about 25 consecutive years.... Was a merchant for a number of years
prior to the War. Methodist.

March 3, 1877
    MRS. POWHATAN ROBINSON, wife of our talented citizen, MAJ.
POWHATTAN ROBINSON of this city died on Mon. morning last, the 26th
Feb. of pneumonia after a very brief illness.... From Church of
Nativity, REV. DR. BANISTER officiating.

March 10, 1877
    MRS. MARGARET M. TONEY of Triana died at her residence in that
place on 28 Feb. last in her 65th year.

March 17, 1877
    Married at the residence of the bride's father, CAPT. W. M. ROPER
in Madison Co. on Wed. 14th by REV. M. E. JOHNSTON, MR. JOHN T. PAUL
and MISS CARRIE V. ROPER all of this county.
    JESSE G. JORDAN a former resident of this city died at the residence
of his son in Aberdeen, Miss. in 77th year. He was a useful citizen of
Huntsville for a great many years.

March 24, 1877
    Married in this city on Wed. the 22 Mar. by REV. R. M. TINNON,
MR. THOMAS S. McCALLEY and MRS. TULLEOLA POWERS (wid of WM. H), all of
Huntsville.
    MME. OCTAVIA WALTON LeVERT died at the residence of a relative near
Augusta, Ga. on Tue. at age of about 88; daughter of COL. GEORGE
WALTON, a native of Prince Edward Co. Va. who was the second son of
GEORGE WALTON, one of Signers of Declaration of Independence. She was
born at Bell Vue near Augusta and when a child moved with her parents
to Pensacola. She married 1836 DR. HENRY LeVERT of Mobile whose father
had been Fleet Surgeon under Rochambeau.

March 31, 1877
    Married in the Cumberland Presbyterian Church in this city Mar. 27
by REV. R. M. TINNON, MR. FREDERICK O. SCHAUDIES, JR. to MISS HENRIETTA
B. OTTO, all of this city.
    Died at her late residence at Cave Springs near Vienna, AMANDA COBB
wife of BRYANT COBB.

April 6, 1877
    COL. EDMUND TONEY died at his residence in Triana Tue. night and
remains brought to this city and interred.
    Died in this city Fri. morning of consumption on 6th, MRS. ALICE
LEE YOUNG, wife of DANIEL B. YOUNG. Leaves husband and large family
of children.

April 14, 1877
        DR. C. A. JORDAN, a dentist, for many years a citizen of Huntsville
died in Memphis one day last week.
        ELISHA L. CHUNN, a most worthy and estimable citizen who lived in
neighborhood of Whitesburg died of pneumonia on 24 Mar. aged 37.
        JOSEPH HAMBRICK, Esq. died at his residence in this county in the
neighborhood of New Market on 21 Mar. last aged about 80. Had been
a resident of Madison Co. for more than 60 years... Methodist Church.
        COL. EDMUND TONEY died at his residence in Triana on 3rd in his
72nd year.... Not a churchman.

April 21. 1877
        Married on 12 April at residence of MR. J. M. ELDRIDGE, MISS MATTIE
J. ELDRIDGE and MR. G. NEWMAN JONES by REV. Z. A. PARKER, all of Madison
County.

April 28, 1877
        GEORGE A. ELGIN died at his father's residence in this city on
Wed. night last after a painful illness of several weeks in 25th yr.
        History of Madison Co.
        THOMAS FREEMAN and HUNTER PEALE were two surveyors.
        WILLIAM ACKLEN was born in Tazewell, Claiburn Co. Tenn. Dec. 1802.
His father came from Va. and married a daughter of JOHN HUNT. After
a residence of some years in Tenn. he removed with his family to
Huntsville in 1808. WILLIAM, the son, received his education at
Greenville College, Tenn. and read law in office of EBENEZER TITUS in
Huntsville in 1822.... He died May, 1872.
        JOSEPH ACKLIN:
A brother of WILLIAM was also a man of energy and ability. Became
Federal district attorney for Ala.
        JOHN ACKLIN:
        Another brother was a useful citizen of Madison and sheriff of the
county. The most celebrated of HUNT's grandsons was
        GEN. JOHN HUNT MORGAN:
        Calvalry Commander who was Maj. General in late war; was a native
of Madison Co. 1825 but removed to Ky. while a child. He was killed
in a disgraceful manner at Greenville, Tenn. Sept. 24, 1864 near former
home of his grandfather. (Mistake corrected in later issue--His mother
was a HUNT but not daughter of JOHN HUNT)
        (Letter from MRS. JACK T. ROARK, 700 Forrest Park La, Nov. 11,
1959. "My husband is a desc. of LEVI COLBERT, the son of LOGAN COLBERT
& an Indian woman whose name is unknown to us. We will try to find out
more about LOGAN & his wife later but right now we are trying to find
out names of LEVI COLBERT's children. His 1st wife was MINTEHOYAS of
the Chickasaw nation & his 2nd wife was DOLLY. We have 4 lists of
these clin & none of them agree! LEVI d. at his dau's place at Buzzard's
Roost, Ala. in 1834. She was m. to a KILPATRICK CARTER. We understand
that Ala. has a Colbert Co. supposedly named for this COLBERT family.
Is this a fact or fiction?
        A distant coz sent the fol list of clin:
        LEVI's clin by MINTEHOYA:
        MARIAH (from whom my husband descended), ROBERT, ALEX, CHAS.,
ADAM, DAUGHTERITY (WINCHESTER), CUMMODORE, ABIJAH, PHILISIS, LEMUEL,
LEWIS, VICY, SUSAN, CHARITY, ACY, MARTIN
        My husband's ggm gave this list:
        LEVI's clin: MARTIN, ADAM, BEN, MORGAN, ABIJAH, LEWIS, ALEX, LEE,
MACH, CHAS., COMMODORE, ELSIE, CHARITY, PHYLLIS (PHALISHTA), MARIAH.
        A great-aunt lists them this way:
        MARTIN, LEMUEL, CHARLIE, BENJ. MAXWELL, PHYLLIS (PHILISIA), CHARITY,
ACY or ELSIE, ELZISA, MARIAH
        By DOLLY:
        ADAIR, ALEX, MORGAN, DOUGHTERY (WINCHESTER), ABIJAH, COMMODORE.
        and the last list was sent by a coz. Vol. 8 MISS HIST see
publication LEVI's clin: MARTIN, CHAS, ALEX, ADAM, LEMUEL, DAUGHTRY,
EBIJAH, COMMODORE, LEWIS, CHARITY, MARIAH, PHALISITA, ASA.")
        (Letter from MRS. HELEN M. JACKSON, Liberty, Mo--1956 "I am a
desc. of LEVI COLBERT & I have been informed that there are descendants
of GEORGE COLBERT living in Tuscaloosa. Where was COLBERT's Ferry & why
was it named? LEVI COLBERT was the grandson of JEAN BAPTISTE COLBERT
of France.")

March 31, 1877
     History continued--On 23 July 1805, JAMES ROBERTSON of Tenn. and
SILAS DINSMORE of N. H. in behalf of U.S. purchased from GEORGE and
LEVI COLBERT a small triangular district south of Tenn. line containing
515 square miles.

April 6, 1877
     History continued--MRS. COYLE, an old widow lady owned the first
mule ever brought to the county. Green Bottom Inn (MR. ALFRED ELLIOTT's
place) was 4 miles north of Huntsville.

April 21, 1877
     History continued--ANDREW BEAN was a companion of HUNT's. Also of
Irish birth. On 1 Sept. 1802, JOHN HUNT and ANDREW BEAN left their
cabin in West Tenn. JOHN HUNT was born in Ireland about 1790. One
CHRISTOPHER BLACK, an Irishman who assisted HUNT is removing his family
from East Tenn.

May 5, 1877
     COL. JOHN FORSYTH, editor of Mobile Register died in that city on
Tue. last aged 66. One of oldest editors in Ala.
     ANDREW J. SIMLER, one of proprietors of Monte Sano Coal Mines in
this vicinity was killed yesterday morning while working in the mine.

May 12, 1877
     Died--ROBERT E. McMULLEN, son of MR. J. H. McMULLEN died at his
father's residence near Maysville in this county on 28 Apr. aged 23.
Cumberland Presbyterian.

May 19, 1877
     Married in this city at residence of MRS. M. M. BLOUNT on Tue. 15th
by REV. DR. OLIVER, MR. WILLIAM J. McCALLEY and MISS MISSOURI FORD.

May 26, 1877
     JOHN M. CROWDER, Esq. who has been on a visit to his old home in
Va. has returned.

June 2, 1877
     Estate of JANE POWER, deceased. R. A. PETTEY, administrator.

June 16, 1877
     History continued--The first settlement made where New Market now
stands was that of two brothers, GEORGE and JACOB BROILES. They came
to this country in 1806 and selected that spot for their home. First
employed themselves in deadening timber and clearing land and in course
of year or two had a pretty little farm. Settlers came in rapidly and
other industries than farming were demanded. GEORGE BROILES built the
first blacksmith shop in that part of what is now Madison Co. In 1808
the first tan yard in the county or state was begun by one TRUMP in
vicinity of BROILES' farm. From 1808 to 1818 the first inn or tavern in
this section was kept by one ROWAN.... One GEORGE SMITH bought land
extending from Main St. in New Market to old Indian boundary line and
built first store house in village; next came MOSES POARE, an old soldier
of the Revolution and built a cabin where DR. TALIAFERRO now lives.
FRED JONES made a settlement at the Berry (Fuqua) Spring and did a
good service for the county by planting out an orchard of fruit trees,
first ever planted in Madison Co.... DUDLEY DAY established the first
saddler's shop. One JAMES BROWNING opened the second store in New Market
but was unsuccessful in business and soon closed up. (We are indebted
to JOSEPH RICE, Esq. and W. B. JONES, Esq. for valuable assistance in
writing this history)

June 23, 1877
     History continued--About 1818 at instance of GEORGE SMITH, a man
by name of BURNS was employed to survey land now forming the site of
New Market. About 1819 New Market received a useful citizen in JOHN
MILLER, ancestor of the MILLER Family now owning property around New
Market. MILLER bought the inn and property of ROWAN and built the
first mill ever erected in the neighborhood. He also built the first

frame house in New Market and perhaps the first in the county. GEORGE
SMITH built the house in which DR. GREENLEE now lives. About 1825,
W. D. HAYTER and JOHN W. ESTELL opened the 3rd store house. In 1833,
STAPLES and PATRICK came to New Market with a stock of goods. HOLDEN
and ECHOLS built the CRINER store and sold goods there in 1834. The
same year, WILLIAM HILL built a residence near the MILLER home. A
man by name of DRAKE first lived where A. HAMBRICK now resides. About
this time DR. HUMPHREYS came to New Market and opened an office.
DR. NORRIS and DR. CABANISS arrived soon after, 1st physicians in
New Market. The first machine shop belonged to MESSRS. J. and D. SIBLEY.
The first saloon was used by one AB. BROWN. The first taylor's shop
was opened by JOSEPH BROWN.

June 30, 1877
        MISS CARRIE M. LACY died in Madison Co. Ala. 8 May 1877. Born in
Franklin Parish, La. Nov. 13, 1860. Methodist Episcopal Church.
        Died in Huntsville on 20 June, FANNIE CORA FOSTER, daughter of
MR. J. D. FOSTER of this city aged 6 years.
        We learn of the death of MR. J. W. TROTMAN of typhoid in Dallas,
Tex. on Thurs. morning last. WILL was a former resident of Huntsville,
Ala.
        History continued--The first mill ever erected on Flynt River was
built by JOHN BYRD in 1808. Soon after, LEVI HINDS, father of MR. LEVI
HINDS and MRS. HENRY RIGNEY, erected an excellent water power mill.
In 1835, DR. WILLIAM H. GLASCOCK was candidate for Congress. GEN.
BENJAMIN F. RICKETTS was killed in a difficulty with ROBERT CLOPTON.
In 1810, a man by name of BOSHART built a grain mill where Bell Factory
now stands.
        It is a matter of much dispute whether the CRINERS or HUNT first
made a permanent settlement in Madison Co. It is certain that HUNT's
visit in 1802 and the discovery of the "Huntsville Big Spring" antedated
the coming of the CRINERS. It is equally true that ISAAC CRINER,
JOSEPH CRINER and STEPHEN McBROOM came to this county and cleared land
and began planting in 1804 or 1805. It was in the summer of 1804 as we
have seen that JOHN HUNT commenced permanent improvements at his settlement near the "Big Spring." The CRINERS and McBROOM brought their
families to this county in the latter part of the year 1805 or the early
part of 1806. ISAAC CRINER settled on what is now the northern part of
GEORGE F. STRONG's land.

July 7, 1877
        ISAIAH DILL died by his own hand. One of our oldest and most
esteemed citizens.

July 14, 1877
        MR. W. R. JOHNSON, an old and respected citizen of Madison died at
his residence in that place on Monday last. Buried with Masonic
honors.

July 21, 1877
        MRS. KATE GRIMBALL, wife of JOHN GRIMBALL, Esq. of N.Y. late
MISS KATE MOORE of this city died at Iuka, Miss. on Tue. last 17 July
1877. Remains brought to Huntsville. Church of Nativity.
        Tribute of respect on death of ISAIAH DILL by Madison Lodge #25
I.O.O.F. He was born in Gettysburg, Pa. Dec. 25, 1806. After reaching
manhood he removed to Indiana and thence to Bellefonte, Ala. where he
practiced law for some years. In 1842 or 3 he removed to Huntsville
where he has resided ever since. Elder in Presbyterian Church.

July 28, 1877
        Died in this city on Sunday the 22nd, WALTER SYDNEY, infant son of
MRS. HENRY LANDMAN aged 11 mo.
        Remains of CAPT. F. P. WEBER were brought to Huntsville for
interment on Thurs. last he having died the day before with bilious
fever. Was connected with U.S. Coast Survey and had been engaged on
Tenn. River for nearly a year past.
        MR. WILLIAM HORTON, an old and highly respected citizen of Blount
Co. was killed a few days ago by jumping from his wagon whilst the team
was running.

August 8, 1877

Funeral of G. J. DAWSON Wed. Aug. 8. Methodist Church.

Married at the Methodist Church in Meridanville on 25 July by REV. Z. A. PARKER, MR. JAMES GRAHAM and MRS. ISSABELLA KINKLE.

Died of congestive chill near Helena (or Bobbie), Ark. JOHN DEMENT BURRUS, son of LUCIEN and MATTIE BURRUS, formerly of Madison Co. Ala.

August 15, 1877

Last Sat. evening HIRAM HUTTON and his son were drowned in a well, which they were engaged to dig.

Died at her residence in Big Cove on 10 Aug. of typhoid fever, MRS. NANCY (AGNES in some rec) BROWN (d of RICHD HOLUGES), widow of the late JOHN P. BROWN in her 79th yr.

August 22, 1877

Died at his residence in this city Sunday evening the 19th, MR. THURSTON LUMPKIN, one of the oldest citizens of Huntsville aged about 70 years. He was, we believe, born in Richmond, Va.

August 29, 1877

Married in this city on Wed. last, the 22nd, DR. J. M. BUCKHANAN of Scottsboro to MISS MARY DYER.

Died in this city on 24 Aug. MISS ELIZA W. STEELE, daughter of COL. MATT. W. and MRS. CATHARINE E. STEELE aged 24. Presbyterian.

Died on Mon. eve. last the 27th at his home in this place, MR. JOHN O'KEEFE, an old citizen aged about 50. For many years has been employed by M. & C.R.R. as car inspector at this place.

September 5, 1877

Died in this city Sat. the 1st, MILO, infant son of MR. and MRS. ROBERT C. SMITH.

WILLIAM H (S?) McCALLEY died Sat. eve. last aged about 60. Native of Spotsylvania Co. Va. Funeral took place at Methodist church.

September 26, 1877

MISS MARY COOPER, an estimable young lady living in Gadsden fell dead while sitting in a chair Sat. of last week.

MRS. KATE T. BARHAM, wife of MR. THOMAS M. BARHAM died at the residence of her mother, MRS. JOLLY in this city on 20th. Leaves a husband and two children.

Married in this city Mon. morning last, 24th Sept. by ROBERT W. FIGG, Esq. CAPT. THEOPHILAS F. HAYNES and MISS EMME A. HIRSHBRUNER, all of Huntsville.

October 3, 1877

MAJ. JAMES ROBINSON, one of the oldest and most esteemed citizens of Huntsville as well as one of the oldest and ablest members of the Bar is dead. Passed away yesterday morning 2nd Oct. at 8 o'clock in his 72nd year. Native of Tenn. having been born we believe near Sparta (White Co.), but had been a citizen of Ala. nearly all his life.

October 10, 1877

MISS MARY SUE WINSTON, daughter of STEPHEN P. WINSTON of Tex. and niece of MR. and MRS. JAS. L. COOPER of this city died in Tuscumbia one day last week.

Resolutions on death of MAJ. JAMES ROBINSON by Mayor and Alderman of Huntsville. States he was born near Sparta, White Co., Tenn. in 1805. Emigrated to Huntsville at an early period. Also resolutions by Huntsville Bar.

October 17, 1877

Married in Huntsville on Oct. 15 by REV. W. FRANKLIN KONE, COL. EDMOND EPPS of Memphis, Tenn. to MRS. TENNESSEE DUPREE of Huntsville.

BENJAMIN F. McCRAVEY, an old citizen of Huntsville died very suddenly on morning of 13th. On evening of same day, O. H. BENJAMIN, who was serving as night policeman also fell dead in beer saloon of WM. STRUVE. Middle aged man of quiet, unobtrusive manners. Leaves wife and several children.

October 24, 1877
    Married at First Methodist Church in Memphis Oct. 10 by REV.
S. B. SURATT, MR. FERDINAND N. HOLT of Huntsville to MISS ELLA PEYTON
of Memphis.
    Died at residence of her husband near Meridianville in this county
on 7 Oct. 1877, MRS. ELIZABETH STRONG, wife of MR. ROBERT H. STRONG
in her 44th year. Cancer. Lived happily with her husband 28 years
and bore 6 children, all save one had preceded her to the grave.

October 31, 1877
    REV. W. E. MUNSEY, D.D. of M. E. Church South died suddenly in
Jonesboro (Wash'n Co.), Tenn. on 23 Oct. One of most distinguished and
ablest pulpit orators in U.S.

November 21, 1877
    Another notice of death of JAMES B. ROBINSON says the funeral
took place from the Cumberland Presbyterian Church.

November 28, 1877
    Married at the residence of MRS. BLOUNT in this city on Thursday
last, the 20th, MR. PONDER and MRS. JOSEPHINE PENNEY.
    Married at the residence of MR. J. O. KELLY on 22 Nov. by REV. Z. A.
PARKER, MR. JAMES H. BURWELL to MISS M. SUE KELLY, all of Madison Co.
    Died at the residence of MR. CHARLES COLLIER near Triana on 21st,
MR. SAMUEL DENNIS, an old and highly respected citizen in his 78th
year. He was, we believe, a minister in the Christian Church.
    Died on Monday last the 26th, WASHING POE MOORE, son of JUDGE
WILLIAM H. MOORE of this vicinity. Funeral this afternoon at 3 from
the Methodist Church.

December 12, 1877
    DR. SAMUEL W. COONS, one of the oldest and most respected citizens
of this county died last Wed. morning at his residence near Triana
aged about 54. We understand he was on the eve of marrying one of
Madison's fairest daughters.

December 19, 1877
    MRS. SALLIE WRIGHT aged 90 died at her home near Maysville in this
county on 3 December having lived a member of the Methodist Church 52
years.

February 19, 1879
    Ex-Sheriff JOSEPH P. DOYLE died of appoplexy Sat. Was well
advanced in life and a long resident of this place. Held high position
of sheriff, first by appointment in 1868.

March 19, 1879
    Died at Hartsell, Ala. (Morgan Co.) on March 11th, MRS. ANNIE L.
SMITH, wife of DR. A. B. SMITH, formerly of Huntsville. Remains brought
to this city.
    Died in this city Saturday last, MRS. VIRGINIA MARTIN, wife of
MR. JOSEPH MARTIN, cashier of the National Bank, of appoplexy.
    Late WILSON HAMILTON died at the residence of J. T. LOWERY near
this city last Friday morning March 15th in his 65th year, of heart
disease. Had been a citizen of this city and county nearly all his
life....

June 11, 1879
    MAJ. ALEXANDER R. WIGGS of this city died after a protracted illness
on the evening of the 9th.... Born near Winchester, Tennessee, and was
about 54 years old. Married MISS HAWKINS, daughter of JUDGE HAWKINS of
Tennessee when quite young. Member of Cumberland Presbyterian Church.
His first wife died, in 1864 he was again married to MISS ANNA JACKSON
of Jefferson, Texas.... Edited Huntsville Independent since 1854,
also later, the Advocate.... (had bro WM. H. of Guntersville & sisters
ELIZ. m. PETER KILPATRICK, CLARISSA = RICHARDSON, CIVIL = CHRISTIAN,
CONNIE = VAUGHN.)

July 30, 1879
    LEVI HENRY HOTZ died July 28, 1879 of typhoid fever aged 19 years
11 months and 10 days. Born in Freesburg, Snyder Co., Penns. September 18,
1859. The father of the deceased came from Sumner County, Ohio in 1872
and settled within 2 miles of Huntsville, where he has since been known
as a highly respected gentleman....

October 8, 1879
    Died in Atlanta, Georgia Saturday September 27th, REBECCA J.,
wife of HON. JOHN ERSKINE and daughter of the late GABRIEL SMITH, Esq.
of Limestone County, Alabama aged 46.
    Died at Bloomfield, Madison County, Ocrober 2d. MR. D. M. CLOUD
in his 63rd year.
    MRS. MARY C. PATTON (@ 24 in 1850), wife of MR. WILLIAM R. PATTON
(@ 32) died at his residence on Meridianville Pike on Sunday night last.
    Died in this city last Friday evening after a brief illness,
MISS KATIE M. JOHNSON, daughter of MRS. E. K. JOHNSON.

November 12, 1879
    FREDERICK ELGIN, aged and well known citizen of this city died a
few days ago in Corinth, Mississippi after a painful illness of
several months, in his 79th year. Member of Cumberland Presbyterian
Church, ordained an elder in 1836....
    MRS. ALICE MURRAY, wife of A. F. MURRAY died in this city....

November 19, 1879
    Died at the residence of her husband, J. N. BLAIR in Dardanelle
(Yell Co), Arkansas on the 18th instant, MRS. HARRIET P. BLAIR aged 37
years 9 months and 9 days. Born in Jackson (to Christian) County,
Alabama and married in her 17th year to J. N. BLAIR in Marion County,
Tennessee. Joined Methodist Episcopal Church South in Huntsville in
1861 where lived until 1870 at which time she came with her husband to
Arkansas. Leaves husband and 7 children.

November 26, 1879
    MISS MATILDA ALLEN, young daughter of MRS. E. C. ALLEN died at the
residence of MR. THOMAS CAIN near Madison on the 23rd.... Short time
since, had to mourn the loss of her father.

December 3, 1879
    "Died in Marianna (Lee Co.), Dec. 2nd MRS. MARY A. RUSSELL aged
45, relic of the late R. F. RUSSEL, Esq. of Huntsville, Ala. Leaves
3 children, HARRY, ROBERT and LULA (MRS. J. P. WRIGHT)..." Marianna
(Ark.) Index.

January 19, 1881
    DR. ALVA DeBOW has left for his new home near Lagrange, southern
Texas.

January 26, 1881
    Died in Madison County on the 20th of January of pneumonia,
CHARLES ALLEN DAVIS in his 21st year.
    At her residence in this city Saturday, January 22nd after a
lingering illness, MRS. JANE E. WEEDEN.
    Died January 17th, KATY FEARN aged 19. eldest daughter of
MRS. ELIZA FEARN.
    MR. C. H. HALSEY of this city received a telegram from near
Charlotte, North Carolina telling of the death of his brother, T. R.
HALSEY (well known here as DICK HALSEY) in a railroad disaster. He
was conductor on a train. Leaves a wife and three small children.

February 16, 1881
    Died, MR. JAMES A. WILLICK, merchant of this city after an illness
of four days. Died Monday the 14th instant. He was born in Baltimore,
Md. and was about 56 years old. Settled in Huntsville 25 years ago.
Was a member of the Cumberland Presbyterian Church.

March 2, 1881
    Died, MR. JOHN W. WASHBURNE, an old resident of Madison County.

He died near his home near Meridianville about noon yesterday of apoplexy.

March 9, 1881
Died at her home near Alexandria, Fairfax County, Virginia on the 1st instant, MRS. D. C. HUMPHREYS, wife of the late JUDGE D. C. HUMPHREYS, who was for many years a resident of this city. Prior to his death, her husband was a Judge of the Supreme Court of the District of Columbia.

March 16, 1881
MRS. ANNIE HUTCHINSON BONE died at the Huntsville Hotel on March 11th. Wife of CAPT. J. H. BONE. Remains taken to Lebanon, Ohio by her husband and son for interment in the family burying ground.

March 23, 1881
Died Friday, March 18th at the residence of his brother the late REV. JOHN M. ROBERTSON, VANS MURRAY ROBERTSON in the 70th year of his age.
Died at the residence of her son, THOMAS O. LOVE, Esq., near Cluttsville on the 21st instant, MRS. MARGARET A. LOVE in the 73rd year of her age.

March 30, 1881
Died at her residence in this city on Thursday, March 24th in her 64th year, MRS. MARY TURNER MASTIN.
Died in this city March 25th, EMMA L., wife of J. WALTER LAXSON in her 24th year.
Died at the residence of her son, MR. TATE LOWRY near this city on the 27th, MRS. ELIZABETH LOWRY in her 86th year. Born in Logan County, Kentucky and moved to this county early in life. Married SAMUEL LOWRY October 31, 1816. Member of the Cumberland Presbyterian Church.
Died March 25th after a lingering illness, MRS. CEMANTHE P(ARKER) GRUBBS, devoted wife of L(UCIUS) H. GRUBBS aged 48 years.

April 6, 1881
Died in McMinnville, Tennessee on April 2nd, MRS. FRENCH (nee MISS L. VIRGINIA SMITH); born in Virginia, she married quite young, MR. JOHN L. FRENCH, wealthy stockman of Tennessee. She leaves her husband, two daughters and one son, also a cultured and gifted sister, MRS. NILES MERRIWEATHER of this city.
Died Wednesday, March 30th of pulmonary complaint, MATTIE TAYLOR, wife of ALEXANDER ERSKINE aged 23 years.

April 20, 1881
MR. NASH MALONE (note: NASHVILLE MALONE), well-known citizen of this county came to an instantaneous and terrible death on Friday last, April 15th. He had been suffering from mental aberration. Had been hunting, but returned and went to the woods with his brother, MR. LOU MALONE, where they cut and dressed some posts. Borrowed a gun and shot himself. Was in his 53rd year. Interred in the city cemetery at Huntsville.

May 4, 1881
Died at his father's home 8 miles west of Huntsville yesterday morning at 6½ o'clock, FULTON CLEMENT LANIER. Had been ill several weeks of tubercular meningitis. Was in his 15th year. Funeral will take place from the residence of his father, BURWELL LANIER, Esq.

June 1, 1881
MR. JAMES H. BURROW died at his residence in this city on Friday, May 27th. Born in Raleigh, North Carolina on January 21, 1805 and was therefore in his 77th year. His residence in this city dates back to 1836. Two sons and three daughters survive.

July 13, 1881
Died of apoplexy Monday afternoon after an illness of a few hours, MRS. M(ARTHA) A(NN) CAYTON (w of STEPHEN S) in her 74th year. Born in Goochland County, Virginia in 1808. Funeral took place from the

residence of her cousin, MRS. BETTIE DELP with whom she had resided.

August 3, 1881
     Death of JOHN G. RUSSELL, prominent citizen of Athens (Limestone County)--died Tuesday morning.

August 24, 1881
     Died--MR. BRYANT COBB, who has been a resident of this county for about 40 years, died at his residence at Cone Spring Sunday evening. He was 80 years of age and was a soldier of the War of 1812.
     JOHN H. TABER died Friday morning August 19, 1881 at the residence of his grandson, DAVIS RICE 1 mile southwest of New Hope in this county. The deceased was 92 last February. Had been a citizen of this county for a number of years. Served in the War of 1812-14 and was at the battle of New Orleans.

August 31, 1881
     Death of CAPT. A. J. FLANNIGAN, native of Madison County is announced in the Vicksburg Herald of the 28th. He was for a number of years Sheriff of Warren Co. Miss. Died of consumption.

September 7, 1881
     Died in this city Tuesday the 6th instant at an advanced age, MRS. DELIA SALE, relict of CAPT. DUDLEY SALE. Funeral at 5 o'clock from the residence of MRS. S. A. JOHNSON. Services by REV. DR. BRYSON.
     Died in this city of apoplexy Wednesday morning at the residence of MRS. M. A. RUSSELS, MRS. MISSOURI W. McCALLEY aged 53.

October 5, 1881
     Died in this city Thursday morning September 29, 1881, AUGUSTUS FRANCIS, infant daughter of WILLIAM F. and M. C. STRUVE aged 6 months and 4 days.
     MRS. FLORA A. FORD, wife of DR. HOWARD FORD died near Dexter, Missouri September 5th. She was born in Huntsville and was the daughter of A. E. MILLS, first president of the Memphis and Charleston Railroad.
     Died Sunday, September 2nd after a lingering illness, JOHN PHILLIPS.

October 12, 1881
     A postal from MAJ. W. R. WHITMAN of New Market brings intelligence of death of JAMES JONES, promising young son of COL. W. B. JONES at the residence near New Market.
     JAMES S. CLARK died Saturday the 8th instant at his home in Decatur (Morgan County) in his 53rd year. Left a wife and children. Was a prominent member of the Legislature.
     Died at his home in New Market Friday the 7th instant, of heart disease, COL. J. M. HAMBRICK.

December 7, 1881
     Died on the 5th instant at the Stegall Hotel, CYRUS MOORE in his 35th year; died of typhoid malarial fever. Bereaved mother and brother reached here Sunday afternoon and carried the remains to his former home, Oak Hill, Lincoln County, Tennessee.

July 25, 1883
     MR. WALTER S. FLETCHER and MISS MARY ELLEN BEASLEY were married by the REV. JOHN A. THOMSON at 3 p.m. Monday July 23 at the residence of the bride's father, DR. JAMES A. BEASLEY near Huntsville.
     Jackson, Miss. July 1st, 1883. JOHN B. FEARN, an old resident of this place but since the War a resident of New Orleans died here this morning. He was First Lieutenant, Co. K. BURT Rifles, 18th Regt. during the war and was disabled from service by a severe wound received at the Battle of Leesburg, Va. He was a gallant soldier and one of nature's noblemen. MR. FEARN was a native of Huntsville the son of MR. GEORGE FEARN, who removed hence to Mississippi with his father long before the War between the States.

August 1, 1883
     JAMES W. HAWKINS and MISS MAY CHEEK of Jefferson Co. Ala. were married July 28th by REV. J. A. B. LOVETT. The parties ran away from Birmingham and were married in Tenn. just across the State Line.

MRS. HARRIET A. WOODRUFF of Mooresville, Alabama died at Tullahoma (Coffee Co.), Tennessee on Saturday morning July the 28th. Her remains were brought to Huntsville and after funeral services in the Baptist Church, were deposited in the City Cemetery. Her family have lost the tender, loving ministrations of a devoted wife and mother.

August 19, 1883
A. WHITED, Esq. of New Hope has just returned from a visit to friends and relatives in East Tennessee. His mother, 73 years old, came home with him. While in Tennessee the family record was made, showing C. P. WHITED married LUCY LOWRY in 1829. The first child, A. WHITED, born October 18, 1830, the oldest of 14 children, 5 sons, and 9 daughters, all living but 2 daughters.

August 22, 1833
Thursday Morning, August 16, 1883, MR. EDWARD S. O'BEIRNE of Elgin, Ill. was married to MISS LENA S. MOORE, daughter of JUDGE WM. H. MOORE at his residence near Huntsville.

MRS. SARAH NEELY, wife of the late JAMES NEELY and mother of GEORGE M. and JOHN N. NEELY, after an illness of six months, died at her residence in this city on Monday, August 20, aged 73 years. She had resided here over 50 years.... Methodist.

COL. JOHN VAN VALKENBURG died at his residence in Huntsville on Saturday night, August 18, 1883 aged about 61. COL. VAN VALKENBURG was a citizen of Indiana and in the War between the States served in the U.S. Army first as a captain of a company and afterward as a colonel of a regiment with distinguished gallantry. After the War, he settled in Madison County...was a kind and indulgent husband and father. His funeral took place at the Episcopal Church and his remains were deposited in the City Cemetery.

September 5, 1833
Married at the residence of the bride's father, MR. A. A. BAKER, Tuesday night, Sept. 4, 1883 by REV. W. F. KONE, MR. WM L. SEAT to MISS BESSIE A. BAKER, all of Huntsville, Ala.

October 10, 1883
MRS. EMILY B. HILL of Huntsville went a few weeks ago to South Ala. to be present at the nuptials of a relative. She met MR. SAMUEL LEWIS CRESWELL, a brother-in-law of her sister JULIA...they were married by REV. JOHN CORLEY at Harpersville, Shelby County October 4, 1883. MR. CRESSWELL was our classmate at the University of Alabama in 1836-37.

MR. CHARLES C. MARTIN, son of MR. JOSEPH MARTIN, cashier of the First National Bank of Huntsville, and MISS ADA JAMAR, daughter of MR. THOMAS JAMAR, neither of whom had lived a score of years, on Saturday October 6 went to Fayetteville (Tenn.) and married.

Died at "Sweetwater" residence of his father, ex-Governor ROBERT M PATTON, near Florence, Ala. Sunday, October 7, ANDREW BEIRNE PATTON, aged 24. His brother, JOHN BRAHAN PATTON accompanied the reminns to Huntsville.

October 17, 1883
Married at the residence of the grandfather of the bride, MR. W. C. WINSTON, by REV. J. F. GOLDMAN at 12:30 p.m. Wednesday, October 17, MR. GEORGE P. DAVID to MISS ALICE ROWTON...left on a train for Memphis.

October 31, 1883
HON. TAUL BRADFORD died at his home in Talladega on Sunday last. He was born in Alabama and illustrated his native state by gallantry and heroism as an officer in the Confederate army, and his distinguished ability and fidelity as a lawyer...member of the State Legislature and represented the 3rd district in the United States Congress, 1874-76.

November 17, 1883
WILLIAM J. FRANKS, son of City Marshall Franks, died Friday. November 9th after a long illness.

SEBRING NEAL, son of the late GEORGE W. NEAL died of a chronic disease Nov. 12, 1883.

MRS. FRANCES NEAL, widow of the late STEPHEN NEAL died of pneumonia
Monday night November 12th aged 96 years. MRS. NEAL was, we believe,
the oldest living resident of Huntsville, having come here when Alabama
was a Territory. She was an affectionate mother and a Christian in the
Presbyterian Church. She and her grandson SEBRING were borne to the
cemetery in the same procession.

November 21, 1883
      MR. JAMES R. ROUTT of Fayetteville (to Naller) and MISS ROSALIE
O'NEAL of Huntsville were married by the REV. J. G. WOODS in this city
Nov. 20, 1883.
      J. W. CALDWELL, Esq. of Knoxville, Tenn. and MISS KATIE M. BARNARD
were married by REV. DR. BANNISTER at the Church of Nativity, in
Huntsville November 20, 1883...reception at the residence of COL. R. B.
RHETT, the bride's stepfather.
      MR. W. H. STYLES of Cartersville (Barton Co.), Georgia and MISS
LIZZIE CHADWICK were married by REV. DR. BARR at the residence of the
bride's father, MR. JOHN D. CHADWICK in Huntsville, Ala. at 2 p.m.
Nov. 21st. (MISS FANNY CHADWICK d @ 86, May 22, 1953, dau of JOHN D.
& FANNY COX CHADWICK)

November 28, 1883
      MR. W. A. PARKS and MISS VASHTI SWAZEY were married by REV. A. B.
JONES at the residence of the bride's father, MR. JOHN SWAZEY on Thursday
night, Nov. 22nd, all of Huntsville.
      MR. J. R. STEGALL and MISS EMMA ORGAIN were married by the REV.
J. A. THOMPSON at the residence of the bride's father in Huntsville,
Ala. Nov. 27, 1883.
      MR. JOHN H(ARDYMAN) DUNN (28 NC), a well known citizen (son of
JOHN of Idale Co, see Vol. 104), died at Madison, Ala. on Monday last,
Nov. 25, 1883 at an advanced age.

December 12, 1883
      MR. LARKIN P. SULLIVAN died at his residence in Madison County,
Alabama on Dec., 1883 aged 71 years.

December 19, 1883
      CAPT. WILLIAM M. ROPER died at his residence in Madison Co. Ala.
on Sunday Dec. 12, 1883 aged over 80 years. CAPTAIN ROPER was one of
the oldest and most estimable citizens of this county.

December 26, 1883
      Married on Thursday, Dec. 20, 1883 at the residence of the bride's
father, MR. W. L. GOODWIN in Huntsville, MR. H. M. RANDALL of Georgia
to MISS MOLLIE GOODWIN by REV. JOHN A. THOMPSON.
      MR. HUGH N. MOORE, an old and respected citizen of Huntsville went
several years ago to Mexico, Texas and died there Dec. 7.
      MR. JOHN C. DRAKE, a worthy son of MR. JOHN R. DRAKE of this city
died of consumption at Mariana a few weeks ago.
      An account of the accidental death of ALFRED HAMBRICK "an old and
respected citizen of New Market, who we hear was going to visit his son,
MR. JOSEPH M. HAMBRICK." He was killed near Brownsboro by the M. & C
passenger train "last night between 1 and 2 o'clock" The deceased was
about 71 years old.

NORTH ALABAMA REPORTER 1875

May 29, 1875
      Died on Tuesday night of this week, MR. IRVIN WINDHAM after a
brief illness at the ripe old age of 76. MR. WINDHAM had been one of
the most useful citizens of Huntsville for over 50 years.

June 12, 1875
      Resolutions of respect on death of DR. L. D. CARTER, who died
May 6, 1875.

July 29, 1875
   Died on the 30 of June at the residence of his daughter, MRS. SIBLEY
in this county, MR. MILLS RENKINS aged 70 years.   Leaves wife and large
number of relatives and friends.

HUNTSVILLE DEMOCRAT

Huntsville, Ala.
Vol. I #4

October 28, 1823
   Died at Phila on 18 September COM. JOHN SHAW, of the U.S. Navy.
   Notice of slave taken off by LETITIA BEADLES, wife of ABRAHAM
BEADLES.

November 4, 1823
   Died in Franklin Co. (Ky) after a painful illness GENERAL MARTIN D.
HARDIN as a member of the Bar a statesman and a gentleman of integrity
and electing worth, the deceased had few superiors.   His death will be
extensively felt and sincerely regretted.

November 11, 1823
   Nothing

November 25, 1823
   Murder of WM. JONES by brother JACK JONES, a young man of this county.
(Alabama Gazette)
   Administrator's Notice--SAMUEL D. SHERRELL, deceased

December 2, 1823
   Nothing

December 16, 1823
   Nothing

January 6, 1824
   Nothing

January 13, 1824
   Died in hour on 8th inst. CAPT. JOHN M. LYNCH, Ca 26 years of age, a
native of Pendleton District, S.C. MR. LYNCH was taken sick in the neighborhood of Knoxville came down the river, and died soon after reaching
this place. At his request it was intended to have removed his remains to
his native state, but his nephew, who received this charge, was prevented
by indisposition.

January 27, 1824
   Married on Wed. evening last instant, by REV. DR. A. A. CAMPBELL, (also
MITTEN WARREN) MR. WARNER T. BOLING, to MISS HARRIET E. SMITH, daughter of
GEORGE S. SMITH, Esq. of this county. On same evening D. THOMPSON, MR.
ISAAC WMS, MISS ELIZA L. M'LARAN?, both of Huntsville

February 24, 1824
   Married on 19 instant by REV. W. BLUNT PECK, MR. JASON L. JORDAN to
MISS CHARITY W. HOBBS, both of this county.
   Died in this place on Tuesday evening last, MAJ. EBENEZER TITUS,
attorney at law

March 2, 1824
   Married on 20th ult., MAJ. JOHN McKINLEY of Florence to MISS ELIZABETH
ARMISTEAD of this place.
   Also married on same evening by REV. W. BLUNT PECK, PULASKI DUDLEY,
Esq. of Tuscumbia to MISS SUSAN M. BASS, of this county.

March 9, 1824
   Funeral sermon of CAPT. WALTER OTEY will be preached at his late
residence near Meridianville on 3rd Sunday of this month by REV. DAVID
THOMPSON.

March 30, 1824
    Lawrence County Alabama--Executor's notice--WM. GREEN, dec--SOLOMON
GREEN of Warren Co., N.C., executor--March 27, 1824
    Married on 24 inst. by REV. MR. PECK, MR. NICHOLAS HOBSON to MISS
SARAH ANN SMITH, daughter of CAPT. GEORGE S. SMITH all of this county.
    Died after a protracted illness at his lodgings in this city yesterday,
the HON. WILLIAM LEE BALL? aged about 45. For several past & time of his
death a Representative in Congress from State of Virginia. United to
social and amiable qualities role made him the delight of his friends,
powers of intellect, who tho' seldom called forth, were effective whenever
exerted in his public station.
    Notice: The late WILLIAM GREEN. This is to give notice to all whom
it may concern that WM. GREEN late of Lawrence County Alabama is dead and
that at court held for County of Warren, State of N.C. in Feb. Court
SOLOMON GREEN, Esq. qualified as executor to will of said deceased.
                          signed DENNIS O'BRYAN agent for executor
                          of WM. GREEN deceased March 27, 1824

April 6, 1824
    REV. JOHN ALLAN will preach on a funeral occasion at house of JOHN
VINING's on 3rd Sabbath in April.
    Married on the ultimo by REV. E. TAYLOR, MR. JOLIN HAMER to MISS
SARAH E. DILLARD, all of this county. (SARAH L. in marriage record)

April 13, 1824
    I, WILLIAM COZBY of Madison County and State of Alabama do hereby
certify that I was appt Agent for my father, R. COZBY, a Pensioner of the
U.S., in the year 1822 to receive pension from the agent in Huntsville and
applied to said agent in 10 Ca the 1st of June, the pension having been
due from the 10th of March preceding, in the year 1822, amounts to $48;
when the agent informed me that he has no funds to pay the pension and
advised me to a(--faded) at Huntsville again in about 2 weeks; when I did,
and was again put off with the same excuse, and so from time to time 3 or
4 times until I think sometime in July, I again applied from his informing
me by mail that I could draw my father's pension upon application & rec'd
from said agent $48 in depreciated bank bills on Tenn and Huntsville banks,
which I received for my because I believed I could get no better money
having understood the agent would pay in --(faded). I further certify
that I afterwards drew said pension for my father, ½ yearly til Sept. or
Oct. 18 when I drew the last, my father now being dead all of which I
received in Tenn & Huntsville bank note a greatly depreciated value
because I could get no better.
    At the receipt of all the installments the agent gave his check on the
Huntsville bank and that 1 of times the cashier of the bank asked the agent
when the agent replied, "in Huntsville or Tenn. notes," given under my
hand this 31st of January 1824.
                          WILLIAM COZBY
Certified by GEORGE T. JONES, J.P.
    Died in this place on 7th inst. MR. JOHN MILLER of the Firm of CAIN
& MILLER.
    I, WILLIAM PARKER, do hereby certify that I was formerly a private in
CAPT. MUHLENBURG's Co. of the 4th Regt., U.S. Inf. and agreeably to my
certificate bearing date 6 Sept. 1820 am entitled to receive $8 per month
to commence on 11th March 1819. I do also further certify that I applied
to the pension agent in Huntsville, COL. POPE (about the month of Oct.
1821) for the amount of my pension then due when he, the said agent paid
me the sum of $237.00 or thereabouts (this being the 1st time I had
applied for my pension) in depreciated, Tenn. bank bills. I demanded U.S.
funds of the said agent but he positively refused paying such. I then
required of him Huntsville bank notes, which were considered about 10%
better than Tenn but he even refused to pay me in that paper and concluded
by saying that if I would not take the Tenn notes I might go unpaid as
he had drawn that description of money to pay the pensioners which I very
reluctantly received as I lived in Mobile where it was of little or no
value. I do also further certify that his money was paid me in the bank
of Huntsville and in the presence of the cashier, who in my presence
requested COL. POPE.
    Given under my hand 25 February 1824
                          WILLIAM PARKER
Certified by THOMAS HUMES, J.P.

April 20, 1824

April 27, 1824
Died on Friday last CAPT. FRANCIS ANDERSON, an old and respectable
citizen of this county.

May 4, 1824
Married in Huntsville on 19th ult. by REV. MR. ALLEN, MR. HENRY H.
DEDMAN of this county to MRS. HANNAH SHAW of S.C. (HENRY C. in marriage
record) (HENRY H. is correct)
Funeral--The REV. MR. BESTER will preach at the house of MAJ. JAMES B.
HOLMAN on Sunday the 15th on a funeral accasion.
Died on 26 April RICHARD RILEY Esq. of Cherokee Nation.
After a long and lingering illness which he bore with Christian
firmness, he died firm in the faith of the hope of gospel leaving behind
him a bright example of piety and real excellence.

May 11, 1824
Married on 6th inst. by REV. MR. PECK, MR. THOMAS BINFORD of Virginia
to MISS HARRIET B. TURNER of this county.

May 18, 1824
Married in Tuscumbia on 13th inst. by REV. MR. PECK, COL. BARTLEY COX
of Huntsville to MISS ELIZA I. N. FREEMAN of Tuscumbia.
Married on Tuesday evening last by REV. JESSE BUTTER, MATHEW CLAY,
Esq. to MISS FRANCES ANN daughter of REV. TURNER SAUNDERS, all of
Lawrence County.

May 25, 1824
State of Alabama--Jackson County at Circuit Court held 2 Monday in
April
    JOHN SNODGRASS   )
        vs   ) Chancery
    NATHAN ABBOTT   )
    NATHAN ABBOTT is a non-resident of this state

June 1, 1824
Nothing

June 8, 1824
Obituary: Died in this place on Friday morning last after a short
illness, MRS. ELIZA M. CONSORT of MR. ELIAS P. SMITH of Huntsville....
"To her to die was gain, but an affectionate husband and 2 small children
are left to mourn the loss, which to them is irreparable."

June 15, 1824
Nothing

June 22, 1824
Died on 1st instant at Marietta, GEN. RUFUS PUTNAM aged 86. REV.
PATRIOT. Born Sutton, State of Massachusetts etc.

June 29, 1824
Nothing

June 30, 1826
Departed this life at her residence in Madison County, Sunday the
18th in 18th year of her age, MRS. EMILY E. C. HARWOOD consort of

July 6, 1824
Nothing

July 13, 1824
Nothing

July 20, 1824
Married on 12th instant by REV. MR. PECK, MAJ. LARK F. WOOD of
Nashville to MISS ELIZA ECHOLS, daughter of COL. WM. ECHOLS of this county.

```
State of Alabama  )  ELIZABETH GALLOWAY by her next friend
                  )                vs
Madison County    )  JAMES GALLOWAY.  Bill for divorce
State of Alabama  )  DEBORAH DICKSON by next friend
                  )                vs
Madison County    )  SAMUEL DICKSON.  Bill for divorce.
                     Marriage Records    SAMUEL DICKSON--DEBORROUG
                     HORTON January 1816
```

August 3, 1824
  Nothing

August 10, 1824
  Married in this place on Thursday 29th July by REV. MR. ALLAN, COL.
JAMES J. PLEASANTS, Secretary of State to MISS EMILY JULIA BIBB, daughter
of THOMAS BIBB.

August 17, 1824
  Died in Lawrence County on Saturday the 8th inst. REV. JESSE BUTLER.

August 24, 1824
  Ad--JOHN C. FINLAY--tailor

August 31, 1824
  Married on 16th at house of CAPT. FRILEY JONES in this County by
REV. S. G. GIBBONS, MR. JOHN BROOKS, merchant of Meridianville to MISS
PENELOPE GARRET, late of North Carolina.
  Died on 25 of August after an illness of 4 weeks, CHARLES KING, JUNIOR,
a young man in the bloom of life...kind and affectionate son to his
parents, tender and affectionate to his brothers and sisters....

September 7, 1824
  Nothing

September 14, 1824
  Married on Sunday evening 22 August in Prince George County Maryland
by REV. ALOYSIUS MUDD, MR. LUKE HOWARD, Merchant of Alabama to MISS
HARRIET, youngest daughter of late HENRY BROOKE, Esq. of said county.
  Died on evening of 12 in this place MR. BENJAMIN PHILBRICK after a short
but severe illness.
  In Richmond Virginia on 21 August DR. WM. FOUSHEE after a lingering
illness of more than 9 months.
  On same day, COL. J. TAYLOR, of Caroline, Virginia a Senator of the
United States.
  In Franklin Missouri, JOSEPH JONES MONROE, Esq. brother of Pres. of
U.S., JOSEPH JONES "a brother of mine" fined for Sabbath (bocahiry ?)
GEO. T. JONES.

September 21, 1824
  Married on 16 instant by S. G. GIBBONS, JOHN VINING Esq. to MRS.
ELVIRA SHELTON, all of Madison County.
  On Thursday evening 16, by HENRY RIGNEY, Esq., MR. JOSH (JOHN in
marriage record) RANDOLPH to MISS FRANCES COOPER, all of this county.
  State of Alabama--Madison County--Bill for divorce--ABRAHAM BEADEL
vs. LATITIA BEADEL
  Depositions of WM. BAKER, RICHARD ELLETT, SAMUEL EVANS, BANISTER
WINN wife SALLY and others

September 28, 1824
  Obituary:
  Died in Madison County on --- MRS. FRANCES JEFFRIES, consort of
--- JEFFRIES aged 52 years.
  Died on Sunday 4th instant after severe illness of 24 days, ELIZ.
ADKINS daughter of MAJ. HENRY ADKINS of Morgan County Alabama, late of
Sussex, Virginia aged 5 years and 4 months. Though she was but an
infant she has left 2 affectionate parents, 2 brothers and a sister
with all that knew her to mourn so promising an ornament to society.

Died at his residence near Haysborough, Tenn. on 10th inst. the REV.
THOMAS B. CRAIGHEAD, in the 71st year of his life.
Died in Madison County, MRS. FRANCES JEFFRIES, consort of --- JEFFRIES,
aged 52 (note: ALEXANDER JEFFRIES).
Died the 4th inst. ELIZABETH, daughter of MAJ. HENRY ADKINS of
Morgan County, late of Sussex County, Virginia aged 5.
Died at his residence near Maysborough, Tenn. on the 10th instant
REV. THOMAS B. CRAIGHEAD in his 71st year.

October 12, 1824
Died the 30th September MRS. MARY, wife of CAPT. JOHN TATE of
Limestone County. Left children.
Died the 17th of September 1824, MISS NANCY CHEEK, aged 25 years.
Died on 30th September MRS. MARY TATE, wife of CAPT. JOHN TATE of
Limestone County Alabama.... (mentions left children)
Died on Friday 17 September the worthy and much esteemed MISS NANCY
CHEEK aged 25 years.

October 19, 1824
Married on 13th instant by REV. DAVID THOMPSON, CAPT. JOHN F. NEWMAN
to MISS ELLENER ROSE, daughter of DR. ROBT. H. ROSE, all of this county.
Died on Saturday 21 August about 12 at night, MR. JOHN HATCH in the
25th year of his age. Native of Charlotte County Virginia having lost
his parents at an early period of life, he resolved to tread the flowery
and enameled paths of literature and after going thru an academical course
in the best preparatory schools, he entered as a student at U. of N.C....
Left numerous relatives.

October 26, 1824
Nothing

November 2, 1824
Estate of SAMUEL GLAIZE deceased. WILLIAM JOHNSON and TIMOTHY W.
McCARTY, Morgan County October 27, 1824.

November 5, 1824
Died in Morgan County, Alabama on the 13th instant after a short
illness, MRS. MARY P. MURPHY, aged 36 years, consort of MR. GEORGE
MURPHY. Left five little children.
Died 21st of August, MR. JOHN HATCHETT in Limestone County. Native
of Charlotte County, Virginia. Having lost his parents in early period
of his life, he emigrated to this county last spring and boarded with
a private family. He was an orator

November 9, 1824
GEORGE T. JONES, in an open letter declares that MR. HAYS made a
report just before the last election for representatives, amongst his
friends at Ditto's Landing to the effect that "I, as a Justice of
Peace, sat on a trial between my brother, JOSEPH JONES and himself
and had given judgment in favor of my brother against him on a plain
note of hand, merely because the note was executed on Sunday. This
report I proved to be a base falsehood in all parts." JOSEPH JONES
had agreed to sell JAMES YOUNG a steer, but testified he never got
paid etc.

November 16, 1824
Petition for divorce:
State of Alabama, Jackson County Circuit October 1824
EDWARD MAXWELL   )
        vs   )   Defendant is not a resident of this state
SUSAN MAXWELL   )

November 23, 1824
Nothing

November 30, 1824
    Married in this county on Thursday evening last by MR. THOMPSON, MR.
JOHN M. CALDWELL, merchant of this place to MISS EMILY BELL.

December 7, 1824
    Nothing

December 14, 1824
    Married on Tuesday evening 16th, instant by REV. MR. CARSON, MR. DAVID
S. McINTOSH of Huntsville, Alabama to MISS CAROLINE MATILDA, daughter of
MR. THOS. FOSTER of this county. Adams County, November 25, 1824--
Mississippian.
    On Thursday the 9th instant by REV. WM. McMAHAN, MR. FRANCIS E. HARRIS,
JR. to MISS SARAH M. eldest daughter of BENJAMIN ELLIS, Esq. all of
Madison County.

December 21, 1824
    Married on Thursday 9th instant by REV. MR. BOOTH, MR. JOHN BROOKS
to MISS ELIZA MILLER, all of this place.

December 28, 1824
    Nothing

January 4, 1825
    Nothing

January 11, 1825
    Died on 6th instant at residence of WM. POWERS, in this county
ROBERT POWERS, eldest son of the late MADISON POWERS.

January 18, 1825
    Married in Courtland on Monday evening the 10th instant A(NDERSON)
HUTCHINSON, Esq. of Huntsville to MRS. MARY M. MITCHELL of the former
place (Vol. 22, p. 16).

January 25, 1825
    Nothing

February 1, 1825
    Died in Triana on 24 ultimo, DR. JOHN A. H. HERRING, in the 23rd (?)
year of his age. Died in the beginning of his manhood.... (see marriage
to MISS SARAH E. WEEDON 1284--daughter of DR. F. WEEDON)
    DR. WEEDON gratefully acknowledges to the citizens of Triana for
their kind and unceasing attention to his son, DR. JOHN A. H. HERRING
during his last illness.
    Died on 25th ult. at his residence in this county MR. FREDERICK W.
JAMES, a highly respected citizen in the 53rd year of his age.
    Administrator's sale--estate of THOMAS ARNETT, deceased of Triana.

February 8, 1825
    Nothing

February 15, 1825
    Nothing

February 21, 1825
    Died in Triana on 24th ult. DR. JOHN A. H. HERRING in his 23rd year.
    Died on 25th ult. at his residence in this county, MR. FREDERICK W.
JAMES in his 53rd year.

February 22, 1825
    Married on 9th instant by REV. MR. THOMPSON, ELIZABETH M. BROWNING
of this county.
    Married on 11th instant by REV. MR. ALLAN, WILLIAM G. HILL, Esq. of
this town to MISS MARY (C or G?) HALL, daughter of E. S. HALL, Esq. of
Nashville, Tennessee.
    Married on 9th instant by REV. S. G. GIBBONS, MR. JAMES LEE of
Madison County to MISS CYNTHIA A. HODGES, daughter of MR. JAMES HODGES
of the above county.

March 1, 1825
    Nothing

March 8, 1825

Died in this county on 21st ult. CAPT. JOHN GRAHAM in the 71st year of his age. CAPT. GRAHAM was an officer of the Rev. and distinguished himself under that gallant sol, GEN. MARION in S.C. He was taken captive by the British and confined 8 or 10 weeks in Camden jail where he endured the privations and sufferings incident to such a confinement. After his release, he joined the American army again and continued gallantly to sustain the cause of his country thruout the war. CAPT. GRAHAM was a gentleman of amiable disposition--respected and admired by all his acquaintances. He has descended to the grave full of honors and left a numerous progeny to deplore his loss. There are few men whose descendants count so numerously. He has left 11 children, 6 sons and 5 daughters; 90 grandchildren and 27 great-grandchildren, 13 sons-in-law and daughters-in-law making altogether 141.

March 22, 1825

Married on 13th inst. by REV. SAMUEL G. GIBBONS, JAMES MULLINS, Esq. to MISS MARTHA MURRAY, both of Madison County.

On 16th instant by REV. S. G. GIBBONS, MR. WILLIAM HARTON of Hazel Green to MISS NICY POWER, daughter of MAJ. NATHANIEL POWER, deceased.

March 29, 1825

Nothing

April 5, 1825

Nothing

April 12, 1825

Nothing

April 19, 1825

Married on 23rd July, in Greenburgh, Kentucky by REV. MR. HODGINS, BYRD BRANDON, Esq. of this town to MISS MARY JANE CALDWELL of the former place.

Married on the 14th instant by REV. MR. HOLLAND, MR. WILLIAM McCAY, to MRS. SARAH O'RILEY, both of this place.

Died on the 18th instant, MRS. ELIZA, wife of DR. HENRY CHAMBERS.

Married on 23rd ult. in Greensburgh, Kentucky by REV. M. HODGINS, BYRD BRANDON, Esq. of this town to MISS MARY JANE CALDWELL of the former place.

Married on 14th instant by REV. J. H. HOLLAND, MR. WILLIAM McCAY to MRS. SARAH O'RILEY, both of this place.

Died on 18 instant MRS. ELIZA CHAMBERS, wife of DR. HENRY CHAMBERS.

April 26, 1825

Married on 21st instant by REV. DAVID THOMPSON, MR. WILLIAM W. HARRIS of Limestone County to MISS MARY JANE, daughter of DUDLEY SALE, Esq. of this county.

May 3, 1825

Died on Thursday 28th instant MRS. MARTHA TURNER, consort of CAPT. THOMAS TURNER of Madison, formerly of Greenville, Virginia.

May 10, 1825

Married on Thursday evening 28th ult. by REV. J. BURNS, MR. ROBERT BLACK of House of Black and Webb, of Florence, to MISS ELIZ. BAGLEY of Franklin County.

May 17, 1825

Married on Tuesday the 3rd instant by REV. THOMPSON, MR. RICHARD B. HARRIS, to MISS ANN H., daughter of WILLIAM H. CLOPTON, Esq. all of this county.

State of Alabama--Decatur County: OC--May 5 1825--The administration of estate of ALEXANDER W. DALANEY, deceased, filed vouchers.

May 24, 1825

Nothing

May 31, 1825

Nothing

June 7, 1825

Nothing

June 14, 1825
Nothing

June 21, 1825
Nothing

June 28, 1825
Nothing

July 5, 1825
Married on 20 June by REV. JOHN BLACKBURN, MR. SEANAH SMITH of this place to MISS MARGARET B. WEST of Williamson County, Tennessee.

July 12, 1825
Nothing

July 19, 1825
Nothing

July 22, 1825
Nothing

July 29, 1825
Citations:
OC Limestone County. 3 Mon July 1825--Admnr. of WOODSON C. MONTGOMERY deceased. It is ordered that WM. L. MONTGOMERY, JAMES K. MONTGOMERY, JORDAN MONTGOMERY, RICHARD H. LEE, husband of PATSEY LEE, who was late PATSEY MONTGOMERY, WILLIAM F. LEE, husband of JANE LEE, JANE MONTGOMERY, WILL BROWN, husband to SOPHIA BROWN "SOPHIA", AUSTIN CEPATA? MONTGOMERY and MARY LOWRY, infants by ROBERT AUSTIN their guardian who are the next heirs of W. C. MONTGOMERY deceased be cited to appear before the court at Athens on -- Mon of August next.

August 5, 1825
Nothing

(Newspaper date unknown)
CLAUDIUS F. HARWOOD. Born in lower part of State of Virginia and lost her mother before she reached her third year; care of her grandmother and aunt reared her to age of 17, when she married MR. HARWOOD on 14 July 1825.... Gavie birth to a still born child.

July 7, 1826
Died on 5th, MRS. SARAH CARUTHERS of this vicinity.
On 5th at residence of R. B. PURDOM, MISS RUTHER JANE 2nd daughter of ARCHIBALD RHEA of Tuscumbia in 12th year. (He married CATHERINE daughter of GEN. JOHN SEVIER)
State of Alabama Madison County. Circuit Court. ROBERT PRYOR and ANNA his wife, WILLIAM KIRLY (K. copied this KIRBY in Chan-rec), HENRY KIRLY, and JAMES KIRLY versus ELIZABETH SIMPSON. SARAH KIRLY, SAMUEL BUCHANAN and wife SARAH, MICAJAH MUCKLEROY (married RACHEL SIMPSON 1815 Madison) and wife RACHEL, POLLY KERMER, MICHAEL DITTO (married PEGGY SIMPSON 1817) and wife MARGARET, WILLIAM SIMPSON, RUTH SIMPSON and JOHN SIMPSON by their guardian, ELIZABETH SIMPSON.

July 21, 1826
Departed this life at her residence on 10th after a lingering and severe illness, MRS. JERUSHA consort of MR. CHARLES WILLIAMS of this county in her 39th year.
Died in the vicinity of this town on 18th and 19th, MRS. ELIZABETH consort of CAPT. NICHOLAS WARE (m. SARAH E. THOMPSON 1821), and MRS. ELIZABETH (KATHLEEN then name), consort of REVD. DAVID THOMPSON. MRS. W. has left a husband and two small children; MRS. T. who only survived her daughter 33 hours, has left a husband and 6 children.
In Jackson County on 11th July of pulmonary disease, MISS LOUISIANA CHEEK, youngest daughter of MR. JESSE CHEEK, JR. leaving mother, relatives and friends....

August 11, 1826
Departed this life on 4th about 8 miles Southwest of Huntsville after a very short illness, MR. GEORGE HOLLOWAY, lately from Orange County, Virginia. In prime of youth.

August 25, 1826

Died in Carnesville, Geo. on 28 July after a long illness, HEZEKIAH TERRELL in her 52nd year. Many years a resident of that village being among the lst settlers.

September 15, 1826

Died on Sat. last at residence in this county, MICAJAH C(LARK) MOORMAN, a native of Virginia and for the last 3 or 4 years a citizen of this state. (wife was ESTHER ALEXANDER--ancestors of MRS. LYDIA GRAYDON, Berkeley, Cal., g-son of ACHILLES MOORMAN, REV. SOL.)

In Limestone County about 9 o'clock, MRS. NANCY HARDING in her 53rd year.

January 5, 1827

Nothing

January 26, 1827

Funeral of BRO. HENRY H. EDMONDS will be preached at house of MR. SUGAR TURNER on 28th. Helion Lodge #1--Masons.

January, 1827

Married 23rd of December MR. LEVI RAGSDALE to MISS CATHERINE, daughter of ALEXANDER WASON, all of this place.

Married on 28th, WILLIAM ROUNTREE, Esq. to MISS HARRIET SHERWOOD of Limesteon County.

Married 4th January 1827 JAMES J. THORNTON, Esq. Secretary of State to MISS MARY GLOVER of Marengo County.

January 9, 1827

Died last Friday evening, WILLIAM G. SEAY in 38th year.

Died in Sparta, Tenn. Sunday, ALEXANDER CRAIGHEAD, Esq. attorney aged 36.

February 9, 1827

Funeral of SAMUEL TINDALL, deceased. Formerly a citizen of Huntsville, will be preached at Methodist Church 2nd Sabbath by REV. L. GARRET of Maury County, Tenn.

Married Tuesday by REV. MR. ALLEN, MR. E. T. PALMER of Tenn. to MISS FRANCES E. DYER, daughter of CAPT. JUSTIN DYER of Madison.

Married in Botetourt Co. Va. Dec. 20 last by REV. JOSHUA BURNETT, MR. J. LEFTWICH of North Alabama to MISS CAROLINE SNODGRASS of Botetourt.

March 9, 1827

State of Alabama--Limestone Co. Estate of WILLIAM HERNDON deceased. JOHN FAVER, JR. adm'r.

State of Alabama--Limestone County. County Court Feb. 24, 1827. WILLIAM COWAN and wife NANCY, late NANCY HALL, administrator and Administratrix of estate of WILLIAM HALL, filed vouchers.

State of Tennessee--Paris 9th District October Term 1826.

JAMES HARRIS et al)
versus) Original bill
JAS. McCOLLUM et al)

Bill states amongst other things that complainants are heirs and legal representatives of EDWARD HARRIS, deceased and that said EDWARD HARRIS died some years ago and left the complainant and JOHN McCLURE and wife REBECCA, formerly REBECCA SLOAN, JAMES McCOLLUM and wife MARY (formerly HARRIS) as heirs at la and legal representatives. EDWARD HARRIS died seized of land in western district of Tenn.

State of Alabama--Limestone County. 20 February 1827. Estate of JOHN FOOTMAN WALKER, deceased. J. N. S. JONES, admr.

Limestone Co.--State of Alabama. Estate of EATON P. VAUGHAN, deceased. FRANCIS EPPES, executor.

Married Tuesday the 6th by THOMAS SCOTT, Esq. MR. THOMAS CLARKE to MISS HESTER MOON, all of Madison Co.

Wednesday the 22nd, by WILLIAM WRIGHT, Esq. MR. JESSE McBROOM to MISS NANCY MEDLEM (MEDLEY in Marriage rec), all of this county.

Thursday the 1st by REV. MR. ROWE, MR. JOHN HAGES (HAZAY in mar rec) to MISS ELIZABETH SCRUGGS.

Departed this life on Sat. night the 24th February, DR. WILLIAM C. GIBSON aged 30 years of age.

March 16, 1827
State of Alabama--Limestone County. WILLIAM SHORES, executor of will of JANE PISSES, deceased.
State of Alabama--Limestone County. County Court Mar. 6, 1827. RICHARD H. M'NEES, administrator of JAMES M'NEES filed accounts for final settlement.
State of Alabama--Limestone County. ALLEN URQUHART, administrator of estate of MARGARET PHILLIPS, deceased.

March 30, 1827
Married in Franklin County, Tenn. by REV. JAMES ROWE, 22, MR. OLIVER J. LINDSEY of this place to MISS SARAH M. daughter of CAPT. LEWIS CLARKE of the former place.
Married on 15th inst in Lincoln County, Tenn. MR. ISAAC H. WALL, of Huntsville to MISS SUSAN P. SMITH daughter of RICHARD SMITH, Esq. See our Vol. 203 p 17.
ISAAC H. WALLS deeded lot to SARAH SMITH 1826.
Married on Tuesday evening, by REV. HENRY W. SALE, MR. JAMES DRAKE of Athens to MISS HONORA G. ROOTES of this county. Note: she was dau of PHILIP JENNINGS ROOTES & wife SARAH DAVIS).
Married 15th inst. in Limestone County by PAUL HILDREATH, Esq. MR. GEORGE LYNES of this town to MISS MARTHA LOVE of former place.
Married on Thursday, 15th inst. by REV. HENRY W. SALE, MR. JOHN BYRN to MISS MARTHA JOHNSON, all of this county.
Died on Thursday morning last in this place, MRS. ROSANNA FEENEY in her 74th year.

April 6, 1827
Married Thurs. 29th by REV. JAMES ROWE, MR. IRVIN WINDHAM to MISS ANN SADLUN (BADLUN in Sou Adv) all of this place.
Died at Red Oak Flat this Co. the 31st CATHARINE FRANCES, youngest daughter of MAJOR ROBERT WALTON aged 11 months.
Died at Athens the 24th DR. JOHN R. BEDFORD, late of the House of Bedford, Breedlove and Robeson, New Orleans.
Died on 4th inst. MR. DAVID WILLIAMSON for some years a citizen of Alabama.

April 13, 1827
State of Alabama--Limestone County. JAMES MILLER deceased. WILLIAM MILLER and MARGARET MILLER, admrs.
State of Alabama--Limestone County. WILLIAM M'GEHEE, deceased. NAN(?) McGEHEE, executrix. L. S. McGEHEE, her agent.

April 27, 1827
Married on Thursday evening the 19th by REV. JOHN M'FERRIN, MR. WILLIAM EARNEST to MISS AGNESS P. daughter of REV. JOHN T. NELSON, all of Madison County. (yes, it is in mar rec "C"--see our vol 119, p 20)
Died at Whitesburg on 18th inst. ROBERT BEATTIE, a native of Dumfries-shire Scotland aged 34.

May 4, 1827
Funeral sermon of MRS. ELIZABETH LEWIS, wife of CAPT. JOHN T. W. LEWIS will be preached by REV. DAVID THOMPSON on 13th at the residence of MRS. MARGARET ROBINSON.
Married on Thursday the 26th by JOHN C. GRAYSON, Esq., MR. RICHARD MEDLEN to MISS LUCINDA P. CHILDRESS, all of this county. (yes, it is in mar rec "C"--see our Vol. 119 p. 20)

May 25, 1827
Died on 17 after a short illness, MR. SAMUEL MITCHELL, one of the earliest settlers of this town.
Married on 17th by REV. WILLIAM EDDINS, MR. SOLOMON GEORGE (one SOLOMON GEORGE lived in Greene Co. 1842 & 1846) of Franklin County to MISS FRANCESS CRUTCHER of Limestone.

Married on evening of 10th by REV. JOHN H. THOMPSON, MR. DAVID
BAILEY to MISS LOUISA BLEDSOE (LOUISIANA in marriage records), both of
Madison County.
    On Tue. evening the 15th, by REV. JAMES ROWE, MR. A(DKINSON)
STEWART to MISS MARY M. WALKER, all of Huntsville.

June 1, 1827
    GOVERNOR ISRAEL PICKENS died in Cuba on 23.
    Died on 22 in 18th year, RICHARD E. PETTUS, son of MR. DAVID PETTUS
of this county.
    State of Alabama--Limestone Co. ANDREW J. EDMONDSON, administrator
of estate of ISAAC HALL, deceased.
    State of Alabama--Limestone Co. WILLIAM ROWNTREE, administrator
of SAMUEL MITCHELL.

July 13, 1827
    Departed this life on evening of 4 July, MRS. KING, wife of
COL. HENRY KING and daughter of MAJOR ISAAC WELLBORN...left her aged
father, mother and husband and 4 small children. REV. McMAHAN will
preach her funeral sermon at the residence of MAJ. ISAAC WELLBORN a
half mile south of Hazlegreen on 1st Sabbath in August.
    Died at Florence on 27 June last, MR. DAVID COBB in his 68th year
with lingering disease which he patiently laboured under for about three
months and then closed his eyes with perfect resignation. He served as
a faithful soldier in the Revolutionary War under GEN. DICKSON and also
under GEN. CARROLL at N. Orleans, where he discharged every duty of a
brave soldier in defence of his country. We have no hesitation in
saying that he is now reaping the reward of his labour.

September 7, 1827
    Married 5th inst. by REV. ANDR. J. CRAWFORD, MR. WILLIAM D. HAYTER
to MISS JANE, daughter of CAPT. WILLIAM EVANS, all of Madison Co.
    Died at Village Springs on Saturday last in 17th year of her age,
MRS. MARTHA, wife of R. MUNSON and daughter of MAJOR DAVID CONNER.
Note: St. Clair Co. Ala. Marriages: RANSOM MUNSON-MARTHA CONNER Oct. 5,
1826. He moved to Jefferson Co. Ala. & M. again.
    Died 28th July in Jessamine Co. Kentucky, SAMUEL H. WOODSON, Esq.
of this place.
    JOHN WYCHE, recently from Brunswick Co. Va. informs public that he
can cure stammering.

November 23, 1827
    Married on 8th inst. by REV. A. J. CRAWFORD, MR. GRANVILLE CRINER
to MISS MARTHA BARNES, all of this county.

December 7, 1827
    Married Nov. 20th MR. ANDA DAVISON of Lawrence Co. to MRS. MARTHA
RICE of this county.
    Married on 29th, MR. JOHN R. TEAGUE of this county to MISS BIDDY
JONES of Limestone Co.
    Another Revolutionary patriot gone. Departed this life at his
residence in this county, MR. SAMUEL AYERS, SR. in 81st year. Was one
of MORGAN's celebrated riflemen. How long he continued in the war, the
writer does not recollect to have heard him say. He was at the defeat
and capture of GEN. BURGOYNE and many other battles. At the close of
the war, he married and settled in Cumberland County, Va. until the
fall of 1818, when at the advanced age of 72 he emigrated to this county.
Left six children and several grandchildren. Richmond Enquirer please
copy.
    Died at her father's residence near Huntsville Dec. 2, 1827
SUSAN RUFFIN, eldest daughter of WILLIAM H. T. and SUSAN C. BROWN aged
4 years and one month.
    Died 29th Jan. MRS. ELIZABETH ATKINSON, daughter of the late
REV. A. K. DAVIS. (ISABELLA in Sou. Adv)

December 15, 1827
    Died 15th, ISAAC LANIER in 61st year. Native of Anson County,
North Carolina.

January 11, 1828

Married on 1st, MR. MILES WOFFARD to MISS ELIZABETH BELL, all of Meridianville.

Married in Greensborough on 20th, MR. DAVID HARDING of Madison County to MISS MARY S(TUART) ALSTON, only daughter of COL. ABSALOM ALSTON.

January 18, 1828

Married 15th, MR. MARTIN WEATHERLY of Huntsville to MISS MARTHA BALL, eldest daughter of SPENCER BALL, Esq. of Madison County.

Died at his residence in this county on the 12th instant MR. JOB KEY in 62nd year of his age. He was a citizen of Madison County for many years. He has left an aged widow and a large family of children.

March 21, 1828

Married on the 19th instant, HUBBARD H. FENNELL to MISS MARY SMITH, all of Madison County.

April 11, 1828

Married on the 3rd instant, MR. AMERICA FOWLER, JUN. to MISS PARTHENA MOONEY, all of Madison County.

Died at his residence in this place on Friday last, MRS. MARY READ, consort of COL. JOHN READ in her 38th year. She has left a husband and four small children, three of whom are daughters.

THE DEMOCRAT

Abstracts published at Huntsville, Alabama

April 18, 1828

Died, CAPTAIN WILLIAM JEFFRIES at the residence of JAMES A. WALL in Morgan County in his 42nd year. He was a native of Greensville County, Va. and left numerous relations. (See Tyler's Quarterly JAMES AUGUSTUS WALL to REBECCA JEFFRIES, Greensville, Va. 3 Sept. 1808. 1850 Census Madison Co. Ala. WALL, JAMES A. 65 Va.; REBECCA 55 Ala & children)

Obituary:
Departed this life on the 6th inst. in her 7-th yr. MRS. ANN HARRIS, consort of MR. FRANCIS E. HARRIS of Madison County, Alabama. A concurrence of felicitous circumstances by the will of the divine Providence were conferred on this excellent woman, which are rarely the lot of mortals here on earth. She lived in all comfort and harmony of conjugal bliss with a worthy, intelligent and kind husband for over a half a century. She had seen long before her death, her children settled in the world with flattering prospects, esteemed and respected. She was the center of a numerous and very respectable circle of friends, whom she loved and for whom she entertained the most cordial regard and who most sincerely revered her. She possessed the means and it was her glory, her delight to receive, to entertain and to cherish the weary, wandering Pilgrims of her much beloved Jesus; her heart was open, her hands liberal to give the deciples more than a "cup of cold water." She bestowed on them the best she had. But the last, the greatest blessing in the cup of human felicity RELIGION she prized above all the rest; she delighted more in the smiles, in the apprebation of her God than in every earthly enjoyment--her piety was rational, deep, solid, and genuine. She was an ornament to religion and to the Methodist Church for about 40 years, during which time she manifested a steadiness and constancy, which clearly declared that her religion was not of the hand but of the heart. The writer of this narrative has been acquainted with her for 34 years. He visited her in her last illness and he bears witness to her fortitude, patience, resignation and victory, the triumph of Faith, the Grace of Jesus, cheering the dying Saint. She died as she lived, a Christian. Note: She was nee MACON, dau. of HENRY & REBECCA (MAYO) MACON. ANN's husband FRANCIS EPPES HARRIS left a will in Madison Co. Ala. in 1828. FRANCIS & ANN are great-great grandparents of PAULINE JONES GANDRUD.

April 25, 1828
Married on 22d, DAVID SPECK to MISS MARTHA, daughter of THOMAS HUMES, Esq. all of this place.
Died in Florence, Ala. on the 15th inst. WILLIAM McBROOM, Esq. of Huntsville, formerly Sheriff. He was on his way from New Orleans.

May 9, 1828
Married on 1st inst. MARCUS L. DISMUKES to MISS DELIA WATKINS, all of Madison Co.

May 16, 1828
Married on 1st inst. SAMUEL BIGHAM, formerly of Lawrence County to MISS ANN MARIA WHITE, daughter of MRS. MARY WHITE of this county.
Married in Williamson County, Tenn. on 24th inst., MAJOR WILLIAM LEDBETTER of Murfreesboro to MISS ELIZA A. WELBORNE.

May 23, 1828
Died on 17th ult. here, FRANCIS C. LEWIS on 19th year of his age.
Died on 19th inst. MRS. MARTHA URQUHART, wife of DANIEL URQUHART, Esq. Left a husband and four small children.

August 1, 1828
Died in Madison County on 30th of June, WILLIAM A. TOMLINSON, a native of Greensville Co. Va. in the 27th years of his age. Left wife and four small children.
Died in Richmond, Va. July 9th, MATTHEW WOODSON in the 50th year of his age.

August 15, 1828
Married on Thursday, the 17th inst. MR. JACOB H. PIERCE to MISS CHARLOTTE W. SIMMONS, all of Madison Co. Note: She was dau. of JOHN, who left a will in Madison Co.

August 22, 1828
Married on Wed. last by REV. JOHN ALLAN, MR. PHARES T. POSEY to MRS. ELIZABETH HUTCHINGS, both of this place. Note: She was widow of STOKELY D. HUTCHINGS--m. in Madison Co. Ala. 1816 ELIZ. ATWOOD.
Died on 18th inst. in her 9th year, MARY ANN, eldest daughter of JAMES G. SCOTT.

September 5, 1828
Married on Tuesday last, THOMAS BRANDON to MRS. W. OWEN. BRANDON is Clerk of County Court.
Married on Wed. JOEL M. SLEDGE, formerly of North Carolina to MISS NANCY HILL of this county.

September 12, 1828
Married on 3rd inst , ROBERT ALEXANDER to MRS. ELIZA A. McFARLAND, all of this county.
Married on Aug. 28, THOMAS H. HARGRAVE to AMANDA WILLIAMS, daughter of CAPT. CHARLES WILLIAMS, all of this county.
Died at Winchester, Tenn. on 30th, MRS. CAROLINE PATTON TAUL, aged 21 years and 3 months, wife of THOMAS P. TAUL, of the Bar of this place.
Died on the 4th inst. HENRY, son of JOHN G. JORDAN.
Married on 28th Aug. 1828 near Montgomery, JOHN W. FAULKNER to MISS M. L. BYRD. (see our Vol. 135 p 40).
Married on 16th inst. JOHN HARRIS to MARGARET CRADDOCK, daughter of DAVID CRADDOCK near Hazel Green.
Married on 4th Sept. 1828, COL. ALLEN WALLS to MISS ELENOR COX, all of this co.

October 3, 1828
Died in Tuscaloosa on 24th inst. RICHARD SELBY in 34th year of his age, a native of England. He was at the battle of Waterloo.

October 10, 1828
Married on 2d inst. WILLIAM B. DENNETT to AMANDA BIBB, eldest daughter of WILLIAM BIBB.

October 17, 1828
    Married on 9th inst. PITMAN FLINT to MISS NANCY MOLOY, all of this co.

October 24, 1828
    Married on 16th inst. ROBERT J. KENNEDY to MISS MARTHA HILL, all of this co.
    Funeral of J. W. URQUHART
    Died on 21st inst. WILLIAM FACKLER, young gentleman.

October 31, 1828
    Married on 27th ult. BENJAMIN S. ROGERS to MARY HILLIARD, daughter of J. HILLIARD, all of Madison.
    Married on 26th inst. EDWARD E. SURGINE to MISS SARAH CRAIGHEAD both of Bellefonte. (Note: He was son of MAJ. JAMES & MARGARET (ERWIN) SURGUINE; gr-son of EDW'd ERWIN. SARAH was dau of THOS. CRAIGHEAD (1781-1839; & gr-dau of ROBT CRAIGHEAD of Knox Co. Tenn.)

November 14, 1828
    Married on 6th inst. WILLIAM BAKER to MISS MARY ROBERT, all of Madison.

November 28, 1828
    Died on 22d inst. in her 33rd year, MRS. MARY ANN CAMP, consort of COL. JAMES W. CAMP.
    Married on 20th inst. REV. ALBERT G. GIBSON of Lincoln County, Tenn. to MISS SARAH ERWIN of Hazel Green.

December 5, 1828
    Died on 16th inst. JOHN RICHARD ALEXANDER, eldest son of WILLIAM HARRIS, Esq. of this county in his 12th year.

December 19, 1828
    Died on 6th inst. JAMES B. CUNNINGHAM in his 52nd year. Left widow and numerous connections.

December 24, 1828
    Married on 18th inst. MR. JOHN L. SMITH to MISS JANE ANNE, eldest daughter of CAPT. WILLIAM ROUTT, all of Madison.

January 9, 1829
    Died on 18th ult. in 35th year, WILLIAM C. ANDERSON, a native of Amelia Co. Va.

January 30, 1829
    Married on 22d inst. SAMUEL W(ALKER) WALTON of Lawrence Co. to MARY, daughter of GEORGE A. LOE of Madison.
    Married in Tuscumbia on 20th inst. ARMSTEAD BARTON to AMANDA C. COOK, daughter of CAPT. HENRY COOK, all of that place. (In Anderson Co. Tenn. there is a deed dated Apr. 10, 1832 which mentioned one ARMSTEAD BARTON "now of Ala.")

February 6, 1829
    Died on 29th ult. JOSHUA and JANE HIX, the former being 82 years of age and the latter 67. There were 13 hours between their deaths. Lived together 52 years and were the parents of 17 children. Natives of Ireland.

February 13, 1829
    Married on 2nd ult, COL. OGLESBY SCRUGGS of Madison to MRS. ANN M. HEWLETT, of Nashville (Tenn.).
    Died in Limestone Co. on 27th in 66th yr. JOHN MASSIE, formerly of New Kent Co. Va.

February 27, 1829
    Died at Bellefonte, JAMES HURT in 26th year, on 14th Feb. was married.

April 10, 1829
     Married on 18th inst. CAPT. RO. B. ARMISTEAD to MISS MARY L. BASS,
daughter of the late URIAH BASS, all of Madison. (Note: Tract book
shows ROBERT BURBAGE ARMISTEAD patented land in Sec. 10, Twp 3 Range 1 W.
in 1833.)

April 24, 1829
     Died 22d Feb. JOHN, son of ROBERT and SARAH HANCOCK, born in
Lancaster District, SC and when small, his father migrated to this
country. Died in 31st year.

May 15, 1829
     Died on 10th, MRS. MARY ROSE, wife of NEAL B. ROSE in her 46th
year. Was a Methodist. Raleigh, NC papers please copy.
     Died on 8th, PETER FAGAN, barber and fiddler.

May 22, 1829
     Married May 15, DR. MILES S. WATKINS of Huntsville to MISS SALLY D.
B. SHELBY of Sumner Co. (Tenn).

June 19, 1829
     Died 17th, ROBERT THOMPSON in 76th year. Was a Revolutionary
soldier; born in Amelia County, Va. Emigrated to Petersburg, Ga. Died
at Bellmina, Ala. at residence of THOMAS BIBB.

July 24, 1829
     Candidate for Commissioner of Roads and Revenue--GEORGE T. JONES.

July 31, 1829
     Died on 16th in Limestone Co. EDWARD H. LEWIS, a native of
Virginia.
     Died in Tuscumbia on 30th at residence of her son-in-law, CAPT.
L(UKE) HOWARD, MRS. HARRIET BROOKE, late of Prince George County, Md.
in her 48th year. Catholic (LUKE HOWARD m. 1824 HARRIET BROOKE. She
was widow of HENRY BROOKE.)

August 28, 1829
     Married Wed. H(IRAM) A. G. ROBERTS to MISS EMILY E. JONES, both
of Limestone.

September 4, 1829
     Died Aug. 26th, THOMAS P. TAUL, Esq. in 27th year. He was born
in Wayne County, Ky. March 7, 1803.

October 9, 1829
     Married Oct. 1, HOWEL D. EASON to MRS. MAYS, all of this county.
     Died on 7th inst. MRS. JANE E. BARBER, consort of ELIAS BARBER
in her 23rd year. Left two small children. (One ELIAS BARBER was in
1850 Census Jefferson Co. Ala. ae 51 b Va.)

January 3, 1833
     JOHN F. GILLESPIE, of Natchez, Mississippi, advertises for runaway
slave.
     LARKIN VENABLE of Moulton (Lawrence County, Ala) also advertises
for runaway slave.
     Notice of taxes due, by A. A. ROWAN, Tax Collector of Madison Co.
     Land for sale, by ROBERT DORTCH; White Sulphur Springs in Morgan
Co. Ala, twenty four cabbins, dining room 60 x 30, tavern with four
large rooms, etc.
     Advertisement: Armstead's Castor Oil, $2.00 per gallon by IRBY
and SMITH, followed by statement that the castor oil manufactured by
MR. R. B. ARMISTEAD is of superior quality and equal to any we have
ever used. (Endorsed by D. M. WHARTON, FLEMING JORDAN, GEORGE R. WHARTON,
F. H. NEWMAN, E. PICKETT, WM. ANDERSON, ALFRED MOORE and JOHN Y BASSETT
(note: these were all physicians here at the time).

January 10, 1833
     Advertisement of THOMAS H. POPE, of a tavern at Tuscumbia.

January 17, 1833
        Married on Monday the 10th instant by the REV. JAMES ROWE, MR.
THOMAS STRONG to MRS. ELVIRA NUNNALLY, all of this county.

January 24, 1833
        Notice: MARY SUBLETT, administratrix of WILLIAM SUBLETT dec'd,
qualified in Jackson County, Ala. August, 1832. Note: Census of 1830
Jackson Co. WILLIAM SUBLETT--2 m -5 1 m 15/20 1 m 40/50 1 f -5 1 f
5/10 1 f 10/15 1 f 30/40 1 f 80/90.

January 31, 1833
        Advertisement of JOSEPH WALLIS who has purchased White Sulphur
Springs in Morgan Co.
        Married, on Wednesday evening the 16th instant by the REV. MR.
MORRIS, MR. HENRY R(ICHARD) FARLEY to MISS ELIZA, daughter of WILLIAM
READ, Esq. of Morgan Co. see our Vol. 32 p. 27.
        On Thursday evening the 24th instant by JUDGE WILLIAM J. ADAIR,
MR. THEOPHILUS HARDISON to MISS SALINA ANN LEWIS, all of this co.
See our Vol. 147 p. 36.
        At Salem on Sunday the 27th instant by the REV. WM. CRUTCHER,
MR. LODRICK GRAVIT to MISS MALVINA PURVIN, all of this co. See our
Vol. 127 p. 23.
        ROBERTSON BREWER of Triana has taken up a small negro boy who
says he belongs to THOMAS HENLEY of Tuscumbia.
        Advertisement of JAMES NEELY, who has for six years been superin-
tendent of the Huntsville water works, to make pumps.
        Sheriff's sale. Jackson County. Property of NACY RIGGINS by
DANIEL LUCAS, sheriff, MOSES JONES, deputy. Also one of land belonging
to JOHN M. DIRWIN.
        Land for sale, in Jackson County. 10 miles west of Bellefonte
by ALEXANDER RIDDLE.
        Ran away or kidnapped--slaves from JAMES DASWELL, Point Chicot,
Washington Co. Mississippi.

February 14, 1833
        E. HANSBROUGH, Bellefonte, Ala. attorney at law.
        Notice: A. JONES of Bolivar (Jackson County?) wife MARTHA has
left bed and board--not responsible for debts.
        Married on Thursday evening last the 5th inst. by the REV. ISAAC W.
SULLIVAN, MR. GEORGE H. GRAHAM to MISS JULIA ANN, duaghter to THOMAS
CAIN Esq. all of this place.
        In Limestone County on Thursday evening the 7th instant by the
REV. JOHN H. THOMPSON, DR. H(UTCHISON) DENT of Triana to MISS ANN R.
LONGSTREET. See our Vol. 21 p. 50.

March 14, 1833
        St. Clair County. MORDICAI FULLER, administrator of MORDICAI FULLER
SENR. dec'd will make final settlement.
        St. Clair County. THOMAS H. LEISTER and FANNY LEISTER Executor &
Executrix of MOSES LEISTER dec'd will make final settlement.
        St. Clair County. JOHN LOLLY, administrator of SAMUEL LOVE dec'd
will make final settlement.
        St. Clair County. Stray mare taken up by HANIBAL HAYS near Turkey
Town.
        Plantation for sale by JOHN S. RHEA 1 mile south of Tuscumbia.
        HENRY F. SCRUGGS, attorney at law, Bellefonte, Ala.

March 18, 1833
        Died, on 11th instant at his residence near Hazel Green in this
county, DR. RICHMOND H. CARROLL. Note: See Marriages of Hancock Co.
Ga. One RICHMOND CARROLL m. there 1806 SARAH DRIVER. DR. R. H. seems
to be son of GRIEF CARRIEL (see our Vol. 61).
        Announcement of COL. WM. WOFFORD, MAJOR JOHN C. GRAYSON and
JASON L. JORDAN as candidates for COLONEL COMMANDANT of 62nd Regiment
Alabama Militia.

March 21, 1833
        Sheriff's Sale; Jackson County; land of WILLIAM RUSH to satisfy
Fi Fa in favor of WILLIAM DICKSON vs WM. and BENJAMIN RUSH and others.

DANIEL LUCAS, sheriff J. M. EVANS, deputy. Also the land of JAMES SMART for WILLIS WARD.

Jackson County. JOHN M. DARWIN vs JACOB T. BRADFORD, administrator of LYMAN JONES dec'd, appointed 19th March, 1831.

May 9, 1833
Died, in this county, on the 20th ult. JOHN WILDY, a native of the Northern Neck of Virginia in the 36th year of his age. The deceased, it is supposed, came to his and either by accident or design as he was found shot with his gun lying by his side. He has left a wife and one child. Note: His wife was FRANCES dau of PEYTON POWELL, Rev. soldier; she m. 2. JOHN M. ELDRIDGE, Feb. 1835.

May 16, 1833
Married, on Tuesday the 7th instant by the REV. MR. DONALD, MR. ELI M. DRIVER to MISS JULIA SOPHIA, daughter of GROSS SCRUGGS, Esq. all of this co. See our Vol. 133 p. 14.

May 30, 1833
Died suddenly on Friday the 24th instant at her residence MRS. MARY PRUIT, wife of VALENTINE G. PRUIT of this co...deprived...her husband of a devoted wife and her children of a most intelligent and affectionate mother.

On Saturday the 25th instant after a long and painful illness MRS. SARAH E. McCLUNG, daughter of JOHN MITCHELL, Esq. late Governor of Georgia, and consort of JAMES W. McCLUNG, Esq. of this town. "Five innocents who survive her.:

On 21st instant ATTICUS LYNN SKILLERN, aged two years, three months, son of MR. ISAAC SKILLERN of this place.

JOHN B. BIGHAM departed this life on the evening of the 26th instant in 7th of his age...scarlet fever.

June 6, 1833
Notice of Regimental Parades. Staff: ROBERT J. MANNING, adujant, SAMUEL HATTON, Paymaster, JAMES MASON, Quartermaster, SAMUEL BRECK, Surgeon. WILLIAM T. YOUNG, First Sergeant's Mate, ALBERT RUSSEL, 2nd Sergeant's Mate. HENRY L. BROWN, Sergeant Major. 1st Battallion 33rd Regiment A.M. will parade at Triana--ED TONEY, Lt. Col.

June 13, 1833
Jackson County: The administrator of the estate of ELISHA STAYTON dec'd will make final settlement.

Departed this life on the 6th instant ROBERT ANDERSON infant son of WILLIAM and MARY ANN GORMLEY of this place.

July 15, 1833
Married 18th by REV. JAMES MOORE, MR. WILLIAM B. GILMORE, of Montgomery to MISS ANN T. McGEHEE, daughter of the late THOMAS McGEHEE of Madison Co. Ala.

July 11, 1833
Married at Halifax, North Carolina on 4th inst. MR. WILLIAM T. T. AVENT of Huntsville to MISS MARY ELIZA M'LEMORE.

Died in this town on 5th inst. after a very short illness, MRS. ZIBBIAH MITCHELL, consort of JAMES MITCHELL in her 36th year. Was a member of the Cumberland Presbyterian Church; left 6 small children, 5 of whom are daughters.

Died suddenly on Friday, 21 ult, at residence of her husband in this county, MRS. NANCY WRIGHT, consort of MAJ. DANIEL WRIGHT in 71st year. Resided 21 years in this county and was married 52 years.

Died in Limestone County, WILLIAM T. KEY in 28th year.

Died in Limestone County of scarlet fever, MR. EDWARD R. DAVIS aged about 27.

Died near Elkton, Tenn. on night of 24th, MR. JOSEPH COLEMAN, formerly of Kentucky, aged about 21.

Died in Clinton, Miss. on 26th, E. P. CATLETT, Esq. Editor of Mississippian.

July 18, 1833
    Died on 28th after protracted illness of 9 months, MRS. ELIZABETH
NOWLIN, wife of JAMES P. NOWLIN of this county. Native of Hanover
County, Virginia. Richmond Enquirer please copy.
    Died recently in New Orleans of malignant cholera, MR. WILLIAM V.
CHARDAVOYNE, commission merchant of that place and formerly a resident
of the city of New York.
    Died in New Orleans of cholera on 24th, SAMUEL DAVIS.
    And on 10th from sprain of the ankle at his father's, PHILIP NEWTON
DAVIS, both sons of GEORGE DAVIS of Madison Co.

August 8, 1833
    Married at SIMON KEMPER's on 31st ult. by SQUIRE ROGERS, ALEXANDER
ROGERS to MISS SUSANNA MILLER, all of this county.
    Married on Wednesday evening 31st ult. by REV. ISAAC SHOOK,
DR. JOHN C. SPOTSWOOD of Athens to MISS LOUISA C. CALDWELL of this place.

August 15, 1833
    Married at Preston's Ridge on Tuesday evening, 23rd ult. by
REV. JOHN EARLY, DR. DAVID MOORE of Huntsville to MISS MARTHA L.
daughter of COL. BENJAMIN HARRISON of Brunswick Co. Va.

August 22, 1833
    Married Tuesday evening, 13th inst. by REV. JAMES SHOOK, MR. ALBERT
J. WATKINS of this county to MISS MARIA LOUISA CLIFTON of Huntsville.

August 29, 1833
    Married Wednesday evening 21st inst. by REV. JOHN M. TAYLOR,
DR. ROBERT W. WITHERS of Greene County to MISS MARY D(OROTHY) M. WITHERS
of Madison Co.
    Died 12th inst. at his residence near Randolph, Tenn. of spasmodic
cholera, DR. ROBERT H. ROSE, a native of Virginia and for many years a
resident of this county. DR. ROSE was well known in North Alabama.
    Died Wednesday, the 26th inst. in his 36th year after a protracted
and painful illness, LEVIN POWELL, Esq...left a widow and one child.
People of Tyscaloosa will miss him.

September 5, 1833
    Died 22nd inst. in his 53rd year WILLIAM ROSS, living about 11
miles Southeast of Moulton, after illness of several months. Secluded
farmer. Left wife and children.
    Died Friday morning, 30th inst. at 9 o'clock at residence at
MR. DAVID PETTIS in Madison County, STANDHOP P. SMITH in his 22nd year.
Left wife and aged mother, a brother and two little sisters. Editors
of Athens, Ala. and Richmond, Va. copy.

September 17, 1833
    Died near Meridianville on 6th inst. after illness of nine days
of bilious fever, ROBERT A. BELL, Esq. Tax Collector of Madison County.
Left wife and several small children.
    Died at residence in Hickory Flat on 29th, MRS. ELIZABETH ANDREWS
aged about 60. Kindly mother. Richmond Enquirer please copy.

September 19, 1833
    Married in this town on 11th inst. by REV. MR. SLOSS, MR. DONALD
CAMPBELL of Mooresville to MISS ELIZABETH M'KINLEY, eldest daughter of
COL. JOHN M'KINLEY. Note: The license was in Lauderdale Co. Ala.

October 3, 1833
    Married Thursday evening, 12th inst. by REV. JAMES ROWE,
MR. BENJAMIN D. ELLIS to MISS CAROLINE A. WATSON, daughter of REV.
JOAB WATSON, all of this county.
    Also on Thursday evening, 26th inst. by same, MR. ALGERNON S.
PORTER of Winchester, Tennessee to MISS MARY V. VINING, daughter of
JOHN VINING, Esq. of this co.
    Married Wednesday the 16th inst near Nashville by REV. MR. GREEN,
REV. JOHN B. M'FERREN of Tennessee Conference to MISS ALMIRA A. PROBART
of Davidson County. Note: He was son of REV. JAMES McFERRIN according
to WEST's History of Methodism in Ala. Published 1893.

Married Tuesday evening, 10th inst. (says the Mississipian) at residence of her father by REV. DONAN, MR. SAMUEL C. FAULKNER of firm of GARLAND & FAULKNER, merchants of this town to MISS MARY ANN VIRGINIA, only daughter of MAJOR FRANCIS FLOURNOY of this co.

Died suddenly at residence of DR. WHARTON of this town, MR. WILLIAM GRAY, native of Washington County, Penna. in his 29th year and graduate of Jefferson College.

October 17, 1833
Married in this town on Thursday evening by HON. JOHN M. TAYLOR, MR. SAMUEL SPENCER to MISS CAROLINE R. R. CAIN, daughter of WILLIAM CAIN, all of this place.

Married Wednesday the 9th inst at residence of MR. TODD, in Lincoln County, Tenn. by ESQ. CLARKE, MR. MAJOR CUMBY to MISS MALINDA HARPERALL of this place.

October 24, 1833
Married on Tuesday evening last 1st inst. by REV. JAMES ROWE, MR. ROBERT D. MALONE of Limestone County to MISS CHARLOTTE M. HEWLETT, daughter of JOHN W. HEWLETT of this co.

Died at Monticello in Pike County on 5th ins. HORATIO G. PERRY, Judge of 2nd Judicial Circuit of this State.

October 31, 1833
Married on Tuesday evening, the 22nd inst. in Maury County, Tennessee by REV. MR. ARNOLD, MAJ. WILLIAM H. TURNER of this county to MISS CAROLINE WEBSTER of the former place.

Married the 24th inst. by the REV. FINIS E. HARRIS, MR. LeROY M. BARNETT of this county to MISS MARY W. BALLEW, daughter of MR. PETER BALLEW of Limestone Co. Note: This is BARNES in Census of 1850 and BARNETT in marriage record. See our Vol. 21 p. 47.

On same evening by JAMES SIMPSON, Esq., MR. MATTHEW H. BARNETT of this county to MISS FIDELIA J. SIMPSON, daughter of MR. THOMAS SIMPSON of Limestone Co. (See our Vol. 21 p. 47)

Died at MR. JAMES BARRETT's in Limestone County on 18th ult. and in 14th year of age, PERSONS TURNER, nephew of MRS. BARRETT, under short but violent attack of bilious fever. Left no surviving father or mother.

Died 22nd inst. at residence of son in this place, CAPT. HENRY HARRIS in his 75th year, native of Richmond County, Virginia. Enlisted at Fredericksburg, Va. in COL. BAYLOR's Regiment of Dragoons.

November 14, 1833
Died on 7th, BYNUM TURNER, son of CAPT. JOHN B. TURNER. He was born September 30, 1829.

November 28, 1833
Married in Macon, Geo. on 30th ult. BENJAMIN RUSH MONTGOMERY, Esq. attorney at law, formerly of East Tennessee to MISS MATILDA HARDIN, youngest daughter of HON JOHN HARDIN, formerly of Augusta.

Married on 22nd by J. S. CALVERT, Esq., MR. WILLIAM DEDMAN to MISS MARY BLANKENSHIP, all of Madison Co.

Died on 18th inst., MRS. M. A. ROWE, consort of REV. JAMES ROWE, Principal in Montesano Female Academy in her 34th year of chronic rheumatism. She was a native of Lexington, Kentucky, but for many years was a resident of Ohio. Cincinnati copy.

Morgan County: Sheriff will sell land of JONATHAN RIDGWAY for WILLIAM CAMPBELL's benefit. JAMES B. GRAHAM, Clerk & Master. Note: Pittsylvania Co. Va. Marriages: One JONATHAN RIDGEWAY m. ELIZ. SHIELDS, 12 Sept. 1788.

Runaway slave committed to jail in Madison County; says belongs to JAMES DUPREE of Hinds County, Mississippi.

Land for sale; in Limestone County by ALFRED BLACKBURN, at CLEMENT BLACKBURN's.

Regimental orders: in consequence of the removal of CAPTAIN BISHOP from this county the company under his command is without an officer, and the muster roll is lost or destroyed...

December 5, 1833
Married Thursday the 28th by REV. PLEASANT B. ROBINSON, MR. JOHN H.
ROACH of Huntsville to MISS MARY P. STEGER of this co.
On same evening by W. GRAVES BOULDIN, Esq. MR. ROBERT WALTON of
Lawrence County to MISS ELIZABETH P. LEE, daughter of CAPTAIN GEORGE A.
LEE of this co.

January 9, 1834
Married on 2 Jan. 1834 by REV. JOSHUA BUTCHER, W. H. ROBERTSON,
Esq. to MRS. ELIZABETH G. LASSLEY, all of this county, Columbus, Mis.
Copy.

January 23, 1834
Married Wednesday evening the 15th inst. by REV. ISAAC SHOOK,
MR. JAMES O'NEAL to MISS ROSANNA FEENEY, all of this place.
State of Alabama--Jackson County. Orphans Court 3 Feb. 1834,
Executor and executrix of estate of BARTELL ANDERSON, deceased ordered
to appear in Court.
Died on 3rd inst. at her father's residence, MRS. LOUISA AUGUSTA
SUMNER, consort of the late THOMAS J. SUMNER of Huntsville and daughter
of REV. WILLIAM LANIER of Madison County. She was born in Anson
County, North Carolina November 28, 1804.
State of Alabama--Jackson County. Orphans Court. 7 Jan. 1834
MARY SUBLETTE, administratrix of estate of WILLIAM SUBLETTE, deceased.
State of Alabama--Morgan County. Orphans Court. 23 Dec. 1833.
Letters of administration on estate of COOLEY WHITNEY deceased granted.
White Sulphur Springs, Morgan Co.

February 20, 1834
Married on the evening of the 30th by REV. JAMES ROWE, MR. FRANCIS
McGEHEE to MISS NANCY MOORE, daughter of MR. JAMES MOORE, all of this
co.
Married on Tuesday evening, 11th inst. by REV. LORENZO D. OVERALL,
MR. CORTEZ D. KAVANAUGH to MRS. CATHARINE LEWIS, both of this co.

February 6, 1834
State of Alabama--Jackson County. Orphans Court. 27th January 1834.
JOB WILHELMS, administrator of estate of TOBIAS WILLHELMS, deceased
and RICHARD WILLHELMS, JACOB WILLHELMS, JOHN WILLHELMS, WILLIAM
McCULLOUGH in right of wife, formerly AILSEY WILLHELMS, DAVID McNABB,
in right of wife, formerly CATHARINE WILLHELMS, JACOB BRADDY in right
of wife, formerly ELIZABETH WILLHELMS, WILLIAM TINDLE in right of wife
formerly SALLY WILLHELMS, heirs of deceased and GEORGE F. BULMAN as
guardian of JACOB WILLHELMS, ELIZABETH WILLHELMS, MARIA WILLHELMS, and
JAMES A. WILLHELMS, who are minor heirs of ANDREW WILLHELMS, deceased.
All cited to appear in Court in Court.
Married Thursday evening last, 30th inst. by REV. R. BREWER,
Esq. MR. THOMAS TUDER to MISS ANN WILLIAMS, eldest daughter of MR. JAMES
WILLIAMS of this co.
On same evening by REV. ISAAC W. SULLIVAN, MR. URIAH BASS to MISS
CYNTHIA, daughter of CAPTAIN JOHN HUNTER, all of this co.

February 13, 1834
Died at residence in Fayette County on 17th day of November 1833
CAPTAIN CHRISTOPHER HUNT, aged about ---- years.
Died in Madison County at the house of her parents, DAVID and
ELIZABETH PETTUS on Friday morning, 7th inst. MISS MARTHA JANE PETTUS
in her 16th year.
MISS MARTHA JANE PETTUS in her 16th year.

March 4, 1834
Died about meridian in the city, WILLIAM WIRT, Esq. aged about 62.

March 27, 1834
Died on 26th in New Orleans of cholera MARY W. MARTIN aged about
7 years, daughter of JOHN MARTIN late of this place.
Died Friday the 15th inst. MARY ELIZA aged 2 daughter of GEORGE
STEELE of this place.

April 3, 1834
Died on 10th inst. at the age of about 70, CAPTAIN BENJAMIN PEETE of Limestone County; native of Virginia.

May 1, 1834
Died on 11th inst. in Lawrence County, ALEXANDER AUSTIN in his 84th year. Moved to this state from South Carolina and was a lieutenant in the Revolution, and continued in service throughout arduous struggle.
Died on 23rd inst. MRS. REBECCA J. wife of DR. ALFRED MOORE at residence in this county, Daughter of the late DR. PETER J. BEASLY of Brunswick County, Virginia; she died in her 24th year. Like her mother and grandmother she died after a premature parturition of her first child. The infant survives.
State of Alabama--Jackson County. Orphans Court, 7 May, 1834. ROBERT H. BROYLES filed petition in Court setting forth that he purchased from JOHN BASHAM of said county certain land and said JOHN BASHAM died without making deed to said BROYLES. THENY BASHAM, administratrix of estate of said JOHN BASHAM.
Died on 6th inst. MRS. ELVIRA VINING, wife of JOHN VINING, Esq. at Oak Grove, his residence in this county in her 33rd year.
Died in Huntsville Friday evening, 10th of May, MR. ZACHARIAH PRICE in his 30th year; native of Charles County, Maryland, but for few years past has resided near Murfreesboro, Ten.
Died on ---- inst. JAMES P. NOWLIN at an advanced age. Moved to this state from Hanover County, Virginia and for last 12 or 15 years has resided in the vicinity of Huntsville.

June 5, 1834
DANIEL B. TURNER and JARED I. SAMPLE announce as candidates as sheriff.
JEFFERSON HAYTER, CAPT. JAMES TAYLOR and CAPT. ROBERT W. DAVIE are candidates for Colonel of the 2nd Regiment Alabama Militia, because of the resignation of ELIAS WELLBORN.
W. GRAVES BOULDIN and WM. T. T. AVANT are candidates for tax collector; for Representatives, COL. WM. FLEMING, JOHN D. PHELAN, Esq. COL. SAMUEL WALKER, COL. JOHN K. DUNN.
DONALD CAMPBELL advertises residence in Morresville for sale.
Land for sale, Marengo County; 720 acres; see R. INGE near Erie or PETER or PETER MARTIN Esq. near the premises.
St. Clair County; THOMAS M. BARKER, executor of the will of MALCOLM McCRANEY dec'd will make final settlement.

June 12, 1834
Town property for sale; Jamestown, Sumter County; ABRAHAM McGEHEE, HENRY JOHNSON, BLAKE LITTLE, WM. SMITH, J. MOORE, JR.
Runaway slave, from JOHN ROBERTS of Erie, Greene Co. Ala.
Died Saturday the 31st ult. at residence near this place WILLIAM BIBB, SEN. Esq. in his 51st year, a respectable citizen of this country. Left a family and large circle of relatives.
Died on Sunday the 24th inst. MRS. ABIGAIL WHITE, consort of HON. JOHN WHITE of Courtland.
Died on 5th inst. WILLIAM EPPES, infant son of DANIEL HARRIS, Esq. of this county.

June 19, 1834
Died in this county on 3rd of June of bilious pleurisy MRS. ELIZABETH POWEL, consort of CAPT. PEYTON POWELL to her 66th year. Member of the Methodist Church, Richmond Enquirer copy.
Died ELIZA NEWMAN, infant daughter of CAPTAIN DANIEL B. TURNER.
State of Alabama--Jackson County. Orphans Court. 26 May 1834. Administration on estate of JOHN W. LONG, deceased filed.
State of Alabama--St. Clair County. Orphans Court 17 May, 1834. THOMAS M. BARKER, executor of will of MALCOM McCRANEY, deceased, late of said co.
Land for sale: Lincoln Co. Tennessee by ISAAC HOLMAN.
Jackson County, administrator of the estate of JOHN W. LONG dec'd will make final settlement. R. B. CLAYTON, Clk. C. C.
Runaway slave committed to jail in Madison County; says belongs to THOMAS SULLIVAN of Athens, Ala.

June 26, 1834

Died on the night of the 22nd inst. WM. R., infant son of WM. R. HUNT of this place.

Sale: Residence and 190 acres adjoining town of Courtland W. H. WHITAKER.

Account (from Columbus, Ga. Sentinel of May 31st) of murder of BEVERLY G. G. A. LUCAS, Esq. Clerk of the Superior Court of Russell County, by CROOKS, in Macon County; the account given by one OSBORN S. ECHOLS who was with him, but escaped. A MR. BOWLES also present. Candidates from Morgan County; for the Legislature; JOHN T. RATHER, HORATIO PHILPOT, ROBERT F. HOUSTON, A. HEWLET. For Sheriff; THOMAS PRICE, JAMES FERGUSON, WILLIAM CAMPBELL, WILLIAM BURISS, WILLIAM SKIDMORE, WILLIAM R. CHUNN, JOHN S. BROOKS, JOHN KING. For Tax Collector; JOHN SAWYERS and JOHN TATOM.

July 3, 1834

Sale of the Railroad Hotel at Courtland by W. H. WHITAKER and J. J. ORMOND, subject to the lease of R. A. TAYLOR which will expire Jan. 1, 1837.

Talladega County; Letters testamentary on estate of MICAJAH T. COTTEN granted 6 May 1834 to PEGGY COTTEN Executrix and A. J. COTTEN, Executor.

Advertisement by SUSANNAH HUGHES for arrest of one HENRY JACKSON CARTER who with JAMES HUGHES left his residence in Carter County, Tennessee in February; was seen with CARTER at Gunters Landing. HUGHES' son returned home. Later CARTER returned, apparently prosperous, and expressed surprise that HUGHES had not arrived before him. She had heard of an unidentified body being found at Coxe's Ferry and believes it to have been that of HUGHES.

Died at the residence of JOHN P. FORD in Plymouth, Mi. on 11th inst. MISS LOUISA E. T. JEFFERSON in her 16th or 17th year.

State of Alabama--Jackson County. Orphans Court. 21 June 1834. Administrator of estate of LYMAN JAMES, deceased, late of said county, ordered to appear.

July 10, 1834

State of Alabama--Jackson County. Orphans Court 14 June 1834. Estate of THOMPSON B. BAILEY, late of said county deceased. Administrator ordered to appear in Court.

Married Wednesday evening 2nd inst. JAMES W. McCLUNG, Esq. of this place to MISS ELIZABETH SPOTSWOOD, daughter of MR. ELLIOT SPOTSWOOD of this co.

Died in Florence on Saturday evening last after a short illness, GENERAL JOHN GRAHAN, old and respected citizen of Huntsville.

RICHARD McANULTY will give a barbecue at McANULTY town.

Jackson County: Sheriff will sell land of E. O. D. PRUIT to satisfy JACOB KENNAMORE; also land of RICHARD DAVIDSON.

Runaway slave committed to jail, Madison Co. by WM. R. HUNT, Jailor--says belongs to RICAHRD SYMS of Bedford County, Tennessee.

July 17, 1834

Funeral of JOHN "BRAHAM"--conveyed to his farm on Sweetwater.

Died on 9th inst. of scarlet fever, ROBERT PEYTON aged 4, only child of MRS. FRANCES WILDY.

July 23, 1834

Married on Tuesday evening last by the REV. P. B. ROBINSON, MR. NEWTON FORD of this place to MISS APPLESS FRAZIER of this county.

July 24, 1834

Died yesterday JOHN D. WALLER, member of the Huntsville Guards.

July 30, 1834

Died on Friday July 11th at house of CAPT. J. STEEN in Knox County, MR. SLADE, Representative from Illinois.

Jackson County; DAVID BAILEY on 28th September purchased land from WILLIAM SUBLETTE who has since died without making title; MARY SUBLETTE, the widow, is administratrix.

August 6, 1834
    Departed this life on Monday the 21st of July MISS MARY H., daughter
of the REV. ZADOK W. BAKER of Marengo County, Ala. formerly of Madison
County, in the 15th year of her age, of a painful illness of 8 days.
    Advertisement: Giles County, Tennessee--MARSHALL MOODY vs
JOHN DUKE MENEAR and wife JOANNA B. Both defendants are non residents
of this state; in the year 1830 complainant executed note to JOANNA B.
MOODY widow of a deceased brother and also guardian of his children.
Complainant with one DAVID SHELTON was security of said JOANNA B. who
was appointed guardian of her said children by the County Court of
Mecklenberg County, Va. where SHELTON still resides. Said JOANNA B.
and her present husband JOHN DUKE MENEAR are disposing of property...
(Note: is this the name the one now spelled DUKEMENIER?)
    Letter from WARNER WASHINGTON of St. Clair County; Is about a
fence dispute; states was feeling infirm when came to this country and
gave MR. WILLIAM GARRET control over his affairs, who with his brother
JOHN GARRETT, closed a lane leading to the house of a MR. MEANS.
After the trouble arose "MR. GARRETT ordered me from his house...unkind
treatment from a son-in-law." Whereupon he went to the house of
MR. MEANS. "MRS. WASHINGTON and her son went to support her rights."
"I have passed the meridian of life."

August 20, 1834
    Land for sale; having determined to move further south"...6 miles
northeast of Florence...WILLIAM M. BURTON.
    Died, on the morning of Saturday, the 9th inst. MARY LOUISA,
daughter of MR. RICHARD A. WIGGINS of this village, aged 4 years
(Triana, Aug. 16, 1834).
    Hazelgreen, August 14, 1834. Departed this life on Tuesday the
12th instant JAMES WALKER in the 48th year of his age, after a confinement
of short duration. Left a large family.
    St. Clair County; petition to sell land by WILLIAM LITTLE,
administrator of JAMES LOVING dec'd.

August 27, 1834
    A funeral sermon over the late MRS. CONNALLY will be preached by
the REV. WILLIAM McMAHAN at the residence of JOHN CONNALLY on Monday the
1st of Sept.
    Died 23rd inst. MRS. SARAH BINGHAM, consort of MR. JOHN G. BINGHAM
in her 28th year. Methodist. Lynchburg, Va. copy.
    Died on 13th inst DOLLY McCLELLAN, consort of MATTHEW W. McCLELLAN,
leaving a husband and four little daughters.
    Died 9th inst. MRS. ELIZABETH THOMASON, consort of JAMES THOMASON
of Pink Hill, in 52 year. Was on a visit to her daughter two miles
from home.

September 3, 1834
    Notice by REUBEN CRUTCHER of a note drawn by WALTER SELBY and
sent to MASON WOOD of Jackson County; lost.
    Married Wednesday, 13th ult. by REV. PLEASANT B. ROBINSON,
THOMAS P. COLLINS, Esq. to MISS ADALINE B. M'CAY, daughter of
MR. WILLIAM M'CAY, all of this place.
    Married on 28th inst. by REV. A. G. GIBSON, REV. O. D. STREET of
Winchester, Tennessee to MISS MARY ANN ADKINS, daughter of THOMAS ADKINS,
Esq. of Madison Co.
    Died in Jacosn County Thursday 14th of August, MR. WILLIAM JONES,
a Revolutionary soldier, aged about 86 years. Left several children.
    Died in Columbia, Tenn. of cholera, REV. LORENZO D. OVERALL,
minister in the Methodist Church.
    Died Friday at his residence, MR. JAMES HAM, one of the oldest
settlers of the county.
    Died at Meridianville on the night of 27th of August DR. WILLIAM H.
WYCHE, late of Mississippi. Left widowed mother, brothers and sisters.
    Died on 1st inst. at residence in Amherst near Lynchburg, REV.
STITH MEAD of Methodist Church in 68th year, leaving widow and seven
children; native of Virginia (Lynchburg, Virginia, Aug. 7).

September 10, 1834
    Died at residence of her father in Limestone County, MRS. JANE A.
JONES, wife of HARDEMAN F. JONES, Esq. of MADISON JONES, aged 31 years
1 mo.

Estrays taken up in Jackson County; one by WILLIAM COFFEY on north side of the Tennessee River, and another by GEORGE FRAZIER, Estill's Fork, Paint Rock.

Sworn to before WM. SOUTHERLAND and JESSE McELZEE, J.P.'s Sheriff (ALEXANDER RIDDLE) of Jackson County will sell the lands of JAMES LATHAM dec'd in the hands of ARCHIHELD WOODS and JONATHAN LATHAM his administrators, the land of JOHN BALL and the land conveyed by WILLIAM WRIGHT to JONATHAN LATHAM and the land to THOMAS BRADSHAW, to satisfy THOMAS WILSON and HOLDEN W. PRUIT.

September 17, 1834

Indian Queen Hotel in Tuscumbia for sale by THOMAS R. BOLLING.

"Texas Fever" Will sell plantation in Talladega County, 8 miles north of the county seat. BENJAMIN SMITH.

Died on 19th Aug. near Clinton, Mississippi, JAMES WILSON IRWIN, formerly of Madison County; left a father, mother and six brothers.

Died on 31st August, MRS. MARY RANDOLPH in her 49th year. Member of the Methodist Church.

Died in New Orleans on 27th ult. HON. WILLIAM KELLY, formerly a citizen of this place and member of the United States Senate.

October 8, 1834

Died on 4th at residence near Hazlegreen, MRS. ANN TATE, in her 61st year.

October 15, 1834

Married Wednesday evening by REV. WILLIAM McMAHON, MR. A. J. WITHERS to MISS MARY J. daughter of P. WOODSON, all of Huntsville (note: PHILIP WOODSON)

Married recently in Franklin County, Tenn. MR. JAMES H. MOSLEY, merchant of Columbus, Miss. to MISS ANN F. IKARD.

November 22, 1834

Died at his mother's residence in Orange County, North Carolina on 16th of October of Bilious fever, ARCHIBALD HARRIS, Esq. attorney at law of Athens.

Died on 4th Nov. 1834 at Oak Grove in Madison County at residence of his father, JAMES H. eldest son of JOHN VINING, Esq.

November 26, 1834

State of Alabama--St. Clair, Orphans Court. 14 Nov. 1834. Petition to WILLIAM J. WHISENANT, administrator of estate of HENRY WHISENANT, deceased.

Died on 10th inst. at his residence near Winchester, Tennessee, CAPTAIN WILLIAM B. HARRIS, a native of Virginia and for many years a resident of Madison Co. Lynchburg, Va. copy.

December 3, 1834

Married Wednesday evening 26th ult. by REV. JAMES ROWE, JOHN ROWE, JR. Esq. to MRS. MARIA JANE COSBY, all of this co.

December 10, 1834

Married Thursday evening by REV. JOHN ALLEN, MR. JEREMIAH CLEMENS to MISS MARY L., daughter of COL. JOHN READ all of this place.

December 24, 1834

Married Tuesday evening 14th inst. by REV. SAMUEL HARRIS, MR. PLEASANT W. WEAVER of Huntsville to MISS LUCINDA J. WEAVER of this co.

Married on Thursday evening in this place by REV. MR. FERGUSON, MR. JOHN MITCHELL to MRS. LATITIA McGRAW, all of Huntsville.

December 31, 1834

State of Alabama--Jackson County. Orphans Court. 12 Dec. 1834. Estate of JOHN HILL, deceased; also estate of MARY KING, deceased.

January 7, 1835

Married on 27th December last by REV. THOMAS W. COX, of Tuscaloosa, MR. JAMES THOMASON of Springville to MRS. ELIZABETH COWAN, both of St. Clair Co.

January 21, 1835
State of Alabama--Jackson County. Orphans Court. 13 Jan. 1835.
BRYANT B. THOMPSON and NATHANIEL WILDER, guardians of NANCY and
WILLIAM WILDER, minor heirs of NATHANIEL WILDER, SR. deceased and heirs
at law of DANIEL McDUFF, deceased. Land in Jackson Co.
State of Alabama--Limestone County. Orphans Court. 17 Jan. 1835.
ZADOCK HILLIARD petitions that MARTHA GARRISON, deceased in her lifetime
sold him land, and died before completing title to same.
Died Wednesday morning at residence near Florence, MRS. CHARLOTTE
THOMSON, wife of CAPTAIN ALLEN C. THOMSON in her 64th year.
Died RICHARD B. BRICKELL, Esq. Editor of Athenian.

January 28, 1835
Another Revolutionary soldier gone! COL. JOHN McCUTCHEON.

February 4, 1835
Died at residence in Limestone County on Monday, Jan. 20th, MR.
JOHN F. MOORE, aged 52 years; died of bilious pleurisy.

February 18, 1835
Married 11th inst. by REV. MR. FERGUSON, DR. FRANCIS H. NEWMAN
of this place to MISS MARY E. POWERS, daughter of MR. WILLIAM POWERS
of this county.

February 25, 1835
State of Alabama--Jackson County. Orphans Court 28 Feb. 1835.
Estate of DANIEL PRICE, late of said county, deceased.
Died 10th of February in 31st year, OLIVE, consort of MR. HILLIARD
PETTY of the County of Lincoln, Tenn. Left husband and three small
children.
Died in this town Tuesday, MR. GEORGE H. MALONE aged about 38
(Little Rock paper).
Died at his residence in Columbia, S.C. on Wednesday evening,
4th inst. GENERAL WADE HAMPTON in his 81st year.

March 4, 1835
State of Alabama--Jackson County. Orphans Court. ELIZABETH
STARNES, formerly ELIZABETH RAINEY, administratrix of estate of JOSIAH
RAINEY, deceased.

March 11, 1835
Died in Madison County on the 27th of January, MRS. PETTUS,
consort of MR. DAVID PETTUS in her 50th year. Left husband and five
children. Richmond Enquirer copy. Note: She was dau of JOHN BOSWELL
of Va. see GOODSPEED's History of Southern Ark. She was b in Lunenburg
Co. Va. and m. 1802.

March 18, 1835
Died on 11th inst. SUSAN CATHARINE, wife of WILLIAM H. T. BROWNE
in her 42nd year. Left husband and four children.

March 25, 1835
Married on 3rd inst. by REV. DAVID M. DANCY of the Methodist
Episcopal Church, MR. ALFRED H. ELLETT of Morgan County to MISS MARY
M. E. A. HEWLETT, daughter of MR. JOHN HEWLETT of this co.
Died at his residence near Versailles on Tuesday (March 3) MAJOR
JOHN McKINNEY, JR. Clerk of the Circuit Court of Woodford, Kentucky.
Died on 18th of February at his residence in this place. JOHN D.
CARRIEL, Esq. formerly of Florence, but for last three years a resident
of this place.

April 1, 1835
Married on 12th of March by REV. F(INIS) E. HARRIS, MR. THOMAS S.
MAXWELL to MISS AMANDA W. LEWIS, all of this county. Bolivar Free
Press Copy.
Died in this village on Thursday morning last, MRS. ISABELLA M.
HALL, wife of DR. MOODY HALL, late a Missionary to the Cherokee Indians.
Died on 15th of February near Fife Post Office, Talladega County,
SARAH THOMASON FOREMAN, daughter of JOHN W. and MARY FOREMAN aged 7 years

1 mo 24 days. (Note: 1 JOHN W. FOREMAN m. in St. Clair Co. Ala., Sept. 4, 1823 POLLY CONNER.)

April 8, 1835
    Died in Montgomery, Alabama on 5th ult. MR. THOMAS GRANTLAND, Primer. Formerly of Huntsville.

April 15, 1835
    State of Alabama--Jackson County. Orphans Court. April 8, 1835. Petition for conveyance. JOEL D. LEWIS, administrator of estate of WILLIAM BABB, late of said county, deceased.
    Married on Wednesday evening last by JUDGE JOHN C. THOMPSON in this place, MR. ORVILLE EASTLAND of Tuscaloosa to MISS EVALINA A., daughter of MAJOR THOMAS McCRARY of this county.
    Lists of unclaimed letters, Huntsville, WM. ATWOOD, P.M. TRIANA, CALEB TONEY, P.M., ST. HELENA (Madison County), URIAH BASS. P.M.
    Advertisement: N(ATH'L) C. POWER states his wife ELIZABETH POWER has left his bed and board, and he will pay no debts of her contracting.
    Jackson County: J. B. STEPHENS, appointed administrator of JOHN McCUTCHEN dec'd, on 23rd February last.
    Jackson County: Runaway slave committed to jail; says belonged to GREEN SISNEY of Buncum County, NC and was purchased by JOHN HOWELL or JASON WILSON. TYREE RIDDLE, Jailor.
    St. Clair County: JOHN ROBERTSON, administrator of CALEB CAPS dec'd petitions to sell land.
    Oak Grove for sale; being desirous to remove further south--600 acres. JOHN VINING.
    Jackson County: Sale of land of JAMES LATHAM, dec'd; ELDRED W. WILLIAMS, JOHN BRIDGES, RICHARD C. CAMPBELL, commissioners.
    NATHAN SHUFFIELD advertises for stolen horse, return to him or to WM. ARNOLD of Jacksonville, Benton Co.

April 22, 1835
    State of Alabama--Talladega County. Orphans Court. Jan. 17, 1835. AQUILLA PEARCE, deceased. ROBERT JEMISON filed petition.
    State of Alabama--Jackson County. Orphans Court. Dec. 30, 1834. Administratrix of estate of HARDY DAYAL, late of said county, deceased summoned to court.
    Married Thursday, the 16th inst. by REV. JOSHUA BUTCHER at the house of REV. JOHN MOORE in Limestone County, JOHN D. PHELAN, Esq. of this place to MISS MARY ANN, daughter of THOMAS K. MORRIS of Tennessee, deceased.
    Married on same evening by REV. MR. THOMPSON, MR. ALFRED A. ROWAN to MISS MARY BINFORD, daughter of CAPTAIN PETER BINFORD, all of this co.
    Died in this village on the morning of the 20th of typhus fever, WILLIAM DYSON, recently from Abingdon, Virginia.

May 12, 1835
    Died Wednesday morning, 23rd of April, AMANDA VIRGINIA, infant daughter of J. D. FENNEL, Franklin County, Tennessee of measels aged about 13 months, 14 days.
    Died in Franklin County on 20th inst. in 40th year, FREDERICK CARELOCK. Left wife and four children.

May 20, 1835
    Married Thursday the 14th inst. by HENRY C. DUNN, Esq. CAPTAIN PATRICK LEONARD to MISS FRANCESS BROWNLEY, eldest daughter of JAMES BROWNLEY, Esq. all of this co.
    State of Alabama--Talladega County. Orphans Court. Apr. 9, 1835. ELIZABETH HARDWICK, administratrix of estate of GEORGE HARDWICK, late of said county deceased.
    JOSEPH CASTLEBERRY, administrator of estate of JAMES HOWARD, dec'd.

May 27, 1835
    Married on Tuesday evening 19th inst. by REV. P. B. ROBINSON, MR. JOHN G. BINGHAM to MISS MARIA, eldest daughter of MR. JOHN FISHER, all of this place.
    Married at the residence of MR. ALFRED HOWELL by REV. DAVID DANCY on Thursday, 21st inst. MR. THEOPHILUS LACY of Decatur. to MISS MARY W. HARRIS of this county.

June 10, 1835
Married at the residence of MRS. HATTON on 4th inst. by REV. DAVID M.
DANCY, MR. JAMES LANDMAN to MISS JULIA HATTON, all of this co.

June 17, 1835
State of Alabama--Jackson County. Orphans Court. 8 June 1835.
Administratrix of estate of CLAUGH A. SHELTON, deceased summoned to
court.
State of Alabama--Jackson County. Orphans Court. JOSEPH McCUTCHEON,
one of heirs of JOHN McCUTCHEON, deceased.
Married on 14th inst. MR. JAMES GIFT to MISS ELIZABETH daughter of
CAPT. SAMUEL DOUGLASS, both of Shelby Co. Tenn.

June 21, 1835
Married Thursday evening, 18th inst. in Limestone County, by
REV. F. E. HARRIS, MR. JAMES LOGAN of Madison County, to MISS NANCY
NEISBIT. See our Vol. 21 p. 85 & Vol. 61 p. 1 (marriage contract).
Died on 26th of May at MRS. MOSBY's after a short illness,
MRS. JANE P. MOSBY, relict of WILLIAM O. MOSBY, deceased and daughter
of CAPTAIN WOODSON of the county of Hanover (Va).
Died on suceeding Friday, MISS JUDITH R. daughter of CAPT. PHILIP
WOODSON.
State of Alabama--Jackson County. Orphan's Court. June 13, 1835.
JOHN CAMPBELL, deceased.

August 19, 1835
Married in Limestone County on Wednesday 5th inst. by REV. J. M.
ROBERTSON, MR. HICKMAN LEWIS of this place to MISS VIRGINIA, daughter of
COLONEL WILLIAM LINDSAY of the United States Army. Note: LEWIS was
in Seminole War, d 1843, See our Vol. 21 p. 85.
Married Thursday evening 6th of August by REV. WILLIAM McMAHAN,
H(ARDY) H. MOORE, Esq. to MISS PENELOPE N. KING, all of Madison Co.
Died on 9th inst. at residence of his father, DUDLEY SALE, MR.
THOMAS D. SALE aged 18.

August 26, 1835
Died on 14th inst. DAVID M. WOOD, Esq. aged about 38, native of
Virginia and has lived in or near Abingdon. Was a carpenter. Lived in
this neighborhood 8 or 9 years as a grocer. (Tombstone shows D. M. WOOD
d 1835 aged 38 Gray cemetery in Madison.)
Died at Harrodsburg Springs, Kentucky on 9th, COLONEL CHARLES
McCLUNG of Knox County (Tenn.) in 75th year. Native of Pennsylvania.
Took up residence in East Tennessee. Was father of JAMES W. McCLUNG of
this place.

September 16, 1835
Died on Sunday, 30th of August at residence near here in 36th
year of age, MRS. ANN LAVINIA EASON, consort of MAJ. WILLIAM EASON.
Filled the role of wife and stepmother gracefully. Left seven children
the youngest about 9 months old. Note: She m. Nov. 1820 in Madison
Co. & was dau of PHILIP J. ROOTES.
Died on 1st, MRS. CATHARINE E. MALTBIE in her 27th year.
Died in Decatur on 31st, CHARLES J. GILLESPIE.
Committee of Vigilance, Lawrence County: JOHN J. ORMOND, BENJAMIN
SHERROD, ROBERT H. WATKINS, RICHARD JONES, JAMES E. SAUNDERS, THOMAS
GIBSON, JOHN F. MOSELEY, JACK SHACKELFORD, ALEX. SALE, DR. A. B.
WASHINGTON, TURNER SAUNDERS, A. M. DEGRAFFENRIED, J. W. BAKER, JACOB K.
SWOPE, AMOS JARMAN, W. B. WHITAKER, W. W. HARPER, THOMAS S. EARLY,
JONATHAN GRAY, JOHN M. SWOPE, G. W. FOSTER, ELISHA MADDEN, CLAIBURNE
SAUNDERS, JAMES FERGUSON, THOMAS FOSTER; D. S. BYNUM, President.
Died, in Decatur on the 31st ult. CHARLES J. GILLESPIE.
Died, on Sunday the 30th of August at her residence near this place
in the 36th year of her age, MRS. ANN LAVINIA EASON, consort of MAJOR
WILLIAM EASON....obligations of wife, mother, stepmother.... Left
seven children, the youngest an infant about nine months old.
(Huntsville, Sept. 6, 1835). Note: m. in Madison Co. 26 Nov. 1820
ANN LAVINIA ROOTES. See our Vol. 119 p. 2.
The Richmond Enquirer will please insert the above.

Died on Tuesday the 1st instant MRS. CATHERINE E. MALTBIE in the 27th year of her age.

Departed this life on Tuesday the 8th instant of bilious fever MISS ADELINE eldest daughter of JOHN WRIGHT, Esq. of this co. in 16th year. Left father, mother, brothers and sisters.

St. Clair County: LEWIS CUNNINGHAM administrator ex officio of EVAN NICHOLSON deceased will sell property.

JOHN C. LITTLE advertises for JOSHUA LOWRY accused of murdering HENRY LITTLE, a citizen of Blounty County, Ala. on February 28th.

September 23, 1835

Land for sale; farm on which I lived three miles east of Tuscaloosa, 880 acres. B. A. JONES

Land for sale in Morgan County 720 acres 9 miles above Decatur by E. H. THOMPSON.

Advertisement, HENRY GARRETT has taken charge of the tavern at Madison Springs.

Land for sale: Homestead plantation on Cypress Creek four miles from Florence. See H. D. SMITH who lives five miles below Florence. Signed J. L. D. SMITH, H. D. SMITH, Lauderdale Co.

Jackson County: sheriff will sell land of Shelby Ussery.

Land for sale; 960 acres on Town Creek, Lawrence Co. G. G. WILLIAMS.

Land for sale; 400 acres 7 mi. NE of Mooresville, by ELIZABETH ASKEW; see JOEL W. BLACKWELL.

Runaway slave, from LEWIS J. MOORE of Selma.

Dissolution; in consequence of the death of SEYMOUR PLUMMER the partnership heretofore existing under firm of PLUMMER & BOGGS is dissolved. JOHN B. BOGGS, Florence, Ala. July 29, 1835.

Died on 12th inst. HEZEKIAH BAYLES, old and respectable citizen in his 80th year. Revolutionary soldier; born in New Jersey when an infant, his father emigrated to Maryland, then to London County, Va. where he married MISS JANE EVANS, who survives him; in 1779 emigrated to Washington County, East Tennessee; in 1787 to Knox County, north of Knoxville, where he lived twenty years. In 1807, he made a partial settlement in this county; in 1808, a permanent residence here. Was a Baptist.

Died on 10th of September at the residence of W. B. JOHNSON in his 68th year, WILLIE BLOUNT, Tennessee Governor.

Married in this place on Wednesday last, MR. ALCUEN EASON to MISS MARTHA M., daughter of MR. WILLIAM POWERS, all of this county.

September 30, 1835

Married in Marietta, Ohio on 6th inst. REV. ISAAC SHOOK, formerly of this place to MISS MARIA SHIPMAN of the former place.

Died on 20th, MRS. NANCY HIGGINS, widow of the late GENERAL HIGGINS (Decatur Sentinel).

By reference to our obituary head it is seen that JUDGE ISAACKS who represented this District in Congress for ten years, died at the residence of his father-in-law in Western District on 31st of August last.

JOHN CAMPBELL reports estate insolvent.

Committee for drawing up rules for the Committee of Vigilance, Madison County, Ala. DANIEL WRIGHT, Chairman, COL. E. HAMMOND, CAPT. LEWIS TALIAFERRO, COL. JOSEPH TAYLOR, COL. JAMES W. CAMP, CAPT. DAVID COBB, DR. THOMAS FEARN, WM. SMITH, A. F. HOPKINS, THOMAS BRANDON, WM. J. MASTIN.

Order to parade: 62nd regiment commanded by COL. EDMOND L. SCRUGGS, JOHN TAYLOR, Adjutant.

3rd Regiment, commanded by COL. JOHN R. H. ACKLEN, JOHN B. PHELAN, Adjutant.

Land for sale; in accordance with the will of WILLIAM E. DUPREE; at his late residence in Lauderdale County on the Tennessee River, 820 acres. JAMES E. DUPREE, executor (I live on adjoining land).

October 7, 1835

Committee of Vigilance, Jackson County. COL. JAMES SMITH, JOHN B. STEPHENS, DAVID LARKIN, COL. SAMUEL McDAVID, ELDRED WILLIAMS, DAVID CAWFIELD, HUGH P. CAPERTON, JACOB GROSS, R. T. SCOTT, HENRY F. SCRUGGS, JOSHUA KIRBY, WILLIAM WELLBOURN, A. C. BEARD, THOMAS MANNING,

BENJAMIN SNODGRASS, JOHN COWART, R. ROLLINGS, ALFRED MOORE, JACOB TALLY,
HIRAM ALLEN, CHARLES L. ROACH, JOHN HOLLAND, PETER ROBINSON, JAMES
DORIN SR. and JEREMIAH BROWN.
    Meeting at Springville; Committee of Vigilance: G. W. PATRICK,
LEWIS S. RIGGS, J. D. RIGGS, JAS. M. MEANS,
      1850 Census Ouachita Co. Ark. L. S. RIGGS 53 SC
                                  EDNEY   43 SC
                                  E J   22 Ala
                                  etc
AN. MEANES, WILIE TRUSS, HENRY BRADFORD, F. BRADFORD, W. P. HOOKER,
M. FULLER, TILMAN THRASHER, L. PATRICK, HARVEY PEARSON, E. B. LOVETT,
J. THRASHER, JAMES THOMASON, J. SEAMANS, A. WOODALL, J. T. RANDOLPH,
JAMES KING, E. RIGGS, JAMES PEARSON, T. KING, J. WASHINGTON, E. WASHINGTON,
C. F. PATRICK, W. HALL, D. H. MORROW, D. SELLERS, W. SEAMANS, S.
SEAMANS, Benton County: Committee of Vigilance: WARREN HARRIS, THOMAS
C. HINDMAN, COL. GEORGE FLEMING, C. A. GREEN, DR. M. SMITH, JAMES LYLE,
EDWARD L. WOODWARD, BENJAMIN HOLLINGSWORTH, R. D. ROWLAND, JAMES WOOD,
MOSES W. BENSON, THOMAS HENDERSON, CARTER W. SPARKS, JOHN RAINEY,
DOCTOR A. SHELTON, WILLIAM GREEN, WILLIAM B. MARTIN, DR. A. THOMAS,
NEIL FERGUSON, WILLIAM ARNOLD, and JOHN B. PENDLETON.
    Land for sale: Flint Mills--wish to remove further south.
URIAH BASS.
    Runaway slaves: from GEORGE REESE of Lowndes County, Ala. and
FRANCIS LEWIS of same neighborhood.
    State of Alabama--Jackson County. Orphans Court June 27, 1835.
ARCHIBALD WOODS and JONATHON LATHAM, administrators of estate of
JAMES LATHAM, deceased.

October 14, 1835
    Died on 28th ult. at father's residence at Hickory Grove, St. Clair
County, JOHN L. P. KELLEY, son of GEORGE A. and SARAH KELLEY; left aged
parents and numerous relations. Was born in Franklin County, Georgia
in 1812. His parents emigrated to Madison County the same year. His
father was a deacon in the Methodist Church; several other children
died in infancy (Communicated). (GEO A. KELLEY's will is in DeSoto
Co. Miss. 1844)
    Died on Friday last at the residence of MRS. BLACK in Big Prairie
after illness of two or three days, MR. GEORGE A(LLEN) LEE, a respectable
citizen of Hot Springs County and late from Alabama aged about 50 years
(Arkansas Gazette, Sept. 22) Note: His mother was MARTHA WILKINSON &
his father was JESSE LOE, Rev. soldier. Data from a descendant.
    State of Alabama--Jackson County. Orphans Court. Oct. 10, 1835.
Estate of JESSE TRIM, deceased.
    Land for sale: 920 acres 4 miles south Greensborough on Warrior
River. See JOHN ERWIN, Esq. of Greensborough. WILLIAM YOUNG
    JAMES B. DAVIS and DRURY ROBERTSON, administrators of HOLLAND
DAVIS, dec'd qualified in Williamson County, Tennessee, will sell
property at late residence of said DAVIS six miles east of Franklin.
(Race horses, etc).
    Jackson County: administrator of TOBIAS WILHELMS dec'd will make
final settlement.

October 21, 1835
    Courtland: JOHN GLAZE and JACK SHACKELFORD, executors of the will
of JOHN EVANS deceased, will sell Planters Hotel etc.
    Jackson County: administrator of JESSE TRIM will make final
settlement.
    Runaway slave, from WILLIAM HODGES of Lawrence County.
    Notice: Records of the War Dept. show MAJOR T. R. BROOM holds
pension certificate issued in the name of the subscriber on 11th May
1819, and he knows not where to find said BROOM to obtain it. This is
to request him to enclose it to me at Claysville, Jackson County, Ala.
MAJOR BROOM is supposed to be living in Baltimore, Md. or some southern
state. THOMAS T. DOTY.

November 4, 1835
    THOMAS FONDREN advertises land in Jackson County, 640 acres 5 miles
north of Bellefonte. See A. FINLEY of Bellefonte.

RICHARD FORD advertises 471 acres thirteen miles north of Athens, in Limestone Co.

Jackson County. Petition to sell land; ELIJAH R. BERRY, administrator of MILES BERRY, deceased; WILLIAM H. BERRY and JOHN G. BERRY, legatees are non residents of the state.

J. W. F. LOWRY, administrator of LEVI A. H. LOWRY will sell property (county not stated).

ELISHA MEREDITH advertises his farm seven miles east of Tuscumbia.

DAVID KELLER advertises plantation two and a half miles south of Tuscumbia. Note: He d. 2 May 1837 wife was MARY FAIRFAX MOORE, dau of ALEX. SPOTSWOOD MOORE & wife of JAMES MASON. See below:

Married on Sunday evening last by REV. DR. EDGAR, HON. JOHN BELL to MRS. JANE YEATMAN of this place (Nashville Republican).

Died Friday evening, 30th October in her 19th year MISS MARTHA EMILY, daughter of CAPTAIN SIMON TURNER of this co. Note: From Richmond Times Dispatch May 11, 1908 "JOHN TURNER d in Greensville Co. Va. in 1796-97 leaving following children: JOHN BLOUNT, SUGARS, SIMON, THOMAS & MARY & ANN, all the sons except WM. & JAS. settled in North Ala."

Departed this life on 20th of September, FREEBORN G. SMITH in 19th year, son of GEORGE and SARAH H. SMITH.

November 11, 1835
Married Thursday, 29th of October at residence of COLONEL LEWIS of Franklin County, Tennessee by REV. MR. SORRELL, MR. LEVI SCOTT of Huntsville to MRS. SOPHIA M. PRICE.

Died on 26th ult. MRS. ELIZA W. HEREFORD, wife of MR. THEODORIC M. HEREFORD of this county in her 39th year. Richmond Enquirer copy.

November 18, 1835
Married in Cumberland County, Kentucky on 29th by REV. THOMAS CROPPER, JOHN VINING, Esq. of Madison County to MRS. LUCY WASH of the former place.

Married Tuesday evening, 3rd inst. by REV. MR. SULLIVAN, MR. ARCHIBALD B. JAMES to MISS ANN E. M. HARRIS, all of this co.

State of Alabama--Jackson County. Orphans Court, Oct. 24, 1835. ELIJAH R. BERRY, administrator of estate of MILES BERRY, deceased. WILLIAM H. BERRY and JOHN G. BERRY, legatees are non-residents.

Funeral of the late MAJ. ROBERT WALTON will be preached by REV. WILLIAM M'MAHON at his late dwelling Sunday the 22nd.

GEORGE MASON advertises tract in Morgan County, one mile east of Wallace's Springs. See JAMES E. MASON who resides on the premises.

WM. ECHOLS, SR. being desirous of removing further south, wishes to sell land in Madison Co.

WM. THOMPSON advertises 642 acres where he lives six miles west of Florence, Ala.

Fayetteville, Tenn. Nov. 12th (YEOMAN) Difficulty between WILLIAM McCLUSTY and JOHN YERGER at MR. TODD's. McCLUSTY, who was YERGER's brother in law, shot and killed him.

Tuscumbis, November 14th. COL. WYATT of Huntsville left this place on yesterday evening with thirty odd volunteers on their way to Texas.

November 25, 1835
Aberdeen, Mississippi (extensively and very generally known as Martin's Bluff) lots to be sold. ROBERT GORDON, ABNER PREWETT, THOMAS N. NILES, O. D. HERNDON, JAMES DAVID, H. ANDERSON, JOHN C. WHITSETT, P. R. PROUT, A. P. BALDWIN, JOHN WIGHTMAN, trustees. (Columbus)

Nov. 6th. Notice: Letters of administration granted 28 Oct. 1835 to BENJAMIN F. CFARK (CLARK?) on the estate of GREEN D. HOWSE deceased, Lincoln County, Tennessee.

State of Alabama--Jackson County. Orphans Court. Nov. 14, 1835. ALEXANDER RIDDLE, administrator with will annexed of JAMES LUSK, deceased.

Married Thursday evening last by REV. JOSHUA BUTCHER, REV. PLEASANT B. ROBINSON to MISS ELIZA C. NEWMAN of this place.

Married Thursday last (19th) by REV. BENJAMIN S. FANT, MR. ASA DOSSIT to MISS SARAH A. LEONARD of this county.

Married on 19th inst. by REV. JAMES ROWE, MR. BENJAMIN F. ANDERSON to MISS MARTHA A. BRYANT, all of this county.

December 9, 1835
Married on 26th by REV. MR. McPHERSON, MR. ANDREW RICE to MISS SARAH ELIZABETH, daughter of STEPHEN S. EWING, all of this co.

On the same evening at JAMES GRAY's by REV. ROBERT DONALD (DONNELL), MR. JOHN G. RUSSELL of Athens to MISS ELIZA, only daughter of the late SAMUEL McALISTER of Mooresville.

Died suddenly in Triana, Ala. HON. WILLIAM I. ADAIR, Judge of 5th Judicial Circuit in that state.

December 16, 1835
Married on 10th in Honey Comb Valley, Jackson County by EDMUND BRIDGES, Esq., MR. ANANIAS VANN of Madison County to MISS JANE T. daughter of JAMES BARCLAY of the former place.

A. G. McNUTT, Vicksburg, Miss. advertises large tracts of land in Washington County, Mississippi adjoining W. W. BLANTON, Esq., part owned jointly with WILLIAM H. SIMS, Esq. part adjoining COL. PERCY's.

Jackson County: ALEXR RIDDLE administrator of HIRAM JACKSON dec'd reports estate insolvent.

"Subscriber having purchased land in Talladega County and determined to move to it by the 1st of March" sell 640 acres four miles south Vienna. JAMES WALKER

Runaway slave committed to jail in Blount County by JOSHUA K(ITTRELL) ROBERTS, Sheriff & Jailor; says belongs to a trader WILLIAM MANOR who purchased him of BARNABAS IVY of Duplin Co. NC. Note: Letter to us from E. R. HUBERT, McCOOK, Neb. July 3, 1962. "ISAAC ROBERTS m. ANN THOMASON in NC 1795 or so. son JOSHUA KITTRELL ROBERTS b NC 1799 next heard of in Blount Co. Ala. 1830 Census. Blount Co. Ala. shows JOSHUA K. ROBERTS. In 1846-48 he moved to Tenn, & to Ark & Tex in 1853" Note: by GANDRUD: He was in 1840 Census Marshall Co. Ala. We find 1 ISAAC in 1830 St. Clair Co. & 1840 Jef. Co.

Land for sale in Perry County, N Y. HOWZE, Marion, Ala.

December 23, 1835
St. Clair County. JOHN ROBERSON, administrator of THOMAS JOHNSON JR. dec'd will make final settlement.

St. Clair County. Estray: taken up by C. C. BARNES, sworn to before C. C. MALONE, Esq.

Married on Thursday evening, 17th inst. at the residence of HOOD HASLETT near Whitesburg by J. B. TURNER, Esq. MR. WILFORD CRUDGETON to MISS ANN MOORE, all of this county.

Died, JOHN C. TAYLOR, native of Maryland and emigrated to this state in the winter of 1834; took charge of private school; within a few weeks past, when removed to Somerville to commence law practice.

State of Alabama--Jackson County. Orphans Court. Nov. 21, 1835. JOHN ROBERSON, administrator of estate of THOMAS JOHNSON, SR deceased

December 30, 1835
Married on 22nd inst. by F. L. HAMMOND, Esq. MR. JAMES GORDON to MISS MARY ANN SANDERSON, daughter of MR. JAMES J. SANDERSON, all of this county.

Also on 23rd by same, MR. CALVIN H. SANDERSON to MISS ELEANOR T. daughter of MR. WILLIAM CARNES, all of this co.

Benton County: contract to be let on January 20th for court house. WM. ARNOLD, M. M. HOUSTON, M. W. BENSON, trustees.

Land for sale near Gainsville, Sumter County, where I reside. JOHN A. WINSTON.

January 6, 1836
Married on 20th December last by REV. JOSHUA BUTCHER of Limestone County, MR. JOHN J(EFFERSON) STEGER to MISS ELIZABETH P. SALE, daughter of CAPT. D(UDLEY) SALE of this co.

Married Thursday evening the 24th inst. by REV. MR. WARREN, MR. WILLIAM HOWARD HOWARD to MISS MARTHA R. MALONE, all of this county.

January 13, 1836
Married on 27th December 1835 at MAJ. ROBERT W. DAVIE's by SAMUEL LOWRY, Esqr. MR. BERRY THOMPSON to MISS TULLINA M. L. WELLBORN (looks like SALLINA in marriage record & SELINA in census).

State of Alabama--Jackson County. Orphans Court Nov. 14, 1835.
ALEXANDER RIDDLE, administrator with will annexed of JAMES TURK,
deceased.

January 20, 1836
    Jackson County: Estray: taken up by JOHN CHILDRES, south side
of Tennessee River. Appraised by C. SULLERELL and C. BYFORD.

January 27, 1836
    ALEXANDER RIDDLE, administrator of estate of HIRAM JACKSON,
deceased.
    Married Thursday evening 21st inst. by REV. MR. ANDREWS, MAJ. NEIL B.
ROSE to MRS. MARTHA T(URNER) MOODY, both of this place. Note: she
was dau of PAUL MITCHELL of Limestone & m 1. (11-1-1832 ROBT H. MOODY &
3. -----SOLOMON. Data from a descendant MRS. ADELLE WHITBY OLNEY, 1974.
    St. Clair County: B. GREEN, administrator of B. GREEN, deceased
will sell property.

February 3, 1836
    Jackson County: ALEXANDER RIDDLE, administrator with the will
annexed of JAMES TURK reports estate insolvent.
    Died, in Florence, Ala. on the 26th instant MARY F. consort of
DR. WADDY TATE of Limestone County. She was for many years...a member
of the Methodist Church, her husband, three children..(edge torn)
    Jackson County: WILLIAM STEPHENS administrator of TOLIVER ADAMS
will make final settlement.

February 10, 1836
    PINES R. INGRAM will continue to practice law in the courts of
Jackson and Marshall Counties; will keep his office in Claysville,
Marshall County.
    Runaway slave, from JAMES J. PALMER of Meridianville, Ala.

February 17, 1836
    JAMES C. MARTIN, being about to remove from Huntsville.
    Died at Seneca Agency west of Mississippi on 31st of December,
1835 in his 50th year, CAPTAIN GEORGE VASHON, Sub-Agent to Western
Cherokee Nation; native of Virginia and distinguished officer of the
late war; was a Captain of the 7th Regiment of Infantry in 1815 and
served as much with that Regiment until 1819 when he resigned command.
Remains brought to Fort Gibson on 5th instant.

February 24, 1836
    WILLIAM S. WOODS and JOHN T. JONES, late of Albemarle County,
Virginia, attorneys have located at Helena Arkansas and will locate and
enter land etc. References WM. H. GLASSCOCK, M.D., Madison County,
SEPTIMUS D. CABINESS, Esq., Madison County, PETER R. BOOKER, Esq.,
Maury County, Tennessee, JEREMIAH S. HELMS, M.D., Tuscumbia, Ala.
    SWIFT AUSTIN, attorney, Claysville, Ala. Marshall County.

March 2, 1836
    Subscribers have established themselves at Gunter's Landing on
south side of Tennessee River; general commission, receiving and
forwarding business. EDWARD GUNTER and JOHN G. ROSS.
    Jackson County. Attachment: LEVI BRYAN assignee versus JOSEPH
SMART; GEORGE SWINK, Clerk. (note: this is probably BYRAM; the
BYRAMS went from Madison to Jackson and LEVI was a favorite name,
coming from intermarriages with the HINDS family.)
    Died on Saturday, 20th inst. at residence in this place MR. RICHARD
BULOCK. Had lived among us many years. Left wife and three small
children. Methodist.
    Died Wednesday, 24th ult. after a painful illness, WILLIAM BARKER,
Esq. in his 56th year of age, formerly of Fredericksburg, Virginia, but
for a number of years a citizen of this place. Kind husband and father.
    State of Alabama--Jackson County. Orphans Court Feb. 20, 1836.
MOSES SWAIN, deceased.

March 9, 1836
    Died in this place on the 21st instant of pulmonia consumption
MR. EDWIN HUNTER in the 25th year of his age. (Tuscaloosa Flag)

Jackson County: JAMES HUGHS administrator of DAVID HUGHS dec'd reports estate insolvent.

Jackson County: ROBERT H. BROYLES and JUDITH WINE, executor and executrix of ALEXANDER WINE deceased petition to sell land.

Limestone County: J. BELL, JOHN FAVOR and S. STEPHENSON commissioners, will sell land of JOHN WATERSON dec'd, widow's dower excepted.

Jackson County: estray: taken up by MARTIN ALLEN on Paint Rock; appraised by HUGH McELYEA and GEORGE RIGGS.

March 16, 1836

WILLIAM H. T. BROWNE was on the 8th instant appointed by his HONOR G. W. LANE, clerk of the circuit court of Madison County vice P. S. WYATT who had vacated his office by absence from the state four months.

Teacher wanted: apply to EDMUND PRINCE or ALEXANDER ALEXANDER lving seven or eight miles southeast of Demopolis, Marengo Co. Ala.

March 23, 1836

Runaway debtors: JOHN J. PLIMPTON, dentist; understand he has gone to the state of New York. H. N. PIPER, cabinet maker, originally from Baltimore, Md.

St. Clair County: JOHN F. DILL, guardian of WILLIAM SLOAN, lunatic, will sell property.

March 30, 1836

Married in Brownsborough, Madison County on 27th inst. JOHN HADEN, Esq. MR. JAMES LAWLER to MISS LOUISA, daughter of CORBIN LEWIS, all of this co. See our Vol. 179 p. 74.

Died in this place on Sunday morning, 27th inst. of bilious pleurasy, in 72nd year of her age, MRS. MARTHA BAILEY, widow of the late CAPTAIN THOMAS BAILEY of Woodford County, Kentucky. She came to this place in the early part of last fall on a visit to some relations. Presbyterian.

State of Alabama--Jackson County. Orphans Court. Feb. 20, 1836. JAMES HUGHS, administrator of estate of DAVID HUGHS, deceased.

April 6, 1836

Married on Thursday evening last by REV. MR. ANDREWS, MR. FRANCIS T MASTIN, JR. to MISS ELIZA JANE, daughter of B. POPE, Esq. all of this place.

Died on Saturday last, MR. LEWIS WOOD, for many years a resident of this place.

Died Tuesday morning, the 15th inst. DR. JOHN W. WITHERS, late of Madison County; emigrated to this state and settled in Clinton in the Spring of 1034.

April 12, 1836

Runaway slave; from my plantation in Marengo County; took free papers of DANIEL PATTERSON, a black man who was apprenticed to ALBERT RUSSEL in 1807, recorded Madison County 1820. JAMES B. CRAIGHEAD, Huntsville.

Notice: Letters of administration granted JOHN W. F. LOWRY on estate of LEVI F. LOWRY dec'd, St. Clair County, 1835. Will make final settlement.

April 19, 1836

Blount County: DAVID HENDRIX SR., PHILIP D. CLARK and JAMES HENDRIX, commissioners, to sell property of WILLIAM JONES deceased. ALVAH JONES, adm'r.

Departed this life on Monday the 4th instant at his residence four miles south of Bolivar, Jackson County, Ala. COL. GEORGE CAPERTON, for advanced in his 60th year, after an illness of ten days...left numerous family in easy circumstances. Was commander of a company in the last Creek and Seminole War in which at many places, Tallahatchee, Talladega and others, but particularly the latter, he distinguished himself as an officer and a good soldier. It was there at the commencement of the battle (the most doubtful crisis of a soldier's feelings) that is exhibited that deliberation and firmness which characterizes the American Soldier. Our army was moving slowly toward the enemy in battle array; COL. CARROLL INSPECTOR GENERAL riding in front and being more elevated than some part of his men first discerned the Indians crouched down in the shrubbery. He halted. Gave the precautionary commands, then fire. COL. CAPERTON, then CAPT. CAPERTON, not being sufficiently high to see the enemy exclaimed to his company, "Stop boys--don't fire until you see the object that you shoot at." Their fire was reserved--but twas for a short time for the firing of the first company caused the Indians to rise from their ambushade with hideous yells and gestures as they rushed toward our encampment, when CAPT. CAPERTON repeated the COLONEL's orders to his company, the Indians were shocked and checked in their impetuous course and filed off in a different direction. (See "History of the Middle New River Settlements & Contigious Territories, page 388.)

April 26, 1836
Blount County. Estrays: taken up by CORNELIUS GILLESPIE and HENRY TIDMORE.
St. Clair County: Estray: taken up by WILLIAM CLARK sworn to before G. G. BEASON Esq. appraised by WM. LOWE and GILES DUBERRY.
St. Clair County: JOEL CHANDLER SR. administrator of E. G. BISHOP deceased petitions to sell land.
St. Clair County: WILLIAM H. SHOTWELL, administrator of WINN B. GOWEN deceased will make final settlement.
Married in Pulaski, Tennessee on the 15th inst. by REV. MR. COLLINS, MR. PLEASANT J. MITCHELL to MISS JANE A. BLACK, both of Huntsville. Note: Is this PLEASANT JONES MITCHELL b. Apr. 19, 1815. Bible rec in poss. of MRS. ADELLE OLNEY, 1974.
Died at the residence of her husband in Madison County on the 15th inst. MRS. ELIZABETH CALHOUN; deceased has left two small children, one an infant at breast. JOHN CALHOUN, the late husband of deceased, being absent on business and place of destination unknown. Papers of Morgan, Madison and adjoining counties are requested to copy in order to find said husband.
State of Alabama--St. Clair County--Orphans Court. Mar. 7, 1836. WILLIAM H. SHOTWELL, administrator of estate of WINN B. GOWEN, deceased; also JOEL CHANDLER, SENR. administrator of estate of H. G. BISHOP, dec'd.

May 3, 1836
Departed this life on Monday evening the 11th of April in the 68th year of her age MRS. FLORA KEY, consort of the late JOB KEY. MRS. KEY was born in the state of Maryland, when small moved to the county of Sullivan, Tennessee, and to this county in 1812. She has left seven children. Knoxville Register requested to publish the above.

May 17, 1836
Jackson County: JAMES G. McELYEA purchased land from JOHN P. McELYEA who has departed this life, JESSE McELYEA, adm'r.
WILLIAM GREEN of Bolivar, Jackson County, states his wife SARAH has withdrawn from his abode.
State of Alabama--Jackson County. Orphans Court. May 6, 1836. JAMES G. McELYEA petitions for title to land bought from JOHN P. McELYEA, now deceased. JESSE McELYEA, administrator of estate of said JOHN P. McELYEA, deceased.

May 24, 1836
Jackson County: FULDEN A. HANCOCK, administrator of LEWIS HAYNES will make final settlement.
Died, at Columbus, Mississippi on the 4th instant CAPT. BEVERLY B. PRYOR aged 20 (or 29-blurred) years 7 months; was an only child.
Runaway slave--Commited to jail at Jasper, Tennessee. Says he belongs to DAVID WILLIAMS near Natchez, Miss.

May 31, 1836
Estray taken up by GILES C. JONES, three miles south of the Tennessee River on road from Blountsville to Deposit.

June 7, 1836
Died in this place on Friday morning last, MR. ANDREW CROSS, an early settler in this place.

June 14, 1836
   Runaway slaves committed to jail on Lawrence County; one belongs
to WILLIAM McMILLON, other to MR. O'RILY of Franklin County. D. H.
VALLIANT, sheriff.
   Morgan County: THOMAS PRICE, sheriff will sell property of
WILLIS GRIFFIN for lease Lane.
   Departed this life on the 10th inst. at her residence in Triana,
MRS. MARTHA A. WILLIS, consort of the late JOSHUA WILLIS...left six
small children--devoted member of the Methodist Episcopal Church. Note:
She was dau of REV. ISAAC HALL.

June 21, 1836
   Long letter from COL. BARTLEY COX to JOHN J. McMAHON, Courtland,
date New Orleans, 7 June; "We had arrived last evening from Texas and
to my astonishment ISAAC HAMILTON of the Red Rovers and JAMES LAMPKINS
came passengers. HAMILTON was wounded in the massacre of Shackelford's
men...LAMPKINS was saved by the General of the Mexicans. LAMPKINS
informs me our friend DR. SHACKELFORD was alive the 15th of May."
   Runaway slaves from NATHANIEL EVANS of Morgan County; one was
raised in Jefferson County, Tennessee, and one by MR. SPESART of
Botetourt County, Va.

June 28, 1836
   Married on Tuesday evening at the City Hotel by the REV. DR.
EDGAR, LEROY P. WALKER Esq. of Huntsville, Ala. to MISS ELIZABETH
HUDNELL of Mississippi (Nashville paper).

July 5, 1836
   Married Tuesday the 28th of June by REV. MR. BELL, MR. WILLIAM C.
JAMES to MISS NANCY F. VINING, daughter of JOHN VINING, Esq. both of
this county.

July 12, 1836
   Jackson County: estrays: taken up by JOEL D. LEWIS; by CHARLES
PARTON; by LAZARUS FLETCHER near BOZE's old mill.

July 19, 1836
   Married Thursday evening 7th inst. by JOHN T. HADEN, Esq. MR.
JESSE LAWLER to MISS JULIET C. daughter of BENJAMIN RAGAN all of this co.
   Letter from DR. JACK SHACKELFORD (Courtland) late CAPTAIN of the
Red Rovers, with a long list of the killed and wounded of his company.
   St. Clair County; AMOS ROLAND appointed administrator of ANDREW
SMITH on 12th March 1836.

July 26, 1836
   "Another swindler out." "One WILLIAM SPILLMAN borrowed $500 from
my father in law ARCHIBALD COBB of Knox County.... CLAYTON T. ABERNATHY,
Morgantown, E. T. (Note: There are several advertisements some
signed by SPILLMAN and some by ABERNATHY; controversy seems to have seen
over which had the right to prepare and sell a certain remedy.)
   Plantation for sale; two and a half miles south of Russelville,
lately property of COL. RICHARD S. JONES, residence late property of
JOHN B. NOE Esq. deceased, and occupied by MR. P. O'REILLY. MR. JOHN P.
IRWIN manager on the premises. Martin, Pleasants & Co.
   Franklin Female Institute: Trustees, PETER WALKER, JOHN HOGAN,
JOHN BRADLEY, JACOB HAIGH*, CHAS. COOPER, ISAAC WINSTON, WM. HUDSON,
C. T. BARTRON, M. TARVER, A. S. CHRISTIAN, G. W. CARROLL, N. J. HOUSTON.
*Miss. Memoirs (Goodspeed, pub. 1890; JACOB HAIGH b ca 1788, merchant
in Tuscumbia, Ala. at 1 time; moved to Miss. ca 1836; moved to Arkansas Co.
Ark. in 1857 where he d 1870. dau. ELIZ. b Tuscumbia Ala. ca 1818
raised in Miss. m. CALVIN A. TAYLOR in Tishomingo Co. Miss).
   Athens Female Academy; J. L. McIRLIN, A. DEDUS, WM. RICHARDSON,
JAMES CRAIG, WILLIAM T. GAMBLE, MICAJAH THOMAS, J. K. MURRAH.
   Mooresville Female Academy. Trustees J. M. S. JONES, J. H. GAMBLE,
T. H. THACH, ED WALTON, W. K. ADAMS, WM. DeWOODY.
   IRWIN SMITH of Greene County advertises runaway slave.

August 2, 1836
   Noxubee County, Mississippi; HEZEKIAH W. FOOTE versus SIMEON GERON,
attachment.

Departed this life, MRS. MARTHA A. POWELL, consort of BENJAMIN H. POWELL of Cartersville, Cumberland County, Virginia, who died at the residence of MAJOR JOHN HATCHERS her father, on Sunday the 26th instant in the 31st year of her age...was...mother... Signed GEORGE W. NOLLEY.

August 9, 1836

Runaway slaves, from HENRY PEDEN, Pikeville, Marion County; one raised in Fayetteville, NC and the other formerly belonged to COL. RIEVES of Sparta, Tennessee.

St. Clair County; JOEL CHANDLER SR. administrator of HARRIS G. BISHOP dec'd petitions to sell property.

Marshall County, P. M. BUSH, sheriff will sell land of ROBERT WALKER.

WILLIAM M. BURWELL of Franklin Co. will sell two and an eighth sections in Marengo Co. see JOHN BURWELL, Esq. of Demopolis.

Subscriber being desirous of moving farther south, will sell tract 13 miles west of Huntsville. STEPHEN W. RUTLAND.

Runaway slave from WILLIAM THOMPSON near BOTELOR's ferry. Morgan County; also one belonging to my son R. A. THOMPSON.

Married on 28th inst. at house of MR. JOHN B. WRIGHT by F. L. HAMMOND, Esq. MR. ISAAC BEAN to MISS CHARLOTTE WRIGHT, all of this co. Note: she was dau of JAMES DAVID WRIGHT (named in his will)

Died in Haynesville, Lowndes County on Monday the 11th inst. (July 11, 1836) COL. JOHN K. DUNN, formerly of New York and late of Huntsville in his 44th year of age.

Died on Sunday, the 24th inst. at his residence in Lincoln County, Tenn. AQUILLA QUICK, Esq. aged 55. Richmond Enquirer and Fayetteville, Tenn. copy.

August 30, 1836

Died on 10th ult. MR. HUGH BLACKWOOD, merchant of Vienna, Madison County, Louisvilla Journal and Nashville papers copy.

Died Sunday, 21st inst. EDWARD TRENT, infant son of DANIEL HARRIS, Esq. of this co.

The subscriber having determined to remove to Mississippi, land on which I reside in Lincoln Co. Tennessee. STEPHEN HIGHTOWER.

NANCY WELBORN (note: WILBURN) of Athens advertises for news of her son ROBERT WELBORN between 12 and 13; left house of her brother WILLIAM W(ASHINGTON) MATTHEWS but did not go to school; was seen in the taverns at Huntsville.

JOHN COX SR. of Marshall County advertises regarding note given to SWIFT AUSTIN "who has left the country." SWIFT AUSTIN advertises has removed to Tuscaloosa.

St. Clair County: SHADRACK MORRIS, administrator of RICHARD SULLIVAN.

Runaway slave from HENRY BURROUGH, Pikeville, Marion Co. subscriber having determined to settle in Texas--1040 acres in Marengo and Perry Counties. WILLIAM K. PAULDING.

September 13, 1836

Subscriber intends to emigrate to the Chockasaw country; ¼ section of land in Ashburn's Cove; immediately adjoining Brownsboro where I reside. MARY TAYLOR.

September 20, 1836

SWIFT AUSTIN and G. W. SAINT CLAIR, proprietors of the Indian Queen Hotel, Tuscaloosa.

A. J. WITHERS, having determined to remove to the southern part of the state, will sell stock of goods. (General merchandise, apparently).

Married on 6th inst. by REV. JOSHUA BUTCHER, the REV. THOMAS D. HARWELL to MISS ANN, eldest daughter of JUDGE JAMES RUSSELL of Jackson Co.

Married on 30th of August by BENJAMIN STEGER, Esq. JAMES LOSSANDGAIN to the amiable MISS MATILDA RAINCROW, all of this co.

Died at his residence on the evening of the 15th inst. MR. WILLIAM ATWOOD, citizen of Huntsville nearly twenty years, being Post Master most of that time. He was 55 years old; kind husband and father. Left wife and five children.

Died on Tuesday last, WILLIAM EASON, planter of this county in the
56th year of his age.
Died on Friday the 2nd inst. MARGARET CORNELIA, daughter of
JOHN D. FENNELL of Vienna of this county. Aged 1 year and 8 days.

September 27, 1836
Land for sale by WILLIAM DYE, 8 miles west of Fayetteville,
Lincoln Co. Tenn.

October 4, 1836
JOHN G. AIKEN, attorney, has removed to Mobile.
Runaway slave, was purchased in the Cherokee Nation about three
weeks ago from COL. JAMES LAMAR near Newman's Store, Will's Valley,
Address Stickard & Goff, Lawrence burg or Mt. Pleasant, Tennessee.
For sale, at old Ft. Deposit, ferry and House of entertainment:
RICHARD GRIFFIN.
Died on the evening of 16th inst. at residence of his father-in-
law (MR. JAMES BAILEY) in Madison County, JAMES ABERNATHY in 24th year
of his age. Formerly of Giles County, Tennessee but for the last two
years and nine months, a resident of Limestone Co. Ala.

October 11, 1836
Married in Smyth County, Virginia on Thursday, 15th of September
by REV. MR. SNEED, GEN. BENJAMIN PATTESON of Huntsville to MISS SARAH T.
SAUNDERS of the former place. Note: 2nd wife & usually written
SARAH ANN SANDERS. His 1st wife was FANNY WEAKLEY.
Married by rt REV. RICHARD CHANNING MOORE on Thursday 22nd inst.
at the residence of MR. GEORGE L. SAMPSON in this city, DR. ALFRED MOORE
of Huntsville, Ala. to MISS MARY JANE WATSON, daughter of MATTHEW WATSON,
deceased (Richmond Enquirer).

October 18, 1836
Administrator's Sale. Residence of GEORGE CAPERTON deceased in
Jackson County. GEORGE CAPERTON and A. H. CAPERTON, administrators of
estate.
Runaway slave from SAMUEL CONNOR, Columbus, Miss. Purchased 1832
from JOHN KEY of Franklin Co. Tenn.
Runaway slave from B. B. SMITH, Louisville, Winston Co. Miss.
Jackson County: GEORGE and A. H. CAPERTON, administrators of
GEORGE CAPERTON dec'd will sell property.
Land for sale by DAVID A. SMITH of Courtland.

October 25, 1836
Runaway slave, from A. B. WASHINGTON, Lagrange, Ala.
Runaway slave, committed to jail in Lawrence Co. says belongs to
SOLOMON NEWMAN of Natchez, Miss. H. H. VALLIANT, Jailor.
Married on Thursday evening last by REV. P. B. ROBERTSON (ROBINSON),
D.R H(ENRY) A(RTHUR) BINFORD to MISS SARAH E. BRANDON; also MR. JAMES H.
HAUGHTON to MISS CAROLINE F. BRANDON, daughters of THOMAS BRANDON, Esq.
of Huntsville.
Married on Tuesday 18th inst. at residence of COL. JAMES N FLETCHER
in this county by REV. WELLBORN ALLEN, DR. A. S. HARRIS to MISS MUSIDORA
V. CHEATHAM.
At the same time and place and by the same minister, MR. CARGILL J.
MASSENBURG to MISS ANN CHEATHAM, Note: 1 Dr. CARGILL J. MASSENBURG d.
in Wake Co. NC Nov. 1, 1809 (Raleigh Register Nov. 23, 1809).
Died on Wednesday 12th Dist MRS. HENRIETTA COOPER, wifc of
MR. ALLEN COOPER of this place.

November 1, 1836
Departed this life Thursday the 13th ult. in Madison County, Ala.
MRS. BELINDA T. DARVIN (DARWIN), consort of CAPT. GEORGE DARVIN in her
32nd year... left husband. 5 children member of the Cumberland Presby-
terian Church. (Note: this name is DARWIN)
Meeting of Executive Committee: North Ala. Jockey Club; Present
JAMES W. CAMP, SAMUEL RAGLAND, WILLIAM FLEMING and WILLIAM H. GEE.
J. H. WILSON, secretary.
Broke jail: two negro men who said they belonged to JOHN C. McCRUE
and RICHARD WELBORN of Sumpter County. THOS. PRICE, Sheriff, Morgan Co.

November 8, 1836
Runaway slaves from POLLY REECE, 9 miles north of Fayetteville,
Lincoln Co. Tenn.
Land for sale: subscriber having purchased land in Mississippi
and intending to emigrate thither, offers 157 acres near Brownsboro;
if a physician would settle there will also dispose of my shop furniture
and medicines. WILLIAM ANDERSON
ARTHUR TRUSS has been appointed administrator of SAMUEL TRUSS
(no county given).
Advertisement: DANIEL SCOTT and DORCAS his wife emigrated many
years ago from Caswell County, North Carolina to the western country,
supposed to be in Alabama, Tennessee or Mississippi, if alive; DORCAS
was formerly DORCAS CANNON; if they or their heirs will write ANN SCOTT,
sister of DANIEL SCOTT at Danville, Virginia (she aged and infirm),
it will be to their advantage (note: Probably estate to be settled).
DR. WHITE of Benton County, Alabama leads to the altar as bride,
MISS JANE NETTLE aged 15. He is about 89.

November 15, 1836
Married on 30th ult. near Cross Roads by REV. J. B. CRAIG, DR.
MOODY HALL to MRS. CHARLOTTE D. DILLON, all of this co. See our Vol. 147
p. 45. She was widow of GEO. DILLARD (see that marriage in our Vol. 153
p. 5 10 Mar. 1823 dau of EDW'D & CATH. (DIGGES) HARRIS).
Departed this life at ½ after 8 o'clock on evening of 4th inst of
pulmonary disease, HNERY JORDAN in his 38th year--for many years a
resident of this co.
"In camp near Tallahassee, Florida 22 Oct. 1836. MAJOR WILLIAM M.
KING; Sir: We are requested as a committee appointed by the Battalion
of Jackson County (Ala) Volunteers to respond to your note of yesterday.
It is the unanimous desire of the officers and privates of this
Battalion that you do not resign your seat in the State Legislature.
DAVID CAWLFIELD, JOHN SMITH, M. PRICE, JOSHUA SCURLOCK, A. COFFEY,
H. POGUE, JAMES P. POSTON, WILLIAM A. McCRARY, THOMAS HOLLAND, JOHN
BRIDGES.
Land for sale, by JOHN F. MOSELEY of Courtland, or see MR. JAMES M.
PEARSALL of that place.

November 22, 1836
Married on 8th inst. by JOHN W. IRBY, Esq. MR. WILLIAM ANDERSON
to MISS CARRENE TIPTON daughter of ISAAC TIPTON, all of this co. See
our Vol. 71 p. ? which says CYRENA TIPTON.
Married in Limestone County on Tuesday evening, 15th instant by
REV. F. G. FERGUSON, MR. JOHN C. BROWN to MISS REBECCA WEBB, eldest
daughter of MR. WILSON WEBB. See our Vol. 21 p. 48.
Account of the murder of MR. THOMAS HUSKY and WILLIAM WRIGHT of
Shelby County, Tennessee, near MR. FENTER's in Hot Springs County,
Arkansas. MR. EDWARD CALVERT found the bodies and went back to MR.
JAMES MARTIN's later discovered one of their negroes had killed them.
JOHN W. JONES and J. HAIGH, executors of CAPT. ARTHUR JONES dec'd
will sell his residence, 720 acres and 48 negroes 1 mile east of
Tuscumbia.
JOHN L. TOWNES, executor of the will of the late E. P. WADDELL will
hold sale at his late residence in Franklin County.
St. Clair. EDWARD EDWARDS, administrator of THOMAS EDWARDS will
sell property at Asheville, that county.

November 29, 1836
Married, on Tuesday evening the 6th instant by the REV. L. D.
MULLENS, MR. HEZEKIAH BAILEY of Limestone County to MISS LOUISA C.
GOOCH of this county.
Died at Greensboro, Alabama on Sunday the 13th instant after a
lingering illness MRS. MARY WILLIAMS, in the 58th year of her age, wife
of MR. BENJAMIN M. WILLIAMS, formerly of Courtland and more recently
a citizen of this place.

December 6, 1836
From the Alabama Mercury we learn that the honorable SAMUEL W.
MARDIS died at his residence in Talladega County on Monday the 14th

instant. MR. MARDIS has for some years past taken as active part in the politics of the country...was as elector on the White ticket and died on the very day of the election.

December 13, 1836
        Married, on the 1st instant by MR. JOEL D. LEWIS, MR. ABNER G. WHITELY of Madison County to MISS ELIZABETH, daughter of SAMUEL LEE of Jackson County.
        Departed this life on the 7th instant at the residence of JOHN D. ROBINSON, Esq. in this county, MISS SUSAN M. HART in the 17th year of her age...only daughter of the late DR. HART, formerly a resident of Huntsville.

December 20, 1836
        Departed this life on the 27th ult. at her father's MISS HENRIETTA ELIZABETH, youngest daughter of CAPT. RICHARD and MARY BURKE, of Madison County, in the 14th year of her age.

December 27, 1836
        Married on the 16th instant by JOHN DEMENT, Esq. MR. JOHN A. HILLIARD to MISS MARTHA B. daughter of CAPT. LEWIS B. SANDERSON, all of Madison County.
        ELDRED W. WILLIAMS was elected Colonel Commander of the 52nd Regiment A. M. Jackson County; MAJOR JOSHUA SCURLOCK and CAPT. ARCHIBALD W. COLLINS were also candidates.

January 3, 1837
        Marshall Co. P. M. BUSH, sheriff will sell land of GEORGE LOYS.
        St. Clair County; estray' taken up by JOHN MORGAN SR. and GEORGE WOOD, sworn to before T. M. L. LESTER, J.P.
        St. Clair County: LEWIS CUNNINGHAM, administrator of LEWIS CAPPS will make final settlement.
        Carroll County, Mississippi; JAMES MEEK, administrator of SAMUEL MEEK dec'd will sell land there.
        JOHN D. PHELAN, attorney, has removed from Huntsville to Tuscaloosa.

January 10, 1837
        Married on the evening of the 3rd instant by J. W. IRBY, Esq., MR. WILLIAM PARKER of Morgan County to MISS ELIZABETH A. C. RUFFIN of Madison.
        Notice: JOHN B. MIZE by O. MIZE, regarding note to ISAAC HAMBRICK for land in District of Tuscaloosa. He has left the state.

January 17, 1837
        Married in this city on Tuesday evening the 17th instant by the REV. MR. LEWIS of the Protestant Episcopal Church PERCY WALKER, M.D. to MISS ELLEN, daughter of JUDGE A. S. LIPSCOMB, all of this city. (Mobile Register Dec. 17th?)
        Obituary of ROSANNA S., daughter of NEIL THOMPSON, aged about 14 who had been reared in the family of DAVID MOLLOY of Jackson County.
        Departed this life on Sunday the 1st day of January, 1837 in La Grange, Ala. at the residence of MRS. ANN DENT, her mother MRS. PATIENCE A. W. TARTT, wife of THOMAS TARTT, aged 42. MR. and MRS. TARTT recently returned from Philadelphia where they resided the last four or five years (Note: Tombstone at LaGrange, Colbert Co. Ala. PATIENCE A. W. TARTT, wife of THOMAS E. TARTT who departed this life Jan. 1, 1837 aged 44-2-15) superintending the education of their two daughters. She was a Baptist and the first individual Baptized in La Grange, in 1826.
        Died in this county on the 1st instant at his residence near Huntsville, WILLIAM ROWNTREE Esq. an old and highly respectable citizen.
        Adv. Town of Hopkinsville, on Paint Rock River, Jackson County-- SAMUEL McDAVID and A. J. LINDSEY, proprietors.
        Land for sale, have bought elsewhere; plantation near Woodville, Perry County. FRANCIS M. PHILLIPS, Pleasant Valley, Dallas Co.

January 24, 1837
    Married on the 10th instant by the REV. JAMES H. GILLESPIE
COL. JESSE B. BEAUCHAMP to MISS LOUISA, youngest daughter of JAMES
DINSMORE Esq. all of Morgan Co. See our Vol. 74 p. 4.
    Marshall County; sheriff will sell property of JOHN BLACKWOOD.

January 31, 1837
    Married on Thursday evening the 12th instant, by the REV. W. H.
WILLIAMS, MR. JONES M. WITHERS of Huntsville to MISS REBECCA ELOISA,
daughter of MAJOR DANIEL M(ORGAN) FORNEY, of this place (Tuscaloosa
Flag). See our Vol. 25 p. 8.
    On the 19th instant by the REV. J. WILLIAMS, MR. THOMAS PATTESON
to MISS MARGARET E. daughter of MR. MARTIN MILLER, all of this place.
See our Vol. 64 p. 15.
    On Thursday the 12th instant by JUDGE RECTOR MAJOR JAMES MUNDY to
MISS JULIA S. daughter of B. S. JONES, Esq. all of Jackson County.
    In Jackson County, Ala. on the 17th instant by SAMUEL EVANS Esq.
CAPT. ROBERT ALLISON of this county to MRS. MARIA GRIFFIN of Whitely
County, Kentucky.
    Washington County, Arkansas. JAMES C. BELL, administrator with
the will annexed of JOHN WILSON dec'd
    W. A. DODDY of Somerville to sell property.
    Persons holding claims against the estate of DAVID GILLESPIE dec'd
of Blount County to present them to J. E. ROBERTS, sheriff of Blount
County. Also claims against GEORGE HOPPER dec'd.
    Advertisement--to sell the estate of DAVID GILLESPIE at the
late residence of JOHN GILLESPIE where R. H. ROGERS formerly lived.

February 28, 1837
    Morgan County: runaway slaves committed to jail; one says belongs
to DRURY OWEN near Courtland, one to DR. DAVIDSON living near "Big
Black" one to widow HUDSON eight miles below Tuscaloosa and one to
JAMES MALONE of Mobile County.
    Land for sale; Lauderdale County; J. C. FUQUA, Commissioner.

March 7, 1837
    Married on the 21st ult. at the residence of ELDRED W. WILLIAMS,
Esq. by JUDGE RECTOR, COL. JOSEPH P. FRAZIER to MISS LUCINDA A. WILLIAMS,
all of Jackson County.
    On Tuesday the 21st ult. by the REV. J. ELLETT, MR. JAMES M. GREEN
to MISS ZORADID W. McCLUNG, all of this county (ZORADIA--see our Vol. 4),
also Vol. 127 pp. 23, 66.
    Advertisement for lost pocket book in Morgan Co. by ROBERT B. BILES.
    Advertisement--On 5th of this month was felonously taken and
carried off out of possession of PERMELIA CARTER of Jackson County
Tennessee a slave...by RICHARD CARTER, about 34 years old...is expected
to take slave to Arkansas or a southwestern state...to apprehend him
will be an act of charity to a young woman who has neither mother nor
father living to protect her. DALE CARTER.

March 14, 1837
    Runaway slave; from FRANCIS DURRETT of Lexington, Lauderdale
County; ran from yard of JOHN DONAHOO, Esq.
    Married, at Oakville, Ala. on Thursday evening the 2nd instant by
the REV. MOSES MORRIS the REV. MADISON ANDERSON late of Madison County,
Ala. to MISS EMILY KILLUM, formerly of Connecticut.

March 21, 1837
    Died in this place on the 12th instant, WILLIAM PHILLIPS son of
MR. WILLIAM E. PHILLIPS.
    On the 16th inst. MRS. LANG, consort of MR. JAMES LANG of this
place. MRS. LANG was originally from Richmond, Virginia and with her
husband located in Huntsville at its early settlement...member of the
M. E. Church.

March 28, 1837
    Departed this life on the 18th instant, JOHN HUNTER, after a
protracted illness of some months. He was a native of Virginia but
for many years a resident of the vicinity of this place.

On the 20th instant WILLIAM McCAY SR. an early resident of this place and well known to the old settlers of Richmond and Petersburgh, Virginia in which cities he formerly resided. He had just recovered from severe wounds received accidentally whilst travelling on a railroad near Philadelphia and survived his recent attack but a few days.

On the 22nd inst. WILLIAM C., son of MR. GEORGE LYNES of this place.

Grand Jurors of Morgan County: G. BURNETT, foreman, W. N. GILLESPIE, P. H. LYLE, JOHN ORR, JOHN F. BANKS, JOHN SHARP, HENRY FENNEL, JOHN TROUP, WILLIAM M. DUTTON, EDWARD HUNTER, D. H. PALL, AARON PERRY, BENJAMIN SANDLIN, MILTON McCLANAHAN.

April 4, 1837

Land for sale, by PITMAN COLBERT, 18 miles west of Tuscumbia, in Franklin Co.

Land for sale, forks of Mulberry Creek, Lincoln County, Tenn. WILLIAM F. SMITH.

Runaway slave, from J. C. CABINESS, Tuscaloosa, Ala.

Runaway slave from B. C. SHIELDS, White Hall, Marengo County, purchased from MR. C. S. PATTERSON of Tuscaloosa.

April 11, 1837

Notice: GEORGE T. JONES, JOSEPH RICE and RICHARD FORSEY commissioners to contract for and superintend building of a bridge across Flint River at Three Forks. Bridge at Tuscaloosa will be taken as a model.

Panola, Mississippi, lots for sale. WILSON T. CARUTHERS and RICHARD BOLTON, trustees.

April 18, 1837

Married on Wednesday evening the 5th instant at the house of MAJOR FENNER near Courtland MR. THOMAS B. TABB of Mississippi to MISS LAURA E. TAYLOR of Courtland.

The REV. MR. HAWKINS will preach the funeral sermon of WILLIAM EASON deceased at his late residence on the 2nd Sunday in May next.

April 25, 1837

Marshall Co WILLIAM RITCHIE, administrator of ABNER VAUGHAN will sell property.

Selma Free Press--account of a difficulty between MR. WILLIAM BLEVINS and DR. JAMES R. DICKINSON; latter stabbed and died.

Marshall County; petition for title; WILLIAM C. THOMAS on 14 December 1831 contracted to purchase land from JOHN HILL has since died without making title. Little D. DOBHART then of Jackson, now of Marshall County, was appointed administrator by Jackson County Court.

May 2, 1837

RACHEL R. MITCHELL and WILLIAM J. YOUNG, appointed administrators of FRANKLIN MITCHELL deceased, Marshall County.

May 16, 1837

Marshall County: ALFRED MOORE appointed administrator of PATRICK BURK, deceased.

Died in Huntsville on 16th of April in 13th year REUBEN CARMICHAEL, son of MR. DANIEL CARMICHAEL of this vicinity; by blow from stone thrown by a black boy.

JAMES WILLIAMS, Esq. Candidate from Jackson County for the Legislature.

Regimental orders: 1st Battalion 3rd Regiment commanded by LT. COL. JOHN H. WEBSTER will parade at New Marker; 2nd Battalion same regiment commanded by MAJ. WILLIAM B. LUSK will parade at JOHN HEATH-COCK's/ WILLIAM M. ROPER, Adjt. 3rd Regt. A.M. by order of COL. BENJ. F. RICKETTS.

May 23, 1837

Blount County; runaway slave committed to jail; says belongs to RICHARD WALTHOL of Perry County. JOSHUA K(ITTRELL) ROBERTS, Sheriff.

For sale: "Somerville's Mills" five miles west of Russelville on the Pontotoc Road, apply to ALEXANDER SOMERVILLE on the premises, D. R. GARLAND at Russelville or to CHARLES A. STEWART (attorney for WILLIAM SOMERVILLE) at Florence.

May 30, 1837
    DR. ALFRED MOORE has removed to Huntsville.
    St. Clair County: WILLIAM THWEATT, administrator of JOSEPH HOWARD.
    Runaway slave from MATTHEW TRUSSELL, Clinton, Alabama.

June 13, 1837
    Married, on 4th instant by SAMUEL EVANS, Esq., MR. REUBEN IRVIN
to MISS HANNAH, daughter of MR. WILLIAM MAPLES, all of Jackson Co.
    Died in this place on the 5th instant, MRS. WILLIAM STREET, wife
of MR. WILLIAM STREET, in the 44th year of her age.
    Died, in Mardisville, Alabama on the 23rd of May last MRS. MARY
McLEOD, wife of GEORGE McLEOD Esq. formerly of this county but now a
resident of the above place.
    Marshall County: Sheriff, P. M. BUSH, will sell property of
MARIAH L. CHEEK; JAMES BOGGESS, JOHN C. JOHNSON, EDMOND BRIDGES.

June 27, 1837
    Died, on Sunday the 11th instant JAMES M. McFARLANE, merchant, of
Claysville, Marshall County. "On the Sunday of his death he went in
company with several of his friends for the purpose of acting as mediator
between opposing claimants to a valuable improvement in the Cherokee
Country. He thought he had affected his object of peace and kindness
when he was suddnely and cruelly shot by one of the contending parties
and died almost immediately. Editors of the Knoxville Register and the
Richmond Va. papers will please insert the above.
    Runaway slave from J. L. COLBORN of Lincoln County, Tennessee see
(Prospect Hill).

July 4, 1837
    Marshall County: Sheriff to sell property of NATHANIEL STEELE.
    Married, on Tuesday evening last MR. WILLIAM H. CLOPTON to MISS
MINERVA C. daughter of WILLIAM E. PHILLIPS, Esq. of this place. See
our Vol. 141 p. 39.
    Departed this life on Sat. 24th of June, MARTHA ELIZA, daughter of
MR. WILLIAM BAKER of this county, in her 4th year.
    Blount County: CALEB MURPHREE administrator of JESSE BYNUM.
    Marshall County: W. W. McFARLANE, administrator of JAMES McFARLANE.
    Runaway slave from ADAM BELL, ten miles east of Pulaski, Giles
County, Tennessee.

July 11, 1837
    Letter from BENJAMIN TANNER; "sometime before my departure for
the south."
    Married, at Claysville on Thursday the 29th of June by LOUIS WYETH
Esq., WILLIAM N. MORGAN, M.D. to MISS MARY, daughter of WILLIAM WELLBORN,
Esq. all of Marshall County.
    Departed this life after a distressing illness of four weeks, on
the 3rd instant, at the residence of his son JOHN G. BENTLEY in Madison
County, Ala. COL. EFFORD BENTLEY in the 78th year of his age, formerly
of Amelia County, Virginia in his very boyhood he entered into the military service of his country, during our revolutionary struggle; on
which subject he dwelt with more than ordinary interest...he has left
a companion, eight children, and a numerous circle of relations...
(See our HARRIS AND ALLIED FAMILIES p. 98) also Robertson's POCAHONTAS &
HER DESCENDANTS. The Editors of the Richmond Enquirer and Whig will
please notice the above.

July 25, 1837
    Departed this life on the 12th instant at his residence in Lauder-
dale County, Ala. BRICE M. GARNER, formerly of Tennessee. Fayetteville,
Tennessee papers please insert the above and oblige the bereaved rela-
tions of the deceased.
    Candidates:
    For Congress: REUBEN CHAPMAN, GABRIEL MOORE, WILLIAM H. GLASSCOCK.
    For House of Representatives, Madison County. (State Legislature?)
JOHN E. MOORE, THOMAS V. PROVINCE, WM. BRANDON, JAMES W. McCLUNG, JOHN
VINING, PARHAM B. BOOKER, WILLIAM SMITH, RODAH HORTON.
    For Sheriff: C. D. CAVANAUGH, WILLIAM C. JAMES

Jackson County. For the Senate: P. H. ARMBRISTER, J. P. FRAZIER.
House of Representatives: BENJAMIN RUSH, SAMUEL McDAVID, M NANCY
HARRIS, THOMAS WILLISON, BOOKER SMITH, WILLIAM H. GRAZIER, JAMES SMITH,
JOHN BAXTER, WILLIAM M. KING, JAMES WILLIAMS, R. T. SCOTT, JABEZ
PERKINS, DANIEL LUCAS, CHARLES M. CROSS.
For Sheriff: HENRY NORWOOD, R. C. CAMPBELL, BENJAMIN SNODGRASS.
WILLIAM BAILEY of Uniontown, Perry County, advertises for pocket
book lost in Huntsville.

August 1, 1837
Died, on the 23rd instant, SARAH ELIZABETH, eldest daughter of
W. D. HOLLOWELL.
Departed this life on the 25th instant infant daughter and only
child of ANDREW J. and SARAH E. RICE.

August 8, 1837
Limestone County; G. S. B. WILKINSON administrator of JOHN B.
WILKINSON.
Limestone County: Runaway slave from SAMUEL D. WHITE of Mooresville.

August 15, 1837
Died in this place on the 5th instant MRS. MARY ANN GHORMLEY,
consort of WILLIAM CORMLEY, after protracted illness.

August 29, 1837
Married, in Tuscaloosa on Wednesday evening the 16th instant by
the REV. MR. WILLIAMS, MR. JOHN B. READ of this place to MISS SUSAN W.
CHILDRESS of Tuscaloosa.
Died, on the...instant after a short illness MR. N. T. PACKARD,
an old resident of this place.
On the 23rd instant FRANCES, aged two years, daughter of MR. GEORGE
LYNES (note: he was a carriage maker).
Blount County. WILLIAM and G. W. COWDEN executors of ELIJAH COWDEN
dec'd.
Runaway slave from WILLIAM R. STANSELL of Pickens County.

September 5, 1837 (Is dated August 29 outside but Sept. 5 inside,
                       latter date correct)
Chancery sale: Winchester, Tennessee. WALLACE ESTELL, administrator of RALPH CRABB dec'd. THOMAS G. CRABB and others, heirs of said
CRABB, are complainants versus GEORGE W. and JOHN T. CRABB, defendants
(see Centenniel History of Alleghany County, Virginia, O. F. MORTON
p. 200.)

September 12, 1837
Died, at the home of JOSEPH RICE on the 28th ult. MRS. JANE BAYLES
aged 76 years, consort of the late HEZEKIAH BAYLES. Their early
attachement took place on the banks of the Potomac. For 56 years they
enjoyed everything which promised a life without trouble, not only
united in their earthly pursuits but lived united in the Baptist
Church for fifty years... She lies by him she loved...(note: The name
is not spelled BAYLESS. HEZEKIAH BAYLESS was a soldier of the Revolution,
and drew a pension for his services)

September 19, 1837
Died, at his residence in Mississippi on the 26th of August,
WILLIAM HEWLETT late of this county, aged 29 years of a short illness
of eight days, leaving an affectionate wife and three children (communicated).

September 26, 1837
Marshall County; WILLIAM GRIFFIN and J. O. FEEMSTER, executor of
JOHN GRIFFIN.

October 3, 1837
Died on Friday the 1st instant at Hunter's Old Stand in Campbell
County, MR. WILLIAM LEWIS in the 62nd year of his age, of Buckingham
County..."tenderest parental and conjugal affections"...(Enquirer)
Note: This evidently copied from the Richmond Enquirer--must have been
related to LEWIS family here.

October 10, 1837
        Marshall County: JOHN NEELY administrator of JAMES BROOM.

October 24, 1837
        Married on the 17th instant by the REV. MR. McCOWEN, MR. JAMES P.
DRAKE of Madison County to MISS MARY A. daughter of MR. JAMES BRIGHT
of Fayetteville, Tennessee.
        Married on Thursday evening last by the REV. MR. KING, MR. ROBERT
BRANDON to MISS ISABELLA, daughter of MR. JAMES CLEMENS, all of this
place. See our Vo. 136 p. 32.
        Died, on the 1st instant, WILLIAM B. S. infant son of JOSHUA BARKER
of this place.

October 31, 1837
        Runaway slave from WM. PHELPS of McNairy, Tennessee.
        Runaway slave from N. B. TATE of Florence, his wife is owned by
MRS. ROWNTREE near Loweville. (See our Vol. 4)
        Runaway slave, from CHRISTOPHER H. RUSSELL, of Morgan County.
        Land for sale in Big Cove (Madison County), subscriber having
purchased land in Mississippi. JOS. COPELAND.

November 7, 1837
        (Communicated) Departed this life on Monday the 30th day of
October ROBERT W. DAVIS, Esq. a planter of this county, in the 28th
year of his age...kind and affectionate husband and father...dutiful
son. Nashville Tennessee and Milledgeville Ga papers requested to
publish.
        Vienna (Madison Co.) FARRAR MASSENGALE was murdered on Sunday
the 29th of October at ROBERT DICKEY's grocery by SILAS RANDALS; $300
reward. REUBEN TATE, JO. B. TATE, GEORGE LOY.
        Married on Sunday evening the 29th ult. by the REV. MR. DONALD,
CAPT. ALLEN C. THOMPSON, SR. of Lauderdale to MRS. E. M. FOX of Limestone
County. (Note: she was wid. of JOHN FOX. See our Vol. 24 p. 55 &
Vol. 40 p. 57)
        In Courtland on the 11th ult. by the REV. ALEXANDER SALE, DR.
A(RCH'D) F. E. ROBERTSON, formerly of Richmond, Va. to MISS MARY,
daughter of the late WILLIAM BANKS.

November 14, 1837
        Died, in Nashville, Tennessee on the 3rd instant of inflammatory
fever MRS. OLIVIA F. consort of MR. E(DWIN) R. GLASCOCK; left mother,
sister, husband to whom she had been married only a few mo.
        Jefferson County: ENOS TRUSS and JOHN TRUSS, admrs of WARREN TRUSS.

November 18, 1837
        Died, on Sunday evening the 29th of October at Tuscumbia where she
had been sent to school MISS AMANDA M., daughter of BENJAMIN and
MARY ANN HARRISON, formerly of Brunswick County, Virginia, on her 14th
year...left father, mother, two brothers, five sisters. Petersburg
Constellation please insert for information of numerous relations in Va.
        Departed this life on Sunday the 12th instant WILLIAM HENRY
youngest son of PRESTON YEATMAN of this place, about four years of age.

November 25, 1837
        Resolutions of Respect by 2nd Regiment, 1st Brigade, 1st Division
A.M. on recent death of ADJUTANT MAJOR ROBERT W. DAVIS; COL. W. GRAVES
BOULDIN, LT. COL. MATTHEW DAVIS and MAJOR THOMAS M. MOSELEY be a committee
to communicate to the family of the deceased, and to his father, a
Revolutionary soldier, the sentiments of this meeting...W. GRAVES
BOULDIN, Chairman, SAMUEL D. J. MOORE, Secy.
        Married at the residence of MAJOR JOHN L. McRAE in this county on
the evening of Thursday the 9th instant by the REV. JAMES O. STEDMAN,
MR. L. D. ALSOBROOK, late merchant of this place to MISS DOROTHEA,
oldest daughter of JOHN H. STONE, Esq. of Dickson County, Tennessee
(North Alabamian).
        Married on the 2nd instant by J. NIXON, Esq., MR. J(AMES) M. GEE
to MISS LOUISA, daughter of JAMES STANDIFER, all of Marshall Co. See
our Vol. 65 p. 61.

Died, on Tuesday the 7th instant at the residence of her mother in Marengo County, MRS. L. M. MAULDIN, consort of LITTLEBERRY MAULDIN, late of La Grange, North Alabama.

ANOTHER REVOLUTIONARY SOLDIER GONE

Departed this life at his residence in Madison County, Ala. on Monday November 20th, 1837 MR. ROBERT CLARK. He was born in Halifax County, NC on the 23rd of February 1756. He had for the last twenty odd years been a resident of this county...an upright, a kind neighbor and affectionate parent. The Milledgeville (Ga) Journal and Nashville Republican Banner will confer a favor by giving the above an insertion.

Died at the residence of S. J. HOUSE on the 22nd inst. MR. JOSEPH SAWYER at the advanced age of 101 years 8 months 11 days. MR. SAWYER was a native of Prague, Bohemia. He emigrated to the United States in the year 1776 during the Revolutionary Struggle in which he took an active part being attached to COL. WASHINGTON's Cavalry. Beside several engagements of minor importance he was in the Battle of Eutaw Springs, SC. After the Revolution he returned to his native city on a visit. On his return to the United States he was seized by a press gang in London and placed on board a man of war where he remained three years. Through the agency of a smuggling vessel he made his escape to Holland, from thence he took passage to the United States. He emigrated to the state about fifteen years ago and remained in the county until his death.

December 2, 1837

Married on Tuesday the 28th instant at the house of F. P. ROSE by the REV. J. H. GILLESPIE, A(LEX.) P. MORROW Esq. to MISS MARGARET S. BAPTIST, all of Morgsn County. The Raleigh NC papers please insert the above.

Died, in Mobile on the 12th instant, JOHN C. FINLEY, proprietor of the Shakespeare Hotel.

Land for sale. 8 miles south of Greensborough, adjoining the lands of CAPT. JAMES PICKENS and H. TINCKER by WM. LAWRENCE.

Runaway slave from NEEDHAM WHITFIELD, while on way from Aberdeen to Russellville.

December 9, 1837

Land for sale by DAVID GRAY who "contemplates leaving this county."

December 16, 1837

Married on Tuesday the 12th instant by the REV. JAMES ELLIOTT of Athens MR. HENRY MOORE, JR. to MISS NANCY N. daughter of JOHN HILLIARD of this co. See our Vol. 48 p. 17.

Married on the 9th ult. by the REV. M. HUTCHINSON COL. JOHN B. WILLIAMSON to MRS. C. W. J. PETTWAY, all of this county (Vicksburg Register).

Departed this life on the 9th instant MR. WILLIAM DIXON LANIER for many years a resident of this county; had not yet reached his 40th year; by accidental bursting of a gun in his hands; devoted husband and fond father.

December 23, 1837

Married on the 13th instant by the REV. MR. WILLIAMS, MR. J. G. WALKER of Chulahoma, Mississippi to MISS AMANDA M. daughter of COL. DYE of Fayetteville.

Married at the residence of MRS. BETTS in this county on the 20th instant by the REV. J. WILLIAMS, MR. JOHN JAMES LOCKHART of Tuscumbia, formerly of Northampton County, NC to MISS OCTAVIA F. daughter of the late CHARLES BETTS. See our Vol. 155 p. 21.

Departed this life on the 14th instant MRS. ELMIRA CLOYD wife of J. P. CLOYD and daughter of MR. JAMES DRAKE, all of this co.

Runaway slave committed to jail in Blount County; says belongs to WM. McMILON of Noxubee Co. Miss.

December 30, 1837

JAMES C. MAXWELL of Blount County advertises for lost pocketbook, lost between Ditto's Landing and Huntsville.

January 12, 1839

Marshall County: Chancery Court: MARTHA ANN KING by next friend JOHN HAMPTON versus JOHN M. KING who is not a resident of Alabama; JOHN O. FEEMSTER, Clk. C C Marshall Co. UNICY D. WILLIAMS, administrator of JAMES WILLIAMS dec'd will make final settlement. R. C. RANDLES, Clk. C C.

Married on Thursday the 27th day of December 1858 by F. L. HAMMOND, Esq. MR. THOMAS LINDSAY of Mississippi to MISS AVERILLA, daughter of MAJOR JOHN TUCK of this co. See our Vol. 155 p. 21.

Marshall County: P. M. BUSH, Sheriff to sell following property: of SILAS RANDLES; of EDMUND BRIDGES; of MARTIN S. KYLE to satisfy fi fa in favor of HANNAH JOHNSON administratrix of JAMES JOHNSON dec'd; of FIELDING L. RECTOR; of ELI CAMPBELL; and of T. B. RECTOR.

"Texas" S. D. CABINESS will leave Huntsville in February next for Texas with the intention of becoming a permanent citizen of that republic; will devote attention to practice of law.

Runaway slave from S. G. STEWART of Greene Co.; formerly belonged to MRS. ELIZABETH ASHE of Greensboro.

Runaway slave committed to jail, Jefferson Co. by HUGH MORROW, Esq. Says belongs to a trader. M. KELLY, Sheriff.

Runaway slave from THOMAS B. STONE, Oleander, Morgan Co.

Land for sale, by THOMAS GRAY, in Limestone Co.

Land for sale, by THOMAS B. RECTOR, Marshall Co.

January 19, 1839

Card of DR. WM. H. ELDRIDGE at medical shop of NEWMAN & BASSETT.

Unclaimed letters: lists signed by - LOWEVILLE, W. M. STEWART, postmaster; Triana, ED TONEY, postmaster; Claysville, WM. H. E. WHEELER, postmaster

Died on the 8th from wounds received by the accidental discharge of a gun, JOHN WALKER, son of MR. JOHN WALKER SR. of Marshall Co.

Departed this life at the city of Houston, Texas, on the 9th of December last in the 27th year of his age, REV. SAMUEL W. FRAZIER of the Presbyterian Church, officiating chaplain to the Senate of the Texian Congress.

Died in this town on Monday the 10th of December after a severe affliction of eight days MRS. ELIZABETH BISHOP consort of CAPTAIN N. C. BISHOP, in the 39th year of her age; left affectionate husband and five children (North Alabamian) m Note: North Alabamian was published in Tuscumbia, Franklin Co. Ala.

A. C. and JAMES H. BEARD of Claysville dissolve partnership.

Land for sale; by decree of the Chancery Court of Greene County; land belonging to the heirs of JAMES TEMPLE, four miles below Elkton. M. L. TEMPLE, Comr.

Land for sale: Courtland; belonging to the estate of THOMAS POINTER dec'd. GEORGE SADDLER and A. M. WALL Comrs.

January 26, 1839

Morgan County. Trust sale: HENRY PENDLETON, JOHN T. RATHER and JOHN TATOM, trustees of WILLIAM SHARP.

Courtland; unclaimed letters. THOS. B. JONES, postmaster.

February 2, 1839

THOS. B. MURPHY has removed stock of goods from Triana to Decatur.

Runaway slave committed to jail, Jefferson County, by L. ROBINSON, Esq. belongs to CHARLES COOPER or JAMES BIRD living in Columbus, Mississippi.

Land for sale: "Cottonville" 363 acres in Jackson County by E. BRIDGES.

February 9, 1839

Departed this life on the 10th instant in the 52nd year of his age PETER BINFORD...within a few short days his beloved daughter ELIZABETH PATTON fell a victim to the resistless mandate of death; had been but a few weeks married...interred by the side of her father on the 30th instant. (Dated 31st Jan. 1839)

Married on Wednesday evening the 30th instant by the REV. ROBERT DONALD, MR. GEORGE GOOCH of this county to MISS ELIZABETH, eldest daughter of STEPHEN B. NELSON Esq. of Limestone Co. See our Vol. 187 p. 2.

If HENRY NEGLEY who was a stage driver in Huntsville in 1833 or 1834 will make known his present residence to DANIEL B. TURNER, postmaster in Huntsville he will hear something to his advantage. He is a son of PHILIP NEGLEY formerly of Mercer Co. Ky and is believed now to reside in the southern or middle part of the state of Alabama.

Notice: Mortgage by DANIEL W. O'BAR 10th Jan. 1838 recorded in Jefferson County; land in Tuscaloosa Land District, JACOB TATE

February 16, 1839

Married on Thursday evening the 31st ult. by F. L. HAMMOND, Esq., MR. THOMAS G. ROCHELL to MISS REBECCA ANN daughter of MR. PHILEMON HILLIARD, all of this co. See our Vol. 76 p. 16.

Land for sale: by JAMES M. BOSTON on Blue Water 17 miles from Florence.

Marshall County: trust sale; land of MINOR B. FEEMSTER and wife MARTHA B. by SIMEON NICHOLS, trustee.

Bellefonte: Feb. 7th. Shocking occurrence; on Friday last a dispute arose between TIMOTHY MESSHON and BENJAMIN BUSH Esq. which resulted in the death of the latter gentleman; stabbed in the abdomen and died in 24 hours; MESSHON is in the Jackson County jail (Courier).

February 23, 1839

Died at his residence near Eddyville (Kentucky) on Sunday the 27th of January 1839 GEN. MATTHEW LYON in his 46th year. Left widow and six children; native of Rutland County, Vermont and emigrated to this county in 1801 with his father COL. MATTHEW LYON dec'd, for many years a member of congress from Vermont and this state. Has been for many years postmaster at Eddyville and for the last twenty years a member of the County Court (Princeton Examiner).

Married on Wednesday evening the 13th instant by the REV. B. S. FANT, MR. HIRAM RAINBOLT to MISS HESTER ANN FORTNER all of this co. See our Vol. 76 p. 16.

Marshall County: WILLIAM W. McFARLANE executor of the last will and testament of JAMES McFARLANE will make final settlement.

Marshall County: JOHN O. FEEMSTER, administrator of ELI R. FEEMSTER dec'd reports estate insolvent.

Marshall County: WILLIAM GRIFFIN and JOHN O. FEEMSTER, executors and SARAH GRIFFIN, executrix of the last will and testament of JOHN GRIFFIN dec'd will make final settlement.

March 2, 1839

Died, at his residence in this county, the venerable JOHN DRAKE aged 91 years. He was a soldier of the Revolution. He removed from Virginia and settled near this place many years ago...member of the Baptist Church...left a large family connexion...The Fincastle Democrat will please copy the above.

Died on the 21st of January at his residence near Meridianville in his 62nd year MR. JOSEPH SALE, an old and respectable inhabitant of this county to which he removed from the state of Georgia in 1814.

Died on the 18th ult. at Van Buren, Marshall County, MRS. SUSAN McFARLANE, consort of WALTER P. McFARLANE, in the 24th year of her age... fever.

If THEODORIC RAGSDALE will make known his residence to the subscriber in Madison County, Ala. or to WILLIAM S. NIBLETT of Virginia he will learn of a legacy coming to him from the estate of his grandfather, WILLIAM NIBLETT dec'd. Said RAGSDALE is a son of PETER RAGSDALE, late of Athens, Limestone Co. Ala. JOHN MORGAN. Editors in Arkansas and Missouri please copy.

March 9, 1839

Married on the 20th of February by the REV. A. FRAZIER, MR. JAMES H. KING to MISS TULLETHA BRAZELTON, all of Madison Co. See our Vo. 124 p. 45.

March 16, 1839

Notice: S. D. CABINESS will continue to practice law in Huntsville.

Regimental orders; 3rd Regt 1st Brigade, 1st Division A.M. ordered to parade by batalions as follows:

1st Battalion commanded by COL. JOHN H. WEBSTER at New Market.

2nd Battalion commanded by MAJOR G. W. PETERSON at JOHN HATHCOCK's SENR. By orders of COL. BENJAMIN F. RICKETTS, J. W. FANT, Adjt.

Runaway slave, from Volney Peel of Marshall County, Miss. Was raised by HUNTER PEEL of Huntsville.

Runaway slave from JAMES CRUTCHER of Marshall Co. Ala.

Died on the 11th instant at the residence of her father near this village MRS. LUCY C. consort of MR. B. BRASHIERS and daughter of MR. JAMES and MRS. NANCY YOUNG, in her 23rd year; left husband and only son.

March 30, 1839

Departed this life on the 3rd instant MRS. ELIZABETH C. consort of THOMAS A. SCOTT, Esq. in the 54th year of her age--pulmonary disease. Left husband, two children. Yorkville, SC paper will please copy.

April 6, 1839

JOHN McGUILL of New London, Walker Co. Ala. advertises regarding note given BURGES TANKISLEY.

Land for sale by ANTYONY WINSTON of Gainesville, Ala.

April 13, 1839

Married on Tuesday the 9th instant by the REV. MR. HALL, JUDGE LOUIS WYETH of Marshall Co. to MISS EUPHEMIA, daughter of the REV. JOHN ALLAN. See our Vol. 153 p. 476.

Same evening, by the REV. MR. ALLAN, LEROY POPE, JR., Esq. of Memphis, Tennessee to MISS MARY E. daughter of P. A. FOOTE, dec'd. See our Vol. 64 p. 36.

Regimental orders:

62nd Regiment 1st Brigade, 1st Division

1st Battalion commanded by LT. COL. R. J. KELLY will parade at Loweville.

2nd Battalion commanded by MAJOR JABEZ L. DRAKE will parade at Vienna. By orders of COL. WM. C. McBROOM, JOHN RUBY, adjt.

June 29, 1839

Another Revolutionary patriot gone. Died at his residence near Pickensville, Ala. on the 31st ultimo OBADIAH HOOPER SR in the 84th year of his age. MR. HOOPER was born in Lunenburg County, Virginia on the 25th day of December, 1755 where he resided until the outbreak of that glorious struggle which gave us our independence. He early engaged in that struggle and was a regular soldier until the close of the war. He heard the Declaration of Independence when first read by the immortal JEFFERSON. He fought at the Battle of Bunker Hill. He was also at Trenton and was one of those who gave a new impulse to the cause of freedom by gaining that important battle. He was one of those who crossed the Delaware under the godlike eye of the immortal WASHINGTON to attack the British and Hessians at Princeton. Here, he has often been heard to say, the blood marked the ground as it trickled from his shoeless feet. He was at the storming of Stony Point; he was at GATES' defeat and had charge of the ammunition wagons on that occasion, but blew them up in order to prevent them from falling into the hands of the British. He was at the memorable Siege and Battle of Yorktown and had the honor of seeing CORNWALLIS surrender his sword. He was likewise at the Battle of Brandywine and was wounded twice in that engagement, once from a musket ball and once from the stab of a bayonet, and there is no doubt but that the wound received on that occasion hastened somewhat his death even at this remote period...has left an affectionate wife and a large number of children and grandchildren (South Alabamian).

Runaway slave committed to jail, Autauga County: says belongs to PETER B. ROBERTSON of Lowndes County. ALLEN RAY, Jailor.

Candidates: Clerk of the county court; WILLIAM H. JONES and RICHARD B. PURDOM. Senate: WM. FLEMING, DANIEL B. TURNER. Representatives: PARHAM N. BOOKER, DAVID MOORE, JEREMIAH CLEMENTS. Tax Collector: THOMAS M. MOSELEY, OTHNEIL RICE, WM. WRIGHT, WALTER T. KEEBLE, JABEZ LEFTWICH, THOMAS H. HALL.

Moulton: Chancery: THOMAS BELL' heirs vs HENRY HORN, JOHN ALLEN, JOHN KIKRLE, STEPHEN TRIBLE and JOSEPH H. SEVERS; HENRY HERN a non resident of the state.

Mobile County: Runaway slaves committed to jail, by WM. MAGEE, Sheriff; one says he belongs to JOHN JONES near Tuscumbia, one to JAMES WOOD of Chester District, SC; one to HENRY MINOR of Greene County; and one to JOSEPH JOHNSTON of Clarke County, Ala.

Land for sale, where I reside, nine miles north of Bellefonte. Jackson County. JOHN A. HANCOCK

Land for sale: by M. T. CHUNN and DAVID GARDINER, Executors of ELISHA BELL of Morgan County.

Jefferson County; DAVID MONTGOMERY versus MATTHEW T. MONTGOMERY who is a non resident of the State of Alabama.

January 11, 1840

Franklin County: land for sale 10 miles NE of Salem by ABRAM VAN ZANT.

Married on the 2nd instant by SLAUGHTER C. HARRELL, Esq., LYTTLETON Y. HARDIN of Limestone County to MISS SARAH W. daughter of CAPT. GILES and MARY NANCE of this co.

New firm, ALFRED HOWELL, JOHN DOE, and ASA SHELTON.

Advertisement regarding a horse thief; property taken from him at the home of J. F. DAVEE, DeKalb Co., J. F. DAVEE, S. C. NEWMAN and W. P. CASEY.

Runaway slave committed to jail in Mobile County by WILLIAM McGEE, Sheriff; belongs to RICHARD ODOM formerly of Demopolis, or to JACOB ODOM of Clark Co.

Marshall County: JOSEPH E. MAY, trustee will sell property of GEORGE W. ALLEN.

Warren County, Tennessee; Commissioners' sale; where late JESSE COFFEE resided; WILLIAM WHITE, guardian of the heirs, and commissioner. Also at same time W. C. SMART and GEORGE STROUD, administrators of ANN COFFEE will sell property.

Runaway slave from SAMUEL M. STEWART, northwest corner of Dallas County, 18 miles from Marion.

Land for sale 2 miles NW of Courtland by JAMES E. SAUNDERS, agent for JOHN GARRETT.

Morgan County, administrators sale; WM. H. GEE, executor of JOHN H. LUNDY dec'd.

Runaway slaves committed to jail.

Mobile County: belongs to JOHN HARTWELL near Columbus, Miss.

Jefferson County. Belongs to MIDDLETON KELLY, Jefferson Co. Mississippi. M. KELLY, Sheriff.

St. Clair County by JOSHUA W. HOOPER, Esq; belongs to SAMUEL NUNN near Columbus, Ga. THOMAS ALFORD, Sheriff

Blount County. belongs to WILLIAM McMILLON of Sumter Co. WM. H. BRASSEAL, Sheriff

Franklin County: belongs to JOSEPH DABNEY of Louisa County, Va.-- left ALEXANDER ALLEN near Natchez. SAMUEL STEPHENS, jailor

Lawrence County. Belongs to WILLIAM H. MOORE of Virginia who was on his way to Mississippi. D. H. VALLIANT, Sheriff

Marion County: one to WILLIAM DUBEAS of New Orleans and one to WILLIAM DENNIS, Rankin Co. Miss. B. L. SHANKLE, Shf.

Madison County: belongs to MIDDLETON KELLY of Jefferson County, Mississippi.

January 18, 1840

Married in the Big Cove on Thursday the 9th instant by JOHN T. HADEN, Esq. MR. JOHN LAMBERSON, JR. to MISS SUSAN ANN FORTNER all of Madison Co. See our Vol. 155 p. 2.

Marshall County. WILLIAM H. E. WHEELER, trustee, to sell property of ROBERT H. ANDERSON.

Limestone County. Petition for dower. JAMES HOLESAPPLE in right of wife SUSAN P. HOLESAPPLE, adm'x of THOMAS COLE, dec'd. for her dower in COLE's land. Note: JAMES HOLESAPPLE m. in Limestone Co. 27 Aug. 1839 SUSAN P. COLE

Marion County: runaway slave committed to jail who says he belongs to BENJAMIN HADLEY of Adams Co. Miss.

January 25, 1840

Married on Thursday the 2nd instant by the REV. JAMES C. ELLIOTT, MR. JAMES SANDERSON to MISS MARTHA ELIZA, daughter of JESSE HARRIS, all of Limestone Co.

On Tuesday the 14th instant by JAMES IRWIN Esq., MR. SILAS STARKY to MISS JULIA ANN LANDERS all of Madison Co. See our Vol. 103 p. 59.

On Tuesday evening the 14th instant by the REV. M. B. FEEMSTER, MR. JOHN W. HUDSON to MISS SARAH S. NETHERLAND, all of Jackson Co..

On the same evening by the REV. CHARLES L. ROACH, MR. WILLIAM H. GREEN of Mississippi to MISS TAMPA, daughter of CAPTAIN FRANCIS RENSHAW of Jackson Co.

On the 24th of December last by the HON. PATRICK SCOTT, DR. THOMAS L. REED of DeKalb County to MISS ELIZABETH, eldest daughter of MR. JOHN YIELDINGS of Blount Co.

Departed this life at the residence of her father in Limestone County on the 25th ult. at 4 a.m. MISS MARY JANE, daughter of WILLIAM K. PARHAM...complication of diseases...in her 18th year. On the same day about 1 o'clock p.m. after long and lingering pulmonary disease MR. WILLIAM K. PARHAM in his 67th year...tender father and favoriate daughter lying dead in the same room at the same time.

February 1, 1840
Advertisement for stolen horses from BENJAMIN WILENARD near JOHN BAXTER, Esq. of Marshall County, also one from MR. B. SMITH of same place.

Fair Warning: JOHN CONNALLY of Greenbottom Inn complains of persons killing his tame deer; if continue will turn names over to a committee "some of whom wear short breeches": THOMAS JOHNSON, J. E. B. ELDRIDGE, D. SALE, M. MILLER, S. SMITHER, R. HAMLET, R. SHOTWELL, S. S. EWING, D. HUMPHREY, R. FOWLKS, E. HAMMOND, R. HARRIS, SR. (it is family tradition that RICHARD HARRIS wore knee breeches until his death).

Marshall County: Sheriff will sell property of BENJAMIN OLIVER and DANIEL S. DICKSINSON.

February 8, 1840
Married on Thursday evening the 23rd ult. by BENJAMIN STEGER Esq. MR. CHARLES C. TIPTON to MISS ELIZABETH eldest daughter of WILLIAM MILLIKEN, all of this co. See our Vol. 151 p. 22.

Departed this life on the 21st day of Jan. last at the residence of MRS. MARY HEWLETT in this county, her eldest daughter MRS. NANCY SCOTT, widow of the late THOMAS W. SCOTT of Jackson County in the 34th year of her age. "Tears of seven orphan children." Disease of long continuance.

Bibb County: runaway slave committed to jail; belongs to JAMES HUGHES of Cherokee County. MICHAEL H. GOSS, Jailor

February 15, 1840
Morgan County: land for sale. H. EASTON

Tuscaloosa County; runaway slave committed to jail; belongs to THOMAS WARD, Decatur, DeKalb Co. Ga.

February 22, 1840
Married on the 13th instant at the residence of the late CAPT. JAMES CUNNINGHAM by W. GRAVES BOULDIN Esq., MR. JEREMIAH SANDERSON to MISS SARAH ANN CUNNINGHAM, all of this co. See our Vol. 103 p. 62.

WM. H. PEEVY of Pope County, Arkansas advertises regarding note made between 1826-1830 to RANDOLPH PALMER of Lauderdale Co.

Marshall County: JOHN STARNES administrator of WILLIAM G. CAMPBELL will make final settlement.

February 29, 1840
Married on the 18th instant by the REV. JAMES C. ELLIOTT, MR. NEWTON STEELE of Limestone Co. to MISS MARY A., daughter of MR. JOSEPH STEELE of Madison Co. See our Vol. 103 p. 62.

Jefferson County: M. KELLY, Sheriff appointed administrator of OWEN FRANKLIN LENIOTT.

Greene County: runaway slave committed to jail, trying to pass as an Indian; belongs to the estate of WILLIAM RAY, dec'd of Hillsborough, NC. JAMES C. LOCK, Sheriff

March 7, 1840
St. Clair County: Executors sale; land at the foot of Sand Mt. belonging to the estate of the late JOEL CHANDLER; SARAH CHANDLER, JOEL CHANDLER and JAMES HAMPTON, Executors.

        Marshall County: BARTON S. CLAPP, administrator of WM. CLAPP,
dec'd.
        Mobile County: Runaway slave committed to jail; belongs to
SAMUEL THOMPSON of Warren County, Miss.
        Madison County: Runaway slave committed to jail; belongs to
JOHN KIDD of Shelby Co. Ala.

March 14, 1840
        Tuscaloosa: Fatal Occurrence: difficulty between WASHINGTON MOODY
Esq. and MAJOR JOHN CANTLEY both of this city led to a most tragical
issue on Thursday last the 5th inst. "It is said MAJOR CANTLEY threatened
the life of MR. MOODY." MAJOR CANTLEY died of his wounds; funeral
service preached on Friday afternoon in the Episcopal Church by REV.
MR. KNAPP attended by the Masonic Fraternity after which the deceased
was buried with the usual solemnities of that ancient order. MAJOR
CANTLEY...left a wife and several children (Monitor).
        Negroes for sale at MR. JOHN M. JACKSON's at Moulton--by JAMES
MADISON. Forced to sell by dire necessity--prefer selling to one or
two persons and will not separate families.
        Marshall County: JOSEPH M. CARTER, executor of the will of JOHN M.
CARTER will make final settlement.
        Blount County. LEWIS WHITE trustee will sell land of CALEB
HARTGRAVES.
        Marshall County. L. D. BOSHART and J. W. BARTON, administrators
of GILBREATH BARTON, dec'd.

March 21, 1840
        Another veteran of the Revolution gone. Departed this life on the
12th of February 1840 MR. ANTHONY PHILLIPS in the 86th year of his age.
He served in the Revolutionary war as a soldier and was entitled to a
pension but would not be prevailed on by his friends to avail himself
of the same. He alleged as the reason of his refusal that he had enough
and did not think it right under such circumstances to draw a pension
from the Government. MR. PHILLIPS emigrated from Charlotte County,
Va. in the year 1818 and settled in Limestone County, Ala. where he
continued till his decease. He was a pious and orderly member of the
M. E. Church and had been for upwards of fifty years.... He left five
children and a numerous circle of friends and acquaintances...(communicated). P.S. The Richmond Enquirer will confer a favor on the friends
of the deceased by copying the above.

March 28, 1840
        Married in Philadelphia on the 11th instant at Christ Church by
the REV. BENJAMIN DORR, DR. WILLIAM HEATHE ELDRIDGE of Alabama to
MARY JAY, eldest daughter of CAPT. F. A. PARKER of the U.S. Navy.

April 4, 1840
        Died on the 29th ult. after a long illness ALEXANDER ERSKINE,
only son of P. T. POSEY of this place aged eight years one month five
days.
        Died in this place on the 26th ult. of consumption MR. ARCHIBALD
RUSSELL, a native of Scotland. If he has any relatives in this country
it is uncertain where they live--are supposed to reside near Cincinnati,
Ohio. Cincinnati papers will confer a favor by giving the above an
insertion.
        Married on Sunday morning the 22nd ult. before breakfast by the
REV. WM. LYLE, MR. SAMUEL STARKEY to MISS MARTHA LANDERS, all of
Madison Co. See our Vol. 103 p. 62.
        Died on Tuesday morning last, THOMAS, third son of COL. THOMAS G.
PERCY of this town, in his 17th year.
        Marshall Co. JACOB DERRICK advertises that horses left with him by
ISAAC DANIEL and WILLIS MENEFEE will be sold for their keep.
        St. Clair County: Letters of administration granted JAMES H. ALLEN
on the estate of JOHN R. ALLEN.

April 11, 1840
        (Communicated) Departed this life on Saturday the 4th instant at
her residence 9 miles northeast of Huntsville MRS. PERMELIA SCRUGGS in
the 35th year of her age after a lingering illness...affectionate and
agreeable companion and fond and indulgent mother.

Died in this place on the 6th instant JOHN DILLARD, infant son of
JOHN and ELEANOR MURRELL aged 9 months and 6 days.
Another Revolutionary soldier gone. Died at his residence in
Madison County, Ala. on the 18th ult. after a painful illness of fourteen
days MR. JAMES TRIBBLE in the 84th year of his age. He died greatly
lamented by an affectionate wife and seven children and a large number
of grand and great-grandchildren; he was beloved and respected by all
who knew him as a gentleman and an honest man. MR. T. was a native of
Maryland; he moved to Virginia in 1766 where he lived until 1785. He
then moved to Lancaster Dist. SC where he lived until 1819 when he
moved to Alabama where he remained until his death. He was one of that
gallant band who fought under GENERAL GREENE at the Battle of Guilford,
and for several years past had drawn a small pension from the government.
He had been a member of the Baptist Church for 46 years, in which he
was a faithful member and died with a full assurance of meeting his
God in peace.
The paper printed in Lancaster District SC will please publish the
above.

April 25, 1840
Married on Thursday the 16th instant by the REV. JUSTINIAN WILLIAMS,
COL. ROBERT HANCOCK of this county to MISS JULIA ANN daughter of
MAJOR RICHARD SHARP of Winchester, Tenn.
Died at his residence in this county on the 13th instant of
consumption in the 37th year of his age GEORGE J. WEAVER. MR. WEAVER
was a native of Virginia and removed to this county in the latter part
of 1814. Lynchburg Virginian please publish the above.

May 2, 1840
Another Revolutionary soldier gone. Died at his residence in
Marshall County, Ala. on the morning of the 18th of April instant
MR. PHILIP FRY in the 83rd year of his age. MR. FRY was a native of
Pennsylvania from whence he emigrated to Virginia, thence to East
Tennessee and thence to Alabama. He was one of that glorious band of
patriots who under God assisted in achieving for us the liberties we
now enjoy; he was truly the kind husband, affectionate father, the
obliging neighbor, the honest and industrious citizen. MR. FRY had
many trials through life having buried an affectionate wife and six
children, but he is now gone leaving a disconsolate widow, nineteen
children, one hundred and thirteen grand and great grandchildren
together with a numerous circle of friends to mourn his irreparable
loss...
Maridon County; runaway slave committed to jail; says belongs to
DUGALD McALPIN of Marengo Co.

May 9, 1840
Married on Wednesday evening the 22nd ult. MR. J. B. CLOYD to
MISS LUCINDA, daughter of THOMAS McCRARY all of this co.
Land for sale; 900 acres in Limestone; also lands in Mississippi,
blooded horses etc. WADDY TATE
M. J. HALL of Oak Grove, Jackson County, advertises for lost
horse.
Marshall County; JOEL HIGGINS, sheriff, adm'r of JOHN BEADLE.

May 23, 1840
JESSE SEARCY departed this life 8th of May, 1840 in the 56th year
of his age, in Huntsville, Ala. Left affectionate wife.
Candidates: For sheriff: WM. H. T. BROWNE, AUGUSTUS H. FORD.
Morgan County: For sheriff: JOHN TATOM and JOHN STUBBS.
E. L. KIMBROUGH of Erie, Greene Co. advertises for runaway slave.
Letter from DAVID GOODNER (note: several letters preceded this,
both from GOODNER and others, it seems someone charged that GOODNER
had had two orphan boys in his care and had punished them cruelly by
pretending to hand them. MR. GOODNER presented affidavits to show the
boys were most unruly and no other means availed; that the boys were
not injured, and the correction did help them. He offered one affidavit
from one of the boys, omitting signature but attested by JOSEPH RICE
that he knew the man and that it was his signature. In no place did I
find the names of the boys). "The boys were committed to my care on the

1st Saturday in March, 1817 at a company muster by THOMAS MILLER Esq.
of this county then Overseer of the Poor in the district that included
his residence. The oldest, supposed to be nine years old, I took as
an apprentice and was the lowest bidder to maintain the youngest, only
about seven years old, twelve months at the expense of the county."
     Testimony of SAMUEL DURRELL SANSOM: On the 4th of last May I
came to MR. GOODNER's where I have ever since resided.... MR. GOODNER
had with him and has yet a couple of boys.... Sworn to before ABR. KING,
J.P. 10 Sept. 1817.
     Testimony of SAMUEL CRAGG; has lived with MR. GOODNER more than
two years...sworn to 17 July 1817 before BENJAMIN FRANKS, J.P.
     Testimony of WILLIAM WADE, has lived with MR. GOODNER since 17th
last February...sworn to before BENJAMIN FRANKS, J.P. 17 July 1817.
     Testimony of WILLIAM D. EVANS; has lived with MR. GOODNER since
last of last March. Sworn to before BENJAMIN FRANKS J.P. 17 July 1817.
     MR. MILLER recollects the grandfather of the boys requested him
not to bind the boys to me...12 months later I was asked to take the
younger as an apprentice.
     Also testimony of REUBEN SHOTWELL and STEPHEN GRIFFITH they being
only ones remaining who were heads of families in the neighborhood at
that time.

May 30, 1840
     Letter from JOHN D. PHELAN of Tuscaloosa to MAJOR N. TERRY of
Limestone County. "In a conversation you had with MR. DAVID RHODES he
informed you that in a conversation with his father (DR. H. W. RHODES)...
     JAMES C. ELLIOTT, MR. GEORGE W. HAGEA to MRS. CAROLINE R. R. SPENCER,
all of Huntsville. See our Vol. 147 p. 49.
     On the 26th instant by the REV. MR. JACKS, MR. BENNETT CLOYD of
Casey County, Ky to MISS LUCINDA J(ANE) daughter of NEELY DRAKE, all
of Madison Co. See our Vol. 141 p. 42.
     Died at his residence in Madison County on Tuesday the 12th instant
after a painful illness MR. STERLING STANBACK in the 35th year of his
age...left amiable wife and two interesting children. MR. STANBACK had
a native of Virginia but has for some years resided in this state.
     Notice: DR. WM. A. WHARTON, New Market, Ala.
     Mobile Co. Runaway slave committed to jail by MOSES RYAN, J.P.
Belongs to SAMUEL THOMPSON of Warren Co. Miss.

June 6, 1840
     Candidates: WM. WRIGHT and THOMAS M. MOSELEY for Tax Assessor
and Collector. WM. R. CHUNN for sheriff of Morgan County; and JAMES M.
ADAMS and THOMAS M. GRIFFIN to represent Marshall County in the
Legislature.
     DR. JOHN W. KING has located 8 miles NW of Huntsville.
     Married on the 21st instant by the REV. J. ALLAN, D.D. MR. WILLIAM
D(ONALD) GARDNER, of Madison County to MISS RHODA H. daughter of
MR. DAVID BUSH of Morgan Co. See our Vol. 74 p. 28.
     Departed this life on the 30th of May at her mother's residence in
Madison County, MISS MARY JANE HARRIS aged 19 years and some months...
member of the M. E. Church. P. B. ROBINSON.
     Died at the residence of MR. JOHN TANNER in this county after an
illness of 12 months his son HARVEY TANNER in the 31st year of his age.

June 13, 1840
     Departed this life in Huntsville, Ala. in the 22nd year of her
age MRS. JANE CATHERINE BRADFORD, consort of COL. LARKIN BRADFORD. She
was born in Cumberland Co. Va. and emigrated to this county in 1834...
united with the Presbyterian Church in Virginia...devoted wife, kind
mother.
     (Communicated) Died at her residence in Huntsville, Ala. MRS.
MARGARET HALL, aged 70 years. She was born in Ireland, moved to the
United States in early life; embraced religion about fifty years before
her death...for the last five years a member of the M. E. Church in this
town...left six children. P. B. ROBINSON.
     (Communicated) Departed this life on the 30th of May, 1840
MISS WINNIFRED ELIZABETH THOMSON in the 17th year of her age...left
father, brothers, sisters. P. B. ROBINSON.

(Communicated) Departed this life on the 24th of May at the residence of her mother, in her 23rd year, MRS. ELIZABETH MALONE, consort of ALEXANDER MALONE...left affectionate husband and three children...attacked with that fatal disease, consumption, interred on the 25th in the family burying ground.

Died at the residence of her father, MR. WILLIAM HUDSPETH in this county on the 12th ult. after an illness of 17 days, MRS. NANCY CATHERINE DERRICK in the 23rd year of her age. (Bellefonte Courier)

Died at her residence in Pickens County, Ala. on the 10th of May last MRS. MARTHA SMITH, consort of COL. NATHAN SMITH, of a protracted illness. She was in the 46th year of her age, and thirty one years of that time a worthy member of the Baptist Church...left affectionate husband and finve children.

LOUIS WYETH, candidate for the Legislature, Marshall Co.

Morgan County. EDWARD WISE, executor of the will of JACOB ORR dec'd will make final settlement.

Chancery Court: Blountsville, Ala. NANCY GORMAN by her next friends, NICHOLAS EASLEY sues WILLIAM GORMAN who resides out of the state, for divorce. JOHN H. HENDERSON, Register

Marshall County: Sheriff will sell property of ABRAHAM G. HOLT for JOSEPH G. GARRETT.

Marshall County: JAMES TIDWELL, trustee will sell property of WILLIAM TIDWELL for L. D. BOSHART.

Dallas County. Runaway slave committed to jail; belongs to THOMAS HODGE of Lowndes County. JACOB HOOT, Jailor

June 20, 1840

DR. WILLIAM H. ELDRIDGE has located at the residence of his father 9½ miles NW of Huntsville.

OTHNIEL RICE, candidate for tax assessor and collector.

Married, on Wednesday evening the 10th instant by WILLIAM C. ARMSTRONG, Esq., MR. JAMES H. MOORE of Winchester, Tennessee to MISS MARY E. daughter of STEPHEN CARTER, Esq. of the vicinity of Bellefonte, Ala.

Died, in Jackson County, Alabama on the 11th instant, MRS. SARAH C. RIACH, consort of the REV. CHARLES L. ROACH in the 28th year of her age...left husband and four small children.

June 27, 1840

Democratic Meeting: at meeting of the citizens of New Market and its vicinity on the 19th instant GEORGE T. JONES, Esq., was called to the Chair, and GEN. B. M. LOWE and COL. ANTHONY H. METCALF appointed assistant chairman, GEORGE D. NORRIS secretary, JOHN C. THOMPSON, assistant secretary--resolutions opposing HARRISON--ABNER TATE, A. H. METCALF, GEORGE T. JONES, P. N. BOOKER, JOSEPH RICE, PETER C. WEBSTER, THOMAS V. PROVINCE, GEORGE ANDERSON, JOHN VINING, A. H. WEATHERLY, RANDOLPH SULLIVAN, JAMES McDAVID, ALLEN WALLS, JOSEPH TAYLOR and SAMUEL WALKER be appointed a committee to meet with such other committees as may be appointed in this county, to be styled Madison Democratic Committee.

Distressing casualty: On Thursday last our town was thrown into an unusual degree of excitement by the accidental death of MR. JOHN H. WALPOLE. In company with MR. T. SCOTT he had rode out for the purpose of shooting squirrels and while passing alongside of a mountain among the rocks he was thrown from his horse, his gun discharged in the fall and shot him in the front part of the thigh and severed the demoral artery. He died in a few minutes. Had been for some years a resident of this place--left lady and five small children. (Inquisitor)

Letter headed Brooksville 15 June 1840...in compliance with a call on the candidates of Blount County...I am in favor of the re-election of MR. VAN BUREN. JOHN SIVELEY.

July 11, 1840

Letter (political) from SAMUEL STEPHENS of Russelville.

Married on Tuesday evening the 2nd instant by the HON. T. M. RECTOR, CAPT. THOMAS J. HAWKINS of Bellefonte to MISS CELIA, daughter of CAPT. JAMES HAWK, all of Jackson Co.

WILLIAM A. AUSTIN, postmaster at Bellefonte advertises unclaimed letters.

Marshall County: ROBERT S. PIERCE administrator of E A D PIERCE.

July 18, 1840

Limestone County: commissioners sale of the lands of ABNER E.
ASKEW dec'd; comrs: SAMUEL JORDAN, NATHANIEL TERRY, R. A. HIGH.
Madison County: runaway slave committed to jail; belongs to
CHARLES TUCKER of Morgan County.
Madison County: chancery; ELIZABETH ELLETT versus JAMES MONROE
ELLETT, non resident of the state--divorce.

July 25, 1840

Democratic Meeting: Bellefonte, June 30th. COL. CHARLES M. CROSS
called to chair, JOHN BERRY, Esq. and CO. JAMES SMITH assistant,
chairman, DR. JAMES BURRUS secretary and DAVID H. HARRIS, Esq. ass't
sec'y Committee: H. A. ANTHONY, JOHN W. REYNOLDS, THOMAS SNODGRASS,
A. HARGESS, JOHN BERRY, F. RENSHAW, JAMES CAMPBELL, JOHN HOLLAND,
JOHN CUNNINGHAM, WM. D. PARKS, C. L. ROACH, THOMAS EUSTACE, THOMAS J.
HARDWICK, D. M. MARTIN, ALVA FINLEY, JAMES BURNS and BENJAMIN SNODGRASS.
Also mentioned are JOHN McREYNOLDS, JOHN SNODGRASS, DANIEL M. MARTIN,
WYATT COFFEE and COL. BENJAMIN SNODGRASS.
Democratic meeting at Larkinsville, Jackson County, July 1st;
JOHN BERRY Chairman, JAMES WOODSEY and JACOB GROSS vice chairman;
WYATT COFFEE and JAMES W. CANNADAY secretaries. Committee: JEREMIAH
BROWN, COL. JAMES SMITH, JAMES B. WRIGHT, SAMUEL C. DAVIDSON, JOHN
JONES and WILLIAM G. LONG. Another committee: DAVID LARKIN, COL.
JAMES SMITH, JOHN JONES, JOHN LINDSEY, U. B. WARREN, S. B. RODES,
BROOKS SMITH, JOHN D. ALLEN and THOMAS WOODS. Signed JAMES WOOLSEY,
Sec'y.
Marshall County: Democratic meeting: RICHARD GOLDEN Esq. to the
chair; ARCHIBALD BAXTER and BOOKER SMITH secretaries: LOUIS WYETH
offered resolution; committee MICHAEL DITTO, R. A. FOWLER, CHAS. KENNEDY,
JEHU HIGGINS, JOHN W. ANDERSON, JOHN NEELY, ROBERT S. PEARCE, JOHN H.
BERRY, REUBEN HENSON, BENJAMIN MERRELL, B. B. RAMSEY, PETER KILFOYLE,
ESTELL W. SCRIVENER, JAMES SCHRIMSHER, GEORGE CHENNAULT, ANDREW ICE,
JOHN BAXTER, LEWIS MARTIN, FREDERICK ICE, BENJAMIN JOHNSON, C. W. ROGERS,
JOEL DIXON, HUGH SINCLAIR, WM. McEWEN, JAMES McDANIEL, BOOKER SMITH.
Signed: RICHARD GOLDEN PREST, PERCIVAL M. BUSH, EDWARD COX, WILLIAM
YOUNG, WILLIAM H. CALLOWAY, SAMUEL LOWRY, ISHAM H. FENNELL, ISHAM
WRIGHT, JOHN B. FINLEY, BURGES McGAHA, JOSEPH G. GARRETT, WILLIAM BARCLAY,
JOSHUA K. ROBERTS, JOHN DOSS, GEORGE W. ALLEN and ALEXANDER DONALDSON,
Vice Presidents.
Democratic meeting: Brooksville, Blount County, 4th July, 1840.
MAJOR JESSE WHARTON called to chair, MAJOR EMORY LOYD assistant chairman,
COL. E. ELDRIDGE and JOSEPH JOHNSON Sec'ys; committee on resolutions;
ISAAC WHARTON, WILLIAM MOORE, H. W. BOOKS, G. SHELTON, MAJOR R.
GRIFFITH, Meeting addressed by COL. WM. MUSGROVE.
Jefferson County: Elyton. Democratic meeting 13th July; on notice
of COL. MOSES KELLY, JAMES McADORY Esq. was called to the chair, on
motion of SAMUEL A. TARRANT, JAMES P. LACEY was appointed secretary.
Committee on resolutions WALKER H. BAYLOR, OCTAVIUS SPENCER, ENOS
TRUSS, SAMUEL A TARRANT, NATHANIEL SELF, JOHN SMITH, ISAAC B. NABORS,
JOEL DICKERSON, JAMES K. JACKS, STEPHEN HODGES and MOSES KELLY.
Paint Rock Valley (Jackson County) Trenton, 2 July 1840. Demo-
cratic meeting. BENJAMIN FRANKS Esq., chairman. WARREN P. ROBERTSON
Esq. and COL. JAMES McDAVID, vice presidents. MAJOR R. K. DRAKE and
ROBERT AUSTIN secretaries. Committee on resolutions. CAPT. MALCOLM
THOMPSON, CAPT. JOHN H. BRITAIN, ABRAHAM VANZART, Esq., JAMES McCORD,
JONATHAN LATHAM, Esq., JOHN J. CAMPBELL, WM. H. DAVIS, JOEL D. LEWIS,
Esq., JONATHAN C. CAMP, SALENES P. PADGETT, ROBERT BRIDGES and THOMAS
BRIDGES.
St. Clair County, Springville. 4th July, Democratic Meeting:
DR. JOSHUA W. HODGES, President. JAMES H. MEANES and T. M. BARKER,
secretaries. Committee on resolutions; COL. G. W. PATRICK; COLS.
JOHN MASSEY and ORAN ROBERTS, HENRY BRADFORD, Esq., CAPT. JAMES M.
EDWARDS, JAMES H. MEANS and T. M. BARKER.
Morgan County. Somerville; 18th instant. Democratic Meeting.
HON. HORATIO PHILPOTT, chairman, JAMES B. GRAHAM secretary. Committee
on resolutions; CHARLES McLAREN, C. P. RICE, C. E. B. STRODE, D. A.
PHILPOTT, WM. READ, F. M. ROBY, D. STOVALL, JAMES MURPHY, WM. SYKES,

D. C. HUMPHREYS, JESSE ROAN, A. B. DELOACH, T. A. STRAIN, R. S. DAVIS,
Central committee at Somerville; JAMES B. GRAHAM, JOHN SHARP, JUNR.,
NATHANIEL EVANS, CARLISLE HUMPHREYS, WM. READ, L. GARNER, S. M. J. BENSON,
E. T. McALEXANDER, A. B. DELOACH, F. M. ROBY, B. A. PHILPOTT, THOMAS
PRICE, WM. PATTON, C. E. B. STRODE, G. P. RICE, M. W. TROUP, W. H. CAMPBELL,
JOHN HARRIS, T. H. MILWELL, D. C. HUMPHREYS. At Decatur: CHAS. McLAREN,
WM. SYKES, JAMES L. SMITH, HENRY BIBB, RO. ARMSTRONG, JAMES M. MURPHY,
JAMES FENNELL, EDMUND KIMBLE, JOHN P. MOSELEY, PETER STOVALL. At
Crowdabout: D. STOVALL, ED. RICE, JONATHAN ORR, W. W. ROBY, JOHN H.
BIBB, THOMAS D. SIMMS, JAMES WIGGINS, SAMUEL DAVIS, MILTON McCLANAHAN,
ROBERT JOHNSON. At Haile's: GEORGE W. HAILE, THOMAS STONE, NATHAN
NEWSOM SENR., SIMPSON BLACK, BEN ALLEN, HIRAM WRIGHT, JAMES CROUCH, SENR.,
D. KING, EDMUND WEBSTER, THOMAS BRISCOE. At Ryan's: E. THOMPSON,
THOMAS RYAN, WM. SKIDMORE, E. WINDS, H. ST. CLAIR, JESSE ROAN, WM.
WADKINS, ED. HUNTER, JOHN BELVINS (BLEVINS), S. A. DILLARD. Bluff
Spring: THOMAS A. STRAIN, JONA. BURLESON, ALEXANDER NESMITH, ROBERT A.
THOMPSON, TH. NESMITH, JOHN McCLANAHAN, WILLIAMSON JOHNSON, DANIEL KIRKLAND,
E. McCLANAHAN, JAMES STRAIN. Gandy's Cove: JOSEPH TURNEY, R. S. DAVIS,
P. KEY, ALBION TAPSCOTT, DANIEL TURNEY, DANIEL GANDY, J. STINSON,
THOMAS P. COOK, J. D. KEY, NEIL PATTERSON. White Sulphur Springs:
P. T. MANNING, L. CHUNN, TURNER CHAPMAN, SAMUEL W. WINTON, DAVID DRAPER,
WALTER GRANTLAND, WILLIAM GRANTLAND, WM. R. CHUNN, WM. DAVIDSON, JOHN J.
SCOTT. "Resolved, that the thanks of the meeting be tendered the ladies
who have favored us with their company."
        Obituary: Departed this life at the residence of her son MR. JOHN
G(AY) BENTLEY of Madison County on the 28th day of June 1840 in the 67th
year of her age, MRS. ELIZABETH BENTLEY, relict of COL. EFFORD BENTLEY,
formerly of Cumberland County, Virginia. Descended from a large and very
respectable family in Virginia...united herself to the Presbyterian
church in Cumberland County some 30 years since. The Richmond papers
will please insert the above notice. (Note: see ROBERTSON's POCAHONTAS
and her Descendants, also our HARRIS AND ALLIED FAMILIES. She was dau
of DR. WILLIAM GAY & wife FRANCES TRANT.)
        Departed this life on the 17th of July 1840 at his residence 4 miles
east of Huntsville MR. NICHOLAS SHEFFIELD in the 52nd year of his age,
of a slow and painful disease...left widow and six children. "Was not
one of those busy bodies who meddle with other men's matters."
        Departed this life after a protracted illness of three months at
his residence in the vicinity of this place on the morning of the 9th
instant at ½ past 1 o'clock CAPT. JESSE H. POSEY in the 58th year of
his age...disconsolate wife and children. Also on the morning of the
10th instant of consumption JOHN W. POSEY aged 18 years, 3 months (son
of CAPT. POSEY). Voice of Sumter.

August 1, 1840
        Letter from corresponding committee of Lauderdale Co. Tippecanoe
Club. 1 July 1840; SAMUEL W. PROBASCO, ROBERT M. PATTON, JAMES JACKSON,
THOMAS KIRKMAN, JOHN CHISHOLM and ROBERT H. MADRA.
        Died, near Huntsville on the 26th instant MISS ELIZABETH A. HURD
of Bridgport Vermont. aged about 20...a desire to be useful in the
world drew her from the happy and enviable place which she occupied in the
bosom of her father's family and induced her in the spring of 1839 to
become a teacher in the Female Seminary of this town.
        Died at his residence in this county on the 27th instant GEN.
WM. A. AIKEN.
        Died at his residence in Jackson County, Ala. on the 20th instant,
WILLIAM R. VAUGHAN in the 42nd year of his age after a severe illness
of 13 days...left widow and large family of helpless children.
        Also at his residence in Jackson County, Ala. on Friday evening the
24th instant NATHANIEL BYRD, after a few days illness...left widow and
six children.
        Died in the 26th year of her age, at this place on Wednesday the
15th instant after a painful illness of 16 days MRS. ELIZABETH G. wife
of SAMUEL MARTIN, merchant. The deceased was a native of Botetourt
County Virginia, and daughter of FREDERICK W. and DOROTHY ANN JAMES late
of that place, whence she early emigrated to Madison County, Ala. and
thence in 1836 to this place where she has since resided (Mason Mississippi Intelligencer). Note: FREDERICK W. JAMES died in Madison County
in 1824 leaving eight children. ROBERTSON's POCAHONTAS and Her Descendants

p. 36 gives ANN DANDRIDGE m. FREDERICK JAMES- 1 son- and on page 460 of
ANN DANDRIDGE's children who married, P. JAMES....m....UTZ, FINCASTLE.
One of FREDERICK W. JAMES' daughters married an UTZ in Virginia as can
be seen by Cumberland County Marriage Bonds published 1931 in the
D A R Magazine, giving consent of JOHN R. B. ELDRIDGE, her guardian
(who was of this county). While it is possible FREDERICK JAMES was
married more than once, it is also possible that this daughter is of
the DANDRIDGE line. There were many of the POCAHONTAS blood among
Madison County's early settlers.
    Died, this morning at her residence in the vicinity of this place,
MRS. SARAH POSEY in the 43rd year of her age. But a few days ago we
were called upon to consign to earth the last remains of her beloved
husband, CAPT. JESSE H. POSEY and on the next morning the son followed
his father to a premature grave. (Voice of Sumter).
    Marshall County: PERCIVAL M. BUSH, administrator of JAMES GULLIAN
reports estate insolvent.
    Chancery Court, Huntsville; JAMES R. FOX et al. versus ROBERT A.
HIGH and wife, ABNER TATE and GREENVILLE BURNETT et al; GREENVILLE
BURNETT resides out of the state.

August 8, 1840
    Died, on the 28th ult. after a short illness MRS. ELIZABETH HOLMES,
widow of the late RICHARD HOLMES of this county, in the 82nd year of her
age. She was a most estimable lady and for a long time a member of the
Presbyterian Church.
    Greene Academy: Exercises will be resumed 7th Sept. next. MR.
JOHN D. WILES, one of the teachers having resigned...his place has been
supplied by the REV. THOMAS F. SCOTT late of Columbia, Tenn. who will
be associated with MR. THOMAS S. FARNSWORTH...present board of trustees,
COL. PERCY, Prest. REV. DR. ALLAN Vice Prest, J. J. TACKLER, Treas.,
J. BOARDMAN, Secy Messrs. HOPKINS, ROBERT FEARN, G. STEELE, WATKINS,
McCLUNG, ERSKINS, DONEGAN, MASTIN, WALLACE and BIERNE.
    Democratic Committee: Tuscumbia, Franklin County. August 8th;
PETER WALKER, Esq. Chairman, JOHN BRADLEY, Sec'y. Barbecue planned;
correspondence committee, JAMES B. LOCKHART, JAMES BAKER, JOHN A. NOOE,
C. T. BARTON, P. G. NORMAN; Committee on contributions: THOMAS SUGG,
TEMPLE SARGENT, P. O'REILLY, JOHN M. STEWART, ANDERSON BEAN, CLAIBORNE
LITTLE, THOMAS EAST, JAMES S. THOMPSON, WM. T. WELDON, PEYTON BURGESS,
JOSEPH F. COOK, JOHN P. RICHARDSON, JAMES GOOCHER, WM. WINSTON, JOHN P.
PRIDE, JOSEPH SHEFFIELD, WM. BYRD, WARREN HOOKS, WM. DICKSON, JESSE
BROWN, DAVIS GURLEY, W W. PEDEN, JOHN BRADLEY, JOHN G. SHINES, WM. H.
REESE, J. J. LOCKHART, JAMES W. RHEA, G. W. MALONE, F. G. NORMAN,
JOHN L. TOWNES, H. A. PROUT, Committee on arrangements: JOHN P. RICHARDSON,
WM. HUDSON, GEORGE D. CLERE, JAMES SNOW, JOHN THARP, R. S. JONES, W. S.
JONES, JAMES W. LIGON, ROWLAND HESTER, WM. WELDON, CYRUS BENSON, L. B.
VINCENT, WESLEY BATES, BENJAMIN HARRIS, ISAAC JAMES, ENOCH McNATT,
THOMAS J. ALLEN, SAMUEL STEPHENS, REESE HAMILTON, WM. VINCENT, C. T.
BARTON, D. C. TYNAN, WM. H. REESE, N. B. JONES, MICHAEL MATTHEWS,
A. C. MATTHEWS, ISAAC WINSTON, ALFRED PURYEAR, G. W. CARROLL, JOHN
BRADLEY, CHAS. TENNANT, L. G. GARRETT, J. H. BRADFUTE, JOHN PORTLOCK,
CULLEN HOOKS, J. J. LOCKHART, W. B. RATHER, JOSEPH COMPTON, WM. T.
DUNCAN, ASA COBB, JR., L. M. GUY, HIRAM ANDERSON, AMOS JOHNSON, W. E.
DANCY, ARMISTEAD BARTON, D. FURGUSON, J. V. JOHNSTON, JOHN ALLEN, A. M.
KELLER, G. W. MALONE, HENRY HIDE, J. L. McRHEA, RICHARD CLARK, JOHN L.
TOWNES, BURT HARRINGTON
    Democratic Committee: Selma, Dallas County. 6th August 1840.
MAJOR JOHN M. STRONG, Chairman, JOHN L. JEFFRIES, Sec'y Committee on
invitation: COL. GEORGE W. GAYLE, MAJOR JOHN JOHN F. CONOLEY, MAJOR
JOHN M. STRONG, P. H. DELAINE, JAMES CANTEL and JOHN M. MILLER, Esq.
    Died at his residence in St. Clair...Thursday the 6th day of August...
HOLLOWAY, SENIOR of the prevailing fever after an illness of 9 days,
in the 72nd year of his age. The Little Rock Gazette will please publish
the above.
    Died on the 6th of August 1840 in the vicinity of Huntsville,
PATRICK HENRY, son of THOMAS and SARAH MARTIN, aged 1 month, 23 days.
    ELDRED RAWLINS announces as candidate for state treasurer.
    Land for sale: Franklin County: 1280 acres 16 miles below
Tuscumbia, the late residence of PITMAN COLBERT. WM. S. MOORE
    Marshall County, Sheriff JOEL HIGGINS will sell property of
ABRAM BIRDWELL and JAMES FINDLEY.

337

Morgan County: JAMES VEST administrator of FELIX KENNEDY will make
final settlement.
J. GIBSON of Greene Co. advertises for runaway slave.
Stewart County, Tenn. Committed to jail, runaway slaves; 1 belongs
to ANDREW JONES of Ala. and one to JOSEPH SMITH near Florence.
WM. COOK, Jailor

August 22, 1840
Letters testamentary with the will annexed granted the undersigned
by the Judge of the County Court of St. Clair County on the estate of
WILLIAM HOLLOWAY, SENIOR, dec'd on the 10th instant. GEORGE HOLLOWAY,
executor.
Executors' Sale; land in St. Clair County also a tract in Blount
County, being lands of JOEL CHANDLER SR. dec'd, SARAH CHANDLER executrix,
JOEL CHANDLER, JR. and JAMES HAMPTON, executors.

August 29, 1840
Death has again visited our land and consigned to the tomb an
honorable citizen, JAMES H. REEVES who emigrated from Georgia and was
for many years a citizen of this county--12 years a member of the Baptist
church--left dear and affectionate wife and six children. Morgan County,
August 21, 1840.
Headquarters, Marshall Co. Aug. 20. The regiments composing the
18th Brigade 9th Division A.M. commanded to parade.
74th Regiment commanded by COL. THOMAS M. BELL
79th   "   "   "   COL. JOHN M. HENDRICKS
86th   "   "   "   COL. A. R. RAWLINS
75th   "   "   "   COL. JAMES LAMAR
83rd   "   "   "   COL. A. DONALDSON
The commanders, officers and volunteers of the Brigade will parade
at Lebanon, Dekalb County on Monday Oct. 5th provided with necessary
perquisites for three days encampment. By order of BRIGADIER GENERAL
JAMES M. GEE, JAMES M. ADAMS, Asst Adjt.
Cherokee County: ABRAHAM WHORTON and ISAAC WHORTON granted letters
testamentary on estate of BENJAMIN WHORTON.
Blount County: Commissioners sale. Lands of WM. ANDERTON dec'd
adjoining Blountsville; JOHN H. HENDERSON, ELIJAH McPHERSON and CALVIN
J. BEASON commissioners.
Marshall County: JOEL HIGGINS, administrator of EDWARD BEASON will
make final settlement.
Marshall County: PERCIVAL M. BUSH, administrator of SAMUEL HENRY
dec'd reports estate insolvent.

September 5, 1840
Land for sale 3300 acres in Marengo County by BENJAMIN GLOVER of
White Hall, Marengo County, or see HON F. S. LYON, B. N. GLOVER, Esq.
or B(ENJ) G(LOVER) SHIELDS of Demopolis, or E. A. GLOVER, Esq. at
Spring Hill.
Died at his residence in Springfield, Greene County, on...inst.
THOMAS RIDDLE, Esq. senator from that county in the Legislature of this
state.
Six and a fourth cents reward! Ran away, or was stolen by his
mother REBECCA RIGDON from the subscriber living in Marshall County,
RILEY RIGDON, a bound boy. STEPHEN BAXTER
Brigade orders: 1st Brigade, 1st Division, A.M.
Regiment No 2, commanded by COL. THOMAS M. MOSELEY
"   " 3,   "   "   COL. B. F. RICKETTS
"   " 63,   "   "   COL. LARKIN BRADFORD
Officers and Volunteers will assemble at The Grove near Huntsville
on 1st of October for a three day encampment. By order of GEN. B. M. LOWE,
D. M. BRADFORD, Asst. Adjt.
Madison County: Runaway slave committed to jail; belongs to
WM. MOHAWK near Beaufort--doesn't know state but supposed to be South
Carolina.
Ordinance No. 108, City of Huntsville--E. H. RICE, Mayor, WM. H. T.
BROWNE, Clerk.

September 12, 1840

Died in Bellefonte, Jackson County, on Thursday the 27th ult. WYATT COFFEE Esq. late editor of the Bellefonte Courier in the 34th year of his age.

Mobile County: Runaway slave, belongs to JAMES COX of Montgomery County, Ala. Committed to jail by WALTER SMITH, Esq. Recorded of the City of Mobile.

September 19, 1840

DT. JOHN D. SALE having recently returned from the Louisville Marine Hospital has located himself at the Cross Roads, Madison County.

Notice: application to be made for duplicate receipt issued 20 February 1821 to THOMAS BLACK of St. Clair County for certain land assigned to me 23rd Jany 1822 and burnt in my house. LAWRENCE SCOTT

Regimental orders, signed by FERD. HAMMOND, Adj. 2 Regt. 1st Brigade, 1st Division A.M.

Morgan County: HENRY FENNELL administrator of THOMAS SUTHERLAND will make final settlement.

Morgan County: H. D. MORROW sheriff and administrator of DAVID BALLEW dec'd reports estate insolvent.

Marshall County: JOEL HIGGINS, sheriff, administrator of WM. FORSYTH dec'd; also of ROBERT DICKEY dec'd.

Jackson, Mississippi, September 1. Died at his residence in Jefferson County on Sunday the 23rd of August MAJOR GENERAL THOMAS HINDS, native of the State of Mississippi, aged about 58 years. During the late war GENERAL HINDS commanded a regiment of Mississippi Cavalry and served under GENERAL JACKSON in the Creek War. In the fall of 1814 he returned home and in December of that year received orders to repair by forced marches to New Orleans. He assembled his soldiers consisting of four companies, one from each of the counties of Jefferson, Amite, Adams and Wilkinson at Woodville and marched 75 miles per day thence to New Orleans and arrived just in time to participate in the bold attack on the British encampment on the night of the 23rd of December. During the period intervening between that engagement and the glorious and decisive victory of the 8th of January he frequently led his troops up to the British lines and charged them with distinguished success and in the language of the order of the day "excited the astonishment of one army and the admiration of the other" GENERAL HINDS represented this state in the U.S. Congress three sessions...wife died many years since and he leaves an only child, a son.

September 26, 1840

DR. E. M. HUSSEY having been Physician and Surgeon in the Cincinnati Hospital 12 months and afterwards attended a full course at the Alma House of Philadelphia will now faithfully attend to the duties of his profession when called on in Mooresville or its vicinity.

Died at her residence in this county on the morning of the 11th ult. MRS. SARAH STEELE late consort of JOSEPH STEELE in the 60th year of her age. MRS. STEELE was born in the State of N. Carolina--early attached herself to the Methodist Episcopal Church...she has left a husband and two children.

Died at his residence near New Market on the 18th instant MR. REUBEN DONABY, a respectable and honest citizen.

Departed this life on the 13th instant in Limestone County, Ala. MRS. CHARLOTTE F. LANKFORD, consort of WILLIAM LANKFORD; became a subject of converting grace in the 14th year of her age and soon after united herself to the M. E. Church; she left a husband and four children.

Departed this life on the 16th instant in Madison County, Ala. MRS. SUSANNAH ROUTT in the 48th year of her age, consort of CAPT. ROUTT... left husband and a large family of children.

Departed this life on the 15th instant in Madison County, Ala. MARY TURNER TAYLOR, infant daughter of MARTHA A. TAYLOR. aged about four years.

Executor's sale; Estate of MAJOR JOHN DUNN dec'd known as the residence of the late L. D. SMITH, lying 4 miles NW of Florence adjoining JAMES JACKSON and P. F. ARMISTEAD, 1200 acres. WM. B. DUNN, RICHARD A. WIGGINS, DAVID F. BLACKWELL, executors.

Marshall County; RICHARD BOWHANNON, administrator of NEWTON BUCHANAN will make final settlement.

October 3, 1840
From Columbia Democrat; Slander of the Dead; (it was charged the grandfather of JAMES K. POLK was a Tory) His grandfather was EZEKIEL POLK and the following is the certificate of CAPT. JAMES JACK who was bearer of the message of the Mecklenberg meeting to Congress; EZEKIEL POLK and THOMAS POLK were brothers, the one the grandfather the other the great uncle of JAMES K. POLK. The ALEXANDERS were his maternal ancestors. CAPT. JACK's certificate: "Having seen in the newspapers some pieces respecting the Declaration of Independence by the people of Mecklenberg County in the State of North Carolina in May 1775 and being solicited to state what I know of that transaction I would observe that for some time previous to and at the time those resolutions were agreed upon I resided in the town of Charlotte, Mecklenberg County, was privy to a number of meetings of some of the most influential and leading characters of the country on the subject before the final adoption of the resolutions, and at the time they were adopted; among those who appeared to take the lead may be mentioned HEZEKIAH ALEXANDER who generally acted as chairman, JOHN McNITT ALEXANDER as secretary, ABRAHAM ALEXANDER, ADAM ALEXANDER, MAJOR JOHN DAVIDSON, Major, afterwards general, WM. DAVIDSON, COL. THOMAS POLK, EZEKIEL POLK, DR. EPHRAIM BREVARD, DUNCAN OCHLETREE, WM. WILSON, ROBERT IRVIN. Nearly all the names here given were the blood relatives of JAMES K. POLK. The next portion that we have of EZEKIEL POLK's history is that he was a captain in the S C Line and our information is that he was engaged in several actions with the British. He was not so distinguished in the war as his brother or his nephew--all cannot be equally distinguished. The grandfather of JAMES K. POLK on the maternal side was CAPT. JAMES KNOX who served his country in the Revolutionary War, was a brave soldier and a good officer. Our neighbor CAPT. DAVID DOBBINS, a good revolutionary Whig and Democrat served with him.
Resolutions by the teachers and pupils of Franklin Academy on the death of two lovely sisters PERMELIA and MARTHA JANE CLAYTON. E. N. HUDGINS, JAMES J. DORAN, JAMES E. TATE, ESTHER HOGE, SARAH C. NICHOLSON and ELIZABETH E. FEEMSTER to present copies to parents. B. R. WEBB and WM. J. KELLY to forward copies to Jackson Republican and Huntsville Democrat. M. B. FEEMSTER, chariman, N. L. CUNNINGHAM, Secy.
Died, in Limestone County on Monday the 14th ult. MRS. PHEBE WEBB, consort of ROBERTSON WEBB, in her 45th year...member of the Baptist church.
In Marshall County, Ala. at the residence of the late JEREMIAH RODEN on the 22nd ult. JOHN RODEN JR. in his 22nd year.
On the 5th ult. in Johnson County, Arkansas after a protracted illness MR. RICHARD T. BANKS, a native of Culpaper Co. Va.
Limestone County: REUBEN CRUTCHER, administrator of LEVI CUMMINGS.
Jefferson County: M. Kelly, sheriff, appointed administrator of the estates of WM. J. DENTON and NICHOLAS ALLENDER.
Morgan County, H. D. MORROW, sheriff to sell property of JESSE BOWERS. Also of KENDALL AXTON.
Notice: HARVEY CORNELIUS of Blount County states he will not pay a note given JAMES CRUTCHER.
Morgan County. Committed to jail, runaway slave, belongs to SAMUEL BOYD of Benton County.
Fayette County: Runaway slave committed to jail; belongs to RALEIGH WHITE of Noxubee Co. Miss. R. H. POSE, sheriff, also one belonging to BRYANT GRICE of Greene Co.
Morgan County; land for sale by E. EASTON

October 10, 1840
Died in Jackson County on the 23rd ultimo MELVILLE BENTON BILES, son of STEPHEN BILES, aged 11 years.

October 17, 1840
Departed this life on the 3rd of October at COL. B. COX's, MRS. MARY A. G. LANE after a long and painful illness. North Carolina papers will confer a favor by publishing. Brown's Ferry, Limestone Co. Oct. 3, 1840.
Married on Tuesday evening the 6th instant by the REV. ROBERT DONNELL, MR. RODNEY PARKER to MISS ELEANOR DILLON all of this place. See our Vol. 64 p. 16--bride's name DILLARD.

Bibb County. Runaway slave committed to jail; belongs to MR. HUNT near Greensborough; also to MR. CARY WATTS of Hamburg, Perry County. LINDSEY RUCKER, jailor.

Commissioners' Sale--lands of JACOB ORR dec'd, in Morgan County; MILTON McCLANAHAN, JOHN TATOM, HENRY T. PENDLETON, DAVIS NEAL, MARK LINDSEY, commrs.

Land for sale--preparing to move to landing and steam mill on Warrior River will sell tract where now live in Greene Co. ROBERT W. WITHERS

October 24, 1840
On July 15, 1812 a great meeting was held in Fansuil Hall which denounced the war and vilified JAMES MADISON. The most prominent actors in that meeting were DANIEL SARGENT, HARRISON GRAY OTIS and JOSIAH TURNEY. The are now living, two in Boston and one in Cambridge. On 15 July, 1812 a meeting of Federalists in Middlesex County, denounced the war. Four are now living and all ardent whigs, viz: SAMUEL S. P. FAY, Judge of Probate, father of R. S. FAY, NATHANIEL AUSTIN, agent of WARREN FREE BRIDGE, REV. MR. RIPLEY now living in Concord, ISAAC FISKE Register of Probate.

Rebel Convention held in Boston Aug. 6, 1812. COL. SUMNER (now ex-Ad.j GEN. SUMNER) as above was secretary. Among the delegates now living are CHARLES JACKSON, as above, ARTEMUS WARD just resigned as Chief Justice of the Court of Common Pleas, WILLIAM PARSONS, son of Chief Justice PARSONS, WARREN DUTTON and BENJAMIN GORHAM ex-Whig Members of Congress, LEVERETT SALTONSTALL, member of Congress was also a delegate.

Worcester Convention against the War, August, 1812; FRANCIS BLAKE, not now living, at its head. Of the 80 members 40 are known to be dead and 20 probably are. Those living: ELIJAH BURBANK of Worcester; NATHANIEL P. DENNEY of Leicester, NATHANIEL CHANDLER of Petersham; RUFUS BULLOCK of Ryalston (Justice); WM. DRURY of Holden (Justice); SAMUEL READ of Uxbridge (Whig Member of Legislature 1837); NATHAN HOWE of Shrewsbury (Justice); PHILIP DELANO of New Braintree; SOLOMON STRONG, now Judge of Court of Common Pleas; WM. CRAWFORD of Oakham, County Commissioner; AARON TUFTS of Dudley (Justice); JAMES DRAPER of Spencer; AARON WHITE of Boylston; NATHANIEL CROCKER and DRADDOCK LIVERMORE of Paxton; DANIEL TURNEY (Justice); ARTEMAS BULLARD and JONATHAN LELAND (Justice) of Sutton, JONAS KENDALL of Leominster (of the Quorum); and SALEM TOWNE of Charlton (Justice). JOHN DAVIS of Worcester now Harrison Federal Candidate for Governor being then at New Haven.

Jackson County: F. M. KIRBY, administrator of MILTON KIRBY.
Jackson County: Notice of election; JOHN R. COFFEY, Sheriff.
IRA CARLTON of Greene Co. advertises for runaway slave.
Runaway slave, from the late residence of J. C. HALEY dec'd Roane County, Tenn. Notify CHARLES HALEY, Marion County, Tenn.
Jackson County. WM. A. CHRISTIAN administrator of CHARLES L. CHRISTIAN, dec'd.
Morgan County. HENRY DAVIDSON and WM. DITTO, admrs. of WM. DAVIDSON.

October 31, 1840
Marshall County. JOHN W. KIRKSEY, adm'r of HENRY KIRKSEY
Jackson County. A. FINLEY, admr of NATH'L BYRD.
Marshall County: Sheriff to sell property of JOSEPH B. TATE

November 7, 1840
Marshall County: Sheriff to sell property to JAMES M. SUTTON.
Land for sale, 2½ miles of Demopolis. JOHN M. CHAPRON
Jefferson County: A. D. TARRANT, administrator of DR. JOHN T. SANBORN.
Jefferson County: JAMES P. LACEY administrator of NIMROD F. RANDOLPH and PHILIP LACEY.
Jefferson County: M. KELLY administrator of DR. JAMES KELLY.
St. Clair County. GEORGE W. PATRICK, administrator of CHARLES F. PATRICK.
Land for sale on which I now live in Franklin Co. WM. S. MOORE.
Jackson County: Sheriff will sell property of SAMUEL McDAVID.

November 14, 1840
Married on Tuesday the 3rd by REV. MR. ROBINSON, MR. WM. J. HALSEY to MISS MARTHA A(NN) daughter of THOMAS CAIN, Esq. all of this place. See our Vol. 147 p. 50.

Died, on the 15th of September last in the Parish of Caddo,
Louisiana, MRS. ANN W. wife of MR. JOSEPH TROTTER. 1830 Census Lawrence
Co. Ala. JOSEPH TROTTER p. 36 1 m 10-15 1 m 20-30 3 m 30-40 1 f 15-20
1 f 20-30 late of Courtland, Ala.

Land for sale--subscriber being determined to move to Louisiana;
1388 acres where now lives 10 miles west of Tuscumbia. JESSE BROWN

Land for sale--1600 acres on Tombigbee River in Sumter County.
NANCY THOMPSON

Jackson County; sheriff will sell property of J. H. THOMAS

November 21, 1840
Jackson County: HIRAM ALLEN and WILSON L. ALLEN, executors of
ANANIAS ALLEN.

Limestone County; PAUL ROBBINS, administrator of WM. TOWNSEND dec'd
petitions for sale on interest of dec'd in certain tract in Section 12,
Twp 3 Range 7 West, said interest being 1/3rd. Heirs of said WILLIAM
TOWNSEND to be cited; KEZIAH CAIN wife of WILLIAM CAIN, heirs of the
dec'd are not residents of the state. ROBERT AUSTIN, JR. Clerk.

DR. DAVID SHELTON has located on Sand Mt. 5 miles from Gunters
Landing.

November 28, 1840
Died at his residence in Jonesborough, Jefferson County on the
morning of Tuesday the 21st of October, 1840 of the prevalent fever of
the country after an illness of four weeks DR. JOHN T. SEABORN in the
45th year of his age. He was a native of the town of Guilford, New
Hampshire and had been a resident of Jonesborough about a year. Left
amiable wife, son, and little daughter. The New Hampshire Patriot and
State Gazette will please copy the above.

The Alabama State Association of Teachers will hold their first
semi-annual meeting at Benton, Lowndes Co. on the 29th of December.
M. L. GRAY, Recording Secretary.

Jackson County, Sheriff will sell property of ISAAC PRUIT; of
WALTER ORMES; of JOHN NEWBERRY; of GEORGE FRAZIER of C. B. Saint Clair;
of NOEL B. WARREN of Marshall County; sheriff will sell property of
ABRAHAM BIRDWELL.

December 5, 1840
Departed this life on the 27th instant after a lingering pulmonary
disease in the 63rd year of her age. Note: she was ANN BROOKS m. in
Botetourt Co. Va. 1850, b July 6, 1778 Albemarle Co. Va. dau of JAS. &
ELIZ. (WOODS) BROOKS.

MRS. ANN CLOYD, consort of MR. JOSEPH CLOYD, formerly of Virginia.
MRS. CLOYD was an exemplary member of the Presbyterian church for the
last 26 years. Was an affectionate wife and one of the kindest and
best of mothers...The Richmond Enquirer and Fincastle Democrat will
please insert the above.

Died at the residence of her uncle MR. JOHN M. ROWLETT in the
County of Lunenberg, Virginia, on the 18th of September 1840 MISS
LOUISIANA P. HARDING daughter of FRANCES and JOHN HARDING, aged 22
years. Huntsville Democrat will please copy the above. Enquirer

Jackson County: SARAH CARROLL administratrix of JAMES CARROLL,
dec'd.

Masonic notice: Athens Lodge no 1 will bury late brother THOMAS
WEST. THOMAS C. TYSON, sec'y.

Jackson County: sheriff will sell property of STITH DANIEL.

Limestone County: sheriff will sell property of WASHINGTON MEADOWS.

December 12, 1840
Democratic Meeting: GEORGE T. JONES, chairman; Committee on
resolutions, JOHN C. THOMPSON, Esq., CAPT. GEORGE STEELE, COL. ROBERT
HANCOCK, MAJOR WILLIAM FLEMING, COL. WILLIAM GRAVES BOULDIN, COL. WILLIAM
CALVIN McBROOM, COL. RUSSELL J. KELLY, COL. JOSEPH TAYLOR, CAPT. DAVID
BRADFORD, CAPT. WILLIAM LESLIE, JOSEPH WARD and STEPHEN S. EWING.
C. C. CLAY, JR., Sec'y

Marshall County. RALEIGH PENDERGRASS, adm'r of BENJAMIN OLIVER.

Jackson County: HUGH P. CAPERTON, adm'r of HENRY NORWOOD.

Jackson County: Sheriff JOHN COFFEY by deputy WM. A. ANDERSON will
sell property of H. P. DELANEY.

December 19, 1840
    Died at the residence of MR. P. T. POSEY on Sunday the 13th instant
MARY ELIZABETH, infant daughter of MAJOR A. J. and ELIZABETH COFFEE
aged 7 months 17 days.
    Jackson County: PLEASANT BASHAM, adm'r of WILLIAM P. CHILDRESS
reports estate insolvent.
    Pickens County: runaway slave committed to jail--says he is free.
JOHN F. NABORS, sheriff
    Tuscaloosa County--runaway slave committed to jail--says he belongs
to WM. WARREN of Macon, Ga. To be sold for jail fees and legal charges.
R. W. BARBER, jailor
    Land for sale Marengo County by GEORGE S. GAINES Spring Hill near
Mobile or see W. H. LYONS Esq. on the premises or see GEORGE W. GAINES
at Mobile.
    Pocketbook lost in Huntsville by J. J. RAMSEY of Fayetteville,
Tenn.

December 26, 1840
    Married on Wednesday evening the 16th instant by the REV. MR. MADDIN,
MR. THOMAS W. WHITE of Abingdon, Virginia to MISS SUSAN W., daughter of
MAJOR JAMES BRADLEY of this place.
    Died on the 23rd of November last MARY JANE, eldest daughter of
MAJOR JAMES MUNDAY in 3rd year...scarlet fever. Bolivar, Ala. Nov. 29,
1840.
    On the 27th of November MARY ELIZA, daughter of MR. GEORGE TAYLOR
in 3rd year of scarlet fever.
    At his residence in Jackson County on the 8th of December BENJAMIN S.
JONES, Esq. in his 54th year.
    Morgan County. Hiring and renting: TURNER and COLEMAN agents of
WM. H. GEE of the will of JOHN LUNDY.

--Overlooked--
January 4, 1840
    Married on Friday the 27th ult. by WILLIAM EAST, Esq. MR. ZADOK
HILLIARD of Madison County to MISS CASSANDRA S. GRAHAM of Limestone Co.

HUNTSVILLE DEMOCRAT

These are items that I have copied from Huntsville, Ala. Democrat in
addition to items already copied for those dates.

January 22, 1845
    Married on 8th by REV. M. H. BONE, MAJ. JOHN M. HUMPHREY to MISS
ELIZABETH F. eldest daughter of JOSIAH REDDICK, Esq., all of this co.
    Married on 9th by REV. P. B. ROBINSON, MR. A. H. THURSTON to
MRS. MARTHA FREEMAN, all of this place.
    Married on Thur. 9th by REV. B. ASKEW, CAPT. JOSEPH LENOW, merchant,
of firm of J. & J. LENOW of Hickory Wythe, to MISS FRANCES CATHARINE,
daughter of the late FRANCES E. BROUM (BROWN or BROUN?), deceased, all
of Fayette County, Tennessee (Somerville, Tenn. Spy).
    Notice--Orphan's Court of Madison Co. Ala. SARAH TAYLOR, deceased.
         "   "   "   "   "   "   " WILLIAM M. BARTON, dec'd.
    STEPHEN DEBOW, administrator.
    JAMES M. GEE of Marshall Co. Ala. claims an undivided interest
with JOSEPH G. GARRELL, administrator ex officio de bonis non of
JAMES EDWARDS, deceased, tract of land in county afresaid. 10 Jan. 1845.

July 9, 1845
    State of Alabama--32 Chancery District. HENRY JORDAN et al by
next friend versus WILLIAM BLAKE et al. BILL states that complainants,
HENRY JORDAN, ANDREW JORDAN and JAMES JORDAN are the only children and
heirs of HENRY JORDAN, late of Madison Co. Ala. deceased; that their
grandfather, BATT JORDAN, father of said HENRY, deceased on 26 October
1836 made a deed of gift conveying to one WILLIAM BLAKE, then of said
county the following negro slaves...

October 22, 1845

Married on Thur. the 7th at house of RICHARD NOELL by REV. DANIEL K. HUNTER, MR. HENRY W. PICKENS to MISS LUCY W. NOWLIN, daughter of the late WADE H. NOWLIN, Esq. all of Madison Co.

Married on Tuesday evening the 14th at the residence of MR. WM. WILSON in this place, by REV. MR. CHAPMAN, of the Cumberland Presbyterian Church, JOHN MOSELEY (64 V), Esq. of this county to MRS. EPSY B. GASTON (37 T; EPSEY had sisters ANN, PRISCILLA (m ALLEN CHRISTIAN), MARTHA & MARY) of Huntsville (she m. 1. 1832 WM. GASTON; 2. 1845 JOHN MOSELEY; 3. JAMES BAILEY (1858)), daughter of MR. HENRY AVENT (m. SARAH daughter of THOS VINING, Rev sol.) of Madison Co.

Departed this life at his residence 4 miles Northwest of Huntsville on 9 October 1845, COL. JAMES W. CAMP. Born in Greensville, Va. 28 June 1789 and removed to this county at an early age, where he resided to the time of his death...At one time member of Ala. Legislature. Nashville Union and Washington Union please copy.

State of Alabama-Marshall County. Orphan's Court. DAVID NEWSOM, deceased. SOWEL NEWSOM (37 yrs. old in Ky.), administrator.

MARY, wife of RICHARD BROOKS, ELIZABETH W. wife of GEORGE W. BROOKS and MARTHA wife of JOHN N. JACKSON are heirs and live beyond the limits of the state.

HUNTSVILLE DEMOCRAT

Published every Wednesday by PHILIP WOODSON, JR.

January 14, 1846

Married on the 24th inst. by REV. P. B. ROBINSON, MR. WILLIAM J. (T in Census) GRANTLAND to MISS NANCY M. BRANSFORD, daughter of ABRAHAM BRANSFORD (see minors), all of this county. (vol. 127 p. 29)

On the 8th by same, MR. JOSEPH C. PETTUS to MISS PAMELIA C. FOULKS, daughter of RANSOM FOULKES, all of this county. (JOS C was son of DAVID & ELIZ (BOSWELL) PETTUS; gs of DAVID PETTUS & of JOHN BOSWELL)-- See Goodspeed's History of South Ark. (1890)

On the evening of the 8th inst. by REV. WILLIAM D. CHADDICK of Fayetteville, Tennessee, DR. ISAAC B. HUNT (36 T) of Warrenton to MISS M(ARTHA) A. G. COLE (24 A), daughter of JOHN COLE, Esq. all of Marshall County. (vol. 96 p. 75)

At the residence of JAMES A. FITZ on the 22nd by REV. THEOPHILUS SAUNDERS, MR. OBEDIAH D. GRAVETT of Limestone County to MISS SARAH FRANCES EDWARDS of Madison County, Tenn.

Died Saturday the 11th of scarlet fever, UDORER, second daughter of ISHAM H. and SUSAN HOBBS aged 2 years and 22 days.

Departed this life in Madison County, Alabama, ASA STRATTON of Vermont and late of Florence, Ala. aged about 40. Highly respected gentleman..(see ts in Vol. 64)

January 21, 1846

Married by P. B. ROBINSON on the 13th inst. DR. JOHN T. DEBOW to MISS MARIA M. RIGNEY, all of Madison County. (vol. 133, p. 21)

February 4, 1846

Married on the 14th by REV. A. DODSON McCORD. MR. SAMUEL M. THOMPSON (36 T) of Lawrence County, Ala. to MISS CAROLINE R. (25 A), daughter of WILLIAM V. TUNSTALL, Esq. of Morgan County.

Departed this life on the 28th Oct. 1845, MRS. MARGARET COTTEN, wife of the late MICAJAH T. COTTEN, deceased in her 71st year. She was born in Hyde County, N.C. and from thence removed to North Alabama and from there to Talladega, where she died. She lived to a very old age and for the last 6 or 8 years of her life has been a devoted member of the Methodist Church...

Died at his residence in this county on Thursday morning the 29th, JAMES WILBORN in his 58th year. For many years a resident of this county and a member of the Methodist Episcopal Church. (see tombstone--born Jan 10, 1789 d Jan 29, 1846--wife SALLY (WYCHE) WILBURN b 1790 d 1857)

February 11, 1846
    Died on the 9th of January in New Orleans, RICHARD CLARKE aged
24, son of the late WILLIAM CLARKE of this county.

February 18, 1846
    (From Richmond Enquirer). Departed this life on the 24th of January
at his residence, Allen's Creek, Hanover, CAPT. PHILIP WOODSON, SR. in
his 79th year. Confined to his languishing bed and sickroom about two
months previous to his dissolution... For about 15 years he was a
zealous Christian, a Baptist... Left a widow with whom he lived for
nearly 56 years.

February 25, 1846
    Married on the 19th at the residence of MR. JAMES LANDMAN by REV.
JAMES W. ALLEN, MR. JOHN McQ. LYNCH (40 T) to MISS NANCY HATTON (37 NC),
all of this county. (Vol. 155, p. 25)

March 4, 1846
    Died at the residence of her husband in this county on the night
of the 18th after a painful and lingering illness...in her 39th year,
MRS. AMELIA W. HOLDING, consort of MR. RICHARD HOLDING and daughter of
CAPT. WILLIAM MARTIN.... Left bereaved companion and tender offspring.
Triana. Feb. 23, 1846.
    Died of pneumonia Sunday morning the 22nd of Feb. at his residence
in this county, JOHN ALLEN WAYLAND leaving a wife and child besides
numerous friends and relatives.

March 25, 1846
    Married Monday evening the 16th by REV. RICHARD TALIAFERRO, COL.
ABSALOM BROWN of Fayetteville, Tenn. to MRS. ELIZABETH E. HIGH of this
county.

April 29, 1846
    Married Wednesday the 22nd by REV. MR. LAIRD, MR. HENRY C. CHAMBERS
of Jackson, Miss. to MISS VIRGINIA, daughter of the late CAPT. CHARLES
BETTS of this county. (vol. 141, p. 50)

May 13, 1846
    Departed this life on Sunday morning the 10th at the residence of
his brother, WILLIAM POWERS near Huntsville, YANCEY POWERS after a
protracted and painful illness of rheumatic affection of about 9 years,
a greater portion of which time he was confined to his bed. Died in his
62nd year. We have known MR. POWERS from our boyhood, being natives of
the same county (Goochland, Va.).... On leaving his native state, he
located in Tennessee, where he remained a few years and from thence to
Madison County, Ala. in 1818 where he continued to his death. Richmond
Enquirer please copy.

May 27, 1846
    Died of cholera morbus after an illness of a few hours on Monday the
4th of May, GEORGE WILLIAM, oldest child of W. W. McCUTCHEN, Esq. aged
5 years 9 months.

June 3, 1846
    Married on the 31st in this county by P. B. ROBINSON, ALEXANDER J.
COYLE of Arkansas to MRS. MARY ANN ACKLEN. (vol. 141, p. 51).

June 10, 1846
    Married on the 18th by REV. JOHN HAMER, MR. SAMUEL WOODRUFF (40 Va)
to MISS MINERVA HARRISON (25 Marshall Co., Ala) both of this county.
    Married in Shelby County, Tenn. on the 26th by REV. J. WILLIAMS,
MR. J. T. LOWRY of Marshall County, Alabama to MISS O. E. ALLEN,
daughter of the late MATTHEW ALLEN of Shelby Co.

June 17, 1846
    Information reached here on Monday morning last of the death of
COL. JOHN R. H. ACKLEN on the evening previous at the residence of
MR. J. V. A. HINDS near Salem, Tenn. When our paper was put to press,

his remains had not reached Huntsville, where they will be interred with Masonic honors.

State of Alabama--Madison County--June Term 1846.
     Orphan's Court
JESSE BENDALL's administrator etc.
     versus
JESSE BENDALL's heirs
     Said heirs are: POLLY BROWN, RICHARD BENDALL, ISAAC J. BENDALL, MARGARET BENDALL, GEORGE BENDALL, MARTHA WOMBLE, JOHN H. BENDALL, HARRIET BENDALL, LUCY ADAMS, MARY ANN WRIGHT, POLLY ZILLS, SUSANAH HAMBLEN, SALLY WRIGHT, THOMAS ADAMS, GEORGE ADAMS, WILLIAM ADAMS, JOHN JONES, WINFIELD JONES, CHRISTIANA SMITH and NORMAN JONES, all non-residents.

July 1, 1846
Died on the 8th inst. at the residence of COL. BEN. HARRISON, NUBBIN RIDGE, VIRGINIA JANE, only child of W. L. and LUCY M. HARRISON aged 8 months.

Died in Warrenton (Marshall Co.) Tuesday the 2nd of June at 4 P.M. the infant son of ISAAC H. and LUCY THOMASSON aged 1 mo.

July 8, 1846
Died in this county at the residence of his brother, A. L. GARNER on Friday the 19th, ROBERT C. GARNER in his 48th year. Had resided for some time in Tuscaloosa then in Mobile then in Sumter County this state, from which place he moved to Kemper Co. Miss.... Had been in bad health for some years and was on a visit to his brother when the disease seized upon him. Left an aged mother, two sisters and five brothers. (From North Alabamian; Franklin Co.)

Died of consumption on the night of the 26th of June at her residence in Jackson County, Alabama, MRS. LUCINDA FRAZIER, wife of GEN. JOSEPH P. FRAZIER (48 years old in Tenn.) in her 31st year. Her sufferings were extremely severe....

July 22, 1846
Married on Wednesday evening the 15th by REV. MR. WALKER, MR. WILLIAM W. CRAYTON to MISS PAMELIA F. COOPER, all of this place. (vol. 141, p. 51)

Wednesday evening the 15th by REV. C. P. WING, MR. W. G. SELLECK to MISS MARY ANN, daughter of the late WILLIAM PATTON. (vol. 103 p. 84)

In Franklin, Tenn. the 7th, MR. SAMUEL J. WATKINS of Alabama to MISS MARTHA JANE, daughter of ROBERT C. FOSTER.

M. in Jackson County the 22nd, REV. W. W. ADAMS to MISS ELIZABETH, daughter of JOSHUA KIRBY, Esq.

Died at the residence of SAMUEL B. HUDSON Friday July 3rd of consumption, MR. JOHN DARBEY. The deceased was born in Madison County, Ala. 18 August 1821 and would have been 25 on the 18 of Aug. next.... From Florence Gazette.

August 12, 1846
Married Thursday Aug. 6th by W. GRAVES BOULDIN, Esq., MR. WOODWARD BAUGHHAUGH (27 A) to MISS TREMANDA GRAHAM (see Vol. XXI) all of this county. (vol. 100 p. 10; WOODWARD H. "BAUGHA" to AMANDA W. GRAHAM)

Departed this life 18 July in Philadelphia, WYATT H. ELLIS, merchant of Huntsville, on his way to Boston to replenish his store. Having arrived at Philadelphia, he died of congestion of the brain. A Presbyterian since 1841. Left a wife and children. Telegraph.

September 2, 1846
Married in Slough Beat at Bethlehem Church, Limestone County August 26, 1846 by REV. F. G. FURGUSON, MR. MAGNESS S. TEAGUE to MISS MUSIDORA P. V. only daughter of the late THOMAS MORGAN of Virginia. (vol. 187 p. 69)

September 9, 1846
Married on the 3rd by REV. H. P. TURNER, MR. HAMMOND BOULDIN to MISS MARTHA JANE BOULDIN, all of Madison Co. (vol. 100 p. __)

In Pickens County the 26th by REV. J. W. LANEY, JOHN W. GARNER (34 V), formerly of Madison Co. to CAROLINE M. (23 A), daughter of ISAAC TAYLOR of Pickens Co.

September 30, 1846
    Died of congestive fever at his residence on the 22nd, HON. S. C.
SMITH, native of South Carolina. His father, WILLIAM C. SMITH emigrated
to Madison County, Alabama many years since, where the subject of this
memoir was raised and married to MISS NORMAN in 1833. He emigrated to
Dekalb County in 1836; was elected Clerk of County Court 1837; elected
to Representative branch of the state Legislature 1839; elected Senate
from Dekalb Co. and Cherokee Co.; served in that body two sessions and
in 1844 was re-elected to the Senate. Left a wife and six daughters and
one son. Was a Methodist for the last 3 years.
    Died at his residence in this county on the 13th, GEORGE DAVIS in
his 83rd year. Had long been afflicted with a painful disease--rheumatism.
Member of the church for 50 years. For last 35 years a consistent
member of the Cumberland Presbyterian Church. The Huntsville Democrat,
Banner of Peace at Lebanon, Tenn. and the prints at Greenville and
Jonesboro, Tenn. copy. (From Athens Chronicle--Limestone Co.)

October 7, 1846
    Died Sunday night last at his residence near this place, ROBERT
HAMBLET, an early settler in this county and much respected as a most
worthy citizen. He was, we believe, a native of N.C.

October 14, 1846
    Departed this life suddenly on the 6th inst., CLARKSTON LIGHTFOOT
(note: in previous records, we have found it written CLACKSTON or
CLAXTON) in his 56th year; of dropsy of heart of which he had a severe
attack some four years ago.... Native of Brunswick County, Va. and
from which he emigrated to Madison County, Ala. in the spring of 1823
and where he continued to reside up until the time of his death....
Amassed a considerable estate... Kind husband. Left a widow and a large
number of neighbors and friends to mourn his loss. Never professed
religion. Southern Advocate and Petersburg, Va. Intelligence copy.

October 21, 1846
    Married on the 18th inst. by REV. P. B. ROBINSON, MR. JOHN C. WELLS
to MISS SARAH A. EDWARDS, daughter of MR. ROBERT EDWARDS, all of
Huntsville. (vol. 153 p. 49)

October 28, 1846
    Died of consumption on the 2nd in his 21st year near Buzzard Roost,
Ala. DANDRIDGE B. SPENCE, son of MR. WILLIAM W. SPENCE of the Western
District, formerly of Madison Co. Ala. Sometime last spring he took a
trip to the Western District to pay his father and relations a visit and
on the way contracted a severe cold settling in his lungs....
    Departed this life in Washington (Hempsted Co.) County, Arkansas
MRS. SUSAN B. PURDOM (wife of RICH'D B. PURDOM), formerly of Huntsville
and daughter of JAMES SEVIER of Washington County, East Tennessee,
aged 46 years. The deceased was among the oldest members of the
Methodist Episcopal Church in Huntsville. In 1819 she joined the church.
For some months prior to her departure from Huntsville, her health was
declining. When she arrived in Arkansas, it seemed to improve up until
the 30th of Sept. last when she was suddenly attacked with a hemorrhage
of the lungs. She died a few days later...
    (From Knoxville Register 15 Dec. 1818. Married on Thursday evening
the 26th ult, MR. RICHARD PURDOM, merchant of Huntsville (AT) to
MISS SUSAN SEVIER, daughter of JAMES SEVIER, Esq. of Washington Co.
Tenn.)
    Died at his residence in this county on the 7th inst. ROBERT DAVIE
in his 89th year after a protracted and painful illness. The Southern
Advocate and Lincoln Journal copy.

November 4, 1846
    Married on 28th October by REV. P. B. ROBINSON, MR. ROBERT S. NANCE
to MISS MATILDA D. SALE, daughter of CAPT. D(UDLEY) SALE, all of Madison
Co. (vol. 53 p. 5)
    Died in Madison Co. Friday the 29th of Oct. MARY CAMP, daughter of
JAMES B. and INDIANA S. TURNER aged 4 years and 6 months.
    Died in Baltimore, Md. Sunday the 18th of Oct. EDWARD ANDERSON
aged 49 years 10 months and 12 days. Native of Montgomery Co. Md. who
resided many years in this county; late of Oktibeha Co. Miss.

Died on 16th inst. at his residence in Mullins Flat, Madison Co.,
LEWIS HERRALD aged 76 years, a native of N.C.

November 4, 1846
    Married 5th, at Mooresville (son of JOHN & EMILY G.) (Limestone Co.)
by REV. MR. KIRKLAND, MR. JOHN H(ENRY) CALDWELL of that place to MISS
MARY D. GREER of Fayetteville, Tenn. (vol. 187 p. 71)
    Married Thursday the 5th inst. by REV. T. B. WILSON, MISS ELIZA J.,
daughter of WILLIAM WRIGHT, deceased of Madison Co. and COL. J(OHN) T.
ABERNATHY of Limestone County, Alabama. (vol. 71 p. 8)
    Married by P. B. ROBINSON in Madison Co. Ala. Tuesday night, MR.
GEORGE B. WRIGHT to MISS HULDAH RIGNEY of Madison Co. (vol. 153 p. 49)
    Married by same on Thursday night the 5th inst. DR. J(OHN) DAVID
MALONE, Limestone County to MISS SUSAN C(ATHERINE) SPOTSWOOD of Madison
County near Huntsville (d of ELLIOTT & SALLY DANDRIDGE ((?)   Spotswood;
vol. 48 p. 26)
    Married at Oakendale on Thursday by REV. MR. HUBBARD, MR. RICHARD S.
ROBERTSON of Virginia to MISS MARY JANE, daughter of LUKE MATTHEWS,
Esqr. (vol. 76 p. 19; "Revolutionary Soldier")

November 25, 1846
    Married on the 11th by REV. MR. BONE, MR. DANIEL H. HOLMES to MISS
VIRGINIA ANN A(DELINE) RUTHERFORD, all of this county. (vol. 147 p. 57)
    Married on the 22nd by REV. JAMES C. ELLIOT, MR. SIMEON P. BRYAN
to MISS MAHALA JANE REEDY, all of this city. (vol. 100 p. 10)
    Departed this life on 29th of October at the residence of her
daughter, MRS. MARY S. LANIER of this county, LOUISA McCRAB in her 78th
year. Born in Pennsylvania and emigrated to this county at an early day
along with her father's family (MR. JOHN SHELBY, formerly of Tennessee)
to what was then called "the far west." Widow of MR. ALEXANDER McCRAB,
who died many years since in Montgomery County, Tennessee.... Presbyterian. Patriotic achievements of her paternal family.... Nashville
papers please copy. (Signed) JAS. W. ALLEN
    Departed this life Tuesday the 17th after a few days illness,
JOHN BLUNT TURNER, second son of MAJ. JOHN B. TURNER of Madison County
aged 20 years and 19 days....

December 2, 1846
    Married Thursday the 26th of Nov. by W. GRAVES BOULDIN, Esq.,
MR. WILLIAM A. PIKE to MISS ELIZA JANE, daughter of WILLIAM JOHNSTON,
all of Madison Co. (vol. 64 p. 26)
    On the evening of the 10th by ELDER J. M. CUMMINGS, MR. ANDREW
DRAKE of Madison Co. to MISS FRANCES CAMPBELL of this vicinity.
(Independent Spectator)
    Married by REV. P. B. ROBINSON in Huntsville (vol. 151 p. 26) on
the 26th inst. MR. JOHN B. TROTMAN to MRS. MARIA A. JONES. (she m. 1.
ALBERT H. JONES, Feb. 16, 1836--was dau of WM. H. CLOPTON)
    State of Alabama--Madison County.
    THOMAS McGEHE's administrator)
        versus   )   Petition to sell land
    THOMAS McGEHE's heirs   )
(letter from M. L. DAVIS 10502 Chadwick St., Houston, Tex 1954 asking
abt these McGEHEE's)
    SARAH McGEHE, wife of JOHN McGEHE, THOMAS McGEHE, FRANCIS M.
McGEHE, WILLIAM McGEHE, WILLIAM ACKLEN who intermarried with MILDRED
CARROLL, formerly McGEHE, are heirs. CHARLES S. (L in other rec)
McGEHE, the petitioner.
    Married by P. B. ROBINSON Dec. 1, 1846, MR. ASA H. HARRINGTON to
MISS ARABELLA N. CHUNING (d of THADEUS), all of Madison Co.
    By same on 3rd Dec. MR. JOHN McLARAN to MISS LUCY ANN HAZELWOOD,
all of Huntsville. (vol. 48 p. 26)
    Died, DR. EDMUND ROGERS. Born in Philadelphia Sept. 26, 1822 from
whence he moved to Huntsville in 1836. There he entered a drug store.
Continued in that employment until the summer of 1844 where he visited
the city of his nativity for the purpose of attending a course of
medical lectures, again in 1845 attended medical lectures. In the
spring of that year, he was induced by a friend, DR. HAUGHTON, to visit
this city. He entered partnership with DR. HAUGHTON in the drug business.
Left a widowed mother, a sister and two brothers...

Departed this life in this county at his residence on the night of
the 13th inst. of pneumonia, MR. WILLIAM PROVENCE in his 74th year.
Native of Pennsylvania but in his early life emigrated to the West.
In his 34th year, he embraced religion.--Methodist Society...Kind husband
and father....

Departed this life on 21 Nov. 1846, DELILAH LEFTWICH, consort of
JABEZ LEFTWICH (Sol of 1812) aged 80 years 8 months and 5 days. He
emigrated from Bedford County, Virginia to Madison Co. Ala. in 1827
where he resided until Sept. 23, 1846 and then moved to Russel Valley,
Franklin County. Labored under protracted illness 5 or 6 months...
Joined Presbyterian Church in 1787 and has been an affectionate
wife and tender mother.... Left numerous family of children, grandchildren and great-grandchildren.

Departed this life on 2 December 1846, MRS. POLLY N. FLETCHER in
her 66th year, of pulmonary complaint. Born in Nottoway County Virginia
May, 1781 and was the relic of MR. NATHAN FLETCHER, late of Brunswick
County, Va. Moved to Alabama some years since with her three sons, who
settled in Limestone County, where at her son's, JOHN JAMES FLETCHER's,
she closed her earthly pilgrimage.... Left an only sister, three sons
and many grandchildren.... Also numerous connections.... Never belonged
to any branch of the church but eminently possessed that Catholic
spirit which induced her to harmonize with all. Richmond Enquirer copy.

December 23, 1846
Married by REV. P. B. ROBINSON on 15th of December, MR. JAMES
LAWLER to MISS SUSAN A(NN) THOMSON (THOMPSON in mar rec vol. 155 p. 25),
all of Madison Co.

By same on 16th of December, MR. HENRY M. POLLARD to MISS MALINDA
JANE MORGAN all of Huntsville. (vol. 64 p. 26)

State of Alabama--Morgan County. Orphan's Court.
Special Term 9 Dec. 1846 before HON. W. H. CAMPBELL. Petition to
sell land.

ALEXANDER BOTELER, Surviving adm'r
versus
ALEXANDER BOTELER's heirs

Of ALEXANDER BOTELER's heirs, MARY CRABB, WILLIAM A. EDMUNDSON,
ROBERT K. EDMUNDSON and ELIZA EDMUNDSON are non-residents.

January 27, 1847
Married on the 21st by REV. R. TALAFARO, MR. DAVID M. HOBBS to
MISS EMILY B., daughter of G. L. SANDIDGE, Esq. all of this county.
(vol. 147 p. 57)

Departed this life on Wednesday the 13th of January at the residence
of his father about 8 miles Northwest of Huntsville of affection of the
heart after a painful and protracted illness, GABRIEL EDWARD MOORE,
second surviving son of EDWARD and JANE MOORE of Madison Co. aged about
34 years. Native of Moore County, North Carolina, where many of his
surviving relatives still reside. From that state he emigrated with his
father's family to Alabama and settled in Madison Co. in 1822....

Died in Madison Co., WILLIAM THOMAS and SOPHIA MARGARET, infant
son and daughter of GREEN C. and LAVINIA E. BRAZLETON. The former died
on the 8th of last month at 3 o'clock P.M. and the latter on the 9th
at 4 o'clock, A.M. THOS. was near 21 months and SOPHIE 3 months and
10 days old. Banner of Peace please copy.

(From Moulton Sentinel--Lawrence Co.). Departed this life on
January 11, WILLIAM P. HODGES after a painful and protracted illness of
nearly four weeks. His distressed mother, MRS. PREWIT, had but six
weeks before consigned to the tomb a younger son, FRANK, who died in
Triana, Madison Co. while on a visit to relations.... The deceased was
22 years old and left an affectionate wife to whom he had been wedded
5 months.

February 10, 1847
Died in DeSoto County, Miss. on 2 Jan. DAVID MAXWELL, formerly a
citizen of this county.

March 17, 1847
Married in Giles County, Tennessee on the 26th inst., MR. ROBERT H.
JACKSON to MISS EASTER ANN ELLIOTT, all of Athens, Alabama (Limestone Co.)

Died at the residence of her husband, MR. J. B. TATE LOURY, of
Marshall Co. on the 4th, MRS. O. E. LOURY aged 19 years.... Memphis
papers copy.
    In Lawrence County on the 13th instant, MRS. SUSAN M. WATKINS,
consort of MR. W. M. WATKINS in her 35th year, leaving a husband and
5 small children.
    In Clarksville, Tex. on the 9 January, DR. JOHN J. PETERS in his
39th year of age, formerly of Lawrence Co. Ala.
    State of Alabama--Morgan County--Chancery Court
    ELIZABETH K. WILBER, by   )
    next friend, GEO. FRANCIS   )   Bill for divorce and alimony
          versus   )
    EZRA WILBER   )
    The defendant is a non-resident.
    State of Alabama--Madison County. Orphan's Court. March Term, 1847
    JAMES WALKER's adm'r   )
          versus   )   Petition to sell land
    JAMES WALKER's heirs   )
    CYNTHIA THOMPSON, wife of HENRY THOMPSON, VIOLET ANN SULLIVAN wife
of SEABORN SULLIVAN, TAYLOR WALKER, JANE ALLEN wife of PHILIP J. ALLEN,
MARTIN WALKER, WILLIAM W. WALKER, PORTER WALKER, MINERVA SALES wife of
WILLIAM SALES, SARAH C. WALKER, ELIZABETH E. SALES wife of ROBERT SALES,
MARY W. WALKER and JOHN M. WALKER, heirs of said deceased are non-
residents.

March 24, 1847
    Died Friday last, JOHN HAMBLEN, an old and highly respectable
citizen of this county.

March 31, 1847
    Departed this life on the 24th inst. ROBERT WRIGHT, SR., a patriot
of the Revolution aged 85 years and 17 days. Native of Amherst County,
Virginia. Was at the seige of York and assisted in the capture of
CORNWALLIS. Emigrated to Madison Co. Ala. in 1818 where he continued
to reside until the day of his death, greatly esteemed and beloved by
large circle of friends and acquaintances. Southern Advocate and
Richmond Enquirer copy.
    Departed this life in this county, JOHN HAMBLEN aged 80 years 1
month and 19 days. Born in Virginia and from thence he removed to East
Tennessee and became a resident of this state and county many years
since, where he has resided, beloved and respected by his fellow
citizens... (MR. PRENTISS PRICE says "JOHN HAMBLEN mar.Huntsville 1834.
He was born 1760-70 & took off for Ala in 1807 leaving wife HANNAH
b 1768 in Hawkins Co. & also son THOMAS b 1788. HANNAH was alive in
Hawkins. I think JOHN had another family in Ala." He certainly did!
His will names wife MARGARET, sons SAM'L & JOHN; daus ELIZABETH BISHOP,
SARAH BISHOP, SUSANNAH MOREL & 4 grandchildren, sons of JOHN.)

March 31, 1847
    Departed this life--ROBERT WRIGHT on 24th, a Patriot of the
Revolution aged 85 years and 17 days. He was a native of Amherst Co.
Va. emigrated to Madison Co. in 1808.
    Departed this life at his residence in this county, JOHN HAMBLEN
aged 80 years 1 month 19 days. Born in Va. and from thence removed to
East Tenn. and became a resident of this State and county many years
since, where he has resided beloved and respected by his fellow citizens.
    Died near Somerville, Morgan Co. Ala. on Wed. 26th Mar. the infant
daughter of WILLIAM P. and MARY L. TERRY aged 3 mo 16 days.
    Chancery Court of Morgan Co. Ala.--SUSAN WEST by next friend
WILLIAM A. LAMONS
          versus
    JOSHUA WEST--divorce suit. Defendant's residence is unknown.
(m. in Morgan Co. Mar. 27, 1833 SUSAN LAMONS--vol. 32 p. 30; JOSHUA in
1850 Cen. JOHNSON Co. Ark.)
    HISTASPAS STEWART, administrator of ALCY ROAN, deceased--Morgan Co.
Ala.
    Morgan Co. Ala. ELIZABETH K. WILBER by next friend, GEORGE FRANCIS
          versus
    EZRA WILBER--divorce suit. Defendant's residence unknown.

(1840 Census Morgan Co. Ala. E. WILBER--1 m 5-10 1 m 20-30, 1 f 20-30; same
page GEORGE FRANCIS 2 m-5, 2 m 5-10, 1 m 10-15, 1 m 15-20, 1 m 40-50, 1 f
30-40; HISTASPAS STEWART same page)
    Morgan Co. Ala.   Estate of STEPHEN C(HANDLER) PENN (b May 5, 1800,
son of STEPHEN, Rev.pen Gr-son of WM. CHANDLER PENN, Rev.sol), deceased.
Letters of administration granted Feb. 13, 1847 to EASTHER PENN (48 T)
and WILLIAM PENN, administrators with will annexed.
    State of Alabama 35th Chancery
        JAMES M. GEE
            versus
    RICHARD S. RANDLES, JAMES BOGGESS, TIMOTHY BOGGESS, HENRY W.
BOGGESS and POLLY BOGGESS et al. The defendants, TIMOTHY BOGGESS,
HENRY W. BOGGESS and POLLY BOGGESS reside beyond the limits of the
state. TIMOTHY BOGGESS resides in St. Francis Co. Ark. (not there in
1850 Cen) and POLLY BOGGESS in the State of Texas. PETER KILFOYLE,
Register and master of said court. Substance of bill: Commissioners
Court of Roads and Revenue for Marshall Co. obtained license to keep a
public ferry across Tennessee River. That one JOHN S. BOGGESS and
RICHARD S. RANDLES had prior to that time kept a public ferry. That
JOHN S. BOGGESS has departed this life some time in the year 1842
leaving the following brothers and sisters his heirs at law towit:
JAMES BOGGESS (43 T) and ELIZABETH BOGGESS intermarried with ELI CAMPBELL
of Marshall Co. Ala., TIMOTHY BOGGESS who resides in St. Francis Co.
Ark., HENRY W. BOGGESS and POLLY BOGGESS who reside in Texas...
    State of Alabama--Madison Co. Orphan's Court. JAMES WALKER's
administrator versus JAMES WALKER's heirs. JOSEPH TAYLOR, administrator
of JAMES WALKER, late of said county deceased. Heirs: CYNTHIA wife
of HENRY THOMPSON, VIOLET ANN wife of SEABORN SULLIVAN, TAYLOR WALKER,
JANE wife of PHILIP J. ALLEN, NARTIN WALKER, WILLIAM W. WALKER, PORTER
WALKER, MINERVA wife of WILLIAM SALES, SARAH C. WALKER, ELIZABETH E. wife
of ROBERT SALES, MARY W. WALKER and JOHN M. WALKER, non resident heirs.
    Died near Somerville, Morgan County on Wednesday the 26th of March,
infant daughter of WILLIAM P. and MARY L. TERRY aged 3 months and 16
days.

April 7, 1847
    Married on 30th inst. by REV. JAMES C. ELLIOTT, MR. NATHANIEL G.
MINGES of Limestone Co. to MISS VIRGINIA DICKSON of Madison Co. (vol. 48
p. 19)

April 14, 1847
    ELIZABETH BELL, relict of the late THOMAS BELL of Limestone Co.
departed this life on 25 March 1847 Daughter of the late JAMES IRWIN
of East Tennessee. She was born January 5, 1784 in Pennsylvania. In
1802, she professed religion and joined the Presbyterian Church in
Blount County, Tennessee. In 1811 or 1812 she moved to Madison County,
Alabama where she united with the Cumberland Presbyterian Church at
Canaan In 1814, then under the care of REV. ROBERT DONNELL who had
organized a C. P. Church at that place... Slough Beat, Limestone Co.
March 29, 1847. (Signed by J. P. I.)
    Died suddenly on the 4th inst. RICHARD M., infant son of ROBERT
and JULIA J. HANCOCK of Madison Co. Ala. aged 7 months 17 days.
    (From Nashville Union, Mon. 27 Apr. 1841. Married at Clover Hill,
Franklin Co. Tenn on evening of 16 Apr., COL. ROBERT HANCOCK of Madison
Co. Ala. to MISS JULIETT JANE SHARP, dau of MAJ. RICHARD SHARP.)

April 21, 1847
    Died on the 9th inst. after a long and painful illness, COL.
EDMUND A. WEBSTER, a well known member of the legal profession in this
place and formerly a member of the Legislature and Secretary of State.
    Died off Tampico, Gulf of Mexico on the 7th of February last,
WILLIAM A. MICHIE, a native of Madison Co. Ala. in his 19th year...
    Departed this life, LIEUT. JOSEPHUS J. TATUM of CAPT. DELAY's
Company of Mississippi Volunteers, aged about 24 years, native of
Madison Co. Ala. where he became an artist under tutelage of his brother.
In the fall of 1845 or spring of 1847, he settled in Oxford, Miss....
In May, 1846 there he joined the Volunteers for the Mexican War...
Remembering the wrongs and sufferings inflicted on his brother while in
chains in castle of Perote whence he had but a short time been released,

he volunteered to avenge his brother's sufferings... He was taken sick
at Monterey where his physician ordered him to return home on furlough...
Since a battle was expected at Victoria, he refused to come home. At
this battle, he was attacked with pleurasy which with his former sickness
terminated in consumption of which he died at Linares on the 20th of
January.... Huntsville, Tuscumbia, Florence, Athens, Ala.; Holly
Springs, Columbus, Miss. and Nashville, Tenn. copy. (From Aberdeen,
Miss. Advertiser)

April 28, 1847
     Married by REV. PLEASANT B. ROBINSON in Huntsville, Ala. REV.
PLEASANT J. ECKLES to MISS MARTHA ISABELLA POWELL of Hillsboro, Illinois
(vo. 119 p. 5)

May 5, 1847
     Married on the 22nd inst. by REV. DAWSON PHELPS, MR. HUGH S. SMITH
to MISS ALSERENA T. ROBERTSON, daughter of WILLIAM H. ROBERTSON, Esq.
all of this county. (vol. 103 p. 65)
     Masonic Obituary:
     Resolutions on the death of DANIEL WHITMAN, Past master....
GEORGE D. NORRIS, Secretary of New Market Lodge #52.
     State of Alabama--32d. Chancery District
     NATHANIEL CLARDY & wife)
          versus   )
     SARAH MINOR & others   )
     Defendants ALBERT HIGH (30 in Virginia) & wife SARAH (35 in Virginia),
GOODWIN COLES & wife JOANNA COLES, THOMAS W. KENDRICK (43 Virginia,
1850) & wife FRANCES (26 V), and WILLIAM R. W. MINOR reside beyond the
limits of this state.... Bill states that WILLIAM MINOR died at his
residence in Madison County, Alabama about the month of June, 1844
intestate leaving a widow SARAH MINOR and REBECCA, DANIEL, SARAH, JOANNA
WHITE, FRANCES, WILLIAM R. W. and SALUDA ANN JANE, his children. The
will was admitted for probate. Said supposed will was dated at Halifax
Court House, Virginia on 16 November 1832. In said will, he gave all
of his estate to his widow during her natural life and on her marriage
she to have such part as the law entitled her to. Said will was afterwards revoked by said WILLIAM MINOR. Bill states that he wrote on the
same sheet of paper in the presence of said SARAH and several of his
children these words: "This is not my will" and signed his name
thereto; that since that time the half sheet containing the words of
cancellation has been torn off and that it was done by said WILLIAM
R. W. MINOR for fraudulent purposes of destroying the evidence of said
cancellation.
     (see Probate Minutes 31 p. 14; 1850 Census Limestone Co. Ala.
District 3 Family #57; KENDRICK, THOMAS 43 Va
                                 FRANCES 26 Va
                        MINOR,   SARAH 60 Va
                                 WM. 9 Va
                                 THORNTON 8 Va
                                 WILEY 6 Va
                                 NANCY 3 Va
                                 MARY 11/12 Ala)
     State of Alabama--Madison County--Orphan's Court--Feb. Term 1847
JESSE G. JORDAN   )
     versus   ) Petition for conveyance
JOHN R. B. ELDRIDGE)
     On petition of JESSE G. JORDAN to compel JOHN R. B. ELDRIDGE,
administrator with will annexed of MARIA A. THOMPSON, deceased, to make
title to said petitioner to certain land. In the last will and testament
of HENRY JORDAN, deceased, the land was bequeathed to said MARIA A.
THOMPSON, who was formerly MARIA A. JORDAN.

May 12, 1847
     Died of quinzy after a few hours illness at his residence in
Morgan County, Alabama 17th of April, WILLIAM F. BLANKENSHIP aged 37
years leaving a wife and 4 small children.
     Departed this life on 13th of February last, MRS. H. A. EDWARDS,
native of Madison County, Alabama. With her husband she emigrated to
Texas in 1838 where she died in her 28th year. She embraces religion in
the 12th year of her age. The Memphis Ark Copy.

May 19, 1847

Died in this county Friday the 14th inst. MARY BROOKS ROPER,
daughter of WILLIAM M. and MARY ANN ROPER aged 2 years 5 months and
19 days.

Died on April 27th of consumption in his 24th year, in New Orleans,
SAMUEL A. LYNES, son of GEORGE LYNES formerly of Huntsville. His remains
were attended to the Protestant burial grounds of Orleans by 5 lodges
of the Society of Odd Fellows. It was hoped that his sojourn from
Florida to New Orleans should have renovated his health....

May 26, 1847

Departed this life in Huntsville, Alabama on the 22nd instant,
MARY BRANDON, consort of COL. WILLIAM BRANDON in her 63rd year. The
deceased was born in Bucks County, Pennsylvania August 25, 1784 and
was among the earliest settlers in Huntsville... Embraced religion 26
years ago, and was a member of the Methodist Episcopal Church. Southern
Advocate and Christian Advocate, Nashville copy.

Died the 3rd of May at her residence in Chicot (he, not there in
1850) County, Arkansas in her 60th year, MRS. NANCY TAYLOR, wife of
JUDGE JOHN M. TAYLOR and daughter of the late WILLIAM FOOTE of Fauquier
County, Va.

Died on April 30th last at the residence of JAMES SHROCKS, Leake
Co. Miss., AMMON SANDERS, formerly of Jefferson Co. Ala.

Died in Austin Co. Texas in February last, WILLIAM B. HORTON,
son of JOHN B. HORTON of this county in his 27th year. Emigrated from
this county to Texas in 1839.

Died on the 18th in Lawrence County, Alabama, GEORGE T. SADLER,
old and much esteemed citizen.

Death seems to have made sad havoc in the family of ROBERT and
ELMIRA FREEMAN of the vicinity of Lowesville, this county. They have
lost three children whose deaths occurred within a few days of each
other. On the 15th inst. their son ALDIGONDA died aged 3 years 9 months
and 27 days. On the 16th, their son CLEMENT CLAY died aged 1 year 9
months and 4 days and on the 21st, ROBERT aged 7 years 6 months and 29
days died.

Died on the 1st inst. aged about 50 years, HON. JESSE SPEIGHT,
late U.S. Senator from Mississippi at his residence in Lowndes County,
Miss.

June 9, 1847

Married on the 1st inst. by P. B. ROBINSON, MR. JONATHON MAHEW to
MRS. ELIZA A. M. STRONG, all of Madison County. (vol. 48 p. 19)

Departed this life, MRS. NANCY H. SALE, wife of our esteemed
citizen, CAPT. DUDLEY SALE on May 1st in her 58th year. Native of
Elbert County, Georgia and has resided in this county to which CAPT. SALE
was among the first settlers since 1815. Professed religion in 1823
and belonged to the Methodist Episcopal Church. She lived to have her
husband and most or all of her children (6 of whom she left to mourn
her loss) to unite with the church.... J. W. A. Charleston Advocate
copy.

In Chancery Court at Huntsville, May Term 1847.
W. GRAVES BOULDIN
versus
JOSIAH W. MARSHALL et al.

The defendant, JOSIAH W. MARSHALL resides in Lincoln Co. Tenn.
Brief:

Bill states that the complainant recovered a judgement in the
Circuit Court of Madison Co. against JOSIAH W. MARSHALL on 23 October
1837. Said MARSHALL removed to Tennessee about the year 1837 and has
no effects in Alabama of which said judgment can be satisfied.

June 16, 1847

Departed this life in triumphs of Christina faith, MRS. ELIZABETH
A. C. PARKER of Trenton, Ala. (Jackson Co.) in her 38th year. Belonged
to the Cumberland Presbyterian Church several years, though she was
deaf and dumb. Left many friends, several children and her husband.

June 30, 1847
    In Chancery at Huntsville, May Term 1847
    WILLIAM PARKER
        versus
    JOHN W. OTEY, JAMES W. HOWARD et al.
    Defendant JAMES W. HOWARD resides in Tenn. county unknown.
    Brief:
    Bill states that complainant and JAMES W. HOWARD about 1 April 1837
formed a partnership under the firm name of PARKER and HOWARD for the
purpose of Buying and selling groceries. Partnership continued until
1839. Said HOWARD is one of the children and heirs at law of said
deceased (who?).

July 21, 1847
    Died in this county on the 7th inst. THOMAS L. MOON aged 22 years
and 16 days.

July 28, 1847
    Married Thursday evening the 22nd ult. by REV. JAMES C. ELLIOTT,
MR. WM. M. DERRICK to MISS JANE D. KENNEDY, all of this county. (Vol.
133 p. 22)
    Died in this place Friday evening the 23rd, WADDY TATE in his 20th
year. Had resided several years in the capacity of clerk in mercantile
establishments in our town. About 10 days before his decease, he was
seized with bilious fever....
    Died on the 24th inst. MRS. MOORE, wife of HUGH N. MOORE of this
place.

August 18, 1847
    Departed this life, RANSOM FOWLKES. Born in Nottoway County Virginia
October 9, 1798, emigrated to Madison Co. Ala. in 1817. Visited his
native state in 1818 at which time he was married to CYNTHIA L. HAMBLEN
of Prince Edward County, Virginia. Returned to Madison Co. Ala. in
autumn of that year where he resided until the morning of August 5,
1847 when he died, of dropsy of the chest.... Left his wife and children.
Banner of Peace, Lynchburg Virginian and Richmond Enquirer copy.
    Departed this life in Madison Co. of pulmonary consumption in the
67th year of her age, MRS. LYDIA BRAZELTON on June 22 last. She and
her husband were among the first settlers to this country. Raised a
large and respectable family of children, all of whom except one are
professors of religion and belong to the Cumberland Presbyterian Church...
Banner of Peace at Lebanon Tenn. copy.

August 25, 1847
    Departed this life August 12th at the residence of COL. BENJAMIN
HARRISON of Limestone County, MRS. MARY ANN HARRISON, wife of said
COL. BENJAMIN HARRISON in her 62nd year. Born in Brunswick County,
Virginia in 1786. She has been greatly afflicted for many years.
Has been a Methodist for many years. Was raised by religious parents.
Left her husband and children to mourn her loss. Petersburg and
Richmond Enquirer copy.
    Died in Huntsville on the 15th inst., MISS SARAH ANN GRAHAM,
lacking only 4 days to complete her 18th year....

September 1, 1847
    Married on the 19th inst. by REV. P. B. ROBINSON, MR. ALFRED ELLETT
to MRS. RACHEL O. CONNALLY (nee BEAL; she was widow of JOHN), all of
Madison Co. Ala. (vol. 119 p. 13)
    Married August 19th by REV. HENRY P. TURNER (vol. 100 p.11),
MR. RICHARD G(RAVES) BOULDIN to MISS MARY JANE CAPSHAW, all of Madison
Co. (dau of DAVID G. 22 Sept 1823, d 24 Dec. 1859; CAPSHAW by 2nd wife
MARY McCRACKEN he d 10 Feb. 1860)
    Married on the 25th by REV. JAMES C. ELLIOTT, MR. ROWLAND C.
STEWART of Mississippi to MISS VIRGINIA C., daughter of SAMUEL SMITHERS,
Esq. of this county. (vol. 103 p. 65)
    Died at his residence in Madison County on the night of August 10th
after 5 days illness, MR. RICHARD LIPSCOMB in his 47th year.... For
17 years a member of the Baptist Church.... Left wife and children.
Tennessee Baptist and papers in Richmond, Va. copy.

Departed this life on the 17th at his residence in Lauderdale County, JOHN DONOHO, Esq. Was once a citizen of Huntsville, but for the last 25 or 30 years has been a resident of the county in which he died. Was born in East Tennessee (to PP) in 1785 and died after a lingering illness....

Died of paralysis on 21st of August last at his residence in Madison Co. Ala. WILLIAM EAST aged 71 years 5 months and 29 days. Born in Halifax Co. Va. February 23, 1776, emigrated from that state to Middle Tennessee in 1808 and thence to this county in 1809 where he resided until his death. Raised a large family.... Richmond and Petersburg Va. papers and Nashville, Tenn. copy.

September 8, 1847
Married in Slough Beat, Limestone County, Alabama Thursday evening at 4 o'clock by REV. JAMES C. ELLIOTT, MR. WILLIAM H. MOORE (43 V), formerly of Sussex County, Virginia (vol. 187 p. 81) to MISS RUTH LODUSKIA LEWIS (23 A), formerly of Madison Co. Ala.

At the residence of MR. A. H. FORD near this place on Wednesday morning, 1st instant by REV. S. S. MOODY, DR. WILLIAM W. HUMPHRIES of Columbus, Miss. to MISS REBECCA ANN JONES, daughter of CAPT. FRILEY JONES (vol. 147 p. 582; vol.86 p. 30)

Suicided in Goldsboro, N.C. R. A. HARRISON, just arrived from Tuscaloosa, Ala. It was supposed he had delirium tremens as he acted queer.

September 15, 1847
Married Thursday evening last by REV. P. B. ROBINSON, COL. JOHN TROUP (41 SC) of Morgan County to MISS ELIZABETH J. E. FENNELL (32 A) of Madison Co. (vol. 151, p. 26)

Departed this life on the 4th ult. MARY GEE, only child of JOEL W. and MARTHA C. JONES aged 2 years and 16 days.

Departed this life August 31st at the residence of her brother-in-law, MR. JOSEPH HOBBS of Huntsville, MRS. FRANCES LEONARD, consort of MR. THOMAS D. LEONARD after a week's illness. Born in Pittsylvania Co. Va. When quite young she left her native state and removed with her brother in law, MR. THOMAS MARTIN, to Madison Co. Ala. where she resided until 1846 when she removed to Lawrence Co. Ala. with her husband and was on a visit to Huntsville to see her relatives when she died.... Baptist.... Left her husband and 3 small children to mourn her loss. Thus died FRANCES, daughter of WILLIAM H. IRBY. Tenn. Baptist and papers in Richmond copy.

October 27, 1847
Died on March 15, 1847 at her residence in Madison Co., MARY BEVILL in her 84th year and on the 20th of September 1847, EDWARD BEVILL, SEN., her husband, died at the same place in his 88th year. They emigrated from Virginia to Mecklenburg Co. N.C. about 1805 and from there to this county about 1823. EDWARD BEVILL, SR. was a Revolutionary soldier and drew a pension at the time of his death....

December 15, 1847
State of Alabama--Madison County. Orphan's Court.
November Term, 1847.
SARAH LIGHTFOOT and MARY WESTMORELAND)
      versus   ) Petition to sell land
CLAXTON LIGHTFOOT, ex'r.)
Petition of SARAH LIGHTFOOT and MARY WESTMORELAND, two of the heirs of CLACKSTON LIGHTFOOT, deceased for sale of land. REBECCA, wife of HARRISON HARTWELL, heir of CLACKSTON LIGHTFOOT, deceased, is a non-resident.

February 9, 1848 (papers between Dec. 15 and Feb. 9 missing)
Died at his residence in Madison Co. Ala. on the 28th inst. MR. MARCUS LAFAYETTE HIGH in about his 65th year, of pneumonia, leaving his widow and 7 children. Native of Wake County, North Carolina and moved to Madison Co. Ala. in the fall of 1843, where he resided until his death. The deceased served 12 months in the service of his country under ANDREW JACKSON in the Indian Wars and is believed to be a true patriot.... Raleigh, N.C. papers copy.

February 16, 1848
    Married on ---- inst. by REV. P. B. ROBINSON, MR. NATHANIEL MOON
to MISS SUSAN A. H. CULP of Huntsville. (vol. 48 p. 19)
    Departed this life on Wednesday morning, 2nd inst. at her residence
in Limestone County, MISS LOUISA COLEQUIT KEY in her 51st year. A
lady of smooth disposition.... Member of Methodist Episcopal Church
South....

January 12, 1848
    Died at his residence near this village Sunday morning, December
26th in the 49th year of his age, MR. CALEB TONEY.... Left a wife and
5 children. Triana, Ala. Jan. 1, 1848.
    Died near Huntsville on the evening of the 25th of December, 1847,
RODERICK GRAVETTE aged 39 years 9 months and 10 days. Born in Virginia
March 15, 1808 but was principally raised in Madison County, Alabama
where he left many friends, relatives, an affectionate wife and 8 little
children....

January 19, 1848
    Married December 23rd by REV. JAMES C. ELLIOTT, MR. ROBERT M. PRUIT
of Madison Co. Ala. to MISS MARGARET J. CONNOR of Noxubee Co. Miss.

January 26, 1848
    Married on the 16th inst. by REV. D. K. HUNTER, DR. A. S. (ANDREW G.
in Cen; 28 A) PICKENS of Warrenton, Marshall Co. to MISS S(USAN) R.
WRIGHT (21 A) of Madison Co.
    On the 12th inst. by REV. G. A. COLLIER, MR. L(EONARD) F(ITE)
LAMBERSON to MISS F(RANCES) C(ATHERINE) PICKENS, all of Madison Co.
(vol. 155 p. 27)
    On the 20th ult. by REV. P. B. ROBINSON, MR. JAMES H. GREGORY to
MISS INDIANA I. (J?) RUTHERFORD, all of Madison Co. (vol. 127 p. 2?)
    Death of a Soldier:
A soldier by name of REUBEN McCANE belonging to CAPT. H. L. CLAY's
Company, died in this place Tuesday the 28th inst. Brought to this
place on a steamer, seriously indisposed and died on the bridge as he
was being removed for medical aid. From papers in his possession, we
learn he was a private in CAPT. CLAY's company, that he was honorably
discharged at Vera Cruz on December 2 by reason of surgeon's certificate--
inability. It furthermore appeared from his discharge that he was about
25 years of age and was born in Clarke County, Georgia. He was decently
buried by our citizens. (From Florence Gazette)

March 22, 1848
    Married on the 7th inst. by REV. DR. SULLIVAN, J(AMES) A. FINDLEY,
M.D. of Marshall Co. to MISS MARY ELIZABETH, daughter of REV. JOHN H.
HAMER of Madison Co. Ala. (vol. 122 p. 8)
    Departed this life on the 18th, COL. WILLIAM BRANDON in his 60th
year. In 1810, the deceased emigrated from Tennessee to this state and
became a resident of Huntsville, where he resided for more than 30
years. Amassed a large amount of the world's goods.... Methodist
Episcopal Church. Left a large circle of friends and children.
Nashville Christian Advocate copy.

March 29, 1848
    Married Thursday March 16th by REV. PROF. PENTLAND of La Grange
College, DR. J. M. CONNER of Tuscumbia, Ala. to MISS MINERVA BIRD of
Lawrence Co. Ala. (Franklin Democrat) (m. in Lawrence Co.)
    Died Friday the 3rd inst. at the residence of her husband in this
county, MRS. ANN V. HAMMOND, daughter of MR. FRANCIS BLACKBURN and wife
of MAJ. FERDINAND L. HAMMOND. Afflicted many weeks with a most painful
disease.... Devoted wife and mother. Tuscaloosa and Houston (Tex.)
papers copy.

November 18, 1857
    State of Alabama--Madison Co. ROBERT D. WILSON, next friend of
HOUSTON LEE BELL and CHARLOTTE BELL, infant children of FRANCIS BELL
late of said county, deceased. Will named the following persons, grandchildren and heirs, towit: WILLIAM BELL, SARAH BELL (a lunatic),
JOSHUA BELL, SUSAN WILKINS wife of WILLIAM WILKINS (THOMAS in Vol. 100),

formerly SUSAN BELL, DUDLEY BELL, MARTIN BELL, MARY BELL and HARDY BELL,
children of TYRUS BELL, deceased, son of deceased, who died in his
father's lifetime. They reside beyond the limits of the state--
towit in Miss.

May 7, 1858
Married at the residence of bride's father in Chickasaw Co. Miss.
on Tue. 12 Apr. inst. by REV. MR. JONES, JOHN CURRY, Esq. of Tuscumbia
to MISS MARY A. daughter of JOHN J. THOMPSON, Esq.
Married in Russellville on eve. of 21st by REV. MR. MULLONS,
MR. JAMES HANCOCK of Florence to MISS PAULINE, daughter of COL. N. R.
LADD of the former place.
Married on Tue. morning the 20th by REV. R. H. RIVERS, D.D.,
HON. JAMES H. TRIMBLE, Judge of Franklin Co. to MISS ANN S. daughter
of JOHN W. HARRIS, SR., Esq. of Russell Valley.

July 14, 1858
State of Alabama--Morgan Co. Probate Court. 30 June 1858.
JAMES FORD, administrator of JOHN McDANIEL (78 Scot) SR., deceased.
State of Alabama--Morgan Co. Probate Court. June 26, 1858.
CHARLES W. PRICE, executor of MARY ANN E. NEVILL, deceased.
Died on 10 July 1858 MRS. MARION SHELBY, widow of the late JUDGE
ANTHONY B. SHELBY at the residence of her son, DR. DAVID SHELBY in
Madison Co. Ala. Brandon, Miss. and Gallatin, Tenn. papers copy.
Ala. Items:
CHARLES G. EDWARDS (45 NY), a distinguished lawyer of Dallas Co.
Ala. died in the city of New York on 17th the day after his return from
Europe whither he went with his wife in 1856 in pursuit of health.
Ill health had caused his retirement from the bar. He was a descendant
of REV. JONATHON EDWARDS, the distinguished Presbyterian divine. He
represented Dallas Co. in the State Legislature about 1848.

August 4, 1858
State of Alabama--Morgan Co. Probate Court. Estate of THOMAS
NeSMITH (47 SC), deceased.
Obituary:
Died, MRS. SARAH ELIZA BINFORD (30 A), wife of DR. HENRY A. BINFORD
(38 NC) of this place and daughter of COL. THOMAS BRANDON of Aberdeen,
Miss. MRS. BINFORD was born in Huntsville May 26th, 1829 and died
July 19, 1858.... Leaves husband and affectionate children.
Died near McKinley in Marengo Co. Ala. Tue. 13 July, COL. HENRY KING
aged 64 years. The deceased was a native of North Carolina but early
removed to Madison Co. Ala. Upon the breaking out of the War of 1812
he enlisted as a private in the ranks of GEN. JACKSON's army and was
with the old hero at the celebrated battle of New Orleans. He returned
to his home not long, however, to enjoy retirement for his fellow citizens
soon elected him, as one of the members of the Electoral ticket for the
State at large during JACKSON's first Presidential campaign. With a
well balanced mind and a vigorous intellect, he inflicted stalwart
blows upon the opposition, and did much to secure for old Hickory a
glorious victory. He was nine consecutive sessions a member of the
State Legislature from Madison Co. and was ranked as one of its most
efficient members. Here his political career ended, the filthy pool of
politics had and for him no charms and the remainder of his life was
devoted to agricultural pursuits. He remained unwaveringly attached to
the cause of Democracy and always exercised the privilege of the
elective franchise. He was a warm friend, with a heart ever open and
ready to afford assistance to the needy. (Poem)

September 8, 1858
State of Alabama--Morgan Co. EDWIN S. PRICE, deceased. W. PRICE,
adm'r.
Married Aug. 26, 1858 by REV. N. T. POWER, MR. W(ILSON) S. McDAVID
of Noxubee Co. Miss. and MISS NANNIE J. daughter of WILEY THOMPSON
(53 NC), Esq. of this co.
Died on 4th CLARENCE HERBERT, son of J. WITHERS and MARY F. L. CLAY
aged 22 months and 29 days. Baptized into Church of Christ.
Died at mother's residence in this county Aug. 15, 1858, MARY ANNA
MAYHEW, daughter of the late ZACHARIAH (deceased) and ELVIRA MAYHEW aged
19 years 2 months.

Died at mother's residence in this county Aug. 22, 1858, FRANCIS GREENVILLE McCAAX (MARY; 4 A) aged about 13 years.

January 19, 1859
Married on 5th by REV. R. P. RIDDLE, GEO. G. THOMPSON to MISS HARRIET A. RAY, all of Limestone Co.
Married on 9th by REV. JAMES C. ELLIOTT, JOSEPH J. ADAMS to MISS ALMYRA A. L. MALONE all of Limestone Co.
Married in Fayetteville, Tenn. on 30th by J. T. GORDON, Esq., JOHN MINGEA to MISS MARGARET V. GRIZZARD.

October 11, 1859
Married on 22nd by REV. W. D. CHADICK, MR. ZACHARIAH N. DRAKE (21 A; ELIJAH & ELIZ.) to MRS. ROSANNAH SHANNON--all of Madison Co.
Married on 2nd by DICKSON COBB, Esq., MR. JOSEPH CLARKSTON (15 A; DAVID) to MRS. SUSANNAH HERRON--all of Madison Co. (vol. 141 p. 66)
Married on 22 September by elder G. A. MORRING, MR. L. W. TAYLOR to MISS MARTHA M. DAVIS--all of Jackson Co.
Died on 26th by R. B. ELGIN, Esq. at residence of MRS. WITCHER, MR. THOMAS DORS of Autauga Co. Ala. to MISS ANGERONE DERRICK (13 A) of Marshall Co.

November 16, 1859
Nothing

November 23, 1859
Married on 16th by JUDGE J. H. SCURGGS, MR. B. W. BLAKE to MISS SARAH R. M. HAIL (mar rec 4-B says SARAH R. M. HALL) both of Huntsville.
Died on 9th, MRS. MARTHA ROBINSON, wife of JOHN H. ROBINSON of Madison Co.

December 7, 1859
Married in Somerville on 23rd by REV. H. M. WELCH, MR. F. M. BROWN to MISS N. J. McKEE, all of that place.
Married on 3rd inst. in Conway Co. Ark. by REV. W. C. STOUT, DR. P. O. HOOPER of Little Rock and MISS GEORGE, daughter of COL. G. W. CARROLL.
Married on 24th in Decatur, by REV. J. A. EDMONDSON, MR. H. R. CRAWFORD, formerly of Bellefonte and MISS MARTHA E. DRAIN of Decatur.
Married on 28th by E. R. HANES, J.P., MR. J. M. STRICKLIN to MISS MARTHA BARNS, all of Blount Co. (Blount Co. WPA mar show WM. STRICKLIN m. MATILDA BARNS same date as above 11-28-59. 1860 Cen shows 1 W. STRICKLAND 27 H; Martha 25 La & 1 J M 31 T ELIZ 27 A)
Married on Tue. 29th Nov. by WILEY W. IRWIN, Esq., MR. JOHN T. RENFRO and MISS NANCY M. A. SWISHER, all of Jackson Co. Ala.
Married on Thursday Nov. 24 near Columbus, Ga. by REV. C. C. WILLIS, MR. J. A. WILLIAMS of Stevenson, Ala. to MISS MOLLIE R. DAVIS.
Died on Sunday morning December 4 after a lingering illness, MISS SUE WELLS PATTESON (13 A), eldest daughter of GEN. BENJAMIN PATTESON of this vicinity.

December 14, 1859
Married on 31 by REV. P. B. ROBINSON, MR. BENJAMIN R. NANCE to MISS REBECCA M(ASON) WILLBURN (SALLY M.; 18 A) all of this co.
Married on Thursday the 1st by REV. W. D. CHADICK at residence of the bride's mother, at Woodville, Jackson Co. Ala. DR. THOMAS A. WRIGHT to MISS CHARLOTTE F. DILLARD--all of Jackson Co.
Died on 7th of pneumonia near Madison Station, MISS MOLLIE BLACKBURN. She was a pupil of Huntsville Female College.
Died in Athens, on Monday last the 5th, MRS. ELIZA J. N. ALLEN aged about 40 years.
Died on the 7th, JOHN GARNER, an old and respected citizen of this county. Native of Virginia and moved to this county in 1818. Leaves many friends to mourn his loss.
Died in Moulton 23 November at 11 o'clock, A.M., MRS. MARY G. BOYD (55 NC) aged 65 years 6 months 10 days. Typhoid fever. (widow of WILLIAM)

December 21, 1859
Married in Jackson Co. on 14th by REV. MR. GRUBBS, MR. GEORGE M. HARRISON of Germantown (Shelby Co.), Tenn. to MISS B. E. HARRIS of Jackson, Ala.

Married on 13th by REV. S. D. HUNTER, D. S. NOWLIN, Esq. of
Marshall Co. Ala. to MISS EMILY NICHOLSON of DeKalb, Ala.

Married at the residence of the bride's father near Mt. Hope,
Lawrence Co. Ala., by REV. DR. A. McCORD, REV. JAMES HENRY PATTERSON
to MISS FLORA ELLA BRIGGS.

Married on Sunday morning last, by REV. W. G. HENSLEY, MR. WM.
BULLINGTON to MISS ANNA IRVING, all of Athens.

Married at Spring Creek, Coffee Co. Tenn. on 20 Oct. 1859 by
H. W. CARROLL, JAS. WALKER aged 78 years to SARAH MATTHEWS aged 84
years.

Died at her residence in Hickman Co. Tenn. on 5th, MRS. DOLLY
GORDON, relative of JOHN GORDON, deceased, Captain of Spies in 1812-14
in the Creek War under GEN. JACKSON aged 83 years.

December 28, 1859

Married in Franklin Co. Ala. on 11th by REV. MR. ABERNATHY, MR.
JAMES C. HOOKER and MISS FRANCIS J. WALLACE.

Married on 15th by same, MR. JOSEPH B. BRITNELL and MISS SUSANNA F.
RICHESON.

Married Dec. 21, 1859 by REV. F. A. ROSS, D.D., B. M. LOWE, JR.
of firm of B. M. LOWE & Co. New Orleans, and MISS FANNIE (12 A), daughter
of BENJAMIN JOLLEY (40 V), Esq. of Huntsville, Ala.

Married on 20th near Whitesburg by REV. J. W. MORRIS, MR. LOUIS J.
ROSS and MISS E. A. JONES, both of Madison Co.

Married near Petersburg (Lincoln Co.), Tenn. on 13th by REV. W. A.
GILL, MR. W. T. GILL to MISS MOLLIE F. LLOYD of Huntsville.

Married on 14th near Petersburg (Lincoln Co.), Tenn. by same,
MR. C. A. GILL to MISS MARTHA A. LLOYD, both of this place.

Married on 6th at residence of MR. SIMS SMITH, by G. L. BRINDLEY,
J.P., MR. H. J. CHANDLER to MRS. SARAH A. WAITS of Blount Co.

January 4, 1860

Married, on 22nd December, in Decatur by REV. J. A. EDMONDSON,
MR. D. A. RAMSEY, conductor on the M & C R R to MISS MOLLIE CRAFT,
of Jonesboro, Ala.

On December 22nd by the REV. E. STRODE, MR. HENRY F. HALSEY to
MRS. CATHERINE G. SMITH, all of Huntsville.

On December 13th (15th in Bible record) by REV. MR. IRWIN, MR.
WILLIAM S. (J) BARRY (BERRY?; 12 A, SAM'L G) to MISS SARAH R(EBECCA)
JONES (10 A), all of Madison County.

Died, on January 2nd, PATTON BRADFORD (12 A), eldest son of MRS.
JOSEPH G. (B) BRADFORD (45 V) of Huntsville--young man.

Departed this life on Tuesday, December 27th BENJAMIN S. POPE
(66 Del) aged 77 years. MR. POPE was a native of Delaware and in early
youth engaged in commercial pursuits in Savannah, Georgia, whence he
removed to this county in 1815, where he remained a planter until his
death. During twelve years of this time he was Register of the Land
Office for the Huntsville District. How sorely must the husband and
father be missed. He died away from home, but not among strangers. At
the residence of his son, DR. CHARLES A. POPE of St. Louis he breathed
his last.

Died, December 16th, in Huntsville, MARY LEA, infant daughter of
MRS. LAVINIA VINCENT.

January 11, 1860

Married, on the 28th of December at the residence of DAVID GARDINER
(40 SC) in Whitesburg, Ala. by REV. ALEXANDER PENLAND, MR. D. W. PARKER
to MISS ELIZABETH J. GARDINER (13 A).

On the 28th of December, at the residence of DAVID GARDINER in
Whitesburg, Ala. by the REV. ALEXANDER PENLAND, MR. DAVID S. BLACK to
MISS MARY A. CHUNN (6 A).

On the 3rd instant by REV. J. G. WILSON, RAWLEY CARTER, Esq. to
MISS MARY S. HARRELL, all of Madison County.

On December 31st by REV. MR. HUMPHREY, MR. R. C. TUCKER of Memphis,
Tennessee to MISS E. A. WEATHERFORD of Limestone County (sent to Jean).

On December 30th by REV. G. W. MITCHELL, DR. JOHN R. HOFFMAN to
MISS FRANCES C(AROLINE) JONES (10 A), daughter of MR. HAMILTON JONES
(55 V), all of Limestone County. (sent to Jean)

On the 3rd instant by REV. W. D. CHADICK, MR. WILLIAM RAFORD of Nashville to MISS NELLIE E. BARRON of Rochester, New York.

On December 22nd by DICKSON COBB Esq., WILLIAM EVANS to MISS SARAH J. RANDALS (12 A; THOS), both of this county.

Obituary: DR. A. R. ERWIN, D.D., member of the Tennessee Conference, Methodist Episcopal Church South and President of the Huntsville Female College died of consumption at his residence in this place yesterday morning about 9 1/4 o'clock. He was a native of Louisiana. Had he lived, he would have been 40 years old tomorrow.

January 25, 1860

Land for Sale. Having purchased lands West and decided to move my hands there--plantation on Triana Road. WM. MATKIN

Married, on the 18th instant by the REV. THOMAS MADDEN, D.D., MR. W. J. LAWLER to MISS OCTAVIA WYCHE, daughter of JOHN BYRNE, all of Maysville, Ala.

On the 15th instant by the REV. G. W. MITCHELL, MR. J. HURD to MISS NANCY J. WILLIAMS, all of Athens, Ala. (sent to Jean)

On the 15th instant, by the REV. A. D. McCORD, MR. GEORGE W. HURLEY to MISS LUCY A. NOLEN, both of Franklin Co. Ala.

On the 15th instant by ELDER J. C. ROBERTS, MR. SIMEON D. SIMMS (24 A) to MISS MARTHA E. HEFLIN (20 A; JOS P.) all of Lawrence County Ala.

In Morgan County at the residence of REV. T. A. STRAIN on the 18th, by REV. S. E. RANDOLPH, MR. J. LAWSON GILL (18 T; DAN'L) to MISS ISABELLA H. HODGES, all of that county.

On the 15th instant by REV. J. J. BURDINE, MR. JOHN C. FOWLER to MISS LOUISA A. SHARP, all of this county.

Died on the 18th, very suddenly at the McCartney Hotel in Decatur, MRS. ANN N., consort of MAJ. WM. DeWOODY, in the 60th year of her age.

At his residence in Giles County, Tenn (sent to JEAN SMITH) on the 3rd of January, JOHN WATKINS, aged 104 years, 2 months, 8 days.

On the 15th instant MR. THOMAS L. MOON (44 T) aged about 55 years, of Madison County.

February 1, 1860

Married, on the 25th instant by REV. E. STRODE, MR. J. W. P. KELLY to MISS CORNELIA W. (7 A), 3rd daughter of JOSHUA H. BEADLES (37 T), Esq. all of Huntsville.

On the 27th instant by REV. DR. ROSS, HENRY C(LAY) SPEAKE, Esq. of Decatur, Ala. to MISS CARRIE O. MAYHEW, of the Huntsville Female Seminary.

On the 8th instant in Cripple Deer, Miss. by JOHN M. THOMPSON, Esq. COL. JAMES H. THOMPSON of Iuka, Miss. to MRS. MARY JANE DERRICK, of the former place, late of Alabama.

Died, in Jefferson County, Arkansas, in Pine Bluff, MRS. LAVENIA C. TWEEDY (35 T), wife of the late JOSEPH M. TWEEDY (44 V) of Lawrence County, Ala.

In Marshall County, Alabama on the 17th instant COL. ALEXANDER GILBREATH in his 80th year (68 V). (We have tombstone--b. Aug. 26, 1778 d Jan. 17, 1860--buried in Cox County, Rt. 1, Guntersville, Ala.)

February 8, 1860

Married, on Thursday, second instant at 5 p.m. in the Church of the Nativity, Huntsville, by RT. REV. N. H. COBBS, D.D., REV. ANASTASIUS MENACOS of Claiborne, Ala. to MISS MARIA WITHERS of Huntsville.

On the 16th ult. by REV. P. M. MUSGROVE, MR. ROBERT I. CHAMBLEE to MISS LOUVICY CALLAHAN, all of Blount County.

On the 29th ult, by E. R. HANES, J.P., MR. MILTON A. ROBINS to MISS MILDY HOLLY, all of Blount County.

On the 2nd instant by REV. MR. MOONEY, MR. JAMES H. McCAMPBELL of this place to MISS ANN HEARN of New York.

On the 1st instant by REV. W. D. CHADICK, CPT. JOHN T. PATTERSON to MISS MARY ANN (18 A), daughter of DAVID T. KNOX (56 Del), Esq. both of this place.

On the 26th instant by REV. G. W. HENSLEY in Giles County, Tenn. MR. JAMES M. ROGERS to MRS. DOROTHY WHITE, daughter of HENRY HOLT (his wife was DOROTHY; 50 NC), Esq., all of Limestone Co. (sent to JEAN)

Died, on the 20th, suddenly, MRS. EDITH (69 NC) SCRUGGS, mother of MRS. O. D. SLEDGE, of this place, in her 80th year.

On the 4th instant JOHN H. McCRAVEY (should be McCRARY; 12 A), son of MR. BENJAMIN McCRAVEY (45 G) of this place.

In Decatur, Alabama on the 3rd instant, MRS. ELIZA ALLEN LOCKE (48 V), aged 58 years.

February 22, 1860

Married, in Somerville, Ala. on the 9th instant by HON. GREEN P. RICE, Judge of the Probate Court, MR. THOMIS C. WELCH (13 A; CHRISTOPHER A.) to MISS MARY C. FOWLER (8A; JOHN), all of that place.

On the 9th instant in Rogersville, Ala. by D. W. HARAWAY, Esq., MR. FELIX TROUSDALE to MISS MARTHA J. WEAVER.

At the WORSHAM House, on the 16th instant by REV. DR. DAVIS, MR. C. C. DUBOSE of LaFayette Co., Ark., to MISS LUCY A. FREEMAN of Glenville, Ala.

On the 15th instant by REV. S. M. CHERRY, MR. JAMES N. FARLEY of Moulton to MISS ESTHER A. DINAMORE (10 A; DAVID S.) of the same vicinity.

Died, in Coffeeville, Clarke County, Alabama on the 14th instant MRS. ELIZABETH WALKER FIGURES (63 G; Clarke Co--daughter of THOS & ELIZ (WALKER) COLEMAN), wife of MAJOR THOMAS FIGURES (63 NC) and mother of the Editor of the Southern Advocate, in the 74th year of her age. She was a member of the Baptist Church. Her aged companion through a lifelong pilgrimage, eventful and arduous, lingers disconsolate, and her children and descendants will revere her memory.

February 29, 1860

Married, in Philadelphia on February 8th by the REV. J. WHEATON SMITH, MR. JOSEPH E. YOUNG of Huntsville, Alabama to MISS LIZZIE BURGIN of Philadelphia.

By REV. W. G. HENSLEY on the 16th instant MR. J. D. FLANAGAN to MISS MARY E. HENDERSON, all of Limestone County. (sent to Jean)

On the 15th instant by REV. G. W. MITCHELL, REV. JAMES B. LENTZ and MISS MARTHA W. SMITH, all of Limestone County. (sent to Jean)

In Somerville, Ala. on the 15th instant by REV. H. M. WELCH, MR. W. C. TRAVIS (Printer's devil) to MISS MARY V. SHARP, all of that place.

In Nashville on the 22nd instant by REV. DR. A. L. P. GREEN, MR. JOHN L. RISOM (11 A; ARCH'D) of Huntsville, Ala. to MISS TENNIE ERWIN, daughter of the late REV. A. R. ERWIN of this place.

On the 21st instant by J. F. ELLIS, Esq. MR. CHAS. W. HOLLOWAY, to MISS SARAH J. HOLLOWAY (18 A), daughter of REV. JOSEPH H. HOLLOWAY (52 V), all of this county.

Died in Huntsville, February 17th, of consumption, MRS. E. A. ERWIN, wife of J. A. ERWIN, in the 37th year of her age--member of the Cumberland Presbyterian Church.

Suddenly, in Arkansas on the 21st instant MRS. AGNES T. KINKLE (20 A), aged about 30 years.

March 14, 1860

Married, on the 1st instant by A. R. CRAWFORD, Esq., MR. ISAAC HAMBY to MISS SUSAN C. THROWER (15 A: SION) of Limestone County. (sent to Jean)

In Tuscumbia on the 2nd instant by JOHN N. GREEN, Esq., MR. EDWARD E. MURPHY to MISS MARY ROBINSON, all of Lauderdale County.

Died, on Monday, March 12th, MRS. MARTHA EASON (32 V, d of WM. POWERS; m. 1835), wife of ALOUIN EASON (37 NC) of the vicinity of Huntsville.

On the 6th instant MRS. FRANCES LANDMAN (72 Va), mother of MRS. J. H. BEADLE of this place, in the 87th year of her age--Methodist. (tombstone b 1773 Campbell Co. Va., d Mar. 7, 1860; DOROTHY JOHNSON says she was FRANCES LOUISE MOORE; she was wid of WM. LANDMAN--see his will & Minor's Reports).

In Limestone County on the 3rd instant, JAMES F. JOHNSTON (51 G), aged 61.

On the 1st instant, HALEY DUPREE of the same county, aged 70 years.

On the 5th instant, MRS. CATHERINE R. J. GOODWIN, wife of THOMAS GOODWIN, aged 20 years, of the same county.

March 21, 1860
        Married, on the 9th of March, 1860 by E. C. WILLIAMS, Esq.,
MR. W. M. SKELTON to MISS S. H. WILLIAMSON, daughter of MR. R. A. WILLIAMSON,
all of Jackson County.
        Died, on the 10th instant at the residence of his son in law
JUDGE C(HRISTOPHER) C. GEWIN (39 NC; he m. 2 of WM. BOYD'S daus - w in
1850, was artimacy @ 21 A), CAPT. WILLIAM BOYD (53 SC) of Moulton in the
64th year of his age.

March 28, 1860
        Married, in Athens, Ala. on the 23rd instant by REV. J. R. PLUMMER,
ARTHUR W. ROBINSON, Esq. of Huntsville to MISS REBECCA O. WILBURN (12 A)
of Athens.
        On the 21st instant, CHARLES J. TIPTON and MISS MARGARET A. MORROW,
both of this county.
        On the 15th instant by REV. W. MOONEY, REV. Z. PARKER of the Ten-
nessee Conference to MRS. LOUISA SANDERS, all of this county.
        On the 13th instant by REV. E. STRODE, MR. T. J. ROBERTSON to
MISS MARY J. NORTHCUT (24 A; MARTHA (PEARSON) & GIDEON NORTHCUT), both
of this place.
        In Florence, Alabama on the 20th ult. by the REV. J. H. WEAVER,
MR. POWEL W. WILLIAMS of Huntsville, Ala. to MISS ELIZABETH BUTLER of
Florence.
        Died, on the 23rd instant, MR. HENRY C. CLARKE of the firm of
SPIVEY & CLARKE of Memphis, formerly of Huntsville, aged 27 years.

April 4, 1860
        Died, on the 2nd instant, after a short illness, DR. JOHN D. BARNARD
of this place.
        In Limestone County on the 26th ult. MISS REBECCA N. ELLIOTT,
aged 20 years.

April 11, 1860
        Married on the 5th instant by REV. R. M. HUMPHREY, MR. BARNETT
KING to MISS LUCINDA HOLBROOKS, all of Morgan County.
        In Fayetteville, Tenn. Friday the 30th ult. by REV. M. B. DeWITT,
MR. JOHN L. CLARK to MISS JULIA M. O'NEAL, both of this place.
        Died on March 28th at the residence of her mother MRS. HANNAH McBROOM
in Ash Cove, Madison County, Ala. MRS. NANCY M. SPINEY who leaves a
large family to mourn her loss. (Bible record shows NANCY M. SPIVEY
(28 A) (daughter of STEPHEN and HANNAH McBROOM) died March 28, 1860,
K. P. J.)
        In Limestone County on Friday last MR. JAMES BRANDON (27 T) aged
about 36.
        On the 3rd ult. JAMES LATTY (90 V), an old citizen of this county
in the 102nd year of his age. He was a native of North Carolina but had
lived on the headwaters of Brier Fork for two generations. He volunteered in the Revolutionary War, but his father being in a helpless
condition, furnished means for a substitute for his son.

April 18, 1860
        Married, at the Church of the Nativity in this place on the 7th
instant by REV. R. H. COBBS, MR. JOSEPH W. KEIL and MISS LOUISA PLATT.
        On the 10th instant by REV. ALEXANDER PENLAND, MR. H. W. GRANTLAND
and MISS LIZZIE EDWARDS, both of Triana.
        On the 5th instant by REV. R. M. HUMPHREY, MR. BARNETT KING to
MISS LICINDA HOLBROOKS, both of Morgan County.

April 25, 1860
        Married on the 19th instant by REV. J. A. EDMONDSON at the residence
of CAPT. MAT TODDS in Decatur, MR. GEORGE W. JOHNSON of the M & C RR
to MISS VIRGINIA A. PARKER (12 A; ELIZA) of Decatur.
        On the 19th instant by REV. DR. ROSS, MR. JAMES P. ASHFORD of
Mississippi to MISS CATTIE (CATHERINE J.) J. BRADFORD (14 A; JOS. B.)
of Huntsville.
        Died, at his residence in Huntsville on the 20th instant, MR. MARTIN
MILLER (70 Pa) at the advanced age of 80 years.

May 2, 1860
    Married on the 24th ult. by REV. W. D. CHADICK, MR. J. H. KELLY to
MISS VURGINIA A., daughter of GEN. JOHN N. DRAKE, all of this county.
    Died, suddenly, of disease of the heart on the 9th ult., at his
residence near Madison Cross Roads, MR. JOHN BAYLESS (70 V) in the 80th
year of his age. MR. B. came from Washington County, East Tennessee
to this county about the year 1810, where he has resided ever since...
consistent member of the Baptist Church...left widow and large family
of children.
    At the residence of her husband in Huntsville at 2 o'clock on the
morning of the 1st of May, MRS. PALMYRA JANE COLEMAN, wife of JOHN J.
COLEMAN, Esq. in the 38th year of her age.

May 9, 1860
    Married on the 1st instant at the residence of J. W. HOLT by
MR. ROBERT P. RIDDLE, MR. N. J. MEADOWS to MISS MARY F. HOLT, all of
Limestone County.
    On the 3rd instant at the residence of the bride's father, COL. C. W.
PRICE, by REV. DR. E. SAMMS, REV. R. M. HUMPHREY to MISS MATTIE A. PRICE
(10 A; CHAS W.), all of Morgan County.
    Died last night, suddenly, MR. WILLIAM WEAVER (43 T), a well known
cabinet maker of this place, aged 53 years.

May 23, 1860
    Married on the 9th instant by REV. THOMAS J. DAVIDSON, HON. ALBURTO
MARTIN to MISS HARRIET L., daughter of HON. WM. S. MUDD, all of Elyton.
    Died, on the 14th instant, MRS. ELIZABETH WESSON (77 V) after a
very short illness. She was born in Brunswick County, Virginia in the
year 1776 and removed to Madison County Alabama in 1819. She joined the
Methodist Episcopal denomination at a very early age and remained in
it, a consistent Christian, until the time of her death.
    At his residence, Mountain Home (Lawrence Co.?), Ala. on the 6th
instant, after a long and painful illness, MR. PHILIP POINTER (44 Va.;
Lawrence Co.) in the 55th year of his age.
    Near Whitesburg, Ala. on the 21st instant, JOHN MORRIS (70 NC),
SR., in his 80th year.

May 30, 1860
    Married on the 23rd instant by REV. DR. ROSS, MR. B(ALTHAZAR)
TARDY of Mobile to MISS MARY R(OROZIE) SPOTSWOOD (ELLIOTT) of this
city. (g-parents of MATTHEWS TARDY, & of LILIAN ROSE CHOCHRAN & MARY
BURTON HALE)
    Died on the 23rd instant in Huntsville, MRS. CATHERINE McDANIEL,
aged 75 years.

June 6, 1860
    Married on the 23rd ult. at the residence of O. KING, Esq., the
bride's father, COL. GEORGE C. HUBBARD to MISS MAGGIE KING, both of
Lawrence Co.
    On the 3rd ult. in the Cumberland Presbyterian Church by REV. WM.
CHADICK, JOHN JORDAN, Esq. of Marshall Co. to MISS NANNIE BENDLE of
Huntsville, Ala.
    Died on the 29th ult. MR. WILLIAM IRWIN (52 Va; ERWIN in census),
aged 69 years, an old and respected citizen of Athens, Ala.

June 13, 1860
    Married on the 30th ult. at the residence of the bride's father,
REV. WILLIAM C. WALKER, MR. WILLIAM S. BLAIR (15 A; JOHN S.) of Limestone
County to MISS P. C. WILLIAMS, of Lauderdale County.
    On the 5th instant in Courtland by REV. J. H. LORAM MR. D(ANIEL)
B(EAUFONT) CAMPBELL of Augusta, Ga. to MISS KATE F(RANCES) JAMES (12 A)
of Courtland. (dau of WESTWOOD WALLACE JAMES & CATHARINE CONWAY WALLACE)
    On the 27th ult. at the residence of THOMAS JOHNSON by WILLIS IRELAND,
Esq., MR. WILLIAM JOHNSON to MISS MARGARET LAFEVERS (16 Ky; GILLUM),
all of Lawrence County.
    Died, on the 4th instant at the residence of GEN. THOMAS M. MOSELEY,
MR. ALLEN McCARGO (46 V), formerly of this county, aged about 55 years.
    Died, on the 6th instant, MR. JOHN HALSEY (69 V), aged about 79
years.

Died, on the 7th instant, MR. JAMES CLEMENS (72 Pa) in the 84th
year of his age.
Died on the 7th, at the residence of her brother WILLIAM J. ROSS,
MRS. AMANDA M. WALL, wife of DR. A. A. WALL, aged 28 years.
On the 26th of May, in this county, MRS. CATHERINE A. wife of
JOHN DOUGLASS, Esq. aged 58 years.

June 27, 1860

Married on the 14th instant by the REV. SAMUEL D. OGBURN, THOMAS F.
ALLEN (17 A; JAS W.) to MISS ELIZA A. (12 A; WM.) PARHAM, both of
Limestone County.
On the 19th instant by REV. R. P. RIDDLE, GEORGE W. EVANS to MISS
MARY L. CURRY, all of Limestone County.
Died, at Brownsboro, Madison County, Ala. June 19, 1860, A. R.
FRANKLIN, aged about 26 years, from near Rogersville, Tennessee. His
remains were brought to this city and interred with Masonic Honors by
the Lodge at Maysville. (copied for Prentiss Price)
At the residence of MRS. SARAH A. SHERROD (32 T) near Courtland,
Ala. on the 17th instant, HENRY CLAY SHERROD (10 A), aged 20 years
3 months nine days.
On the 25th instant at the residence of MR. A(NDREW) J. JOHNSON
(34 Pa) in this place, MRS. LUCY G. HILL (52 V) in her 66th year.
On the 16th instant, MARY SCOTT, infant daughter of WM. J. and
M(ARTHA) A. HALSEY.

July 18, 1860

Married, by REV. J. J. BURDINE, on the 26th of June, MR. JAMES M.
FREEMAN to MISS NANCY A. DALTON, all of Madison County.
Died, on the 4th instant in Fayetteville, Tenn., MR. GARLAND
B(URLEIGH) MILLER aged 44 years...was a native of this county. (son of
THOS, see vol. 48 p. 72, 73)
On the 12th instant in Limestone County after a short illness,
B. CARTER MALONE in his 26th year.

July 25, 1860

Died on the 21st instant of typhoid fever MR. HUGH BINFORD of
Madison County, Ala. aged 74 years. He was born in Northampton Co.
N.C. but was for many years a resident of North Alabama.

August 1, 1860

Married on the 17th ult. by REV. J. TURRENTINE, MR. JAMES D.
GRIFFIN to MISS EMILY HOLT, all of Limestone County.
On the 19th ult. by REV. W. MOONEY, MR. OLIVER HUBBARD of Athens,
Ala. to MISS AMANDA M. SMART of this county.
Died, in Tullahoma (Coffee Co.), Tenn. COL. W(ILBURN) G. BARTON
(50 G) aged 61 years. COL. BARTON was married in 1823 in this county
to MISS MARY ANN PENNICK (42 V). He was a citizen of Madison County
for about 30 years. (vol. 100 p. 7)

August 8, 1860

Married on the 25th of July, in Limestone County by A. R. CRAWFORD,
Esq., W. C. BEARD to MISS MARY E. WALKS.
On the 25th of July by the same, MR. JACOB HARLING to MISS MARTHA
WOODARD.
On the 25th of July by REV. W. G. HENSLEY, MAJOR JOHN R. HARRIS
(38 V) to MRS. ELIZA M. GARRETT (was she ELOUISA M. (GREER) wid of
EDMUND A GARRETT?)
On the 17th of July by REV. J. TURRENTINE, MR. JAMES D. GRIFFIN
to MISS EMILY HOLT, all of Limestone County.
On Thursday the 26th ult. in Fayetteville, Tennessee by K. FARQUHAR-
SON, Esq., MR. THOMAS B. STRONG to MISS WILLIE ELLETT, both of Alabama.
On the 5th of June, 1860 by REV. J. C. CLICK, MR. ANNANIAS KENNAMER
(13 A; DAVID) to MRS. NANCY LUSK, all of this county.
On the 9th of July by the REV. J. C. CLARK, MR. NATHANIEL WHITAKER
(18 A; WM.) to MRS. REBECCA STANLEY, all of this county.
On the 15th of July by the same, MR. JOHN ATCHLEY to MISS ADELINE
PENCE, all of this county.
Died, at his residence in Tuscumbia on July 31st, COL. JOHN HOGUN
(65 NC) in the 77th year of his age.

Obituary: Communicated. A dear and beloved friend once a resident of Huntsville, died suddenly of paralysis on the 21st ult. at Nashville, Tenn., MATILDA G. R., wife of MR. SAM D. MORGAN.

Resolutions of Respect by the Mayor and Aldermen of Huntsville on the death of JAMES GASTON (19 A) who for a long period of his life was a faithful and efficient officer of the Corporation of Huntsville.

B. T. MOORE, Clerk

August 22, 1860

Died on the 5th instant at Valley Head (Dekalb Co.), MARY WINSTON, daughter of COL. W. O. WINSTON in her 17th year.

On the 21st instant in Jackson County AMELIA SKELTON (43 T), wife of ROBERT B. SKELTON, Esq. in the 49th year of her age. (MRS. PROCTOR of Scottsboro says this AMELIA was AMELIA VANCE & said to be daughter of 1 of Governors of N.C.)

On the 18th instant in Jackson County ROBERT B. SKELTON (47 G) in the 57th year of his age.

August 29, 1860

Married on the 20th instant by ELDER JOHN CHASTAIN, MR. JOHN SCOTT to MISS SARAH ANN CAMPBELL.

On the same day at the residence of JOHN IRBY, Esq. by the same, MR. ALFRED CAMPBELL to MISS ELLEN IRBY (13 A; JUS W), all of this county.

On the 23rd instant by REV. J. ELLIOTT, WM. A. ATKINS to MISS MARTHA G. GILES, both of this county.

On the 22nd instant by REV. D. PISE, FRANK JAY McLEAN, Esq. of Kentucky to MISS SUE A. PILLOW, only daughter of MAJOR G. A. PILLOW of Maury Co. Tenn.

Died, on the 13th instant MRS. JANE McGAHA, wife of G. W. McGAHA aged 26.

On the 26th instant CHARLES WILLIE, infant son of DR. HOLBERT S. and FANNIE P. DAVIS, aged 10 months, 24 days.

September 5, 1860

Married on the 23rd ult. by JOHN R. FLANNAGAN, MR. P. C. McBRIDGE (McBRIDE) to MISS SARAH E. FOOTE (14; WM), all of Lawrence County.

On the 22nd ult. in Chattanooga, Tenn. by REV. J. N. BRADSHAW, MR. T. F. MARTIN of Huntsville to MISS JENNIE MARTIN of West Tennessee.

September 12, 1860

Died on the 18th ult. of consumption in Cotleeville, Clarke Co., Ala. MISS MARGARET T. FIGURES aged 47 years---wife and mother---Methodist Episcopal,

September 19, 1860

Married on the 5th instant by REV. W. MOONEY, MR. MEREDITH B. CANNON (should be CAMERON) of Jackson County (11 Jackson Co; son of HENRY) to MISS LUCY ANN NORTHCUTT (22 A) of this city. (dau of GIDEON & MARTHA (PEARSON) NORTHCUTT, orig. from Pettsylvania Co. Va.)

On the 4th instant by REV. R. B. C. HOWELL at Fairfield near Nashville, Tenn. at the residence of the bride, J. D. B. DeBOW, Editor of DeBow's Review to MISS MARTHA E., daughter of the late JOHN JOHNS of Nashville.

On the 5th instant by REV. MR. MITCHELL, MR. WILLIAM A. DeWOODY to MISS LUCY TANNER (8 A; PETERSON) of Athens.

On the 4th instant by REV. MR. HENSLEY, MR. WILLIAM A. MINGA (15 A) to MISS LOU ECKERBERGER (14 A; SAM'L), both of Athens, Ala.

September 26, 1860

Married on the 29th inst. by REV. J. SHACKELFORD, MR. W. D. McDANIEL to MISS SARAH JANE PREWETT, all of Lawrence County.

On the 11th instant by A. G. WESTMORELAND, Esq., MR. THOMAS H. SCOGGIN (11 T; RICH'd G) to MISS MARY F. FAULKNER, all of Limestone County.

On the 12th instant by REV. M. G. MILLIGAN, MR. JAMES T. DAVIDSON to MISS SARAH J. GRAYSON, all of this county.

On the 13th instant by REV. E. STRODE, MR. JOSEPH W. ELLETT to MISS MARY A. KELLY (8 A), daughter of H(AMPTON) W. KELLY, Esq. all of this county.

On the 19th instant by REV. WM. CHASTAIN, MR. WILLIAM YOUNG to MISS NANCY JONES, all of this county.

October 3, 1860

Killed--We learn that a difficulty took place in Fayetteville, Tenn. on Saturday night the 29th ult. between JAMES M. DAVIDSON, Esq. and MR. JAMES B. CARTY, in which the former was killed by three pistol shots. MR. DAVIDSON formerly resided here where he has many friends. He was a man of fine culture and much ability. He leaves an interesting family.

Fratricide. We learn with sorrow that yesterday on his father's plantation, REUBEN G. VINCENT, a youth of about 18 or 20, shot and killed his brother, JOHN, 22 or 23 years old. We have not ascertained the provocation. They are sons of our respected fellow citizen CLEMENT VINCENT.

Married, on the 21st instant at the residence of M. J. WARREN, Esq. by the REV. DR. MITCHELL, MR. JOSEPH MILNER of Florence to MISS MARGARET A. WOODALL of Tuscumbia.

In Mooresville at the residence of the bride's brother on the 27th ult. by REV. MR. HENSLEY, MR. JOHN H. GAMBLE (11 A; JAS. H.) to MISS FANNIE E. SMITH.

On the 27th ult. at the residence of M. C. SMITH, Esq. by REV. F. A. KIMBELL, MR. ED. N. G. KIMBELL to MISS ADA H. SMITH, all of Mooresville.

On the 27th ult. by REV. D. K. HUNTER, MR. JOHN W. BROWN to MISS MARY E. SADDLER (10 A; WM. H.), both of this county.

Died, R(EBECCA) M. M. NANCE (18 A), daughter of JAS. and SALLY M. WILBURN (59 V), was born Sept. 10, 1830, married to B. R. NANCE December 1, 1859, died September 5, 1860.

October 17, 1860

Married, on the 2nd instant by W. A. HOOD, Esq., R. O. HENSHAW to MISS ISABELLA JANE REED (10 A; ALEX H), all of Jackson County.

On the 3rd instant by the REV. JOSEPHUS SHACKELFORD, WM. F. McKELVEY, Esq., to MISS KITTY E. ALEXANDER, all of Lawrence County.

On the 4th instant by REV. J. TURRENTINE, MR. WILLIAM R. CALVIN (d 1868 m. 31 yr; 13 A; THOS) to MISS MARY JANE MOORE, all of Limestone County.

On the 23rd ult. by REV. A. R. WATSON, JOHN R. GAMBLE to MISS M. L. HANBY, both of Walker County.

On the 10th instant at the Presbyterian Church by REV. F. A. ROSS, MR. JAMES W. ATKISSON of Knoxville Tenn. to MISS FANNIE M. PEEBLES of Philadelphia, Pa. Knoxville and Philadelphia papers please copy.

Died on the 4th instant MR. AB. H. THURSTON, aged about 40 years.

On the 6th instant MRS. ELIZABETH JUDE (1788-1860 w of GEO 1786-1872) aged 79 years.

On the 8th instant JOHN R. B. JOHNSON, Esq. (55 V) aged 66 years.

October 24, 1860

Advertisement of the Crutchfield House, Chattanooga, Tenn. (Hotel) "In consequence of the death of my brother in law and partner, the late JOHN H. LUMPKIN of Georgia...." TOM CRUTCHFIELD.

Died on the 19th instant at her residence near Meridianville in this county, after a long and protracted illness, MRS. ELIZA E. POPE (40 V), relict of the late BENJAMIN S. POPE, in the 60th year of her age--for many years a member of the Methodist Church.

November 7, 1860

Homicide. At Guntersville on election day JAMES CRITCHER, ex-member of the Alabama Legislature shot and killed instantly a young man named DAVENPORT, son in law of S. K. RAYBURN, well known Circuit Clerk of Marshall County. We understand there was an old grudge between them.

November 14, 1860

Married, on the 1st instant by REV. J. D. BARBEE, MR. ISAAC WHEATLY of Holly Springs, Miss. to MISS ELIZABETH THOMAS of Tuscumbia.

In Moulton on the 6th instant by REV. JOS. SHACKELFORD, MR. JOHN N. CRADDOCK of Tuscumbia to MISS LUCY W. OWEN of the former place.

On the 8th instant by the REV. W. G. HENSLEY, MR. ROBERT N. MALONE to MRS. ANN E. MALONE, all of Athens.

On the 23rd ult. at the residence of MILTON R. BRASSFIELD near Forkland, Greene County, Ala. by the REV. J. W. (J. C. in newspaper), MISS
MARY A. HARRIS to MR. WM. A. SORSBY, all of Greene County.

Died on the 7th instant, MRS. ELIZABETH ATKINS (is this 29 A, w
of JOSEPH?), of consumption after a long and painful illness. The
deceased united with the Baptist Church in 1854, at Mt. Zion, Madison
County, Alabama. She adorned all the relations of life--as a Christian
sincere and devoted, as a wife kind and affectionate, and to her children
a mother indeed. E.S.

November 21, 1860
        Married on the 14th instant by the REV. F. A. KIMBELL, MR. WILLIAM
SPRAGUE to MISS SUSAN T. (9 A), eldest daughter of REV. P(LEASANT) B.
ROBINSON (45 T) all of this city.
        On the 14th instant by the REV. MR. BARBER in Tuscumbia, MR. JOHN
GOODWIN of Aberdeen, Mississippi to MISS SARAH A. COOPER (9), daughter
of WM. COOPER, Esq. (48 T) of Tuscumbia.
        In Nashville, Tenn. at the residence of the bride's father by the
REV. DR. HOWELL, MR. P. LINDSLEY NICHOL to MISS SUE M. SHAFFER.
        Died on the 16th instant, ANNIE EMERY RUCKMAN, daughter of MRS.
MARY C. RUCKMAN of the Huntsville Female College in her 5th year.
        On the 5th instant at his father's residence in Madison County,
Ala. RICHARD MARION MARTIN (21 A), son of RICHARD (60 V) and LYDIA
(55 V) MARTIN, aged 32 years.

November 28, 1860
        Married on Tuesday the 30th instant in Tuscaloosa Mississippi by
REV. S. W. MOORE, DR. W. T. THATCH of Limestone County, Ala. to MISS
CATHERINE GIRAULT.
        On the 14th instant by the REV. W. H. ADAMS, MR. ROBERT RUSSELL
to MISS ELLA MORRISON (ELLEN in cen; 7 A; JOHN A. or N?), all of
Bellefonte.
        By the REV. W. H. BALDRIDGE, MR. JAMES G. DEMENT (16 A?) of
Limestone County to MISS ELIZA JANE (8 A), daughter of HODGE L. STEPHENSON,
Esq. (47 T) of Lawrence County.
        Died suddenly on the 26th, WILLIAM MURPHY of this place aged about
35 years.
        November 18, 1860. CAPT. THOMAS GREEN (48 NC) in the 59th year of
his age. CAPT. GREEN at the time of his death was contractor for
carrying the U.S. Mail between Tuscaloosa and Courtland, Ala. and will
be greatly missed by the country as well as by his family and friends.
        At Hopston, Yates Co. N.Y., on the 9th instant, MRS. ANN CARY,
wife of ABRAHAM DOX, Esq. and eldest and last surviving daughter of the
late HON. JOHN NICHOLAS, in the 68th year of her age. She was a native
of Virginia and for more than 50 years a communicant of the Protestant
Episcopal Church.

December 19, 1860
        Married on the 11th instant by REV. J. SHACKELFORD, DR. A(UGUSTIN)
J(ENKUIS) JENNINGS (23 A) to MISS JULIA BLASSINGAME (8 A; ROBT), all
of Lawrence County.
        On the 16th instant by REV. F. A. KIMBELL, MR. ROBERT BAILEY to
MISS ELIZABETH MOORE, all of this city.
        Died on the 9th instant MRS. NANCY ABLES (46 T) aged 58 years;
she was born in South Carolina, married in Tennessee in 1820 and came
to Madison County in 1821, where she resided in Huntsville till her
death--lived and labored for her children.

January 16, 1861
        Resolutions of Respect, Church of the Nativity, Huntsville, signed
by J. M. BANISTER, rector, on the death of REV. NICHOLAS HAMNER COBBS,
D.D., Bishop of the Diocese of Alabama who died at his residence in
Montgomery, Ala. on Friday last January 11.

February 13, 1861
        Married on the 29th ult. in Decatur Ala. by REV. F. P. SCRUGGS,
MR. THOMAS A. TAYLOR of Chickasaw, Ala. to ANNIE LEDINGHAM (9 A; WM.)
of Decatur.

Died at his residence in Tuscumbia on the 31st ult. MR. JAMES JACKSON
(56 V), an old and highly esteemed citizen of this neighborhood. (Bible
record says b in Middle Tenn 1802, d in Colbert Co. Ala. of heart failure
1862, aged 60)
     On Thursday the 31st ult. in Decatur, Ala., MRS. BURTON, consort of
MR. ALLEN BURTON, aged about 50 years.

February 20, 1861
     Died, MRS. ELIZABETH J. MARTIN (26 A), wife of THOMAS W. MARTIN
and daughter of J(OHN) B. HORTON. She was born September 24, 1823, and
when quite young attached herself to the Missionary Baptist Church at
Triana. She was on the first day of February, 1842 united in marriage
with THOMAS W. MARTIN--long afflicted with consumption--her only regret
was leaving her husband, daughter and two little sons. On the 10th day
of the present month she fell quietly asleep--died near Madison X Roads.
     In Somerville, Ala. on the 15th ult. ALFORD V. TARNEY (ALFORD F.
TURNEY in census, 6 A; PLEASANT J.) aged 16 years.
     On the 8th instant WILLIAM B. BLACKBURN (33 V) of Morgan County.
     On the 27th ult. MRS. S. GIBSON wife of WILLIAM GIBSON of Marshall
County.

March 6, 1861
     Married at the bride's residence by the REV. P. B. ROBINSON, MR.
W. W. ALEXANDER of Fayetteville Tenn. to MRS. H(ILLA) H(INE) TOWNSEND
of Madison County.
     At the residence of the bride's father HON. R. M. PATTON of Florence,
Ala. on the 21st ult by the REV. DR. W. H. MITCHELL, J. J. McDAVID, Esq.
of Huntsville. Ala. to MISS MARY J. PATTON.
     On the 21st ult by REV. J. G. WILSON, MR. W. H. EGGLESTON, of
Tennessee to MISS M(ARY) C. BIBB (9 A), daughter of PORTER BIBB (36 A),
Esq. of Limestone County, Ala.
     On the 19th ult. in Athens by REV. J. M. BANISTER, DR. JOHN W.
WITHERS of Arkansas and MISS PATTY HAYWOOD of Limestone County.
     On the 18th of February by REV. R. M. HUMPHREY, J. D. DRAKE and
MISS SARAH E. NICHOLSON of Limestone County.
     On the 28th ult. by REV. F. A. KIMBLE, MR. JAMES A. PICKARD (9T;
HENRY J.) of this place and MISS ESTHER E. BOLDMAN of Knoxville.
     MRS. SELINA POE, relict of late WASHINGTON POE, at home of her
dau. MRS. W. H. MOORE; b July, 1812 & was oldest citizen of Macon & Bibb
Co. (Ga.) having moved here with her widowed mother, MRS. NORMAN & brother-
in-law HON. OLIVER H. PRINCE who was appt by Reg. of 1822 to lay off
Bibb Co. & city of Macon. 1st Presb Ch.1825 m HON. WASHINGTON POE
Dec. 1829 & was present at reception to GEN. LaFAYETTE. He was an
orator, scholar, & an elder in Presb Ch. Bro-in-law MORTIMER H. WALLACE
was 1st P/M of Bibb Co. MRS. POE had 10 chn--3 of whom survive her.
OLIVER POE of Columbus, Ga., MRS. W. H. MOORE of Hs Ala , JUDGE W. A. POE
of this city (Macon Telegraph)

March 13, 1861
     Married, on the 28th ult. in the city of Macon, Georgia by REV.
MR. WILLS, COL. WILLIAM H. MOORE of this city to MISS MARY F. daughter
of HON. WASHINGTON POE of Macon.
     Died, on the 9th instant, COL. JOHN READ (59 Va; t. says 1784-1861),
suddenly, aged 76 years.
     On the 4th instant in Moulton, Ala. WILLIAM B. REED (30 T) aged
48 years.
     On the 24th ult. in Franklin, Ala. MRS. SARAH GARNER, wife of
A. L. GARNER (43 SC).
     On the 9th instant after a long illness at the residence of
COL. J. C. BRADLEY in this place MRS. JANE SANDERS wife of FRANCIS A.
SANDERS of Memphis, Tenn.

March 20, 1861
     Married on the 14th instant by the REV. E. STRODE, MR. JAMES J.
COLT of Athens, Georgia to MISS MINERVA M. NUCKOLLS (16 A), daughter of
S(AM'L) O. NUCKOLLS (46 V), Esq. of this county.
     On the 18th instant MR. ALBERT H. JONES of Arkansas to MISS SARAH J.
(10 A), daughter of MR. JOHN M. ELDRIDGE (38 A) of this county.

On Tuesday the 12th instant at the residence of DR. THOMAS DAVIS
in Franklin County, North Carolina, by the REV. JOHN THOMAS, WALTER S.
SHERROD, Esq. to MISS LAURA DAVIS, all of Alabama.
    Died, in Huntsville on the 16th instant JOSEPH W., second son of
J. W. and MARY HOBBS, aged 2 years, 5 months.
    At her residence near Stevenson, Ala. on the 7th of March, MRS.
JANE M. GRIFFIN, consort of P. G. GRIFFIN.
    On the 28th ult. at his residence in Morgan County REV. THOMAS A.
STRAIN (49 V), in the 62nd year of his age.

April 10, 1861
    Resolutions by teachers and pupils of the Sunday School of the West
Huntsville Station on the death of Superintendent T. C. HAMBRICK (24 A),
who died on the 4th instant.
    Married on the 28th of March REV. WILLIAM J. GLADISH at the resi-
dence of the bride's father, WILLIAM H. WRAY of East Tennessee to MARY
S. E. CURTIS (11; JAS M. or N.) of Madison Station, Ala.

May 29, 1861
    Married on the 15th instant at the residence of the bride's father,
JONATHAN McDONALD (43 K) in Limestone County, by REV. DR. RIVERS,
MR. JOHN E. LOGWOOD of Memphis to MISS HETTIE McDONALD (is this
HENRIETTA? yes; 9 A)
    On Wednesday the 15th instant at the residence of the bride's at
Claysville, Ala. GEN. S(AM'L) K. RAYBURN (37 T) of Guntersville to
MRS. EVERGREEN FINLEY (29 A; nee RAINEY--she m. 1836 SAM'L FINDLEY)
    Died, on the 18th instant at his residence in this county, DAVID
WADE, SR. (66 V) in his 78th year.
    On the 22nd instant MRS. RUTH GARNER, relict of MR. JOHN GARNER
in the 76th year of her age--had been a member of the Methodist Church
60 years.

June 12, 1861
    Died at his residence in the Northeastern portion of the county
on the 28th of May, 1861, WILLIAM POWER (70 SC) aged about 85 years.

June 26, 1861
    Died on the 18th instant at Easley's Hotel in this city of consump-
tion MAJOR THOMAS W. STATON (33 T) aged about 50 years, a citizen of
Blount County and for some years a Senator in the Alabama Legislature.
    Married on the 11th instant at the residence of the bride's father
HON. W. T. HAWKINS by REV. DR. RIVERS, MR. H. M. WELLS to MISS MARY
HAWKINS of Florence, Ala.

July 3, 1861
    Married on the 18th instant by the REV. MR. ALLGOOD at the residence
of the bride's father MR. JOHN P. CRUMP (9 A; WM.) to MISS MARTHA J.
MURPHREE, all of Blount County.
    On the 17th instant by S. M. THITT, Esq. at the residence of the
bride's mother in DeKalb Co. Ala. MR. A. M. BEARD of Guntersville to
MISS M. F. COX.
    Died on the 1st instant, MRS. SALLIE JAMES (m. 1850; SARAH A.
HOWARD), wife of MR. RICHARD (B.) JAMES (30 A).

August 7, 1861
    From the Nashville Union: Obituary--JAMES CAMP TURNER (12 A) of
Huntsville, Ala. (son of CAPTAIN DANIEL D. TURNER (see m. VOL V p. 5;
49 V) and grandson of MAJOR ROBERT SEARCY, dec'd, one of GENERAL JACKSON's
aides in the Creek War) was shot through the heart at Manassas.

August 28, 1861
    Married on the 18th instant by REV. H. P. TURNER, MR. W. S. PHILLIPS
to MISS SUSAN F., daughter of MR. ED D. HUMPHREY all of this county.

September 4, 1861
    Died near Cookeville (Noxubee Co.), Miss. August 10 MRS. VIRGINIA C.
BEALLE, wife of MR. JOHN R. BEALLE of Mississippi, and daughter of
COL. JOHN D. KING (55 V) of Madison County, Ala. She was a woman of
admirable traits of christianity, beloved by many friends in this
vicinity.

GEORGE T. ANDERSON (7 A), eldest son of GEORGE ANDERSON (44 V) of this county was killed at the Battle of Stone Bridge on Sunday the 21st in his 18th year.

September 18, 1861
    Married on the 15th of August LT. THOMAS B. HILLS (son of ARCH'D E. & ALMIRA (BIBB) MILLS, gs of GOV. THOS BIBB) of the Confederate States Army to MISS CARRIE S. GOODWIN (9 A), daughter of DR. A. G. GOODWIN (42 SC) of Autauga County.
    Died at Mt. Hope, Ala. September 1st RUFUS McVAY of typhoid fever.

September 25, 1861
    Died near Courtland, Ala. on the 11th of Sept., MRS. JANE S. ELGIN ASHFORD (53 K), wife of THOMAS ASHFORD (59 V), Esq. in her 65th year.
    Married, on the 10th instant by N. J. CARTER, Esq., MR. J. RUSSELL NOBLE (11 A) to MISS REBECCA JANE WILSHER (6 A; JOHN D.) of Marshall County.

October 9, 1861
    Died, on the 3rd instant, MRS. LUCY D. TERRY (32 T) of this place.
    On the 2nd instant ALEXANDER MILLER, of consumption.

October 23, 1861
    Departed this life at his residence in Phillips Co., Ark. on the 29th ult. COL. ROBERT FREEMAN (41 NC), formerly of this county, of congestion of the stomach. COL. FREEMAN was born in Warren County, N.C. in the year 1809, and moved to Madison County, Alabama in his youth, where he lived for many years. He removed to the West in the spring of 1860, where he died leaving a large circle of relatives and friends to mourn his loss. "He leaves a grief stricken family."

October 30, 1861
    Married on the 23rd instant at the residence of DR. H. A. BINFORD in this city by REV. J. R. PLUMMER, MR. J. HALL, Esq. of Harrison Co. Texas to MRS. JULIA A. HAUGHTON, daughter of the late THOMAS BRANDON of Aberdeen, Mississippi.
    Died, October 12, MRS. SARAH TROTMAN (b May 8, 1824), wife of DR. THOMAS TROTMAN (b Jan 8, 1822, d. Mar. 18, 1855). (she was SARAH CATH. FARLEY, ½ sis of MICHAEL FARLEY; she m. DR. THOS BARBEE TROTMAN)
    On the 9th instant of typhoid fever, MR. WM. M. GOOCH (39 V), aged about 50 years. He leaves an interesting family.
    In Bellefonte, Alabama, on the 6th instant DR. WILLIAM O. HAYNES (47 V), aged about 60 years.

November 6, 1861
    Died at his residence in Lawrence County on Tuesday the 20th of October, PAUL J. WATKINS (35 (55) G), Esq., aged 66 years less 5 days.
    In Madison County, Ala. on October 12 of typhoid fever, MRS. RACHEL E. SPRINGER (38 T), wife of JOSIAH SPRINGER (41 T), aged 50 years 8 months 1 day. She was born in the State of North Carolina March 11, 1811. She leaves a husband and many friends.
    In Memphis on the 28th ult. JAMES R. MALTBIE, Esq. for many years a citizen of Huntsville.

November 13, 1861
    Died on Monday night November 11th at the residence of his mother-in-law, MRS. PICKETT near Mooresville, MR. THOMAS BIBB in his 51st year.

December 4, 1861
    Died on the 30th ult. at her residence in this place, MRS. LUCY A. M. HORTON (44 V; dau of WALTER OTEY), relict of the late RODAH HORTON.

December 25, 1861
    Died at the residence of her husband, "Woodgreen" near Huntsville Ala. December 19, 1861, aged 46 years, MRS. MARY WOODSON WITHERS (34 V), wife of COL. AUGUSTINE J. WITHERS (44 V), and only daughter of PHILIP WOODSON, Esq.

July 10, 1861
    Married on the 1st instant in the Methodist Church in Russellville,
Ala. by REV. J. D. BARBES, MR. L. C. ALLEN of Marion City to MISS
MARTHA A. HARRIS of Franklin County.
    On the 24th ult. by ELDER G(ENNETT) A. MORRING, DR. A. C. STEPHENSON
to MISS SARAH BENSON, all of Jackson County.
    On the 25th of June at the residence of the bride's father, MR.
WILLIAM J. THOMPSON, by REV. WM. B. BLACKBURN, MR. JOHN R. BELL and
MISS JOSEPHINE E. THOMPSON, all of the vicinity of Frankfort, Ala.
    Died on the 4th instant after a short illness WILLIAM WATKINS
(old Free State says (1788-1859), Esq. aged about 62 years. He was a
native of Georgia and had resided in Madison County from early manhood.
Leaves many relatives.
    On the 29th ult. MR. JOHN N. MILLER an old and respected citizen
of this place.

July 17, 1861
    Married on the 11th instant by REV. M. E. JOHNSTON, DR. ROBERT T.
SEARCY of Fayetteville, Tenn. to MRS. CORNELIA J. HERRIFORD of Meridian-
ville.
    Died on the 7th instant after a long illness, JOHN P. BROWN (59 V),
Esq. aged about 72 years.

August 14, 1861
    Married on the 4th instant by A. W. HADEN, Esq., MR. JONOTHAN WILLIAMS
to MISS AILSEY KIRKPATRICK (10 A; JOS.), all of Jackson County.
    Died on the 10th instant, DR. H(OLBERT) S. DAVIS, a most exemplary
and worthy citizen of this place, leaving hosts of friends to mourn
his untimely death.

February 11, 1874 (1875?)
    Died in this city Tuesday, GEORGE S. WILSON, a native of Chester-
field, England and since 1848 a resident of Huntsville, aged about 50.
    Died in this city Tuesday February 9, 1875 of pulmonary consumption,
MRS. HATTIE M. IRBY, wife of MR. P. M. IRBY, aged about 38 years.

February 25, 1874 (1875)
    Married in Mobile on the 26th inst. by REV. DR. J. A. MASSEY,
MR. R. H. SMITH, JR., son of COL. ROBERT SMITH of Mobile and MISS ALICE A.
MOORE of Mobile, daughter of the late COL. SYDENHAM MOORE of Eutaw
(Greene Co.).

March 11, 1874 (1875)
    Died on Friday March 5, 1875 MRS. LAURA RICE HELM, daughter of
MR. JOHN PATTON and wife of MR. THOMAS HELM. Member of the Protestant
Episcopal Church....

March 18, 1874 (1875)
    Died at the residence of HON. F. L. HAMMOND near Madison Cross
Roads March 13, 1875, MRS. NANCY O. BLACKBURN, widow of the late FRANK
BLACKBURN at an advanced age.

April 1, 1874 (1875)
    Resolutions of Respect--Society at Bethlehelm Church on 28 March
1875 loss of late pastor and Brother, AMBROSE F(LEMING) BRISKILL.
    Died at Madison in this county Tuesday March 30, 1875, MRS. MOLLIE J.
DRAPER, wife of DR. N. W. DRAPER.

April 8, 1874 (1875)
    Obituary: MRS. MARTHA A. O'NEAL, wife of B. W. O'NEAL and daughter
of DUDLEY and ANN SALE was born in Elbert County, Georgia March 4, 1815.
Her father moved to Madison County, Alabama when she was quite young.
She was married in 1838, professed religion in 1842 and united herself
with the Methodist Episcopal Church. She moved with her family from
Madison Co. Ala. to Milam County, Texas in the fall of 1872. Was
confined to her bed with consumption. Left one brother and one sister,
MRS. M. D. WANCE, a husband and 4 children. (Written by H. P. TURNER)

April 15, 1874 (1875)
     It is our painful duty to announce the death of DR. HENRY A.
BINFORD.

April 22, 1874 (1875)
     Died at New Market, Alabama on the 22 March, 1875, MISS ANGIE
HAMBRICK.
     (For other notes from 1875 numbers of "The Democrat" see Volume
XLII.)

January 7, 1875
     Died in New York City January 4th, 1875 MRS. FELICIA CHAPMAN HUBARD,
daughter of ex-Governor REUBEN CHAPMAN and wife of BOLING HUBARD, Esq.,
who had only recently settled in New York to practice his profession,
the law. Left an infant daughter.

January 14, 1875
     Tribute of respect, Hazel Green Grange #251, Patrons of Husbandry--
to Worthy Master and Brother, JOHN B. CORN who died the 3rd of January,
1875.

May 20, 1875
     Died near Huntsville, Alabama, Thursday May 13, 1875, MRS. CAROLINE
MATILDA McCALLEY, wife of THOMAS S. McCALLEY in her 55th year. MRS.
McCALLEY was a daughter of the late ROBERT LANFORD and was born and
reared in this county and in 1838 she married MR. McCALLEY. Self-
sacrificing mother and wife, pious and devout Christian.

May 27, 1875
     Died on the 28th of April last in the 73rd year of his age at the
residence of his son, JOHN M. TATE in Phillips County, Arkansas,
ABNER TATE, who was for many years a prominent citizen of northern
part of this (Madison) County, where he continually resided from early
boyhood until the year 1863. He was born in Logan County, Kentucky in
1802. His parents were among the early settlers of Hazlegreen district.
He survived his wife, who died in 1859, and all his children except
two sons.

July 22, 1875
     Died of paralysis at the residence of his daughter, MRS. SIBLEY
in Madison County, Alabama, MR. MILLS JENKINS, who was born January 13,
1805 and died June 30, 1875 aged 70 years 3 months and 13 days. Leaves
wife and large circle of relatives and friends.

July 29, 1875
     Tribute of respect, Oliver Lodge #280 S.O.C.T., New Market--
JAMES C. DAVIS who died July 24th.

July 29, 1875
     MRS. SUSAN CAIN KNOX died at the residence of her son-in-law,
JOHN T. PATTERSON July 26, 1875 aged 77. Born in Petersburg, Virginia
July 26, 1798, moved to Knoxville, Tennessee 1816 thence to this city
in 1818. Member of the Methodist Episcopal Church until 1840, then
joined the Cumberland Presbyterian Church.

August 5, 1875
     Death of MR. LUKE MATTHEWS. This old and highly respectable citizen
of Huntsville died at his residence on Sunday night last. Born in
Campbell County, Virginia September 10, 1796. He settled in Limestone
County, Alabama in 1824. He married MISS JUDITH E. PEETE March 8, 1826
and by her had 8 children. She died and on January 26, 1843, he married
MISS LUCY ANN SPOTSWOOD by whom he had 8 children. He removed from
Limestone Co. to Madison Co. in 1846. He was a soldier of the War of
1812.

August 11, 1875
     Resolutions of respect by Oliver Lodge #280--death of our beloved
brother, JAMES C. DAVIS, who died at his home in New Market July 24th.

August 25, 1875
    Died at the residence of his brother-in-law, DR. PULLIAM in
La Grange, Tennessee, August 21, 1875, ALGERNON S. BEASLEY in his 22nd
year, son of DR. JAMES A. BEASLEY of Huntsville, Ala.

October 6, 1875
    Died in Huntsville, Alabama September 24, 1875, MRS. ANNIE BUSSEY,
wife of REV. MR. BUSSEY of the Baptist Church. Her remains were taken
to Columbus, Georgia.

November 3, 1875
    Died last night, November 2nd at about 9 o'clock, COL. NICHOLAS
DAVIS at his residence in this city after about a week's illness with
Typo-malarial fever in his 52nd year. He was a man of more than ordinary
ability as a popular orator and made his mark as an advocate. He has
been a state soldier, member of the state legislature, delegate to
Secession Convention, member of Provisional Congress. Leaves a widow,
3 sons and a daughter.

November 3, 1875
    Died in Phillips County, Arkansas, September 21, 1875, D(ANIEL) H.
SEVERS, an old citizen of this county, aged 73.
    Died at his residence in Holmes County, Mississippi October 18, 1875
of chronic diarrhea, WILLIAM C. BINFORD, formerly a resident of this
county, a faithful husband and father.

November 10, 1875
    MRS. SHACKLEFORD, the venerable widow of DR. JACK SHACKLEFORD of
Texas fame and mother of MAJ. W. V. CHARDAVOYNE died recently near
Courtland aged 66 years. (Lawrence Co.)

December 1, 1875
    Resolutions of respect by Ebenezer Grange Lodge #503 on death of
W. C. BINFORD, who died on the 18th at the residence near Ebenezer,
Holmes County, Mississippi aged 48 years. He leaves a bereaved family.
    Died at his residence in Leake County, Mississippi about the 1st
of October last, WILLIAM M. ELDRIDGE, formerly of this county.
    Died at his residence in this county November 27, 1875, GEORGE
WHITFIELD DRAKE, an old and respectable citizen, having nearly completed
his 62nd year. He was born and reared in this county. Affectionate
husband and father.

December 22, 1875
    Obituary: JULIA HUTTON (should be HATTON) was born in North
Carolina about 1799, emigrated to Alabama in early life with her parents
and located in Madison County; was united in marriage to JAMES LANDMAN
June 6, 1835 and died November 27, 1875 aged 76 years. Good wife,
affectionate mother, kind neighbor.
    Died in Huntsville this morning (December 22nd) at about half
past 2 o'clock, MRS. MATTIE LEE STEVENS, wife of MAJ. J. R. STEVENS and
daughter of the late DR. CHARLES H. PATTON aged 32.

July 27, 1877
    We regret to note the death of two estimable ladies of Madison,
MRS. THOMAS CAIN aged 40, and MRS. SARAH FARLEY, in her 81st year.
    Also MAJOR ARTHUR C. BEARD (40 K) who died Wednesday the 17th instant
at Guntersville; he was well known as Commissary of old 4th Alabama
Regiment.

January 9, 1878
    Died after an illness of severest suffering lasting nearly 5 years,
MRS. ANN HARDIN, only daughter of REV. HENRY P. TURNER and wife of
MR. BENJ. L. HARDIN. Departed this life at family residence in this
county on 31 December 1877. She was born Nov. 2, 1839, joined the
Methodist Church in September 1850 and was married 22 Feb. 1866. She
leaves two interesting children, a son and a daughter too young to
realize the irreparable loss of an affectionate mother.... (we had
copied her death date as 1887 on ts, but 1877 has to be rt)

January 16, 1878
    Died at residence of JOHN GANO WINTER, Montgomery, Ala. on night
of Jan. 14, 1878, MISS FLORIE BETTS LEWIS, daughter of the late JOHN H.
LEWIS of Huntsville. Her remains will be interred in the Huntsville
city cemetery, after funeral service at Church of Nativity.

January 23, 1878
    Died at her residence in Huntsville, Fri. Jan. 18, 1876 (misprint
for 8 I suppose), MRS. HARRIET MARIA CRUSE, widow of the late SAMUEL
CRUSE in her 79th year. MRS. CRUSE was born in 1799. She married and
came to Huntsville in 1819 and has lived ever since, respected and
beloved.... She was buried with the impressive services of the
Episcopal Church by REV. DR. BANISTER on Sun. morning last...
    Died at residence of CAPT. JOHN GANO WINTER, Montgomery, Ala. on
morning of 15th Jan. 1878, MISS FLORIDA BETTS LEWIS, daughter of the
late JOHN H. LEWIS.... At age of 17 she set out to earn her livelihood
as a teacher.

February 13, 1878
    Our community was startled yesterday evening by sudden death of
ANDREW J. JOHNSON, a respected citizen since the year 1843. He had
been affected with heart disease and complained yet of rheumatism in
one hip. While sitting with his family he fell back and in a few
minutes was dead. He was quiet, unobtrusive, liberal in his opinions
and noted for his business integrity. He was in his 61st year.
    Last week was announced the killing of JASPER J. JONES, an estimable
lawyer and register in Chancery of Scottsboro, Ala. by REN R. FRANKS.
CAPT. JONES was a graduate of University of Ala. and a gallant capt. in
Confederate army.... CAPT. JONES married MISS MADGIE WARWICK, daughter
of MR. GEOR. H. WARWICK of Huntsville a year or more ago. His wife,
orphan child and other relatives survive.

February 20, 1878
    Married on 14 at residence of bride's mother by REV. MR. WATTERSON,
of Winchester, Tenn. MR. LaFAYETTE ORR to MISS SALLIE MALONE, all of
this county.

February 27, 1878
    Died at or near Senatobia, Miss. Feb. 23, 1878 after a short illness,
LARKIN W. ECHOLS, native of Huntsville, but long a resident of Miss. and
highly esteemed in both states for his many virtues. Leaves a widow and
a large family connection. His remains were brought to Huntsville and
interred in our city cemetery.
    In Huntsville Sun. night Feb. 24 of catarrh after 4 weeks illness,
MRS. ELLEN LAUGHLIN, wife of J. B. LAUGHLIN and daughter of the late
JOSEPH CAROTHERS, one of the most amiable and lovely of women, and a
devout Christian and member of the M. E. Church for many years. Leaves
a husband, little son and a large circle of friends.
    In this city Feb. 25, LOUIS GUSCIA, a native of Switzerland, but
a resident of Huntsville for several years.

March 6, 1878
    Died in this city March 5 of whooping cough, JOHN M. infant son of
JOHN M. CROWDER.
    Married at Baptist Church, Nashville, Tenn. Feb. 26, OSCAR R. HUNDLEY,
Esq. of Huntsville, Ala. to MISS ANNIE E. THOMAS of Nashville.

March 13, 1878
    Died at residence of JOHN A. ERWIN in Huntsville, March 8, of pul-
monary consumption, JAMES B. STRODE aged about 20 years. Son of REV.
EUGENE STRODE (gf of HUDSON STRODE) the 1st pastor of Baptist Church
of this city. He resided in Columbus, Ky. and came here about 3 weeks
ago for benefit of his health. Native of this county...
    Died in Hale Co. Ala. on 19 Feb. MRS. MARY G. WITHERS, wife of
ROBERT W. WITHERS, Esq... (Greensboro Watchman)
    Died at her residence in Huntsville Sat. Mar. 3 (tombstone says
Mar. 3) after a short illness, MRS. ADELINE BRADLEY, widow of the late
JAMES BRADLEY in her 72nd year. Member of M. E. Church South....

Married in Huntsville Mar. 12 by REV. W. F(RANKLIN) KONE, of
Baptist Church, MR. JOHN J. DELP to MISS KATIE GIBSON, daughter of
MADAME HELEN d'APERY all of Huntsville.
Married at residence of MR. JAMES GROOMS, the bride's father,
near Huntsville Mar. --- MR. A. L. WHITELY of Maysville to MISS PATTIE
GROOMS.

March 20, 1878
Married in Maysville Mar. 19 by REV. GEO. W. F. PRICE, MR. HENRY S.
BRADFORD to MISS DORA HEREFORD all of this county. (MRS. VASSER ALLEN's
parents DORA was daughter of THEODORE M. & ANNE ELIZA CHAMBLESS. HENRY S.
son of HAMILTON G. BRADFORD).
Cadet WM. WILLIAMS ALSTON, son of DR. L. & MRS. SARAH F. ALSTON
of Dallas aged 17 yrs 7 mo was shot and killed on 22 Mar. Episcopalian...

March 27, 1878
State of Ala--Madison Co. In Chancery
R. M. SLEDGE, ex'r of O. D. SLEDGE dec'd
vs
ALFRED O. WILLIAMSON et al.
Defendants MONROE M. CHEATHAM and wife EDITH R., ELLEN NANCE,
WILLIAM H. NANCE, JR. and ERSKINE S. HELM are non-residents. All reside
in Nashville except WILLIAM H. NANCE, who resides in Shelby Co. Tenn.
and ERSKINE S. HELM, under 14, resides with his father, THOMAS HELM in
Jackson, Miss. 18 Feb. 1878.

April 3, 1878
Married in this city on April 2 by REV. MR. KONE of Baptist Church,
MR. ELIJAH CHADDICK to MISS MARGARET TROXSTER.
At residence of bride's father, NICHOLAS SANDLIN, near Hazel Green
Mar. 27 by GEO. M. FOWLER, J.P., MR. MARTIN A. TOWRY to MISS SARAH E.
SANDLIN, all of this county.

April 10, 1878
Died in this city Sun. morning Apr. 7 of pneumonia, MR. JOHN HUEY,
an old citizen aged about 75. MR. HUEY was an Irishman by birth and
came to Huntsville to reside about 1835 afterwards married here and has
made his record as a man of sterling integrity, a faithful and devoted
husband and father and an humble, upright Christian, Presbyterian,
mason.
Died in this city Tue. eve. Apr. 9, after a long and lingering
illness from paralysis, MRS. CATHERINE MOLONEY aged about 77. Sister
of COL. J. J. DONE and MRS. WEAKLEY and has resided in Huntsville for
many years.... Roman Catholic Church.

April 17, 1878
Died Apr. 12, MR. GEORGE SHOENBERGER. Born in Glarus, Switzerland
1820. Aged 58. Assassinated.
Died in this city on Sat. Apr. 12 of lockjaw, MRS. NARCISSA C.
BALDRIDGE, wife of DR. M. C. BALDRIDGE aged about 43. Cumberland
Presbyterian.
In this city Apr. 12 after a short illness, MRS. CAROLINE JOLLY,
widow of the late BENJAMIN JOLLY aged about 60 years. Presbyterian.

April 24, 1878
Obituary:
MR. GEORGE SHOENBERGER born in Switzerland May 8, 1820. Married
Mar. 1871 MRS. FANNIE DAVIS (who had been MISS STRONG). His mother died
in Switzerland several years since, his father more recently, while a
brother and sister with families survive in Switzerland....

May 15, 1878
Married at MRS. SHOENBERGER's near Huntsville May 15 by REV. G. W.
MITCHELL, DAVID K. WEST of Giles Co. Tenn. to MRS. SUSAN E. McCLELLAN,
daughter of the late CHARLES STRONG of Madison Co.
Died in Huntsville May 15, MRS. LOUISA A. HEREFORD, wife of
CHARLES W. HEREFORD and daughter of FREDERICK ELGIN aged 42. Cumberland
Presbyterian.

In the vicinity of Huntsville, tombstone says May 14, May 13, of bladder disease, MR. ALFRED H. ELLETT aged over 70. Had been a highly esteemed citizen of Madison Co. for many years. Leaves a family and numerous friends.

May 22, 1878
Married at residence of W. A. BLAIR in Huntsville May 22 by the grandfather of the groom, REV. BENJAMIN GRAVES, MR. JAMES H. MAYHEW to MISS MAY L. FRENCH....

Died near Triana, May 21, MRS. ELIZABETH M. COLLIER, wife of CHARLES E. COLLIER, SR. Born Dec. 16, 1812. Member of Christian Church....

May 29, 1878
Died at residence of her father-in-law, THOMAS W. WHITE in Huntsville, May 27 after less than a week's illness, MRS. MARIA WITHERS WHITE, wife of DR. ALEX'R. L. WHITE and daughter of the late AUGUSTINE J. WITHERS in her 27th year.

June 19, 1878
Died at residence of his son-in-law, S. J. MAYHEW, in Huntsville, June 17, June 16 tombstone says, REV. BENJAMIN GRAVES nearly 82 years old. Born in N.Y. and went to Ohio in early life and resided there till 1870 when he came to Huntsville to live with his daughter, MRS. MAYHEW. Licensed as a Presbyterian minister 1842 and preached the Gospel 54 years. (Tombstone says b. July 4, 1796)

Married on Thursday June 13 at 10:15 a.m. in Methodist Church, Huntsville, by REV. G. W. F. PRICE, MR. HENRY ADAMS of Tuskegee to MISS IDA WHITEHURST of Huntsville.

At same time and place by same, both of Huntsville, LAWRENCE COOPER, Esq., MISS ELIZA PRICE.

June 26, 1878
Married June 12 in Big Cove by JUSTICE ALLEN, MR. SAMUEL WEB to MISS DICEY TUCK, youngest daughter of HENRY TUCK.

Died at his residence near Seneca Lake, N.Y. June 13, JOHN NICHOLAS DOX, twin brother of HON. P(ETER) M(YNERT) DOX. (latter b. Sept. 11, 1813, Genero, N.Y.; d. Apr. 3, 1891. his son ABRAHAM & (MISS NICHOLAS) DOX; grandson JOHN NICHOLAS (Owen's III, p. 504).

In this city June 25. HARRY CHRISTO son of DR. and MRS. C. A. ROBINSON, aged about 18 mo. old.

July 3, 1878
Died at Wood's Mill June 27 of malarial fever A. J. WOOD aged about 60 yrs. old and useful citizen....

In this city June 27 after a long suffering with chronic rheumatism, JOHN F. ADAY aged probably 65. Pump maker by trade....

July 17, 1878
Died in Huntsville Tue. night July 16 of pulmonary consumption after a few months illness, MRS. FANNIE MASTIN, daughter of the late THEOPHILUS LACY and wife of WILLIAM J. MASTIN in her 27th year.

State News

Regret the death of HENRY W. KIMBALL (35 NC), an old and respectable citizen of Limestone from pneumonia near Mooresville July 6. (married 1840 ANN ELIZA GAMBLE.

CAPT. ARTHUR H(ENLEY) KELLAR, Editor of Tuscumbia North Alabamian, was married in Memphis July 1 to MISS KATE ADAMS, daughter of HON. CHARLES ADAMS of that city. (note: Parents of HELEN KELLER)

August 7, 1878
Died at residence of DR. J. P. HAMPTON, near Meridianville, Ala. Aug. 2, 1878 EMMA MAY, infant daughter of R. V. and MARGARET HORTON of Limestone Co. Ala. aged 9 mo. 13 days.

August 14, 1878
Died at Memphis, Tenn. July 31 of congestive fever, FREDERICK O. SHAUDIES, JR. son of MR. F. O. SHAUDIES of Huntsville aged 23. Estimable young man, sober, industrious, frugal and honest. Left a wife and child. Body was brought to Huntsville for burial.

State of Alabama--Madison Co. Aug. 5, HUGH L. CLAY, administrator
of JOHN C. LOGEMAN, deceased.
Tribute of respect by Church of Nativity to REV. JOHN MURRAY ROBERTSON
who departed this life at his residence in vicinity of Huntsville on
Wednesday night Aug. 7...devoted minister for about 47 years. Signed
by J. M. BANISTER, rector. JOSEPH MARTIN, Sec'y.

August 21, 1878

Within the past month, Alabama has lost two of her most prominent
men--Early in the month JOHN A. ELMORE, an able and leading lawyer of
Montgomery died after long suffering with cancer of the tongue. A few
days since, HON. JOHN BRAGG, of Mobile, long a leading lawyer and Judge
of Circuit and once a member of Congress, died at an advanced age.
The Nashville American brings news today of HON. BALIE PEYTON near
Gallatin, Tenn. a prominent politician and member of Congress.
We regret to learn that MITCHEL RICHARDSON, a brother of HON.
WILLIAM RICHARDSON died in Nashville on Monday nite last of pulmonary
consumption. His remains were taken to Athens, his native home for
burial.
On Sunday last in this city, MRS. HUNT, the venerable mother of
the MISSES HUNT aged 82 fell off her back porch and broke her arm and
thigh.
MR. SELDON WATKINS, a native of Huntsville, who left here 28
years ago is in our city.
State of Alabama--Madison Co. Estate of NANCY A. DOUGLASS, deceased.
JOHN A. DOUGLASS, administrator, presents petition representing that
MRS. MARY W. ROBINSON, THOMAS H. DOUGLASS, trustee, JOHN A. DOUGLASS,
all of whom reside in Madison Co. and MARTHA J. DOUGLASS, who resides
in DeSoto Co. Miss.--own a certain tract of land.

September 11, 1878

Married at Methodist Church in Huntsville Wed. Sept. 4 by REV. DR.
OIVER (OLIVER?), DR. HENRY McDONNELL to MISS ADA FENNELL, daughter of
ISHAM J. FENNELL, all of Madison Co.

September 18, 1878

Married at Presbyterian Church, in Huntsville, Tue. night Sept. 17
by the Pastor, REV. J. DeWITT BURKHEAD, MR. MALCOLM J. GILCHRIST of
Courtland to MISS FLORENCE BURKHEAD, daughter of the Pastor. (Lists
attendants etc.)
Died at Big Cove in this county Sept. 7 of convulsions, MAMIE,
infant child of the late FRED O. SCHAUDIES, JR. aged 3 mo. She was
brought back from Memphis and MR. and MRS. F. O. SCHAUDIES, SR. took
her camping and nursed her till its death, fearing it might be yellow
fever.
Huntsville was deeply saddened by a dispatch from Memphis announcing
the death of DR. JOHN HENRY ERSKINE (son of ALEX) yesterday Sept. 17
at 5:40 a.m....victim of yellow fever. Native of Huntsville, reared in
our midst.

September 25, 1878

Died at residence of her daughter, MRS. SALLIE P(OLK) SALE in this
city, Sept. 14, MRS. R(ACHEL) O. ELLETT, widow of the late ALFRED H.
ELLETT. Member of the Methodist Episcopal Church.

October 2, 1878

Married at residence of DR. SAML J. WITHERS in Mooresville, Ala.
Sept. 18 by REV. MR. McDONNELL, DR. J(OHN) W. KEYES of Iola, Fla. to
MISS MARIANNE HENTZ of Ala.
In Memoriam
MISS SOPHRONIA WHITE was born in Winchester, Tenn. (daughter of SARAH)
but removed when quite young to Ala. and has been a resident of Madison
Co. for 35 years. She embraced religion in her 12 year. Methodist.
Died Sept. 30, 1878 just at close of day....
MISS SARAH HICKMAN LEWIS, daughter of MRS. JOHN H. LEWIS of
Huntsville, Ala. died at Houston, Texas on Thurs. Sept. 26 after a
congestive chill a few hours before. Well educated and accomplished,
she set out to earn her livelihood as a teacher....

Died in Tuscumbia, Ala. Mon. eve. Sept. 30 of congestion of the
brain, MRS. AMY BOLDMAN, widow of the late H. H. BOLDMAN of this city
aged 73.

At Holly Springs, Miss. Sept. 27 of yellow fever, LUCY, youngest
daughter of J(AMES) and MARTHA FORT aged 17....

Yellow fever--Died at Madison in this county yesterday, MRS.
JENNINGS, a sister of MISS PLEDGE, who recovered. Both were from
Memphis.

October 9, 1878

Married at residence of ARCHIBALD McDONNELL, SR. the bride's father
in Madison Co. Wed. Oct. 9, by REV. C. D. OLIVER, MR. JOHN D. ROBINSON
of Morgan Co. to MISS MARY E. McDONNELL.

At residence of bride's mother, MRS. ----VAUGHAN, near Triana, by
the REV. MR. THOMPSON, of Florence, Ala. Tue. nite Oct. 1, 1878,
DR. W. T. HENSLEY to MISS MARY BYRD LEFTWICH, all of Madison Co. Ala.

Died at her residence near Brownsboro, Madison Co. Ala. on Mon.
Oct. 7, 1878 at 3 a.m., MRS. RHODA LAWLER, widow of the late BENJAMIN
LAWLER aged 79.

October 16, 1878

Died in Huntsville suddenly Oct. 10, MR. WHORLEY WHITE, an old and
well known citizen.

In Huntsville Oct. 15, MR. CYRUS STAMATE, an old and well known
citizen.

Tribute of Respect on death of ROBERT HERSTEIN, -- by Mayor and
Alderman.

Yellow fever--Tuscumbia--DR. DISPREZ has died.

Huntsville--Two refugees from Decatur died Sun.--MR. JONATHON FISHER
and a negro woman.

October 30, 1878

State of Alabama--Madison Co. Estate of MARY H. GARNER, deceased.
THOMAS W. MARTIN, admr. WILLIAM L. GARNER who resides in Waco, Texas,
JOHN T. GARNER, who resides in Aberdeen, Miss., REBECCA SULLIVAN and
her husband, who reside near Clarksdale, Coahoma Co. Miss., ROBERT H.
GARNER and WALTER B. GARNER, who reside near Germantown, Shelby Co.
Tenn., MOLLIE E. GARNER and OLIVER G. GARNER, whom also reside near
Clarksdale, Coahoma Co. Miss.

November 6, 1878

Married in Grace Church, New Market, Md. Oct. 29 by REV. MR.
STEPHENSON, WILLIAM L. CLAY, Esq. of Huntsville to MISS LOUISA JOHNSON,
eldest daughter of DR. JAMES THOMAS JOHNSON, formerly of Frederick Co.
Md....

Death of WILLIAM Y. POLLARD--yellow fever on Mon. night last.
Interred in Huntsville by Huntsville Steam Fire Co. on Tue. eve.

November 13, 1878

Married at residence of MR. JAMES A. PICKARD in Huntsville on Mon.
morning Nov. 11 by REV. W. C. HEARN, MR. THOMAS H. McALLISTER to MISS
AMIE STINE, all of this county.

November 20, 1878

Married at residence of bride's father at Elkton, Tenn. by REV.
W. WEAKLEY, DR. JOHN W. BARCLAY of Madison Co. Ala. to MISS LAVINIA P.
BAUGH of Elkton.

Died 16 Oct. KATIE V. HALL aged 22-11-15 wife of DR. P. M. HALL of
New Market.... Left husband and a sweet child, VIRGINIA.

November 27, 1878

Died in Huntsville Fri. Nov. 22 of pulmonary consumption, MRS.
MATTIE MASON daughter of JAMES W. POLLARD and wife of JOHN R. MASON.

December 4, 1878

Married in Church of Nativity in Huntsville Thurs. Nov. 28 by
REV. J. M. BANISTER, MR. W. J. WHITSELL to MISS SALLY W. MARTIN,
daughter of MR. JOSEPH MARTIN all of this city. Left Thursday for their
home at Gainesville, Ala.

December 25, 1878
     Died in Huntsville, Dec. 19, of softening of the brain, MRS. MARY
ELIZABETH NEWMAN, daughter of the late WILLIAM POWERS and widow of the
late DR. FRANCIS H. NEWMAN aged 61. Methodist....

DEMOCRAT

January 3, 1883
     Married, December 21, 1882 at the residence of DR. JAMES HANKIN
at Belle Mina by REV. MR. McDONALD, DR. WM. F. JORDAN of Maysville to
MISS M. A. DEASON of Trenton (Gibson Co.), Tenn.
     MR. JAMES McFARLAND of Gurleysville and MISS LAURA J. HUEY,
daughter of the late JOHN HUEY of this city were united in marriage at
the residence of the bride's mother at 2 p.m. Wednesday, January 3, 1883.
     Died, at the residence of his sister MRS. JOSEPH C. BRADLEY (m.
1838 ISABELLA CLARKE; 29 Va; vol. 16, p. 3; vol. 35, p. 100; d of
WM. & SUSAN CLARK), Huntsville, Ala. January 3, 1883, CAPT. WILLIAM
CLARKE (app. 84) in his 63rd year. CAPT. CLARKE was a native of Madison
County. He was a gallant, chivalrous Confederate soldier, and for four
years served as captain in the 17th Tennessee Regt. commanded by COL.
(afterwards Governor) MARKS. He was planting last year in the Mississippi bottoms below Memphis, was taken ill a few weeks ago with malarial
fever, taken to Memphis and was so prostrated that his son RICHARD
CLARKE brought him to his sisters' last Saturday, where he died today.
     HON. FRANK S. LYON, one of the most distinguished men in Alabama
died suddenly at his residence in Demopolis, Ala. last night, aged 83.
He..faithfully served his people in the U.S. House of Representatives,
as Commissioner to wind up the State Banks, and in the State Legislature.

January 10, 1883
     Contains long Tribute of Respect to DR. FLEMING JORDAN (46 G),
dec'd, by the Medical Society of Madison County. "On Sunday the 24th
of December, 1882, in the 79th year of his age, DR. FLEMING JORDAN,
honorary member of this society and the oldest practitioner of medicine
in this County ceased his earthly labors...he was a native of Georgia
and moved with his parents to this county in early childhood. He
graduated from the Medical Department of the University of Pennsylvania
in March, 1829 and in July of that year married MISS LUCY J. MOORE....
     Married, in the Church of the Nativity by the rector REV. DR. J. M.
BANNISTER, MR. STERLING LANIER of Birmingham to MISS MARY LOU BANNISTER,
daughter of the rector.
     Died, at the residence of his son in law JAMES E. FLETCHER (12 A;
EDWD A.), in Huntsville, January 5, 1883, MR. SAMUEL MATTHEWS in his
85th year. MR. MATTHEWS (51 V) was born in Brunswick County, Virginia
December 12, 1798 and came to Madison County about 1818-19, afterwards
removed to Limestone County, and became a citizen of Huntsville in
1858...member of the Presbyterian Church...left a large circle of friends
and relatives.
     Died, at Decatur, Ala. January 6, 1883, DR. FRANCIS W. SYKES (31 NC)
of Lawrence County, Ala. DR. SYKES was a native of North Carolina and
at an early age came to Morgan County, Ala., afterwards settling near
Courtland, Lawrence County. He represented Lawrence County repeatedly
in the Legislature and in the Constitutional Convention of 1875. A
Democratic Legislature elected him to the U.S. Senate since the War but
a radical senate refused him his seat.

January 17, 1883
     One JOHN BROAD, an Englishman, died in Atlanta in 1881 leaving
240,000.... JONATHAN BROAD, a brother and MRS. TOMMY MAYNARD, a sister,
and heirs of 2/5 of the property live in the vicinity of Huntsville.
JONATHAN BROAD and TOMMY MAYNARD, coal miners on the mountain adjoining
Huntsville employed JOHN J. McDAVID to represent their interests.
     Died, near Whitesburg January 12, 1883 MRS. CAROLINE R. McGEHA
wife of JAMES M. McGAHA (21 A; JAS), aged 48...devoted wife and
mother...member Methodist Church.

January 24, 1883
	CAPT. WALTER A. GOODMAN died at his residence in Memphis on Saturday, January 20, after a brief illness; last year he was elected presiding Judge of the County Court of Shelby County. He was exemplary as a husband, father, friend, citizen and as a gallant Confederate soldier.

January 31, 1883
	Died in Memphis, Tenn. Jan. 25, 1883 MR. SAMUEL RIDGLEY CRUSE (20 A; SAM'L) in his 53rd year. MR. CRUSE was born in Huntsville, Ala. December 23, 1829, and was married to MISS BESSIE NEWMAN (14 A), daughter of DR. FRAS. H. NEWMAN (48 MD) November 25, 1858. He entered the Confederate service as a First Lieutenant in CAPT. J. J. WARD's Battery in 1861, and when his gallant captain was killed by his side in GEN. JOS. E. JOHNSTON's retreat from Dalton, Ga. he succeeded to the Captaincy and served gallantly till the close of the War. In 1865 he succeeded his father SAMUEL CRUSE, who died during the War, as Secretary and Treasurer of the Eastern Division of the M. & C. RR....
His body was removed from Memphis to Huntsville in a special car draped in mourning, and accompanied by his family, his wife and three sons, and a number of friends...funeral held from the Church of the Nativity, and buried in the City Cemetery.
	Married at the residence of the bride's mother by REV. A. L. DAVIS, on the 16th of Jan. 1883 MR. W. H. MITCHELL of Limestone County and MISS MAGGIE E., daughter of the late WYLIE F. BOULDIN (18 A; Morgan Co.).

February 7, 1883
	Died at her home in Big Cove, January 15, 2883 after two years illness MISS MILDRED EVALINE SCHRIMSHER (18 A; SARAH) in her 51st year.
	Died suddenly at Wheeler, Lawrence County, Ala. Feb. 3, 1883 COL. RICHARD JONES (57 V), aged 89 years. COL. JONES was father-in-law of GEN. JOSEPH WHEELER.

February 7, 1883
	Died at the house of his father, JAMES A. PAUL, in Madison County, Alabama, February 4, 1883, WILLIAM PAUL, aged about 26 years...a most estimable young man, a model son and brother.
	MR. JOHN F. MARTIN, agent of the M & C RR at Stevenson Alabama for 15 years was run over by a train from Chattanooga Friday night...he died on Saturday.

February 14, 1883
	Married February 6, 1883 in the City of New York by REV. H. H. WARTE, MR. J. H. GOODWIN, author and accountant of New York to MISS FRANKIE LAMBERT. The bride, a native of Huntsville will be remembered here as a sweet and sprightly lass, grown to womanhood since she left here.

February 21, 1883
	Died in Huntsville, Alabama February 19, 1883, MRS. MARY E. STEGALL, wife of J. R. STEGALL of this city...member of the Cumberland Presbyterian Church.
	In memory of JOSEPH RICE, deceased.
	JOSEPH RICE, Esq. died at the residence of his brother-in-law W. R. JONES near New Market, Ala. of acute bronchitis on Monday, February 12, 1883 at 12:15 p.m. in his 86th year. The deceased was born Nov. 5, 1797 in Cooke (Cocke?) County, Tennessee, whither his parents removed to Buncombe, N.C., and in 1806 to the vicinity of what is now New Market in Madison County, which was organized as a County by the Mississippi Territorial Legislature in 1805. His father, SPENCER RICE, dying in 1808, his mother went back to North Carolina taking JOSEPH and his younger brothers LEVI and GEORGE with her. In a few months she died, leaving these little boys to the care of her sister, MRS. SARAH McCATHY. The subject of this sketch and his brother LEVI, young as they were, wishing to live in Alabama, set out on foot and in less than two weeks were again at the present New Market where JOSEPH RICE has since resided, except for six years when he lived in Dallas County, Ala.
	In 1813, when about 16 years old he served under GENERAL JACKSON as a volunteer in the Creek War and (a friend informs us) was one of a

body of volunteers sent from Fayetteville, Tenn. by GENERAL JACKSON to defend Huntsville from a threatened Indian raid, and they came at a double quick, reaching Huntsville, 30 miles distant, in five hours.

On the 18th of February, 1818 he was married to JOHANNA BAYLESS, daughter of HEZEKIAH BAYLESS, Esq. who in 1805 settled on the place where JOHN A. FANNING now lives. This union was blessed with nine children, four sons and five daughters, of whom only one son, DR. FRANCISCO RICE, and three daughters survive him.

In the fall of 1841 he made a profession of faith in Christ but did not attach himself to any Church for several years, when he united with the Baptist Church at New Market, and ever after lived a consistent Christian.

He was of a cheeful, lively disposition, very humorous, having a pleasant smile and word for every one, polite and curteous to the most lowly as to the most honored, liberal in the distribution of his means in the aid of churches and schools, and never turning the poor and needy empty away. In his pursuits as a private citizen and in his official capacity as a Justice of the Peace a love of right and justice was his ruling trait. Few men, if any were more respected than he for these eminent Christian virtues. He died in peace with God and man with a blessed hope of a resurrection of the just...May he rest in peace and rise in Glory.

(NOTE: MR. CARTER RICE, a grandson of JOSEPH RICE, now dead, told us a number of years ago that JOSEPH's father, SPENCER RICE, a Revolutionary Soldier, died here before the county records began. This is the first proof we have found of SPENCER RICE's residence, since he died before land in this county was placed on sale by the Land Office. He had a number of sons, OTHNIEL being another.)

March 17, 1883
Married in Huntsville Thursday night, March 1st, 1883 by REV. DR. J. H. BRYSON, MR. WILLIAM B. VAN VALKENBURG to MISS EMILY BRADLEY, daughter of the late COL. JOS. C. BRADLEY.

Died suddenly of heart disease at the family residence in Maysville at 10 p.m. March 1, 1883, MRS. ANN BARKER STEWART (34 V), wife of MR. WILLIAM STEWART (46 V), aged about 68 years....wife and mother. Her sister MRS. M. C. GALLOWAY of Memphis, Tenn. came up on Saturday to attend her funeral. We extend to her venerable husband and other relatives our sincere sympathies.

March 14, 1883
We were gratified a few days ago to receive from our old and gallant friend CAPT. HUGH L. McCLUNG of Brenham, Texas, a subscription to The Democrat.

Died, March 2, 1883 at New Market, Ala. of pulmonary consumption, MRS. ELIZA M. TALIAFERRO, wife of DR. E. T. TALIAFERRO.

Died, in Huntsville, Ala. March 8, 1883, MRS. MARY SAXON (42 T), aged about 76 years, an old resident (w of JAMES) of Huntsville... member of the Baptist Church.

Died in Huntsville, Ala. March 9, 1883, MR. BENJAMIN H. BAILES (9 A; ELDRIDGE), aged about 38...devoted husband and father...member of the Baptist Church.

Died in Huntsville, Ala. March 9, 1883, MRS. MARY MURPHY (believe should be NANCY, I believe), widow of the late JERE MURPHY in her 82nd year. MRS. MURPHY was born in North Carolina Oct. 22, 1801. She came to Madison County about 66 years ago...devoted wife and mother and member of the Methodist Church. Her husband died in '61. Of nine children four survive her, of whom are ROBERT E. and JERE MURPHY.

March 21, 1883
Died in Huntsville, Ala. March 18, 1883 MRS. CLARA A(NN) SIVELEY (nee MARSHALL; 25 A), widow of the late JOSEPH SIVELEY (33 A) of Madison County, aged 38 years. MRS. SIVELEY was the mother of MRS. GEORGE P. LANDMAN of this city. She died in the triumphs of Christian faith and was buried in the City Cemetery, REV. J. A. B. LOVETT performing the ceremony.

April 4, 1883
MR. THOMAS McFARLAND, formerly of McFARLAND's Mills in this county died of pneumonia at his home in Gurleysvolle, Ala. March 22, 1883.

He was born in Scotland and came to Alabama about 26 years ago.

MRS. ELLEN N. WEAKLEY (42 IRE), widow of the late JAMES H. WEAKLEY (52 V) of Florence, Ala. and sister of the late JAMES I. DONEGAN of this city died of pneumonia at St. Cecelia Academy, Nashville, Tenn. March 30, 1883, aged 81 years. MRS. WEAKLEY was born in Cork, Ireland and came to the United States when about 18 years old, landing at Baltimore. Afterward she came to Alabama, and married Judge WEAKLEY, who died many years ago. She lived in Huntsville during the greater part of her widowhood but left here several years ago to reside in Nashville better to enjoy the religious privileges of the Roman Catholic Church.

MRS. MATILDA C. FLETCHER, (38 V) widow of the late JAMES N. FLETCHER (62 V) died at her home near Madison, Ala. on Sunday April 1, 1883 aged about 75 years. MRS. FLETCHER was born in Chesterfield County, Virginia in 1808, married in Manchester, Virginia in 1826 and came to Madison County, Ala. in 1833. Before and after her husband's death her home was the happy abode of a large family.... Methodist Episcopal Church of which she was a devoted member 50 years...leaves a large family of children, grandchildren, other kindred and many friends.

MRS. MARTHA H(ARVIE) BONE (48 G), relict of the late REV. MATTHEW H. BONE (48 K) of the Cumberland Presbyterian Church died at her home in Madison County, Ala. April 3, 1883 in the 81st year of her age.

April 11, 1883

MR. THOS. N. MARTIN (36 A) died April 3, 1883 at his residence at Madison X Roads, Ala. in his 69th year. 'SQUIRE MARTIN was born in Madison County Nov. 20, 1814. He was a good and useful citizen, a prominent man in his neighborhood, esteemed for his blunt honesty of speech and integrity of conduct, kindness and hospitality to friends, and devoted affection to his family. He was for many years a Justice of the Peace, and also post master at Madison X Roads. May he rest in peace and rise in glory.

April 18, 1883

REV. FREDERICK A. ROSE died of pneumonia at his residence in Huntsville, April 13, 1883, aged 86 on December 25, 1882.

DR. ROSS was a native of Virginia, and educated at the Moravian School at Nazareth, Pa. and at Dickinson College, Carlisle, Pa. and entered the ministry of the Presbyterian Church when about 28 years old...he began his ministerial life in Southwestern Va. and remained there until about 1853/4, was then called to a church in Chattanooga, remained there a year or two, then accepted a call to the church in Huntsville, and remained in its charge about 20 years. His family has our sincere sympathy in their bereavement of devoted husband and father.

April 25, 1883

Married in the City of New York at the residence of the bride's father, MR. HORACE E. GARTH by REV. D. HALL, MR. WINSTON F. GARTH of Huntsville to MISS LENE GARTH.

In Opelika, Ala. April 10, 1883 REV. DR. ANSON WEST of the North Ala. Conference to MRS. Z. A. SWEARENGEN.

MRS. ELIZA BRANDON SEELYE (7 A; MARY J.), after a long illness died at the residence of her brother CAPT. JOHN D. BRANDON (14 A) in Huntsville, Ala. April 19, 1883 aged about 50 years. MRS. SEELYE was a dutiful and affectionate daughter, sister, wife and mother...member Methodist Church.

MRS. ABBY E(MMA) SPENCE (30 NJ), widow of the late WILLIAM SPENCE (35 V), died after a few days illness at her residence in Huntsville, Apr. 24, 1883 at an advanced age. Methodist.

MRS. (MARIA) FRANCES BAILEY (26 A), widow of the late JOSEPH BAILEY (31 MISS (F.)) died at her residence on the Huntsville & Whitesburg turnpike April 20, 1883. Methodist.

May 9, 1883

MRS. CHERILL B. VAN DE VENTER, wife of DR. JOHN VAN DE VENTER died at the residence in Huntsville Friday night, May 4, 1883...she was faithful in loving ministrations to husband, children and friends... member of the Presbyterian Church.

May 30, 1883
MRS. ELIZABETH KELLY (48 SC), widow of the late HAMPTON W. KELLY
(40 G) and mother of J. W. POLK KELLY of Huntsville died at the residence of her son in law PETER SIMMONS at Hazel Green, Ala. May 25, in
her 84th year. She was a Christian in the Baptist Church. Her remains
were buried in our City Cemetery on Sunday last.

June 6, 1883
MRS. EMILY JOHNSON, widow of DR. JAMES T. JOHNSON dec'd, died
May 29, 1883 at the residence of her daughter MRS. WILLIAM RICHARDSON,
in Frederick, Md.
MRS. MAHALA WINSTON, wife of MR. ISAAC N. WINSTON died May 20,
1883 at Bell Factory Ala. aged about 57 years. MRS. WINSTON was a
most exemplary wife and mother and a Christian in the communion of the
Methodist Church.

June 13, 1883
MR. REAVIS J. TERRY of Birmingham and MISS LENI L. ELLIOTT of
Huntsville were married by REV. J. A. B. LOVETT in this city May 12,
1883.
MRS. MARY MORRIS who was, perhaps, the oldest person in Jackson
County, died at the residence of her son in law WM. POTTER in Maynard's
Cove on the 21st day of May last at the age of 96 years. She had been
married 76 years, and a member of the Baptist Church 76 years. Her
youngest daughter, wife of WM. POTTER, is 51 years of age. The deceased,
it is said, told her daughter and the family of MR. POTTER about 15 days
before she died that an angel had appeared to her and informed her she
would died on the 20th or 21st of May at furtherest. (Scottsboro
Herald.)

June 27, 1883
LARKIN A. WORTHAM (A is right; H. in census; 23 T; WM. H.) died at
his home in Maysville, Ala. June 25, 1883. Methodist.
LOGAN B. REEDY (6 A; JOHN A.) died in Huntsville June 25, 1883.
MR. REEDY was a native of Huntsville, and went to Texas 7 or 8 years
ago. A few weeks ago he returned to his mother's in this city with a
chronic complaint of which he died. We condole with his family in their
loss, especially with his two little fatherless and motherless children.

July 18, 1883
MRS. MARY WOODSON HUFF (10 A), wife of HENRY P. HUFF and daughter
of the late AUGUSTINE J. WITHERS (44 V) died of heart disease at
Salem, Va, July 23 (13?), 1883, aged about 42 years. MRS. HUFF was
born and brought up in Madison County, member of the Episcopal Church...
remains brought to Huntsville and deposited in the city cemetery.
We are grieved to learn that our old friend JOHN C. BRAHAN died
last week at Como (Panola Co.), Miss...earnest Christian in the Episcopal
Church. He was a son of GEN. JOHN BRAHAN, one of the earliest settlers
of Huntsville, brother of MRS. PATTON, wife of GOV. PATTON, and uncle
of MRS. JOHN D. WEEDEN and MRS. J. J. McDAVID...devoted husband and
father.

ALABAMA RECORDS---VOLUME 173

Compiled by

KATHLEEN PAUL JONES and PAULINE JONES GANDRUD

September, 1957

Madison County Newspapers:
Huntsville Independent 1878
Huntsville Mercury 1825
Huntsville New South
Huntsville Mercury 1890
Huntsville Mercury 1891
Huntsville Mercury 1883
Huntsville Mercury 1892

ALABAMA RECORDS

MADISON COUNTY NEWSPAPERS

The Independent, 1878   (Continued from a previous volume.)

October 3, 1878
        Married on the 9th, by the REV. WILLIAM HIGHTOWER, MR. G. B.
FALKNER and MRS. RACHEL T. KEYES, all of Lawrence County (Moulton
"Advertiser.")
        Died in the Big Cove, 4th September 1878 HETTIE D. (30 Kentucky)
wife of JAMES L. WEBSTER (35 Alabama) in the 59th year of her age.
Pulaski, Tennessee papers please copy.
        A dispatch was received by DR. FENNELL of Triana last Friday from
Holly Springs, Mississippi. "Drs. G. M. FENNELL and J. W. FENNELL both
dead." These two noble specimens of men had many relatives in this
section. They stood at the post of danger. They did their duty.
        MRS. AMY BOLDMAN, an aged and highly esteemed member of the
Methodist Church of Huntsville, died at the residence of MR. B. F. STINE
in Tuscumbia last Monday. The funeral was from the Methodist church
yesterday. The deceased was the wife of the late H. H. BOLDMAN and
mother of MRS. JAMES A. PICKARD.
        MISS SOPHRONIA WHITE died five miles from this city Monday night
of erysipelas and was interred in the City Cemetery yesterday.
        The remains of MISS SARAH H. LEWIS, daughter of MRS. JOHN H. LEWIS
of Huntsville, were brought from Houston, Texas, and interred in our
City Cemetery Sunday.
        It was found necessary to amputate the limb of MRS. CORINNE
GOODMAN above the knee. DRS. SAUNDERS, ERSKINE, ROBINSON and LOWRY.
        In Memoriam. MRS. AMY BOLDMAN was born in Lee County, Virginia,
and died in Tuscumbia September 30, 1878. She was converted and
joined the Methodist Church when quite young. She leaves four daughters.
W. C. HEARN, her Pastor.

October 17, 1878
        Decatur.
        MRS. W. G. GILL is dead of the fever.
        DR. DEAGNES of Florence is dead of the fever.
        JOHN RAGSDALE died at Florence a few days ago.
        HIRAM A. HIGGINS (15 Alabama, Lst., son of HIRAM H. HIGGINS),
formerly of Athens died at National Cemetery, Tennessee of yellow fever,
September 30. He was a member of WARD's Battery.
        ARCHIBALD STRANGE (35 Virginia; Limestone County) one of the oldest
and most respected citizens of Limestone County (to Jean) died at the
residence of his brother EDMUND S. STRANGE on the 8th instant. He
was a native of Fluvanna County, Virginia.
        DR. GEORGE H. MOORE, who died of yellow fever in Memphis, was a
brother of the late GEN. SYDENHAM MOORE of this state.
        MR. JONATHAN FISHER (38 Virginia, Limestone County) who came here
from Decatur on Wednesday died Saturday night at the residence of
MARSHALL BAKER in this city, of yellow fever. He was 67 years of age.
There was not a kinder, more honest man in North Alabama than MR. FISHER.
His wife has the sympathy of all. He was a native of Virginia.
        Died of apoplexy, in Huntsville, Thursday the 10th of October 1878
WORLEY WHITE (33 North Carolina; WHORLEY on tombstone--WORLEY in
census) in his 65th (tombstone says 60th) year. He was a native of the
State of North Carolina and moved to Huntsville about 40 years ago.
Unmarried.
        In Memoriam. MARY ELLETT. She laid her down in peace September 5,
1878...a Carolinean by birth but for many years a resident of Madison
County.... To her children she was all that made life lovely--let this
be balm to the hearts of her children and grandchildren.

MR. GEORGE T. RATHER, who contracted yellow fever in Memphis,
died at Tuscumbia last week.

The death of MRS. MARGARET E. HORTON, wife of R. VAN HORTON,
which occurred at the residence of DR. J. P. HAMPTON, is spoken of
most pathetically in an In Memoriam in the Athens (to Jean) "Post."

Married, in Limestone County (to Jean) September 25th, WILLIAM A.
GARRETT to MATILDA M. daughter of CLEM W. JOHNSON.

October 24, 1878

COLONEL LEE BREWER (is this LEROY? 28 Alabama) will soon leave
Jackson County to make his home in Texas.

MR. WEAVER, shot at Hazel Green by one TALLENT, is dead.

GABE HOLLOWAY, stabbed by his brother, will likely recover.

REVEREND JOEL W. WHITTEN, pastor of the Methodist Church at
Decatur, died of the yellow fever. (cemetery at Florence--REV. JOEL W.
WHITTEN born December 27, 1823, died October 20, 1878 of yellow fever.
ELIZA MERCER WHITTEN born 1827-1911--a devoted wife, mother and friend)

Married at Maysville, September 17, 1878, THOMAS BLANTON and
MRS. LIZZIE POLLARD, all of this city.

Frost at last! Meaning end of the yellow fever epidemic...
October 31 MRS. RODGERS, wife of the old gentleman who died of the
yellow fever, is also dead.

Married at the residence of the bride's father COL. JAMES M.
McGAHA on the Huntsville and Whitesburg Pike 10th of October by
REV. L. F. WHITEN, MR. PRYOR B. FARLEY to MISS SUE V. McGAHA.

Married at Triana, October 11, 1878 DR. W. T. HENSLEY to MISS
BIRDIE LEFTWICH, daughter of the late DR. WILLIAM LEFTWICH of Huntsville.

Married, Tuesday the 29th at Grace Church, New Market, Frederick
County, Maryland WILLIAM L. CLAY of Huntsville to MISS LOUISA JOHNSON.

It was a mistake, about the death of DR. GEORGE T. MOORE; he was
very ill, but is recovering.

DR. ALEXANDER ERSKINE of Memphis has been on a visit here.

November 7, 1878

MRS. MAGGIE TOWNSEND, wife of HON. JOHN M. TOWNSEND, died at their
home in Limestone County October 13th.

Married at Elkmont, by REV. C. W. MITCHELL, H. C. REDUS to
MISS ANNIE McWILLIAMS, also on October 24th, F. RAYBURN DALY to
MISS REBECCA, daughter of COL. THOMAS REDUS of Elkmont.

HON. BANTON SANDERS (21 Alabama, Limestone County) has had the
hand of affliction laid upon him. A few days since we learned of the
death of his brother Oliver P. Sanders who lived near Granada, Mississippi, then the wife of his brother and his daughter. Athens "Post."

November 14, 1878

NICHOLAS PERKINS of Pulaski and ELILAH F., daughter of J. C.
HUNTER, REUBEN ELLIS and MARGARET DALTON, CHARLES HOLLINGSWORTH and
LAURA V. HORTON, GEORGE W. WATTS and MARY M. THOMAS were recently
married, all in Limestone County.

The death of Postmaster HENRY at Decatur is announced--yellow
fever.

WALKER COLEMAN of New Orleans has been (visiting) in Huntsville.

November 21, 1878

Married November 12 at the residence of the bride's father at
Elton, Tennessee, DR. J. W. BARCLAY of Madison County to MISS GLOVINA P.
BAUGH.

Marriage of MR. J. W. McCLUNG to MISS JOSEPHINE A., youngest
daughter of R. BEVERLY COLE...the bride is a charming and accomplished
lady, as San Franciscans well know and her father is a distinguished
physician and surgeon. MR. McCLUNG is one of the famous McCLUNGS of
the South and is Assistant Secretary of the San Francisco Stock and
Exchange Board. San Francisco "Stock Report"

The Shelby "Sentinel" was in mourning for W. W. McMATH.

MRS. JACK HAY, daughter of JOHN ADAY, died a week or two ago at
McComb City, Louisiana of yellow fever. JACK HAY had died some weeks
previous of the same disease. They left five helpless children who
will be brought here and cared for by MISS KITTIE MANN. (note on
page 5, volumn 173--re JACK HAY--MISS KITTIE MAN reared TIM HAY

385

children--including ANNIE and KATIE. "Democrat 6-3-96 MISSES ANNIE
and KATIE HAY have received tickets from their aunt MRS. HADDICK of
Sunderland, England to come to England to visit relatives." You
remember MR. TOM HAY and MR. JOHN, who was CARROLL HAY's father. I
can't think of #5, if ever I knew--may have died too)
    MRS. ANNA BUTTERFIELD, formerly of this city, died recently in
Montgomery.

November 28, 1878
    Died in this city the 22nd instant of consumption MATTIE L. MASON,
wife of JOHN R. MASON and daughter of JAS. W. POLLARD (22 in Alabama).
    JOHN CARLTON died at Stevenson the 18th instant.
    Married, in South Florence Sunday evening the 17th instant at
the residence of the bride's stepfather C. P. CONWAY, Esq., MR.
DeFORREST HYDE of Florence to MISS MARTHA R. DAVIS.

December 5, 1878
    Died of congestion, in Madison County November 29, 1878 MRS.
ELEANOR R. SCOTT, wife of SAMUEL SCOTT deceased, aged 46 years, 9 months,
12 days, leaving seven sons to mourn her loss. She was a native of
Limestone County...professed religion in 1848. A Friend.
    R. W. AUSTON, son of the late JOHN H. AUSTIN of Decatur, is
a practicing attorney in Washington City.
    MRS. MARYLAND HENRY, wife of the late postmaster of Decatur, who
died of yellow fever, has been commissioned to take charge of the
Decatur post office.

December 12, 1878
    MR. CREED L. TAYLOR an old and respected citizen of Marshall
County was adjudged insane last Monday and ordered sent to the asylum
at Tuscaloosa. MR. TAYLOR was for many years a citizen of this county.
    MR. W. B. GLOVER, JAMES I. HADEN and MAY I. BAKER from over in
Big Cove have located in Cameron, Milan County, Texas. (Note--"MAY I"
may be MAI. HPJ)
    Married at the residence of the bride's father COL. JOSEPH W. NIX,
MR. T. D. MITCHELL to MISS SALLIE NIX, at Talladega, Alabama November 26.
MR. MITCHELL, formerly of Madison County is now of Waco, Texas.
    Married at the residence of the bride's father REV. GEORGE W.
CARMICHAEL near New Market on the 20th instant MISS BETTIE CARMICHAEL
to MR. B. F. COOLEY of Knoxville, Tennessee.
    On the 4th instant at the residence of DR. G. E. KUMPE at
Leighton, Alabama MR. GEORGE E. KUMPE to MISS NINA BARCLAY.
    DR. MONROE BANISTER was commissioned in the Surgeon's Department
of the U.S. Army...is spending a few days with his father's family
here...will soon enter on his duties.

December 26, 1878
    Died, EDWARD ORR, formerly of Morgan County.
    JAMES ARNOLD, formerly of Decatur, died suddenly in Limestone
County last week.
    W. R. TAYLOR, who went to Texas from the Paint Rock Valley, is
dead.
    CHARLES G. ROSS, son of DR. F. A. ROSS, was admitted to the
practice of law.
    Died at his residence near Russellville, Alabama 5th November 1878
DR. FREDERICK H. ANDERSON in her 76th year.
    In Memoriam, MARY ELIZABETH NEWMAN, wife of the late DR. FRANCIS H.
NEWMAN, was born in Hanover County, Virginia September 17, 1817 and
died in Huntsville, Alabama December 19, 1878. The deceased was one of
the only two children raised, both the same age, of CAPT. WILLIAM
POWERS, who served his country in the War of 1812. The deceased came
to Alabama in infancy, married young, and shortly after connected
herself with the Methodist Church. She was the mother of thirteen
children of whom there are eleven surviving.

January 4, 1885
    REV. PETER M. MAPLES (to pp.) died of paralysis at his residence
near Bethel Church in this county on Wednesday, January 7, 1885 in
his 81st year. He was a native of East Tennessee and one of the
pioneer settlers of New Madison, coming here in the year 1830. Shortly
afterward he purchased his present homestead at the public land sale
and resided there until his death. He was the beloved pastor of the
Primitive Baptist Church at Bethel about thirty years.
    WILLIAM ROUTE and family from Meridianville leave tonight for
Texas, their future home.
    MR. JOHN T. PATTERSON died at his residence in this city last
Wednesday night, in the 58th year of his age...buried in the City
Cemetery Friday morning from the Cumberland Presbyterian Church under
the auspices of the Order of the Odd Fellows, participated in by the
Knights of Pythias and Knights of Honor "each of which he was a member."
MR. PATTERSON was one of the few surviving veterans of the Mexican
War, in which he contracted a chronic disease of dearrhoe and never
recovered. He leaves a widow and several children.

February 11, 1885 (inside page marked February 4...they often failed
                    to change)
    Died at Mt. Adams, Arkansas 23 January 1885 MR. WILLIAM B. BRADLEY
in his 51st year. MR. BRADLEY was born and reared in Huntsville, a
brother of MR. JOHN BRADLEY and MRS. THOMAS W. WHITE of this city.
He moved to Arkansas a number of years ago.
    Died in this city Sunday morning DR. DAVID D. SHELBY in the 71st
year of his age. He was buried Monday morning, with funeral services
at the grave by DR. BANISTER. Some time before his death he had
practically retired from active practice of medicine. As a husband
and father he was kind, affectionate and indulgent...one of the most
thoroughly and punctiliously honorable men the world ever knew.

February 18, 1885
    Mooresville. DR. J. W. and C. C. WITHERS, twin brothers and sons
of DR. J. S. WITHERS, have been up on a visit from their Arkansas home.
    We regret to learn of the death of MRS. COLEMAN in Athens Monday
night, full of years...she was the venerable mother of MESSRS. DAN and
FRANK COLEMAN of this city.
    Died, Monday afternoon, MARTHA EASON GORDON, wife of GEORGE S.
GORDON...buried from the Church of the Nativity.

March 4, 1885
    Died in this city Sunday morning NICHOLAS DAVIS, of tubercular
menengitis. He leaves a wife and two children, SHELLY and RODNEY.
(Half a column, Resolutions by the Huntsville Bar; W. L. CLAY's tribute
stated that before the age of 19 he was admitted to practice in the
Supreme Court of the State.)
    Died at his home near Florence last Saturday morning ex-Gov.
R. M. PATTON in the 78th year of his age. Funeral services were held
in this city last Monday at the Presbyterian Church, conducted by
DR. J. H. BRYSON. (Gives copy of funeral oration.)

March 17, 1885
    Died, February 9, 1885, MRS. JANE JENKINS aged 83 years 11 months.
SISTER JENKINS had been a consistent member of the Cumberland Presbyterian Church for 68 years.   F. J. TYLER

March 26, 1885
    Died Saturday, MR. ENOCH CARLTON ELLIOTT in his 23rd year.
    The remains of MRS. WALTER ROBINSON reached here Sunday night from
Georgia and buried from the Methodist Church Sunday noon, REV. JOHN A.
THOMPSON officiating. MRS. ROBINSON was MISS BIRDIE MOORE. To the
bereaved husband and the family we extend sympathy. (note--daughter
JUDGE WM. HENRY MOORE, great-niece of GABRIEL MOORE. KPJ)
    MRS. F. M. TAYLOR, lately a resident of this city died in Memphis,
Tennessee Saturday. The remains were brought to Huntsville and buried

from the residence of MR. J. B. BEADLE. MRS. TAYLOR was a daughter of
MR. JOSHUA H. BEADLE of this city.

April 1, 1885
Died at New Market March 20, 1885, MRS. NICIE RODGERS (volume 76,
page 12), widow of MR. ROBERT RODGERS. She was born in 1814, married
in 1831, and in 1859 joined the Cumberland Presbyterian Church.

April 8, 1885
Married at Madison at the residence of the bride's mother,
MRS. BETTIE FLOYD PERKINS, MR. WILLIE T. DOUGLASS of Marshall County,
Alabama to MISS LILLIE PERKINS.

April 15, 1885
Florence Gazette, April 11. With deep regret we announce the
death of MR. JACKSON VAN BUREN RICE (18 in Alabama, Morgan County,
son of GREEN P.) which occurred Saturday morning. He was 54 years of
age, a native of Morgan County but had been residing in Florence 35
years. He leaves a wife and several children.

May 6, 1885
Marriage of a former Huntsville girl. (Taken from the Waco
(Texas) Daily Examiner) MR. CLAY CLARK to MISS CLARA L. DAVID.

May 13, 1885
Died in this city Sunday night at the BEIRNE residence, MISS
ELIZA GRAY BEIRNE.
MR. PERRY L. HARRISON, SR. died this morning at his home in this
city in his 56th year. He was born near Viena and lived in Madison
County nearly all his life. He filled the offices of County Commis-
sioner and Tax Collector. About a year ago he affiliated himself with
the Cumberland Presbyterian Church. He leaves a widow and six children.

May 20, 1885
Friends of DR. ISAAC F(OX) DELONEY will regret to know he has
moved to Ednaville, Texas.
News reached the city from Birmingham that MR. WILLIAM BRADLEY
had seriously shot MR. HENRY BARNARD...know nothing of the real facts.
Died at his home in this city, MR. HENRY MOTZ Tuesday morning;
came here many years ago from Ohio.

May 27, 1885
Mooresville. MR. and MRS. MISER from Blount County, East
Tennessee are visiting their daughter MRS. R. H. HAFLEY. MRS. GRAY
from Williamson County and MISS KENNARD from Maury County, Tennessee
are visiting--the former is the mother and latter a sister of MRS.
J. N. McDONALD.
We were grieved to hear last week of the sudden death of MR.
W. G. LAXSON (30 in Tennessee) of New Market, while quietly seated in
his chair, his wife reading to him. MR. LAXSON was an old, esteemed,
and valuable citizen, long a resident of Madison County.

June 3, 1885
Married Saturday morning May 25th at seven o'clock at the residence
of the bride's mother in Maysville MISS MARIA JOHNSTON to CAPT. BRAME
of West Point, Mississippi.
Married, at the residence of the bride's mother in this city
Tuesday, June 2, MR. J. D. DAVIS of Iowa to MISS ANNA McANALLY.

June 10, 1885
Died in this city Friday, MRS. PERCY M. SLOSS at the residence of
JOSEPH H. SLOSS, Esq. She leaves a devoted young husband.

June 17, 1885
MRS. CAROLINE HORTON and daughter MISS ANNA of Aberdeen, Mississippi
are visiting the family of DR. J. J. DEMENT.
We learn with regret of the death of MR. PETER WHITE last Saturday
at his home in Bell Green. He was Editor of the Franklin County News
and a native of Lawrence County, aged 43 years. He was a brother of the
MESSRS. WHITE, editors of the Moulton Advertiser.

July 8, 1885
    In Memoriam. Haden, Alabama July 4. Died July 2, 1885, MRS.
E. J. McGAHA in her 61st year. Cousin BETSY JANE was born and raised
in the Cove. Her maiden name was BRAZELTON. She joined the Cumberland
Presbyterian Church when young...consumption...her husband and four
children preceeded her, only two left.

July 15, 1885
    From Rep. With regret we learn through the Decatur News of the
death of MR. WILLIE CRAIG of Floral City, Florida. He left Madison
a little over a year ago...leaves a wife and little daughter.
    MISSES ANNE and BESSIE MARTIN of Huntsville got here yesterday to
visit their grandfather, GEN. S. D. WEAKLEY. Florence Gazette
    Married, at the residence of the bride's father on Franklin Street
Tuesday morning, MR. SAMUEL L. NELSON of Mississippi to MISS ADDIE B.
HUNT.

August 19, 1885
    MRS. MARY PITMAN RICE died at her residence in this city this
morning, aged 83. Born in Virginia, only child of LUELLEN and NANCY
JONES, in early life came to Huntsville, married ELISHA HICKMAN RICE,
who died several years before the war. MRS. RICE leaves no children.

September 23, 1885
    MR. MICHAEL WELLS, living near Leon, Crenshaw County, died a few
days ago, between 75 and 80 years of age. He had lived in that county
since 1840; Deacon in the Primitive Baptist Church.

October 7, 1885
    Died at Nashville, Tennessee October 3rd, MRS. MARY FLIPPIN, aged
85 years. MRS. FLIPPIN was for more than half a century a resident of
this county. She was born in Virginia but her family moved here when
she was yet a girl. Some are still honored citizens of Madison County.
The remains of MRS. FLIPPIN were interred in the family burying ground
near Bethel Church, Sunday October 4. (Census of 1850, Madison County,
shows FRANCIS FLIPPEN, 61 born in Virginia; MARY FLIPPEN, 52 born in
Virginia and their children. She was a DOUGLASS.)

October 21, 1885
    Mooresville, REV. J. N. McDONALD was called to Athens Tuesday last
to attend the funeral of MRS. JUDGE McCLOUD. She was a daughter of the
late DR. HUSSEY of this place, who preceeded the daughter just three
years to the day.

October 28, 1885
    MRS. JOSEPHINE E. BENTLEY died Sunday morning at her residence at
Meridianville. She was a native of this county and the only daughter
of the late JAMES N. HARRIS. In 1865 she married A. J. BENTLEY.
Surrounded by sorrowing friends, her loving husband and two children,
she died. She was an active member of the Methodist Episcopal Church.

November 18, 1885
    Mooresville. November 16. Our town was shocked early Saturday
night at the sad intelligence that MRS. DR. H. W. HILL had suddenly
died. She was a sister of MRS. R. C. GAMBLE and MRS. DR. THACH. Her
maiden name was GIRAULT. Friends tender sympathy to DR. HILL. Interment took place at the GAMBLE family graveyard. While there MR.
GAMBLE planted (pointed?) out a row of eight graves, all his own
children.
    MR. NATHAN A. BESTIE of New Market has gone to Arkansas where he
proposes to reside in the future.
    Notes regarding New Market, states it has DRS. J. C. BLANTON,
G. E. BLANTON, D. LIPSCOMB, J. A. R. JONES and F. RICE, also G. D.
NORRIS, E. T. TALIAFERRO and P. M. HALL, retired.

December 9, 1885
    Died Monday night at his home near Princeton, Jackson County,
Alabama MR. RUSSELL M. CLAY (39 in South Carolina; RUSSELL W. in
census; Jackson County). MR. CLAY had lived beyond the allotted time

of man being eighty years of age. He was a man noted for many of the noblest traits. MR. CLAY had acquired a large estate and was one of the wealthiest citizens of Jackson County. He leaves a widow, three married daughters and an only son, MR. M(ARTIN) A. CLAY (5 in Alabama). MRS. CLAY is far advanced in years and in very feeble health.

Rep. MR. E. E. KEY and family leave today for Manor, Texas, where he will make his future home.

December 16, 1885

Talladega, December 9. The community was saddened by the death of MRS. TAUL BRADFORD yesterday. She was a sister of the late JAMES T. HARDIE of Montgomery.

MR. THOMAS DAVIS, a most excellent citizen, died yesterday at the residence of his daughter, MRS. H. B. HARTZ.

In Memoriam. MRS. ADDIE TATE RICE, wife of our brother DR. FRANCISCO RICE, born March 25, 1838, died October 30, 1885. They were married March 25, 1860 and eight children were born to them. Five survive her. By Cumberland Lodge I. O. O. F., New Market, Alabama.

December 23, 1885

Haden's. December 21. Died...MRS. JERUSHA MEDLIN whose maiden name was GRAYSON, sister of HON. J. W. GRAYSON, a devoted member of the Cumberland Presbyterian Church. The next death was MRS. PARLIE MOON whose maiden name was BRAZELTON. (note--PARALEE MOON elsewhere.)

MRS. S. D. PICKENS was with us a few days last week. The sun always shines when she is with us. She is very old, 82, but full of life and religion. She has been a member of the church for 64 years, and all that time going about doing good. (Note: SELINA BRAZELTON PICKENS, wife of JOSEPH PICKENS. KPJ)

On December 2nd JAMES B. KENNEDY was united in marriage to MRS. TEXANA McKINNEY. (Column signed by "SOLO.")

December 30, 1885

Mooresville. MR. THOMAS COLLIER and family from Arkansas are visiting relatives.

NEW SOUTH 1885

January 10, 1885

Died two miles east of New Hope at the residence of his father J. A. F. VANN on January 3, WALTER A. VANN, born August 8, 1858. An affectionate husband, kind to his parents and forgiving to his brothers and sisters.

Died in this city January 5, LOUIS LUCET, for many years Professor of French in the schools here.

February 14, 1885

Died, WILLIAM G. (BARLOW) BRADLEY at Mt. Adams, Arkansas. The deceased leaves a wife and three children; he was born and raised here.

Died, DR. DAVID SHELBY at his residence in Huntsville Saturday in his 71st year.

February 21, 1885

Died at Athens 16th February 1885 MRS. ELIZABETH COLEMAN, relict of JUDGE DANIEL COLEMAN. She was born in Northampton County, North Carolina May 22, 1811. In the death of this grand and noble old lady the country has lost another of those magnificent women who belong to a generation which is nearly extinct, and which were noted for their motherly wisdom, their womanhood, and nobility of character. We extend sympathy to her stricken sons and daughters.

February 28, 1885

MR. JO PARTON, now a citizen of Waco, Texas, is on a visit to Huntsville.

Died, MR. WILLIAM MARTIN, an old and highly respected citizen of Limestone County, in Mooresville last week.

March 7, 1885
    Died in Huntsville, Alabama February 28 NICHOLAS DAVID in his
31st year. As a son he was perfection, as a husband he was gallant,
tender and true, and as a father he was affectionate; the Bar has lost
its brightest member. (Half a column of obituary, and three columns
of resolutions.)
    A historical sketch of Huntsville started, and continued.

March 28, 1885
    Died, MRS. FANNIE TAYLOR, wife of MAJOR FELIX TAYLOR at the
residence of her daughter, MRS. W. G. TAYLOR in Memphis, Saturday
March 21, 1885, of consumption, aged 45. The funeral took place from
the residence of her father MR. JOSHUA H. BEADLE Sunday, March 22nd,
conducted by the REV. F. J. TYLER.
    REV. HERMON HUMPHREY of the Methodist Episcopal Church South died
at Troy, Alabama March 23, 1885. He was a brilliant scholar, of deep
learning, and profoundly devout.
    MRS. MARGARET ROBINSON, wife of MR. WALTER B. ROBINSON and
daughter of JUDGE WILLIAM H. MOORE, died at the residence of her sister
MRS. JENNIE CONNOR at Macon, Georgia March 20, 1885 aged 33.

April 4, 1885
    The History of Huntsville says schools were here as early as 1807...
about the time WYATT BISHOP taught a school here, and MRS. POSEY about
the same time. In 1819 MRS. SARAH McCAY established a school. In
1850 there was a disastrous fire...including the handsome hotel known
as the Caldwell House, and in 1855 another consumed the Bell Tavern.

May 9, 1885
    T. E. CAIN of Lake Charles, Louisiana is visiting his family in
Madison.
    MRS. DR. DAVID MALONE has left for Hurrican Springs, Tennessee
owned by her son-in-law MR. IKE MILLER.

May 16, 1885
    Died at his residence in Huntsville May 13 MR. PERRY L. HARRISON
in his 56th year; he was born and reared in Madison County, a noble
husband, indulgent and kind father.
    Died, at the residence of her mother in this city May 10th,
MISS ELIZA GRAY BEIRNE; funeral from the Church of the Nativity.

November 28, 1885
    MRS. ELIZABETH WALKER, consort of GEN. L. P. WALKER, died in this
city Thursday. We extend sympathy to her only son, L. P. WALKER, of
New York City.
    Jackson, Mississippi. "Clarion." St. Andrews Church was packed
last night...MISS MAI BIRD HILSHEIM was united in marriage to MR.
GRAHAM McF. TINDALL, of Huntsville, Alabama.

December 12, 1885
    MR. PERRY HARRISON and MISS MAMIE VAUGHAN were married in
Pulaski, Tennessee last Monday.

MERCURY, 1890

Page 18A, Volume 173

March 12, 1890 (piece of DeLESSEPS' canal)
    " re loading cotton barges on the streets of New Hope April 20,
Wetumpka. DR. M. G. MOORE, one of the oldest citizens of this place,
was found dead in bed this morning; resident of Wetumpka nearly half
a century; before the war was for many years warden of the penitentiary.
    A/c of the burning of the Donegan House

May 7, 1890
    Re Maysville...was named after Maysville, Kentucky about 50 years
ago. It was Loweville, but was incorporated as Maysville . DANL K

(note not clear) HOLMES, from Maysville. Ky was its first mayor.
After the war he went to Texas. Present biard are DR. LAYMAN, mayor,
with F. A. GILLIAM, J. W. SPRIGGS, J. E. DANIEL, A. J. BYRNE and W. L.
JONES, aldermen. The 1st church built was Ewing Chapel (organized?)
July 19, 1846 by REV. M. H. BONE of the Tennessee Presbytery.
On last page, piece re Monte Sano Ry

June 11, 1890
More about Monte Sano Ry

June 18, 1890
Monte Sano Hotel. List of stockholders of cotton mill

July 29, 1890
The telephone company now has 41 subscribers and prospects are
good for an increase.

July 30, 1890
Roster of Huntsville Guards, CAPT. EGBERT J. JONES, and North
Alabamians; also next page 4th Alabama Infantry and Calvary, and
U.S. Vets.

September 3, 1890
Oil well at New Market down to 500 feet.

September 17, 1890
MRS. DAVID BUSH of near Lacey Springs died on the 8th instant...
husband..d..s.. (too hurried to be careful. Must go back.) (This may
be some of CATHERINE's husband's people.)

MERCURY 1890

January 1, 1890
The death of MRS. ROBERT TYLER of Montgomery is announced. She
was daughter of the tragedian THOMAS _OOPER (torn) and MARY FAIRLIE,
a celebrated _h_le of New York. In 1840 she married ROBERT TYLER,
eldest son of PRESIDENT TYLER, and at the special request of the
President and his wife, an invalid, was the presiding lady of the
White House during the first three years of his term. At her death she
was 74 years of age.
MRS. MARY KEITH, aunt of HON. THOMAS J. TAYLOR, Probate Judge,
died suddenly at his residence on the night of Monday last of heart
disease. MRS. KEITH was an old resident of the county and had been
married and widowed twice. For over ten years she had made her home
with her nephew, JUDGE TAYLOR. The funeral took place today in
Maysville.
(Tombstones, Maysville. JOHN R. DRAKE, son of RUFUS and MARY A.
DRAKE, born February 4, 1850, died December 7, 1878. MARY A. KEITH
born December 3, 1819, died December 30, 1889. JOHN R. was her only
child. KPJ)

January 15, 1890
COL. CHARLES MASTIN received a dispatch from St. Louis announcing
the death of MR. FRANK O'FALLEN, son of JOHN and CAROLINE O'FALLON.
He has been ailing for some time; he leaves a wife and two children,
boys.
Died, DAVID BRADLEY of Bell Mina, January 10th. Buried in the
family burying ground.

January 22, 1890
Died January 13 MRS. C(HARITY) C(AROLINE) GRAYSON, nee PENLAND,
the youngest daughter of REV. ALEX PENLAND of Tirana who in the last
few years has buried his wife and three daughters. She was the wife
of CAPT. J. W. GRAYSON.

January 22, 1890
Resolutions of Respect. L. M. SULLIVAN died at his residence near
Hazel Green January 7, 1890. Pleasant Valley Lodge No. 89 I.O.O.F.

January 29, 1890
    A letter was received in Atlanta Friday stating that MRS. BANKS
WINTER was thought to be dying in Montreal with gripps. She went only
a short time ago with her babe to join MR. WINTER. She was born and
reared (in Huntsville.)

February 3, 1890
    In Memoriam. MRS. MARGARET GRAYSON was born February 18, 1841
and died January 30, 1890. She was a member of the Methodist Church
from her youth up. She left an affectionate husband, three children,
a sister and three brothers. "A Niece." (Is this MRS. N. B. GRAYSON,
shown in the book of death certificates as died January 29th aged 40?)

February 12, 1890
    MR. ISHAM H. HOBBS died at his home near this city Monday at the
advanced age of 75 years. His death was caused by paralysis. In the
death of MR. HOBBS our county loses a time honored citizen, the
Methodist Church a valuable and consistent member and his family a
fond husband and a loving father.
    Wedding account. February 15, 1890 at the residence of MR. A. A.
BAKER, father of the bride, MR. JAMES M. LOVETT to MISS EMMA MAI BAKER,
Prof. J. A. B. LOVETT, assisted by DR. A. B. JONES officiating. The
groom is the junior partner in the firm of J. A. B. LOVETT & Son.

February 18, 1890
    COL. R. R. TOWNS (died) at Athens Sunday. He was a brother-in-law
of HON. C. P. LANE of this city.
    Died, Thursday night, MR. JOHN R. SISK, aged 48.
    Friday night, MRS. JANE W. REEDY, aged 74, a lifelong member of
the Cumberland Presbyterian Church. Her children will keenly feel
their loss.
    Copy of the memorial address, DR. GEORGE D. MORRIS, at his burial,
February 14th. DR. GEORGE D. NORRIS was born at Baltimore, Maryland
October 25, 1811 and died February 12, 1890 aged 78 years, 3 months and
17 days. He graduated at Yale in 1829 in a class of 20, graduated in
medicine at the University of Maryland in 1831, and in 1832 came to
New Market and married MISS MARTHA W. RAGSDALE in 1833, and second to
MISS LUCRETIA J. MARTIN in 1864 who is left to mourn her loss. He
was a Trustee of the Alabama Insane Asylum up to his death...an
enthusiastic member of the Order of Free and Accepted Masons, taking
33 degrees, twice Grand Master of the State of Alabama and Representative of the Grand Lodge of England, commissioned by the Prince of
Wales. He professed religion in 1841 and became an organic member of
the New Market Baptist Church in 1847. He left a wife and children.

February 26, 1890
    Obituary. JOHN W. McGAHA, son of JAMES M. and CAROLINE R. McGAHA
born December 22, 1868.

March 5, 1890
    Resolutions of Respect, MRS. M. A. CAREY, by the Mission Sunday
School.
    MR. JOHN M. McMULLEN died at his home in Meridianville March 2nd...
one of the oldest residents of the county. He had reached the advanced
age of four score. A member of the Cumberland Presbyterian Church...
buried in the family burying ground near Meridianville.
    There is a letter in the Madison (Missouri) Advance, written by
HON. W. S. MILLER, born in Triana 74 years ago. JUDGE and MRS. MILLER
were in Huntsville recently. He moved from this county when only ten
years old.

March 12, 1890
    In Memoriam. ISHAM H. HOBBS (son of JOBN; 36 in Virginia) was
born in Virginia October 22, 1814 and died in Huntsville February 10,
1890. MR. HOBBS moved to Alabama at an early age and spent the greater
part of his life in or near Huntsville. He was married twice, first to
MISS SUSAN S. SANDIDGE (25 in Georgia; daughter of GARRETT), August 24,
1841. His second wife, who survives him was MISS ELLEN PARKER, to
whom he was married April 14, 1872. Both marriages took place in

393

Madison County. He leaves a widow and eight children. He was for many years a member of the Methodist Church. "A Friend."

Madison County Journalism. In 1806 CAPT. JOHN HUNT erected the first log cabin and six years later the first newspaper was published, called the Madison Gazette and a MR. PARHAM who came here from Nashville, Tennessee was the Editor and Publisher. In 1816 MR. THOMAS B. GRANTLAND took over the Gazette and called it the Huntsville Republican. The Republican was merged in the Southern Advocate and the Advocate absorbed by the Mercury.

In 1823 the Democrat was established by PHILIP WOODSON and the first issue appeared October 8th. MR. WOODSON was succeeded by J. WITHERS CLAY in 1849.

The Huntsville Independent was established December 1, 1855 by JOHN J. DEW and JOHN J. YOUNG...MR. DEW went to Memphis and MR. YOUNG was forced to the wall, and it was then taken in charge by W. P. NEWMAN and FRANK COLEMAN. When the Advocate was absorbed by the Mercury MAJOR SLOSS attempted to start a new Advocate but was unsuccessful and sold the plant to CHARLES P. LANE who started a Republican weekly called the New South but it went down unhonored and unsung. Two decades ago MESSRS. CARUTHERS and WRENCH started the North Alabama Reporter but it was not a success.

JAMES WESLEY FARLEY (20 in Alabama; son of MICHAEL and SARAH) died at Madison Station Tuesday. He was born July 12, 1829 (59?), and was nearly 61. When only 16 he united with the Methodist Church. He leaves a wife and five sons. He will be buried this afternoon at the family burying ground on his place. (tombstone--JAMES WESLEY FARLEY born July 12, 1829, died March 11, 1890; FANNIE A. FARLEY born July 19, 1834, died August 6, 1906; married FRANCES ANN CRUTCHER February 9, 1853).

Died--last evening, ALICE HARDIE SEAY at the residence of her mother on West Holmes Street, wife of MR. THOMAS SEAY...leaves her husband, and four children.

March 19, 1890
In Memoriam. On the morning of February 12th in a collision of trains, E. P. DOOLITTLE, engineer for the A. C. S. Left a wife, father, sister...aged 38. Remains were carried to Madison, his father's home for interment.

Monday, at his brother's residence on East Holmes Street, MR. JAMES P. WARWICK. He was born in Philadelphia over 85 years ago, in which city he followed the avocation of merchant tailoring. He has been a citizen of Huntsville 15 years. He was a widower, and his children are all married and settled down, in the East.

Madison, Alabama. The last issue announced the death of MR. J. W FARLEY. This week it is our painful duty to chronicle the death of his oldest son, MR. P. B. FARLEY, of pneumonia. He leaves a wife and five little children. On Sunday morning last his body was taken to the family burying ground.

We regret to announce the death of MRS. HARRIET HARDIE at six o'clock last evening at the family residence on West Holmes Street. (Death Certificate: HARRIET HARDIE, born in Alabama, aged 59, died in Huntsville March 18, 1890; a widow.)

March 26, 1890
In Memoriam. THOMAS GEORGE died March 19, 1890 on his plantation in Madison County, Alabama. He was 65 years of age and a lawyer by profession, a native of the state of Virginia. He graduated at the University of Virginia at the age of 21 and that same year married MISS MARGARET LEE, a daughter of CHAPMAN LEE of the renowned LEE family, and moved to New York; the same year two children were born, LAURA and HELEN. LAURA married your fellow townsman, JAMES H. BONE, late of the Federal Army. HELEN was a member of St. Mary's Episcopal Sisterhood of New York and with two other sisters, was sent to Memphis in the yellow fever epidemic of 1878 to assist stricken orphans in the Episcopal orphanage; a few days after her arrival she died with the fever. His wife died about 1873 and about four years ago he married MISS HAMMOND of Madison County and since has resided on the plantation where he died. He practiced in New York, served two terms on the bench in Orange County, and about fifteen years ago went to Denver.

<u>April 2, 1890</u>

On Thursday, March 20th, at the residence of the parents of the bride, MR. and MRS. J. HENRY LANDMAN, MR. GORDON C. GREENFIELD of Pine Bluff, Arkansas (was married) to MISS LIZZIE W. LANDMAN.

Died, MRS. A. M. NAIL, Monday, at her residence in Big Cove. She was a sister-in-law of MR. J. W. POTTS, Tax Collector.

<u>April 9, 1890</u>

In Memoriam. Died at his home in Madison County, February 24, 1890 MR. J. M. KING, at a ripe old age. He was born and reared near the place where he died; he was in his 74th year. He gave much good advice, even to his grandchildren, exhorting them to live like Christians....   R. A. THOMPSON

<u>April 16, 1890</u>

At 1 o'clock Thursday, at the residence of his brother and sister, MR. and MRS. GEO. W. HUNT, MR. WILLIAM RICE breathed his last at the age of 90 years. He was born near Nashville, Tennessee March 18, 1800, a son of JOEL L. and ELIZABETH RICE, and one of sixteen children, only two of whom survive him, MRS. GEO. W. HUNT of this city and MR. A. J. RICE of Florida. The funeral took place Friday morning, conducted by REV. J. H. BRYSON, D.D. (Death certificate; WILLIAM M. RICE aged 90 born in Tennessee, died in Huntsville May 10, 1890, single.)

Married in Fayetteville April 12, MR. DAN POWELL to MISS MATILDA NANCE, both of Madison County.

MR. JAMES S. McDONNELL, youngest son of A. McDONNELL, SR. Esq. of this county, was married Tuesday last at Althmier, Arkansas to MISS SUSIE BELLE HUNTER of that place.

<u>April 30, 1890</u>

On Monday, April 14 MR. JAMES L. BROWNING died at his home in the Lone Star State, aged 78. He was the father of MRS. G. M. NEELY of this city.

Married. Wednesday April 28th at the home of the parents of the bride, MR. JOSEPH GOLIGHTLY of Florence to MISS KATIE LEE, eldest daughter of MR. and MRS. GEO. M. NEELY of this city. The flower bearers were sisters of the bride, MISSES CARRIE and GEORGIA NEELY.

An invitation was received by MR. GEORGE B. GILL to the wedding of his nephew J. O. GILL, formerly of this city, on April 24th to MISS WINNIE TERRY of Dallas, Texas; he is the son of CHARLES O. GILL.

Died, at her home in New Market on April 22, 1890, MRS. EMMA LOVE, wife of MR. F. C. LOVE...born in May, 1855...left husband and five daughters.

<u>May 21, 1890</u>

F. P. WARD, Esq., an old and highly esteemed citizen of Huntsville (died) in Nashville Wednesday. He began life as a physician, then was a builder and contractor and then finally settled on the legal profession. He was born in one of the Carolinas about 65 years ago and has been living in Huntsville the past 45 years.

<u>May 28, 1890</u>

In Memoriam. MRS. F. A. ROSS, died in Rogersville, Tennessee May 29, 1890. Signed by "The Pupils of the Synodical College."

Resolutions of Respect by Lodge 309, Knights of Honor, in the death of ABRAHAM NEWMAN.

<u>June 4, 1890</u>

THOMAS W. WHITE (33 in Virginia), born in Abingdon, Virginia (died 30 May 1890) the 15th of August, 1817 when a young man, moved to Huntsville. Here in our midst he built a character and led a life full of honor, full of kindness and full of affection. As a husband and father he was perfection, as a citizen he was an ornament to any community.

<u>June 11, 1890</u>

New Market Notes. June 10, 1890. MR. JOE PIKE, one of the oldest residents of this place died Sunday morning. He was a member of the Methodist Church...was buried in the old Davis Cemetery.

June 18, 1890
        We learn of the sudden death of MR. JOHN CRUTCHER at Triana
yesterday of heart disease. He was a brother-in-law of MRS. HENRY B.
DILLARD.

July 23, 1890
        A shooting scrape this morning JOHN A. STEELE, JR., Mayor of the
city and son of JUDGE JOHN STEELE was instantly killed by JOHN W.
GOODWIN, and the latter injured by TOM STEELE, brother of the Mayor.
(Dispatch from Tuscumbia, July 18th.)
        News of the death of MR. C. Q. WHITE at his residence near
Hazel Green Saturday has reached the city. Funeral services were held
at his late residence Sunday morning and the remains brought to this
city for interment.
        Died at his residence on Spragins Street yesterday evening,
DANIEL C. CLARK of consumption.

August 13, 1890
        Friends of MR. JAMES H. WARE will be pained to learn of his
sudden death Wednesday night, in his 79th year. He came to this county
from Virginia when a young man. The bereaved family have the sympathy
of the entire community.

August 20, 1890
        Died at the residence of his father, JOHN A. ERWIN, August 14th,
GEORGE T. ERWIN, aged 38. Baptist.
        In Memoriam. MRS. JOHN W. WALKER, born June 1, 1855, died August 13,
1890 aged 35. On November 18, 1880 she married MR. JOHN W. WALKER,
a merchant, of Plevna....

September 3, 1890
        Scottsboro. Died at Larkinsville September 1st, MR. DAVE LARKIN,
married only a few months. There were two deaths in Scottsboro of
heart disease last week, MRS. J. B. McCORD and MISS BURROWS.

September 10, 1890
        Relatives and friends of WILLIAM LAWLER will regret to hear of
his death August 20, 1890 at Camden, Wilcox County, Alabama. He was a
native of Madison County.
        In Memoriam. Died at the residence of her parents in New Market,
August 26, 1890, MISS FANNIE D. FUQUA.
        La Grange. Account of a shooting affair Monday in which MR.
THOMAS B. BEASLEY was shot in a difficulty with a painter working for
him; MR. BEASLEY died.

September 17, 1890
        Article re the National Farmer Congress selecting the golden rod
as the national flower...the movement was started by MRS. AURORA PRYOR
McCLELLAN, wife of HON. R. A. McCLELLAN of Athens and eldest daughter
of ex-Senator (U.S.) LUKE PRYOR.
        MRS. PARTHENIA BROWN, wife of MR. THOMAS W. BROWN (died) Tuesday
at her residence on Meridian Pike...buried in the City Cemetery.

September 24, 1890
        MR. DAVID JACKS and wife, of Larkins' Fork, visited their daughter
MRS. RICE. (from New Market notes)
        The death of JOHN P. SPENCE occurred Monday night from a pistol
wound by his own hands. He was born in this city April 30, 1847 and
has been married about 21 years. He leaves a wife, four girls and two
boys. For many years he has been Engineer of the City Fire Department.

October 22, 1890
        JOHN PERVIN, an aged farmer who lives between Madison and
Cluttsville, was shot through the heart by his nephew JOHN BALCH...an
old family feud...both parties have many friends who will regret to
hear of the sad affair.

November 12, 1890
        MR. JOHN E. BENTLEY of this city died this morning at McMinnville,
Tennessee of typhoid fever. MR. BENTLEY came to Tennessee in his youth

from Alabama...was a member of the firm of FIFE, LYLES, DAVIS and
Company. He was 42 years of age, and leaves a wife and two children.
Nashville Banner. The deceased was well known in this city, and a
brother of A. J. BENTLEY, who was with him when he died, having been
called by telegram.

November 19, 1890
        Married at the residence of the bride's mother, MRS. ELIZABETH
SHEFFEY, Wednesday, MR. DAVID K. COLLINS of Bryson, North Carolina to
MISS ELLEN H. SHEFFEY.

November 26, 1890
        Resolutions of Respect. Chestnut Grove Farmers' Alliance No. 64,
Berkley, Alabama on the death of G. W. GLOVER who died November 9,
1890. The bereaved family has lost husband, father, brother.

December 3, 1890
        Early Monday morning MRS. ANNIE R. CONWAY, wife of Alderman
JAMES CONWAY, died. Funeral was from the Catholic Church.
        MR. J. R. McKINNEY, an aged and highly respected citizen of the
county, died near Brownsboro, yesterday morning. (Death Certificate--
J. R. McKINNEY, born in Alabama, aged 65, married, died December 2,
1890 at Meridianville.)

December 31, 1890
        Died, COL. HUGH LAWSON CLAY. He was born in Huntsville January 16,
1822, educated at Green Academy, University of Alabama, University of
Virginia, Captain in the War with Mexico, Captain of U.S. 13th Infantry,
March 5, 1847, Company H, COL. R. M. ECHOLS commanding the regiment.
In May 1855 he married MISS CELESTE COMER of Macon, Georgia. Served
in the Confederate Army. (No child survived.) (Death Certificate 69)

January 7, 1891
        Died, MRS. NANNIE MAXWELL, daughter of MR. J. MURRAY ROBERTSON,
at her father's residence, Sunday. The remains were brought to this
city and funeral services held from the Episcopal Church.

January 14, 1891
        MRS. SALLIE S. TAYLOR, born December 5, 1867, joined the Cumberland
Presbyterian Church at Union Chapel in the fall of 1885, was married
to W. S. TAYLOR in this city. February 19, 1890 and died January 9,
1891.
        In Memoriam. NANNIE D. MAXWELL, eldest daughter of J. MURRAY
ROBERTSON, aged 34.
        MRS. AGGIE PHARR, after a pleasant visit, left yesterday for her
home in Arkansas. She is a sister of J. L. and W. R. RISON.

January 21, 1891
        In Memoriam. DR. WILLIAM E. RIVERS died at his home near New Hope,
Alabama December 17, 1890. He was born February 10, 1826 and was
married just forty years lacking one day. DR. RIVERS was of a high
order of intellect, proud spirited, high minded and richly endowed with
all those principles that are calculated to engender love and respect
of his fellowmen. T.L.O.
        At Brundidge, Alabama MR. COLLIER, an aged citizen about 80
years of age, fell dead Sunday morning of heart disease.
        At Monroeville BOB GRAHAM shot and fatally wounded JOHN L. STALLWORTH,
brother of HON. N. J. STALLWORTH, member of the Legislature.
        MAJOR JESSE ADAMS of Tuskeegee died Sunday afternoon. He left a
wife and a large family, including J. R. ADAMS, railroad conductor and
N. K., WILL and FRAZER ADAMS, all engaged in the express or railroad
business, and FRANK ADAMS of Huntsville. MAJOR ADAMS had been an
express agent for forty years.
        Meridianville notes. MRS. AGGIE PHARR, nee JONES, from Arkansas,
made a visit to her sister, MRS. JOHN FORD.
        Our community is saddened by the death of MRS. OTEY. We sympathize
with the family. The loss of a mother is indeed a great loss. (OTEY
graveyard, old home near Meridianville, Highway 431: OCTAVIA AMELIA,
wife of WILLIAM M. OTEY and daughter of WILLIAM HENRY and REBECCA WYCHE,
born August 13, 1831, died December 30, 1890.)

After a brief illness, MRS. ALICE VAN VALKENBURG _YAN departed
this life yesterday morning...a loving young wife and gentle mother.
(Left) husband and four little children.

January 28, 1891
MRS. SARAH J. HUBERT, widow of the late GEORGE HUBERT, received
from the Knights of Pythias, $2000 insurance. (Death certificate,
GEORGE HUBERT, aged 45 born in Tennessee died in Huntsville December 15,
1890, of a railroad accident. Married.)
Resolutions of Respect on the death of GEORGE HUBERT by Huntsville
Post #3, G. A. R. signed by W. C. WELLS and ED. E. GREENLEAF.
On Monday night at his residence on Walker Street MR. THOMAS B.
WINSTON departed this life, from double pneumonia. The deceased
gentleman was universally known and highly esteemed by the entire
community. Funeral services will be held at the Methodist Church this
morning. (Death certificate: THOMAS B. WINSTON, born in Alabama,
aged 64, died Huntsville January 6, 1891, married.)

February 4, 1891
MR. PERCY DARWIN editor of a newspaper at Gainsville, Texas, is
on a visit to relatives, guest of DR. JAMES L. DARWIN.
Died near New Hope, January 24, 1891, MISS CALLIE HAMER, born
February 26, 1841.... J. C. HUNKAPILLAR. (He was a minister. KPJ)
New Market. At 4 o'clock yesterday MR. JOSEPH WALKER died of
pneumonia. He leaves a large family, and a circle of friends and
relatives to mourn his sudden death.
MR. and MRS. DAN POWELL of Cluttsville Precinct left yesterday
for Gainesville, Texas where they will make their future home.
MRS. ALEX JOHNSON and granddaughter MISS MAY TALBOT have returned
home after spending several weeks at Scottsboro, guests of MR. ROBERT
HAMLET and family.
MRS. CORA ROLFE, wife of W. T. ROLFE, was born at McMinnville,
Tennessee January 13, 1854, married at Bell Factory June 16, 1872, and
died of pneumonia February 4, 1891. (by Her Pastor, V. L. HERRING.)

February 11, 1891
Resolutions of Respect. JOSEPH R. WALKER, born February 2, 1850,
and happily married to MISS MARY D. SLOAN in early manhood. They were
blessed with seven children, who with their mother, are left to mourn
their loss. He was a consistent member of the Locust Grove Baptist
Church. Order of Prayer Meeting and Sabbath School, at Rice's School
House. BETTIE POWER, ELLA FANNING, NANNIE SMITH and NELLIE JONES,
Committee.
News reached the city yesterday of the death at his home near
Deposit of MR. WILLIAM W. McCRARY, a highly esteemed and worthy gentle-
man, of pneumonia.
The remains of MRS. WILLIAM JONES, sister of DR. FRANCISCO RICE
of New Market, arrived in the city from Tuscaloosa early in the morning
and left on the Eldro train for New Market where they will be interred.
She had been in Tuscaloosa about a month. (WM. R. JONES married
January 21, 1852 GILLIANN RICE).

February 18, 1891
MRS. _LLIE DUNNINGTON, wife of MR. L. H. DUNNINGTON, died at her
residence on Washington Street after a prolonged illness...devoted
wife and mother.
Scottsboro. MR. P(ETER) GULLATT, a highly respectable citizen of
near Bellefonte was killed by a falling tree Monday.
Death of our oldest citizen. Yesterday the soul of MR. JAMES
SCOTT winged its flight...MR. SCOTT resided in Huntsville all his life,
and at the time of his death lacked but a few months of being 92 years
of age. He was probably the oldest citizen of the county. The funeral
will be held at the Methodist Church this afternoon. (Note: he evidently came as a child...there were no white people here until at
least 1804. Death certificate gives: JAMES G. SCOTT, born in Virginia,
aged 91 years 9 months 7 days, died in Huntsville February 17, 1891.
Married.)

February 25, 1891
     The remains of MR. W. A. LOVE, who died suddenly at his home in
Madison Saturday afternoon, were interred in the Far_ey burying ground
near Madison yesterday morning...none knew him but esteemed him.
     Monrevia. We regret very much to hear of the death of MRS.
WILLIAM ALLEN of Fayetteville.
     MRS. ANNA SMITH of Reedyville, Tennessee is guest of her mother
MRS. P. O. SCHAUDIES.

March 4, 1891
     Whitesburg notes. MR. JACKSON LEE, in his 70's, is visiting
relatives in Decatur, his first railroad ride was from your city to
Decatur.
     MR. J. W. FLYAN, an aged citizen living in the eastern part of
the county died Friday...pneumonia. (Death Certificate: JOHN W. FLINN,
born in Tennessee aged 63, died February 28th at Whitesburg. Married.)
     In Memoriam. Died at his residence in Madison County, 21 February
1892, W. W. McCRARY, of pneumonia. He left an aged mother, a wife,
and a large family of children. He was born 63 years ago in the house
where he died...a man of rare ability, honesty and integrity. For
eleven years he had been a member of the Christian Church. L. C. LITTLE.
(Earlier report of death was premature, his tombstone shows "WILLIAM
WRIGHT McCRARY, born October 1, 1827, died February 21, 1891.")
     DR. F. L. ANDAMS of Tuskeegee, brother of FRANK ADAMS (druggist),
returns to his home. We are glad this young dental surgeon has
decided to locate in Huntsville for the practice of his profession.

March 11, 1891
     Friends of MR. ISAAC FIELDS will be shocked to learn of his being
drowned. He ran a ferry at this place...on the opposite side of the
river he got off the ferry, got on his horse and started home. The
supposition is the horse ran off the bridge and he fell in Long Pond,
and drowned. MR. FIELDS was a prosperous farmer, a good citizen,
highly respected, and a good friend to the poor and needy. His wife
died last April. He leaves three children, two boys and one daughter.
(Whitesburg notes.)

March 18, 1891
     Resolutions of respect. COL. LIONEL W. DAY, by the Huntsville
Bar; also by the I. O. O. F.
     In Memoriam. Y(ANCY) P(RESTON) TROTMAN (22 in Alabama; SAM'L),
born November 15, 1828, married MISS SARAH E. CRUTCHER June 20, 1871,
died February 4, 1891. We have known PRESTON TROTMAN from early
manhood...when the war broke out he joined CAPT. JOHN COLTART's
Company and went to Pensacola, Florida where taking sick, he was discharged. The following spring he joined CAPT. JOHN S. DICKSON's
Company, principally made up in Huntsville before going to La Grange
College and joining the 35th Alabama Regiment commanded by COL.
ROBERTSON, president of the college. After the war he returned and
devoted his life to farming. There was never a more true and devoted
husband and loving father. W. L. M.
     The many friends and relatives of MRS. LUCINDA HEREFORD will
regret to learn of her death at her home near New Market the 4th of
March, 1891. She was a devoted member of the Cumberland Presbyterian
Church. Having married quite young, her first husband DAVID STRONG
after a few years died, leaving her alone to care for and rear her
three small children, all of whom survive her. After a few years she
was again married, to MR. WILLIAM HEREFORD, with whom she leaves four
children.

March 25, 1891
     MR. F. VARIN died last Monday, after a long illness from diabetes,
in his 73rd year. MR. VARIN was born in Montreal, Canada and moved
to Huntsville in 1853. For 22 years he was employed by the Memphis
and Charleston Railroad as a Master Car Builder. He leaves a widow
and five children.
     Resolutions. J. R. WALKER was born February 23, 1850 and died
near New Market, Alabama February 2, 1891 aged 40 years 11 months and
29 days. He joined the Baptist Church at Locust Grove in August, 1890.

His companion in life (was) MARY D. SLOAN whom he married March 3,
1871...God gave seven children who survived their father.

A telegram from Memphis yesterday morning announced the death of
MRS. J. C. FAVER nee MISS MARY NEELY formerly of this city. The
remains reached the city this morning and will be interred in the
City Cemetery today.

April 1, 1891

MRS. STERLING LANIER of Birmingham (is visiting) her father's
family, DR. J. M. BANISTER.

The funeral of MRS. W. C. FAVOR of Memphis was held at the residence of W. T. HUTCHENS. The community sympathizes with the husband,
mother and sister of the deceased.

MRS. MARY W. FRANKS, wife of City Marshall BRITTAIN FRANKS died
at the residence of her husband on Green Street Friday morning. MRS.
FRANKS was an aged lady and had been in feeble health several years.
MR. and MRS. FRANKS married in November 1832. The Mercury extends
sympathy to her husband and other relatives. (Death Certificate says
aged 79, born in Georgia. MARY W. FRANKS.)

April 8, 1891

MRS. JOE MACON, nee MISS RICE, daughter of DR. FRANCISCO RICE,
of New Market, who lives at her father-in-laws DR. J. S. MACON near
Bell Factory, was accidentally shot in the face by a pistol which was
under the pillow of her bed; as she removed the bed clothing it dropped
to the floor and discharged...a frightful but not a dangerous wound.

Resolutions of Respect. JUDGE PETER M. DOX, by the Huntsville
Bar.

In Memoriam. Died at the residence of MRS. R. W. WALKER on
Thursday, April 2nd, JUDGE PETER M. DOX in the 78th year of his age.
Though not a native of Huntsville, he had lived so long among us he
was completely identified with us...Senior Warden.

Resolutions of Respect, by Vestry of the Church of the Nativity;
On Thursday, April 2, 1891 JUDGE PETER M. DOX, the Senior Warden of
this Church departed this life in the 79th year of his age. He was
a member of the Vestry continuously from 1875. To his widow and
friends, we tender heartfelt sympathy.

April 15, 1891

An Unfortunate Accident. At Madison Wednesday, MRS. NANCY MARTIN,
wife of GEORGE W. MARTIN and mother of MR. BERRY L. MARTIN (the agent),
attempted to cross the track in front of an approaching locomotive...
injuries feared may prove fatal.

Dies of her injuries. It is with profound regret we chronicle
the demise of MRS. NANCY MARTIN in Madison Friday night. She leaves an
aged husband and a large family of grown children. The funeral took
place Saturday afternoon.

In Memoriam. Cumberland Lodge No. 49 I.O.O.F., New Market,
Alabama...Brother J. W. WALKER (died.) To his wife and children, our
sympathy. W. A. BRITTON, THOS. O. GILL, W. F. LAXSON, Committee.

At her residence on East Holmes Street yesterday morning MRS.
ELIZABETH SHEFFEY passed quietly away. She leaves three daughters
and two sons, three brothers and a sister. The funeral will take place
from the Presbyterian Church tomorrow afternoon, conducted by DR.
J. H. BRYSON.

Gretna Green. A telegram from Fayetteville, Tennessee announces
the marriage in that city of MR. FRANK DAY of Baltimore to MISS LILLIE
SPENCE of this city, eldest daughter of MRS. SUE SPENCE. The groom
and his father will open a music store in this city.

Whitesburg. MRS. P. C. JOINER, after a long illness, died last
Tuesday leaving a husband and two little children. Her remains were
laid to rest in the old burial ground near this burg. (Ebenezer
Church? If so, stone not found. Death Certificate: MRS. P. C. JOINER,
born in Alabama aged 35 died April 13, 1891 at Whitesburg.)

April 29, 1891

Died, Thursday morning, MR. WALKER WOOD of pneumonia. Leaves a
wife.

MRS. MALINDA SISK (39 in North Carolina), an aged lady of probably 85 years, died Thursday at the residence of her daughter, MRS. REUBEN STREET.

Died at the residence of HON. MILTON HUMES in this city on the morning of the 24th of April, 1891, REUBEN CHAPMAN in his 33rd year, native of this place, a worthy son of his distinguished father, GOV. REUBEN CHAPMAN. His mother was MISS PICKETT. (also another account, in the same paper says "a few months ago" he led to the altar MISS ROSA SHEFFEY, the sweet companion of his life...the young wife and mother is left bereft. Reuben was the only male representative of an illustrious family. He (has been) taken from a loving wife, three little children, devoted sisters and admiring friends.)

May 6, 1891
Died at Decatur, Wednesday April 29th, MRS. REBECCA HUGHES, wife of MR. JOHN HUGHES, formerly of this city, aged 40. Remains brought to this city for burial. The Mercury extends sympathy to her husband and little son.

New Market. MR. J. N. KENNEDY, an estimable citizen and good farmer, about 60 years of age, died of heart failure while smoking his pipe before breakfast.

MR. JOHN ROBINSON of Hurricane died of consumption.

MRS. ELLA (ELIN in 1850) DARNABY (44 in North Carolina), aged 84, came overland in a buggy 30 miles last week to spend a short time with her daughter, and did not complain of fatigue...is as vigorous as she was ten years ago. (This was also in the New Market notes.)

MR. G. H. BERRY of the firm of BERRY & WALKER, died at New Market yesterday. He has been ill several months at the residence of his father-in-law, MR. G. L. TERRY...consumption. Will be buried in New Market Thursday morning.

May 12, 1891
Our community was shocked Thursday evening when it became known MR. T. B. HENRY, son-in-law of MRS. SUE SPRAGUE, had passed suddenly away, only being ill a few hours. MR. HENRY has been a resident of this city a year or two, moving here from Guntersville.

Resolutions of Respect. T. B. HENRY, Madison Lodge #25, I.O.O.F.

May 27, 1891
MR. and MRS. NEWTON BURDINE will celebrate their golden wedding at their home in the neighborhood of Hazel Green today. MR. BURDINE lives within fourteen miles of this city but has not made a visit to town since 1861.

City Marshall BRITTAN FRANKS will leave for Florence today to visit his sister at that place.

June 3, 1891
News reached the city yesterday of the death near Paris, Texas, of MR. BALDRIDGE, the venerable father of our townsmen DR. M. C. and CAPT. W. F. BALDRIDGE. The deceased lived to be quite an aged gentle-man, and was held in high esteem by all acquaintances.

Married last Thursday evening at the residence of the bride's parents, MR. and MRS. WM. J. KELLY, MR. MARSHALL CARR to MISS ADA KELLY.

REV. R. T. BENTLEY, of Spring Garden, Cherokee County, is a guest of his brother A. J. BENTLEY, Esq., Holmes Street.

MR. MORGAN FARISS arrived in the city from Texas yesterday, on a visit to his mother.

MR. JAMES PHELPS of Jackson, Mississippi is a guest of MR. SMITH CERTAIN, he was in the past a resident of Huntsville and this is his first visit in fifteen or twenty years.

New Market: MRS. MARY MACON...was cut riding this week. With hearts of gratitude, we welcome her back to her large circle of relatives and friends.

June 10, 1891
MRS. MILDRED JAMAR, daughter of MRS. PANKEY of this city, died at her home in Tuscumbia Sunday afternoon.

From the Gadsden Times-News. Long account--On Monday night DR. D. A. BAKER shot and killed his father-in-law COL. R(OBT.)

ABERCROMBIE; (was lying in wait for a chicken thief and mistook the Colonel for the prowler.) The remains were carried to Tuskeegee, his former home, for interment. (tombstone: born September 17(?), 1838, died June 8, 1881)

July 1, 1891
    OSCAR STRONG, aged 19, killed by lightning...son of THOMAS R. STRONG.

July 15, 1891
    MR. CHARLES M. FENNELL died suddenly at Woodville. He was a brother of MRS. GEORGE F. SCRUGGS. MR. FENNELL recently resided at Bessemer, but he and his family have been in Huntsville for several weeks, visiting relatives. A day or so before his death he went to Woodville on business; found dead in bed. Supposed to have been heart failure (complained the night before of pains.) The remains were brought to this city and interred in the Cemetery Monday.
    The News reached the city last evening of the death of MR. TOM CAWTHORN (43 in Tennessee) at his home near Maysville last Friday. MR. CAWTHORN was about 80 years of age. The deceased was a good man and had a legion of friends who will regret to hear of his death.
    DR. HUMPHREY received a telegram announcing the death of EDIE HUMPHREY at Aspen, Colorado on the threshold of manhood. Buried in Mt. Olivet, Nashville. (mentions friend in this city, his former home.)
    In Memoriam. CHARLES MARIAN FENNALL. Another wife lost her husband, another little son was bereft of his father. He died at Woodville, Alabama July 12, 1891, born March 7, 1855 at Belle Fonte, Jackson County, Alabama, married November 28, 1879 to MISS SUSIE H. HOBBS. Funeral services were conducted by REV. J. D. SIMPSON at the home of his brother-in-law, MR. GEORGE F. SCRUGGS. A Friend.
    MR. CRANSTON NASH, pharmacist at the drug store of MR. JOHN L. RISON, received a telegram from Parkersburg, West Virginia bearing the sad intelligence of the sudden death of his father at that place yesterday. (See "HARRIS and Allied Families.")
    MR. JAMES McGAHA, formerly of this place but for 18 months of Texas, is visiting relatives and friends.

July 22, 1891
    Whitesburg. MRS. MATTIE LOGAN of Corinth, Mississippi is visiting relatives in the Green Grove community.
    MRS. WALLACE JAMAR of Corinth, Mississippi is visiting her parents, DR. and MRS. J. W. MORTON.
    MR. THOMAS DRAKE of Fourth Alabama fame and MISS SALLIE and MASTER RICHARD were visiting relatives in the community Sunday.
    MRS. NARCISSA COBB of Argenta, Arkansas is visiting relatives.

July 29, 1891
    The remains of MRS. SALLIE DILLARD, wife of MR. JAMES Q. DILLARD, were laid to rest in the Triana Cemetery Monday afternoon. The deceased was a beloved sister of the MESSRS. HALSEY of this city.
    News of the death of MRS. MARIA KINKLE, which occurred at Scotts- boro last Sabbath evening aroused much tender sympathy in our city. MRS. KINKLE was an old woman, 92 years of age. She was one of the pioneers of our land, and no one ever lived and died in Huntsville who was worth of greater honors than this grand old lady. MRS. KINKLE leaves many descendants who have loved and cherished her throughout the infirmities of all her old age. She also leaves an entire community who honored and esteemed her for her many noble characteristics, but not least in a long life of usefulness nearly entirely spent in our city she leaves a name and character above reproach, one that is honored and respected by everyone.

July 29, 1891
    News was received in Huntsville yesterday of the death in Clarksdale, Mississippi of MR. WILEY P. DRAKE, a former citizen of this county, which occurred at that place early yesterday.
    MR. WILLIAM SCHAFER died at his home on Arms Street yesterday. MR. SCHAFER had been a resident of Huntsville for a long time; he was

an industrious shoemaker and a quiet, clever citizen. He had been married
twice, and by the second wife who survives him, two children had
blessed their union. The death of the first wife left him with three
children, he leaving behind five children and a devoted mate.

August 12, 1891
     The sad tidings of the death of DR. J. J. DEMENT flashed over the
wires from Lithia Springs, Georgia where he died suddenly from heart
failure. As a physician, DR. DEMENT stood at the head of his profession;
he was a man of brains, a careful, a prudent and safe thinker, a man
whose intelligence was impressive. As a husband and father he was
generous, tender and loving. When the war cry sounded through our
land, DR. DEMENT responded and for four years nursed the wounded and
dying. Huntsville feels her loss...every household weeps....
     Death of an Honorable and Beloved Citizen. The many friends of
JUDGE WILLIAM H. MOORE were pained to learn last Friday evening of the
death of this honorable and honored gentleman, which occurred at his
residence near the city about six o'clock.... The deceased was in his
69th year and was a man who filled responsible positions, and who
possessed the confidence and esteem of all who knew him. JUDGE MOORE
was elected a member of the Board of the Huntsville Female College in
the year 1850 and held that position up to his death. He was a man
whom everyone liked. (See M/S "Some of the Descendants of JOHN MOORE,
JR., MATTHEW MOORE and ANN MOORE HAMNER" etc. DAR Library. JUDGE WM.
HENRY MOORE was a son of EDWARD MOORE and a nephew of GABRIEL MOORE)
     MR. EDWARD MOORE returned last night to his Mississippi home,
having been called to this city on the death of his father, JUDGE WM. H.
MOORE.
     Memorial. MR. GEORGE EMORY HUNT, born May 15, 1825, died
August 2, 1891. He was a man of many excellent qualities of character:
he was a true husband, an indulgent parent, a man and a citizen above
reproach, and a lover of our Lord and Savior Jesus Christ. He professed
religion in early life and joined the Baptist Church...(consumption)...
He leaves a wife and eight children. He was laid to rest in the
Neil Chapel Cemetery.
     In Memoriam. MRS. SALLIE H. DILLARD, wife of JAMES Q. DILLARD,
died in the village of Triana July 26, 1891...she had long been a
faithful member of the Methodist Episcopal Church South. She was a
faithful wife, fond and affectionate mother and true and steadfast
friend. (1/2 a column.)
     Triana, August 8, 1891. MR. HARRIS TONEY left for Hot Springs,
Arkansas where he will visit COL. and MRS. RUGG. MRS. RUGG is a sister
of MR. TONEY.
     REV. G. L. HERRING, one of our promising young ministers of the
Hazel Green Circuit has been visiting his aunt, MRS. McINTOSH.
     MR. JOHN WITHERS, formerly of Mooresville, but now of Arkansas
has been visiting his uncles, WILLIE and CHARLES COLLIER.

August 19, 1891
     Resolutions of Respect. Monrovia Alliance, on the death of
W. H. BAUGHER, July 27th.
     CAPT. HARRY H. ESTES of Heningway, Mississippi is on a visit to
his mother at the home of B. F. LUDWIG.

August 24, 1891
     We learned last evening of the death yesterday of MR. ALFRED
HAMBRICK at his home near Maysville. MR. HAMBRICK was 78 years old and
had been ill with slow fever for some time. He was buried in the
burying ground of that place today was surely a confusion of names;
ALFRED HAMBRICK, BRADFORD HAMBRICK's brother and the only one of that
generation of that name, died in 1883. (Death Certificate shows
BRADFORD HAMBRICK, aged 78, born in Alabama, died August 25, 1891,
Maysville...married.)

September 2, 1891
     Died at New Market. Last Monday at her residence one and a half
miles east of New Market, MRS. LOUISA C. HAMBRICK breathed her last.
She was 76 years of age and greatly beloved for her many noble qualities.
(Death Certificate: LOUISA C. HAMBRICK, born in Virginia aged 76 years,

8 months, died August 31, New Market...widow...married 1) HEZEKIAH,
2) JOSEPH VIER. She was the last wife and widow of JOSEPH HAMBRICK,
father of BRADFORD and ALFRED.)

September 30, 1891
     MR. MILSON G. YARBROUGH of Cherokee is a guest of his relative
DR. J. D. HUMPHREY. MR. YARBROUGH, a native of this county, left here
soon after the war.

September 23, 1891
     HON. EDWARD CHAMBERS BETTS died September 18th at the residence of
MR. TANCRED BETTS, aged 71 years on August 21st. In law, politics and
literature JUDGE BETTS held for half a century the position of one of
the representative men of the south. Admitted to the Bar at eighteen
years of age, his fine legal mind having received the best culture of
the North and the South.... Another item in the same paper: Died at
the residence of his son, JUDGE TANCRED BETTS, ...he was born in June,
1819 and was in his 73rd year...was a Member of the Legislature from
Madison County several times, Judge of Probate during the administration
of GOV. CHAPMAN, first Commissioner of Agriculture. Funeral services
were held at the Church of the Nativity Saturday afternoon.
     In Memoriam. EMILY JOHNSTON BLAIR, daughter of DR. T. JOHNSTON
married 11 months ago to MR. CAREY M. BLAIR.

October 14, 1891
     News reached the city Saturday evening of the death of MRS. NANCY F.
GRAHAM, an aged and much beloved lady of Pond Beat.

October 28, 1891
     In Memoriam. Died in this city Saturday the 24th, MRS. ELIZABETH,
wife of HON. WILLIAM RICHARDSON. (1/4 column)
     MR. JOHN C. HAMBRICK and family of St. Louis are on a visit to
relatives in New Market. MR. HAMBRICK formerly resided in this county.

November 4, 1891
     Resolutions, Confederate Veterans' Association, on the death of
ROBERT W. FIGG.
     CAPT. ROBERT W. FIGG died suddenly of heart failure last Friday,
in his 72nd year. He was born near Petersburg, Virginia and came to
this state when a youth. A dentist by profession, he lost an arm in
the army....
     Died at his residence at Madison Station Wednesday the 7th of
October 1891, HON. C(HRISTOPHER) G. GEWIN (39 in North Carolina,
Lawrence County), aged 81 years, 2 months 9 days. He was born in
Anson County, North Carolina July 28, 1810 and while a youth came to
Madison County with his father. After reaching manhood he removed to
Moulton, Lawrence County, Alabama where on May 6, 1834 he married
INDIANA PINKSTON. A few years later he was elected Sheriff of Lawrence
County, and later to the General Assembly of Alabama. Losing his wife
about this time, he married ARTEMISSA (21 in Alabama), daughter of
WILLIAM BOYD of Moulton and half sister of his first wife. In 1857 he
was appointed Probate Judge of Lawrence County to fill out the
unexpired term of HON. CROCKETT McDONALD who had died in June of that
year. In 1869 he returned with his family to Madison, Madison County,
Alabama. Postmaster, magistrate, mayor.... In 1882 he was united with
the Christian Church in which he was an Elder. God bless his widow
and children.

November 11, 1891
     Sabbath morning last, at his home in New Market, MR. PETER MERTZ
breathed his last, aged about 66 years. He had been a resident of
New Market for a number of years and was an industrious worker at his
trade, that of a shoe maker...a consistent member of the Cumberland
Presbyterian Church for the past ten years. The remains were brought
to this city Monday and interred in the City Cemetery.
     Died at the home of her father in Cherokee Saturday, MISS ELLA
YARBROUGH; she had been on a visit to her aunt MRS. J. M. HUMPHREY of
this county and had returned only a few weeks ago.

November 18, 1891
     Died at Shelby, North Carolina Sunday November 15, 1891, MR.
CHRISTIAN FROMM, aged 63. The deceased formerly resided in this city
and was the father of MRS. ROSE DAHN, wife of MR. HENRY DAHN of
Huntsville.

December 9, 1891
     Sunday night, CAPT. JOHN D. BRANDON, who has been a sufferer
from illness several months, passed quietly away at his home on East
Holmes Street. CAPT. BRANDON was born in this city December 18, 1837,
the youngest of a family of two sons and three daughters. At the age
of 15 the deceased accompanied his mother to St. Louis; he took a law
course, graduated at Cumberland University and returned to St. Louis
but in 1859 he came to Huntsville. In April 1861 he enlisted as a
private in Company I, 4th Alabama and served to the close of the war.
After the First Battle of Manassas he was promoted from the ranks 2
Second Lieutenant and in April 1862 was advanced to Captain. CAPTAIN
BRANDON married in 1863 MRS. ROSALIE C. CHRISTIAN, daughter of DR.
JOHN D. CALDWELL. His wife died in 1869 leaving only one child, a
daughter. Methodist, Knight of Pythias, Knight of Honor.
     Last Wednesday afternoon MRS. ISABELLA BRADLEY, relict of the
late JOSEPH C. BRADLEY, quietly passed away, surrounded by her loving
children and friends. (1/5 column)

December 16, 1891
     Whitesburg. MRS. BETSEY GIBSON, nearing her 90th year, lives with
her son-in-law MR. THOMAS MAN in the southeast part of the County,
post office Bell, Alabama.

                         MERCURY 1883

              ADVOCATE January 3 through March 14

                    MERCURY rest of the year

January 3, 1883
     The venerable MR. SAM MATTHEWS is quite ill at the residence of
his daughter MRS. JAMES ED FLETCHER.
     JAKE FRANKS son of our worthy City Marshall is quite ill. (Con-
sumption. His father was BRITTAIN FRANKS.)
     CAPT. WILLIAM CLARK is hopelessly ill at the residence of his
sister MR. JOE BRADLEY. CAPT. CLARK has for some time been engaged in
planting, in Mississippi. He came here last week, very ill, in care
of his son DICK CLARK of Memphis. His daughter MRS. HASKELL of Atlanta
is at his bedside. CAPT. CLARK is uncle of City Clerk ED. I. MASTIN.
Later, CAPT. WILLIAM CLARK died at 3 a.m. Deceased was about 62 years
of age. He served with distinguished gallantry in the 17th Tennessee,
GOV. MARKS' troops, during the late war.
     MR. JAMES T. SKELTON. We are sorry to chronicle the death of this
leading citizen and merchant of Scottsboro, which occurred at his
home on the 24th of December. MR. SKELTON was born in this county on
the 16th of September 1829.
     Notice. My son W. R. VAN VALKENBURG is admitted as a partner in
the Hardware and Implement Business. J. VAN VALKENBURG.

January 17, 1883
     Marshall County. On the 9th instant MR. G. W. C. NEILL of
Nashville led to the altar MISS BELLE FENNELL of this county.
Guntersville Democrat.
     Lauderdale County. MR. JOHN COFFEE, a good man, died last Friday
night at his home near Center Star, of consumption.
     Married, on Tuesday morning, January 9th at the residence of COL.
JOSIAH PATTERSON in Memphis, Tennessee by REV. MR. CALDWELL, WILLIAM
JACKSON to SALLIE J., daughter of JOHN B. WEAKLEY, all of Florence,
Alabama. Florence Gazette.
     Morgan County. The impressive Masonic ceremonies over the remains
of DR. F. W. SYKES were conducted by CAPT. J. W. JONES, Worshipful

Master of Rising Sun Lodge #29. There were present members of the
Trinity and Town Creek Lodges, the deceased being a member of the
latter lodge.

CARRIE MAY WOODALL, wife of J. J. WOODALL, died Tuesday, the 8th,
after an illness of more than three months. MRS. WOODALL was connected
with some of the most prominent families of Morgan County.

Died, at the residence of MR. JAMES H. McGAHA (21 in Alabama),
near Whitesburg, January 12, 1883, MRS. CAROLINE McGAHA (at 48 years
at death).

January 24, 1883

Lauderdale County. On the 24th instant GEORGE W. MARTIN of
Tennessee was married to MISS MARTHA M. THREAT.

On the 17th instant, JOHN McKINNEY of Madison County to MISS
ELIZABETH LAMBERT. (Lauderdale County notes)

MR. WILLIAM D. CROW, an old Florence boy, died Wednesday in
Paducah, Kentucky where he was resting, on his way home, from several
years exposure in the Colorado mines.

Jackson County. MR. REUBEN SCOTT of Madison County is clerking
for C. M. FENNELL. MR. W. T. GRAHAM committed suicide at his home
near Larkinsville last Tuesday. MR. GRAHAM was a well-to-do farmer,
out of debt, and got along well with his family. The only reason his
friends assigned is that he has been in bad health for some time. He
was a sober man, a good citizen.

January 24, 1883

From the Memphis Avalanche we take the following notice of the
death of MR. WALTER A. GOODMAN, in that city on the 20th instant.
MR. GOODMAN was highly esteemed in this community, where he married
his wife, the former MISS CORINNE ACKLEN, a beautiful woman and belle
of this city: "MR. WALTER A. GOODMAN died last night after a brief
illness. For many years MR. GOODMAN has been prominent in Memphis
business circles and was universally esteemed. Last November he was
unanimously elected a magistrate for the city and subsequently
Chairman of the County Court....

Account, from the Chattanooga Times, of the murder of JAMES McCABE
a merchant of Town Creek, by a TOM MATHIS, who was drunk.

January 31, 1883

From the Atlantic (Iowa) Messenger: MRS. ROBERT MAJOR, one of the
most highly esteemed ladies of Atlantic, died on Wednesday evening of
consumption. MR. and MRS. MAJOR came to this city in 1878 from
Huntsville, Alabama and since that time the gentleman has been one of
our leading lumber dealers. MRS. MAJOR was a leading member of the
Presbyterian Church.

MRS. SARAH STRAUSS of New York is the guest of her brother
MR. OSCAR GOLDSMITH.

The Cullman Independent says MRS. KATE D. THOMPSON of Birmingham
is visiting her sister MRS. DR. SEARCY.

REV. DR. ROSS and wife enjoyed the 24th anniversary of their
marriage Saturday last, the 27th. The occasion was beautifully
remembered by the teachers and young ladies of the Seminary and a few
friends, who gave a delightful surprise party to the esteemed couple.

McCABE of Town Creek, reported shot, is slowly getting well.

COL. S(AMUEL) R(IDLEY) CRUSE (20 in Alabama). The telegraphic
dispatch on Thursday that COL. CRUSE had died suddenly at his home in
Memphis was a painful shock to this community. He was a son of the
late SAMUEL R. CRUSE. COL. CRUSE, at an early age, fell under the
spell of the "gold fever"...returning from California he was appointed
teller in the old Northern Bank of Alabama which position he held until
the beginning of the war. He served gallantly throughout the long
struggle as an officer of the battery commanded by the much lamented
JAMISON WARD. In 1865 he was called to the Treasureship of the Memphis
and Charleston Railroad. COL. CRUSE was in his 52nd year, leaves a
wife and three sons, two in business in Memphis and the other in
school. The remains arrived in this city Friday morning on a special
train; funeral was held from the Church of the Nativity.

February 7, 1883
    The terrible death of MAJOR JON's MARTIN at Stevenson. MAJOR
J. F. MARTIN, for more than thirty years Agent of the Memphis and
Charleston RR, and of the Express Company, at Stevenson, was run over
by the incoming train Friday night and was so injured that he died at
8 o'clock next morning. MAJOR MARTIN was about 60 years old, a man
of splendid physique and proverbial high character. MAJOR MARTIN
leaves a wife and four children, two of whom are grown.
    MISS GLENN ORR, daughter of HON. J. G. ORR of Danville was
enrolled as a pupil and boarder at the Seminary last week.
    MR. WILLIAM PAUL, son of MR. JNO A. PAUL of this county died
Sunday afternoon from shock caused by amputation of leg. (JAMES
ALEXANDER PAUL was his father. KPJ)
    COL. RICHARD JONES. This old and well known citizen of Lawrence
County died at the residence of his daughter, MRS. JOSEPH WHEELER,
last Saturday morning. For many years prior to the war COL. JONES was
prominently identified with the history of North Alabama. A man of
considerable wealth and influence, he was a power in his day. He was
ninety one years of age.

February 14, 1883
    Account of "a shooting" between FISHER OLDFIELD and DANIEL MOSELEY,
well esteemed citizens and merchants at Hazel Green. OLDFIELD's clothing
was penetrated with 117 birdshot but he escaped unhurt. MOSELEY did
not escape so well...2 buckshot in left breast and one in the stomach
but reported getting well.

February 21, 1883
    MRS. FINNEY, wife of J. W. FINNEY the son of JONATHAN FINNEY died
suddenly on Tuesday last in the vicinity of this place. Scottsboro
Herald.
    We regret to hear of the death of MR. BENJAMIN SANDLIN (50 in
South Carolina, Morgan County) which occurred near Hartsell on Friday
the 9th instant. He was about 65 years old. Decatur News. (died
December 9, 1883, born September 4, 1800; auc. of J. T. MACK, Marks,
Mississippi)
    MRS. SARAH H. BOURLAND, relict of HON. BAYLES R. BOURLAND died
at the residence of W. J. T. STAPLER, Esq. in Rogersville Wednesday
last the 7th instant. Lauderdale News.
    Our whole community was shocked last Sunday morning on hearing of
the death of DR. J. Y. CANTWELL which occurred at the residence of his
niece, MRS. R. D. HORTON, on Bank Street (Decatur)
    The beautiful MRS. WADE HAMPTON, JR. nee MISS KATIE PHELAN, is
visiting her cousin, DR. JAMES R. BEASLEY.
    DR. W. F. McMULLEN, a former Huntsville boy, is visiting his
family and friends. DR. McMULLEN has been living for some time in
Drew County, Southeast Arkansas.
    The Scottsboro Citizen of last week (tells that) WILLIE SPOTSWOOD,
his sister, and also an aunt, who reside in Huntsville, recently fell
heir to 5000 acres of valuable land near San Antonio, Texas. MISS
LUTIE SPOTSWOOD, married, as our people know, the REV. CHARLES E.
CABANISS, late of Huntsville, but now in charge of a flourishing
Episcopal Church in San Antonio, Texas. The people of Scottsboro
will be pleased to learn of the success of WILLIE and LUTIE SPOTSWOOD.
    The Commencement Exercises of Hospital College, Central University
at Louisville were held the 14th instant. First on the list of gradu-
ates is WILLIAM M. BANISTER...received a gold medal...third son of
REV. J. M. BANISTER.
    Died at the Stegall Hotel Monday, February 18th, MARY K. wife of
J. R. STEGALL...consumption...daughter of MRS. THOMPSON residing near
Meridianville. She was a devoted member of the Cumberland Presbyterian
Church.

February 28, 1883
    Alabama Courier (Limestone County). In Vancent County, Texas,
MR. OSCAR L. JOHNSON, formerly of this county, was united in marriage
to MISS FANNIE HILL, on the 12th instant.
    JOHN HAMMERLY (50 in Virginia) was born in Leesburg, Louden County,
Virginia September 11, 1799 and died at Athens, Alabama February 16,

1883 aged 83 years, 5 months and 5 days. (Goodspeeds, Mississippi
Memoirs, 1891--JOHN HAMMERLY born in Berkeley County, Virginia in 1799,
moved to Alabama and then married SARAH PRICE in 1825. Died in Athens,
Alabama in 1882 (obituary says 1883). She was born in 1800 in Tennessee,
daughter of WM. and NANCY (REED) PRICE. She died 1883. WM. PRICE
born in 1770 in North Carolina. His family moved to Tennessee while very
young, married NANCY REED, moved to Limestone County in 1821, children(?)
of JOHN and SARAH HAMMERLY: GEO(?) born in Limestone County 1829. In
1851 moved to Eastport, Mississippi. In 1874, Iuka, Mississippi. In
Civil War, married MARY A. SCRUGGS 1858. Lived in Iuka, Mississippi
1891, LYDIA M. born between 1826-36; NANCY R. born between 1826-36,
married WM. HENDRICKS; WM. G. born between 1826-36, died in Alabama
1860; see 1850 Census of Limestone County, Alabama.
        MR. ALBERT HARVEY of Slough Beat died Saturday with pneumonia.
        Lauderdale News. Died at the residence of her father, MR. J. H.
HARDWICK at Woodland in this county, MRS. D. McENTYRE, relict of the
late ANDREW McENTYRE.
        MR. JAMES R. BILLINGSLEY, born and raised in this county, died
at his home in Coshoma County, Mississippi of pneumonia, 26th of January.
        MR. SOLOMAN W. RAVES died at Paducah, Kentucky on the 14th instant;
he was formerly a resident of this county.
        New Court House at Center, replacing one that burned.

March 7, 1883
        ALCUIN RASON of Mississippi is visiting his family and friends.
        Married at the residence of the bride Monday evening, MR. JAMES M.
BONE and MRS. LAURA GUNNEL. CAPT. BONE is U.S. Commissioner, a Northern
man who has come amongst us and made many friends. MRS. GUNNEL is a
daughter of JUDGE THOMAS GEORGE of Colorado.
        Married Tuesday night at Madison, MR. P. M. FAUGHT to MISS ANNIE
WIGGINS. The groom is a druggist of Denton, Texas.
        In Memoriam. Died, March 2nd, MRS. ELIZA M. TALIAFERRO, wife of
DR. E. T. TALIAFERRO of New Market. Only a few months since, passed
away MR. J. B. BATTLE, brother of the now deceased...consumption.

IT IS HERE THAT THE ADVOCATE CEASES AND THE MERCURY BEGINS.

March 14, 1883
        Scottsboro Citizen. MRS. TOONS enjoyed her 93rd birthday yester-
day, the 4th instant.
        Died Thursday afternoon MRS. MARY SAXON. The funeral services
were conducted by REV. JOHN A. THOMPSON from her late residence on
Holmes Street...she had seen her early friends sink into earth's quiet
green breast....
        Friday, MR. BENJAMIN E. BALES (cancer) Services from the Baptist
Church Sunday by REV. J. A. B. LOVETT. MR. BALES was for years one of
our best contractors and builders. He was buried with fraternal
honors by the Knights of Pythias. He leaves a wife and several small
children.
        Friday evening, MRS. NANCY MURPHY, the verable mother of MESSRS.
JERE and ROBERT E. MURPHY. Funeral services were conducted by REV.
JOHN A. THOMPSON; deceased was 91 years of age.
        Tribute to MRS. IDA WESTMORELAND who died at her old home in
Limestone County 24th of February...one so young, a loving mother,
affectionate sister, devoted daughter... J. C.
        Jackson County. MRS. TOONS enjoyed her 93rd birthday today, it
being the 4th.
        MR. WADDY SCRUGGS left this morning for St. Louis, Missouri where
he expects to make his future home.

March 21, 1883
        North Alabamian, 10th. MR. KIRK JACKSON, son of the late COL.
JAMES JACKSON of Florence, has been appointed Clerk to the Railroad
Commission of this State.
        HON. JOSEPH B. McDONALD died at Athens Sunday morning, March 11th
in his 48th year. He was a skillful lawyer, a scholar of unusual
culture and attainments, and a man of conspicuous integrity, generosity
and nobility of mind.

Died, Sunday evening at her residence, MRS. CLARA A. SIVLEY, of pneumonia. Funeral services were held from the Cumberland Church, by REV. J. A. B. LOVETT.

Died at her home in Meridianville, MRS. JOHN STUART nee MISS SAUNDERS...she had been married only a short time.

Resolutions of Respect, Monte Sano Lodge #1 Knights of Pythias, for B. E. BAILES, deceased.

March 28, 1883

MR. JOHN W. SCRUGGS, one of our most excellent young men, is roughing it on a cattle ranch near Richmond, Texas. Success to him in his new enterprise.

Died, Thursday, MR. JAMES T. ESSLINGER...consumption.

MRS. ANNIE D. WHITAKER, daughter of MRS. J. E. LAUGHINGHOUSE died at her home near Fayetteville, Tennessee...buried in the Huntsville Cemetery Sunday...only a short year ago she was married....

April 4, 1883

HON. THOMAS H(ORD) HERNDON (21 in Alabama), Representative in Congress for the First Alabama District, died at his home in Mobile the 28th of March in the 55th year of his age. COL. HERNDON was born in that part of Greene County, now Hale, in 1828, graduated at the State University at Tuskaloosa, and after studying a course in law at Harvard began practice in Eutaw in 1849. In 1857, having removed to Mobile, he represented that county in the Legislature, but returning to Greene, he went from that County as Delegate to the Constitutional Convention in 1861. He was Colonel of the 36th Alabama Regiment. He returned to Mobile in 1878, was elected to Congress, and when he died, was on the threshold of his third term.

Rep. March 29. It is with no ordinary sadness I chronicle the death of one of our most worthy young men, R. A. GOOCH, who a little over a month ago left here with wife and babe, for Hope, Arkansas (Hempstead County) where he died the 15th of menengitis. He leaves a widowed mother, brothers and sisters. He married the youngest daughter of your townsman, MR. RICHARD JAMES.

Died, Thursday, March 29th, at the residence of MRS. JOSEPH C. BRADLEY, MARY ST. JOHN, infant daughter of W. E. and JENNIE B. STANAGE.

Died in Huntsville, March 29, 1883, MRS. ACHEAH L. LAKIN, wife of REV. A(RAD) S. LAKIN (Methodist) and mother-in-law of CAPT. JOHN W. RAINES...member of the Presbyterian Church...fond mother, devoted wife.

April 11, 1883

Gretna Green. MR. RICHARD COYLE led the fair MISS LORENA LEBOW over the border, into Pulaski, Tennessee where they were made man and wife.

April 18, 1883

Tuscumbia Alabamian. (Died) On the 11th instant MRS. PRISCILLA YOUNG, wife of the late E. S. YOUNG, in her 68th year. MRS. YOUNG was one of the oldest citizens of Tuscumbia, and for many years a member of the Presbyterian Church. MRS. MANLEY and MRS. B. P. STINE are her nearest relatives, MRS. STINE having been adopted by her.

Moulton Advertiser. MR. W. J. GIBSON, an old citizen of this county, died at his home near Courtland Monday last.

Athen Courier. DR. RUFFIN COLEMAN of Clarksdale, Mississippi is visiting his mother in Athens.

Guntersville Democrat. JUDGE WYETH moved to this county 47 years ago the 29th of this month and knows, perhaps, more of its history than any other one man.

MR. GEORGE W. MORROW died last Sunday. He was an old citizen of Morgan County, and highly esteemed.

April 25, 1883

Moulton Advertiser; There is a general demand for plow boys in this section. MR. REASONA LE YOUNG wants a half a dozen good boys to whom good wages will be paid.

Another landmark has been wiped out by the Angel of Death, another mother, grandmother and great grandmother gone; MRS. MARGARET ELLIS (48 in Tennessee, wife of GEO, daughter of ANDREW NELSON, Respen), aged 81 years, died near Moulton on the 13th.

May 2, 1883
    Scottsboro citizen. THOMAS NEWTON, SR. of Copenhagen, Jackson
County writes us his son, THOMAS NEWTON, JR., aged 16, left his
parents on the 16th instant. He was born in England, is small and
very talkative. Should anyone meet up with such a boy his anxious
parents would be greatly obliged by learning his whereabouts.

May 9, 1883
    Moulton Advertiser. The courthouse was honored with the stately
form of MR. WILLIAM COOPER of Tuscumbia, now in his 82nd year.
    Died in Huntsville May 4, 1883, MRS. G. B. VANDEVENTER, wife of
MR. J. D. VANDEVENTER, for years a devout member of the Presbyterian
Church.

May 16, 1883
    Death of CAPT. R(UFUS) K. BOYD, on Thursday, the 18th. Week
before last his friends in Huntsville were delighted to see him.
Friday week he returned to Guntersville, and (fording Honeycomb Creek,
buggy went in a hole, wetting him.) He was attacked by a congestive
chill from which he died. Of North Carolina blood, CAPT. BOYD was
born in Wilkinson County, Tennessee and moved with his parents to
Missouri during his childhood. When a boy he travelled in Europe with
his father. He left with the gray eyed man of destiny to conquer
Nicaragua. Surviving that he sought the gold fields of California.
He joined the Confederate Army of Missouri in 1861. In 1865 he came
to Guntersville and married his attractive wife. In 1870 he was elected
to the General Assembly of Alabama, and in 1878 elected Secretary of
State. (Half a column.) (No Wilkinson County in Tennessee...either
WILSON or WILLIAMSON)

May 23, 1883
    From the Scottsboro Citizen, account of the "foul murder of
JOHN CARTER" about 21, son of W. A. B. CARTER; he leaves a wife and
one child.
    Died in this county, Saturday May 19, 1883, MRS. WINSTON, aged
wife of MR. ISAAC WINSTON, after a life of devotion and beautiful
Christian deeds.
    (Died) Young MRS. CARTER, wife of MR. B. C. CARTER.
    MRS. GUNN, venerable mother of our townsman, MAJOR J. R. STEVENS,
came up from Mississippi last week.

May 30, 1883
    Died May 26, 1883 MRS. ELIZABETH KELLY, aged mother of MR. POLK
KELLY. Services were conducted by REV. J. E. CARTER and REV. W. F. KONE,
of the Baptist Church.
    Died in this city, May 24th, MR. JAMES PRICKETT, a native of
Indiana, a young man just entering on the duties of life.

July 7, 1883
    We have a wedding card of MR. S(AM) J. KENNERLY, formerly of this
place, now of Gainesville, Texas, and MISS CALLIE BIRD.
    MR. JOHN M. CROWDER, a former citizen, is with us a few days
from Talladega.
    MR. JOE BRADFORD, a former resident of Huntsville, now of
Jackson, Mississippi (is visiting).
    MR. HENRY CLARK, an ex-Huntsville boy, arrived from St. Louis (for
a visit).

June 13, 1883
    MRS. MARY MORRIS, perhaps the oldest woman in Jackson County, died
at the residence of her son-in-law WILLIAM POTTER in Maynard's Cove
the 21st of May last aged 96 years. She had been married 76 years and
a member of the Baptist Church 76 years. Her youngest daughter, wife
of WILLIAM HOTTER is 51.
    Decatur News? The family of HON. W. C. SHERROD arrived Monday
from Mississippi. We hope they will settle in Florence permanently.
    A long account of the wedding of S. J. KENNERLY and MISS CALLIE
BIRD, at the parents of the bride, MR. and MRS. GEORGE Y. BIRD,
Wednesday evening last (from the Gainesville (Texas) paper).

Florence Gazette. MR. SIMPSON WALKER, a native of Florence and son of the late HON. R. W. WALKER was here Friday on a short visit to his uncle R. T. SIMPSON.

L. W. HUMES, son of GEN. W. Y. C. HUMES of Memphis and law partner of his father is in the city.

MASTER JOHN ERSKINE, son of the lamented DR. XAN ERSKINE of Memphis is visiting relatives.

DR. J. L. WATKINS, a young physician of Nashville, of talent and promise, has been visiting in our city.

MISS ELLA YARBROUGH of Cherokee is (visiting) her aunt MRS. GEN. HUMPHREY, near Rep.

June 20, 1883

Moulton Advertiser. MR. GRAHAM (probably LYDDA wife of JOHN GRAHAM, she was 53 in 1850 and died after 1880), said to be nearly 100 years old, died a few miles northwest of Moulton Monday night of last week.

Decatur News. Our venerable friend. MR. JOHN F. BANKS, in his 93rd year, is on a visit to his friends in town...in sound health.

June 27, 1883

LARKIN A. WORTHAM died at Maysville on the morning of June 26, 1883. He was born near Lebanon in the State of Tennessee and was about 50 years of age.

MR. LOGAN B. REEDY (6 in Alabama; son of JOHN A.) died in this city Monday last, June 25th. He was a native of this county but for the past 18 or 20 years has resided in Texas, reaching home only some few months ago. MR. REEDY passed away in the very meridian of life.

July 11, 1883

MR. OSCAR W. SULLIVAN, son of DR. C. R. SULLIVAN of Madison, was fatally stricken by a bolt of lightning Wednesday...a young man of 19 or 20.

MISS ELLA LEE WITHERS, daughter of DR. SAMUEL J. WITHERS of Mooresville, is visiting at the home of COL. H. L. CLAY.

MR. and MRS. W. H. TANCRE and daughter have gone to Chicago to visit MR. WILLIAM TANCRE, a son and brother.

July 18, 1883

Scottsboro Citizen. MRS. JONES, who lives at Bridgeport, will celebrate her 100th birthday Saturday next. Her descendants numbering near 200 are expected to be present.

MRS. PATSY FLYNT of Mississippi (widow of PERRY FLYNT?), who formerly lived in the Hazel Green country, is visiting friends in the county. She is the venerable aunt of J. T. McDAVID, Esq is about 80 years of age and is wonderfully preserved.

MRS. SARAH BARRETT of Mississippi is visiting relatives in the city.

MAJOR CHARLEY COXE has returned to Louisville, Kentucky.

The remains of MISS SALLY CLARK, the daughter of MR. SAM CLARK, for many years a resident of this county, were brought from Nashville for burial Monday.

The remains of MRS. MARY WOODSON HUFF were brought to this city for burial Sunday. She was a native of Madison County but was living in Salem, Virginia at the time of her death; she was a devoted wife and mother, and communicant of the Episcopal Church.

Legal Advertisement; non resident notice, to ARTHUR HOPKINS BEARD of Lee County, Arkansas (Circuit Court in Equity, Wilson Sewing Machine Co. vs. ARTHUR HOPKINS BEARD.)

July 25, 1883

MR. ARTHUR HAMMOND, brother of JUDGE F. L. HAMMOND, is visiting relatives. He is now a resident of Mississippi but lived in Texas for a time.

In Memoriam. Death twice last week visited our community and cut down two of our friends, on Tuesday MRS. ANTOINETTE PETTUS and on Friday MRS. ANN M. BROWN; both were interred in the family burying ground on MR. R. E. PETTUS' place. MRS. BROWN, relict of the REV. HARTWELL BROWN (tombstone ANN M. BROWN our mother--wife of REV. H. H. BROWN--died July 20, 1853 @ 79-1-20), died in her 79th year, July 20th,

at the residence of her son-in-law DR. W. D. PETTUS. She was a devoted
member of the Methodist Episcopal Church (to REV. MOSELEY) for more
than half a century. She leaves one sister older than herself, two
daughters, and many grand and great grandchildren. On the morning of
the 17th of June MRS. ANTOINETTE PETTUS, wife of MR. S(AMUEL) W(ILBURN)
PETTUS, died. She professed faith at 15 and connected herself with
Mt. Zion Church. May her dear old father, sorrowing husband and children
find comfort in that she is at rest. Funeral services were performed
by the pastor, J. W. HILLIARD. Brother. (Tombstone: ANTOINETTE
LOUISA wife of SAMUEL WILBURN PETTUS, October 29, 1848, July 17, 1883
(daughter of JOSEPH ATHENS) SAMUEL WILBURN PETTUS October 4, 1847,
July 9, 1916) (note: married December 3, 1868)
    CORONER FRANKS has been searching for the remains of a MR.
McLESLOSKEY and son, whose family resides in Pennsylvania, and are
desirous of removing the remains to the city graveyard. They were
buried in what was a few years since the Roman Catholic graveyard
situated on the place of MR. HENRY MOTZ. So far the search has been
futile.
    MRS. WASHINGTON POE of Macon, Georgia is visiting MRS. W. H.
MOORE.
    MR. JAMES S. McDONNELL, our lifelong friend and college chum is
at his home for a few weeks. He is now a thriving merchant of Cotton
Center, Arkansas.
    Died in this county July 29, 1883, MISS SARAH NICHOLS, daughter
of W. C. and MARGARET NICHOLS...just budding into womanhood.
    The remains of MRS. WOODRUFF of Mooresville, a native of this
city, were interred in our cemetery Sunday afternoon.

August 8, 1883
    Scottsboro Citizen. WILLIAM HARPER who lived near Fackler,
veteran of the War of 1812, died recently aged nearly 90 years. He
was, we believe, the last survivor in Jackson County who was engaged
in that memorable struggle.

August 15, 1883
    Scottsboro Citizen. Account of armed robbery of a MRS. TOWNSEND
of Greasy Cove, widow of DANIEL TOWNSEND alone except for her small
children; disguised men searched and found $300.
    A prowler entered the residence of MR. THOMAS W. SMITH and stole
$20 from MR. LANE, brother of MR. SMITH's wife.
    Died, Friday, August 10, little JAMES P., second son of MR. and
MRS. E. R. MATTHEWS. (He was accidentally shot by BLAIR BANISTER,
young son of DR. BANISTER.)
    MR. JAMES BROCK was called to Prescott, Arkansas on account of the
illness of his son EMANUEL BROCK.
    ROBERT H. WILSON, Esq. and two little boys have gone to Wooleys
(Wooley Springs, in Limestone County.)

August 22, 1883
    MR. XAN ERSKINE, a handsome young man of Memphis, is visiting
relatives.
    MR. W. T. RAYMOND, from Selma, is visiting relatives.
    MR. W. M. BURTON of Florida, nephew of THOMAS O. BURTON, is
visiting relatives.
    MR. ARTHUR ROBINSON from Memphis, is visiting relatives.
    MR. BERRY L. MARTIN, formerly of Madison, now of Calera, was in
the city Saturday.
    "A Shooting Affair at Brownsboro." GREEN McMULLEN shot and
severely wounded ZIMRI SPELTZ. The parties married sisters and for
some time there has not been friendly relations. On Friday, it is
reported, an indictment was found by the Grand Jury vs. McMULLEN for
assault and battery on his wife, on the evidence of his wife and
SPELTZ. Both are well known and respected...a very unfortunate affair.
(Note: This name is usually spelled SPELCE.)
    MR. J. R. LOCKERD died at Scottsboro August 6th of pneumonia. He
was road inspector for the M & C RR and a member of Monte Sano Lodge,
Knights of Pythias, insured for $3000. He leaves a wife and three
children.
    Died Thursday, ROBERT S., infant son of MR. and MRS. R. S. HALSEY...
funeral from the residence of MR. GEORGE P. LANDMAN Friday.

412

Died Monday, August 20, MRS. SARAH NEELY (40 in Tennessee, nee
HAGEY, widow of JAMES NEELY), the venerable mother of MESSRS. G. M. and
J. H. NEELY. She was buried from her late residence on Green Street
yesterday afternoon, services conducted by REV. JOHN A. THOMPSON. The
deceased came to this country in 1820 and had reached the green old
age of 74 years; she joined the Methodist Church at 12 years. (Death
Certificate: SARAH NEELY, born in Tennessee, aged 72, died August 20
at Huntsville--a widow.)
     Died Saturday August 18, COL. J. VAN VALKENBURG; burial was from
the Church of the Nativity Sunday afternoon, REV. J. M. BANISTER
officiating. COL. VAN VALKENBURG was an officer in the Federal Army
and came to Huntsville after the War...Mason, Knight of Honor, Knight
of the Golden Rule. (Death record: JOHN VAN VALKENBURG, born in
Pennsylvania, aged 60, died in Huntsville August 18. Married.)

August 29, 1883
     Athens Courier. MRS. THOMAS JEFFERSON FOWLER was killed by
lightning Tuesday, also a little girl two years of age. MRS. FOWLER
and her two children had been visiting a neighbor; on the way home were
overtaken by a storm and took refuge under a tree. The 3 months old
child in her arms was unhurt.
     Decatur News. JOHN PROCTOR, digging a well near Brooksville last
week, died from the effects of foul air.

September 12, 1883
     Decatur News. MR. GEORGE BLEVINS of Cedar Plains has made a
second attempt at a suicide...so far, he has failed.
     Scottsboro Citizen. MR. McGUYNN, aged 80, living on Sand Mt. was
struck by lightning and killed last Monday (sitting under a tree).
     Died at the residence of CAPT. HUMES, GEN. W. Y. C. HUMES of
Memphis, Tennessee, a distinguished member of the Memphis War. The
remains were taken to Memphis for interment. (An earlier paper said
he was taken ill in Virginia; CAPT. HUMES, finding him able to travel,
had brought him as far as Huntsville.)
     Died on the 10th at Bell Factory, WILLIAM H. AYRES, about 60.
His family have the sympathy of the neighborhood, where he has lived
for a number of years.

September 19, 1883
     New Hope, Alabama. September 4, 1883. Death took our little
friend AZUBAH DICKEY, third daughter of J. B. and MRS. C. B. DICKEY,
aged 11 years, 1 month.
     Decatur News. MRS. WALLACE and MR. PENN of Huntsville, daughter
and son of the late MR. PENN, of great culture and much fame as a
ripe scholar, great authority as a Mason and one of the founders of
that order in Alabama, are teaching here.

September 26, 1883
     Mounton Advertiser. MR. REASON YOUNG was bitten by a furious
hog on one of his arms; will have to be amputated.

October 3, 1883
     MR. WM. FACKLER and wife have gone to Hot Springs, Arkansas where
he has employment.

October 10, 1883
     Account of the murder of WILLIAM J. STREET, policeman, in attempting
to arrest WES. BROWN and CHARLES ADAMS, (COL.) BROWN was lynched,
ADAMS escaped.

October 17, 1883
     MR. JOSEPH JONES died very suddenly last week. His remains were
taken to his old home at New Market.

October 24, 1883
     Married last Tuesday, the 23rd instant MR. WILLIAM LOVE and
MISS MARY LOVING, at the residence of the bride on West Clinton Street,
by REV. J. A. B. LOVETT ("a lovely affair.")

October 31, 1883
Talladega, October 28.   COL. TAUL BRADFORD died of consumption
here this morning at 1 o'clock and was buried this afternoon at 3.
A large concourse of citizens attended his burial.   No ceremonies were
observed.   He was a member of the 44th Congress.

December 12, 1883
Died at his home in Memphis, MR. FRANK H. CRUSE--double pneumonia.
MR. CRUSE, a native of Huntsville, was born in April, 1860.   Burial was
from the Church of the Nativity.
Died at his residence in this city Saturday, MR. LARKIN P.
SULLIVAN in the 72nd year of his life.   The deceased was a native of
South Carolina but at the age of 4 he came with his parents to this
county and settled near Hazel Green.   About the time he was grown he
removed to Texas, for 4 years.   On his return he went to the old home,
and in 1867 came to Huntsville.   Member of the Methodist Church.
MRS. MILLER of Hot Springs, Arkansas nee FEARN, is visiting the
home of COL. GARTH.

December 19, 1883
Guntersville Democrat.   JAMES POWERS, an old citizen living near
Claysville, was found dead in bed Saturday.
WESLEY CURRY of Friendship dropped dead.   He had been living in
the county 8 years; left a wife and five children.
Scottsboro Herald.   J. W. McKAY, an industrious and upright
citizen was found dead, head mashed...evidently his team had run away
and thrown him from the wagon.   He left a widow and a large family of
children.
MR. FEARN PENN and MRS. V. A. WALLACE, teaching at Madison were
in Huntsville Saturday.
MRS. LEE (nee McDEVITT) is visiting, from Chattanooga.

December 24, 1883
MR. MATTHEWS ERSKINE, who made his home at Richmond, Virginia a
few years ago, is visiting his family.
Death Record: CLARA SIVELY, born in Alabama, aged 58, died in
Huntsville March 18, 1883...widow.

MERCURY 1892

January 6, 1892
We clip the notice of the death of a former Huntsvillian from a
Maryland paper.   MR. MULLONS erected the two story brick houses on
Washington Street which still belong to his estate.
"WILLIAM C. MULLENS died at Rock Springs, Cecil County, Maryland
Sunday night in his 65th year; born in Hopewell, Chester County;
in 1856 he went to Philadelphia, and about two years before the war
he went to Huntsville, Alabama and in 1868 he came to Rock Springs."
News was received in Huntsville yesterday of the death of MR.
THOMAS JAMAR (33 in Virginia) at his home in Green Grove Monday night.
MR. JAMAR was formerly a merchant and business man of this city and no
man was estimated higher for his just and fair dealing.   He was 75
years of age, and for the past few years has conducted a large farming
interest in the southern portion of the county.   His funeral and burial
will take place this morning from his old home in Mullons Flat.   He
leaves a large family circle.

Sheet dated December 23, 1891 (probably merely failed to change date.)
Wednesday afternoon at 5 o'clock the soul of MR. HENRY JACKSON
(35 in North Carolina) PICKARD winged its flight....   MR. PICKARD was
76 years old last April and had been a citizen of this city all his life.
He was well and favorably known in our community.   He leaves an aged
wife, a sister MRS. SARAH HILLIARD of Nashville, MRS. NANCY WHITE of
Columbia, Tennessee who is a half sister, and a number of grandchildren.
(Death record: JACK PICKARD, born in Tennessee aged 76 died in
Huntsville December 31st.   Married.)

January 13, 1892
    Died, MRS. MARGARET McCLUNG, aged widow of the lamented COL.
JAMES W. McCLUNG, who, during his life, filled a number of high
positions and offices within the gift of the people of his native
county and State. He was a lifelong resident of Madison County.
(Note: He was from East Tennessee. KPJ)

January 20, 1892
    Resolutions of Respect by the City Council, on the death of
City Marshall BRITTON FRANKS (41 in Tennessee). (Death Record:
BRITTON FRANKS, aged 84, born in Tennessee, City Marshall, died in
Huntsville December 27, 1891. Widower.)
    Yesterday morning at 5 o'clock at the residence of MR. ROBERT S.
LANDMAN, MRS. JANE STEELE, relict of MR. JAMES W. STEELE, passed away.
The deceased came to this city with her husband in 1853. Funeral
services will take place this afternoon at the Baptist Church.

January 27, 1892
    Died Sunday last at the residence of his uncle, MR. JOHN S. NANCE,
Adams Avenue, HENRY S. PICKETT, aged about 23, second son of MR.
STEPTOE PICKETT, a resident of Madison till his death. He was a loving
son, a source of comfort and joy to his widowed mother.
    Died, MR. J. LAWRENCE WATKINS Sunday, at the residence of his
nephew, MR. S. W. HARRIS. MR. WATKINS was in his 78th year.
    With regret the Mercury notes the death of MR. GEORGE WILLIAM
CAIN. MR. CAIN was born and reared in Limestone, County, Alabama, a
gallant soldier, a useful and prominent citizen, and at the time of
his death a candidate for the Probate Judgeship of Limestone County.
    Married, yesterday afternoon at the home of the bride, MR. J. W.
COYLE of Molly Springs, Mississippi to MISS FANNIE M. STRONG of New
Market.

February 3, 1892
    The remains of the late WILLIS P. WOODALL (were brought to) this
city from New Market and interred in the City Cemetery. (Death Record:
WILLIS P. WOODALL, aged 70, born in Alabama, died January 29, 1892 at
New Market. Married. Note. the widow was a second wife.)
    Whitesburg. MRS. JOHN TRAVIS died at the residence of her
husband in the McDONALD settlement in this county, January 21, aged 45,
and was buried in the family burying ground in the Green Grove community;
her husband and daughters have the sympathy of friends.
    Died, on Sunday last at his residence near Green Grove, MR.
RICHARD A. JAMAR, 88 years of age and brother of the late THOMAS JAMAR.
His remains were brought to this city and interred yesterday.
    Another aged and good citizen, MR. SAMUEL J. PETTUS, died at his
home in Rep Saturday. He was over 80 years of age, and uncle of MR.
R. E. PETTUS. The deceased came to this county from Virginia when but
a young boy.

February 10, 1892
    News reached the city yesterday of the death of MISS ELLEN HUNT
in St. Louis (following a surgical operation.) Burial will take place
this afternoon, REV. J. H. BANISTER officiating.
    In Memoriam. MRS. E. TRAVIS, nee WOODWARD, was born near
Whitesburg, Alabama January 3, 1843, married JOHN W. TRAVIS January 3,
1867 and died near McDONNELL's Chapel January 21, 1892. Wilson's
Chapel Church has lost a faithful member, her husband a devoted wife,
her daughters a loving mother, her brothers a kind sister.
    Macon, Mississippi. February 6, 1892. About 7:30 o'clock last
night JOSEPH S. L. HAMBRICK a prominent farmer and stock raiser of
this county, was assassinated while visiting his relative MR. E. R.
CONNOR of this place. (He was sitting by the fire and the shot was
fired through the window.) MR. HAMBRICK is a son of MR. CALVIN
HAMBRICK of New Market, where the deceased lived until he moved to
Mississippi, a few years ago.

February 17, 1892
    Last Monday morning at his home near Hazel Green MR. WILLIAM
McDAVID TAYLOR breathed his last. MR. TAYLOR, usually called "SHANKS

TAYLOR" was 70 years of age, and was a man who commanded the respect and esteem of all his acquaintances. He was the father of MR. SHELL TAYLOR.

MRS. P. HOLMES DRAKE, wife of COL. JAS. P. DRAKE, died at her residence near this city Thursday, February 11th, a native of Indianapolis, Indiana, but a resident of this county more than a score of years. (Death Record: PRISCILLA H. DRAKE, aged 79 years, 8 months, born in New York, died Huntsville February 11, 1892; widow).

A Tribute. On the morning of February 1st the spirit of SAMUEL J. PETTUS (38 in Virginia) took its flight...he was, perhaps, one of the oldest residents of this county, having moved here from Halifax County, Virginia with his father's family in 1832. He died in his 81st year on the same place he had lived more than half a century. He was married in 1836 to MARTHA BROWN ALLEN (volume 24, page 1), in Limestone County, Alabama, who passed away only about two years ago. Having survived his other brothers a number of years he was especially kind to their sons. To his surviving son and daughter and grandchildren, we would say "Weep not..." (Death Record: SAMUEL J. PETTUS, born in Virginia aged 80 years, 7 months, 24 days died at Cluttsville February 1, 1892...widower)

March 2, 1892
Died--CHARLES E. PEEBLES, of Mooresville, Saturday. Sympathy is extended to his brothers and sisters.

March 9, 1892
Died at the residence of JASON M. BRAZELTON, February 26th, JOHN H. McGAHA, in his 20th year, son of ROBERT S. and FANNIE C. McGAHA. He died away from home, while visiting relatives.

Whitesburg. We had the pleasure of meeting in your city last Friday our friend MR. THEO LACY formerly of Huntsville, but for 20 years making his home in South Alabama.

March 23, 1892
One of the best, as well as the most loved women in the county has just passed away at her home near Monrovia in the 78th year of her age. This was MRS. MARY A. PETTUS, aunt of MR. R. E. PETTUS and mother-in-law of MR. JAMES THOMPSON. Burial took place Monday in the family burying ground. (MRS. MARY A. C. PETTUS born January 2, 1815, died March 20, 1892; 1850 Census; 35 in Virginia, wife of THOS. W.)

Died--Sunday morning, MR. SAM HOLLOWAY, a resident of Huntsville for a few years.

March 30, 1892
MR. W. H. HALSEY, an old Huntsville boy, now at Atlanta, Georgia spent yesterday in our city, guest of his cousin MR. THOMAS W. SMITH.

Anniston Hot Blast. The Hot Blast had a visitor yesterday. REV. B(ENJ) D(ENNY) TURNER (39), one of the most interesting men of the day. He is nearing his 82nd year, moved here in 1832 when this was known as the Creek Purchase. In the fall of that year it was made Benton County. The old gentleman informs us Alexandria was then known as Coffeytown, and it was there our county site, Jacksonville, was first proposed. His present wife was an infant at one of his first sermons...he afterward married her to her first husband. Eleven years ago she became his wife, after a widowhood, and now he exihibits the wonderful curiosity of a smiling, prattling six months old boy and a hoary headed father four score years. He does not look over 60.

Died, at Decatur Wednesday, MORGAN T. McGAVOCK about 38; left two brothers, business men of Athens.

April 6, 1892
MRS. LIZZIE THOMPSON a most estimable lady, died Wednesday night at the residence of MRS. ROBERT H. WARE, Meridian Street.

A letter from Greenville, Texas dated March 25, 1892, stating "Lately I came across the muster roll of CAPT. PEYTON S. WYATT's Co. of Huntsville, Alabama. Volunteers who came to Texas, in December, 1835 I think, to assist...in throwing off the despotism of Maxico. Over 56 years have passed and it is doubtful if a single one survives for most of them were with FANNIN at Goliad and were massacred. Among

416

the names is that of F. PETRESWICK who distinguished himself as an
Artillerist.... Another of the same name, A. PETRESWICK joined this
Company February 25, 1836. The two are supposed to be brothers.
GEORGE THAYER, 2nd Sergeant, whose name was W. J. THAYER was another
to win fame in the battle only to lose his life in the massacre.
J. TYLER was JAMES TYLER, I believe. A. G. LEMOND was transferred to
CAPT. DUVALL's Kentucky Company and was also killed in the massacre.
Muster Roll, WYATT's Company. B. T. BRADFORD, First Lieutenant,
OLIVER SMITH, 2nd Lieutenant, WM. WALLACE, 1st Seargent, GEORGE THAYER,
2nd Seargent, HENRY SHELKY, 3rd Seargent, J. D. RAINS, 4th Seargent,
OLIVER BROWN, Ordnance Master, ALLEN PETERS, musician. Privates:
GABRIEL BUSH, JAMES CORNELIUS, N. DEBRISKI, HENRY DIXON, T. B. FRIZEL,
J. H. FISHER, ED. D. FULLER, FRED GIBENRATH, JAS. HAMILTON, E. D.
HARRISON, J. KIRTIKY, . MIXON, WM. A. McLENNDER, J. F. MORGAN, F.
PETRESWICK, WM. S. PARKER, CHAS. PATTON, A. PETRESWICK, JOHN R. PARKER,
WM. R. SIMPSOM, J. C. STEWART, FRED SIVERMAN, ALLEN WRENN, J. TYLER,
A. G. LEMOND. Those whose names I have called have estates in Texas,
granted for their heirs, after the war...I have been in Texas over 40
years. FRANK TEMPLETON.
    Whitesburg. Died--MRS. ELIZABETH PARKER, at her home in Gardener
Settlement. She left three children, two daughters and one son.
Funeral services were held Sunday by her pastor for more than 40 years
and remains laid in Evenezer Burying Ground. (Death Record: ELIZABETH
PARKER, born in Alabama, aged 55, died April 2, Whitesburg, buried
Ebenezer Church. Widow. Note--did not find a stone when copied those
there. KPJ)
    Died Monday at the home of her mother MRS. W. H. WATKINS on
Rand Street, MRS. IDA GILLESPIE; leaves a devoted husband, little
daughter, mother and several brothers.

April 20, 1892
    It is with profound regret we announce the death of MRS. SUSAN C.
ERSKINE on Sunday last, April 17th at the residence of her son-in-law,
MRS. JAMES H. HASTIN. MRS. ERSKINE was in the 88th year of her age,
and one of the oldest residents of Huntsville. She had lived here since
early childhood, her father, COL. ALBERT RUSSELL, a Pennsylvanian by
birth and LT. COL. in the Revolutionary Army having moved from Loudon
County, Virginia* to Alabama in 1816 when she was quite young. She
was born near Leesburg, Virginia in the year 1805, her mother's maiden
name being ANN FRANCES HOOE. In the year 1820 she was married to
DR. ALEX ERSKINE whose name has long been identified with the history
of Huntsville as one of its earliest and most prominent physicians.
By this marriage there was a large family of children of whom most of
the surviving members are yet residents of this place. She was of
Scotch Irish descent, a Presbyterian by ancestry, and has been for over
65 years a member of the Presbyterian Church of this city.... Peaceful
be her last sleep! (* DAR Lineage Book 142, page 132 gives ALBERT
RUSSEL's rank in the Revolution as Lieutenant only. He lived in
Maury County, Tennessee for a time, before coming to Madison County,
having gone to Maury County in 1807.)

April 20, 1892
    DR. BRYSON received a dispatch from the officers of the Presbyterian
Church at Montgomery informing him of the death of DR. (DEWITT)
BURKHEAD Monday evening and asking him to conduct the funeral service.
DR. BURKHEAD had charge of the Presbyterian Church here from June,
1876 to May, 1879. He was a native of North Carolina, a graduate of
the Theological Seminary, Columbia, South Carolina, Chaplain in the
Confederate Army and for several years pastor at Athens, Georgia.
From here he went to Paris, Texas and spent several years. His last
charge was Montgomery, Alabama. His family will have the sympathy of
friends in this community.

April 27, 1892
    With sorrow we announce the death of ARTHUR HARRIS, only child
of DR. GEORGE M. HARRIS, at his residence Sunday night. "Whatever
sins he was guilty of were only sins against himself." He was devoted
to the wife and baby he leaves behind. (Death Record: ARTHUR LEE
HARRIS, aged 35, born in Alabama, "no occupation," died in Huntsville
April 25, 1892...married.)

417

May 18, 1892
    MR. JOHN P. TURNER of Texas, just out of Medical College at
Louisville, is visiting his brother MR. A. H. TURNER, whom he has not
seen since boyhood days.
    About ten o'clock Monday morning MR. DAN SCHIFFMAN passed peacefully
away; was a few months over 50. He was born at Hoppstadton C. H.
Oldenburg January 1, 1842, and moved to Huntsville in 1868. Odd
Fellow--merchant; leaves a large family circle.
    Fatal Shooting at Tuscumbia. JOHN GOODWIN killed by THOMAS STEELE...
was an effect of a shooting affray about two years ago when JOHN STEELE,
JR. lost his life, and THOMAS STEELE and JOHN GOODWIN were wounded.
(THOMAS STEELE is also dead) Both parties are highly connected and
both were single.
    Below we repeat an article from the Calvert (Texas) Courier, on
the death of JUDGE THOMAS MARTIN, brother of MR. JOSEPH MARTIN,
Cashier of the First National Bank.... "occurred at his home in this
city (Calvert) April 25th last. He had passed more than 60 milestones
on the journey of life.... To the sorrowing family, the Courier
expresses sympathy."

May 25, 1892
    On Sunday morning last MR. JAMES M. HUTCHENS breathed his last
at his home on Henry Street. MR. HUTCHENS came to Huntsville from
Tennessee in 1851 and for years was engaged in the contracting and
building business. The deceased was a soldier in the late war. The
funeral took place at the residence Monday afternoon, REV. J. W. CALDWELL
officiating. (Pastor of the Cumberland Presbyterian Church.) Peace
to the ashes of the lamented dead who, if during more than fifty years
of life, had an enemy, we never heard of it.
    MR. W. R. HUMPHREY, editor of the Platt City (Illinois) Republican
is guest of his cousin, DR. J. D. HUMPHREY.

June 11, 1892
    Your correspondent was at the wedding of H. B. LANSDEN to
MISS CAMERON, at Flintville, Tennessee (New Market notes.)
    Yesterday a telegram was received by W. J. POTTS from Helena,
Arkansas, informing him that TOM E. AUSTIN had been killed at that
place the day before, particulars not given. MR. AUSTIN was a brother
of MRS. A. L. BLUNT.

June 15, 1892
    Death of an aged lady. Last Saturday at the home of MR. O. B.
LAXSON, MRS. BINEY PEEBLES breathed her last...interment in the
Pettus graveyard.
    From New Market. We partook of dinner with our venerable soldier
friend COL. JACK NANCE and his genial and courteous wife, where we
met REV. MR. PERSINGER, mother and AUNT POLLY HAMBRICK who will soon
pass her four score years is hale, hearty and vivacious. (note:
something seems omitted. "AUNT POLLY HAMBRICK" is quite evidently
mother of MRS. NANCE, RUTH, daughter of BRADFORD and MARY HAMBRICK.
KPJ)
    Whitesburg. MRS. MAGGIE MORTON, wife of DR. J. W. HORTON, died
at her home Friday evening...consumption.
    MR. HENRY McGEE is dead; born in Perryville, Pennsylvania 1836,
moved to Huntsville 1866, proprietor of the McGee Hotel; left one
child, MISS MOLLIE. (note--she never married. KPJ)

June 29, 1892
    MESSRS. W. T. and ROBERT DUNCAN of this city received the sad
intelligence of their mother's death at her home in Buckingham County,
Virginia, in the 70th year of her age. She left four grown sons to
mourn her loss.
    Friday a telegram from New York informed friends of the death of
MRS. KRAUS. Her husband, with his eldest son, was in Louisville and
left immediately for New York. Last January she went to that city for
treatment.
    J. W. C. STEGER, JR., prescriptionist, from Franklin, Kentucky will
arrive Saturday to spend a few days with his mother, MRS. F. E. M.
STEGER, and his sister MRS. J. S. HUNT of Brownsboro.

July 6, 1892
    MR. JESSE L. FERGUSON was down from Brownsboro last week and
informed the Mercury of the death of MRS. JESSE MILLETTE Wednesday.
MR. MILLETTE is an honest, hardworking farmer; friends extend sympathy.

July 13, 1892
    Sunday night at her home on Meridian Street MRS. H(ENRY) J(ACKSON)
PICKARD (35 in North Carolina) passed away. The deceased was born in
Tennessee July 15, 1820 and married to her late husband January 14,
1836. She had been a resident of Huntsville a long period, and long
a faithful member of the Cumberland Presbyterian Church. Peace to
her noble ashes. (Death Record: MARIA WALKER PICKARD (27 in Tennessee),
born in Tennessee, aged 72 years 11 months 25 days, died July 10, 1892,
Huntsville, Alabama. Widow.)

July 20, 1892
    Last Saturday night Alderman JOHN G. BAKER (died); 42 years of
age, born and raised Oswego, New York, came to this city December, 1875,
married about 13 years and leaves a devoted wife, 3 little daughters
and a son, 1 brother and two sisters, MRS. WHEELER of Portland, New
York and MRS. BARRATT of Pennsylvania. (Death Record: JOHN G. BAKER,
born in New York aged 48 years 3 months died July 16, Huntsville,
Alabama. Married)
    This morning, at the residence of her husband, about 9 miles from
town, MRS. CHARLEY POWELL breathed her last. Funeral services were
held at the Methodist Church Friday.

August 3, 1892
    Notice of the death at Dallas, Texas July 24, 1892, of RAYMOND,
infant son of ROBERT P. and NELLIE P. LYON, nee PARISS, Signed "Grandma."

August 17, 1892
    MRS. WALTER O. CARPENTER died at the residence of her husband at
Owens X Roads Wednesday.
    On Wednesday last, August 10, 1892 HUGH OTEY, eldest son of MR.
and MRS. A. G. NOWLIN, who reside a few miles from town, died of typhoid
fever, aged 24.

August 24, 1892
    A telegram from Athens last Saturday gave the information that
COL. L. R. DAVIS died at 4 o'clock. The deceased was a man of strong
and ennobling traits of character and was an intellectual and prominent
citizen.
    MR. R. W. YOUNG is up from Mississippi on a visit to relatives.
    Whitesburg, August 23. Last Saturday morning Esq. J. D. W. SMITH,
after a long illness, breathed his last. Services were held at the
residence Sabbath afternoon conducted by REV. B. F. BELLINGER and the
remains laid to rest in the family burying ground.

August 31, 1892
    FRED GREEN, 19, son of MR. and MRS. TOM GREEN of Meridianville
died Sunday--typhoid.
    A letter from Jackson, Tennessee received by the family of DR.
A. B. JONES, informs them DR. JONES father is extremely ill.
    DR. J. C. STEGER, an intellectual and polished gentleman from
Dover, Tennessee arrived in the city yesterday for a few days.

September 7, 1892
    THOMAS W. LYNE, now located at Lone Junction, Texas, is spending
a few days in the county with relatives.
    MR. WALTER MORRISON, formerly of Huntsville, now of Memphis,
Tennessee is visiting relatives.
    NEWT COPELAND was killed by a posse near Blevna, escaping from
custody.

September 14, 1892
    GEORGE M. COPELAND, brother of NEWT COPELAND, swore out warrants
against JOHN ORMAN and CYRUS McFARLAND, charging them with murder.

Talladega. Sect. 10. GEN. LEVI W. LAWLER died at his home _?_
miles from Talladega this evening; his remains will be taken to
Mobile for burial. Funeral services will take place at the St.
Francis St. Baptist Church, Mobile, Monday evening. GEN. LAWLER was
about 70 years of age. At the time he died, he was a member of the
Railroad Commission of Alabama. (In the Editorial column, commenting
on him, the Editor said "GEN. LAWLER was a native Alabamian and was
about 76 years old.")

September 28, 1892
    The sad news reached the city last Friday of the death of MRS.
R. O. KELLY. She leaves a devoted husband and four small children to
mourn an irreparable loss. MRS. KELLY is a daughter of the late
COL. RIP DAVIS of Athens. The burial of the deceased took place in
the cemetery at Athens. (Note: was a child of LAWRENCE RIPLEY DAVIS
and his first wife, a MISS ABERCROMBIE of Talladega. See Owens Bio-
graphical Dictionary, which errs however in stating COL. DAVIS' daughter
MALVINA married a JACKSON; she married JOSEPH HASTIN JACKS of Madison
County, grandson of REV. DAVID JACKS. KPJ) See below.

October 5, 1892
    Died recently in New York City, MR. HORACE TENNANT, only son of
W. H. and LUCIA B. TENNENT, only grandson of HORACE UPSHAW, Senator
from Virginia, and only brother of MRS. MARY L. DRAKE who resides near
Huntsville, Alabama. He married MISS VIRGINIA BOYD; four lovely
children were given to them, all of whom preceeded their father to the
grave.

October 12, 1892
    MR. J. M. McGAHA, who had been in charge of the second toll gate
on the Whitesburg Pike for some time, died Saturday morning; remains
interred in the Love Cemetery near Whitesburg Sunday afternoon. (Death
record: JAMES MADISON McGAHA, aged 63, born in Alabama, died October 7,
Whitesburg. Married.)
    Death Record: JANE KELLY, born in Alabama, aged 42, died at
Cluttsville September 23, 1892, buried at Athens. Married.
    JAMES McDONNELL Esq. returned to Pine Bluff, Arkansas yesterday.
He was called to this city Sunday (to attend) the funeral of his father.
(Death record: ARCHIBALD McDONNELL, born in Alabama, aged 77 years
7 months 7 days died October 15th at LANIER's...widower.)

October 19, 1892
    Died at Gurley Wednesday night MR. JOHN KING, highly esteemed by
all who knew him. Left a wife and two children.

November 30, 1892
    A letter from HENRY NOVATT, Bird City, Kentucky wanting information
of the whereabouts of AMOS WINTER, who lived in Huntsville in 1861 with
father, mother, sister and brother. He was about ten years old and
with some other boys ran away and went into the Confederate Army,
joining the Lower Mississippi Regiment commanded by COL. BRECKENRIDGE,
and when last heard of was carrying dispatches between the lines.

ARGUS 1893

January 26, 1893
    MR. JOHN HARRIS, a venerable and respected citizen of the Mays-
ville Precinct, visited the city yesterday. He was anxious to transact
his business quickly as he had promised to return to his mother as
soon as possible. Noting his appearance, someone asked how old his
mother was, and he replied she was 101 years of age. (Cameron Church,
Hurricane Creek. JOHN HARRIS, October 5, 1824. October 20, 1917.
His wife, DORCAS P. HARRIS, April 24, 1823. October 21, 1902.)

February 16, 1893
    MR. J. W. COOPER breathed his last at his residence on Randolph
Street last night. Last week his children were called home and all

were present when he died except CARROLL, who was in Memphis. The
deceased was one of the city's merchants of ante-bellum says. At
the time when the office sought the man he was elected Sheriff. He
was a member of the Methodist Church.

MR. RISON yesterday was recipient of a telegram from Memphis
stating MRS. STRATTON died at her home there, February 15. She was
the mother of MRS. WM. B. LEEDY, formerly of this city, and now of
Birmingham.

February 23, 1893

DAVID A. RAMSEY, one of the earliest employees of the M & C RR,
died at Memphis Sunday February 19. The deceased belonged to this
city and the remains will arrive here for burial this morning. MR.
RAMSEY antedated every conductor on this division, he having been with
the road since its inception. When through transit between "Bluff
City" and Chattanooga first began to make through trips, in 1856, he
was a conductor. Only when age began to tell did the officers of the
road conclude to reward the faithful attache with an easier position
at Memphis. He was a member of the Masonic fraternity, Delphic Lodge
of the Knights of Honor and Monte Sano Lodge #1 of the Knights of
Pythias.

March 2, 1893

In Memoriam. DAVID A. RAMSEY died February 19, 1893 at Memphis,
Tennessee in the 65th year of his age. He joined the Lodge December 2,
1877...copy of Resolutions be furnished the family of Brother RAMSEY.
Delphic Lodge #306, Knights of Honor. (Also Resolutions by the
Knights of Pythias..."a true citizen, a kind and affectionate husband
and father.")

MRS. LUCY W. DAVIS died suddenly at the house of a friend on the
mountain road leading to Maysville, Thursday morning last, of paralysis.
She was the mother of C. M. and SEP DAVIS; funeral today from the
Methodist Church. (Death record: LUCY C. DAVIS, aged 69, born ...,
died (Beat 11; Meridianville) February 23, 1893, buried at Huntsville.
Reported by J. P. BURKE, M.D. (note: MRS. CHARLES DAVIS, nee LUCY
ALLEN. See "Harris & Allied Families." Another death record: LUCY W.
DAVIS, born in Alabama aged 68 died February 23, 1893 in Beat 12
(Hazel Green) buried in Huntsville, reported by C. M. DAVIS...widow)

Yesterday morning LESLIE MOORE DONEGAN (died) at the residence of
his uncle, W. R. MOORE. His father and brother JAMES had been summoned
from Memphis and his sister MARY from Nashville. The funeral will
take place at the Church of the Nativity tomorrow, DR. BANISTER
officiating.

MESSRS. WM. SILVESTER and FRANK MITCHELL, son and son-in-law of
TOM SILVESTER arrived in Town Saturday and removed their father to his
home in Danville. It was a risky move in a wagon but MR. SILVESTER
was anxious to get home. We hope the trip was made in safety.

March 9, 1893

(Died) Thursday March 2, 1893, MRS. W. H. McANELLY; the death of
EMILY NEWMAN McANELLY occurred in the morning of her fresh young life...
(Death report. EMILY J. McANELLY, born in Alabama, aged 30, died
March 2, in Huntsville. Married.)

Died of pneumonia at the home of her son-in-law MR. JOHN BRADLEY
yesterday afternoon, MRS. W. VINCENT. The recent death of her daughter
weighed on her mind (she died of pneumonia). The deceased was a sister
of CAPT. FRANK GURLEY of this county and shortly after the death of
her husband about 5 years ago she came to this city and made her home
with her son and daughter. After the death of the latter she devoted
herself to caring for her grandchildren...for the second time these
little ones are bereft. (Death record: JENNIE VINCENT, aged 60, died
in Huntsville, March 2) (LOUISA JANE ELIZ 17 in Alabama, daughter of
JOLENO GURLEY)

MRS. EMMA STUBBS died in this city yesterday and will be buried
on the SIMPSON place in Pond Beat. She was a sister of MR. HENRY
SIMPSON.

March 16, 1893

Resolutions of Respect, Meridianville Lodge #625 F & A. M. Died,
at the residence of his son, DAVID GRAHAM in Huntsville, Alabama on

the 25th of February 1893, JOHN CALVIN GRAHAM...Brother JOHN C. GRAHAM
was an industrious man, a kind father, a generous neighbor, a charitable
citizen.

March 30, 1893
      Died at Nashville, MRS. MOLLIE MATTHEWS ERWIN, wife of MR. ALEX
ERWIN, on Tuesday, March 28th. Sister of MR. LUKE MATTHEWS. Funeral
will be held this afternoon from the Methodist Church in this city.
      We regret to announce the death of MR. JOHN CLIFT yesterday
morning at his residence near Madison. MR. CLIFT was a time honored
citizen of this county, loved, honored and respected by all who knew
him. He was a kinsman by marriage to MRS. J. W. WALL. (see tombstone
in Volume 235, p. 63--"JOHN H. CLIFT born September 5, 1821, died
March 25; MARY CLIFT born August 4, 1820, died June 24, 1897)
      A telegram was received yesterday by MR. CHRIS McDONALD from
CAPT. ZACH THOMAS of Washington bearing news of the death of his wife
MARTHA SLACK THOMAS Friday. The deceased was a native of Huntsville,
daughter of the late CHARLES SLACK who was a confectioner in this
city. She was married to CAPT. THOMAS in the reconstruction period and
for many years their home has been at the Capitol. In 1889 and 1890
CAPT. and MRS. THOMAS resided in Huntsville, CAPT. THOMAS filling the
office of Government Superintendent of the public building here during
its erection. (This name was SCHLACK.)

April 13, 1893
      Died...MRS. BURNEY FOWLKES of Monrowia.

April 20, 1893
      SAMUEL W. SHACKELFORD died at Courtland yesterday in his 77th
year. He was a noble Southern gentleman. His father was the historic
DR. JACK SHACKELFORD who carried a company from the Tennessee Valley,
known as the "Red Rovers" to Texas in the war between Texas and
Mexico, of which only three returned.
      The funeral of MRS. SUE SPRAGUE took place from the Methodist
Church yesterday. She was greatly beloved here in her old home where
nearly all her life was spent. Of the children of the highly esteemed
DR. P. B. ROBINSON, of which she was one, MRS. DYSART of Jackson,
Tennessee, MRS. REAGAN of Memphis and MRS. SMITH of Chicago still
survive. All of MRS. SPRAGUE's children came to the burial.
      We regret to learn of the critical condition of ROBERT D. WILSON
Esq. of this city, at the residence of his daughter MRS. MOSELEY in
Decatur. MR. WILSON was for many years a Justice of the Peace here.
      The death of MRS. MARY E. STEGER of Nashville on Sunday last is
announced by the Banner of Monday as follows: MRS. MARY E. STEGER,
wife of DR. F. E. H. STEGER, died yesterday afternoon. She was
mother of CAPT. T. M. STEGER and DR. R. W. STEGER and sister of
DRS. T. J. and J. W. MADDEN. Funeral services will be conducted by
BISHOP FITZGERALD and DR. BARBEE at the residence on Farrell Street
this afternoon and burial will take place at Mt. Olivet. (See
"Harris & Allied Families")
      Sad News from Afar. MR. EDWARD CRUTE, eldest son of MRS. W. H.
WATKINS, who sustained serious injuries from being run over by the
cars at Washington Friday, died yesterday. To his sorrowing mother
and sisters the Argus extends sympathy.
      COL. J. R. H. CUMMINGS of Washington, Arkansas was introduced to
an Argus man yesterday by MR. A. D. RODGERS. COL. CUMMINGS' father
settled in this then utterly wild section in 1807 and COL. CUMMINGS
knew this immediate region when it was scarcely more than a hamlet.
He lived many years in the eastern portion of Limestone County. He
was a volunteer in CAPT. SAM FRENCH's Company, COL.   H. ACKLEN's
Regiment, GEN. BEN PATTERSON's command. The late HON. Z. P. DAVIS was
a fellow soldier with COL. CUMMINGS. He pointed to a spot about 50
feet east of the First National Bank and said "I remember as if it
were but a short while ago when we were mustered out right where I am
showing you."

May 4, 1893
      Scottsboro Citizen. A marriage license was procured here last
week for MR. M. A. CLAY, the handsome and wealthy bachelor of Princeton,

and MISS MARTHA MOORE, an amiable and lovely young lady. (Note--later papers carried an account of a suit of breach of promise, brought by another young lady vs. MR. CLAY.)

May 11, 1893
In Memoriam. MRS. LUCRETIA J. GILES who removed from Madison County to Texas in 1891, died December 3, 1892. The deceased was born in Madison County January 27, 1843 and was one of the Constituent members of Locust Grove Baptist Church at its organization. She leaves a husband, two sons and one daughter; an aged father, two sisters and five brothers mourn her loss. BETTIE POWER.

An account of the elopement of WAT TONEY, son of HARRIS TONEY of Triana, and MISS LUCY, daughter of COL. D. R. HUNDLEY; young TONEY is 19, MISS LUCY 18. Accompanied by JOHN TONEY and MISS MILDRED TONEY (they walked the railroad bridge across the Tennessee River) and were married in Pulaski, Tennessee.

Died, MISS EFFIE P. DAVIS...consumption.
In Memoriam, DAVID C. HUNT...a young man...of New Hope.

May 18, 1893
On Sunday morning, May 14, MRS. LOUISA M. HAR is exchanged the sorrows of earth for the joys of Heaven. The deceased was born in Petersburg, Georgia December 28, 1819 and was 73 years 4 months and 15 days of age. She was MISS WATKINS and descended from a family of Virginians. She was married at Courtland, Lawrence County, Alabama to the late S(TEPHEN) W(ILLIS) HARRIS (32 in Georgia) and after her marriage came to Huntsville. She had four children, two sons and two daughters, but only S. W. HARRIS JR. survives her.

Death of MRS. JOSEPH JONES. The westbound train last Sunday brought the remains of MRS. MADGE JONES, daughter of MR. GEORGE W. WARWICK, and widow of the late JOSEPH JONES Esq. a brilliant member of the Alabama Bar, whose tragic death at Bridgeport some ten years ago is still fresh in the memory of those who knew him. MRS. JONES went to Bridgeport about two weeks ago and died Sunday of heart disease. MRS. JONES was a consistent member of the Episcopal Church. She leaves one daughter.

Yesterday afternoon MR. JOHN S. NANCE, venerable father of MR. HARRY NANCE died at his residence on Adams Avenue. Before the war MR. NANCE was Receiver of Public Moneys in the U.S. Land Office, and later engaged in the mercantile business. He had passed three score years and ten. The funeral will take place from the Methodist Church this afternoon.

The venerable CAPT. JOHN REED is dangerously ill.

May 25, 1893
MR. J. C. VANN of this city was at a reunion of his family at Owens X Roads Sunday, complimenting his father and mother, both of whom have passed three score. It was the first reunion of the Vann family in 18 years and the number present footed up to over 150 souls. In addition to MR. and MRS. J. C. VANN of this city, there were present GEORGE, THOMAS, JOS. NEWTON and DEE VANN and their sister MRS. MARY CARMACK.

MR. J. A. GAINES a prominent citizen of Winchester, Tennessee died suddenly Thursday of heart disease.

June 1, 1893
At an early hour yesterday morning MR. GEORGE H. WARWICK (40 in Pennsylvania) quietly passed into rest eternal. MR. WARWICK, at the time of his death, was one of the oldest citizens of Huntsville. Prior to the war he carried on business as a cabinet maker. He was one of the charter members of Madison Lodge #25 I.O.O.F., installed April 4, 1848. He was the soul of integrity. The funeral will take place this afternoon, REV. DR. BANISTER officiating in the absence of DR. BRYSON, the pastor of whose church the deceased was a member (i.e., the Presbyterian Church.)

The funeral of the late JOHN J. FORD will take place this afternoon from the Cumberland Presbyterian Church. The deceased was born in this county, his father being one of the wealthiest planters here prior to the war. Of the family, but two members survive, a brother and a

sister of the deceased, WILLIAM B. FORD of Chattanooga and MRS. BURWELL
LANIER of Madison. At the beginning of the war the deceased was one of
the first to answer the call, and joined the 4th Alabama. He leaves a
wife.

June 8, 1893
     Death of MRS. ELIZA J. REEDY. Shortly after 6 o'clock last
evening the soul of the venerable MRS. REEDY, beloved mother of
MESSRS. GEORGE and HENRY LANDMAN, slipped away...bowed with the weight
of years. She was a consistant member of the Methodist Church.
(Death record: ELIZA REEDY, aged 78 years, 3 months, 16 days, born in
Virginia, died July 1, 1893, Huntsville. Widow)
     Died in Texas. DR. J. H. DIOUS, Treasurer of Jackson County, died
at San Antonio, Texas Tuesday. The remains will be interred at
Scottsboro.
     News has reached Huntsville of the sudden death in Santa Ana,
California of MR. WILLIAM B. LACY, a native of Huntsville.

June 29, 1893
     MR. CORNELIUS McNEIL died at his residence near Gurley last week
at the age of 92. MR. M. came of a family remarkable for longevity.
A day or two ago one of his kinsmen, MR. GEORGE DOUGLASS, 82, was in
the city looking remarkably robust; he can read without the aid of
glasses.

July 2, 1893
     MRS. PRISCILLA D. PHELAN, daughter of the late JUDGE SHELBY and
widow of the late JUDGE JOHN D. PHELAN of the Supreme Bench of Alabama,
died in Nashville Sunday night, July 2nd, in her 78th year.

July 13, 1893
     News of a terrible tragedy at Mint Springs, near Hosters' Creek
Saturday; JOHN W. WALKER, a sheep farmer of near Plevna and once a
leading merchant there, was found at the spring, almost disemboweled
with knife wounds. (He was not dead, but died. KPJ) (Volume 35,
page 51--tombstone JOHN W. WALKER November 28, 1858, died July 10,
1893)
     In Memoriam. Hall of the Huntsville team Fire Company No. 1.
Sympathy to BROTHER A. N. WOOLDRIDGE on the death of his mother,
MRS. MARY WOOLDRIDGE who died July 8, 1893. O. K. STEGALL, Chief;
ABE W. WISE, Ass't Chief. (Note: Death report shows MRS. PARALEE T.
WOOLDRIDGE died July 8, 1893, born in Tennessee, aged 74 years, 7
months, 16 days. Tombstone also shows PARALEE T. KPJ)
     The Plevna Tragedy. MR. JOHN W. WALKER was a highly esteemed
citizen. REV. MR. WALKER of Plevna was in town and detailed what
facts he was in possession of to the Sheriff.

July 20, 1893
     WILLIAM CAMPBELL, business partner and alleged slayer of JOHN W.
WALKER, surrendered.
     MR. ISAAC PARKER, an elderly and much respected citizen who lived
in about two miles of New Market, was killed yesterday by a runaway
team; his daughter who was with him, was only slightly hurt.
     The remains of the late JAMES LEFTWICH arrived from St. Louis
yesterday and were interred in the City Cemetery. The deceased was a
native of Huntsville and son of the late JABEZ N. LEFTWICH; a brilliant,
talented young man. He leaves a wife and child now residing here.
     GEN. JAMES T. HOLTZOLAW died at his home in Montgomery Tuesday in
his 60th year; he was a Brigadier General in the Confederate Army.

August 3, 1893
     The whole county of Madison will be sorrowful to learn of the
death of DR. E. T. TALIAFERRO near New Market yesterday. DR. TALIAFERRO
came to Madison County from West Tennessee in 1865 and entered into
practice of his profession. In 1884 he was elected to the Legislature.
He would have been 73 years of age his next birthday--he was three
times married. From the first and second marriages there were four
children, EDWIN T. TALIAFERRO of New York, CHARLES P. TALIAFERRO and
PAUL TALIAFERRO of New Market and MRS. R. S. PULLEY of Huntsville.

His last wife was MISS FANNIE PATTERSON who survived him. The funeral
will take place in this city from the Baptist Church.

We have to chronicle the death yesterday morning of MR. JOHN D.
SWASEY. It is not known when he will be buried as the family wish to
have his son present, now on his vessel on the Gulf. JOHN DUSTAN
SWASEY was born in Bethlehelm, New Hampshire September 28, 1826,
married in Patterson, New Jersey MISS JEANNETTE WILSON and came south
in 1865, first to Macon, Georgia, and entered the employ of the M & C
Railroad. His wife died nearly twenty years ago. There were four
children, two dead. Living are JOHN E. SWASEY of New Orleans and
MRS. W. A. PARKS of Huntsville...a worthy member of the M. C. Church
South.

MRS. FIFE, a lady of advanced years died yesterday in this city,
at her home on the corner of Washington and Madison Streets. (Death
record: MARTHA FIFE, born in Alabama, aged 69, died July 27. 1893 in
Huntsville, a widow.)

DR. L. C. PYNCHEON received a telegram announcing the death of his
only sister. MRS. CARRIE BROYSACHER, at Little Rock. The deceased
was well known and greatly beloved in Huntsville.

Limrock, July 30. On the mountain above Pt. Rock, THOMAS WILLIAM
REAY shot and killed THOMAS J. ERWIN, a merchant, and a HOUSTON
SUMMERS (in a dispute over location of a land entry.) Sympathy of the
public is with REAY.

MRS. COCHRAN, wife of DR. R. E. COCHRAN of New Hope, died on the
2nd instant. She was a daughter of JOHN LEDBETTER, aged 52, and a
member of the Primitive Baptist Church.

August 10, 1893
MRS. CALLIE DICKEY died at New Hope yesterday. She was a most
excellent lady and greatly beloved. (Death record: MRS. J. B. DICKEY
aged 50, born in Alabama. died August 9, 1893, "Beat 5.")

August 17, 1893
Died in Marshall County GEORGE BARRETT working in a well near
Cushing, was overcome by foul air.

MISS EMMA K. HENRY of Philadelphia (telegraph operator in
Huntsville) died of consumption.

On Sunday, August 13 MR. W. N. DAVIS died at his home in New Market
of typhoid fever. At the funeral of DR. TALIAFERRO he was a pall
bearer; one of his sons is still suffering from typhoid. The deceased
was about 65 years of age and was highly esteemed by all who knew him.
He served as Tax Collector one term...a consistent member of the
Cumberland Presbyterian Church, a fond husband, a gentle father   The
remains were laid to rest in the family burying ground in New Market.

August 24, 1893
Death of MRS. JOSEPH N. GATES. At two o'clock yesterday MRS. SUSAN
GATES, mother of MRS. A. B. JONES of this city, died at the residence
of her daughter on Randolph Street in her 70th year; remains taken to
Jackson, Tennessee for burial in family burying ground at that place.

August 31, 1893
MRS. AGATHA LEFTWICK will open a kindergarten on Franklin Street.

Sad News. Death of MRS. ANNIE E. HUNDLEY, wife of HON. OSCAR P.
HUNDLEY, at Waukesha, Wisconsin yesterday; the remains will reach the
city today and the funeral will take place from her late residence.

(Died) EUGENE KELLY, son of HON. and MRS. THOS. B. KELLY of
Cluttsville, August 20; had just reached the age of maturity.

Died--MRS. W. J. POTTS, wife of the late Tax Collector Saturday
afternoon at her residence in Meridianville. The funeral took place
Sunday at the family burying ground.

September 7, 1893
MRS. C. C. CLARK died at her home in Cluttsville Wednesday night
after a long illness.

MRS. MARY A. HERZ died yesterday. The deceased was a native of
Mobile, a lady of rare accomplishments. The funeral will take place
from the Church of the Nativity this afternoon.

MISS SERENA BRONAUGH, known by those to whom she was endeared as
AUNT SI, died at the residence of HON. G. C. SAUNDERS at Meridianville
yesterday morning. The remains were interred Sunday in the family
burying ground. (Anderson Cemetery buried April 1963 by W. F. SPARKMAN--
west of HAMMUND graveyard; in memory of CYRENIA M. BRONAUGH July 3,
1815 - September 2, 1893; GEO. C. SAUNDERS 1827-1903; OCTAVIA SAUNDERS
1834-1915 (nee ANDERSON) see Volume 76).
     The many friends of the late THOMAS L. SEAY will learn with regret
of his death yesterday morning...consumption. MR. SEAY lost his wife
a few years ago. He leaves a family of young children. Methodist;
Knight of Pythias. (Death record: THOMAS SEAY born in Alabama,
aged 47, died September 5, 1893, in "Alabama". Widower.)

October 12, 1893
     Three columns on death of WALTER H. RHETT, of Atlanta; son of
R. BARNWELL RHETT and JOSEPHINE HORTON of Huntsville; baptized in the
Episcopal Church by his uncle REV. JOSEPH WALKER, D.D. at Beaufort,
South Carolina...lost his mother before he was 3 1/2--father was a
widower 7 years; as a child he lived with his grandfather RHETT. In
1888 he married MISS ANNIE RAYMOND REID, daughter of DR. REID and
granddaughter of DR. CALDWELL...when he died was boarding with
MRS. JOHN H. JONES, his mother-in-law.
     From the Charlotte (Virginia) Gazette: JUDGE R. H. MARSHALL left
Friday for Chicago in the interest of the heirs of the late ELISHA E.
HUNDLEY...2000 feet on Lake View Shore claimed by the City of Chicago
is also claimed by the HUNDLEY Estate. The wife of our old friend
COL. D. R. HUNDLEY, was a daughter of ELISHA E. HUNDLEY and one of his
heirs.
     Yesterday morning just as the eastbound train was pulling out of
Belle Mina Conductor ALEX PERRYMAN was siezed with a violent hemmorhage
of the lungs and expired in a few minutes. The funeral will take place
today in Tuscumbia.
     On Friday morning MR. GEORGE W. BRYANT breathed his last; formerly
an employee of the M & C Railroad, then in business in Madison County.
     On Sunday, October 16 the soul of ESTELLE ADLER slipped from its
earthly prison...funeral from the Synagogue.
     Suddenly, at the home of her daughter MRS. AMELIA DILLARD, MRS.
MYERS passed away. (Death record: MARY E. MYERS, born in New York,
aged 55, died October 16, Huntsville, Alabama. Married.)

October 26, 1893
     MAJ. B. W. TIPTON, well known hotel manager of Guntersville,
died Friday...he is to be buried at Scottsboro.

November 2, 1893
     THOMAS MADISON WHEELER, the reverend and venerable father of
DR. W. C. WHEELER died yesterday at the ripe age of 84 years. The
deceased was a native of Kentucky and moved to Tennessee with his
parents when quite young, and came to Alabama when about 21. He was
married in Colburt County and four children blessed his union, two of
whom survive, DR. W. B. WHEELER of this city and MRS. BENSON of
Cherokee. For over 50 years he was a member of the Methodist Church.
(Death record: THOMAS M. WHEELER, born in Kentucky, aged 83 years,
10 days, died in Huntsville October 30, 1893. Widower)

November 9, 1893
     Yesterday evening MR. C. G. SPELLMAN died at his residence on
Washington Street aged 62. A bereaved wife and daughter mourn their
loss. MR. SPELLMAN was born in Virginia January 12, 1831 and came to
this city in 1857. He was a carpenter and builder. Shortly after
coming here he married MISS MARY, daughter of THOMAS O. GILL. Of two
children only MISS LUCY is living. Methodist, Knight Templer....
     The funeral of the late CHURCHILL GORDON SPELLMAN took place
yesterday.... (Death record: born in Virginia...aged 62 years,
9 months, 20 days).
     On Friday, November 3rd MRS. MARY A. COLLINS, mother of IRA F.
COLLINS of this city, died at the residence of her son, DR. G. M. COLLINS
in Tipton, Indiana in the 84th year of her age.

November 16, 1893
        CAPT. HENRY B. ROPER received a telegram yesterday from his brother-
in-law, HON. WILLIAM H. CLOPTON of St. Louis, announcing the death of
his wife. She leaves two sons and a daughter. (A fuller account is
given on another page, taken from the St. Louis Republic; committed
suicide while deranged on the subject of religion, and found by her
daughter EMILY.

November 23, 1893
        Athens. MRS. McWILLIAMS who died at Elkmont yesterday was the
wife of WALTER McWILLIAMS, and eldest daughter of CAPT. DAVID PHILLIPS,
one of our most wealthy citizens.
        W. R. HANSARD, SR. who died near Elkmont a few days ago was one of
our oldest and best citizens, and at one time a member of the General
Assembly of Alabama.

December 7, 1893
        MRS. D. W. TERRY died at her home in Marshall County yesterday.
Her remains will be interred at Ebenezer Church at Whitesburg this
afternoon. (Tombstone: ELIZABETH C., wife of D. W. TERRY, born
October 6, 1850, died December 2, 1893.)

December 31, 1893
        A dispatch from Dallas, Texas brings news of the death at that
place, on the 13th instant, of JUDGE ALECK WHITE aged 78 years. This
is our own "Bonnie Blue Flag White." JUDGE WHITE gained this appelation
by his famous apostrophe to the Confederate Flag when the state seceeded...
in the dark days of reconstruction he went against us being one of the
leaders...in the Legislature of 1872. In 1874 he was appointed by
GENERAL GRANT to fill an unexpired term as Chief Justice of the
Territory of Utah. He afterward moved to Dallas and practiced law. He
was a brilliant, but erratic, man.

EARLY ALABAMA NEWSPAPERS

Madison County, Alabama

1819-1824, 1862-1863, 1875, 1880 and 1882

HUNTSVILLE REPUBLICAN

(Madison County)

Printed and published every Saturday by J. BOARDMAN at Huntsville,
Alabama.

January 9, 1819
        Advertisement of MRS. M'CAY, mantua maker and milliner.

February 6, 1819
        Died at the house of MAJOR WALKER on the 4th instant, CAPTAIN
JOSEPH COLEMAN, long a respectable citizen of Nashville (Tennessee)
and its neighborhood.

February 13, 1819
        The Bell Tavern in Nashville has rented the Huntsville Inn,
lately occupied by MR. CLAYTON TALBOT, now the property of JOHN M'KINLEY,
Esq. The house has been fitted up and is ready for business. (Signed)
                                        E. BAKER
        JOHN LAYMAN states he is not responsible for the debts of his
wife, REBECCA LAYMAN, she having left his bed and board (1 REBECCA
LAYMAN in 1820 was former widow of LEVI BYRAM).

February 27, 1819
        REV. ROBERT DONALD will preach a funeral sermon at DR. PROUT's on
the first Sabbath in March (probably SARAH (PROUT) as she died in
January 29, 1819).

March 20, 1819
    DR. JOHN A. GREEN, having become a resident of Madison County
tenders his professional service to the public. He may be consulted
at the house of DR. WILLIAM B. GREEN two miles above Three Forks of
Flint River on the road leading to Winchester (Tennessee).
    Dissolution of partnership of WILLIS H. BREWER and RICHARD
RISON--gin making business.

April 3, 1819
    Married on the 18th by REV. MR. DAVIS, MR. SAMUEL HAZARD of
Philadelphia to MISS ABBY C. HETFIELD of Elizabethtown, New Jersey.
(see marriage record in Volume 147, page 7--in which her name appears
as "HITCHFIELD.")
    Died on the 25th instant in this town, JOHN BUTLER, late a soldier
in the 13th Regiment of the United States Infantry. An Irishman by
birth, a shoemaker by trade and about 30 years of age. His heirs, if
any there are in the United States or representatives can have his
patent for military bounty land by applying to the Postmaster of
Huntsville, Alabama Territory. It is said he has a sister living in
Saratoga County, New York but he was last from Fincastle County,
Virginia. His death was caused by a shot received in a fray three
weeks ago, since which time he has been delirious and unable to give
any account of his relations or affairs. The Editors of newspapers
in New York and Virginia may do the heirs of Butler a service by
inserting the above notice.

April 17, 1819
    Died suddenly on the 12th instant, CAPTAIN NATHAN JONES, late of
Surry County, Virginia in the 74th year of his age. (Rev. sol--q.v.)

April 24, 1819
    Limestone County, Alabama--Orphan's Court. Letters of administra-
tion on the estate of BENJAMIN C. BENHAM, deceased, granted to JOHN
CUNNINGHAM and JOHN MONTGOMERY. March Term 1819.
    EBENEZER TITUS has settled in Huntsville and will practice law.

May 29, 1819
    Slave stolen from WILLIAM BROWN on the 8th instant living on
Richland Creek, Giles County, Tennessee.

June 5, 1819
    Married on Tuesday last by REV. MR. BURRUS, MR. ROBERT A. BELL
(son of HENRY, Rev. sol), merchant of this place to MISS MARTHA
WATKINS (volume 100, page 3), daughter of MR. ISHAM WATKINS of this
county.
    At Nashville (Tennessee) on the 27th instant by REV. MR. HUME,
MR. SAMUEL CRUSE, merchant of Huntsville to MISS HARRIET MARIA COLEMAN,
daughter of the late CAPT. JOSEPH COLEMAN of the former place.

June 12, 1819
    Married on Thursday, the 3rd instant, CAPT. BOWLER ("BOWLES" in
Bible Record) FARISS to MRS. SARAH BROWN, both of Giles County,
Tennessee.

August 21, 1819
    NELSON ROBINSON, attorney-at-law

September 4, 1819
    JOHN E. REVIERE--confectioner, distiller and baker.

September 18, 1819
    Candidates for Governor:
    WILLIAM W. BIBB
    MARMADUKE WILLIAMS
    Candidates for Congress:
    DR. HENRY CHAMBERS
    JOHN CROMWELL, Esq.
    Candidates for Senate:
    LeROY POPE
    GABRIEL MOORE

428

Candidates for House of Representatives:
SAMUEL CHAPMAN
DAVID MOORE
GRIFFIN LAMKIN
THOMAS ELDRIDGE
JOHN LEIGH TOWNES
ROWLAND CORNELIUS
WILLIAMS WRIGHT
JAMES G(ILLISPIE) BIRNEY
SAMUEL WALKER
JOSEPH MASON
JOHN M. LEAK
EPPS MOODY (1 EPPES MOODY married August 6, 1811, Franklin County,
North Carolina, Bulletin page 68; ancestor of MISS BIRDIE YOUNG
1410 Pennsylvania Avenue, Ft. Worth, Texas--April, 1953 who says
EPPES MOODY married MATILDA RAWLINGS JOHNSON August 6, 1811)
     State of Alabama--Limestone County. Orphan's Court: LEMUEL ROGERS
versus ELIZABETH MARDIS, administratrix and JOSEPH D. HEACOCK, administra-
tor of SAMUEL MARDIS, deceased. Petition for conveyance. Obligation
dated 18 November 1817. September Term, 1819.

October 30, 1819
     State of Alabama--Madison County. Orphan's Court. BENJAMIN WILSON,
administrator of the estate of DANIEL WALL, deceased.

December 25, 1819
     Died suddenly at Ditto's Landing on the 19th instant, MR. THOMAS
AUSTIN, one of the oldest settlers in this county.

February 19, 1820
     JOHN MARTIN, Esq. and HENRY STOKES nominate themselves for
Justice of the Peace.
     COL. GRIFFIN LAMKIN of this county is candidate for Major General
of the 1st Division of Militia composed of counties of Jackson,
Madison, Limestone and Lauderdale.
     State of Alabama--Cotaco County. February Term 1820. TOBIAS
GRIDER (1 TOBIAS S. GRIDER was in 1840 census of McNairy County,
Tennessee) and ELIJAH HOGAN (1 ELIJAH HOGAN married MARY ELIZ. of
WM. LAMKIN; see G and H April 1940) assignees versus MARIAN GILLESPIE,
administratrix and THOMAS D. CRABB, administrator of estate of ROBERT
GILLESPIE, deceased.

February 16, 1820
     Married on Tuesday evening, the 7th instant by REV. DAVID THOMPSON,
NICHOLAS HOBSON, merchant of this place to the amiable MISS SUSAN A.
LANIER, daughter of REV. WILLIAM LANIER (Volume 147, page 7).
     Departed this life on 26th February last at MAJ. ROBERT DAVIE's,
SELTON (should be SHELTON) WELBOURNE in his 41st year, son of MAJ.
ISAAC WELBOURNE. MR. WELBOURNE was attempting to cover a corn crib
and unfortunately fell across a rib pole on the house and was so seriously injured by the fall that he expired in about one hour--before
he could have the satisfaction of bidding adieu to his wife and little
children. MR. WELBOURNE had lately emigrated to this country from the
state of Georgia, where he held many responsible offices, both civil
and military and discharged the duties of them with credit to himself
and honor to the country. In fact, such was the confidence of the
community in him that he solicited no appointment that was not promptly
and almost immediately and unanimously conferred upon him.
     In the death of such a man, we may well say, society has lost one
of her brightest gems.
     MR. WELBOURNE has left a disconsolate wife and six little children
and a numerous host of friends and acquaintances to mourn their
irreparable loss.

April 29, 1820
     Died at her residence in Limestone County on Friday evening,
21st instant, after an illness of 3 days, MRS. JULIA M. TATE, wife of
DOCTOR WADDY TATE and eldest daughter of the late CAPT. JOSEPH COLEMAN
of Nashville (Tennessee).

July 21, 1820

Married Tuesday evening, July 11th by REV. MR. SALE in Lawrence County, MR. JAMES SEARCEY to MISS MARTHA BOOTH, daughter of MR. WILLIAM BOOTH, all of that county.

On Thursday evening, July 18th, by same, MR. ALBERT F. KEEBLE of Rutherford County, Tennessee to MISS SARAH McCOLLOCH, daughter of MAJOR ALEXANDER McCULLOCH.

July 28, 1820

Paper in mourning for GOVERNOR WILLIAM W. BIBB.

Married on the 13th instant by REV. DAVID THOMPSON, MR. JOHN OLIVER of Petersburgh, Georgia to the truly amiable MISS RUTH ANN WEEDON of this county (volume 53, page 7).

August 11, 1820

Died in Sommerville (Morgan County) on the 3rd instant, JOHN GILLASPIE, Esq., Clerk of the Circuit Court of Cotaco County aged 21 years.

September 1, 1820

Married on 17th of August, MR. PARKER PHILLIPS to the accomplished MISS ELIZABETH HAMNER, daughter of HENRY HAMNER, Esq. all of this county.

On the 24th, MR. JOHN CULP to the amiable and accomplished MISS CATY CROMER, daughter of MR. DAVID CROMER, all of this county.

Died at Blakeley on the 4th of August, MR. HORATIO S. BUTLER aged 27, son of REV. DAVID BUTLER of Troy, New York. He was a young man of great mark. (Note: Blakely is in Baldwin County)

A Methodist Camp Meeting will commence on Friday in the neighborhood of BATT JORDAN's.

September 29, 1820

State of Alabama--Limestone County. Circuit Court, August Term, 1820.

JOHN W. SMITH   )
     versus   )   attachment
JOSEPH CREASEY   )

October 6, 1820

WILLIAM McBROOM, Tax Collector for Madison County states he will attend the Muster ground of CAPTAIN MONTGOMERY's company on Monday the 9th of this month for the purpose of collecting state and county tax for 1820; at Muster ground of CAPT. SIVELY'S company on the 10th; at Triana on 11th for CAPT. BAKER's Company; on 12th at ARCHIBALD McDANIEL's for CAPT. BASKERVILLE's company; on 13th at MARCRAM's shop for CAPT. FARRIS's company, at Ditto's Landing for CAPT. McWHORTER's company on the 14th; at SAMUEL VEST's on Monday the 16th for CAPT. NEWMAN's company; at house of EPPES MOODY on Tuesday the 17th for CAPT. ROPER's company; at 16th, at Section 18 for CAPT. M'NULTRY's company.

THE ACA-REPUBLICAN

Huntsville

October 13, 1820

JOHN P. NEAL is appointed PostMaster of this town, vice S. D. HUTCHINGS, resigned.

November 3, 1820

Died at the seat of MR. RICHARD HARRIS, near Huntsville, on morning of 25th October, MRS. RACHEL I. M'MAHAN, consort of REV. WM. M'MAHAN after a long, severe and lingering illness....

ABSTRACTS FROM ALABAMA REPUBLICAN

Published weekly in Huntsville, Madison County, Alabama

November 1, 1820
    MRS. ANN I. FOOT, consort of CAPT. GEORGE FOOTE of this county died
on 21st of November surrounded by a family of lovely children, a fond
husband, many friends....

December 1, 1820
    Married at Nashville on 12th October, MR. ANDREW ERWIN, JR. of
Bedford County, Tennessee to MISS ELMIRA JULIAN SEARCY, daughter of
MAJ. ROBERT SEARCY, deceased.

January 19, 1821
    Married Wednesday 10th instant MR. ELISHA H. RICE of this place to
MISS MARY P(ITMAN) JONES, daughter of LEWELLEN JONES of this county.
    Died near Knoxville on 18th December on his way from Gloucester
County, Virginia to this state where he was about to settle, CAPT.
WILLIAM A. ROGERS in the 50th year of his age.

May 18, 1821
    Married near Nashville 3rd instant JOHN N. S. JONES, Esq. of this
county to MISS ELIZA HAYWOOD, daughter of HON. JOHN HAYWOOD of
Tennessee.

June 22, 1821
    Died on Sunday the 10th instant BENJAMIN CASH, Esq. aged about 39.
    Died in Jefferson County (Jones' Valley) on 13th instant MR. JOHN
YORK.

July 20, 1831(?) 1821
    Married on 11th instant by REV. JOHN P. HARTON, CAPT. WILLIAM GRAVES
BOULDIN to MISS ELIZABETH P. HAMMOND.

July 27, 1821
    Married on 19th instant, Thursday, COL. JONATHON L. OWEN to
MISS ESTHER STEUART, both of Morgan County.

August 17, 1821
    Married on the 9th instant, by REV. WILLIAM WOODS, MR. WILLIAM P.
ROBINSON of this county to amiable MISS FRANCES H. CALLOWAY, daughter
of COL. RICHARD CALLOWAY of Franklin County, Tennessee.

August 24, 1821
    Died on 10th instant, PHEREBA BRAGG, consort of WILLIAM BRAGG
of Morgan County.
    Died on 14th instant at his father's seat in Morgan County, MOSES
McCARLEY, aged 21.

September 21, 1821
    Married on 20th August last in Troy, New York, MR. HENRY ADAMS of
Huntsville, Printer, of Alabama Republican to MISS MARY S. FAIRCHILD of
the former place.

October 26, 1821
    Married in this town Thursday 11th instant by REV. MR. M'MAHAN,
MR. MATTHIAS MUNN to MISS ROSANNAH FEENEY, both of this place.
    In Bedford County, Tennessee on 11th instant HENRY HITCHCOCK, Esq.
Attorney General of Alabama to MISS ANN ERWIN, daughter of COL. ANDREW
ERWIN of the former place.
    Died at his seat in this county on the 19th instant MR. JAMES
G(IBSON) FLOURNOY.

November 16, 1821
    Married 8th instant by REV. MR. THOMPSON, MR. BENJAMIN TILLER and
MISS ANN TIBBS, both of this county.

November 23, 1821
   Married on Wednesday evening 16th instant by MR. THOMPSON,
MR. HENRY JORDAN to MISS LANEAR, daughter of REV. WILLIAM LANEAR, all of
this county.

November 30, 1821
   Died 19th November MRS. ELIZABETH BURRUS, consort of COL. CHARLES
BURRUS of Madison County in her 40th year.

December 28, 1821
   Married 1th instant in Smith County, Tennessee, DR. RICHARDSON
OWEN of this town to MISS TABITHA M. ALLEN of the former place.
   Married on 20th instant, DR. J. B. SANDERS of Fayetteville to
MISS M. L. KENNEDY of Lincoln County, Tennessee.

January 18, 1822
   Married in Courtland, Lawrence County, on 8th by REV. JOHN C.
BURRUS, MR. WILLIAM MARSH to MISS MARY D. HINES, both of said town.
   Married on Tuesday 15th by REV. MR. THOMPSON, MR. GEORGE FOOTE and
MISS SARAH, daughter of CAPTAIN PEYTON POWELL.
   Married at Winchester (Tennessee) on 12th, MR. CHARLES J. GILLESPIE
to MISS LILY THOMAS, daughter of COL. RALPH CRABB.

February 1, 1822
   Married 24th January, MR. WILLIAM L. HATHAWAY to MISS ELIZABETH
HARLAN, both of this county.

January 22, 1822
   Died on Saturday 16th, MRS. SOPHIA TATE, wife of CAPTAIN JOHN TATE
of Limestone County. She left four small children.

May 10, 1822
   Married at residence of JESSE SEARCY, Esq. near Huntsville on
Wednesday eve, last by REV. MR. DAVIS, MR. DANIEL B. TURNER, of the
firm of MORGANS and TURNER, merchants, to MISS SYSAN B. SEARCY, daughter
of MR. ROBERT SEARCY of Nashville, Tennessee.

May 31, 1822
   Married Thursday 23rd by REV. J. ALLEN, THOMAS McELDERRY, Esq. to
MISS ELIZA BOTELER, daughter of COL. ALEXANDER BOTELER, all of Morgan
County.
   Married in this town on Wednesday evening the 29th by REV. MR.
ALLEN, MR. GEORGE H. MALONE, merchant, to MISS HYLDAH BROWN, all of
this town.

June 14, 1822
   Married in Washington County, Tennessee on 7th of May by REV.
JOHN C. HARRIS, MR. JOHN JONES of this town to CLARISSA C. SEVIER,
daughter of JAMES SEVIER, Esq. of the former place.
   Married in this town on Wednesday evening 12th instant by REV.
MR. DAVIS, WILLIAM B. WALLACE, Esq. to MISS ELIZA M'DOWELL, all of
Huntsville.

August 2, 1822
   Died on 26th July, MR. WILLIAM CAMPBELL, JR. aged about 20.
   Died Wednesday evening 30th July, MR. WILLIAM LAVANS, a young man,
who was a native of Ireland.

August 9, 1822
   Married Thursday evening 1st, by REV. ANDREW K. DAVIS, MR. THOMAS W.
SCOTT, son of CAPTAIN WILLIAM SCOTT, to the amiable and much admired
MISS NANCY HEWLETT, daughter of MR. JOHN W. HEWLETT, all of this county.
   Died in this town yesterday the 8th, MRS. FRANCES RATHER, consort
of MR. DANIEL RATHER.

August 16, 1822
   Married Thursday, MR. BENJAMIN E. HARWOOD to MISS RACHEL SHARP,
all of Morgan County.
   Died on Wednesday last, JOSIAH BRANDON, brother of the BRANDONS of
Huntsville.

March 29, 1822
    Died in the neighborhood of Huntsville at the residence of MR.
WILLIAM B. HARRIS on the morning of 22nd of March MISS CAROLINE M.
GILLASPIE in the 17th year of her age, daughter of MRS. FRANCES GILLASPIE
of Franklin County, Tennessee.

September 6, 1822
    Died in this county on Friday the 30th ult. MR. WILLIAM LAMKIN in
the 49th year of his age. (Note: wife was ROSANNAH WOODS, married
December 4, 1798 in Washington County, Tennessee. He was son of
WM. and JANE (MOORE) LAMKIN. See Genealogy and History. April 1940)
    Died near Huntsville on Wednesday the 4th instant MRS. ELIZABETH
BADLUN aged 43, the wife of MRS. WILLIAM BADLUN.
    Died on 26th of August at his residence in Tuscaloosa, COL. JOHN
JOHNSON INGE, a member of the Alabama Bar and a native of North Carolina.

September 13, 1822
    Married in this town on 3rd instant by REV. DAVID THOMPSON, MR.
JIHN MARTIN to MISS CLARINDA GLASGOW, daughter of the late COLONEL
JAMES GLASGOW of Tennessee.

September 20, 1822
    Died on the 27th at Sulphur Springs in Blount County, Alabama,
WILLIAM DUNN, Esq., Judge of the County Court of said county--a useful
and enterprising man and a pious Christian.

September 27, 1822
    Died in this county on Friday the 20th, COLONEL LITTLEBERRY
ROBINSON, an old and respectable resident of this county (widow was
PAULINE--children: JOHN, MARTHA, WM., CHERRY married RODAH H____,
FANNY married JOHN DICKERSON; CHERRY dead in 1834).
(In Volume 35, page 11, change that date on LITTLEBERRY ROBINSON to
1822. You show the paper just before this as 1822, and I am positive
it is a typographical error, as in ORc 2, page 362 24 September 1822
LITTLEBERRY ROBINSON, late of this county, has died without will and the
widow of said deceased has waived her right of administration on said
estate and signified to the court her wish that WILLIAM PATTON should
administer in her place. (Bond, $50,000, with HENRY COOK and RODAH HORTON,
securities.)
    Also...that tombstone of EZEKIEL MOORE and wife MARY JONES (its
page 84 of the T/S volume, and I think is in some others too, was
copied by either H or BOYCE while on a survey--and 1855 is wrong--it's
1852, for her administrator was appointed then and the PSL says she
died April, 1852, when TS says May. The 1852 newspaper notes don't
list either her death or that of WM. ROBINSON; I guess they weren't
subscribers.)
    At Coosawda, Alabama Monday the 9th instant, MISS CAROLINE HITCHCOCK
after an illness of 18 days, which terminated in typhus fever.
    Died while on a visit at St. Stephens (Washington County) the much
lamented MR. DAVIS H. MAHEW, Rector of the Coosawda Academy and formerly
of Hampshire County, Massachusetts.
    At Cahawba (Dallas County) on Monday evening, September 9th,
COL. ROBERT H. DRAUGHON of Claiborne (Monroe County). (See lawsuit
in Monroe County giving all family history)

    See Volume VI for papers between 1820-1822.

October 4, 1822
    Died in this county on Thursday evening the 26th, COL. THOMAS
ELDRIDGE aged 44 years.
    Died in this town on Friday last, MR. AUDLEY M'CAUSLAND aged 36
years.
    Died on Monday evening last, WILLIAM, son of JOHN M. TAYLOR aged
about 9 years.
    On Wednesday morning last, MR. GREEN MALONES.
    Died near Russelville, Alabama (Franklin County) on the 25th
ult. JENKIN WHITESIDE, Esq. of Nashville (Tennessee), a lawyer of great
eminence.
    In the Territory of Arkansas lately, COLONEL MATTHEW LYON.

At Warm Springs, Virginia whither he had gone for benefit of health, on 4th, SPENCER ROANE, Esq. one of Judges of Appeals in that state.

October 11, 1822
Another Patriot Gone!
Died Wednesday last at Locust Grove in this county, MAJOR WILLIAM CROHAN in his 70th year. MAJOR CROHAN was a native of Ireland and emigrated to America in his early life. He was one of those patriots who raised this country to honor and to empire. During the whole memorable conflict which resulted in the dismemberment of one and the creatoin of another empire, he discharged the duties of an ardent and gallant officer in the dangers as well as glories of that eventful period he largely participated. From Louisville Post.

November 1, 1822
Died in Florence on Tuesday the 22nd, MRS. JULIA McKINLEY consort of JOHN M'KINLEY, Esq. late of this town.
Died in Limestone County on Friday the 25th, MRS. TITUS, wife of CAPT. JAMES TITUS.

November 15, 1822
Died in this town on Saturday evening last, CAPT. WILLIAM P. OWENS aged about 30 years and on Sunday was buried by Masonic brethren of this town.
At Arkansas on 25th September MAJ. GEORGE M'GLASSIN, late of the U.S. Army. He was recently appointed Factor at Spadre Bluff in the Cherokee Nation.

December 6, 1822
Died on the 27th instant, at Pleasant Grove Academy, JOHN ALLEN STOKES aged 8 years, son of C. A. STOKES of Huntsville.

December 20, 1822
Died in this county on the 15th instant, MRS. ELLENOR GRAY, consort of MR. WILLIAM GRAY aged 65.... Affectionate wife, kind mother to her children. Her disease was lingering, her pain acute.

HUNTSVILLE REPUBLICAN

Published Each Friday by HENRY ADAMS

January 10, 1823
Married on 1st instant at Hazelgreen (volume 141, page 13) by REV. MR. DONNEL, MR. ALEXANDER W. COTTEN (he had boys ALLEN and MONTFORD), merchant of Athens to MISS MARY H. ERWIN, daughter of MR. ROBERT ERWIN (and SALLY (LEAVITT)) of the former place.

January 17, 1823
Married 31st instant in Tuscaloosa County, MR. HARDY CLEMENTS (66 in North Carolina) late of Tennessee to MISS PATSY HARTGROVE, daughter of REV. DUDLEY HARTGROVE (1st wife).
On Thursday evening the 9th instant MR. JAMES M'CLARRAN of Huntsville to MISS SUSAN, daughter of CAPT. ELI HAMMOND of this county (volume 48, page 9).
Died in this town Wednesday night last of consumption, MRS. NANCY RAWLINS, consort of ELDRED RAWLINS, Esq.
House and Sign Painters--HENRY SPRAGUE and JOHN TILLER.

February 7, 1823
State of Alabama--Limestone County. September Term 1823
JOHN G. EASON versus PHILIP T. NORRIS
State of Alabama--Limestone County. September Term 1823
JOHN McALISTER versus PHILIP T. NORRIS (Defendant is not an inhabitant of this state.)
State of Alabama--Limestone County. September Term 1823
WILLIAM BELL   )
    versus   ) In Chancery
GEORGE BELL and others)

GEORGE BELL, ISAAC BOON and SOLOMON CENTER and wife NANCY are not inhabitants of this state.

State of Alabama--Limestone County. September Term 1823
JAMES M. GRAY   )
    versus   ) Defendants are non-residents
THOMAS J. REED and WILLIAM CARROLL)
State of Alabama--Limestone County. September Term 1823
BETSEY C. MIDDLETON   )
    versus   ) Circuit Court
ENOS TATE, JOHN A. VERDELL and CHARLES COX)
ENOS TATE and JOHN A. VERDELL are non-residents

February 28, 1823
HENRY CHAMBERS of Limestone County, candidate for Governor.
WILLIAM T. GAMBLE, candidate for Clerk of Circuit Court of Limestone County.
EDWIN JONES, RICHARD B. PURDOM, JAMES BIBB and THOMAS BRANDON, candidates for Clerk of County Court of Madison County.

March 7, 1823
REV. JACOB C. LATTA will preach at the Court House in Huntsville on the last Sunday in this month.
JOHN L. TOWNES, candidate for Clerk of Circuit Court of Lawrence County.

March 14, 1823
Died on Friday evening, February 7th in her 75th year, MRS. SUSAN, consort of MR. WILLIAM STAINBACK of Brunswick, Virginia.

March 28, 1823
Married Thursday evening the 20th by REV. MR. THOMPSON, MR. B. M. LOWE, merchant of Hutnsville to the young, amiable and highly accomplished MISS SARAH, only daughter of DR. JAMES MANNING of Madison County.

April 18, 1823
Funeral sermon of the late MRS. LEFTWICH will be preached by REV. WILLIAM EDDINS (Baptist) at the house of JAMES DRAKE, Esq. 3 miles south of Huntsville on the fourth Sunday of this month.
ARCHIBALD McROBERT, resident of Athens (Limestone County), candidate for Clerk of the County Court of Limestone.
Advertisement for Coffee House--IRBY JONES, proprietor.
Following are candidates for House of Representatives: WILLIAM MOORE, HENRY KING, CHRISTOPHER HUNT, ROBERT H. ROSE, DAVID COBB and JOHN HAMNER.
Trustees of Athens Famale Academy: ROBERT BEATY, President, DANIEL COLEMAN; JOHN D. CARRIELL; JOSHUA L. MARTIN; ANDREW FOSTER; BEVERLY HUGHES; and JOHN W. SMITH.

May 9, 1823
Died lately at the house of JAMES ELLIOTT near Blountsville, Alabama ROBERT DIXON, late of Tennessee in the 79th year of his age.

May 21, 1824 (1824 is right--see page 27 and volume 5, page 25)
LANCELOT CHUNN, JR. states he is not responsible for the debts of his wife, MATILDA S. CHUNN, she having left his bed and board. (married MATILDA REID October 12, 1822; volume 27, page 6).
Married in Tuscumbia on 18th by REV. MR. (JACOB) PECK, COL. BARTLEY M. COX of this town to MISS ELIZA I. N. FREEMAN of the former place.
At the same place by REV. DR. FAVORS, DR. CASTLETON B. A. AKE to MISS RACHEL SIMS, all of Tuscumbia (see volume V--says married in Limestone County).
At the residence of JESSE SEARCY, Esq. near Huntsville on Tuesday evening, GEORGE FEARN of this town to MISS ELIZABETH, daughter of the late COL. CHARLES BURRUS (volume 122, page 4).

June 6, 1823 (right)
TEMPE WILLIAMS by next friend) Decatur County.
    versus   ) Petition for divorce.
GEORGE WILLIAMS   )

Original bill states that said TEMPE was married to the said GEORGE WILLIAMS in 1813 and that he abandoned her in 1821. He is a non-resident.

June 20, 1823
Died in this twon Sunday last, MR. THOMAS M'GLATHERY, a baker.
The account in a few of our last papers of the death of CAPT. CARROLL, we are glad to say was incorrect--it was a hoax upon the editors of this paper.

June 27, 1823
Married on the 12th in Limestone County by REV. DR. A. A. CAMPBELL, MR. ELISHA W. HARRIS of Montgomery County, North Carolina to MISS ANN ELIZA A. MOORMAN, daughter of MR. M(ICAJAH CLARK) MOORMAN.

July 4, 1823
Married on Monday evening last by REV. MR. ALLAN, NELSON ROBINSON, Esq., attorney at law to MISS JANE E. SWANN, all of this town (volume 76, page __, married 1823).

July 25, 1823
Died on the 18th at the residence of DR. CAMPBELL, MISS CATHARINE, daughter of MR. JOHN BROWN of Cherokee Nation.... Was moved from her father's residence to DR. CAMPBELL's in Limestone County.
To the Public:
We have been neighbors of MAJ. SIMEON GEREN since his settlement in Madison County and can say that his conduct is excellent and we think him qualified to represent this county in the Legislature. (Signed) J. P. HAUGHTON, WILLIAM DERICK, HENRY RIGNEY, AUGUSTIN HEWLETT, J. W. HEWLETT, JOHN HAMNER, ISAAC SKILLERN, STEPHEN S. EWING, and WILLIAM ROUNTREE.

August 8, 1823
Married in this town Thursday the 31st of July by REV. DAVID THOMPSON, MR. ROBERT CARUTHERS to MISS SARAH RATHER, daughter of DANIEL RATHER of Huntsville.
Married in Nashville (Tennessee) on the 24th instant by REV. MR. DALES, MR. JAMES B. WALLACE of Alabama to MISS CAROLINE C., daughter of P. CRADDOCK of the former place. (Note: She is daughter of PLEASANT CRADDOCK and they are buried in Tuscaloosa County. See Volumes III and VIII.)

August 22, 1823
Died near Huntsville on Sunday evening last, MARY, the only daughter of HENRY STOKES, Esq. aged about 7 years.

August 29, 1823
Married at Tuscumbia on the 21st by REV. MR. WOOD, MR. RICHARD B. BRICKELL, junior proprietor of the Alabamian of this town, to MISS MARGARET COMANS, late of this county.
Died near Greensboro on the 16th, MRS. PICKENS, consort of GOVERNOR ISRAEL PICKENS.

September 26, 1823
Died in this place on the 19th instant in his 25th year, MR. JOHN M. HUNTER, formerly of New York....
Letters of administration on the estate of WILLIAM HINTON, deceased, granted to JOSEPH W. AYRES.

October 10, 1823
Died in Chesterfield County, Virginia a few days ago, JOHN W. EPPES, Esq. aged about 50 years.... His first wife was a daughter of THOMAS JEFFERSON, President of the United States.

October 17, 1823
Tribute of respect on death of HON. HENRY Y. WEBB, Judge of the 3rd Judicial District. HUME R. FIELD, chairman.
Married in Newark (Delaware) on Saturday evening 20th of September by REV. MR. ENGLES, MR. ROBERT ORRELL of Trisna, Alabama to MISS SARAH MATILDA, daughter of MR. THOMAS PHILLIPS of the former place.

In Lexington, Kentucky on the 24th instant by REV. MR. CHAPMAN,
COL. CALVIN C. MORGAN of Huntsville to MISS HENRIETTA, daughter of
MR. JOHN W. HUNT, merchant of the former place.
In Lexington, Kentucky on the 25th by REV. MR. CHAPMAN, MAJ.
ALEXANDER G. MORGAN of Huntsville to MISS AMERICA HIGGINS, daughter of
MR. RICHARD HIGGINS, merchant of the former place.
Property of the late JOHN YATES, deceased, to be sold.
Advertised for sale by WILLIAM COWDEN (68 in South Carolina),
Blount County, Alabama (wife was CATH. YATES, according to tombstone
in Blount County; 61 in Virginia)

November 14, 1823
State of Tennessee--Humphrey County. Circuit Court, September
Term, 1823
THOMAS HOLLAND
versus
ELIZABETH PARKER, JOSHUA PARKER, RICHARD PARKER, DELILA PARKER,
WILLIAM PARKER, BAILEY HOOPER and wife FRANCES, SAMUEL PARKER, JR.,
THOMAS GRAY and wife LUCY, heirs at law of SAMUEL PARKER, deceased.
Defendants RICHARD, DELILA, WILLIAM, SAMUEL PARKER and THOMAS and LUCY
GRAY are inhabitants of Alabama.

November 28, 1823
Married in this county on the 23rd instant by REV. RICHARD
SHACKLEFORD, MR. THOMAS McCRARY (volume 48, page 9) to MISS NANCY W.
WRIGHT, daughter of COL. WILLIAMS WRIGHT, all of Madison County (married
November 23, 1823)
In Blount County, Alabama on the 16th instant by WILLIAM COWDEN,
Esq., CAPT. YARBROUGH to MISS ELIZABETH LANE (WPA Marriages has
BEAUFORD YARBROUGH and ELIZABETH LOCKHART), both of Turkey Creek,
Jefferson County.

December 5, 1823
Died yesterday morning, 4th instant between 8 and 9 o'clock,
MR. ARTHUR M. HENDERSON, Esq. in the 29th year of his age. He commenced
to practice law in this place in 1819.
State of Alabama--Tuskaloosa County. Special Court of Prob--(faded)
WILLIAM Y. GLOVER, sheriff, administrator of) Petition for sale of
PAULSER INGLE, deceased   ) real estate
versus
JACOB INGLE, PETER INGLE, and GEORGE INGLE, SALLY and DAVID WAGGONER,
BETSEY and JOSEPH MURRY, POLLY INGLE and the heirs of JOHN INGLE,
deceased, to-wit: RASON (EASON?), BETSEY, JOHN, GEORGE, JAMES and
NANCY, distributees of the estate of said intestate.

December 26, 1823
Married on Tuesday evening last (married December 24, 1823;
volume 103, page 54) MR. GEORGE STEELE (born in Beauford County,
Virginia April 11, died October 21, 1855; came to Madison County in
1817) of Huntsville to MISS ELIZA ANN WEAVER (from Campbell County,
Virginia), daughter of MAJOR MATHEW W. WEAVER of this county.

January 9, 1824
Died in this place Saturday evening last, PEYTON DANDRIDGE BIBB,
infant son of THOMAS BIBB, Esq. aged 4 months and 22 days.

January 16, 1824
Died in this place on the 8th instant, CAPT. JOHN M. LYNCH of
Pendleton District, South Carolina aged about 26 years.
On Tuesday the 13th ult. of consumption, MISS NANCY IRBY aged ---

January 23, 1824
Married on Wednesday evening last by REV. MR. THOMPSON, MR. ISAAC
WILLIAMS to MISS ELIZA L. M'LARAN, both of this town (volume 153, page
17; married January 22).
On the same evening by REV. MR. CAMPBELL, MR. WARNER (WARREN in
other records: volume 7, page 73 for deed--WARREN T. in deed,
WARREN T. in marriage record, WARNER T in 1830 Census) T. BOLLING to
MISS HARRIET E. SMITH, daughter of GEORGE S. SMITH, Esq. (volume 100,
page 7) all of this county (married January 21).

437

February 20, 1824
Married on the 28th instant by REV. MR. ARCHER, DR. JOHN A. HERRING
(see his obituary in 1825) of Petersburg, Georgia to MISS SARAH E.
WEEDON, daughter of DR. F. WEEDON of Blount County, Alabama.
Died in this town Tuesday last, 17th instant, EBENEZER TITUS,
attorney-at-law, aged about 27.

March 5, 1824
Married in this place Thursday evening, 26th instant by REV. JOHN
ALLAN (volume 48, page 9), JOHN M'KINLEY, Esq. of Florence, Alabama to
MISS ELIZABETH M. ARMISTEAD of Loudon County, Virginia.
On the same evening by REV. MR. PECK, PULASKI DUDLEY, Esq. of
Tuscumbia, Alabama to MISS SUSAN M(ARIAH) BASS, daughter of the late
URIAH BASS of this county (a descendant, MRS. A. B. McLEAN, Mobile,
Alabama says PULASKI DUDLEY was born 1793, son of SAM'L born 1761--
PULASKI born Edgecomb County, North Carolina).
In Lawrence County on the same evening, CAPT. MORGAN SMITH of this
county to MISS SARAH, daughter of COL. NICHOLAS JOHNSON of the former
place (volume 22).
In this town Tuesday evening last by REV. MR. PECK, MR. COLIN
BISHOP to MISS SARAH M'CAY, both of this place (volume 136, page 7;
married 3 March 1824).
Died at the house of THOMAS WILSON in this county on the 3rd
instant, MRS. JANE CARUTHERS aged 49 years.

April 2, 1824
Married on the 24th instant by REV. MR. PECK, NICHOLAS HOBSON, Esq.
to MISS SARAH ANN SMITH, daughter of GEORGE S. SMITH, Esq. all of this
county (volume 147, page 17).

April 9, 1824
Married on the 2nd instant in this town by R. B. PURDOM, Esq.
MR. WILLIAM STEADMAN to MISS MARGARET TURVIN, both of Decatur County
(TURNER in marriage record, volume 103, page 54).
REV. JOHN ALLAN will preach on a funeral occasion at the house of
JOHN VINING on the third Sabbath in April.

April 30, 1824
Died Friday the 23rd instant CAPT. FRANCIS ANDERSON, an old and
respectable inhabitant of this county.

May 7, 1824
Died in this town yesterday morning, MR. DANIEL RATHER in his 63rd
year. One of the oldest citizens of Huntsville.

May 21, 1284
Married in Tuscumbia on the 13th instant by REV. MR. PECK, COL.
BARTLEY COX of this town to MISS ELIZA I. N. FREEMAN of the former
place.
At the same place by REV. DR. FAVORS, DR. CASTLETON B. AKE to
MISS RACHEL SIMS, all of Tuscumbia.
At the residence of JESSE SEARCY, Esq. near Huntsville, on Tuesday
evening last, GEORGE FEARN, Esq. of this town to MISS ELIZABETH BURRUS,
daughter of the late COL. CHARLES BURRUS (volume 122, page 4; married
19 May 1824).

May 28, 1824
Died in Woodville, Decatur County, Alabama on 19th of May, MRS.
SEBRINA HAINEY, consort of MR. WILLIAM HAINEY, in whom he lost an
affectionate wife and his children a tender mother.

June 11, 1824
Died in this town Friday morning last after a short illness,
MRS. ELIZA M. SMITH, wife of MR. ELIAS PRESTON SMITH.

June 25, 1824
Married Tuesday evening last by REV. MR. THOMPSON, REV. WILLIE
BLOUNT PECK, Pastor of the M. E. Church of this town to MISS ANN J.
RIVERS, daughter of REV. ROBERT RIVERS of this county. (Letter from

MRS. OSCAR HORTON, Guntersville, Alabama, November 27, 1954 "I have
the will of THOMAS RIVERS who lived in Montgomery County, Tennessee.
He has a son, ROBERT RIVERS, who was a preacher and was first President
of Athens College after Methodists took it over. He was a first
cousin of my ROBERT, who was father of ELDRIDGE KENNON RIVERS, my
ancestor. My ROBERT RIVERS came to Alabama in 1823. Was from Amherst
County, Virginia where he left a will."
     On Tuesday the 15th by REV. MR. DAVIS, MR. THOMAS LYLE (46 in
North Carolina, Morgan County) of Morgan County to MISS AMERICA M.
ALLISON, daughter of JOHN ALLISON, Esq. of this county. (volume 155.
page 8)

July 9, 1824
     Married in Harrisonburgh, Virginia on the 10th instant, CAPT.
WILLIAM M'CAUSLAND, merchant of this town to MISS HARRIET KYLE,
daughter of JEREMIAH KYLE, Esq. of the former place. (From Richmond
Enquirer 18 June 1824--married in Harrisonburg on 10th instant by REV.
JARED MORGAN, CAPT. WM. McCAUSLAND of Huntsville, Alabama to MISS
HARR--(faded), daughter of JEREMIAH KYLE, Esq. of that place.)

July 23, 1824
     Married on the 13th instant by REV. MR. PECK, MAJ. LARKIN F. WOOD
of Nashville, Tennessee to MISS ELIZA ECHOLS, daughter of COL. WILLIAM
ECHOLS of this county (volume 153, page 18).
     Died on the 21st ult. at Bellefonte (Jackson County), DOCTOR
THOMAS J. HARRIS aged 27. His death was occasioned by being thrown
against a tree from a horse at full speed.

August 6, 1824
     Married in this place Thursday the 29th of July b6 REV. MR. ALLEN,
COL. JAMES J. PLEASANTS, Secretary of State, to MISS EMILY JULIA BIBB,
daughter of THOMAS BIBB, Esq. (volume 195. page 92).
     Died in this town on Saturday the 31st instant MR. THOMAS GILLIAM
aged 33, formerly of Richmond, Virginia.
     On the 2nd instant in this place, SARAH JANE, infant daughter of
ALEXANDER and JANE WILSON, aged 15 months and 11 days.

September 10, 1824
     Died on the 23rd at the residence near Washington, Mississippi
after a short illness, HON. LEWIS WINSTON, Judge of the 2nd Judicial
District of that state.

October 8, 1824
     Died in this town Wednesday night last, MR. JOHN B. COX aged about
20.
     Departed this life on the 30th of September, MRS. MARY TATE, wife
of CAPT. JOHN TATE, Limestone County, Alabama.

October 22, 1824
     Died on the 22nd instant in Jefferson County, Mississippi, MR.
JAMES MACKEY of the firm of BEDFORD and MACKEY, merchants of New
Orleans and late of this town.

October 29, 1824
     Died on the 27th instant at Elizabethtown, New Jersey, MRS.
SARAH C(LARK) POPE, wife of WILLIS POPE, Esq. (son of LEROY) of this
town in her 36th year. (nee SARAH CLARK HETFIELD; married October 21,
1812 ELIZ.; ancester of MRS. A. P. WHITE, 1965).
     In Cincinnati on the 3rd, MR. ABRAHAM S. THEW, formerly of this
town.

December 3, 1824
     Married Thursday evening the 25th by REV. MR. THOMPSON, MR. JOHN
M(ADISON) CALDWELL of this town to MISS EMILY BELL of this county.
(son of DAVID CALHOUN and LUCY (CABANESS) CALHOUN--EMILY and GARRET BELL
daughter of HENRY and __ (GEE) BELL, volume 141, page 16).
     On Tuesday evening last in Limestone County, MR. PRESTON YEATMAN
of this town to MISS AGNESS N(ELSON) A(NDERSON) MASSIE of the former
place. (Note. daughter of JOHN MASSIE, 1812 sol, who died in

Limestone 1829, January 29 and wife JUDITH MOSS who were married in
New Ke--(faded) Virginia, 1792--see 1812 pension)
    Died in Jackson County on the 23rd instant, MR. SAMUEL WEAVER,
aged about 50. Though he was generally considered a respectable man,
yet to those who are excessively intemperate in use of ardent spirits,
his death affords a warning. While intoxicated, his clothes caught
fire....

December 10, 1824
    Died in Courtland, Alabama (Lawrence County) on the 5th, MR.
JAMES M. TILFORD aged about 23, brother of JOHN W. TILFORD of this
town.
    State of Alabama--Jefferson County
    ELIZABETH C. LANE   )
        versus   ) Bill for divorce
    SIDENCE W. LANE (should be TIDENCE))

December 17, 1824
    Married near Natchez, Mississippi on the 16th, MR. DAVID ST. C.
McINTOSH of this town to MISS CAROLINE MATILDA FOSTER, daughter of
MR. THOMAS FOSTER of Adams County, Mississippi.
    In this county Monday evening last, MR. JOHN B. SANNONER of this
place to MISS MALINDA VANHOOK of this county (volume 103, page 55).

December 24, 1824
    A. D. VEITCH has just received 70 boxes of candles.
    EDWIN JONES, administrator of ANN IRBY, deceased (kin--see will
of NATHAN JONES)

HUNTSVILLE CONFEDERATE 1862

November 12, 1862
    Died on the 29th ult. in the 72nd year of his age, MR. JOHN GIDDENS
(54 in North Carolina), a respectable citizen of Madison County, the
people of which repeatedly indicated their sense of his probity by
electing him Tax Assessor.
    Died August 20, 1862 in Richmond, Virginia of wounds received in
the Battle of Seven Pines on the 31st of May last, HON. SYDENHAM MOORE,
COLONEL of the 11th Alabama Volunteers in the 46th year of his age. He
was born in Tennessee and carried to Alabama in his infancy. He volunteered as a private in the Creek War in 1836, raised a company and
served as Captain in the War with Mexico.
    Jackson County. W. C. DAVIDSON as administrator for SAMUEL C.
DAVIDSON, advertises, as does JOHN W. ELLIS, administrator of ANN H.
HARRIS and W. D. PARKS as administrator of RICHARD SANFORD.

November 26, 1862
    Died at Berkley in this county on Wednesday last, the 19th of
November, in the 33rd year of her age MISS MARIA E. NORMENT (21 in
North Carolina) daughter of J(OHN) H(AYWOOD) NORMENT (50 in Georgia)
of that place. Raleigh, North Carolina and Tallahassee, Florida papers
please copy.
    Legal advertisements. Jackson County. JAMES M. GULATT administra-
tor of JOHN P. HARPER.
    Jackson County. WILLIAM H. CHRISTIAN offers will of SAMUEL JAMES
for probate, he being named as executor. WILLIAM P. JAMES an heir at
law of said decedent resides in Marion County, Tennessee.

December 3, 1862
    Married in Huntsville, Alabama on Thursday, November 27, 1862 by
ELDER E. STRODE of the Baptist Church MR. GEORGE W. KENNARD, Printer of
the Confederate office and MISS MAGGIE F. PRYOR (10 in Alabama),
daughter of MRS. MARTHA PRYOR (35 in Virginia), all of this city.

December 31, 1862
    Legal advertisements from Jackson County; WILLIAM WASHINGTON as
administrator of MATHEW WASHINGTON (41 in Virginia): ELIZABETH MANNING
as administratrix of GEORGE MANNING.

January 7, 1863
        Obituary of JOHN HEARTWELL COLEMAN (9 in Alabama), of Sharpshooters,
Woods' Brigade, aged 28 years 4 months 11 days, a son of the late
DANIEL COLEMAN (48 in Virginia; Limestone County Census) of the Supreme
Court Bench.
        Limestone County legal advertisements: FRANCIS M. CANTRELL
executor of the will of AMANDA C. CANTRELL; BRICE M. TOWNSEND, adminis-
trator of HOWELL C. FEATHERSTONE (54 in South Carolina); and WILLIAM
C. NICHOLS (26 in North Carolina) administrator of POLINA E. NICHOLS
(21 in Alabama, wife of WM. C.).

January 14, 1863
        Died of congestive fever at the residence of MR. HIRAM WILLIAMS,
St. Helena Parish, Louisiana August 8, 1863, LT. WILLIAM M(ATT) REDUS
of Company C. 35th Regiment, Alabama Volunteers. LT. REDUS was born
in Giles County, Tennessee January 13, 1814. When a small boy his
family removed to Limestone County, Alabama where the subject of this
notice has since resided. On the 18th of January, 1841 he married
MISS PARALEE ATKINSON of this county. In 1857 he was elected to the
State Legislature. On the 7th of April last he bid adieu to a beloved
and tender wife and five interesting children. T.C.P.

January 28, 1863
        Jackson County. JAMES E. VERNON produces the will of ISAAC C.
DIBLEE of which is named executor.... DIBLEE, an heir at law is a
resident of the Kingdom of Great Britain.

February 4, 1863
        Obituary. Departed this life at Huntsville, Alabama January 31,
1863 in the 36th year of her age, MARY MARGARET, consort of ROBERT H.
WATKINS and daughter of DR. BENJAMIN CARTER of Pulaski, Tennessee. She
was snatched from devoted husband and now motherless children.

February 12, 1863
        Another young hero gone. JAMES W. FRANKS, son of BRITTON FRANKS,
fell mortally wounded at Parkers Cross Roads December 31, 1862.
        COLONEL GEORGE WALTON, son of one of the Signers of the Declaration
of Independence died in Petersburgh, Virginia a few days since aged 73.
He was formerly Territorial Governor of Florida and later in life Mayor
of Mobile. He was father of the amiable and accomplished MRS. OCTAVIA
WALTON LeVERT of this city. Mobile Register and Advertiser. Obituary:
COL. GEORGE WALTON died in Petersburg Virginia on the 3rd instant. He
was born in Augusta, Georgia during the Revolution; he had in his
illustrious father, the Signer of the Declaration of Independence and
a gallant officer and eminent jurist, and in his accomplished mother
(MISS CAMPER) who has been well styled one of the heroines of that trying
period the best exemplars of intellectual, social and patriotic worth.
He graduated at Princeton College, and when barely of age (1812) was
elected to the Georgia Legislature. In 1821 he was appointed Secretary
of the Territory of Florida while JACKSON was governor, and succeeded
him in that office; in his administration founded the city of Tallahassee
and bestowed its name. He removed to Mobile in 1837 or 1838 and was
elected mayor. For several years he has resided in Washington and
Virginia. In early manhood he married MISS SALLIE MINGE WALKER, daughter
of an eminent lawyer of Georgia, who preceeded her husband to the grave
by two years. They had two children, MAJOR ROBERT WALTON, whose
untimely death bore to the tomb promises of a brilliant career, and our
fair townswoman.

March 12, 1863
        Died near Huntsville on the 11th of February, JOHN SEAY (63 in
Virginia), native of Amelia County, Virginia and a resident of Madison
County since 1816, aged 77 years 2 months 5 days.

March 19, 1863
        Advertisement--Jackson County: ELIZABETH STEPHENS and JAMES M.
HUDGINS administrators of SOLOMAN STEPHENS (35 in Tennessee); also of
JANE KEITH as administrator of JAMES A. KEITH.

441

April 2, 1863
    Obituary: DR. THOMAS FEARN (55 in Virginia) died in Huntsville,
Alabama 16 January, 1863 in the 74th year of his age. He was a native
of the State of Virginia and emigrated to Huntsville in the year 1811.
He left a family consisting of seven daughters.

April 9, 1863
    Advertisement--Jackson County: JOSEPH WILSON administrator of
DAVID P. SKELTON; also THOS. WILSON, administrator of JAMES McKINNEY.
    Advertisement--Limestone County: MARTHA J. EASTER, administratrix
of FANNY N. EARLY.

April 16, 1863
    Advertisement--Jackson County. P. H. HELTON, administrator of
JOHN COLLINS; WILLIAM STOCKTON, administrator of SAMUEL CUNNINGHAM-
MARTIN CUNNINGHAM, one of the heirs at law lives in Tennessee:
R. C. AUSTIN, administrator of ADAM L. HYDER.

May 7, 1863
    Advertisement--Limestone County: B(RICE) M. TOWNSEND, administrator
of RICHARD J. FEATHERSTONE.
    Advertisement--Jackson County: W. B. MASON and J. G. MASON
administrators of WINFIELD S. MASON; P. BROWN, administrator of
ISAAC TETERS (46 in Virginia).

May 28, 1863
    Died in Madison County, Alabama on the 26th of April, 1863 MRS.
MARY SULLIVAN (60 in South Carolina), consort of RANDOLPH SULLIVAN
(66 in South Carolina), in her 74th year. She was born in Laurens
County, South Carolina in 1789--a devoted wife and loving and kind
mother.
    Deaths in the Huntsville Hospital: On Friday May 22nd 1863
THOMAS D. ELKINS, private in COL. SHACKELFORD's Company, COL. RODDY's
Regiment Alabama Cavalry. Native of Lawrence County. Leaves wife and
children.

HUNTSVILLE WEEKLY INDEPENDENT

Huntsville, Alabama--A. R. WIGGS and Company Proprietors

January 2, 1875
    Married at the residence of the bride's mother in middle Tennessee
on 22 December 1874 by REV. W. T. GILL, MR. ISHAM H. GILL of Athens,
Alabama to MISS LUCY FISHBACK of the former place.

January 9, 1875
    Married in this city on Thursday evening the 7th by REV. DR.
BANNISTER, MR. J. LAWRENCE WATKINS, JR. and MISS BETTIE MATTHEWS, all
of Huntsville, at the Church of Nativity. Attendants were MR. J. P.
MATTHEWS and MISS LUCY and SUSIE MATTHEWS.

January 16, 1875
    Tribute of respect to memory of THOMAS T. BINFORD by Madison
Lodge No. 25 I. O. O. F.

January 23, 1875
    At Indianopolis, Indiana on 16th, MRS. AGGIE NEAL, wife of MR.
FRANK NEAL of this city; amiable, accomplished and beautiful woman.
She bloomed in northern soil until gathered by her Southern lover at the
close of the war....
    In this city on Sunday last, January 17, of diptheria, EUGENE,
youngest child of JOHN A. and BETTIE F. ERWIN aged about 18 months.

January 30, 1875
    Died in Dayton, Ohio Monday January 18, MR. DAVID BARNARD aged 72.
Was father of our fellow townsman, MR. HENRY BARNARD. It will be
remembered that MR. BARNARD spend several months on a visit to his son
last year....

February 13, 1875
    Died in this city on 9th of pulmonary consumption, MRS. HATTIE M.
IRBY, wife of MR. P. M. IRBY aged about 38.   Baptist.
    In this city after a brief illness, GEORGE S. WILSON (26 in
England) aged 50.   Native of Chesterfield, England but since 1848 has
resided in this place.
    Died near Mobile December 23, 1874, ALEXIS H. TARDY, native of
Mobile aged 31....   Left a widow and orphaned little ones and a
brokenhearted father.

March 6, 1875
    Married near Winchester, Tennessee on 23 by REV. A. A. ALLISON,
MR. JOHN L. GRAHAM of Meridianville and MISS ELLA P. COOVER of the
former place.

March 20, 1875
    HON. ROBERT S(TITH) SPRAGINS (26 in Alabama) is dead.   Died at his
residence in this city Sunday evening last, the 14th instant in his
53rd year.   Left a widow and four children.   Elected Circuit Court
Clerk for Madison County in 1848, which held til the close of the war.
Then he   practiced law.   Then was Probate Judge.

March 25, 1875
    MRS. N. O. BLACKBOURN, wife of the late FRANCIS BLACKBOURN died at
the residence of her son-in-law, HON. F. L. HAMMOND in Madison County,
Alabama March 13, 1875.   Maiden name was ROLFE and she was born in
Virginia 1797.   Married in early life and soon after removed to
Madison County, Alabama.   Lady of purest and noblest life.   Kind and
affectionate.   Mother of 5 children.   FRANK died young; three survive
her, a son and two daughters.   Her oldest daughter, wife of F. L.
HAMMOND died years ago leaving three children.   From her two grand-
daughters she would never consent to separate long at a time....   After
the eldest sister reached her from middle Alabama, neither left her
until saw her deposited in the grave...   H. P. TURNER

April 1, 1875
    Tribute of respect to memory of AMBROSE F(LEMING) DRISKILL (48 in
North Carolina) by Society at Bethlehem Church.
    Died, LAURA PATTON HELM March 5, 1875.   Episcopalian.

April 8, 1875
    Died Wednesday 31 March 1875 at her residence 3 miles west of
Vienna in Madison County, MRS. JANE McMILLAN (48 in Georgia, wife of
WM.) aged 74 years and 11 days.

April 15, 1875
    Died in this city, LILEA LEE, daughter of JOHN and ELLEN FARISS.

April 22, 1875
    Died in Woodland, Freestone County, Texas January 23, 1875,
MRS. CHILDRESS, wife of W. P. CHILDRESS.   Daughter of JONATHON (had
brother GREEN) and KATY COLLIER of this county where she was born and
raised.
    Tribute of respect to memory of DR. H. A. BINFORD by physicians and
druggists.

May 13, 1875
    Died at the residence of her father near Meridianville in this county
on the 3rd, MISS POCAHONTAS, daughter of JOHN M. ELDRIDGE, Esq.   She
was a young lady of sweet disposition and endowed with many of womanly
and Christian graces, which won the love and esteem of all who knew
her.
    Married in this city on 6th by REV. R. M. TINNON, MR. HENRY FORD
and MRS. I. M. HAWKINS.
    Married on the 6th, MR. C. S. LUCAS and MISS ELLA WILLIAMS.
    In Iuka (Tishomingo County), Mississippi on the 4th, MR. B. F. McRAE
and MISS JIMMIE, daughter of JAMES H. DORAN.

May 20, 1875

Died, MRS. CAROLINE M. McCALLEY, wife of MR. THOMAS S. McCALLEY at the residence of her husband in this vicinity Friday the 14th after a painful illness of two or three months in her 55th year. Funeral took place at the church of Nativity Sunday evening last REV. DR. BANISTER officiating. Native of this county, daughter of ROBERT LANFORD, one among the oldest settlers in Madison County.

May 27, 1875

Another old citizen gone! MR. IRVIN WINDHAM (49 in Virginia) died at his residence in this city Tuesday night last after a very brief illness of paralysis in his 76th year. Has been a worthy citizen of this county about 55 years. Methodist.

June 3, 1875

DR. L. D. CARTER, an old citizen of this city died May 6 after a long and serious illness.

June 10, 1875

Died near Huntsville, May 19, HENRY, infant son of JAMES and ELVIRA PAUL aged 4 months and 6 days.

June 17, 1875

Died in Knoxville, Tennessee June 10, 1875 of consumption, MRS. MARGARET E. STINE, wife of MR. B. F. STINE of this city aged 39. Had been in wretched health for many months and went to Knoxville (home of her childhood) on a visit to her sisters. Methodist.
    Obituary:
    MRS. SAPHRONIA E. MARTIN died of consumption at Madison Station May 29. 1875. Second wife of MR. E. T. MARTIN, a very highly respected citizen of Madison.... W. T. ANDREWS

June 24, 1875

REV. JAMES ELLIOTT was born 1799 and died June 5, 1875. For 50 years he was actively engaged in preaching as a minister in the Cumberland Presbyterian Church. Although denied privileges of education, he did great good. Throughout middle Tennessee and north Alabama, he was well known. Out of a large family, he leaves only a widowed daughter. His wife and 8 children had "gone before."

July 1, 1875

Died in Triana, Alabama June 18, 1875 of consumption, MRS. LIZZIE P. GRANTLAND....
    Obituary:
    POCAHONTAS, daughter of JOHN M. and FRANCES ELDRIDGE died at her home in Madison County near Huntsville one evening of May 3, 1875....

July 8, 1875

Died in Trianna June 19, MRS. LIZZIE P. GRANTLAND, wife of CAPT. H. W. GRANTLAND and daughter of W. B. and M. E. EDWARDS. Born October 10, 1843; married CAPT. H. W. GRANTLAND April 10, 1860.

July 15, 1875

Married at the residence of ex-Mayor B. M. SOWEL in Athens on Monday July 5, 1875 by REV. F. T. J. BRANDON, MR. CLEMENT G. CAPSHAW to MISS EMMA C. DUPREE.
    Died July 8 after a brief illness, MRS. LUCY JOHNSON RUBLEE, daughter of MR. and MRS. A. J. JOHNSON....

July 22, 1875

Died in this county on 30 June of paralysis at residence of his daughter, MRS. SIBLEY, MR. MILLS JENKINS (45 in North Carolina) aged 70 years 5 months and 13 days.... Leaves a wife and large circle of relatives and friends.
    Married in this city on 19th in Church of Nativity by REV. DR. BANISTER, MR. JAMES M. GILBERT and MISS BELLE REYNOLDS, both of Gilbert Sisters Dramatic Troupe.

July 29, 1875
    Married in this city Tuesday, July 27, 1875 by MOYER MURPHY,
MR. JOHN NEELY and MISS BELLE JOHNSON, both of Huntsville.
    Died in this county on 24 after a brief illness of brain fever,
MR. JAMES C. DAVIS, son of COL. WM. DAVIS of New Market.
    MRS. SUSAN KNOW (52 in Virginia), relict of the late DAVID KNOX
(56 in Delaware), one of the oldest citizens of Huntsville died on
26th at residence of her son-in-law MR. JOHN T. PATTERSON of this
city on her 77th birthday.
    MRS. TRECY, mother of REV. FATHER J. F. TREECY, died in this city
on 26th aged 84.
    DR. A. M. BARCLAY died at his residence near Triana in this county
on 21st.
    Obituary of LUCY RUBLEE.
    Obituary of NASHVILLE MALONE; born Caswell County, North Carolina
January 2, 1800, died at his residence in the vicinity of Huntsville on
July 1, 1875 aged 75 years 6 months. Was 18 when he came to Madison
County, Alabama. Successful farmer....

August 5, 1875
    Died, LUKE MATTHEWS, one of the oldest citizens of Huntsville at
his residence in this city Monday evening last in his 79th year.

August 12, 1875
    Golden wedding of ELLIS MURPHREE (48 in Alabama) and wife JINNIE
MURPHREE (45 in South Carolina) July 20 in Murphree's Vallen, Blount
County, Alabama. Among those present were REV. DeFOREST ALLGOOD and
JEREMIAH ELLIS and MRS. PATSEY ELLIS, who were witnesses of their
marriage. MRS. ALLGOOD, who is their step-mother, who is 93 was present
with them together with 18 children, sons, sons-in-law, daughters-
in-lay, 40 grandchildren and 11 great grandchildren. All grandchildren
present except 3 who are in Texas.

August 19, 1875
    Died, MR. BRIANT REEDY (72 in Tennessee), one of oldest citizens
at the residence in this vicinity on Monday morning last aged about 75.

August 26, 1875
    A. SIDNEY BEASLEY, son of DR. JAMES A. BEASLEY (35 in Virginia)
of this city died at LaGrange (Fayette County), Tennessee on 18th.
Remains brought to Huntsville and buried in Huntsville Cemetery Sunday
last. Aged about 20.
    MISS MOLLIE MUDD, daughter of JUDGE MUDD died at Blount Springs
on Sunday last of consumption aged 21.

September 2, 1875
    Died of consumption at the residence of MR. T. M. (FRANCIS M.?)
SANFORD (18 in Tennessee) on August 11, MISS MARGARET SANFORD (16 in
Alabama; JOHN) aged 35.
    Of asthma, near Brownsboro Thursday August 26, MR. BYRON SKELTON
(41 in Alabama; heir of SAMPSON SKELTON) aged 65.
    Near New Market, Alabama August 30th, 1875, MRS. M(ARTHA) WOODJON
MOORE, wife of MR. WM. H(ENDERSON) MOORE and youngest daughter of
MR. ISAAC CRINER.

September 9, 1875
    Died in this city on the 5th of congestive chill, WILLARD SAWYER
aged about 20 years.

September 16, 1875
    Death of a former highly esteemed citizen of this county, a native
in fact, MR. JAMES Q(UINN) DILLARD (34 in Tennessee), father of our
respected citizen, HENRY DILLARD (14 in Alabama) died at his residence
in Aberdeen, Mississippi on the 4th in his 60th year. MR. DILLARD
was a former resident of Triana.

September 30, 1875
    MRS. ANNIE BUSSEY, wife of REV. B. W. BUSSEY, Pastor of the
Baptist Church in this city died Friday night last after a long and

tedious illness. Remains forwarded to Georgia for interment amongst
friends and relations there....
        AUSEY SMOOT? (AUSBURN in census; 9 in Alabama), son of the late
WYATT P. SMOOT (58 in Virginia) died in this county recently.
        Married on the 22nd by REV. MR. WEAKLEY, MR. MIKE WHITE of this
city fo MISS LIZZIE HUFFMAN of Shelbyville, Tennessee.
        Died near New Hope in this county on Monday night September 20
of congestive chill, GEORGE CHILDRESS aged 15.
        Near New Hope in this county on Saturday last, MR. J. T. CHILDERS
aged about 27. Promising young school teacher, and but a few years ago
was married to MISS BUTLER of this county.

October 14, 1875
        Died in Madison County October 4, MR. WINN THOMAS after a short
illness. Had been in our midst but a few short months having removed
to this county from near Wartrace, Bedford County, Tennessee in
January, 1875.

October 21, 1875
        Married in this city on the 19th at the residence of MRS. E. P.
DAVID by REV. B. W. BUSSEY, MR. THOS. SMITH and MISS CALLIE LANE, all
of this city.

October 28, 1875
        Died in Phillips County, Arkansas September 21, 1875, D(ANIEL) H.
SEVERS (52 in Tennessee) aged 73 years and 2 months. Formerly an old
citizen of this county.
        Married on the evening of the 21st by REV. DR. BANISTER, DR. C. A.
ROBINSON and MISS JOANNA ROBINSON (2 in Alabama), daughter of MAJ.
JAMES ROBINSON (45 in Tennessee), all of this city.
        CAPT. A. D. BENNETT, one of the oldest citizen of Gadsden died a
few days ago.

November 4, 1875
        COL. NICHOLAS DAVIS (25 in Alabama, Limestone County) died at his
residence in this city Tuesday evening last after an illness of one
week. Born in Limestone County January 14, 1825.... Brilliant lawyer....
Volunteered and was an officer in the Mexican War.

November 11, 1875
        MRS. SARAH, wife of JAMES W. WARREN died on 20 October 1875 in
Giles County, Tennessee, Missionary Baptist....
        Died at Bolton, Mississippi Tuesday October 10th, LAWRENCE WATKINS,
son of CHARLES L. and JENNIE P. ROBINSON aged 6 years and 6 days.

November 19, 1875
        Married November 11 at the residence of the bride's father, MR.
JAMES SANFORD by REV. F. M. PROCTER, MR. JAMES S. MATTHEWS and MISS
JENNIE W. SANFORD, all of Madison County.

November 25, 1875
        MRS. JULIA LANDMAN (44 in North Carolina), wife of JAMES LANDMAN
(49 in Virginia) of this vicinity died on Saturday last of pneumonia
aged about 77. Funeral took place Sunday evening last, REV. R. M.
TINNON of the Cumberland Presbyterian Church officiating.
        If MARGARET ANN DAVIS and WILLIAM DAVIS will come to the front
now and will communicate with VANDERBILT L. BAXTER, JR. they will hear
something pleasant. Their mother, MRS. ANN DAVIS is dead and MR. BAXTER
is looking for the heirs. His address is 289 Greenwich Street.
Southern and Western newspapers please copy.

December 2, 1875
        Died at his residence 3 miles west of New Hope, Alabama on the 8th,
MR. JOHN T. HARRISON aged 76.
        GEORGE WHIT(FIELD) DRAKE (35 in Alabama), one of the oldest citizens
of this vicinity died at his residence on Saturday morning last the
27th instant in his 61st year; died of asthma.
        Death of HON. JOHN FOSTER at his home in Jacksonville--a distinguished
citizen of Alabama.

December 9, 1875
    Death of MR. WILLIAM R. DELP (8/12 Alabama; HENRY) at his father's residence in this city Wednesday morning....

December 30, 1875
    Married on 16th by REV. J. G. WALKER, MR. HOLMAN of Valley Head, Dekalb County, Alabama to MISS ELLEN HOLT, daughter of DR. W. L. HOLT of Guntersville.
    Near Buck-Horn Tavern in this county Tuesday, December 21st, by REV. E. C. GORDON, MR. GEORGE T. ERWIN of this city to MISS GEORGIA WELLS.
    Died on December 12th, 1875 in Madison County, MRS. ANN M. PENNEY (52 in Virginia), widow of JOHN PENNEY (58 in Virginia) and mother of the late WALTER O. PENNY (ALEX; 28 in Virginia). Died within six days of completing her 79th birthday. She was the daughter of MR. and MRS. HUMPHREYS of Spotsylvania County, Virginia. Born December 18, 1797 in the above county and state. Married JOHN PENNEY of said county March 22, 1818. Baptist. Emigrated to Madison County, Alabama about 1836. She had two children, both of whom died before her.

HUNTSVILLE (ALABAMA) ADVOCATE

January 19, 1872
    Married in Tuskaloosa on the 27th at the residence of DR. SEARCY by REV. MR. ROBERTSON of Huntsville, MR. S. L. ROBERTSON to MISS I. D. NORRIS, both of Elyton.
    From Livingston (Alabama) Journal Sumter County, Alabama. May 18, 1877: DR. SAM PARSONS of Jefferson County is 83 years old, was a soldier of 1812, has 12 children, 45 grandchildren and 34 great-grandchildren.
    From Livingston (Alabama) Journal February 9, 1877 copied from Birmingham Independent. Married by ALLEN BLIVINS, J.P. on Saturday at the residence of the bride's father 3 miles from Morris Station on South and North Road in this county, MR. WM. LASSITER, late of Georgia and MISS VASHTI R. EDWARDS. He is 22 years old and the bride was 10 years and 13 days old.

January 26, 1872
    ALFRED H. ROEBUCK, an old citizen of Jefferson County, Alabama died last week.

July 12, 1872
    MR. J. L. MORAGNE of Gadsden was married on the 25th of MISS S. C. ROEBUCK of Jefferson.

HUNTSVILLE WEEKLY INDEPENDENCE

    DR. WILLIAM TYLER YOUNG born in James City County, Virginia November 7, 1796, died... (I found that death notice.) 1852. He married ELLEN GORDON STEWART born November 11, 1800, died April 4, 1849. (doesn't quite agree with date we have, in a May 4th paper, saying she died the 2nd.) She was born in Petersburg, Virginia. She was daughter of ROBERT STEWART born in Scotland April 4, 1756, died in Madison County, Alabama November 17, 1840. He married AMY GOODWIN RAINES born January 14, 1773 in Sussex County, Virginia, died October 7, 1840, Madison County, Alabama. The STEWARTS were apparently living with DR. YOUNG in 1830. DR. YOUNG died at house of CHAS. E. COLLIER, he was apparently father of AMY RAINES COLLIER who married WM. HY PICKETT. JAMES EDWARD COLLIER, I believe it was, married ELIZABETH GOODWYN STEWART...sounds very much as if they were sisters of ELLEN GORDON, doesn't it? I don't find ROBERT STEWART in the S's. Is he on the master index? Probably buried in Collier graveyard as not found in Triana.
    Make a note--DR. WM. T. YOUNG was WM. TYLER YOUNG from Augusta, Georgia. His daughter ELLEN T. married JOHN JAMES WARD...folks from Chatt hunting them the other day...she was a lovely person. Just started it recently and having loads of fun. She was all thrilled over

FRANCIS E. WARD's estate, but he was mostly interested in trying to find out if J. J. WARD built MRS. BOLLING's old house. I knew he was killed in the war--it was at the Battle of Atlanta. After I came home I found the p of a to FRANCIS E. WARD of Martin County, North Carolina, and his TS for them. Oh--you want the address for your magazine... WILLIAM I. REILLEY, 407 Sweetbrier Avenue, Chattanooga, Tennessee.

January 1, 1880
Died in this city at the residence of MR. WILSON POLLARD on the evening of December 18th, W. T. MORRIS aged 24, son of WILLIAM and ELIZABETH J. MORRIS, both of whom preceded him to better land. Written by his aunt, ELIZA P.
MARY G. HASTIN, daughter of WILLIAM J. and MARY MASTIN died at the residence of her mother in Huntsville on the night of December 26th. Catholic.

January 22, 1880
Died on the morning of the 11th at the home of W. T. BUSH near New Hope, DR. P. M. BUSH in his 74th year. Born in Virginia, married in this county in his young days, moved to Marshall County a half century ago. Elected Sheriff and to State Legislature.

January 29, 1880
PURNELL LEE HAMMOND, son of JUDGE FERDINAND L. HAMMOND died at the State Asylum for insane January 16th aged about 37. Was a Confederate soldier.

February 5, 1880
MRS. ELLEN T. WARD, wife of the late CAPT. JOHN JAMISON WARD and daughter of the late DR. WILLIAM T. YOUNG died suddenly at her home in Huntsville February 1st aged 56. Leaves 6 children.

February 12, 1880
Died in this city on the 7th instant, MRS. ALICE J. HAWK, wife of JOHN HAWK, Esq.

March 4, 1880
MR. LEROY H. JONES, a well-known citizen of this county died at his home near Meridianville last Friday. The deceased was born within a mile of the place where he died and was in his 67th year. He went to Arkansas in 1858 and returned to Madison County in 1870. Among his relatives are MRS. WILLIAM RISON, MRS. JOHN J. FORD, MRS. R. A. JONES.
MRS. ANN ELIZA LeVERT, wife of the late FRANCIS JOHN LeVERT died at her residence in Huntsville Sunday, February 29, 1880 aged 72. She was one of the children of JOHN WITHERS of Virginia. Born in an old fort near Nashville, Davidson County, Tennessee in 1808 and came to Alabama early in life.
REV. HENRY P. TURNER died suddenly at his home near Madison Cross Roads.

March 11, 1880
JOHN BROWN, an old and respected citizen of this county died of cerebral abscess of brain. Brother of CAPT. JAMES H. BROWN of this city and of BEN. BROWN of Nashville.
MRS. DOLLY THOMPSON, wife of MR. WILLIAM THOMPSON, City Engineer, died last week.

March 25, 1880
Death of MRS. G. W. JONES: MRS. JONES, wife of the late MAJ. G. WASHINGTON JONES and daughter of DANIEL JONES (should be DANIEL HARRIS-- P.J.G.) died in this county and was deposited by the side of her husband in our city cemetery.

April 22, 1880
Died in this city on the 18th instant at the residence of her son, MR. SMITH CERTAIN, MRS. ELIZA CERTAIN (wife of JACOB--census nee LEWIS, daughter of JOSEPH and ELIZABETH (SMITH) LEWIS) in her 76th year. She was one of our oldest residents and a member of the Methodist Church.
MRS. SARAH FANNING, wife of MIDDLETON FANNING departed this life April 13th of pulmonary consumption in her 63rd year. She was born in

Virginia and came to Alabama when a child. In 1836, she was married.
In her 19th year, she professed religion and was a member of the
Primitive Baptist Church.

May 13, 1880
        ROBERT McBRIDE, son of ROBERT and ZARILDA McBRIDE died April 25,
1880 of meningitis; was born January 6, 1855.

May 27, 1880
        Death of DR. JOHN T. LOWE of Aberdeen, Mississippi. Oldest child
of COL. B. M. LOWE and brother of HON. WILLIAM MANNING LOWE.

June 3, 1880
        MRS. ELIZA TROTMAN died May 16. Born at Madison Station November 29,
1854 married to F. M. TROTMAN February 4, 1873. Her maiden name was
SARAH ELIZA MAGAHA. Leaves her husband, three boys, father, mother,
brothers and sisters.

June 17, 1880
        Died in this city the 15th instant of consumption, MRS. E. T. HUSSEY
aged about 65. Mother of MRS. CHARLES CUMMINS and a member of the
Cumberland Presbyterian Church.

June 24, 1880
        Died June 19th, SALLIE IRBY STRODE after a long and painful illness
(grandparents of HUDSON STRODE). Born in Madison County, the daughter
of THOMAS MARTIN, Esq. In 1854 she married ELDER EUGENE STRONE,
1st pastor of Enon Baptist Church at Huntsville, MR. STRODE removed with
his family to Mississippi and resided there until his death in 1872,
after which MRS. STRODE removed her family to this place.
        Died in Sharpe's Cove Monday the 7th instant of consumption,
JOHN C. CARTER aged 48. Leaves a wife and 7 children.

July 1, 1880
        Died June 29th in this city, MRS. ADELAIDE B. BREWSTER, wife of
MR. HIRAM BREWSTER of the Memphis and Charleston Railroad, after a
long and painful illness.
        MRS. SUSAN TULETA HANNAH, wife of A. J. HANNAH died of cancer
of the breast, near Owens X Roads May 12th. Leaves 3 little children.
Was a member of the Cumberland Presbyterian Church.

July 8, 1880
        CHARLES P. CABANISS died on the 5th instant aged 64.

July 29, 1880
        Died, RUCKER, infant daughter of JUDGE WILLIAM RICHARDSON at his
home in Huntsville Wednesday July 21st after a brief illness.

August 12, 1880
        HARRIET R. TAYLOR, wife of MORRIS K. TAYLOR died at their home in
the country at 4 a.m. Tuesday, July 20th in her 67th year....
Belonged to Missionary Baptist Church....
        GUSTAVUS LYLE MASTIN died at his home on Franklin Street at 3:30
p.m. Tuesday, August 10th after a most painful illness. He was born in
Fincastle, Virginia January 1, 1815, was taken to Tennessee when a
small child and remained in that state under the care of his grandfather,
SOLOMON HOGE until Jane (January or June?), 1827 when he moved to
Huntsville. He has resided in Huntsville ever since. Was one of the
earliest of University of Alabama students. In 1833, he entered the
mercantile business.... Since 1858, he has been a planter in Madison
County. Was a leading member of one of the most numerous and highly
respected families in the South. Leaves a large family.
        Death of CHARLES W. HEREFORD (son of THEODORIA--Census). Died at
his late home in this city August 7th in his 46th year. Born May 15,
1835. Commenced business under MR. HASTIN in 1851 and remained under
him 7 years. Then he entered the employ of MR. SLEDGE for one year
after which he went into business as a member of the firm of HEREFORD
and LEFTWICK and afterwards HEREFORD and TIMBERLAKE. He first married
1855 LOUISA A. ELGIN, whom died in 1878. On October 2, 1879, he married
MRS. N. W. BINFORD, who survives him.

August 19, 1880
　　OSCAR HUNDLEY, Esq. was suddenly called to Nashville yesterday by the death of his wife's sister, MISS EMMA THOMAS.

September 9, 1880
　　Married at the Baptist Church at 9 p.m. Thursday, September 2nd, 1880 by REV. W. FRANKLIN KONE, ARTHUR L. HARRIS and MISS L. E. WEAVER...
　　Died, THOMAS K. BEAVES (BEAVERS?) at San Antonio, Texas of consumption. The deceased was a great favorite during his sojourn in Huntsville as express agent.
　　DR. JOHN S. BLAIR, well known in Madison and Limestone Counties for more than a half century died recently at the residence of his son, DR. FRANK BLAIR, who lives near Gurleysville in this county. Native of Logan County, Kentucky and was nearly 73. His parents first resided near Mooresville from which they were forced to move by unfriendly Indians. The deceased practiced medicine for many years in Southwestern portion of Limestone County.

September 16, 1880
　　CAPT. JAMES W. POLLARD died September 11th at his late home. Born in Madison County November 14, 1828. In early life, he was a grand muster of COL. BLUNT's militia regiment and lost an arm while loading a cannon. In 1859 he was elected Superintendent of Streets and Water Works of Huntsville.... Left wife and children.
　　CAPT. JUSTIN D. TOWNER, hotel proprietor of fame, died at Blount Springs September 9th of gall stones. Had left Huntsville a day or two before in perfect health. Native of Illinois and commanded an Illinois company in the late war. Married a second time, his last wife being a MISS BUGG, daughter of a prominent citizen of Giles County (Tennessee). CAPT. TOWNER was about 40 years of age....

September 23, 1880
　　MR. WILLIAM C. McPHERSON died at the Huntsville Hotel Tuesday night last. Was in the employ of Southern Express Company here. Native of Hopkinsville, Kentucky and son of COL. JOHN W. McPHERSON.
　　MISS LOUISA J. BRICKELL died....
　　Death of JUDGE A. R. MANNING (see vol. XXXIX) Friday the 17th instant in New Youk City. Accompanied by his wife, two daughters, a son-in-law, COL. DUNN of Alabama, he went to New York for his health. Born in Perth Amboy, New York 1810. Came to Alabama with his uncle, JAMES MANNING.

September 30, 1880
　　Died Friday, EDMUND TONEY, second son of EDMUND TONEY of Triana.
　　MISS KATE THOMPSON died at the residence of J. R. STEGALL September 28th.
　　MRS. NANCY WINSTON, sister of the late THOMAS and WILLIAM BRANDON (wife of ISAAC), who were well-known in early history of the community, died at the residence of her son, MR. ISAAC WINSTON near Meridianville in this county Sunday the 26th of September 1880. Born in Burke County, North Carolina in 1790, she was the mother of 11 children, 5 of whom have gone before her. When in her 16th year, she became a member of the Methodist Church and for 74 years remained a devout member... Was 90 years of age at her death....
　　MR. SEHUYLER HARRIS, residing within 1½ miles of Harris Station, Limestone County, died at his home Wednesday, September 22nd after a brief illness...was an excellent citizen....

November 4, 1880
　　Died at the residence of R. M. THOMPSON on the 19th of October, MRS. E. S. GARVIN aged 69....

November 11, 1880
　　MRS. SARAH CAWTHON, wife of THOMAS CAWTHON resided near Brownsboro died Sunday November 7th aged about 79 years, of consumption.
　　Died near Madison on the 28th of October in her 46th year, MRS. KATE HUGHES, wife of E. J. HUGHES, Esq.

December 2, 1880

Died near Maysville November 23, 1880 LYDIA RIGNEY, daughter of LEVI and HULDAH HINDS. Born in Knoxville, Tennessee January 1, 1794, came with her parents to Madison County, Alabama about 1809. Married HENRY RIGNEY September 28, 1817 and was left a widow March 30, 1832...

December 16, 1880

Remains of the late JOHN B. HARDIE buried in city cemetery at Huntsville Friday, December 10, 1880. Native of Huntsville about 32 years ago. Truly an excellent officer....

December 23, 1880

Died Tuesday December 14th at his home about 8 miles from Huntsville in Pond Beat, MR. JOSIAH SPRINGER at advanced age of about 75. The deceased came to Madison County in a comparatively early period... All residents of the county of more than 40 years will remember him.

COL. J. J. GIERS died very suddenly in a barber's chair while getting a shave. Was a German of high attainments...

December 30, 1880

SARAH, infant daughter of COL. L. H. SCRUGGS died in this city December 27....

January 5, 1882

Died January 1, 1882, MR. JOHN R. JOHNSON of typhoid fever, son of RICHARD A. JOHNSON and a native of Albemarle County, Virginia. Leaves a mother and two sisters in Lynchburg, Virginia.

January 12, 1882

Died on Washington Street Tuesday, January 10th, JASPER PRICE.

Died at his residence in Marshall County near Whitesburg, MR. HENRY DAVIDSON aged 78.

Died--MR. JOHN FRAZIER in Athens (Limestone County) last Friday night; was more than 80 years old.

February 2, 1882

THOMAS McBROOM, a straight-out Republican has been appointed Postmaster of Scottsboro (Jackson County). He is a nephew of PERRY L. HARRISON.

March 2, 1882

Died--MRS. ROBERT PEEBLES of Mooresville (Limestone County) February 25th.

Died--SALLIE A. BOONE, young daughter of COL. O. C. BOONE.

Died--MISS ELIZABETH HODGES at the residence of GEORGE P. LANDMAN about 6 a.m. February 27th. Had resided in Madison County for many years.

Died--PROF. J. Y. BRISTOL in this city February 28th aged about 35. Came to Huntsville from Kentucky about three months ago. The father of deceased lives in Pennsylvania. He leaves a wife and a step-son.

Death of MARCUS A. ERWIN, son of the distinguished Methodist minister. He was born August 16, 1849 and died February 27, 1882. As a minister, he was connected with the Tennessee Conference of the Methodist Episcopal Church South for five years and with the North Alabama Conference one year.

March 16, 1882

Died in Huntsville March 14, 1882, MARION ROSNAYNE, wife of DR. JUSTIN ROSNAYNE.

March 23, 1882

MRS. CORNELIA WILLIAMS, wife of JOE D. WILLIAMS died near Sulphur Rock (Independence County), Arkansas February 21st of scarlet fever in her 45th year. Moved from the vicinity of Madison Station about 12 months ago.

March 30, 1882

Died at her home in Big Cove March 14th in her 25th year, REBECCA E. MILLER, wife of HENRY C. MILLER and daughter of W. A. MILLER.

Death of JOHN SHELBY CORBITT Friday, March 24, 1882 aged 33. He resided here more than 9 years. Left a wife and two children. Born near McMinnville, Tennessee.

April 27, 1882
Died, FRANK MASTIN SCRUGGS, son of JAMES WADDY SCRUGGS, of consumption at the residence of his brother-in-law, E(LIOTT) R. MATTHEWS, April 21st. Born November 5, 1861. (married September 24, 1869 FANNIE SCRUGGS.)

May 4, 1882
J. D. BATTLE died at DR. HAMPTON's, his brother-in-law, last Saturday night. Was 25 years old.

May 11, 1882
Died May 4 at the residence of his father near Madison, JOHN G. BOWERS, born November 28, 1850.

May 18, 1882
COL. ISAAC D. WANN died Saturday night May 13 about 2 miles north of New Hope. Had lived in Madison County about 40 years and was more than 60 years old.
MRS. ELIZA LANE, widow of JAMES LANE of Athens (Limestone County) died Tuesday at an advanced age. She was a sister of the late COL. SAMUEL PEETE of Huntsville. (BERY-PEETE was their father--see will in Limestone County--our volume 21 and 32)

May 25, 1882
B. FRANKENBERGER died at his late residence on Pulaski Road. Came to Huntsville from Pennsylvania about 4 years ago and was 72 years old.
MRS. FANNIE MOORE THOMPSON, wife of REV. JOHN A. THOMPSON died May 23rd aged 28.

June 8, 1882
MR. THOMAS McALLISTER died...left a wife.

June 15, 1882
MRS. JANE HAMILTON CHILDS died May 22nd. (see obituary in volume 165, page 59)

June 29, 1882
Death of FLEMING WHITE (tombstone--FLEMING BATES WHITE born 1802, died June 26, 1882) at his home about nine miles northwest of Huntsville, June 26th. Was one of the oldest citizens of Madison County-- aged 83.
Death of MR. JAMES JOHNSTON June 27th. Leaves wife and several children.

July 13, 1882
MAJ. POWHATTEN ROBINSON died near Florida coast July 7th. Civil Engineer of the Department of U.S. engaged in work upon several streams in southern portions of Mississippi, Alabama and Florida. Native of Virginia.

July 20, 1882
Died--the wife of CHARLES A. GILL at Dallas, Texas July 9th. Leaves an infant of three weeks.

July 27, 1882
DR. WILLIAM PATTON WATKINS born in Huntsville December 9, 1854 and died here July 22, 1882 after a brief illness. Graduate of Washington and Lee College, Virginia and afterwards of University of Virginia, then went to New York. Only son of JAMES LAWRENCE and ELIZA WATKINS. Died at the residence of his aunt, MRS. LOUISA HARRIS.

August 24, 1882
Died August 15th after a long illness at the residence of her husband, MR. WILLIS WOODALL near New Market, MRS. SUE H. DOUGLASS WOODALL in her 45th year.

August 31, 1882
Died--MR. STEPTOE PICKETT, one of our best known citizens at
Madison Tuesday, August 29th in his 66th year. For many years he has
been a respectable citizen of this county.

September 7, 1882
CAPTAIN WILLIAM L. MUDD died at Birmingham (Jefferson County)
Friday, September 1st of typhoid fever.

September 14, 1882
REV. DAVID JACKS died August 27th at the residence of his son,
J. H. JACKS, Mt. Fork about 6 miles north of New Market. He was born
in North Carolina in 1795. Has lived a highly esteemed citizen of
Madison County since 1832. Leaves many friends and relatives.

September 21, 1882
Died--MRS. MARY M. BRECK, wife of DR. BRECK, who lived in Hunts-
ville many years ago. Died at Canton, Mississippi September 14th after
a brief illness.
Died on the night of September 10th at the home of MR. M. BONE,
MISS JENNIE LEE, only daughter of A. D. LANEDEN.

October 5, 1882
MR. A. P. HOXTER, whose nigh unto 75 years of youth blossomed as
he took the train from Decatur (Morgan County) to Huntsville, where he
first saw MRS. PARMELIA MURRELL, ripe relict of the late ANDY MURRELL.
The effect was electrical, he proposed marriage within one hour and
they were married at once.

October 26, 1882
MRS. ELIZABETH ANGELL, relict of the late JOSEPH ANGELL for many
years a resident of Huntsville died at the residence of her son,
ALBERT H. ANGELL in Brooklyn, New York Wednesday, October 18th in her
74th year. When here, she was a member of the Cumberland Presbyterian
Church, but later of the Baptist Church.
Died WILLIAM M. BRANDON, formerly a resident of Huntsville, in
Little Rock (Pulaski County), Arkansas, November 12th of typhoid fever.
Known here as MAC BRANDON, brother-in-law of our sheriff.
WILLIAM CRUSE COLES died Friday in Huntsville November 10th in his
29th year having been born September 25, 1853.
Died at New Market Monday night October 2, 1882, JOE CALVIN, son
of W. F. and F. E. LAXSON aged 2 years 3 months and 16 days.

November 23, 1882
DR. HENRY WILLIS BASSETT was killed November 20th. Left a wife
(nee CARRIE NEAL) and two little boys.

November 30, 1882
MR. JAMES LANDMAN died at the residence of his son-in-law,
MR. WILLIAM F. BALDRIDGE, southwest of Huntsville, Tuesday November 28th.
He was about 82 and had spent a greater portion of his life in Madison
County. Leaves behind him many relatives and friends.

December 7, 1882
Death of JAMES ANDERSON, son of our esteemed fellow citizen,
JOHN B. ANDERSON at Decatur (Morgan County) Saturday night December 2.
Leaves a young wife (nee DICKSON).
Obituary of JAMES LANDMAN (see page 61). Born in Virginia in 1801
and moved to Madison County, Alabama some time in 1809 and has resided
here ever since. On June 4, 1836 (1835, should be) he married MISS JULIA
HATTEN. They had several children but only two are now living, his
wife having died some years ago....

December 21, 1882
Died at her home in Madison County December 18th, in her 65th
year, MRS. ELIZABETH T. McMAHAN. She was married February 11, 1845 to
JOHN McMAHAN and had but one child, a daughter, who died nine months
ago. Nashville Christian Advocate please copy.

May 6, 1825
"MESSERS JOSEPH MOORE, late soldier in ALLAN's Company of 17th Regiment of Infantry and ROBERT HIGGINS, late soldier in CAPT. PHILIPS Company of Artillery and their legal representatives are informed that on authority of papers intrusted to my charge, I have obtained patents for their bounty land, situated in Arkansas Territory. Not knowing by laws of the Territory their lands will at a certain period be liable to be sold for the taxes, I have thought proper to convey to those interested the above information."
April 14th   GABRIEL MOORE

May 2, 1825
State of Alabama--Morgan County. Orphans Court
NEILL PATTESON, administrator of JOHN PATTESON, deceased.
ISAAC TELLER, merchant
WILLIAM McCAY, JR., lawyer
THOMAS B. TUNSTALL, lawyer
A. D. VEITCH, merchant
SAMUEL COLTART, merchant tailor
DR. D(ABNEY) M(ILLER) WHARTON announces partnership with DR. GEORGE R. WHARTON, graduate of Transylvania University. Note: DR. D. M. WHARTON born Powhatan County, Virginia 10 October 1780, died 20 May 1966 Hinds County, Mississippi. Married May 1809, Powhatan County, Virginia ANNE T. SWANN daughter of CO. SAML. SWANN. She died 1843 Madison County, Alabama. DR. D. M. WHARTON, son of JOHN and RHODA MORRIS WHARTON.

May 10, 1825
EZEKIEL CRAFT, county treasurer
JAMES B. CRAIGHEAD and H. ORLANDO ALDEN, law partners
DAVID T. KNOX, watchmaker

September 2, 1825
Departed this life Tuesday the 30th ult., MR. QUENTIN MARSHALL, aged about 23 years. Deceased, we are informed was a native of Prince Edward County, Virginia from whence he removed in the year 1822 to this place, where he has been engaged in the mercantile line up until his death. He was a Mason.

September 16, 1825
Married on the evening of Wednesday the 7th instant at the house of DAVID MUNRO, Esq. by REV. MR. THOMPSON, JOHN T. DISMUKES, Esq. of Davidson County, Tennessee to MISS ANN MUNRO, daughter of WILLIAM MUNRO of Florence, Alabama.
Died of cramp on the 28th ult. ELIZABETH, daughter of MAJ. M. W. WEAVER in her 7th year.

October 7, 1825
Married at Pulaski, Tennessee on Friday the 23rd by REV. MR. DAVENPORT, MR. JAMES M. MOORE to MISS ARABELLA JONES, daughter of MAJ. WILLIAM JONES, all of this county.
Departed this life on the 26th ult. at 10 minutes to 9 a.m. and in 26th year of his age, at residence of REV. BOOTH MALONE of Limestone County, the REV. ARTHUR McCLURE, who fell a victim of an inflammatory billious fever.... He was a man of superior talents. He sustained the office of an itinerant preacher with great acceptibility, a Methodist. He was far from parent or brother.

September 30, 1825
Departed this life Saturday morning September 24, at her residence in this place, MRS. BROWN, aged about 75. She left behind many relatives and friends. REV. JOHN ALLAN preached her funeral sermon etc.

October 21, 1825
Married at the residence of MR. JAMES JACKSON at Florence the 12th ult. by the REV. S. WALL, MR. ALEXANDER POPE, merchant to MISS ANN HANNA of Lauderdale County.

November 11, 1825
    Died on the 8th instant, in this place after three days illness,
GEORGE W. LEE, formerly of North Carolina, but for many years a highly
respected citizen of this town.

November 18, 1825
    Married on Friday the 11th instant by THOMAS HUMES, Esq. MR.
RICHARD H. CHAMPION to MISS ELIZABETH COBB, all of this town.
    Died on the 11th instant WILLIAM ANTHONY AUGUSTUS, aged 4 years,
son of WILLIAM HARRIS, Esq. of this county. Suffered intolerable pain
for the last three months from a schrophulous affection, producing hard
and enlarged tumors of the abdomen and caries of the jawbone. He
evinced extraordinary firmness etc.

January 13, 1826
    Died on Saturday night last in this place, MAJ. THOMAS BANISTER,
aged 78, formerly of Jamaica, Long Island, New York. Much regretted
by friends and acquaintances.
    Married on the 17th instant by REV. JOHN ALLEN, MR. JOHN A. FACKLER,
merchant to MISS ELIZABETH TURNER, all of this city.
    Married at Fairfield, Tennessee the seat of WILLIAM B. LEWIS,
Esq. on Thursday evening last, ABRAHAM P. HENRY, Esq. Editor of Nashville Republican to MISS MARY CLAIBORNE.

March 31, 1826
    Married on Wednesday evening by WILLIAM ROUNTREE, Esq. MR. JOHN C.
FINLAY to MISS CYNTHIA, eldest daughter of MR. ROBERT HAMBLET, all of
this county.
    Died on the 13th ult. at his residence in Blount County, Alabama
GEN. GABRIEL HANBY, aged about 40. He was a member of the Convention
that framed the Constitution.
    OWEN's Dictionary of Alabama Biographies Volume III page 739 says
GABRIEL HANBY lived in Henry County, Virginia until ca. 1817 when he
moved to Blount County, Alabama. Married NANCY, of North Carolina
daughter of NICH. and REBECCA (BADGETT) HORN.
    Letter to us from MISS AMELIA PORTER, Route #1, P.O. Box 529,
Guntersville, Alabama May 22, 1961 "Wanted: Information on GABRIEL
HANBY, 1 of delegates from Blount County to Constitutional Convention
1819 and our 1st State Senate."

April 14, 1826
    Married on Tuesday the 4th instant at the house of THOMAS LOVE,
Esq. by REV. ALLEN, MAJ. JOHN F. FARLEY to MISS MARY ALLEN, all of
Limestone County.

April 28, 1826
    Died on Thursday morning the 27th instant, in the 20th year of
his age, WILLIAM LEE HAMMOND, eldest son of CAPT. ELI HAMMOND of
this county.

May 12, 1826
    Married on Tuesday evening the 25th ult. In Tuscaloosa by REV.
MR. CURTIS, HENRY W. COLLIER, Esq. to MISS MARY BATTLE, all of that
place.
    Died in the vicinity of Huntsville on Saturday the 15th ult.,
MRS. MINERVA P. CLEMENS, aged about 32 years. She left a husband and
four small children.
    Died on Wednesday the 26th of April, GEORGE P. HARRELL, Esq. in
his 52nd year, an old and respectable citizen of Madison County.
    Died on Friday the 5th instant in Jackson County, MAJ. DANIEL
PEYTON in his 64th year.
MRS. PHEBE JOHNSTON
Limestone County, Alabama
    Died.--On the 6th instant at the residence of JOHN B. WILKINSON,
Esq. in Limestone County, MRS. PHEBE JOHNSTON in 114th year of her age.
MRS. JOHNSTON was born in Bermuda in 1712, was married in 1732 to
CAPT. JOHNSTON in the British service, who removed to Georgia with
GEN. OGLETHORP at the first settlement of that state, where he remained
until the close of the revolution, when he removed to the Bahama Islands

where he died. After his death, his widow, the subject of this notice,
came back to Georgia and resided with a daughter who was married in that
State, with whom she lived until the death of her daughter, when she
took up her residence with her grand-daughter, the wife of JUDGE WILKINSON,
with whom she removed to this State.
    MRS. JOHNSON retained her faculties in an eminent degree to the
last, and died with the most perfect composure and resignation after a
short illness. She never used spectacles until she was 100 years old,
and in her latest days conversed with great accuracy of the scenes and
occurrences of her early life.
    SEE: Southern Advocate
          Huntsville, Madison County, Alabama
          June 30, 1826 - Page 3, Column 3
    Filed in Department of Archives and History Montgomery, Alabama.

August 18, 1826
    Died on Monday last the 14th instant, CAPT. BENJ. JOURDON in the
29th year of his age, son of FLEMING JOURDAN, Esq. of a tedious illness
of some months.
    Died on Thursday the 10th, 3 miles west of Huntsville, of fever,
MRS. MARTHA, consort of REV. JOSEPH AKE, deceased of Bedford County,
Tennessee.
    Died on Thursday the 10th instant after a short illness, LOUISA
MATILDA, aged 5 years and 7 months and on 13th instant MARY ELIZABETH
aged 3 years and 9 months both daughters of ARBHIBALD McNEIL.

September 1, 1826
    Died on the 15th instant at her residence in Morgan County, MRS.
MARTHA, consort of LANCELOT CHUNN, JR. formerly of Frederick County,
Maryland in her 55th year.
    Died Wednesday 15th of August at her residence in Roane County,
Tennessee COL. RUFUS MORGAN aged about 45 years. He was one of our
most active citizens.
    Died in the parish of West Baton Rouge 15th of August THONAS EVANS,
painter, late from England.

September 8, 1826
    Died at the house of MR. FLEMING FREEMAN, Autauga County 15th of
last month in 68th year of age, MRS. SALLY S. BARNETT. Was left a
widow at an early period of her life with several children. Note:
Will of one HOLMAN FREEMAN, Wilkes County, Georgia probated 1817 names
a son FLEMING.

September 22, 1826
    Died on Tuesday 12th instant at residence of DR. WADDY TATE in
Limestone County in 17th year of her age, MISS ELIZABETH, daughter of
MR. GROSS SCRUGGS of this county.
    Died at the residence in this county on 18th instant of prevailing
fever, MR. THOMAS H. BODDIE, aged 30.
    Died Sunday night in this town, MR. ALLEN BLEDSOE, printer, aged
24, formerly of Raleigh, North Carolina.

October 27, 1826
    Married on 26th instant in Bardstown, Kentucky, MR. JOHN H. POLIN
of Limestone County to MISS NANCY, daughter of MR. EDWARD HAYDEN of
that place.
    Died on Tuesday the 24th instant at his residence, Locust Grove
in Limestone County, BENJAMIN FOX in his 42nd year a native of Greenville
County, Virginia. Note: One BENJ. FOX married in Greenville County,
Virginia. 8 March 1813 FRANCES H. WALKER; Surety: WM. FOX.

November 3, 1826
    Died 30th instant in 3rd year CALEDONIA, only daughter of SAMUEL
COLTART.
    Died 25th instant last month at Sommerville, Morgan County,
MRS. BARBARA W. consort of JOHN T. RATHER, Esq.
    Died at Somerville, Morgan County 29th of last month, DR. WILLIAM S.
GOODHUE in his 35th year, a native of Vermont. Graduated at Union
College.

November 17, 1826
    Married 2nd instant by REV. MEEKS, MR. ROBERT SHOTWELL to MISS
MARY E. H. daughter of CAPT. L. B. TALIAFERRO, all of this county.
    Died in Mobile 28th of October DR. CHARLES J. LEWIS, formerly
of this place.

December 1, 1826
    Died at his father's residence in Madison County on 18th instant
EZEKIAH HERVY WEBB EASTLAND, aged 7 months, youngest son of MAJ.
JOSEPH EASTLAND.

February 16, 1827
    Died 31 ult at residence in Madison County, MR. JOEL W. JONES in
40th year of age, formerly of Buckingham County, Virginia. Left wife
and 5 children.
    Died at residence in Lawrence County 30 ult. MATTHEW CLAY, Esq.
native of Virginia. Born of wealth. A few years since, he emigrated
to Alabama. Was a member of the legislature.
    Died at Mooresville on 19th ult. MRS. ELIZABETH, wife of COL.
G(RIFFIN) LAMKIN. Note: She was BETSY CLARK daughter of JAMES and
SUSAN said they married December 24, 1800.
    Died near Vicksburg, Mississippi 19th BEVERLY HUGHES, Esq.

March 30, 1827
    Married on the 8th in Limestone County (see letter from MRS. LOUISE
S. CHELF, Roanoke), by REV. JOHN THOMPSON, CAPT. WILLIAM EASTLAND of
this county to MISS ANN P(ANNEL) BRONOUGH. (she was daughter of
SAML and NANCY (MASSIE) BRONAUGH)
    Married Tuesday evening last by REV. HENRY SALE, MR. JAMES W. DRAKE
of Athens to MISS HONORA G. ROOTES of this county. (volume 133, page 9--
1 marriage record says married 27 March 1827; one says 8 May 1827)
    Died Thursday morning last in this place, MRS. ROSANNA FEENEY in
her 74th year.

April 6, 1827
    Married Thursday the 29th by REV. JAMES ROWE, MR. IRVIN WINDHAM
to MISS ANN BADLIN ("BADLUM" in marriage records) of this place (note:
BADLIN written "SADLUN" in Huntsville Democrat. P.J.G.)
    Died at Athens, Alabama on 24th, DR. JOHN R. BEDFORD of Lauderdale
County. He died suddenly and before his afflicted wife, who hastened
upon hearing of his dangerous illness, could reach him Remains brought
to his plantation and interred in family burial ground on Monday the
26th Left a widow and children. For many years ,he was an eminent
practitioner of medicine, his latter days devoted to management of his
extensive mercantile business, formerly of house of BEDFORD and MACKEY,
and until his death, connected with the firm of BEDFORD, BREEDLOVE and
ROBESON of New Orleans....
    Died at Red Oak Flat in this county on the 31st, CATHARINE FRANCES,
youngest daughter of MAJ. ROBERT WALTON, aged 11 months.
    Death of MR. JOHN M'ALISTER, merchant of Franklin (Williamson
County), Tennessee, formerly a resident of Jonesboro (Washington County),
East Tennessee. Drowned in Barren River near Bowlinggreen, Kentucky
on night of 26th...(Nashville Republican).
    State of Alabama--Jefferson County. BENJAMIN MATTISON, administra-
tor of estate of BENJAMIN S. SIMS, deceased.

April 27, 1827
    Married on 11th at Spring Grove, Madison County, HENLY DRUMMOND,
Esq. to MISS MARY, 2nd daughter of CAPT. WILLIAM MUNROE. (see volume 29,
page 18--and next Tennessee County volume after 99, volume 133, page 9)
    Married on 18th by REV. JNO. H. THOMPSON, MR. FRANCIS W. BRADLEY
of Mooresville to MISS SUSAN M. daughter of WILLIAM FISHER, of Limestone
County.
    Died at Whitesburg on the 18th, ROBERT BEATTIE, a native of
Dumfriesshire, Scotland aged 34....

May 11, 1827
    Married on 5 April last in Erie, Greene County, by JUDGE MOODY,
MR. WM. P. HUDNELL (60 in Virginia; Choctaw County), late of this place

to MISS MELISSA B., daughter of REV. JAMES MONETTE of the former place.

Died at his residence in this county on Thursday, 3rd instant, in the 40th year of his age, MR. JOHN P. POWELL of an illness of but a few hours continuance. Left a widow and five small children.... Native of Powhattan County, Virginia and emigrated to this country about 11 or 12 years ago. Richmond Enquirer please copy.

May 18, 1827

Departed this life in Huntsville Tuesday morning last, MRS. JANE WHEELER, late consort of HENRY J. WHEELER. Left a husband who is now absent on business in the western district of Tennessee, also a numerous family....

State of Alabama--Limestone County. In Chancery--March Term
Circuit Court
NANCY HAINEY)
   versus   ) defendant is not a resident of this state.
EMANUEL HAINEY)

State of Alabama--Jefferson County. Orphan's Court 3rd Monday in April 1827. JANE HUNT, administratrix versus Heirs of ISAIAH HUNT, deceased. JANE HUNT, administratrix of will. Land described as W½ of NE¼ of Section 2 Township 20 Range 4 West and NE¼ of Section 3 Township 20 Range 4 West of Meridian of Huntsville with exception of one acre sold to JORDAN BA--; set aside for dower.

June 1, 1827

State of Alabama--Blount County. April Term 1827.
JESSE HOLMANK)
   versus   ) In Chancery--The defendant,
THOMAS M. BIBB, WINFIELD HAMNER) THOMAS M. BIBB is not an inhabitant
and JOHN FRY   ) of this state

State of Alabama--Madison County. May Term 1827. CHARLES DEMOSS, deceased.

Orphan's Court 19 March 1827. On application of SARAH NABORS and JAMES BARTON, administratrix and administrator of FRANCIS NABORS, deceased, to settle administration at Court House at Elyton (note: Jefferson County)

June 8, 1827

State of Alabama--Jefferson County. Orphan's Court 3rd Monday in May, 1827. ANNA McSHAN, administratrix of WILLIAM McSHAN, deceased.

June 15, 1827

State of Alabama--Jefferson County. 3rd Monday in May, 1827. FRANCES LAWLEY, administratrix of estate of ELIJAH LAWLEY, deceased.

June 22, 1827

Died in this place on the 10th, MRS. JUDITH POPE in the 58th year of her age, wife of COL. LeROY POPE.... Native of Virginia from which state she emigrated to Georgia in early life. From Georgia she removed to this place in 1810 and was the first and oldest female inhabitant of the town. Leaves a bereaved husband and children.

June 29, 1827

Married on 20th by REV. DAVID THOMPSON, MR. JAS. S. SMITH to MISS MARY ANN, daughter of MR. JAMES E. BROWNING, all of this county.

Died at his father's residence in Madison County, on the 21st, MATTHEW MOORE, Esq. in his 21st year.... Finished his education at Chapel Hill, University of North Carolina.

State of Alabama--Jefferson County. 3rd Monday in June 1827. JAMES HALL, administrator of JOHN B. LUCIOU-, deceased.

July 6, 1827

State of Alabama--Morgan County. Orphan's Court June 30, 1827. RICHARD PRIDDY and WINNAFRED PRIDDY, executors of the will of WILLIAM PRIDDY, deceased.

State of Alabama--Morgan County. Orphan's Court June 30, 1827. PETER COUCH, administrator of estate of ANAHEL BULLARD, deceased.

August 3, 1827
    State of Alabama--Jackson County. July Term 1827. GEORGE W.
HIGGINS and STEPHEN CARTER versus JANE RILEY, administratrix of estate
of JAMES RILEY, deceased. Petition for conveyance. Set forth that
JAMES RILEY in his lifetime bound himself by penal bond dated 3 October
1820.... JAMES RILEY has since departed this life.
    State of Alabama--Jefferson County. 23 July 1827. AGNES GEE,
administratrix of estate of WILLIAM J. GEE, administrator of estate of
JOSEPH R. FINDLEY, deceased.

August 17, 1827
    Departed this life suddenly on the 5th July in his 52nd year,
REV. ANDREW K. DAVIS. Descended of a pious ancestry...(very long)
    State of Alabama--Limestone County. MRS. JANE SCOTT, deceased.
SAMUEL JORDAN, executor

August 31, 1827
    Departed this life on Sunday evening last, CAROLINE DYER aged about
5 years 11 months; also on Tuesday morning following, MARY ANN DYER,
aged about 8 years and 4 months, children of MAJOR JUSTIN DYER,
residing in this county about 8 miles from Huntsville. Bilious fever.
    State of Alabama--Madison County. DANIEL ADKINS, deceased.

September 7, 1827
    Died in this place Wednesday last, GEORGE M. infant son of MR.
WM. ATWOOD aged about 12 months.
    State of Alabama--Jefferson County. 16 August 1827. BENJAMIN
LONG, late administrator of SOLOMON HENSON, deceased.
    State of Alabama--Blount County. Orphan's Court Special Term 1827
20 August. LEWIS WHITE, administrator of estate of PETER WHITE, late
of Blount County deceased.

September 21, 1827
    State of Alabama--Limestone County Court. WILLIAM DEWOODY,
administrator of JAMES R. PATTESON, deceased.

September 28, 1827
    Married on Thursday the 20th by REV. DAVID THOMPSON, MR. DANIEL
HARRIS to MISS ELIZA G. daughter of COL. EFFORD BENTLEY, all of this
county (note: my great grandparents. P. J. GANDRUD)

October 5, 1827
    Died on 3rd HARPOLYCE, daughter of JOHN W. LANE of Limestone
County aged one year 11 months 14 days. The Southern Recorder,
Milledgeville (Baldman County), Georgia please copy.

October 12, 1827
    Departed this life on the 10th, MRS. ELIZA BRANDON, consort of
THOMAS BRANDON, Esq. of Huntsville in the 35th year of her age. Left
behind a disconsolate husband and 6 little daughters. Died at 7 o'clock
at night.... Funeral will be preached by REV. WILLIAM McMAHON at the
Methodist Church in Huntsville on first Sunday in November.
    Died in Natchez (Adams County) on 21 Setpember, MR. RICHARD R.
HENLEY, formerly of this place.

October 19, 1827
    Departed this life on 2 September in 16th year, PHILIP D.,
second son of CAPT. NICHOLAS and MARTHA DAVIS of Limestone County....
    Died suddenly on Saturday evening last in her 13th year, SARAH E.,
daughter of COL. OGLESBY SCRUGGS of this county.... Left a fond parent,
3 brothers and a sister.

November 2, 1827
    Married on Thursday evening last by REV. DAVID THOMPSON, MR. JAMES
MANNING, JR. to MISS INDIANA, daughter of DR. ASA THOMPSON, all of this
county.
    State of Alabama--Madison County. County Court. 26 October 1827.
JOHN FRANKLIN, deceased.

November 9, 1827
	Married on the 7th by REV. DAVID THOMPSON, MR. ELISHA E. DISMUKES
of Sumner County (copied for Jean and P.P.), Tennessee to MISS SARAH E.
daughter of MRS. MARY A. WATKINS of this county (married in original
marriage book and skipped in later)
	Married on 9 October by REV. JOHN WOODVILLE, MR. ISAAC HERRON of
Traveller's Rest, aged 101 to MISS ANN SIMPSON aged 70 of Culpepper
County, Virginia.
	Departed this life in 15th year on Friday night last after a
severe illness of a few days, MISS ELIZA EDINGTON, only daughter of
MR. JAMES EDINGTON of Limestone County....
	State of Alabama--Jackson County. October 19, 1827. WILLIAM B.
GREEN, guardian of heirs of ALEXANDER W. DULANEY, deceased.
	State of Alabama--Jackson County. October 19, 1827. MARTHA
MITCHELL and ELIZABETH MILLER, guardians for the minor heirs of
STEPHEN RUSSELL filed accounts and vouchers.

November 23, 1827
	Sheriff advertises for arrest of WILLIAM McMAHAN who killed
JESSE DUNN in Madison County, three miles from Whitesburg. McMAHAN
described as being about 25 years of age.

November 30, 1827
	Died on Tuesday evening the 20th in Morgan County, Alabama,
WILLIAM B. LILE in his 26th year. Member of the Methodist Episcopal
Church.... Raleigh Star to copy.
	State of Alabama--Madison County. County Court. 28 November 1827.
THOMAS GLASCOCK, deceased.

December 7, 1827
	Died on the 3rd at the residence of her parents, SUSAN RUFFIN,
eldest daughter of WILLIAM H. T. and SUSAN C. BROWN aged 4 years
1 month--of croup....

December 14, 1827
	Married on Thursday the 6th by REV. MR. SULIVEN, MR. ELDRED W.
WILLIAMS to MISS HARRIET L. daughter of JOHN ALLISON, Esq. all of this
county.
	Died on the 29th, MRS. ISABELLA (written ELIZABETH in Huntsville
Democrat. P.J.G.) ATKINSON, daughter of REV. A. K. DAVIS...leaving
behind a tender infant and afflicated husband. (volume 71, page 4--
marriage record of AMOS A. ATKINSON to ISABELLA M. DAVY, 1826 but
DAVIS is right)
	Died on the morning of the 12th, December about 7 o'clock,
JOHN LAFAYETTE only son of NICHOLAS C. and ELIZABETH BISHOP in 4th
year of his age--of croup.

December 28, 1827
	Married on Wednesday the 12th instant at Quaker Springs, Columbus
County, Georgia by REV. MR. KENNEDY, MR. JOHN H. WALPOLE of this place
to MISS MARY ANN (28 in Maryland), daughter of MR. JAMES LYNES of the
former place.

January 4, 1828
	Died on Sunday morning, 23rd, at residence in this county, in 52nd
year, DR. ASA THOMPSON, late of Elbert County, Georiga.... Left a
widow and 7 children.
	State of Alabama--Morgan County. Orphan's Court December 29, 1827.
NATHAN BUSBY and GABRIEL CROW, administrators of JOHNSON CROW, deceased.
	State of Alabama--Morgan County. Orphan's Court December 29,
1827. WILLIAM BURRIS, and JOHN GANDY, administrators of estate of
ROBERT TAPSCOTT, deceased.

January 11, 1828
	Married in Greensborough on 30th (marriage record says married
21st), DAVID HARDING of Madison County to MARY S(TUART) on daughter of
COL. ABSALOM ALSTON. (also in volume 5, page 22; volume 17, page 69)
	State of Alabama--Jefferson County. Orphan's Court December 24,
1827. ELIJAH BROWN, administrator of estate of THOMPSON BROWN, deceased.

January 18, 1828
Married on Tuesday evening last by REV. J. W. ALLEN, MR. MARTIN
WEATHERLY (57 in Virginia) of this place (Talladega County 1850) to
MISS MARTHA (42 in Alabama), daughter of MR. SPENCER BALL of this
county.
Note: From HAYDEN's Virginia Genealogies page 143. "W. H.
WEATHERLY, Anniston, Alabama writes: 'MOSES BALL born ca. 1740-50
had a son SPENCER, whose daughter MARTHA says he was born ca. 1770.
MARTHA was born 1808, living 1889. They moved 1820-30 from Alexandria,
Virginia to Alabama. MARTHA married -------- WEATHERLY and had the
writer, W. H. WEATHERLY.'"
Died at his residence in this county on 12th instant, MR. JOB KEY
in his 62nd year. Had been a citizen of Madison County for many years
and was highly respected by his neighbors as an honest, upright man.
As a husband and father...etc.

February 6, 1828
Deed of trust dated on 17 January 1825 and recorded in Madison
County also in Blount County by LUTHER MORGAN, ANN C. MORGAN, SAMUEL D.
MORGAN, MATILDA MORGAN, CALVIN C. MORGAN, HENRIETTA MORGAN, ALEXANDER G.
MORGAN, and AMERICA MORGAN, land in Blount Springs, 320 acres.
Died on 22nd at her father's residence in Limestone County after
a lingering and painful illness, ELIZABETH FIGURES COE, eldest daughter
of MAJOR JESSE COE in her 18th year. (long)
State of Alabama--Jackson County. STEPHEN HORN, deceased.
Orphan's Court. SAMUEL VAUGH (VAUGHN or VAUGHT?), deceased
January 29, 1828.

February 29, 1828
Married on Friday evening the 22nd instant by REV. JAMES W. ALLEN,
MR. GEORGE W. JOHNSON to MISS MARTHA WILKINSON (sent to CAPT. EV (faded))
Married on Tuesday evening the 26th instant (marriage record says
27; volume 130, page 9), MR. LEWIS ROFFE to MISS MARTHA, daughter of
GROSS SCRUGGS, Esq. (volume 76, page 11).
On Wednesday evening the 27th instant, MR. WM. M. WILBURN to MISS
NANCY L. daughter of MR. RICHARD FORD. (volume 153, page 25)
On the same evening, MR. WM. McDOWELL, merchant of this place to
MISS PRISCILLA WITHERS of this county (volume 48, page 11).

March 7, 1828
Departed this life on 23rd ult after a sudden and short illness,
MRS. ELIZABETH consort of MR. JAMES COLLIER of this county....

March 21, 1828
Married Wednesday last by RICHARD B. PURDOM, MR. HUBBARD H. FENNELL
to MISS MARY SMITH, all of this county (volume 122, page 2; 1850
Marshall County he 43 in Virginia)

April 4, 1828
State of Alabama--Madison County. JESSE CHILDRESS (son of DAVID),
deceased.

April 25, 1828
Married on 22nd by REV. JAMES W. ALLEN, DR. DAVID SPECK to MISS
MARTHA, daughter of THOMAS HUMES, Esq. all of this place (volume 103,
page 57)
Died on 15th in this place, WILLIAM M'BROOM, Esq. of Huntsville,
former sheriff of Madison County. He was on his way to New Orleans
two days previous to his death he reached the Florence Hotel from aboard
the Steam Boat Friendship in extreme ill health. Medical aid was
called and every possible attention paid him without effect (Florence
Gazette)

May 9, 1828
Died on Wednesday night the 7th after a lingering illness of 20
months, MR. ALEX. WASON, an old and respectable citizen and for many
years a resident of this place.

May 16, 1828
     State of Alabama--Jackson County. April Term 1828. JOHN O. BURTON,
sheriff and administrator of SOLOMON COLLINS, deceased.

May 23, 1828
     Departed this life on Saturday morning the 17th about 2 o'clock
MR. FRANCIS C. LEWIS in his 19th year....
     Died on Monday evening last, MRS. MARY, consort of DAVID URQUHART,
Esq. in 28th or 29th year.
     In Meridianville, on Saturday 10th, JAMES ASA, son of ROBERT J.
MANNING aged 2 years 7 months.

June 13, 1828
     Died on 1st in vicinity of this place, MRS. ELIZABETH consort of
JOHN HAYS after a short but severe illness. Left a husband and 5
children. Member of Methodist Church.

June 27, 1828
     Died in this town Tuesday the 27th ult. MRS. LUCINDA P. BIRDSEYE,
consort of MR. EZEKIEL BIRDSEYE, merchant in her 33rd year. Native of
Cornwall, Connecticut, where she resided much esteemed, until about 2
years ago, when she accompanied her husband to this place.

July 4, 1828
     Died in Triana on the 25th, SARAH FRANCES, youngest daughter of
EDWARD W. PARKER.
     Died in this place Sunday last, MRS. MARTHA ANN PAYNE ELY consort
of HENRY B. ELY, formerly of Campbell City, Virginia aged 23 years.
Lynchburg, Virginia papers please copy.
     Died on Friday the 20th at house of MR. CLAIBORNE SAUNDERS in county
of Lawrence, COL. WILLIAM W. PARHAM after a brief but truly distressing
illness in his 34th year. Native of Brunswick County, Virginia but
greater portion of his life was spent in southwest country having emigrated to Tennessee before he had fairly attained manhood. After spending
a few years in Nashville, he removed to this state in the year 1812,
established the first paper ever published in Huntsville, was one of
the earliest citizens of Tuscumbia, and has resided here constantly
for the 10 years past.... Member of legislature.

July 11, 1828
     State of Alabama--Jackson County. HUGH McCLYED, deceased.

July 18, 1828
     Died in this county on 19th, MRS. ELIZA, consort of DR. ALFRED
MOORE, leaving a bereaved husband and 7 small children.

July 25, 1828
     Married by REV. JAMES WALLER on evening of 23rd instant, MR.
LAWRENCE S. BANKS (46 in Virginia, Morgan County) of Triana to MISS
ISABELLA M. daughter of the late FREDERICK W. JAMES of this county.
(volume 136, page 19--he married again 1834 MARGARET J. NOBLE)

August 1, 1828
     Died in this county on Monday last, JAMES, only child of THOMAS
GRAY aged 10 months.

August 15, 1828
     Married on Thursday the 7th, by REV. A. J. CRAWFORD, MR. JACOB A.
PIERCE to MISS CHARLOTTE SIMMONS, all of this county (volume 103, page 9)

August 22, 1828
     Married on Wednesday evening last by REV. JOHN ALLEN, MR. PHARES
T(OWNZEN) POSEY (born December 8, 1806, died October 2, 1841) to MRS.
ELIZABETH HUTCHINGS, all of this place (son of JESSE HAMILTON and
ELEANOR BROOKS POSEY (see POSEY Bible) volume 64, page 9)

August 29, 1828
     Married Tuesday the 19th at residence of MR. JESSE SEARCY, COL.
EDWIN JONES to MRS. SARAH COLEMAN, all of this county (Athens Athenian)

Died Tuesday evening last after a short illness of 7 days,
ANDREW D. VEITCH, merchant of this place aged 38 leaving a wife and
5 small children.

September 5, 1828
    Married on Tuesday last by REV. MR. KING, THOMAS BRANDON, Esq.
clerk of county court of this county to MRS. MARY OWEN both of this
place. (Volume 136, page 19; 2nd wife--nee GLASGOW--she married 1.
WM. PURNELL OWEN)
    Married on Wednesday 3rd instant by REV. DAVID THOMPSON, at the
house of MR. JAMES FRAZIER, MR. JOEL M. SLEDGE of this place to MISS
NANCY HILL of this county (volume 103, page 56)

September 12, 1828
    Married on 3rd at residence of DANIEL H. TILLINGHAST (marriage
record says married 4th), Esq. near Triana, by REV. J. L. SLOSS, MR.
ROBERT ALEXANDER to MRS. ELIZA A. McFARLAND, all of this county (volume
71, page 4)
    Died in this place on 3rd, JOHN JAMES, infant son of MR. S(AMUEL)
K. M'GRAW.
    Died on 4th instant ALEXANDER, infant son of MR. JOHN HAYS.
    Died at Winchester, Tennessee on 30th, MRS. CAROLINE PATTON TAUL
aged 21 years 3 months wife of MR. THOMAS P. TAUL of this place.

September 19, 1828
    Married on Thursday 4th instant by REV. WM. EDDINS, COL. ALLEN
WALLS to MISS ELEANOR COX all of this county (volume 153, page 26;
COCKE in marriage record)

October 3, 1828
    Died in Tuscaloosa on 24th ult after a lingering and painful
illness of 20 days, MR. RICHARD SELBY, formerly of this place in the
34th year of his age native of England; was in the battle of Waterloo
and there received a wound in his neck

October 10, 1828
    Married on Thursday evening 2nd instant by REV. DAVID THOMPSON,
WILLIAM B. DENNETT to MISS AMANDA N. (A. in marriage record) daughter
of WILLIAM BIBB, Esq. all of this county (volume 133, page 11)

October 17, 1828
    State of Alabama--Jefferson County. CATHARINE LAWLEY and ELISHA
COCKERHAM, administrators of estate of LEWIS LAWLEY, deceased.

October 24, 1828
    State of Alabama--Morgan County. ATOLALTPA STUART, administrator
of BENJAMIN STEWART, deceased.

November 7, 1828
    State of Alabama--Morgan County. JOHN FENNEL, administrator of
NANCY TAYLOR, deceased.

November 14, 1828
    Married on Thursday evening the 6th by REV. MR. OVERALL, MR. WM.
BAKER to MISS MARY HERBERT, all of this place (HEBERT in volume 6;
marriage record volume 136, page 19)

November 28, 1828
    JAMES M. M. WHITE departed this life in Tuscaloosa on 10th aged
25, son of HON. HUGH L. WHITE of Knoxville, Tennessee. Affectionate
husband, devoted father.
    Departed this life on 22nd, MRS. MARY ANN CAMP, amiable consort of
COL. JAMES CAMP in her 33rd year.
    Married on Thursday the 20th instant by REV. ROBERT DONALD,
REV. ALBERT G. GIBSON of Lincoln County, Tennessee to MISS SARAH
daughter of ROBERT ERWIN of Hazlegreen (volume 127, page 5)

December 5, 1828
    Departed this life on 14, MRS. EMILY G. wife of MR. WILLIAM COLLIER
of Triana. Born in Petersburg, Virginia 11 March 1802. Married MR.

WILLIAM COLLIER on September 1, 1825. Became seriously ill about 9
days before her death.... Died in 27th year of her age.

December 12, 1828
Married on 4th by REV. JOHN THOMPSON, WM. J. GLADDISH (44 in
North Carolina) of Limestone County to MISS SARAH SANDERS of this
county (volume 127, page 6)

December 24, 1828
Married on Thursday evening the 18th by REV. MR. SULLIVAN, MR.
JOHN S. SMITH to MISS JANE ANN, eldest daughter of CAPT. WILLIAM ROUTT
all of this county (volume 103, page 56)
Died in Sommerville on morning of the 10th, in her 30th year,
MRS. ESTHER H. HOUSTON, wife of M. C. HOUSTON, Esq...pulmonary consump-
tion...(tombstone in Sommerville Cemetery illegible except for "daughter
of")
Died on Thursday last in this place, after a protracted illness,
MR. WILLIAM C. ANDERSON in his 35th year, a highly respectable citizen
of this county for the last 4 or 5 years, formerly of Amelia County,
Virginia.
Information wanted of MAJ. CALEB B. HUDSON, a native of Prince
Edward County, Virginia and lately from Halifax County, Virginia.
Signed by DAVID G. LIGON, Lawrence County, Alabama, Moulton.

January 9, 1829
WILLIAM I. ADAIR, attorney-at-law

January 16, 1829
CASWELL R. CLIFTON, attorney-at-law

January 30, 1829
Information wanted of the present place of residence of MAJOR
CALEB B. HUDSON, a native of Prince Edward County, Virginia and lately
from Halifax County, Virginia (he lived in Jackson County, Alabama
1830-31; son of JOHN and LUCY (BAKER) HUDSON) (Signed) DAVID G. LIGON,
Moulton, Lawrence County, Alabama December 10, 1828

February 6, 1829
JOHN PIPKIN, administrator of the estate of THOMAS H. PIPKIN,
deceased. Madison County, Alabama.
Married on Thursday the 22nd instant by REV. MR. CRUTCHER,
CAPT. NEILLY DRAKE to the amiable MISS ELIZA, daughter of COL. JABEZ
LEFTWICH, all of this county.
On Tuesday evening last by REV. JOHN ALLEN, MR. GEORGE W. SMITH
of the firm of BRADFORD and SMITH, merchants, to MISS MARTHA PATTON,
daughter of MR. WILLIAM PATTON, merchant, all of this place. (volume
103, page 56)

February 13, 1829
Died at his residence in Limestone County, Alabama on Thursday
the 27th instant in his 66th year, MR. JOHN MASSIE, formerly of New
Kent County, Virginia. Attack of pulmonary consumption, which he bore
for several months with fortitude... Kind husband and father. From
the Athenian of February 5 (Limestone County)
DAVID SPECK since the late fire has removed his shop to the north
side of the Public Square to carry on his tailoring business.
State of Alabama--Morgan County. January 31, 1828. WILLIAM DARWIN,
in behalf of his wife, late CELIA PECK, administratrix of GEORGE PECK,
deceased, has filed accounts.
Morgan County, Alabama--WILLIAM BYRD, administrator of DAVID
DEVAULT, deceased.

February 20, 1829
Married in Fayette County, Tennessee by REV. MR. KESTERSON,
CAPT. WILLIAM H. FARISS to MISS MARGERY B., daughter of MR. JAMES
MAXWELL, late of Davidson County, Tennessee.
On Monday evening, 2nd instant, by REV. DR. JENNINGS, COL. OGLESBY
SCRUGGS of Madison County to MRS. ANN HEWLETT of Nashville, Tennessee.

February 27, 1829
    Married on Tuesday evening last by REV. MR. DONNELL, MR. WILLIAM
DICKSON LANIER of this county to MISS LUCY ANN CALDWELL of this town
(volume 155, page 15)
    Died lately at his residence in this county at an advanced age,
MR. REUBEN SIMMONS. Was well known in this place and universally
esteemed.... Left a numerous train of children and grandchildren...

March 13, 1829
    Died in the vicinity of Courtland (Lawrence County) on the 25th
ult. MRS. ANTOINETTE SWOOPE, consort of J. K. SWOOPE, merchant of that
town and daughter of COL. BENJAMIN SHERROD of Lawrence County. She
was well known in this town where she completed her education a few
short years ago....
    THOMAS B. TUNSTALL, attorney-at-law
    DUDLEY CURLE, attorney-at-law
    ROBERT M. RICHARDS states he is not responsible for the debts of
his wife, ELIZABETH H. RICHARDS, she having left his bed and board.

March 20, 1829
    Married on the 11th instant at Flower Hill near Winchester,
Tennessee by REV. MR. HENDERSON, MR. THOMAS RAWLINS, merchant of
Danville, Virginia to the amiable and accomplished MISS EMILY D.,
youngest daughter of WILLIAM HAUGHTON, formerly of Madison County.
    Died in this town at the residence of MR. WILLIAM H. T. BROWN,
JOHN W. CHRISTIAN, Esq. in his 28th year. Native of Charles City
County, Virginia, from whence he emigrated three years ago, to this
county. Graduate of WILLIAM and MARY and he qualified himself for
profession of law.

March 27, 1829
    Died on the 6th instant at his residence in Madison County, MR.
LEWELLEN JONES, formerly of Buckingham County, Virginia. Richmond
Enquirer please copy.

April 17, 1829
    Married on Thursday the 9th instant by REV. JOHN M'CLURE, MR.
JOHN G. WARD to MISS SALLY H. CLARK, all of this county (volume 153,
page 27)
    On Wednesday evening the 8th instant by REV. MR. NICHOLAS, MR.
ABNER G. PETTY of Limestone County to MISS MALVINA M., daughter of
WILLIAM G. LONG of this county.
    Died lately at his residence in Morgan County, GEN. THOMAS D.
CRABB. For many years an estimiable citizen of that county and lately
a Senator from that county in the Legislature of the State.

April 24, 1829
    Information wanted:
    THOMAS HAY, a native of Ireland, at present aged about 28 years,
has not been heard of by his brother for some time past. The last
letter received, dated July 28, 1825 stated he was teaching school in
Huntsville, Madison County, Alabama. In 1824, he was teaching school
in Georgia. He has been in the United States about 7 years.

May 1, 1829
    Married Tuesday evening last by REV. THOMAS M. KING, MR. JOHN F.
MILLS to MISS CALEDONIA R., eldest daughter of THOMAS BRANDON, Esq.
all of this place (volume 48, page 12)

May 15, 1829
    Died at his residence in this county, near Hazel Green, DAVID M'COA
(M'CAA) aged 64. Left a wife and nine children. Member of Cumberland
Presbyterian Church.

May 29, 1829
    Married Friday last, May 15, by REV. WILLIAM HUME, DOCT. MILES S.
WATKINS (1812 sol) of Huntsville to MISS SALLY D. B. SHELBY of Sumner
County. From Nashville Republican. (Goodspeed's Miss. says moved to
Jax. Mem. 1891; Mississippie 1850 and died 1866)

June 12, 1829
    Married at Triana on Wednesday, 3rd instant by REV. MR. PERRIN,
MR. RICHARD B. FARRINGTON to MISS SARAH ANN PARKER, all of this county.

June 26, 1829
    Died at Belmina, the residence of THOMAS BIBB, Esq. in Limestone
County on the morning of the 17th, CAPT. ROBERT THOMPSON in his 76th
year. Born and educated in Amelia County, Virginia; at an early age
joined a band of patriots who fought for and finally obtained liberty
of their country. The Revolutionary struggle being over, he emigrated
to Petersburg, Georgia where he engaged in active life...from thence at
an early day, he moved to this county....
    Died on 28 May in Hamilton, Ohio after a protracted illness, JOHN
CLEVES SYMMES, author of Theory of Open Poles and Concentric Spheres.

July 3, 1829
    Married Tuesday evening the 30th by REV. JOHN M. TAYLOR, DOCT.
FLEMMING JORDAN to MISS LUCY JANE M. MOORE, daughter of WILLIAM H(ARVIE)
MOORE, Esq. all of this county.

July 24, 1829
    Died in this town Thursday the 16th after a painful illness of
nearly 8 months, MRS. FANNY PATTESON (see tombstone born May 6, 18--;
died July 16, 18--), consort of BENJAMIN PATTESON, Esq. in her 29th
year. (1st wife--they married in Nashville December 21, 1818. He
married 2--SARAH ANN SANDE (faded). She is buried in Maple Hill--
born 6 May 1800; died July 16, 1829)

October 16, 1829
    Died on Wednesday the 7th of October at ½ past 11 o'clock p.m. at
her husband's residence near Bellefonte, Jackson County, MRS. JANE E.
BARKER in the 23rd year of her age and consort of MR. ELIAS BARKER
("BARBER" in Huntsville Democrat--BARBER in 1840 Jackson County) from
Fauquier County, Virginia. Left an affectionate husband and two small
children. U.S. Telegraph and Richmond Enquirer please copy. (his
tombstone says BARBER)
    On Monday the 28th ult. at Blount Springs after an illness of three
months, MRS. HARRIOT HOWARD aged 26 years, consort of MR. LUKE HOWARD of
Tuscumbia.
    State of Alabama--Madison County. County Court. WILLIAM VEITCH,
administrator of ANDREW D. VEITCH, deceased.
    Circuit Court of Madison County, Alabama
    RODAH HORTON and other
        versus
    ELIZABETH BROCK, administratrix, and the heirs of REUBEN BROCK,
deceased. ELIZABETH and the minor heirs are non-residents.
    County Court of Madison County, Alabama.
    WILLIAM H. CAMPBELL, one the administrators of THOMAS HART,
deceased.
    JOHN HARDIE, administrator of JEPTHE BEAKEY, deceased.

October 23, 1829
    Died on the 24th of September at JUDGE MARTIN's on Coosawatie,
in the 28th year of his age, GEORGE W. M'GEHEE, Professor of Mathematics
in the University of Georgia. Received his appointment in August and
with his family was returning from Pulaski, Tennessee where he formerly
resided, to take up his permanent residence in Athens, Georgia. Attacked
with a violent fever in Cherokee Nation to which was subsequently added
jaundice. Left an amiable and interesting widow and an orphan son.

October 30, 1829
    Died in this county on Monday the 19th instant after a short
illness, MRS. PARMELA DRAKE, consort of MR. ANDREW DRAKE aged 42 years,
leaving a husband and 8 children. Lynchburg Virginian please copy.

November 13, 1829
    THOMAS J. SUMNER and JAMES PENN, law partners.
    Died in Tuscumbia Wednesday evening 23rd of September, DR. WILLIAM
CLAY, native of East Tennessee and aged about 32. Has lived amongst
us as a physician for 6 years...Mason...left a widow.

In Mooresville, Alabama (Limestone County) on Sunday night last, MRS. MARY THACH, consort of MR. THOMAS H. THACH, merchant of that place and daughter of CAPT. BENJAMIN PEETE of Limestone County.

November 27, 1829
Married in this town Tuesday evening last by REV. WILLIAM McMAHAN, MR. BULLOCK B. MITCHELL to MISS REBECCA WILLIAMS, daughter of THOMAS H. WILLIAMS, Esq. of East Tennessee.
Died at the residence of DOCT. TATE in Limestone County on 23rd instant MR. WILLIAM B. SCRUGGS in the 34th year of his age...
In this place, on Monday the 16th instant after a short illness, MR. THOMAS RATHER in his 27th year.
HENRY F. SCRUGGS and THOMPSON M. RECTOR--attorneys-at-law, Jackson County, Alabama
County Court of Madison County, Alabama.
MARGARET HARPER, executrix of DANIEL HARPER, deceased

December 11, 1829
Married in Tuscaloosa Thursday evening the 26th ult. by REV. ROBERT CUNNINGHAM, MR. ERASMUS WALKER, editor of the Intelligencer to MISS ANN P. CHILDRESS (not there)
Died at Lexington, Kentucky on the 25th ult. HON. THOMAS B. REED, Senator in the Congress of the United States from the State of Mississippi.

December 18, 1829
Married on Tuesday evening the 8th by REV. T. PERRIEN, MR. WILLIAM E. COLLIER to MRS. JANE O. SLAUGHTER, both of Triana (volume 141, page 26)
ELIZABETH JONES (nee ELIZ. COWDEN), executrix of OBADIAH JONES (born 1763 in North Carolina; died 1825 in Madison County), deceased. Offers house and lot at auction. (ancestors of MRS. VANDAMAN, Rosedale, Mississippi; sketch in Owen's varies greatly; says born in Virginia 1783 and married 1810 instead of 1802)

December 25, 1829
LEARCHUS VANHOOK, administrator of EDWARD W. COSBY, deceased. Madison County.

January 1, 1850
Married on Thursday the 24th instant in Courtland (Lawrence County) by REV. HUGH BARR, JOHN J. COLEMAN (son of JOHN and ELIZABETH (WALKER) COLEMAN; see THOS FAY), Esq., Editor of this paper to MISS EMELINE R. WILLIAMS of that place.
Died on Sunday the 13th ult. at his father's residence in Madison County in his 33rd year, MAJOR SHUBAL STEARNS WELLBORN of Jackson County, Alabama. Plain, intelligent, upright citizen...member of our last legislature from Jackson County. Firm Republican. Affectionate husband. Severely afflicted for last nine months with a pulmonary affection. Left an affectionate wife and aged parents. Augusta Chronicle and Georgia Courier copy.
At his residence in Jackson County, Alabama at 1 o'clock in the morning of the 16th instant MAJ. WILLIE COTTON of a disease of the breast. Emigrated thither from North Carolina about 10 years since... left wife and several small children.... Tabroro, North Carolina "Free Press" copy.
Died at Brandenburg, his residence, December 18th after a protracted illness, PATRICK HENRY DARBY, Esq., counsellor-at-law, formerly of Nashville and Frankfort. A man of genius and of considerable acquirements.
Departed this life at 11 o'clock on Sunday morning last, MRS. MARGARET PEEL, wife of MR. HUNTER PEEL of this county aged 45 years and 3 months of a violent pulmonary affection. Had been in delicate health for several years...a loving wife and affectionate mother. Had been married nearly 27 years. Leaves a husband and 10 children.
State of Alabama--Limestone County. ISAAC SKILLERN, surviving executor of WILLIAM GULLIFORD (ancestor of MRS. W. R. CARTER, Minneapolis, 1961), deceased.

January 8, 1830
    Died on the 4th instant at the residence of ARTHUR F. HOPKINS, Esq. in his 33rd year, JOHN P. CARTER, Esq. after a protracted illness.... The widow and orphan, though far distant, were objects of his tender solicitude...native of North Carolina from which state he but recently removed....
    Died on Saturday the 2nd instant after a short but painful illness occasioned by wounds received from the accidental bursting of a musket, FRANCIS B. BASSETT aged about 22 years, a native of Baltimore. Had been a resident of our town but a short time.... The Guards resolved to wear crape on the left arm for 30 days in respect.
    Died of a pulmonary consumption on the 19th instant at the residence of MRS. CALLAWAY in the county of Bedford, CALCHILL MENNIS aged 33 years, late a member of the Convention of Virginia.

January 15, 1830
    JOHN K. DUNN, auctioneer
    State of Alabama--Morgan County.
    JAMES S. TURRENTINE, executor of the will of NANCY TURRENTINE deceased, filed accounts and vouchers. December 30, 1829.

January 22, 1830
    Died at the residence of COL. THOMAS G. PERCY, 10 miles from Huntsville, on the 12th instant DR. SAMUEL BROWN, late Professor of Theory and Practice of Medicine in Transylvania University. Was in 61st year of his age; occupied many and important relations in society. A polished gentleman, a scholar...etc.
    DR. ALEXANDER ERSKINE and DR. EDMUND IRBY drew up resolutions on the death of DR. SAMUEL BROWN.
    Died in this town on Sunday last of a pulmonary affection, MR. JACOB BARKMAN, originally from Maryland but for many years past, a resident of this place.... Let his distant friends then repose in confidence that tears of regret have flowed over his lonely grave. (see our volume 100, page 37 for his will)
    On Monday the 18th instant at the residence of her father, CAPT. ELI HAMMEND (HAMMOND) in this county, after a protracted illness of 18 months, MRS. SUSAN C. M'LARAN, wife of MR. JAMES M'LARAN aged 23 years.
    State of Alabama--Morgan County.
    THOMAS CROW, administrator of DAVID CROW, deceased.
    JOHN MORRIS, administrator of ROBERT J. MORRIS, deceased.

January 29, 1830
    Married on Tuesday evening the 12th instant by REV. JOHN MORGAN (Cumberland Presbyterian), PAUL HILDRETH, Esq. of Athens (Limestone County) to MISS ELIZA OTEY, daughter of the late CAPT. WALTER OTEY of this county. (volume 147, page 33)

February 5, 1830
    Died in this town on Sunday night last the 31st ult. after a lingering illness, MR. LAWRENCE R. WARREN, a native of Ireland and for many years a citizen of this place.
    State of Alabama--Morgan County.
    HORATIO PHILPOTT and GEORGE W. CRABB, administrators of THOMAS D. CRABB, deceased.

February 12, 1830
    Died at his residence in Brownsborough on the 8th instant in his 40th year, GRANT TAYLOR, Esq., a U.S. Pensioner. Severely wounded at the battle of Emuckfaw on the 22 of January 1814, which wound was the immediate cause of his death. Left a wife and 6 children....
    State of Alabama--Morgan County.
    PETER STOVEALL, executor of the will of FEATHERSTON WALDEN, deceased.

February 19, 1830
    Died at his residence in this county on Saturday last of dropsy, JOHN M. LEAKE, Esq. aged about 59. He was one of the earliest settlers here and for several years represented Madison County in the House of Representatives of Alabama.

Died in this county on Friday last, MR. JAMES FRAZIER, an old and respectable resident.

Died in Murfreesborough (Tennessee) on Wednesday evening the 3rd instant COL. JOHN NELSON of Washington County in his 42nd year. Member of the Legislature of this state and was returning home from a late session when taken ill.... Was county surveyor for many years, was also Colonel Commandant of regiment in which he lived. (From Nashville Banner)

February 26, 1830

Married on Thursday evening the 11th instant by REV. D. P. BESTOR, MR. WILLIAM SWINNEY of Tennessee to MISS ELIZABETH, daughter of MR. EDWARD NEWELL of LaGrange, Alabama (Franklin County)

On Tuesday evening, the 17th instant by REV. ROBERT DONNEL, MR. ROBERT TINNIN, Principal of Athens Male Academy to MISS MARGARET S. TATE, eldest daughter of DOCT. WADDY TATE, all of Limestone County. (see will in Lauderdale County, volume 104, page 41)

On the 10th instant in Franklin County, Kentucky at the house of A. ALEXANDER, Esq. by REV. J. T. EDGAR, the REV. JOHN POPE TROTTER of Lexington to MISS PAMELA BRASHEAR of Mercer County, Kentucky.

March 5, 1830

Married in Augusta, Gerogia on the 2nd ult. CAPT. WILLIAM WEEDON (1812 sol) of this county to MRS. JANE E. WATKINS of that city.

Died in Triana Tuesday the 23rd after a short but distressing illness, MRS. MARIAN I. BANKS, consort of MR. LAWRENCE S. BANKS and daughter of the late MR. FREDERICK JAMES of this county. She died at the early age of 19 years and left a disconsolate husband...

March 12, 1830

Married on Wednesday evening last by REV. MR. KENDRICK, MR. ALEXANDER S. MALONE to MISS ELIZABETH, daughter of the late NICHOLAS READY, all of this county (married March 10; volume 48, page 13)

State of Alabama--Morgan County

NICHOLAS LEWIS and JOHN C. NUNALLY, administrators of HARDIN P. LEWIS, deceased.

March 19, 1830

Married at Tuscaloosa on Friday evening the 5th instant by REV. MR. KENNON, LEVIN POWELL, Esq. late President of the Senate of Alabama to MISS JANE MOODY, both of that place (not recorded in Tuscaloosa County)

Died on the 10th instant in Lawrence County, Alabama COL. BENJAMIN B(RAUCH) JONES, a worthy member of the Methodist Episcopal Church and one of the trustees of LaGrange College, (married December 31, 1818 Nashville, MARTHA, daughter of JOHN HAYWOOD. She later married DR. AUGUSTINE BURKET WASHINGTON. See letter from MRS. ALBERT EWING, who worked up a sak line for a client)

March 26, 1830

State of Alabama--Morgan County.

JAMES LYNN, administrator of the estate of EDLEY LYNN, deceased.
BANYAN PAYNE, executor of the will of NANCY PAYNE, deceased.

JOHN R. GIBSON, one of the executors of will of JOHN GIBSON, deceased.

April 2, 1830

Married on Thursday evening, the 25th instant by REV. WILLIAM KENDRICK, MR. WILLIAM GORMLEY to MISS MARY ANN FEENEY, all of this town (volume 127, page 9 "FENNEY")

Died in Athens (Limestone County) on Tuesday the 23rd of March, MRS. MARGARET HARRISON, widow of the late COL. MICHAEL HARRISON in her 65th year, after a few days illness.... Left four daughters.

April 9, 1830

Died in Mooresville, Alabama (Limestone County) on Saturday evening, March 27, MR. WILLIAM VINCENT, brother of MR. AMOS VINCENT of that place.

April 16, 1830
     Died on the 10th instant in this town, MRS. MARY TALBOT, consort
of MR. CLAYTON TALBOT in the 60th year of her age. Her illness was
painful. Was a Presbyterian about three years....
          State of Alabama--Morgan County.
          JOSEPH LANE, executor of JOSEPH LANE, SEN., deceased.

April 23, 1830
     Married in this place on Thursday evening 15th instant by REV.
MR. KENDRICK, MR. WILLIAM TABLER to MISS ANN EVERSOLL, all of this
town. (He was son of MICHAEL and MARY ANN (ROBERTS) TABLER--w and
ann later moved to Marshall County--see footnote volume 151, page 36)

April 30, 1830
     Married near Courtland (Lawrence County) on the 15th by REV.
H(UGH) BARR, MR. RICHARD PURYEAR to MRS. MARIA WOODFIN. (ALFORD A. in
WPA copy of marriages; MARIAH B. in marriage record. There was an
ALFRED "PURRUR" in 1830 in Lawrence County; 1 m-5 1 m 10-15 1 m 20-31
1 f 5-10 1 f 30-40)

May 7, 1830
     Died at his residence in this vicinity on Sunday morning the 2nd
instant in his 51st year, THOMAS TURNER, Esq. a native of Greenville
County, Virginia but for the last 10 years of this state...Richmond
Enquirer please copy. He had but recently returned from Virginia where
he had united himself to a most excellent lady.
          State of Alabama--Morgan County.
          DUDLEY BROOKS, deceased. MILTON BROOKS, administrator.
          J. L. OWENS, administrator of EDMUND PATRICK, deceased.
          JAMES B. McNOSKEY (McCROSKEY?), administrator of JEREMIAH HOOD,
deceased.

May 7, 1830
     Died, THOMAS TURNER, Esq. on May 2, a native of Greenville County,
Virginia but for the last ten years a citizen of this state. Was in
51st year of his age.
     Married on Wednesday evening last by HON. JOHN M. TAYLOR, THOMAS
J. SUMNER, Esq., Editor of the Democrat, to MISS LOUISA A. LANIER,
daughter of REV. WILLIAM LANIER. (see volume 6, page 45 for her
obituary; volume 103, page 57)

July 31, 1830
     Married on 20th instant by REV. JOHN MORGAN, the rt. REV. SAMUEL M.
COWAN to MISS NANCY E. daughter of BENJAMIN CLEMENTS of Lincoln County,
Tennessee.
     Died at Tyree's Springs on 20th instant MR. GEORGE W. SMITH.

August 21, 1830
     Died at Blount's Springs on 29th July, DR. WILLIAM AUGUSTUS KING,
Professor of Chemistry at the University of Alabama aged about 27.

August 28, 1830
     Died at the residence of her father, MR. BENJAMIN S. JONES, on
17th instant MISS PRUDENCE E. JONES in her 19th year.

September 4, 1830
     Died on Saturday last, MRS. PEETE, aged consort of CAPT. BENJAMIN
PEETE, of this county.
     Married on 26th ult. by REV. GABRIEL CHALON of Mobile, MR. JAMES H.
WEAKLEY of Florence to MISS ELLEN M. DONEGAN of this place.
     Married on Thursday (or Tuesday?) evening the 31st ult. by REV.
JOHN MORGAN, MR. WILLIAM WILSON to MISS AMANDA M. RICE, both of this
place.
     Married on Tuesday the 17th near Cahawba, MR. THOMAS H. WILEY,
Editor of Tuscaloosa Intelligencer to MISS LOUISA PERRY of Dallas
County.

September 11, 1830
     Died on 31st August, MRS. MARY HARRIS HARTON, wife of REV. JOHN P.
HARTON and daughter of CAPTAIN PEYTON POWELL of Alabama of a violent
bilious fever, which she bore with patience and fortitude.

October 9, 1830
Married in this town Tuesday, the 5th instant by REV. JOHN ALLAN,
MR. WILLIAM H. POPE to MISS JANE R. daughter of MR. WILLIAM PATTON,
all of this town.
On same evening by REV. JAMES ROWE, MR. JOHN L. KEMPER to MRS.
ELIZABETH BROOKS, all of this county.

October 16, 1830
Died on 2nd instant at his residence in Morgan County in his 63rd
year, CAPT. GREEN BOULDIN. He was a native of Henry County, Virginia
and for some years prior to his decease, resided in this state. Having
been favored with a large family of descendants, he departed this life.

October 23, 1830
Married on 17th by REV. WILBURN ALLEN, MR. WILLIAM HENRY SALE of
this county to MISS FRANCES R. HARRIS, daughter of MR. JOHN HARRIS of
Limestone County.

October 30, 1830
Died in this county Monday evening 18th instant MRS. ANN CHEATHAM,
aged 48, consort of the late WILLIAM CHEATHAM, Methodist.

November 6, 1830
Died in this town Thursday morning last, THOMAS HUMES, Esq.
aged about 54. Was a citizen of this place, about 12 years.

November 13, 1830
Married on Tuesday evening 2nd instant at Bellefont (Jackson
County, Alabama) by REV. WILLIAM POTTER, REV. TIMOTHY ROOT to MISS LUCY
JANE PATTON, of Lincoln County, Kentucky. (In 1850 Census, one TIMOTHY
aged 48 born in Vermont, wife Mary 45 born in Connecticut. LEWIS FAMILY
OF AMERICA "TIMOTHY ROOT of Tuskegee married LUCY PATTON, daughter of
WM. and SARAH THOMAS (LEWIS) PATTON.)
Died on Saturday a.m. last MR. ROGER STEPHENS, native of Ireland,
formerly of New York, but for many years a resident of this place.

November 27, 1830
Died at the residence of COL. LeROY POPE on 23rd instant, MRS.
JANE SALE, aged upwards of 80 years.

December 11, 1830
Married on 2nd instant by REV. MR. PERRIN, MR. ALBERT I (or J)
SADLER to MISS POCOHONTAS FRANKLIN, all of Triana.

January 8, 1831
Married on Wednesday last by REV. JOHN MORGAN, MR. OLIVER D. SLEDGE,
merchant of Meridianville to MISS EDITH SHOTWELL, daughter of REUBEN
SHOTWELL, all of this county.

February 5, 1831
Died on Sunday evening last aged about 70 years, PETER FRANCISCO,
Esq. sergeant-at-arms to House of Delegates and a Revolutionary Hero,
justly celebrated for his personal prowess.
Died at the residence of MAJ. J. P. HICKMAN in this county on 19th
instant MRS. ELIZABETH RICE, consort of MR. JOEL RICE of Alabama.
Died at the residence of his father in this county on Saturday
29th ult. MR. WILLIAM ALLISON, in 23rd year of his age. Surviving
relatives are consoled....

March 5, 1831
Married on Wednesday evening last by REV. J. B. McFERRIN, MR. JAMES
A. JOHNSON of Franklin County to MISS ELIZABETH ELLETT, daughter of
MR. RICHARD ELLETT of this county.
Married on Thursday evening (3rd instant) by REV. JOHN ALLAN,
MR. WILLIAM PATTON to MISS MARY ANN MILLER, daughter of MR. MARTIN
MILLER, all of this place.

March 19, 1831
Died at his residence in this county on 9th instant HUNTER PEEL,
Esq. a native of England, but for many years a highly respectable citizen

of this county, MR. PEEL was a man of genious and of no ordinary
attainments, and held the appointment of county surveyor for many
years, which part he filed to the period of his death.

March 26, 1831
        Died at his residence in this vicinity on 8th instant after an
illness of two weeks, MR. JOSHUA FALCONER, aged about 45 years....
        Died on 18th last, of a cancer in the breast, LUCY NEAL, consort
of WILLIAM GRAY, SR. of this county in her 55th year of age.

April 16, 1831
        Died at his residence in Madison County on 7th instant at an
advanced age, WILLIAM MOORE, SEN., Esq. SQUIRE MOORE emigrated to this
state from North Carolina and had for many years previous to his death
resided in vicinity of this state.
        Died recently at his residence in this county, CAPT. ISAAC JACKSON,
formerly of South Carolina, but for many years a respectable citizen of
this place.
        Died recently at LaGrange, Franklin County, DR. SIDNEY S. PRINCE
of that place.

April 23, 1831
        Married in Washington City on 5th instant by REV. MR. MATTHEWS,
COL. FRANCIS W. ARMSTRONG, of Alabama to MISS ANN M. MILLARD, daughter
of MR. MILLARD, merchant of the former place. Note: he was son of
JAS and SUANNAH (WELLS) ARMSTRONG. His 1st wife was ELIZ. C. AYLETT
born 1805 in King Wm. County, Virginia; died 31 August 1823 at Knox
County, Tennessee. ANN was 2nd wife. She married 2. GEN. PERSIFER SMITH.
After his death, she entered a convent and became a Mother Superior.
        Married on Thursday evening last by REV. MR. ROWE, DR. JOHN Y.
BASSETT of this place, formerly of Baltimore to MISS ISAPHOENA P.
THOMPSON, daughter of DR. ASA THOMPSON, late of this county.

May 14, 1831
        Married on Tuesday evening, 10th instant by the REV. JAMES ROWE,
MR. JESSE G. SCOTT, merchant of this town to MISS AGATHA P. RICE,
daughter of JOEL RICE, Esq. of this county.
        Died at her residence in the vicinity of this place on the morning
of the 6th instant after a short illness, MRS. MARY COLEMAN in the
65th year of her age.

June 4, 1831
        Married on 26th ult. by HON. S. CHAPMAN, DOCT. A(LFRED) G. VAUGHAN
to MISS MARY O. WALTON, daughter of MAJ. ROBERT WALTON, all of this
county.

June 11, 1831
        Died in this county on 9th instant after a lingering illness,
PHILIP A. FOOTE, Esq. aged about 38; for many years a highly respected
citizen of this town.

July 30, 1831
        Married on Tuesday evening last by REV. MR. THOMPSON, MR. JACOB
SIVELY to MISS SARAH ANN SCRUGGS, all of this county.
        Died at his residence in this county on Saturday the 23rd instant
at 3 o'clock p.m. after a short and severe illness, JAMES McCARTNEY,
Esq. in the 48th year of his age, leaving a wife, two children and
many relations.
        Died at Chunn's Springs, Morgan County on Tuesday last, the 27th
instant after a lingering illness, DR. JOHN R. LUCAS, of Limestone
County.
        Died at her father's residence on Thursday afternoon last, after
an illness of four weeks, MISS PAMELIA B. SCRUGGS, daughter of GROSS
SCRUGGS, Esq. of this county; she recently finished her education at
Salem, North Carolina and was just entering her 17th year.

August 6, 1831
        Married on Thursday last, 4th instant in this place by REV. HUGH
BARR, DAVID A. SMITH, Esq. of Courtland to MISS ELIZA E. ALLAN,
daughter of REV. JOHN ALLAN of this town.

August 20, 1831
    Died in the vicinity of Meridanville on Tuesday, 9th instant
MRS. ELIZABETH WATKINS, consort of MR. ALBERT WATKINS in the 25th year
of her age, after an illness of 10 or 12 days of bilious fever.
    Died on Friday evening 12th instant after a short illness in his
68th year, FLEMING JORDAN, Esq., an old and respectable inhabitant of
this county.

August 27, 1831
    Married on Tuesday evening last, 23rd instant by REV. JOHN B.
McFERRIN, MR. PEYTON E. WHEELER of Huntsville to MISS MARIA VEITCH of
this county.

September 3, 1831
    Married on Tuesday 16th ult. by ELDER JOSEPH LANE, DANIEL FISHER,
Esq. of Murfreesboro, Tennessee to MISS SARAH MARGARET F., second
daughter of COL. FRANCIS DANCY of Decatur.
    Married on Tuesday evening, 30th ulto. by REV. THOMAS M. KING,
MR. WILLIAM JONES to MISS MARIA L. C. BRANDON, daughter of COL. WILLIAM
BRANDON, all of this county.

September 10, 1831
    Married Thursday, 4th ult. by REV. FIFE, MR. FONTAINE C. BOSTON,
of Alabama to MISS CYNTHIA B. RAGLAND, daughter of MR. DUDLEY RAGLAND,
of Goochland County, Virginia. (From Richmond Enquirer)
    Married on Tuesday evening last by REV. MR. MALONE, MR. JOHN C.
WEAVER to MISS ANN FORD, all of this county.
    Married on Thursday evening last by REV. JAMES ROWE, MR. GEORGE
MITCHELL to MISS EMILY PEEL, daughter of the late HUNTER PEEL, deceased,
all of this county.
    Died at the residence of her grandfather, in her 3rd year,
MARY SOPHIA, eldest child of JAMES MANNING, JR.
    Died at residence in this county, 24th of August, JAMES WIGGINS,
Esq. aged 58 years. He emigrated from Martin County, North Carolina
in the early settlement of this state and has ever since lived among
us.
    Died on Wednesday last at Bell Factory in this county JAMES, son
of GERMANICUS KENT, aged about 2 years.
    Died Thursday night the 25th of this month at the residence of
her father in this vicinity, MRS. MARGARET ANN W. ALEXANDER aged 21
years and 9 months, wife of EBENEZER ALEXANDER, Esq. and daughter of
HON. HU. L WHITE

September 17, 1831
    Died on Monday last at Blount Springs in this state, MAJOR WILLIAM
M. MARR, a respectable citizen of this town in his 49th year, MAJ. MARR
was born in Pittsylvania County, Virginia and emigrated to Tennessee
in the year 1798, where he married and resided more than twenty years.

September 24, 1831
    Married on Monday evening, 12th instant in Fayetteville, Tennessee
MR. NAPOLEON B. GARNER of Selma, Alabama to MISS ANN L. McCONNELL,
daughter of the late JOHN P. McCONNELL of the former place.
    Married on Tuesday evening, 20th instant by REV. JAMES ROWE,
MR. EDWIN DABBS of Limestone to MISS ELIZABETH LEWIS, daughter of
MR. CORBIN LEWIS of Madison County.
    Died on Wednesday, 21st instant after a lingering illness, MISS
ELIZA JULIA TATE in the 17th year of her age, 2nd daughter of CAPT.
WADDY TATE of Limestone County. Educated at MRS. DeVENDEL's Academy
in this town.

October 1, 1831
    Married on Tuesday, 13th ult. in Henry County, Tennessee COL.
JAMES W. CAMP of this town to MRS. MARY J. TATE of the former place.
    Died on 22nd. SARAH ELIZA. infant daughter of JARED L. SAMPLE,
aged 22 months, 11 days.

October 8, 1831
    Married on Tuesday evening last, 4th instant in this place by REV.
MR. COPP, MR. JOSEPH B. BRADFORD to MRS. MARTHA SMITH, daughter of MR.
WILLIAM PATTON, all of Huntsville.

Married in Greene County on 27th instant MR. ROBERT CARUTHERS to MISS BELINDA HATTER, both of Tuscaloosa.

Died recently in Limestone County, MR. THOMAS MATTHEWS, and a respectable and worthy citizen.

October 15, 1831
Married on Wednesday evening last at residence of MAJOR ROBERT WALTON in this county by REV. JOHN B. McFERRIN, JOHN R. H. ACKLEN of Huntsville, Sheriff of Madison County to MISS HAMLET H. CASH.

October 22, 1831
Married Tuesday evening 18th instant by REV. JOHN B. McFERRIN, MR. WILLIAM WITHROW to MISS MARY ANN MORRISS, all of this county.

Married on Thursday evening last by REV. J. B. McFERRIN, MR. LEWIS M. KENNARD to MISS CATHARINE SPENCE, daughter of MRS. JANE SPENCE all of this place.

Died on morning of 15th instant, MRS. HARRIET MOORE, wife of DR. DAVID MOORE of this county, daughter of the late JUDGE HAYWOOD of Tennessee, formerly of North Carolina and was born in the latter state on 23rd day of April, 1790. Educated in most approved schools of her native state. Remains will be entombed in the family burying ground of REV. JOHN MOORE, father of her husband.

October 29, 1831
Married Thursday evening last by REV. MR. COPP, COL. THOMAS McELDERRY of Morgan County to MRS. FRANCES S. EDMONDS. Also at the same time, MR. JOHN HENRY TURNER to MISS MARY B. TURNER, both ladies being daughters of SUGARS TURNER, Esq. of this county.

November 5, 1831
Married on 26th instant by REV. MR. SULLIVAN, CAPT. JAMES W. BOULDIN of Morgan County to MISS M(ARY) TABITHA J. HAMMOND, daughter of CAPT. ELI. HAMMOND of this city.

Married in Falmouth on Wednesday evening last by REV. E. C. McGUIRE, JAMES INNIS THORNTON, Esq., Secretary of State of Alabama, to MISS ANNE AMELIA, daughter of the late GOVERNOR GEORGE SMITH, Esq. of Dumfries.

November 19, 1831
Married on Wednesday evening last, 16th instant by REV. JAMES ROWE, MR. STERLING STAINBACK of Huntsville to MRS. MARIA F. PATTIE, daughter of MR. HARRISON OWENS of this county.

Married on Wednesday evening, 9th instant at the residence of MR. JOHN S. BROOKS in Morgan County, MR. WILLIAM B. PATTON to MISS ELIZABETH LEWIS, all of said county.

Died at Courtland, on 3rd instant, after illness of many months, MRS. MARIA D. BLUNT in 23rd year, wife of MR. HENRY R. BLUNT of that place and daughter of MR. BENJAMIN M. WILLIAMS of Marengo County.

Died on 28th ult. MRS. ISABELLA WATKINS, consort of MR. JAMES C. WATKINS in her 26th year.

December 10, 1831
Married in this place Thursday evening, 1st instant, by REV. THOMAS M. KING, MR. HENRY JORDAN to MISS MARIA A. GLASGOW, all of this county.

Married Thursday evening, 24th November by REV. DR. DELANEY, CHARLES INGERSOLL to SUSAN CATHARINE, only daughter of the late DR. SAMUEL BROWN of Alabama.

Died in Nashville, Tennessee a few days since, MR. ERNEST BENOIT, for many years a respectable citizen of this place. Note: His wife was FRANCES, daughter of HENRY and ELIZ. BELL. FRANCES born October 1, 1795.

December 17, 1831
Married Wednesday evening last by REV. JOHN H. THOMPSON, MR. SIMEON DOUGLASS of Mooresville to MISS MARY W. BROWN, daughter of HENRY BROWN of this county.

Died at his residence in this county on 5th instant HUME R. FIELD, in 59th year of age, formerly Judge of County Court of Tuscaloosa and for several years president trustee of University of Alabama.

January 14, 1832
Married on Thursday evening, 5th instant by W. GRAVES BOULDIN,
Esq. MR. MATTHEW DAVIS to MISS SARAH, daughter of MR. WILLIAM WALLS,
all of this county.

February 4, 1832
Married on Tuesday evening last by REV. JOHN ALLEN, MR. ROBERT
PATTON, merchant of Florence to MISS JANE, daughter of GEN. JOHN BRAHAN
of this place. On same evening by REV. ISAAC SHOOK, MR. WILLIAM SYDNOR
to MRS. ELIZABETH SPRAGUE of this place.
Died Tuesday evening, 31st instant after some weeks illness,
MRS. JANE R. POPE, consort of MR. WILLIAM H. POPE and eldest daughter
of WILLIAM PATTON of this place.

February 11, 1832
Married at Montevallo, Shelby County by REV. JOAB LAWLER, WILLIAM
ACKLEN, JR., Esq. of Huntsville, to MISS LOUISA H. KING of the former
place.
Married on 9th instant in this place, MR. JESSE JORDAN to MISS
MARGARET BRANDON, daughter of THOMAS BRANDON, Esq.
Died on 27th ult. in Limestone County, MR. WELBORN PHELPS.
Died on 7th instant, MRS. ELIZABETH McDANIEL, widow of the late
ARCHIBALD McDANIEL of Madison County (note: probably M cDONNELL)
Died on 2nd instant in St. Louis, formerly of Florence, MR. A. W. H.
CLIFTON, for many years a highly respected citizen of this place.

February 25, 1832
Married 2nd instant MR. ROBERT L. CLARK to MISS MARTHA MALONE,
daughter of MR. HARPER MALONE, all of this county.
Died on 19th instant at residence of his father in this county,
COL. REUBEN G. HEWLETT, esteemed citizen.

March 3, 1832
Died on 29th ult. MR. THOMAS CAVETTE and on 1st suddenly, MR.
WILLIAM MOORE, JR. both worthy citizens of this county.

March 17, 1832
Married in Davidson County, Tennessee on 6th instant DR. JOHN P.
FORD of Florence, Alabama to MISS ANN S. JEFFERSON.
Died on 14th instant MR. PHILIP FLANAGAN, a resident of this
place.
Died at Montgomery, Alabama on 1st, MR. JESSE D. NOBLE.

March 31, 1832
Died at Oak Grove in Madison County, Alabama on 23rd of March,
MATTHEW H. VINING, son of JOHN VINING, Esq. aged 20 years, 11 months,
18 days.

April 7, 1832
Died on 30th ult. at his residence in this county, HENRY RIGNEY
an old and respectable citizen, who came to his death from a stab
inflicted by a man named KENNEDY who is now in jail.

April 21, 1832
Married on Sunday evening, 15th instant by REV. ASHLEY B. ROZELL,
MR. ARCHIBALD CAMPBELL of this county to amiable and accomplished MISS
MARY ELLISON of Huntsville.

May 19, 1832
Married in Davidson County, Tennessee on 10th instant MR. PHILIP
SCHETTER to MISS VIRGINIA A. WHARTON.

May 26, 1832
Married Thursday evening last by REV. JAMES ROWE, MR. JOSHUA BARKER
to MISS LUCY MARIA MASON, both of this place.
Died Friday morning 18th instant at residence of MR. ALLEN STEGAR
in this county, MISS TEMPERANCE E. WILLIAMS in her 20th year of age.

June 2, 1832
Died on Wednesday morning last on 30th ult. at residence of his brother in this place, MR. JAMES POPE, aged about 60.

June 9, 1832
Died on 28th of May at his residence in this vicinity, MR. WILLIAM WATKINS, SEN. aged 76 years. Native of Virginia, but at early period of his life moved to Georgia, whence he removed to west about 23 years ago. Kind and affectionate husband and father (From Courtland Herald June 1st)

June 16, 1832
Died on Friday, 3rd instant at his residence in this county, CAPT. EDWARD HARRIS aged about 40 years, an old and respected citizen. (Re-checked and age is 40, but a descendant says this is wrong--that he was supposed to be 56 and born in Amherst County, Virginia)
Died on 10th, MRS. MARTHA G. RATHBONE, consort of RUFUS C. RATHBONE, Esq. of this county. Native of Warren County, North Carolina and resided for many years in Kershaw District, South Carolina. Note: In 1835 he married ELIZ. MASON. He died 1842 in 62 or 67th year and she married 1843 ELI DEAN. In 1843 ELIZ. DEAN and RATHBONE children were in Monroe County, Mississippi. See our volume 76.

June 23, 1832
Died Thursday last in this place after lingering illness, THOMAS J. SUMNER, Esq., Senior Editor of the "Democrat." Left wife and one child.
Died on 27th of May in Sullivan County, Tennessee HON. JOHN RHEA, aged 79.

June 30, 1832
Married in Fayetteville, Tennessee 25th instant by REV. MR. COWAN, MR. HENRY L. BROWN of Huntsville to MISS LOUISA P. MOSELEY, eldest daughter of CAPT. W. H. MOSELEY, of Mooresville (Alabama).

July 14, 1832
Died on 27th instant in New Orleans, after illness of four days, MR. DAVID L. WAYLAND of this place aged 27.

July 21, 1832
Married Thursday 21st instant at residence of COL. WILLIAM HODGES in Lawrence County, Alabama by REV. CARSON P. REID, the REV. ROBERT DONNEL to MISS CLARISSA W. LINDLEY, late Principal of Oakville Female Academy.
Died at Bedford, Pennsylvania on 1st instant MR. JAMES I. HOGE, late of House of P. T. MASTIN and Company and for 14 years a resident of this town.

July 28, 1832
Married near Courtland on Tuesday 17th instant by REV. MR. BESTER, MR. WILLIAM V(ERMILIA) CHARDAVOYNE to MARTHA, daughter of the late WILLIAM WATKINS, Esq.

August 25, 1832
Died on 17th instant after protracted illness, MRS. CAROLINE R. H. SPENCER, wife of MR. SAMUEL SPENCER of this place.

September 15, 1832
Died on Sunday last, 10th instant, at his residence three miles from this place, MAJOR WILLIAM JONES aged about 55 years, formerly of Virginia and for a number of years a citizen of this county, Richmond Enquirer requested to copy.

September 29, 1832
Married Wednesday evening, 19th instant by REV. MR. DOUGLAS, MR. WILLIAM W. FLOYD to MISS MARGARET ANN FRIER of Limestone County.
Married on Tuesday evening last, 25th instant by REV. AASHLEY B. ROZELL, MR. CLEMENT WOODWARD to MISS MARTHA ANN MARTIN, daughter of MR. WOODY MARTIN, all of this town.

October 6, 1832
      Married on 13th September by W. GRAVES BOULDIN, Esq. MR. RAINARD A.
WOOLLY of Limestone County to MISS ELMIRA ROBERTS, daughter of MR.
RICHARD ROBERTS of this county.
      Died at Red Sulphur Springs, Virginia on 19th instant in her 49th
year, MRS. MARY SCRUGGS, wife of GROSS SCRUGGS, Esq. of this county.
Lynchburg papers please copy.

October 20, 1832
      Died in New Orleans on 26th September after a few days illness,
MR. HUGH FINDLEY, late a merchant of South Florence.
      Died in Tuscumbia on 7th instant MR. LUKE HOWARD.
      Died near Montgomery on 5th instant MR. DAVID R. ALSOBROOK.
      Married 26th ult. near Greensborough by the REV. MR. WESTMORELAND,
COL. JAMES B. HOLMAN of Marengo County to MISS CHARLOTTE H. OSBORNE of
Greene County (note: See will of JAS. B. HOLMAN in Marengo County,
Alabama; see our volume 29, page 35; volume 28, page 28)

November 3, 1832
      Died in this county 25th January last in 87th year of his age,
MR. JEREMIAH GOGERS, a soldier of the Revolution. Honest, upright and
highly respectable citizen.

November 17, 1832
      Married Tuesday evening on 6th instant by REV. MR. SULLIVAN,
DR. GEORGE R. WHARTON to MISS ELIZA P. HARRIS, daughter of MR. RICHARD
HARRIS, all of this county.

December 1, 1832
      Married on 8th November by REV. F. K. TALMAGE, MAJ. FELIX A. M.
SHERROD of Alabama to MISS MARGARET McGRAN of Augusta (George Courier)
      Married on 28th by REV. JAMES W. ALLEN, MR. ALBERT DANCY to MISS
JANE DANCY, daughter of COL. DAVID DANCY, all of Limestone County.
Note: ALBERT GALLATIN DANCY and JANE EATON DANCY were cousins, says a
descendant, FENTON M. DANCY, 107 Green Street, Decatur, Ha. July, 1956.

December 22, 1832
      Married on Wednesday last, 19th instant by REV. JOHN ALLAN,
MR. GEORGE COX, JR. to MISS ELIZABETH PATTESON, both of this place.
      Died at his residence of consumption, JAMES TAYLOR, Esq. of house
of MESSRS. TAYLOR and WOOD, merchants of this city. Has long resided
among us.

December 29, 1832
      Married 15th last in Morgan County, Alabama, MR. CHARLES M.
M'LARAN of Tuscumbia to MISS ELIZA THURMAN.
      Married on Thursday, 20th instant in Morgan County by JOHN S.
BROOKS, Esq. MR. ANDREW B. PATTON to MISS ELIZABETH O. FOWLER, both of
Morgan County.

January 5, 1833
      Died at Louisville, Kentucky HON. THOMAS T. CRITTENDEN, Judge of
5th Judicial District in Kentucky, formerly a resident of this place.

January 26, 1833
      Married Friday evening, 18th instant by REV. JOHN ALLEN, D.D.,
DOCT. EDMOND IRBY to MISS MARY G. MASTIN, only daughter of MR. FRANCIS T.
MASTIN, all of this town.

February 2, 1833
      Married Tuesday evening last by REV. JOHN ALLAN, MR. GEORGE I.
WEAVER of Huntsville to MRS. MARTHA H. McCARTNEY, all of this county.

February 9, 1833
      Married Tuesday evening last, 5th instant by REV. ISAAC W. SULLIVAN,
MR. GEORGE H. GRAHAM to MISS JULIA ANN, daughter of THOMAS CAIN, Esq.
all of this place.

February 16, 1833

Married on 6th instant by REV. J. H. THOMPSON, MR. WILLIAM VALIANT to MISS MARGARET HUSSEY, all of this county.

Married on 8th instant by REV. BRADSHAW, DR. W. W. HUMPHREYS to MISS MARGARET S., daughter of MAJ. ROBERT WALTON.

Married on 7th instant DR. H. DENT to MISS ANN R. LONGSTREET.

February 23, 1833

Married on 16th instant by REV. MR. ROZWELL, MR. JOHN P. HARRISON of Limestone County to MISS MARTHA A. FOWLKS of this county.

Married in Florence on Thursday evening 14th instant by REV. MR. SLOSS, SYDNEY C(HERRY) POSEY, Esq, Editor of Florence Gazette to MISS HARRIET CALISTA DePRIEST. Note: We have Bible record. He was son of JESSE HAMILTON and ELEANOR (BROOKS) POSEY; born May 4, 1803, died December 22, 1868 in Florence, Alabama. HARRIET was daughter of DR. HORATIO DePRIEST.

Died on 20th instant ELVIRA ELIZABETH, daughter of CAPT. DANIEL B. TURNER, aged 16 months.

March 2, 1833

Died on 22nd instant at his residence three miles from this place in his 43rd year. CAPT. WILLIAM CLARKE, native of Chesterfield County, Virginia and for last 14 years a citizen of North Alabama. Kind husband and father.

March 9, 1833

Married on 28th February by REV. JAMES ROWE, LEVI HYNDS to MISS ANN R. HUNT, all of this county.

Died yesterday morning after illness of 1½ days of scarlet fever, ARTHUR HOPKINS, son of MR. JAMES G. BIRNEY of this town, aged about 6 years.

Died in this town on 27th of February, DOCT. JAMES ROANE.

March 16, 1833

Married on 12th instant by REV. J. BUTCHER, MR. DAVID M. DANCY, minister of the Gospel in the Methodist Church of Morgan County to MISS JANE E. MASON, daughter of GEORGE MASON, Esq. of this county.

March 30, 1833

Died at the residence of ELI HAMMOND, JAMES TROTTER aged about 55; native of New Galloway in Scotland. Emigrated to the United States about 34 years since and settled in Petersburg, Virginia, where he resided for some years. Later came to Tennessee, thence to this state, where he was a teacher.

Died on 28th instant GEORGIANA, daughter of MR. GEORGE LYNES of this place, aged 2 years, 11 months.

Died on 20th, JOHN TAYLOR, son of JARED I. SAMPLE, aged 9 months 6 days.

April 6, 1833

Married Wednesday evening last by REV. ROBERT DONNELL, COL. CYRUS S. AIKEN to MISS MILDRED NOBLE, both of Triana.

Died Friday, 29th instant of scarlet fever, JULIA POPE, youngest daughter of MR. B. S. POPE, aged about 3 years.

Died on 30th instant MYRA LOUISA, daughter of E. R. WALLACE, aged 6 weeks.

Died on 31st, SARAH E. M., daughter of MRS. L. L. PATTON, aged about 8.

Died on Monday night last, MARY MARGARET, daughter of MR. GEORGE LYNES, aged 8 years 2 months.

April 13, 1833

Married Wednesday evening last by REV. TURNER SAUNDERS, MR. WILLIAM MANNING to MISS ELIZABETH, daughter of MR. WILLIAM WEEDON, all of this county.

Died on 1st, MISS SARAH H. CALVERT in 14th year, daughter of MR. J. S. CALVERT of this county.

Died suddenly at his residence in this county on 30th instant MR. JOHN AMONIT in his 82nd year of his age. Thus another Revolutionary spirit has sunk to rest.

Died on 11th ult. MARTHA R. infant daughter of J. G. BIRNEY.

April 20, 1833
Married on 2nd instant DR. SAMUEL B. MALONE of U.S. Navy to
MISS ELVIRA ANTOINETTE, only daughter of COL. JOHN D. BIBB of Columbus,
Mississippi.
Married on 9th in this county by REV. JOHN Y. BALLAD, DR. GEORGE D.
MORRIS, late of Baltimore to MISS MARTHA W. RAGSDALE of Tennessee.
Died in this town Wednesday evening 17th instant CAPT. MANNING
CARPENTER in his 35th year, Cincinnati Gazette please copy.

April 30, 1833
Died on 16th, MRS. MARY M. HUTCHISON in 29th year, consort of
ANDERSON HUTCHISON, Esq. of this place. Afflicted since 1828 with
chronic disease. Member of Presbyterian Church; wife, mother, daughter.
Died on 7th, at 7 p.m. at her residence in Huntsville, MRS.
ELIZABETH, consort of W. L. HATHAWAY in her 31st year. Member of
Methodist Church.

May 7, 1833
Married on Wednesday evening last, 1st instant by REV. FINIS E.
HARRIS, MR. DANIEL M. GRAY of Limestone County to MISS ISABELLA,
daughter of MR. WILLIAM MUNROE of this county.
Died Tuesday, the 16th of April near Danville, Pittsylvania
County, Virginia, MRS. WHITMOLE TUNSTALL, eldest daughter of MR.
JOHN F. GONEKE in her 18th year.
Died at Female Academy of MR. and MRS. M'CAY in this place on 27th
instant, SARAH ELIZABETH, eldest daughter of MR. WILLIAM L. HATHAWAY
in her 10th year.
Died on Saturday the 20th at residence near Triana, CAPT. NATHANIEL
RAGLAND in 70th year, native of Albermarle County, Virginia whence he
emigrated to this state in 18--(blank)

May 14, 1833
Married on 3nd at Lexington, Kentucky by REV. BISHOP SMITH,
DR. CAMPTON J(ESSE) POSEY, formerly of this place to MISS MARY ROBERT
of Lexington. (POSEY Bible) H. J. died October 1878, son of JESSE.
Died Tuesday evening, JAMES H., only son of MR. BENJAMIN PATTESON
of this place aged 7 years, 3 months.
Died on 11th instant ISAAC ANDERSON, son of MR. ISAAC SKILLERN.

May 21, 1833
Married Tuesday, 7th instant by REV. MR. DONALD, MR. ELI M(OORE)
DRIVER to MISS JULIA SOPHIA, daughter of GROSS SCRUGGS, Esq. all of
this county.

May 28, 1833
Died suddenly Friday the 24th at her residence, MRS. MARY PRUIT,
wife of MR. VALENTINE G. PRUIT of this county; affectionate wife and
mother.
Died Saturday the 25th, MRS. SARAH E. McCLUNG, daughter of
JOHN MITCHELL, Esq. late Governor of Georgia, and consort of JAMES W.
McCLUNG, Esq. of this town.
Died on 21st, ATTICUS LYNN SKILLERN, son of MR. ISAAC SKILLERN of
this place; aged 2 years, 3 months.
Died on 25th instant JOHN B., eldest son of JOHN G. and SARAH
BINGHAM aged about 6.
Died Friday the 8th in this city, CATHERINE H. and ANN C. MORGAN,
infant daughters of C. C. MORGAN, Esq. of this county.
Died in this city Tuesday evening last, MISS CATHARINE G. HUNT,
aged 18 or 19, daughter of MR. JOHN W. HUNT (From Kentucky Reporter
of the 16th)
Died of cholera on Tuesday the 7th of May, JANE, EMILY and
JULIET, daughters of DR. J. W. HAGEMAN. One of these was to have been
married to MR. RUEL A. WATSON, who died on the same day.

June 4, 1833
Died in this town Thursday May 23rd, REV. WILLIAM HUME.
Died on Friday last, WILLIAM, son of CAPT. WILLIAM HOWSON aged
5 or 6.

Died on Saturday last, ALEXANDER, son of MR. JAMES NEELY of this place, aged about 6.

June 11, 1833
Died in this place Tuesday evening last, CAROLINE MARIA, infant daughter of MR. L. WOOD.

Died on Thursday last, ROBERT ANDERSON, infant son of MR. WILLIAM GORMLY.

June 25, 1833
Married on 11th June by REV. JAMES ROWE near Brownsborough in this county, MR. ROBERT FREEMAN of Limestone County to MISS ELMYRA T. daughter of JOHN W. HEWLETT, Esq. of the former place.

Married on Tuesday evening last by REV. JAMES ROWE, MR. CHARLES L. McGEHEE to MISS SARAH V. ACKLEN, all of this county.

Another Revolutionary soldier gone! Died Saturday morning 22nd instant at residence in Big Cove, of lingering illness, JOEL RICE, Esq. in his 71st year, one of first settlers of country.

Died in Maury County, Tennessee on 13th instant MRS. CATHERINE LITTLEFIELD, consort of DR. LITTLEFIELD, formerly of this place.

July 9, 1833
Died near Elkton, Tennessee of cholera on night of 21st instant MR. JOSEPH COLEMAN, formerly of Kentucky but since last fall, a resident of this county had been on a visit to Kentucky and was on his way home. Was about 21 years old and was married a few months since to a young lady.

Died Friday, the 21st at residence of her husband in this county, MRS. NANCY WRIGHT, consort of MAJ. DANIEL WRIGHT in 71st year. Resided 21 years in this county, was 46 years a member of the Baptist Church and enjoyed 52 years of married life.

Died Wednesday last, MR. WILLIAM T. KEY in 29th year of his age.

Died Thursday last, MR. EDWARD R. DAVIS, aged about 27, eldest son of CAPTAIN NICHOLAS DAVIS.

Died in this town on 5th instant MRS. ZIBBIAH MITCHELL, consort of MR. JAMES MITCHELL in her 36th year; was a Cumberland Presbyterian.

September 11, 1833
Died in Madison County, MRS. BARBARY, wife of REV. FINIS E. HARRIS September 11, 1833.

April 26, 1844
Married in Fayetteville, Tennessee on Friday 18th instant by WILLIAM NEALE, Esq., REV. W. H. MUSE to MISS MARTHA A. ECHOLS, both of this place.

May 3, 1844
Married on 25th instant by REV. DR. ROBINSON, MR. SAMUEL MATTHEWS of Limestone County to MISS SARAH SPOTSWOOD of Madison County. Note: She was daughter of ELLIOT and SALLY DANDRIDGE (LITTLEPAGE) SPOTSWOOD.

May 19, 1844
Married in this place on Thursday, the 2nd, by REV. JAMES C. ELLIOTT, CAPTAIN WILLIAM M. GOOCH to MISS MARIA H. COMBS.

Died on 27th, JAMES BRADLEY, son of MR. and MRS. JOSEPH C. BRADLEY in his 2nd year, of this place.

May 24, 1844
Died at the residence nine miles west of Huntsville on May 1, 1844, MRS. PRISCILLA W. PIKE, consort of JAMES A. PIKE and daughter of WILLIAM EAST aged 30 years 7 months and 20 days. Died of measles.

Died near Mooresville, Limestone County, Alabama on 26th of April, 1844, SUSAN FRANCES, only daughter of JESSE and MARY GRAVET aged 10 years, 10 months and 25 days.

May 31, 1844
Died in Huntsville on Saturday the 25th instant THOMAS, son of MR. THOMAS BRANDON, aged 7 years and 2 months.

June 7, 1844
    Married on 16th by REV. M. H. BONE, MR. WILLIAM STEWART of
Loweville to MISS ANN B. BARKER, all of this county.
    Married in Huntsville on 20th by REV. DR. ROBINSON, DR. JOHN
HARDIE to MISS HARRIET H. SEXTON (SAXON in marriage record)
    Died in New Orleans on 11th May, ARTHUR F. HOPKINS, son of
ARTHUR M. and ELIZA P. HOPKINS aged 3 years and 9 months.
    Died in this county on the 23rd ult. in his 85th year, CAPTAIN
PEYTON POWELL, formerly of Virginia, but for the last thirty years
of this county. He was a lieutenant in the Revolutionary army, and did
his duty nobly. He was greatly respected by all.

August 9, 1844
    Married on 30th of July by REV. THOMAS M. KING, DR. WILLIAM G.
RODES, formerly of Lexington, Kentucky to MRS. MARY E. ROPER of Jackson
County.
    Died on 2nd, MARIA, youngest child of A. J. and MARY W. WITHERS
aged 2 years and 17 days.
    Died near Bellefonte on 30th, DR. HENRY S. CHANDLER, formerly of
this county in his 27th year.
    Died in Madison County, Mississippi on 12th of July of congestive
fever, DR. BENJAMIN F. JONES, formerly of this county in his 24th year.
    Died in Tuscumbia on 24th, HON. PETER WALKER aged about 51.

August 2, 1844
    Died in Tuscaloosa on 18th instant MR. WILLIAM M. WOMACK, printer,
aged 24 years a native of Virginia. For a few years back, he has been
a resident of this place.

August 30, 1844
    Married on 18th instant MR. ROBERT J. MENDUM to MISS SARAH BREECE,
all of this county. Marriage record says REECE--see our volume 187,
page 51.
    Married on 15th instant MR. WILLIAM C. NICHOL to MISS PERLINA,
daughter of MAJ. H. C. FEATHERSTON, all of this county. See marriage
record in our volume 187, page 50.
    Married on 15th instant by REV. HOWELL PEOPLES, SR., JEREMIAH
FRENCH to MISS MARIETTA DAVIS, both of this place.
    Married on 21st ult. A. M. SWEANY (Sheriff) to MISS ----- JAMES,
daughter of HARDY JONES. (Athens Chronicle) Note: Will of HARDY JONES
names daughter ABIGAIL SWEANY.

September 6, 1844
    Died on 28th of consumption, MRS. SUSAN ELDRIDGE consort of JOHN
R. B. ELDRIDGE aged 56.
    Died on 23rd instant, WILLIAM D. THOMAS aged 66, a citizen of this
county since 1821.
    Died on 31st near this place, MR. ELIJAH WARREN, old citizen of
this county.
    Died on 1st instant in this place, MARY LOUISA, infant daughter
of MR. and MRS. E. R. WALLACE.

September 13, 1844
    Married in Nashville on 2nd instant JOHN R. BLOCKER, Esq. of Mobile
to MISS ANN E. youngest daughter of MICHAEL C. DUNN, Esq. of Davidson
County (Tennessee).

September 20, 1844
    Married on Thursday evening 12th instant by REV. JOHN M. ROBERTSON,
MR. JOEL W. JONES of Pickens County to MISS MARTHA C. GEE, only daughter
of WILLIAM H. GEE, of this county. See our volume 130, page 19.
    Died in Memphis on 3rd instant MR. A. F. BERRY, formerly of this
place.

October 4, 1844
    Died on 29th instant MISS VIRGINIA JANE, aged ---, daughter of
MR. BENJAMIN HARRISON of Limestone County.
    Died on 29th instant MARIA WITHERS, youngest daughter of WILLIAM
and PRISCILLA W. McDOWELL aged 4 years, 10 months and 11 days.

October 11, 1844
Married on the evening of 7th in this place by REV. M. H. BONE, DR. CHARLES H. WILLIAMS of Jackson County to MISS ELIZABETH J. GREEN of this place.

October 15, 1844
Married October 1, 1844 by REV. MR. LAPSLEY at the residence of COL. ROBERT WEAKLEY, REV. WILLIAM FRED M'REE of Selma to MISS ANN ELIZA, daughter of the late GENERAL JOHN BRAHAN of North Alabama.
Died at the residence in Huntsville in her 38th year, MRS. SARAH consort of GEN. B. M. LOWE.
Died in Knoxville, Tennessee on 5th instant COL. MATTHEW McCLUNG in his 49th year; brother of our townsman, COL. McCLUNG and much respected.

October 25, 1844
Married in Marshall County on 6th instant by REV. J. W. JAMES, MR. JEROME C. CORNELL to MISS MARY C. FIELDS.
Died in this place on morning of 20th instant NANCY C. WALSH, native of Dublin, Ireland, aged about 45. For many years past, has been a citizen of this country and this place. A musician well-known over the south.

November 1, 1844
Married in Jackson County on Wednesday, 16th of October by REV. O. L. ROACH, MR. JOSEPH McCALEB, formerly of Madison County to MISS MARY JANE, daughter of HENRY ROACH of Jackson County.
Died at Loweville in this county on Friday the 18th instant ELIZABETH THOMPSON, relict of JOHN THOMPSON, Esq. of that place in her 53rd year. Ill nine days.

November 8, 1844
Died at the residence of MAJOR SAM RAGLAND in this county on 18th instant, JOHN E. son of THOMAS and RHODA SHESHANE in his 20th year.
Died in Morgan County on 21st, JAMES M. BOULDIN.
Died on 11th instant ANDREW ARMSTRONG aged 53, an old settler of Lawrence County.

November 29, 1844
Married on 31 of October by REV. N. R. GARRETT, JOHN S. KENNEDY, Esq. of Florence to MISS MARY E. KENNEDY of Marshall County, Mississippi (Holly Springs Guard).
Died in Texas on 26th of September, MR. JOHN BRADLEY, formerly of this place and late a prisoner in Mexico.

November 6, 1844
Married on 3rd instant by REV. P. B. ROBINSON, JOHN R. B. ELDRIDGE, Esq. to MRS. MELLICENT T. HARRIS, all of this county.
Married in Fairfield, Pickens County on 21st instant by REV. MR. HANSHAW, MR. H. D. RHODES to MISS MARY B. WICKS.
Married at residence of COL. A. D. CHRISTIAN in Tuscumbia on 27th instant by REV. J. O. STEDMAN, MR. ROBERT BIBB of Huntsville to MISS ANN, daughter of the late COL. JOHN BRADLEY of Texas.
Married Thursday, 21st of November by REV. F. G. FERGUSON, MR. JOHN A. JOHNSON (one of publishers of Athens Chronicle) to MISS MARY JANE, daughter of REV. JAMES C. ELLIOTT of this vicinity (Athens Chronicle).
Married on 7th by REV. H. H. BROWN, MR. WILLIAM L. HARRISON to MISS LUCY M. SANDERS, all of Limestone County.
Married on 20th instant by REV. J. BUTCHER, WILLIAM W. MATTHEWS to ANN D. WILKERSON, all of Limestone County.
Died at Nashville Inn, Wednesday the 27th instant after severe illness, ELLIS WARE PERCY, youngest son of the late COL. THOMAS PERCY of Huntsville aged 7 years.

December 13, 1844
Married on 25th instant MR. JAMES W. SLOSS of Athens to MISS MARY ANN BIGGER, daughter of JOSEPH BIGGER, Esq. of this place (Florence Enquirer).

Married on Sunday 24th ult. by FRANCIS E. HARRIS, Esq., MR. SAMUEL
H. CLAYTON to MRS. MARY WILLIAMSON, daughter of THEOPHILUS PENNINGTON,
Esq. all of Jackson County.

Married in Mobile, HON. SAMUEL CHAPMAN of Sumter County to MRS.
E(LIZA) M. CENTER.

December 20, 1844
Married on December 9th by REV. F. G. FERGUSON, MR. LEWIS GOLDIN
of Madison County to MISS LUCINDA, daughter of MR. THOMAS J. STONE of
this vicinity (Athens Chronicle).

Married on 4th instant WILLIAM E. HARAWAY, M.D. of Lauderdale
County to MISS ELIZA BONNER of this county (Athens Chronicle).

Married in this place, on 12th instant by REV. P. B. ROBINSON,
MR. ANDREW J. JOHNSON to MISS SARAH N. HILL, all of this county.

December 27, 1844
Married Wednesday, 18th instant by REV. JOSHUA BOUCHER, MR. JAMES M.
CLEVELAND of this county to MISS SOPHIA A. DAVIS of Limestone County.

Married on 12th instant in this county by REV. JAMES O. (C?)
ELLIOTT, MR. WILLIAM H. MARDIS to MISS ELIZABETH E. HICKS.

In this county on 12th, by same, MR. JAMES J. WILBURN to MISS
SUSAN E. BOULDIN, daughter of COL. W. GRAVES BOULDIN of this county.

Married on 12th instant by REV. MONROE F. MOSES, MR. JOSEPH HAMBRICK
of Madison to MISS MARY A. R. MAXWELL, of Limestone County.

On 17th by REV. R. H. RIVERS, MR. J(OHN) M. DAVIS to MISS MARTHA
DANFORTH all of Limestone County.

Married on 12th instant by REV. JOSHUA BUTCHER, MR. A(BNER) H.
BINFORD to MRS. ELIZABETH ALLEN, all of Limestone County.

Married on 15th instant by REV. MR. FERGUSON, MR. G. W. GRIFFIN
to MISS ANN E. MONTGOMERY of Lawrence County.

Married on 19th instant at residence of WILLIAM CORNELIUS by
REV. F. B. ROBINSON, MR. WILLIAM M. ELDRIDGE to MISS MARY CARSON,
all of Madison County.

Married on Saturday evening, 7th instant by W. G. BOULDIN,
MR. JEFFERSON SANDERSON to MISS SUSAN, daughter of SANDY (TANDY)
LEWIS all of this county.

Married on 4th instant MR. RALCIJAH SPRAGINS to MISS LOUISA BIBB,
all of Madison County.

Married on 18th instant at residence of VINCENT GRAVETT, MR.
ALEXANDER COSBY to MISS SARAH, eldest daughter of RICHARD MARTIN all
of this county.

January 3, 1845
Married on 19th instant by REV. MR. BRYANT, MR. THOMAS W. GREEN
to MISS MARTISHA, daughter of B. B. ROGERS, Esq. all of this county.

Married on 31st instant by REV. MR. ROBINSON, WILLIAM H. MOORE,
Esq. to MISS MARGARET C. HARRIS, daughter of MR. B. D. HARRIS, all of
this county.

Married on 21 of December by REV. J. C. ELLIOTT, MR. ELCANAH
HUSSEY to MISS ARAMENTA B. JONES of Limestone County.

Married on 23rd of December by REV. ELLIOTT, JOSEPH M. PETTY to
MISS AMERICA K. HIGGINS, all of Limestone County.

Married on 19th instant by REV. ELLIOTT, MR. JOHN JACKSON to
MISS MARY A. JOHNSON, all of Limestone County.

January 10, 1845
Married on 24th in Rutherford County (Tennessee) at residence of
COL. THOMAS RUCKER by REV. JOSEPH LINDSY, MR. OLIVER B. BODDIE of
Marengo County, Alabama to MISS JOSEPHINE B. RUCKER, daughter of DR.
EDMUND RUCKER, of this place (Lebanon Tennessee Chronicle).

Died Sunday, 5th instant of spasmodic croup, SAMUEL ROOSEVELT,
youngest child of REV. F. H. L. LAID aged 19 months and 9 days.
(should be LAIRD)

Died on 2nd instant MRS. JUDITH ELIZA BEAL, wife of HENRY BEAL
of this place (communicated).

Died on Saturday, 4th instant at the residence in Madison County,
MRS. CAROLINE R. HOBBS in her 34th year, wife of MR. JOHN F. HOBBS
and second daughter of the late WILLIAM BIBB. Left a husband and three
small children, one of whom was an infant eight weeks old, and four
sisters and two brothers.

January 17, 1845
    Married on 26th of December by REV. F. C. FERGUSON, MR. R(ICH'D) M.
GREEN to MISS MARTHA COE, all of Athens.
    Married on January 1st, 1845 in Madison County by REV. F. G.
FERGUSON, MR. ROBERT M. BOUCHER of Limestone County to MISS SUSAN E.
CLEVELAND.
    Married on 26th of December by REV. J. C. ELLIOTT, MR. JOSEPH W.
FINN of Limestone County to MISS CLARISA M. GIBSON of Lawrence County.
    Married on 5th of January by REV. J. C. ELLIOTT, JESSE M. EGGER
of Mississippi to MISS ELIZABETH R. HODGES of Limestone County.
    Married on 6th instant by same, MR. SAMUEL CONNER to MRS. MARTHA
DAVID, both of Madison County.
    Married on 7th instant by REV. J. C. ELLIOTT, MR. JAMES A. MONTGOMERY
of Lawrence County to MRS. LOUISA V. HOLMAN of this county.
    Married on 8th instant by REV. MR. BONE, MR. JOHN M. HUMPHREY to
MISS ELIZABETH REDDICK, all of this county.
    Died on 10th instant MR. RICHARD GREEN HAMLET in the 37th year of
his age.
    Died Wednesday 1st instant at her residence in Madison County of
a painful illness of 18 days, MRS. SARAH ALLISON, consort of DAVID
ALLISON, in her 33rd year.
    Died on Tuesday, 7th instant ANN L. THOMPSON, infant daughter of
JOHN C. and HENRIETTA THOMPSON.

January 24, 1845
    Married on 19th instant by REV. P. B. ROBINSON, MR. A(BRAHAM) H.
THURSTON to MRS. MATILDA FREEMAN, all of this place.
    Married on Monte Sano on 23rd by REV. R. D. WILSON, MAJ. ELIJAH
STANDEFER to MRS. ELIZABETH SCHRIMSHER, all of this county.

January 31, 1845
    Married Thursday evening 9th instant by REV. E. CALLOWAY, DR.
WILLIAM D(URHAM) LYLES of Macon to MISS MARY BIBB of Huntsville.
    Died on 22nd ult. in Limestone County, MRS. JUDITH MASSEE. She
was born in Newkent County, Virginia March 27, 1777 and was 73 when
she died. Was an affectionate mother....

February 14, 1845
    Married on 10th instant by REV. P. B. ROBINSON, MA----ES to
MISS ------, all of this place (scratched out).
    Married on Tuesday evening by REV. MR. LAIRD, EGGLESTON D. TOWNES,
Esq. of Tuscumbia to MISS MARTHA C. BETTS of this place.
    Married Sunday evening, 26th instant by REV. SAMUEL HENDERSON,
MR. THOMAS J. CROSS to MISS ELIZA EDWARDS, all of that place. (In 1850
Census Talladega County, Alabama he 27 Alabama, she 22 in North Carolina
with them, LEAH EDWARDS 60 in South Carolina. They married in Talladega
County with consent of her grandchildren, H. G. CUNNINGHAM.

February 28, 1845
    Married on 11th instant by REV. THOMAS W. DORMAN, DR. WILLIAM
HENRY COLEMAN to MISS MARGARET ALLISON, daughter of COL. ROBERT G.
ALLISON of Sumer.
    Married on 11th instant by REV. CHARLES HODGES, COL. J. R. H.
CUMMINGS of Limestone County to MISS SOPHENIA DONALSON of Madison
County. (SOPHIA in Census)

March 7, 1845
    Died on the morning of the 18th instant at his residence in this
county, MR. ROBERT D. MALONE (Athens Chronicle)
    Died on 9th of February after severe illness, ELISHA H. RICE, JR.
son of COL. E. H. RICE of this place
    Died on 12th of February, JOHN KINKLE, Esq. ---for last twenty-five
years a citizen of this place. He was born in Shenandoah County,
Virginia January 15, 1797 and moved to this county in 1820. For the
last seven years he had rheumatism....
    Died on 25th ult. at his residence in this county, MR. JOHN G.
JORDAN, an old and worthy citizen.

March 21, 1845
    Died in Madison County, Alabama on 5th instant MRS. MARY C. consort
of RICHARD A. JAMAR, JR.
    Died on 27th of February near Huntsville, PLEASANT B. CAROTHERS,
son of JOSEPH and MARY CAROTHERS aged 11 years.
    Married in Mooresville on 11th instant by REV. J. C. ELLIOTT,
MR. JAMES M. HAFLEY to MISS MARTHA ANN ATKINSON, both of Triana.

March 28, 1845
    Married on Thursday, 20th instant by REV. P. B. ROBINSON, MR.
AARON H. H. ROUNTREE, formerly of Illinois to MISS ELIZA A. WALPOLE
of this place.

April 4, 1845
    Died at the residence of ROBERT G. McMAHON, Gainesville, Sunday,
March 16th instant COL. ANDREW BEIRNE of Monroe County, Virginia in his
74th year. He was a native of Ireland and landed in New York about
1791....
    Died in Huntsville on 2nd instant MISS MARGARET RUSSEL aged about
50 years and 2 months.
    Died on Sunday last, ALBERT, son of CAPTAIN FRED ELGIN of this
place--a promising boy.

April 18, 1845
    Married in Morgan County on 3rd instant HENRY TURNER (TURNEY in
marriage record and census) to MISS JANE M. STRAIN. See our volume
105, page 34.
    Married in Somerville on 9th ult. J(ACKSON) I. CRABB to MISS
MARTHA EVANS. See our volume 105, page 39.
    Married in Florence on 8th instant A(LEXR) W. ENSOR to MISS
MARY BRADLY. See our volume 230, page 43.
    Died in Demopolis on 2nd instant JONES C. LUCY proprietor of
Blount Springs.

April 25, 1845
    Married by PLEASANT B. ROBINSON in Huntsville on 11th instant
MR. JOHN F. HOBBS of Madison County to MISS LOUISA ANN BIBB of
Huntsville.

May 23, 1845
    Died on 13th ult. JAMES PATTERSON, infant son of JOHN W. SCRUGGS
aged 6 months and 10 days.
    Died in DeSoto County, Mississippi on 9th instant MR. JOSEPH
JOHNSTON, formerly of Limestone County in his 59th year.
    Died in Russell's Valley on 12th instant the REV. THEOPHILUS
SKINNER aged 65 years, formerly of the State Legislature and a zealous
minister.
    Died in Walker County on 14th instant CAPT. JACOB PRUETT, formerly
of this county, aged about 80.
    Married on 15th instant by REV. JAMES GAINES, MR. JOHN N. MALONE,
Esq. of Athens to MISS MARY LUCY KERNACHAN of Lauderdale County.
See our volume 230, page 42.
    Married in Montgomery on 1st instant by HON. H. W. HILLIARD,
MAJ. JOHN C. BATES, one of Editors of Journal to MISS SARAH, daughter
of the late THORNTON TALIAFERRO.
    Married near Memphis (Tennessee) on 8th instant CAPT. ALEXANDER
McGOWIN of Pittsburg to MISS MARGARET T. ODELL of Athens, Alabama.

May 30, 1845
    Married on 20th instant by REV. PHILLIP W. ALSTON, MR. WILLIE B.
MILLER, of this city to MISS LOUISA E. POPE, daughter of JOHN POPE,
Esq. of this county.

June 4, 1845
    Died on 27th instant at his residence in this county, in 64th
year, CAPTAIN JESSE RANDALL, formerly of Sussex County, Virginia but an
early settler of Madison County, Alabama.
    Died May 23rd at his residence in this county, JOHN L. LIGHTFOOT
in his 40th year.

Died on 1st instant CATHARINE S., only child of SEPTIMUS D. and
VIRGINIA CABANISS, aged about 9.

June 20, 1845
Died on 5th instant MRS. SARAH ANN TRUE, consort of MR. ROBERT
TRUE of Madison County in her 25th year.
Married by BISHOP JOHNS on Thursday evening at the residence of
WILLIAM H. MACFARLAND, Esq. in Richmond, Virginia, MR. WILLIAM F. TURNER
of Jefferson County to MISS ELLEN BEIRNE, youngest daughter of HON.
ANDREW BEIRNE of Monroe County, Virginia.

June 20, 1845
Married in Limestone County on 19th instant, MR. SCHUYLER HARRIS
to MISS M. E. DEWOODY, daughter of MAJ. W. DEWOODY. (ANN in marriage
record)
Died near Rodgersville, Lauderdale County on 6th instant MR.
WILLIAM SHOALER aged 61 years. He was one of early settlers of the
county.
Died on 7th instant in Athens, MRS. MARY R. VASSER aged 97 years.

July 4, 1845
Died at his residence near Courtland on Saturday morning, 21st
of June, MAJ. FELIX A. M. SHERROD leaving afflicted wife and three
children.
Died on 29th instant, LUCY JULIA WINN, daughter of J. W. and
CORNELUA D. WINN aged one year and eight months, Lexington, Kentucky
required to copy.
Died on 26th instant by REV. B. C. CHAPMAN, MR. GEORGE H. WARWICK
to MISS JANE GASTON, daughter of JAMES GASTON all of this place.

July 10, 1846
Died in Franklin County on the 19th of June, MR. ROBERT C. GARNER
aged 48 years.
In Jackson County on 26 June, MRS. LUCINDA FRAZIER, wife of
GEN. JOS. P. FRAZIER (48 in Tennessee) aged 31 years.

July 3, 1846
ELIJAH L. NEELY departed this life in Franklin County on 14 June.
Born in Williamson County on 14 October 1814 (Franklin County, Tennessee.
Review)

June 22, 1846
JOHN R. H. ACKLEN of Madison County, Alabama died at the house of
his brother-in-law, JAMES V. A. HINDS in Tennessee on 14. (born in
Tennessee 23 Ja-- (faded), 1800 and brought to this country by his
parents 18-8.)

August 7, 1846
Departed this life 18 July in Philadelphia, WYATT H. ELLIS, a
merchant of Huntsville on his way to Boston to replenish his store....
In November 1841, he was a member of the Presbyterian Church of
Murfresborough.
Died of congestive fever on 26 at his residence 10 miles north of
Huntsville, CHARLES McCAA in his 56th year. Left a wife and children.
Died in Franklin County on 28 MAJ. JOHN L. TOWNES aged 62 formerly
of this county.
Died in Madison County, Alabama on 17th, MRS. E. E. POOR, consort
of WM. H. POOR aged 19-4-8.
MR. WILLIAM WILHOITE to MISS -------LITTLE, daughter of JOSEPH
LITTLE, Esq.

September 4, 1846
Married in Slough Beat at Bethlehem Church, Limestone County,
Alabama August 26 by REV. F. G. FURGASON, MR. MAGNESS S. TEAGUE, to
MISS MUSIDORA P. V. only daughter of the late THOMAS MORGAN of Virginia.

August 28, 1846
Died in Morgan County on 11, MR. GEORGE MURPHY, a native of
North Carolina aged 73.

In this place on Sunday last, HOWARD, infant son of COL. J. W. McCLUNG.

August 21, 1846
Died Friday last 14th, LUCY infant child of COL. J. J. PLEASANTS of this place.

September 11, 1846
Married in Franklin County, Tennessee on 10 by JOHN THOMAS SLATTER, Esq. MR. WILLIAM WILHOITE to MISS ----LITTLE, daughter of JOSEPH LITTLE, Esq.

September 25, 1846
RODAH HORTON departed this life on Thursday the 10th in 54th year. A Virginian by birth and removed to (from) Russell County to this place in 1817. Twice married and left a large family....

October 9, 1846
Died on Sunday night MR. ROBERT HAMLET aged 84 years. One of oldest settlers and a native of North Carolina. Left a wife and several children.
    On Tuesday last of apoplectic fit, MR. CLACK LIGHTFOOT an old and very much esteemed citizen.
    Died on 22nd, MR. GRANVILLE L. COOKRELL (COCKRILL?) of Tuscumbia.
    At La Grange on 25th, MRS. ELIZABETH HART. (note: MR. JAMES says her tombstone says she died on 25th August)
    Died in Dekalb County on 22, HON. SOLOMON C. SMITH, formerly of this county, Represented Dekalb County for several years. Methodist. Left wife and 6 children.
    In Limestone County on 13, MR. GEORGE DAVIS aged 83.
    In Lauderdale County on 22, MR. JOHN LORANCE aged 60.

October 16, 1846
Died in Morgan County on 19, MRS. MARY E. NEVILL aged 21 years.
    On 29th, MR. JAMES K. EDMONDSON of Decatur aged 37 and on 10th MR. W. B. GREGORY aged 47 of Morgan County.

October 29, 1846
Died in Franklin County on 2 of consumption, DANDRIDGE B. SPENCE of this county.
    Died at his residence in this county on 7th, ROBERT DAVIE in his 89th year (rev sol qr)
    Died on 5th at his residence near Huntsville, ROBERT HAMLET, 8 (faded) native of Virginia and one of oldest citizens.

November 5, 1846
Died in Baltimore, Maryland on Sunday 18th October EDWARD ANDERSON aged 49-10-12. Native of Montgomery County, Maryland who resided many years in this county; late of Oktibeha County, Mississippi.
    In Madison county on Friday 29th, MARY CAMP, daughter of JAMES B. and INDIANA S. TURNER aged 4 years 6 months.
    On 16th, at his residence in Mullins' Flat, Madison County LEWIS HERRALD aged 76 years, native of North Carolina.
    Married on 28th by REV. P. B. ROBINSON, MR. ROBERT S. NANCE to MISS MATILDA D. SALE, daughter of CAPT. D. SALE, all of Madison County.

November 19, 1846
Departed this life on 15th, SUSAN BLUNT, daughter of JAMES and INDIANA S. TURNER of Missouri aged 8 years 8 months.
    Departed this life on night of Monday 9th at residence of her mother in immediate vicinity of this town, MRS. SARAH JEMIMA HILL consort of MR. ROBERT HILL and second daughter of MRS. SUSAN POLLARD aged 20 years 14 days.

November 26, 1846
Departed this life on 29 October 1846 at residence of her daughter MRS. MARY S. LANIER of this county, LOUISA McCRAB in her 78th year.
    Departed this life on Tuesday 17th after few days painful illness, JOHN BLUNT TURNER, 2nd son of MAJ. JOHN B. TURNER of Madison County, Alabama aged 20 years 19 days. (May 17, 1908 of Richmond Times Dispatch

states that JOHN TURNER died in Greenville County, Virginia in 1796-97 leaving the following children: JOHN BLOUNT, SUGARS, SIMON, THOS., MARY and ANN, all sons except WM. and JAMES settled in North Alabama)

Wednesday, 25th, CHARITY JANE, aged 6 years, daughter of MR. E. T. PARKER of this place.

December 10, 1846

Departed this life on 21 November DELILAH consort of JABEZ LEFTWICH aged 80-8-5. She emigrated from Bedford County, Virginia to Madison County, Alabama in 1827 where she resided until 23 September, 1846 and then removed to Russel Valley, Franklin County. Joined Presbyterian Church in 1787. Left numerous children, grandchildren and great grandchildren.

Departed this life at his residence in this county on night of 13 of pneumonia, MR. WILLIAM PROVENCE in 74th year.

Departed this life on 2 December 1846, MRS. POLLY N. FLETCHER in 66th year of pulmonary complaint. Born in Nottoway County, Virginia 1781 and was relic of MR. NATHAN FLETCHER, late of Brunswick County, Virginia.

December 17, 1846

Died in Tuscumbia on 6th, MR. MARCELLOUS W. HARVEY aged 20 years. The captain of the Jackson County Guards in a letter from Rio Grande announces the deaths of SILAS GEORGE, JOHN R. INGLES, and HERVEY S. (HENRY S.; see pension) FLIPPO, members of that county of Alabama Regiment.

June 22, 1846 (omitted before)

Died in Harrison County, Texas on 18th April MR. JAMES E. BROWNING aged 65, formerly of this county.

Died in Decatur on 15th, MR. JOHN PARKER aged 63.

In Dallas County on 16th, GEN. GILBERT SHEARER aged 57.

December 24, 1846

Departed this life on 26th in Limestone County WILLIAM H. BLACKWELL after illness of 10 days aged 54. Native of Fauquier County, Virginia from which his family emigrated to Columbia County, Georgia.

January 22, 1847

Died in Triana on 30th, MR. WILLIAM KIRBY aged 52. Born in North Carolina but raised in Tennessee. In 16th year entered the army under GEN. JACKSON and continued in it during the war and fought bravely at New Orleans. Settled in Triana in 1824 where he resided up to his death.

On Monday morning the 11th, of whooping cough, JANE, eldest daughter of DR. CHARLES H. PATTON of this place aged about 10 years.

At her residence in this county on the 31st, MRS. ELIZABETH E. SMITH, consort of H. SMITH, Esq. in her 64th year. Born in Rutherford County, North Carolina. Emigrated to Alabama where she continued to reside until her death. Member of Methodist Episcopal Church.

In Lawrence County, on the 11th, MR. WILLIAM P. HODGES aged 22.

January 29, 1847

Departed this life on Wednesday the 13 of January at the residence of his father about 8 miles northwest of Huntsville, of an affliction of the heart, after a painful and prostrated illness, GABRIEL EDWARD MOORE, 2nd surviving son of EDWARD and JANE MOORE of Madison County aged about 34 years, native of Moore County, North Carolina where many of his surviving relatives still reside. From that state he emigrated with his father's family to Alabama and settled in Madison County in the year 1822....

Died in Talladega County on 17th, WILEY P. SAUNDERS aged 44, formerly a citizen of Jackson County.

February 12, 1847

Died in DeSoto County, Mississippi on 2 January DAVID MAXWELL, formerly a citizen of this county.

February 26, 1847

Died at his residence in Elyton, Alabama, February 13, 1847, JAMES MUDD, Esq. in his 57th year. Native of Maryland and in early life removed to Kentucky where he married, from thence to North Alabama, and in 1829 he settled in Elyton, where he resided until his death.

Died at Tampico, Mexico on 17 January MR. JOHN EDWARD SMITH, aged 18 years of Tuscaloosa. Student at University. Joined Alabama Regiment and died of yellow fever.

At Point Isabel on 1st December last, ARCHELOUS A. COCHRAN of Greensboro aged 20 years and a volunteer.

In Courtland on 27 January last, MRS. LUCINDA McLEMORE in 48th year of age.

March 5, 1847

Died near Courtland on 25, COL. BENJ. SHERROD, an old and well known citizen of Lawrence County.

In this county last week at his residence near Triana, MR. JAMES HATTON, a good citizen.

March 12, 1847

Died in Lawrence County on 13, MRS. SUSAN M. WATKINS, consort of MR. W. M. WATKINS in her 35th year, leaving a husband and 5 small children.

In Clarksville, Texas on 9 January DR. JOHN J. PETERS in 39th year of his age, formerly of Lawrence County.

March 19, 1847

Died in Tuscumbia on 7th, COL. JOHN K. FERGUSON, merchant of that place.

On 9th, MRS. MARY CRAWFORD BLAIR, consort of DR. JOHN S. BLAIR (47 in Kentucky) of Limestone.

At residence of her husband, MR. J. B. TATE LOURY of Marshall County on 4 MRS. O. E. LOURY aged 19.

March 26, 1847

Died on Friday last, JOHN HAMLEEN, an aged and highly respectable citizen of this county.

April 2, 1847

Died near Rodgersville on 21, MR. BENJAMIN FRENCH aged 84, an old and faithful Revolutionary soldier.

Another patriot gone

Departed this life on 24 ROBERT WRIGHT, SR. a Patriot of the Revolution aged 85 years 17 days, native of Amherst County, Virginia. Was at Seige of York and assisted in capture of CORNWALLIS. Emigrated to Madison County in 1808....

Died near Somerville, Morgan County, Alabama on Wednesday 26th, the infant daughter of WILLIAM P. and MARY L. TERRY aged 3 months 16 days.

At Linares, Mexico on 20 January last, LT. JOSEPHUS I. TATUM, of Mississippi Volunteers aged 24 years and a native of Madison County.

April 9, 1847

Died on 28th, MR. ROBERT AUSTIN for many years clerk of Circuit and County Courts of Limestone County; on 31 in same place, MRS. REBECCA DAVIS.

April 16, 1847

Died on 25th MRS. ELIZABETH BELL, relict of the late THOS. BELL of Limestone County aged 63 years.

On 8th, MARY MARGARET infant child of MR. HUGH L. VEAL of this place.

On 9th after a long and painful illness, COL. EDMUND A. WEBSTER, a well known member of legal profession.

April 23, 1847

Died off Tampico, Gulf of Mexico on 7 February last, WILLIAM A. MICHIE, a native of Madison County, Alabama in 19th year.

In Upsher County, Texas on 4th of March, 1847, PHILIP D(EDMAN) CLACK of Marshall County, Alabama. Died far from home. (married in Blount County, Alabama January 1, 1824 MARY A. HENDERSON, daughter of WM. HENRY HENDERSON and wife MARY H.)

March 19, 1851
    Died on 23, MR. JOHN A. HALL for many years the principal teacher
of Bellefonte Academy.
    Skipped marriages.

May 21, 1847
    Died in Athens on 8th instant MR. WILLIAM McCRACKEN aged 54 years.

June 11, 1847
    Married on Wednesday evening 9th instant by REV. MR. RIGGS, MR.
WILLIAM McM. BRANDON to MISS THERESE E. THOMAS, all of this county.
(1860 Census Hempstead County, Arkansas he 33 in Alabama, she 28 in
Alabama)
    On 1 by REV. R. B. ROBINSON, MR. JONATHON MAHEW to MRS. ELIZA A. M.
STRONG, all of Madison County.
    Died on 29th in Franklin County, MR. ARMSTEAD BARTON aged 47.
    MRS. NANCY H. SALE, wife of CAPT. DUDLEY SALE departed this life
on 1st of May in 58th year of her age.

July 16, 1847
    Married at Flower Hill, Lawrence County, Alabama on 7th by
REV. EDWARD WADSWORTH, D.D., EPHRAIM H. FOSTER, JR., Esq. of Nashville,
Tennessee to MISS SUSAN A. WATKINS, 2nd daughter of PAUL J. WATKINS,
Esq.
    Died on 7th in this county, THOMAS L. MOON aged 22 years 10 days.
    On 13, M. LOUISE, infant daughter of JOSEPH B. and MARY BRADFORD.

July 23, 1847
    Died on 15th, MR. REUBEN ROGERS, a native of this county and for
many years a citizen of the town, leaving a wife and 4 small children.
    On 16th, MR. REUBEN SHOTWELL, an old and respected citizen of this
county.

July 30, 1847
    Died in this place on Friday evening 23rd, WADDY TATE in his 20th
year. Deceased had resided for several years in capacity of clerk.
Bilious fever.
    Died on 24th, MRS. MOORE, wife of HUGH N. MOORE of this place.

August 13, 1847
    Married near Abingdon, Virginia on 22, CAPT. RICHARD W. JONES of
Bellefonte, Alabama to MISS CORNELIA J. daughter of MR. THOS. THURMON.
    Died in Moscow, Tennessee on 13th of July last, MR. JOHN H. ROACH,
formerly of this place.
    In Nashville, Tennessee on 2nd instant MRS. MARIA PERCY, relict of
the late COL. PERCY and 2nd daughter of the late venerable COL. LEROY
POPE, both of Huntsville, Alabama...(Christian Record).

August 27, 1847
    Departed this life 12th of August at residence of COL. BENJAMIN
HARRISON of Limestone County, Alabama MRS. MARY ANN HARRISON, wife of
COL. B. HARRISON in 62nd year of her age. She was born in Brunswick
County, Virginia in the year 1786. Has been greatly afflicted for many
years. Methodist...Petersburg papers please copy.
    Departed this life on 18th of August JULIA CESARIA JONES, daughter
of JOHN N. S. and ELIZA JONES.

September 3, 1847
    Married on 19th by REV. P. B. ROBINSON, MR. ALFRED ELLETT to
MRS. RACHEL O. CONNALLY, all of Madison County.
    On 25th by REV. JAMES C. ELLIOTT, MR. ROWLAND C. STEWART of
Mississippi to MISS VIRGINIAN C. daughter of SAMUEL SMITHERS of this
county.
    Died at his residence in Madison County on night of 20 August after
5 days illness, MR. RICHARD LIPSCOMB in 47th year. Baptist.
    Died in Athens on 25, GEORGE MALONE aged about 64, an old and
much respected citizen of Limestone County. (auc. of MRS. HARSH)
(Thanks, but GEORGE MALONE's and JOHN N's re all the estates I contracted
to copy; will send notes only on other collateral MALONES. I have

490

GEORGE's death date from MRS. SMITH's notes--26 August 1847; so that
PM I am working on ought to show either pro of will or appointment
of administrator. I am confident if a will, it was in lost Will Book 8.
I am working on PM 1843-47. I see I worked "S" 1850/53. Wonder if
1847/50 is lost? Probably. They must have lettered those books at
random. There is the 1st or C I don't have but you say you do, from
MRS. SMITH. I copied 1830/34 - 1835/40 - 1840/43, now 1843/47, then
would come the 1848/50 gap--and then the 1st lettered one "S" is
1850/53...then comes "D" 1854/56...then "T" 1857/60...and then starts
over with "A" 1865/66. I reckon if there was one 1860/65 it burned.
I'll take a look for 1847/50 as I feel sure that would be estates that
were in Book 8. We will have to check the ones mentioned in this
1847 book versus WB 7, and anything not in it must have been in 8.
      Since MRS. HA---(faded) is so eager to learn GEO. M.'s parents,
and he was evidently close kin to THOMAS C. (perhaps a brother),
should I refer her to MR. NOLAN...if he worked on THOS. C.'s family,
may have his ancestry. If so, give me the address. She said an ancestor
said to be COUNTESS CHAPPELL. "The name has come down in the THOMAS
MALONE family. I think they were the THOMAS (H?) MALONES of "Recluse-
ville" who later went to Nashville. I would like to know if he was
a brother to GEORGE. The COUNTESS may have been a common ancestress."
Hmmm...wonder if that's old Nashville of HV's ancestress? Once I had
something you sent, that I though indicated the Tennessee father of
Nashville and HARPER and remember getting it out, to tell FRANCES DAVIS
to check it but now I can't find it any more. Oh for a filer!)
      In 3rd Dragood Hospital, Matamoras, Mexico on 15 July, ROBERT S.
CAPSHAW, a private in Company F. 13 Regiment of the U.S. Army.
      Departed this life on the 17th at his residence in Lauderdale
County, Alabama JOHN DONOHO, Esq.
      Died of paralysis on 21 August last at his residence in Madison
County, Alabama WILLIAM EAST aged 71-5-29.
      Administrator's sale. Orphan's Court of Morgan County, Alabama.
Estate of JOHN TROUP, SEN. late of said county, deceased. JOHN TROUP
and M. W. TROUP, administrators.

September 10, 1847
      Married in Slough Beat, Limestone County, Alabama on Thursday
evening at 4 o'clock by REV. JAMES C. ELLIOTT, MR. WILLIAM H. MOORE,
formerly of Sussex County, Virginia to MISS RUTH LODUSKIA LEWIS,
formerly of Madison County.
      At the residence of MR. A. F. FORD (near this place; see volume 147,
page 58) on Wednesday morning, 1st instant by REV. S. S. MOODY,
DR WILLIAM W. HUMPHREYS of Columbus, Mississippi to MISS REBECCA ANN
JONES, daughter of CAPT. FRILEY JONES.

September 17, 1847
      Married on 8th instant by HENRY STANLEY, Esq. MR. JAMES M.
STOGSDILLE (probably son of NANCY (BROWN) by first husband, WM. STOGSDILLE)
to MISS ELLEN M. YANCY (Madison County 1850; ELEANOR in Census; 21 in
Virginia), at same time and place, MR. WILLIAM B. TIDWELL (probably
son of NANCY (BROWN) by second husband, EDWARD TIDWELL) to MISS MARTHA
ANN YANCY, all of Limestone.
      In Morgan County, on 8th by REV. JOHN S. WILLIAMS, MR. G(EO.) W. A.
ROGERS (24 in Alabama) to MISS CAROLINE STRAIN (21 in Alabama); at
same time and place, MR. JOHN W. ROGERS to MISS FRANCIS STRAIN.
      In Madison County, Alabama on 2, by REV. S. S. MOODY, REV. JOHN S.
WILLIAMS to MISS MARY P. TURNER.
      Died on 14, GEORGE COOPER aged 23 months, 3 days, son of BOLING C.
BLACKWELL of Limestone County.

September 25, 1847
      Died on 7 at residence near Shoalford in this county, MR. JOHN
DONALSON aged 68 years.
      In Madison County on 4, MARY GEE, only child of JOEL W. and
MARTHA C. JONES aged 2 years 16 days.
      Married
      Thursday evening last by REV. P. B. ROBINSON, COL. JOHN TROUP (41
in South Carolina) of Morgan County to MISS ELIZABETH J. S. FENNELL
(32 in Alabama) of Madison County, Alabama.

In Morgan County on 8th instant by REV. JAMES C. ELLIOTT, MR.
JOSEPH S. BENSON of Limestone (see footnote and marriage in volume 105,
page 51--they moved to Burleson County, Texas) to MISS CATHARINE N.
BENSON of Morgan.
On 2 by ALBERT WALLS, Esq., MR. GEORGE W. HOLT to MISS REBECCA M.
LONG.
On 14 by REV. MR. SEALS, JOHN W. CRENSHAW to MISS JANE JONES.
On same day by REV. J. C. ELLIOTT, MR. BROOKS McKINNEY to MISS
HARRIET JONES, all of Limestone County.

October 2, 1847
Died on 9 of last month of pulmonary consumption in Madison County,
Alabama WILLIAM F. OWEN in 56th year of his age. Member of C. P.
Church. May the Lord care for his widow and orphans.
Died on 30th of last month in Madison County in 21st year, of
congestive fever, MR. MADISON ANYAN.
Died at residence of her husband in this county on 16 September
1847, MRS. MARTHA JANE EAST, wife of ALEXANDER H. EAST and daughter of
JAMES GORDAN, aged 18-5-10.

October 9, 1847
Died on 23rd ult. at his residence on Mountain Fork in this county,
ALFRED CRINER (oldest son of ISAAC and NANCY (McCAIN) CRINER), a worthy
and exemplary man, leaving a widow and four children and a large family
connection to mourn his loss.

November 6, 1847
Died in Memphis, Tennessee on the way to his home in Texas on 24th
ult., COL. PEYTON S. WYATT, formerly of this county, and well-known by
most of our citizens. He was well noted for his fine social qualities,
warm feelings and generous nature.
Married on Thursday the 4th by REV. S. S. MOODY, MR. SAMUEL J.
SHANKLIN to MISS LUCY ANN, daughter of WM. EASTLAND, Esq. all of this
county.
Married on 19 in Franklin County by HON. D(AVID) G(REENBELL) LIGON,
REV. R(ICHARD) B(YRD) BURLESON (28 in Alabama; son of JONATHON and
---(illegible) (BYRD)) to MISS SARAH (21 in Alabama; 1850 Census
Lawrence County; 1st wife--he married 2. MISS HOLBERT and died in Waco,
Texas), daughter of REV. W(ILLIAM) LEIGH. (Letter from a gen--
MRS. NETTIE LEITCH MAJOR, Washington, D.C. 1957. "I proved WM. LEIGH
Baptist preacher of Florence and have gotten about 10 members into DAK
on his father, ZACHARIAH LEIGH. I hit the jackpot with a Bible! No
one ever learned of all the children of REV. WM. LEIGH, and I have added
4 to those daughters who were known descendants. The sons went to
Texas.")

November 20, 1847
Died at the residence of CAPT. DAVID BRADFORD, MRS. NANCY MARTIN
aged about 80 years, and relict of the late ANDREW MARTIN. Baptist for
last 20 years.
Died at residence of his sons in Madison County, Alabama on 26th
ult. WILLIAM C. MAPLES in 81st year of his age.
Married
On 27th by REV. JAMES SHELTON, MR. ANDREW C. LEGG to MRS. TERRY A.
WALKER, all of Limestone County.
On 24 by G. GREENWOOD, Esq., MR. CALVIN BROWN (24 or 21 in Virginia)
of Decatur to MISS CAROLINE MATISON (21 in Tennessee) of Marshall
County, Alabama (1850).
Married on 13 by REV. PLEASANT J. ECKLES, MR. GEORGE W. LEWIS to
MISS ELIZABETH JOHNSON, all of Madison County.

November 27, 1847
Married in Columbus, Mississippi on 9th, SAMUEL B. MALONE to MISS
WINFIELD, daughter of JAMES T. SYKES.
In this place on Thursday morning 25, by REV. MR. MOODY, COL.
ANDREW ERWIN of Tennessee to MRS. MARY J. CAMP of Huntsville.

December 11, 1847
Married near Whitesburg, Alabama on 3rd by REV. JAMES H. LORANCE,
MR. NATHANIEL EVENS (55 in Virginia) of Somerville, Alabama to MISS

SARAH JANE RICHARDSON (RICHARDS in marriage record; daughter of STEPHEN) of Whitesburg.

Married on 30 by J. W. IRBY, Esq., MR. CRAWFORD HARR, son of MR. JOHN HARR to MISS MARY JANE LUSK, all of McNulty Beat, Madison County.

On 5th by REV. TH. F. KEY, at residence of MRS. RACHEL PROVINCE, MR. JOHN SHARPE of McNulty Beat, to MISS MARY A. CARROLL (MARY JANE in marriage record) of Killensworth Cove, Madison County.

By REV. JAMES W. ALLEN at Triana, in this county on 2nd, MR. THEOPHILUS C. HYMAN to MISS HARRIETT ELIZABETH WARD, both of Martin County, North Carolina.

On 28 October by REV. M. H. BONE, MR. JOHN HALL to MISS A(RTIMISSE) BALES (daughter of ELD--(faded) BAILES), all of this county.

By the same, on 18th, MR. JEFFERSON JENKINS to MISS MARTHA JENKINS all of this county.

By same on 24, MR. BENJAMIN W(ILSON) LAWLER (28 in Alabama, Sumter County) of Sumter County, Alabama to MISS TERRISA LAMBERTSON (24 in Alabama), daughter of MR. JOHN LAMBERTSON, of this county. (she died in Greene County July 20, 1853)

December 25, 1847

Died, ELIZABETH ANDERSON JENKINS on Wednesday the 15th, daughter of STEPHEN and MARY KILLINGSWORTHS and a native of Knox County, Tennessee. Member of M. E. Church. Became the wife of REV. WARREN L. JENKINS in April 1833, whom she left with 4 interesting children.

January 1, 1848

Died in Nashville, on 29th instant MR. STEPHEN S. CHEEK aged about 57 years.

On 26 of pneumonia, MR. LODWICK GRAVETT, a well-known citizen of this county.

Departed this life in the Town of Somerville on 16, after severe illness of 17 days, THOMAS SERVALLEN, only son of TOM (42 in Tennessee) and MARTHA A. PRICE (41 in Georgia) aged 3 years / months.

January 15, 1848

Died at his residence near this village on Sunday morning on 26th December in 49th year of his age, MR. CALEB TONEY, Triana, Alabama January 1, 1848 (long obituary).

Died near Huntsville on evening of 25th December, 1847 LODERICK GRAVETTE aged 39-9-10. Deceased was born in the State of Virginia March 15, 1808 but was principally raised in Madison County. Left an affectionate wife and 3 little children.

January 29, 1848

Died in Decatur on 12 of consumption, MRS. PENELOPE DANCY (she was nee MITCHELL, married 1836), wife of MR. WILLIAM M. DANCEY (33 in North Carolina).

February 5, 1848

Died in Franklin County on 21st, MR. HUGH FINLEY aged 67 years. First white man who settled where Tuscumbia now is.

February 12, 1848

Died at his residence in Madison County on 28th, MR. MARCUS LAFAYETTE HIGH in about the 65th year of his age, of pneumonia. Left a widow and 7 children.

February 19, 1848

Died very suddenly at the residence of her son in Limestone County January 31st 1848, MRS. JANE WORD, consort of WILLIAM WORD, SR. in 75th year of her age.

In Mexico in December last, CHRISTOPHER C. BUDD, corporal of Company F, 13th Infantry. Sick only 2 days.

April 8, 1848

Died in Hutnsville, Alabama April 1, 1848 JEREMIAH C. JONES, son of LEROY H. and MARY A. JONES aged 4 years 2 months 4 days.

At his residence near Berkley in this county on Tuesday the 28th after a violent attack of pleurisy, BURGESS COLBERN, a man much esteemed by his neighbors and a worthy citizen.

493

JAMES BASCOM WARD, son of JOHN and SARAH WARD formerly of Albemarle County, Virginia, died at his father's residence near Huntsville, Alabama on the 26th aged 15 years 7 months.

Died on 31, MR. WILLIAM TAYLOR aged about 35 years, a worthy, honest and industrious citizen of this place.

Very suddenly on 1st at residence of her brother, CAPT. GEORGE STEEL, MRS. ELIZABETH G. DICKEY, for many years a pious member of the Cumberland Presbyterian Church.

WILLIAM H. POPE died on his plantation in Washington County, Mississippi on Wednesday the 22 March in his 42nd year.

April 15, 1848
Departed this life on the 5th instant in Loweville, Madison County, Alabama in 36th year of her age, MRS. HARRIET WILLIAMS, consort of COL. E. W. WILLIAMS and daughter of the late JOHN and present DUANA ALLISON. She was raised in Madison County.

May 20, 1848
Died in Jackson County on 2nd, MRS. RACHEL MITCHELL, consort of A(RCH'D) S. MITCHELL, Esq. (42 in Tennessee) in 5th (4? 5th? 1st figure blurred, but 45 would be right) year of her age. Deceased was from and raised in Madison County and has left a large circle of friends.

June 10, 1848
Married on 30th ult. by REV. G. A. COLLIER, MR. JOEL P. LEDBETTER (31 in Alabama) of Warrenton, Marshall County, Alabama to MISS JANE C. (20 in Alabama), daughter of DR. DILLARD of Jackson County, Alabama.

June 24, 1848
Died at his residence near Lamar, Marshall County, Mississippi on 9th instant CAPT. E. DUPUY in 59th year.

On 17th MR. ELIJAH DRAKE of this county. He was born on 16th of May, 1793.

Married at residence of A. G. HOOK, Esq. in Fayette County, Tennessee by REV. JOSEPH E. DOUGLASS, MAJ. J. J. STEGER, Representative of Marshall County, Mississippi to MISS EMELINE RAIFORD.

August 12, 1848
Married on Thursday evening the 3rd, MR. THOS. ESSLINGER to MISS ELIZA ANN SCOTT.

Died in this place of a very protracted and lingering disease MRS. SUSANNAH BURROW in 38th year of her age. Born in Knox County, Tennessee, raised principally in Lincoln County, same state where she married JAMES BURROW. Cumberland Presbyterian Church. Left a husband and seven children.

September 2, 1848
Died at his residence in Talladega County on 17, MR. JOHN HARDIE, in the 51st year of his age. Deceased was well-known in this community and was an honest, upright, kind hearted sensible man. (He lived 1st in Madison County where he married in 1828 MARY MEADE HALL, daughter of REV. ISAAC HALL).

September 9, 1848
Died in Moulton on 27, REV. WM. GOULD about 40 years of age.

In Tuscumbia on 23 ult., MR. WILLIAM NORTHCROSS. (WILSON NORTHCROSS died August 24, 1848 (see CROXTON Bible; 2nd husband of MARY JANE MISSOURI CROXTON daughter of ELIJAH CROXTON).

October 6, 1848
Married in this place on Tuesday evening last the 3rd instant by REV. S. S. YARBROUGH, CAPT. DUDLEY SALE of this county, to MISS DELIA COLEMAN of Huntsville.

Also at the resience of CAPT. DUDLEY SALE in this county on Wednesday evening last on 4th instant by REV. S. S. YARBROUGH, MR. LEVEN POWELL to MISS FRANCES A. E. HARRIS, only daughter of MR. WILLIAM W. HARRIS and granddaughter of CAPT. SALE, all of Madison County.

October 27, 1848

Died in Russellville, Alabama on 7th instant DR. NOBLE R. LADD in 25th year of his age.

Died at his residence in this county on 15th instant MR. ISAAC POWELL aged about 45 years.

November 17, 1848

Married on 24 instant by REV. JAMES C. ELLIOTT, GEN. JAMES M. LANE to MRS. ELIZA A. F. ANDERSON, all of Limestone County.

On 2 by REV. BETHEL BRYAN, MR. JOHN VARNEL (22 in Tennessee) of Lauderdale County, Alabama (1850 Lauderdale County) to MISS ELIZABETH KATHARINE (20 in Tennessee), daughter of REV. SAMUEL EDMONSON of Limestone County (ancestor of SAML D. F. CANAGAN, Athens, Alabama 1966-- he says SAML married REBECCA HICKS, daughter of JAS. HINSON HICKS and ---- (KNIGHT)).

On Thursday evening 2nd instant by REV. JEPTHA HARRISON, D.D., MR. FERDINAND SANNONER (26 in Alabama) to MISS MARGARET BIGGER (24 in Alabama; Lauderdale County; daughter of JOSEPH), both of Lauderdale County.

December 1, 1848

Died in this county on 30 ult. MRS. MARY DANCY DOUGLASS, daughter of HOLMAN SOUTHALL (he was son of ROBT. CLARK's wife).

In Tuscumbia on 15th, MR. R. T. R. GILLESPIE aged 25 years on 24th, MR. FREDERICK O. SHERROD.

Married on 16 in this county by REV. J. W. ALLEN, COL. DAVID R. SCOTT to MRS. ALMENA A. EARNEST, daughter of W. ROBERTSON, Esq. (see volume 119, page 1 for marriage of AARON EARNEST to ALMENA A. ROBERTSON 8 April 1835.)

On 14th instant by REV. MR. HUSBANDS, MR. H(ENRY) A. SKEGGS to MISS MARY J. HUNT, all of this place.

December 22, 1848

Married on 28th instant, MR. JOHN W(ESLEY) DICKEY (27 in Alabama) of Marshall County to MISS SALINA NEAL (22 in Alabama) of Madison (ancestors of MRS. ROBERT RICKETTS, Jefferson City).

Died on 17 at residence of her father in Huntsville, MISS MARY ANN TABLER aged 17 years 10 months. (she was daughter of WM. TABLER and grand-daughter of MICHAEL TABLER).

Died in Nashville on 9 in 29th year of her age, MARY JANE HENRIETT wife of MR. CHARLES C. PERCY, formerly of this place.

December 29, 1848

Died in Florence on 17th, MRS. ELIZABETH WALKER, wife of GEN. L. P. WALKER in 28th year of her age.

January 5, 1849

Married at Buzzard Roost on 21st instant by REV. W. D. F. SAWRIE, MR. JOHN L(EWIS) MALONE (23 in Alabama; Franklin County) to MISS MARY JANE (20 in Alabama), daughter of the late ARMSTEAD BARTON.

January 19, 1849

Married on 16th day of January, 1849 by REV. B. C. CHAPMAN, MR. JESSE J. SHEID of Franklin County, Tennessee to MRS. CYNTHIA WILKINSON of Madison County, Alabama. (She was daughter of ROBT. HAMLET and married 3 times in Madison County, Alabama. 1. JOHN C. FINLAY--March 29, 1826, 2. JOHN M. WILKINSON--May 6, 1839, 3. JESSE J. SHEID; see will of one JESSE J. SHEID in Sumter County 1861; 2nd wife CYNTHIA--In 1850 he was 38 born in Tennessee; CYNTHIA was 40 born in North Carolina; see volume 158, page 65; and volume 146, page 54 for tombstone of CYNTHIA HAMLETT, born 1810--buried in Jackson County)

January 26, 1849

Died at New Orleans of cholera on 29th, MR. HUGH THOMSON, merchant of Florence.

February 9, 1849

Died in Tuscumbia on 1st REV. J. B. GALLAGHER.

On 22 in Farmington, Mississippi, LEWIS ROFFE, formerly of Franklin County, Alabama aged 58 years.

February 23, 1849
Died in Tuscaloosa the 7th instant DR. JNO. OWEN for many years a resident of Tuscaloosa. DR. OWEN was a minister of the Gospel of Protestant Methodist Church.

March 2, 1849
Departed this life on the 21st at his residence near Somerville, Morgan County, Alabama COL. JAMES B. GRAHAM in the 55th year of his age. Born in Bath County, Virginia on 15th September 1795 and removed to this county nearly 30 years since. Elected clerk of Circuit Court 1824 and continued in office with the exception of 4 years until October 1847....

March 23, 1849
Died on 15th, MR. SAMUEL R. BROOKS aged 22 years.

March 30, 1849
Died in Limestone County on 19th, MR. SAMUEL LENTZ, an old and much respected citizen.
In Madison County at his residence on 23 March 1849, EDWARD DOUGLASS in 74th year of his age after 7 months of extreme suffering with rheumatism. Born and raised in Virginia, moved to this county in 1823. Member of C. P. Church at Liberty.

SOUTHERN ADVOCATE

Published at Huntsville, Alabama

W. B. FIGURES, Editor and Proprietor

April 6, 1849
Married on the 28th instant by REV. W. W. WRIGHT, MR. PATRICK H. POTTER (24 in Virginia to MISS JANE R(EBECCA) HOOSER (25 in Virginia), all of Mooresville, Alabama (Limestone County; see volume 205, page 4).
Married on the 29th instant by REV. P. B. ROBINSON, MR. JOEL R. LOVE to MISS HARRIET McLEOD, all of Madison County (volume 155, page 27)
Married on the 27th instant MR. COVINGTON EDMONDSON (54 in Virginia) to MRS. MAHALA A. H. FAVER (38 in Tennessee), all of Limestone County (volume 205, page 4).
Died in Florence (Lauderdale County) on the 24th instant, MR. HENRY BURROW aged 48.
Died a few days since in Marshall County, MR. SIMEON NICHOLLS, an old and esteemed citizen.

April 13, 1849
Married on the 29th instant, MR. JAMES A. OGLESBY to MISS MARGARET ANN BRUNDIDGE, all of Limestone County (volume 205, page 5).
Died in this county of consumption after protraction of nearly two years, on 16 March 1849, JOSEPH CLOYD, JR. formerly of Botetourt County, Virginia in his 35th year (this is JOS., JR.).... Belonged to the Methodist Episcopal Church South. Left wife and two children, together with many relatives. Lynchburg Virginian please copy.

April 20, 1849
Died on the morning of the 17th ult. at the residence of MRS. CHILDS, MISS VIRGINIA WILSON of Washington County, D.C. aged 21.
Died in this county at the residence of her son, JAMES GORDON (58 in South Carolina) on the 7th of April after a protracted illness, MRS. ELIZABETH GORDON, aged about 83.
Married Thursday evening the 12th instant, by A. L. LOGAN, Esq., MR. JOSEPH HILL to MISS MARIA LEE (MIRA in census and marriage records), daughter of REDDEN LEE, Esq. all of this county in the vicinity of Whitesburg. (volume 147, page 60)
Married on the 10th instant by REV. WILLIAM G. HENSLY, REV. THOMAS A. STRAIN to MRS. MARY C. ROGERS, relic of the late DR. CHRISTOPHER ROGERS and daughter of the HON. HORATO FILPOT, all of Morgan County (volume 105, page 63).

Married on Sunday the 18th of March by REV. MARTIN PUTNAM,
MR. R(ANDOLPH) IVY, Esq. to MISS NANCY L. COLLINS, all of Marshall
County, Alabama (volume 139, page 2).
    Married on the 8th instant, W(INSTON) P. PETTUS to MRS. EVELINE B.
SETSINGER (LETSINGER in marriage record). Also on the 8th, ELIJAH J.
MATHENY to MISS MARY ALEXANDER (see marriage in volume 227, page 65 in
Lauderdale County). On the 10th, S. A. M. WOOD to MISS LELIA LEFTWICH.
On the 10th, REV. J. B. F. SMITH to MISS ELLEN O. ARMSTEAD, all of
Lauderdale County (volume 227).

April 27, 1849
    Died of pleurisy March 8, 1849 MRS. MARGARET MATHKIN (MATKIN)
consort of WILLIAM MATHKIN daughter of ACHIBAD (should be ARCHIBALD) and
ELIZABETH McDONALD (should be McDONNELL) aged 48 years 11 months 19
days. Cumberland Presbyterian.

May 4, 1849
    Died in Limestone County on the 5th, MR. ADAM BIRNEY aged about
84 years. (see letter from MRS. MECCA D. McCOY asking about him)
    Departed this life on Wednesday morning on 2, MRS. ELLEN GORDON
YOUNG, wife of WILLIAM T. YOUNG in 49th year. Born in Petersburg,
Virginia....

May 11, 1849
    P. W. WEAVER, formerly of this place departed this life 20 April
1849 near Naconnah, Tennessee at 12 a.m. Born 1811 in the State of
Virginia. Moved to this State and resided in Huntsville for some time
after which he moved to the western district where he resided for many
years past. M. E. Church....

May 18, 1849
    Died on Wednesday 18, ELLEN GALT MARTIN, daughter of the late
JOHN MARTIN, merchant of this city....

May 25, 1849
    Died on Friday 11th instant in Triana, Madison County after a
short illness, JOHN ARCHER COCKE, a native of Goochland County,
Virginia bur for many years a resident of Madison County, Virginia?
(Alabama?).

August 3, 1849
    Departed this life on Wednesday 25 July MR. ROBERT GRAHAM aged
about 50 years. Born in Monaghan, North of Ireland and for the last
25 years a resident of Huntsville   Kind husband and father.
    Died in Somerville, Morgan County, Alabama on Monday the 16th of
July, HARRIET EUGENIA, daughter of WILLIAM P. (40 in Virginia) and
MARY LOU (32 in Virginia) TERRY aged 5-2-6.
    At Sherwood, Lunenburg County, Virginia, on the morning of July 18,
ROGER ATKINSON, son of HENRY C. and ELIZA W. LAY of this place aged
nearly 14 months.
    Suddenly on 25, MR. WM. BEALE of this place aged about 23.
    At Bell Factory on 22, MRS. ELEANOR TABER, wife of MR. WM. TABER.

August 17, 1849
    Died at Mammoth Cave, Kentucky on 18th, MR. WM. EAKIN of Nashville
of firm of W. and T. EAKIN and Company.
    State of Alabama--Morgan County. 29 July 1849 Orphan's Court.
WILLIAM MORROW, administrator of WILLIAMS HAWKINS, deceased.

August 24, 1849
    Resolutions on death of JAMES J. PLEASANTS, which took place at
his residence yesterday.

August 31, 1849
    Died in Lawrence County on 17th, MR. ALEX'R ROSS aged 67.
    In Lowndes County, Mississippi on 5th, MR. A. S. HOGAN aged 72,
formerly of Franklin County, Alabama.
    On 21st, BENJ. D. WALKER of Tuscumbia aged 22.

September 7, 1849
    Died in Forence on 27 July after a lingering illness of 3 months,
ANN ELIZABETH, eldest daughter of ABRAM and E. M. DEAN aged 11 years
10 days.
    At Cahawba, on 17th, JOSEPH BRYAN, a well known Steam Boat Captain
for many years on Alabama river.
    In Athens on 28th, MR. JONATHON J. VASSER aged 33 years, a popular
merchant and good citizen.
    On 29, MRS. REBECCA W. PETTUS wife of W. R. PETTUS of Limestone.

September 14, 1849
    MRS. EMILY J. PLEASANTS died at Huntsville September 2 aged 41.
Daughter of GOVERNOR THOMAS BIBB and PAMELIA THOMPSON and was born in
Petersburg, Virginia on 20 November 1808.... Married 30 July 1824
COL. JAMES J. PLEASANTS....
    Died in Dallas County MRS. MARGARET O. BLEVINS (see Bible record),
wife of MR. JOHN BLEVINS aged 41. Formerly a resident for many years
of this place where she was raised. Episcopalian.
    Died on 27, DR. JOHN V. McKINNEY of Fayetteville, Tennessee in his
60th year.
    On 31st, MR. JAS. GRIGSBY, an old citizen of Limestone.
    Married on 9th at residence of MRS. DEMENT's by REV. R. W. CRUTCHER,
MR. PHILIP DEDMAN to MRS. MARY C. VAUGHAN all of this county.

September 21, 1849
    Died in Lauderdale County (will in volume 104, page 47) on 3rd,
MR. LEVI CASSITY of Cypress Factory aged 50 years.
    In Franklin County on 11th, CAPT. GEORGE COCKBURN, an old citizen.

September 28, 1849
    Died on 9th after a short illness, MRS. MARTHA HALL, consort of
the late CAPT. THOMAS H. HALL of Triana in 58th year. Native of
Charlestown, Virginia, where she came to womanhood.
    Departed this life September 22 at Huntsville, Alabama at the resi-
dence of her son, NEILL McCORD, MRS. JENET McCORD, consort of AZEL
McCORD, who was born in Warren County, Kentucky February 5, 1795,
aged 54 years.
    On 25th, in this place, MARGAERT ELLEN aged about 13 years,
daughter of MRS. MARY WALPOLE.

October 5, 1849
    Died at her residence, MARY HOLLOWELL, consort of WM. D. HOLLOWELL
on 1st instant at 7 a.m. after a lingering illness of 18 weeks, in her
40th year. Baptist 9 years. Holly Springs copy.
    Married on the 20th instant in New Market by REV. M. H. BONE,
M. WILLIAM DOUGLASS to MISS MARY JANE LAUGHINGHOUSE, all of Madison
County. (volume 133, page 23)
    Died at her residence, MARY HOLLOWELL, consort of WILLIAM D. HOLLOWELL
on the 1st instant at 7 a.m. after a lingering illness of 18 weeks....
Died in her 40th year, after having been a member of the Baptist Church
nine years. Holly Springs papers please copy. (Tombstone--MARY
HOLLOWELL, wife of WM. D. HOLLOWELL and daughter of WM. ECHOLS, SR.--
born March 29, 1810, died October 1, 1849--and three HOLLOWELL children.
Her husband and several children are buried in Maple Hill, Huntsville
and while she and these children are buried in the ECHOLS cemetery)

October 12, 1849
    Died on 30th, MR. J. A. MONTGOMERY aged 24 of Athens (probably she
same as ANDREW J., died October 1, 1849 at 23 buried in Garden cemetery)

October 19, 1849
    Died on 14 after a short illness, MR. THOMAS D. BRADFORD aged 34
leaving many friends and relations to mourn his loss.

October 26, 1849
    Married in this place on the 18th instant by REV. E. C. SLATER,
MR. JOHN C. YERGER to MISS MARIA F. KINKLE (volume 113, page 97).
    Married at the residence of MR. C. C. GERON in this place on the
18th instant by REV. E. C. SLATER, MR. JOHN H. BINFORD to MISS AMELIA
MATILDA ALLEN of Limestone County (volume 100, page 13).

Married on the 25th instant in this place by REV. P. B. ROBINSON, CHARLES W(ILLIAM) ROBINSON, Esq. to MISS FANNY M. DAVIDSON, both of Ramelton, Ireland (volume 76, page 20).

November 2, 1849
     Died of an affliction of the lungs in this vicinity the 26th October 1849, MR. A. T. MADDERA. Born in Surry County, Virginia August 10th, 1792 making him over 57. Resident of this county for 30 years....
     Died of pneumonia, 20th October, MR. JOHN FORD in his 62nd year. Born in Amelia County, Virginia on 15 April 1788 and lived in his native state until the year 1819 when he emigrated to Madison County, Alabama where on 24 June 1823 he was married to MISS MARIANNE ROPER, with whom he lived until his death. Methodist Episcopal Church.
     Died at Bellefonte on 24 MR. H. F. DELANCY aged 45, a worthy citizen.

November 9, 1849
     REV. P. B. ROBINSON will preach the funeral sermon of B. D. SCHRIMSHER at the Baptist Meeting House in Big Cove on the third Sunday of this month at 11 a.m.
     Died October 9, 1849 at the residence in Panola County, Mississippi, CAPT. ALEXANDER BOTELER, formerly a resident of Morgan County in his 41st year, leaving a wife and nine children and numerous relations....
     Died suddenly on the 5th instant, MRS. MARY EWING, wife of MR. STEPHEN S. EWING of this vicinity.

November 16, 1849
     Married on the 25th instant by REV. MR. COLLIER (daughter of GEORGE), MR. JOHN TAYLOR (24 in Alabama) to MISS NANCY DILWORTH (29 in North Carolina), all of this county (volume 151, page 27).
     Married on the 21st instant at the residence of SAMUEL McMURRY, EDWARD G. MUSGROVE to MISS NANCY McMURRY, all of Blount County, Alabama.
     Married on the 12th instant by REV. J. C. ELLIOTT, MR. ROBERT LEWIS to MISS MARY P. daughter of PLEASANT STRONG, all of this county (volume 155, page 28).
     Died on the 28th of October, MRS. JANE H. KELLEY, consort of COL. RUSSEL J. KELLEY of Madison County, Alabama in her 39th year.
     Died in Athens (Limestone County) on the 1st instant, MRS. MARY LUCY MALONE, wife of MAJ. JOHN N. MALONE.
     At the same place on the 3rd instant, MRS. ELIZA MALONE, wife of DR. T. STITH MALONE and daughter of CAPT. NICH. DAVIS, aged about 27.
     Died on the 9th in his 4th year and on the 16th in her 10th year, JOHN and BETTIE, children of JOHN F. and FRANCIS E. BANKS of Somerville, Alabama (Morgan County).
     Departed this life on the morning of the 7th instant in her 32nd year, MRS. SARAH E. THOMPSON, wife of ROBERT THOMPSON, Esq. of Somerville, Alabama (Morgan County) Florence Gazette copy.

November 23, 1849
     Married on the evening of the 15th instant by REV. WILLIAM JONES, MR. BARTLEY C. JOHNSON (son of JOSHUA) to MISS ELIZABETH L. DITTO, all of Marshall County, Alabama (volume 139, page 9, 265).
     Married on the 8th instant by REV. B(ENJ) H. HUBBARD, MR. FERDINAND P. MADDIN (21 in Tennessee) to MISS MATTIE A. R. MALONE (18 in Alabama), daughter of THOMAS H. MALONE, Esq. all of Limestone County.
     Married on the 8th instant by REV. M. H. BONE, MR. JOHN T. LOWRY of Mississippi to MISS VIRGINIA H. MILLER, daughter of the late JOHN MILLER of New Market, Alabama. (volume 155, page 28)

November 30, 1849
     Married by REV. DR. COSSITT on the 20th ult. COL. LOUIS J. DUPREE of Macon, Mississippi to MISS AMELIA M. JONES, daughter of GOV. JAMES C. JONES of Lebanon, Tennessee.
     Married on the 8th instant, MR. T(OLIVER) L. FERGUSON (39 in North Carolina) to MISS ELIZABETH WALTON (19 in Virginia), all of Marshall County (volume 139, page 8).
     Died in Limestone County on the 29th of October, CHARLES VICKRY aged 85 years; on October 30, POLLY VICKRY aged 75 years; on November 1st, ANNA VICKRY aged 79 years.

December 7, 1849
        Married on the 27th instant MR. SAMUEL A. SLAUGHTER of Madison
County, Alabama to MISS MARTHA E. CLABORNE of Lincoln, Tennessee.
        Married on the 6th instant, ROBERT C. WINTHROP, late Speaker of
the House of Representatives to MRS. WELLS, a wealthy and fashionable
lady of Boston.
        Died on the 17th instant in Vienna (Alabama) in his 22nd year,
MR. THOMAS L. BAINS...Methodist.
        Died in Athens (Limestone County) on the 21st instant, JAMES
ALLEN, son of REV. J. W. ALLEN.

December 14, 1849
        Married on the 29th instant, MR. SAMUEL SEAY to MRS. RACHAEL R.
HUDNELL, both of Nashville.
        Married by REV. M. H. BONE on the 5th instant, DR. WILLIAM D. ALLEN
to MISS MARTHA ACKLEN, all of Loweville, Madison County (volume 71,
page 8).
        Married on the 8th instant by REV. J. LEROY HARRIS, MR. JOHN T(HOMAS)
DILWORTH to MISS MARGARET A(NN) SMITH, all of this county. (volume 133
page 23).
        Married on the 29th instant by same, MR. HOWARD A(LEX) TORBET
(26 in Tennessee) to MISS CYNTHIA ANN GARDNER (20 in Alabama), all of
this county. (1st wife--MRS. HUBERT M. NORWOOD (client of MISS CLAIR
WRIGHT) is descendant of 2nd wife, MARTHA NAVE. TORBETS in 1850 census
Madison County, 1860 census Perry County, married MARTHA NAVE, Perry
County March 15, 1859, volume 151, page 27, 35)
        Departed this life, AMANDA NOWLIN COLEMAN, born in Davidson County,
Tennessee on July 11, 1809 and so was in her 41st year. Daughter of
WILLIAM and SARAH BIBB, both of whom lived for many years and died in
the immediate vicinity of this place.... When she was a mere girl,
her parents removed and settled down within sight of Huntsville. At
the age of 16 or 17, she joined the Methodist Episcopal Church. She
married on October 2, 1828 WILLIAM B. DENNETT by whom there were two
children, WILLIAM and JAMES. Her first husband died September 18, 1839
and she was again married to JOHN J. COLEMAN, Esq. on June 6, 1841 and
departed this life most suddenly Friday morning December 7, 1849 at
5 o'clock. She left two little children by her last husband--JOHN WILLIAMS
WALKER and AMANDA NARCISSA GRAVES, the former upwards of 6 and the latter
under 3 years....
        Died on the 29th instant, at Cairo, COL. JOHN H. WILSON, formerly
commander of the Steamboat Huntsville.

December 21, 1849
        Died at 10 p.m. at the residence of RICHARD MARTIN in Madison
County, MRS. SUSANNA FITZ aged 90 years.
        In Florence on 7th, MR. JOSEPH ALEXANDER aged 44 years.

January 16, 1850
        Died near Marianna, Florida on 18, JUDGE S. W. CARMACK of
Fayetteville, Tennessee.

January 30, 1850
        Died in Athens on 17, MRS. MARTHA A. IRWIN, wife of WM. IRWIN
aged about 49 years.
        On 19th, in same place, WM. BROWN aged 15.
        In Columbus, Mississippi on 27, RUFFIN COLEMAN aged 51.
        In Madison County on 3rd, JAMES THOMAS and on 10th, FEODORAH S. L.
infant children of MR. R. E. BRISTER.

February 13, 1850
        Died in Memphis on 31 ult. of cholera, MR. A. H. CLIFTON aged 50.
        Married on 6th, MR. STEPHEN A. HUNT to MRS. SARAH L. TRAVIS, both
of Athens (SARAH LOUISA TRAVIS was divorced from HENRY TRAVIS in
Limestone County 1846).

February 20, 1850
        Died on 27 in Madison County, DR J. A. FINDLEY aged 27 of consump-
tion formerly a resident of Philadelphia.
        Departed this life on 10th at residence of her son-in-law, COL.
J. N. FLETCHER, MRS. MARY CHEATHAM, daughter of the late STEPHEN BEASLEY

of Nottoway County, Virginia and widow of the late BRANCH CHEATHAM of Manchester, Virginia aged 65 years.

February 27, 1850
Died on 19th, MR. JESSE G. SCOTT, an old and highly respectable citizen of Huntsville.

March 6, 1850
Died on 27 KATE ERSKINE, daughter of JAMES H. and MARY JANE MASTIN aged 5 years.
In Athens on 25th, MRS. L. M. G. SWAIN aged 41.
In same place on same day, MISS MARY A. T. WARD aged 12.

March 13, 1850
Departed this life at her residence in Madison County 21st February, MRS. FRANCES COSBY in her 68th year and a native of Louisa County, Virginia.
Died on 26th, MRS. ANN B. WHITMAN, wife of COL. W(ILLIAM) F(ENNO) WHITMAN, near New Market, Alabama (1st wife--he married 2. UNITY MILLER, 3. DOROTHY JONES)

March 20, 1850
Died in Benton County on 10th ult., JOHN CHANDLER aged 104 years, a revolutionary soldier. (last payment of pension says he died February 19, 1850)
In Camden, Arkansas on 16th in 71st year of his age, REV. PORTER CLAY, last surviving full brother of HENRY CLAY.

April 10, 1850
Died in this county on 8th (married 1849 LUVISA ACKARD), after a long and painful illness, MRS. LEVISA CAMPBELL, wife of MR. GEORGE W. CAMPBELL aged about 25.

April 24, 1850
Married on the 6th, MR. GEORGE J. ISOM to MISS ELEANOR E. HARRISON, both of Limestone County.
Died on Sunday morning, 17th of last month, MRS. MARY FRANCES PICKETT, wife of MR. STEPTOE PICKETT of Limestone County and only sister of MR. JOHN J. WARD in 21st year of her age....
Died on 17th, MR. JOHN M. CULP for many years a citizen of this county.
On 22nd, JAMES PLEASANTS, infant son of BENJAMIN and CAROLINE JOLLEY.
On 23, MR. WM. A. McKINZIE of consumption; left wife and relations.

May 1, 1850
Died in Madison County on 18th, MRS. EMMA J. wife of WILLIAM LANFORD. Born in North Carolina on 20 April 1811. In the year 1818 moved to this country. In 1831 or about that time married to DR. DUARMON of Madison County, where she resided a number of years. After his decease, she remained a widow for several years. In 1844 on 16 July she married WILLIAM LANFORD of this county. In 1842 joined the M. E. Church.... (Letter from MR. d'ARMAND--February 27, 1952--"I have identified BENJ. DUARMON as a son of HUGH DEYARMON, SENIOR, of Uniontown, Fayette County, Pennsylvania. Also BENJ. had 3 brothers: ALEXANDER, HUGH, JR. and MELHERD. 1830 census for Madison County, Alabama shows him as head of a household --- (faded) only 3 m 20-30; 1 m 15-20. These correspond to ages of his brothers. Also, I have a notation that his father died at age of 45 by a fall from a horse. His 1st child was born 1798, so we can assume he was grown which would bring his death before 1830. It is possible and probable that BENJ.'s younger brothers were with him temporarily in 1830. A family letter says that a nephew saw BENJ. in Uniontown in 1835; probably on a visit. His title as a doctor also agrees as another letter said he went at an early age to Knoxville to study medicine and later became an M.D. MRS. VA P. LIDWIN, Crystal, Texas 1957 says EMILY J. AULD wife of BENJ. DUARMON was daughter of JOLIN and NANCY (ANN JACKSON) AULD; granddaughter of DR. ISAAC and MARY JACKSON of Madison County. She was widow of BENJ. DUARMON, who was dead in 1837. ROSCOE d"ARMAND says "I have identified BENJ. DEARMON as belonging to the family of HUGH DeGARMON of -50-Pennsylvania."

May 8, 1850
  Died at his father's residence in this county on 15th after a long
and protracted illness, HENRY MARTIN in 25th year of his age.

May 29, 1850
  Died on 25 at his residence in Macon, DR. ARCHIBALD M. CLEMENS,
a resident physician of that place aged about 33. Native of Madison
County....

June 5, 1850
  Died in Tuscaloosa on 16, CAPT. JOHN PHELAN, for many years a
citizen of Huntsville.
  In Nashville on 28th ult., MRS. MARTHA MEAD in her 66th year,
formerly of this place. (HARRIS book says aged 61)

June 12, 1850
  Died in Talladega County on 27, COL. MICAH TAUL, formerly of
Franklin County, Tennessee.
  In Tishomingo County, Mississippi on 28th, CAPT. HENRY COOK,
many years ago a resident of Huntsville.

June 17, 1850
  Died in Limestone County, Alabama, May 8, 1850, MRS. MARY LOUISA
BINFORD aged 20 years. United to THOMAS BINFORD, Esq. in marriage
July 29, 1849. Member of M. E. Church....
  Married on 8th, MR. JOHN L. VERNON to MISS ELIZABETH E. CRAWFORD,
both of Limestone.
  On 9th, MR. EDMUND J. WRIGHT (26 in Alabama) of Lawrence to MISS
MARY E. COPELAND (15 in Alabama) of Limestone.
  On 12 by REV. J. C. ELLIOTT, MR. JOSHUA O. KELLY (23 in Alabama;
son of DAVID (census)) to MISS SARAH B. daughter of MR. CHARLES STRONG
(15 in Alabama), all of this county.

July 3, 1850
  Died of cholera at Shelbyville, Tennessee on 11th while returning
home from New Orleans, MRS. LUCINDA WYCHE, consort of DR. JOHN F. WYCHE
of Madison County, Alabama in her 48th year. Professed religion 1823,
M. E. Church. Left a husband and 6 children. Her remains were brought
immediately home and entered in the family burying ground of her father,
the late MAJOR DANIEL WRIGHT.
  Died in Huntsville June 22, 1850, ENOCH ELLIOTT, who was born 7th
of July 1775 in Randolph County, North Carolina. In early life he was
associated with Quaker church in which church he was a member till the
year 1809, at which time he emigrated to the State of Tennessee, Maury
County. In the year 1818, he settled in Tuscaloosa in this State in
which place he united himself with the M. E. Church. In the year 1838
he became a resident of Huntsville, Alabama where he spent his last
days.... Aged 74-11-15. Left a wife and a number of children.
Tuscaloosa papers please copy.
  Died in the 2nd instant of congestive fever, at his residence in
this county, RANDOLPH SULLIVAN, Esq. in his 63rd year. Native of
South Caroline, Lawrence District and emigrated to this State in the
fall of 1816 and pitched his tent at his late residence.... Left a
widow and large family of children.

July 10, 1850
  Died in the vicinity of Huntsville on 28 ult. JAMES STREET aged
about 28 years....

July 19, 1850
  Married on 27 by REV. S. R. CALDWELL, MR. WM. MATKINS of this
vicinity to MRS. MARGARET A. TATE of Limestone.

July 26, 1850
  Died on 17th in this place after a painful illness, COL. BENJAMIN
HARRISON aged about ---- years, a native of Virginia, but for many
years a citizen of this county. Most amiable, upright, worthy man and
much esteemed by all who knew him.
  Died in Eutaw on 16, COL. H(ILLIARD) M. JUDGE aged 32 and on 18th,
HON. ALEXANDER GRAHAM.

August 2, 1850
    Died July 16, 1850 after a protracted illness of 4 weeks on Monte
Sano, KATE, daughter of MR. and MRS. WM. H. THOMSON aged 1-9-16.
    In Tuscumbia on 21 at residence of his father, WM. COOPER, Esq.
in 25th year of his age, LANGSTON COOPER, Esq. of Memphis.
    In Courtland, on 10th, MR. NATHAN J. CALLAWAY (43 in Georgia),
aged about 40.
    On 20th in Marshall County, MRS. MARTHA HIGHTOWER (37 in North
Carolina), wife of J(OHN) C. HIGHTOWER (38 in South Carolina).
    In Athens on 28th, MRS. SARAH A. B. MENDUM (married in Limestone
County 1844; marriage record says SARAH REECE, newspaper says SARAH
BREECE), wife of ROBT. J. MENDUM, in her 26th year. In same place on
30th, WM. PARROTT, son of GEN. G. S. HOUSTON in his 5th year. In same
place, on same day, RICHARD OWEN, son of JOHN A. LEE, in his 3rd year.
    In this place on Monday last after a very short illness, ROBERT S.
CHAMBERS, a young gentleman of unblemished reputation and greatly
esteemed by a large circle of acquaintances.
    Departed this life on 26th, APPELLUS AUGUSTA, infant daughter of
JOSHUA H. and PAULINA S. BEADLE aged 2 years.
    Married on 22 near Vienna, Madison County by REV. G. A. COLLIER,
MR. A. W. ARNOLD (41 in South Carolina; married before) of Summit,
Blount County, Alabama to MISS F(RANCES) E. A. RIVERS.
    On 28th by REV. JOSEPH WHITE, MR. AUGUSTUS M(EED) HEWLETT of
Madison, to MISS NARCISSUS (VENILA) CROXTON of Franklin (daughter of
ELIJAH CROXTON).
    On 24th, MR. WM. H. WIGGS (34 in North Carolina) to MISS NANCY
McCAIN (31 in Tennessee), both of Marshall County.

August 9, 1850
    Married on 29 at Robinson's Springs, Autauga County, by REV.
A. MORRISON, HON. L(EROY) P(OPE) WALKER (33 in Alabama) of Florence
(Lauderdale), Alabama to MISS ELIZA DICKSON PICKETT (18 in Alabama),
daughter of the late JUDGE PICKETT of Montgomery.
    On 6th by REV. B. C. CHAPMAN, MR. JOHN R. GARDNER (see letter from
MRS. CHELF) of Rutherford County, Tennessee, to MISS EMMA B. EASTLAND
of this county (she was daughter of WM. and ANN PANNEL (BRONAUGH)
EASTLAND; grand-daughter of SAM'L and NA--- (faded) (MASSIL) BRONAUGH).
    On 30 July at residence of MR. DAVID ALLISON, Madison County, by
REV. J. LEROY HARRIS, REV. A(LEX) PENLAND of Courtland, Alabama to
MISS ISABELLA L. ALLISON, eldest daughter of MR. DAVID ALLISON.
    Died at residence in Limestone County, Alabama on 28th of July,
in the 93rd year of his age, MR. JOHN WEBB, an old and respectable
citizen of that county. Baptist for about 30 years.

August 16, 1850
    Obituary of ROBERT S. CHAMBERS. Died in this place Monday 29
July. Son of DR. HENRY CHAMBERS....
    Died in Moulton, Alabama on 1, MR. JOHN M. JACKSON (51 in Virginia).

August 21, 1850
    Married on 14th, MR. JAMES T. PETTIT of Memphis to MISS JANE FOSTER,
daughter of WM. COOPER, Esq. of Tuscumbia.
    On 15th, MR. J(OSHUA) S. DITTO (24 in Alabama) to MISS RHODA
GARRISON, all of Marshall County.
    Died on 16th, MR. WM. HIGGINS, an old citizen of Huntsville.

September 4, 1850
    Married on 15 by REV. MR. LAY, MR. JAMES M. WILSON to MISS MARY E.
MILLER, both of this county.
    Died on 16 in city of New York, MR. JOHN B(RISCOE) LEFTWICH
(44 in Virginia, Lauderdale County), citizen and merchant of Florence.
    Tribute of respect to brother F. M. JONES, who died suddenly
Union Division No. 14, S. of T. To citizen of Florence, who so kindly
administered to our stranger brother; to his widowed mother towards
her first born.

September 11, 1850
    Married on 25, THOMAS S. TWEEDY (21 in Alabama; son of JOS M.) of
Lawrence County to MISS ELIZA PEEBLY of Athens.

On 3, MR. JONATHON FISHER to MISS MARY S. SNEAD, both of Limestone.
On 29 by S. LEROY HARRIS, MR. RICHARD HOLMES to MISS FRANCIS A.
ASHBORN (marriage book 4B says FRANCES ASHCRAFT), all of Madison
County.
Departed this life at his residence in this county, ROWLAND GOOCH,
an early resident and most estimable citizen. Born in Albemarle County,
Virginia on 22 April 1778 and at time of death was 72-4-7 years.
Methodist Episcopal Church.
In Tuscumbia on 29, DR. ALEXANDER SPOTSWOOD MOORE (62 in Alabama)
aged 61 years.

September 18, 1850
JOHN VANHOOZER died near New Market, Tennessee on 1st aged 122
years!

September 25, 1850
Married on 17th at Walnut Springs, Woodford County, Kentucky,
by REV. THOMAS CLELAND, REV. J. H. ZIVLEY, Pastor of Presbyterian
Church, Huntsville, Alabama to MRS. MARY SUTTON of Woodford County,
Kentucky.
On 12, W. W. PHILLIPS of Giles County, Tennessee to MISS ELIZA CLAY
of Limestone County, Alabama.
On 4, by REV. G. A. COLLIER, GEORGE RUSSELS, Esq. to MISS H. S.
MILLER, all of this county.
Died in Athens on 12, HENRY M. ECKENBURGER aged 35. Also on 12th,
only daughter of GEN. GEORGE S. HOUSTON. Also on 12, MRS. SARAH COMPTON
aged 35 wife of W. R. COMPTON.
In Limestone County, Alabama on 16, ADAM POWELL (he was son of
JOHN) aged 34.
In Morgan County on 16, MRS. SALLY ANN FLETCHER (24 in Alabama)
aged 26, wife of DR. NATHAN FLETCHER (38 in Virginia; married in
Limestone County 19 September 1840; SARAH A. SMITH).

October 2, 1850
Married on 25, MR. DAVID H. HALSEY (30 in Virginia) to MISS MARY
WOOD (21 in Alabama). On 24, MR. JAMES M. ALLISON to MRS. MARTHA NEIL,
all of Tuscumbia, Alabama.
Died in Galveston, Texas on 9, MRS. ELIZA ANN, wife of MR.
W. T. M. SMITHSON, formerly of this place aged 34.

October 9, 1850
Married on Wednesday morning the 2nd, by REV. E. C. SLATER, MR.
ROBERT J. HART to MISS MARY E. daughter of MR. JOHN HALSEY this vicinity.
On 3rd, JAMES JACKSON, Esq. (Lauderdale County), to MISS ELIZABETH
PERKINS (18 in Tennessee), all of Lauderdale.
Died on 3rd near Whitesburg, GEORGE McLEOD, Esq. an old and respec-
table citizen of this county.

October 17, 1850
Married on 26 by REV. G. A. COLLIER, MR. JOHN D. W. SMITH to
MISS SARAH M. DILWORTH--all of this county.
By same on 1st, MR. R(OBERT) A. WALTON to MISS M(ARGARET) T(ALITHA)
PICKENS--all of this county.
By same, MR. JOSEPH COBB to MISS MARY J. RUSSEL, all of this county.
Died near Pulaski, Tennessee on 19 September after a protracted
protracted illness of 4 weeks, MR. ISAAC SKILLERN in his 63rd year.
(letter from MRS. ETHELMSE CARTER, Minneapolis, Minnesota 1961--"ISAAC
CAMPBELL SKILLERN died September 18, 1850--moved from Lee County,
Virginia about 1832. Her ancestor was a MR. EATHERLY who married
MISS SKILLERN whose daughter SUSANNAH EATHERLY born 1801 Tennessee,
Davidson County, MR. JOS. GULLIFORD) Born in the State of Virginia and
removed to this place in the year 1817, where he was long a merchant
noted for industry and business integrity. In the spring of 1848, he
removed to this county and settled near Pulaski, Tennessee where he
remained until his death. Presbyterian. Kind husband and father.

October 30, 1850
Married on 17, MR. JAMES SKEETERS to MISS ELIZA E. HANEY all of
Limestone.

Died on 27, ROBERT MICAJAH, infant of MR. and MRS. WM. McBRANDON.
In Selma on 9th at residence of her father, COL. P. J. WEAVER,
MRS. MARY BLEVINS, wife of MR. WM. A. BLEVINS aged 23.
On 17, MISS ANN MARIA HENDRICKS aged 17.
On same day, MRS. ELIZA SKEETERS wife of WILLIAM SKEETERS, JR.
aged 17 all of Limestone.
On 20, MR. ELIJAH HOBGOOD (54 in North Carolina) an old citizen of
Franklin County.
In Nashville, on 23, MR. CHARLES B. PERCY, formerly of this
place and had many virtues and many friends.

November 20, 1850
    Married on Wednesday evening the 6th at the residence of JUDGE
PRICE in Somerville by REV. J. LEROY HARRIS, DR. JAS. M. JACKSON (23
in Tennessee) to MISS A. E(LIZA) D. WILKINSON (21 in Alabama), both
residents of that place.
    On the 7th, by REV. GABRIEL MOORE, DR. J. N. BLEDSOE of this place
to MISS AMANDA M. PARVIN of Bourbon County, Kentucky.
    In Lawrence County, Alabama at the residence of J. H. S. DONNEL on
7th by REV. DAVID BRIDENTHALL, HON. TRUMAN SMITH, Senator in Congress
from Connecticut to MISS M. A. DICKINSON, formerly of Litchfield,
Connecticut.
    On 7th, DR. SAMUEL D. DELOATE to MRS. ELIZABETH S. CLAIBOURNE
(daughters of JAS N.) and on same day, MR. SAMUEL TILLMAN (21 in Alabama)
to MISS CORNELIA F. NOEL (16 in Alabama, daughter of JAS.,sister),
all of Lauderdale.
    Died at his residence in Huntsville on 17th, DR. FRED JONES aged
about 50 years, after a few days illness. Born and raised in North
Carolina. Educated at Chapel Hill. For some years was a resident of
Tennessee in the year 1816, became a resident of Huntsville, Alabama.
From Huntsville, he removed to Mississippi where he passed several
years in practice of his profession and then moved back to Huntsville.
Left a large and respectable family.
    On 3rd of influenza or cold at his residence in Big Cove, Madison
County, Alabama, HARRY BUFORD (HARVY in another record; HENRY in census;
69 in Virginia) in 71st year. Born in Virginia and emigrated to this
country in early day and settled on the plantation where he died....
    On 13, MR. JAMES NOEL (70 in Virginia) of Florence. On 11th,
MR. T. LACY aged 24 of Limestone County.
    In Tuscaloosa on 29, at advanced age of 80, HON. MARMADUKE WILLIAMS,
long and favorably known in political history of Alabama.

November 27, 1850
    Married on Tuesday evening the 19th by REV. W. D. F. SAWRIE,
MR. GEO. W. YUCKLEY to MISS MARY R. C. CHEWNING, all of this county.
    On 14, near Hillsboro (Lawrence County), Alabama by REV. DR.
ROBINSON, DR. ALEXANDER A. WALL of Madison to MISS AMANDA M. ROSS
(20 in Alabama; ELIZ).
    On 7th, MR. HARVEY N. JIMASON (18 in Alabama) of Lawrence to MISS
MARTHA A. MITCHELL of Franklin.
    On 13th, MR. JAMES J. HOGG of Tuscumbia to MRS. MARTHA J. SCOGGIN
of Louisville, Kentucky.
    On 14th, MR. W. E. HOKE to MISS MARY P. THOMPSON, both of Limestone.
    Died in Tuscumbia on 15, MRS. DOLLY B. PRYOR of this place aged
62 years.
    On 17, in same place, REUBEN TONEY (23 in Alabama) aged 23.

December 4, 1850
    Died on 27 after a short illness, MR. SAMUEL HATTON aged about
52 years. Native of North Carolina, but has resided in this county for
last 30 years. Kind hearted citizen, amiable man, a good citizen and
death much regretted.
    Died at his father's residence in Big Cove, Madison County,
Alabama CLEMENT CLAY (1833-50) SCHRIMSHER in 18th year....

December 11, 1850
    Died in Decatur, on 1st, MRS. ELIZABETH S. ROGERS (30 in Virginia)
aged 30 years wife of DR. G(EO) W. A. ROGERS (45 in Virginia). Baptist.

December 18, 1850
    Married on Thursday evening the 12th, by REV. THOMAS WOODARD,
MR. RICHARD CHEWNING to MISS SCYNTHA N. SPENCE all of this county.
    On 5th, GEORGE W. BARKSDALE to MISS MARY S. HICKS, both of
Limestone.

January 1, 1851
    Married in Aberdeen, Mississippi on 19th, DR. JAMES A. WIMBUSH
formerly of Halifax County, Virginia to MISS MINERVA, daughter of
COL. JOHN F. MILLS.
    On same evening, MR. SAMUEL WHITFIELD to MISS MARGIA, daughter of
COL. THOMAS BRANDON.
    On 18th, MR. ROBERT WILLIAMSON of Tuscumbia to MRS. ELIZA MARTIN
daughter of GOV. McVAY of Lauderdale.
    On 18th, DR. THOMAS MATTINGLY (32 in D.C.) to MISS FRANCIS WALKER
(19; daughter of PETER), both of Florence.
    On 18th, MR. J. H. THOMAS of Florence to MISS AVERY ANN BLASSENGAME
of Moulton.
    Died on 11th of cholera on board of the Saxon near Byou Sara,
MR. WILLIAM ARTHUR JONES, formerly of this place. Died while on his
way to Texas where he had recently settled. Amiable young man.

SOUTHERN ADVOCATE

Published at Huntsville, Alabama

by WILLIAM B. FIGURES, Editor and Proprietor

January 8, 1851
    Married on the 26th instant MR. W. B. GLOVER of Lawrence County,
Tennessee to MISS A. E. RICH of Limestone County, Alabama.
    Married on the 28th of November, MR. ROBERT L. HARPER (21 in
Alabama) to MISS REBECCA M. MAXWELL (21 in Alabama), all of Limestone
County, Alabama (daughter of REBECCA; volume 205, page 26).
    Married on the 18th of December, DR. DAVID W. BLACKBURN to MISS
MARTHA SUSAN DUBLIN (21 in Alabama), both of Madison County (daughter
of JAS.).
    On the 26th of December, MR. NATHANIEL M. GOUCH (GOOCH) (30 in
Alabama) to MISS SUSAN LIGHTSEY of Madison County.
    On the 31st by REV. M. H. BONE, MR. JAMES SANFORD to MISS MARIANA,
daughter of MILLS JENKINS, Esq. all of this county (ancestor of MRS.
KATIE SANFORD JONES, Huntsville, Alabama, 1957).
    On the 1st instant by same, MR. MATTHEW JORDAN to MISS IBBY HALL,
all of this county.
    On the 26th instant by REV. P. B. ROBINSON, MR. JAMES B. WARE to
MISS MARGARET J. CLEVELAND, all of this county.
    Married on the 17th ult. by REV. G. A. COLLIER, R(EV) J(OHN) J.
BURDINE (36 in Georgia) to MISS ELIZABETH C. HODGES, all of Madison
County, Alabama. (volume 42, page 2. R. J. J. BURDINE must be meant
REV. J. J. BURDINE as A4 has first J. J.; 14 ROBT. W. CHAPPELL in A4).
    Died at his father's residence in Limestone County December 7, 1850,
EDWARD B. LEWIS (30 in Alabama) aged 30 years 11 months and 8 days,
death occasioned by wound received December 21, 1846 in the battle of
Monterey.

MEMPHIS EAGLE

    Died at 3 o'clock on the morning of 24th, MISS MARIA F. PICKETT,
second daughter of MRS. ANN F. PICKETT of this city. Accidentally
came in contact with flame of candle and was burned to death....
    Died recently in Jackson County, REV. THOMAS M. KING (57 in
Georgia), an old and well known citizen.

January 15, 1851

Died on 27 in Jackson, GEN. CHARLES M. PRICE, long and favorably known in the state as Editor of the Mississippian.

Married on 11th, PETER E. McCAIN to MISS TRANQUILLA KING, all of Marshall County (skipped other marriages).

Married on evening of 3rd by REV. H. P. TURNER, MR. SETH CASON to MISS ANN GRUBB- all of this county.

Married by REV. H. P. TURNER, on evening of 4th ult. MR. JEROME PERKINS to MISS MARTHA ANN BLANKENSHIP--all of this county.

By same, on 18th, MR. CHARLES A. HATCHETT of Limestone to MISS SOPHRONIA B. ELDRIDGE of this county (volume 147, page 63).

By same on 4th, MR. THOMAS B. CARROLL ANN to MISS MARY E. CLARK-- all of this county (volume 141, page 82; license in volume 141, page 51; "CARRELL" and "CLARKE")

Married on 9th by C. B. HILL, Esq., ARCHIBALD S. MITCHELL to ELIZABETH KIRKPATRICK--all of Jackson County.

Married on 11th (born Rhea County, Tennessee), RUFUS M(ORGAN) THOMPSON (26 in Tennessee; Marshall County; married in Marshall County, Alabama) to MISS MARY E. GARVIN--on 22nd, JOHN HAMPTON to ROANNA WALKER and C. G. GILLETT to MISS MARY BISHOP--all of Marshall County. (RUFUS M. THOMPSON was son of JOSEPH and MARY (HOPKINS) RHEA; MARY E. was apparently daughter of HENRY A. GARVIN in 1850 census).

These are marriages previously skipped because of lack of time.

January 22, 1851

Married on 8th by REV. JAMES H. OTEY (Episcopalian), MR. CHARLES J. COLCOCK of South Carolina to MISS LUCY FRANCES, daughter of the late RODAH HORTON of this place (volume 141, page 57).

Married on 24th in Marengo County (married 24 December 1850), DR. EDWARD WARDSWORTH, President of LaGrange College to MISS MARY WINIPED (WINIFRED) SLEDGE.

Married on 5th in Columbus, Mississippi, PROF. THOMAS G. RICE, of LaGrange College to MISS JULIA A. YONGUE.

Married on the 12th, JOHN J. SLAUGHTER of Tuscumbia to MISS MATILDA F. PEARSON of this vicinity.

Married on 8th, JAS. T. TURNLEY, to MISS FRANCES L. HOUSTON-- both of Lauderdale (license in volume 233, page 43).

Married on 9th REV. JAS. R. PLUMMER of Tennessee Conference to MISS SARAH A. E. FORD of Athens.

Married on 9th, MR. ROBERT PEARCE to MRS. MARY A. CLACK.

On 15th, MR. WM. NIXON to MISS PHEBE ANN McWILLIAMS--all of Marshall County.

January 29, 1851

(These marriages are to be found in our volume 42)

Married on the 13th instant, MR. HENRY W. WARREN to MISS PRISCILLA McKELVEY, both of Moulton, Alabama (Lawrence County).

In Nashville (Tennessee) on the 19th, JOHN A. NOOE, Esq. of Tuscumbia (Alabama) to MISS HARRIET E. CROWDUS of Simpson County, Kentucky.

Married on the 1st instant, MR. S(AMUEL) B(OVELL) HUMPHREYS to MISS ISABELLA BURLESON, all of Morgan County.

January 29, 1851

(see marginal note in volume 74, page 49)

February 5, 1851

Died on the 13th instant near Bellefonte (Jackson County) MR. JOHN F. COWAN (49 in Tennessee), formerly Sheriff of Jackson County.

On the 9th ult. DR. HENRY COBB (28 in Virginia; Dallas County) of Dallas to MISS AMANDA, daughter of GEORGE B. MALONE, Esq. of Clarke County (married in Clarke County).

On the 22nd instant MR. WILLIAM G. ROBINSON to MISS LOUISA FANT (10 in Alabama), both of Franklin (daughter of GEO. D.).

On the 26th ult. MR. A. L. WHITE to MISS ELIZABETH IRVIN, both of Athens (Limestone County).

On the 28th by REV. P. B. ROBINSON, MR. WILLIAM T. READ to MISS
JANE, daughter of the late WILLIAM WEEDON, all of this place.
On the 23rd, MR. JOHN ALEXANDER of Lawrence to MISS ELMIRA T.
CROSS of Lauderdale County (18 in Alabama; daughter of BENJ.).

February 19, 1851
Married in Fayetteville (Tennessee) on the 4th instant, MR. ROBERT
HILL, late of this place to MISS MARY E. McCONNELL (see Tennessee IV,
page 59).
Married on the 15th instant by REV. B. C. CHAPMAN, MR. BENJAMIN S.
TIPTON to MISS ELIZABETH PIERCE, all of this county.
Died Thursday morning last, 13th instant at the residence of
DR. JOHN Y. BASSETT of a lingering pulmonary complaint, MISS MARGARET
BASSETT (50 in Maryland)...no ordinary woman...gifted...attached to her
brother and to the cultivation of his children....
At Vienna in this county on Sunday the 9th of influenza, MRS. MARY
BAINS in the 54th year of her age, wife of LEMUEL C. BAINS...(LEMUEL C.
BAINS married MARY EVERETT 24 April 1817--see volume 50, page 76;
he was son of GEO. and SARAH (CHARLTON) BAINS).

March 5, 1851
On the 19th instant, MR. JACOB K. SWOOPE (see volume VII, page 26)
to MISS ELIZABETH T. HAYLEY, all of Lawrence County.
On 19th instant, MR. RICHARD F. GRIFFIN (21 in Alabama) to MISS
SARAH A. RYAN, all of Marshall County.
Died on the 26th ult. MISS SARAH WOODWARD of Athens, Alabama
(Limestone County) aged 17 years.

March 12, 1851
Married in New Orleans on 29th of January at Christ Church by
REV. MR. NEVELL, GEN. MIRABEAN L. LAMAR to MISS HENRIETTA, daughter of
the late J. NEWLAND MAFFIT, both of Texas.
On the 25th instant, MR. THOMAS W. MATTHEWS to MISS MARY E. ROBINSON,
both of Limestone County.
Died at his residence in Selma (Dallas County) on the 23rd instant
JOHN BLEVINS in his 57th year. He was a native of Tennessee (son of
DILLEN BLEVINS) and emigrated to Alabama in his boyhood (see his Bible
record). Served under JACKSON in Indian campaigns and participated in
many of his most distinguished battles. Extensively known throughout
the state...leaves a large and interesting family of children, some of
them of very tender years...
At Grove Hill in Clarke County on the 3rd instant MRS. HANNAH S.
PATTESON (34 in South Carolina), wife of GEORGE R. B. PATTESON aged 36
years. She was an old schoolmate of the Editor of the Advocate.
Fond wife and good mother.

April 9, 1851
Married on the 26th instant by REV. J. C. ELLIOTT, MR. JOHN C.
THOMAS to MISS SUSAN E. COCHRAN, both of Madison County.
On the 23rd of January last, MR. GEORGE W. SCALLERN to MISS FRANCIS C.
RICE, both of this county.
Died in Richmond, Virginia after a few hours illness, REV. JOHN
SCHERMERHORN in his 68th year. He was an officer under JACKSON's
administration, as Indian Agent in Western States and was at the time
of his death attending lands he had recently gained in a suit in Richmond.

April 23, 1851
Married on the 9th instant MR. MAJOR A. BROOKS to MISS MARY J.
STANLEY, all of Limestone County.

April 30, 1851
Died on the 22nd instant of apoplexy (tombstone says died 22 August
1851, born May 13, 1797) near Bellefonte (Jackson County), MR. SAMUEL GAY
(50 in Tennessee) aged 60 years.
Married on the 19th instant MR. ALFRED J. TUCKER to MISS CALEDONIA F.
CAMPER, all of Athens, Alabama (Limestone County).
Married on the 15th instant by J. T. HADEN, Esq., MR. DAVID D.
HARLESS to MISS NANCY W. LAWLER, all of this county.

Married on the 23rd instant by REV. P. B. ROBINSON, MR. ROBERT WADE to MISS MARY BOGGESS, daughter of MRS. ELIZA L. BOGGESS, all of this county.

May 7, 1851

Married on the 19th instant MR. JOSEPH S. MENIFEE of Tennessee to MRS. SARAH J. COPELAND of Limestone County, Alabama (see MINOR's-- widow of --- COPELAND--1 child, SARAH M. and 3 others; MENIFEES removed to White County, Tennessee; volume 88, page 79).

Married on March 24th MR. ARTHUR A. ACKLEN of Courtland, Alabama (Lawrence County) to MISS SUSAN J. WATKINS of Seguin, Texas.

Died on the 20th instant in Aberdeen, Mississippi, MRS. SARAH ANN LEEDY aged about 30, wife of LORENZO D. LEEDY, formerly of this place.

Died in Limestone County on the 18th instant MRS. AGNESS WILLIAMS, aged about 70.

May 14, 1851

Died in this place on Saturday last about 4 o'clock p.m. CATHARINE CALEDONIA, eldest daughter of MR. SAMUEL COLTART in her 19th year.... Presbyterian....

May 21, 1851

Married on the 7th instant by REV. P. B. ROBINSON, MR. JAMES T. ALFRIEND to MISS ELEANOR J., daughter of MR. W(M) H. ROBERTSON, all of this county.

Married on the 12th instant MR. THOMAS J. COX (18; son of BARTLEY) to MISS MARY FRANCES TYUS (17; daughter of THOS. G.), all of Limestone County (volume 205, page 33).

Died on the 12th instant MR. WILLIAM H. MOORE (43 in Virginia) aged 45; and on the 17th instant (married 1847) RUTH LADOISKA (23 in Alabama), his wife, aged 24, both of Limestone County. (nee LEWIS; family of Madison County)

May 28, 1851

Married on the 8th instant by REV. J. M. ROBINSON, MR. HENRY LEONARD of this place to MISS MARIA E. WHITE of Limestone County.

Married on the 15th instant by REV. T. H. WOODWARD, MR. ISAAC D. WANN to MISS LUCINDA E. OWEN, all of Madison County.

Died in Cass County, Texas April 12th, DR. JOHN Y. WILKINSON, formerly of Limestone County, Alabama in his 33rd year.

June 4, 1851

Married in Elkton, Tennessee on the 23rd instant MR. A. D. COE to MISS EMILY C. KENNAMER, both of Athens (Limestone County)

Married on the 22nd instant J(OHN) W. RICE, Esq. of Mississippi to MISS AUGUSTA HOPKINS, daughter of HON. A(RTHUR) F. HOPKINS. (Goodspeed's Miss Memoirs--AUGUSTA HOPKINS born about 1834 in Huntsville, Alabama; daughter of ARTHUR F. HOPKINS (born about 1801, Justice of Supreme Court of Alabama). She married 1851 JOHN W. RICE born about 1815 in Chester District, South Carolina; son of JOHN S. and NANCY (HERNDON) RICE. JOHN W. moved to Alabama, Captain in Mexican War. Moved to Oktibbeha County, Mississippi. He died 1857. Their son DR. ARTHUR H. RICE born in Talladega County, Alabama August 21, 1852 married FANNIE M. SMITH 1879; lived in Oktibbeha County, Mississippi 1891.)

Died on the 27th instant in her 27th year, VIRGINIA ANN, consort of MR. GEORGE W. DRAKE of this place. Columbia Tennessee papers please copy.

Died on the 22nd instant In Athens (Limestone County) MRS. MARY FRANCES COX, wife of MR. THOMAS J. COX aged 18 years.

Died suddenly in this vicinity on 23 May 1851, YANCEY S. EAST aged about 47.

June 11, 1851

Married on 22nd instant by GABRIEL MOORE, Esq. MR. JESSE WITT of Chattanooga (Tennessee) to MISS MARTHA C(AROLINE) ROBINSON of Marshall County, Alabama (see volume 139, page 27).

Married on the 15th instant MR. A. G. BENTON to MISS MARY ANN RUSSELL, both of Morgan County (volume 105, page 79).

Married in Elkton, Tennessee on the 2nd instant MR. WILLIAM S. SARTIN (20 in Tennessee) to MISS CLARA D. ELLIOTT, both of Athens (Limestone County).

Died in Athens on the 3rd instant MISS MARGARET RICHARDSON, an amiable and lovely young woman.

June 18, 1851

Married on the 4th instant at Woodlawn, Fayette County, Tennessee by REV. MR. HARRIS, JAMES L. PENN, Esq. attorney at law of Memphis to MISS MARTHA O. WILLIAMSON, only daughter of COL. BENJAMIN W. WILLIAMSON.

Died at his residence in this county on Monday evening the 9th instant after twelve months illness with cancer in the face, JOSEPH STEELE in his 75th year, a native of North Carolina and emigrated to this county in 1811 where he had lived ever since. Presbyterian.... He has left his children and the community to mourn his loss.

Died in Athens (Limestone County) on the 6th instant REV. A. G. KELLY aged about 28.

Died in Rogersville (Lauderdale County) on the 5th instant MISS MARY JANE BONNER aged 17.

June 25, 1851

Married Thursday evening the 12th instant by REV. MR. ZIVLEY, MR. WILLIAM NATCHER of this place to MISS MARTHA H. MARSHALL of Madison County.

Married on 18th instant MR. EDWARD GOODWIN of Aberdeen (Mississippi) to MISS ANN KING, daughter of the late HARTWELL KING of Lawrence County.

Married on the 15th instant MR. WILEY F. MITCHELL to MISS MARY AMONETT; and on the 19th instant MR. ELIJAH McLAUGHLIN to MISS CATHARINE SHROPSHIRE, all of Lauderdale County.

July 2, 1851

Married in Giles County, Tennessee on the 24th instant MR. HENRY M. STANLEY (20 in Alabama) of Athens (Limestone County) to MISS SARAH JANE BROWN.

Died on the 24th ult. MRS. LOUISA BROWN, wife of MR. R. H. BROWN of Athens, Alabama.

July 9, 1851

Married on 1st instant by REV. M. H. BONE, MR. WILLIAM C. VINCENT to MISS LUOISA J. E. CURLEY, all of this county.

July 16, 1851

Married on the evening of the 4th instant by REV. JAMES C. ELLIOTT, MR. SAMUEL M. VEST to MISS MARGARET SPRINGER, all of this county.

July 30, 1851

Married on the 17th instant MR. HENRY T. LOVE to MISS JANE WOODWARD, all of Limestone County.

Died in Athens (Limestone County) on the 17th instant MR. SAMUEL T. CRENSHAW (60? in North Carolina).

Died in Athens on the 19th instant WILLIAM A. ROGERS aged about 12 years.

Died in Limestone County on the night of the 22nd instant DR. GEORGE RICHARDSON aged about 22 years.

Died in Limestone County on the 13th instant, MR. JACOB NORTON aged about 35 years.

August 6, 1851

Married on the 20th instant MR. JAMES McKINLEY to MISS JULIA A. ADAMS, all of Decatur (Morgan County).

August 20, 1851

Married on the 6th instant by REV. EDWARD WADSWORTH, WILLIAM F. SALE, Esq. to MISS ANN ELIZABETH (18 in Alabama), only daughter of the late MRS. LUCINDA McLEMORE; and WILLIAM S. BANKHEAD, Esq. to MISS MARTHA JANE WATKINS (17; she died 25 April 1852 at 20), daughter of MR. PAUL J. WATKINS, all of Lawrence County, Alabama.

August 27, 1851
     Married on the 13th instant by REV. J. C. ELLIOTT, MR. WILLIAM R.
PETTUS of Limestone County to MISS CHARLOTTE H. DAY of Madison County.

September 3, 1851
     Married in Athens (Limestone County) on the 26th instant DR.
J(OHN) P. A. DAVIS of Newmarket, Alabama to MISS ELIZA ANN MARTIN
(volume 205, page 38).
     Died on the 22nd instant MRS. MARGARET THOMAS aged 24; died on the
29th instant MISS MARY ANN MYERS aged 16 years--both of Limestone
County (15 in Alabama; daughter of CHRISTOPHER).

September 10, 1851
     Resolutions on the death of MAJ. JAMES BRADLEY by Alderman and
Mayor of Huntsville.

September 17, 1851
     Married on the 2nd instant by REV. B. C. CHAPMAN, MR. ROBERT W.
CAPPELL to MISS MARY M. COMBS, all of this place.
     Married on the 4th instant by REV. JAMES C. ELLIOTT, MR. WILLIAM H.
ODOM, JR. to MISS JULIA P. WORTHAM (16 in Tennessee), daughter of
WILLIAM H. WORTHAM, all of this place.
     Married on the 9th instant MR. ALEXANDER MONTGOMERY (39 in
Tennessee) to MISS PRISCILLA JOHNSON (31 in Alabama), both of Limestone
County. (volume 205, page 39;   in 1840 PRISCILLA HOLT married
DAVID JOHNSTON).
     Married on the 11th instant by REV. M. H. BONE, MR. WILLIAM H.
JOHNSON of East Tennessee to MISS LUCILLA A. FORD of this county
(daughter of MARIANNA and JOHN--see census).

September 24, 1851
     Died on the 17th instant after a short illness, MR. WILLIAM L.
BIBB of this vicinity, a quiet, trustworthy man and a good citizen.
     Married on Wednesday evening the 10th instant by REV. J. W. PURVIS,
COL. H. A. NUNNALLY to MISS LIZZIE, eldest daughter of JUDGE M. L. FITCH
of Holmes County (Mississippi). From Yazoo Whig.

October 1, 1851
     Married in Athens (Limestone County) on the 21st instant MR. EMORY
WADIL (38 in North Carolina) to MRS. NANCY M. BROADWATERS, both of
this county. (volume 205, page 39)
     Died near Louisville, Kentucky at the residence of F. G. EDWARDS,
Esq. on the 6th instant MRS. SALLY B. GRAY aged 52 years, only surviving
daughter of the late COL. RICHARD TAYLOR and sister of the late
ZACHARY TAYLOR, President of the United States.

October 8, ,1851
     Married on the 24th instant MR. WILLIAM S. HARVEY to MISS MARY E.
CLEM, all of Limestone County (volume 205, page 40).
     Married in Limestone County on the 22nd of September ANDREW M.
WHITE to MISS SARAH V. HOLT, all of that county (volume 205, page 40).
     Married on the 25th ult. DR. THOMAS S(TITH) MALONE to MISS HARRIET
B(OLLING) PRYOR, all of Limestone County (volume 205, page 40; 2nd
wife--daughter of LUKE and ANNE BATTE (LANE) PRYOR).
     Died at his residence in Madison County September 16, 1851, MR.
JAMES LAWLER, aged 25.
     Died near Athens 26th of September, STITH T. MALONE, son of
THOMAS H. and ELIZABETH T. MALONE in the 22nd year of his age.
     Died on the 24th instant at his residence in Limestone County,
COL. JOHN MAPLES, an old and highly respected citizen.
     Departed this life on the 23rd of September, PAULINA L. infant
daughter of J(OSHUA) H. and PAULINA G. BEADLE aged 10 months and 18
days.
     Died September 25th aged 18 months and 8 days, FRANK WARD PICKETT,
only child of the late MRS. MARY FRANCES PICKETT (3/12 in Alabama),
wife of STEPTOE PICKETT.

October 15, 1851
     Married on Thursday the 9th instant by REV. JOHN M. ROBERTSON,
COL. R. BARNWELL RHETT, JR. of South Carolina to MISS JOSEPHINE B.
HORTON, daughter of the late RODAH HORTON, Esq. of this place.

Married on the 9th instant by REV. B. C. CHAPMAN, MR. JAMES R.
BLUNT to MISS MELVINA M. LEWIS, daughter of CORBON LEWIS of this
county (volume 169, page 74).

Married in the Circuit Court Office on the 13th instant by THOMAS H.
EANES, Esq., MR. JAMES BROMLEY to MISS CANDIS HICKMAN, both of Jackson
County. (bet she was a widow aged 27 in North Carolina in 1850 with 2
HICKMAN children with her and JOHN BROMLEY 26)

Departed this life at her residence in this county on the 9th
instant after a short but painful illness, MRS. ANN THOMAS in her 68th
year. Native of "Lowden" County, Virginia, but has been a citizen of
this county for the last 30 years. Member of the Methodist Episcopal
Church.

Died in Memphis on the 6th instant MR. ELI M. DRIVER, well known
to many of our citizens, in his 54th year.

October 22, 1851

Died on the 12th instant at the residence of MRS. E. F. COLES in
this place, her daughter, MARY FEARN COLES in her 21st year....

Died September 15 at her residence in Hardeman County, Tennessee
in her 50th year, MRS. ELIZABETH H. GRAVETTE, formerly of this county.

Died in Limestone County on the 8th instant, ALEXANDER P. EASTHAM
(44 in Virginia), a respectable and useful citizen.

Died on the same day, JESSE CRAFT, aged about 65 years.

Died in Shelby County, Tennessee on the 8th instant, ASBURY
CRENSHAW, formerly of the House of FEARN, CRENSHAW and Company in his
70th year.

State of Alabama--Madison County. Probate Court, October Term,
1851

ISAAC WELLBORN, SENR.   )
         versus   )   Petition to sell land
ISAAC WELLBORN's heirs)
ISAAC WELLBORN, WILLIAM WELLBORN, SARAH DAVIE, ROBERT O'HERRON,
ELIZA O'HERRON, ISAAC WELLBORN, WILLIAM N. MORGAN and wife MARY, ISAAC
JONES, WILLIAM S. JONES, ------ BARRON and wife MARY, ------- HARRISON
and wife EUGENIA, ------- BARRON and wife JUDITH and CHARLES C. WELLBORN,
distributees of said estate are non-residence of Alabama.

October 29, 1851

Died on the 8th instant, VIRGINIA, infant daughter of GEORGE W.
DRAKE aged 4 months and 28 days.

November 5, 1851

Married Thursday October 23 by REV. JOHN M. ROBERTSON of Huntsville,
MR. GEORGE W. KARSNER (23 in Alabama) of Florence (Lauderdale County)
to MISS ELIZA J. KELLY of Madison County.... From Florence Gazette
(volume 124, page 35; marriage record says married P. B. ROBINSON)

Died at his residence in Madison County, Alabama on the 14th of
October, BROTHER ADAM DALE in his 84th year. He was born in Worcester
County, Maryland July 14, 1768; married POLLY HALE February 24, 1790,
left Maryland in the spring of 1797 and settled in Davidson County,
Tennessee, where Nashville is now situated; removed to Smith County,
Tennessee October, 1801 and united with the Presbyterian Church known
as Craigheads; from Smith County he moved to Columbia, Maury County,
Tennessee in 1829 and realizing he had never been baptized, he joined
a church known as Miller's Church; from Maury County, Tennessee, he
moved to Madison County, Alabama in December, 1840.... Deacon in Baptist
Church...left several children and grandchildren as well as an aged
consort.... This aged wife he leaves behind was POLLY HALE, daughter
of JORDAN and SOPHIA HALE, who resided in Delaware, Sussex County.

Brother DALE at the age of 15 years was a volunteer in a company
raised in his county consisting wholly of boys of his age or near about
it to endeavor to arrest progress of CORNWALLIS; he commanded a company
of volunteers raised in Tennessee and fought bravely and successfully
in the Creek War and at the battle of Horseshoe. He was wounded, his
company in the thickest of the fight and stood whole force of enemy for
40 mintues until reinforced by JACKSON. His son, THOMAS DALE was a
volunteer with him in the same war.... Tennessee Baptist, Nashville,
Tennessee, Sign of the Times-Middle Town, Orange County, New York;
Maury Intelligencer, Columbia, Tennessee and Aberdeen Independent
please copy.

Died in Winchester, Tennessee on the 26th instant, DR. ELISHA SIMS aged 69; also on the 29th instant MR. LEVI SCOTT aged 50, formerly of this place.

Died on Saturday night the 1st instant at his residence in Lincoln County, Tennessee, BENJAMIN M. WILLIAMS aged about 70 years. Native of North Carolina, but for many years a resident of Courtland, Alabama (Lawrence County).

November 12, 1851
Married on the 29th instant (marriage record says married 5 November) by REV. B. C. CHAPMAN, MR. JOHN W. O'NEAL to MISS MARGARET M. GRAHAM, both of this place (volume 53, page 9).

Married on the 5th instant, by REV. DAVID JACKS, MR. JOHN LAWLER to MISS SOLINA W. STONE, all of this county (volume 155, page 29).

Married on the 30th instant at the residence of WILLIAM WILLIAMS near this place by JOHN T. HADEN, Esq., MR. JOHN A. (H) MILLER to MISS MARTHA ANN BROOKS (volume 48, page 22).

Married in Athens on the 29th instant, FOUNTAIN E. OGLESBY (19 in Tennessee, son of W. H.; H in census, H in marriage record) to MISS LUCINDA E. LEWIS.

Married in the Circuit Clerk's Office on the 11th instant by REV. WILLIAM GREEN, MR. JAMES GILES to MISS ELIZABETH GRIFFIN, all of this county (volume 127, page 26).

Died on the 4th instant, MAJOR A. BROOKS aged about 23 years, and MR. JOHN M. CLEM, aged about 30 years, both of Limestone County.

November 19, 1851
Married in Tuscumbia on the 14th instant, MR. S. W. BARTON to MISS ELIZA JANE MURPHEY, both of Florence (Lauderdale County).

Married in this place on the 13th instant by REV. MR. LAY, ELLIOT W. GREGORY, Esq. of New Orleans to MISS CHARLOTTE G. SELLECK (volume 127, page 29).

Died near Memphis (Tennessee) on the 5th instant, GENERAL ISAAC WILBORN (WELBORN), well known in this county.

Died in Tuscumbia on the 13th instant CAPT. WM. C. FRANCIS, a well known steamboat captain on the Tennessee River.

In the same place on the 11th instant, MR. THOMAS E. CUMMINGS of Lawrence County.

December 3, 1851
Married on the 4th of September by A. L. LOGAN, Esq., JOSEPH R. MORRIS (son of JOHN, SR.) to MARTHA J. BAINS, all of this county (daughter of LEMUEL--see census; volume 48, page 47; 22).

December 24, 1851
Married on the 19th instant by REV. J. H. ZIVELY, WILLIAM S. BAR-(hole punched in paper), Esq. of Mississippi to MISS SARAH L. FEARN, daughter of DR. THOMAS FEARN of Huntsville (volume 100, page 15). (note: We have checked with the marriage records in Madison County and the name should be WILLIAM S. "BARRY")

December 30, 1851
Married on the 26th instant MR. BYRD HAMLET to MISS ELIZABETH E. VAN HOOK, both of this county (volume 147, page -64 which says married December 24).

Married on the 11th instant (son REV. DANIEL K), by REV. G. A. COLLIER, MR. J(AMES) A. M. HUNTER to MISS MARY C. McGAH(A?), all of Madison County (volume 147, page 64).

Married on the 2nd instant (son of WILSON) by REV. G. A. COLLIER, MR. FLEMING PUTMAN (18 in Alabama) to MISS ELIZABETH JENKINS of Madison County.

Married on the 16th instant by REV. WILLIAM EGGLETON, MR. PHILIP P. GILCHRIST of Alabama to MISS ELLEN A. PHILIPS, youngest daughter of HON. JOSEPH PHILIPS of Rutherford County, Tennessee.

December 31, 1851
State of Alabama--Madison County. Petition to sell land. WILLIAM M. GOOCH, administrator of ROWLAND GOOCH, deceased. RUFUS PETTY and wife MARY E. PETTY (daughter of deceased) of full age are non residents of Alabama.

January 7, 1852

Married on 17th, MR. MURRAY C. SMITH to MISS LOUISIANA J. TISDALE,
all of Limestone County. (1850 Census shows LOUISIANA J. TISDALE aged
21 born in North Carolina, daughter of SHIRLEY TISDALE; also in Fayetteville,
Tennessee Observer).

Died at the residence of DR. FELIX MANNING of Aberdeen, Monroe
County, Mississippi, 22 December 1851, MADAME S. D. BODE, formerly of
Huntsville.

January 21, 1852

Married on 30 December 1851 by REV. N(ATHAN) J. FOX, MR. L. Q. .
AYRES of Huntsville to MISS VIRGINIA P. HUTCHINS of Winchester,
Tennessee (note: 1850 Census shows LEVY Q. AYRES aged 21 born in
New York).

Married on the 8th by REV. P. B. ROBINSON, MR. FRANCIS A. WATSON
(29 in Alabama, son of JOAB) of Phillips County, Arkansas to MISS
SOPHIA E. CLEVELAND of Madison County, Alabama (note: 1850 Census
shows SOPHIA aged 22, daughter of MARTHA CLEVELAND; see 1850 Census
Phillips County, Arkansas for her; also in Fayetteville, Tennessee
Observer).

Married in Limestone County on 8th by JOHN A. JOHNSON, Esq.
LEMUEL JOHNSON to MISS MARTHA L. FRENCH.

January 28, 1852

Married on 20th by REV. R. A. YOUNG (also in Fayette (Tennessee
Observer) February 5, 1852), MR. JOS. W. DURYEE to MISS MILLIE NUNNALLY,
both of this place. (1850 Census shows MILDRED J. NUNNALLY aged 21
born in Alabama).

Married on 21st by REV. R. H. TALIFARRO, MR. WILLIAM JONES of
Franklin County, Tennessee to MISS GILLIANN RICE, daughter of JOSEPH
RICE, Esq. of Madison County, Alabama (1850 Census shows GILLIANN RICE
aged 18 in Alabama).

Died in Limestone County on 9 January, ROBERT STEEL aged 85 years
(1850 Census, aged 83 born in Pennsylvania).

Died on 2 after a short illness, ROBERT WILLIAM aged 5 years,
son of MR. and MRS. JOHN HUEY of this place...

State of Alabama--Madison County. Probate Court October Term
1851. WILLIE COTTON's heirs versus REUBEN SHOTWELL's executors.
FRANCIS EDWARD COTTON, MARGARET JANE COTTON and JOHN COTTON, heirs of
WILLIE COTTON, deceased; suit to compel RACHEL SCRUGGS, executrix and
GROSS SCRUGGS, executor in right of his wife, of will of REUBEN SHOTWELL,
deceased, to make title to land in Jackson County.

February 4, 1852

Married on the 1st by REV. M. H. BONE, MR. GREEN B. MORROW
(36 in Tennessee) of Maysville, Alabama to MISS MARY S. CONNELL of
same vicinity.

Married by REV. M. H. BONE on 22nd in Ewing Chapel, Maysville,
Alabama, MR. JAMES HALL to MISS MARGARET ARCHEY.

Married on 21 by REV. J. C. ELLIOTT, COLUMBUS B. McKINNEY and
MARY A. JONES; on 8th by REV. J. C. ELLIOTT, ALFRED M. OLSTEEN (OSTEEN)
and LUCY A. F. E. BATTS; on 22 by REV. R. P. RIDDLE, A(NDREW) J.
JOHNSON and MARY E. WITTY; on 22 by J. A. JOHNSON, Esq., JAMES M. NEWBY
and SARAH A. BARKSDALE, all of Limestone County (volume 205, page 49).

Married on 22 VINCENT SMITH of Bedford County, Tennessee aged 73
to MRS. MARY E. KEELING of Coffee County, Tennessee aged 74.

Died in this county on 25 of typhoid fever in 24th year, MRS.
SUSAN REBECCA, consort of DR. A. G. PICKENS and daughter of WILLIAM
WRIGHT, Esq. She died at her father's house surrounded by her husband,
parents, brothers and sisters.... On 27 of last November, she witnessed
the death of her little son, GEORGE WILSON aged 3 years.

February 11, 1852

Married on 28th by REV. G. A. COLLIER, MR. ELIAS A. HODGES to
MISS MARY A. MILLER, all of Madison County.

Died on 2, JAMES LINCOLN, infant son of MAJ. and MRS. JAMES
ROBINSON.

Death of MRS. FRANCES M., wife of A. H. SIBLEY of Madison County,
Born 1815 and departed this life 24 January 1852 aged 37. In 1844,

she professed religion in the Methodist Episcopal Church at Jordan's Chapel.... (1850 Census shows ABRAM H. SIBLEY aged 45 born in Virginia; FRANCES aged 30 born in Alabama).

Died in Madison County on 10 December last, HENRY BRAZELTON in 75 year, one of first who emigrated to this county.... 1850 Census aged 73 born in Maryland.

February 18, 1852
Married on 9th at Hines Hotel, Fayetteville, Tennessee by REV. W. C. DUNLAP, MR. JOSPEH C. HENDRICK to MISS MARTHA A. GILL, all of Huntsville, Alabama (also in Fayetteville (Tennessee) Observer February 12, 1852).

Married on 5th by REV. JAMES C. ELLIOTT, MR. JOHN W. WEBB of Limestone to MISS CASSANDRIA A. DILLARD of Madison County. (also in Fayetteville (Tennessee) Observer, February 19, 1852)

Died of pulmonary consumption at Jacksonville, Florida on 22 December last, FRANKLIN H. MORGAN of House of Morgan, McCLUNG & Company, St. Louis. Formerly a resident of Nashville and member of the firm of MORGAN ALLISON & Company.

Died in Guntersville on 6th, MR. JAMES A. HARRISON aged 22, formerly of this county.

Died on Saturday evening last at his residence 4 miles East of Huntsville, DANIEL HARRIS, an early settler of this county, and a man greatly esteemed by all who knew him. (note: my great grandfather, son of FRANCIS EPPES HARRIS and wife, ANN MACON. P.J.G.)

February 25, 1852
Married on 12 at residence of MR. SAMUEL MATTHEWS in Limestone County by REV. B. H. HUBBARD, MR. E. S. HINE to MISS MARY E. BOWEN.

State of Alabama, Madison County. Petition to sell land. DAVID PETTUS' administrator versus DAVID PETTUS' heirs.

State of Alabama--Madison County. T. W. HINE, administrator of DAVID PETTUS, deceased. REBECCA, wife of WILLIAM HERBERT; DAVID G. PETTUS, JOHN W. PETTUS, JAMES H. PETTUS and THOMAS E. PETTUS are non-residents.

March 3, 1852
Married on 27th at the residence of MR. JOSEPH B. BRADFORD by REV. J. H. ZIVLEY, MR. FREEMAN GOODE (also in Fayetteville (Tennessee) Observer March 25, 1852) of Lawrence County to MISS MARTHA CURLEY of Huntsville, Alabama (1850 Census shows FREEMAN GOODE aged 50 in South Carolina).

Married on 4th by H. G. LENTZ, Esq., BROWDER PICKET and MISS PARTHENIA COODY; on --- instant by same, SAMUEL LENTZ and ANGELINE SHOEMAKER (Fayetteville (Tennessee) Observer March 4, 1852; marriage record shows married 11 December 1851), JAMES COODE and MALINDA C. LENTZ; on 12th by same, A. H. WINSETT and HARRIET E. STOKES, all of Limestone County, Alabama (1850 Census shows ANGELINE 16 in Alabama, daughter of WILLIAM SHOEMAKER (other records say RICHARD); HARRIET E. aged 23 in North Carolina, daughter of CREACY STOKES.

Married on 12th by REV. JACOB SWOOPE, MR. JAS. L. WALL of Courtland to MISS MARGARET BARBEE of Lawrence County, Alabama (1850 Census shows MARGARET aged 16 in Alabama).

Died at his residence in Lawrence County on 22 of typhoid fever, COL. JOHN F. LIGHTFOOT aged 46. This is JOHN FRAZIER LIGHTFOOT born in 1850 in Davidson County, Tennessee; died 1852 in Lawrence County, Alabama. Married 1833 in Giles County, Tennessee MALEANA JONES McKISSACK. He was son of DR. THOMAS LIGHTFOOT and wife SARAH ALLEN, and grandson of DAVID ALLEN, Revolutionary pensioner of Lawrence and Franklin Counties, Alabama. (1850 Census--aged 44 in Tennessee).

State of Alabama--Madison County. Bill for divorce. MAHALA FANNING versus JAMES FANNING. Defendant is a non-resident of Alabama (1850 Census shows MAHALA 30 in Virginia and JAMES 30 in Tennessee).

March 10, 1852
Married on 9 February 1852 by REV. H. H. STEVENSON, JOHN B. ELDRIDGE (45 in Virginia), clerk of Circuit Court of Madison County to MISS SUSANNAH ELIZABETH EDDINS of same county.

Married in Mobile on 26, MAJ. HENRY D. BLAIR to MISS MARY LOUISA, daughter of JAMES E. SAUNDERS, Esq.

Died in Warrenton on 26, MR. JOHN D. WILCHER, an old and highly respectable citizen of that place.

March 17, 1852
Married on Thursday evening by REV. MR. INGRAHAM, HON. F. M. ROGERS to MISS INDIANA V. SYKES, daughter of REV. S. B. SYKES, all of Aberdeen, Mississippi.
Died in Decatur on 5th, JAMES C. WILLIAM aged about 50 years.
Died on 11th, HAMBLEN REAR of Morgan County aged about 45.
(married 11 September 1851 JULIA STRADFORD)

March 24, 1852
Married on 11th by ESQUIRE MARTIN BRIDGES, MR. EDMUND BLANKENSHIP to MISS MARY ANN HALE, all of Marshall County.
Married on 18th by REV. R. W. CRUTCHER, MR. DAVID W. HILLIARD to MISS ELIZA JANE, daughter of MR. LEDNEY RODGERS, all of this county.
Died on Friday morning the 19th, MRS. SUSAN P. wife of DR. CHARLES H. PATTON aged about 38....(1850 Census shows DR. CHARLES H. aged 42 in Virginia; SUSAN P. 35 in Virginia).

March 31, 1852
Married on 6 March 1852 by SMITH ADAMS, ESQ., MR. WM. McKENNIE to MRS. RHODA ANN PEMBERTON--all of Montesane, Madison County.
Married on 13th by REV. J. C. ELLIOTT, MR. DEWITT C. KINCAID (21 in Alabama) to MISS MARIA ISAACS--all of this county.
Married on 16th, MR. WALTER GLENN, JR. to MISS LOUISA J. BUTLER-- all of Lauderdale County, Alabama.
Departed this life on Wednesday March 10, at the residence of CHARLES E. COLLIER near Triana, DR. WILLIAM T. YOUNG in his 56th year. Native of James City County, Virginia and one of the early settlers of Triana, having located there in 1823 as a physician...kind husband and father. Richmond papers copy. (1850 Census shows him aged 50, born in Virginia).
Died March 20, 1852 at the residence of her son, ALFRED COLLINS in Limestone County, MRS. ELIZABETH COLLINS, relict of SOLOMON COLLINS, a revolutionary soldier, aged about 88 years (1850 Census shows her aged 82, born in North Carolina and ALFRED aged 56, born in South Carolina).
Died in Athens on 19th after a protracted illness, ELIJAH M. BROWN (8 in Alabama), son of R(ICHARD) H. (S in census) BROWN aged 9 years 8 months.
Died in Florence on 18, MRS. MARTHA ANN BARKER (26 in Alabama), wife of B(AYLER) B. BARKER, Esq. (32 in Virginia) aged 30 years.

April 7, 1852
Married on 22 by REV. GEORGE W. COONS, MR. HENRY C. WALKER of Nashville (of firm of S. O. NELSON and Company, New Orleans) to MISS LIZZIE A. TRIGG, daughter of JOHN TRIGG, Esq.
Died on 2, GEORGE, son of MR. and MRS. GEORGE W. NEAL aged about 4 years. (1850 Census shows GEO. W. NEAL aged 35, born in Alabama; GEORGE, 3 in Alabama)
Died in New Market, Alabama on 21 March, MRS. SARAH E. (21), wife of DR. M. P. ROBERTS aged about 26 (Democrat and Memphis Eagle copy).
Died at the residence of E. W. GRIGSBY, Limestone County, on the 25th, MRS. SARAH ADAMS aged about 85. (1850 Census shows EDWARD W. GRIGSBY aged 42, born in South Carolina and SARAH ADAMS aged 83, born in South Carolina).

April 14, 1852
Married in Athens on 31 March by REV. D. B. HALE, WILLIAM P. TANNER (18 in Alabama; son of SAM'L) to MISS SOPHRONIA M. RAGSDALE (Fayetteville (Tennessee) Observer, April 15, 1852).
Married on 23 March, MR. WILLIAM D. WARD to MISS ELIZABETH M. HEITH both near Larkinsville, Jackson County.

April 21, 1852
Married on 30th, MR. JOSEPH P. ELLIS of Madison County, Alabama to MISS EMMA DAVIS of Fayette County, Tennessee.

Died at his residence in Huntsville on 15th after a brief illness,
MR. ROBERT M. KINKLE aged 30 years 4 months 10 days...(1850 Census shows
him aged 28, born in Alabama).
Died on 16th, CAPT. WILLIAM LESLIE, an old and highly respectable
citizen of this county. (1850 Census shows him aged 75 in North
Carolina)

May 12, 1852
Married on 6th by REV. W. D. F. SAWRIE, A. H. SOUTHALL, Esq. of
Allsboro (Colbert County), Alabama to MRS. LOUISA M. COCKRILL, of
Tuscumbia. (1850 Census of Franklin County, Alabama shows him aged
39, born in Virginia; shows her 32, born in Virginia)
Married in New Orleans on 22, CAPT. WILLIAM H. BERKSHIRE of New
Albany, Iowa to MISS H. T. WHITE, daughter of N. H. WHITE, Esq. of
Lawrence County, Alabama. (1850 Census shows HYPEPPILE aged 19 in
Tennessee, daughter of NELSON H. WHITE aged 53, born in Virginia)
Died in Athens on 29th, MRS. TURNER, wife of COL. WILLIAM H.
TURNER. (1850 Census shows WILLIAM H. TURNER aged 40 in North Carolina;
wife CAROLINE S. TURNER, 37 in Tennessee)
Died in Athens on 30th, JAMES E. MASON (41 in Virginia).
Died near Athens on 2, MISS MALONE, daughter of THOMAS H. MALONE.
Died at the residence of her father in Courtland on 25 April,
MARTHA JANE BANKHEAD, consort of MR. WM. S. BANKHEAD and daughter of
PAUL J. WATKINS, Esq. aged 20 years...(1850 Census shows WM. S. BANKHEAD
24 in Virginia; MARTHA 17 in Alabama)

June 9, 1852
Married near Triana on 2 by ELDER SAMUEL DENNIS, MR. JAMES H.
LEWIS to MISS MARY STREET.
Died at her father's residence in Limestone County on 14 of May,
VIRGINIA, daughter of COL. NATHANIEL TERRY aged 7 years 6 months.
(1850 Census shows NATHANIEL TERRY aged 51, born in Virginia; VIRGINIA
TERRY aged 3, born in Alabama)
Died at same place on 29 May, MARY JANE, eldest daughter of above,
she having 11 days before, attained her 21st birthday.
Died on 1, THOMAS H. EANES, a resident of this place for many
years. (1850 Census shows him aged 43 in Virginia)
Died on 30 May, at his residence near Woodville, Jackson County,
DR. F. L. DILLARD in his 53rd year. Lynchburg Virginia papers please
copy. (1850 Census shows FRANCIS L. DILLARD aged 50, born in Virginia)
Died on 13 May of consumption, HULDAH, consort of CHARLES BRADLEY,
deceased, only daughter of WILLIAM and MARTHA RIGNEY aged 24 years 7
months 24 days. (Arkansas Republican)
Died on Friday 29 May aged 11 years, MARY CHAMBERS BRADLEY, infant
daughter of the late JAMES BRADLEY of this place. (1850 Census shows
him aged 55, born in Virginia; her aged 9, born in Alabama)

June 23, 1852
Died on the 16th, MR. MOSES CAVATT, an old citizen of this county.
(Note: his tombstone says he was aged 65)

June 30, 1852
Married on 27th by REV. M. SELLERS, MR. JAMES SNOW, aged 14
years, to MRS. MARIA EDGMAN, aged 35, all of Roane County, Tennessee.
Married on Saturday evening the 12th by REV. R. M. WHALEY,
MR. GEORGE SMITH aged 16 to MISS REBECCA HEADLY aged 40, all of Knox
County, Tennessee.
Died at the residence of her husband on 1 June, MRS. VIRGINIA A.
consort of MR. BENJAMIN R. NANCE, and daughter of T. M. HEREFORD, Esq.
in 26th year. Left a husband and 2 helpless infants.
On 21 May in this county, JAMES WYCHE, son of GEORGE and MARY A.
WILBURN. Born 27 March 1846.
On 2 in Franklin County, Alabama, MRS. ALVIRA, wife of L. P.
LEDBETTER and daughter of GEORGE HERIN in 34th year.
On 22 in this place, SUSAN CORNELIA DORRISS aged 8 years 2 months
and 13 days.
Died in Athens on 16th after an illness of near 3 weeks, MRS.
ELIZABETH JOYNER, consort of GEORGE W. JOYNER (1850 Census shows him
29 in Alabama, her 26 in Virginia)

July 7, 1852
    Died in Decatur on the 23rd, MR. GEORGE W. A. ROGERS, SR. aged
47--a very respectable citizen of the place.
    Died in Tusbumbia on the 26th, COL. A. A. JOHNSON (is this AMOS at
JJ North Carolina in 1850?) aged 57.
    Bill for divorce--VIRGINIA MINGA versus NATHANIEL G. MINGA.
Defendant is a non-resident of Alabama. Note: VIRGINIA DICKSON married
March 30th, 1847 NATHANIEL G. MINGA of Limestone County. In 1850 census
of Madison County she was 38 and born in Virginia; with her was
MARGARET A. MINGA aged 2 born in Alabama (volume 129, page 6).

July 14, 1852
    Died on the 5th after a protracted illness of 6 weeks, WILLIAM
THOMAS, son of A. O. and ELIZABETH WEAVER aged 11 years 10 months.
Columbia Tennessee copy.
    Died on Saturday the 26th in Aberdeen of typhoid fever, MR.
CHARLES C. EWING in his 34th year.

July 21, 1852
    Married in Belle Fonte on the 7th MR. JOSHUA STEPHENS to MISS
LOUISA WILLIAMS.
    Married on the 4th by A. L. LOGAN, Esq. MR. THOMAS WILKINS (25;
WILHELMS in marriage record; WILHELMS is right) to MISS JANE PARKER
(16; WM.; living next door in census) all of this county.
    Married in Mooresville on the evening of the 30th by REV. J. C.
ELLIOTT, MR. CALVIN BLEDSOE to MISS ANN S. GANTT (GRANT in Marriage
record; volume 205, page 55).
    Married in Limestone County on the 8th by REV. R. P. RIDDLE,
NATHAN COPELAND, to MISS PERMELIA J. MURRAH (volume 205, page 55).
    Died on the 5th IRA E. infant son of ISHAM H. and SUSAN HOBBS
aged 9 months 12 days.
    Died in Limestone County on the 9th of consumption DAVID M.
CRAWFORD an old and highly respected citizen.
    Died in Limestone County on the 5th, MRS. MARY M. consort of
D. A. CANNON aged 26-3-2.
    Died in Lawrence County on the 28th, MR. JAMES M. DOWNS aged 27.

July 28, 1852
    Married in Decatur, Alabama Wednesday 21 July by REV. THOMAS J.
NEELY, CAPT. JAMES M. TODD to MISS S. F. PARKER.
    Died in this place Wednesday the 21st, WILLIAM J. infant son of
MR. RICHARD CHEWNING aged 9 months 3 weeks and 4 days....
    Died on 23rd, MAJ. SAMUEL RAGLAND of this county aged about 80
years. Native of Virginia and distinguished for his kindenss of heart
etc....(Census of 1850 shows him aged 66, born in Virginia)
    Died on the 15th, JOHN WITHERS, infant son of J. WITHERS and
MARY F. L. CLAY aged 2-2-18.
    Died 17th June at 4 o'clock at the residence of his father,
JOHN WATKINS TROUP, son of COL. JOHN TROUP of Morgan County aged 9
years 6 days.
    Died in Matagorda, Texas on the 1st, ELBERT A. THOMPSON aged 37
years formerly of this state.
    Died in South Florence, Saturday the 17th after a short illness,
COL. HENRY R. BLOUNT. (1850 Census shows him aged 49, born in Virginia).

August 4, 1852
    Married on the 28th by REV. G. A. COLLIER, MR. JOHN S. BALDWIN of
Mississippi to MISS ISABELLA C. A. PARKER of this county. (Census of
1850 shows her aged 15, born in Alabama, daughter of EDWARD T. PARKER;
volume 100, page 16; she married 2. WM. D. COLLINS 1857)
    Died on Friday night July 23 CARALISA, only daughter of J. WITHERS
and MARY F. L. CLAY aged 5 years 20 days....
    Died on 30th LILLY VIRGINIA aged about 4 years, daughter of S. D.
and VIRGINIA C. CABANISS.

August 11, 1852
    Married on Thursday the 5th by REV. DR. HALL, MR. WILLIAM C. SUGG
of Franklin County to MISS MARIA FANNIE STONE of this place (also in
Fayetteville (Tennessee) Observer August 19, 1852 and says WM. E.)

Married on the 4th by REV. P. B. ROBINSON, MR. J(AMES) R. KIDD of
Aberdeen, Mississippi to MISS CALLIE E. (CALEDONIA), daughter of
MR. JESSE G. JORDAN of this place. (Census of 1850 shows her aged 17,
born in Alabama; JESSE G. JORDAN, 50 in North Carolina; also in
Fayetteville (Tennessee) Observer August 19, 1852)
    Married at the residence of CAPT. THOMAS PATTERSON near Guntersville
on the 22nd by REV. P. S. WOODS, MAJ. RICHMOND (RAYMOND in marriage
record) NICKLES of that place to MISS SARAH A. PATTON, daughter of
W. M. PATTON, Esq. (Census of 1850 shows her 17 in Alabama; her
father 45 in Virginia; volume 139, page 38).
    Married on 29th, MR. ALLEN J. HOGAY (HAGEY in marriage record,
volume 147, page 65) of Tennessee to MISS MARY E. daughter of MR.
JAMES BURROW of this place. (1850 Census shows her 17 in Tennessee;
her father 46 in North Carolina)
    Married on the 20th by REV. WILLIAM GREEN, MR. LEWIS MILLER to
MISS SARAH CARPENTER (also in Fayetteville (Tennessee) Observer
September 9, 1852; volume 48, page 23).
    Died on 27 July, EVELINE, daughter of ROBERT TRUE of Madison County.
(Census of 1850 shows her aged 7, born in Alabama; her father 36,
born in Alabama)
    Died in Athens on 30 July, WILLIAM HENRY, infant son of JOHN and
MARY F. LEVESQUE aged 1 year 5 months and 18 days.
    In Athens on the 1st, EGBERT JONES, son of JUDGE THOMAS G. and
ANN M. TYUS aged 10 years 1 month 19 days. (1850 Census shows him
8, born in Alabama; his father 50, born in Virginia)
    Died on the 27th, LUCY, daughter of LOGAN D. and SARAH A. BRANDON
of Monroe County, Mississippi aged 3 years 6 months.
    Died in Philadelphia on the 2nd, MRS. LYDIA VEITCH, wife of
MR. WM. VEITCH, formerly of this place.

August 18, 1852
    Died--MRS. MARY E. HAMBRICK, consort of THOMAS C. HAMBRICK on
27 July of typhoid fever; daughter of SAMUEL and MARY CONNER and was
born in Madison County where she lived and died.

August 25, 1852
    Died in Limestone County Thursday the 5th, MRS. LUCY A. E. G.
BATTE, consort of JOHN H. BATTE aged 36 years 3 months and 2 days.
(1850 Census shows her aged 35, born in Virginia; her husband 40 in
Virginia)

September 1, 1852
    Married on the 25th by REV. J. LEROY HARRIS near Whitesburg,
MR. JOHN Q. A. CARTER to MISS MILDRED A(NN) RICHARDS, all of this
county. (1850 Census shows her aged 14, born in Alabama, daughter of
STEPHEN M. RICHARDS; volume 141, page 58)
    On 10th by REV. G. A. COLLIER, MR. GROVES SAMMONS to MISS KEZZIAH J.
TRUE, all of this county (daughter of SAM'L TRUE, deceased; grand-
daughter of KEZIAH DOUGLAS; volume 48, page 69)
    Married on 16th, MR. HENRY HOLLOWAY to MISS MARY MARSHALL.

September 8, 1852
    Married on Tuesday evening the 31st in this place by REV. DR.
HALL, MR. JOHN W. ROBINSON of Jackson (Hinds County), Mississippi to
MISS MARY JANE (16 in Alabama), daughter of JOS. B. BRADFORD (see
Goodspeeds' Mins Memoirs, says she was daughter of B. M. BRADFORD;
volume 76, page 22), Esq. (Fayetteville (Tennessee) Observer September 16,
1852 says MARTHA JANE--it's MARY JANE in census)
    Married in Limestone County on 11 August by REV. WILLIAM LEVESQUE,
COL. MOSES GAGE of Panola, Mississippi to MISS CAROLINE S. EVES. (1850
Census shows her aged 18, born in Alabama; volume 205, page 57;
Fayetteville (Tennessee) Observer, September 9, 1852).
    Married on the 26th by REV. P. B. ROBINSON, MR. PENHAL REBMAN
(BERNHART in marriage record; 27 in Germany) to MISS MARY E. MIDDLETON,
all of this place. (Fayetteville (Tennessee) Observer September 16,
1852, volume 76, page 21; BERNARD in 1850 Census).
    Died on the evening of the 30th after a few weeks illness,
WILLIAM F., infant son of MR. GEORGE W. and MARY C. YUCKLEY aged 11
months 7 days.

Died on Sunday 22 August at the house of a near relation in Columbus,
Ohio of pulmonary consumption, DAVID REEVE ARNELL of Columbia, Tennessee
after a lingering illness.

Died in Courtland August 31, MISS MARY A. (18 in Alabama) eldest
daughter of MR. J(OHN) M. (52 in Virginia) and MRS. CYNTHIA A. SWOOPE
(38 in Georgia) aged 31 years. Census of 1850 shows MARY A. aged 18,
born in Alabama; JOHN M. SWOOPE aged 52, born in Virginia; CYNTHIA 38
in Georgia.

Died on 23 August 1852 at his father's residence in Lawrence
County, WILLIAM GREENBERRY ALEXANDER in his 23rd year.

Died in Decatur on the 27th, CELIA MALVINA aged 9 months and
13 days and on the 3rd, DANIEL GRIFFITH aged 2 years 4 months 15 days,
daughter and son of JOSHUA and MARY COLLIER. Died of measles and
whooping cough.

Died at his residence in Morgan County August ----, MAJ. JOHN ORR
for many years a citizen of this county (Census of 1850 shows him 63,
born in Georgia).

Died in Decatur on 2nd, MRS. JULIA CRIDER.

September 15, 1852

Married on the 4th in Centenary Church, Richmond, Virginia, by
REV. JOHN EARLY, D.D., THOMAS H. HOBBS, Esq. of Athens, Alabama to
MISS INDIANA E. BOOTH of the former place. (1850 Census shows THOMAS H.
HOBBS aged 22, born in Alabama)

Married in Limestone County on 29 August by JOHN A. JOHNSON, Esq.,
WILLIAM R. CHRISTOPHER to MISS LUCY VINSON. (Census of 1850 shows him
28 in Virginia; her 18 in Alabama; volume 205, page 57)

Married on Thursday, 2nd, at the residence of MR. DONALD,
Lawrence County, by REV. A. PENLAND, DR. A. W. BENTLEY of Courtland
to MISS JULIA B. PETERS of Litchfield, Connecticut. (Note: This is
ALEXANDER WILLIS BENTLEY, son of EFFORD and ELIZABETH (GAY) BENTLEY;
EFFORD BENTLEY was a Revolutionary soldier, who died in Madison County,
Alabama. This was the second marriage of A. W. BENTLEY, his 1st wife
being MARGARET NEWMAN. P.J.G.)

September 22, 1852

Married in Athens on 12 by JOHN A. JOHNSON, Esq., JAMES B. STEWART
to MISS VIRGINIA ANN STANLEY. (1850 Census shows him aged 39, born in
Tennessee; her 22 in Alabama; volume 205, page 58; Fayetteville
(Tennessee) Observer)

Married yesterday morning the 16th by REV. JOS. CROSS, H. K. WALKER,
Junior editor of True Whig to MISS MARY JANE AUSTIN, all of this city
(Nashville Banner).

Married Tuesday morning August 24 in Cass County, Texas by
REV. B. B. DYE, SAM F(OUNTAIN) MOSELEY, Esq. (son of JOHN and 1st wife
ELIZABETH WAKEFIELD, grandson of GEO. MORE and 1st wife JONES LUCY M.)
of Jefferson to MISS ELIZA J. (IRBY), daughter of SEABORN J. WILKINSON
of Caddo Parish, Louisiana. (great-grandfather of FORREST M. SMITH, JR.,
1960; SEABORN JONES WILKINSON married ELIZ. ANN JONES, daughter of
IRBY and REBECCA BROWN EDWARDS JONES on March 19, 1828, Limestone
County, Alabama. She was born April 29, 1812 and her parents married
February 20, 1810, he Surry County, Virginia; PHOEBE JOHNSON, great-
grandson of SEABORN J. WILKINSON died June 6, 1826, Limestone County at
112 according to JANE BIBB)

Died in Madison County at the residence of ALCUIN EASON, Esq.,
MISS MINERVA MARIAH POPE aged about 22 years. Born and raised in
Limestone County but for some time previous to her death had resided
at MR. EASON's..."as left an orphan"...

Died--MISS HELLEN G. WALL...at the residence of her mother on
Monday evening. (Census of 1850 shows her 20 in Alabama, daughter of
MARY)

Died in Athens on the 9th, WILLIAM AVERY aged about 23 years.
(1850 Census shows him 21, born in Mississippi)

Died in Athens on 14th, ROBERT H. CLARK aged about 20 years.

September 29, 1852

Married on Wednesday evening the 22nd, at Church of Nativity by
REV. HENRY C. LAY, MR. GABRIEL JORDAN, JR. of Virginia to MISS ELLEN,
daughter of JOHN H. LEWIS, Esq. of this place. (volume 130, page 22;
Fayetteville (Tennessee) Observer October 7, 1852)

Died on 26th, MR. JOSEPH CAROTHERS, an old and worthy citizen of this place, leaving a large family. (Census of 1850 shows him 52 in North Carolina)

Died on 26th, JANE ANN, infant daughter of B. C. and CATHERINE MOORE aged 2-2-4.

Died at his residence in Jackson County recently, MR. W. A. CHANDLER.

Died on 16th at residence of her son in Lauderdale County, Mississippi, MRS. SARAH, consort of ROBERT SIMPSON aged 82 years 2 months. Presbyterian for 40 years...left numerous friends and relatives.

October 6, 1852

Married at the residence of JOHN TURRENTINE, Esq. on the 23rd by REV. S. W. MOORE, DR. GEORGE FORD to MISS N. JANE HIGGINS all of Athens. (volume 205, page 59; Fayetteville (Tennessee) Observer October 7, 1852)

Died September 14th at the residence of COL. MATT T(HOMAS) CHUNN (grandson of LAUNCELOTHER, son of LAUNCELOT, JR.) in Morgan County, his wife, MRS. CHARITY STRATFORD CHUNN, daughter of the late ELISHA BENN, SEN. and ELIZABETH STRATFORD BELL of the same place. She was born in Camden, South Carolina July 24, 1818, from which place her parents moved to North Alabama while she was quite young....

Died at Spring Dale, Mississippi on 10 September, the infant child of JESSE ADDINGTON aged 2 weeks and 18 hours.

Died in Athens on 24 September, BENJAMIN F. ROBERTS, Esq. aged about 23.

October 13, 1852

Married on 3rd at Mooresville, Alabama (volume 205, page 59) by SHIRLEY TISDALE, Esq., J(AMES) B. HOLLINGSWORTH to MISS SARAH E. OLIVER. (1850 Census shows her 18 in Virginia; daughter of MORDICA OLIVER)

Died on 25th, MR. WILLIAM TIMMINS, one of the oldest residents of Fayetteville, Tennessee.

Died in Athens on the 3rd, ROBERT WILSON, son of ALEXANDER and SUSAN RODGERS aged about 4 years.

Died in Athens on 30th, WILLIAM J. RICHARDSON of the firm of SLOSS, RICHARDSON and Company.

Died on the 8th, HENRY, infant son of DR. L. B. and ELIZABETH W. SHEFFEY of this place.

October 20, 1852

Died on 25 September at the residence of COL. NAT TERRY in Limestone. MILTON WALKER JONES, infant son of JOHN M. and CORNELIA JONES aged nearly 7 months.

Died on 25 September last, JOHN E., infant son of A. L. and MARY S. LOGAN aged 12 months 21 days.

Died in Decatur on 14th, COL. JAMES L. DANCEY. (1850 Census shows him aged 36, born in North Carolina)

Died on 11th, infant child and only son of WOODWARD and TEMANDRIC (LEMANDRA in Census) BAUGHER aged about 12 months.

October 27, 1852

Married on 18th by REV. R. W. CRUTCHER, MR. LOGAN R. GLOVER to MISS MARY JANE McELHANEY--all of this county.

On 20 instant by REV. MR. CRUTCHER, MR. DAVID GILHART of Limestone County to MISS ELIZABETH ANN PETTUS of this county.

Died, EDWIN J. RUSSELL at residence of his father in Limestone County on 4th instant. Born July 8, 1830.

MRS. JANE BAKER, relict of the late CAPT. WM. BAKER of Madison County, Alabama died on 30th August last after a painful illness of 11 days at residence of her son, T. WOODRUFF BAKER, Esq. in Monroe County, Mississippi.

November 3, 1852

Married in Tuscaloosa on 14th instant by REV. DR. MANLY, GEORGE W. BENAUGH, Professor of Mathematics in University of Alabama, to MISS MARY W. eldest daughter of His Excellency H. W. COLLIER.

Married on 21st instant by REV. JAS. C. ELLIOTT, MR. JAMES JOHNSTON to MISS SARAH E. FOWLKES (daughter of RANSOM; Fayetteville (Tennessee) Observer November 4, 1852; volume 130, page 12)

Near Athens on 26 by REV. S. W. MOORE, MR. SAMUEL HENDERSON of
North Carolina married MISS FRANCES H. MALONE (22 in Alabama; JAS. C.,
Fayetteville (Tennessee) Observer November 4, 1852; volume 205, page 61)
    Married in Limestone County on 7 by REV. R. P. RIDDLE, LEWIS
MORRIS to MISS SARAH E. HUGHEY (Fayetteville (Tennessee) Observer
November 4, 1852; volume 205, page 60 (or 61?))
    On 7 October by same, J. R. SPARK to MISS VIRGINIA R. TOONE
(JAMES R. SPARKS in marriage record and VIRGINIA G.; voluem 205, page 60)
    On 12 October by same, MR. THOMAS HARGRAVE to MISS REBECCA A.
McWILLIAMS (HARGROVE in marriage record).
    On 24 October in Giles County, Tennessee MALACHA GREENHOW to
MISS LUCY A. R. ANDREWS, both of Limestone County.
    Died at residence of her son-in-law, R. S. ELLIOTT in Huntsville,
Alabama, MRS. ELISA ANN BISHOP aged 43 years 6 months 28 days. Member
of Presbyterian Church for number of years. Kind and affectionate
mother and highly respected by all who knew her.
    In Hinds County, Mississippi on 4, MRS. PAMELIA HOPKINS, wife of
JUDGE ARTHUR F. HOPKINS of this city (Mobile Tribune).
    Died in Limestone County on 9th instant MRS. FRANCES MARTHA WYNN,
consort of MAJ. J. W. I. WYNN in her 48th year.
    Died in Mooresville on 21, SAMUEL J. HOLT in 26th year of his age.
    Adv. of New Market Infirmary--ROBERTS and RICE.

November 10, 1852
    Died on 25, COLUMBUS HILLIARD aged 29 years and a few months.
    Also on 27 ult. WM. AMERICUS HILLIARD, borthers. They were kind
and accommodating and beloved by every one that knew them. They left
many relatives and friends.
    Died at her residence in Madison County in her 51st year,
MRS. CELIA DEMENT, consort of JNO. J. DEMENT, deceased....

November 17, 1852
    Died on the 7th, JOHN PRESTON, son of I. H. and SUSAN S. HOBBS
aged 6 years 11 months.

November 24, 1852
    Married on Tuesday the 16 by JOHN T. HADEN, Esq., MR. JOHN GRAYSON
to MISS MARY JANE KIRKSEY--all of this county (volume 127, page 29).
    In Morgan County, Alabama November 9 opposite ROGERS' well in the
public road by GEORGE W. A. ROGERS, Esq., MR. ROBERT SEXTON, aged 80
to MRS. BETTY PIERCE aged 75, both from Forsyth County, Georgia
emigrating west.
    Died on the 8th at his residence near Jackson, Mississippi after
an illness of several weeks, COL. JOHN J. LOCKHART, formerly a citizen
of North Alabama.
    Departed this life on 2nd instant, MRS. MARY ANN TRUE, wife of
MR. ROBERT TRUE of Madison County, Alabama. MRS. TRUE having been left
an orphan when quite young, was principally raised and educated by
MRS. HARRIET BOYD, sister of the late DR. ALLAN of Huntsville.
MRS. BOYD bestowed upon her all a mother's care and pains in the
cultivation of both her mind and morals and MARY ANN, having the inclina-
tion and capacity to receive and appreciate both and possessing
inherently an amiable, modest and unassuming disposition was, when
matured in age, a most lovely and interesting young lady...Cumberland
Presbyterian Church at Bethlehem held her membership.

December 1, 1852
    Died on 19th in this place, MR. ROBERT S. LIPSCOMB, a very worthy
young man and very highly esteemed by all who knew him.
    Died at his residence near Athens on 10th, ARTHUR M. SWEANY aged
54 years, of a protracted illness of Flux. (1 ARTHUR M. SWEANEY
married in Limestone County 11 March 1847 MARTHA S. ST (faded);
ARTHUR M. SWEANEY married in Madison County, Alabama 1850 ELIZ. M.
DAVIS; ARTHUR M. SWEANEY, son of ABIGAIL SWEANY and grandson of HARDY
JONES; ARTHUR M. SWEANEY 1850 Census Limestone County 51 in North
Carolina)

December 8, 1852
    Married on Tuesday morning last, the 30th November ult., at the
residence of MRS. ELIZABETH ACKLEN in vicinity of Town by the REV.

W. R. J. HUSBANDS, JOHN JAMES COLEMAN, Esq. attorney at law of
Huntsville to MISS PALMYRA JANE ACKLEN of Madison County (Com).
(volume 141, page 58)
    Died, MRS. ANN BIBB, wife of MR. ROBERT BIBB, formerly of
Huntsville, Alabama but more recently of Jackson, Mississippi.
Departed this life on 25th instant at the Madison House in Montgomery,
Alabama.
    Died on 23 ult., MR. ABRAHAM RICKS, aged 63, an old and highly
respectable citizen of Franklin County, Alabama.
    On 25 of Typhoid fever, at the residence of her father, H. MOORE,
in Limestone County, MISS ELIZABETH MOORE aged 27 years.

December 15, 1852
    Married on 1 by REV. M. H. BONE, MR. A(BNER) D(ELANEY) LANSDEN of
Maysville to MISS M(ARTHA) W. FORSEY of this county (volume 155, page
30).
    On 3rd instant by REV. MR. HODGE, MR. JOHN W. L. CRAWFORD to
MISS MARTHA E. HOLT--all of Limestone County (volume 205, page 62).

December 22, 1852
    Married on 16 by REV. W. D. F. SAWRIE, MR. ERBY E. SPOTSWOOD to
MISS LUCY ANN, daughter of JOHN M. CALDWELL (volume 103, page 70).
    At same time and place, DR. GUSTAVUS A. WYCHE to MISS ELIZABETH
daughter of JOHN M. CALDWELL, by same (volume 153, page 55).
    On same day by REV. ----, MR. HILLARY Y. GARRISON to MISS ELIZA C.
BEALE (volume 127, page 25).

December 29, 1852
    Married on evening of 21st instant by RT. REV. BISHOP MILES,
MR. W. F. ELLIOTT of Huntsville, Alabama to MRS. MARY P. CALLAGHAN of
Nashville.
    Near Athens on 22 by REV. S. W. MOORE, MOSES S. HURT of Cornersville
(Marshall County), Tennessee to MISS MARTHA E. CAIN, daughter of
A. C. CAIN, Esq. of Limestone County (volume 205, page 65).
    Died in Little Rock (Pulaski County), Arkansas on 22nd day of
November 1852 TOLIVER B. DAWSON formerly a resident of Limestone
County.

January 5, 1853
    Married at Southern Hotel on 28th by REV. W. D. F. SAWRIE,
MR. LANDEN CARTER of Huntsville to MISS HENRIETTA TOWNS of the City
of Nashville.
    On 27th by same, MR. JAMES L. HALL to MISS MARY JANE WELLS of
this place.
    On 2, MR. BYRAM MILLER to MISS CATHARINE J. daughter of ABRAM
MILLER--all of this county (volume 48, page 25).
    On Wednesday evening 15th ult. at 8 o'clock by REV. MR. McTEYNE at
residence of her father, MISS MARY GAYLE, daughter of HON. JOHN GAYLE,
Judge of U.S. District Court of Alabama to GEN. H. K. AIKIN of
Fairfield District, South Carolina.
    At residence of COL. JAMES LAMAR on Wednesday 15th ult. by
JUDGE GILBREATH, JAMES E. PEEBLES, Esq., Editor of the Marshall Eagle
to MISS MARY E. NICHOLSON, all of Marshall County (volume 139, page 42).
    In this county on 12 by REV. J. C. PUTNAM, MR. JAMES C. MATKINS
(18 in Alabama; son of DURHAM or DENHAM) to MISS E. J. CHILDERS--all
of Morgan County.
    On 21 ult., by REV. W. J. THOMPSON, MR. F. P. HOOD to MISS SARAH P.
ALEXANDER all of Morgan County.
    Died in this place on 17 of typhoid fever, MISS MARTHA A. R.
LIPSCOMB in her 27th year. She was the daughter of the late ROBERT
LIPSCOMB of this county. Her death was a sad bereavement to her
widowed mother, who a few weeks previous followed a beloved son to the
grave, a victim of the same disease....
    In Decatur on 12 ult., ALFRED G. SMITH aged 21 years 1 month,
27 days.
    On 28 ult., EDWARD P(RIDE) LANE (19 in Alabama), only son of
COL. ISAAC LANE (63 in North Carolina, Franklin County 1850) in his
22nd year, after a painful and protracted illness of more than 90 days.

January 12, 1853
    Married in Triana on 23 December by ELDER SAML DENNIS, MR. MERRIMAN
J. LEDBETTER of Franklin County to MISS PRUDENCE E. AUSTIN of Madison
(volume 155, page 30).
    Married on 30 ult near Whitesburg by A. L. LOGAN, Esq., MR. THOMAS E.
WADE to MISS DORDEANNAH KELLY--all of Madison County (DORA in marriage
record; volume 153, page 55).
    On 7 instant by same, MR. RANSON SHAVER to MISS NANCY WEBSTER--
all of Madison County (volume 103, page 70).

January 19, 1853
    Married on 13 by REV. FINCH P. SCRUGGS, CHARLES J. LANE to
MISS ELLEN R. CROCKETT (2nd wife; related to PERKINS of Nashville,
Tennessee) all of Morgan County. (Methodist minister--volume 82,
page 34; JONATHAN and MARIA PRICE GILLESPIE; ancestor of MISS AMELIA
LANE, 1933).
    On 6 by REV. B. C. CHAPMAN, REV. JOHN H. DRAKE (Cumberland
Presbyterian) of Madison County, Alabama to MISS NANCY J. WORTHAM of
Franklin County, Tennessee (Fayetteville (Tennessee) Observer January 27,
1853; married in Madison County; volume 133, page 20)
    On 11 by REV. S. W. MOORE, MR. WILLIAM E. CAGE (son of ALFRED and
ELIZA) to MISS SARAH A. (E in marriage record) ROGERS all of Athens
(volume 205, page 67).
    On 30 November by REV. R. P. RIDDLE, GREEN C. ROBINSON to MISS
ELIZA A(NN) ROCHELL. (volume 205, page 62) On 20 (30 November, says
marriage record) December by same, WM. I. PHILPOT (volume 205, page 64)
to MISS MARTHA E. HOLMES. On 23rd December by same, JAMES H. HUGHEY to
MISS MARTHA M. SIBLEY (volume 205, page 64). On 27 December by same,
NATHANIEL A. GREEN (marriage record says GREESON) to MISS ELVIRA N.
ANDREWS. On 3 December by same, HENRY E. WILEY to MISS SARAH F.
MALONE--all of Limestone County (volume 205, page 66).
    Died in Huntsville, Alabama December 29, 1852, MRS. ISABELLA
BRANDON wife of ROBERT S. BRANDON and daughter of JAMES CLEMENS, Esq.
MRS. BRANDON was born in Huntsville, Alabama June 9th, 1821...to her
brothers and sister she was always kind. In the year 1837 she married
ROBERT S. BRANDON...wife and mother....
    In Decatur, December 12, ALFRED G. SMITH aged 21 years. In
Franklin County EDWARD P. LANE aged 22 years.

January 26, 1853
    Married on Tuesday by ELDER REUBEN W. CRUTCHER, MR. FRANCIS M.
SANDEFER of Lowndes County, Mississippi to MISS LUCY ELIZABETH ELLIS
of Madison County, Alabama (volume 103, page 70).
    At Memphis on evening of 12, by REV. GEORGE W. COONS, MR. CALVIN M.
FACKLER, formerly of Huntsville to MISS ANNA S., eldest daughter of
JOHN KIRK, Esq. of Memphis.
    On 20 by REV. MR. MOONEY, MR. JAMES L. COOPER to MISS MARY K.
daughter of WILLIAM WINSTON, Esq. all of Tuscumbia.
    Died at his residence in Madison County, Alabama on 8th instant of
typhoid fever, JOSIAH REDDICK. The subject of this brief notice was
born in Nansemond County, Virginia on 10th July 1796. He emigrated to
Madison County, Alabama in June, 1825, and professed the religion of
Jesus Christ at a Camp meeting held at Blue Spring August 10, 1829.
During the same year, he attached himself to C. P. Church.... He has
left 5 children to mourn his loss--4 daughters and 1 son....
    On 14th instant, MARY ANN wife of CHARLES D. ANDERSON of Limestone
County in her 38th year. She was born in Brunswick County, Virginia in
November 1815 and was the daughter of the late COL. BENJAMIN HARRISON
of this place. Left 3 little children, one an infant scarce 1 month
old....
    At his residence in Tuscumbia on 12, COL. SAMUEL MEREDITH in 67th
year of his age.
    At his residence in Franklin County, Alabama on 15th instant
JAMES G. MHOON in 61st year of his age.

February 2, 1853
    Married in Hernando (DeSoto County), Mississippi on 23 ult. by
REV. WILLIAM CAREY CRANE, MR. JAMES ARMSTRONG of Moulton, Alabama to
MISS LUCY J. McKISSACK of DeSoto County.

At Franklin, Tennessee on 19th instant by REV. A. M. CUNNINGHAM, MISS NARCISSA H., daughter of R. C. FOSTER of that place and MR. JOHN W. McALISTER of Florence, Alabama.

In Nashville on 27 by REV. DR. EDGAR, MR. G. H. SCRUGGS, late of Huntsville, Alabama (and of the firm of BALLOWE and SCRUGGS) to MISS E. C. SIMPSON of Nashville.

February 9, 1853

Married on Thursday, 27th ult at residence of WILLIAM ROUTT, Esq. by REV. H. P. TURNER, DR. B. F. HAMMOND to MISS OLIVIA ROUTT--all of this county.

On 25 by REV. JAMES C. ELLIOTT, MR. AUSTIN L. D. BENHAM and MISS CHRISTIANA C. P. McCLUNG--all of Madison County, Alabama (volume 100, page 16).

In Athens on 27 by REV. J. W. ALLEN, BENTON SANDERS (son of WM.), Sheriff of Limestone to MISS ELIZA F. THACH (volume 205, page 68).

On 29 in Whitesburg at end of Turnpike Road by A. L. LOGAN, Esq. MR. JAMES ANDERSON to MISS BRITAINA FIBERR--all of Anderson County, Tennessee emigrating to Missouri (volume 71, page 9; we copied marriage record BRITTANNY PYBNOR).

Died at her residence in Madison County, Alabama 14 January 1853 after a protracted illness of 2 weeks, MRS. ELIZABETH SCHRIMSHER, consort of WILLIAM SCHRIMSHER in 73rd year of her age. Born in Virginia and emigrated to South Carolina with her father, CAPT. BENJAMIN MERIT, where she lived till she was married to WILLIAM SCHRIMSHER and then (in 1818) emigrated to Alabama and in 1825 joined the Cumberland Presbyterian Church...mother and wife.

Departed this life at residence of her son, WILLIAM M. OTEY on Monday 25 January, MRS. MARY OTEY in 73rd year of her age. Born in Roanoke County, Virginia 30 January 1780. She was married to CAPT. WALTER OTEY in 19th year of her age after which she went and resided with her husband in village of Liberty, Virginia where she remained until the year 1817, after which they removed to this county and settled on the farm where she continued to live until time of her death. Mother of 4 sons and 5 daughters. At her funeral she was surrounded by all but one of these (who was absent in South Alabama)....

Died in Madison County, Alabama January 23, 1853 CAPT. RICHARD HARRIS. Born in Powhatan County, Virginia 20 November 1758. (A full account has been published previously by us. B.J.G.)

Died at his residence in Limestone County January 20, 1853, MR. FREEMAN CRENSHAW, one of the oldest and most respected citizens of the county. Born in Nottoway County, Virginia in 1776, removed to North Carolina 1795, thence to Georgia 1810 (thence to Tennessee in 1811). Soon after the War of 1812 in which he served 3 tours of duty he removed to Limestone County where he resided till his death. He was an unostentacious man, but all who knew him, admired his unswerving uprightness and untarnished integrity.

Died at his residence near Newburg, Franklin County, Alabama, REV. JAMES SMITH (Methodist) in his 62nd year. He was a native of South Carolina but has resided in that county upwards of 20 years. 30 years a minister in M. E. Church.

February 16, 1853

Married on 8th by REV. D. B. HALE, JAMES M. COLE of Lincoln County, Tennessee (also in Fayetteville (Tennessee) Observer February 17, 1853) to MISS SARAH A. ARLEDGE of Limestone County. (volume 205, page 68)

Died at residence of DR. ANGEL of this place, MR. HENRY ERNE, a native of Zurich, Switzerland in 24th year of his age.

At his residence in Madison County on 17 January, after a short illness of 1 week, MR. JOHN CRENSHAW in his 76th year. Born and raised in Virginia and emigrated to this state in 1817 where he lived up to the time of his death.

At the same time and place on 24 January 1853 after an illness of one week, MRS. POLLY CRENSHAW, consort of JOHN CRENSHAW, Esq. in 65th year of her age. Affectionate wife, tender mother....

February 23, 1853
    Married on 8th by REV. ROBERT B. WHITE, W. W. WATKINS, Esq. to
MRS. MARTHA M. WHITING, all of Tuscaloosa, Alabama (nee MURRELL,
widow of RICH'D WHITING; volume 81, page 15; volume 25, page 18).
    Died at his residence in Madison X Roads of typhoid fever on
8 February 1853, MARTIN COLE, JR. aged about 40 years leaving behind a
large family to mourn their loss. Highly respectable citizen....
    On 25 of January last near Ocala, Marion County, East Florida,
REV. E(THALBERT) H. HATCHER of Columbia, Tennessee (was M. E. minister
in Athens, Alabama 1844)....

March 2, 1853
    Married on 8 of February by REV. DR. HUTTON, BREVET COLONEL
CHARLES A. MAY of USA to MISS JOSEPHINE, daughter of GEORGE LAW, Esq.
of New York.
    On evening of 22 by REV. S. S. YARBROUGH, DR. LUCIAN MINOR to
MISS ANN ELIZA MOSELEY, daughter of REV. J. P. MOSELEY (M. E.), all
of Morgan County.
    On 24 by REV. B. C. CHAPMAN at residence of MR. RISON, WILLIAM C.
ELLIOTT of this place to MISS EMILY BABCOCK of Oswego, New York
(volume 119, page 12).
    Died on 23 at residence of MRS. POSEY, WILLIAM, infant son of
MR. and MRS. W. P. BEDLOCK aged 5 months 10 days.

March 9, 1853
    Died in Pike County, Alabama on Sunday, the 20th December last,
MR. WM. WICKER. The deceased was about 106 years. He served as a
soldier in the revolutionary war. He was in the battle of Eutaw
Springs and was engaged in several skirmishes with the British and
Tories under GEN. MARION of South Carolina (Spirit of the South).

March 16, 1853
    Died in Athens on Monday, March 7 of consumption, MR. ARCHER ALLEN
JOHNSON aged 29-6-13 (also in Fayetteville (Tennessee) Observer
March 24, 1853).

March 23, 1853
    Married in Rogersville on 3 by REV. MR. BRADSHAW, MR. LUTHER DUNN
(21 in North Carolina, son of GRAY) to MISS ELIZABETH NANCE (16 in
Alabama, daughter of STERLING) all of Lauderdale County.
    On 16th by REV. JAMES WALSTON, MR. W. B. TAYLOR to MISS HANNAH A.
ISBELL of Lauderdale County.
    On 10th by REV. JAMES KIRKLAND, MR. DANIEL T. WELLBORN (22 in
Alabama) to MISS MIRA E. TATE (ELMIRA; 15 in Alabama) both of Madison
County.
    Funeral sermon of MISS SARAH BIBB will be preached at Jordan's
Chapel on 4th Sabbath in this month at 11 o'clock by REV. MR. PLUMMER.

March 30, 1853
    Married on evening of 16th by REV. H. S. PORTER at residence of
MR. THOMAS HOLTON, A. C. RUSSELL, Esq. of San Francisco, California to
MISS CATHARINE E. PICKETT, daughter of DR. EDWARD PICKETT of Jackson,
Mississippi (Memphis Appeal 17th).
    On 22 by REV. JAMES C. ELLIOTT, WILLIAM B. ELLIOTT to MISS JANE S.
STANLEY, all of Athens (volume 205, page 70).
    On 23 instant at residence of JOHN H. ELLIOTT by REV. JAMES C.
ELLIOTT, MR. R(ICHARD) H. BROWN to MISS SARAH S. REEDY of Madison
(married in Limestone County; volume 205, page 70).
    On 24 by SMITH ADAMS, Esq., MR. GEORGE W. CAMPBELL to MISS
LUTECIA ACORD (LOUISA in marriage record; LUVIEA in obituary), 2nd
daughter of MR. DAVID ACORD of this vicinity (volume 141, page 55).
    (obituaries evidently clipped out of this paper)

April 6, 1853
    Married on Thursday evening by REV. DR. HALL, JAMES T. MOORE, Esq.
of Helena (Phillips County), Arkansas to MISS NARCISSA FRANCIS OTEY,
daughter of the late HON. JOHN W. OTEY of this place (volume 48, page 2).
    On 22 at Sommerfield, Alabama by REV. W. H. PLATT, the HON. BEN.
EDWARDS GREY of Kentucky to MRS. E. F. CARSON.

Died at his residence in Bellefonte, Jackson County, Alabama on
8th instant J (or I) A. C. EATON aged 30 years. Formerly published
and edited Jackson County Democrat. For many years afflicted with a
severe pulmonary complaint. Left a wife and 5 small children. At time
of decease, held office of Register in Chancery and Tax Assessor for
the county.
    State of Alabama--Madison County. Probate Court March Term 1853.
Administrator versus heirs and distributees of THOMAS WILLIAMS,
deceased. JAMES WILLIAMS resides in Morgan County, Alabama, SUSAN, wife
of WILLIAM HOLLIS, MARTHA, wife of ------ BELL, who resides in Jackson
County, Alabama and the following grandchildren of his deceased daughter,
wife of EZEKIEL MILLER, who resides in Limestone County, Alabama towit,
JAMES E. MILLER, a minor over 14, AMANDA JANE MILLER and MARGARET
MILLER under 14.
    State of Alabama--Madison County. Probate Court March Term 1853.
JOHN W. SCRUGGS and JAMES H. SCRUGGS, executors versus Heirs and
distributees of JULIA S. DRIVER, deceased. ELIZABETH HUNT, wife of
WILLIAM R. HUNT resides in Panola County, Mississippi, WILLIAM DRIVER
resides in Knoxville, Tennessee and JULIA MOORE DRIVER resides temporarily in Charleston, South Carolina, heirs of above.

April 13, 1853
    Died on 18 March 1853 at residence of her husband CAPT. NICHOLAS
DAVIS of Limestone County, Alabama MRS. MARTHA DAVIS aged 63 years,
7 months, 11 days. Born in Virginia 7 September 1790...she was married
to CAPT. NICHOLAS DAVIS in the year 1806 (whole column long).
    In New Orleans on Saturday (26th) of March after a long and
painful illness, MRS. JANE C. RATHER of Decatur.
    On 1st, KATE, infant daughter of MR. LEWIS M. KENNARD of this
place.

April 20, 1853
    Married on 5th at residence of GEN. MOORE in Lincoln County by
REV. MR. COWAN, MR. JOEL B. SMITH, formerly of Nashville to MISS BETTIE
daughter of the late GOV. YELL of Arkansas.
    Died in Huntsville April 5 aged 9 years BETTIE COLLEY, second
daughter of JUDGE LANE of this place....

April 7, 1853
    Married on Monday --- March by HON. REUBEN ESTES in Wills Valley
(Dekalb County), Alabama, JULIA ROSALIE, daughter of HON. B. F. PORTER
to JOHN PRATT, Esq., 2nd son of HON. JOHN PRATT, late of Union District,
South Carolina now of Cherokee County, Alabama.
    Died on 18 of consumption, MR. EDMUND TOWNSEND, an old and well
known citizen of this county.
    On same day, MR. PLEASANT STRONG, a worthy citizen of this county.

May 4, 1853
    Married at Southern Hotel, Huntsville, Alabama (Fayetteville
(Tennessee) Observer May 5, 1853; says HOLMES P.) by REV. P. B.
ROBINSON on 21 April 1853, MR. HOLMES H. HOPKINS of Pulaski, Tennessee
to MISS JULIA A. MORRIS (HOLMES H. in marriage record) of Jackson
County, Alabama (volume 147, page 64 for marriage record).
    On 19 by REV. G. A. COLLIER, MR. JOHN A. F. VANN to MISS MARY J. E.
HUGGINS all of this county (volume 124, page 4).
    On Tuesday 26 April by JOHN T. HADEN, Esq., MR. ROBT. H. OWEN to
MISS OBEDIENCE A. CHILDRESS--all of this county (volume 53, page 10).
    Died at his residence in this county on 19th instant, MR. PLEASANT
STRONG, son of GEORGE and MARY STRONG, and was born in Goochland
County, Virginia 14th July 1798. Moved in 1806 to Davidson County,
Tennessee and from there to Bedford County 1807. In 1819 he removed to
Lauderdale County, Alabama, where he remained until 1822 during which
year he settled in this county, where he spent remainder of his life.
Married three times and leaves a wife and 10 children, 5 by the 1st wife
and 5 by the last....

May 11, 1853
    Married on 28th by REV. B. C. CHAPMAN, MR. ABRAM H. SIBLEY to
MISS EMELINE JENKINS, all of Madison County (volume 103, page 70).

Died of disease of the heart, at his residence in Lawrence County on evening of 28th REV. DAVID M. DANCEY in 46th year of his age.

May 18, 1853

Died on 13th, JOHN MOSELEY, Esq., an old and highly respected citizen of this county. Left a large circle of friends and relations... good and honest man and a christian (son of GEO and 1st wife LUCY MOORE--see Bible record, GEO was her sol--)

In vicinity of Russellville on 21 April, MR. JOSEPH McCULLOUGH in 66th year of his age.

Married on 10 by REV. B. C. CHAPMAN, MR. JAMES WILLIAMSON, late of New York to MISS SUSAN A. GUNTER of Madison County, Alabama (volume 153, page 56).

May 25, 1853

State of Alabama--Madison County. Last will and testament of EDMOND TOWNSEND, deceased. The following heirs, being children of his deceased sister, JINCEY TOWNSEND, namely, ELIZABETH wife of ARCHIBALD TOWNSEND, JANE wife of UPTON CROW, RUTHA wife of JONES CROW, CELIA wife of THOMAS SMITH, MARY ANN TOWNSEND, LOUISA TOWNSEND, JOSEPH TOWNSEND, THOMAS and DANIEL TOWNSEND, reside beyond the limits of the state.

Information wanted

DAVID DUNKIN, who was born in Virginia and died February 1852 in Madison County, Alabama, left the undersigned executors of his will. By his will his property was bequeathed to heirs of POLLY DONEGAN, formerly POLLY DUNKIN, to heirs of AMOS DUNKIN; to heirs of NANCY BAKER, formerly NANCY DUNKIN; to heirs of JOSEPH DUNKIN, to be equally divided among heirs and widows of AMOS and JOSEPH, if said widows are yet living. Executors want information as to heirs of AMOS DUNKIN and NANCY BAKER.

June 1, 1853

Married at Aberdeen, Mississippi on evening of 19 May ult by BISHOP R(ORBERT) PAINE, BAYLOR B. BARKER, Esq. of Florence, Alabama to MRS. C. EWING of Aberdeen.

Married in Limestone County on 25 instant by REV. R. DONNELL, MR. HARVEY CUNNINGHAM of Madison County to MISS ELIZABETH E. SWEANY of that county (volume 205, page 71).

Died at Athens on 21, MRS. SARAH S. BROWN consort of R. H. BROWN in 22 year of her age.

June 8, 1853

Married on Thursday 26 by REV. M. H. BONE, BURWELL C(LINTON) LANIER, Esq. to MISS LAURA P. A. FORD, daughter of the late JOHN FORD, all of this county (volume 155, page 30).

Died at the residence of his mother in this place on the night of 31 May, JAMES PLEASANTS BRADLEY aged about 17 years, son of the late MAJOR JAMES BRADLEY....

In Monroe County, Virginia on 17 May, MR. JAMES H. BUDD (married in Limestone County; married January 1846 HARRIET ANN MASSI (faded); volume 187, page 66) of consumption, died. Was about 40 years of age and a native of Virginia. He moved from his birthplace some years ago, and the last 8 years of his life was spent in Pulaski, Tennessee. Left his residence 5 or 6 weeks ago in hope to regain his health... left wife and orphan son. Democrat please copy.

Died at his residence in Decatur, Alabama on Wednesday 1st instant, ALEX. PATTESON, SR. in 75th year of his age. Resided in this place for many years prior to his removal to Decatur and was always regarded as an upright citizen and honest man.

Died very suddenly in Tuscumbia on Tuesday night, 23rd May, MRS. MATILDA BARCLAY, wife of DR. A. M. BARCLAY of that place, and daughter of HARRIS TONEY, Esq., deceased, late of this county.

June 15, 1853

Married in Baptist Church in Tuscumbia, on 23rd instant by REV. J. GUNN, MR. D. F. EDINGTON of Arkansas to MISS MARY A. LONG of that place.

Died, JOSEPH CLOYD. Born in Botetourt County, Virginia where he remained until fall of 1837 at which time he emigrated to Madison County, Alabama with a large family, several of whom have preceded him to the grave...M. E. Church South February 1848. Died at residence of his son-in-law, MR. JOHN R. F. HEWLETT on 30 May aged 74-6-12.

Died of consumption at her mother's residence in Madison County MRS. ELIZABETH DELANY in --- year of her age. Cumberland Presbyterian Church in Huntsville since summer of 1847....

Died on 3rd after a lingering and painful illness, at his residence in the vicinity of Tuscumbia, EDWARD PEARSELL, Esq. (66 in North Carolina), one among the oldest and most esteemed citizens of Franklin County.

Died in Demopolis, Marengo County on 27th, JOHN W(OODSON) HENLEY, Esq. (28 in Georgia) an able lawyer and well known throughout the state.

Died in Nashville, Tennessee on Tuesday the 17th, MR. WM. H. WEAKLY, long a citizen of Florence.

June 22, 1853
Died at his mother's residence (MARTHA H. BONE's) in Madison County, Alabama on 12th after a painful and protracted illness, FLEMING A. McCARTNEY in 24th year of his age and youngest and last son of the late JAMES McCARTNEY....

Died in Rogersville, Alabama on Sunday morning, 5th of June after a very short illness, MRS. ELIZA T. TWEDY. Cholera morbus.

On 22 May, MARY ELMIRA SAWRIE aged 16 months.

Died at Florence on 8th, MR. J. D. COFFEE aged 43 years.

June 29, 1853
On 10 June, by JOHN A. JOHNSON, Esq., MR. WM. H. DUPREY to MRS. MARY JANE PAINE, all of Limestone County (volume 205, page 71).

On 20 June by JOHN A. JOHNSON, Esq., MR. WM. HENDRICKS of Tennessee to MRS. MARY RAY of Limestone County.

Departed this life on 11th in 31st year of her age, MRS. MARY ANN HADEN, wife of JOHN T. HADEN, Esq. Born and raised in Madison County. Professed religion in 1839 at Mt. Pleasant Camp Ground. United herself with C. P. Church. On 31 May 1842, she was united in marriage to BROTHER JOHN T. HADEN....

Died in Marion on 30th of dysentery, C. PERRY JONES, Professor of Natural Science and of Modern Language in Judson Female Institute aged 28.

July 6, 1853
On 12th by JOHN W. IRBY, Esq., ANDREW J. PROVENCE to MISS SARAH L. daughter of JAMES RAGSDALE--all of Madison County (volume 64, page 67).

On 28 June last by REV. B. C. CHAPMAN, MR. ANDREW C. McCARTNY of Tennessee to MISS MARY P. DONALDSON of Madison County (volume 48, page 24).

Died in this place on Thursday morning last, 30 June after a brief illness of about 36 hours, FLORA aged about 4 years, second daughter of WILLIAM B. and HARRIET S. FIGURES.

Died--at his Iron wroks near Talladega on 15th instant COL. WALTER RIDDLE. Born and raised in Pennsylvania...Presbyterian There remains but one brother and a sister, MR. JOHN C. RIDDLE of Montevallo and MISS S. E. RIDDLE of Presbyterian Collegiate Institute, Talladega.

Died at his father's (blurred) residence in this place, June 26 about 8 o'clock p.m. JEREMIAH CLEMONS, son of JOHN and JANE READY. Brain fever, lasted about 14 days. Aged 7 years 9 days.

Died on 30 of congestive chill, MR. JAMES RAGSDALE. Well known and much respected. Was at time of death a candidate to represent Madison County in the legislature.

Departed this life Thursday 22nd in Marion County, Alabama, A. A. ALLEN aged 33 from effects of two aortal wounds inflicted with a knife in left breast by M. S. BRIGHT.

July 13, 1853
Married on 20th in Tallapoosa County by HON. MARK LANE, MR. BENJAMIN GARDNER, Junior Editor of Montgomery Journal to MRS. HARRIET L. SUMNER formerly of Elizabeth City, North Carolina.

On 22 June last by REV. MR. LAWRENCE, MR. WILLIAM L. JONES to MISS CALEDONIA M. LAWLER, all of Madison County, Alabama (volume 130, page 19).

In Franklin County, Tennessee on 26 June by REV. MR. LARKINS,
MR. J. P. HIMMO of Nashville, Tennessee to MISS A. E. HUGHES, daughter
of the late SAMUEL HUGHES, Esq. of this county.
On 29th by REV. J. H. HOLLOWAY, SOCRATES D. GLAZE to MISS AMANDA C.
HATCHETT all of Limestone County (volume 205, page 72).
In Elkton, Tennessee on --- ult by ESQUIRE BAUGH, JOHN D. HAYES
to MISS MARTHA C. McWILLIAMS, both of Limestone County.
In Morgan County on 29 June by REV. E. F. WHITE, MR. WM. G. SHARP
to MISS MARTHA HOLDING, all of that county.
In Decatur on 5th by REV. B. F. WHITE, MR. PATRICK H. POTTER to
MISS ELIZA B. HURT, all of Decatur, Alabama.
Married on 26 June by ELDER WILLIAM J. THOMPSON, MR. LEVI F.
WARREN to MRS. NANCY A. BONE, all of Lawrence County, Alabama.
On 7th by REV. MR. SAWRIE, MR. ANDREW J. HENTZ to MISS JULIA E. M.,
daughter of SAMUEL SMITH, Esq., all of this county (volume 147, page 66).
Died at residence of his father (EDMOND KIMBELL) in Morgan County
on 5th instant WILLIAM R. B. KIMBELL aged 32 years 3 months.
In Town of Gilmer, Upshur County, Texas on 2 ult. after a pro-
tracted illness of 11 months, MRS. ELIZABETH WARD in 83rd year of her
age. She was a native of State of Georgia and emigrated with her husband
to Alabama in 1811 and from thence to Texas in 1849.
On 8th REBECCA JANE aged 3 years, daughter of MR. JOHN B. BRANDON...
In Maysville on 9th, WILLIAM LEWIS aged 10 months, infant son of
GEORGE H. POTTER, late of Baltimore....

July 20, 1853
Married on 7 instant by REV. DR. PAGE, MR. LEWELLYN C. LAMBERT
to MISS MARY E. RAGLAND, daughter of DR. N. RAGLAND, all of Shelby
County, Tennessee.
At same time and place, MR. C. DEVER DUNLAP of Louisiana to MISS
SARAH VIRGINIA RAGLAND.
Died on 30 near Helena (Phillips County), Arkansas in his 41st
year, MARTIN SIVLEY, a native of Madison County, Alabama from whence
he moved in 1849. Left a family of 6 children. (SIVLEY, Martin 38 in
Alabama, farmer 3840; ANN 35 in Tennessee; SARAH E. 10 in Alabama;
ELIZA J. 8 in Alabama; MARTIN H. 1 in Arkansas; LUCY H. 3 in Alabama;
MARTIN was son of ANDREW; mentions MARTIN died before his father leaving
children SARAH, ELIZA, OCTAVIA, LUCY and MAR-- (faded)).
On 16th at Oakley, the family residence, MISS CORNELIA, daughter
of CAPT. WILLIAM and NAOMI LESSLIE after a long and painful suffering.
Died at her residence near New Market, Madison County, Alabama,
MARTHA T. HEREFORD, daughter of ROBERT and LUCY STRONG on 24 day of
June, 1853 aged 24 years 6 months leaving 4 children, 3 sons and 1
daughter. She was a member of Cumberland Presbyterian Church.
Died at her father's residence in Madison County, Alabama,
SUSAN STRONG, daughter of ROBERT and LUCY STRONG on 6 day of July 1851
aged 7 years 9 months.

July 27, 1853
Died of typhoid fever at residence of her father in Madison County,
Alabama MRS. MARY ADALINE HODGES, daughter of MOSES and REBECCA MILLER.
Born January 10, 1830 died July 10, 1853 aged 23 years 6 months....
Died at residence of his father near Whitesburg, Alabama on 20th
of cholera, DR. D. C. B. GARDINER aged 22 years 6 months 11 days.
Presbyterian.
Died on Friday the 15th MRS. MARY SHERROD wife of JOHN SHERROD
of Lauderdale County.
Died on 13th MR. A. A. WESTMORELAND, an old and useful citizen
of Lauderdale County.
Died on 15 in Decatur, Alabama of typhoid fever, JNO. W. CAGE
(son of ALFRED) and ELIZA; 187) aged about 20 years 6 months.

August 3, 1853
Married in Decatur on 26th by REV. H. H. BROWN, MR. HENRY C.
JORDAN of Madison County to MISS LUCY E. MARTIN (26 in Alabama) of
Decatur (Dabney).
Died at Bailey's Springs near Florence, Alabama of a sudden
illness on 30th June, ADDIE PLEASANTS, daughter of the late J. J.
PLEASANTS of this place.... Richmond papers copy.

Died in Choctaw County on 6th, MR. JOHN EGELL aged 55 years.
Kind and affectionate husband.
CAPT. BENJAMIN JOHNSON (55 in Virginia) died at his residence in
vicinity of Decatur Monday 25th ult in 59th year after a brief illness
of 24 days (Decatur Advocate).

August 10, 1853
Died on 21st at residence of MR. T. A. COMBS 6 miles north of
Buzzard Roost in Franklin County MRS. NANCY A. WALKER.
Died at his residence near Russelville, Alabama on 25 July
CHARLES DAVENEY (61 in Tennessee) in 64th year.
Died in Morgan County on 2nd, aged 51 years, RICHARD M. BOALDIN
(49 in Virginia).

August 17, 1853
Married on 4th by REV. MR. MIZELL, MR. JESSE G. W. LEFTWICH of
Louisiana to MISS MARIA AGNES, daughter of MR. JOSIAH POLLOCK of
Florence, Alabama.
On 2nd by REV. W. D. F. SAWRIE, MR. WM. H. PACE to MISS JULIA G.
GRAHAM, all of this place (volume 64, page 23).
On 7th in Wichester, Tennessee MR. JOHN H. GUTHRIE to MISS MARINDA
MARKHAM all of McNulty, Madison County, Alabama.
Died at his father's residence on 9th of typhoid fever, MR. JOHN D.
MURPHY in his 27th year....
On 25th July at residence of MR. W. E. ROBERTSON in Limestone
County MR. JAMES M. CARMICHAEL of this county aged 39 years....
Died in Athens of typhoid fever on 6th, MR. ALFRED D. COE aged
about 23.
In Athens on 7th MISS MARGARET J. ECKEBERGER, daughter of MR.
SAMUEL ECKEBERGER aged about 25.
Died in Athens on 8th MRS. ELIZABETH HOLT, widow of the late
WM. H. HOLT.
Died in this city on 5th, MR. JOHN C. SIMPSON in 39th year. Had
long been a resident of this city and for several years had transacted
business in New Orleans.... Kind husband and father (Tuscaloosa
Enquirer).

August 24, 1853
Married on 6th by REV. DR. P. B. ROBINSON, MR. EDWARD Y. POLLARD
to MISS FANNY A. McCOY, all of this place (volume 64, page 23).
Died on 7th August MRS. ANN A. HINDS at residence of MR. A. J.
ESSLINGER, daughter of MR. SAMUEL and ELIZABETH KNOX and was born in
North Carolina, Anson County on 3 March 1804. Moved to this county in
1825. Educated in best seminaries in North Carolina. Member M. E.
Church.
Died in Vienna, Madison County, Alabama SISTER NANCY JANE NOWLIN,
consort of DAVID S. NOWLIN and daughter of EPHRAIM and HESTER LEDBETTER
born in Madison County January 4, 1827. Was married January 23rd,
1845 departed this life July 28, 1853 aged 26 years 6 months and 24
days.
Departed this life on 6th in 24th year, MRS. LOUISA CLOUD, wife
of JAMES CLOUD, of Madison County, Alabama. Left husband and 4 small
children.
Departed this life on 3 August 1853 in Cloud's Cove, Madison
County, Alabama in 26th year, MRS. ELIZABETH A. TURNER, wife of
SIMON N. TURNER. Left husband and 3 small children....
Died in Lauderdale County on 16th, after a short illness, MR.
THOMAS HICKS in his 96th year.
Died at his residence in Colberts Reserve on 10th of chronic
diarrhea, MR. ROBERT SHERROD aged 64.
Died in Limestone County on 15, HENRY DWIGHT only son of JAMES L. R.
and SARAH F. LEONARD aged 3 years.

August 31, 1853
Married at residence of JOSEPH HERRING, Esq. in Morgan County
on 17th at 12 o'clock midnight by A. A. HULETT, Esq., MR. CALEB COLLINS
to MRS. MARTHA E. JOHNSON, all of Morgan County.
Married on 11 August by JAMES SILIVAN, Esq., MR. JOHN CARSON SMITH
to MISS MARY M., daughter of JAMES and NANCY JOHNSON all of Morgan
County.

Married on 30 July by REV. R. E. SAUNDERS, MR. SOL. K. SCRUGGS to
MISS MARTHA K. PENDERGAST, all of Limestone County, Texas.
On 16th by J. H. THOMASON, Esq., MR. WILLIAM ROBINSON and MISS
MARGARET A. CAMPBELL, both of Somerville, Alabama.
Died, HESTER SUSANNA HUGHS NOWLIN, born 6 October 1852, departed
this life 18 August 1853, youngest child of DAVID S. NOWLIN.
MRS. LOUISA H. BLEVINS, wife of GEORGE P. BLEVINS, Esq. of
Selma, Alabama died at Shelby Springs on 10 August 1853 aged 26 leaving
a daughter and son. Second daughter of HON. ARTHUR F. HOPKINS of
Mobile and a native of Huntsville.
Died on 22nd after a short illness, MR. ROBERT S. NANCE aged about
42 leaving a wife and 2 children....
Died on 26th of measles, MR. THOMAS J. BIBB, a highly respected
and worthy citizen of this county.

September 7, 1853
Died at the residence of her father in Somerville, Alabama
August 19 LOUISA PERKINS RICE, youngest daughter of HON. GREEN P. RICE
and ANN E. RICE (GREEN P. RICE married ANN E. TURNER in Lawrence
County 1826).
Died in Guntersville, Alabama on --- August last after a lingering
illness of many weeks, MRS. NANCY WIGGS, consort of WILLIAM H. WIGGS
in her 33rd year.

SOUTHERN ADVOCATE

Huntsville, Alabama (Continued from Volume 101)

September 7, 1853
Married on 1st at Church of Nativity, Huntsville, by REV. HENRY C.
LAY, MR. ARCHIBALD J. IRWIN (46 in Pennsylvania) to MISS MARIA S.
HUNTON.
Married on 18th by JOHN TURRENTINE, Esq., WM. S. HARVEY to MISS
SARAH A. CLEM, all of Limestone County.
Married on 30th at Presbyterian Church by REV. MR. MITCHELL,
REUBEN G. SCOTT (18 in South Carolina) of Madison County to MISS
MARY ANN TOWNSEND of Athens.

September 14, 1853
Married in Giles County, Tennessee on 3rd by SQUIRE HOLLOWAY,
MR. JOHN H. JOHNSON to MISS MARTHA J. COPELAND (13 in Alabama,
daughter of BRANCH), both of this place.
Died on 30th at his residence in this county, MR. JOHN SHARPE
(63 in Kentucky) aged about 60 years--one of the oldest settlers of
the county.
Also on 6th, MR. GEORGE SHARPE (17 in Alabama), son of the former,
a young man of promise, cut down in the vigor of manhood.... Dated
from McNulty, September 1853.
Died of measles at her father's, RICHARD PEETE (26? in Virginia)
in Harrison County, Texas on 28 July last, after an illness of 11
days, MISS MARY L. PEETE (12 in Alabama), 15 years of age....
Died at Tuscumbia, Alabama (REV. MOSELEY has it Tuscahoma,
Choctaw County) on 26th of yellow fever contracted in New Orleans,
REV. JAMES O. WILLIAMS (M. E. Church) aged 43.
Died on 2 August at residence ofhis mother 10 miles north of
Huntsville, CHARLES D. McCAA (15 in Alabama). Born in Madison County,
Alabama, the place of his death, on 22 September 1835.
Also at same place on 27 August, JAMES P. McCAA (21 in Alabama),
born October 13, 1828--only son of the late CHARLES McCAA. They left
a widowed mother (MARY 47 in Virginia) and six sisters, nearly all
small.

September 21, 1853
Married on 8th by REV. D. B. HALE (son of --- (faded) and NANCY
(COLEWART) LEGG), MR. ANDREW C. LEGG (30 in Alabama; 1st wife TYRA ANN)
to MISS MARTHA GRAY (2nd wife), all of Limestone County (daughter of
LEVEN and SARAH --- (faded)).

Married in Davidson County, Tennessee on 9th by REV. J. B. McFERRIN,
MR. JOHN O(SBORNE) FRIEND (22 in Alabama; son of SANDERS), of Madison
County, Alabama to MISS ELLEN WEBB, daughter of MR. JOHN WEBB of
Davidson County, Tennessee.
    On 15th by REV. M. P. BROWN, MR. M. I. SWANN of Knoxville,
Tennessee to MISS MARY MORRISON (14 in Alabama; daughter of JOHN, ANN?)
of Bellefonte, Alabama.
    On 15th, at Beechwood, Bedford County, Tennessee by REV. JOHN T.
EDGAR, GEN. LUCIUS J. POLK of Maury County, Tennessee to MRS. ANN POPE
(26 in Alabama), formerly of Huntsville, Alabama and daughter of
COL. ANDREW ERWIN.
    Died in Lincoln County, Tennessee on 3rd, MRS. SUSAN wife of
WILLIAM C(ALVIN) SOLOMON aged about 33. 3rd wife.

September 28, 1853
    Married on 15 by REV. G. A. COLLIER, JOHN T. HADEN (1st wife
MARY A. died 11 June 1853?), Esq. to MISS CLEMENTA J. (18 in Alabama),
daughter of JOSEPH PICKENS, Esq. (55 in South Carolina), all of this
county.
    On 20th by REV. D. B. HALE, MR. GEORGE W. GRAY to MISS MARGARET
SMITH, all of Limestone County.
    On 14 by JOHN A. JOHNSON, Esq., MR. JOSEPH M. GRIFFIN (21 in
Alabama, son of JOHN W.) to MISS MINERVA E. GLAZE, all of Limestone
County.
    In Clarksville, Texas on 16 August by REV. SAMUEL CONLEY, MR.
CHARLES L. DILLAHUNTY (18 in Alabama, son of HARVEY), formerly of
Florence, Alabama, to MISS FANNIE A. NORWOOD, of Warrenton, Warren
County, North Carolina.
    On 22 by S. A. M. WOOD, Mayor of Florence, MR. ANTHONY T. LIOBER(?)
to MISS CYNTHIA E. CULLOM (15 in Tennessee; daughter of WM), all of
Florence.
    On 20 by REV. JAMES C. ELLIOTT, MR. GEORGE L. TERRY to MISS
MARY B. DARWIN, all of this county.

October 5, 1853
    Married at MERIDITH MILLER's on Thursday evening, 22nd by ELDER
G. W. CARMICHAEL, MR. W(M). F. WHITMAN (41 in Virginia) to MISS
UNITY MILLER (20 in Alabama), daughter of MRS. MARGARET MILLER, all
of this county.
    Also by same on 8 September, MR. JOHN ROGERS to MISS MARGAERT F.
MILLER (12 in Alabama).
    On 14th by REV. PETER J. WALKER, MR. JOHN L. BARNARD to MISS MARY A.
HOGE (18 in Tennessee, JAS) all of DeKalb County.
    On evening of 21 ult, by HON. H. W. HILLIARD, W. D. MOSS, Esq.
to MISS ROSA WADDEL, daughter of MRS. L. M. WADDEL of Montgomery.
    On evening of 21 at residence of HON. JAMES ABERCROMBIE, in
Russell County by REV. MR. EVANS, JAMES H. CLANTON, Esq. (22 in
Alabama) of Montgomery to MISS PARTHENIA (16 in Alabama), daughter of
HON. JAMES ABERCROMBIE (50 in Georgia).
    Long column cut out--could be obituaries
    State of Alabama--29th Chancery District. BRYANT P. READY and
JOHN A. READY versus JAMES T. CAMP and others.
    The defendants, ELIZABETH FLOURNOY, ANDREW J. MARCHBANKS and wife
MARTHA MARCHBANKS, DAVID FLOURNOY, CHARLES FLOURNOY, MARTHA FLOURNOY
and MARY C. FLOURNOY, ANDREW ERWIN and wife MARY JANE ERWIN, are
non-residents of Alabama (married MARY J. CAMP 25 November 1847).

October 12, 1853
    Married in Shelbyville, Tennessee on Tuesday evening, MR. W. S.
SOUTHWORTH, merchant of Fayetteville to MISS MARTHA A. GILLILAND,
daughter of SAMUEL E. GILLILAND of Shelbyville.
    In Winchester on 4th by REV. N. J. FOX (is this REV. NATHAN J. FOX,
Cumberland Presbyterian--cred Greene County 1835?), MR. JOSEPH C.
TAYLOR of Madison County, Alabama to MISS JULIA A. WAGNER of Winchester.
    In Winchester on 30 by JOHN T. SLATTER, Esq., PROFESSOR HENRY
HARIG, late of Baltimore, Maryland to MISS MUSIDORA DRAKE, of Hillsborough,
Coffee County, Tennessee.
    On 22nd by A. L. LOGAN, Esq., MR. SIMON N. TURNER (25 in Alabama)
to MISS MARTHA ANN ASHBURN, all of this county.

Died on 8, MR. CHARLEY JONES (36 in Kentucky) of this place after
a short illness. He was well known to a large number of people....
Died in New Orleans on 13 August of yellow fever, SARAH E., daughter
of JOHN B. and SARAH GROVES.
On 28 August of yellow fever, MARY T., 3rd daughter of same.
On 18 August of yellow fever, ELLEN, youngest daughter of same.
On 23 August of yellow fever, FRANCES B., eldest daughter of same.
On 1st September of yellow fever, JOHN B. GROVES, merchant of
this city, formerly of Columbia, Tennessee. (New Orleans paper)
In Limestone County on 27th, MRS. REBECCA HALDANE aged 80-8-19.
Died in Montgomery on Saturday the 10th at 8 o'clock p.m., MRS.
ANN ELIZABETH BAGBY (2nd wife), consort of Ex-Governor ARTHUR P. BAGBY
and daughter of CAPT. SIMON CONNELL (died September 1857, buried in
Mobile), formerly of Darlington District, South Carolina. (ancestor of
MRS. HARRY B. BROWN, 1964; a P. BAGBY married 1. EMILY STEELE, 2. (1828)
ANN ELIZ. CONNELL. Then daughter ADELAIDE 1832 Tuscaloosa, married
THOS HAMLET WILSON, A. P. BAGBY died September 21, 1858, buried in
Mobile. Old Claiborne Cemetery, Monroe County, Alabama. Consecrated
to the memory of EMILY N. B. BAGBY, consort of ARTHUR P. BAGBY who
departed this life on the 28th day of May 1825.)
JAMES FLETCHER ROPER (4 in Alabama), son of WILLIAM M. (49 in
Virginia) and MARY ANN ROPER (34 in Virginia), born June 7, 1846 died
August 19, 1853.
Died on 3 of consumption, COL. HOUSTON H. LEA, a well known and
worthy citizen of this county.

October 19, 1853
Married on 12 by REV. P. B. ROBINSON, MR. CHARLES THOMAS to MISS
EMILY SULLIVAN (22 in Alabama, daughter of RANDOLPH) all of this county.
On 12 in Harrodsburg, Kentucky, MR. WILLIAM A. BRONAUGH of this
place to MISS LUCIE J. COLEMAN of the former place.
On 2 October by JAMES H. POOR, Esq., MR. CHARLES RUBY (21 in
Alabama) to MISS MARGARET J. (14 in Alabama), daughter of CHARLES
(63 in North Carolina) and ENNIS CONLEY (EUNICE P. in census) (38 in
Alabama), all of this county.
Died at his residence in this county on 3, MRS. MARY E. RUSSEL
(MARY E. PRUIT married 1847; 22 in Alabama), wife of ROBERT F. RUSSEL
(25 in Alabama) in her 25th year....
Died at residence of his father (NASHVILLE MALONE) on 11th of
typhoid fever, MR. ROBERT MALONE (born December 19, 1830, died October 11,
1853), aged about 24 years. He was a young man of generous impulses,
frank and social disposition, left many friends.
Departed this life at his residence on 3rd, COL. H. H. LEA (44 in
Tennessee) aged about 48 years. COL. LEA was a native of Jefferson
County, Tennessee but for several years past, a resident of this county.
Presbyterian...Elder of Church at Whitesburg...Democrat and Knoxville
papers copy.
Obituary:
RICHARD R.'JEFFRIES who died at his residence near this place on
the 30th instant of a chronic disease, which had been undermining his
constitution for several months.
In a short obituary like this....
MR. JEFFRIES was born in the County of Culpepper in the State of
Virginia on 4th of August 1803 and emigrated with his father about the
year 1817 to Madison County in this state and remarried there until
December, 1839 at which time he removed to this section--he leaves a
wife, 2 sons--1 grown and other near his majority--22 little grandchildren,
offspring of a daughter who died about 18 MRS. SEVY Uniontown October 1,
1853. Huntsville papers will please copy.
Died in Perry County on 30, MR. RICHARD R. JEFFRIES (46 in Virginia)
aged 50 years. Formerly resided in Madison County.
Died at Warrenton, Marshall County, Alabama on morning of 3rd of
an affection of the throat, EMILIE, daughter of DR. A. MOORE aged
8-7-27.

October 26, 1853
Married on Thursday evening 20th, at Oak Place by REV. C. FOSTER
WILLIAMS, MR. RICHARD H. WINTER of New Orleans, to MISS SALLIE F.
(20 in Alabama), daughter of GEORGE STEELE, Esq. (52 in Virginia) of
this county.

Married in Athens on 19 by REV. G. W. MITCHELL, JAMES E. BLAIR
(20 in Alabama, daughter of JOHN SIR F.?) to MISS ANN V. FRIEND (17 in
Alabama, daughter of DAVID H.) all of Limestone.

Died in Lewisburg near New Orleans on 13 September of yellow fever,
MRS. SALLIE F. PARKER, wife of REV. LINUS PARKER and daughter of REV.
ALEXANDER SALE (70 in Virginia) of Lawrence County, Alabama....

Died at Cottage Hill near Mobile on Friday the 20th, HENRY T.,
twin son of SEYMOUR R. and OCTAVIA W. LONGLEY aged 2 years 3 months.

Died in Gainesville on 22, MR. J. PAXTON McMAHON of Courtland,
Alabama in 29 year. Born 26 January 1852 (sic--1822?) in Rockingham
County, Virginia and in year 1838 removed with his father (JOHN J.)
to this state.

Died in Limestone County after a long and lingering illness,
MALCOLM THOMPSON (46 in North Carolina) aged 51...worthy citizen.

November 2, 1853

Married on 12th by REV. T. H. WOODWARD, MR. THOS. C. HAMBRICK to
MISS SARAH E. KELLEY, all of Madison County.

Died on 25 at his father's residence near Lowesville, MR. WILLIAM L.
JONES aged 21 years. Young man of much promise...had been married but
a few months.

Died of typhoid fever on 3 August, CHARLES D. McCAA aged 17 years,
at his mother's residence near Meridianville.... The widowed mother has
given up her eldest, her only son, JAMES P. McCAA who departed this life
27 August. When quite a small boy, he was bereft of an indulgent
father....

Died in Bellefonte on 11th, MRS. ELIZA J. (21 in Alabama) wife of
COL. J(AMES) M. HODGINS (HUDGENS in Census; 26 in Alabama), and on 20th,
MR.(S) AMANDA (35 in Virginia), wife of MR. W(M) F. HURT (37 in Virginia)
of Jackson County.

November 9, 1853

Married in Newburyport, Massachusetts on 11th by REV. MR. FELLS,
MR. JOHN E. BLUNT of Decatur to MISS AUGUSTA E. WOOD of Newburyport.

On 18 by REV. JUSTIN WILLIAMS, MR. W(ILLIAM) D. CAROTHERS (34 in
Tennessee) to MISS FRANCES A. HURT, all of Decatur.

On 27th by REV. DR. FINLEY, REV. B(ENJ.) F. WHITE, of Tennessee
Annual Conference, to MISS SALLIE M. WYNN (16 in Alabama, daughter of
JOHN H. J.) of Limestone County.

Married on 31, MR. J. A. BULTON to MRS. POLLY CAVETT of this
county.

Married on 1, MR. JOHN M. CLARK (21 in Alabama, son of ROBT M.)
to MISS VIOLET P. JACKSON (19 in Alabama, daughter of JOHN M.). At
same time, COL. JOHN H. HANSELL to MISS CAROLINE CLARK (18 in Alabama;
daughter of ROBT. M.), all of Lawrence County.

Married in this county on 20th, by REV. MR. CARMICHAEL, MR. EDWARD
NICHOLS (19 in Alabama, son of ELIZA) of Marshall to MISS SARAH OLD of
Madison County.

Near Leighton, Alabama October 30, by REV. E. A. STEVENSON,
H(ORATIO) V. PHILPOTT (24 in Alabama), attorney at law, Somerville,
to MISS ELOISE THOMPSON, of Lawrence County.

Died on 31 of consumption at residence of MR. E(LIAS) P. SMITH
(56 in New Jersey), MISS MARGARETTE THOMPSON (27 in Pennsylvania),
native of Pennsylvania, but had resided here for several years prior
to her death.

Died in Athens on 20th, MRS. JANE OGLESBY (43 in Tennessee, wife
of W. H.) in her 48th year. She was 30 years a member of the M. E.
Church...kind wife, mother, friend and neighbor.

Died on 23rd, MR. WM. BRIGHT aged 85, one of the oldest and most
respected citizens of Lincoln County, Tennessee.

Died near Triana on 25th, MR. JOEL M. WATKINS (78 in Virginia)
aged 86, a worthy citizen.

Died at Joppa, near Decatur, Alabama, MARY (22 in New Jersey),
daughter of CEPHUS (52 in England) and MARY HALL (50 in New York) and
wife of JACKSON FINERTY (28 in Virginia). Born in Patterson,
New Jersey and died October 26, 1853 aged 26 years 3 months.

Died in Decatur on 29 of October, HENRY L. KILPATRICK, late of
Pontotoc, Mississippi in 25th year of his age.

State of Alabama--Madison County. LOUISA C. HAMBRICK and JOSEPH HAMBRICK in right of wife, said LOUISA, executrix of last will and testament of HEZEKIAH BAILEY, late of Madison County deceased. Division among devisees of will. JASPER BAILEY, MARTHA BAILEY, MARY PRIDE wife of ------ PRIDE, and JULIA MAXWELL, wife of JOHN MAXWELL, children and heirs apparent of MATTHEW M. BAILEY, and the husbands of said MARY and JULIA reside without this estate....

State of Alabama--Madison County. SARAH LIPSCOMB, administrator of ROBERT LIPSCOMB, administrator of RICHARD LIPSCOMB, deceased.

November 16, 1853
Married on 10 by REV. MR. MITCHELL, MR. LUCIUS LORANCE of Florence, to MISS MARY SUSAN (20 in Alabama), daughter of MR. WM. WATKINS (52 in Georgia), of this vicinity.

Died in Grove Hill (Clarke County, Alabama) on 30 ult of yellow fever, after an illness of 9 days, JAMES T. FIGURES (28 in Alabama), brother of the editor of the Advocate, aged about 29 years. One of the editors of Grove Hill Herald....

Died at residence of his brother-in-law, MR. R. J. ALLISON on 26th, DR. WM. HENRY COLEMAN (38 in Tennessee, Sumter County) aged about 42 years. Had long resided in this place and in the vicinity. DR. COLEMAN was a man of intelligence. About 2 years ago he removed to Butler, Choctaw County...leaves an affectionate wife and four children (Sumter Whig).

Died in Athens on 7th, GEORGE LYNES (57 in Maryland) aged 61 years 26 days. Leaves a large family and numerous friends.

November 23, 1853
Married at Church of Nativity Thursday evening, November 17, by REV. HENRY C. LAY, MR. JAMES P. COLES to MARIA PERCY (18 in Alabama), daughter of SAMUEL CRUSE, Esq. (53 in Maryland), all of Huntsville, Alabama.

In Bellefonte on 16 by REV. W. H. ADAMS, MR. WM. STEWART of Somerville to MISS VIRGINIA MARTIN, of that place.

Married in Guntersville on 6th by JUDGE GILBREATH, MR. THOMAS WORD to MISS MARTHA RAYBURN.

Died in Columbus, Mississippi on 27th ult aged 23, MRS. MARY JANE wife of W. R. SMITH of Tuscaloosa district.

November 30, 1853
Married on 15th by REV. JAMES C. ELLIOTT, MR. WM. SMITH to MISS ANN CLARKE (14 in Alabama), daughter of WM. CLARKE (42 in Virginia) of the neighborhood of Madison Cross Roads.

Married on 17th by JOHN W. IRBY, Esq., MR. HAMILTON WALKER (22 in Alabama) of Limestone County to MISS MARY (16 in Alabama), daughter of MR. SHEDRICK GOLDEN (44 in Georgia) of Madison County.

Married on 24 by REV. MR. SAWRIE, MR. WALTER W(ELLS) TROUP (born October 8, 1830, died in Mississippi August 13, 1864) of Mississippi to MISS MARY E. (16 in Alabama), daughter of STEPHEN S. EWING, Esq. (61 in Virginia) of this vicinity. (ancestor of MRS. CORINNE BASKIN NORFLEET, Winston-Salem, North Carolina 1957)

On the same day by REV. MR. LARKINS, MR. R. C. McCORD to MISS MARTHA TIDWELL (18 in Alabama), both of this county.

Died in Madison County, Alabama 27 October 1853 MRS. JANE MOORE (72 in North Carolina), wife of EDWARD MOORE (81 in North Carolina) and daughter of BENJAMIN and ANN TYSON. She was born 6 July 1777 in Moore County, North Carolina and with her husband and family removed and settled in Madison County, Alabama in 1822 where she remained until her death. For more than 50 years she bore the love of her husband....

Tribute of respect by I. O. O. F. for their beloved brother, PEYTON T. MANNING (39 in Alabama).

December 7, 1853
Died at the residence of his son, COL. WM. GARRETT in Coosa County, Alabama on 20th ult, REV. WILLIAM GARRETT for many years a citizen of Nashville and Recorder of the city, aged 80 years.

State of Alabama--Madison County. Court of Probate. CHARITY LEA, executrix of will of HOUSTON H. LEA, late of said county, deceased. Heirs at law who reside beyond the limits of this state are: CASWELL LEA,

ALFRED LEA, ANN J. INMAN, PLEASANT J. G. LEA, PRESTON LEA, WILLIAM P. LEA and PRYOR N. LEA.

December 12, 1853
Married by BISHOP GREEN on Thursday 24 November, MR. JAS. R. PUTNAM of Vicksburg and MISS E. M. BURWELL of Jackson, Mississippi.
Married on evening of 7th, by JOHN W. IRBY, Esq., MR. JEFFERSON K. GOLDEN to MISS ESTHER HONEY all of Madison County, Alabama.
Died of typhoid fever at the residence of her father in Madison County, Alabama MRS. JANE BUFORD (24 in Alabama; married September 1847 HOPKINS O. BUFORD), daughter of THOMAS (57 in Virginia) and NANCY HODGES (46 in South Carolina) in 28th year. Joined C. P. Church 1840....

December 21, 1853
Married on 30th by REV. H. P. TURNER, MR. JOHN A. SAUNDERSON to MISS SOPHRONIA CLARK (15 in Alabama; daughter of CHAS CLARKE) all of Madison County.
Died on 12, WILLIAM P., son of MR. and MRS. SAMUEL H. ALLISON aged about 2 years.
Died in this county on 12 after a protracted illness, MRS. SUSAN N. WRIGHT (28 in Alabama), consort of MR. ALBERT WRIGHT (31 in Alabama), in her 32nd year, leaving 5 children and a devoted husband....
Died on the 8th, WILLIAM HENRY (17 in Alabama), son of SAMUEL CRUSE, Esq. (53 in Maryland).
State of Alabama--Madison County. LUTHER M. GIBSON, administrator versus LUTHER M. GIBSON's Heirs
NAPOLEON B. GRAYSON, administrator of estate of LUTHER M. GIBSON, deceased. Included is a lot in the town of Vienna, Madison County.

December 28, 1853
Married on 21 by REV. B. C. CHAPMAN (Cumberland Presbyterian), MR. JOHN T. PATTERSON to MISS JOSEPHINE B. KNOX (15 in Alabama; daughter of DAVID T. Her sister MARY ANN married him 1860), all of this place.
By same on 20th, MR. JOHN C. HOLLOWAY (22 in Alabama) to MISS VIRGINIA M. REDDICK (22 in Alabama; daughter of JOSIAH), all of this county.
By same, on 20, MR. JOHN M. CROSS (21 in Alabama; son of RUTHY) to MISS LUCY P. PHIPPS (T. in census; 16 in Virginia; daughter of MARTHY G.), all of this county. (He married 2. 1874 MISS SUSAN A. LEA)
On 15 by REV. G. W. MITCHELL, DR. N. B. WALLACE of Triana, Madison County to MISS MARTHA A. HIGGINS of Athens.
On 22 by JOHN W. IRBY, Esq., MR. DRURY M. COOPER to MISS CATHARINE SPELTS, all of this county.
Died in the town of Huntsville on the night of the 13th, of typhoid fever, JOHN WALTER OTEY (18 in Alabama), son of CHRISTOPHER C. OTEY of Madison County aged 21 years 11 months 2 days...born 11 January 1832; belonged to Cumberland Presbyterian Church.

January 4, 1854
Married in Bolivar on 21st instant by REV. MR. BATEMAN, MR. LEONIDAS TROUSDALE, Junior Editor of Memphis Appeal, to MISS VIRGINIA F. JOY of Bolivar, Tennessee.
Near Camden, Alabama on afternoon of 4th, by REV. J. C. JONES, FRANCIS P. M. GILBERT (Junior Editor of the Temperance Register) to MISS MARY ELIZABETH CHANDLER--both members of Social Degree in connection with WILCOX TEMPLE of Honor no. 18.
On 21st by REV. ALEXR PENLAND, MR. JOHN R. GRANTLAND, to MISS HAIDENIA A. CLEVELAND (20 in Alabama; daughter of MARTHA), all of Madison County, Alabama.
In Whitesburg on 29th by I. H. THOMASSON, Esq., MR. ISAAC A. McADAMS to MISS MARTHA J. PARKER (13 in Tennessee; daughter of WM.), all of this county.
Married in Cloud's Cove, Madison County, Alabama on 31 December 1853 by A. L. LOGAN, Esq., MR. JAMES CLOUD (32 in South Carolina) to MISS MARY HAMONS both of said county (1st wife died 6 August 1853!).
Died in Madison County, Alabama on 12 December 1853 MARTHA C. F. MILLER (12 in Alabama), daughter of MOSES (49 in Virginia) and REBECCA MILLER (41 in Tennessee) aged 16-2-12. Cumberland Presbyterian Church.

January 12, 1854
        Married on 25 December by J. A. JOHNSON, Esq., MR. AMOS B. FRENCH
to MISS MARTHA A. MITCHELL, all of Limestone County.
        Married on 27 by same, MR. BARNETT McNELLY of Giles County,
Tennessee to MISS SARAH E. MARSHALL of Limestone County, Alabama
(volume 205, page 84).
        Married on 22 by REV. R. P. RIDDLE, MR. BRYSON HUGHY (22 in
Tennessee; son of EZEKIEL?) to MISS HARRIET E. LEWIS (14 in Alabama;
daughter of WM.), all of Limestone County (volume 205).
        Married on 6 by JAMES H. POOR, Esq., MR. BENJAMIN H. GLOVER to
MISS MARTHA COOPER, all of this county.
        Married on 5 by JAMES H. POOR, Esq., MR. HENRY VANN to MISS ELIZABETH
COOPER, all of this county.
        State of Alabama--Madison County. Estate of JOSEPH CAROTHERS
(died 26 September 1852), deceased. WILLIAM H. THOMPSON, administrator.

January 18, 1854
        Married at First Presbyterian Church in Nashville by REV. DR. EDGAR
at 8½ o'clock Sunday morning 14th instant, DR. A. M. BARCLAY (1st to
MATILDA N. TONEY, died 1853) of Tuscumbia, Alabama to MISS MILLIE A.
TONEY (14 in Alabama; daughter of CLAUSSA) of Madison County, Alabama.
        Married in Athens, Alabama on 12 by REV. MR. MITCHELL, MR. WILIE F.
BOULDIN (18 in Alabama) of Morgan County to MISS LAURA B. FOOTE (12 in
Alabama) of Athens.
        Married on 10 by JAMES H. POOR, Esq., MR. ALLEN LANDERS (17 in
Alabama; daughter of LEWIS) to MISS ELIZABETH C. GASS.
        Also on same day, MR. GEORGE W. POOR to MISS JUDY E. LANDERS,
all of this county.

January 25, 1854
        Married on 4th by REV. DR. WELCH, COL. M. T. CHINN (should be
CHUNN; 41 in Maryland; 1st wife died 1852) to MISS MARIAH S. BOWLIN,
all of Morgan County.
        Married on 16 by REV. ISAAC MILNER, MR. DAVID H. WALKER of Moulton,
Alabama to MISS VIRGINIA A. (14 in Alabama), daughter of MACLIN SLEDGE
(47 in North Carolina), Esq., of Franklin County, Alabama.
        Married on 10 by REV. WILLBORN MOONEY, MR. JOHN E. DONLEY (20 in
Alabama; son of JAS.) to MISS MARTHA J. M. ATKISSON, all of Franklin
County, Alabama.
        Married on 10 by WM. J. BULLOCK, Esq., MR. GEORGE M. GHOLSON to
MISS MARY E. PATTON (14 in Alabama; daughter of AARON), all of Franklin
County, Alabama.
        Married at Church of Nativity, January 12, 1854 by REV. HENRY C.
LAY. GEORGE A. GORDON, Esq. of Savannah, Georgia to MISS ELLEN C.
GRAY (1839-85), oldest daughter of GEORGE P. BEIRNE (1809-81), Esq. of
Huntsville, Alabama.
        Died of pneumonia on 11th, at his residence near LaGrange, Fayette
County, Tennessee, MR. RICHARD C. PERKINS, formerly of Lawrence County,
Alabama in his 53rd year.
        State of Alabama--Madison County. SARAH LIPSCOMB (47 in Virginia;
widow of RICH'D) versus RICHARD LIPSCOMB's Heirs
        Petition for dower. MARY E., wife of EDMUND E. BYRD (married 21
November 1849), one of the heirs of said RICHARD LIPSCOMB, deceased, is
not a resident of Alabama, but resides in the State of Texas.

February 1, 1854
        Died at his residence in this county, CAPT. STEPHEN McBROOM, one
of the first settlers of the country. He came to this county in 1804 and
was born in Hawkins County, East Tennessee the 26th March 1784. He
bore his last illness with a firm mind and was willing to die, and
retained his mind to the last. (Bible record states he died January 6,
1854. He was son of THOMAS and ---- (CRINER) McBROOM, and grandson of
JOHN CRINER, who died in Hawkins County, Tennessee before 1808.)

February 8, 1854
        Married on 23rd by JOHN W. IRBY, Esq., MR. JASON G. HAMBRICK to
MISS MARY CAMPBELL, all of this county.
        Married in Wetumpka on 24th by REV. OTIS SAXTON (M. E.), DR. M. G.
MOORE, one of the Lessees of the Alabama Penintentiary to MISS GEORGIA
SPRATLIN (16 in Georgia) of Wetumpka.

State of Alabama--Madison County. Administrator's Sale. Estate of
JAMES THOMAS, deceased. Property 4 miles north of New Market.

February 15, 1854
Married on 8th by REV. B. C. CHAPMAN, MR. WILLIAM S. KERR to MISS
ELIZABETH COMBS, all of this place.
Married by REV. JOHN G. WILLIAMS on 5th, MR. A. LANCASTER (ALLEF
LANCASTER, 36 in Tennessee; wife NANCY A. 1850) of Marengo County to
MRS. MARY E. KEEL (28 in Alabama, wife of JNO. C.) of Clarke County.
On 25 by REV. F. W. WHITE, MR. E. F. S. COLYER of Franklin County,
Tennessee to MISS HARRIET S. SMILEY of Morgan County, Alabama.
Married in Decatur on 8th by ELDER JACKSON GUNN, MR. LEWIS HOBART
to MISS MARY SUSAN WELLS all of Decatur.

February 22, 1854
Married on 8 February by ELDER D. N. HALE, MR. BENJAMIN C. PEETE
(19 in Alabama; son of BERY B.) to MISS JANE F. MALONE, all of Limestone
County.
Died on 23 December at residence of THOMAS BIBB, Esq., NIMROD
FIELDER (80 in North Carolina) aged 83 years. He moved to this place
30 odd years ago and had an eventful life and was well known to all.
Died on 20th in this vicinity, MR. ANDREW SIVLEY (68 in Virginia),
one of the earliest settlers in this place and quite an old man.

March 1, 1854
Departed this life on 10th at residence of MR. E. W. DRAKE, MISS
MARY C. WORTHAM of Winchester, Tennessee after a protracted illness of
one month. MARY was left an orphan for several years...Cumberland
C. P. Church.

March 8, 1854
Married in vicinity of Columbia, Tennessee on 1st by REV. MR. MACK,
ROLFE S. SANDERS, Junior Editor of Knoxville Register to MISS ELIZA
ANDERSON of Maury.
On 28th in Morgan County by REV. H. M. WELCH, MR. JOSEPH G. BROWN
to MISS ELIZABETH KEY (17 in Alabama; daughter of PLEASANT).
On 16th by JAMES H. POOR, Esq., MR. COLUMBUS R. BLACKBOARN to MISS
ELIZABETH C. VANN, all of this county.
Died on 2 at residence of MR. WM. GORMLEY in this place, MISS ANN I.
HALL, amiable young lady, much esteemed and beloved by her friend.
Died on 3, MR. CHARLES SCHLACK (42 in Germany) after a short
illness at this place, quiet and unobtrusive in his department; left an
interesting family.

March 15, 1854
Married on 2 by JUDGE J. G. DIXON, NELSON ROBINSON, JR. (20 in
Alabama; NELSON, SR.) of Bellefonte to MISS SYDNEY METTS of that
vicinity.

March 22, 1854
Married on 5 at Robinson Springs, Alabama, MR. J. A. WATTERSON,
Principal of Deaf and Dumb Institute to MISS CHARITY THOMAS of Barbour
County both deaf mutes.
Married in this place on 8th, by REV. D. K. HUNTER, DR. A. G. PICKENS
to MISS EMILY C. CONNELLY (17 in Alabama), all of this county.
Died on 8 at residence of her husband, J(OSEPH) C(HAMBERS) STEELE
in Madison County, Alabama, ANGELINE C(ORNELIA) STEELE (30 in Alabama),
daughter of ANDREW and ELIZABETH McWILLIAMS of Limestone County aged
34 years, 2 months, 2 days. She was born in Limestone, professed
religion at New Garden and joined the C. P. Church. After she married,
she moved to Madison, becoming a member of the church at Liberty. Left
a bereaved companion and four children...her remains now lie in grave by
her two children who died last year (see her tombstone in volume 76,
page 89 and STEELE generation in volume 191, page 100).

April 5, 1854
Married in Chattanooga on board the steamer Chattanooga on 29th by
REV. W. H. BATES, MR. J(OHN) L. McINTOSH (16 in Tennessee) of Triana,
Alabama to MISS LAURA J(ANE) FARISS (14 in Alabama; daughter of DANDRIDGE)
of Huntsville, Alabama.

Married on 17th by REV. ALEXANDER PENLAND, MR. R. A. SMITH to
MISS ELIZA REYNOLDS, all of this county.
Married on 23 by REV. J. GUNN in the "Honey-cut Academy" MR.
FRANKLIN BELL to MISS ELIZABETH AUSTIN, all of Morgan County.
Married on 16 by JOHN W. IRBY, Esq., MR. GEORGE W. WILDER (14 in
Tennessee; son of HESIKIAH) to MISS MARY FRANCES MARKHAM, all of this
county.
Married on 28 by JOHN T. HADE, Esq., MR. NOAL KEEL (16 in Alabama;
son of WM.) to MISS SARAH WHITINGBURG.
Married on 30, MR. WM. MILLS to MISS REBECCA OWENS, all of this
county.
Died in Huntsville March 22, 1854, after a painful illness of four
weeks, MARY LUCINDA (9 in Alabama), daughter of MR. and MRS. JACOB
CERTAIN (45 in Tennessee) aged 12 years 10 months....

April 12, 1854
Married on 23 by G. GREENWOOD, Esq., MR. THOS. C. HALE (17 in
Tennessee; son of THOS.) to MISS SARAH E. CRITCHER (CRUTCHER in Census;
17 in Alabama; daughter of JAS), all of Marshall County.
Married in this place on 4 by REV. MR. SAWRIE, MR. JASPER N. BRAY
to MISS ALICE C. JONES (10 in Alabama), daughter of the late CHARLEY
JONES (36 in Kentucky) of this place.
Married on 5 at residence of COL. J. C. BRADLEY by REV. J. W. HALL,
MR. FRANCIS A. SANDERS of Charleston, South Carolina to MISS JANE M.
CLARK (19 in Alabama; daughter of WM. and SUSAN) of Huntsville, Alabama.
Died on 27 March, OSCAR D., infant son of MAJ. JOHN M. and
ELIZABETH F. HUMPHREY aged 4 months.
Died in Madison County on March 31 at residence of her uncle,
DR. A. A. WALL, LAURA AMANDA WILLIAMS, daughter of DR. CHARLES and the
late MARY BELL WILLIAMS aged 7 years 17 days after a short illness of
24 hours.
State News--JOHN WOODS (66 in North Carolina), an old and respected
citizen of Clarke County, Alabama committed suicide a few days ago.

April 19, 1854
Married in Decatur on 12, by REV. J. GUNN, MR. JAMES T. SAWYERS
(19 in South Carolina; son of JAMES) to MISS SARAH A. INLOW.

April 26, 1854
Married on 20 April 1854 by ELDER G. W. CARMICHAEL, Elder G(ENNETT)
A. MORRING to MISS MARTHA C. VANN (16 in Alabama), daughter of MR.
EDWARD (57 in North Carolina) and MRS. ELIZABETH VANN (44 in South
Carolina), all of Madison County, Alabama.
State of Alabama--29th Chancery. CAROLINE P. ROBINSON et al.
versus AUGUSTUS H. FORD et al.
AUGUSTUS H. FORD (married 1835 MARY E. JONES), WILLIAM K. THOMASSON,
SALLY D. THOMASSON, CAROLINE P. THOMASSON, IDA THOMASSON, JOHN C. WEAVER
and wife ANN M., and JOHN P. FORD are non-residents of Alabama.

May 3, 1854
Married on 18 at residence of COL. RICHARD WHITE of Nashville,
DR. JAMES LIGHTFOOT of Alabama to MISS ELIZABETH WHITE, eldest daughter
of COL. R. WHITE, formerly of Fayetteville.
Died at her residence in Mobile, Alabama Tuesday 4 April after a
lingering illness of chronic rheumatism, MARY JANE FEARN, wife of
DR. RICHARD LEE FEARN of that city and eldest child and only daughter of
the late HON. JOHN W. WALKER of Madison County...born in Huntsville
1 December 1810, consequently was in her 44th year. Her early life
(with exception of 4 years at school in Philadelphia) was spent in
Madison County. On 15 January 1829 she married, her husband now surviving her. In 1834, she removed to Mobile. An only son (now absent
in Europe) and five affectionate brothers also survive. Protestant
Episcopal Church.
On 25th at his residence in this county, JOHN KINNEBRUGH, Esq.
(62 in Virginia), an old and highly respected citizen died. Honest and
good man.

May 10, 1854
Married on Thursday 20 April by J. A. JOHNSON, Esq., MR. DAVID M.
ELLIOTT to MRS. ANN E. CARPENTER, all of Limestone County.

Married on 20 at Pine Grove, Maury County, Tennessee by REV. D. G.
DOAK, REV. C. FOSTER WILLIAMS of Tuscumbia to MISS BETTIE F., daughter
of SAMUEL HENRY ARMSTRONG, Esq. of the former place.

Died of dropsy at residence of his father in Choctaw County,
Alabama on 11th, SAMUEL T. PORTER, late editor of Pickens Republican and
formerly apprentice in Democrat office.

Died in vicinity of Huntsville on 22, JOHN MARTIN.

Died at his residence in Limestone County after a long and painful
illness, MR. LEMUEL SMITH (54 in South Carolina) aged 55 years 6 months.
Native of Madison County, Alabama (!) but for the last three years a
citizen of that county.

May 17, 1854

Married in this place on 10th by REV. HENRY C. LAY, MR. HENRY
WILLIAMSON of Savannah, Georgia to MISS SUE S. (15 in Alabama), only
daughter of CAPT. D(ANIEL) B. TURNER (49 in Virginia).

Married on 10 by REV. C. FOSTER WILLIAMS, MR. SAMUEL FINLEY to
MISS LETITIA J. DOYLE, all of Tuscumbia, Alabama.

Married on 11th by REV. S. C. POSEY, MR. ROBERT T. KERNACHAN (23 in
Alabama) to MISS A. E. E. SIMMONS, daughter of MRS. REBECCA SIMMONS, all
of Lauderdale County, Alabama.

Married in this place on 11th by REV. MR. ROBINSON, GEN. THOMAS
M(ADISON) MOSELEY (41 in South Carolina) to MISS MINERVA JANE LIPSCOMB
(21 in Virginia; daughter of SARAH), both of this place.

Died last Monday, H. L. WARD, at W. G. MUSTIN's Hotel in this place
of inflamation of stomach, after illness of 5 days. MR. WARD came to
this place in 1843 and entered in the practice of law. Had his faults....

Tribute of respect to memory of ARCHIBALD E. MILLS (36 in Kentucky),
deceased by Huntsville Bar.

May 24, 1854

Married on 18 by REV. P. B. ROBINSON, COL. JOHN R. PRICE, of
California to MISS MARY ELIZABETH (23 in Alabama), daughter of COL.
JOHN D. KING (55 in Virginia) of this county.

Died in Limestone County on 17, MRS. INDIANA E. HOBBS (married
4 September 1852), wife of MAJ. THOMAS H. HOBBS.

State of Alabama--Madison County. THOMPSON M. VAUGHN, deceased.
JOHN BYRNE, administrator.

May 31, 1854

Married on 18 by REV. C. FOSTER WILLIAMS, DR. J. RAGLAND to MISS
EMMA L. MEREDITH (14; daughter of SAML), all of Tuscumbia.

Married on 23rd by same, MR. WM. ANDERSON to MISS FRANCIS M.
(12 in Alabama), daughter of the late HENRY B. OLD (51 in Virginia),
all of Tuscumbia.

Married on 21 by REV. WELBORN MOONEY, MR. SAML DAVIS (he died 1880
Magnolia, Louisiana) to MISS CLARENA U. MORGAN (16; CLARA W. in census),
all of Tuscumbia. (She was daughter of JOHN S. and ISABELLA (WEST)
MORGAN, granddaughter of REV. JOSHUA and HANNAH (PRENTICE) WEST.)

Married on 23 by REV. ISAAC MILNER, DR. ALBERT EDMONSON of Pontotoc,
Mississippi to MISS MARY F. (25 in Alabama), daughter of REV. ALEX. SALE
(70 in Virginia) of Lawrence County, Alabama.

Died in Huntsville 20 May MISS MARY E. WORTHAM (14 in Tennessee)
aged 17 years 6 months, daughter of W(M) H. (48 in Tennessee) and
L(UCY) K. WORTHAM (41 in Tennessee).

Died near Coffeeville (Clarke County) on 9 of measles, HUBERTA
SUSAN, youngest daughter of C. C. and E. Y. FIGURES aged 1 year 10
months.

June 7, 1854

Married on Tuesday evening the 6th by REV. J. W. HALL, DR. GEORGE G.
STEELE of Austin, Texas to MISS ADA (19 in Alabama), daughter of DR.
THOMAS FEARN (55 in Virginia) of Huntsville, Alabama.

On 25th by REV. JEREMIAH DAILY (Baptist), MR. ALFRED C. MATTHEWS to
MISS VALERIA A. (19 in Alabama), daughter of CAPT. EDMUND LITTLE (43 in
Tennessee) all of Franklin County.

Married on 31 by REV. T. A. MORRIS, HON. FRANK GILBREATH (22 in
Alabama) to MISS SALLIE R. MOORE, all of Marshall County.

On the same evening by REV. T. A. MORRIS, DR. T. CLIFFORD MOORE to
MISS VIRGINIA C. PATTON, all of Marshall County.

Died on 28th at residence of her mother, MRS. MARY B. ACKLEN in this place, MARY T., daughter of the late COL. JOHN R. H. ACKLEN of Madison County in her 17th year.

Died on the 5th after a long illness, MRS. SALLIE D. SPOTSWOOD, an old and highly esteemed lady of this vicinity.

June 14, 1854
Married on 8th by REV. W. D. F. SAWRIE, COL. E. J. JONES to MISS MARY ECHOLS (18 in Alabama), daughter of WM. ECHOLS, JR., Esq. (50 in Virginia), all of this place.

Died in Decatur on 1st, MISS SUSAN GRIFFITH.

Died in Decatur on 3rd, MR. NATHAN R. CAMPBELL.

Died in Decatur on 3rd, MISS SARAH E. SHARP.

June 21, 1854
Married on 11th by REV. JAMES C. ELLIOTT, MR. JAMES C. WEAVER to MISS SARAH H. NABORS (19 in Alabama; daughter of NATHAN), all of this place.

Married on 7 at residence of HENRY M. STANLEY by REV. JOHN G. RAY, MR. JULIUS M. A. GEORGE of Lincoln County, Tennessee to MRS. MARIA J. BROOKS of Limestone County.

Died at residence of MR. EDWARD WISE in Morgan County on 15th by REV. JACKSON GUNN, MR. B. H. COLLIER to MISS MARY JANE WOOD (16 in Alabama).

Died at her residence in Madison County, Alabama June 5, 1854 MRS. SALLY D., wife of ELLIOTT SPOTSWOOD, deceased. MRS. S. was born in Hanover County, Virginia June 5, 1790 moved to this county in the year 1819 and continued to reside near this place where she died for a period of 35 years. 15 years (died 1839) prior to her death, MRS. S. lost her husband and was left a lone widow in moderate circumstances, with a large family of children. She educated her children and accumulated additional property...M. E. Church.

June 28, 1854
Married on 14 by ELDER R. W. CRUTCHER, MR. D. J. HILL to MISS MARY A. R. HOLLOWAY, youngest daughter of ELDER J. H. HOLLOWAY.

Married on 14 by REV. MR. GUINN, MR. M(ONTGOMERY) M. KILFOYLE (17 in Alabama; son of PETER) to MISS MARY E. TAYLOR, all of Warrenton, Marshall County, Alabama.

Married on 14 by REV. J. P. RILLS, COL. S. K. McSPADDEN to MISS CHALSEA (CHARLSEY in census) A. GARRETT (17 in Alabama; daughter of MARY), all of Cherokee County. (daughter of WM.? and MARY (HALE?) GARRETT)

Married on Tuesday morning the 20th by H. V. BROWN, C. P. M. ETIENNE LAMBERT to MISS CATHARINE (14 in Alabama), daughter of MR. H(UGH) EASLEY (40 in Georgia) of this place.

Married on 21, MR. W. F. HEREFORD to MISS M(ARY) R(ICE) FLIPPEN (25 in Alabama; daughter of FRANCIS), all of this county.

On 27 by REV. B. C. CHAPMAN, MR. JOHN E. BEAUCHAMP of Smithland, Kentucky to MISS MARTHA L. BURROW (13 in Tennessee; daughter of JAS. H.) of Huntsville, Alabama.

Died in Jackson, Mississippi Friday morning the 2nd, P. P. ROBINSON, a native of Chenango County, New York in his 22nd year...he came to reside among us in the fall of 1850....

Died in Tuscumbia on 11th, MRS. ELENOR (42 in England), wife of DAVID DESHLER (50 in Pennsylvania) in her 47th year.

July 5, 1854
Married on 28 by REV. P. S. WOOD, MR. JOHN RYAN, Esq. attorney-at-law to MRS. JOANNA MOORE (22 in Alabama; wife of GABRIEL M. MOORE), all of Marshall County.

Married in Bellefonte, on 29 by HON. JUDGE J. G. DIXON, MR. LEWIS KINSTLAER of Nashville, Tennessee to MISS SUSAN AKE of that place.

Died on 24 at residence of her father, G(ARRET) L. SANDIDGE (58 in Virginia), Esq. in Madison County, Alabama, MRS. LAURA WHITAKER (17 in Alabama), wife of MR. THOMAS WHITAKER of Franklin County, Tennessee, in her 19th year, 3 months after her marriage....

Died on 25 June in this county, MRS. LAURA N. MOORE after a short illness in her 17th year and only about 9 months after marriage.

Died of typhoid fever after an illness of 24 days, near Huntsville, Alabama, at the residence of her mother, on 20 June, MISS LOUISA MATILDA JONES. Born April, 1834....

July 12, 1854
Married on Thursday evening July 6 by REV. W. D. F. SAWRIE, MR. JOHN T. BRUCKNER to MISS MARY J(ANE) (16 in Alabama, eldest daughter of DR. GEORGE R. WHARTON (46 in Virginia).

July 19, 1854
Married in Fayetteville, Tennessee on 4th by WM. PRYOR, Esq., MR. JAMES B. CARTY, of that place to MISS BETTIE ELLIOTT of Huntsville, Alabama.
Married on 28th by LORENZO RUSSELL, Esq., MAJ. J. F. MARTIN to MISS TALITHA (TABITHA in census; 15 in Alabama), daughter of MR. WM. McMAHAN, Esq. (39 in Tennessee) all of Jackson County, Alabama.
Married on 13 by REV. MR. CHAPMAN, MR. JAMES W. HOBBS (25 in North Carolina) to MISS MARY (17 in Alabama), daughter of MR. HENRY BEALE (50 in Alabama), all of this county.
Married on 5th by REV. MR. CHAPMAN, MR. ROBERT HAMLET (13 in Alabama) to MISS MARY E. (14 in Alabama), daughter of MR. JAMES M. COCHRAN (45 in North Carolina), all of this county.
Died on 3, R(EUBEN) J. (G. in census) JORDAN (1 in Alabama), son of FLEMING (46 in Georgia) and L(UCY) J(ANE) (MOM) JORDAN of Maysville, Alabama. Born 16 September 1849.
Died in Livingston, Alabama on 30th, DR. A(LFRED) B. DELOACH (40 in Tennessee) in his 42nd year (son of JOHN of Jefferson County).

July 26, 1854
Married on the 20th instant by REV. THOMAS MADDIN, MR. WM. E. SPOTSWOOD to MISS MARTHA E., daughter of WILLIAM WATKINS, Esq. (14 in Alabama), all of this place and vicinity.
Married at the residence of CAPT. NICK DAVIS on the 18th by REV. J. B. WILSON, MR. J(OHN) J. FLETCHER (44 in Virginia) to MRS. MALVINA DAVIS (35 in Alabama), all of Limestone County.
Married on the 18th by G. GREENWOOD, Esq., MR. JOSEPH CUNNINGHAM to MISS NANCY NEWMAN, all of Marshall County.
Married on 13th by REV. ISAAC MILNER, REV. E. A. STEVENSON to MISS EMILY E. (20 in North Carolina), daughter of NATHAN COOK, Esq. (61 in North Carolina), all of Lawrence County.
Married on the 5th by REV. WILLIAM SCOTT, MR. JOHN T. FACKLER (JOHN J.?) (22 in Alabama) of New Orleans to MISS JANE C., daughter of MR. THOMAS REED of Boyle County, Kentucky.
Died in Petersburg, Lincoln County, Tennessee of typhoid fever on the 13th instant, MR. BARNET METCALF, formerly of this place.

August 2, 1854
Married on 26th by REV. THOMAS MADDIN, MR. BENJAMIN D(UKE) MATTHEWS to MISS MARY C. KINKLE (15 in Alabama; daughter of ROBT. M.), all of this place (father of BEN MATTHEWS born 1861).
Married on 20th by REV. J. W. SULLIVAN, MR. W. H. FOGG to MISS E. J. COLLIER, all of this county (volume 122, page 14).
Married in Choctaw County, Alabama on 12th by REV. WILEY BURGESS, F. S. DENSON, Esq. (24 in Alabama), Editor of Alabama Standard to MISS OCTAVIA OLIVIA CHANEY (14 in Alabama; daughter of G. B.), all of Choctaw.
Married on 10th by REV. J. GUNN, MR. WM. ROYER (16 in Alabama; son of CHAS.) to MISS NANCY PUTMAN, all of Morgan County.
Married on 20th by REV. J. GUNN, MR. L. AUSTIN to MISS MARY HUTSON (24 in Alabama, daughter of ROBT.), all of Morgan County.

August 9, 1854
Married on the 27th by JOHN S. MORGAN, Esq., MR. PETER GILL (26 in Alabama) to MISS MARY E. BOWLES, all of Franklin County.
Married in Huntsville, Alabama on the 19th by REV. T. MADDIN, MR. JOHN A. FLIPPO to MISS LUCY H. EVANS.
Died in Memphis, Pickens County, Alabama on the 13th, THOMAS R. COLEMAN in the 23rd year of his age, a native of Morgan County, Alabama.
Died in this place on the 30th of typhoid fever, JOHN M., second son of MR. ROBERT P. FINNEY of Fayetteville, Tennessee aged 10 years 3 months.

August 16, 1854
    Married on the 27th near Claiborne by REV. WILLIAM C. SMITH,
HON. ROBERT G. SCOTT, of Virginia, U. S. Consulate to Rio Janiero to
MRS. MARY W. DELLETT (30 in Virginia) of Monroe County.
    Married in Athens on 3rd by REV. G. W. MITCHEL at residence.of
MRS. C(UZZY) SNEAD (43 in Kentucky), MR. SAMUEL L. HALSEY of Decatur,
Alabama to MISS MARTHA G. SNEAD (15 in Alabama) of Athens, Alabama.
    Died on 27 July last in Greensboro, JOHN CRUTCHER, 4th son of
DR. THOMAS C. (32 in South Carolina) and MRS. HARRIET C. OSBORNE (22 in
Alabama; Greene County) aged 15 months, 2 days.
    State of Alabama--Madison County. SALLY D. SPOTSWOOD, deceased.
Next of kin--LUCY ANN (37 in Virginia) wife of LUKE MATTHEWS, EDWIN P.
(should be "B") SPOTSWOOD, SARAH E., wife of SAMUEL MATTHEWS, SUSAN,
wife of DAVID MALONE, WILLIAM E. SPOTSWOOD, JOHN C. SPOTSWOOD, MARY R.
SPOTSWOOD, IRBY E. SPOTSWOOD, all over 21, PEYTON W. SPOTSWOOD, JAMES W.
McCLUNG and SPOTSWOOD McCLUNG, infants under 21, all residents of Alabama
except IRBY E. SPOTSWOOD.

August 23, 1854
    Married on Thursday evening last, 17 August by REV. W. D. F. SAWRIE,
MR. ROBERT F. RUSSELL to MISS MARY A., daughter of ROBERT FREEMAN, Esq.
all of this county.
    Married on the 13th by HON. J. G. DIXON, at the residence of
THOMAS SNODGRASS, Esq., COL. BENJAMIN SNODGRASS to MRS. NANCY CHANDLER,
all of Jackson County.
    Married at the residence of MAJ. JOSEPH H. GREER, in Lincoln on
the 9th, by REV. MR. COWAN, MR. SAMUEL A. SLAUGHTER of Marshall County,
Tennessee to MISS JOSEPHINE EDMONDSON of Lincoln.
    Died at his residence near Huntsville, Alabama on the 17th of
hemorrhage, ROBERT S. BRANDON (33 in Alabama) aged about 38 years.
Born, raised and educated in this community...member of the Methodist
Episcopal Church. Left orphan children.
    In Bellefonte, Alabama on the 16th, CHARLIE J., son of MR. and
MRS. W. J. GREENE, died.
    Accidental death of MR. HENRY GILDER, an old gentleman 66 or 67
years of age, well known in this and some of adjoining counties as a
school teacher...(Jacksonville Sunny South).

August 30, 1854
    Married on 8th by JAMES H. POOR, Esq., MR. WILLIAM L. McDUFF to
MISS MARY WATSON (12 in Tennessee; HARDIN), all of this county.
    Married 9th by JAMES H. POOR, Esq., MR. LEWIS C. LEMLEY to MISS
SUSAN T. SEWARD, all of this county.
    Married on 23rd at residence of REV. F. P. SCRUGGS by REV. B. F.
WHITE (died July 5, 1855 at 24), MR. P(HINEAS) T. SCRUGGS to MISS BETTIE
MURPHEY (13 in Alabama), all of Decatur.
    Married at "Somerville Inn," Somerville, Alabama on the 23rd by
REV. JOEL TURRENTINE, MR. B. SPOTS to MRS. SARAH SAWYERS (41 in South
Carolina; wife of JAMES), both of Decatur.
    Married on the 22nd by REV. W. MOONEY, SAMUEL W. L. McCLESKY (40
in Tennessee), Esq., of Frankfort, Alabama to MISS MARY A. MATTHEWS of
Tuscumbia.
    Died in Huntsville at the residence of his son-in-law, THOMAS
MARTIN, Esq., on 8 August, WILLIAM H. IRBY (73 in Virginia) at the
advanced age of 79. He was born in Pittsylvania County, Virginia where
he resided until 1825 at which time he removed to Madison County,
Alabama.
    Died on the 12th at residence of his father, in Morgan County,
WM A. S. DAVIS (10 in Alabama) in the 13th year. Eldest son of RILEY S.
DAVIS (47 in Kentucky) and FRANCES S., deceased--formerly FRANCES S.
SLAUGHTER (dead 1850--evidently widow COLLIER), only daughter of the
late JOHN SLAUGHTER of Virginia.
    Also at the same house on 17th, RHODA ANN, second daughter of
ELISHA BELL, deceased and NANCY P., now NANCY P. DAVIS.
    Died at her residence in Limestone County, Alabama on Friday 4
August MRS. ELIZABETH PETTY (73 in South Carolina) in the 77th year of
her age. Methodist.

September 6, 1854
Died at his residence in Montgomery, Texas the 15th after a short
illness, REV. THOMAS CHILTON, Pastor of the Baptist Church of that
place.

September 13, 1854
Married in Franklin County, Kentucky on 31st by REV. CHARLES TOMES,
MR. ALFRED M. WATKINS of the firm of GILLILANDS, HOWELL and Company,
Charleston, South Carolina to MISS JANE D. CROWDUS of the former place.
Died at her residence in Huntsville on the 23rd, MRS. MARTHA
HAMBLIN (49 in East Tennessee) aged 53 years 11 months, daughter of
NICHOLAS and ELIZABETH REEDY, the latter surviving still in the vicinity
of Canaan meeting house in Madison County, Alabama. Her husband died
previous to our acquaintance in the family. He was the son of the much
respected JOHN HAMBLIN. She was left a widow with five children, three
of whom still live here. In 1840 or '42 she professed religion....
An aged mother has lost a dutiful daughter, two kind brothers and 2
sisters have lost a sister....
Died on the 5th after a short illness, MRS. PAMELIA BIBB (66 in
Virginia), relict of the late THOMAS BIBB, Esq., aged about 70 years.
She was among the early settlers in Huntsville; was noted for her piety
and charitable deeds and was beloved by all. She leaves many relatives
and friends to mourn her loss.
Died in Athens, Alabama on the 4th, ARCHIE SNEAD (CUZZY; 17 in
Alabama) aged 22 years.
Died on the 30th, ISAAC HYDE (51 in South Carolina), an old and
respectable citizen of Limestone County.
Died on Florence, Alabama on the 30th, OLIVER P(ERRY) ASHER (25
in Alabama) of firm of M(ONTGOMERY) P. and O(LIVER) P. ASHER in the 30th
year of his age.

September 20, 1854
Married on the 7th by E. S. MASTERSON, Esq., CAPT. JOEL M. TERRILL
to MISS NANCY A. WOOD all of Lawrence County, Alabama.
Married on the 29th by REV. ISAAC MILLNER, MR. S(IGMUN) BROCK to
MISS MELVINA E. SIMMS (SIMMONS in marriage record; SIMMS is right), all
of Lawrence County.
Died in St. Francis County, Arkansas on 5th, COL. EDWIN JONES
aged 63 years. Born in Surry County, Virginia September 2, 1791 whence
in 1817 he emigrated to Huntsville, Alabama; thence in 1831 he removed to
Mississippi County, Arkansas and finally within the past 18 months to
St. Francis County where, after a painful and protracted illness,
---(?) he died Possessed of a peculiarly happy degree of those nice,
social qualities that endeared him to old and young....(Memphis Eagle
and Enquirer of the 12th; In 1850 Mississippi County, Arkansas--EDWIN
JONES 58 in Virginia alone).
Died at his residence in Jackson County, Alabama on the 26th of
typhoid fever, MR. ISAAC FRIDDELL aged about 37, leaving a wife and 3
small children.
Died in Sommerville on the 19th of consumption, MARY L. MORROW
(43 in Tennessee), consort of COL. H(UGH) D. MORROW (50 in South Carolina)
aged 47 years. Note: see our volume 27, page 3 for marriage of HUGH D.
MORROW to POLLY L. LYNN on December 31, 1821 (her tombstone says died
23 September 1853).
Died on 13 September at residence of JOHN HALSEY, TABITHA (18 in
Alabama), wife of JAMES O. HALSEY (26 in Alabama) aged 22 years.

September 27, 1854
Married on 5th in Glasgow, Missouri by ELDER A. PROCTOR, MR. CHARLES
H. LEWIS, late of Huntsville, Alabama to MISS ANNIE E., daughter of
WM. P. ROPER, Esq. of that city.
Married on 6th by REV. MR. HUMPHREYS, ELDER E(UGENE) STRODE of
Chattanooga to MISS SALLY J., daughter of THOMAS MARTIN, Esq. of this
county. (note: grandparents of HUDSON STRODE, famous author of the
University of Alabama)
Died in this place on the 19th, DR. ROBERT W. WITHERS (52 in
Virginia) of Greene County, Alabama.
Died in this place on 23rd, MARIA HALLOWELL, daughter of DR. and
MRS. A. L. WILKINSON aged about 2 years.

Died on 24th instant at residence of her father, near this place, SARAH aged 3½ months, infant daughter of REUBEN and FELICIA A. CHAPMAN.

October 4, 1854

Married in the city of Montgomery on evening of the 28th, by the RT. REV. BISHOP COBBS, JOHN W. SHEPHERD, Esq., to MISS MARY SOMMERVILLE (17 in Alabama; ANN E.).

Married in Hardeman County, Tennessee on the 14th by REV. MR. GREEN of Somerville, MR. JOHN T. MORROW of Fayette County to MISS MARGARET F. MARCH of the former county.

Married in Montgomery on the 29th at residence of MR. JOHN P. GIGH? by REV. O(LIVER) R(UFUS) BLUE, MR. GEORGE W. NOBLE to MISS BARBARA J. DICKINSON (25 in Virginia), all of that city.

Died at his residence in Madison County, Alabama on the 13th instant JOHN W. MITCHELL in the 39th year of his age. Native of this county, son and only child of MARGARET and OBADIAH MITCHELL. Kind husband and father. Left a wife and 4 little children....

Died on the 20th in Clarke County after a lingering illness, MR. JAMES THORNTON (63 in South Carolina) aged about 66 years...husband and father.

Died on the 28th, WILLIE J. (1 in Alabama) son of MR. and MRS. WM. J. McCALLEY of this vicinity aged about 6 years.

Died on the 29th in this place, ALEXANDER ERSKINE, infant son of DR. and MRS. A. L. WILKINSON. In less than one week, their two children were cut down by death....

Died on 20 of typhoid fever in this place, MR. GREEN PICKARD aged about 55 years. He was a good man, a true man, an honest man and a christian. He was respected and esteemed by all who knew him. Leaves a large family.

VIRGINIA E. LILE (23 in Alabama), wife of JOHN A(LLISON) LILE (24 in Alabama; THOS), and second daughter of JOHN and MARIANNE FORD, was born in Madison County on 25 April 1827; was married on 13 December 1849 and removed to Morgan County. On 16 September 1854 she died after severe attack of malignant fever.

Departed this life in Somerville, Alabama at the residence of JOHN F. BARKER September 23, MRS. SUSAN H. RATHER (42 in Virginia), wife of CAPT. JOHN T. RATHER of Decatur in her 49th year. Daughter of PHILAGAETIUS and MARGARET ROBERTS of Culpepper County, Virginia. She came to Alabama with her brother-in-law, MR. BANKS in 1826. Was united in marriage to her surviving husband October 29, 1830. Joined M. E. Church in 1829.

Died on 26th, ELISHA B. SMITH for many years cashier of Planters Bank of Tennessee at Pulaski.

State of Alabama--Madison County. JOHN WRIGHT, administrator of AUGUSTUS SPAIN, deceased.

October 11, 1854

Died in Decatur, Alabama on the 24th, MRS. MARTHA E. COLLINS, wife of MR. CALEB COLLINS in 25th year of her age.

Died in Decatur, Alabama on 25th after a lingering illness of 9 weeks, NANCY WILES (45 in Virginia) aged 64.

Married on the 18th by REV. RICHARD TALIAFERRO, MICAH TAUF, Esq. of Talladega, Alabama to MISS LOUISIANA (14 in Alabama), daughter of REV. C. L. ROACH of Jackson County, Alabama.

Married on the morning of the 2nd by JOHN W. IRBY, Esq., MR. JOSEPH SPENCE to MRS. ARAMINTA V. MILLER--all of this county.

Married on the 14th by JAMES H. POOR, Esq., MR. JEFFERSON WALKER of East Tennessee to MISS ELIZABETH A. McKINNEY, of this county.

Married on the 21st by JAMES H. POOR, Esq., MR. A. B. LEDBETTER to MISS NANCY C. GRAYSON, all of this county.

Married on the 21st by JAMES H. POOR, Esq., MR. JOHN C. GRAYSON to MISS L. M. BUFORD, all of this county.

Married on the 28th by REV. B. C. CHAPMAN (volume 129, page 99; volume 134), MR. P(INCKNEY) M. IRBY to MISS SUSAN E. HAMBLIN, all of this county. (she was grand-daughter of JOHN HAMBLIN).

Married on Wednesday evening the 4th instant by BISHOP ROBERT PAINE, NICHOLAS DAVIS, JR., ESQ. to MISS SOPHIA (21 in Alabama), eldest daughter of GEN. B(ARTLEY) M. LOWE, all of Huntsville, Alabama.

Married on the morning of 5th by REV. J. G. WILSON, DR. WM. TELL
SANDERS of Limestone County to MISS ANNA E. (14 in Alabama) daughter
of RICHARD A. WIGGINS, Esq. (40 in North Carolina) of this county.
Married on the evening of the 5th by REV. DR. J(OHN) W. HALL
(Presbyterian), DR. ALBERT R. ERSKINE of Huntsville, Alabama to MISS
MARIA D. daughter of LUKE MATTHEWS, Esq. of this county.
Married on 28th by REV. WELLBORN MOONEY, MR. G. W. GILES to MISS
CALLIE (CALIFORNIA in census) M. CLAYTON (17 in Alabama), all of
Tuscumbia, Alabama.
Married on 28th by JOHN T. HADEN, Esq., MR. RICHARD MOON (marriage
record shows RICHARD MOON married OLIVE JENKINS and JACKSON MOON married
FRANCES JENKINS. In 1843 they were daughters of BARBRY JENKINS,
FRANCES 17 in Alabama, "OLIPH" 15 in Alabama) to MISS FRANCES D. JENKINS.

October 18, 1854
Married on 3rd by REV. B. C. CHAPMAN, MR. FRANCIS L. BELL to
MISS MARY J. LAMBERSON, all of this county.
Married in Athens, on 4th by ELDER D. B. HALE, MR. J. H. DOAN,
of East port Mississippi to MISS EMILY J(ANE) TANNER of the former
place (volume 205, page 73).
Married on 5th by REV. J. N. MULLENS (probably ISAAC N.; methodist),
MR. LUCIUS H. GRUBBS of Giles County, Tennessee to MISS CEMANTHA P.
MULLENS (18 in Alabama; WM.) of Lawrence County, Alabama.
Married on the 10th by REV. WM. McGAUGHEY, MR. ROBERT J. WARREN
to MISS CATHARINE J. CLARK, all of Lawrence County.
Married on the 11th by REV. DR. J. W. HALL, MR. DAVID CRESWELL of
Louisiana to MISS JULIA PLEASANTS (22 in Alabama), daughter of the late
COL. JAMES J. PLEASANTS of Huntsville, Alabama.
Married on the 12th by REV. P. B. ROBINSON, MR. PETER N. DOX of
New York to MISS MATTIE W., daughter of B. S. POPE, Esq. of vicinity of
Huntsville, Alabama.
Died in New Orleans on 5 October of yellow fever, JAMES ATWOOD
aged 22 years 3 months 1 day. Born and raised in Huntsville....
Died in New Orleans on 8th, MRS. ANN (38 in Tennessee; Franklin
County), wife of the late JOHN T. CHRISTIAN (32 in Virginia).
Died in Decatur, Alabama on 10th of flux, MARY, only daughter of
W. D. S. and D. V. COOK aged 2 years 2 months 17 days.

October 25, 1854
Married on Thursday evening October 19, 1854 by REV. P. B. ROBINSON,
H. C. BRADFORD, Esq. of this place to MISS ANNIE (16 in Alabama),
second daughter of WILLIAM WATKINS, Esq. of this vicinity.
Married on the 14th by REV. WELLBORN MOONEY, HON. R(OBERT) B(URNS)
LINDSAY, to MISS SARAH M(ILLER) WINSTON (18; WM), all of Tuscumbia.
Married on the 14th by REV. WELLBORN MOONEY, DR. J. L. BURT of
Courtland, Alabama to MISS CATHARINE B. WINSTON of the vicinity of
Tuscumbia.
Married on the 17th by REV. WELLBORN MOONEY, MR. P. A. ROSS to
MISS JULIA A. JONES, all of Tuscumbia.
Married on 11 October by REV. D. K. HUNTER (volume 141, page 60),
MR. JOHN W. CAMPBELL (13 in Alabama) to MISS SARAH E. MOORE, daughter
of DR. DAVIS MOORE (50 in North Carolina), all of this county.
Married on 19th, by ELDER SAMUEL DENNIS, MR. WM. WILLIAMS of
Limestone County to MRS. SARAH WILLIAMS of this county (volume 153,
page 57).
Married on 10th by JOHN TITTADEN, Esq., MR. GEORGE H. ANYAN (19 in
Alabama; BENDALL S.) to MISS FERTIMA A. SARTIN, all of this county.
Married on the 12th by same, MR. JOHN C. POTTS (20 in Alabama)
to MISS RUTHA ANN (12 in Alabama), daughter of MR. JOSEPH R. JENKINS
(K in census; 39 in North Carolina), all of this county.
Married on the 17th at Hotel of PETER PURYEAR in Courtland, by
REV. T. MILLER, MR. THOMAS T. TWEEDY to MISS LABARREARE of Lawrence
County.
Married on the 4th by REV. R. PATE, J. R. WEST, M.D. of Alabama to
MISS MELISSA BURGESS, daughter of CHARLES BURGESS of Itawamba County,
Mississippi.
Died at his residence in Madison County on the 9th, DAVID McLEHANY,
Esq. (64 in Virginia) in the 68th year of his age, after a short but
painful illness of 24 hours...more than 30 years a resident of Morgan
County.

November 1, 1854
    State of Alabama--Madison County. Heirs of GREEN PICKARD, deceased.
SPENCER PICKARD, JOSEPH F. HALBROOK and wife LUCINDA HALBROOK, JOHN
PICKARD, ELIZABETH PICKARD, ANDREW McCANN and wife MARY McCANN, JAMES
PICKARD, MARTHA PICKARD, MARGARET PICKARD, WILLIAM PICKARD, PETER PICKARD,
ISAAC PICKARD, GEORGE PICKARD and SARAH PICKARD; JAMES, MARTHA, MARGARET,
WILLIAM, PETER and JOHN and JAMES PICKARD who are non-residents of
Alabama.
    Married in Tuscaloosa on the 17th by REV. B. MANLY, D.D., DR. WM. A.
JONES of Greensboro to MISS MARGARET (19), only daughter of the late
THOMAS D. KING (Georgia) of Tuscaloosa (volume 3, page 79).
    Married on the 19th by REV. DORSEN (DAWSON) PHELPS, NATHAN W.
COPELAND (21 in Alabama) to MISS CAROLINE GRISBY (17 in Alabama;
EDWD. W.), all of Limestone County (note: should be "GRIGSBY").
    Married on 25th by REV. W. D. F. SAWRIE, MR. WILLIAM LAWLER of
Huntsville, Alabama to MISS MATTIE, daughter of MR. JOHN BYRN of near
Maysville, Alabama.
    Died in Tuscaloosa on the 15th, WM. BANKS ORMOND (14 in Alabama),
second son of HON. J. J. ORMOND.
    Died on 26th in Limestone County, MR. AMOS M. VERNON (21 in Alabama)
aged 26.
    Died on 17th in Madison County after an illness of twenty-one days,
WILLIE WALTON, infant son of THOMAS H. and JANE S. HEWLETT aged 9
months.
    Died in Decatur on 17th, MR. EDMOND KIMBELL (71 in North Carolina),
an old and respectable citizen.

November 8, 1854
    Married in Marietta, Georgia on 25 October 1854, SMITH D. HALE,
Esq. (26 in Tennessee) of Huntsville to MISS S. E. PYNCHON, daughter of
MR. E. E. PYNCHON of the former place.
    Married on the 5th by JOHN A. JOHNSON, Esq., MR. J. W. FRENCH to
MISS MARY ANN JOHNSON. On the 10th by same, JAMES F. JOHNSTON to MISS
MARTHA CLEM. On 17th by same, JAMES C. PEACE (12 in Alabama; WM.) to
MISS ---- GREENHAW. On 20th by same, JAMES G. MARTINDALE to MISS W.
HENRIETTA TOONE, all of Limestone County.
    Married on the 25th by REV. J. G. WILSON, REV. THOMAS J. LACY of
Louisiana Conference, to MISS MARY E. GLADISH of Limestone County.
    Married on the 25th by REV. R. H. RIVERS, MAJOR JOHN N. MALONE of
Limestone County to MISS REBECCA SIMMONS of Lauderdale County, Alabama.
    Married in Tuscumbia on the 30th by REV. C. F. WILLIAMS, MR.
F. H. G. TAYLOR of Madison Parish, Louisiana to MISS ANN TROUP CARTER
of Franklin County, Arkansas.
    Married on 30th ult. by REV. THOMAS MADDIN, MR. EDWIN B(OSWELL)
SPOTSWOOD to MRS. MARTHA A(NN) WILLBURN, all of this vicinity (she was
daughter of DANIEL HARRIS and widow of FREDLE B. WILBURN).
    Married on 1st by REV. JOHN T. EDGAR, COL. VERNON K. STEVENSON,
President of Nashville and Chattanooga Railroad to MISS MARIE LOUISA,
daughter of JOHN M. BASS, Esq., all of Nashville.
    Died at his residence in Limestone County on 22nd, MR. DAVID R.
CRAIG in 31st year.
    Died in Tuscumbia on 29th, NAT. A. F. RAGLAND, Esq. (47).

November 15, 1854
    Married on 2nd in Franklin County, Alabama by REV. JUSTINEAN
WILLIAMS, SR., R. E. BRINKLEY, Esq., President of Bank at Memphis, and
MISS ELIZABETH M. (22 in North Carolina), daughter of the late COL.
JAMES G. MHOON of Shelby County, Tennessee.
    Married on 2nd by REV. G. G. D. GWINN, MR. LEWIS M. SEAT to MISS
MARY E. DICKEY (11 in Alabama; MOSES), all of this county.
    Died--WILLIAM RUSSELL (16 in Alabama), third son of ALEXANDER
RUSSELL, Esq. (42 in Virginia) of Limestone County, Alabama; was born
23 January 1833 and departed this life 15 September 1854 in Lowndes
County, Mississippi whither he had gone to visit relatives.
    Died at his residence in Limestone County, Alabama on 30th, MAJ.
EDMUND WALTON (60 in Virginia; EDWD in census) in 65th year (son of
DAVID born 1760 buried in Limestone County; ancestor of MRS. WM.
MIZELL, Folksten, Georgia 1954).
    Died in Decatur, on 17th, MR. EDMUND KIMBELL, an old and respectable
citizen.

November 22, 1854

We find the following marriage notice in Baltimore Patriot of the 10th instant. HON. ARTHUR F. HOPKINS of Mobile, Alabama was married last evening at St. Thomas Church to MISS JULIET A. GORDON of Fort Hamilton, daughter of the late HON. H. I. OPE of Virginia.

Married on the 8th by REV. T(IMOTHY) ROOT, MR. JOHN T. HARDIE of New Orleans to MISS W. E. GARY (ANN; 14 in Alabama) of Tuskegee, Alabama (daughter of WM. L).

Married on 14th in Marshall County, MR. JOHN F. EDDS (14 in Alabama) to MISS MARTHA JANE ALLEN, both of Jackson County.

Married on 15th by WM. ARMSTRONG, Esq., MR. WM. JENKINS to MISS MARGARET CLARK, all of Jackson County.

Married on 15th by REV. JAMES AUSTILL, MR. SAMUEL MEAD to MISS SUSAN HANCOCK (14 in Alabama; A. F.), all of Jackson County.

Married on 16th, MR. J. A. TIPTON to MISS LUCINDA MEAD (16 in Alabama; SAM'L), all of Jackson County.

Married on 7th by REV. THOMAS A. MORRIS, MR. ROBERT B. HARRIS to MISS PRUDENCE E. HURT (14 in Alabama; W. F.), all of Jackson County.

Married on 31 October by REV. N. T. POWER, COL. JAS. M. SHEAD to MISS SUSAN A. RICE of this county.

Married on the 8th by REV. N. T. POWER, MR. J. C. STEELE to MISS MARTHA STEELE, all of this county.

Married on 12 by REV. JAMES A. WOODALL, MR. ARCHIE M. VEST (21 in Alabama) to MISS MATILDA SUMMERFORD (17 in Alabama; ISAAC C.), all of Morgan County.

Married in the Church of Nativity on 16th by REV. HENRY C. LAY, MR. JOHN D. BARNARD, of Georgia to MISS HARRIET H., daughter of the late DR. DAVID MOORE of this place.

Died on 11th, GEORGE, infant son of MR. and MRS. GEORGE H. WARWICK of this place.

Died at his residence in Hickory Flat in this county, on 6th after a short illness, MR. THOMAS E. SPRAGINS (29 in Virginia) in his 34th year.

Departed this life at his residence in this county on 18 October ROBERT H. HEREFORD (19 in Alabama; THEODORE) in the 24th year of his age. Born in this county September 29, 1830 and was united in marriage to MISS CORNELIA J. DEMENT on 3 September 1851.

Departed this life at her residence in this county, MRS. ANN THOMPSON in the 75th year of her age. Born in Brunswick County, Virginia in the year 1779 (tombstone says 1789 in Pittsylvania County, Virginia) where she resided until the year 1835 when she emigrated to Madison County, Alabama, where she died November 5, 1854.

November 29, 1854

Married on 9th at the residence of MERRIWETHER LEWIS, Esq. in Triana, by REV. DR. FINLEY, MR. JAMES M. GALOWAY of Limestone County to MISS JULIA LEWIS of Madison County, Alabama (volume 127, page 30).

Married on 26 October MR. JAMES HARGROVES to MISS SARAH F. MARTIN, all of Limestone County.

Married on 16th by JOHN TURRENTINE, Esq. at his residence in Athens, MR. JAMES G. SCOTT to MISS ELIZABETH JANE BRADLEY of Huntsville, Alabama.

Married on 21st by RT. REV. BISHOP MILES, at Sylvan Hall, MR. J. FELIX DEMOVILLE and MISS MARY, daughter of WM. D. PHILIPS, Esq. (Nashville Banner).

December 6, 1854

Married in Decatur, Alabama on Sunday evening, 19th instant, by JAMES M. MEANS, Esq., MR. D(AVID) R(USSEL) ROMINES to MISS ARRENA M(ALINDA) EDGE all of that place. (Letter from MRS. FLORENCE W. CRANDELL, 216 South Hobson Street, Mesa, Arizona, April 1, 1960--daughter of FLORENCE (ROMINE) WAHL, grand-daughter of DAVID RUSSEL ROMINE born in Alabama December 3, 1835, died 4 June 1888 in Clarksville, Tennessee and wife IRENE MALINDA EDGE born in Alabama October 24, 1834, died 5 July 1917 in Saginaw, Michigan; she was daughter of JAS T. and MARY EDGE; D. R. R. was son of JEREMIAH ROMINE; FLORENCE (ROMINE) WAHL, born June 6, 1879 in Clarksville, Tennessee on 25 February 1903; ALBERT LUIS WAHL).

Married on the morning of 30th November at residence of COL. JOHN
REED by REV. CHARLES B. KING, of Augusta, Georgia MR. THOMAS EDWARD KING
of Roswell, Georgia to MISS MARY READ CLEMENS, only daughter of HON.
JERE CLEMENS of this place.

Married in Memphis, Tennessee on the 27th by REV. DR. PAGE,
HON. WM. C. DAWSON, U.S. Senator from Georgia to MRS. ELIZA M. WILLIAMS
of that city.

Married on 16 November by REV. T. ELLIOTT, MR. PARKS S. TOWNSEND
(16 in Alabama) of Madison County, Alabama to MISS SALLIE L. COOVER of
Franklin County, Tennessee.

Married at Summerfield, Alabama on 22nd, REV. BISHOP ANDREW of
Methodist Episcopal Church South and MRS. CHILDERS.

Died on 29 after lingering illness, MRS. ELIZABETH POSEY (56 in
Virginia) aged about 60. Had resided in Huntsville many years. Presby-
terian. (she was nee ATWOOD--her 1st husband was STOKELEY DONELSON
HUTCHINGS; 2. (1828) PHARES J. POSEY)

December 14, 1854
Married in Courtland, Alabama by REV. R. A. COBBS, EDWARD C. BETTS
of Huntsville to MISS VIRGINIA (14 in Alabama), youngest daughter of
JOHN M. SWOOPE, Esq. of Courtland, Alabama.

Married on 30 November by REV. W. M. TURNEY, MR. THOMAS H. STEPHENSON
of Lawrence, to MISS ELIZABETH A. HAMILTON of Morgan.

Married on 22nd by REV. H. A. PHILPOTT, MR. GABRIEL L. BRINKLEY
of Blount County to MISS MARY S. WILSON of Morgan County.

Married on 29th by REV. JAMES S. LANE (Methodist), N. G. SHELLEY,
Esq. (25), Editor of Selma Reporter to MISS SARAH FRANCES (19 in
Alabama), daughter of CAPT. JACOB D. SHELLEY of Talladega.

Married on 29th by REV. MR. WELCH, the HON. NOAH H. AGEE of the
Claiborne (Monroe County) Southerner to MISS ANN C. HUNLEY of Shelby
County.

Died on 9th instant after a short illness, MR. WILLIAM G. SELLICK
(38 in Vermont) aged about 42 years, native of Vermont but had resided
in Huntsville many years.

Died on 4th, MARY HARDIE (9 in Alabama), youngest daughter of
GEN. JACOB T. BRADFORD of Talladega.

Died near Mooresville on December 1st, of typhoid fever, E. B.
TAYLOR aged 27 years 2 months 17 days.

Died at his residence in Limestone County on 6th after a very long
and painful illness, DAVID ELLIOTT (56 in North Carolina).

December 20, 1854
Married on 30th by REV. B. C. CHAPMAN, MR. JAMES E. SEAT, of this
place to MISS MARY J. BRAND of this county.

Married on 7th by REV. R. P. RIDDLE, MR. WM. McCORMICK to MISS
MARGARET M. LEWIS, all of Limestone County.

Married in Selma on the morning of 11th by REV. W. H. PLATTE,
MR. R. B. COOK (or firm of SAYRE, COOK and Company) to MISS PARALEE P.
BLEVINS, all of that place.

Died on 5th, OTIS AINSWORTH, only child of J. M. H. and ELIZABETH M.
SMITH aged 10 months 8 days.

Died in Courtland on 23rd, OCTAVIUS BYRD (18 in Alabama; MARTHA)
aged 23.

Died in Franklin County on 5th, E. H. NEWSOM (NEWMAN in census)
aged 51.

Died in Tuscumbia on 9th, WM. D. GORDON aged 46.

December 27, 1854
Died at 12 o'clock on night of 18th, JAMES ERSKINE O'NEAL of
scarlet fever. Born August 8, 1849.

January 3, 1855
Paper torn and part of it missing

February 6, 1855
Married at residence of WILLIAM H. TURNER, Esq. in Madison County,
Alabama, January 16, 1855 by REV. P. B. ROBINSON, AUGUSTUS BATTE, Esq.
of Nashville, Tennessee to MISS MARY ANN HANCOCK of Giles County,
Tennessee.

Married on 18th by REV. R. B. ROBINSON, MR. WILLIAM L. MARTIN to MISS SARAH N. WEBB all of this place.

Married in Greensboro, Alabama on 30th by REV. JAMES C. MITCHELL (Presbyterian), JUDGE FRED TATE of LaGrange, Texas to MRS. LUCY CROOM of Wharton County, Texas.

Married on 24th by REV. DR. EDGAR, at residence of O. B. HAYS, in vicinity of Nashville, W. L. B. LAWRENCE, Esq. to MISS CORINNE HAYS.

At the same time and place by same, GEORGE SHIELDS, Esq. of New Orleans and MISS LAURA HAYS.

Married on 31st by REV. W. S. BARKSDALE at residence of HON. E. D. TOWNES in Tuscumbia, MR. JOHN L. EGGLESTON (40 in Virginia) of Lawrence County to MISS MARY R. EGGLESTON of Tuscumbia.

Married by REV. MR. CLARK on 1 February, MR. JOHN D. WHITTINGTON (28 in Virginia) to MISS MARTHA ANN ROACH (15 in Alabama). Also at the same time and place by same minister, MR. JAMES T. WALL (16 in Alabama; MARY) to MISS MARY ELIZA CAWTHON, all of Madison County.

Died on Saturday the 3rd of August H. MORRISON (32 in Maryland) aged 37.

Died on 4th at the residence of MILLS JENKINS, Esq. after a painful illness, MR. ALBERT WRIGHT aged about 36 years.

Died in Tuscumbia on the 24th after a long illness, THOMAS BROWN, a native of Lancaster, England, aged about 80 years.

Died on 28th January at his residence in Warrenton, Marshall County, Alabama, JOHN C. ASHWORTH (20 in Aladama, Madison County) aged 24 years.

Died on 3rd of scarlet fever, EMMA (3 in Alabama), daughter of JAS. H. and MARIA SCRUGGS aged about 8 years.

February 14, 1855
Married on 8th by REV. MR. COWAN, V(ALENTINE) GREEN PRUIT (19 in Alabama) to MARY A. OTEY (14 in Alabama), all of this county.

Married on 1st by REV. DR. F. A. ROSS, MR. JOHN O. NOBLE to MISS ELIZA ANN HOPKINS, both of this place.

Married on 8th by REV. DR. ROBINSON, MR. CRAWFORD W. HUMPHREY to MISS MARTA L. McGRAW, all of this county.

Married on 7th by REV. B. C. CHAPMAN, MR. JORDAN H. SCOTT of Giles County, Tennessee to MISS SARAH A. GORDON (14 in Alabama; JAMES) of this county.

Married on 7th by REV. W. M. SHAW, MR. LUCIEN B. BURRUS of Winchester, Tennessee to MISS MARTHA E. DEMENT of this county.

Married on 7th of February 1855 by JAMES H. POOR, Esq., JAMES GIBSON to MATILDA MANN, all of this county.

Married in Macon, Georgia on 30th by HON. KELIN COOK, MR. ISAAC B. PILGRIM, Printer, to MISS MARY G. CASH, both of Atlanta.

Died at his residence in Madison County, Alabama on morning of 11th January, 1855, JOHN WARD (50 in Virginia), an old and worthy citizen of this county. Born in Albemarle County, Virginia December 6, 1798 and was born again in 1820--Methodist Episcopal Church. Left a widow and an only daughter.

Died at Angola Plantation, Louisiana on the morning of Thursday the 25th ult of scarlet fever, LAURA VICTORIA, twin daughter of COL. JOSEPH A. S. and ADELICIA ACKLEN aged 2 years and 3 months.

Died at Buzzard Roost, Franklin County, Alabama on 24 January after a lingering illness, R(OBERT) M. WHITE (70 in Virginia) in 74th year. (ancestor of MRS. WM. S. JOHNSON, Spruce Pine, Alabama, 1963)

Died on 3rd, WILLIAMETTA E., eldest daughter of R. D. and M. E. ELLIOTT aged 3 years 2 months and 24 days.

February 21, 1855
Married on 14th by REV. JNO. D. BARBEE, GEORGE W. JOYNER, Esq. to MISS S(ARAH) M. STRAIN, all of Morgan County.

Married on 18th by REV. DR. ROBINSON, MR. HENRY LAWRENCE (12 in Tennessee) to MISS ZUALDA (ZERILDA in census) E. CASEY (18 in Tennessee; MICAJAH), all of this place. (Looks like ZERILDA in census record; in marriage record 4--says URILDA).

Married on 6th by REV. THOMAS MADDIN, MR. CHRISTOPHER C. McBROOM (22 in Alabama; STEPHENS) to MISS AMANDA M., daughter of DANIEL JOHNSON, Esq., all of this place.

Died on 15th of consumption, MR. NICHOLAS P. McKINZIE (26 in Alabama; son of NICH. and AMELIA) of this vicinity, a most amiable young man.

February 28, 1855

Married on Tuesday the 13th by REV. J. G. WILSON, MR. JAMES BIBB to MISS LAURA E. DILLARD, all of this county.

Married on 20th by REV. B. C. CHAPMAN, MR. JOHN BRAND (37 in Virginia; married before) to MRS. MARY S. DIFFEY (34 in Alabama), all of this county.

Died on 22 MR. STEPHEN S. CAYTON (38 in North Carolina) of this place.

March 7, 1855

Married on 18th by MR. JOSEPH RICE, ROBERT WILSON to ISADORA COOK, all of Morgan County.

Married on 28th by JAMES H. POOR, Esq., MR. JAS. BESHERS (BARSHEARS) to MISS MARTHA WILLIAS (WILLIAMS), all of this county (volume 136, page 38).

Died of scarlet fever at Angola Plantation in parish of West Felicianna, Louisiana, on Thursday 25 January, LAURA VICTORIA and on Sunday the 11th February of same disease, CORINNE ADELICIA, aged 2 years 3 months. (children of JOSEPH A. S. and ADELICIA ACKLER)

Tribute of respect--JOHN P. JOHNSON (55 in Virginia) departed this life on 21st aged 61 years 9 months 12 days. Maysville Lodge #158 publishes resolutions on his death.

March 14, 1855

Married on 28 by REV. DR. FENNELL, JOHN D. RIVERS, Esq., to MISS MARY E. KINNIBRUGH (11 in Alabama; JOHN) of Madison County.

Died in Madison County on 14 February 1855, MRS. CATHARINE HARRIS (73 in Virginia), widow of the late EDWARD HARRIS; deceased. MRS. HARRIS was in the 80th year of her age and had been for many years a member of the Baptist Church. She was an affectionate mother, a kind neighbor, devoted friend and an indulgent mistress. Having attained an age which few reach, and with the respect and love of all who knew her, she has been called to the rest which remaineth for the people of God-- A Friend. Note: Her tombstone states that she died February 14, 1855 aged 77 years and a descendatn, JUDGE WILLIAM LOGAN MARTIN, Birmingham, Alabama states her age on tombstone is correct and not the obituary.

March 21, 1855

Married on 14th at the residence of COL. NELSON, in Athens, by REV. I. R. FINLEY, DR. SHEGOGG of Leighton, Alabama to MRS. MARIA LEONARD of this county.

Married on 10th by JAMES H. POOR, MR. ANDREW McMINN to MISS SUSAN CAMERON (13 in Alabama), all of this county (she was sister of JOHN CAMERON; volume 197, page 88; volume 145, page 26).

Married in Lauderdale County on 6th by REV. R. H. RIVERS, DR. ALBERT H. JONES to MISS REBECCA BODDIE.

March 28, 1855

Married on 21st by REV. A. L. P. GREEN, MR. ALEXANDER WHEELESS of Tennessee to MISS ELIZABETH T. MALONE of Athens.

Married on 8th by JOHN A. JOHNSON, Esq., MR. ZACHARIAH CLARK to MISS MARGARET E. GRAY, all of Limestone County.

Married on 21st by REV. DR. KIMBLE, MR. EDWARD A. G. KIMBLE (EDWIN in census; 23 in Alabama; NANCY) of Morgan County to MISS JANE H. BRUNDIDGE (15 in Alabama; JAS. M.) of Athens.

April 4, 1855

Died near Aberdeen, Mississippi on 18th, LOGAN D. BRANDON, formerly of this county.

Died in this place on 26th, CAPT. WM. R. HUNT aged 65, one of the earliest settlers of Huntsville and the place took its name from his father.

Died in Whitesburg, Alabama on the 1st, MRS. CYNTHIA A. TORBETT (20 in Alabama), wife of MR. H. A. TORBETT. Presbyterian. (note by P. J. G. She was CYNTHIA ANN GARDNER)

Died on 3rd, MR. NATHAN NABORS (43 in Tennessee) of this place.

April 11, 1855
Married on 28 March by REV. WILLIAM HOWARD, MR. JAMES A. KING of Pickens County to MISS MARY A. BINION of Noxubee County, Mississippi.

Married in Elkton (Giles County), Tennessee on the 4th, MR. ISHAM A. WILSON to MISS MARY J. BAUGH.

Married in LaFayette, Chambers County, on the 3rd, by REV. H. WILLIAMS, COL. CHARLES McLEMORE to MRS. MARY GEORGE.

Died at the residence of WILLIAM ECHOLS on the 8th after a long illness, MRS. MARY JONES, wife of COL. E. J. JONES aged 23 years 2 months and a few days.

Died in Greene County at Morven, the residence of her husband, on 17th, MRS. MARY VIRGINIA LIGHTFOOT (31), wife of DR. PHILIP L. LIGHTFOOT in the 37th year of her age.

Died on 19th in this county, MARY A. ACUFF aged 19. Since September 1851, she has been a member of the Cumberland Presbyterian Church in Ewing Chapel Congregation.

Died at the residence of MR. W. H. POWERS in this place on the 23rd, MISS CORDELIA C. VINCENT (10 in Alabama; CLEMENT R.), born December 24, 1839.

Died near Whitesburg, Alabama on 14th after a short illness, MRS. ELVIRA J. BELL (32 in Virginia), wife of MR. FRANCIS H. BELL (33 in Alabama), Methodist.

Died in Jackson County, Alabama on the 8th, SAMUEL J. JONES, only son of DR. S. J. and MRS. V. A. JONES aged 1 year and 8 months.

April 18, 1855
Married on 27th by JAMES E. VERNER, MR. ISAAC S. HOLT of Stevenson, Alabama to MISS NANCY J. SCRUGGS (14 in Alabama), daughter of CAPT. JAS. SCRUGGS (60 in Tennessee) of Jackson County, Alabama.

Married in Morgan County, Alabama on the 8th by REV. ZACHARIAH PARKER, JAMES H. SHARP, of Decatur to MISS N(ANCY) B. DAVIDSON (13 in Virginia; EDWARD T.) of Morgan County.

Married on the 12th by REV. W. D. F. SAWRIE, MR. JAMES F. PHELPS to MISS ELIZABETH CERTAIN (14 in Alabama), daughter of MR. JACOB CERTAIN (45 in Tennessee), all of this place.

Married on the 12th, by REV. ED M. RICE, MR. TILLMAN L. McGEHEE to MISS SARAH BEVELL (14 in Alabama; LEWIS), all of this county.

Married on 12th by REV. J. M. ROBINSON, MR. C. L. LEWIS to MISS MARTHA A. HILLIARD, all of this county.

Married on 8th by REV. W. M. REED, MR. F. C. DOWNS of Waco, Texas to MISS VIRGINIA A. WILSON, near Leighton, Alabama.

Died in Coffeville, Clarke County, Alabama on the 6th after a short illness, MR CHARLES C. FIGURES (elder brother of the editor of the Advocate) aged about 39...leaves wife and 3 children.

April 25, 1855
Married on 17th in Memphis by REV. DR. PORTER, MR. J. H. McNEIL to MISS APLESS P. SLEDGE, daughter of DR. JOEL M. SLEDGE.

Married in Parrottsville, Cock County, East Tennessee, on the 12th by JUSTICE KANYAN, MISS MARTHA G. WINNIFORD to COL. JAS. M. HUDGINS (26 in Alabama) of Jackson County, Alabama.

Married at Green Bottom, Madison County, Alabama, on the 17th by REV. MR. CLARK, MR. J. PEARCE KELLY to MISS MOLLIE C. (14 in Alabama), daughter of the late JOHN CONNALLY.

Married on the 17th by REV. J. R. HOWELL, MR. THOMAS W. SCOTT to MISS MARY L. CHAMBLESS (12 in Alabama; JOEL H.), all of this county.

Departed this life April 16, 1855 in Triana, Alabama, MRS. JULIA A. (34 in Alabama), wife of JAMES Q. DILLARD and daughter of HENRY and NANCY BROWN. Born in Huntsville, Alabama March 16, 1816....

May 2, 1855
Married in Lincoln County, Tennessee on the 18th, DR. GEORGE M. STRONG to MISS MARGARET B. MOORE, daughter of GEN. WILLIAM MOORE.

May 9, 1855
Died in this place on Sunday morning 29th April, MRS. JOSIE B. PATTERSON (15 in Alabama), wife of CAPT. JOHN T. PATTERSON and daughter of MR. and MRS. DAVID T. KNOX (56 in Delaware) aged 20 years 9 months and 4 days. Member of Cumberland Presbyterian Church.

May 16, 1855

Married in Mobile on Wednesday morning the 25th by REV. MR. MASSEY, MR. THOMAS J. GOLDSBY, Esq. of Dallas County to MISS AGNES WINSTON, daughter of GOVERNOR WINSTON.

Died, JAMES J. McCLELLAND (35 in Pennsylvania) on the 12th of consumption in his 39th year. Born in Pennsylvania 23 September 1816, removed to Huntsville 1839. Left a wife and 2 children.

Died in St. Louis, Missouri of asiatic cholera on 4th, PERCY BRECK (15 in Alabama; SAM'L C.) in his 19th year.

May 23, 1855

Married in this county on 10th, by REV. J(OHN) G. BIDDLE (Cumberland Presbyterian), MR. J. H. YOUNG of Winchester, Tennessee to MISS INDIE (INDIANA in census) T. McBRIDE (16 in Alabama; L. A.) of Madison County, Alabama.

Died on 14th, ELIZABETH SCRUGGS, daughter of MR. J. W. and NARCISSA SCRUGGS of this place.

Died in Athens, on 16th, of pneumonia, MELVINA, wife of EBENEZER JOHNSON aged about 34.

Died on 13th in vicinity of Athens of scarlet fever, BREVIER N. L. (5 in Alabama), eldest daughter of JOHN A. and MARY J. JOHNSON aged 9 years 3 months 18 days.

Died on the 18th in the vicinity of Athens, ALICE L. (2 in Alabama), daughter of A(LEX) L. and MARY McKINNEY aged 7 years 3 months 22 days.

May 30, 1855

Married on 20th by THOMAS BLACK, Esq., MR. MARKHAM G. COFFMAN to MISS MINERVA ARLEDGE (27 in South Carolina; grandparents of HENRY EARL ADAMS, Athens, Alabama 1962; grand-daughter of ELISHA BELL), all of Limestone (daughter of ISAAC? 65 in South Carolina; see volume 98, page 55).

Married on Sunday the 13th just after dinner, after a short courtship of about 6 years (years or hours?) by WILLIAM C. MAPLES, Esq., MR. S. E. KENNEMORE of Pruitt's Ferry to MISS SELINA DERRICK of Woodville all of Jackson County, Alabama.

Died on 14th at the residence of her father in vicinity of Triana, MISS E. BOLEYN COLLIER, born April 8, 1831.

Died on 15th after a short but painful illness, HENRY W. BRAZELTON (21 in Alabama), son of SILAS M. and MARGARET BRAZELTON of this county aged 26 years 5 months 14 days. Left a young wife and infant children.

Died in Eastport, Mississippi on 13th, JAMES LANSDOWN, for many years a citizen of Morgan County. Leaves a wife and several children.

June 6, 1855

Died in Fayetteville, Tennessee on 24, MR. JOHN T. MORGAN aged 70.

Died on 9 May in 27th year, MRS. CHARLOTTE C. (22 in Alabama), wife of MR. FRANCIS BELL (70 in Alabama) of this county...leaves husband and 3 little children.

Died in this place on 2nd, FRANK E., infant son of MAJ. and MRS. JAMES ROBINSON.

June 13, 1855

Married in Macon, Georgia on 31st by REV. MR. REESE, CAPT. H. L. CLAY of Alabama and MISS CELESTE, daughter of MAJ. ANDERSON COMER of the former place.

Married at Bethany, Virginia on 19th by PRES A. CAMPBELL, MR. JOHN H. HUNDLEY, formerly of North Alabama, to MISS A. C. daughter of HON. J. M. MEEK of Bethany.

Also, at same time and place, by PRES A. CAMPBELL, MR. BENJAMIN F. CAWTHON, formerly of Thomaston, Georgia to MISS C. M. COLTART, daughter of DR. A. C. COLTART of Bethany.

Died June 1 at residence of GOV. CHAPMAN, near Huntsville in her 13th year, JULIA FELICIA (8 in Alabama), second daughter of RICHARD O. (30 in Virginia) and FANNY L. PICKETT (27 in Pennsylvania) of Lawrence County.

Died on 21 May last in 39th year, MRS. ELIZABETH C. CRITCHER (34 in North Carolina), wife of JAMES CRITCHER, Esq., former Representative from Marshall County in State Legislature (CRUTCHER in census).

June 20, 1855
      Departed this life on 3rd, MARY ANN STEGER (11 in Alabama) in her
16th year, eldest daughter of K. H. and MARY E. STEGER.
      Married on Wednesday morning the 13th by REV. THOMAS MADDIN,
MR. JOHN H. SWIFT (40 in New York), formerly of Rochester, New York,
to MISS SARAH ELIZABETH VENABLE (14 in Tennessee), daughter of MR.
JAMES M. VENABLE (40 in Virginia), all of this place.
      Married on Sabbath after 10 by REV. DR. FINLEY, MR. JOHN H.
WILLIAMSON (40? faded) of Giles County, Tennessee to MISS MARTHA C. FINN
of Limestone County.
      Married on evening of 12th at the residence of A. M. HOPSON, Esq.
of Memphis, by REV. J. O. STEADMAN, MR. WM. KENAN HILL of Memphis and
MISS EMILY BIBB PLEASANTS (12 in Alabama), daughter of the late J. J.
PLEASANTS of Huntsville, Alabama.

June 27, 1855
      Married on Thursday evening the 21st by REV. F. A. ROSS, WILLIS W.
GARTH, Esq. (23 in Alabama) of Decatur, to MISS MARIA, daughter of
DR. THOMAS FEARN of this place.
      Married in Morgan County, Alabama on 12th by REV. ZACHARIAH PARKER,
MR. JOHN M. SHARP of Decatur, to MISS MILDRED C. DAVIDSON of that
county.
      Departed this life on 7 June at residence of COL. WM. H. MOORE,
in this place, MRS. MARY E. WRIGHT (27 in Virginia), wife of JOHN M.
WRIGHT (37 in North Carolina; married 1844) and daughter of BENJAMIN D.
HARRIS. Born in Nelson County, Virginia educated at Staunton and
afterwards removed to Madison County, Alabama. Baptist.
      Died in this place Friday the 22nd, MARY SUSAN, infant child of
CAPT. JOHN T. and JOSIE B. PATTERSON aged 8 months 20 days.
      Departed this life September 29th sister MARY SUTTON (49 in
Georgia; wife of PHEELAN SUTTON) born May 20, 1802 her age was 52 years
4 months 29 days. Baptist. Leaves husband and children.
      Departed this life in Decatur, Alabama, Sunday evening last,
EMILY, wife of LEVI SUCARS, Esq. lacking but one day of being 23 years
old.

July 11, 1855
      Married by REV. R. A. COBBS at Kenlock, Alabama on 27th, MR. WM. C.
HENDERSON, Esq. of Aberdeen, Mississippi to MISS CALEDONIA, daughter of
HON. DAVID HUBBARD, Esq.
      Married on 5 July by R. D. WILSON, Esq., MR. MORRIS BERNSTEIN to
MISS JENETTA NEWMAN, all of this place.
      Married on 27th by REV. JAMES C. ELLIOTT, MR. JOHN W. HAFLEY to
MISS VIRGINIA L. (16 in Alabama), daughter of F(REDERICK) R. SHELTON
(45 in Virginia) of Mooresville, Alabama.
      Married on 20th by REV. F. P. RIDDLE, DR. JOHN T. DANIEL to MISS
MARY J. E. CORPER, all of Limestone County.
      Married on 27th by REV. W. R. J. HUSBANDS, MR. R. H. BROWN to
MISS MARTHA A. CARTER, all of Limestone County.
      Married in Decatur, Alabama on 5th by REV. J. D. BARBEE, MR.
WM. E. MURPHEY to MISS MARY JANE COLLINS, all of that place.
      Married on 5 July by JAS. H. POOR, Esq., MR. THOMAS MANNS to
MISS MATILDA A. GIBSON, all of this county.
      Died on 1st, after a long illness, JOEL SHOTWELL, son of MR. and
MRS. O. D. SLEDGE of this place aged 23 years....

July 18, 1855
      Nothing of importance.

July 25, 1855
      Died on 8th, WILLIAMETTA, daughter of MR. and MRS. ALCUIN EASON,
born 20 November 1853.
      SAMUEL HECTOR RICHARDSON (13 in Alabama), son of WILLIAM and
ANN M. RICHARDSON of Athens, Alabama died in his 19th year on the 14th.
Born 10 February 1837.

August 1, 1855
      Married in Triana, Alabama on 16th by REV. J. D. BARBEE, MR. THOMAS
A. SHARP of Decatur to MISS MARY C. DILLARD (12 in Alabama; JAS. Q.) of
Triana.

Married in Moulton, Alabama on 22 by C. McDONALD, Esq., MR. CALEB
COLLINS of Decatur to MRS. MARY T. WALKER of Moulton.
Married on 26th by JAMES H. POOR, Esq., MR. JOHN M. HORNBUCKLE
(14 in Alabama; HARRIS F.) to MISS JANE CLARK, all of this county.
Died at the residence of his father, REV. F. P. SCRUGGS in Decatur,
Alabama on 15 PHINEAS T. SCRUGGS in his 24th year.

August 8, 1855
Married on 14th by REV. JAMES C. ELLIOTT, MR. RICHARD W. SURGINNER
and FANNY A. LEWIS.
Married on Thursday morning the 24th by REV. A. J. STEEL, WM. E.
TAYLOR, Esq. to MISS MALINDA J., daughter of HON. HOPKINS L. TURNEY.
Married in Florence on 26th by REV. MR. MITCHELL, MISS CORNELIA
MARGARET, daughter of the late HON. E. H. FOSTER and MR. JAMES SIMPSON.
Married on Monday morning the 6th by REV. HENRY C. LAY, MR. HYMAN
HILZUZIN (HILZHEIM is right) of Jackson, Mississippi to MISS JANE GREY
(17 in Alabama), daughter of COL. D. M. BRADFORD of Huntsville, Alabama.
Married in Philadelphia on Tuesday morning 31 July, MR. WILLIAM
VEITCH (formerly of this place) to MISS SARAH S. HAMERSLY, all of
Philadelphia.
Died at the residence of her father, JOHN McCROSKEY, 4 miles from
Somerville, Alabama on 25th, MISS NANCY McCROSKEY aged 18 years 2 months.
Died on 28th, MR. JOHN C. BLEVINS of Dallas County.

August 15, 1855
Died at the residence of JOHN H. HUNDLEY in Limestone County,
Alabama on the morning of 24 July, EDWIN CLAUDE HUNDLEY, infant son of
D. R. and M. A. HUNDLEY aged 11 months 5 days.
Died on 3rd in Athens, WM. B. ALLEN (22 in Alabama; JAS. W.),
born 20 February 1829 in this county, represented Limestone County in the
last Legislature. Was a man of talents.
Died on 4th in this county at the residence of ISHAM J. FENNELL,
Esq., COL. JOHN TROUP (41 in South Carolina) of Morgan County aged
about 47.
Married on Sunday evening July 29 by REV. MR. HUSBANDS, MR. ROBERT S.
ATKINSON (18 in Alabama) to MISS MARY R. ROWE (15 in Alabama; JANE M.),
all of this county.
On 2nd by REV. J. G. WILSON, MR. RICHARD M(ATTHEW) FLETCHER (19 in
Virginia; JAS. N.) to MISS REBECCA MASON, all of Limestone County.
Married at White's Springs, Giles County, Tennessee on 30th July
last, by REV. ISAAC MILNER, MR. THOS. O. BURTON to MISS MINNIE A.
BRANDON (10 in Alabama; ROBT. S.), all of this county.

August 22, 1855
Died in Morgan County, Alabama July 7, MARY FRANCES, infant daughter
of JOSHUA and ANN E. BELL aged 6 months 29 days.
Died in Nashville, Tennessee on 10th at residence of her mother,
MRS. SUSAN BARR, ANNA, wife of MR. J. BOLIN of Huntsville, Alabama.
Died at Wayland Springs, Lawrence County, Tennessee on 25 July of
dropsy, MR. WILLIAM MORRIS of Madison County, Alabama.
Died on 18th after a short illness, CHARLIE C. aged about 4 years,
son of MR. and MRS. JOHN B. TROTMAN of this place.
Departed this life on 4th, JAMES LEE, infant son of DR. HENRY and
SARAH E. BINFORD.
Married in Lincoln County, Tennessee on 31st by JOHN T. GORDON,
Esq., MR. WM. DOSSEY (16 in Alabama; JAS. H.) and MISS PIETY WEAVER
(11 in Georgia; JETHRO), all of Morgan County, Alabama.
Married on 15th by REV. SAML DENNIS, MR. SAMUEL M. VEST to MISS
SARAH A. WATKINS, all of this county.
Married on 15th at residence of CAPT. RICHARD HARRIS by REV. W. H.
ADAMS, W. F. HURT and MISS ELIZA J. HARRIS, all of Jackson County.
Married on 9th August, 1855 by JAMES H. POOR, Esq., MR. WILLIAM
GIBSON to MISS ANNA M. MANN, all of this county.

August 29, 1855
Married on 26th by JOHN W. IRBY, Esq., MR. ANDREW J. HAWKINS to
MISS ADALINE, daughter of MR. JOSEPH SHARP, all of this county.
Died on 17 May last at Octagon Villa, city of St. Johns Antigua,
ANDREW COLTART, Esq., brother of S(AM'L) COLTART, of this place, merchant

there, third son of the late JOHN COLTART, manufacturer, Gate-house-of-Fleet, Scotland. He emigrated to Antigua in 1818....
Died in Tuscumbia on 10th in her 41st year, MRS. NANCY C. PATTERSON (33), wife of COL. JAMES A. PATTERSON and daughter of DABNEY MARTIN (73 in Virginia) of Morgan County, Alabama.

September 5, 1855
Died on 24 of typhoid fever at residence near courtland, Alabama, MR. DANIEL GILCHRIST in his 66th year.
Died in Athens on 27th, MRS. MARTHA A., wife of S. O. NELSON of New Orleans aged 39.
Died in Marshall County, Tennessee, JOHN N. SMITH aged 76 years, long a resident of Limestone County.
Died in Jackson County on 24th, WM. HOUSTON aged 55.
Died on 29th, CAPT. DAVID BRADFORD (61 in North Carolina) of this vicinity in 68th year, one of early settlers of Huntsville. He formerly represented Madison County in Legislature.
Died on 28th after a long illness, MRS. NATHAN NABORS (35 in North Carolina; 43 in Tennessee (MARY)) of this place.
Married in Fayetteville, Tennessee on 2nd by MR. NEELEY, MR. FRANK BELL to MISS MARY (11 in Alabama), daughter of MR. HENRY P. GRIZZARD (45 in North Carolina), all of this county.
Married in Decatur, Alabama on 20th August by J. M. MEANS, Esq., MR. WILLIS M. LIPSCOMB (20 in North Carolina; THOS.) to MISS REBECCA E. STRADFORD (10 in Alabama; NANCY), all of that place.
Married on 28th MR. JOHN E. HAMEL to MISS MARTHA J. PICKARD, all of this place.
Married on Moulton on 15th by REV. B. P. WHITE, MR. JEROME GIBSON (WPA; JEREMY in marriage record), editor of Moulton Standard to MISS ELIZABETH C. McGHEE of that place.
At Allisonia, Franklin County on 23rd by REV. DR. EDGAR, RANDALL W. McGAVOCK, Esq., member of Nashville Bar to MISS SERAPHINA, youngest daughter of late MR. WM. DEERY, long resident of Sullivan County, Tennessee.

September 12, 1855
Nothing

September 19, 1855
Died in Franklin County on 11th, JAMES NANCE, Esq., in 70th year.
Died in Lawrence County on 10th, JAMES ARMSTRONG, Esq. He was Democratic Elector in last Presidential canvass.
Married on 13th by HON. JNO. G. DIXON, MR. L. C. COULSON to MISS CAROLINE BRYANT, all of Jackson County.

September 26, 1855
Died in Limestone County September 3, MRS. ELIZABETH BARRETT, wife of JAMES BARRETT.
In Mooresville on 4th, MRS. HENRIETTA (19 in Virginia), wife of JOHN N. MARTIN (M.; 26 in Alabama) aged 25.
Marriages (didn't finish)

SOUTHERN ADVOCATE

Huntsville, Alabama

Continued from our Volume 116 (Volume 148)

September 26, 1855
Married in Cleveland, Ohio on 17th at Grace Church, by DR. PERRY, DR. S. D. GILSON of Huntsville, Alabama to MISS LOUISA A. WHITE of the former place.
Married on the 12th instant by REV. ALEXANDER PENLAND, MR. ELISHA JOINER to MISS MARTHA WATKINS, all of this county.
Married on 11th in Talladega by REV. THOS. A. COOK, MAJ. N. W. SHELLEY, editor of Selma Reporter to MRS. E. R. CAMPBELL.

October 3, 1855

Married on 18th, LEWIS L(EANDER) POATS (descendants spelled it
POATES but he didn't), editor of Rogersville (Tennessee) Times to
MISS ANNIE (should be ANNIS) A. McCARTY of that place (PRENTISS PRICE
says she was ANNIS, daughter of JAS. P. McCARTY and grand-daughter of
WM. and RACHEL (KYLE) McCARTY).

Married in this county on 20th September by REV. S. ROSBORO, MR.
JOSEPH C. BUCHANAN to MISS MARY J. HAMBRICK.

Married on 22nd by REV. W. D. CHADICK, DR. DeKALB LIPSCOMB to
MISS MARY, daughter of COL. ELIAS WILBOURN, all of Madison County,
Alabama.

Died on the 4th in Parkersburg, West Virginia, MATILDA A. NASH,
daughter of MR. EDMUND L. SCRUGGS, late of Madison County, Alabama.

Died at his residence in Madison County, Alabama on the morning of
the 11th instant after a short illness, in his 77th year of his age,
JAMES IRWIN, Esq. He had been a citizen of Madison County for more than
40 years; he lived respected and died lamented by all who knew him.
(Note: 1850 Census Madison County, Alabama shows him aged 72, born
in Pennsylvania).

October 10, 1855

Married in Madison County on 20th by REV. W. D. F. SAWRIE, MR.
P. L. HARRISON of Cherokee to MISS ELIZABETH C. DANIEL of Madison.
Note: This is PERRY LEWIS HARRISON; ELIZ. was daughter of KIBBLE T.
DANIEL.

Married at Longwood on 26th September by REV. MR. OSBORNE,
ALBERT G. McGEHEE, Esq. of Alabama and MRS. AGNES CATHERINE VENABLE
of Prince Edward County, Virginia.

Married on September 20th, by JOHN R. HENDRICK, the REV. JOHN T.
EDGAR, D.D. of Nashville to MRS. ANN CRITTENDEN, daughter of JOHN MORRIS,
Esq. of Davidson County.

Married on 27th at Beechwood at residence of COL. ANDREW ERWIN,
by REV. DR. LAPSLEY, JAMES WOODS, Esq. of Nashville to MRS. ISAAC ERWIN
of Alabama.

Married on 3rd at residence of DR. NAPIER, Lawrence County, Alabama,
by REV. W. M. REED, JOHN G. STEPHENSON, Esq. of Jefferson, Texas and
MISS MARY A. NAPIER.

Married on 25th at residence of MRS. COX, Brown's Ferry, Limestone
County, by REV. E. M. SWOPE, MR. JOHN PURYEAR of Courtland to MISS
VIRGINIA B. HAWKINS of Mississippi (volume 223, page 54).

Married at the residence of THOS. B. COLLIER in Limestone County
on 24th by REV. J. P. MOSELY, DR. D(EWIT) C. KIMBLE of Decatur to
MISS MARY ANN, daughter of DR. DENT of Mississippi (volume 223, page 54).

Married on 2nd by REV. MR. ----, MR. N. K. MAGUIRE of Maury County,
Tennessee to MISS MARY COLLIER of Florence, Alabama.

October 17, 1855

Died on 7th of consumption, MRS. ADALINE WILLIAMSON of this vicinity.

Died on 8th of consumption, MR. HENRY POLLARD of this vicinity
aged about 30 years.

October 24, 1855

Married on 18th by REV. MR. BARTEE, REV. MR. GEO. D. GUYNN to
MISS ELIZA J., daughter of DR. SULLIVAN, all of this county. Note:
her name was ELIZA MILLICENT SULLIVAN.

Died in this place on 15th, C. C. HAMBLEN, infant son of WILLIAM M.
and MARY C. HAMBLEN.

October 31, 1855

Married at Christ's Church, Holly Springs, Mississippi on 4th by
REV. J. W. ROGERS, GEN. H. E. WILLIAMSON and MISS DARTHULA O. BRADFORD,
daughter of GEN. A. B. BRADFORD, all of that place.

Married on 18th by REV. WM. GREEN, MR. BENJAMIN F. DICKSON to
MISS MARY A. GREENE, all of this county.

Married on 25th at residence of CAPT. DUDLEY SALE, by REV. P. B.
ROBINSON, JOHN S. NANCE to MISS MOLLIE SALE, all of this county.

Married in Decatur, Alabama on 23rd by REV. F. P. SCRUGGS, J. M.
MEANS, Esq. to MISS SARAH, eldest daughter of CEPHAS HALL, all of that
place.

Died on 25th of croup, WILLIE, in his 4th year, son of WM. ROLLSTON, editor of Tuscumbia North Alabamian.

CAPT. GEORGE STEELE was born in Virginia, Beford County, on 1st day of April 1798, removed to Huntsville in 1818 where he resided up to his death on 21 instant in his 58th year...kind hsuband and father.... (long obituary)

November 7, 1855

Married on 16th by REV. M. H. BONE, MR. SAMUEL W. SANDFORD to MISS ELIZA J. MORROW, all of this county.

Married in Eastport, Mississippi on 17th by SAMUEL LEWOODY, Esq., MR. BENJ. GLEADALL of Tuscumbia to MRS. CORNELIA HICKMAN of Eastport. (1850 Census shows him aged 50, born in England)

Died at her residence in this county on Tuesday the 9th, ELIZABETH ASHWORTH, consort of JOSEPH ASHWORTH, aged 37 years 5 months. (1850 census shows her aged 32, born in Virginia; him 29, born in Tennessee)

November 14, 1855

Married on 16th at residence of PAUL J. WATKINS, Esq., JAMES H. BRANCH, Esq. of Arkansas to MISS MARY E. WATKINS, daughter of PAUL J. WATKINS of Lawrence County, Alabama.

November 21, 1855

Married on 1st by REV. T. A. MORRIS, MR. R(OBERT) S. McREYNOLDS of New Orleans to MISS MARY HOGAN, daughter of COL. JOHN HOGAN of Bellmont near Tuscumbia, Alabama. (in 1850 census shows JOHN HOGAN aged 65, born in North Carolina; her 14 in Alabama)

Married on Saturday morning, St. John's Church, by REV. MR. GEORGE CLARK, MR. THOMAS B. CLARK of Knoxville, Tennessee to MISS ELIZA JESSIE CRISP, elder daughter of MR. WM. H. CRISP of Savannah (Hardin County).

Married on 8th by REV. G. W. CARMICHAEL, MR. ZACHARIAH R. PETTY to MISS REBECCA A., daughter of COL. W. F. WHITMAN, all of this county.

Married in Selma on 6th, by REV. MR. PLATT, MR. A. E. BAYAL of Greene County to MISS KATE BLEVINS of Selma, daughter of the late JOHN BLEVINS.

Married on 11th at residence of THOMAS SNODGRASS, Esq. by HON. J. G. DIXON, MR. WM. L. SHELTON to MISS ELIZABETH J. SNODGRASS, all of Jackson County.

Married on 12th by REV. W. C. JOHNSON, REV. J. B. McFERRIN, D.D., editor of Nashville Christian Advocate to MISS CYNTHIA TENNESSEE, daughter of JOHN McGAVOCK, Esq. of Edgefield, Tennessee.

Died in Cass County, Texas on 14 October 1855, MRS. LUCY C. THOMAS, wife of the late JAMES THOMAS of Madison County, Alabama aged 45 years. Woman of strong sense, kind feelings and lived in and for her family. She has many friends and relations in this county....

Died at his residence in Greene County on 6 November of hemmorhage of the bowels, MR. CALVIN B. SNEED aged 34 years.

Died at residence of COL. H. H. HIGGINS in Athens on 12th, JOHN B. ELLIOTT, about 90 years of age. (1850 census shows one JOHN ELLIOTT aged 72 born in Ireland.)

November 28, 1855

Married on 13th by REV. P. B. ROBINSON, MR. JOHN H. MILLER to MISS MILDRED JOHNSTON, all of this county.

Married on 23 October MR. ALEXANDER JORDEN of Marshall County to MISS MARY L. THWEATT of St. Clair County.

Married on 15th by REV. WM. GREEN, MR. WM. COBB to MISS TABITHA RUBY, all of this county.

Married on 21st by REV. W. D. F. SAWRIE, MR. A. D. LIGHTON to MISS ELIZA ALLEN, all of this place.

Married on 13th by REV. F. P. SCRUGGS at residence of REV. J. P. MOSELEY, MR. WILLIAM MOSELEY to MISS MARTHA PRIOR KIMBLE, all of Morgan County.

Married on 20th by ELDER J. GUNN, MR. W. H. DAVIS of Decatur to MISS MARTHA JANE MATKIN, all of Madison County.

Married on 30th in Hopkinsville (Christian County), Kentucky by REV. DR. RIDLEY, DR. ALBERT G. LONG of Tuscumbia, Alabama to MISS JOSEPHA STURDIVANT of Montgomery County, Tennessee.

Died on 2nd, THOMAS REUBEN, son of JOHN M. and MARGARET SCOTT aged 2 years 3 months 2 days.

River land for sale--Probate Court Jackson County. 20 October last. Administrator of JOHN PARKS, deceased. Late residence of deceased. 250 or 300 acres about 7 miles south of Bellefonte.

December 5, 1855

Married on 22nd near Elkton, Giles County, Tennessee by REV. JAMES C. KIRKLAND, MR. LOUIS L. FREEMAN to MISS MARGARET V. GARRISON, all of Giles County, Tennessee.

Married on 15th by REV. MR. FANNING, MR. SAMPSON BOBO and MISS JOSEPHINE E. C., daughter of E. M. EGGLESTON, Esq., all of Franklin County.

Married on 8th in Sumpter County, Alabama by REV. MR. SCHAFFER, MR. ABRAM RICKS, of Tuscumbia to MISS SALLIE POPE.

Died in Franklin County on 25th, WILLIAM PRIDE, an old citizen (note: 1850 census shows him aged 49, born in North Carolina).

Died in Courtland on 27th, JOHN T. LECKEY aged 36 years.

December 12, 1855

Married on 28th by REV. J. C. WILSON, MR. ALEX'R. S. EMBREY of Winchester, Tennessee to MISS LOUISA P. CAIN of Limestone County, Alabama (volume 223, page 56--descendant says married at residence of A. C. CAIN).

Married on 29th by same, MR. WM. W. WATKINS, to MISS MARTHA M. ROWE, all of Madison County, Alabama.

Married on 5th by REV. C. FOSTER WILLIAMS, MR. MATTHEW H. THOMPSON and MISS ELLEN C., daughter of W. G. THOMPSON, Esq., all of Tuscumbia.

Married on 29th by REV. JUSTINIAN WILLIAMS, DR. A. T. GOODLOE of Arkansas to MISS SARAH L. COCKRILL of Allsboro (Colbert County, Alabama.

Married on 2nd by REV. THOMAS A. WARE, COL. SAMUEL I. BUNCH (the popular Conductor of Memphis and Charleston Railroad) to MISS SALLIE COE, daughter of the late LEVIN H. COE, Esq. of Memphis, Tennessee.

Married on 5th by REV. F. M. HICKMAN, MR. JOHN WILLIAMS of Chattanooga, Tennessee to MISS SUSAN E. J., only daughter of JARED I. SAMPLE of Jackson County.

Died in Russellville on 3rd, MRS. PORTIA HILLMAN, wife of JOSEPH HILLMAN and daughter of COL. N. R. LADD. Her life had been one of continual sickness...devoted wife and daughter and sister. (1850 census shows PORTIA aged 22 born in Alabama; her husband aged 30 born in Germany)

December 19, 1855

Married on 28th November at residence of D. G. CURRY, Esq. by REV. W. J. ELLIS, COL. WILLIAM WALTER HORTON and FANNIE, second daughter of J. C. VANDYKE, Esq., all of Marengo County.

January 2, 1856

Died near Aberdeen, Mississippi, December ---, THOMAS BIBB BRADLEY in 27th year...(long obituary).

Died in Petersburg (Lincoln County), Tennessee of inflammation of stomach, Saturday 15th, MRS. JOSEPHINE, wife of MR. S. A. SLAUGHTER aged 23.

January 9, 1856

Married in the vicinity of this place on 3rd by REV. P. B. ROBINSON, MR. JOHN T. YEATMAN and MISS ANNA JANE, only daughter of the late CAPT. DAVID BRADFORD, all of this place. (1850 census shows YEATMAN aged 22, born in Alabama; ANNA BRADFORD 17 in Alabama; her father, 61 in North Carolina)

Married on 19th by REV. H. M. BONE, MR. WM. C. HALL to MISS MARTHA E., daughter of MATTHEW JORDAN, Esq., all of Maysville, Alabama.

In Camden, Wilcox County on Thursday morning, the 13th, HON. ALEXANDER WHITE of Talladega to MISS NARCISSA RODGERS of the former place. (1850 census shows him aged 34 in Alabama; her 16 in North Carolina)

Married in Greenville on 13th by REV. G. F. PAGE, HON. DAVID T. PATTERSON, Judge of First Judicial Circuit to MISS MARTHA, daughter of GOVERNOR ANDREW JOHNSON of Tennessee.

On 3rd, by JOHN T. HADEN, Esq., MR. WM. H. BRAZELTON to MISS SARAH ANN GRAYSON, all of this county.

January 10, 1856
    Married on 20th by REV. JOHN A. ELLIS, MR. JOHN A. SHELTON of
Bellefonte, Alabama to MISS JULIA G. FINLEY of Cumberland Iron Works,
Tennessee.
    Died on 23rd in Belleftone at residence of his uncle, R. H.
McCRAVEY, BENJ. A. GREEN of consumption aged 22 years.

January 23, 1856
    Married on 19th by REV. M(OSES) M. HENKLE, GEN. WM. B. BATE of
Nashville, Tennessee to MISS JULIA, daughter of SAMUEL PEETE (1812 sol
(gr)), Esq. of this place (1850 census shows her 16 in Alabama).
    Married on 6th by E. M. RICE, Esq., MR. GOODWIN FISK to MISS
MARY E. SEVEL, all of this county.
    Married on 16th, MR. HENRY FRANKLIN to MISS JANE E. MORRIS, both of
this county.
    Died in Belleftone on 6th of consumption, JOHN A. MORRISON, aged
20 years. Worthy young man--has left a father and mother, three sisters
and a large circle of friends (1850 census shows him aged 16 born in
Alabama).
    Died in Limestone County, Alabama on 7th, DR. ALFRED MOORE aged
65 years. Highly respectable and honorable physician and gentleman.
(1850 census shows him aged 58 in North Carolina).
    Died on 13th at his residence in this county, WILLIAM F. PAYNE of
pneumonia aged 61 years 7 days (1850 Census shows him aged 55 born in
Kentucky).

January 30, 1856
    Died--MRS. NAOMI LESSLIE, relict of the late CAPT. WILLIAM LESSLIE
of Madison County, Alabama, departed this life on 7th of pneumonia.
MRS. LESSLIE was about 75 years of age, was born in Brunswick County,
Virginia and her maiden name was HARRISON. (1850 Census shows her
68 in Virginia) (Brunswick County, Virginia marriages--5 February 1801--
WM. LASHLEY--NAOMY HARRISON--SUR. ROBERT HARRISON---1 February by
REV JAMES MEACHAM--page 126)
    MRS. MARY ANN DORTCH, relict of ROBERT DORTCH departed this life
on 14th aged about 49. (1850 census shows her 35 born in South Carolina.
She was daughter of the above WM. and NAOMI LESSLIE.)

February 6, 1856
    Married on 20th by REV. W. H. ADAMS (Methodist minister 1832-1918),
MR. THOMAS B. PARKS (18 in Alabama; JOHN and 2nd wife RUTH BROWN, page
115) to MISS MARTHA A. HUDGINS (16 in Alabama; BENJ.), all of Jackson
County.
    Married on 22nd by REV. THOMAS MADDIN, MR. JAMES M. JONES and
MISS MARTHA E. SCRUGGS, all of this county.
    Married on 28th by REV. D. K. HUNTER, MR. BURGESS MILLER, Esq. to
MISS BETTIE MARCRUM, all of this county.
    Died in the neighborhood of Guntersville on 16 December 1855,
MRS. MISSOURI CONNER BROOKS, wife of MR. WILLIAM BROOKS and on 23
December 1855, MRS. SARAH E. JORDAN, wife of MR. DAVID JORDAN, all of
Marshall County; who, with husbands and father, in space of little over
a week was called upon to lament the death of a second daughter and
grandchild, the son of MRS. BROOKS, aged about 10 months, who followed
his mother within three days. The three were victims of scarlet fever.
(1850 census shows DAVID JORDAN 22 in Alabama; SARAH E. 16 in South
Carolina)
    Died at the residence of EDWARD D. MOORE of Marshall County on
27th, IDA MONTGOMERY, infant daughter of MR. FRANK and MRS. SALLIE R.
GILBREATH, aged about 7 months.
    Died at the residence of her mother in Lawrence County, Alabama
on 15 January 1856, of typhoid pneumonia, MISS ANNIE E. WALLIS aged
16-1-10.

February 13, 1856
    Married on 4th by REV. MR. HUSBANDS, MR. JOHN W. WEST to MISS
ELIZABETH OWENS, all of this county.
    Married on 5th by REV. MR. COWEN, DR. C(AD) A. CRUNK of Tennessee
to MISS ELIZABETH G(AY) FRIEND of this county. (note: she was born
1833, daughter of DANIEL B. FRIEND and wife MARTA BUCHANAN BENTLEY.)

Married on 31st by DAWSON PHELPS, Esq., MR. W(ILLIAM) W. COLLIER
to MISS MARTHA A. WALLS, all of Limestone County (volume 223, page 58;
daughter of ALBERT WALLS).

Married on 31st by REV. G. W. MITCHELL, MR. JAMES G. BARKSDALE
(volume 223, page 58) to MISS SUSAN V. NEWBY, all of Limestone County.
(1850 census shows him aged 21, born in Tennessee, son of DANIEL; her
16 in Virginia, daughter of MARTHA; married at daughter of MRS. ANN
NEWBY)

State of Alabama--Chancery District--29th Chancery District at
Huntsville:

ELIZABETH LANGLEY   )   SAMUEL H. LANGLEY, POLLARD LANGLEY
        versus   )   and THOMAS LANGLEY, defendants
SAMUEL H. LANGLEY et al.)   the last two are infants aged about
                             14 years, and residents of Pitt County,
                             North Carolina.

February 20, 1856

Married by REV. F. JOHNSON, A.M. on 5th, MR. A. L. DAVIS of North
Carolina to MISS ANN L. FENNEL, daughter of the late COL. JAMES FENNEL
of Morgan County, Alabama. (1850 census shows her aged 10 born in
Alabama)

Married on 11th by ELDER T. G. SELLARS (volume 223, page 59),
MR. H. B. VAUGHN of Gallatin (Sumner County), Tennessee to MRS. MARY A.
IRVIN of Athens, Alabama.

Married on 10th by JAMES A. JOHNSON, Esq., MR. GEO. E. BARKSDALE to
MISS MARY W. FRENCH, all of Limestone County. (1850 census shows him
aged 22, born in Tennessee; volume 223, page 59)

On 12th instant, GREEN B. STROTHER, Esq. to MRS. DOLLIE T. CLOYD,
all of this county (1850 census shows one GREEN B. STROTHER aged 46 in
North Carolina).

Died at residence of WILLIAM R. DAVIS (41 in Kentucky; son-in-law;
married in Morgan County 1833 NANCY M. PHILPOTT) of Freestone County,
Texas 5th January, MRS. HARRIET PHILPOTT of aforesaid county late of
Morgan County, Alabama, after an illness of three weeks in her 64th
year. (1850 census shows her aged 58, born in Virginia; HORATIO PHILPOTT
married 1) ANNE ALLEN, 2) about 1810 HARRIET PAXTON in Botetourt County,
Virginia, nee Lone State State, cousin of SAM HOUSTON)

Died in Marshall County on 4 January 1856, EPHRAIM REAGAN aged
64 years (ancestor of MRS. JAS. L. NANCE, 1976). MR. REAGAN was born in
East Tennessee in July, 1762 and emigrated to Alabama in 1829. (Note:
I am sure 1762 is an error for 1792, as he was aged 58 in 1850 and born
in Tennessee, and in 40's in 1840--MRS. NANCE says he was 1812 soldier)

February 27, 1856

Married on Tuesday evening the 19th in this vicinity by REV.
F. A. ROSS, EDWARD D. TRACY, Esq. of Macon, Georgia to MISS ELLEN E.,
daughter of the late CAPT. GEORGE STEELE of Huntsville, Alabama. (1850
census shows her 16 in Alabama)

Married at the residence of MRS. PEARSALL near South Florence on
21st by REV. WM. H. MITCHELL, GEN. JOHN D. RATHER of Morgan County to
MISS SARAH LETITIA PEARSALL of Franklin County.

On 13th by JOHN A. JORDAN, Esq., JOSEPH M. GILL to MISS MARY M.
ANDERSON, all of Limestone (volume 148, page 60; "Dres of MRS. BLUE";
volume 223, page 60).

On 14th, by REV. JESSE SEALS, JAMES E. DAVID to MISS J(OICE) E. (A?)
HENDERSON, all of Limestone County. (volume 223, page 59)

Married on 24th by JOHN W. IRBY, Esq., WILLIAM K. SPELTS to MISS
SARAH A. FOWLER, all of this county.

Married on 17th by REV. JESSE SEALS, ANDREW J. STINSON to MISS
SARAH A. C. HENDERSON, all of Limestone (volume 223, page 59).

Died near Huntsville, Alabama on 3 February 1856, MR. ELIAS A.
HODGES in 28th year. The gentlemanly conduct of the deceased...left a
lovely little daughter (who but a few years ago was deprived of a
mother's love) an aged father and mother, brothers and sisters....

Died on 18th in Franklin County, JOHN MARTIN aged 38, a native of
Ireland and late a merchant in Tuscumbia. (1850 census shows him 28
in Ireland)

Died in Fulton (Itawamba County), Mississippi on 9th, JOHN McMECHAN
(see volume 197, page 25--wife was SARAH JANE, daughter of ROBT. COMAN
of Madison County), formerly of Franklin County.

Died in Athens on 17th, MRS. SALLIE BETTIE, wife of DR. L. H.
BINFORD of Limestone County. (1850 census shows her 19 in Alabama;
LITTLEBERRY H. BINFORD 23 in Alabama)

March 5, 1856

Married on 21st by REV. H. P. TURNER, MR. GEORGE W. HUMPHREY and
MISS ELLIE ROGERS, all of this county.

Married on 19th February 1856 by REV. WILLIAM J. HOLT, MR. THOMAS J.
VANN to MISS SARAH M. SANDERS, all of this county.

Married at Powellton (Corsa County), Alabama on 21st by REV. MR.
PHELAN (married LAURA POWELL, sister of COL. JAS. R. POWELL), JAMES H.
WEAVER, Esq., Secretary of State of Alabama to MISS MAGGIE E. POWELL.
(1850 Coosa County: POWELL, CATHERINE R. 57 in Virginia; JAMES R(OBT.),
35 in Virginia; MARGARET E., 24 in Virginia; ALLISON, 17 in Virginia;
Coron County marriages--JAMES H. WEAVER--MARGARET E. WEAVER 20 February
1856)

Married on 21st by ELDER J. SEALS, MR. JOHN P. FARRAR to MISS
ABIGAIL T. CRENSHAW, all of Limestone County (1850 census shows him
aged 18 in Alabama; her 14 in Alabama).

Married on 19th by REV. D. L(?) or D(?) MITCHELL, MR. STRODDER A.
McWILLIAMS to MISS NARCISSA M., daughter of JAS. HARGROVE, all of
Limestone County. (note: looks like "STRANDER A" in census, aged 14
born in Alabama; Prob. Min. 1865, page 16; MRS. NARCISSA McWILLIAMS
filed petition--estate of STRANDER McWILLIAMS, deceased; it's STROTHER
in marriage record)

Married on 24th by JOHN TURRENTINE, Esq., MR. JESSE RAMBO to
MISS EALANDER H. (A?) BRADSHAW, all of Limestone County (married
2 February; volume 223, page 60).

Died in Bellefonte on 24th, MR. JOHN W. CROMER of pneumonia.

March 12, 1856

Died at his own residence in Madison County, Alabama on night of
19th February 1856, JOHN L. KING, son of JOHN KING, on 20th before his
burial, his funeral was preached by REV. M. H. BONE. JOHN L. KING was
born December 28, 1825, married February 1851 and departed this life at
above named time aged 31 years 1 months and some days. Professed religion in 1846 and joined the Cumberland Presbyterian Church. (1850
census shows him aged 24, born in Alabama; his father 72 in North Carolina)

March 19, 1856

Married on 9th by E. S. MASTERSON, Esq., MR. A(LEX M.) N. SMITH
to MRS. LEONORA NeSMITH, all of Lawrence County (WPA Copy Lawrence
County, Alabama, ALEXANDER M. SMITH to LOUISA NESMITH March 9, 1856).

Married on 5th by REV. FRANK KIMBLE, MR. R(ICHARD) B. NEVILL of
Morgan County to MISS AMERICA W. BRUNDIDGE of Limestone County (volume
223, page 60). (1850 census shows her aged 13, born in Alabama;
daughter of JAMES M. BRUNDIDGE)

Married on 28th by REV. DR. EDGAR, DR. JOSEPH A. DUNCAN of Branwell
(Barnwell? C. H., South Carolina and MISS MADILINE ALLISON, daughter of
S. D. MORGAN of Nashville.

Married on 5th by GEO. RUSSELL, Esq., MR. ANDREW WOODEY to MISS
MARTHA WATTERSON, all of this county.

MR. MARTIN G. MILLIGAN married MRS. HYPASIA H. COLLIER. (1850
census shows her 36 in Alabama, widow of GREEN A. COLLIER.)

Married, MR. GILES SANDIDGE to MISS SARAH WILLIAMS.

Died in this place on 15th after a short illness, LUTHER, youngest
child of MR. WM. D. HOLLOWELL, aged about 4 years.

Died in Elkton, Tennessee on the 6th, MAJ. ROBERT B. HARNEY.

Married in Columbus (Muscogee County), Georgia on 8th, OLIVER TOWLES,
formerly of this place.

Died after a short illness on 9th at advanced age of 77 years,
PETER LOONEY for many years a citizen of Lawrence County. (1850 census
shows him aged 69 in South Carolina)

March 26, 1856

Married on 25th February by REV. J. R. MORRIS, MR. MILAS RUSSELL
to MISS LUCINDA H. SHOOK, all of Jackson County.

Married on the 16th by HON. M. GILBREATH, MR. JAMES CRUTCHER to
MISS E. R. PHILLIPS, all of Marshall County.

Died on 28th of pulmonary consumption, at Oleander, Marshall
County, Alabama, ELIZA HENDERSON, fourth daughter of LUCINDA and
GEORGE W. HALE, Esq. in the 25th year of her age. (1850 census shows
her aged 17 born in Alabama; her father 55 in Tennessee; mother 34 in
Tennessee)

April 2, 1856
Died near Huntsville, Alabama, MRS. ELIZA WADE, consort of DAVY
WADE in her 58th year...(long obituary).

April 9, 1856
Married on 16th at 9 o'clock a.m. by HENRY W. PICKENS, Esq.,
MR. LAFAYETTE BURGER to MISS RENA GARNER, all of Cherokee County,
Alabama (1850 census shows him aged 18 in Alabama, son of JACOB).
Died near Woodville, Jackson County, Alabama on the 20th, JOHN P.
HAWKINS, an old and respectable citizen. MR. HAWKINS served his country
during several campaigns, and always acquitted himself honorably and
left testimonials to prove this fact. (1850 census shows him aged 60,
born in Virginia)
On 2nd, of pneumonia, MRS. CAROLINE CHILDRESS aged 34 years.
Left five little children and a bereaved husband. Belonged to Methodist
E. P. Church. (1850 census shows one RHODA CAROLINE, wife of JOHN F.
CHILDRESS as aged 25)
Died on 26th, JOHN EDWARD, infant son of THOMAS J. and LOCKEY T.
TAYLOR aged 7 months and 24 days.

April 16, 1856
Married in Lynchburg, Virginia on 19th March by BISHOP EARLY,
HON. THOMAS RIVERS, Member of Congress from Memphis, Tennessee District
and MISS LUCETTA, daughter of COL. THOMAS DILARD?
Married on 10th by REV. MR. SALE, MR. THOMAS LIGHTFOOT to MISS
MARTHA ANN TWEEDY, all of Lawrence County.
Died in Larkinsville, Jackson County, March 2nd, 1856, of croup,
JOHNNIE BAINS MORRIS, son of REV. J. R. and MARTHA J. MORRIS aged 2-7-3....
Died in Lafayette County, Mississippi on 21st, MR. JOEL TATUM aged
about 75 years, formerly of Morgan County, Alabama.
Died in this place on 7th, of consumption, MRS. ANN ELIZABETH,
consort of MAJ. JOHN L. BUNCH in her 28th year.

April 23, 1856
Married on 18th at 8 a.m. at Jackson Inn, Bellefonte, by HON. J. G.
DIXON, MR. A. M. SAXON to MISS ELLA ACKLIN, both of Jackson County.
Married on 14th at 5 o'clock p.m. at Court House by ROBT. D. WILSON,
Esq., MR. S. D. BLANKENSHIP to MISS E. A. MAPLES, all of this county.
Married on 6th by J. M. MEANS, Esq., WILLIAM AUSTIN to MISS FRANCES
HUTSON, all of Morgan County. (1850 census shows one FRANCES HUTSON
aged 16 in Alabama; daughter of ROBERT HUTSON)
Married at Lewisburg, Conway County, Arkansas on 13th, DR. ROBERT T.
ABERNATHY of Tuscumbia and MISS CALLIE, daughter of G. W. CARROLL, Esq.
Married on 15th by SMITH ADAMS, Esq., MR. THOMAS BROWN of East
Tennessee to MISS MARY ANN BROWN of this place.
Died in Limestone County on 4th, MARY E. STINNETT, consort of
CLAY STINNETT aged 32 years. (1850 census shows her aged 26 in Alabama;
him 34 in Alabama)

April 30, 1856
Married on 16th by REV. P. B. ROBINSON at W. H. WORTHAM's Hotel,
in Huntsville, MR. F. A. JORDAN of Mississippi to MISS M. E. MAZARK
(see later).
Married on 11th by REV. SAMUEL DENNIS, MR. P. H. BONN to MISS
MARY L. SPRINGER, all of Madison County.
Married on 15th by REV. ALEXANDER KIRKLAND, MR. K. L. DENNIS of
Courtland to MISS MARTHA A. WARREN near Triana, Alabama (not in
marriage record, Madison County).
Married on 17th by REV. W. D. F. SAWRIE, MR. HENRY M. FLIPPOE to
MISS CALHE C. COPELAND, all of this place. (1850 census shows one HENRY
FLIPPO aged 17, son of CLOEY FLIPPOE)
Died on 20th of consumption WILLIAM A., third son of MR. and MRS.
OLIVER D. SLEDGE of this place aged about 20 years...seems to be
WILLIAM W. SLEDGE in other records.

Died on 27th CHARLES, infant son of MR. and MRS. A. J. JOHNSON of this place.

Died in Athens on 22nd, R. H. BROWN aged about 32 years, a highly respected citizen. (One RICHARD H. BROWN in 1850 census aged 48 in North Carolina)

Died on 22nd WILLIE D., infant son of SAMUEL J. and LUCY A. SHANKLAND of this vicinity aged 17 months 10 days.

May 14, 1856

Married on evening of 1st by REV. MR. MITCHELL at Spring Hill, MR. F. ROBERTS of Limestone County to MISS SUSAN V. BURWELL of Madison.

Died in Guntersville at the residence of his son, A. G. HENRY on 29th April, MR. HUGH HENRY aged 60 years and 18 days. (1850 census shows him 55 in Tennessee)

Died on Monday at 11 p.m. April 27th of malignant scarlet fever, FANNIE, daughter of R. O. PICKETT, Esq. in her 11th year.

Departed this life on Thursday the 1st at 2 p.m., MR. JOEL CHILDRESS aged 44 years. Reared and educated in Madison County in the neighborhood where he died...left a wife and 8 children to mourn his loss.

Died in this place on 25th, MR. JOHN ADAY aged 61. He was one of the oldest citizens of Huntsville (note: 1850 census shows him aged 50, born in Tennessee; 1812 pen (gr))

May 21, 1856

Married on 8th by REV. MR. BARBEE, DR. J. P. COOPER to MISS ELIZABETH STODDARD, all of Tuscumbia. (in 1850 census, one JAMES PARKER COOPER, son of WILLIAM, was aged 17)

Married on 11th at MOSES MAPLES' (47 in Tennessee?) by REV. S. HAWK, MR. J. E. ADAMS to MISS MARY MAPLES (12 in Alabama), all of Jackson County.

Married on 16th by REV. P. B. ROBINSON, MR. F. A. JORDAN to MISS M. E. MOZART.

Married on 24th MR. BRYANT HANNAH to MISS MARTHA E. HANNAH. (One BRYANT HANNAH was 16 in 1850 census, born in Alabama, son of MARTHA HANNAH)

Married on 23rd, MR. C. H. McLOUD to MISS J. U. RICE.

Married on 10th, MR. JOEL RIGGINS of Jackson County to MISS MARY E. FOWLER of Madison.

Died in Nashville on 4th of paralysis of the brain, MR. PHILIP S. WOODSON, printer, formerly of this place.

In Tipton County, Tennessee on 23rd, DR. HUGH F. ROSE aged 34.

Died in Lauderdale County on 5th, DR. JONATHAN BECKWITH aged 57. (1850 census shows him 52 born in Virginia)

June 4, 1856

Married on 29th by REV. WM. JOHNSTON, HAMPTON S. WAITFIELD or WATTFIELD?,'editor of Tuscaloosa Monitor to MISS NANNIE LEWIS of Clarke County. (Tuscaloosa County marriages--H. S. WHITFIELD to MRS. NANNIE LEWIS 29 April 1856--at residence of JOHN MAXWELL by WM. JOHNSON, M.G.; 1850 Tuscaloosa WHITFIELD, n L 37 in Georgia; H(AMPTON) S(MITH) 25 in Alabama, sons of BENJ.)

Married on 27th by REV. MR. CHADICK, MR. F. S. KIRK of Russel's Valley, Franklin County to MISS S. E. DRAKE, daughter of ANDREW DRAKE, Esq. of Madison County. (Shown as FRANKLIN L. KIRK in other records, son of JAMES M. KIRK; her name was SUSANA JANE DRAKE; in 1850 she was aged 12, born in Virginia)

Married on 27th JOHN H. TABOR to MISS ALICE HANNAH, all of this county. (1812 sol (gr)--he married 1. in Washington County, Tennessee about 1818)

Married on 30th by THOS. W. MARTIN, Esq., MR. WM. A. GULLETT to MISS MARY ANN E. CASON, all of this county.

June 11, 1856

Married in Lincoln County, Tennessee on 22nd by REV. M. MARSHALL, MR. G. M. STEELE and MRS. L. L. WHITAKER.

Died in this place on 1st of consumption, MRS. MARY E. BURROW, consort of W. A. BURROW in her 23rd year.

June 18, 1856
    Married on 30 April by W. W. BAKER, Esq., MR. THOMAS B. OWEN of
Lafayette, Mississippi to MISS MARY A. LIPSCOMB of Coffeeville,
Mississippi, formerly of Decatur, Alabama.
    Married on 3rd by REV. MR. MITCHELL, MR. BASWELL T. MALONE of
Columbia, Tennessee to MISS MARY E. (C?), daughter of DR. JOHN S. BLAIR
of Limestone County. (in 1850 census he was aged 26, born in North
Carolina listed as "BOSWELL Y. MALONE"; JOHN K. BLAIR was 47 in Kentucky
and MARY E. was 9 in Alabama; volume 223, page 61)
    Married in Guntersville on the 5th, MR. SAMUEL BRADLEY of St. Clair
County, Alabama to MISS VIRGINIA STEEL (13 or 17? in Alabama) of Marshall
County (name was ANN JANE, daughter of NATH'L; see volume 65, page 49).
    Died at the residence of his son near Kossuth (Alcorn County),
Mississippi on the 5th, COL. A. McMILLAN, formerly a highly respectable
citizen of Lawrence County, Alabama.
    Died in Bellefonte on 12th of consumption, JOHN W. GREEN aged 26.
    Died on 8th in this county, MRS. NANCY JANE DRAKE, wife of REV.
JOHN H. DRAKE in 25th year. MRS. DRAKE was a worthy member of the
Cumberland Presbyterian Church.

June 25, 1856
    Married on 5th at residence of E. H. McNUTT by E. H. PLAXICO, Esq.,
MR. JOHN BOUNDS to MISS ELIZABETH McNATT, all of Franklin County,
Alabama.
    Married on Monday the 2nd by REV. W. MACK, JOHNSTONE TROUSDALE,
Esq. of Centre Star, Alabama, and MRS. ELIZA P. GOFF of Columbia,
Tennessee.
    Married in Athens on 18th by REV. N. R. GABARD, DR. WILLIAM LESLIE
of Madison County to MISS ANNA BASS, daughter of THOMAS BASS, SR.,
Esq. of this place. (in 1850 census, she is 16 in Alabama; volume 223,
page 61).
    Died on 8th, MR. RICHARD GLOVER aged about 67 years. He was one
of the oldest settlers of Madison County and was an honest, upright
man, and a good citizen, highly respected by all who knew him. Left
a large number of relatives and friends.
    Died in Bellefonte on 19th of measles, HON. JOHN G. DIXON, Judge
of Probate Court 43 years of age. (1850 census shows him 37, born in
Virginia)

July 2, 1856
    Married in Tirana, Alabama by REV. ALEXANDER PENLAND, MR. C. C.
McKINNEY of Fayetteville, Tennessee to MISS ELLEN DENNIS, at residence
of her father, REV. SAMUEL DENNIS (Cumberland Presbyterian).
    Married on 24th by REV. MR. BARBEE, DR. E. B. DELONY to MISS S.
AMELIA JONES, late Principal of Tuscumbia Female Institute.

July 10, 1856
    Married in Tuscaloosa on 24th at residence of her mother by
REV. JOSEPH J. HUTCHINSON (Methodist), WM. T. KING, Esq., of Dallas
County to MISS EVELINA H. COLLIER, daughter of the late GOVERNOR
H(ENRY) W. COLLIER (volume 8, page 39).
    Married on 26 June at residence of ROBERT McGEE, Esq. in Alexandria,
COL. WM. P. DAVIS of Benton to MISS HARWELL of Talladega County.
    Died on Saturday in this place on 5th of brain fever GEORGE, son
on BENJAMIN and CAROLINE JOLLEY in his 10th year.
    Departed this life in Madison County, Alabama, GROSS SCRUGGS, SENR.
aged 84 years. Deceased was born in Bedford County, Virginia January
1770. He removed to Madison County, Alabama in the year 1815, where he
has resided ever since, beloved and respected by all who knew him.
Surrounded by his children and a large circle of friends, he passed his
years pleasantly and happily...in early life the deceased consecrated
himself to God....
    Died at his residence at Cross Roads in Limestone County on 29
June, MR. SAMUEL McCOMB aged 41 years 7 months 12 days. (1850 census
shows him 36 in South Carolina)
    Died at his residence on 29th JOHN M. RICHARDSON, long a resident
of Athens. (1850 census shows him 54 in Tennessee)
    Died on 26th, JOHN FITZHUGH, son of MR. and MRS. H(ENRY) C. LAY
aged about 4 years.

Died on 2nd, MARY ELLA, daughter of MR. and MRS. S. D. CABANISS aged 17 months 3 days.

July 17, 1856

Married on 23rd by REV. JOHN S. MARKS, MR. D. J. JOHNSON to MISS H. A. THOMAS, all of Franklin County.

Married on 3rd by HON. JAMES H. TRIMBLE, CAPT. E. W. HOOPER to MISS LOUISA DAVIDSON, all of Franklin County.

Married on 23rd WILLIAM T. LUCK to MISS ANN JOHNSON, all of this county.

Married on 4th, J. L. CROFT to MISS LUCINDA HUNT, all of this county.

Married on 8th, MR. W. H. JOHNSON to MISS E. F. GUY, all of this county.

Married on 9th, MR. THOS. COBB to MISS R. A. HERRON, all of this county.

Died on 25 June last, EMBERSON M. WANN of Vienna, Madison County, Alabama. MR. WANN was born in 1832 and lived an exemplary life. Left a wife and infant to mourn his loss. (1850 census shows him aged 23 in Alabama, son of ISAAC D. WANN)

Died on 9th, MR. JOSHUA BARKER, long a resident of Huntsville. (1850 census shows him 40 in Virginia)

Died in Talladega on 28th, MISS MARY VANN, daughter of ANAIAS (ANANIAS?) and JANE VANN, formerly of this county, in the 19th year of her age.

July 24, 1856

Married in Somerville, Alabama March 21 by REV. DR. WELCH, THEO' ACKLIN, Esq. of Huntsville, Alabama and MISS HARRIET MORTON GOOCH of Smyrna, Rutherford County, Tennessee. Nashville Banner please copy. (1850 census shows THEODORE ACKLIN aged 17, born in Alabama, son of WILLIAM)

Died in this place on 26th MARTHA CATHARINE, wife of D. S. NOWLIN in 22nd year of her age....

Died on 30th ult. SARAH CATHARINE, only child of DAVID S. and MARTHA C. NOWLIN aged 1 year 1 day.

Died in Jasper, Walker County, Alabama, June 10th, COL. GRIFFIN LAMKIN of Virginia in 75th year of his age.

Died in Athens on 30th, JOHN M. RICHARDSON aged 60.

Died in Limestone County on 10th, WILLIAM B. ELLIOTT aged 28.

Died at residence of E. L. HUSSEY in Chickasaw County, Mississippi on 23 June, JOSHUA M. DILLARD after an illness of 3 days, aged 29 years 4 months. Left a large circle of relations and friends. (1850 census shows him aged 23, born in Alabama)

July 31, 1856

Married on 23rd by REV. J. C. ELLIOTT, MR. ROBERT J. McCALEB and MISS MARY E. GARRISON, all of Madison County, Alabama.

Married on 24th by same, MR. ROBERT B(EASLEY) BARKSDALE of Mississippi and MISS LUCY R(AIRTY) GIDDENS, daughter of JOHN GIDDENS of this county. (1850 census shows her 13 in Alabama; her father 54 in North Carolina; ancestor of ARTHUR O. BARKSDALE, 1968)

Died in Lawrence County, Alabama on 18th, MRS. ELIZABETH WATKINS consort of PAUL J. WATKINS aged 52 years. (1850 census shows her aged 45 in North Carolina)

Died near Huntsville, Alabama at the residence of MR. THOMAS MARTIN July 19, MARY B., daughter of REV. E. and SALLIE J. (IRBY) STRODE aged 9 months....

August 7, 1856

Married by REV. H. M. BONE on 31st, MR. A. J. HOUSE to MISS MARY T. LOWRY, all of vicinity of Maysville.

Died, MRS. ELIZA A. D. JACKSON, wife of DR. JAMES M. JACKSON at the residence of her mother, MRS. PRICE in Somerville, Alabama at 10½ o'clock on Saturday morning the 26th after a painful illness of 6 days. MRS. JACKSON was born December 8, 1826, was married to her surviving husband November 6, 1850, became a member of the Methodist Church in the fall of 1853.

Married by PRESIDENT E. JOHNSON of Lagrange College on 14th instant DR. J. M. LEWIS to MISS HETTY M. JONES, both of Bellefonte, Alabama.

Married on 6th by REV. WILLIAM H. BARKSDALE of Lawrence County, Alabama, MR. CHARLES E. POLK of Kossuth, Tishomingo County, Mississippi and MISS CORNELIA E. FAIRCLOTH (ELIZA FAIRCLOTH in license) of Brickville, Alabama.

Married on 7th at Frankfort, Alabama by REV. MARTIN CLARK, C. G. BOBO of Coahoma County, Mississippi to MISS LAURA E., daughter of JUDGE TRIMBLE of the former place.

Married on 7th by REV. A. W. SMITH, MR. W. T. PRICE of Florence and MISS V. C. BALDRIDGE of Madison County, Alabama.

Married at LaGrange (Fayette County), Tennessee on 16th (or 18th?) MR. R. REINHARDT to MISS SALLIE M. SLEDGE, daughter of DR. J. M. SLEDGE of Memphis.

Died on 7 July ALEXANDER ERSKINE EWING, son of ALEXANDER and MARY JANE EWING aged 1 years 8 months 15 days.

Died on 3 August SUSAN ELLEN EWING, daughter of same aged 8 years 3 months 21 days.

Died on 12th August JOHN JAMES EWING, son of same, aged 3 years 9 months 25 days.

Died on 5 August, WILLIAM B. LILE in his 28th year, of measles.

DR. THEODORIC M. HEREFORD died suddenly in Maysville, this county on 2 August. DR. HEREFORD was born in Loudon County, Virginia on 3 April 1824. His parents moved to this county when he was quite young, where he was reared and educated and has lived ever since. He had many traits of character that exhibited to his associates that he was a noble hearted man. Joined M. E. Church in 1841...he was married to MISS A. E. CHAMBLESS on 7 July 1852...affectionate husband, devoted father.

Died on 7th of typhoid flux, MR. GEORGE D. HUGHEY, a worthy and esteemed citizen of Limestone County. (1850 census shows him 41 in North Carolina)

Died near Athens on 4th very suddenly, MRS. ELIZABETH TUCKER MALONE, wife of THOMAS HILL MALONE aged about 58 years.

Married in Marshall County, Alabama on 12 August 1856 by THOMAS C. BARCLAY, Esq., JOSEPH R. ABRAHAMS, Esq., Chief Engineer on Tennessee and Coosa Railroad to MISS LARUA E., daughter of HON. B. F. PORTER.

Married in Marshall County, Alabama on 14 August, by REV. ABIJAH WATSON (M. E. Minister), LEVI MURPHY, Esq. to MISS MARY F., daughter of SAPPINGTON, Esq. (sic)

Married on 20th by REV. JAMES AUSTILL (Baptist), MR. JOHN R. HAYNES to MISS MARTHA HANCOCK, both of Jackson County.

Married on 6th by JOSEPH MINOR, Esq., JOHN T. WOMACK to MISS MARGARET COUNSEL, all of Jackson County. (if she died 1858 leaving 2 daughters they must have been twins or born close together)

Married at the residence of ROBERT M. RICHARDSON on 20th instant by REV. JEREMIAH DAILY, MR. JOHN C. ENLOW to MISS CYNTHIA ANN RICHARDSON all of Franklin County. (1850 census shows her aged 23, born in South Carolina)

Died on 22 instant THOMAS CARLTON FIGG, eldest son of L(ITTLETON) G. and M. A. FIGG aged 17 years 8 months 5 days.

Died at Tuscumbia Hotel on 15th of congestion of the brain, after an illness of 2 weeks, JOHN W. HAMILTON in 22nd year. Native of Franklin County, a young man of great promise and universally beloved by his acquaintances for sterling qualities of both head and heart.

Married on 27 August at home of COL. SAMUEL J. HUNT, by REV. G. W. MITCHELL, MR. ISAAC N. TEAGUE to MISS INDIANA NOWLIN.

Died in Forence, Alabama, HARRIET WATKINS, wife of WILLIAM WATKINS and daughter of JOHN and MARY ANDERSON. Born in Montgomery County, Maryland May 4, 1801 and died in Florence, Alabama August 29, 1856 aged 55 years 3 months 25 days. Her remains were moved to Huntsville Cemetery Saturday 30 August.

Died near Helena (Phillips County), Arkansas on 18th August MR. AB. J. ELLIOTT, aged 23, formerly of Huntsville, Alabama.

September 11, 1856

Married on morning of 3rd by REV. G. GARRETT, Judge A. B. MEEK to MRS. EMMA D. SLATTER, both of the city of Mobile.

Married on 2nd instant by REV. W. D. F. SAWRIE, MR. ACHILLES NOEL to MISS MARY A. A., daughter of MR. JAMES NEELEY, all of this place.

Died in Jackson County on 28th, CHARLES LEWIS ROACH in his 59th year of age. For 30 years he was a faithful member of the Baptist Church. (1850 Census shows him 52 in Virginia; volume 144, page 56; born in Amherst County, Virginia September 9, 1797, died Jackson County, Alabama August 28, 1856)

Died on 3rd instant after a short illness, MRS. IDELIA SAWRIE, wife of REV. W. D. F. SAWRIE, leaving many devoted to mourn her loss. She was a devoted wife, a faithful mother and a pious Christian. (1850 census shows her 26 in Alabama)

September 18, 1856

Married on Saturday the 7th by REV. MILTON BROWN, MR. ZEPHANIAH GIDEON to MISS ELIZA JANE WOOD, all of Jackson County.

Married on Wednesday morning, September 3rd by REV. J. GUNN, JAS. THROCKMORTON, Esq. to MISS MARY M. ELLETT, daughter of EDMUND ELLETT, Esq., all of Tuscumbia. (This was 2nd marriage for him; he was 41 in New Jersey in 1850 census; she was 21 in Virginia)

Married on 13th by BENJAMIN STEGER, Esq., MR. RICHARD BOWHANNON to MISS MARY PARKER, all of this county.

Died in Wilmington, North Carolina on Wednesday September 3rd, JAMES H. WEAKLEY of Florence, Alabama...he was on his way to Virginia Springs to complete his restoration to health when without a moments warning he was stricken with apoplexy...(1850 census shows him 52 in Virginia).

Died at the residence of MR. JOHN S. BEALLE on 9th, SIMENE EDDINS, infant daughter of JOHN R. and JENNY BEALLE.

Died of apoplexy at residence of CAPT. J. W. RHEA in the town of Tuscumbia, on evening of 1 September, MRS. SARAH BLOCKER, wife of COL. ABNER BLOCKER, deceased in 59th year. (1850 census shows her 46 in North Carolina)

Died on 12th, H. PETWAY, one of the oldest citizens of Nashville.

Died on night of 15th in this place, MR. JESSE LAWLER aged about 19 years.

September 25, 1856

Married on 10th by H. W. PICKENS, Esq., MR. THOMPSON BROWNE to MISS ELIZABETH J. OWEN, both of Black Creek Falls, Cherokee County.

On 10th by REV. T. A. WEATHERSPOON, MR. JAMES H. WOODLIE to MISS LAURA J. PRICE, all of Jackson County.

Married on 10th by REV. WM. GREENE, MR. G(EORGE) P. BRAY, of Jackson County to MISS MARTHA C. GRAYSON of Madison County.

Married on 18th by REV. ALEXANDER PENLAND, MR. SAMUEL HENRY to MISS CHARITY E. FENNELL, all of Marshall County.

Died on 3rd by 10 p.m. at his residence 4 miles East of Vienna, MR. JOHN STAPLER, deceased was born in Columbia County, Georgia and emigrated to this county in the year 1816, where he lived until the day of his death aged 81 years 3 months 3 weeks 4 days, leaving a wife and 4 children, 30 grandchildren and 5 great-grandchildren. (1850 census shows him aged 75 in Georgia)

Died on 10 July last in St. Francis County, Arkansas, WILLIAM EDGAR PEEVY, eldest son of WILLIAM H. and P. F. BAXTER, formerly of this county aged 13 years 1 week 3 days.

Died on 16th MARY TIZZY OTEY, eldest daughter of N. W. and T. A. PEEVY of Limestone County aged 3 years 5 months 8 weeks and 3 days. EDGAR and LIZZY were cousins.

Died on 19th, LEILA PATTON, infant daughter of MAJ. and MRS. J. J. WARD of this place.

Died on 17th, CHAMPION EASTER; on 18th, B(ENJAMIN) F. WILKINSON, both citizens of Limestone County. (1850 census shows CHAMPION EASTER 70 in Virginia; the latter 32 in Alabama)

October 2, 1856

Married on 24th in Huntsville at the residence of BILL SPENCE by REV. P. B. ROBINSON, MR. H. J. LANDERS and MRS. MARY J HALL, all of Madison County.

Married on Wednesday evening the 24th September by REV. DAVID
JACKS, ROBERT S. SPRAGINS, Esq. to MISS SALLIE A., daughter of
REV. WM. CRUTCHER, all of this county. (1850 census shows him 26
in Alabama; her 15 in Alabama)
Married on 23rd by LEVI HINDS, Esq., MR. P. DWIRE to MISS
MARIAH HELE (KEEL in marriage record; 12 in Alabama, daughter of
W. KEEL), all of this county.
Married in Courtland at residence of DR. BENTLEY, by REV. J. H.
LORANCE on July 31, WM. V(ERMILIA) CHARDAVOYNE and MISS LAVINIA
B(ENTLEY) HARRIS.
Died on 26th CORTES HUBBARD, infant son of MR. and MRS. C. D.
KAVANAUGH of this place.
Died on 19th MR. BARNEY MOORE for many years an honest citizen
of this place.
Died in Maysville, this county on 30th, MR. AMOS VINCENT aged
about 60 years.

October 9, 1856
Died in Triana on 26th September MARY E. MARSHALL, daughter of
GEORGE W. and ELLEN F. MARSHALL aged 1 year.
Married on 1st by REV. DAVID JACKS, MR. THOMAS O. LOVE to MISS
LUCRETIA PETWAY, daughter of DR. J. W. PETWAY of this county.
Married on 16th September by REV. W. L. WILSON, MR. JOHN W.
HAGOOD to MISS KITTIE A., daughter of WILLIAM H. STOKES, all of
Jefferson County.
Married on 10th September in Albemarle County, Virginia at the
residence of DR. M. L. ANDERSON, MR. JAMES E. PRIDE of Franklin
County, Alabama and MISS SALLIE PRICE, 2nd daughter of the late
COL. STEPHEN PRICE of Albemarle.
Married on 25th September by R. D. WILSON, Esq., MR. FREDERICK L.
LUDWIG and MISS MARY HOXTER, all of this place.
Married on 2nd by DICKSON COBB, Esq., MR. OVERTON GOODWIN to
MISS SARAH CRAFT, all of this county.
Married on 7th MR. LEVI SUGARS to MRS. M. S. CHUNN, both of Morgan
County. (1850 census shows LEVI SUGARS aged 41, born in Virginia)
Married in Athens on 2nd, by REV. T. G. SELLARS, MR. DUDLEY S.
HARRIS (WM. D. in license) to MISS ANN F. (E.) THOMPSON (volume 223,
page 64).
Married on 1st by JOHN A. JOHNSON, Esq., MR. JAMES D. (L.) MEADOWS
to MISS LUCY A. HASTINGS, all of Limestone County (volume 223, page 64).

October 16, 1856
Married on 9th by REV. (failed to copy name), MR. GEORGE R. STRONG
to MISS SARAH E. JONES, daughter of MR. JOHN T. JONES, all of this
county. (note: He was son of PLEASANT STRONG, and she was daughter of
JOHN TANNEHILL and JANE (LARKIN) JONES; grand-daughter of GEORGE
TANNEHILL and REBECCA CAMPBELL (BROWN) JONES.
Died at the residence of her father in Brownsboro on the morning
of the 12th, MRS. EMILY SMITH, daughter of JOHN SADLER and wife of
WM. SMITH (see his death on page 48), formerly of the vicinity of
Florence and more recently a contractor on Eastern division M. and C
Railroad (Memphis and Charleston Railroad). MRS. SMITH, in company
with her husband was on a visit to her aged parents, with high hopes of
soon meeting with those she so fondly loved...she was in sight of the
home of her childhood, when part of the harness gave way and the horse
became unmanagable and ran away. MRS. SMITH being alarmed sprang out
of the Rockaway and fell to the ground with such force as to produce
concussion of the brain. She remained insensible till the hour of her
death, being about 8 hours after the accident. MRS. SMITH was an
affectionate wife, a dutiful daughter....The Democrat and Florence
papers please copy.
Died October 3rd, 1856 of bilious fever, at her residence near
X Roads, Madison County, Alabama, MRS. SARAH BAILEY, consort of JAMES
BAILEY, Esq. MRS. BAILEY was born in Virginia February 16, 1798,
emigrated to South Carolina with her parents when 8 years old. Was
married to JAMES BAILEY September 11, 1821, emigrated to Madison County
Alabama in 1830...professed religion at an early age, united herself
with Piney Grove Baptist Church, Limestone County, Alabama, August 22,
1854. MRS. BAILEY lived an exemplary Christian life and bore her

sickness with meekness and fortitude. Her husband and 6 children, together with numerous circle of friends, mourn her loss.

Died at her residence on 27 September 1856, MRS. ELIZA JORDAN in Limestone County.

Died at the residence of her husband on 27 September, MRS. ALMENA A. SCOTT, wife of COL. DAVID R. SCOTT. Born in Madison County, Alabama near Huntsville on 8th day of March 1816.

Died on September 28, 1856 at her late residence near Courtland, Alabama, MRS. REBECCA McMAHON (67 in Virginia), widow of the late COL. WILLIAM McMAHON, in 74th year of her age. (Note: In 1850 census Lawrence County, Alabama, she is aged 67 born in Virginia).

Died in Florence on the 6th, ISAAC CAMPBELL aged about 72. (In 1850 census, Lauderdale County, Alabama, he is aged 65 born in Scotland)

Died in Lauderdale County on the 7th, WYATT COLLIER, an old and influential citizen. (In 1850 census Lauderdale County, Alabama he is aged 58, born in Virginia)

October 23, 1856

Married on 25 September by REV. JAMES A LYON, DAVID P. BLAIR to MISS BETTIE E. POPE, daughter of WILLIS POPE, SR., all of Columbus, Mississippi.

Married on 9th, MR. JOHN P. GRIGSBY to MISS OCTAVIA C(LAY) REDUS, all of Limestone County (volume 223, page 64).

Married in Cumberland Presbyterian Church in this place, on Wednesday evening the 15th, by REV. W. D. CHADICK, MR. SYDNEY S. DARWIN and MISS MARY A. D. LANIER.

Died on 8th, MRS. NANCY M. DAVID, consort of WATSON DAVID of Limestone County, Alabama aged 45 years 7 months 21 days. (In 1850 census, she was aged 39 born in Virginia)

Died on 18th, MRS. LUCINDA R. RATHER, consort of WILLIAM B. RATHER, Esq. of Tuscumbia, aged about 50.

October 30, 1856

Married in Nashville, Tennessee on Tuesday evening the 21st, by REV. DR. EDGAR, MR. WM. C(RAWFORD) SHERROD of Lawrence County, Alabama to MISS AMANDA, daughter of SAM D. MORGAN, Esq. of that city.

Married on 15th by REV. D(AWSON) PHELPS, MR. WILLIAM B. (A.) BAUGH to MISS SALLIE GRIGSBY, all of Limestone (volume 223, page 65).

Married in Triana on 14th by ELDER SAMUEL DENNIS, MR. JOHN YEARWOOD of Limestone to MISS MARY F. HERBERT of Madison.

Married in Morgan County on 15th by REV. H. M. WELCH, MR. JAMES P. GORDON to MISS MATT L. HAMILTON.

Married on 20th by JOHN W. IRBY, Esq., MR. WILLIAM PRESTON of Tennessee to MISS SARAH A. READ of Madison County

Died on 19th in Huntsville of a short illness in 67th year of her age, MRS. MARY ANN McDONALD, relict of JOHN N. McDONALD, deceased. MRS. McDONALD was born in Knoxville, Tennessee on first day of January A.D. 1790 and made a profession of religion and attached herself to Methodist Episcopal church in that place when she was quite young. She removed to Madison County some time in 1843 where she resided up to the day of her death, beloved by all who knew her. (In 1850 census she was aged 53 born in Tennessee)

Departed this life at the residence of her husband, DR. WM. H. McCARGO in DeSoto County, Mississippi October 19, MRS. LUCY A. McCARGO. She was born in Madison County, Alabama November 23rd, 1823 and was 2nd child of ROBERT and ELIZA F. PAYNE and was nearly grown when her parents removed to the State of Mississippi. She was married August 10, 1843.

Note: See our Volume 64 page 6 for marriage of ROBERT PAYNE to ELIZA BROWN, 3 June 1819. She was daughter of HENRY BROWN and 2nd wife, NANCY POPE, who was said to be a sister of LeROY POPE, early settler of Huntsville.

Departed this life in Madison County, Alabama on Sunday 5th day of this month, MRS. MARY ANN REEDY, consort of MR. BRYANT P. REEDY in 37th year of her age. MRS. REEDY was at the time of her death, a most worthy and acceptable member of the Methodist Episcopal Church and had been for the last 15 years. (See our Volume 76 page 19 for marriage of BRYANT P. REEDY to MARY JANE BOND 23 December 1846)

Died in Lockhart, Texas September 9th of typhoid fever, WILLIAM H. ROSS, son of REV. F. A. ROSS of Huntsville, Alabama.

Died on Friday morning, October 17th, MARY FRANCES, infant daughter of GEORGE E. and MARGARET E. NAFF aged 1 year 6 days.

Died Saturday morning October 19th at residence in Limestone County MR. SAMUEL MOORE in 56th year. (In 1850 census, he was aged 48 born in North Carolina)

Died on 26th, PATTIE, daughter of MRS. A. BRADLEY of this place.

On 16th, GASTON, infant son of GEORGE H. and JANE WARWICK of this place died.

November 20, 1856

Married on 4th at residence of CHANCELLOR VAN DYKE by REV. G. A. CALDWELL, COL. THOS. B. SAMPLE of Charleston, South Carolina to MISS KATE R., daughter of the late COL. V. M. CAMPBELL of Athens (McMinn County), Tennessee.

Married on 13th by H. H. HAAN, Esq., MR. JAMES A. RUSSELL to MISS NANCY A. CARPENTER, all of Madison County.

Married at Southern Hotel in Huntsvilel on 12th by REV. M. M. HENKLE, MR. JOHN F. DENNIS to MISS CHARITY C. HARRALL of this county.

Married on Monday morning the 17th in this place by REV. W. D. F. SAWRIE, MR. WILLIAM W. LEA of Grainger County, Tennessee to MISS ELIZA L. 2nd daughter of JOHN H. LEWIS.

Died in Courtland, Alabama on the 20th, MISS MARTHA R. McMAHON in her 30th year of age.

Died in this place on 15th, HARRIET N., daughter of the late RICHARD LIPSCOMB in her 14th year.

November 27, 1856

Married on 18th by REV. HENRY C. LAY, DR. JOHN S. PICKETT of Mooresville, Alabama to MISS MATTIE W., daughter of the late WILLIAM BLACKWELL of Limestone County (volume 223, page 66).

Married on 19th by REV. J. C. ELLIOTT, MR. HENRY J. BAILY (FARRAR or FARVAR) to MISS SARAH A. FAVOR of Limestone County (volume 223, page 66).

Married on Wednesday morning at the residence of the bride's father, R(HODERICK) JOYNER, Esq. of Athens, by REV. J. SEAL, WILLIAM BROWN, Esq. of Giles County, Tennessee to MISS MARY P. JOINER (volume 223, page 66).

Married on 19th near Havana, Greene County, Alabama by REV. THOMAS WINN, DR. DAVID T. MORROW (20 in Alabama; Morgan County) of Somerville, Alabama to MISS ELIZA A. (183-81), only duaghter of THOMAS E. (1810-74, born in South Carolina) and JANE W. WILSON (1815-81, born in South Carolina).

Died on Thursday the 20th at his residence, MR. SAMUEL TOWNSEND of this county, aged about 55 years. He was one of the early settlers of this county and was industrious and frugal in his habits. By his strict attention to his own business, he became one of the largest cotton planters in the county. He was well known and leaves many relations to lament his death. (Note: He is buried on the Townsend plantation at Hazel Green, Madison County, Alabama and his tombstone reads: "SAMUEL TOWNSEND born May 12, 1804, died November 19, 1856. Born in Virginia."

Died on 8th October MRS. LETTICE MEACHAM aged about 60 years, a very worthy, pious lady of Limestone County. (Note: See our volume 115 page 74 for reference to HENRY MEACHAM and wife LETTICE in 1816 in Madison County.

Died in Limestone County on 15th October, WILLIAM LOVE in the 82nd year of his age. Born in Southampton County, Virginia, emigrated to Tennessee in 1814 from thence to this county in 1818 where he has since lived, much respected. (1850 Census shows him aged 75, born in Virginia.)

Died at Pulaski House, Tennessee on 23rd, MARY AMANDA, only child of J. M. H. and ELIZABETH M. SMITH aged 14 months.

December 4, 1856

Married on the 20th by REV. MR. KLINE, MR. ROBERT B. TYUS and MISS MARY H. MERIDITH, all of Tuscumbia.

Married near LaGrange, Alabama on the 16th, by REV. MR. WINN, MR. AMMIRALD RICKS of Palestine, Texas to MISS BETTIE LONG of Franklin County.

Married in Limestone County on the 20th by REV. J. SEAL, DR. WILLIAM H. YARBROUGH to MISS ANN A(BIGAIL) JONES, daughter of HAMILTON JONES, Esq. (volume 223, page 66).

Married in Athens, Alabama on 26th by REV. A. L. P. GREEN, D.D., MR. GEORGE S. HOBSON of Nashville, Tennessee to MISS PATTIE C. MALONE (MARTHA), eldest daughter of DR. T. S. MALONE of that place (volume 223, page 67).

Married in Limestone County on the 18th (31st) by L(UKE) G. BULLINGTON, Esq., MR. SYLVESTER B. (F.) DAVIS to MISS MARY J. CHRISTOPHER (volume 223, page 66).

Married on the 20th ult. by REV. A. W. SMITH, MR. ELIJAH TONEY to MISS ANN ELIZA ELLIS, all of this county.

Married, MR. GEORGE S. DILWORTH to MISS SARAH J. ALLISON, all of this county.

Married, MR. LEVI LEWIS to MISS ELIZABETH C. DERRICK, all of this county.

Married on the evening of 26th by REV. D. K. HUNTER, MR. JOHN W. MILLER to MISS MARTHA J. ARMSTRONG, all of this county.

Died at his residence in Harrison County, Texas on the morning of 27th of October, JAMES A. PREWITT, formerly of North Alabama, in his 38th year.

Died near Mooresville, Limestone County on 23rd October 1856, SUSAN BRADLEY aged 5 years 10 days, and on 15th November 1856, MARY COLLIER aged 3 years 23 days, infant children of J. P. and ELIZABETH GRIFFITH.

Died on 19th at residence of JOHN ALLISON, Esq. in this county, NANCY CATHARINE, daughter of MR. J. A. F. and MRS. MARY J. E. VANN aged 2 years 3 months 19 days. (See our Volume 124 page 4 for marriage of JOHN A. F. VANN to MARY J. E. HUGGINS April 19, 1853)

December 11, 1856
Married on 27th by REV. G. W. MITCHELL, MERRIWEATHER A. LEWIS, Esq. to MRS. MARGARET E. JONES of Limestone County (volume 223, page 66).

Married on 3rd instant by JOHN A. JOHNSON, Esq., PLEASANT LENTZ to MISS MARTHA MORGAN, all of Limestone (volume 223, page 67). (In 1850 census Limestone County, one PLEASANT LENTZ aged 23 born in Tennessee.)

Departed this life in Limestone County on the 19th, MRS. FRANCES THOMPSON aged 41 years 8 months; MRS. THOMPSON was daughter of ANDREW and ELIZABETH McWILLIAMS; was born in Madison County, Alabama March 15, 1815. (Note. 1850 census shows her aged 35 born in Alabama, wife of NEEL THOMPSON.)

December 25, 1856
Married in Athens, Alabama on the 16th by REV. A(LEX'R) R. ERWIN (Methodist), MR. CHARLES N. HARRIS of Louisiana to MISS VIRGINIA D., daughter of the late CAPT. NICK DAVIS of Limestone County (volume 223, page 67).

Married on 14th by JOHN W. IRBY, Esq., MR. SAMUEL BARLY to MISS MARY ANN CAMMELL, all of Madison County.

Married near Whitesburg on 18th December1856, by REV. ALEXANDER PENLAND, MR. NEWTON RADFORD to MRS. ELIZABETH J. MORRIS, all of Madison County, Alabama.

Married on 18th by REV. J. J. BURDINE, MR. G. W. FOWLER to MISS M. J. GRIGSBY, all of this county.

Married on 18th by REV. P. B. ROBINSON, MR. SAMUEL A. GILES to MISS MELISSA J. SEVERS, all of this county.

Married, MR. WILLIAM M. MANLY to MISS MARTHA A. HILL.

Married, MR. GEORGE SAUNDERS to MISS OCTAVIA A. ANDERSON.

Married, MR. J. J. CHILDRESS to MISS SARAH COBB.

Married, MR. J. W. MOON to MISS P. A. COBB.

Died near Fayetteville, Tennessee on 5 November, MRS. NANCY BRIGHT in 71st year of her age.

Died on 16th December near Whitesburg, Madison County, Alabama, ISABELLA JANE, infant daughter of REV. ALEX. and ISABELLA J(ANE) PENLAND aged 1 month 2 days.

Tribute of respect by Mayor and Aldermen on death of JOSEPH B.
BRADFORD (ancestor of MRS. FLETCHER KING, 3801 Jackson Boulevard,
Birmingham?, Alabama 1956).

January 1, 1857
Married on 234d by Franklin Springs by REV. DR. T. MADDIN, MR.
P. H. HOBBS to MISS OCTAVIA M. JONES, both of Tuscumbia.
Married on Tuesday evening, December 23rd near Granada at Emerald
Garden, the residence of the bride's father, by REV. S. W. MOORE, of
Bascom Female Seminary, COL. EDWARD PICKETT of Vicksburg (Warren
County) and MISS CORNELIA C. BROWN, daughter of COL. A. S. BROWN.
Married on 18th at residence of REV. W. B. DEVER in Blount County,
by HON. J. C. GILLESPIE, MR. THOMAS W. HENDRICKS to MISS ELIZA J.
DEVER, all of Blount.
Died on Saturday the 29th instant at residence of MRS. DONALDSON
in Limestone County, MR. WM. H. SMITH aged 52 years. Resident of this
county, and was a good citizen and he has left two sons and 1 daughter
and numerous friends to mourn his loss. Had been engaged for some time
past in building bridges for Memphis and Charleston Railroad. (Note:
see wife's death on page 38)
Died on 5th instant of pneumonia at the residence of her husband,
THOMAS LEWIS in Madison County, Albama, MRS. SUSAN LEWIS in the 46th
year of her age.
Died on 19th, MR. HENRIECH LEHMBURH, a Prussian by birth but for
the past 15 or 20 years a citizen of this place. He was an industrious
mechanic.

January 8, 1857
Married on 25 December 1856 by REV. W. H. ADAMS, MR. JOHN H.
NORWOOD of Bellefonte to MISS MARY A. NETHERLAND of that vicinity.
(see their tombstone inscriptions in our Volume 146, page 32)
Married on 13th by REV. J. C. ELLIOTT, MR. BEVERLY W. GIBBS to
MISS MARGARET ODAM, all of Limestone County (volume 223, page 67--
license issued 13th, solemnized 23)
Married on 25th December in Pulaski, Tennessee by REV. MR. PLUMMER,
MR. W. McINARIA to MISS BETTIE JANE CUNNINGHAM, both of Limestone
County.
Married on 18th by REV. R(OBERT) P. RIDDLE, MR. JOHN W. WALLS of
Madison County to MISS NANCY L. (S.) MURRAH (14 in Alabama) of Limestone
(volume 223, page 67--license says married at residence of AMOS MURRAH--
44 in Kentucky).
Married on 25th by BENJAMIN STEGER, Esq., MR. P. G. LOVE to MISS
LUCINDA BARBER, all of this county.
Married on Monday evening, the 5th instant by REV. M. M. HENKLE,
MR. W. N. PRESTON to MISS M. A. GRANT, all of this place.
Died at his residence in Giles County, Tennessee on the 25th of
December last, SAMUEL D. WHITE. He resided for many years in Limestone
County. (Note: 1850 census shows him aged 51, born in Virginia)

January 15, 1857
Married January 1, 1857 by REV. JOHN M. ROBINSON, T(HOMAS) S.
JONES of Huntsville and MISS MARY JONES WITHERS of Limestone County
(volume 223, page 68).
Married on 8th by REV. G. A. MORING, MR. ANQUILLA C. BRAZELTON to
MISS ELIZA ANN HINDS, all of this county. (See our volume 136, page 40
for marriage record. In 1850 census "AQUILLA E" aged 14, born in
Alabama; son of JASON M. BRAZELTON. Tombstone shows AQUILA E. BRAZELTON
born October 7, 1835, died September 29, 1915.)
Married on 11 December 1856 by JAMES KELLY, Esq., MR. H. A. BISHOP
to MISS ELIZABETH BUCHANAN, all of Marshall County.
Married on Thursday the 8th at residence of DAVID BLACKBURN, Esq.,
by REV. J. G. WILSON, MR. E. J. HUGHES to MISS L. C. ABERNATHY, all of
Madison County (not in marriage record, Madison County)
Married in Tullahoma, Coffee County, Tennessee by REV. JAMES
KIRKLAND, MR. HEZEKIAH F. SMART of Warren County, Tennessee and MISS
SALLY E. ALLEN of Tullahoma, formerly of Madison County, Alabama (she
was evidently a CABANISS descendant).
Married on 1st day of January 1857 by REV. WILLIAM N. CRUMP,
MR. STEPHEN B. MURPHREE to MISS CAROLINE E. C. INGRAM, all of Blount
County.

Died--PETER BINFORD, youngest son of MAJ. AD. BINFORD of Lauderdale
County, Alabama, who was born February 22, 1843. (Shown in 1850 census
Limestone County, Alabama PETER was aged 9, born in Alabama. His father,
ADDISON BINFORD was aged 58, born in North Carolina. According to
Bible record, ADDISON BINFORD was born March 1, 1792, son of JOHN MOSBY
BINFORD and wife FRANCES HARDIMAN.
Died on Monday the 5th instant at the residence of MR. J. J.
FLETCHER, on Nubbin Ridge, Limestone County, Alabama, PETER BINFORD
under circumstances deeply afflicting. He had returned after his
holidays in fine health and buoyant spirits to the house of MR. FLETCHER
with whom he boarded. On last Saturday evening he retired to rest in
an office in the yard, which in some way unknown, took fire and ere he
could make his escape, he was severely burned.
Died on the 7th MRS. MILDRED EVELINE, wife of ROBT. D. WILSON,
Esq. of this place in her 42nd year. Humble devoted Christian and through
much bodily suffering has entered into the Joys of her Lord. (1850
census shows her aged 39 born in Alabama; him 42 born in Pennsylvania)

January 22, 1857
    Married in Americus, Sumter County, Georgia on the 12th by
REV. MR. HINTON, MR. GEORGE W. DRAKE of Huntsville, Alabama to MISS
MELVINA JONES of Sumter County, Georgia.
    Married on the 15th by REV. J. H. DRAKE, MR. WILLIAM M. LEDBETTER
to MISS HARRIET E. DILWORTH, all of this county.
    Married on 7th by REV. J. H. DUNN, MR. JOHN H. HURT or HERT? of
Limestone County to MRS. VIRGINIA MARTIN (20 in Virginia; wife of JOHN)
of Franklin County.
    Died in Athens on Friday January 9, 1857, MR. WILLIAM KITRELL.
(1850 census shows him aged 43)
    Died in Hempstead County, Arkansas on 14th December, MR. THOMAS
LOVE of Limestone County, Alabama who was on his way to Texas. (1850
census shows him aged 46 born in Virginia)
    Married on 15th near Memphis, at the residence of the bride's
father (NEWTON FORD, Esq.) by REV. SAMUEL WATSON, SAMUEL RAINES, Esq.
of Mississippi to MISS MARY FORD.
    At the same time and place by same, DR. D(REW) W(ILLIAMSON) BYNUM
of Mississippi to MISS BETTIE FORD, daughter of NEWTON FORD, Esq.
    Married on the 11th by REV. HENRY P. TURNER, MR. COLLIN HOBBS,
to MRS. CHARITY GRIFFIN, all of this county.
    Married on 20th by REV. JAMES C. ELLIOTT, MR. R. L. PULLEY to
MISS GEORGIA STRONG, all of this county.
    Married on 21st by REV. DR. ERWIN, REV. JAMES R. PLUMMER of
Florida to MISS LAURA, daughter of DR. GEORGE R(ANSOM) WHARTON of this
vicinity (see our HARRIS & ALLIED Families)
    Died in Franklin County on 25th ult, WHITMIL RUTLAND in his 75th
year. (in 1850 census aged 68 born in North Carolina)

January 29, 1857
    Married on 21st by RT. REV. MR. RANSOM, DR. F. B. HARRIS of
Bellefonte, Alabama to MISS MOLLIE ALLEN of Athens, Alabama. (See our
HARRIS & ALLIED Families--He was son of FRANCIS E. HARRIS of Jackson
County, Alabama)
    Married on 22nd by REV. NELSON WRIGHT, MR. C. W. McCUTCHEN to
MISS MARTHA A. WILLIAMS, all of Jackson County.
    Married on 22nd instant by REV. P. B. ROBINSON, A. L. HAMILTON,
D.D., President of Shelbyville University, Tennessee to MISS DOLLIE M.,
daughter of ALOUIN EASON, Esq. of this vicinity.
    Married on 14th near Whitesburg by REV. ALEX. PENLAND, MR. ELISHA
BELL to MISS SARAH C. BELL, all of this county.
    Married on 22nd, MR. R(ADFORD) W. HOBBS and MISS AMANDA J. COPELAND,
all of this county. (In 1850 census one AMANDA COPELAND aged 18,
daughter of BRANCH COPELAND)
    Died near Courtland, Alabama at the residence of his father,
MR. SAMUEL W. SWOPE, only son of REV. ADGAR M. and ELMIRA C. SWOPE.
MR. SWOPE was born in Courtland September 23, 1832 and died January 8
at 5 o'clock p.m. 1857 aged 24 years 3 months and 16 days. He made a
profession of religion and joined the Methodist Church in 1847 and
remained a member until God called him to church triumphant.
    Died in Huntsville, Alabama on 15th at the residence of MR. H.
McANALLY, MISS CORNELIA A. HUNT in her 16th year.

February 12, 1857
     Married in Waco, Texas on 29th December 1856 by REV. S. G. O'BRYAN,
MR. R. J. TALLY (formerly of Tuscumbia, Alabama) to MISS H. V. LINKINHOGER,
all of Waco.
     Married on 3rd by REV. ALEX. PENLAND, MR. HENRY W. GRANTLAND to
MISS MARIA F. OWEN, daughter of THOMAS OWEN, Esq., all of Madison
County. (In 1850 census, MARIA was aged 12 born in Alabama and her
father was 39 born in Virginia)
     Married on 3rd by REV. G. W. MITCHELL, MR. WASHINGTON L. NELSON
to MISS MATTIE A. TANNER, both of Athens (volume 223, page 68).
     Died in Tuscumbia on the 5th at about 7 o'clock after a short
illness of pneumonia, FRANCIS H. ROSS in 46th year.
     Died of pneumonia in DeSoto County, Mississippi on the 26th,
MR. WILLIAM THOMAS EASON in 43rd year of his age. Born in North
Carolina but raised in Madison County near Huntsville, where he married
a daughter of HENRY HARRIS. He was endowed with a superior natural
mind...Methodist. (See our volume 119, page 2 for marriage of WILLIAM T.
EASON to LUCY ANN HARLESS 25 July 1838--HARRIS is right.

February 19, 1857
     Tribute of respect--on death of our beloved brother, A. NOEL,
from Madison Lodge No. 25, I. O. O. F.
     Obituary
     Died in Larkinsville on 6th February of congestion of the brain,
EDWARD, only son of MRS. ANN DILLARD aged 4 months 4 days...has gone to
meet his parents, his grandpa, his little brother DAVID LARKIN and
sister MARY ELLEN.
     Resolutions on the death of our brother, WM. H. JONES--Maysville
Lodge No. 158 and Helion Lodge No. 1, of A. Y. MASONS.
     Married on 12th by REV. MR. HARWELL, MR. JOHN M. ALSOBROOK of
Pinetucky to MISS ANN FORSYTH of Tuscumbia.
     Married on 5th by REV. ALEX. SALE at the residence of DR. VAN EATON,
MR. HAMILTON MASK of Corinth (Alcorn County), Mississippi to MISS
JESSIE O. VAN EATON of Moulton, Alabama.
     Married on 2nd by REV. J. H. HALL, MR. JAMES W. ALLEN of Russellville,
Alabama and MISS SALLIE DUNBAR of Wheeling, Virginia.
     Married on 29th by REV. G. W. MITCHELL, MR. P. H. D. NEWBY and
MISS MARTHA J. CRUTCHER all of Limestone County (volume 223, page 69;
license says "at residence of REUBEN CRUTCHER).
     Married on 29th by REV. J. SEAL, MR. F. HARRIS and MISS SALLIE A.
WALLS, all of Limestone County (JAMES F. in marriage record "at residence
of ALBERT WALLS" says license; volume 223, page 69)
     Married in Guntersville, Albama on the 4th by M. GILBREATH,
Judge of Probate Court of Marshall County, C. R. CAPSHAW, Esq. to
MISS ANN ELIZA, daughter of the late JAMES M. ADAMS, Esq. of said
county.
     Married in Tuscumbia on Thursday, February 5, 1857 by REV. MR.
CLINE, E. B. RAGLAND, Esq. of Madison County to MISS THIRMATHIS,
daughter of the late JOHN C. SIMPSON of Franklin County.

February 26, 1857
     Married at Mt. Pleasant on 6th by REV. I(SAAC) MILNER, MR.
RICHARD S. COOK of Franklin County, Alabama to MISS BETTIE BOND of
Spring Hill (Maury County), Tennessee.
     Married on 10th, MISS ELIZABETH J. WILLIAMS to MR. JAMES PERRY,
all of Jackson County.
     Married on Tuesday the 17th by REV. MR. KLINE, MR. WILLIAM A.
NELSON of Memphis, Tennessee to MISS SUSAN H., daughter of WILLIAM
COOPER, Esq. of Tuscumbia.
     Married on 5th by ELDER J. GUNN, MR. WILLIAM MAXWELL of DeSoto
County, Mississippi to MISS MARY A. BURLESON of Morgan County, Alabama.
     Also on 11th by same, MR. D(ABNEY) A(DAIR) BURLESON and MISS
SARAH A. V. ORR all of Morgan County.
     Died near Bellefonte, Jackson County, Alabama on the 15th,
WILLIAMSON R(OLIN) W(INN) FENNELL, son of F(RANCIS) M(ARION) and
ISABELLA FENNELL (nee ALLISON; see FENNELL Bible record) aged 4 years
6 months 10 days. (he was son of JAS. C. and ELIZ. FENNELL)
     Died on 9th in Larkinsville, Alabama of typhoid fever, MR. WILLIAM
PATTON aged 43.

Died on 13th, MR. JOHN McKINNEY of consumption aged about 34.
Died on Thursday night last, WILLIE WATKINS, infant son of MR.
and MRS. WILLIAM E. SPOTSWOOD of this place.
Died at Franklin Female College in Holly Springs, Mississippi on
3rd, MR. T. P. HATCH, Professor of Natural Science in 30th year of his
age. Deceased was formerly a Professor in LaGrange College, Alabama
and afterwards in Florence Wesleyan University.

March 5, 1857
Married on 30th January by REV. J. C. ELLIOTT, MR. JOSEPH L.
PENROD of Decatur, Alabama to MISS MARGARET M(ELISSA) PUTMAN of
Tuscumbia. (Note: Ancestors of MRS. D. J. CONSODINE, 7708 Jarboe,
Kansas City, 14, Missouri. She says MARGARET M. is supposed to be the
daughter of ISAIAH and REBECCA (WELCH) PUTMAN. In 1850 census of
Lawrence County, Alabama was one LADY PUTMAN aged 46 born in North
Carolina with children fairly well checking with list of brothers and
sisters of MARGARET. Two were deaf and dumb, and a relative remembers
that there were two deaf and dumb sisters of MARGARET.)
Married on 18th by THOMAS C. BARCLAY, Esq., MR. JAMES C. HAYS to
MISS ANNA O. MOORE, all of Marshall County.
Died on 25th in Aberdeen, Mississippi after illness of intense
severity, MRS. N. T. SALE, wife of JOHN B. SALE, Esq. and daughter of
COL. JOHN F. MILLS.

March 13, 1857
Married on Tuesday the 10th ult. by REV. B. B. BARKER, MR. CHAS.
C (or O?) DRAKE of this county to MISS EMILY CROCKER of this city
(from Aberdeen paper).
Married in Fayetteville, Tennessee on 26th February by REV.
C. D. ELLIOTT, JAMES B. LAMB, Esq., Memphis, Tennessee and MISS
ELIZABETH F., daughter of DR. WM. BONNER.
Died on Tuesday morning last at the residence of his mother in
this place, DR. ALEXANDER M. KELLER of Beaver Dam Springs, Tennessee
in the 45th year of his age. Deceased was on a visit to his relatives.
when he was attacked with pneumonia--which proved fatal in a few days
(Tuscumbia, Alabama paper).
Died on 26th ult, after a long and painful illness, MRS. LIZZIE
ADAMS, wife of REV. WILLIAM H. ADAMS of Jackson County, Alabama.
Died on 4th of consumption, DR. J. A. MORRISON, an old and
respected citizen of Bellefonte aged about 53.
Died at the residence of her husband near Camden, Jackson County
of measles, NANCY ANN BUTLER in her 26th year. Leaves a husband and
3 infant children.

March 19, 1857
Married on the 10th by H. H. HADEN, Esq., MR. WM. A. SCRIMSHER to
MISS MARTHA R., daughter of NATHAN WILLIAMS, all of Madison County.
Married on 11th at Goff's Notel by REV. J. R. HARWELL, MR.
JOHN A. PEDEN of Pulaski to MISS MARGARET J. HAMILTON of the vicinity
of Somerville, Alabama.
Married at Brookfield near Lynchburg, Virginia on 25th of February
by REV. MR. WILLMORE, MR. A. L. PERKINS of near Huntsville, Alabama
to MISS BETTIE W., daughter of DR. N. W. FLOYD.
Died on the 6th at his mother's residence near New Market,
MR. JOHN F. JAMES after a lingering illness aged 43 years. Born and
raised in Madison County and died in hope. (1850 census shows him
aged 35 born in Alabama in family of MARTHA JAMES)
Died in Tuscumbia on 10th after a short illness, WILLIAM B. RATHER
in the 56th (or 50th?) year of his age. Among oldest citizens of the
town.

March 26, 1857
Married on the 12th by REV. WILLIAM H. ADAMS, MR. THOMAS A. CAPERTON
to MRS. HARRIET J. OLIVER, all of Jackson County.
Died at the residence of her husband, B. B. ROGERS, Esq. in
Madison County, Alabama on 16th, MRS. ONEY M. ROGERS aged 62 years 9
months 2 days. Born 14 June 1791 in Pittsylvania County, Virginia and
was the daughter of ALLEN and MARTISHA STOKES. Member of M. E. Church.
(1850 census shows her aged 56 born in Pennsylvania)

Died on 15th February at his residence near Marshall, Harrison County, Texas, WILLIAM A. ADAIR aged 35 years. He was son of the late JUDGE ADAIR of 5th Circuit. He was formerly a citizen of Athens; read law under JUDGE COLEMAN. Married in 1844 (married in Limestone County 1 June 1843), OCTAVIA ISABELLA, 2nd daughter of the late JOHN N. S. JONES. Removed to Texas in 1849. (see marriage record in Limestone County, volume 187, page 40)

Died on 19th in Bellefonte of apoplexy, NELSON ROBINSON, JR. aged about 27 years.

Died on 15th ult at the residence of her husband in Florence, Alabama, MARY SUSAN, wife of W. L. LORANCE, Esq. and oldest daughter of WILLIAM WATKINS, Esq. of Huntsville, Alabama.

JOHN BLEVINS   ) Bill for divorce
    versus   ) 23 February 1857
AGNES BLEVINS   ) 30th Chancery District

April 2, 1857

Married on 19th by REV. J. B. McFERRIN, D.D., the REV. J. RUFUS HARWELL, Pastor of the Methodist Church, Tuscumbia, Alabama, to MISS ANN L., daughter of JOHN HUFF, Esq. of Nashville, Tennessee.

Died in Decatur on the 15th at half past 4 after a short illness, SOFRONIA LOCKE, wife of W. G. LOCKE in her 32nd year. (she was SOPHINA WILDS, married January 1846--see our volume 49, pge 63; 1850 census shows her as aged 27 born in Tennessee, wife of WILLIAM G. LOCKE; see page 73 for death of their infant)

April 9, 1857

Married on 29th by REV. W. H. ADAMS, MR. JOHN CUNNINGHAM to MRS. ELIZABETH DICKSON, all of Jackson County. (Note: She was evidently the widow of JOHN G. DIXON, who died in 1856)

Married on 25th March, by JOHN W. IRBY, Esq., MR. JOHN WICKS to MISS MARTHA A. FOWLER, all of Madison County.

Married on --- instant by B. STEGER, Esq., NATHANIEL JENKINS of Giles County, Tennessee to MISS NANCY M., daughter of CASWELL B. DERRICK.

Died on Sunday morning last in this place after a lingering illness of several months, MRS. ROWENA HUDGIN, wife of MR. WESCOM? HUDGIN, and daughter of REV. DR. ROSS, Pastor of the Presbyterian Church, all of Huntsville. (volume 113, page 31; deed of gift from FREDK A. ROSS for love and affection--to grand-child THEODOSIA TEMPLE "only child of my deceased daughter ROWENA HENGEN, formerly ROWENA TEMPLE; if she died without heirs, then to my son CHARLES G. ROSS--8 February 1858--DB BB page 348.)

Died near Bellefonte on 24th March of inflammatory pneumonia, MRS. MILLEY WILSON, wife of MAJ. THOMAS WILSON of Jackson County.

Died in New Orleans of dropsy of the head, WILLIAM W. THOMPSON aged 22 years 1 month 1 day.

Died at Athens, Limestone County on Saturday afternoon of 28th March, LAURA HUSBANDS aged 8 years 4 months.

Also at same place on Saturday morning, the 4th, ELIZABETH PALMYRA HUSBANDS aged about 15 months. They were the oldest and youngest children of REV. WILLIAM R. J. HUSBANDS of Tennessee Conference and grandchildren of MRS. ELIZABETH ACKLEN of the vicinity of this place. (Note: see our volume 147 page 58 for marriage of WM. R. J. HUSBANDS to CHRISTIANA B. ACKLEN 1 September 1847. She was daughter of SAMUEL BLACK ACKLEN and wife ELIZABETH HUNT, and granddaughter of JOHN HUNT, for whom Huntsville was named)

April 16, 1857

Died, MRS. MARTHA ANDERSON, daughter of THOMAS and ELIZABETH CHAPPELL. Born Sussex County, Virginia 15 June 1778 and died at Athens, Alabama at DR. STITH MALONE's April 6, 1857. A member of M. E. Church for 57 years. (Sussex County, Virginia marriages--JAMES ANDERSON to MARTHA CHAPPELL, daughter of THOS CHAPPELL, married 20 February by REV. STITH PARHAM, Security THOS MALONE,Witnesses TEMPLEY HEATH and PHOEBE TUCKER; Sussex County, Virginia marriages--20 August 1772 THOMAS CHAPPELL and ELIZ. MALONE, infant (under age) Security DANIEL MALONE, witness MICHAEL MALONE)

April 23, 1857
    Married on 12th by JOHN A. JOHNSON, Esq., M. A. B. EWTON to
MISS ARTY M(ACY) FALKNER, all of Limestone County (volume 223, page 70;
license A. B. EWTON to ARTY MACY FOLKNER--at residence of W. FOLKNER).
    Married in Jacksonville, Illinois on Wednesday the 8th by REV.
MR. GLOVER, PROF. C. H. OAKES, Principal of Musical Department of
Huntsville Female Seminary to MISS KATE A. JONES of that place.
    Died at his residence in Limestone County on 9th, COL. SIMPSON B.
FLANNEGAN. Born in Fluvanna County, Virginia August 1798. Moved to
Limestone County, Alabama at early day and has ever maintained the
character of an upright worthy citizen. (1850 census shows him aged
51 born in Virginia)
    Died at his residence in Limestone County on 14th, ROBERTSON WEBB
aged about 67. One of oldest citizens of Limestone County. (1850
census shows him aged 65 born in Virginia)
    Died at his residence in Madison County, Alabama on 15th,
WILLIAM ROGERS in 89th year. Member of old Baptist Church near 60
years. Moved to this county from Virginia in the year 1832. (1850
census shows him aged 65 born in Virginia. A descendant tells us he
was son of JOSEPH and ELIZABETH ROGERS. He married twice, his second
wife being SARAH SALMON of Pittsylvania County, Virginia)
    Departed this life on 1 April 1857, LUCIEN MOORE BLEVINS, son of
the late COL. JOHN and MARGARET O. BLEVINS aged 20 years 8 months 21
days.
    Departed this life at the residence of her husband in Larkinsville,
Alabama March 28, 1857 after a short but painful illness of pleural
pneumonia, MRS. MARTHA ANN, consort of MR. PHILIP P. MURRAY in the
21st year of her age.

April 30, 1857
    Married in LaGrange (Fayette County), Tennessee the 22nd, at
residence of P. A. GORMAN, Esq. by REV. DR. GRAY of Memphis, MR. CHARLES
McCLUNG of Huntsville, Alabama to MISS LAURA M. BUNCH of East Tennesee.
    Married in Marshall, Texas on the 9th by REV. T. B. WILSON, MR.
KLEBER VAN ZANDT to MISS MINERVA J. PEETE, formerly of Limestone
County, Alabama.
    Married in Athens on the 20th by REV. J. SEAL, MR. CHANDLER to
MISS MARY MINGEA (volume 223, page 70; ROBERT CHANDLER to MARY A.
MINGEA at house of M. MINGEA).

May 7, 1857
    Married on 28th April by REV. J. R. HARWELL, MR. DANIEL A. GOFF
to MISS ANNIE E., daughter of THOMAS I. SMOOT, all of Tuscumbia.
    Married on Tuesday morning the 5th, by REV. W. D. CHADICK,
DR. WM. L. LEFTWICK of this place to MISS FANNIE, daughter of MR. JAMES
LANDMAN of this county.
    Died at her residence on Bear Creek, Franklin County, Alabama,
on April 2nd, MRS. ANN M. WILLIAMSON, wife of E. M. WILLIAMSON and
daughter of JOHN and MARY GIBBS.
    Died in this county on the 20th, MR. BRICE M. LYNCH (volume 113,
page 49; BRUCE LYNCH deceased; JOHN M. LYNCH administrator).
    Died on 3rd, MR. DAVID E. KELLY, a highly respected citizen of
this county.
    Died at his residence in Tuscumbia on the 27th after a protracted
illness, WILLIAM WINSTON, Esq. in the 70th year of his age. MR. WINSTON
had long been a resident of that vicinity and ranked among the most
wealthy and respectable planters. He was father of the present Governor
of the State.

May 14, 1857
    Married at Christ Church on the 2nd by REV. B. B. LEACOCK,
HENRY ALLEN LOWE, Esq. to CORNELIA C., daughter of JUDGE A. E. HOPKINS
both of Mobile.
    Married in Decatur, Alabama by REV. JACKSON GUNN, REUBEN W.
JOHNSON of Nashville, Tennessee to MISS MARY L. HIGGINS of Athens,
Alabama.
    Married on the 12th at the residence of MAJ. THOS. McCRARY, in this
county by REV. W. H. BARKSDALE, OSWALD KING, Esq. of Lawrence County
to MISS CYNTHIA WRIGHT of Madison (1850 census shows OSWALD KING aged
44 born in North Carolina; CYNTHIA was daughter of WILLIAMS WRIGHT).

Died in Winchester, Tennessee on the 2nd of consumption, MRS.
ELIZA R. CLOPTON, wife of DR. A. J. CLOPTON and daughter of the late
MAJ. ROBERT WALTON of this county.
Died in Memphis on the 11th, PERCY POPE, son of LEROY and MARY POPE
in 13th year of his age.
Died in New Orleans on the 27th, JACOB G. POINTS aged 52, formerly
of Courtland, Alabama.
Died on Tuesday morning, the 4th, of pneumonia, DR. LEVI TODD,
one of the oldest and most highly esteemed citizens of Florence. (See
our volume 123, page 60 for tombstone inscription. "DR. LEVI TODD
born in Adair County, Kentucky August 28, 1818; died May 5, 1857")

May 21, 1857
Married at the residence of the bride on 29th by REV. G. TAYLOR,
COL. W. M. LEE of Columbus, Georgia and MRS. M. W. MONTGOMERY, of
Bradley County, widow of COL. B. R. MONTGOMERY, deceased of Chattanooga.
Married on the 12th by REV. MR. CLINE, MAJ. JOHN L. BUNCH to MISS
LUCY M. JOHNSTON all of Tuscumbia.
Married on the 7th at the residence of MAJ. JAMES H. WITHERSPOON,
Waterloo, Alabama, by REV. R. H. RIVERS, MR. ROBERT W. HAWKINS of
Florence, Alabama to MISS A. E. WITHERSPOON of Waterloo, Alabama.
Married at Springhill, on the 5th by REV. MR. CHALON, VICAR
GENERAL, ABIN or ADIN? SELLERS to JOSEPHINE, youngest daughter of
E. DE VENDEL, Esquire.
Died on the 15th, HENRY TUTWILER, only son of CARLOS G. and
MARTHA L. SMITH aged 13 months.
Died Sunday night the 10th, at Franklin House in Tuscumbia, of
consumption, DAVID P. ELLIS, native of Kentucky in 26th year.
Died in this county on the 23rd, JAMES B(RUCE) BRONAUGH in his
60th year; good citizen and much respected. (1850 census shows him
aged 52 born in Virginia. According to our information, he was son of
SAMUEL and NANCY (MASSIE) BRONAUGH.)
Died on the 15th May, 1857 in Maysville, Alabama, little MOLLIE,
infant daughter of DR. B. B. and E. C. NUNNALLY aged 1 year and 8 months.
Died in this place on the 9th, IDA MAY, infant daughter of THOMAS H.
and JANE S. HEWLET aged 10 months 4 days.
Died in this county on 3rd at his residence, after illness of 6
weeks, MR. DAVID E. KELLY aged 63 years 11 months 24 days. Native of
Virginia but emigrated to this state in early life and settled in this
county in which he passed the remainder of his days. Plain and
unaffected in his intercourse with his neighbors and of unsullied integrity he gained the respect of all who knew him. About 15 years ago
he made a profession of religion and attached himself to the M. E.
Church...left a wife and 6 children. (See our volume 124, page 97 for
tombstone inscriptions from KELLY graveyard. "DAVID E. KELLY, born in
Brunswick County, Virginia May 9, 1793, died May 3, 1857" and others.

May 28, 1857
Married on the 26th instant by REV. P. B. ROBINSON, M. (MR?)
ALANSON BILLINGS of Tennessee to MRS. MARIA A. PROCTOR of this vicinity.
Died in this place on the 26th after a short illness, MR. GEORGE
DELP.
Died on the 23rd, FANNIE ELLA, daughter of ROBERT F. and MARY A.
RUSSEL aged 6 months 3 days.
Died in Giles County, Tennessee on Tuesday the 5th, MARY ELIZABETH,
infant daughter of JOHN C. and VIRGINIA H. HOLLOWAY aged 9 months 12
days.

June 4, 1857
Married at White Sulphur Springs, Limestone County by JOHN A.
JOHNSON, Esq., MR. JAMES NICHOL to MISS SARAH ELIZABETH CREAMER
(volume 223, page 70 JAMES NICHOLS to SARAH ELIZ. CREAMER solemnized
26 M(arch or May) 1857 at residence of MR. ABERNATHY)
Married on 26th by REV. A. L. KLINE, MR. THOMAS E. WINSTON and
MISS IOWA, daughter of MRS. L. B. MEREDITH, all of Tuscumbia.
Married on 21st instant by REV. JUSTINIAN WILLIAMS, SR., MR.
ROBERT E. CORRY and MISS ELIZA, daughter of the late JAMES HARRIS,
all of Franklin County.

Married in this county on the 28th, by REV. MR. WILSON, ALEX. M.
WYNN, Esq. of Limestone County to MISS MARTHA C(USTIS), daughter of
MR. SAM. WARD, of this vicinity (volume 153, page 60).

Died in Nashville on 27th, SARAH, wife of the venerable BISHOP
SOULE.

Died in this place on 2nd, MISS JANE HALL, for many years a well
known resident of Huntsville.

Died of measles near Whitesburg, May 21st, in her 14th year,
NANCY RICHARDS, daughter of STEPHEN M. and JANE RICHARDS. Born May 24,
1843. Member of Presbyterian Church.

June 11, 1857

Married on the 4th by E. M. FITZ, Esq., MR. JOHN P. PARVIN to
MISS MATTIE A. PIKE, all of this county.

Married at the residence of NICH. PARHAM on 28th of May by JOHN A.
JOHNSON, Esq., MR. JOHN W. BLACK to MISS SARAH F. OWEN, all of Limestone
County (volume 223, page 70; "at residence of NICHOLAS PARHAM").

Married on the 4th, by REV. MR. TOMES, HIRAM J. JONES to MISS
CORNELIA, daughter of DR. J. P. FORD, all of Nashville. (See our
HARRIS and Allied Families page 34, CORNELIA MARTHA LOUISA FORD was
daughter of DR. JOHN PRYOR FORD and wife ANN SMITH JEFFERSON.)

Married on the 4th, by REV. DR. BROWN, HON. JOHN M. BRIGHT of
Fayetteville and MISS ZOURILDA, daughter of A. H. BUCKNER, Esq. of
Mt. Pleasant, Maury County, Tennessee.

Died in Marshall, Texas on the 2nd, SAMUEL FINLEY, a very worthy
citizen.

July 9, 1857

Married in Nashville on 30th of June by REV. F. A. THOMPSON,
MR. BYRD DOUGLAS of Nashville to MISS SALLIE C., daughter of W. J.
CRAGWELL, Esq. of Wilson County.

Married on 28th June by JOHN W. IRBY, Esq., JAMES H. MURRAY to
MISS ELENDER CATHERINE SAMMONS, all of this county.

Married on 28th by REV. J. H. DUNN at the residence of WILLIAM
FOGG, MR. BENJAMIN F. SCOTT to MISS VIRGINIA S. FOGG, both of Limestone
County (volume 223, page 71 for license).

Married near Shelbyville, Tennessee on 1st, MAJ. JAMES RUSS, JR.,
Editor of Shelbyville, Expositor and MISS CLARA J. GREENE.

Died--MRS. MARY A. LAWLER, consort of MR. JEHU LAWLER near
Maysville, Alabama. Eldest daughter of JNO. R. F. and LILA S. HEWLETT...
born April 17, 1839. Methodist Episcopal Church. Joined July 12, 1851.
Died June 23, 1857.

Died at the residence of her husband, DR. WM. B. GREEN in Madison
County, Alabama on 28th June, MRS. SARAH GREEN, in the 58th year of
her age. The deceased was born in Wayne County, North Carolina in the
year 1799 and removed to this county in 1816. She died a Christian.
Raleigh and Newberne, North Carolina papers copy, also Huntsville,
Texas paper. Note: She was daughter of URIAH BASS. See our volume 129
page 69 for tombstones of BASS and GREEN families. "SARAH GREEN born
February 4, 1799, died June 28, 1857."

Died on July 1st in this place, WILLIE MORRISON, infant son of
JOSEPH W. and MILLIE DURYEE.

Died in this place July 2, 1857, ANNIE, infant daughter of MRS.
MARTHA LACKLAND of DeSoto County, Mississippi.

Died in Jackson County on the 24th of scarlet fever, MOLLIE CATE,
daughter of J. P. and JANE C. LEDBETTER aged near 4 years.

Died on the 21st instant SARAH A., wife of JUDGE JAS. H. TRIMBLE
of Franklin County.

Died Thursday, July 2nd of consumption, EMMA HUDGINS, wife of
A(NDREW) HUDGINS, Esq., of Jackson County and daughter of WILLIE
STINNETT, formerly of Limestone County.

July 23, 1857

Resolutions on the death of DR. ALEXANDER ERSKINE.

Died July 19th at the residence of H. E. MORGAN in Shelby County,
Tennessee, MR. MARCUS A. BOTELER aged 23 years 3 months.

Died at 2 o'clock Friday morning the 17th at residence of her
father, MARIA LOUISA, youngest daughter of COL. JOHN READ.

Departed this life at her residence in Madison County on the 5th, MRS. MARY HEWLETT, widow of JOHN W. HEWLETT, deceased, in the 73rd year of her age. Native of Henry County, Virginia. Shortly after her marriage she emigrated with her husband to Tennessee and from thence to Madison County, Alabama, where she resided until her death. Member of the Methodist Episcopal Church. (1850 census shows her aged 68 born in Virginia)

July 30, 1857

Married in Tuscaloosa on 21st by REV. R. D. NEVINS, MISS MARY E(LIZABETH), eldest daughter of HON. J(OHN) J. ORMAND to DR. J(OHN) W. MALLET, Professor of Chemistry at the University of Alabama. (Tuscaloosa County marriage book 1855-1859, page 253; JOHN W. MALLET to MARY E. ORMAND 17 July 1857 (21 July at residence of JUDGE ORMAND by R. D. NEVINS, Rector of Christ Church).

Married in Tuscumbia, July 16th, at the residence of M. J. WARREN, Esq. by REV. J. R. HARRELL, MR. JOHN M. WARREN to MISS ANNA E. HUSTON, 2nd daughter of DR. N(ATHANIEL) J. HUSTON.

Married on Tuesday morning last at the residence of JNO. S. BLAIR, by REV. J. H. DUNN, MR. HOLMAN FARRAR to MISS SALLIE JONES, daughter of HAMILTON JONES, Esq. all of Limestone County (volume 223, page 71; married 21st at residence of DR. JOHN S. BLAIR by T. G. SELLERS).

Died on 23rd instant MR. ROBERT I. HART of this place.

Died on July 6, 1857, FANNIE A. J., daughter of L. G. and M. A. FIGG, in her 14th year.

Died at the residence of her father in Jefferson County, Arkansas on the 10th, FRANCIS N. JENKINS, child of JAMES H. and LOUISIANA JENKINS aged 8 years 3 months 23 days.

Died on the 24th, FRANK ATLEE, infant son of MR. and MRS. ISAIAH DILL of this place.

Died July 24, 1857, ALONZO JAY, infant son of T. J. and E. A. HUCKABEE aged 1 year 7 months 10 days.

Died--MRS. LILA JANE, consort of MR. JNO. R. F. HEWLETT near Maysville, Alabama. Born May 28, 1818, born spiritually September 1837. Member of Methodist Episcopal Church South at Maysville, died 23 July 1857.... The Huntsville papers and Nashville Christian Advocate please copy. Signed R. L. H. Maysville, Alabama. (Note: She was daughter of JOSEPH CLOYD, who died 30 May 1853 aged 74-6-12.)

August 6, 1857

Married in Memphis, Tennessee July 7th by REV. MR. SEADMAN, MR. FRANK A. DUVAL of Grenada (Mississippi) Locomotive and MISS MARY E. A. MABSON.

Married in Blount County on the 9th by REV. N. CRUMP, MR. E(MORY) J. COZBY to MISS MARY JANE COWDEN.

Died at the residence of her husband near this city on the 24th of July 1857, MRS. SARAH J. HALSEY, wife of MR. HENRY HALSEY in the 27th year of her age...devoted wife and mother...presbyterian.

Died in Decatur, Alabama on the 1st, after an illness of some weeks, from teething, FANNY BUCHANAN, infant daughter of W. G. and the late SOPHRONIA LOCKE aged 12 months and 10 days. (see page 61 for her obituary)

Died in Tuscumbia on the 25th, SAML M. GREEN aged 25. Well known citizen and manager of Franklin House of that place.

END OF THAT BOUND VOLUME OF NEWSPAPERS

SOUTHERN ADVOCATE

Huntsville, Alabama

This next bound book of newspapers had 1st few pages torn and exact date could not be read.

August --, 1857

Married on 13th by REV. P. B. ROBINSON, MR. THOMAS CLEM to MISS ORENA, daughter of MR. HUDSON N. ALLEN, all of this place. (note: ROWENA in census)

Married in Tuscumbia on 11 August by ELDER J. GUNN, MR. JESSE BROWN and MISS MINERVA WHITE of Tuscumbia, Alabama.

Died of congestion of the lungs at Corinth, Mississippi on August 5th, WAVERLY, son of JAMES and ELEANOR ALFRIEND (married ELEANOR J. ROBINSON 6 May 1851; volume 7--; see volume 42) aged 4 years 10 months 11 days.

Died, MR. ROBERT ITHUELL HART, youngest and third son of THOMAS and SUSAN HART. Born October 6, 1829 died July 29, 1857 being in his 28th year. Married October 2, 1850 MISS MARY E. HALSEY. Kind husband, father and son. Left a wife and 2 lovely children. I. O. O. F... Tuscumbia North Alabamian copy. (Note: He is buried in Maple Hill Cemetery, Huntsville, Alabama. Census gives Alabama as his birthplace)

Died on 17th, MOSES MILLER, an old and respectable citizen of this county. Native of East Tennessee. Aged about 80 years. (Census gives his age as 49 born in Tennessee and tombstone shows he was born August 14, 1800, died August 17, 1857; buried at Holmes Chapel in Big Cove.)

August 27, 1857
Married on the 20th, by ELDER R. W. CRUTCHER, MR. CLAIBORNE S. ROGERS to MISS SARAH ANN LEWIS--both of this county.

Died in Athens on the 15th, MRS. MARGARET B. CARTWRIGHT, wife of RICHARD H. CARTWRIGHT (married in Limestone County 16 April 1844 MARGARET D. (should be B), volume 187, page 49). Left a husband and 6 children. (1850 Census shows her aged 30 born in Alabama)

Died at Bailey Springs on the 17th, MRS. SARAH D. COOLEY, wife of MR. TIMOTHY COOLEY of Tuscumbia in her 48th year. (1850 Census shows aged 36 born in New York; her husband aged 41 born in Ireland)

Died on the 18th at the residence of D. M. MARTIN, Esq. in Bellefonte, MR. HENRY DAVIS aged about 90 years. (volume 144, page 2; HENRY DAVIS, SEN. born in Mecklenburg County, North Carolina August 27, 1767; died in Bellefonte, Alabama August 18, 1857)

September 3, 1857
Married on 6th August by REV. DR. ERWIN, BENJAMIN B. ROGERS, Esq. to MISS MARGARET S. THOMPSON, both of this county. (1850 Census shows him aged 58 born in Virginia)

Married on 25th of August by REV. J. R. HARWELL, MR. GEORGE A. WOOD to MISS EDMONIA V. WILBURN, all of Tuscumbia.

Married in this place August 26th by REV. P. B. ROBINSON, MR. ROBERT A. LANFORD of this vicinity to MISS ISABELLA A. JONES.

Married on the 27th instant near Bellefonte, MR. A. A. GAY to MISS DELILA ARMBRESTER

Married on the 25th by A. J. JOHNSON, Esq., MR. HOWELL HORTON and MISS AMANDA C. MEADOWS, all of Limestone County (volume 223, page 71).

Married in this place, September 1st, by REV. P. B. ROBINSON, MR. JAMES E. SEAT and MISS MARTHA J. WEAVER.

Died on Tuesday morning August 18th at her residence in this county, MRS. REBECCA M. STEGER, widow of the late JOHN P. STEGER in her 79th year. She had been a member of the Methodist Episcopal Church for a great many years. She left a large circle of relations and friends to mourn her loss. Note: This was REBEKAH MACON HARRIS, widow of JOHN PERRATT STEGER. She was daughter of FRANCI EPPES HARRIS and wife ANN MACON, early settlers of Madison County, Alabama from Powhatan and Cumberland Counties, Virginia. See our HARRIS and Allied Families.

September 10, 1857
Married on 19th at Greenville, Georgia by REV. HENRY W. HILLIARD (Methodist), COL. JOHN COCHRAN to MISS KATE, daughter of COL. ALFRED WELLBORN of Merriwether.

Married on 1st by REV. R. H. RIVERS, D.D., WARREN W. PEDEN, Esq. of Franklin County to MISS SARAH L. MATTISON of Tuscumbia.

Married in San Francisco, California on 4th of August, MR. ALEX P. GREENE to MISS JESSIE EARLY POSEY, formerly of Huntsville, Alabama.

Married September 3rd, 1857 by REV. THOMAS MADDIN, MR. C. C. SALE and MISS SALLIE POLK CONNALLY, all of Madison County.

Married on the 20th at the residence of JACK PHILLIPS, Esq. by REV. WILLIAM ATWELL, RICHARD A. BAILEY to MISS MARY JANE PHILLIPS, daughter of JACK PHILLIPS, all of Lauderdale County.

Died in Athens on 28th, MRS. OCTAVIA MORROW aged 75.
Died in Talladega County on the 26th, JAMES BARCLAY aged 74. He
formerly resided in Huntsville. (1850 Census shows him born in Scotland
and aged 68)
JOHN CLICK died in Jefferson County, Alabama the other day aged 97.
Note: He was a Revolutionary soldier. 1850 Census shows him aged 87
born in Virginia.
REV. L. B. McDONALD of the Methodist Church died in Shelby County,
Alabama on the 23rd. Note: West's History of Methodism in Alabama
page 705 says: "REV. L. B. McDONALD died August 23, 1857, near Columbiana,
Alabama. He was a native of Giles County, Tennessee and was in the
43rd year of his age...he joined the Methodist Episcopal church in
August 1833, and about the same time entered LaGrange College where he
remained as a student until December 1837....

September 17, 1857
Married in Limestone County on 3rd September by JOHN A. JOHNSON,
Esq., MASTIN C. HARVEY to MISS MARY R. CLEM (volume 223, page 72 for
license--MARY C. CLEM).
Died--HENRY ALDEN PEEBLES, eldest son of ROBERT and SOPHIA C.
PEEBLES; was born in Mooresville, Limestone County, Alabama on 30 March
1840 and died of typhoid fever August 30, 1857 aged 17 years 5 months.
Died in Coahoma County, Mississippi on the 6th, ELIZA SMITH
CHAMBERS, daughter of HENRY C. and VIRGINIA CHAMBERS aged 5 years 1
month and 3 days.
Died in this place on the 14th, VIRGINIA OCTAVIA, only daughter of
JOHN H. and MARY V. KNOX, formerly of Winchester, Tennessee aged 15
months 2 days. Winchester and McMinnville, Tennessee papers please
copy.

September 24, 1857
Married September 15th by REV. P. B. ROBINSON, MR. ABNER F. McGEE
of Mississippi and MISS SALLIE M. KING, daughter of COL. JOHN D. KING
of this county. (Written "McGEHEE" in census; and SALLIE W. KING in
census)
Died in Limestone County on 9th of consumption, MRS. JULIA ANN
DAWSON, wife of JAMES J. DAWSON aged 32. (Note: She was daughter of
ISAAC and JEMIMA HYDE)
Died in Franklin County on the 11th, ABNER DICKSON in his 68th
year. (1850 Census shows him aged 60 born in North Carolina)
Died on 10th in Franklin County, MRS. JANE G. BARKER, wife of
AMBROSE BARKER, aged 63.
Died on the 15th in Franklin County, MRS. JESSE BROWN, an aged and
worthy citizen. (1850 Census shows him aged 55 born in North Carolina)
Died in this county on 15th at his residence near Whtiesburg,
MR. FRANK BELL an aged and worthy citizen--Baptist.
MRS. MARY A. CANNON, daughter of MARY and GILES NANCE and wife of
MR. DANIEL A. CANNON was born in Madison County, Alabama January 23,
1827 and died August 31, 1857. (Note: She married 1st 23 August 1843
GEORGE H. WILBURNE and 2nd, January 25, 1853 DANIEL A. CANNON. See
our volume 53, page 12 for will of GILES NANCE.)
Died at her residence in this county on the 14th instant MRS.
ELIZABETH HILLSMAN, widow of the late JOSE HILLSMAN, formerly of
Amelia County, Virginia in her 84th year. Her husband was a soldier of
the Revolution and she was the last Revolutionary pensioner of the
general government in this county. She was baptized in the Episcopal
Church in Virginia the year 1800 and died professing repentenance towards
God and faith in the Lord Jesus Christ."
Died at his residence in Coahoma County, Mississippi September 18th,
MAJOR S. A. BOBO in his 27th year.

October 1, 1857
Married in the vicinity of --------- on 23rd, by REV. W. D. CHADICK,
MR. JOSEPH MARTIN and MISS VIRGINIA O. WHITE.
Married on evening of the 26th by REV. MR. STRODE, MR. RODAH HORTON
to MISS MARGARET E., daughter of JOSIAH D. BATTLE, Esq., all of this
county.
Married in Limestone County on the 24th by JOHN A. JOHNSON, Esq.,
MR. JOHN H. OGLESBY to MISS MARY T. INMAN (volume 223, page 72).

Married in Limestone County on the 17th by REV. R. P. RIDDLE,
MR. WILLIAM W. BATES to MISS M(ARTHA) A. F. SANDLIN (volume 223, page
72).
Married on 22nd by REV. DR. WHITE, of Florence, MR. JOHN A. PERSON
and MISS HELEN, daughter of JAMES THROCKMORTON of Tuscumbia.
Died in this place on 26th, MR. ABRAM BRANSFORD aged 77. Born
in Virginia but removed to this county about 1817 where he has since
resided. Methodist. See our volumes 136 and 137 for marriage and
other records.
Died September 22, 1857 in Giles County, Tennessee of typhoid
fever, MR. JOHN C. HOLLOWAY aged 29 years 7 months 7 days....
Died on the 11th, MRS. FRANCIS HARDY, wife of MR. CHARLES HARDY,
living near Berah, Limestone County.

October 8, 1857
MRS. JANE DINAMORE, a revolutionary relic, wife of the late
JAMES DINAMORE died on 31st August last in Morgan County aged 89 years.
In 1810 with her father, ANDREW McDANIEL she settled near Huntsville.
She was for 50 years a member of the Presbyterian Church and worshiped
with it years ago in the Court House in this place. She was truly a
mother of Israel. (See our volume 32 for pension, Bible records,
etc. In the pension, the name "McDANIEL" applears as McDONALD, and
in Bible as "McDONNELL," which descendants say is correct.)
J. LIPSCOMB, a worthy citizen of Montgomery died a few days ago.

October 15, 1857
Married in Fayetteville, Tennessee on the 8th, DR. H. S. DAVIS to
MISS FANNIE P. STRONG, daughter of CHARLES W. STRONG, Esq., all of this
county.
Married in Maysville on the 11th instant by REV. M. H. BONE,
DAVID S. NOWLIN, Esq. to MISS ELVIRA A. RUTHERFORD, both of this
county.
Married on the 3rd by J. A. JOHNSON, Esq., ALFRED CLEM to MISS
SARAH J. HARVEY, all of Limestone (volume 223, page 72 of ALFRED A.
CLEM to JANE HARVEY).
Married on 7th in Court House in Athens by J. A. JOHNSON, Esq.,
JAMES SCHRIMSHER to NANCY HENRY (volume 223, page 72).
Died on 8th in this county, MR. JOHN WELLS in his 70th year.
Native of South Carolina but has lived in this county ever since 1812
where he enjoyed the respect of all who knew him. (1850 census shows
him aged 60 born in South Carolina)
Died in this vicinity on the morning of the 10th, ALONZO SCOTT,
infant son of W(INSLOW) L. and E(LIZA) A(NN) DYER aged 17 months and
2 days.
Died in Lawrence County on the 15th ult, JOHN L(EE) ASH (24 in
Alabama; son of WM.) aged 31. (1850 census shows him aged 24 born in
Alabama in family of WM. ASH.)

October 29, 1857
Married on Tuesday evening at the residence of the bride's father
by PROF. J. SHACKELFORD, MR. ASA M. HODGES (26 in Alabama) to MISS
MARTHA HODGES (15 in Alabama), daughter of DANIEL HODGES, Esq. (42 in
South Carolina), all of Lawrence County.
On October 14th by REV. L. Q. ALLEN, MR. M. F. AMOS of Larkinsville,
Alabama to MISS AMANDA E. HOLMES, daughter of JAMES G. HOLMES of Dade
County, Georgia. (Letter from MRS. J. B. SHELTON, New Albany, Mississippi,
1956, "JAMES G. HOLMES and ELIZ. B. NEWTON were married in Georgia.
They lived in Jackson County, Alabama but not sure whether they died
there or in Dade County, Georgia)
Married on 21st, WILLIAM S. CHAPMAN, Esq., Editor of the Talladega
Democratic Watchtower, to MISS K. L., daughter of GEN. L. W. LAWLER of
that county. (Note: She was KATHERINE LETTICE, daughter of GEN. LEVI W.
LAWLER)
Married on the evening of the 15th by JOHN W. IRBY, Esq., MR.
JOSHUA ESTES to MISS MARY ANN LANDMAN? (LARD in marriage record) of
Madison County (volume 119, page 17).
Married on the evening of the 20th by JOHN W. IRBY, Esq., THOMAS
WILSON, Esq. of Jackson County to MISS MILDRED ROGERS of Madison County.

Departed this life on the 12th at the residence of her son-in-law, MR. DAVID BLACKBURN in Madison County, Alabama, MRS. SARAH F. BAILEY in the 78th year of her age, leaving a large circle of children, grand-children and great-grandchildren. (1850 census shows DAVID BLACKBURN as aged 40 born in Tennessee)

November 5, 1857
Married on 22nd October by REV. DR. GREEN, REV. W. D. F. SAWRIE of Tennessee Conference to MISS VIRGINIA M. JONES of Williamson County. (1850 census shows WILLIAM D. F. SAWRIE aged 39 born in North Carolina. His former wife died 3 September 1856)

November 12, 1857
Married on 20th October by REV. ALEXANDER SALE, MR. JAMES A. PATTERSON, of Tuscumbia to MRS. MALVINA J. LIGHTFOOT of Lawrence County. (Note: Our records show JAMES A. PATTERSON aged 37 born in Ohio, 1850 census; his former wife died 10 August 1856; MALENCE or MALEANA was widow of JOHN F. LIGHTFOOT)
Married in Triana by REV. SAMUEL DENNIS, MR. WILLIAM H. COWART to MISS MARY E. GORDON. (W. H. COWART seems to have been married before; was aged 27 in 1850, born in Tennessee)
Married on the 3rd by REV. GEORGE F. BULMAN, MR. JOHN H. PENCE to MISS SARAH ANN BULMAN, all of this county.
Married on the 3rd by REV. DR. ERWIN, CALUDIUS A. HARRIS to MISS MOLLIE A. HUSSEY, all of this county. (Note: See our HARRIS and Allied Families. CLAUDIUS A. HARRIS was son of FRANCIS EPPES HARRIS, JR.)
Married in Church of Nativity in this place on the morning of the 11th, by REV. HENRY LAY, MR. THOMAS BIBB to MISS ANNA PICKETT, all of this place. (not in marriage record of Madison County.)
Died--JUDGE AMBROSE CRANE on the 15th in Brownville, Texas aged 70.
Died on 1st near Moulton of flux, MR. F. C. OWEN aged 40; a good citizen. (Note: FRANK CALEB OWEN, aged 32 in 1850, born in Alabama)
Died on 18th in Jackson County, Alabama, MR. ARTHUR FRAZIER, an old and respectable citizen of that county and on the 26th, his widow, MRS. ELIZABETH FRAZIER. (In 1850 census he was aged 55, born in North Carolina and she was 53 born in North Carolina)
Died on Friday night the 30th, MRS. MARY SUSAN BRADFORD, wife of MR. HAMILTON G(EORGE) BRADFORD and daughter of JOHN WARD, deceased, all of this county. (In 1850 she was 24 born in Alabama)
Died in this place on the 1st suddenly of apoplexy, MRS. NORTHCUT, an estimable old lady.

November 19, 1857
Married on the 11th by REV. M. E. JOHNSON, DAVID WADE, JR. to MISS MARY T. SIBLEY, all of this county.
Married on the 12th at the residence of JONATHON MAYHEW, Esq. of this vicinity by REV. DR. ERWIN, PAUL J. WATKINS, Esq. of Lawrence County to MRS. MARY E. MORRISON of Huntsville.
Married in Tuscumbia, Alabama on the 15th by REV. MR. CLINE, MR. J. D. ROSSER of Memphis and MISS SALLIE E. SIMPSON, daughter of WILLIAM SIMPSON, Esq.
Died in his 63rd year on the 6th, WILLIAM WARREN, Esq., an old and highly respected citizen of Lawrence County. (1850 census shows him aged 56 born in Georgia)
Died on the 12th at hotel of D. M. MARTIN, Esq. in Bellefonte, Alabama, MR. YOUNG W. STOKES aged about 36.

November 26, 1857
Married on the 18th by REV. JOSEPHUS SHACKELFORD at the residence of COL. I(SAAC) N. OWEN in Moulton, MR. WILLIAM F(RANKLIN) OWEN to MISS CARRIE N(ORVEL) WALLACE, daughter of HON. JAMES B(RANDON) WALLACE of Tuscaloosa.
Died on the 20th of September, EMMA MASON, daughter of R. G. and MARY A. SCOTT aged 3 months.

December 3, 1857
Married on the evening of 19th by REV. M. H. BONE, COL. JOHN M. WRIGHT to MISS MARY STEGAR, second daughter of ALLEN STEGER, Esq., all of this county. (See our HARRIS and Allied Families)

Married at the residence of MRS. SARAH GOREE in Marion on the 17th by REV. WILLIAM A. STICKNEY, POWHATAN LOCKETT, Esq. to MISS MARTHA J., daughter of his EXCELLENCY, A. B. MOORE, Governor of Alabama.

Married on 25th at the residence of H(OWELL) C. FEATHERSTONE, Esq. in the vicinity of Athens, Alabama by REV. J. G. WILSON, DR. ROBT. (E.) TWEEDY of Courtland, Alabama to MISS HARRIET O(PHELIA) FEATHERSTONE (volume 223, page 73).

Married by REV. JOSEPHUS SHACKELFORD on the 24th, MR. A(UGUSTUS) D. RUSSELL of Louisiana to MISS MOLLIE S., daughter of ROBERT BLASSENGAME, Esq. of Lawrence County, Alabama.

Died on 26th in this place after a lingering illness, JOSEPH N. KENNEDY aged 82. Methodist and old citizen of this county. (1850 census, aged 74 born in Pennsylvania)

Died December 1, 1857 HUGH EASLEY, JR., only son of H(UGH) and M(ARGARET) A(NN) EASLEY aged 5 years 3 months.

December 10, 1857
Married on 24th by REV. ISAAC MILNER, MR. JESSE W. BROOKS and MISS OLLIE E., daughter of HIRAM KENNEDY, Esq., all of Lauderdale County (OLLIVE in 1850 census).

Married on 25th by JOHN W. COMPTON, Esq., G(EORGE) W. LENTON and MISS MARTHA CROWLEY, all of Lawrence County.

Married in Limestone County on 26th of November by JOHN A. JOHNSON, Esq., PLEASANT A. PEACE to MISS FRANCES E. CHRISTOPHER.

Married on 26th of November by JOHN A. JOHNSON, Esq., MR. P(HILIP) G. GILL to MISS MARY L. S. CALVIN, of Limestone County.

Died on 4th of November at the residence of her father in Morgan County, MARTHA L. GORDON, consort of JAMES P. GORDON, aged 21 years 4 months 28 days.

Died in Meridianville on the 8th, MISS MARY FANNIE, daughter of MR. and MRS. BOYLE P. HUMPHREY (Bible record) aged about 19.

December 7, 1857
Died in this place on 10th, MRS. NEELY, wife of R. T. NEELY.

Died in this place on 8th, THOMAS LEONARD. (1850 census shows him aged 35 born in Tennessee)

Married in this vicinity on 1st by REV. P. B. ROBINSON, MR. THOMAS RUTLEDGE to MRS. FRANCIS A. BAILEY, all of this county.

Married on 6th by REV. P. B. ROBINSON, MR. CHARLES F. RALEIGH of Lawrence County, Alabama to MARY A. FRENCH of Decatur, Alabama.

December 24, 1857
Married on December 10th by HON. W. T. HAWKINS, M. J. M. HORNE and MISS MARY H. REED, all of Florence.

Married on 15th by REV. MR. DAVIDSON, MR. M. M. SLAUGHTER, editor of Talladega Democratic Watchtower to MISS ELIZABETH CALLEY of that county.

Died in Meridianville, Alabama December 8, 1857, MISS MARY FANNIE, daughter of MR. and MRS. BOYLE P. HUMPHREY aged 17.

Died on 14th instant near New Market of consumption, JOHN T. JONES, a respectable citizen of this county. (Note: This is JOHN TANNEHILL JONES, born November 16, 1814; Bible record says died December 15th, 1857. He was son of GEORGE TANNEHILL JONES and wife REBECCA CAMPBELL BROWN.)

Died on 8th, COL. ELIAS WILBURN, an old and respectable citizen of this county after a protracted illness. (1850 census aged 54 born in Georgia)

Died in Nebraska Territory on the 5th, MR. WILLIAM L. PARKER, formerly of this place aged 24 years. Promising young man.

Died at his residence in Franklin County, Alabama on 14th of October 1857 after an illness of 13 days, of pneumonia. WILLIAM H. ALSOBROOK in the 50th (or 60th or 30th, not clear) year.

Died on 13th in Lawrence County, DR. JOHN H. MASSIE. Native of New Kent County, Virginia. His parents removed to this county when he was a child. Here he grew up, studied medicine and was a practicing physician up to the time of his death in 50th year of his age. Eminent physician...left a wife and 2 sons. (1850 census shows him aged 42 born in Virginia)

December 31, 1857
　　Departed this life on 6th of December p.m., ROBERT BAULCH of
Lawrence County, Alabama aged 59 years 11 days. (In 1850 census aged
50 born in North Carolina)
　　Died in Marshall, Harrison County, Texas on 24th of November,
WILLIAM D. GOODLETT, formerly of Moulton, Alabama.
　　Married on 24th by REV. W. D. CHADICK, MR. DAVID B. STRADFORD to
MISS ANN E. HUNT, all of Huntsville.
　　Married on 29th, MR. JOHN E. SNODGRASS to MISS MARY DUBLIN, both
of this county.
　　Married on 23rd by REV. MR. MILLIGAN, JAMES H. COLLIER to MISS
MARGARET E. VANN, both of this county.
　　Married on 24th, MONTRAVILLE FRANKLIN to MISS MARY C. MORRIS,
both of this county.
　　Married on 16th, WM. H. WINFREY to MISS MARY F. BINION, both of
this county:
　　Married on 1st by REV. P. B. ROBINSON, THOMAS RUTLEDGE to
MISS FRANCES A. BAILEY, both of this county.
　　Married on 6th by same, CHARLES P. RALEY to MISS MARY A. FRENCH,
both of this county.
　　Married by REV. J. C. JONES at the residence of the bride's father
in Wilcox County, Alabama (copied for DR. SELLERS) on 28th, HON. CHARLES
S. SCOTT (Representative in Congress from California) to MISS ANN V.
GORIN, eldest daughter of G. GORIN, Esq.
　　Married on 16th in the vicinity of Triana, by REV. J. G. WILSON,
MR. JACOB L. HERRING of Mooresville to MISS PAULINA BALL.
　　Married on the 17th by JOHN A. JOHNSON, Esq., MR. WILLIAM M.
SIMPSON (WM. W. in license) to MISS MARY A. McBROOM of Limestone
(volume 223, page 74).
　　Married on 16th by REV. T. W. RANDLE, MR. LARKIN SULLIVAN to
MRS. R. A. CULLOCH (MRS. RHODA CARLOCK), all of this county. (spelling
you haven't noted it, on page 90, SULLIVAN by RHODA CARLOCK. Guess the
Editor spelled it as he heard it!)
　　Married on 16th by REV. T. W. RANDLE, MR. JEHU LAWLER to MRS.
SUE LAWLER (24 in Virginia), all of this county (SUSAN A. THOMPSON
married 15 December 1846 JAMES LAWLER; 2. JEHUE LAWLER 16 December 1857;
volume 155, page 35, 25).
　　Married on 22nd by REV. P. B. ROBINSON, J(OHN) W. SEVERS to MISS
LUCY TILLER, all of this county.
　　Married on 17th December at Laman's Ferry, Madison County by
REV. ALEX. PENLAND, MR. REUBEN WEBSTER to MISS SARAH JANE GRIFFIN.
　　By same on December 23rd in Morgan County, Alabama near Valhermoso
Springs, WILLIAM F. MATHERSON to MISS AMANDA McCUTCHEN.
　　By same, December 24th at STEPHEN M. RICHARDS above Whitesburg,
Madison County, JAMES H. JOHNSON to MISS MARY P. RICHARDS.
　　Married at the residence of CAPT. W(ILLIAM) S(TRATTON) JONES near
Russelville on the 8th by REV. R. H. RIVERS, D.D., DR. JOHN K(ING)
CLARKE to MISS EVIE W. JONES (EVELINA ELDRIDGE WYATT JONES, daughter of
WM. STRATTON JONES and wife ANN HARRIS COX--see COX-JONES Bible).

January 7, 1858
　　Nothing of interest

January 14, 1858
　　Married on the 6th by REV. P. B. ROBINSON, PROF. H. S. SARONI and
MRS. ANNA DILL, all of this place.
　　Married at St. John's Church in Montgomery on the 7th by RT. REV.
N. H. COBBS, MR. JOHN ALEXANDER ELLERBE of Dallas County, Alabama to
MISS MARTHA S. COBBS, daughter of RT. REV. BISHOP COBBS.
　　Married on 7th of January 1858 in Panola County, Mississippi by
REV. R. L. ANDREWS, MR. JOHN A. GILCHRIST of North Alabama to MISS
TEXANA A. JONES.
　　Departed this life (see volume 82, page 1, 2) at her late residence
near Centre Hill, DeSoto County, Mississippi, MRS. SUSAN DEMENT,
daughter of REV. WM. BYRD of North Alabama. Her earlier days were
passed in Alabama where she was married. (See our volume 4, page 4
for marriage of JAMES (MOSELEY) DEMENT to SUSANNAH BYRD, 28 October
1817, Madison County, Alabama.)

January 21, 1858
    Married on Wednesday 30th, at the residence of MR. JAMES PEARING,
by REV. B. B. BARKER, MR. GEORGE EWING, formerly of Huntsville, Alabama
to MISS KATE STEVENS of Noxubee County, Mississippi.
    Married on 7th at the residence of MR. JOHN R. GEORGE by DAVID L.
DINSMORE, Esq., MR. JOHN T. HAMPTON to MISS SARAH ANN CROW, all of
Lawrence County, Alabama. (In license it is JOHN J. W. HAMPTON)
    Married on 7th by REV. P. P. ROBINSON, MR. JAMES GOOCH and MISS
KATE SEVERS, all of this county.
    Married on 20th ult by REV. H. N. PHARR, MR. JOSEPH W. PHILLIPS,
Editor of Chambers Tribune to MISS ELIZA S. (N. in license), daughter
of COL. CHARLES McLEMORE of Chambers County (license says married
December 20, 1857).
    Married in Talladega County on 24th ult. by REV. A. B. McKORKLE,
MR. JASPER E. WILSON to MISS DARTHULA M., daughter of GEN. JACOB T.
BRADFORD.
    Died on 20th December, MR. JOSEPH G. EVETTS of Lawrence County,
Alabama aged 64 years 9 months 21 days. (In 1850 aged 57 born in
North Carolina)
    Died in Rusk County, Texas November 30, 1857, MRS. MARY EUBANK,
wife of THOMAS EUBANK (58 in Virginia; 1812 pension--married in Bedford
County, Virginia 1816--March 7 MARY GIBSON), formerly a citizen of
Lawrence County, Alabama aged about 70 years. (In 1850 aged 55 born in
Virginia)
    Died in this place very suddenly on 1st of November 1857 of
apoplexy, MRS. MARTHA ALLEN NORTHCUT aged 65 years 3 months. Born in
Pittsylvania County, Virginia, married quite young. Moved to Tennessee
thence to Alabama where she remained until time of her death. For
last 10 years a resident of this place. She and 7 daughters composed
her family...Baptist.
    (To be continued in a later volume)

April 10, 1878
    Died in Huntsville Saturday, April 6th of pneumonia, MR. JOHN HUEY
in his 73rd year, an old and esteemed citizen of this county and one
of the eldest members of the Helion Masonic Lodge and for the past 25
years held the position of tylor.

May 15, 1878
    Died in this city early this morning, MRS. L(OUISA) A. HEREFORD,
beloved consort of MR. CHARLES A (should be W.) HEREFORD in her 43rd
year of a painful and lingering illness. Member of the Cumberland
Presbyterian Church...left her husband and two daughters to mourn her
loss.
    Died near this city last night, ALFRED ELLETT in his 70th year.
    Married at Athens, Alabama (Limestone County) Thursday the 9th
instant at the Cumberland Presbyterian Church at 8 p.m. by REV. G. W.
MITCHELL, REV. R. W. BENGE, pastor of said church to MISS HATTIE E.
TYUS (7 in Alabama; daughter of MRS. ANGELINA TYUS).
    Married at the residence of MRS. FANNIE SHOENBERGER in this
vicinity on May 15, 1878 by REV. G. W. MITCHELL of Athens (Limestone
County) MR. DAVID K. WEST of Giles County, Tennessee to MRS. SUE E.
McCLELLAN, daughter of the late CHARLES STRONG of Madison County.

May 22, 1878
    Married at the residence of MR. W. A. BLAIR in this city at
9½ o'clock this morning, MR. JAMES H. MAYHEW and MISS MATILDA S. FRENCH,
REV. MR. GRAVES officiating.

July 3, 1878
    Died Saturday last, 22nd ult. at his plantation near Canton,
Mississippi, HENRY C. G. SHACKELFORD. JUDGE SHACKELFORD held several
positions of honor in his state and was a gentleman of high culture and
dignified deportment. He married a daughter of the late CAPTAIN GEORGE
STEELE. This widow and children have our sympathy.

August 21, 1878
    REV. JOHN MURRYA ROBERTSON departed this life at his residence in
the vicinity of Huntsville Wednesday night August 7th...resolutions of
respect by Church of Nativity, J. M. BANISTER, Rector.

September 11, 1878
      Died of congestion in Phillip(s) County, Arkansas, August 3rd,
MOLLIE, eldest daughter of HARVEY and MARY NANCE, aged 19 years and
1 month.

September 25, 1878
      Died at his late residence on Monte Sano of pernicious bilious
fever Friday, September 20, 1878, ROBERT HERSTEIN in the 47th year of
his age. Born in Grand Duchy of Hesse, Dermstadt, Germany and came to
this country in his teens; located for several years at Leesburg,
Virginia and moved to Huntsville in 1855...merchant. Leaves a widow
and 7 children.

November 13, 1878
      Married in this city November 11 by REV. C. W. HEARN, MR. THOMAS H.
McALLISTER and MISS AMY STINE....

February 25, 1880
      Died at his residence in this city Sunday, February 22, THOMAS S.
McCALLEY, native of Spotsylvania County, Virginia. Born February 13,
1807. Removed when quite a young man to Huntsville. Successful merchant
and planter. Member of Episcopal Church.

June 9, 1880
      Died in this city at the residence of her mother, MRS. CARUTHERS
on Tuesday afternoon, MRS. COLTART, widow of the late ROBERT W. COLTART
after a long illness.

June 23, 1880
      Died the 17th instant at her husband's in Moulton (Lawrence
County), MRS. NAOMI SOPHIA PETERS (28 in Alabama), wife of JUDGE THOMAS M.
PETERS (39 in Tennessee) of that place. The deceased was born in
Lawrence County and was the daughter of WILLIAM and NAOMI LEETCH
(73 in North Carolina). Her mother was the aunt of PRESIDENT POLK.
Educated at celebrated school Southmayd in Huntsville. Married June 26,
1838 in her 18th year to THOMAS M. PETERS, then a young lawyer but
afterwards Chief Justice of the Supreme Court of this state. Presbyterian. Died in her 60th year. Left a husband and 5 children. (see
her mother in 1850 census)

August 11, 1880
      Death of two old and highly r-spected citizens MR. CHARLES W.
HEREFORD, prominent merchant and life long resident of this county, died
after a brief illness at his residence in this city last Saturday
morning in his 46th year. Remains deposited in the city cemetery by
Knights of Honor.
      MR. G. S. MASTIN, leading planter of this county died at his
residence in this city yesterday evening in his 56th year. Both leave
a large circle of relatives.

September 15, 1880
      Died Saturday last, 11th instant at his residence in this city,
JAMES W. POLLARD, an old and respectable citizen. Born in this city
in 1828 and had been continuously connected with municipal government
since 1855.

September 22, 1880
      JUDGE MANNING of Alabama Supreme Court is no more. He died on
the night of 17th in New York. Elected to Supreme Court Bench 6 years
ago and re-elected without opposition last August. Alabama mourns
the loss of one of her noblest sons.
      WILLIAM C. McPHERSON died Tuesday at midnight after illness of
3 days...his father, COL. JOHN W. McPHERSON of Hopkinsville, Kentucky
arrived a few hours before his son's death.

October 13, 1880
      COL. JOSEPH C. BRADLEY died the 6th at his residence in this city.
Born near Abingdon, Virginia in 1810, he removed to Madison County,
Alabama in 1825 and began business career as clerk in large commission

House of JAMES BRADLEY, his brother...paralysis...Presbyterian...was
an affectionate father and husband.

November 3, 1880
       BISHOP DANIEL S. DOGGETT of M. E. Church South died at his residence
in Richmond, Virginia last night, 27th, after protracted illness.
Born in Lancaster County, Virginia 1810. His father was worthy member
of the Bar of that county (New York Herald).

February 1, 1884
       Died January 27, 1884 after a brief illness at her residence in
Limestone County, Alabama, MALINDA ROBINSON HUNDLEY, relict of the late
DR. JOHN H. HUNDLEY being nearly 80 years old. She was born in
Greenville County, Virginia April, 1804, the only daughter of DANIEL
ROBINSON, a most respectable merchant and planter of that county and
state. After her marriage in 1824, she came with her husband to reside
in Alabama, where she has had her home ever since...(Greensville County,
Virginia marriages by Know born September 1824 JOHN H. HUNDLEY and
MALINDA ROBINSON. Surety: SAMPSON ROBINSON, married by REV. JAMES
MORRIS, page 94)
       Died Tuesday the 22nd instant of pneumonia, JOHN L. FARISS, an
old and valuable citizen of this city in his 74th year. Born in Amelia
County, Virginia. Early schoolboy days were spent near Courtland,
Alabama (Lawrence County) and he came to Huntsville in 1826 and worked
in the Southern Advocate Office with his brother, DANDRIDGE FARISS. He
married MISS KATE WILSON in 1835. For awhile resided in Mobile, Alabama
but afterwards moved back to this city and became engaged in the drug
business with the late GEORGE W. NEAL. To his aged companion, consolation
and to her child and grandchildren.

February 29, 1884
       At Green Pond, Lawrence County lives MR. JOSEPH ELKINS (59 in
Georgia), who was born in Wilkes County, Georgia on the 29th day of
January, 1791, consequently he is over 93. He moved to Madison County
in 1817 living 1 mile north of Hazel Green four years when he moved to
Lawrence County. In 1821 he killed three bears in one day. He has
seven girls, two boys, 46 grandchildren, 89 great-grandchildren and a
few great-great-grandchildren.

March 7, 1884
       Died at her residence in Huntsville on Saturday night March 1st
of pneumonia, MRS. INDIA TEAGUE, 46 years old.

March 21, 1884
       Died Saturday at 8 a.m. March 15th at Denver, Colorado, J. C
GREENE, Esq., formerly a well known citizen of Huntsville aged about 26.

March 28, 1884
       Died February 14th, OTHNEL RICE at his home about 4 miles of New
Market on Hester's Creek, aged 88 of erysipalis. Was one of oldest
and most highly respected citizens of Madison County...Mason...had been
Tax Assessor of Madison County and J. P. for 20 years. Raised 10
children, living to bury them all. His wife died about 6 years ago.

April 4, 1884
       Died at her home on Holmes Street March 31 of typhoid pneumonia,
MISS LULA PANKEY, daughter of MRS. W. J. PANKEY.

May 2, 1884
       Died March 10th at his home near Brownsboro, OSCAR J. HARRIS in
his 58th year. Left his widow and orphan.

May 30, 1884
       Died--WALTER S. BARRATT. Born in England in 1842, emigrated to
America and located in the state of New York in 1871. Was happily
married to MISS RUTHA E. BAKER in 1872. Died in Huntsville April 30th
leaving his wife and a little daughter.
       Died at Florence, Alabama Saturday May 24th, JUDGE T. H. LOGWOOD,
formerly of Memphis, late of Austin, Texas. The writer knew him as a

soldier, Judge and citizen...after the war, he was elected Judge of the Criminal Court of Memphis. About 16 years since, he married MISS KATE, daughter of GEN. SAMUEL D. WEAKLEY of Florence. They had 3 boys, two of whom died and only one, 14 years of age, survives.

July 4, 1884
    Died in Huntsville at the residence of his cousin, MRS. BLUNT, on Thursday, July 3rd, ex-governor, DAVID P. LEWIS aged 63.

September 12, 1884
    Departed this life at her home in this city on Sunday, September 7th, MRS. MARY A. McCULLOUGH, wife of A. W. McCULLOUGH, Esq. in her 43rd year. Had been a resident of Huntsville for more than 18 years.

October 3, 1884
    Died at his Huntsville home on Sunday, September 28, 1884, J. E. ERWIN aged 46.

ALABAMA REFERENCES FROM TENNESSEE PAPERS

Contributed by MR. PRENTISS PRICE, JR., Rogersville, Tennessee

NOTES FROM KNOXVILLE REGISTER (TENNESSEE)

Established 3 August 1816

December 7, 1816
    Married at COL. GEORGE W. SEVIER's on Tuesday last, COL. DAVID VERTNER of Natchez to MRS. RUTHA SPARKS, daughter of GEN. JOHN SEVIER, deceased, of this county, and relict of the late COL. SPARKS of the U.S. Army. (volume 1, #19)

December 15, 1818
    Married on Thursday evening the 26th ult., MR. RICHARD PURDOM, merchant of Huntsville (Alabama Territory) to MISS SUSAN SEVIER, daughter of JAMES SEVIER, Esq. of Washington County, Tennessee.

January 11, 1820
    Died at Kymulgee, St. Clair County, Alabama on the 18th December ROBERT SINGLETON, son of MAJ. JOHN SINGLETON of Blount County, Tennessee (volume 4, #181).

September 19, 1820
    Act of Congress for the relief of the legal representatives of HENRY WILLIS; to enter not to exceed 1300 arpents of land in any land office in Mississippi or Alabama in lieu of two tracts on Bayou Sarah which have been sold by the U.S. dated 8 May 1820 (volume 5, #217).

October 2, 1821
    $10 Reward; Runaway on the night of the 5th instant a negro man named JOE, a bright mulatto; formerly belonged to COL. POPE and a servant at the Bank in Huntsville. JOHN J. WINSTON, Madison County September 8 near Triana (volume 6, #271).

October 29, 1822
    Died at the residence of her son in Cotton Fort (Limestone County), Alabama, MRS. HANNAH DEWOODY, consort of WM. DEWOODY, deceased, on the 13th July 1822 aged 54 years. Note: WILLIAM DEWOODY married in Washington County, Tennessee HANNAH ALEXANDER 26 March 1791. See "Suanders Early Settlers" page 106, JOHN SIMMONS and the DEWOODYS into which family he married more than 61? years since descended the Tennessee River in a flat boat. The DEWOODYS landed at a place called Cotton-Gin Port in Limestone County. The DEWOODYS were a very respectable family and descended from WM. DEWOODY who emigrated from Ireland when 18 years of age. His wife was HANNAH ALEXANDER, a Pennsylvanian by birth. They had a large family of children, one of them, JOHN, was a Cumberland Presbyterian preacher. One daughter, ELIZA, married JAS. HUBBARD, another daughter, AGNES G., married JOHN SIMMONS. Ancestors

of MRS. ANDREW HEATON (MARGUERITE), Route 3, Box 674, Mena, Arkansas
January 27, 1965.

October 29, 1822
      Notice from Wilcox County, Alabama Circuit Court September Term
1822.   JOHN LOONEY, agent of DAVID GORDON who is assignee of LEWIS TYUS
versus ALEXANDER S. OUTLAW.

November 5, 1822
      Notice from Circuit Court (doesn't say where: L. MEAD, C.C.
Note: LEMUEL MEAD was Circuit Clerk of Madison County, Alabama.
P. J. G.): JOHN HEMBLEN versus HANNAH HAMBLEN for divorce: publication
ordered in Knoxville Register and in a Huntsville paper (note by
P. P. JOHN HAMBLEN moved from Hawkins County, Tennessee to Madison
County, Alabama).

October 17, 1823
      Married in Athens on Tuesday the 7th instant by the REV. D. P.
BESTOR, MR. ALEXANDER A. McCARTNEY, Editor of the Alabama Gazette to
MISS JANE BEATY, both formerly of Huntingdon, Pennsylvania (1830 census
Limestone County, Alabama ALEX. A. McCARTNEY 1 m 30-40, 1 f 20-30).

October 24, 1823
      MAJ. FRANCIS W. ARMSTRONG of Mobile and formerly of this place is
appointed by the President of the United States, Marshall of the
state of Alabama.

September 24, 1824
      Died the 5th instant in the State of Alabama, DOCTOR BENJAMIN
HARRISON of Kingston after a lingering illness of ten weeks, leaving
a wife and five small children.

October 22, 1824
      Huntsville, Alabama bank robbed 13th ult.

April 10, 1826
      Died Sunday, the 26th ult. in Florence, Alabama, MR. EDWARD S.
CAREY, aged 25, one of the Editors of the Florence Gazette. His father
and other relations reside in this county (volume 10, #503).

September 5, 1827
      $50 Reward. Runaway...the above reward will be given for his being
returned to the subscriber living near Moulton, Lawrence County,
Alabama. THOMAS KYLE

April 20, 1831
      Married on the 5th April in Washington City by the REV. MR.
MATTHEWS, COL. FRANCIS W(ELLS) ARMSTRONG of Alabama to MISS ANN M.
MILLARD, daughter of MR. MILLARD, merchant of that city. (2nd wife--
his 1st wife, ELIZ. AYLETT, died 1823 as a bride, in Mobile; From
National Intelligencer, Washington, D.C. April 8, 1831, "COL. FRANCIS W.
ARMSTRONG of Alabama and ANN M. MILLARD, daughter of JOSHUA MILLARD of
this city were married April 5, by REV. MR. MATTHEWS")

October 5, 1831
      Died in Jackson County, Alabama on the morning of the 16th of
September after an illness of five days, MRS. MARY CLAYTON, consort
of the late DANIEL CLAYTON, deceased, aged about 55 years.

November 16, 1831
      Died in the 48th year of his age, in Lauderdale County, Alabama,
(at his residence), on the 20th of September. ISAAC BROWNLOW, Esq.
Parents of the deceased came from Rockbridge County, Virginia, in early
life. They raised a respectable and intelligent family of sons, three
of whom, viz: WILLIAM, JOHN and ALEXANDER, died officers in the
United States Navy.

November 30, 1831
    Married on the 10th of November, SAMUEL PROCTER, Esq. to MISS
MARGARET DONOTHON, daughter of the REV. MR. DONOTHON, all of Jackson
County, Alabama (see 1850 census of Jackson County, Alabama).

January 9, 1833
    Married at Gunter's Landing, Alabama on the 1st day of November
1832, by the REV. C. PUTNAM, MR. BENJAMIN HENSLEY to MISS CATHARINE
AIKEN, all of McMinn County, Tennessee.

June 12, 1833
    Died on Saturday the 25th instant, after a long and painful
illness, MRS. SARAH E. McCLUNG, daughter of JOHN MITCHELL, Esq., late
Governor of Georgia, and consort of JAMES W. McCLUNG, Esq. of that
town (Huntsville Southern Advocate).

July 24, 1833
    Died at his late residence in the vicinity of Florence, Alabama
on the 8th instant, GENERAL JOHN COFFEE, a distinguished officer of
the late war, in the 62nd year of his age.

August 21, 1833
    Died of consumption at the Knoxville Hotel on Thursday the 15th
instant, CESAR COCLOUGH, Esq. of Montgomery, Alabama.

August 28, 1833
    Married in Clinton on the 22nd instant by the REV. SAMUEL LOWE,
MR. JOHN W. RUTHLAND (RUTLAND?; 41 in North Carolina) of Madison County,
Alabama to MISS MARGARET ANN BARTON (37 in Tennessee), daughter of
DOCTOR HUGH BARTON (76 in Virginia; ancestor of MRS. MARY LOLLAR,
Tuscaloosa, Alabama 1956).

September 25, 1833
    Married in this town on the 11th instant, by the REV. MR. SLOSS,
MR. DONALD CAMPBELL of Mooresville to MISS ELIZABETH McKINLEY, eldest
daughter of COL. JOHN McKINLEY (Florenze Gazette).

January 17, 1838
    Murder of COL. EDWARD WARD of Shelby County, Tennessee December 22nd.
1837 by the brothers, LAFAYETTE, CHAMBERLAYNE, DR. CAESER and ACHILLES
JONES. (note by P.P.--EDWARD WARD moved from Davidson to Shelby
County, Tennessee)

KNOXVILLE ENQUIRER

July 26, 1826
    Died at Tuscumbia, Alabama on the 11th instant MR. JOHN GODDARD
of this county.

November 22, 1826
    MRS. RACHEL CULLEN, wife of JOHN M. CULLEN, late of Knoxville, died
11 ult. (October) at Triana, leaving a husband and six children (from
Huntsville, Alabama Democrat).

NASHVILLE WHIG

June 29, 1813
    Married on Sunday the 22nd instant, MR. JOHN READ of Huntsville,
M. T. to MISS MARY RICHARDSON of Warren County, Kentucky.

May 9, 1821
    Married on Thursday evening last, MR. SPOTSWOOD JONES of Alabama
to MISS ELIZA HAYWOOD, daughter of HON. JOHN HAYWOOD of this county.

NASHVILLE WHIG AND TENNESSEE ADVERTISER

January 16, 1819
   Died lately at Mobile, MADAME MARY FONTINNELLE, at the very
advanced age of 105, and for the last 70 years a resident of that
place.

March 29, 1820
   Married on Tuesday evening 7th instant, NICHOLAS HOBSON, Esq.,
merchant of Huntsville to MISS SUSAN A. LANIER, daughter of the
REV. WILLIAM LANIER, all of Madison County.

July 26, 1820
   Married on the 21st June, GEORGE W. OWEN, Esq. of Claiborne to
MISS LOUISA HOLLINGER of Baldwin County, Alabama.
   Wednesday, 22nd ult., THOMAS ROGERS, Esq., Secretary of the State
of Alabama.

January 2, 1819
   Married on the same evening Thursday last by the REV. MR. HODGE,
CAPT. B. B. JONES of the Alabama Territory, to MISS MARTHA HAYWOOD,
daughter of JOHN HAYWOOD, Esq. of this county.

July 31, 1819
   Died in this county on the 28th instant, BENJAMIN BRANCH.

NASHVILLE REPUBLICAN

December 30, 1826
   Died on Thursday night, 22nd instant, the HON. JOHN HAYWOOD.

December 3, 1835
   Died suddenly in Triana, Alabama, HON. WM. J. ADAIR, Judge of the
5th Judicial Circuit in that State.

January 5, 1836
   Married in Dresden (Weakley County), Tennessee DR. WM. H. JENKINS
of Alabama to MISS ANN GLENN.

June 28, 1836
   Died in the vicinity of this place, MRS. SUSANNAH C. PAINE,
consort of REV. ROBERT PAINE, President of LaGrange College, Alabama.

July 19, 1836
   Died in Florence, Alabama, MRS. MARTHA, consort of THOS. CHILDRESS,
Esq., formerly of this place.
   Died in Sumpter County, Alabama COL. THOMAS HENDERSON, late of
Madison County, Tennessee.

June 13, 1835
   Married in this place on Wednesday morning last (see marriage
record volume 174, page 73), by the REV. MR. CUNNINGHAM, MR. WALTER B.
WRIGHT to MISS PAULINE SNYDER, the armless lady, exhibited throughout
the U.S. (Montgomery Advertiser).

June 4, 1835
   Married in Courtland, Alabama MR. FELIX SHERROD to MISS SARAH A(NN),
daughter of the late COL. JOEL PARRISH of this place (married May 28,
1835).

ALABAMA REFERENCES FROM NORTH CAROLINA NEWSPAPERS

Taken from Bulletin Published by North Carolina State Library

RALEIGH REGISTER

February 20, 1804
  ROBERT COMAN to JANE WADE PROUT--marriage--February 6, Wadesborough
(note: this couple later lived in Limestone County, Alabama).

August 4, 1808
  DR. D. MOORE of Nashville married HARRIET HAYWOOD of this state.
August Tennessee (note: This couple later settled in Madison County,
Alabama).

December 22, 1815
  FRANCIS INGE of Granville County to REBECCA C. WILLIAMS. December.
Warren County. (note: FRANCIS INGE later settled in Greene County,
Alabama where he died).

February 13, 1818
  COL. LEMUEL J. ALSTON (Rev. sol.) of Alabama territory to MRS.
JOSEPH J. WILLIAMS, JR. of Halifax County. February 3. Halifax County.

June 25, 1819
  CAPT. JAMES H. DEARING of Alabama married JULIA ANN SEARCY June 10.

July 7, 1820
  WILLIAM ALSTON of Alabama married MARY HAYWOOD June 22, Halifax
County.

December 22, 1820
  JOHN T. SCOTT of Alabama and this state married MARY KNOX December 5,
Sneedsborough.

January 24, 1821
  MRS. OLIVER FITTS of Mississippi Territory died January 20,
Warrenton.

July 20, 1821
  HENRY B. SLADE of Martin County died July in Alabama.

March 8, 1822
  JAMES BELL of Pitt County died January 26 in Alabama.

August 16, 1822
  GEORGE TUNSTALL of Raleigh married ELOUISA MATILDA MARY TATE of
Alabama July 4.

September 6, 1822
  THOMAS W. SCOTT of Raleigh to NANCY HEWLETT. September, Madison
County, Alabama.

April 11, 1823
  JOHN F. FOREST of Raleigh died March 23 in Alabama (Jefferson
and Madison Counties).

December 31, 1824
  JOSEPH GEE of this state died December in Alabama.

January 14, 1825
  PEYTON H. LILES of Raleigh to MARY C. KIMBELL of Warren County.
November. Alabama. Note: This marriage is in Morgan County, Alabama.

May 10, 1825
  MAJ. WILLIAM RUSSELL of Rutherford County died May in Franklin
County, Alabama.

October 7, 1825
IRA PORTES of Nash County died September 8 in Alabama (Raleigh Register; Clarke County).

November 11, 1825
MAJ. ALEXANDER ROLAND of Robeson County died October 12 in Alabama.

June 23, 1826
LUNSFORD L. ALSOBROOKE of Alabama (of Tuscumbia; see volume 5, page 32) married TEMPERANCE B. EATON June 7 in Warren County.

November 17, 1826
DEMPSEY FULLER of Raleigh died October 18, in Alabama.

December 15, 1826
BENNET B. EASON of Edgecombe county died November 2 in Alabama (1 BENNETT EASON estate 1830 in Lawrence County).

February 2, 1827
MRS. LEMUEL D. BERRY of Alabama died in January in Pitt County.

February 6, 1827
FRANCIS P. CASSO of Raleigh died January 1 in Tuscaloosa, Alabama.

May 1, 1827
THOMAS COLEMAN of Anson County died February 26 in Montgomery, Alabama.

May 11, 1827
REV. WILLIAM TERRY of this state died April 16 in Alabama.

June 26, 1827
MAJ. CHARLES M. RIDDLE of Chatham County died May 8 in Greene County, Alabama.

November 16, 1827
SMITH MURPHY of Alabama married SARAH R. JONES November 13 in Wake County.

March 25, 1828
BRYAN BOROUGH of Moore county died February 19 in Alabama.

July 22, 1828
PETER MAHLER married SUSAN NEAL of Orange County July in Tuscaloosa, Alabama.

September 23, 1828
THOMAS A. WILLIAMS of Cumberland county died August 28 at Claiborne, Alabama.

November 7, 1828
COL. WILLIAM C. WATSON of this state died October 27 in Henry County, Alabama.

November 28, 1828
MR. S. H. GEE of Alabama married MARY T. WILLIAMS November in Warren County.

February 6, 1829
JOHN A. WILLIAMS of Raleigh died January 9 in Greene County, Alabama.

September 4, 1829
MRS. JOHN D. BARR of Greensboro died August 3 in Alabama.

September 24, 1829
RICHARD A. WIGGINS of Madison County, Alabama married ELIZA ANN DUNN (ROULSTONE; tombstone born 5-31-1811; died 8-18-1840) September 17 at Raleigh.

November 5, 1829
     DAVID WARE of this state died in October in Mobile, Alabama.
     REV. JAMES RICHARDSON of Bladen County died September 5 at
Moulter (Moulton?), Alabama.
     MRS. M'LEOD of this state died October 7 in Mobile, Alabama.
     NANCY M'LEOD of this state died October 8, in Mobile, Alabama.

November 12, 1829
     DR. F. W. H. OSBORNE of North Carolina died September 30 in
Mobile, Alabama.

December 10, 1829
     ROBERT HAWKINS of Warrenton died November 14 at Courtland, Alabama.

June 17, 1830
     THOMAS HOLMES of Salisbury (Roman County) died June in Tuscaloosa,
Alabama.
     MRS. GEORGE KERR of Hillsboro (Orange County) died June in
Tuscaloosa, Alabama.

January 27, 1831
     COL. ELISHA YOUNG of Tuscaloosa, Alabama married MARTHA STRUDWICK
of Hillsborough (Orange County), January in Tuscaloosa, Alabama.

May 5, 1831
     DR. SIDNEY S. PRINCE of Chatham County died in May in Alabama.

July 28, 1831
     MRS. FREDERICK B. NELSON of Washington, Beaufort county died
July in Alabama.

October 13, 1831
     THEOPHILUS LACY, SR. of Rickingham County died in October in
Morgan County, Alabama (see tombstone).

May 7, 1833
     ELIJAH WHEALINGTON of Alabama married FANNY MASK of Richmond
County April 21, in Richmond County.

July 16, 1833
     SIDNEY R. HINTON of Wake County died July in Greensboro, Alabama.

November 5, 1833
     JORDAN HILL of Raleigh married MISS CAROLINE MARY BIRD of Orange
County October 24 in Greensboro, Alabama.

April 1, 1834
     DUNCAN WHITESIDES of Hillsborough (Orange County) died March 22
in Marion, Alabama.

May 13, 1834
     ABSALOM WOODALL of Johnston County died February 4 in Greene
County, Alabama.

July 22, 1834
     GAIUS WHITFIELD of Alabama married MARY ANN B. WHITFIELD July 15
in Lenoir County.

August 26, 1834
     CALVIN M. HIGH of Alabama married LAVINA SARAH JETER of Raleigh
August 21 in Raleigh.

September 16, 1834
     DR. GEORGE W. DISMUKES of Chatham county died August 12 in Autauga
County, Alabama.
     ALEXANDER HAMILTON HENDERSON of Rockingham County died August 18
in Sumpter County, Alabama.

September 30, 1834
GEORGE M. JOHNSON of Wake County died September 4 in Greensborough, Alabama.
MRS. DAVID DONLOP of Franklin County died August 7 in Marengo County, Alabama.

November 4, 1834
ALBERT G. M'GEHEE of Alabama married ANN V. PAYNE, November in Caswell County.

July 7, 1835
TIGNAL JONES of Morgan county married SUSAN KING of Lawrence County both formerly of Wake County June 28 in Alabama.

August 4, 1835
MRS. ANN RAMSEY of Chatham County died in September in Marengo County, Alabama.
MRS. A. B. W. HOPKINS of Wake County died July 8 in Greene County, Alabama.

September 22, 1835
MRS. CORNELIUS MOORE of Anson County died September in Autauga County, Alabama.

October 20, 1835
BENJAMIN S. KING of Raleigh died September 29 in Greensboro, Alabama.
DR. DAVID RUSSELL of Vernon (Lamar County), Alabama married LUCY J. DICKSON October 8 in Duplin County.

November 3, 1835
HECTOR McKENZIE of Robeson County died October 13 in Sumpter County, Alabama.

November 10, 1835
BENJAMIN HORTON of Alabama married LUCY BOWLING of Iredell County September 11 in Iredell County.

January 5, 1836
LAUCHLIN CURRIE of Alabama married SARAH M'DONALD December 4 in Richmond County
JOHN J. HUMPHREYS of Talladega, Alabama married ADELIA ARMIDA CHUM December 19 in Asheville (Buncombe County).

March 1, 1836
GEORGE A. DISMUKES of Anson County (Buncombe County) died January 4 in Autauga County, Alabama.

May 3, 1836
BRYAN RICHARDSON of Johnstone County died March 19 in Sumter County, Alabama.

May 10, 1836
ZADDOCK BAKER of this state died April 1 in Greene County, Alabama.

August 2, 1836
COL. THOMAS HENDERSON of Rockingham County died June 22 in Alabama.

August 16, 1836
BOLLING DUNN of Wake County died July 21 at LaGrange, Alabama.

August 23, 1836
G. W. CHARLES of this state died July 25 in Terry (Perry?) County, Alabama.

October 18, 1836
MARY DELAH FARRETT of Edgecombe County September in "Marrengo" County, Alabama.
JOHN S. GORMAN of Raleigh died September 24, in Tuscaloosa, Alabama.

DANIEL BOOKER of this state died in September in Greensboro, Alabama (volume 180, page 35; wife GILLEY).

MILDRED S. CHARLES of Wake County died in September in Tuscaloosa, Alabama.

WILLIAM ROBINSON died in October in Montgomery, Alabama.

October 25, 1836
GEORGE HOOPER of Alabama married CAROLINE MALLET October 7 in Fayetteville (Cumberland County).

November 8, 1836
REV. DR. S. AUTRY of this state married EMILY R. BROWN in October in Madison County, Alabama.

November 22, 1836
MRS. THOMAS BARR of this state died October 27 in Selma, Alabama.

MARGARET A. KITRELL of Chapel Hill died October in Greensboro, Alabama (she was beautiful daughter of BRYANT KITTRELL. Her fiance died and she refused to marry anyone else--see KITTRELL-JONES MMG.).

BENJAMIN H. TURLAND of this state died October 8 in Montgomery, Alabama.

January 31, 1837
MRS. SAMUEL WILKINS of Newbern (Craven County) died January 8 in Mobile, Alabama.

February 14, 1837
REV. JOHN AVERY of this state died January 17 in Green County, Alabama.

March 28, 1837
LEVI W. YOUNG of Alabama married SARAH CLANCY March 17 in Hillsborough (Orange County).

May 2, 1837
WILLIAM C. PALMER of Orange County married AMARENTHA GARY in April in Marion, Alabama.

May 9, 1837
FRANCIS P. CLINGMAN (CLINGHAM in marriage record) married APPHIA ROSE of Stokes County in April in Morgan County, Alabama.

June 19, 1837
COL. CALVIN R. BLACKMAN of Wayne County died in June in Sumpter County, Alabama.

July 17, 1837
JOSEPH SEAWELL married ELIZA C. CAMPBELL of Fayetteville (Orange County) June 24 in Mobile, Alabama.

July 24, 1837
MRS. CHARLES ODOM of Wake County died May 6 in Limestone County, Alabama.

August 14, 1837
JOHN LOCKHART of Greensborough, Alabama married TEMPERANCE HARRIS July 27 in Orange County.

August 21, 1837
WILLIAM D. WEBSTER of Milton (Caswell County) died July 23 in Athens, Alabama.

September 18, 1837
MARTHA ANN ELIZABETH CROSSLAND of Warrenton died August 29 in Greensborough, Alabama.

September 25, 1837
BRYAN HINES of Erie, Alabama married ELMINA HOYLE September 12 in Hoylesville.

BENJAMIN S. KING of Raleigh died August 30 in Greene County, Alabama.

October 23, 1837
    BRYANT KITTRELL (ancestor of EMILY THOMASON PETERSEN, 1958) of Chapel Hill died September 21 in Greensborough, Alabama (see meeting from MARGARET KITTRELL to BRYANT KITTRELL both of Orange County, North Carolina about to remove to Alabama; 1832 Greene County, Alabama).

November 13, 1837
    JACK F. ROSS of this state died in November in Mobile, Alabama.

November 27, 1837
    EDWARD G(RIFFITH) PASTEUR of Newbern (Craven County) died in November in Greene County, Alabama.

December 18, 1837
    HON. WILLIAM D. PICKETT of this state died in December in Montgomery, Alabama.

December 31, 1838
    R. W. COCKERALL of Nash County married WHEATON WILLIAMS December in Greensborough, Alabama.   (AQUILLA W. COCKERALL in marriage record)
    MRS. THOMAS ASHE of this state died in December in Greensboro, Alabama.

January 21, 1839
    JOHN W. MUNDY married ANNE M. C. STEDMAN of Raleigh December 27 in Benton (Lowndes County), Alabama. (From Selma (Alabama) Free Press, December 29, 1838: married in Benton on Thursday evening last by REV. MR. WRIGHT, MR. JOHN W. MUNDY, Esq. to MISS ANN M. C. STEADMAN, all of that place)

March 4, 1839
    MRS. BRIAN HINES of Holeysville, Lincoln County died in February in Greene County, Alabama.

March 30, 1839
    MURPHY W. JONES of Alabama married HENRIETTA C. CAMPBELL March in Cumberland County.

April 13, 1839
    MARGARET ANN PICKETT of Wadesborough, Anson County, died in April in Marengo County, Alabama.

July 27, 1839
    COL. ADAM J. OSBORNE of this state died June 1 at Linden, Maringo County, Alabama.

September 28, 1839
    JOSEPH C. MOSES of Louisburg (Franklin County) died September 11 in Clinton, Alabama.
    ANDREW WALKER of Orange County died in September in Sumpter County, Alabama.

October 5, 1839
    MRS. JOHN W. SMITH of Williamston (Martin County) died in October in Greene County, Alabama.

January 17, 1840
    ISAAC R. HELLEN of Beaufort died in January in Mobile, Alabama.

January 28, 1840
    ABNER FRANKLIN in Statesville, Iredell County, died January in Gainesville, Alabama.

April 7, 1840
    MRS. WILLIAM HAWKINS died March 5 in Somerville, Morgan County, Alabama.

April 10, 1840
WM. GIOHAN (should this be GIVHAN?) of Dallas County, Alabama married MARGARET A. STEDMAN of Raleigh March 12 in Benton (Lowndes County), Alabama.

July 17, 1840
EDWARD STEDMAN of Chatham County, June 19, Spring Hill, Alabama.
HON. WILLIAM SMITH of this state died June 26 in Huntsville, Alabama.
HON. W. B. STREET of Hillsborough (Orange County) died June 20 in Greensborough, Alabama.

August 18, 1840
JAMES B. PALMER of Orange County died July 30 in Perry County, Alabama.
MRS. OBEDIUS COLLIER of Orange County died August 2 in Perry County, Alabama.

September 23, 1840
MISS RUTH A. T. WHITFIELD of Nashville died in September at Gainesville, Alabama.

October 13, 1840
MRS. RICHARD H. LEWIS of Edgecombe County died September 24 in Greensboro, Alabama.

November 6, 1840
JOHN M'LEOD of Montgomery County died in November in Shelby County, Alabama.
MRS. JOHN M'LEOD of Montgomery County died November in Shelby County, Alabama.
MRS. ANN WILLIAMS, Montgomery County, Alabama died in November in Shelby County, Alabama.

November 24, 1840
LOTT BALLARD of Onslow County and Sumpter County, Alabama married MARGARET ANN M'INTOSH November in Noxubee County, Mississippi.

November 27, 1840
MILES CAVIN of Iredell County died November 1 in Marengo County, Alabama.

December 4, 1840
A. D. CAMPBELL of Alabama married FLORA A. M'ARN November in Richmond County.

January 5, 1841
JOSEPH J. LITTLE of Alabama married ELIZA T. GILL November 24 in Franklin County. See 1850 census of Sumpter County, Alabama.

January 8, 1841
BENJAMIN FRANCKLIN PATTON of Asheville died January 1 in Clarkesville, Alabama.

March 26, 1841
DANIEL RENCHER (54 in North Carolina; see Will in Sumter County; volume 164, page 76) of Alabama married CATHARINE J. WARREN (48 in North Carolina) in March in Wake Forest (Wake County; 1st wife was CHARLOTTE).

May 14, 1841
MRS. WILLIAM GIVHAN of Raleigh died April 19 in Dallas County, Alabama.

June 4, 1841
DR. SAMUEL N. SOUTHERLAND of this state died April 30 in Gainesville, Alabama.

June 18, 1841
     GEORGE T. DUNLAP of Anson County died June in Mobile, Albama.

August 17, 1841
     DR. RICHARD INGE of Franklin County died in August in Greene
County, Alabama.

August 27, 1841
     R(OBT.) H. MADRA of this state died August 5 in Florence, Alabama.

September 14, 1841
     WILLIAM F. BENTLEY of Greensborough, Alabama to SARAH DUPRE of
Raleigh September 9 in Wake County. Note: This is WILLIAM FIELD BENTLEY,
son of EFFORD and ELIZABETH (GAY) BENTLEY.

September 17, 1841
     JOHN NORRIS of Wake County died August 20 in Tuscaloosa, Alabama.

October 12, 1841
     DAVID YARBROUGH of Hillsboro (Orange County) died September 23 in
Marion, Alabama.
     DR. HENRY YARBROUGH of Hillsboro died September 8 in Marion,
Alabama.

September 28, 1841
     JOHN GRADY, SR. of Wake County died August 24 in Chambers County,
Alabama.

October 26, 1841
     SIDNEY SMITH of Alabama married ELIZA ANN BRANNOCK in May in
Guilford County.

November 9, 1841
     GEORGE W. BAKER of Fayette County, Alabama died in November in
Salisbury.

December 10, 1841
     JOHN J. COLLIER of Alabama married ANN NELSON HUGHES of Raleigh
December 7 in Wake County.

December 17, 1841
     LODOWICK MOORE, SR. of Person County died December in Sumpter
County, Alabama.

December 31, 1841
     COL. WILLIAM W. INGE of Granville County died in December in
Livingston, Alabama.

February 13, 1842
     MRS. LEVI W. YOUNG of Hillsboro (Orange County) died February at
Demopolis, Alabama.

February 15, 1842
     WILLIAM D. TISDALE of Nash County died February in Livingston,
Alabama.

February 22, 1842
     JAMES H. CURTIS of Fayetteville (Cumberland County) married
ANNA M. BONDURANT in February in Linden, Alabama.

May 20, 1842
     THOMAS E. TARTT of Edgecombe County died May 6 in Mobile, Alabama.

July 12, 1842
     RICHARD WHITING married MARTHA M. MURRELL of Wake County July in
Tuscaloosa, Alabama.

July 26, 1842
     THOMAS W. KORNEGAY of Jones County and Tuscaloosa, Alabama died
in July in Philadelphia, Pennsylvania.

CHARLES L. ROBERTS, formerly of Raleigh and Greene County, Alabama died July 22 at Eutaw, Alabama.

August 19, 1842
ORRIN LEWIS of Connecticut and Chapel Hill died August 3 in Marion, Alabama.

August 26, 1842
JOHN DILLEHAY of Macon County, Alabama married JANE SLEDGE August 10, in Halifax County.

September 23, 1842
BURWELL P. JORDAN of Franklin County died September 20 in Alabama.

September 30, 1842
D. LINDEMAN of Raleigh died September in Mobile, Alabama.

October 21, 1842
HENRY H. MUNDY of Franklin County died October in Pickens, Alabama.
FRANCIS M. ALEXANDER of this state died in October in Mobile, Alabama.
DAVID CANNON of this state died October in Lauderdale County, Alabama.

October 28, 1842
MRS. FRANCES BOWEN of Fayetteville (Cumberland County) died October 2 in Camden, Wilcox County, Alabama.
MRS. JOHN H. FANNIN of this state died in October in Alabama.

November 8, 1842
MARTHA ANN ROBERTS of Raleigh died October 28 in Gainesville, Alabama.

December 2, 1842
COL. WILLIAM BETTS of this state died in December in Montgomery County, Alabama.

May 2, 1843
GEN. JAMES C. WATSON of Cumberland County died in May at Mount Meigs (Montgomery County), Alabama.

May 5, 1843
ASA KING of Newbern died April 16 in Greensborough, Alabama.

August 29, 1843
JAMES H. CALDWELL of Falkland, Alabama married AMELIA CAROLINE CRENSHAW of Wake Forest, August 17.

October 17, 1843
HENRY W. HORN of Fayetteville (Cumberland County) died September 28 in Mobile, Alabama.

November 10, 1843
MARY ANN HUIE of Salisbury (Roman County) died November in Autauga County, Alabama.
COL. THOMAS KENAN of this state died October 22 in Selma, Alabama.

February 13, 1844
JOSEPH HOPKINS of Wake County died January 5 in Greene County, Alabama.

February 27, 1844
SEABORN WILLIAMS (35 in South Carolina) married SUSAN W. MARTIN (32 in North Carolina) of Raleigh February 8 in Tuskegee, Alabama (Macon County census 1850).

March 8, 1844
JOHN T. HAYES of Lincoln County married CYNTHIA J. HUTCHISON of Charlotte in March in Marengo County, Alabama.

April 12, 1844
    DOCTOR BLAKE LITTLE married MRS. ELIZABETH JONES in April in
Sumter County, Alabama.

May 7, 1844
    IREDELL S. JORDAN of this state died May 6 in Dallas County,
Alabama.

July 2, 1844
    JUNIUS ALEX MOORE of Wilmington (New Hanover County) died in June
in Tuscaloosa, Alabama.

August 30, 1844
    CHARLES B. JONES of Fayetteville died July 30 in Marengo County,
Alabama.

September 13, 1844
    ALSEY H. ALLEN of Lowndes married MARY COOPER STEDMAN of Raleigh
June 18th in Dallas County, Alabama.

September 17, 1844
    RICHARD H. ROBERTS of Raleigh died September 1 in Gainesville,
Alabama.

October 4, 1844
    ROBERTS ROBERTS, JR. of Raleigh died September in Gainesville,
Alabama.

October 18, 1844
    GILES KELLY JACKSON of Greensborough, Alabama died October in
Fayetteville.

October 22, 1844
    DUKE H. HUNTINCTON (son of WM. and grandson of ROSWELL HUNTINGTON;
Rev. sol. who died in March, 1836) of Hillsboro died September 6 in
Marion, Alabama.

January 24, 1845
    WILLIAM S. MHOON of Bertie County died December 25, in Alabama.
(Tombstones in cemetery at Mhoontown, several miles to the northward
of Cherokee, Franklin County, Alabama. WILLIAM S. MHOON born in
Bertie County, North Carolina December 25, 1801; died in Franklin
County, Alabama December 26, 1844 aged 43 years. WILLIAM SPINEY MHOON
was the son of JOHN MHOON and MARY his wife. JOHN was born in Martin
County, North Carolina 12th November 1761 and died March 4, 1816. He
was the son of JOSIAH MHOON and MOURNING his wife. MARY MHOON was
born in Bertie County, North Carolina October 5, 1758; died in Tuscumbia,
Alabama October 16, 1838. She was the daughter of MOSES SPIVEY and
JEMIMA his wife (also other MHOON stones in this cemetery.)

April 1, 1845
    MAJOR JOHN LEONARD of Brunswick County and Montgomery, Alabama
died in March in Bladen County.

April 11, 1845
    ADDISON C. HINTON of Wake County died in April in Cedar Bluff
(Cherokee County), Alabama.

June 3, 1845
    REV. JOHN L. GAY married ANNE ELIZA PARKE of Wadesboro in June in
Barbour County, Alabama.

June 10, 1845
    HENRY M'KINNIE of Alabama married MARY E. VICKE of Hertford County
in June in Florida.

July 1, 1845
    MAJOR ALLEN C. JONES of this state married CATHARINE ERWIN June
in Greensborough. (Greene County, Alabama marriage Book B, page 371--

ALLEN C. JONES--MISS CATHERINE ERWIN 6 June 1845 (11 June) by T. R. HANSON, Rector of St. John Church, Greene County)

July 29, 1845
    JOHN BELL of Tuscumbia, Alabama to ELIZABETH DUNN of Wake Forest July 21, in Wake Forest.

August 15, 1845
    WILLIAM D. RICE of Greene County, Alabama married ALEY A. MARRIOTT of Wake County, August 13 at Raleigh.

September 19, 1845
    ALLEN RICHARDSON of Johnston County died in September in Pickens County, Alabama.

December 5, 1845
    GEORGE L. JONES of Newbern (Aanen County) died in November in Perry County, Alabama.

January 30, 1846
    UMSTEAD RENCHER (26 in Alabama) of Alabama (Sumter County; 1850 census) married ELIZEBETH J(EMIMA) PHILPOTT (22 in Alabama) January 11, Person County.

February 6, 1846
    GEORGE F. HUCKABEE (26 in North Carolina; Marengo County 1850 census) of Alabama to WILLIE F. CARTER (married) February in Windsor, Bertie County. (note: She died 1846 in Marengo County, Alabama and he married again. P.J.G.)

February 24, 1846
    HENRY TISDALE of Newbern (Craven County) married HARRIET BANCROFT February in Mobile, Alabama.

May 19, 1846
    JONES FULLER of Mobile, Alabama married ANNA L. THOMAS of Louisburg (Franklin County), May 13, Louisburg.

October 13, 1846
    RICHARD T. HOSKINS of Alabama to ELIZABETH A. LAWRENCE, October, Tarboro (Edgecomb County).

May 25, 1847
    FRANCIS E. CASON of Alabama to A. S. M'ALPHIN, May, Onslow County.

June 18, 1847
    GRAY BRIDGES of Marengo County, Alabama married MARGARET A. BROWN, June, Nash County.

July 8, 1847
    WILLIAM MILLER to OLIVIA BINGHAM of Raleigh, June, Tuscaloosa, Alabama.

August 4, 1847
    RICHARD HUNLEY of Alabama to MARTHA JOHNSTON, July, Lincoln County. (Note: One R. R. HUNDLEY with wife, MARTHA, was living in Lowndes County, Alabama in 1850 census. He was 25 born in North Carolina and she was 23 born in North Carolina)

March 31, 1849
    W. A. RAMSEY of Sumpterville, South Carolina married PAULINA HOOKS of Montgomery, Alabama, March 8, Winnsville, Virginia.
    WM. J. HOUSTON of Kenansville, Duplin County to INEZ HOOKS of Montgomery, Alabama March 8, Winnsville, Virginia.

June 16, 1849
    R. H. LEWIS of Greene County, Alabama to MRS. M. F. FOREMAN of Pitt County. June 5, Pitt County.

October 13, 1849
DRURY THOMPSON of Mobile, Alabama married MARY C. LAZARUS October 9,
Wake County.

October 17, 1849
RUFUS ALEXANDER HENSON of this state to MARY R. DEARING of
Tuscaloosa, Alabama September 26, Tuscaloosa, Alabama.

October 24, 1849
FRANCIS Y. TOWNSEND of Greene County, Alabama to MARY P. DANIEL of
Roxboro, Person County October 9, Roxboro, Person County.

August 23, 1851
J. D. TOLSON of Alabama to CLAUDIA MEREDITH August 19, Raleigh.
(JAS. D. TOLSON married in Greene County, Alabama 19 October 1848
MISS HENRIETTA BOZEMAN. She died May 22, 1849, born in Chowan County,
North Carolina August 3, 1826. He married 2nd--is this DUMOND?
JAS. TOLSON son of FREDERICK, Volume 20, page 5)

August 29, 1851
JOHN PARKER of Mobile married ELIZA J. PHILLIPS of Edgecomb County,
October 15, Edgecomb County.

October 11, 1851
EDWIN G. SPEIGHT of Alabama married MARY SHEPHERD BRYAN October 8,
Raleigh.

November 22, 1851
JOHN W. O'NEAL, formerly of Raleigh, married MARGARET M. GRAHAM
October 29, Huntsville.

May 15, 1852
REV. B(ASIL) MANLY, JR. married MRS. CHARLOTTE E. SMITH April 28,
Marion, Alabama. (1850 census of Tuscaloosa County)

January 1, 1853
B. W. JUSTICE of Wake County married ANN L. GORMAN of Tuscaloosa,
Alabama December 16, Tuscaloosa, Alabama.

June 29, 1853
E. B. PERRY of Perry County, Alabama married SALLIE BURGES, June 22,
Warren County.

November 9, 1853
D. A. F. ALEXANDER of Eutaw, Alabama married CATHARINE J. STOKES,
October 25, Morne Rogue near Wilkesboro (Wilkes County).

December 3, 1853
CHARLES BATRE of Mobile, Alabama married MARY E. P. FORBES
November 30, Newbern (Craven County).

November 29, 1854
DR. J. McD. WHITSON of Talladega, Alabama married REBECCA R. CARSON
November 6, McDowell County.

June 27, 1855
JAMES M. SPENCER of Clinton, Alabama married CORNELIA ANN PHILLIPS
June 20, Chapel Hill (Orange County).

November 7, 1855
RUFUS J. REID of Alabama married SARAH L. REID October, Mt. Mourne,
Iredell County.

February 6, 1846
DAVID R. HENDERSON of Mecklenburg died in January in Alabama.

May 29, 1846
WRIGHT HELLEN of Jones County died in May, Mobile, Alabama.

July 28, 1846
COL. JOHN BELL of this state died July 4 at Tuscumbia, Alabama.

October 16, 1846
MAJ. SAMUEL PERRY of Franklin County died September 8 at Marion,
Perry County, Alabama.

October 23, 1846
DR. A. L. MARTIN of Richmond County died October in Barbour
County, Alabama.

March 26, 1847
COL. BENJAMIN SHERROD of Halifax County died March in Courtland,
Alabama.

July 2, 1847
JOHN P. OWEN of Wilmington died in June, Mobile, Alabama.

July 24, 1847
JAMES SAUNDERS of the state died in July, Greene County, Alabama.

July 31, 1847
LUCY ELEANOR COBB of Alabama died in July, at Wilmington.

October 23, 1847
WILLIAM HINTON of this state died October 3, Greene County,
Alabama.

January 5, 1848
MRS. ELYAH B. PERRY died December 12 at Perry County, Alabama.

March 18, 1848
MRS. ANN E. WADSWORTH of Raleigh died February 26 at LaGrange
College, Alabama.

March 25, 1848
WILLIS SHELTON of Halifax County died March 12 at Macon County,
Alabama.

February 3, 1849
MRS. CHARITY LAWRENCE PRINCE of this state died in Tuscaloosa,
Alabama.

February 24, 1849
MRS. SARAH COBBS of Johnston County died February 6 in Choctaw
County, Alabama.

May 16, 1849
HON. JOHN F. FORREST of Orange County died April 10 in Jefferson
County, Alabama.

July 2, 1851
MRS. P. L. SINK of Salisbury (Rowan County) died June 5 at
Tuscaloosa, Alabama. (1850 census shows MRS. PHILLIP L. SINK aged 34
born in North Carolina; 1850 census Tuscaloosa County--1860 Dallas
County)

August 9, 1851
(Obituary) MRS. RALPH BANKS of Wake County died July 11 in
Tuscaloosa, Alabama.

August 16, 1851
JAMES JOHNSON DONALDSON of this state died July 30 at Mobile.

October 20, 1849
GEORGE B. WITHERSPOON of Hillsborough (Orange County) died
September 5 at Uniontown, Perry County, Alabama.

October 4, 1851
DR. WILLIAM F. STRUDWICK of Demopolis, Alabama died September 24
in Hillsboro (Orange County).

608

June 12, 1852
F. Y. TOWNSEND of Person County died May 16 at Bladen Springs (Choctaw County), Alabama.

June 4, 1853
(Obituary) JAMES G. MHOON of Bertie County died January 15 at Franklin County, Alabama.

November 23, 1853
SEYMOUR R. DUKE of Warrenton (Warren County) died October 22 at Mobile, Alabama.

December 14, 1853
MRS. EDWARD (TYSON) MOORE of Moore County died October 27 at Madison County, Alabama (Obituary).

September 9, 1854
MRS. MARGARET DOYLE WILLIAMS of Craven County died June 3 in McMathis, Alabama.

May 9, 1855
MRS. B. B. LEWIS of Franklin County died April 23 at Mobile, Alabama.

NATIONAL INTELLIGENCER

Washington, D.C.

January 3, 1823
JAMES W. PETERS, 2nd son of GEN. ABSALOM PETERS, of Lebanon, Connecticut aged 31 died 1 January 1823 at Blakely, Alabama. He moved to Alabama in 1815 and was a pioneer settler at Blakely in 1817. His firm, PETERS and STEBBINS, had a large and successful business there. He was elected representative to the Territorial Legislature in 1819 and subsequently was appointed Chief Justice of Baldwin County.

April 21. 1823
HON. JOHN WILLIAM WALKER, late U.S. Senator from Alabama, died in his 40th year.

July 30, 1823
MRS. AMY TOULMIN, wife of JOHN D. TOULMIN, died near St. Stephens, Alabama 3 June 1823. She was born at Falmouth, Cornwall, England 18 May 1789 and out of 4 children lost 3 soon after her removal to America. She was born of a Quaker family and professed the faith of the Friends.

August 20, 1823
MAJ. THOMAS McHENRY of Montevallo died in Jonesborough, Jefferson County, Alabama 7 August 1823. At the time of his death he was a candidate for Congress in the District in which he lived.

September 11, 1823
JOHN S. FULTON died at Russellville, Franklin County, Alabama.

September 11, 1823
CAPT. SAMUEL RIDDLE, late of the army, and last sutler at the Barrancas died at St. Stephens, Alabama 28 July 1823. He was of a humble but respectable family in Pennsylvania. Immediately after the declaration of the War of 1812 he entered his country's service as a Private. He was actively engaged in nearly all of the Northern campaigns.

September 17, 1823
MRS. MARTHA PICKENS, wife of HON. ISRAEL PICKENS, Governor of Alabama, died at her husband's residence 16 September 1823. She leaves a husband and four children.

September 23, 1823
Married Saturday evening the 20th by REV. MR. ENGLES, MR. ROBERT
ORRELL of Alabama to SARAH MATILDA, daughter of MR. THOMAS PHILLIPS of
Newark, Delaware.

September 30, 1823
PROF. ALVA WOODS of Columbiana College, Washington, D.C. and
MISS ELMIRA MARSHALL, daughter of JOSIAH MARSHALL were married in
Boston. Note: This couple later lived in Tuscaloosa, Alabama where
DR. WOODS was President of the University of Alabama. P.J.G.

October 11, 1823
DON MIGUEL ESLAVA, an inhabitant of Mobile died 17 September in
the 83rd year of his age. He was a native of Mexico and entered the
Spanish service at an early period. In Louisiana and the Floridas he
served his country in various civil and military employments for upwards
of 40 years. When the United States took possession of Mobile in 1813,
DON MIGUEL remained there.

November 5, 1823
JAMES ERWIN of Cahawba, Alabama and MISS ANN BROWN CLAY, 2nd
daughter of the HON. HENRY CLAY of Lexington, Kentucky, were married
21 October.

November 14, 1823
MRS. F. T. ROSE, sister of MR. MADISON, late President of the U.S.,
died 4 October 1823 at Huntsville, Alabama.

November 28, 1823
JAMES S. GAINES died at his residence near Cahawba, Dallas County,
Alabama 20 November aged about 45 years.

December 13, 1823
HON. HARRY TOULMIN, late a Judge of the U.S. District Court for
the District of Mississippi died at his residence in Washington County,
Alabama 11 December 1823 in his 57th year. He was descended from a
very ancient and respectable family in England. He was born at Taunton,
Somersetshire. His father was DR. JOSHUA TOULMIN. He became a
dissenting minister at Chowbert, Lancastershire, came to Norfolk,
Virginia in 1793, removed to Kentucky, and in 1794 was appointed
President of the Transylvania Seminary there. He held high offices
in Kentucky, Mississippi and Alabama (long account).

August 23, 1824
CAPT. JOS. H. ASHBRIDGE aged 33 years died 18 July at the residence
of C. FRAZEE in Baldwin County, Alabama. He was formerly of Philadelphia. At a very early age he commanded an East Indiawan but on the
declaration of war, joined the Navy and so distinguished himself with
KEARNEY and LAUGHTON off Charleston in such a manner as to draw from
a number of his senior officers letter of the warmest approbation. On
the return of peace he resigned his commission and had command of some
of the boats on the Mississippi till about two years ago when he was
employed on the Columbus on the Alabama.

September 29, 1824
JOHN CARR died in Autauga County, Alabama 26 September in his
60th year. He was from Albemarle County, Virginia.

January 20, 1825
JOHN BECK died at Cahawba, Alabama 26 December 1824. He was a
Representative in the Legislature from the County of Wilcox.

March 28, 1825
"CAPT. JOHN GRAHAM died in Madison County, Alabama 21 March 1825,
in his 71st year. CAPT. GRAHAM was an officer of the Revolutionary
War, and distinguished himself under GEN. MARION in South Carolina.
He was taken captive by the British, and confined 8 or 10 weeks in
Camden Jail. After his release, continued throughout the war. He has
left 11 children, 6 sons and 7 daughters; 90 grandchildren and 27 great
grandchildren, 13 sons and daughters-in-law."

June 16, 1825
    "ROBERT J. FARRELL of Shelby County and MISS TEMPERANCE WORRILL of
St. Clair County both late of South Carolina were married in St. Clair
County, Alabama 9 May."

May 10, 1825
    "JAMES H. SMYTH died at Cahawba, Alabama 14 April 1825 aged about
35 years. He was a printer and a native of Pennsylvania. The deceased
assisted in the discharge of cannon on the 5th of April, the day on
which GENERAL LAFAYETTE arrived there, and, unfortunately, after a
few discharges in quick succession, and upon the ramming down a
cartridge by the deceased, it exploded, and so much injured him as to
cause his death."

May 21, 1825
    "MAJOR WILLIAM HENRY died in this city 15 May 1825. He was a
native of Virginia and removed to St. Stephens in the state of Alabama
several years ago, where his family now resides. MAJ. HENRY, during
the last war, was an active and intrepid officer. He has left a wife
and several children."

September 12, 1826
    "BEIRNE, CAPT. FRANCIS, a native of Lisle, France, aged 36 years,
died 23 July, 1826, on board the steamboat HERALD, on his passage from
Mobile to Demopolis in Alabama. He was a soldier in Napoleon's Army
and was one of the survivors of the Russian Campaign, in which he was
wounded and made prisoner."

RICHMOND (VIRGINIA) ENQUIRER

October 17, 1837
    Died in Perry County, Alabama on Tuesday the 19th ult of bilious
fever, MEREDITH SLATER, formerly an old and respected citizen at
New Kent County, Virginia.

December 12, 1837
    Married in Courtland, Alabama on the 11th ult by the REV. ALEXANDER
SALE, DR. A(RCH'D) F. (T.) E. ROBERTSON, formerly of Richmond, Virginia
to MISS MARY, daughter of the late WILLIAM BANKS (volume 12, page 45
and license).

NASHVILLE (TENNESSEE) UNION

April 27, 1841
    Married, at Clover Hill, Franklin County, Tennessee, on the
evening of the 16th of April, COLONEL ROBERT HANCOCK of Madison County,
Alabama, to MISS JULIETT JANE SHARP, daughter of MAJOR RICHARD SHARP.

KNOXVILLE REGISTER

Knoxville, Tennessee

November 24, 1849
    Died on 23rd of October at his residence near Bellefont, Alabama,
MR. HYRAM F. DELANEY (1840 Jackson County), formerly a resident of this
place.
    Died, in Athens, Alabama on the 25th of February. MRS. L. M. G.
SWAIN, aged 41 years.

March 2, 1850
    Married in the Methodist Church in this city, on Wednesday evening
February 27th, MR. RUFUS W. COBB of Alabama to MISS MARGARET W. McCLUNG,
daughter of COL. HU L. McCLUNG of this city.

April 13, 1850
    Died, in Tuscumbia, Alabama on the 3rd instant. MRS. LOUISA
VIRGINIA, wife of DR. L. B. THORNTON, in the 22nd year of her age.

MRS. THORNTON was the daughter of JOHN B. and HARRIET T. NOOE, who were among the earliest settlers of this county.

June 22, 1850
    Married in this city, on Tuesday evening, the 25th instant, by REV. J. H. MYERS, MR. B(ENJ.) S. BARCLAY (41 in England) to MISS MARY SWAIN (22 in Virginia), both of Athens, Alabama.

October 24, 1850
    Married, on Thursday evening the 10th instant, by the REV. WILLIAM LUCAS, LAWSON D. FRANKLIN, Esq. of Lead Vale, Tennessee to MRS. CATHARINE SMITH of Morgan County, Alabama.

October 21, 1850
    Married on Thursday evening the 10th instant by the REV. WILLIAM LUCAS, LOSSEN D. FRANKLIN, Esq. of Lead-Vale, Tennessee to MRS. CATHARINE SMITH (46 in Tennessee) of Morgan County, Alabama. (Note by MR. PRICE: Who was she? She was a second wife; CATHERINE McDONNELL, daughter of ARCH'D McDONNELL married in Madison County, Alabama ebruary 13, 1823 JAS. L. SMITH who left a will in Monroe County, Mississippi 1847.)

THE POST

Knoxville, Tennessee

September 11, 1841
    Married, on the 13th instant by REV. ROBERT H. SNODDY, MR. HENRY CRESWELL (68 in Virginia) of Talladega County, Alabama to MISS MARY SNODDY of Sevier County.

HUNTSVILLE (ALABAMA) ADVOCATE

February 9, 1872
    "Married on the 15th, MR. W. G. HOLDEN of Mississippi to MISS MARY E. TARTT of Sumter County, Alabama."

February 23, 1872
    "MAJ. ED. HERNDON of Livingston died there on the 2nd."

March 1, 1872
    "JUDGE GEORGE B. SAUNDERS of Livingston died last week."

TUSKALOOSA GAZETTE

January 27, 1876
    "Married in Livingston on the 16th, MR. ALBERRY W. OWENS and MISS LIZZIE McALPINE."

February 24, 1876
    Married in Sumter County on the 15th MR. A. HINKLE and MISS EUGENIA WILSON.
    Died in Gainesville of typhoid pneumonia last week, JOSEPH HERRING.

May 25, 1876
    Died in Livingston on the 10th, ERNEST HERR aged 10, son of B. F. HERR, Esq., editor of Livingston Journal.

August 24, 1876
    Married in Sumter County on the 2nd, JAMES A. BRAKEFIELD and MRS. M. SWINDLE.

NEWSPAPER UNKNOWN

October 13, 1881
MR. ASA PARKER (46 in North Carolina), one of oldest and best
known citizens of this county, died at his home in Monroeville last
Saturday morning was about 77 years old.

June 8, 1881
DR. JAS. KENT (22 in Virginia), who came to Linden from Petersburg,
Virginia in 1850 and removed to Selma 1855 and to Jefferson County a few
years ago, died in Birmingham the 22 and was buried in Selma.

June 29, 1881
(From Linden Reporter) Died at residence of MR. JOHN HUNTER
near Jefferson, Alabama the 21, MRS. BARBARA SIMMONS, consort of late
LEWIS SIMMONS. Was 64 years old.
MAUD, daughter of MRS. M. A. DUNCAN who removed from this place
to Selma the 1st of the year died the 19th.

July 21, 1881
CALEB WILLIAMS, only son of MRS. MARY E. ALDRIDGE, died of conges-
tion at home of his mother, Saturday the 2nd.
JOEL DEES died at his home near Monroeville last week.
DR. H. P. SMITH, formerly of Monroe, died at Brewton a few weeks
ago.

July 28, 1881
MRS. ELLIOTT, an aged lady died near Linden Saturday night of
some bronchial affection.

August 4, 1881
BENJ. CRISSETT (40 in North Carolina), formerly of Claiborne,
died at his home in Escambia County a few days ago.
MRS. ROBINSON, an aged widow of Claiborne, fell dead from her
chair July 20.

August 11, 1881
JOHN SIMMONS, once sheriff of Monroe County, died in Monroeville
the 28th.

August 18, 1881
MRS. FANNY AGEE, wife of MR. W. L. AGEE, Sheriff of Marengo
County, died Thursday at Linden. Daughter of MR. T. B. GAINES of
Dayton. She was quite young, having been married less than a year.
(From Demopolis News)

October 20, 1881
MRS. SARAH B. ALLEN died near Jefferson on the 8th instant.

October 27, 1881
Died in Coffeeville this county Monday night 24th, J. WALTER MALONE,
son of late NAT MALONE of Coffeeville.

November 3, 1881
Died last week at Rehoboth, Alabama MRS. SALLIE PRICE aged about
68 years, wife of HON. THOS. W. PRICE of Wilcox and mother of MRS.
MARY TIDWELL of this place.

CHOCTAW COUNTY NEWS

September 8, 1881
GEO. C. DELL of Mt. Sterling died 24th. Buried at Mt. Sterling
with Masonic ceremonies.

October 6, 1881
MR. H. STOKES, 1 of oldest and most citizens of the county died
at his home near Bladen Springs.

November 3, 1881
    Died at residence of WRIGHT RICHARDSON, Esq. in Washington County,
Alabama Monday, 17th REV. NOLEN A. GREEN of pernicious fever. Member
of Alabama Conference.

WILCOX NEWS

September 8, 1881
    B. J. KITTRELL, a former resident of Camden, died.

September 29, 1881
    The venerable JUDGE JOHN A. CUTHBERT of Mobile died night of 22nd
in 95th year of his age.

November 3, 1881
    THEODORE WILTZE died at his residence near Rehoboth on October 5.

MONROE JOURNAL

November 3, 1881
    DANIEL ROBBINS, an old and respected citizen, died recently at his
home near Pineville.

November 10, 1881
    WALTER MALONE died October 24, 1881 at his mother's residence,
Clarke County, in 27th year.

CLARKE COUNTY DEMOCRAT

Grove Hill, Alabama

May 25, 1881
    Married on 5 at residence of REV. GEO. FONTAINE, DANIEL McLEAN to
MOLLIE FONTAINE by REV. E. B. PILLEY.
    Also by REV. J. W. McCANN, NATHAN G. DAVIS to FLORENCE ABERNATHY
in Monroe County.

July 14, 1881
    Last week we published a brief announcement of death of this
aged, intelligent and prominent citizen, NAT MALONE. MR. NATHANIEL
MALONE (43 in Tennessee) died 4th instant in his 74th year. Member of
board of county commissioners, member of Ulconush Baptist Church near
Coffeville. Leaves many relatives.

July 21, 1881
    ISHAM KIMBELL deceased--will--letters testamentary granted 4 April
1881, THOS I. KIMBELL and MARY F. KIMBELL, executors.
    ANDREW JACKSON BENSON (34 in Georgia) died at his residence about
5 miles east of this place Friday morning 15th instant aged 67. Native
of Georgia but had resided in this county for over 60 years. Old and
prominent member of Salem Baptist Church; good and popular citizen,
loving husband and father.
    MR. JOHN W. GASTON and family of Wilcox County are visiting the
family of his father-in-law MR. STEPHEN PUGH near this place.

July 28, 1881
    MRS. MARTHA JANE SPINKS (5 in Alabama), wife of WM. H. SPINKS and
daughter of late THOS. CARTER (44 in Georgia), of this place died
in Milam County, Texas 9th instant in 37th year of her age. Left
husband, several children and many relatives in this state and in Texas.

August 4, 1881
    MISS EMMA, daughter of MISS MARY E. and the late T. A. WIMBISH,
died at her mother's residence in Grove Hill the morning of 29th
after a brief but severe illness.

Died at residence of her step-father, MR. W. D. GIBSON, 5 miles west of Grove Hill, the night of 28th, MRS. JANE PUGH, after a protracted illness.

August 11, 1881
W. H. F. WAITE, deceased. N. M. CALHOUN, executor. Letters testamentary granted 9 July 1881.

August 25, 1881
Died in Grove Hill July 29th, 1881 EMMA C. WIMBISH, eldest daughter of MR. T. A. and MRS. M. E. WIMBISH after a painful illness of 7 days. Born May 27, 1857.

September 1, 1881
Obituary

A. J. BENSON (34 in Georgia) died at his home on 15 July last. Born in Hancock County, Georgia December 5, 1813 and came to Clarke County 1814. Married JANE HENDLEY February 5, 1835 and became a member of Baptist Church 22 September 1832...devoted husband and father.

MISS NANCY PHILLIPS, daughter of MR. G. W. PHILLIPS who lives near this place died 29th ult after a brief illness.

September 8, 1881
MRS. SNODGRASS, wife of SAML SNODGRASS of Baski and daughter of MRS. ADALINE and the late H. P. RIVERS, became the mother of 3 little boys weighing about 6 pounds each.

MRS. MATILDA HENDERSON (60 in North Carolina; MALINDA in census) died at residence of her son, MR. J. M. FINCH, some 3 miles south of Suggsville this county 4th instant at 91 years. MRS. HENDERSON was one of early settlers of this county and knew much of history. She was born in Halifax County, North Carolina 22 December 1789 and came to Clarke County 1810 and married HITE FINCH in January 1811. In 1823 she married NATHANIEL HENDERSON and in 1844 again became a widow. She left many relatives and friends.

MR. WM. FLUKER (13 in Alabama; son of GEO.) of Boiling Springs, Wilcox County, Alabama has sent a bundle of flax that was grown by MR. ALEX. CAMMACK on Bassett's Creek near Suggsville this county in year 1815 or 1816. We cannot realize this flax is 65 years old! For many years MR. FLUKES was a resident of this county and the ashes of his parents sleep in our soil.

Died in Lower Peach Tree at 4:30 a.m., little ELLA POME, daughter of D. C. McCASKEY, JR. and MRS. ANNA McCASKEY at 1 year 23 days.

September 15, 1881
Land office--ELIZ. CHRISTIAN, widow of JAS. A. CHRISTIAN, homestead entry number 2325 for SW¼ of SW¼ S7, NW¼ of NW¼ of 18-6 NR3E.

MRS. DR. KROUSE died at her residence 3 miles south of Suggsville this county this night after a protracted illness.

September 22, 1881
Died in Hernando County, Florida near Brooksville August 16, 1881 JOSIAH RUTLEDGE at 69-10-16. Old citizen of this county having moved to Florida last year.

Died on morning of 11, infant of MR. C. C. DAUGHERTY. Also on 15th, IRA BELLE at 2 years, daughter of same.

September 29, 1881
Died near Corsicana, Texas on 5th, CLARA, daughter of L. L. and N. E. DeWITT, formerly of Clarke County.

October 6, 1881
HENRY H. PEEBLES, deceased. JACOB MAYER, administrator.

COMBS (cont.)
  Stephen B. 163, 193,
    196
  T. A. 531
COMEGYS, Catharine 152
  E. F. 152
  Edward F. 152
COMER, Anderson 554
  Celeste 397, 554
COMERFORD, P. F. M. 212
COMFORT, S. W. 155
COMMONS, Margaret 8
COMPERE, Lee 194
COMPTON, John W. 587
  Joseph 337
  Sarah 504
  W. R. 504
CONE, Laura A. 174
CONLEY, Charles 534
  Ennis 534
  Eunice P. 534
  Margaret J. 534
  Samuel 533
CONNALLY, -- (Mrs.) 303
  John 303, 330, 354, 553
  Mollie C. 553
  Rachel O. 354, 490
  Sallie Polk 583
CONNELL, Ann Eliz. 534
  Mary S. 514
  Simon 534
CONNELLY, Emily C. 539
CONNER, Charles D. 153
  David 291
  G. W. 230
  J. M. 356
  Joseph H. 225
  Martha 291
  Mary 519
  Polly 306
  Samuel 484, 519
  Tennie 237
CONNERLY, -- (Prof.) 115
  Allis 247
  Catharine 161
CONNOR, E. R. 415
  Jennie 391
  Margaret J. 356
  Samuel 317
CONOLEY, John John F. 337
CONROE, -- (Mr.) 12
CONROW, Marion 176
CONSODINE, D. J. (Mrs.)
    577
CONSTANTINE, F. L. 45
  Francis L. 45
CONWAY, Annie R. 397
  C. P. 386
  James 225, 397
CONWILL, A. R. P. 173
COOK, -- (Rev. Mr.) 40
  Amanda C. 294
  Ann B. 55
  B. G. 69
  D. V. 547
  Daniel P. 139
  David 136
  Emily E. 543
  F. S. 55
  Henry 294, 433, 502
  Henry H. 55, 58
  Isaac 93, 218, 238
  Isadora 552
  J. M. 73, 104
  J. N. 104
  John 136
  Joseph F. 337
  Joseph J. 87
  Kelin 551
  Lemuel 136
  Mary 547
  Mary E. 104
  Mary Frances 58

COOK (cont.)
  Moses J. 148
  Nathan 543
  R. B. 550
  Richard S. 576
  Thos. A. 557
  Thomas 136
  Thomas P. 336
  W. A. 125
  W. D. S. 547
  Wm. 338
  William H. 136
COOKE, Alexander 178
  Charles 111, 119, 123,
    124
  Susan 123
COOKSEY, W. E. 122
  Wm. 122
  Wm. E. 122
COOLEY, -- (Judge) 132
  B. F. 386
  Emma 251
  Emory 179
  Nancy 173
  Sarah D. 583
  Timothy 583
COONS, Everett 218
  George W. 516, 524
  Martha E. 218
  Samuel W. 218, 275
COOPER, -- 195
  -- (Rep.) 186
  -- (Rev. Mr.) 208
  Allen 237, 317
  Benjamin 13
  Chas. 315
  Carroll 421
  Charles 326
  Duet 159
  Drury M. 537
  Elizabeth 538
  Elizabeth B. 224
  Erasmus 161, 165
  Ettie 251
  Frances 284
  George H. 183
  Henrietta 317
  J. P. 565
  J. W. 237, 420
  J. DeWitt 6
  Jas. L. 274
  Jas. L. (Mrs.) 274
  James L. 237, 524
  James Parker 565
  Jane Foster 503
  John W. 237, 251
  John W. (Mrs.) 269
  L. B. 107
  Langston 503
  Lawrence 376
  Martha 538
  Mary 107, 274
  Pamelia F. 346
  Samuel W. 244
  Sarah A. 367
  Susan H. 576
  Wm. 224, 367, 503
  William 107, 565, 576
  Williams 410
COOVER, Ella P. 443
  Lottie 233
  Sallie L. 550
COPE, W. A. 127
COPELAND, Amanda 575
  Amanda J. 575
  Branch 532, 575
  Calhe C. 564
  George M. 419
  J. S. 140
  Jos. 324
  Martha J. 532
  Mary E. 502
  Nathan 518

COPELAND (cont.)
  Nathan W. 548
  Newt 419
  Sarah J. 509
  Sarah M. 509
CAPP, -- (Rev. Mr.) 155,
    473, 474
CORBETT, John S. 267
CORBIN, James 189
CORBITT, John Shelby 452
CORLEY, John 279
  Nancy 173
CORMLEY, William 323
CORN, John B. 372
CORNELIUS, -- 236, 350
  H. 178
  Harvey 340
  James 417
  Rowland 429
  William 483
CORNELL, Jerome C. 482
CORNETTE, -- (Rev.
    Father) 109
CORNICK, Sophia A. 33
  Tully R. 33
CORNWALLIS, -- 328, 489,
    512
  Lord 171
CORPER, Mary J. E. 555
CORPIER, A. L. 224
CORY, Alice 140
CORRY, Robert E. 580
COSBY, Alexander 483
  Frances 501
  Maria Jane 304
COSEY, Edward W. 467
COSSELIN, Alexander 187
  Mary A. 187
COSSITT, -- (Rev. Dr.)
    499
COST, Henry 202
  Henry (Mrs.) 147
COTTEN, A. J. 302
  Alexander W. 434
  Allen 434
  James L. 131
  Margaret 344
  Micajah T. 302, 344
  Montford 434
  Peggy 302
COTTON, Francis Edward
    514
  Jehial 253
  John 514
  John A. 39
  Margaret Jane 514
  Willie 467, 514
COUCH, A. B. 87
  Daniel 80
  H. V. 87
  Ida 80
  Lavinia D. 48
  Mary 80
  Peter 458
  Sarah C. 234
  W. J. 189
  W. P. 258
  William J. 48, 178
  William Jonathan 48
COULSON, L. C. 557
  P. D. 88
COUNSEL, Margaret 568
COURLIE, R. 191
COUSINS, F. T. 261
COWAN, -- (Rev. Mr.) 476,
    527, 544, 551
  Elizabeth 304
  John A. 30
  John F. 507
  Nancy 289
  Samuel M. 470
  William 289
  William M. 232